Social Psychology

Social Psychology

Irwin A. Horowitz
Oregon State University

Kenneth S. Bordens
Indiana University-Purdue University at Fort Wayne

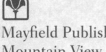

Mayfield Publishing Company
Mountain View, California
London • Toronto

For Kay, my wife and soulmate
I.A.H.

To my wife, children, and parents
K.S.B.

Library of Congress Cataloging-in-Publication Data

Horowitz, Irwin A.
    Social Psychology / Irwin A. Horowitz, Kenneth S. Bordens.
        p.   cm.
    Includes bibliographical references (p.   ) and index.
    ISBN 0-87484-976-4
    1. Social psychology. I. Bordens, Kenneth S. II. Title.
HM251.H675   1994
302—dc20   94-16772
                                                                     CIP

Manufactured in the United States of America
10 9 8 7 6 5 4 3 2 1

Mayfield Publishing Company
1280 Villa Street
Mountain View, California 94041

Sponsoring editor, Franklin C. Graham; *developmental editor,* Kathleen Engelberg; *production editor,* Lynn Rabin Bauer; *manuscript editor,* Margaret Moore; *text and cover designer,* Jeanne M. Schreiber; *cover artist,* Karen Barbour; *illustrators,* Robin Mouat and John and Judy Waller; *art editor,* Susan Breitbard; *photo researcher/editor,* Melissa Kreischer; *manufacturing managers,* Martha Branch and Aimee Rutter. The text was set in 10.5/12.5 Fairfield Light by Progressive Information Technologies and printed on acid-free 45# Mead Pub Matte by R. R. Donnelley & Sons Co.

Acknowledgments and copyrights continue at the back of the book on pages C-1 to C-4, which constitute an extension of the copyright page.

Brief Contents

Contents

9   Obedience and Disobedience   357

10   Group Processes   397

Part Three

SOCIAL RELATIONS   443

Preface

As social psychologists, we have long been impressed with the research and theory that have been developed over the years in our field. When we first learned of Milgram's obedience experiments, for example, we were intrigued by their implications. We wanted to pursue the question of how the results could be applied to obedience behavior in the real world. Similarly, other research and theory inspired us to think about how real-life social behavior is affected by the presence of other people and by the dynamics of interpersonal and group situations. In short, we were excited by the implications and applications of the work being done in social psychology.

As teachers, we also saw that the results coming out of social psychology "laboratories" could help students understand the complexities of the world and the forces that shape history. Over time, we began to formulate the idea of writing a social psychology textbook that integrated up-to-date and classic research and theory with history, current events, and the wider culture.

Putting our idea into concrete terms meant departing somewhat from the formula used in many social psychology texts. They tend to approach the field from the perspective of research and theory, using examples from everyday life or current events to illustrate principles. This book, in contrast, teaches social psychology by tying it to important current and historical events and issues. Examples and applications are an integral part of how the principles of social psychology are presented. The result is a fully balanced and integrated presentation of research, theory, and application. No other text, in our opinion, offers so full an appreciation of the power and usefulness of social psychology for understanding the complexities of human social behavior and of social, cultural, and historical events.

We can summarize our approach in this book by saying that we present social psychological research and theory within the context of a broad sociohistorical perspective. By this we mean, first, that the usefulness of social psychology for understanding social, cultural, and historical events and issues is emphasized throughout. For example, social psychology can help students understand the ethnic conflict in Bosnia, as well as how such a conflict originates, how it leads to intergroup aggression, and how it can be reduced and resolved.

The second dimension of the sociohistorical perspective is its insistence that these events and issues be interpreted within their own particular social, cultural, and historical contexts. For example, the high levels of obedience in Nazi Germany must be examined in the context of a highly regimented, authority-oriented society in which a tremendously high value was placed on conformity and compliance. Similarly, the phenomenon of racism in the United States must be examined within a historical and cultural context that once included the institutionalized slavery of people of African descent.

Teaching social psychology from a sociohistorical perspective can increase student interest both in the field itself and in the kinds of events, issues, and phenomena that occur around them every day in the world. Often, they have never seriously considered many of these events, nor have they had tools for analyzing and understanding them. The sociohistorical perspective as employed in this book thus becomes a powerful tool that students can use to enrich and deepen their own lives.

This approach also helps students gain an understanding of how different disciplines relate to one another because it exposes students to information and data from disciplines outside the traditional scope of social psychology. It helps them see how "book knowledge" relates to everyday life, and it encourages them to develop and use critical thinking skills. In short, students learn that social psychology can help them make sense of their lives and the world.

This text, then, offers a balance and integration of research, theory, and application that we believe cannot be found in other social psychology textbooks. It is also balanced in three other ways. First, there is a balance of everyday, personal examples and examples involving significant social, cultural, and historical events. The text constantly moves back and forth between the personal situation—the interpersonal relationship, the student study group—and the national or world event.

Second, there is a balance of classic research and cutting-edge research. The most important foundational research from the early and middle years of the field is here, as is the latest research from the 1990s. A glance at the reference list will show that the research base of this text is extraordinarily current.

Finally, there is a balance among the three major areas of study in social psychology—social cognition, social influence, and social relations. No area is underrepresented, and extensive coverage is provided of topics in social influence, an area that other texts have tended to slight in recent years in favor of social cognition.

As a discipline, social psychology gives us a perspective on the world that no other field of psychology can. Knowledge of human social behavior informs us about how those in our immediate social environment affect us. It also informs us about a variety of important social and cultural issues, including racial and ethnic hostility, prejudice and discrimination, aggression and violence, persuasion and propaganda, and health and environmental issues. More than any other field of psychology, social psychology offers us a glimpse of what it is to be human. In this book we hope to share that glimpse of human behavior with a broader population of students than we can reach in our own classrooms.

ORGANIZATION AND EMPHASIS

This text is organized into four major parts: Social Cognition (with chapters on the self, social perception, attribution, prejudice, and attitudes), Social Influence (persuasion, conformity, obedience, and group processes), Social Relations (interpersonal attraction, aggression, and altruism), and Applied Social Psychology (applications of social psychology to the law, health, and international conflict). In our experience, thirteen core chapters can be handled adequately in a semester. Instructors may add or substitute chapters to meet their individual needs.

Although the organization of this book is similar to that of other social psychology texts, there are some differences. Chapter 1, for example, avoids the common trap of bogging students down with detailed descriptions of research methods. Instead, we show students how social psychology can be used to make sense of common, everyday events as well as a range of cultural and historical events. The section on research methods focuses only on those issues and topics that will help students understand the research discussed in subsequent chapters of the book.

Another difference is that this book has separate chapters on conformity and compliance (Chapter 8) and on obedience and disobedience (Chapter 9). Too often, coverage of social influence is light compared to coverage of social cognition. We believe that this expanded coverage of topics in social influence provides a broader, more balanced view of social psychology.

FEATURES

In keeping with our goal of teaching social psychology by tying it to important events, we open every chapter with an extended vignette centering on a contemporary event or an event from history or literature. Chapter 13, for example, opens with the story of Seth Conklin, a white man who risked his life to bring a stranger's family out of slavery in 1851. The chapter asks why a person would act so selflessly on behalf of someone he didn't even know. It then helps students understand the dynamics of altruism and the varieties of helping behavior.

Other vignettes focus on the Rodney King trial, the long-term relationship of Gertrude Stein and Alice B. Toklas, the *Vincennes* incident, the massacre at My Lai, Watergate, and the life of muckraking journalist Ida Tarbell. We have not attempted to make the vignettes "timely" because any description of a current event is outdated the week after the event occurs. Instead, we have selected incidents and issues that reflect the timeless nature of human social behavior: What was true one hundred years ago is still true today. Our purpose is to show that the principles of social psychology apply to people's lives regardless of when and where they live.

The chapter-opening vignettes are fully integrated into the chapter; they structure and direct the material that follows. At the end of every chapter, the vignettes are "revisited" in a special section in which the meaning of the vignette for that topic area is reinforced.

The text also includes featured discussions of special, high-interest topics and issues in separate boxes. These discussions, numbering over 50 in all, give students a closer look at themes introduced in the body of the chapter without interrupting the narrative flow of the text. The following sampling of titles suggests the range of these discussions:

- What Motivates Us to Help: Sympathy or Guilt? (Chapter 1)
- The Availability Heuristic at Work: Public Perception of Crime (Chapter 3)
- Interpreting Behavior: The Case of Oskar Schindler (Chapter 4)
- Forming Political Attitudes: The Case of Janet Reno (Chapter 6)
- The Lure of Cults: Persuasion Among the Branch Davidians (Chapter 7)
- Buying a Car: An Exercise in Social Influence (Chapter 8)
- From Newark to Los Angeles: Frustration and American Urban Race Riots (Chapter 12)
- Altruism and Religion (Chapter 13)
- Scientific Jury Selection: The Joan Little Trial (Chapter 14)
- The Dynamics of Intransigence (on the Arab-Israeli conflict; Chapter 16)

Each featured discussion is followed by a series of questions designed to help students develop their critical thinking skills. These questions ask students to think about the boxed material in relation to issues and themes discussed elsewhere in the chapter, in other chapters, or in their own lives. The questions can be used as a means to get students thinking about issues in social psychology and as a starting point for in-class discussions.

Gender and cultural issues are covered extensively in this book, and the coverage is integrated throughout the chapters rather than isolated in a single chapter. Thus, when we discuss stereotyping, we include a discussion of gender role stereotyping and its effects on children. When we discuss conformity, we consider gender differences in conformity. The same is true of the discussions of obedience, aggression, friendship styles, and so on. We also include material on cultural differences where such information is available and relevant, such as in the featured discussion entitled, Are Attribution Theories Culture Bound? The following is just a brief sample of gender and cultural issues covered in the text:

- The origins of stereotypes about African Americans and women in the United States (Chapter 1)
- The influence of culture on the contents of the self-concept (Chapter 2)
- The historical, social, and cultural roots of prejudice against Jews in Europe and against African Americans in the United States (Chapter 5)

- Gender stereotyping and prejudice (sexism): historical roots and social context; gender roles and stereotypes; cognitive roots; the male norm; social roles theory (Chapter 5)
- Gender differences in goals and expectations in romantic and sexual relationships, according to sociobiologists, with relevant research findings (Chapter 11)
- Violence against women: the role of pornography in rape and the effect of film, TV, and magazine violence on the acceptance of the "rape myth" (Chapter 12)
- The impact of race on sentencing decisions and imposition of the death penalty (Chapter 14)

WRITING STYLE AND VISUAL APPEAL

Social psychology is too exciting a field to be described in dry, stilted prose or to be presented to students solely as a research-based social science. Our approach is to set up discussions with relevant examples and then show how social psychological research and theory relate to the issues embodied in the example. We do, of course, provide extensive descriptions of research where needed, but we do not allow these descriptions to drive the discourse. Instead, discussion is driven by the issues and supported with appropriate research and theory.

Because we are dedicated to making social psychology interesting and accessible to students, we have written this text in a friendly, conversational style. We have included as many lively and relevant examples and applications as possible to engage students' attention. We believe this is a book that students will enjoy reading. And along the way, they will learn a bit about history, culture, and current events.

We have also taken care to make the book a pleasure to look at. Nearly 200 photographs, both historical and contemporary, provide a visual accompaniment to the text, reinforcing concepts and meanings. Abundant illustrations—graphs, flow charts, original line art, and cartoons—further enhance the text's accessibility and appeal. The illustration program is designed to provide maximum support for the text, particularly for those students who are more visually oriented in their learning style.

LEARNING AIDS

To facilitate both teaching and learning, we have included a number of learning aids in this text. Each of the four parts opens with a part overview and preview of the general topic. Each chapter opens with a chapter outline orienting the student to chapter contents. Key terms are printed in boldface type within the text, explained in context, and defined in a running glossary in the margin. Terms are also defined in an end-of-book glossary.

Chapter reviews at the end of each chapter provide a quick summary of chapter contents and help students focus on the main points of the text. They are organized in question-and-answer form for maximum accessibility.

All key terms are included in the chapter reviews in boldface type and are used in context.

Also appearing at the end of every chapter are annotated suggestions for further reading for students who wish to follow up on particular topics. We have included a wide range of materials in these sections, including journal articles, popular books on social psychological topics, and additional readings on historical or cultural issues highlighted in the chapter.

Finally, for quick reference, the text includes both a name and a subject index.

ANCILLARIES

This text is accompanied by a comprehensive ancillary package. Central to the package and serving to integrate all the elements is the *Resource Book for Social Psychology: A Teacher's Tool Kit.* The resource book includes a number of tools for organizing and teaching the course, including listings of suggested films, videos, books, journals, and on-line information sources; ideas for classroom activities, demonstrations, and discussions; student handouts and worksheets; transparency masters; an annotated bibliography; and suggestions for teaching with diversity issues in mind.

The ancillary package also includes a student study guide designed to help students get the most out of the text. The study guide includes chapter outlines, learning objectives, key terms reviews, and practice test questions. Also included are "knowledge in action" and "personal assessment" sections with exercises and activities students can undertake on their own to get "hands-on" experience in social psychology.

Additionally, the package includes an extensive computerized test bank of examination questions. As teachers and authors, we feel strongly that test questions must meet the high standards of the text and truly conform to the needs of instructors. Too often a text package is ruined by poor quality, irrelevant examination questions. Therefore, we have taken the time to write the questions ourselves. Although every item might not be perfect—we have all had too much experience creating tests to make that claim—we do guarantee that the questions are well constructed and well written and that they target the most important concepts in each chapter.

Finally, the ancillary package includes an exciting video package featuring films and videos that highlight and reinforce the sociohistorical aspect of the text. Each film or video centers on the life or actions of an ordinary person who becomes part of an extraordinary cultural or historical event that has shaped our social existence.

ACKNOWLEDGMENTS

A project of this scope requires the hard work and support of many people. First and foremost, we would like to thank our families for their support and patience throughout this project. Our wives, Kay Schaffer and Ricky

Karen Bordens, provided much needed love and support while we labored long and hard to complete this book. Our children, Jessica Horowitz, Todd Horowitz, Ilisa Horowitz, Laura Bordens, and Alexander Bordens, were sources of comfort and support. We would especially like to thank Ilisa Horowitz for her assistance in obtaining permissions.

Next, we would like to extend thanks to our colleagues, who provided support and input during various stages of the project. Special thanks go to Kip Williams, Keith Neidermeier, Marty Bourgeois, Sherwin Kepes, and Craig Hill for their comments on drafts of chapters. Their input helped us shape this book into its final form.

We also want to thank a number of students and former students who played a role in the writing of this book. Special appreciation goes to Lynn ForsterLee, David Seguin, Marc Feldman, Kristin Sommer, Gloria Lyons, and Sonja Vest for their efforts.

Finally, this book would not have been possible without the support of the editorial and production staff at Mayfield Publishing Company. First, we want to extend our deepest appreciation to our sponsoring editor and friend, Franklin Graham, for his guidance on this project. His vision and firm hand kept the project on the straight and narrow when it threatened to go off course. Second, we want to thank our developmental editor, Kate Engelberg, for taking a manuscript written by two academics and transforming it into a textbook that students will enjoy reading. Third, our thanks to Lynn Rabin Bauer, our production editor, for molding the manuscript into the finished product. And finally, we want to thank all the others at Mayfield who contributed to this book. Even though we might not have had direct contact with them, we deeply appreciate their dedication and hard work.

REVIEWERS OF *SOCIAL PSYCHOLOGY*

This book also owes its final shape to the academic reviewers who took the time to read drafts of chapters at various stages and who provided us with valuable feedback. Their efforts contributed greatly to the quality and integrity of the contents of this book.

Reuben M. Baron, University of Connecticut

Galen V. Bodenhausen, Michigan State University

Martin Bolt, Calvin College

Meredith Bombar, Elmira College

Paul C. Cozby, California State University, Fullerton

Robert T. Croyle, University of Utah

Lynda Dodgen, North Harris College

William J. Froming, Pacific Graduate School of Psychology

Jayne T. Gackenbach, Athabasca University

(Reviewers continued on next page)

Ranald D. Hansen, Oakland University

Craig A. Hill, Indiana University-Purdue University at Fort Wayne

Marita R. Inglehart, University of Michigan

Donn L. Kaiser, Southwest Missouri State University

Martin F. Kaplan, Northern Illinois University

Mary E. Kite, Ball State University

Hilary M. Lips, Radford University

Angela Lipsitz, Northern Kentucky University

Dan P. McAdams, Northwestern University

Richard E. Petty, Ohio State University

Adrian Rapp, North Harris College

Cheryl A. Rickabaugh, University of Redlands

Tony Riley, University of Massachusetts at Amherst

Jerry I. Shaw, California State University, Northridge

Vaida D. Thompson, University of North Carolina at Chapel Hill

Teddy D. Warner, Iowa State University

Bernard Weiner, University of California, Los Angeles

Bernard E. Whitley, Jr., Ball State University

Social Psychology

Chapter 1

The Field of Social Psychology

ou awaken at your usual time, shower, and get ready for your day. You pick up the morning paper from your front doorstep and scan the headlines as you head into the kitchen for breakfast. The first thing you read is that the president has just announced a plan to overhaul the nation's health care system. As you butter your toast, you read that, according to one political analyst, the president must be prepared to "sell" the plan to the American people and the Congress. You wonder just how this will be done.

Reading on, you find that American troops were sent overseas to intervene in a civil war and assist starving civilians. You are distressed to learn that several American soldiers have already been killed while carrying out this mission. Still farther into the newspaper you read a story about continuing conflict in another part of the world. This conflict involves different ethnic and religious groups whose hostility toward one another goes back several centuries. The origins of the conflict are obscure, but the pictures of killing and destruction are real and disturbing.

You congratulate yourself for having the wisdom to pick ancestors who chose to live in the United States. Your smugness is short-lived, however, when you come to a story about gang violence in your city. You knew that there was gang activity in your city, but you hadn't realized how widespread it was or how near to your home the latest violence occurred.

Just when you think that the only thing worth reading in the paper is the comics, a story in the second section catches your eye. It's about a man who was given 6 months to live after a diagnosis of lung cancer. The man had just become a grandfather. According to the story, he told himself, "No, I won't die in 6 months. I have to live to teach my grandson how to fish and hunt and play baseball. I want to teach him my values, and I want to see him start school." The man's obituary noted that his grandson was now in the first grade. His physician commented that there was something in him—some will, some strength—that helped him survive those years. The physician also commented that while the will to live may have affected the lifespan of this man, many others with similar diagnoses may have the same drive to live and yet die without seeing their dreams realized. You wonder why the best story in the paper is buried in the second section.

Before leaving the house you call the person you've been dating for several months. You've noticed that your initial strong physical attraction has begun to fade. You still enjoy being together, but you see signs of cracks in the relationship. You've decided to bring up some of these problems, and to your surprise, your friend agrees that the relationship has lost much of its ardor. Together you decide to begin seeing other people.

After hanging up, you feel a little hurt. You were surprised to learn that your friend no longer found you exciting. It was one thing for you to feel that way about your friend, but quite another for that person to lose interest in you. A few months ago, you had both been sure that this relationship was it. How could you have been so wrong? Why, you wonder, is it so hard to predict how people are going to feel and act in the future? In any event, there is that new person you're attracted to . . .

Before your first class you must put in 2 hours at your part-time job at a local bookstore. Thinking about it causes your stomach to turn because you've been having some trouble with your manager. You think she's being too demanding about some of the trivial details of the job. In fact, you reflect, quite a few of your supervisors at various part-time jobs have given you a hard time. It crosses your mind that perhaps you really don't like relating to authority figures. But there's no time to think about that; you have more important things on your mind—taking an important exam in two days, making an appointment with your adviser, planning your course schedule for next year. Gulping down your coffee and grabbing your jacket, you're out the door.

This "day in the life" depicts a variety of social events, all of which fall within the domain of **social psychology.** Social psychology is the scientific study of how individuals think and feel about, interact with, and influence each other, individually and in groups. It is the branch of psychology that studies social behavior—the thinking and behavior of individuals as they relate to other human beings.

Social psychology provides tools for understanding the events that occur around you every day. In your personal life, it can help you make sense of your day-to-day interactions—your friendships, love relationships, interactions at work, and performance at school. It can give you insight, for example, into why your most recent romantic relationship did not succeed, and why you find yourself attracted to a person in your afternoon class—but not to another. It can also help you understand why you may behave aggressively when someone cuts ahead of you in a cafeteria line or why you get annoyed when someone sits right next to you in a theater when there are plenty of other seats. Social psychology can also help you understand why *other* people act the way they do.

social psychology The scientific study of how individuals think and feel about, interact with, and influence each other, individually and in groups.

In 1993, in a historic meeting hosted by U.S. president Bill Clinton, Israeli prime minister Yitzhak Rabin and Palestine Liberation Organization leader Yasser Arafat signed an agreement to begin working toward Palestinian self-rule in parts of Israel. Their handshake symbolized the triumph of diplomacy and peaceful conflict resolution over violence and war. Social psychology offers concepts and principles that help us make sense both of international conflict and of conflict resolution.

But your life is touched by events beyond your immediate, day-to-day affairs—events that occur in the community and the nation. Although these events are more distant, you may still feel strongly about them and find a link between them and your personal life. If your friend's father were very sick, for example, you might want to tell him about the man whose determination kept him alive for six years. Perhaps the story would encourage him to keep on with his life. If your city were engulfed in a race-related disturbance, you would experience directly the effects of racial prejudice and conflict. You probably would hear many people decrying the violence and talking about ways to improve relations among different ethnic and racial groups. And if you watch television, you have been the target of countless hours of advertising, designed to persuade you to buy certain products whether you need them or not. You have also been the target of cleverly produced political advertisements designed to "sell" you on policies and programs like the president's health care plan.

International affairs touch you too. You live in a world where conflict is a fact of life, as demonstrated by countless stories in the newspapers. There are also notable cases of conflict resolution, such as the September 1993 meeting between Yasser Arafat and Yitzhak Rabin in Washington, D.C. You may have wondered how this conciliation could have taken place, after so many years of bitter prejudice and hatred between the Israelis and the Palestine Liberation Organization.

In the one form or another, all these events represent recurring themes in human history. No, people haven't always been annoyed by fellow movie-viewers or bombarded by TV ads. But human beings have always had to find ways to live with each other. We have always functioned together in groups; had love relationships; tried to persuade others of our point of view; followed or rebelled against authority; and sought ways to resolve conflicts, whether through negotiation or through coercion. We help each other and we hurt each other. We display prejudice and discrimination; we have even tried to kill entire populations. History has been a tapestry of the best and the worst that human beings can do. Social psychology can help us understand these human social events in their infinite variety.

It's important to note, however, that social psychologists do not simply wonder and speculate about social behavior. Instead, they use scientific methods involving carefully designed and executed research studies to help explain complex, uncertain social issues. Social psychology is first and foremost a science. Through theory, research, and thoughtful application of concepts and principles to real-life situations, social psychologists provide insights into everyday events, both past and present, as well as those monumental events that are the stuff of history.

In this chapter we introduce the field of social psychology. We consider how all the different aspects of everyday life—as well as national and international events—can be better understood through the perspective and tools of this social science. We look at such questions as, Why is it important to know the social and historical context of events like ethnic conflicts abroad and gang wars at home? What models does social psychology offer for interpreting personal interactions like that between a bookstore manager and an employee? For interpreting historical events like the meeting of Rabin and Arafat in Washington, D.C.? For analyzing political speeches designed to sell you a health care plan? For exploring a complex event like the Los Angeles riots of 1992? In its approach to issues like violent conflict between groups, how does social psychology differ from other fields of study? And what are the scientific methods on which social psychological principles and research findings are based? The answers to these questions provide a context—both theoretical and practical—for understanding the topics and issues discussed in subsequent chapters.

USING SOCIAL PSYCHOLOGY TO UNDERSTAND SOCIAL BEHAVIOR

More than any other branch of psychology, social psychology offers a broad perspective on human behavior. Rather than focusing on the personal histories of individuals, or on how individuals respond to their environment, it looks at how people interact with and relate to each other *in social contexts*. As we have seen, a wide range of behavior and events falls within its domain.

The Sociohistorical Perspective

This text takes the broad perspective of social psychology a step further by adopting a **sociohistorical perspective** as a framework for understanding social psychological principles, research, and theory. The sociohistorical perspective has two main features. The first is its emphasis on the social, cultural, and historical contexts in which social psychological phenomena occur. Events can be best understood, according to this view, when the settings in which they are embedded are also scrutinized.

The second feature of the sociohistorical perspective is its interest in a broad range of contemporary and historical events, as well as incidents and characters from literature and the arts, in contrast to a narrower focus on research and theory. This perspective suggests that the principles of social psychology are best used in providing insight into real-life behaviors and problems, and it consistently relates principles and research findings to real-world events. Let's consider a few examples of each of these features.

Understanding Context   The sociohistorical perspective highlights the fact that social behavior may vary depending on an individual's cultural identity and gender as well as the time period in which he or she lives. For example, conformity behavior—going along with a group because of perceived pressure to do so—varies across cultures. Cultures in which a sense of identification with the larger group is high (such as Norway) show higher levels of conformity to commonly agreed upon standards of behavior than is the case in cultures in which such identification is less strong (France, for example). Similarly, gender differences in social behavior vary from one time period to another as a culture evolves. What is true of gender differences today may not be as true tomorrow.

Additionally, understanding the historical roots of events and patterns of behavior helps us understand those phenomena as they exist today. Consider the stereotypes about women and individuals of different ethnic groups that are prevalent in our culture. Various scholars have observed that both women and African American slaves were treated similarly by the law in the first 100 years of the history of this nation. In essence, both were considered to be property: Women "belonged" to their husbands, slaves "belonged" to their masters. The purpose of these laws was to repress and control these elements of society (Friedman, 1985).

Women were denied financial responsibility, access to education, and the right to own property except under some unusual circumstances. The rationale for these restrictions was that women need to be "protected." The "best minds of the day" declared that women possessed "disabilities" or shortcomings that precluded full civil rights. These practices remained in place until the middle of the 19th century when reforms slowly began to occur.

The enslavement of African Americans, similarly, was based on a falsehood—that African American slaves were subhuman. This notion meant that blacks could justifiably be denied all rights available to whites. The slave system deprived and degraded African Americans and then despised them

sociohistorical perspective A framework for understanding social psychological principles, research, and theory that emphasizes the importance of social, cultural, and historical context and the relevance of social psychology to current and historical events.

for how they lived (Friedman, 1985). This is ever the way with ignorance and prejudice: Different ethnic and racial groups are degraded, and then their debased condition is taken as proof of their inferiority. For their own part, African Americans responded to the cruelty of slavery by defying the stereotypes and devising an independent and varied culture "rich in love for one another, in community, and in human meaning" (Hymowitz & Weissman, 1978).

The myths of black and female inferiority have persisted in our culture. Until fairly recently, the doors to independence and advancement have been shut, overtly for blacks, more subtly for women. When we are looking at the phenomena of prejudice and stereotypes in our society (as we do in Chapter 5), knowing this background, this sociohistorical context, gives us a deeper understanding of their roots and their persistence.

Exploring Current and Historical Events   The sociohistorical perspective also highlights the use of social psychological principles in explaining current and historical events. For example, social psychology can help us understand why there is ethnic tension in the former Yugoslavia and, as indicated earlier, why racial tensions continue to exist in the United States. It can give us insight into how juries in rape trials listen to testimony and reach their verdicts. It can teach us the best ways to overcome stereotypes and learn to live more peacefully in a diverse society. These issues and countless others are addressed in the pages that follow. We hope that the insights gained from these explorations will help all of us better understand the events that are played out each day in our communities, our country, and the world.

To get a better idea of how social psychology views events, and particularly of how the principles of social psychology can be applied to real-life situations, let's turn now to a series of events that occurred in California in May 1992.

A Case Study: The Los Angeles Riots

On May 11, 1992, a predominantly white jury in Simi Valley, California, handed down not-guilty verdicts against the police officers accused of beating African American motorist Rodney King. Most people had expected the jury to find the defendants guilty, largely on the basis of a segment of videotape, played endlessly by the news media, that showed the police officers beating King as he lay on the ground. Among those closely watching the case were the residents of South Central Los Angeles.

The city was calm in the moments immediately following the announcement of the jury's verdict. Neighborhood residents gathered at the First African Methodist Church to hear speakers decrying the injustice that blacks endure every day. The speakers noted that the criminal justice system had once again failed the black community, but they pleaded for nonviolence.

In the meantime, the situation was beginning to heat up outside the church. Angry crowds began gathering. Slowly but surely the gathering became more raucous. Seeing that the police were going to do little to contain

Looters ravage Los Angeles stores during the riots of May 1992 (left). Were these individuals criminal by nature, or were they average, law-abiding citizens overcome by the pressures and opportunities of the situation? Similar questions can be asked about the men who pulled Reginald Denny from his truck and beat him (right). What role did circumstances have in this incident, and what part was played by the individual characteristics of his attackers?

their reaction, many of the crowd turned to violence. Bands of rioters began to attack white motorists who happened to be passing through the intersection. They set fires, looted stores, and attacked innocent people.

Although many black-owned businesses were targets of the rioters, many more of the looted and burned shops belonged to Korean Americans. Tensions had been building for years between the African American and Korean American communities. Koreans owned many businesses in the South Central area but employed few local black residents. The black community's sense of outrage was exacerbated by an incident during the previous year in which a Korean grocer named Soon Ja Du shot a 15-year-old black girl, Latasha Harlins. Du accused her of stealing a bottle of orange juice priced at $1.79. Du was convicted of the crime but sentenced to only five years on probation—despite the fact that the store's security camera clearly showed that Du shot Harlins in the back.

As the day progressed, the level of violence escalated. A helicopter hovering above the streets captured on videotape one of the most savage images of the Los Angeles riot: White trucker Reginald Denny, who stopped for a red light, was forcibly dragged from the cab of his truck by at least five black men. Denny was smashed in the head with the fire extinguisher, kicked repeatedly in the head, and shot with a shotgun. His head was bashed in with a brick thrown by one of the men. Eventually, the men left Denny unconscious and bleeding in the street.

In the midst of all of this mayhem, the better side of human nature emerged. Four black residents who had seen Denny being beaten on television came to his aid. They managed to drive his truck to the hospital, where he underwent surgery for several hours. Their actions saved his life. In fact, on several occasions, black residents of South Central Los Angeles risked their lives to protect and rescue total strangers. These incidents were not much publicized by the news media.

The police, who were slow to respond, were largely powerless to stop the looting and violence. They concentrated their efforts on responding to life-threatening situations and protecting Los Angeles firefighters, one of whom had been shot by a sniper while fighting a fire. In fact, police stood by and watched as looters filled their arms with the booty taken from the vandalized stores.

The unrest continued over the next 2 days and then gradually subsided. Eventually, 4,500 federal troops were called in to restore peace. However, it was too late—the damage had already been done. When the smoke cleared, the devastation was staggering. Property damage, estimated in the hundreds of millions of dollars, was evident throughout the South Central area, as well as some other neighborhoods. Over 40 people had died.

This story of the Los Angeles riots raises many questions in our minds. We wonder, for example, how the initial, relatively small-scale acts of violence escalated into a full-scale riot. Would things have been different had the police responded to the early acts of violence and looting in force? We wonder also why Reginald Denny, who had nothing to do with the verdict in the King case, was so savagely beaten. And what of those who beat him? Were they "bad" people, or were they caught up in the rapidly deteriorating crowd situation? A jury appeared to think that Denny's tormentors should not be held totally responsible for their actions. The most serious crime for which the defendants were convicted in their October 1993 trial was "simple mayhem," a misdemeanor.

Other questions arise about the four black residents who came to the aid of Denny and saved his life. How did they overcome the violent situational forces at work? What characteristics did they possess that predisposed them to offer help in such a violent setting? Why were these individuals "responsible" for their actions whereas those who attacked Denny were not entirely responsible? Finally, we might ask what role the racial tensions and prejudice between the African American and Korean American communities played.

These are just some of the questions social psychologists ask when an incident like the Los Angeles riots occurs. To answer such questions, they apply a broad range of concepts, principles, and research findings. Let's consider now a model that can bring some order to these efforts.

A Model for Understanding Social Behavior

Social psychologists are interested in the forces that operate on individuals and cause them to engage in specific examples of social behavior. But social behavior is typically complex and has many contributing causes. Consequently, explaining social behavior is a difficult task. To simplify this task, we can assign the multiple causes of social behavior to one of two broad categories: the situation and the individual. According to a formula first proposed by Kurt Lewin (1936), one of the important early figures in social psychology, social behavior is a function of the interaction of the situation and the individual's characteristics, or

$$\text{Behavior} = f(\text{situation} \times \text{individual characteristics}).$$

Lewin's model of social behavior was inspired by his observation that the individual's perception of a situation is influenced by the tasks he or she has to accomplish. Lewin was a soldier in the German Army during World War I. He noticed that as he came nearer the battlefield, his view of the world changed. Where he once might have seen beautiful flowers and beckoning forests, he now saw boulders to hide behind and gullies from which he could ambush the enemy. Lewin came to believe that a person's perception of the world is influenced by what he or she has to do in that situation. He termed the combination of individual needs and situational factors the *psychological field* in which the individual lives (Pratkanis & Aronson, 1992).

According to this view, individuals with different needs and tasks would come to see the same event in dissimilar ways (Pratkanis & Aronson, 1992). Although Lewin looked at the individual's needs and tasks, he emphasized the importance of social context in producing the forces that control the individual's actions. Lewin was aware that we often fail to take situational factors into account when we try to explain why people behave as they do (Ross & Nisbett, 1991). For example, those who rioted in South Central Los Angeles viewed the situation differently than did those who helped victims of the riot. Their differing needs and interpretations of the situation led to vastly different social behaviors—aggression or altruism—despite the fact that many of each group probably agreed about the outcome of the King case.

Thus far we have seen that the situation and individual characteristics are central to the understanding of social behavior. How do social psychologists define "situation" and "individual characteristics"? Let's take a closer look.

The Situation   For social psychologists the "situation" comprises all influences on behavior that are external to the individual. A situational factor might be any aspect of the physical and/or social environment (the presence of other people, real or imagined). For example, many of the residents of South Central Los Angeles who looted may have done so because they saw others looting. Ordinarily, these individuals may have been law-abiding citizens who would never steal anything from a store. However, in the altered social environment, where looting became the thing to do, they took part. Once the social situation returned to normal, so did their behavior. In fact, many of those who looted later returned the items they had stolen.

Sometimes the situation works on us in more subtle ways. We may modify our behavior even if there is no pressure on us to do so. We may imagine or believe that we are expected to act a certain way in a certain situation, and these beliefs can be as powerful as the situation itself. For example, let's say that you are in a restaurant with a group of friends. You are trying to decide what to order. You are leaning toward the sautéed buffalo, but the stewed rabbit sounds good too. When the waiter comes to the table, you order last, intending to try the buffalo. However, each of your friends orders the rabbit. When your turn comes, you also order the rabbit. You modified your behavior based on your friends' actions, because you didn't want to appear different. You felt and responded to social pressure of your own making!

Situational or social determinants of behavior exist on several levels simultaneously. Sometimes the social environment leads to temporary changes in behavior, as was the case in the restaurant. Ordering the rabbit may be specific to that one situation; you may never order rabbit again. In other cases the social environment is a more pervasive influence and may lead to relatively permanent, enduring patterns of behaviors. The culture within which a person lives exerts a long-lasting influence over a wide range of behaviors. Culture influences the foods we like, how we relate to members of the other sex, the amount of personal space we require (the area immediately surrounding us that we claim and defend), what we plan and expect to accomplish in life, and a host of other behaviors.

Individual Characteristics Individual characteristics include sex, age, race or ethnicity, personality characteristics, attitudes, self-concept, ways of thinking, and so on. In short, individual characteristics consist of anything *internal* to the person that might influence behavior. Physical traits are individual characteristics that are relatively enduring and for the most part known to others. Personality characteristics also tend to be enduring, but they are not necessarily obvious to others. Personality is an area of growing interest in social psychology today (Larsen & Ketelaar, 1991). Other internal characteristics, like attitudes, opinions, self-concept, and so on, can change over time. People often have some choice about how much of these areas of themselves they reveal to others.

Let's consider the Los Angeles riots again. Several residents came to the aid of the victims of violence, despite the danger to themselves. These individuals were subjected to the same situational pressures as those who committed the violent acts and looting. However, they were able to withstand the social pressure to act violently or loot. Did some combination of personal traits and attitudes mix with the situation to produce this altruistic behavior? Since the situation was basically the same for all residents, we look to individual characteristics like personality traits to understand why some acted in violent ways and others helped the victims of violence.

Another important individual characteristic that is somewhat different from personality characteristics is the particular way each individual perceives and thinks about his or her social world. Social psychologists have two terms referring to these processes: *social cognition* and *social perception*. **Social cognition** refers to a general process we use to make sense out of social events, which may or may not include other people. For example, after reading about the Los Angeles riots, you may begin to interpret those *events*, attempting to determine a cause. **Social perception** is a more specific process involving how we perceive other *people* in our social world and form impressions of them. Social perception involves making inferences about the motives of other people and what causes their behavior. For

social cognition The process by which we make sense out of social situations and begin to interpret them.

social perception The process by which we make sense out of people's behavior; it involves inferring motives and attributing causes.

Although some individuals looted and destroyed property in the Los Angeles riots, afterward many others pitched in to clean up and repair the damage (top). Members of different ethnic and racial groups worked side by side in this effort. Group differences also were not a consideration for the four individuals who rescued Reginald Denny from his attackers and drove his truck to the hospital (bottom). What distinguishes the people who helped and rebuilt from those who hurt and destroyed?

example, seeing the image of Reginald Denny being beaten, you begin to form impressions of his attackers and infer from their behavior, mannerisms, and dress why they behaved the way they did.

Social cognition and social perception are central to our interpretation of situations. When we are exposed to a particular situation, how we respond depends on how we interpret that situation. Social cognition gives direction to our interpretation. The decisions we make based on our perception and cognition will influence our response. Every individual has a slightly different view of the world, since everyone has unique personal traits and a unique history of life experiences. This is because each of us actively constructs our own view of our social world, based on interpretations of social information. For example, if you watched the Los Angeles riots on TV, how did you perceive the residents? Before the riots you probably gave little or no thought to those who lived in that area. However, based on the images flashed before your eyes on the evening news you may have formed a negative impression of the residents. But ask yourself this: Would your impression have been different if the news media had pointed out that a very small proportion of residents of the area rioted?

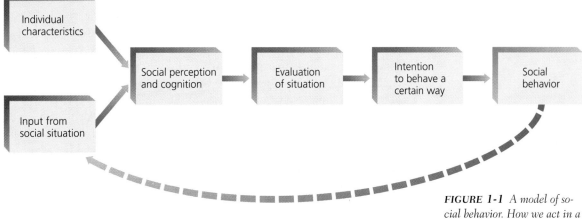

FIGURE 1-1 *A model of social behavior. How we act in a given situation—whether waiting in line at the supermarket, giving a speech, or responding to a disaster—is the product of a complex process. Our evaluation of the situation is shaped by an interplay of situational factors and individual characteristics, mediated by the processes of social perception and cognition. From our evaluation we form an intention to act a certain way, and from this intention our behavior usually (but not always) flows. Once we act, our behavior becomes a new factor in the situation, changing its dynamics both for ourselves and for others.*

What if the media had shown images of residents coming to the aid of victims rather than angry men standing over Reginald Denny, fists raised triumphantly in the air?

Expanding the Model Lewin's model tells us that both the social situation (physical setting, the presence of other people, real or imagined) and individual characteristics (physical traits, personality traits, attitudes and habitual ways of thinking, perceptual and cognitive processes, needs and tasks) influence social behavior. Lewin's model, however, does not specify how situational factors and individual characteristics fit together into a broad, general model of social behavior. We need to expand on Lewin's original model to gain a better understanding of the forces that shape social behavior. An expansion of Lewin's original model is shown in Figure 1-1.

As shown in this model, input from the social situation and individual characteristics do not directly influence social behavior. Instead, they both contribute to how we process information via mechanisms of social cognition and social perception. How that information is processed yields a particular evaluation of the situation. For example, one individual (individual characteristics) might interpret (social cognition) the images of the Los Angeles riots (input from the situation) in a negative way, concluding that the individuals who looted were all criminals (evaluation of the situation). Another person might focus on the social conditions in South Central Los Angeles and conclude that those who looted were driven to it by poverty and social injustice.

According to Figure 1-1, our evaluation of the social situation does not translate immediately into overt social behavior. Instead, based on our evaluation of the situation we form a behavioral intention. For example, one person might form an intention to buy a handgun to protect himself from those he perceives to be criminals. Another person may form an intention to help rebuild the riot-stricken area and work to eliminate poverty and social injustice.

It is important to realize that just because we form a behavioral intention, it does not mean we will act on that intention. Sometimes behavioral intentions are not acted upon. For example, the person who perceived the Los Angeles rioters as criminals might have been thinking about buying a gun for a long time. Interpreting the riots the way he did raised the chances that he will go out and buy one. However, just because he formed such an intention does not guarantee that he will act in the way intended. The individual may never go out and buy the gun, perhaps because he is afraid that a member of his own family might get hurt by it in the future.

This view of social behavior implies that social behavior is a dynamic process. Our monitoring of the social situation does not end with an evaluation of the situation, or the formation of an intention, or social behavior. Instead, we are constantly monitoring the social situation (our own behavior and that of others) and may modify our assessment of it on a moment-to-moment basis. Thus, we fine-tune our behavioral intentions up to the point that we engage in social behavior. So, even though the various processes underlying social behavior are presented in Figure 1-1 in a sequence of discrete boxes, they are really quite fluid and involve constant updating of our evaluation of the situation.

One final aspect of this model needs to be addressed. Notice that there is a dotted arrow going from social behavior to the social situation. In any social situation in which we are directly involved, our own behavior influences the social environment and probably will cause changes in the behavior of others. For example, imagine that you are talking to someone you have just met. Based on the first thing she says, you determine that she is not very friendly. Consequently, you become defensive (you fold your arms, lean away from her) and respond to her in a cold way. She picks up on your behavior and becomes colder herself. This cycle continues until one of you breaks off the conversation. How might this situation have played out if you had interpreted her initial behaviors as nervousness and responded to her in a positive way? You may have made a new friend. Thus, your own interpretations and behaviors had a profound effect on the situation. (These and other complexities of social interactions are discussed in detail in Chapters 3 and 4.)

Social Psychology and Related Fields

We have seen that social psychology is a field of study that seeks to understand and explain social behavior—how individuals think and act in relation to other people. Yet many other disciplines are also concerned with the thoughts and actions of human beings, both individually and in groups. In what ways does social psychology differ from its two parent disciplines, sociology and psychology? And how is it similar to and different from other fields of study, such as biology, anthropology, and history?

To see how these fields differ in their approaches, let's consider a single question: Why do groups of people, including nations, display hostility toward one another? Although social psychologists are interested in this social problem, they have no unique claim to it (nor to others). Biologists, psychologists, anthropologists, sociologists, historians, and others all have explanations for the never-ending cycle of human violence. Let's consider first those fields that look for the causes of violent behavior within the individual, and then we'll move on to fields that focus increasingly on factors in the environment.

Many *biologists* say the answer to the puzzle of human violence resides not in our social situations, organizations, or personalities, but rather in our genetic structure. Recently, for example, scientists have identified a tiny genetic defect that appears to predispose some men toward violence. Geneticists studied a large Dutch family with a history of violent and erratic behavior among many, although not all, of the males. They found that those males who were prone to violence had an enzyme deficiency due to a mutation of a gene carried by the X chromosome (Brunner, Nelon, Breakefield, Ropers, & van Oost, 1993). Since men have only one X chromosome, they were the only ones who manifested the defect. Women may be carriers of the deficiency, but they are protected from expressing it by their second X chromosome with its backup copy of the gene. Geneticists do not argue that genetic defects are the sole cause of violence, but they do say that these factors play a definite role in determining who is violent.

Another biologically oriented view of this question comes from *developmental psychologists* (who study the development of human beings across the lifespan). They suggest that human beings may have an innate fear of strangers. They point out that, beginning at about 4 or 5 months, infants begin to react with fear to novel or unusual stimuli such as the faces of strangers (Hebb & Thompson, 1968). Between 6 and 18 months, infants may experience intense "stranger anxiety." These psychologists, as well as some biologists, argue that fear of strangers may be part of our genetic heritage. Early humans who possessed this trait may have been more likely to survive than those who didn't, and they passed the trait down to us. On a group or societal level, this innate mistrust of strangers might be elaborated into hostility, aggression, or even warfare. Other psychologists, however, are not convinced that fear of the novel is inborn (Hebb & Thompson, 1968).

Along similar lines, *anthropologists* (who study the physical and cultural development of the human species) have documented that some tribal societies view strangers with suspicion and may even attempt to kill them. Some anthropologists argue that hostility to strangers may have benefited early human groups by helping them unite against threats from the outside.

Other scientists emphasize the psychological makeup of individuals as a way of explaining behavior. *Personality psychologists* suggest that aggressiveness (or any other behavioral trait) is a characteristic of the individual. The person carries the trait from situation to situation, expressing it in any number of different circumstances (Derlega, Winstead, & Jones, 1991). Personality psychologists would argue that some internal characteristic drove the rescuers of Reginald Denny to behave altruistically, just as some other personality trait affected the behavior of those who attacked Denny.

One researcher studied the aggressive behavior of adolescent boys in Sweden over 3 years (Olweus, 1984). He found that boys who were aggressive (started fights, were bullies) in the sixth grade were also physically aggressive in the ninth grade. Personality researchers take this as evidence that individual factors are an important determinant of aggression. Over the course of the 3 years, the boys had different teachers, were in different buildings, and had a variety of classmates. Yet their behavior remained consistently aggressive despite the change in their social situation (Derlega et al., 1991).

Hostility and aggressive behavior seem to be an integral part of human experience, but different disciplines seek to explain them in different ways. Social psychologists look at aggression as a function of the characteristics of the individual (such as ability to tolerate frustration) in combination with the characteristics of the situation (such as a violent environment).

Social psychologists study the individual in the social situation. They are concerned with determining what characteristics of a situation increase or decrease the potential for violence. In looking at the question of hostility between groups, social psychologists would focus on the forces both in individuals and in situations that lead to this outcome. The featured discussion "Investigating Intergroup Hostility: A Social Psychological Approach" describes how one social psychologist tackled the question of intergroup hostility, focusing on how he could experimentally manipulate a situation to produce different reactions in individuals.

Whereas psychology (including social psychology) focuses on the role of the individual, other fields look for the causes of behavior in more impersonal and general causes outside the individual. For example, *sociologists* are concerned primarily, although not exclusively, with larger groups and systems in society. A sociologist interested in violence might study the development of gangs. Interviews with gang members, observation of gang activity, or even participation in a gang as a participant-observer, if possible, would be potential methods of study.

Although sociology and social psychology are related, there are important differences between them. The sociologist asks what it is about the structure of society that promotes violence; the social psychologist, in contrast, looks at the individual's particular social situation as the potential cause of violence. The social psychologist is interested primarily in the behavior of individuals or of small groups, such as the jury. Sociology may be empirical in the sense that it attempts to gather quantitative information. A sociologist might compare rates of violent behavior in two societies and then try to determine how those societies differ. Social psychology is much more an experimental, laboratory-based science.

One social psychologist, the late Henri Tajfel, decided to approach the problem of intergroup hostility by gathering data through experiments on in-groups and out-groups. *In-groups* are the groups of which we are members; *out-groups* are groups of which we are not members. Tajfel hypothesized that hostility results from our categorization of individuals into in-group members and out-group members.

Tajfel thought that if he could find out how our positive feelings for our own in-groups got started, he would then be able to expand his work and discover how and why our negative feelings about out-groups evolved. Tajfel's initial idea was to try to find a social situation that was so basic, so minimal, so trivial, that an in-group feeling would not exist. Once he found this minimal group situation, he would, like a cook adding to a recipe, add social factors until he could find out what precisely caused the in-group to reject out-groups.

The subjects of Tajfel's experiments (1981, 1982) were teen-aged British school boys in the city of Bristol. In one study the boys were shown dots on a screen and asked to estimate the number of dots. They were told that no one could accurately estimate the number of dots; consequently, they would either overestimate or underestimate. After each boy made a guess, he was randomly assigned to the overestimators group or the underestimators group—a rather minimal basis for group membership.

In a second part of the experiment, the boys, now in an overestimator or underestimator group, had to give points worth small sums of money to any of the other boys (except themselves) in the room. Now, all a boy could know at this point, besides his own group membership, was whether the others were overestimators or underestimators. Each boy was sitting in his own place and was unseen by anyone else.

As it turned out, the boys followed a basic pattern of in-group favoritism. Underestimators gave more to underestimators, overestimators gave more to overestimators. When each boy was identified with his group label at the end of the experiment, his fellow "group members" cheered. This basic experiment was repeated a number of different ways. Tajfel and his colleagues never found that minimal situation in which some type of group social identity did not form.

If the only study that demonstrated in-group favoritism under minimal social circumstances was Tajfel's original experiment with Bristol school boys, we would hesitate to generalize his findings to the larger population. But Tajfel's experiment has been repeated many times with a variety of subjects in different countries; the results consistently indicate the power of the in-group favoritism phenomenon (Turner, 1987).

What Tajfel added to the debate about intergroup hostility is that there seems to be no basis too trivial for in-group favoritism. Whether this favoritism is due to our biology or our culture, it seems that we have a need to believe the groups we belong to, and the members of those groups, are more worthy than out-groups and their members. Although Tajfel's main focus was in-group favoritism, it is a short leap from in-group favoritism to out-group hostility. His findings suggest that hostility starts with this fundamental individual tendency to favor "our own."

---

*T*ajfel's approach to the issue of intergroup conflict was to look at the dynamics of in-groups and out-groups. What role do you think in-group/out-group thinking played in the Los Angeles riots? What role does it play in hostilities between Arabs and Israelis? In your own life, what groups do you identify as in-groups? What are your feelings toward people you identify as members of out-groups?

Historians take an even broader view of intergroup hostility than sociologists. They are primarily concerned with the interplay of large forces such as economic, political, and technological trends. Historians have shown, for example, that one nation can express power against other nations only if it has sufficient economic resources to sustain armed forces and if it has developed an adequate technological base to support them (Kennedy, 1987; O'Connell, 1989). One historian documented the importance of a single technological advance—the invention of stirrups—in accelerating violence between groups in the early Middle Ages (McNeill, 1982). Before stirrups were invented, knights on horseback were not very effective fighters. But once they were able to steady themselves in the saddle, they became capable of delivering a powerful blow with a lance in full gallop. The use of stirrups quickly spread throughout Europe and led to the rise of cavalry as an instrument of military power.

History and sociology focus on how social forces and social organization influence human behavior. These fields tend to take a "top down" perspective; the major unit of analysis is the group or the institution, whether a nation, a corporation, or a neighborhood organization. Psychology, with its emphasis on individual behavior and the individual's point of view, offers a "bottom up" approach. Social psychology offers a distinct perspective on social behavior. Social psychologists look at how social forces affect the individual's thinking and behavior. Although the field takes a "bottom up" perspective, focusing on the individual as the unit of analysis, behavior is always examined in social situations. Social psychology therefore tries to take into account individual factors, such as personality, as well as social and historical forces that have shaped human behavior.

As indicated earlier, social psychology is a science. The use of scientific methods is the primary contribution of social psychology to the understanding of complex, uncertain social behaviors like intergroup hostility. The scientific dimension of the field is our topic in the next section.

RESEARCH IN SOCIAL PSYCHOLOGY

In January 1992, a celebrity basketball game was held in New York City. There was open seating at a college basketball arena that held a little over 4,000 people. Therefore, the first people in the arena would get the best seats. As the crowd outside the arena grew into the thousands, anticipation built. People began pushing and shoving to get closer to the doors. As the crowd pressed forward toward the arena, the situation got out of control. In the crush that followed, nine people were killed.

If you read about this event in the newspaper, you would probably wonder how it could happen and try to come up with an explanation. You might ask yourself, Could it be that there were thousands of highly aggressive, mean-spirited individuals waiting to see the game? That would be hard to believe. Well then, could the fact that the event occurred in New York City explain it? This also seems unlikely, because similar things have happened in smaller cities with more benign reputations, like Cincinnati, Ohio.

Spectators are left stunned and bewildered in the aftermath of a violent melee among soccer fans. When people become immersed in a crowd, they can lose their sense of personal identity and act in ways they would never act as individuals.

Or could it be that the presence of celebrities, the limited number of good seats, and the excitement of the event somehow influenced the crowd's behavior, causing them to act in ways they wouldn't act as individuals? This seems more likely, but is it true?

When we devise explanations for events like these, based on our prior knowledge and experiences, our attitudes and biases, and the limited information the newspaper provides, we don't know if they're accurate or not. Such *commonsense explanations*—simplistic explanations for social behavior that are based on what we *believe* to be true of the world (Bordens & Abbott, 1991)—serve us well in our day-to-day life, providing easy ways to explain complex events. People would be hopelessly bogged down in trying to understand events if they didn't devise these explanations and move on to the next concern in their lives. Unfortunately, commonsense explanations are usually inadequate; that is, there is no evidence or proof that they pinpoint the real causes of events.

The aim of social psychology is to provide valid, reliable explanations for events such as the one in New York City. Rather than relying on conjecture, rumor, and simplistic reasoning, social psychologists approach the problem of explaining complex social behavior in a systematic, scientific way. They develop explanations for phenomena by applying the **scientific method,** which typically involves four steps:

1. Identifying a phenomenon to study
2. Developing a testable research *hypothesis* (a tentative statement about the relationship between variables)
3. Designing a research study
4. Carrying out the research study

scientific method A method for developing explanations of behavior that involves four steps: (1) identifying a phenomenon to study, (2) developing a testable tentative statement about the relationship between variables, (3) designing a research study, and (4) carrying out the research study.

Only after applying this method to a problem and conducting careful research will a social psychologist be satisfied with an explanation.

Throughout this book we refer to and describe research that social psychologists have conducted to test their ideas, to gain information about events, and to discover the causes of social behavior. We turn now to some of the basic principles of research, including the major research methods, the role of theory in research, the settings for social psychological research, and the importance of ethical conduct in research involving human subjects.

Research Methods

The principal aim of the science of social psychology is to uncover scientific explanations for social behavior. A *scientific explanation* is an interpretation of the causes of social behavior that is based on objective observation and logic and is subject to empirical test (Bordens & Abbott, 1991). To this end, social psychologists use a wide variety of techniques to study social behavior. Generally, they favor two research strategies in their quest for scientific knowledge: experimental research and correlational research. Let's consider the characteristics of each of these methods, along with their advantages and disadvantages.

Experimental Research The goal of research in social psychology is to understand the causes of social behavior. The researcher usually has an idea he or she wants to test about how a particular factor affects an event or a behavior—that is, whether a particular factor *causes* a particular behavior. To establish a *causal relationship* between factors, researchers have to use the research method known as the *experiment*. Because **experimental research** is the only kind of study that can establish causality, it is the method most social psychologists prefer.

An experiment has two essential characteristics. The first is that a variable is manipulated—changed in value—so that one group receives more of it and another group receives less of it. For example, if you were interested in the effects of the drug epinephrine on aggression, you could give one group of subjects a 5-mg injection and another group a 15-mg injection. The variable here is the amount of the drug given to subjects in the different groups. This variable that the researcher manipulates or varies to see if it causes a change in the subject's behavior is called the **independent variable.** The researcher then observes behavior (for example, the number of aggressive acts by members of both groups) and records data about this second variable to see if it changes when the first one does. This second variable is called the **dependent variable;** it is the measure the researcher assesses to determine the influence of the independent variable on the subject's behavior.

The essence of experimental research is to manipulate an independent variable (or two or even more independent variables) and look for related changes in the value of the dependent variable. To see how independent and dependent variables work, let's consider a hypothetical experiment to investigate a situation like the one that occurred in New York City. To design this experiment, you might think about the various factors that

experimental research Research that involves changing the value of a variable suspected of influencing behavior and seeing whether and how much that change affects behavior. Results allow researchers to discover causal relationships among variables.

independent variable The variable the researcher manipulates or varies to see if it causes a change in the subject's behavior.

dependent variable The variable the researcher measures to determine the influence of the independent variable on the subject's behavior.

could, in your opinion, cause irrational crowd behavior. You might think about open seating—in which seats are available on a first-come, first-served basis—as opposed to reserved seating, in which seat numbers are printed on tickets. Your hypothesis might be that open seating causes, or contributes to, irrational crowd behavior in a situation like this. To test this hypothesis, you might design an experiment in which some people are in an open-seating situation and others are not. The independent variable in this experiment—the factor you are manipulating—would be the nature of the seating conditions. The dependent variable would be how your subjects behave under the two different conditions. As you change the independent variable, you observe whether and how the dependent variable changes.

A second essential characteristic of an experiment is that there are at least two groups involved who are comparable at the outset of the experiment. In the simplest type of experiment, one group of subjects receives a treatment (for example, they are told there is open seating). The subjects who receive the experimental treatment comprise the **experimental group.** To know for sure that an experimental treatment (the independent variable) is causing a particular effect, you have to compare the behavior of subjects in the experimental group with the behavior of subjects who do not receive the treatment (they are told nothing about seating arrangements). The subjects who do *not* receive the experimental treatment comprise the **control group.** The researcher then compares the behavior of the subjects in the experimental and control groups. In essence, the control group provides a *baseline* of behavior in the absence of the treatment against which the behavior of the treated subjects is compared.

In the real world of research, the situation is usually more complicated than a simple experimental group/control group experiment. Often there are more than two different levels of the independent variable. For example, in the epinephrine experiment, you might administer 5 mg, 10 mg, and 15 mg to different groups. In other cases, the researcher might manipulate the quality of the independent variable. For example, in an experiment on the effects of the race of a victim on helping behavior, the independent variable would be the race of the person in need (black or white)—a qualitative difference.

In order to establish a clear cause-and-effect relationship between the independent and dependent variables in an experiment, the subjects in the groups must have the same characteristics at the outset of the experiment. For example, in the experiment on race and helping, you would not want all African American subjects in one group and all white subjects in the other. If this were the case, you would not know if it was your independent variable (the race of the victim) that caused any observed differences across groups or the fact that the racial composition of the groups differed.

The best way to ensure that two or more groups will be comparable at the outset of an experiment is **random assignment** of individuals to groups, which means that each subject has an equal chance of being assigned to the experimental or control group. Researchers can then be fairly certain that subjects with similar characteristics or backgrounds are distributed among the groups. In the Tajfel study, for example (highlighted earlier in this chapter), subjects were assigned randomly to the overestimators

experimental group The subjects who receive the experimental treatment.

control group The subjects who do *not* receive the experimental treatment.

random assignment The method of assigning subjects to groups in an experiment so that each subject has an equal chance of being assigned to the experimental or control group.

group or the underestimators group. This ensured that subjects who might be naturally inclined to be more or less competitive would not be overrepresented in one or the other group. If the two or more groups in an experiment are comparable at the outset, the experiment is said to have *internal validity*, and it can legitimately demonstrate a causal relationship.

Researchers are also concerned about another kind of validity, known as *external validity*, or generalizability. When researchers study how experimental treatments affect groups of subjects, they want to be able to generalize their results to larger populations. To do so, they have to be reasonably sure that the subjects in their experiments are representative (typical) of the population to which they wish to generalize their results. For example, if the subjects of a study were all male science majors at a small religious college, the researchers could not legitimately generalize the results to females or mixed populations, to younger or older people, or to music majors. If the researchers have gotten a *representative sample* of their population of interest, then they can legitimately generalize the results to that population, and the study is said to have external validity.

Most of the research studies described in this book are experimental studies. When evaluating these experiments, ask yourself these questions:

- What was the independent variable, and how was it manipulated?
- What were the experimental and control groups?
- What was the dependent variable?
- What was found? That is, what changes in the dependent variable were observed as a function of manipulation of the independent variable?
- What was the nature of the sample used? Was the sample representative of the general population, or was it limited with respect to demographics such as age, gender, culture, or some other set of characteristics?
- Based on the methods and sample used, does the experiment have internal and external validity?

Correlational Research   Although most research in social psychology is experimental, some research is correlational. In **correlational research,** researchers do not manipulate an independent variable. Instead, they measure two or more variables and look for a relationship between them. If changes in one variable are associated with changes in another, the two variables are said to be correlated. When the values of two variables change in the same direction, increasing or decreasing in value, there is a **positive correlation** between them. For example, if you find that crime increases along with increases in temperature, a positive correlation exists. When the values change in opposite directions, one increasing and the other decreasing, there is a **negative correlation** between the variables. For example, if you find that less help is given as the number of bystanders to an emergency increases, a negative correlation exists. When one variable does not change systematically with the other, they are uncorrelated.

Even if correlations are found, however, a causal relationship cannot be inferred. For example, height and weight are correlated with each

correlational research Research in which two or more variables are measured to see if there is a relationship between them.

positive correlation The relationship between two variables when their values change in the same direction, increasing or decreasing.

negative correlation The relationship between two variables when their values change in opposite directions, one increasing and the other decreasing.

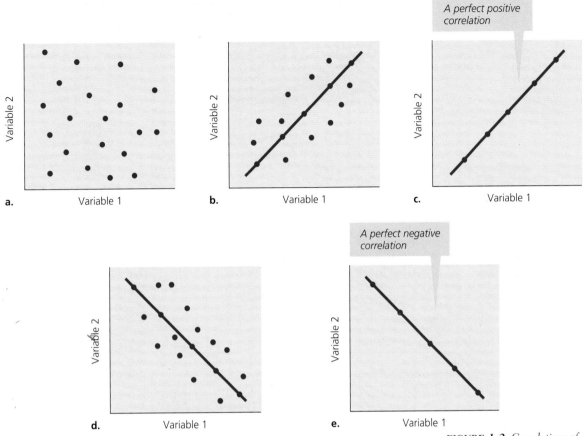

a.   Variable 1

b.   Variable 1

c.   Variable 1

A perfect positive correlation

d.   Variable 1

e.   Variable 1

A perfect negative correlation

FIGURE 1-2 *Correlations of varying strengths and directions. When one variable does not change systematically with changes in another, the two are uncorrelated (a). The tendency to smoke cigarettes, for example, is uncorrelated with height. When one variable changes systematically in the same direction as another variable—as in the case of cigarette smoking and the likelihood of developing lung cancer—they are positively correlated (b and c). When one variable changes systematically in the opposite direction from another variable—as in the case of maternal cigarette smoking and infant birth weight—they are negatively correlated (d and e).*

other—the greater one is, the greater the other tends to be—but increases in one do not *cause* increases in the other. Changes in both are caused by other factors, such as growth hormone and diet. Similarly, aggressive behavior in children is correlated with violent TV viewing, but it isn't known which factor causes the other or if a third factor causes both. Correlational research indicates whether changes in one variable are related to changes in another, but it does not indicate *why* the changes are related. Cause and effect can be demonstrated only by experiments.

In correlational studies, researchers are interested in both the direction of the relationship between the variables (whether it's positive or negative) and the degree, or strength, of the relationship. They measure these two factors with a special statistical test known as the *correlation coefficient* (symbolized as *r*). The size of the correlation coefficient, which can range from −1 through 0 to +1, shows the degree of the relationship. A value of *r* that approaches −1 or +1 indicates a stronger relationship than a value closer to 0.

In Figure 1-2, the five graphs illustrate correlations of varying strengths and directions. Figure 1-2a shows a 0 correlation. Points are scattered at random within the graph. Figures 1-2b and c show positive correlations of different strengths. As the correlation gets stronger, the points start

How do you feel when you pass a homeless person on the street who asks you for spare change? Do you feel sympathy, pity, anger, contempt, embarrassment, shame? If you give the person the change, why do you think you do? Is it because you truly feel for the person asking for help? Or is it because you're afraid if you don't, you'll feel like a stingy, uncaring person for the rest of the day? These questions are all reasonable questions concerning the relationship between our feelings and our likelihood of giving help. What do we know about this relationship?

A correlational study conducted by Nancy Eisenberg and her colleagues (1989) addressed the relationship between subjects' feelings of sympathy and personal distress and their likelihood of helping. Each subject was shown a film depicting a mother talking about an accident in which her children were severely injured and

WHAT MOTIVATES US TO HELP: SYMPATHY OR GUILT?

were having problems adjusting to their injuries. The subjects were led to believe that they were watching the film as part of a study for a public television station interested in reactions to actual, unaired programs. As part of the study, subjects were told that their physiological responses to the film would be measured. Consequently, they were hooked up to a heart rate monitor. The subjects' facial expressions were also videotaped and later evaluated for the expression of several emotions (sympathy, sadness, personal distress, happiness). Independent raters evaluated each of the emotional expressions on scales ranging from 0 (no sign of the given emotion) to 5 (exceptionally strong display).

After viewing this film, each subject was asked to fill out a questionnaire dealing with how he or she felt about the film and the individuals portrayed in the film. The experimenter told the subject that a page of the questionnaire was missing and then left to look for it. The experimenter returned carrying an envelope from the principal investigator of the study. The envelope was addressed to "the student scheduled to watch tape #24" (each subject had been led to believe that he or she would be the only one to view that particular film). Inside the envelope was a request for the subject to help the person portrayed in the film. Subjects indicated their willingness to help by checking off the number of hours they would be willing to donate to the family described in the film. They then completed the remainder of the questionnaire.

Based on this brief summary, you can see that four variables

to line up with each other (Figure 1-2b). In a perfect positive correlation $(r = +1)$, all the points line up along a straight line (Figure 1-2c). Notice that in a positive correlation, the points line up along a line that slopes in an upward direction, beginning at the lower left of the graph and ending at the upper right.

In a negative correlation (shown in Figures 1-2d and e), the same rules concerning strength apply that held for the positive correlation. The main difference is that in a negative correlation, the line representing the points slopes in a downward direction from the upper left to the lower right of the graph. Figure 1-2e shows a perfect negative correlation (-1).

To get a better idea of what positive and negative correlations mean, consider the study described in the featured discussion "What Motivates Us to Help: Sympathy or Guilt?" Here, researchers measured four variables and looked for relationships among them. They were not trying to determine what caused certain kinds of behavior; they were simply interested in associations.

Although correlational research does not demonstrate causal relationships, it does play an important role in science. Correlational research is

were measured: heart rate, facial expressions, subjects' self-reports of how they felt about the film, and subjects' willingness to help the victims depicted in the film. However, notice that Eisenberg and her colleagues did not manipulate any of the variables. Therefore, there were no independent variables.

Eisenberg's findings are summarized in the accompanying table. As you can see, most of the correlations are positive, though modest in size. The correlation between willingness to help and verbal self-reports of sympathy, for example, is .25; the correlation between willingness to help and self-reports of personal distress is .23. In other words, the more sympathetic the subjects reported feeling, the more likely they were to help. Notice that the correlations between willingness to help and happy facial expressions during the film and while reading the request for help are negative

(−.06 and −.15). In other words, the happier the subjects appeared while watching the film and while reading the request for help, the less likely they were to help.

CORRELATIONS BETWEEN FACIAL AND VERBAL INDEXES AND WILLINGNESS TO HELP

Index	r
Verbal	
Sympathy	.25
Personal distress	.23
Facial (during film)	
Sympathy	.20
Sadness	.29
Personal distress	.16
Happiness	−.06
Facial (during letter)	
Sympathy	.01
Sadness	.00
Personal distress	.07
Happiness	−.15

From Eisenberg, Fabes, Miller, Fultz, Shell, Mathy, and Reno, 1989.

This pattern of results suggests that feelings and expressions of sympathy and sadness for a victim are positively correlated with offers of help. That is, the greater the sympathy expressed by the subject, the more likely the subject was to offer help. These findings suggest that we give money to the homeless because we feel sympathy for their predicament, not just because we're afraid it might ruin our day if we don't.

───────────

Correlational studies show relationships among variables but don't establish causality. In what ways does Eisenberg's study differ from an experimental study? How could people's motives for helping be studied experimentally? What advantages and disadvantages do you see in the correlational versus the experimental approach to this issue?

used in situations where it is not possible to manipulate variables. Any study of individual characteristics (age, sex, race, and so on) is correlational. After all, you cannot manipulate someone's age or sex. Correlational research is also used when it would be unethical to manipulate variables. For example, if you were interested in how alcohol consumption affects the human fetus, it would not be ethical to expose pregnant women to various dosages of alcohol and see what happens. Instead, you could *measure* alcohol consumption and the rate of birth defects and look for a correlation between those two variables. Finally, correlational research is useful when you want to study variables as they occur naturally in the real world.

Settings for Social Psychological Research

Social psychological research is done in one of two settings: the laboratory or the field. *Laboratory research* is conducted in a controlled environment the researcher creates. Subjects come into this artificial environment to participate in the research. *Field research* is conducted in the subject's natural environment. The researcher goes to the subjects, in effect taking the

Jane Goodall's early research with chimpanzees involved unobtrusive observations and no direct contact. This type of research method is known as a field study.

study on the road. Observations are made in the subject's natural environment; sometimes independent variables are even manipulated in this environment.

Laboratory Research   Most research in social psychology is conducted in the laboratory. This allows the researcher to exercise tight control over extraneous (unwanted) variables that might affect results. For example, the researcher can maintain constant lighting, temperature, humidity, and noise level within a laboratory environment. This tight control over the environment and over extraneous variables allows the researcher to be reasonably confident that the experiment has internal validity—that is, that any variation observed in the dependent variable was caused by manipulation of the independent variable. However, that tight control also has a cost: The researcher loses some ability to apply the results beyond the tightly controlled laboratory setting (external validity). Research conducted in highly controlled laboratories may not generalize very well to real-life social behavior, or even to other laboratory studies.

Field Research   Field research comes in three varieties: the field study, the field survey, and the field experiment. In a **field study,** the researcher makes *unobtrusive observations* of the subjects without making direct contact or interfering in any way. The researcher simply watches from afar. In its pure form, the subjects should be unaware that they are being observed, because the very act of being observed tends to change the subjects' behavior. The researcher avoids contaminating the research situation by introducing any changes in the subjects' natural environment.

Jane Goodall's original research on chimpanzee behavior was a field study. Goodall investigated social behavior among chimpanzees by observing groups of chimps from a distance, initially not interacting with them. However, as Goodall became more "accepted" by the chimps, she began to

field study A type of field research in which the researcher makes unobtrusive observations of the subjects without making direct contact or interfering in any way.

FIGURE 1-3 *In a field experiment, the researcher manipulates an independent variable and observes changes in the dependent variable, all in a naturally occurring situation. Here, the race of a person who faints on a subway train is the independent variable. The number of people who help and the alacrity with which they do so are the dependent variables.*

interact with them, even to the point of feeding them. Can we be sure that Goodall's later observations are characteristic of chimp behavior in the wild? Probably not, since she altered the chimps' environment by interacting with them.

In the **field survey,** the researcher directly approaches subjects and asks them questions. For example, he or she might stop people in a shopping mall and collect information on which brand of car they plan to buy next. The ubiquitous political polls we see during election years are examples of field surveys.

Field studies and surveys allow us to describe and catalogue behavior. Political polls, for example, may help us discover which candidate is in the lead, whether a proposition is likely to pass, or how voters feel about important campaign issues. However, they cannot tell us what *causes* the differences observed among voters, since we would need to conduct an experiment to study causes. Fortunately, we *can* conduct experiments in the field.

The **field experiment** is probably the most noteworthy and useful field technique for social psychologists. In a field experiment the researcher manipulates independent variables and collects measures of the dependent variables (the subject's behavior). In this sense a field experiment is like a laboratory experiment. The main difference is that in the field experiment, the researcher manipulates independent variables under naturally occurring conditions. The principal advantage of the field experiment is that it has greater external validity—that is, the results can be generalized beyond the study more legitimately than can the results of a laboratory experiment.

As an example, let's say you are interested in seeing whether the race of a person needing help influences potential helpers (Figure 1-3). You might consider a field experiment in which you had someone, a *confederate* of yours (a confederate is someone working for the experimenter), pretend to faint on a subway train. In the experiment you use two different confed-

field survey A type of field research in which the researcher directly approaches subjects and asks them questions.

field experiment A type of field research in which the researcher manipulates independent variables and collects measures of the dependent variables (the subject's behavior) in the subject's natural environment rather than in a laboratory.

erates, one a black male, the other a white male. The two are as alike as they can be (in age, dress, and so on) except, of course, for skin color. You then observe how many people help each man and how quickly they do so. Such an experiment would be very realistic and have a high degree of external validity. Consequently, the results would have broad generalizability.

A disadvantage of the field experiment is that the researcher cannot control extraneous variables as effectively as in the laboratory. Thus, internal validity may be compromised. In the subway experiment, for example, you have no control over who the subjects are or which experimental condition (white or black confederate) they will walk into. Consequently, the internal validity of your experiment—the legitimacy of the causal relationship you discover—may suffer. The experiment also poses some ethical problems, one of which is that the people who purchased a ride on the subway did not voluntarily agree to participate in an experiment. We discuss the ethics of research in a later section of this chapter.

The Role of Theory in Social Psychological Research

On many occasions throughout this book we refer to social psychological theories. A **theory** is a set of interrelated statements or propositions about the causes of a particular phenomenon. Theories help social psychologists organize research results, make predictions about how certain variables influence social behavior, and give direction to future research. In these ways, social psychological theories play an important role in helping us understand complex social behaviors.

There are a few important points to keep in mind as you read about these theories. First, a theory is not the final word on the causes of a social behavior. Theories are developed, revised, and sometimes abandoned according to how well they fit with research results. Rather than tell us how things are in an absolute sense, theories help us understand social behavior by providing a particular perspective. Consider attribution theories—theories about how people decide what caused others (and themselves) to act certain ways in certain situations. Attribution theories do not tell us exactly how people assign or attribute causality. Instead, they suggest rules and make predictions about how people make such inferences in a variety of circumstances. These predictions are then tested with research.

The second important point about social psychological theories is that, often, more than one theory can apply to a particular social behavior. In Chapter 4, for example, we discuss several different attribution theories. Each theory helps provide a piece of the puzzle of social behavior. However, no single theory may be able to account for all aspects of a social behavior. One theory helps us understand how we infer the internal motivations of another individual; a second theory examines how we make sense of the social situation in which that individual's behavior took place.

Theory and the Research Process Theories in social psychology are usually tested by research, and much research is guided by theory. Research de-

theory A set of interrelated statements or propositions about the causes of a particular phenomenon that help organize research results, make predictions about how certain variables influence social behavior, and give direction to future research.

In basic research, scientists design and conduct a study to test a theory, model, or hypothesis. Here, an experimenter observes children in a laboratory setting to gain data that will support or undermine a particular theory (top). Knowledge derived from basic research can be applied to countless real-world situations, such as this decision-making group (bottom), which can be more productive if the leader has some knowledge of group dynamics.

signed to test a particular theory or model is referred to as *basic research*. In contrast, research designed to address a real-world problem is called *applied research*. The distinction between these two categories is not rigid, however. The results of basic research can often be applied to real-world problems, and the results of applied research may affect the validity of a theory.

For example, research on how stress affects memory may be primarily basic research, but the findings of this research apply to a real-world problem: the ability of an eyewitness to recall a violent crime accurately. Similarly, research on how jurors process evidence in complex trials (e.g., Horowitz & Bordens, 1990) has implications for predictions made by various theories of how people think and make decisions in a variety of situations. Both types of research have their place in social psychology.

Theory and Application Application of basic theoretical ideas may take many forms. Consider, for example, the idea that it is healthy for individuals to confront and deal directly with psychological traumas from the past. Although various clinical theories have made this assumption, evidence in support of it was sparse.

In one study, social psychologist Jamie Pennebaker (1989) measured the effects of disclosure on mind and body. The research showed that when the subjects confronted past traumas, either by writing or by talking about them, their immunological functioning improved and their skin conductance rates were lowered. This latter measure reflects a reduction in autonomic nervous system activity, indicating a lessening of psychological tension. In other words, people were "letting go" as they fully revealed their feelings about these past traumas. Those who had trouble revealing important thoughts about the event—who could not "let go" of the trauma—showed heightened skin conductance rates. Pennebaker's work shows that the act of confiding in someone protects the body from the internal stress caused by repressing these unvoiced traumas. Here is an example of basic research that has clear applications for real-life situations.

What Do We Learn from Research in Social Psychology?

Two criticisms are commonly made of social psychological research. One is that social psychologists study what we already know, the "intuitively obvious." The other is that since exceptions to research results can nearly always be found, many results must be wrong. Let's consider the merits of each of these points.

Do Social Psychologists Study the Obvious? William McGuire, a prominent social psychologist, once suggested that social psychologists may appear to study "bubba psychology"—things we learned on our grandmother's knee. That is, social psychologists study what is already obvious and predictable based on common sense. Although it may seem this way, it is not the case. The results of research seem obvious only when you already know what they are. This is called the **hindsight bias,** or the "I-knew-it-all-along" phenomenon (Slovic & Fischoff, 1977; Wood, 1978). With the benefit of hindsight, everything looks obvious. For example, after the Los Angeles riots it seemed obvious to all that the police should have responded more quickly and in greater force when the riot first began. However, the Los Angeles police were concerned that a show of force would cause even more violence. Before the event, it is not as easy to predict what will happen as it would seem in hindsight.

Although the results of some research may seem obvious, studies show that when individuals are given descriptions of research without results, they can predict the outcome of the research no better than chance (Slovic & Fischoff, 1977). In other words, the results were not so obvious when they were not already known!

hindsight bias The tendency to regard the results of research to be obvious only *after* one has found out what the results are.

TABLE 1-1

RESULTS FROM A HYPOTHETICAL STUDY OF HELPING BEHAVIOR

Subject Number	No Bystanders	Three Bystanders
1	Help	No help
2	Help	No help
3	No help	No help
4	Help	Help
5	No help	Help
6	No help	No help
7	Help	No help
8	Help	No help
9	Help	No help
10	Help	No help

Do Exceptions Mean Research Results Are Wrong?   When the findings of social psychological research are described, someone often points to a case that is an exception to the finding. Suppose a particular study shows that a person is less likely to get help when there are several bystanders present than when there is only one. You probably can think of a situation in which you were helped with many bystanders around. Does this mean that the research is wrong or that it doesn't apply to you?

To answer this question you must remember that in a social psychological experiment, *groups* of subjects are exposed to various levels of the independent variable. In an experiment on the relationship between the number of bystanders and the likelihood of receiving help, for example, one group of subjects is given an opportunity to help a person in need with no other bystanders present. A second group of subjects gets the same opportunity but with three bystanders present. Let's say that our results in this hypothetical experiment look like those shown in Table 1-1. Seven out of ten subjects in the no-bystander condition helped (70%), whereas only two out of ten helped in the three-bystander condition (20%). Thus, we would conclude that you are more likely to get help when there are no other bystanders present than if there are three bystanders.

Notice, however, that we do not say that you will *never* receive help when three bystanders are present. In fact, two subjects helped in that condition. Nor do we say that you will *always* receive help when no other bystanders are present. Three of the ten subjects did not help in that condition.

The moral to the story here is that the results of experiments in social psychology represent differences between *groups of subjects,* not differences between specific individuals. Based on the results of social psychological research, we can say that "on the average," groups differ. Within those groups there are nearly always subjects who do not behave as most of the subjects behaved. We can acknowledge that exceptions to research findings usually exist, but this does not mean that the results reported are wrong.

Ethics and Social Psychological Research

Unlike research in chemistry and physics, which does not involve living organisms, research in social psychology uses living organisms, both animal and human. Because social psychology studies living organisms, researchers must consider research ethics. They have to concern themselves with the treatment of their research participants and with the potential long-range effects of the research on the participants' well-being. In every study conducted in social psychology, researchers must place the welfare of the research participants among their top priorities.

Questions about ethics have been raised about some of the most famous research ever done in social psychology. For example, you may be familiar with the experiments on obedience conducted by Stanley Milgram (1963; described in detail in Chapter 9). In these experiments, subjects were asked to administer painful electric shocks to an individual who was

ticipation is a course requirement or an opportunity for extra course credit, an equitable alternative must be offered to fulfill the requirement or obtain the credit. If a person is legally incapable of giving informed consent, the psychologist must still provide an appropriate explanation of the research, obtain the participant's consent, and obtain permission from a legally authorized individual (if the latter is allowed by law).

9. Deception is not permitted in research unless the psychologist can demonstrate that it is justified by the scientific, educational, or applied value of the research and that alternatives to deception are not feasible. Deception is never allowed when it involves information that might affect a participant's willingness to participate (e.g., potential risks, adverse effects, discomfort, physical or emotional

harm). Any deception used must be explained to the participant as early as possible, preferably at the end of participation, but no later than the end of the research.

10. The psychologist must not interfere with the participant or the research environment from which data are collected unless it is warranted by appropriate research design and is consistent with the psychologist's role as a researcher.

11. The psychologist has an obligation to provide participants with a prompt opportunity to receive information about the nature, results, and conclusions of research in which they have participated. The psychologist also has an obligation to correct any misconceptions participants may have about the research. The psychologist must take reasonable measures to honor all commitments made to research participants.

One of the results of some experiments in social psychology is that subjects discover they would behave "just like everybody else," given the right conditions. Self-revelations like this can be profoundly disturbing, especially when the subject deplores the behavior in others. Do you think it's unethical to involve people in experiments in which they might make unpleasant discoveries about themselves? How do you think you would react in such a situation?

Adapted from "Ethical Principles of Psychologists and Code of Conduct," Sections 5 and 6, 1992, *American Psychologist, 47,* pp. 1597–1611.

doing poorly on a learning task. Although no shocks were actually delivered, subjects believed they were inflicting intense pain on an increasingly unwilling victim. Following the experiment, subjects reported experiencing guilt and lowered self-esteem as well as anger toward the researchers. The question raised by this and other experiments with human subjects is how far researchers can and should go to gain knowledge.

Research conducted by social psychologists is governed by an ethical code of conduct developed by the American Psychological Association (APA) (1992). The main principles of the APA code are summarized in the featured coverage titled "Ethical Principles of Psychologists and Code of Conduct for Research with Human Participants." Notice that the code mandates that participation in psychological research be voluntary. This means that subjects cannot be compelled to participate in research. Researchers must also obtain **informed consent** from the participants, which means that they must inform the subjects of the nature of the study,

informed consent The ethical research principle stating that subjects must be fully informed about the nature of the experiment in which they are participating.

the requirements for participation, and any risks or benefits associated with participating in the study. Subjects must also be told they have the right to decline or withdraw from participation with no penalty.

Additionally, the APA code restricts the use of deception in research. Deception occurs when researchers tell their subjects they are studying one thing but are actually studying another. Deception can be used only if no other viable alternative exists. When researchers use deception, they must tell subjects about the deception (and the reasons for it) as soon as possible after participation.

Following ethical codes of conduct protects subjects from harm. In this sense, ethical codes help the research process. However, sometimes ethical research practice conflicts with the requirements of science. For example, in a field experiment on helping, it may not be possible (or desirable) to obtain consent from subjects *before* they participate in the study. When such conflicts occur, the researcher must weigh the potential risks to the subjects against the benefits to be gained.

A LOOK AHEAD

Theory and research in social psychology tend to fall into four major (but interrelated) areas. The remaining chapters of this book are divided into four parts reflecting these major divisions: social cognition (Part One), social influence (Part Two), social relations (Part Three), and applied social psychology (Part Four). For a better idea of what these four areas include, let's consider each one briefly.

Social Cognition   As mentioned earlier, social cognition (how we perceive and think about social situations) is an important mediator of social behavior. Thus, important questions for social psychologists are how and why social cognition processes influence how we think and behave. Part One of this book addresses various topics in these areas: how we build and manage a sense of self in the social world (Chapter 2), the processes by which we construct social reality (Chapter 3), the processes involved in determining other people's intentions and motives (Chapter 4), how we develop and maintain stereotypes and prejudices (Chapter 5), and how we come to hold the attitudes with which we approach the world (Chapter 6).

Social Influence   While researchers in social perception and cognition focus on how internal processes affect behavior, other social psychologists are more interested in how situational factors affect behavior. For example, we must often follow the commands authority figures give us. If our boss tells us to do something at work, we do it or risk getting fired. If a police officer tells us to pull off to the side of the road, we do it or face a stiff penalty. Situational factors influence our behavior across a wide range of circumstances, as we see in Part Two when we consider persuasion (Chapter 7), conformity and compliance (Chapter 8), obedience and disobedience (Chapter 9), and group processes (Chapter 10).

Social Relations Some social psychologists are particularly interested in how people relate to one another; they investigate the internal and external factors that influence these interactions. As an example, consider the case of James McElveen, who was seriously injured after he fell while hiking. His friends, including a particular friend named Benny Milligan, rushed him to the hospital. Milligan knew that McElveen had no health insurance, so he gave his own name and insurance number to the hospital to make sure his friend would receive adequate care. Unfortunately, Milligan's act was illegal. Eventually he lost his job because of the incident, received a 9-month prison sentence, and was ordered to pay back $41,000 to the insurance company. Why would Benny Milligan lay so much on the line for his friend?

Social psychologists interested in social relations study questions like this one. Part Three explores in detail how we relate to others in our social world. This includes why we find each other attractive and how we form, maintain, and dissolve close relationships (Chapter 11). Social psychology also has an abiding interest in when we hurt (aggression) (Chapter 12) and when we help (altruism) (Chapter 13).

Applied Social Psychology Some social psychologists are particularly interested in how social psychological theory, research, and concepts apply to real-world problems and phenomena. For example, trials like the one in the Rodney King case raise several questions about how juries operate. Did the composition of the jury (ten whites and two individuals from different ethnic groups) influence the outcome? Did the jurors' racial attitudes influence how they perceived the evidence? Did pretrial publicity play a part in the outcome of the trial? These and other questions are studied by social psychologists who are interested in applied areas of social psychology.

Part Four covers a broad range of topics relating to applied social psychology, including chapters on social psychology in relation to law (Chapter 14), health (Chapter 15), and international conflict (Chapter 16).

The chapters that follow show that the application of the scientific method to the study of social behavior has been fruitful and illuminating. Social psychologists have crafted intriguing and engaging research and theories about social behavior. Although the results of their research are important, the process by which they get these results is equally important. For this reason, we describe research studies throughout the book, usually briefly, occasionally at some length. In each chapter we explore a few research questions in detail, along with the studies designed and carried out to answer them.

Although social psychology has posed and answered some very interesting questions about social behavior, you shouldn't expect it to answer *all* questions. There are limits to what social psychology (or any discipline) can tell us. For example, social psychology is not very good at predicting how any *one* individual is going to behave, as mentioned earlier. Social situations are complicated, and every individual has a slightly different perception of reality. This makes understanding and predicting people's behavior a tough enterprise. Nevertheless, social psychology *is* fairly good at making predictions about aggregates, or groups of individuals.

Social psychology today is an exciting, dynamic field, filled with bright people doing thoughtful, ingenious research. We, the authors of this book, would like to show you the excitement of social psychology—its unique approach to social behavior, its thought-provoking theories, its creative research, and its wide-ranging applications to our lives. When it comes to understanding why and how people act as they do, we all need every bit of help we can get. So let's begin.

CHAPTER REVIEW

1. *What is social psychology?*
   Social psychology is the scientific study of how we think and feel about, interact with, and influence each other. It is the branch of psychology that focuses on social behavior, specifically how we relate to other people in our social world. Social psychology can help us to understand everyday things that happen to us, as well as past and present cultural and historical events.

2. *What is the sociohistorical perspective?*
   The **sociohistorical perspective** is a framework for using social psychological principles to understand a wide range of events. It has two components. First, it emphasizes that social behavior is influenced by the cultural and historical contexts within which it occurs. Second, it highlights the fact that social psychology can help us make sense out of events in our day-to-day life as well as events that we read or hear about in the news media.

3. *How do social psychologists explain social behavior?*
   An early model of social behavior proposed by Kurt Lewin suggested that social behavior is caused by two factors: individual characteristics and the social situation. This simple model has since been expanded to better explain the forces that shape social behavior. According to modern views of social behavior, input from the social situation works in conjunction with individual characteristics to influence social behavior through the operation of **social cognition** (the general process of thinking about social events) and **social perception** (how we perceive other people). Based on our processing of social information, we evaluate the social situation and form an intention to behave in a certain way. This behavioral intention may or may not be translated into social behavior. We engage in social behavior based on our constantly changing evaluation of the situation. Once we behave in a certain way, it may have an effect on the social situation, which in turn will affect future social behavior.

4. *How does social psychology relate to other disciplines that study social behavior?*
   There are many scientific disciplines that study social behavior. Biologists, developmental psychologists, anthropologists, personality psycholo-

gists, historians, and sociologists all have an interest in social behavior. Although social psychology has common interests with these disciplines, unlike biology and personality psychology, social psychology focuses on the social situation as the principal cause of social behavior. While sociology and history focus on the situation, social psychology takes a narrower view, looking at the individual in the social situation rather than the larger group or society. In other words, history and sociology take a "top down" approach to explaining social behavior, making a group or institution the focus of analysis. Social psychology takes a "bottom up" approach, focusing on how individual behavior is influenced by the situation.

5. *How do social psychologists approach the problem of explaining social behavior?*

Unlike the layperson who forms commonsense explanations for social behavior based on limited information, social psychologists rely on the **scientific method** to formulate scientific explanations—tentative explanations based on observation and logic that are open to empirical testing. The scientific method involves identifying a phenomenon to study; developing a testable research hypothesis; designing a research study; and carrying out the research study. Only after applying this method to a problem and conducting careful research will a social psychologist be satisfied with an explanation.

6. *What is experimental research and how is it used?*

Experimental research is used to uncover causal relationships between variables. Its main features are (1) the manipulation of an **independent variable** and the observation of the effects of this manipulation on a **dependent variable** and (2) the use of two or more initially comparable groups. Every experiment includes at least one independent variable with at least two levels. In the simplest experiment, one group of subjects (the **experimental group**) is exposed to an experimental treatment and a second group (the **control group**) is not. Researchers then compare the behavior of subjects in the experimental group with the behavior of subjects in the control group. Independent variables can be manipulated by varying their quantity or quality. Researchers use **random assignment** to ensure that the groups in an experiment are comparable before applying any treatment to them.

7. *What is correlational research?*

In **correlational research,** researchers measure two or more variables and look for a relationship between them. When two variables both change in the same direction, increasing or decreasing in value, they are **positively correlated.** When they change in opposite directions, one increasing and the other decreasing, they are **negatively correlated.** When one variable does not change systematically with the other, they are uncorrelated. Even if a correlation is found, a causal relationship cannot be inferred. Researchers evaluate correlational relationships between variables with a statistic called the correlation coefficient (symbolized as r). The sign of r (positive or negative) indicates the direction of the relationship between variables; the size of r (ranging from -1 through 0 to $+1$) indicates the strength of the relationship between variables.

8. *Where is social psychological research conducted?*
Social psychologists conduct research either in the laboratory or in the field. In laboratory research, researchers create an artificial environment in which they can control extraneous variables. This tight control allows the researchers to be reasonably confident that any variation observed in the dependent variable was caused by manipulation of the independent variable. However, results obtained this way sometimes cannot be legitimately generalized beyond the laboratory setting.

There are several kinds of field research. In the **field study,** the researcher observes subjects but does not interact with them. In the **field survey,** the researcher has direct contact with subjects and interacts with them. Both of these techniques allow the researcher to describe behavior, but causes cannot be uncovered. In the **field experiment,** the researcher manipulates an independent variable in the subject's natural environment. The field experiment increases the generalizability of the research findings. However, extraneous variables may cloud the causal relationship between the independent and dependent variables.

9. *What is the role of theory in social psychology?*
A **theory** is a set of interrelated statements or propositions about the causes of a phenomenon that help organize research results, make predictions about how certain variables influence social behavior, and give direction to future research. A theory is not the final word on the causes of a social behavior. Theories are developed, revised, and sometimes abandoned according to how well they fit with research results. Theories do not tell us how things are in an absolute sense. Instead, they help us understand social behavior by providing a particular perspective. Often, more than one theory can apply to a particular social behavior. Sometimes one theory provides a better explanation of one aspect of a particular social behavior and another theory provides a better explanation of another aspect of that same behavior.

10. *What can we learn from social psychological research?*
Two common criticisms of social psychological research are (1) that social psychologists study things that are intuitively obvious and (2) that since exceptions to research results can nearly always be found, many results must be wrong. However, these two criticisms are not valid. The findings of social psychological research may *appear* to be intuitively obvious in hindsight (the **hindsight bias**), but individuals cannot predict how an experiment would come out if they don't already know the results. Further, exceptions to a research finding do not invalidate that finding. Social psychologists study groups of individuals. Within a group, variation in behavior will occur. Social psychologists look at average differences between groups.

11. *What ethical standards must social psychologists follow when conducting research?*

Social psychologists are concerned with the ethics of research—how subjects are treated within a study and how they are affected in the long term by participating. Social psychologists adhere to the code of research ethics established by the American Psychological Association. Ethical treatment of subjects involves several key aspects, including **informed consent** (informing subjects about the nature of a study and requirements for participation prior to participation), protecting subjects from short-term and long-term harm, and ensuring anonymity.

SUGGESTIONS FOR FURTHER READING

Agnew, N., & Pike, S. (1994). *The science game* (6th ed.). Englewood Cliffs, NJ: Prentice-Hall.

An innovative, even humorous look at the research methods and concepts used in the social sciences.

American Psychological Association. (1992). Ethical principles of psychologists. *American Psychologist, 47,* 1597–1611.

Details the ethical concerns that researchers should attend to when doing research with human subjects.

Nickerson, R. (1992). *Looking ahead: Human factors and challenges in a changing world.* Hillsdale, NJ: Erlbaum.

A book that examines, in part, what social psychology, and psychology in general, could contribute to solving the challenges of the 21st century. An interesting view for anyone contemplating a career in psychology.

Part One
SOCIAL COGNITION

We have defined social psychology as the study of how people think and feel about, interact with, and influence each other, both individually and in groups. Part One addresses the first of these concerns—how people think and feel about each other. In this diverse and complex social world, how do we make sense of other people's behavior? How do we understand their attitudes and prejudices? How, for that matter, do we understand ourselves?

Part One begins with a consideration of the social self—how we think about and present ourselves in the social world. This discussion leads naturally to a consideration of how we think and feel about others—how we organize information, form impressions, and make judgments about our fellow human beings. The process of constructing social reality has many facets, and some are examined in the remaining chapters of Part One. These chapters explore how we interpret other people's motives, how we develop prejudices and stereotypes, and how we form attitudes.

In all these processes, people tend to make predictable cognitive errors that lead to a skewed view of the social world. So a recurring theme in these chapters is how we can correct these errors to get a more accurate understanding of ourselves and others.

Chapter 2
The Social Self

In one of the most telling moments in F. Scott Fitzgerald's novel *The Great Gatsby,* the title character reveals a flaw in the image he has carefully constructed for himself:

> "I'll tell you God's truth," [said Gatsby]. . . . "I am the son of some wealthy people in the middle-west—all dead now. I was brought up in America but educated at Oxford because all my ancestors have been educated there for many years. It is a family tradition."
>
> He looked at me sideways—and I knew . . . he was lying. He hurried the phrase "educated at Oxford," or swallowed it or choked on it as though it had bothered him before. And with this doubt his whole statement fell to pieces. . . .
>
> "What part of the middle-west?" I inquired casually.
> "San Francisco."
> "I see."

Jay Gatsby has carefully put together a "public self" with which he hopes to impress others. Handsome, young, aloof, he seems to exist only in this persona. We first encounter him as the fabulously wealthy and rather mysterious owner of a magnificent house on Long Island. His chief occupation is throwing lavish parties to attract the beautiful, rich, and famous, who drive out from Manhattan on Saturday nights, eat, drink, and dance, and drive back on Sunday. Some of them don't even know who their host is; he floats among them like some ineffable presence, smiling and silent.

No one really knows much about Gatsby. Clearly he is rich, though how he made his money is unknown. Some say he once killed a man who insulted him; others think he has connections to the underworld. Gatsby himself wants people to see him not only as wealthy but also as aristocratic—refined, well educated, a person of style and taste.

We learn that the goal of Gatsby's behavior is to attract and impress Daisy Buchanan, a woman he once loved who is now married to another man. When she finally visits his house, he takes her on a tour to show her what he is really "worth." The narrator tells us:

> He hadn't once ceased looking at Daisy, and I think he revalued everything in his house according to the measure of response it drew from her. . . . He opened for us two hulking patent cabinets which held his massed suits and dressing gowns and ties, and his shirts piled like bricks in stacks a dozen high. . . . He took out a pile of shirts and began throwing them one by one

before us, shirts of sheer linen and thick silk and fine flannel which lost their folds as they fell and covered the table in many-colored disarray. While we admired he brought more and the soft rich heap mounted higher — shirts with stripes and scrolls and plaids in coral and apple green and lavender and faint orange. . . .

Gatsby defines himself through his silk shirts, his mansion, his parties, his Rolls Royce. He thinks of himself only in terms of what others might think of him. Even his passion for Daisy is heightened by the fact that other men desired her:

It excited him too that many men had already loved Daisy — it increased her value in his eyes. He felt their presence all about the house, pervading the air with the shades and echoes of still vibrant emotions.

Gatsby's sense of self is uncertain. When confronted by Daisy's husband, he becomes less sure of who he really is and how he wants to present himself to others:

"By the way, Mr. Gatsby, I understand you're an Oxford man."
   "Not exactly."
"Oh yes, I understand you went to Oxford."
"Yes — I went there."
A pause. Then Tom's voice, incredulous and insulting:
". . . I'd like to know when."
"It was in nineteen-nineteen. I only stayed five months."

Who was Gatsby, really? Was there anything beneath the polished veneer? We do get occasional glimpses of Gatsby's private self, but most of his attention is focused on his public self, the self he wants to present to other people. He actively constructs that self, changing and altering it when he thinks he can make a better impression. Even as a child he had been dissatisfied with who he was and had worked at becoming something different. We know this because, at the end of the book, after Gatsby's funeral, his father shows the narrator an old copy of a "Hopalong Cassidy" book:

"Look here, this is a book he had when he was a boy. It just shows you."
   He opened it at the back cover and turned it around for me to see. On the last fly-leaf was printed the word SCHEDULE, and the date September 12th, 1906. And underneath:

Rise from bed	6.00 A.M.
Dumbbell exercise and wall-scaling	6.15 – 6.30 A.M.
Study electricity, etc.	7.15 – 8.15 A.M.
Work	8.30 – 4.30 P.M.
Baseball and sports	4.30 – 5.00 P.M.

Practice elocution, poise and how to
attain it   5.00 – 6.00 P.M.
Study needed inventions   7.00 – 9.00 P.M.

GENERAL RESOLVES

No wasting time at Shafters or [a name, indecipherable]

No more smokeing or chewing

Bath every other day

Read one improving book or magazine per week

Save $5.00 [crossed out] $3.00 per week

Be better to parents

"I come across this book by accident," said the old man. "It just shows you, don't it?"

"It just shows you."

Although Gatsby represents an extreme (and fictional) case, parts of his experience are familiar to all of us. He had a private self, unknown to other people, and a public self that he presented to the world. His feelings about himself were strongly affected by what other people thought of him. His construction and presentation of his public self were his attempt to gain control over his life. This need for control is a basic human motivation. When people feel that they do not have personal control over their image of themselves or how others see them, they go to great lengths to recapture or reestablish control (Pittman & Pittman, 1980).

Gatsby had an idea of himself as he really was and an idea of what he wanted to be, as we all do. For Gatsby there was a tremendous gap between these two ideas. Such discrepancies create dissatisfaction and discomfort, and people are motivated to narrow them. Gatsby's inability to narrow the discrepancies in an authentic way contributed to his uncertainty about who he really was.

Gatsby's idea of himself was the basis for all his social interactions, as our ideas of ourselves are for our interactions. Human beings can see the world only through their own eyes. Therefore, if we want to have satisfying interactions and relationships with others, the most important knowledge we can have is self-knowledge. The methods we use to gain self-knowledge are the same tools we use to understand others (Ross & Nisbett, 1991). The errors we make about ourselves we also tend to make about others. The self is the core of our world; all else is filtered through our ideas of what we are and how we think and feel about ourselves. For all of these reasons, the study of social psychology properly begins with the study of the self.

In this chapter we look at the self from a number of different perspectives. We ask, What does a person like Jay Gatsby know about himself, and how does he know it? How does Gatsby's self guide him as he negotiates his way through a world of other selves? How does Gatsby *feel* about himself, when he's alone and when he's with others? And how does he attempt to maintain control of himself and his world by managing the impression he makes on others? From questions like these we begin to get a sense of this complex construct at the center of our lives—the social self.

THE NATURE OF THE SELF

"Who am I?" The answer to this question is the driving force in our lives. If you were asked to define yourself, you would most likely use sentences containing the words I, me, mine, and myself (Cooley, 1902).

The self may be thought of as a structure that contains the organized and stable contents of one's personal experiences (Schlenker, 1987). In this sense, the self is an object, something inside us that we may evaluate and contemplate. The self is "me"—the sum of what I am.

But the self is more than just ideas and knowledge about ourselves. Over 100 years ago, American philosopher William James observed that the self is a doer (1890). The self is an actor, guiding and regulating our thoughts, feelings, and actions. It actively gathers information, organizes that information, and structures our experiences. The self acts as a control device, helping us understand and predict how we and others are likely to act.

The self, then, has various components. It is a cognitive structure, containing ideas about who and what we are. It has an evaluative and emotional component, as we judge ourselves and find ourselves worthy or unworthy. Seeking to bring ideas and actions into congruence, the self guides our behavior as we make our way through the perils and pleasures of social life. It also guides us as we attempt to assert control over our social world by managing the impression we make on others.

SELF-CONCEPT: THINKING ABOUT THE SELF

A significant part of what we call the self is knowledge. All the ideas, thoughts, and information that we have about ourselves—about who we are, what characteristics we have, what our personal histories have made us, and what we may yet become—make up our **self-concept.** These pieces of knowledge comprise the cognitive component of the self.

The Private, Public, and Collective Selves

No matter what the specific content of the self-concept, certain kinds of ideas and beliefs about the self are likely to be more dominant and others less dominant. We all have our private thoughts and evaluations of who and what we are. This is the private self. The thought "I am an honest person" is an expression of the private self. We also have a public self that we present to others; it is revealed by thoughts about how other people view us: "People think I am an honest person" or "Most people think I am very smart." We saw that Jay Gatsby devoted his whole life to cultivating a public self; he defined himself by what others thought of him and relegated his private self to the closet.

self-concept All the ideas, thoughts, and information we have about ourselves.

We all have a private self that defines us to ourselves and a public self, a persona, that we present to others. Some people—like pop star Madonna, shown here on her 1993 world tour—aggressively cultivate a public image designed to create a particular impression. Such an image may be sharply divergent from the private self within.

If the public self reflects how some unspecified "other people" think of us, there is also a self that reflects how we think specific others—family, friends, co-workers—think of us. This *collective self* is reflected in thoughts such as, "In my family I am considered the responsible, studious one." The collective self reflects the evaluation of the self by important and specific groups to which the person belongs (Greenwald & Pratkanis, 1984).

These three selves do not occupy equal space and influence in the self-concept. The relative importance of any of them for an individual is determined in large part by the culture in which the person lives. In some cultures, the private self is dominant. Cultures that emphasize individual striving and achievement—societies that are concerned with people "finding themselves"—produce individuals in which the private self is highly complex, containing many traits and beliefs. Other cultures may emphasize specific groups, such as family or religious community, and therefore the collective self is primary. The public self is most highly developed in cultures that focus on what other people think of you (Triandis, 1989). (For a closer look at how the construction of the self varies in different cultures, see the featured discussion "'Who Am I?' The Influence of Culture on Self-Concept.") In American society, people tend to focus on the private self, especially on traits that make them different from others.

Not only do different cultural forces affect individuals' notions of themselves but so do historical forces. Indeed, it can be argued that the idea of

Nothing, it seems, could be more personal and individual than how we answer the question "Who am I?" But, as it turns out, our answer is powerfully shaped by the culture in which we grew up and developed our self-concept. Some cultures place more emphasis on the uniqueness of the individual—the private self—whereas others focus on how the individual is connected to important others—the collective self.

In a culture that emphasizes the collective self, such as Japan, individuals are more likely to define themselves in terms of meeting the expectations of others rather than of fulfilling their own private needs. In fact, if you asked Japanese subjects to answer the question "Who am I?" (a common technique for investigating self-concept), you would find that they give many more social responses ("I am an employee at X") than do Americans (S. D. Cousins, 1989). In contrast, Americans are more likely to emphasize the content of the private self, defining themselves with such statements as "I am strong-willed." The Japanese view themselves as part of a social context, whereas Americans tend to assume they have a self that is less dependent on any set of social relations (S. D. Cousins, 1989; Ross & Nisbett, 1991).

Individuals in cultures that emphasize the collective self are also less likely to view themselves as the focus of attention in social interactions (Markus & Kitayama, 1991; Ross & Nisbett, 1991). Japanese appear to view their peers, rather than themselves, as the focus of attention. Consequently, social interactions in Japan are quite different from those in a society like the United States.

Private-self societies emphasize "self-fulfillment" at the expense of communal relationships; collective-self societies are more concerned with meeting shared obligations and helping others. In Haiti, for example, where the culture emphasizes the collective self, people are willing to share houses and food with relatives and friends for long periods of time.

Obviously, the thoughts and traits that make up the core of the self of a Japanese or Haitian person are likely to differ from the content of the self of an American. We would expect many more individual attributes to be part of an American self-concept. Japanese or Haitian individuals would probably emphasize attributes that reflect their similarities with others. Americans are more likely to emphasize attributes that make them different from other people.

To investigate some of these cultural differences, Markus and Kitayama (in press) examined self-presentation strategies used by Americans and Japanese to open a speech before an audience. They found that an American was more likely to tell a joke as a speech opening. Telling a clever joke is a way of displaying the self; it demonstrates a self that is independent and self-reliant. The cleverness calls attention to the speaker, and a good joke or story puts the individual and audience at ease. A Japanese person is more likely to open a speech with an apology. This tactic presents the individual as imperfect, a small cog in a large machine. This, says Markus, brings on a sympathetic understanding and promotes a closer connection between the audience and the speaker. The goal of the Japanese speaker is to show a connection, an affinity, with the social context. The goal of the American speaker, in contrast, is to say, "Hey, look at me. I'm different from the rest of you."

We see in this example both the pervasive role of the self-concept in directing behavior and the pervasive role of culture in determining ideas about the self. The self-concept is not just a private, personal construct; culture plays a part in shaping the individual's deepest levels of personal knowledge.

Individuals from different cultural backgrounds may have different kinds of self-concepts. What do you think the impact of such differences is on their interpersonal relations? On a larger scale, how do you think cultural differences affect diplomacy and relations between nations? And on a personal level, how do you think your culture has shaped your own self-concept? How do you answer the question "Who am I?"

an individual self is a rather recent invention. The featured discussion "The Self in the 14th Century" takes a look at the nature of the self 700 years ago.

What Does the Self-Concept Contain?

What are our basic ideas about ourselves? Most simply, we may think of the self-concept as containing a core of attributes, arranged in meaningful ways; memories of what we have been; and ideas about possible selves we may yet become.

Personal Attributes First of all, the self-concept contains ideas and beliefs about personal attributes. A person may think of herself as female, American, young, smart, compassionate, the daughter of a single mother, a good basketball player, reasonably attractive, hot-tempered, artistic, patient, and a fan of Woody Allen movies. All of these attributes—and many more—go into her self-concept.

Researchers have investigated the self-concepts of American school children by asking them the following kinds of questions (McGuire & McGuire, 1988, p. 99):

- Tell us about yourself.
- Tell us what you are not.
- Tell us about school.
- Tell us about your family.

These open-ended probes revealed that children and adolescents defined themselves by characteristics that were unique or distinctive. Subjects who possessed a distinctive characteristic were much more likely to mention that attribute than were those who were less distinctive on that dimension (McGuire & McGuire, 1988).

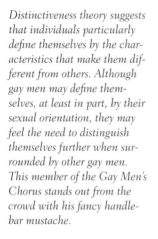

Distinctiveness theory suggests that individuals particularly define themselves by the characteristics that make them different from others. Although gay men may define themselves, at least in part, by their sexual orientation, they may feel the need to distinguish themselves further when surrounded by other gay men. This member of the Gay Men's Chorus stands out from the crowd with his fancy handlebar mustache.

Consider how a person's self-concept might develop in a different historical period, say the 14th century. The structure of medieval society, the strong influence of the church, and the desperately poor economic and social conditions in which most people lived led them to value the *soul* more than the *self*. The quality of one's life was determined by rank and kinship, not by any personal qualities or actions. For most people, life was hard and death came early. But the soul was believed to survive the body after death. Immortal and eternal, the soul was unaffected by one's daily thoughts and experiences (Baumeister, 1987). Any introspection that occurred would have focused on this all-important aspect of oneself.

Historian Barbara Tuchman (1978) has given us some insights into that long-ago time. She observes that medieval art and literature do not often depict children or childhood. "Medieval illustrations show people in every other form of human activity . . . yet so rarely with children as to raise the question: Why not?" (p. 50). One finds books of advice on every subject, but few give advice on how to raise children. Tuchman speculates that people did not value children as we in Western society do today because one or two of every three died in infancy or childhood. Although parents must have loved their children—there were cradles and lullabies—it appears that they did not invest much in their development until the child had survived to the age of five or six.

How might this childhood, without the faith of parents that one would survive into youth and adulthood, have affected the development of the child's self-concept? What did it mean to be taught that the soul apart from the body and physical experience was all that mattered? We can only guess. But it is hard to imagine a child perceiving him- or herself as a valued object. One's thoughts and experiences were irrelevant. Future possibilities, hopes and dreams of what one might become, were dim. Tuchman surmises that "the relative emotional blankness of a medieval infancy may account for the casual attitude toward life and suffering of the medieval man" (p. 52). Just as childhood was emotionally blank, probably so was the self.

Individuals in medieval Europe had less to do with defining their own social world than their 20th-century counterparts. It was not until the Renaissance and the Reformation took hold in the 15th and 16th centuries that the concept of the self drew attention. Philosophers and artists in this period questioned the church's view that every living thing, in heaven and on earth, participated in a "great chain of being," from God to angel to human being to animal to plant to dust. The individual had to confront the universe alone, isolated from others. Discovering who one was gained importance. Self-knowledge became, as it had been for Socrates in ancient Greece, an important and necessary goal.

From a sociohistorical perspective we can see that the meaning of "self" changes over time and place. Even in one lifetime, people experience different cultural influences. A person who "came of age" in the 1950s, an era of relative conformity, would tend to define herself differently and have different thoughts, feelings, and life goals than someone who entered adulthood in the 1960s, when the "counterculture" and peace movement were prominent social phenomena, or in the 1970s, when the women's movement was gaining ground. In what ways do you think your ideas about yourself have been shaped by the time in which you grew up? Your feelings about yourself? Your ideals and goals?

According to *distinctiveness theory*, people think of themselves in terms of those attributes or dimensions that make them different, that are distinctive, rather than in terms of attributes they have in common with others. Recall how Jay Gatsby defined himself: an Oxford man who drove a yellow Rolls. Distinctive, wouldn't you say? Gatsby existed to himself because he was different from other people. So it is with the rest of us. People

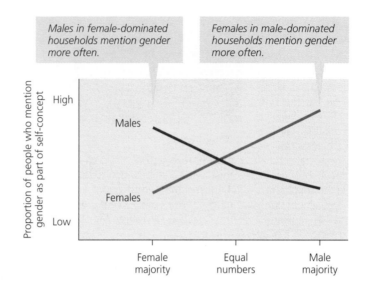

Males in female-dominated households mention gender more often.

Females in male-dominated households mention gender more often.

who are taller than others, for example, or shorter than others, or who wear glasses or are left-handed are likely to incorporate that characteristic into their self-concept.

People usually are aware of the attributes they have in common with other individuals. A male going to an all-male high school is aware that he is male. But being male may not be a defining part of his self-concept because everybody around him has that same characteristic. He will define himself by attributes that make him different from other males, such as being a debater or a football player. At least, being male will not be a defining attribute in that high school. It may certainly be important in another social context, such as when taking part in a debate about changing gender roles in the 1990s.

People who belong to nondominant or nonmajority groups are more likely to include their gender, ethnicity, or other identity in their self-concept than are those in dominant, majority groups (white male, for example). Among the school children in the study (McGuire & McGuire, 1988), boys who lived in households that were predominantly female mentioned their gender more often, and girls who lived in households that were predominantly male mentioned their gender more often (Figure 2-1).

Of course, not all knowledge about the self is conscious simultaneously. At any given time we tend to be aware of only parts of our overall self-concept. This *working self-concept* varies depending on the nature of the social situation and how we feel at the moment (Markus & Nurius, 1986). So when we're depressed, our working self-concept would be likely to include all of those thoughts about ourselves that have to do with failure or negative traits.

Organizing Attributes: Self-Schemas People don't think of themselves as just chaotic masses of attributes. Instead, they arrange knowledge and information about themselves and their attributes into *self-schemas* (Markus, 1977; Markus & Zajonc, 1985). A schema is an organized set of related cognitions—bits of knowledge and information—about a particular person, event, or experience. A **self-schema** is an arrangement of information, thoughts, and feelings about ourselves. It contains information that we believe to be true about ourselves, including information about our gender, age, race or ethnicity, occupation, social roles, physical attractiveness, intelligence, talents, and so on. People have many different self-schemas for the different areas of life in which they participate.

Self-schemas serve a very important function: They organize our experiences so that we can respond quickly and effectively in social situations. They help us interpret situations, and they guide our behavior. Schemas also help us understand new events (Scheier & Carver, 1988). You may have a self-schema about how you act in an emergency, for example. From past experience and from your ideals and expectations about yourself, you may believe that you are a person who stays calm, acts responsibly, and takes care of others—or one who panics and has to be taken care of by others. These beliefs about yourself influence your behavior when an emergency arises in the future. Or perhaps you have a self-schema about being a runner. When you hear people talking about "keeping fit" or "eating the right foods," you know what they're talking about and how it relates to you. In these ways, self-schemas contribute to our sense of control over our social world.

Self-schemas lend order to our past experiences as well. They guide what we encode (place) into memory and affect how we organize and store that memory. Memories that match our self-schemas are recalled more easily than are those that do not (Neimeyer & Rareshide, 1991). Self-schemas also affect how we think we will behave in the future. A person who thinks of himself as socially awkward, for example, may behave inappropriately in social situations. And, based on his behavior in the past, he expects to behave inappropriately in future social situations.

People tend to have elaborate schemas about areas of life that are important to their self-concepts. They have a great deal of information about themselves on those dimensions. Runners pay attention to their weight (they can never be too thin), to their diet (love that pasta), and to all the characteristics that go with that particular lifestyle. They are also very attentive to other people who look like they might be runners: They notice their clothing, their running shoes, their running style, and their way of talking about running. Conversely, people lack schemas for domains of life that don't interest them. A person may not know anything about stereo equipment and may react with indifference when told about the features of an expensive sound system.

People also make self-schematic answers quite quickly. If you are self-schematic about exercise, you will answer right away when someone asks you what your target heart rate is when you work out. This is so because the schematic person has much information available on the topic. Of course, if it is a complicated question, highly schematic individuals might take longer to answer because they have so much information available. If you

self-schema An arrangement of information, thoughts, and feelings that we believe to be true about ourselves. Self-schemas organize our experiences, help us interpret situations, and guide our behavior.

ask a professor of literature what the greatest novel of all time is, she might hesitate for a long time while considering everything from *Tom Jones* to *One Hundred Years of Solitude*.

People have schemas not only for themselves but for other people, for social roles, and for events. We discuss schemas again in Chapter 3 in the context of social perception.

The Self and Memory Besides attributes and self-schemas, the self-concept contains memories. As mentioned earlier, the self actively seeks to establish and maintain control over the social world and over the individual's sense of self. The self is concerned with maintaining positive self-feelings, thoughts, and evaluations. One way it does this is by influencing memory. Anthony Greenwald (1980) suggests that the self acts as a kind of unconscious monitor that enables people to avoid disquieting or distressing information. The self demands that we preserve what we have, especially that which makes us feel good about ourselves.

According to Greenwald, the self employs biases that work somewhat like the mind-control techniques used in totalitarian countries. In such countries, the government controls information and interpretations of events so that the leadership is never threatened. Similarly, we try to control the thoughts and memories we have about ourselves. The self is "totalitarian" in the sense that it records our good behaviors and ignores our unsavory ones or at least rationalizes them away. The self is a "personal historian," observing and recording information about the self—especially the information that makes us look good. Like a totalitarian government, Greenwald claims, the self tends to see itself as the origin of all positive things and to deny that it has ever done anything bad.

Is it true, as Greenwald predicts, that the self is a kind of filter that makes us feel good by gathering self-serving information and discarding information that discomfits us? The study of **autobiographical memory**— memory for information relating to the self—shows that the self does indeed play a powerful role in the recall of events (Neimeyer & Rareshide, 1991). The self is an especially powerful memory system because events and attributes stored in the self have many associations (Greenwald & Banaji, 1989). Let's say, for example, that you are asked to recall whether you've done anything in your life that exemplifies a trait such as "honesty" or "creativity." A search of your self memory system perhaps would conjure up a recent event in which you devised a creative solution to a problem. The memory of that event might trigger similar memories from earlier periods in your history. You probably would be able to generate a flood of such memories.

Most people take only about 2 seconds to answer questions about their traits (Klein, Loftus, & Plog, 1992). This is because we have a kind of summary knowledge of our self traits, especially the most obvious ones. Such a handy summary makes it harder to access memories that conflict with our positive self-concept, however. As noted earlier, memories that match a person's self-concept are recalled more easily than those that clash with that concept (Neimeyer & Rareshide, 1991). If you perceive yourself

autobiographical memory
Memory for information relating to the self.

as an honest person, you will have trouble digging up memories in which you may have behaved dishonestly.

A research study of social memory of everyday life among college students bore out these findings (Skowronski, Betz, Thompson, & Shannon, 1991). Subjects were asked to keep two diaries; in one they recorded events that occurred in their own lives, and in the other they recorded events that occurred in the life of a close relative or friend, someone they saw on a daily basis. The students had to ask the consent of the other person, and they recorded the events discreetly. Subjects made entries in the diaries for self and other for roughly 10 weeks, the length of the academic quarter.

At the end of the quarter, the subjects took a memory test on the events recorded in the two diaries. They were presented with the recorded events from the diaries in a random order and were asked to indicate how well they remembered the event, the date it occurred, and whether it was a unique episode.

The researchers found that subjects recalled recent events more quickly than earlier ones, with faster retrieval of the oldest episodes than of those in the middle. They also found that pleasant events were recalled better than unpleasant ones, and extreme events, pleasant and unpleasant, were recalled better than neutral episodes. Pleasant events that especially fit the person's self-concept were most easily recalled.

Subjects also recalled events that were unusual better than they recalled typical events. This was true of events occurring in the lives of both the self and the other person. This is consistent with the findings mentioned earlier that the self incorporates distinctive events and attributes more readily than neutral or typical attributes. The self, then, monitors our experiences, processing information in ways that make us look good to ourselves. We interpret, organize, and remember interactions and events in self-serving ways, recalling primarily pleasant, self-relevant events that fit our self-concept. Obviously, this built-in bias affects the manner in which we understand our social world and interact with other people. Without realizing it, we are continually constructing a view of the world that is skewed in our favor (Figure 2-2).

Possible Selves In addition to attributes, self-schemas, and memories, the self-concept includes **possible selves**—ideas about what we may be in the future. Social psychologists Hazel Markus and Paula Nurius (1986) describe possible selves as selves we would like to attain and those we want to avoid or are afraid of becoming. Jay Gatsby was motivated by the possible self he wanted to become—a successful, fabulously wealthy playboy. He was also motivated by possible selves he wanted to avoid. He didn't want to be "Mr. Nobody from Nowhere," as Daisy's husband calls him. Notice that Gatsby's possible self played a role in controlling not only how he thought of himself but the way he presented himself to other people. In other words, possible selves influence how we behave.

Possible selves are very real and quite social; that is, we form them by observing others, we maintain them by imagining how others will react to them, and we use them to guide our behavior with others. Consider the

possible selves Selves we would like to attain and those we want to avoid or are afraid of becoming.

FIGURE 2-2 *Thanks to built-in cognitive biases, we all tend to construct a version of social reality subtly skewed in our own favor. We might see ourselves as a little more important, a little more attractive, or a little more charismatic than others would judge us to be, thus pleasantly enhancing our self-esteem.*

case of Mark Lenzi, the gold medalist in springboard diving in the 1992 Olympics. Lenzi, originally a wrestler, watched the 1984 Olympics and decided that he could win a gold in diving. He knew he had the athletic ability to do it. This was a "possible self" for Lenzi. It was real, and it motivated his behavior for 8 years. It was social because this possible self formed when he compared himself with the athletes whom he saw competing in the Olympics.

Many of us spend a good deal of time thinking of ourselves as we want to be in the future (Markus & Wurf, 1987). We may not have such lofty possible selves as Mark Lenzi, but if we "see" ourselves as 20 pounds thinner than we are right now, that possible self is real and social. It is real because we have a full and vivid conception of ourselves wearing clothes we cannot now wear and doing things we do not now do. We have a good idea about how we will look when we reach this "ideal," and we imagine how others will react to us. This possible self guides and controls our behavior as we go about our daily lives, influencing our thinking and decisions about eating, exercising, and buying clothes.

Some individuals have many "possible selves" in their self-concept. Richard Gill is a well-known Harvard economist, teacher, author, and host of a public television course on economics. He is also known for his leading roles as a bass with the Metropolitan Opera. Self-complexity helps people deal with the ups and downs of life.

The Importance of Self-Complexity

People differ in the number of self-schemas, memories, and possible selves that are part of their self-concept. Some people have highly complex selves, others much less complex selves. Jay Gatsby's self was wrapped up in his presentation of himself as rich and mysteriously successful. As far as we know, this is all there was to him. Other people may conceive of themselves in more complex ways. A person may think of herself as a woman, a wife, an engineer, a mother, a daughter, an artist, and an opera lover. She would have many self-schemas and many possible selves.

Self-complexity is important in influencing how people react to the good and bad events in life. Individuals who are high in self-complexity, such as the woman just described, can absorb a negative event without much damage to their overall self-concept (Linville, 1985, 1987). If her latest artistic endeavors meet unfavorable reviews, this woman's sense of self is buffered by the fact that there is much more to her than being an artist. She is still a mother, an engineer, an opera lover, and much more. People who are low in self-complexity may be devastated by negative events because there is little else to act as a buffer. For Gatsby, any challenge to his "rich and famous" self was deadly. After all, that was all he had.

Future self-complexity may also protect people against disappointments and failures (Niedenthal, Setterlund, & Wherry, 1992). If someone has a variety of possible selves, the news that she may not succeed at realizing one of them is not as difficult to accept as it would be for a person with fewer possible selves.

How Do We Know the Self?

Clearly, the self-concept is a complex structure. How does this structure come to exist, and how do we get our information about it? The self is a social construct, something that develops through our interactions and relationships with other people. As such, it is highly sensitive to information obtained from interaction with others.

Three sources of social information help us forge our self-concept. The first is our view of how other people react to us. From earliest childhood and throughout life, these **reflected appraisals** shape our self-concept (Cooley, 1902; Jones & Gerard, 1967). We begin to form these ideas about ourselves in our first relationships, with parents or other adults who care for us. Although self-concept is already quite stable by the end of childhood, the reflected appraisals of others continue to shape our ideas about ourselves as we grow and mature.

We also get knowledge about ourselves from the comparisons we make with other people (Festinger, 1954). We engage in this process of **social comparison**—comparing our reactions, abilities, and attributes to those of others—because we need accurate information in order to succeed. We need to know if we are good athletes or good students or good race-car drivers so that we can make rational choices. Social comparison makes our world more predictable and so functions as a control device.

The third source of information about ourselves is observation of our own behavior (Jones, 1990). Sometimes we don't know why we do things, so we simply observe our behavior and assume that our motives are consistent with our behavior (Bem, 1967). Someone who rebels against authority may see this about herself and conclude, "Well, I must be a rebel."

The Stability of the Self-Concept

The basis of a person's self-concept, the core attributes, is probably quite stable (Markus & Kunda, 1986). We can begin to see why this is so. First of all, people actively search for information that confirms their self-concepts. They also organize self-relevant information into the structures called self-schemas. These organizations of self-knowledge make it easier to remember information related to the self and guide behavior so that it is consistent with the self-concept. If you see yourself as health-conscious, for example, your self-schemas include knowledge and preferences concerning nutrition, exercise, and medical care. They will determine what and where you eat, how you spend your leisure time and with whom, what kinds of vacations you take, and various other aspects of your life. All of these self-schemas will reinforce your basic self-concept and make it relatively resistant to change. As noted earlier, this internal self helps you organize and control your social world.

reflected appraisals Our view of how other people react to us.

social comparison The process by which we compare our reactions, abilities, and attributes to those of others.

SELF-REGULATION: THE SELF AS A GUIDE TO BEHAVIOR

As we have seen, a crucial task of the self is to guide and regulate our behavior so we can control our social world as much as possible. It does this principally through the development and use of various *self-guides*.

Social psychologist E. Tory Higgins (1989) has proposed that people think of themselves from two different perspectives: their own perspective and the perspective of a significant other, such as a parent or a close friend. He also suggests that people have a number of different selves that guide their behavior. The first is the *actual self*, the person's current self-concept. The second is the *ideal self*, the mental representation of what the person would like to be or what a significant other would like her to be. The third is the *ought self*, the mental representation of what the person believes she *should* be or what another person believes she *should* be.

Higgins (1989) assumes that people are motivated to reach a state in which the actual self matches the ideal and the ought selves. The two latter selves thus serve as guides to behavior. When there is a discrepancy between the actual self and the self-guides, we are motivated to try to close the gap. That is, when our actual self doesn't match our internal expectations and standards, or when someone else evaluates us in ways that fail to match our standards, we try to narrow the gap. We try to adjust our behavior to bring it into line with our self-guides. Self-regulation—our attempts to match our behavior to our self-guides or to the expectations of others—is thus a critical control mechanism.

Sometimes, of course, we are simply not capable of behaving in accord with our expectations. We might not have the ability, talent, or fortitude. In this case, we may have to adjust our expectations to match our behavior. And sometimes it seems to be in our best interest not to focus on the self at all. To do so may be too painful, or it may get in the way of what we're doing. For a look at how and why we sometimes avoid self-awareness and "lose ourselves," see the featured discussion "Loss of Self-Awareness: Positive or Negative?"

What factors influence self-regulation? One is the degree to which we are aware of and focus on our own behavior. Another is the degree to which we believe we can change our behavior when we notice a discrepancy. A third is the amount of knowledge we have about ourselves.

Self-Focus

In order to engage in self-regulation, we must first be aware of our behavior (as well as our internal guides). In some situations we are acutely aware of ourselves, monitoring, evaluating, and perhaps adjusting what we say and do. When we are in a minority position in a group, for example, we become focused on how we respond (Mullen, 1986). Other situations that increase self-focus are looking in a mirror, being in front of an audience, and seeing a camera (Scheier & Carver, 1988; Wicklund, 1975).

To maintain a sense of control over the self and the social world, people have to focus on themselves and their behavior. But do people always want to focus on the self? Are there times when it's preferable to avoid self-awareness? In fact, there are many situations in which people would rather not focus on the self—but all of these situations are not the same.

ESCAPE FROM THE SELF

For some people, not paying attention to the self is a way to suppress negative thoughts, low self-esteem, or unwanted memories. In extreme cases, people will go to any lengths to avoid focusing on the self. Suicide may be seen as a permanent escape from self-awareness (Baumeister, 1988, 1990). Sexual masochism may also be motivated in part by an attempt to escape the self (Baumeister, 1988, 1990). By focusing on the intense mixture of pleasure and pain, the sexual masochist does not have to deal with the self, only with these intense sensations.

The abuse of drugs and alcohol is also an example of escape from the self. Alcohol intoxication causes people to focus very narrowly and consequently to engage in riskier behaviors than they would otherwise (Steele & Josephs, 1990). People under the influence of alcohol seem to respond to the most obvious cues in the situation, cues that involve the impulse to do something. They overlook less salient cues, those that have to do with the long-term effects of actions and that therefore inhibit impulsive behavior.

But alcohol has a number of self-enhancing effects. It lowers self-awareness, particularly awareness of negative attributes, such as shyness or awkwardness. It typically leads people to focus more on their positive attributes and to overrate the value of those attributes (Steele & Josephs, 1990). When drunk, most people pay attention mainly to their positive thoughts about themselves and the positive cues they're getting—or think they're getting—from the environment. Alcohol also relaxes inhibitions, allowing people to be more socially assertive, and it reduces stress. This again has to do with decreasing awareness of self. Drunk people simply stop paying attention to themselves. They do not spend much energy thinking negative and inhibitory thoughts, which are stressful.

"Binge eating" may also be motivated by the desire to escape focusing on the self (Heatherton & Baumeister, 1991). Binge eaters tend to be very sensitive to other people's expectations for them. When they fail to meet those expectations, they become anxious and depressed and simply want to forget themselves. Ignoring all of

When people become more aware of themselves, they are more likely to try to match their behavior to their beliefs and internal standards. In one study, two groups of subjects, one in favor of the death penalty, the other opposed, had to punish another subject (a confederate of the experimenter) (Carver, 1975). Some subjects held a small mirror up to their faces as they administered an electric shock (no shock was actually transmitted).

As shown in Figure 2-3, when subjects self-focused (looked into the mirror), they were truer to their beliefs: Their attitudes and their actions were more in harmony. Highly punitive individuals (those who favored capital punishment) gave much more shock when the confederate made errors than did the less punitive, anti–death penalty individuals. No such differences existed when subjects did not self-focus.

Self-focus means that the individual tends to be more careful in assessing her own behavior and is more concerned with the self than with

self-focus The extent to which the individual monitors his or her own behavior and is more concerned with self than with others.

those inhibitions that keep them from "pigging out," they focus narrowly on the immediate sensations of eating and drinking. Binge eating, a total loss of control, is an escape from anxiety and depression and from the self.

POSITIVE LOSS OF THE SELF: PEAK EXPERIENCES

Sometimes a temporary loss of self-awareness is a positive experience, a high point of life. Mihaly Csikszentmihalyi (1990) has studied the phenomenon of "optimal experience," or peak experience, when we are "in the flow" of whatever we are doing. We become so deeply engrossed in an activity that we forget who we are. Emotional problems, worries and concerns, and sense of time all disappear. Freed from distracting and intrusive thoughts about ourselves, we perform to our maximum abilities.

To explore this state, Csikszentmihalyi (1990) used a technique known as experience sampling, in which subjects were given beep-ers and a series of response sheets. Eight times per day the beeper reminded the subjects to show on the response sheets where they were, what they were doing, with whom they were doing it, and how they felt about it.

These studies showed that people were happiest and most likely to experience flow when they were pursuing leisure activities that required few if any material resources but which did demand great involvement, such as gardening, walking, or exercising. People who used expensive equipment in their leisure activities were less happy and less likely to experience flow. Activities that require elaborate equipment and resources tend to demand less concentration.

In general, people report feelings of pleasure, concentration, strength, and alertness when they are in the flow. This state seems to occur when people set goals, profoundly enjoy the activity, do it for its own sake, and become totally immersed. It can happen in a variety of circumstances—when they are trying to solve a problem, playing a sport, talking with a friend, or making love.

Being in the flow is precisely the opposite of being self-focused. As pleasant and desirable as they are, peak experiences can't be scheduled or arranged. They occur only when we give up the idea of control, lose our self-awareness—and forget all about ourselves.

Some people resort to alcohol or drugs when they experience a painful discrepancy between what they are and what they want to be. In what other ways might they deal with this experience? What methods do you use to maintain your self-esteem? And what activities in your life produce peak experiences? Are these experiences similar to those described in the research?

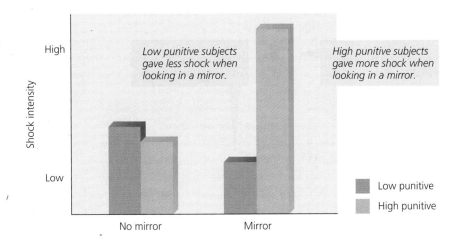

High

Shock intensity

Low punitive subjects gave less shock when looking in a mirror.

High punitive subjects gave more shock when looking in a mirror.

Low

No mirror   Mirror

Low punitive
High punitive

FIGURE 2-3 *The intensity of electric shock given by subjects as determined by the amount of self-focus and their attitudes toward punishment. People who were self-focused (those looking into a mirror) were more likely to be self-consistent: Low-punitive people gave less shock, while high-punitive people gave more shock.* From Carver, 1975.

The presence of an audience increases self-focus for most people, but whether that self-focus inhibits or enhances performance varies from one individual to another. Dallas Cowboy Emmet Smith is a person who enjoys audience pressure and thrives in the spotlight.

others (Gibbons, 1990). Self-focused individuals are concerned with what is proper and appropriate given their self-guides. Self-focused individuals probably have an increased need for accuracy and try to match their behavior to their self-guides. That is, they try to be more honest or moral.

However, it is not always true that self-focus leads to a closer connection between one's beliefs and one's behavior. The effects of self-focus depend on whether the focus is on one's behavior, or emotions, or reasons for acting (Gibbons, 1990). Timothy Wilson and his co-workers (1989) have shown that when you ask individuals to tell why they held certain opinions, they could not give rational reasons. It's not so much that they did not have reasons; they just found it hard to remember what those reasons were. In fact, just focusing on the reasons behind an opinion often made these individuals alter their opinions. We sometimes don't really know why we hold an opinion or behaved in a particular way.

Self-focusing may lead to positive outcomes or negative ones, depending on how difficult it is to match performance with the self's standards and with the expectations of others. Sometimes, for example, sports teams perform better "on the road," especially in important games, than they do on their "home" field or arena. There is a definite home field advantage—that is, teams generally win more games at home than on the road. However, baseball teams win fewer final games of the World Series than expected when they play on their home fields (Baumeister, 1984). Their performance declines due to the pressure of the home fans' expectations ("choking").

Does audience pressure always lead to "choking"? It depends on whether the performer is more concerned with controlling the audience's perceptions or just with living up to internal standards. If concern centers on pleasing the audience, the pressure may have a negative effect on performance. But if concern centers on meeting personal standards, then audience pressure will have less impact (Heaton & Sigall, 1991).

Certain situations make just about everyone more self-conscious. But some people tend to be more self-conscious than others in virtually all situations. This tendency to be a "high self-monitor" is discussed in more detail later in this chapter in the context of impression management.

Self-Efficacy Expectancies

Self-focus may reveal discrepancies between the actual self and the self-guides. What influences how people respond to those discrepancies? According to psychologist Albert Bandura (1986), people have *self-efficacy expectancies* (or beliefs), views about whether they are capable of carrying out a particular action. Bandura's self-efficacy theory states that the stronger a person's belief that she can be effective at a task, the more likely it is she will attempt the task. When a person does not believe she can succeed, she will avoid that area if possible. For example, you might like to date a particular someone and you know that the proper behavior leading to the desired outcome (a date) would be a phone call. Whether you make that phone call depends on your self-efficacy beliefs—your expectation that you are capable of obtaining the desired result.

People who have strong feelings of self-efficacy respond to substandard performance by putting more effort and resources into their performance. In this way, self-efficacy beliefs function as a regulatory control mechanism. One group of researchers studied self-efficacy among participants in aerobic dance classes (McAuley, Wraith, & Duncan, 1991). They found that those who stayed with the program had strong feelings of self-efficacy, as exemplified by their agreement with such statements as, "I believe that I can exercise at my target heart rate for 10 minutes without stopping and that I can exercise three times per week." They were also motivated by their own internal standards. They compared what they were doing with what they thought they were capable of doing and tried to bring their performance into line with those standards. When their performance fell short, they intensified their efforts.

In contrast, participants who did not feel competent in aerobics were motivated by external factors, such as improving their looks or health. Although these are good reasons for exercising, they are not as powerful at motivating people as are internal factors.

People who have strong feelings of self-efficacy set high goals for themselves. The more effort they apply to doing something, the better they become at it and the more success they experience, which in turn increases their feelings of self-efficacy as well as their positive feelings about themselves (Bandura & Jourden, 1991). People who lack feelings of self-efficacy in particular areas tend to avoid those areas, which in turn limits their experience—the very thing they need to increase their feelings of self-efficacy.

Self-Knowledge as a Factor in Self-Regulation

Accurate information about ourselves as we actually are is essential to effective self-regulation (Pelham & Swann, 1989). Such knowledge may lead us to adjust our self-guides—lower our expectations or standards—in order to close the gap between what we are and what we want to be or think we ought to be. Although it is effortful to adjust our standards, it is important to minimize discrepancies between the actual and the other selves. Small discrepancies—that is, good matches between the actual self and the self-guides—promote a strong sense of who we really are (Baumgardner, 1990). This knowledge is satisfying because it helps us predict accurately how we will react to other people and situations. It increases our sense of control over our behavior and our social world. In other words, the stronger our sense of personal identity, the better we feel about ourselves and the more confident we are. It is therefore in our best interest to obtain accurate information about ourselves (Pelham & Swann, 1989).

Research confirms that people want to have accurate information about themselves, even if that information is negative (Baumgardner, 1990). It helps them know which situations to avoid and which to seek out. If you know that you are lazy, for example, you probably will avoid a course that promises to fill your days and nights with library research. There is evidence, however, that people do prefer some sugar with the medicine of negative evaluations. They want others to evaluate their negative attributes a little more positively than they themselves do (Pelham, 1991).

People who are not certain about their attributes can make serious social blunders. If you are unaware that your singing voice has the same effect on people as someone scratching a fingernail on a chalk board, then you might one day find yourself trying out for the choir, thereby making a fool of yourself. Greater knowledge of your vocal limitations would have saved you considerable humiliation and loss of face.

Gatsby behaved in a manner suggesting that he was uncertain of his attributes. He floated among his guests like a mysterious presence. He spoke to few people, knowing that any prolonged conversation might endanger the self he presented to these people. There was a large gap between what he wanted to be and what he really was.

As mentioned earlier, Higgins (1989) assumes that people are motivated to reach a state in which their self-concept matches the two self-guides. Close matches among the selves—actual, ideal, and ought—lead to feelings of satisfaction, and discrepancies among the selves lead to feelings of dissatisfaction. We turn now to these emotional outcomes, as well as other feelings associated with the self.

SELF-ESTEEM: EVALUATING THE SELF

The self is more than a knowledge structure and a guide to behavior. The self also has an affective, or emotional, component that consists of both positive and negative self-evaluations. This is known as self-esteem. We evaluate, judge, and have feelings about ourselves. We are motivated to try to feel good about ourselves, and we actively pursue this goal in both conscious and unconscious ways. We saw earlier in this chapter, for example, that people find it easier to remember positive and pleasant events from the past, incidents that reflect well on them. By continually adjusting perceptions, interpretations, and memories, the self works tirelessly behind the scenes to maintain positive self-feelings and self-evaluations, or high self-esteem.

Self-esteem is affected both by our ideas about how we are measuring up to our own standards and by our ability to control our sense of self in interactions with others. Both of these processes—one primarily internal, the other primarily external—have important repercussions on our feelings about ourselves.

Internal Influences on Self-Esteem

Our feelings about ourselves come from many sources. Some, perhaps most, we carry forward from childhood, when our basic self-concepts were formed from interactions with our parents and other adults. Research in child development indicates that people develop basic feelings of trust, security, and self-worth—or mistrust, insecurity, and worthlessness—out of these early relationships and experiences.

Other feelings about ourselves come from our evaluations of ourselves in terms of our internal standards, our self-guides. The closer the match among our various self-concepts, the better we feel about ourselves. Additionally, the more information we have about ourselves and the more certain we are of it, the better we feel about ourselves. This is especially true if the self-attributes we are most certain of are those that are most important to us (Pelham, 1991). Our ability to self-regulate, to match our performance to our expectations and standards, also affects our self-esteem. In sum, then, we tend to have high self-esteem if we have (1) a close match among our selves; (2) strong and certain knowledge about ourselves, especially if it includes attributes that we value; and (3) the ability to self-regulate.

Close Matches Versus Discrepancies Researchers have investigated how self-esteem is affected by good matches versus discrepancies among the selves. When there is a good match between our actual self and our ideal self, we experience feelings of satisfaction and high self-esteem. When there is a good match between our actual self and our ought self, we experience feelings of security (Higgins, 1989). (Recall that the actual self is what you or another think you are currently; the ideal self is the mental representation of the attributes that either you or another would like you to be or

A good match between actual and ideal selves contributes to a person's feelings of satisfaction, security, and self-esteem. Simply put, such individuals like themselves and feel satisfied with their achievements. U.S. Secretary of Health and Human Services Donna Shalala conveys the sense that her actual and ideal selves are closely matched.

wishes you could be; and the ought self is that which you or others believe you should be.) Good matches may also allow people to focus their attention outside of themselves, on other people and activities. Secretary of Health and Human Services Donna Shalala was once asked how she managed to have so much energy all the time. She responded, "I have no inner conflicts."

But what happens when we can't close the discrepancy gap? Certainly it is not possible for us always to reach our ideals. Most of us must know that there are discrepancies between what we are, what we would like to be, and what we think we ought to be.

These discrepancies, if sizable, lead to negative emotions and low self-esteem. As with good matches, the exact nature of the negative emotional response depends on which self-guide we believe we are not matching (Higgins & Tykocinsky, 1992). When the discrepancy is between the actual self and the ideal self, the result tends to be depressive emotions such as sadness or disappointment. Researchers who asked people what happened when they failed to meet their parents' ideal for them found that the stronger the person's belief that he or she had failed to meet that ideal, the more the person currently experienced depression (Higgins & Tykocinsky, 1992). Discrepancies between the actual self and the ought self, on the other hand, tend to lead to feelings of fear, anxiety, and restlessness. People who indicated that they were punished or criticized by their parents for not being the person they ought to be reported that they frequently felt anxious or uneasy (Higgins & Tykocinsky, 1992).

So, for example, if you wanted to be a rock star and instead became a dentist, or if your father wanted you to be an attorney and you ended up a cab driver, you might feel sad or at least wistful about it. But if your parents

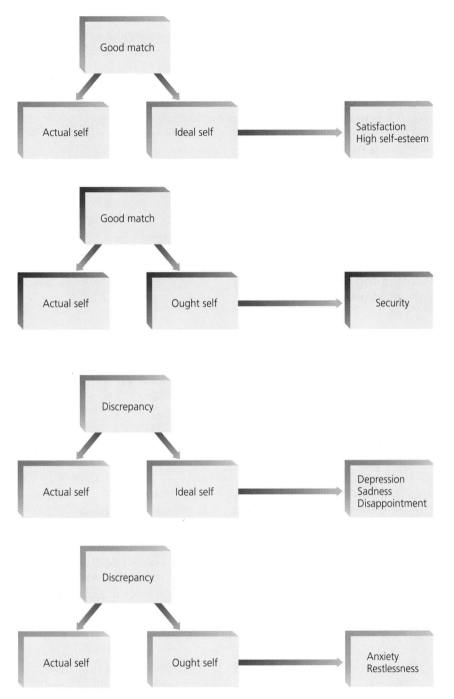

FIGURE **2-4** *Good matches and discrepancies among the selves: emotional outcomes.*

wanted you to be a dutiful son or daughter, maintaining close contact with them after you left home, and you found you would rather establish some distance from them, you might experience anxiety as a result. Figure 2-4 illustrates the outcomes of good matches and discrepancies among the selves.

Integrating Positive and Negative Thoughts   Positive self-esteem does not mean that people have only positive self-evaluations. They do not. When normal people with positive self-esteem think about themselves, roughly 62% of their thoughts are positive and 38% are negative (Showers, 1992). What is important is how those thoughts are arranged. People with high self-esteem blend the positive and negative aspects of their self-concept. A negative thought tends to trigger a counterbalancing positive thought. A person who learns she is "socially awkward," for example, may think, "but I am a loyal friend." This integration of positive and negative self-thoughts helps to control feelings about the self and maintain positive self-esteem.

But some people group positive and negative thoughts separately. The thought "I am socially awkward" triggers another negative thought, such as "I am insecure." This is what happens in people who are chronically depressed: A negative thought sets off a chain reaction of other negative thoughts. There are no positive thoughts available to act as a buffer.

Maintaining Self-Esteem in Interactions with Others

In order to feel good about ourselves, it is not enough to self-regulate. We also need to maintain and enhance our self-esteem in our interactions with others, as well as defend it against the inevitable threats that life throws in our path. When interacting with others, human beings have two primary self-related motives: (1) to enhance self-esteem and (2) to maintain self-consistency (Berkowitz, 1988).

Enhancing Self-Esteem   Obviously, people have a powerful need to feel good about themselves. They prefer positive responses from the social world. They become anxious when their self-esteem is under threat. What steps do they take to maintain and enhance self-esteem?

According to Abraham Tesser's *self-evaluation maintenance* (SEM) theory (1988), the behavior of other people, both friends and strangers, affects how we feel about ourselves, especially when the behavior is in an area that is important to our own self-concept. The self carefully manages emotional responses to events in the social world, depending on how threatening it perceives those events to be. Tesser gives this example to illustrate his theory:

> Suppose, for example, that Jill thinks of herself as a math whiz. Jill and Joan are close friends; Joan receives a 99 and Jill a 90 on a math test. Because math is relevant to Jill, the comparison is important. Therefore, Joan's better performance is a threat, particularly since Joan is a close other. There are a variety of things that Jill can do about this threat. She can reduce the relevance of Joan's performance. If math were not important to Jill's own self-definition she could bask in the reflection of Joan's performance. Jill could also reduce her closeness to Joan . . . then Joan's performance would be less consequential. Finally, Jill could try to affect their relative performance by working harder or doing something to handicap Joan. (Tesser & Collins, 1988, p. 695)

According to self-evaluation maintenance theory, we are threatened by a high achievement in a self-relevant area by a person to whom we are close. This theory predicts that either of these two sisters will feel threatened (rather than proud) if the other surpasses her on the court.

This story neatly captures the basic elements of SEM theory. The essential question that Jill asks about Joan's performance is, What effect does Joan's behavior have on my evaluation of myself? Notice that Jill compares herself to Joan on a behavior that is important to her own self-concept. If Joan excelled at bowling and Jill cared not a fig about knocking down pins with a large ball, she would not be threatened by Joan's rolling a 300 game or winning a bowling championship. In fact, she would *bask in the reflected glory* (BIRG) of her friend's performance; Jill's self-esteem would be enhanced because her friend did so well (Cialdini et al., 1976).

Because Joan's performance in math is relevant to Jill's self-definition, however, Jill engages in a *comparison process* with her friend. If the behavior were not relevant (bowling), Jill would simply reflect on Joan's performance (the *reflection process*). She would feel good for Joan if she did well and sorry if she did not do well (Tesser, 1988).

The comparison process is activated when you are dealing with someone who is close to you. If you found out that 10% of high school students who took the math SAT did better than you, it would have less of an emotional impact on your self-esteem than if you learned that your best friend scored a perfect 800, putting her at the top of all people who took the exam (provided, that is, that math ability was important to your self-concept).

SEM theory is concerned with the self's response to threat, the kinds of social threats encountered in everyday life. Tesser formulated SEM theory by investigating people's responses to social threats in terms of the two

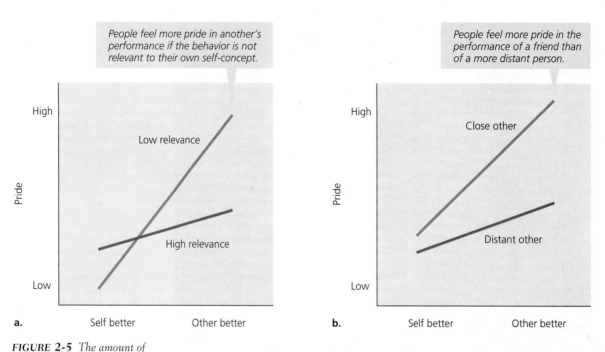

People feel more pride in another's performance if the behavior is not relevant to their own self-concept.

People feel more pride in the performance of a friend than of a more distant person.

a.

Pride

High

Low

Low relevance

High relevance

Self better   Other better

b.

Pride

High

Low

Close other

Distant other

Self better   Other better

FIGURE 2-5 *The amount of pride people show in the performance of either a close or distant other person as determined by the individual's performance and the importance of the behavior to the individual. (a) On tasks that are highly self-relevant, people feel less pride in the performance of another person as compared to when the behavior is not self-relevant. (b) People feel more pride in the performance of a close friend when he or she does well than in the performance of a distant other.*

dimensions just described—relevance of the behavior to a subject's self-concept and closeness of the subject to the other person (Tesser & Collins, 1988). Subjects were asked to remember and describe social situations in which a close or distant other performed better or worse than they did. Half the time the task was important to the subject's self-concept, and half the time the task was unimportant. The participants also reported the emotions they felt during those episodes.

Results indicated that when the behavior was judged relevant to the self, emotions were heightened. When subjects did better than the other, distant or close, they felt happier, and when they did worse, they felt more personal disgust, anger, and frustration. When the behavior was not particularly relevant to the self, emotions varied, depending on the closeness of the relationship. When a close other performed better than the subject, the subject felt pride in that performance. As you would expect, subjects felt less pride in the performance of a distant other. And of course, they felt less pride in the friend's performance when the behavior was self-relevant. Figure 2-5 shows these variations in response to the performance of others.

One conclusion we can draw from this research and from SEM theory is that people are willing to make *some* sacrifices to accuracy if it means a gain in self-esteem. People do undoubtedly want and need accurate information about themselves and how they compare to significant others (Trope, 1983), but they also display an equally powerful need to feel positive about themselves. This need for self-enhancement suggests that in appraising our own performances and in presenting ourselves to others, we tend to exaggerate our positive attributes.

In sum, then, one way the self maintains self-esteem is to adjust its responses to social threats. If a friend does better than we do at something we pride ourselves on, we experience a threat to that part of our self-concept. Our friend's achievement suggests that we may not be as good in an important area as we thought we were. To preserve the integrity and consistency of the self-concept and to maintain high self-esteem we can (1) try to downplay the other's achievement; (2) put more distance between ourselves and the other, since we feel less threatened by the performance of a distant other; or (3) work hard to improve our own performance or try to handicap our friend. In each case, the self subtly adjusts our perceptions, emotions, and behaviors in the service of enhancing self-esteem.

Our personal self-esteem is determined not only by our individual attributes and achievements but also by the status and achievements of the groups with which we identify. Any threats to those groups may be perceived as a threat to ourselves. For a discussion of how the self defends itself in situations like these, see the featured discussion "Self-Esteem and Terror Management."

Maintaining Self-Consistency The second driving motive of the self in social interactions is to maintain high self-consistency—agreement between our self-concept and the views others have of us. We all have a great investment in our self-concepts, and we make a strong effort to support and confirm them. Motivated by a need for **self-verification**—confirmation of our self-concept from others—we tend to behave in ways that lead others to see us as we see ourselves (Swann, Hixon, & De La Ronde, 1992). The need for self-verification is more than just a simple preference for consistency over inconsistency. Self-verification lends orderliness and predictability to the social world and allows us to feel that we have control (Swann, Stein-Seroussi, & Giesler, 1992).

People seek to confirm their self-concepts regardless of whether those ideas are positive or negative. One study showed that people with unfavorable self-concepts tended not to pick roommates who had positive impressions of them (Swann, Pelham, & Krull, 1989). In other words, people with negative self-concepts preferred to be with people who had formed negative impressions of them, which were consistent with their own views of themselves.

Another study tested the idea that people search for partners who will help them self-verify (Swann, Hixon, & De La Ronde, 1992). Half the subjects in this experiment had positive self-concepts, and half had negative self-concepts. All subjects were told that they would soon have the chance to converse with one of two people (an "evaluator") and could choose one of the two. Every subject saw comments that these two people had made about the subject. One set of comments was positive; the other set was negative (all comments were fictitious).

As shown in Figure 2-6, people with negative self-concepts preferred to interact with an evaluator who had made negative comments, whereas people with positive self-concepts preferred someone who had made

self-verification Confirmation of our self-concept from others—we tend to behave in ways that lead others to see us as we see ourselves.

We gain self-esteem not just from our individual attributes and performances but also from the attributes and performances of the groups to which we belong. Remember, the self is a social construct. Our personal self-esteem is determined by our membership in a variety of groups, large and small, and the success of those groups influences how we feel about ourselves as individuals.

Consider some group memberships: You may think of yourself as a Catholic, an opponent of abortion, a member of the local arts society, a U.S. Marine reserve officer, an American, a St. Louis Cardinal fan, and a member of Jack's Deli softball team. Threats to any one of these groups may affect your personal self-esteem.

Sheldon Solomon, Jeff Greenberg, and Tom Pyszczynski (1992) have a theory about how we maintain self-esteem under threat, why people need self-

esteem, and how self-esteem affects our social behavior. They call this theory *terror management theory* (TMT). It suggests that we human beings know we are living in an unpredictable universe—our existence is fleeting and could be ended at almost any moment. When we become aware of this condition, it scares the heck out of us. As individuals and as societies, therefore, we try to devise methods to protect ourselves against, or at least control, the terror that this realization produces.

TMT suggests that cultures provide people with a buffer, a "terror shield," against the ultimate terror (death, nothingness). They do this by allowing us to be-

lieve we are worthy people in a world that is orderly, stable, controllable, and meaningful. Any threat to our culture puts our personal self-esteem at risk. Attacks on cultural values or symbols, such as the flag, increase our anxiety and compel us to react with anger and hostility.

Solomon, Greenberg, and Pyszczynski offer rock music as an example of this kind of perceived attack on American society. In the 1960s, rock music was identified with the "counterculture," with rebellion against the values of mainstream American culture. People proclaimed their contempt for materialism, for business and industry, for the Vietnam War, for the military, for conservative clothes, for "straight" jobs, attitudes, and lifestyles—for the 1950s American way of life. Jerry Rubin threw money from the balcony of the New York Stock Exchange, and Abbie Hoffman pub-

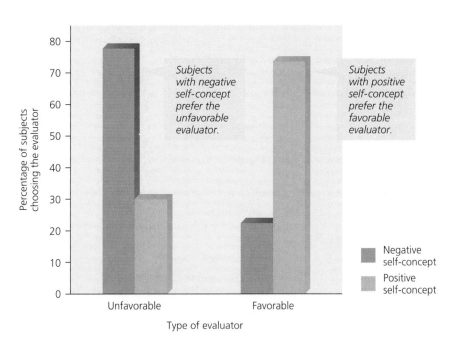

FIGURE 2-6 *Preferences for interaction partners. People tend to prefer interacting with evaluators who verify their self-concepts, whether positive or negative.* From Swann, Stein-Seroussin, and Giesler, 1992.

Subjects with negative self-concept prefer the unfavorable evaluator.

Subjects with positive self-concept prefer the favorable evaluator.

Percentage of subjects choosing the evaluator

Negative self-concept
Positive self-concept

Unfavorable   Favorable

Type of evaluator

lished *Steal This Book*. Psychedelic drugs, "free love," communal living, long hair, and hippie clothes completed the attack on mainstream American cultural values.

The rallying cry of this movement was provided by rock and roll. Standing against the "easy-listening" pop music of the 1950s, it challenged the direction of American political, economic, and social policies. From Bob Dylan's "Blowin' in the Wind" and "Masters of War" to the Beatles' "Lucy in the Sky with Diamonds" to Jimi Hendrix's "Purple Haze," rock music in the 1960s and early 1970s represented an attack on every aspect of American society. For a time, Americans were polarized into two camps. Those in the mainstream directed hostility and hatred at those in the counterculture. This polarization probably reached its height in 1970 when four students at Kent State University were killed by the National Guard, called out to quell a campus protest.

But typically, when a member of a group departs from the group's values, the group will expend great effort trying to recapture that person and bring him or her back into the fold (Schachter, 1951). Both the deviant individual and the group make some accommodation in this process. This is what has happened with rock music. The protest songs of the 1960s can now be heard in shopping malls and dentists' offices. They are today's "easy listening." Rock singers who began their careers as counterculture heroes now sing the praises of America's favorite beers. The Beatles' song "Revolution" became the background music for an athletic-shoe commercial.

The threat that rock music presented to mainstream cultural values has been diluted by accommodation on both sides.

Mainstream culture has accepted and assimilated the sound of rock, shaping it to its own uses. Rock musicians who have "sold out" have no doubt found it hard to resist the enormous amounts of money available for those who play the game. Mainstream culture has succeeded in disarming the massive attack of the 1960s and bringing the whole system into balance.

---

*H*ow valid do you think the notion of terror management is? Do you think some cultures provide a more effective buffer against this kind of existential terror than others do? By what means? What insights does terror management theory provide into warfare and international conflict?

---

positive comments. Why would someone prefer a negative evaluator? Here is one subject's explanation:

> I like the (favorable) evaluation, but I am not sure that is, ah, correct, maybe. It *sounds* good, but the (unfavorable evaluator) . . . seems to know more about me. So I'll choose the (unfavorable evaluator). (Swann, Hixon, & De La Ronde, 1992, p. 16)

In another study, spouses with positive self-concepts were found to be more committed to their marriage when their mates thought well of them. No surprise there. But, in keeping with self-verification theory, spouses with negative self-concepts were more committed to their partners if their mates thought poorly of them (Swann, Hixon, & De La Ronde, 1992).

People with low self-esteem do appreciate positive evaluations, but, in the end, they prefer to interact with people who see them as they see themselves (Jones, 1990). Recall the effort and difficulty Jay Gatsby invested in his attempt to be something he was not. It's easier and less complicated to be yourself than to live up to someone's impression of you that, while flattering, is inaccurate.

People tend to seek self-verification in fairly narrow areas of the self-concept (Jones, 1990). You don't seek out information to confirm that you are a good or bad person, but that your voice is not very good or that you are really not a top-notch speaker. If your self-concept is complex, such negative feedback gives you accurate information about yourself but does not seriously damage your self-esteem.

People not only choose to interact with others who will verify their self-concepts but also search for situations that will serve that purpose. If, for example, you think of yourself as a storehouse of general knowledge, you may be the first to jump into a game of Trivial Pursuit. You have control over that kind of situation. But if you are the kind of person who can't remember a lot of trivial information or who doesn't care that FDR had a dog named Fala, then being forced to play Trivial Pursuit represents a loss of control.

Finally, keep in mind that most people have a positive self-concept. Therefore, when they self-verify, they are in essence enhancing their self-image because they generally get positive feedback. So, for most of us self-verification does not contradict the need for self-enhancement. But, as Swann's research has shown, people also need to live in predictable and stable worlds. This last requirement is met by our need for self-verification.

THE SELF AND OTHERS: IMPRESSION MANAGEMENT

Obviously, most of us have a great investment in how others perceive and evaluate us. We need to protect our self-esteem and maintain self-consistency. We want to have personal control over our social environment (Arkin & Baumgardner, 1986). Therefore, we often carefully consider how we are going to present ourselves to other people. Most of us engage in **impression management,** the process of presenting ourselves in certain ways in order to control the impressions that others form of us (Leary & Kowalski, 1990). For a closer look at this process in a public figure, see the featured discussion "Crafting a Public Image: The Case of Benazir Bhutto."

Some people have a clear idea of the image they would like to convey. Jay Gatsby certainly did. He wanted others to think of him as fabulously wealthy, highly educated, mysterious, and perhaps a bit dangerous. He carefully crafted those images. Other people might not always know exactly what image they want to convey. Nevertheless, most of us, in most situations, are concerned with the impression we make on others.

How People Manage Self-Presentations

Several factors, both situational and personal, influence how and when people try to manage the impressions they make on others. Situational factors include such variables as the social context, the "stakes" in the situation, and the supportiveness of the audience. Personal factors include such variables as whether the person has high or low self-esteem and whether the person has more or less of a tendency to self-monitor.

impression management The process of presenting ourselves in certain ways in order to control the impressions that others form of us.

egotistical bias The tendency of people to present themselves as responsible for success whether they are or not.

self-monitoring Focusing on one's own behavior in a given social situation. The degree, ranging from low to high, to which individuals self-monitor reflects their need to manage and control the impressions they make on others.

Self-Esteem and Impression Management One research study looked at how people with high and low self-esteem differed in their approaches to making a good impression (Schlenker, Weigold, & Hallam, 1990). People with low self-esteem were found to be very cautious in trying to create a positive impression. In general, they simply are not confident of their ability to pull it off. When presenting themselves, they focus on minimizing their bad points. On the other hand, people with high self-esteem tend to focus on their good points when presenting themselves.

As might be expected, people with low self-esteem present themselves in a less egotistical manner than those with high self-esteem. When describing a success, they tend to share the credit with others. People with high self-esteem take credit for success even when other people may have given them help (Schlenker, Soraci, & McCarthy, 1976). Interestingly, all people seem to have an **egotistical bias;** that is, they present themselves as responsible for success whether they are or are not.

Social context makes a difference in how people present themselves, but in different ways for people with high and low self-esteem. When subjects were told to try to make a good impression in front of an audience (Schlenker, et al., 1990), people with high self-esteem presented themselves in a very egotistical and boastful way, pointing out their sterling qualities. People with low self-esteem toned down egotistical tendencies in this high-pressure situation, becoming more timid. It seems that when the social stakes increase, people with high self-esteem become more interested in enhancing their self-presentation, whereas their low self-esteem counterparts are more concerned with protecting themselves from further blows to the self (Schlenker, 1987).

Self-Monitoring and Impression Management Another factor that influences impression management is the degree to which a person engages in **self-monitoring**—that is, focuses on his or her self-presentation according to the demands of the situation. Some people are constantly gathering data on their own actions. These high self-monitors are very sensitive to

Low self-monitors spend less time worrying about impression management and more time enjoying each other's company, as seems to be the case for the group on the top. High self-monitors care about the impression they are making on others and want to be seen with attractive partners. The couple on the bottom may have chosen each other more on the basis of appearance than on the basis of personality or character traits.

How does a modern, Westernized woman manage to become leader of a male-dominated Islamic country? This was the challenge facing Benazir Bhutto when she found herself in a position to become prime minister of Pakistan. Part of that challenge involved creating a public image that would persuade the Pakistani people of her right and her ability to lead the country.

Bhutto was born into a powerful, aristocratic family. Her father, Zulfiqar Ali Bhutto, was the founder of the socialist Pakistan's People's Party (PPP) and the first president of Pakistan to be democratically elected. Benazir grew up in luxury, pampered by servants and favored by her father, on a walled estate of 10,000 acres. In 1969, at the age of 16, she was sent to Radcliffe; after one semester she abandoned her silk native dress for jeans and sweatshirts. She read feminist literature, went to rock concerts, and marched against the war in Vietnam. Impassioned and fiercely intelligent, she became a fiery debater and a defender of Pakistani nationalism.

She went on to Oxford, where her father had enrolled her at the time of her birth, to study politics, philosophy, and economics. She was elected president of the prestigious debating club and became known as a "jet-setting princess" who drove a yellow sports car and was always accompanied by handsome young men. She planned a career in law and the foreign service.

But soon after she returned to Pakistan, her father was overthrown by General Zia ul-Haq of the Pakistan army, jailed, and subsequently hanged. With her mother, Benazir assumed leadership of the PPP and began a campaign to restore democracy to Pakistan. She too was arrested and jailed. Her years of imprisonment included a period of solitary confinement in a notorious desert prison where her guards often left her enough poison to kill herself. She was sustained, she says, by anger (Weaver, 1993, p. 100).

On release in 1984, she went into exile in London, but she returned to Pakistan in 1986 and began a new campaign to force Zia to hold elections. In 1988 she was elected prime minister of Pakistan, only the second person to be popularly elected to that office and the first female prime minister in the Islamic world. She was ousted from her position in 1990, but in 1993 she ran again and was reelected.

How did she do it? How did an expensively educated, Westernized woman win the leadership of a country dominated by a feudal landed aristocracy, a powerful military organization, and Islamic clerics? It is a country where women live in seclusion and appear in public heavily veiled. When Bhutto campaigned, the few women who came to hear her were restricted to separate enclosures, as is traditional in Islamic countries.

Benazir Bhutto is, in the words of a Western diplomat, a "bewildering woman" with a carefully crafted public image. Although she is an aristocrat, she is adored by many as a populist, a public figure who cares about the common people. When she was campaigning for election, tens of thousands of ecstatic supporters—mostly young men—came to hear her speak. She would of-

the social demands of any situation and tend to fit their behavior to those demands. They are always aware of the impressions they are making on others; low self-monitors are much less concerned with impression management.

High self-monitors are concerned with how things look to others. For example, they tend to choose romantic partners who are physically attractive (Snyder, Berscheid, & Glick, 1985). Low self-monitors are more concerned with meeting people with similar personality traits and interests. Most high self-monitors are aware that they fit their behavior to the expecten ask the crowd, "What is the price of meat today? What is the price of flour?" (Weaver, 1993, p. 87).

Bhutto is also honored as the daughter of Zulfikar Ali Bhutto. Although the people had been dissatisfied with his leadership and supported the climate that led to his overthrow, they revere his memory and his name. That he was hanged, and that Bhutto spent long years in prison from the time she was 24, contribute to the family mystique. "Muslims prize martyrdom, and to them suffering is a form of validation" (Watson, 1986, p. 34). During her campaigns Bhutto presented herself as "an orphaned 'sister' seeking justice" for her father's death. She would often tell the crowd, "You are my brothers, I am your sister" (Watson, 1986, p. 33).

The fact that Benazir Bhutto is a woman was perhaps her greatest liability. Most of those with power in Pakistan regard a female leader as unnatural and repellent, and they have tried to undermine her leadership. But Bhutto has cultivated the image of herself as a traditional, God-fearing Islamic woman. After returning to Pakistan in 1986, she began appearing in public in a veil, and she agreed to an arranged marriage. She uses the women's entrance at her family home in Sindh. One observer remarked, she "understands the woman's place in Pakistan. At a . . . campaign stop . . . she spent hours mourning with other women over the death of a young party worker who had been killed by police" (Watson, 1986, p. 34).

Other Pakistanis, more Westernized and liberal, hoped Bhutto would bring reforms to better the position of women. One critic commented, "When Benazir came to power, she could have set the trend, but the first thing she did was to shroud herself in a [veil] . . . and begin praying incessantly at saints' tombs, the most superstitious part of Islam. . . . She could have been a reformer, but she wasn't; she did nothing for women. . . ." More recently, however, Benazir has undertaken some actions designed to improve the lot of Pakistani women. She has ordered that a certain number of civil service jobs be reserved for women and has proposed that special parliamentary seats for women, abolished in 1990, be restored.

Describing Bhutto in 1993, an observer wrote, "One senses in talking to Benazir that the role of Prime Minister was not an easy one for her to adopt, and that she was never quite certain how to protect herself: Should she be the avenging feudal daughter of Sindh? The urbane internationalist? The demure Muslim mother and wife? Or the impetuous aristocrat who, with arrogant ease, could plunge into the maelstrom of political maneuvering and intrigue?" (Weaver, 1993, p. 104).

We might also ask, Is she a master of public image, brilliantly manipulating how people see her? Or is she a complex woman with many identities?

---

*W*hat methods do you think Benazir Bhutto used to manage the impression she made on others? Do you see similar techniques used by other public figures, such as Hillary Rodham Clinton? What special problems do you think public figures have in managing impressions that private individuals don't have to face?

---

tations of others. If they were to take a self-assessment like the one presented in Figure 2-7 (Snyder, 1987), they would agree with the "high self-monitor" statements.

It may be that low self-monitors have less need to manage other people's impressions of them. They may have high self-esteem or strong, consistent self-concepts. Remember, people who know themselves well like themselves more than those who don't have a lot of self-knowledge (Baumgardner, 1990). All of these factors may influence people's need to manage and control the impressions they make on others.

1. *I would probably make a good actor. (H)*
2. *My behavior is usually an expression of my true inner feelings. (L)*
3. *I have never been good at games like charades or improvisational acting. (L)*
4. *I'm not always the person I appear to be. (H)*
5. *I can deceive people by being friendly when I really dislike them. (H)*
6. *I can argue only for ideas that I already believe. (L)*
7. *I find it hard to imitate the behavior of other people. (L)*
8. *In order to get along and be liked, I tend to be what people expect me to be rather than anything else. (H)*

(H) indicates items with which high self-monitors would agree.
(L) indicates items with which low self-monitors would agree.

Self-Presentation and Manipulative Strategies

When people engage in impression management, their goal is to make a favorable impression on others. But sometimes people want to do more than create a good impression: They want to get something out of the interaction. To reach their goals they try to manipulate the people with whom they are interacting, using any of several strategies. Edward Jones (1990) identified five different manipulative strategies (Table 2-1). You probably have encountered some of these strategies in your dealings with others.

Some people use *ingratiation,* an attempt to get you to like them. They agree with you, say nice things about you, and offer you help or favors. Other people are more inclined toward power as a manipulative tool. *Intimidators,* for example, want to be seen as tough and ruthless, as individuals you wouldn't want to "mess with." Their tactic is fear. *Self-promoters* try to project an image of themselves as "winners." They tell you how many widgets they sold on their last sales trip or how high their test scores were. Their goal is to gain your respect. *Exemplifiers* have a lot in common with self-promoters. They try to present themselves as individuals of superior virtue, people who have often suffered in a good cause—whereas you have not. And in fact, exemplifiers often have given themselves over to some cause or banner and have sacrificed for it. Their sacrifice gives them a claim to special virtue. Finally, *supplicators* use the strategy of last resort, the approach used by low-status persons. Supplicators present their weakness, hoping, by their pleas for help, to engage your feelings of obligation toward them.

Table 2-1 indicates that each of these strategies has some serious potential drawbacks. As Abe Lincoln remarked, you can't fool all of the people all of the time. People who use these manipulative strategies on a regular basis are likely to have them backfire at least some of the time.

TABLE 2-1

GOALS AND RISKS OF SOME MANIPULATIVE SELF-PRESENTATION STRATEGIES

Strategy	Goal	Risk	Outcome Sought	Action Used
Ingratiation	Likable	Slavish flatterer	Affection	Flattery
Intimidation	Dangerous	Blusterer	Fear	Threats
Self-promotion	"A winner"	Conceited	Respect	Accomplishments
Exemplification	Worthy	Hypocrite	Guilt	Self-denial
Supplication	Unfortunate	Lazy	Obligation	Call for help

Adapted from Jones (1990).

Creating a Negative Impression: Self-Destructive Behaviors

We have seen that people work hard to create favorable impressions on others. Yet we all know people who seem determined to make a poor impression and to behave in ways that are ultimately harmful to themselves. Do people actually try to harm, defeat, or even destroy themselves in systematic ways?

Investigations of this question have led researchers to identify three models of self-destruction (Baumeister & Scher, 1988). The first, **primary self-destruction,** involves actions that are harmful because the person foresees and desires the pain. The second category, **counterproductive strategies,** involves situations in which people seek positive outcomes but use ineffective or counterproductive strategies to achieve them. These people want to have positive control over their lives and social world, but they pick the wrong strategies for doing so. The third category involves **self-handicapping.** In this situation a person, prior to doing something important (like taking an exam), provides himself or herself with a ready excuse in case of failure. In each case, however, the individual may still be seen as trying to maintain control over his or her social world.

Primary Self-Destruction Little evidence exists to show that people engage in primary self-destruction—at least normal people. It is likely that those who commit suicide or other acts of great self-harm are excluded from experimental samples because they have been labeled mentally ill. People not mentally ill who commit suicide may have decided that death is preferable to an intolerable life. In this sense, they are asserting control over their lives just as much as someone who works hard to create a favorable impression before an audience. For example, a young man recently leapt to his death from the Golden Gate Bridge, the 900th such suicide. His sister told his story: He was a vigorous young man now afflicted with AIDS, brain cancer, and incipient blindness. He did not want to be a burden to his companion or his loving family. After a farewell dinner, he leapt from the bridge. Self-destructive? Yes. Did he have control over his life? You judge.

primary self-destruction
Self-destructive behavior involving actions that are harmful because the person foresees and desires the pain.

counterproductive strategies Self-destructive behavior in which a person seeks positive outcomes but uses ineffective (counterproductive) strategies to achieve them.

self-handicapping When, prior to doing something important (like taking an exam), a person provides himself or herself with a ready excuse in case of failure.

Counterproductive Strategies Situations involving counterproductive strategies are much more common than cases of primary self-destruction. As an example, consider the process of salary negotiation in major league baseball. When a player and a team cannot agree on a salary figure, the dispute may be submitted to arbitration. Each party submits a salary figure, along with supporting arguments, to an arbitrator who considers the case and chooses either one figure or the other. In this situation, overestimating one's value may lead to an excessive and self-defeating demand. Let's say the athlete wants to get $800,000 even though he believes that his "true" worth is $600,000. The team offers $400,000. What figure should the player submit to the arbitrator to get as close to $800,000 as possible? He is likely to choose something like $750,000 since it is closer to his "true" value than is the team's offer. But if he is overconfident about his true value and the arbitrator believes that $575,000 is the fair market price for his talents, then the arbitrator will choose the team's offer of $400,000. A slight miscalculation based on a misjudgment costs the athlete a lot of money (Bazerman, 1986).

As this example shows, counterproductive strategies lead to negative outcomes not because of deliberate self-defeating impulses but because of faulty reasoning. Notice that the problem occurs because the ballplayer overrates his performance compared to the evaluation of more objective observers. He fails to see that other people may have a different view of reality—in particular, of his ability—than he does. This tendency to have positive illusions about the self is a continuing theme in human social interactions, as described in the next four chapters.

Self-Handicapping The third kind of self-destructive behavior is called self-handicapping. Have you ever goofed off before an important exam, knowing that you should study? Or have you ever slacked off at a sport even though you have a big match coming up? If you have—and most of us have at one time or another—you have engaged in what social psychologists call self-handicapping (Berglas & Jones, 1978). People self-handicap when they are unsure of future success and, by putting an obstacle in their way, protect their self-esteem if they should perform badly.

The purpose of self-handicapping is to mask the relationship between performance and ability if you should fail. If you do not do well on an examination because you did not study, the evaluator doesn't know whether your bad grade was due to the lack of preparation (the handicap) or a lack of ability. Of course, if you succeed despite the handicap, then you are evaluated that much more positively. This is a way of controlling the impression people have of you, no matter what the outcome.

Although the aim of self-handicapping is to protect the person's self-esteem, it does have some dangers. After all, what are we to make of someone who goes to a movie rather than studying for a final exam? In one research study, college students negatively evaluated the character of a person who did not study for an important exam (Luginbuhl & Palmer, 1991). The self-handicappers succeeded in their self-presentations in the sense that the students were not sure whether their bad grade was due to lack of ability or lack of preparation. But the students did not think very much of someone

Success can be the ultimate challenge to the self. Some successful people resort to self-handicapping behaviors in order to manage conflicting self-perceptions and the demands of public life. River Phoenix is just one of the many young, talented individuals who have lost their lives to self-destructive behavior.

who would not study for an exam. Therefore, self-handicapping has mixed results for impression management.

Still, people are willing to make this trade-off. They are probably aware that their self-handicapping will be seen unfavorably. But they would rather have people think they're lazy or irresponsible than dumb or incompetent. A study found that people who self-handicapped and failed at a task had higher self-esteem and were in a better mood than people who did not handicap and failed (Rhodewalt, Morf, Hazlett, & Fairfield, 1991).

Self-handicapping can take two forms (Baumeister & Scher, 1988). The first occurs when the person really wants to succeed but has doubts about the outcome. This person will put some excuse in place. An athlete who says that she has had a nagging injury while knowing that she is capable of winning is using this kind of impression management strategy. People will really be impressed if she wins despite her injury; if she loses, they'll chalk it up to that Achilles tendon problem.

The second form also involves the creation of obstacles to success but is more self-destructive. In this case, the individual fears that some success is a fluke or a mistake and finds ways to subvert it, usually by handicapping himself in a destructive and internal manner. For example, a person who is suddenly propelled to fame as a movie star may find himself showing up late for rehearsals, or blowing his lines, or getting into fights with the director. It may be because he doesn't really believe he's that good an actor, or he may fear he won't be able to live up to his new status. Perhaps being rich and famous doesn't match his self-concept. Consequently, he handicaps himself in some way.

The abuse of alcohol and drugs may be an example of self-handicapping (Berglas & Jones, 1978). Abusers may be motivated by a need to have an excuse for possible failure. They would rather that others blame substance abuse for their (anticipated) failure than lack of ability. Like the athlete with the injured leg, they want ability to be discounted as the reason for failure but credited as the basis for success. Since the self-handicapper will be embarrassed if the excuse that clouds the link between performance and outcome is absurd, it is important that the excuse be a reasonable and believable one. Self-handicapping is thus another way people attempt to maintain control over the impression others have of them.

How Public Behavior Affects Private Self-Knowledge

The images we try to convey to other people are not without consequences for what we think about ourselves. When people alter their self-presentations to create a specific impression for others, there is a shift in their own self-concepts in the direction of the managed image (Rhodewalt, 1986). Surely each layer that Jay Gatsby added to his self-presentation altered his self-concept. It may be that the various tricks Gatsby used to construct and convey his image left him with little of his own core self.

Self-presentations are more likely to become part of the person's self-concept when the images conveyed are in line with the person's beliefs about him- or herself. In one study, people with strong and certain self-beliefs were influenced only by self-presentations that were close to their true self-concept (Schlenker & Trudeau, 1990). These people may have tried, for example, to portray themselves as happy-go-lucky at a party, but that was not in keeping with their self-beliefs. The happy-go-lucky self-presentation did not influence their permanent self-concept.

In contrast, people who had weak and uncertain self-concepts were much more influenced by their self-presentations. If they conveyed a "party animal" image, they were likely to incorporate that presentation into their self-concept. The more extreme their self-presentations, the more they changed their self-concept.

What we see is that learning about ourselves is a process that does not end. As theory and research about the self suggest, all of us are constantly negotiating with ourselves and others what identities we feel most comfortable with, what parts of the self we wish to present to others, and what aspects we want to keep private.

GATSBY REVISITED

Jay Gatsby is, of course, a fictional character. Fitzgerald writes in a very lean prose, so we know very little, if anything, of Gatsby's thoughts about himself. We can only make inferences from his behavior and from the responses of others to him. Nevertheless, it's easy to see that many of the same psychological needs shaped his behavior as shape our own.

Gatsby was driven by a sense of his own inadequacy and by his failure to truly become the self he wanted to be. His sense of self was primitive and unstable. His inner emptiness led him to define himself by how others thought of him, especially the elusive Daisy. Self-presentation was all he had. In the end, it was not enough.

LOOKING AHEAD

Chapter 2 is the first of five chapters that focus on how we come to structure and understand our social world. The purpose of this chapter has been to explore how we think about ourselves. We saw that the self is the core of our world, the center from which we interpret and understand other people and events. The self guides our behavior so that we can maintain control over our social world, and it allows us to sculpt reality into a shape that pleases us.

We need a basic understanding of how we understand ourselves before we can begin to understand how we perceive and form impressions of other people. These are the topics of Chapter 3. We see how each of us—each self—constructs his or her own version of social reality, based on personal traits, experiences, needs, and goals. We also see that as important as it is that we form accurate ideas about ourselves and others, the cognitive processes by which we do so are by no means flawless. This chapter showed that we humans tend to see ourselves through rose-colored glasses—we retain those memories that most enhance our self-concept, we overrate what we do, and we assume that others see the world as we see it. In the next chapter we will find that we bring all of these biases along when we enter social interactions.

CHAPTER REVIEW

1. *What is the self?*
   The self is, in part, a cognitive structure, containing ideas about who and what we are. It also has an evaluative and emotional component, as we judge ourselves and find ourselves worthy or unworthy. The self guides our behavior as we attempt to make our actions consistent with our ideas about ourselves. Finally, the self guides us as we attempt to manage the impression we make on others.

2. *What thoughts are in the self?*
   A significant part of the self is knowledge. All the ideas, thoughts, and information that we have about ourselves make up our **self-concept.** These bits of knowledge—or cognitions—comprise the cognitive component of the self.

3. *How is the self organized?*
   People arrange knowledge and information about themselves into **self-schemas.** A self-schema contains information about gender, age, race or ethnicity, occupation, social roles, physical attractiveness, intelligence, talents, and so on. Self-schemas help us interpret situations and guide our behavior.

4. *How does the self affect memory?*
   The study of **autobiographical memory**—memory for information relating to the self—shows that the self plays a powerful role in the recall of events. Researchers have found that subjects recalled recent events more quickly than older ones, pleasant events more quickly than unpleasant ones, and extreme events, pleasant and unpleasant, more quickly than neutral episodes. Pleasant events that especially fit the person's self-concept were most easily recalled.

5. *Do we have more than one self?*

In addition to attributes, self-schemas, and memories, the self-concept includes **possible selves**—ideas about what we would like to be (and like to avoid) in the future.

6. *How do we know the self?*

Three sources of social information help us forge our self-concept. The first is our view of how other people react to us. From earliest childhood and throughout life, these **reflected appraisals** shape our self-concept. We also get knowledge about ourselves from comparisons with other people. We engage in the process of **social comparison**—comparing our reactions, abilities, and attributes to those of others—because we need accurate information in order to succeed. The third source of information about ourselves is observation of our own behavior. Sometimes we simply observe our behavior and assume that our motives are consistent with our behavior.

7. *What does the self do?*

A crucial task of the self is to guide and regulate behavior to allow as much control of the social world as possible. It does this principally through the development and use of various *self-guides*. One self-guide is the ideal self, the mental representation of what the person (or a significant other) would like to be. Another self-guide is the ought self, the mental representation of what the person (or a significant other) believes she *should* be. People are motivated to reach a state in which the actual self (the current self-concept) matches the ideal and the ought selves.

The likelihood of self-regulation is affected by three factors: **self-focus,** the extent to which the individual monitors her own behavior and is more concerned with self than with others; self-efficacy expectancies, the extent to which the person believes she can match her actual, ideal, and ought selves; and self-knowledge, the amount of information the person has about herself.

8. *How do we evaluate the self?*

By continually adjusting perceptions, interpretations, and memories, the self works tirelessly behind the scenes to maintain positive self-evaluations, or high self-esteem. Self-esteem is affected both by our ideas about how we are measuring up to our own standards and by our ability to control our sense of self in interactions with others.

According to Abraham Tesser's self-evaluation maintenance (SEM) theory, the high achievement of a close other in a self-relevant area is perceived as a threat. In response we can (1) downplay the other's achievement; (2) put more distance between ourselves and the other; or (3) work hard to improve our own performance or try to handicap the other.

The second driving motive of the self in social interactions is to maintain high self-consistency—agreement between our self-concept and the views others have of us. Motivated by a need for

self-verification—confirmation of our self-concept—we tend to behave in ways that lead others to see us as we see ourselves.

9. *How do we present the self to others?*
We engage in **impression management,** the process of presenting ourselves in certain ways in order to control the impressions that others form of us. People with low self-esteem are cautious in trying to create a positive impression and focus on minimizing their bad points. People with high self-esteem focus on maximizing their good points. Everyone, however, demonstrates an **egotistical bias,** the tendency to take credit for successes, whether appropriate or not.

Another factor that influences impression management is the degree to which a person engages in **self-monitoring**—that is, focuses on his or her own behavior in a given social situation. High self-monitors are very sensitive to the social demands of any situation and tend to fit their behavior to those demands; low self-monitors are much less concerned with impression management.

10. *Are there circumstances in which individuals try to create a negative impression of themselves?*
Researchers have identified three models of self-destruction. The first, **primary self-destruction,** involves actions that are harmful because the person foresees and desires the pain. The second, **counterproductive strategies,** involves situations in which people seek positive outcomes but use ineffective or counterproductive strategies to achieve them. The third, **self-handicapping,** involves actions that are harmful but that the person believes may produce some positive outcomes. In each case, however, the individual may still be seen as trying to maintain control over his or her social world.

SUGGESTIONS FOR FURTHER READING

Bazerman, M. H. (1986). Why negotiations go wrong. *Psychology Today, 20* (June), 54–58.
An interesting presentation of how we make self-defeating decisions when we overvalue our own performances.

Kernis, M. P., Cornell, D. P., Sun, C.-R., Berry, A., & Harlow, T. (1993). There's more to self-esteem than whether it is high or low. *Journal of Personality and Social Psychology, 65,* 1190–1204.
A somewhat different view of self-esteem. Examines the importance of maintaining a stable level of self-esteem and how this stability affects feelings of self-worth.

Triandis, H. C. (1994). *Culture and social behavior.* New York: McGraw-Hill.
A paperback volume that examines the diversity of social psychological behavior, including our views of the self, due to cultural influences. An important book from a researcher who has devoted 40 years to the study of cultural influences on self and social perception.

Chapter 3

Social Perception: The Construction of Social Reality

$\mathcal{I}$n 1980 Iran and Iraq began a grueling, 8-year-long war of attrition in which millions of people were maimed or killed. The war was sparked by Iraq's claim to the entire Shatt-al-Arab waterway, Iran's only access to the Persian Gulf. Iraq's actions breached a treaty with Iran signed in 1975.

The United States had mixed feelings about the conflict between Iraq and Iran. Iraq was perceived to be a prime source of international terrorism, but Iran was seen as a worse threat—a revolutionary, anti-Western nation whose leaders promised to drive the United States presence out of the Middle East. Iran had been swept by a religious fervor in the late 1970s, culminating in the overthrow of the Shah and his American-supported government. During

the revolution, the U.S. embassy had been overrun and hundreds of Americans taken hostage. The American public watched helplessly as bound and blindfolded hostages were displayed on TV by their Iranian captors. The months-long incident contributed to the defeat of U.S. president Jimmy Carter in 1982 and the election of Ronald Reagan.

Thus, with Iran perceived as more dangerous than Iraq, the U.S. government eventually, and in secret, decided to tilt its support toward Iraq. Direct U.S. involvement began with arms sales to Iraq. Then U.S. warships were sent to the Persian Gulf to ensure the free passage of oil tankers to the oceans of the world. In 1987 an Iraqi fighter plane attacked an American ship, the U.S.S. *Stark,* causing the loss of many lives. The Iraqis claimed it was an accident.

In July 1988 the U.S. guided missile frigate *Vincennes* was on patrol in the Persian Gulf. A state-of-the-art ship carrying the most sophisticated radar and guidance systems, the *Vincennes* became embroiled in a skirmish with some small Iranian naval patrol boats. During the skirmish, Captain Will Rogers III received word from the radar room that an unidentified aircraft was heading toward the ship. The intruder was on a descending path, the radar operators reported, and appeared to be hostile. It did not respond to the ship's IFF (Identify Friend or Foe) transmissions, nor were further attempts to raise it on the radio successful. Captain Rogers, after requesting permission from his superior, ordered the firing of surface-to-air missiles. The missiles hit and destroyed the plane.

The plane was not an Iranian fighter. It was an Iranian Airbus, a commercial plane on a twice-weekly run to Dubai, a city across the Strait of Hormuz. The airbus was completely destroyed and all 290 passengers were killed.

Following the tragedy, Captain Rogers defended his actions. But Commander David Carlson of the nearby frigate *Sides,* 20 miles away, reported that his crew accurately identified the airbus as a passenger plane. His crew saw on their radar screen that the aircraft was climbing from 12,000 to 14,000 feet (as tapes later verified) and that its flight pattern resembled that of a civilian aircraft (*Time,* August 15, 1988). The crew of the *Sides* did not interpret the plane's actions as threatening, nor did they think an attack was imminent. When Commander Carlson learned that the *Vincennes* had fired on what was certainly a commercial plane, he was so shocked he almost vomited (*Newsweek,* July 13, 1992). Carlson's view was backed up by the fact that the "intruder" was correctly identified as a commercial aircraft by radar operators on the U.S.S. *Forrestal,* the aircraft carrier and flagship of the mission (*Newsweek,* July 13, 1992).

Commander Carlson also suggested that the *Vincennes* did not show proper restraint: The ship "hankered for an opportunity to show its stuff." He reported that the *Vincennes* was known as "Robocruiser" because of the crew's very aggressive behavior in war games as well as in the gulf patrols.

What happened during the *Vincennes* incident? How could the crew of the *Vincennes* have "seen" a commercial plane as an attacking enemy plane on their radar screen? How could the captain have so readily ordered the firing of the missiles? And how could others—the crews of the *Sides* and the *Forrestal,* for instance—have seen things so differently?

The answers to these questions lie, in part, in the nature of human thinking and behavior. The captain and crew of the *Vincennes* constructed their own view of reality, based on their previous experiences, their expectations of what was likely to occur, and their interpretations of what was happening at the moment, as well as their fears and anxieties. All of these factors were in turn influenced by the context of current international events, which included a bitter enmity between the United States and what was perceived by Americans as an extremist Iranian government.

The captain and crew of the *Vincennes* remembered the deadly attack on the *Stark* the previous year. Their own recent skirmish with Iranian naval patrol boats was fresh in their minds. They strongly believed that they were likely to be attacked by an enemy aircraft, probably one carrying advanced missiles that would be very fast and very accurate. If this occurred, the captain knew he would need to act quickly and decisively. The radar crew saw an unidentified plane on their screen. Suddenly they called out that the aircraft was descending, getting in position to attack. It didn't respond to their radio transmissions. Weighing the available evidence, Captain Rogers opted to fire on the intruder.

The commander and crew of the *Sides* had a different view of the incident. They saw the incident through the filter of their belief that the *Vincennes* was itching for a fight. From their point of view, a passenger plane was shot down and 290 lives lost as a result of the hair-trigger reaction of an overly aggressive crew.

These different views and understandings highlight a crucial aspect of human behavior: Each of us constructs a version of social reality that fits with our perception and interpretation of events (Jussim, 1991). We come to understand our world through the processes of *social perception*, the strategies and methods we use to understand the motives and behavior of other people.

The crew of the *Vincennes* had to determine the motives and intentions of the "intruder" based on its "behavior" on their radar screen. Similarly, in our everyday lives we need to understand and interpret the behavior of others. Usually, we need only a "good enough" understanding, one that allows us to predict what they will do. We also deal with events and make decisions in some of the same ways that Captain Rogers did. We often operate on automatic pilot and make quick initial judgments of social situations based more on our preconceptions than on the available evidence.

In this chapter we take a look at the tools and strategies people use to construct social reality. We ask, What cognitive processes are involved when individuals like Captain Rogers and his crew are attempting to make sense of the world? What mechanisms come into play when they form impressions of others and make judgments about their behavior and motives? How accurate are these impressions and judgments? And what accounts for the errors in perception and judgment that seem to inevitably occur in social interactions? The answers to these questions shed some light on how all of us go about constructing social reality.

THE STRATEGIES AND METHODS OF SOCIAL PERCEPTION

If we think for a moment of what we must do to understand the behavior of other people—that is, to construct our version of social reality—we see that it can be a daunting task. Much of the time we have limited information about other people and events; we have no direct access to what they are thinking, feeling, or intending. Therefore, we must infer (surmise) their motives from their overt behavior, either what we see and hear with our own eyes and ears or what we learn from secondhand report. Whenever we must make inferences, which means that we have to manufacture an impression from less than perfect evidence, there is the chance that we may be wrong.

We may have false information, for example, or we may be operating from a biased point of view, or we may use an incorrect or inappropriate cognitive process.

To complicate matters further, we often have to try to understand other people's behavior while we are interacting with them. The version of social reality we construct depends on the nature of the interaction and the goals of that interaction. For example, we would have different goals when interviewing a prospective candidate for a job opening than when asking the same person out to dinner. Additionally, during the interview, our goals (as the interviewer) would differ from those of the applicant. Each person uses different strategies and interprets the responses of the other quite differently, based on what each hopes to obtain from the interaction (Neuberg, 1989).

Human beings use a wide range of cognitive methods to construct social reality. These cognitive methods and strategies—ways of noticing, thinking about, interpreting, and understanding—are what we use to create our understanding of the social world in which we live.

Running through all of these processes is a thread that seems to be part of our human makeup: our tendency to prefer the least effortful means of processing social information (Taylor, 1981). This is not to say we are lazy or sloppy; we simply have a limited capacity to understand information and can deal with only relatively small amounts at any one time (Fiske, 1993). We tend to be **cognitive misers** in the construction of social reality: Unless motivated to do otherwise, we use just enough effort to get the job done. In this business of constructing our social world, we are pragmatists (Fiske, 1992). This is the fundamental strategy social perceivers use. Essentially we ask ourselves: What is my goal in this situation, and what do I need to know to reach that goal?

This tendency to interpret the world with the least expenditure of energy possible is seen in all the information-processing strategies described in this chapter. It helps us to function efficiently in the social world, but, as we shall see, it also makes us vulnerable to numerous systematic errors of perception and cognition.

Categorization

Consider the following list of common items: robin, baseball, football, sparrow, golf, duck. Do any of these items belong together? Obviously, you respond, robin, sparrow, and duck go together, as do baseball, football, and golf. Why? Well, you answer, robin, sparrow, and duck are all birds, and baseball, football, and golf are all sports.

The fact that you imposed an organization on these six items illustrates the basic and very powerful human predisposition to categorize. **Categorization** is the process by which we classify items, objects, or concepts, placing them together in groupings on the basis of their similarities with each other. As human beings we categorize things all the time—birds, sports, books, classes, animals, plants. We also classify people into cate-

cognitive miser This label can be applied when a person uses the least effortful means of processing social information.

categorization The process by which we classify items, objects, or concepts, placing them together in groupings on the basis of their similarities with each other.

Category-based expectancies lead us to make certain assumptions about members of a category of people, such as construction workers. These expectancies help us deal with the world, but they also limit our ability to discover individual characteristics. Although we might not expect it, there isn't any reason that one of these construction workers couldn't be an opera lover, a feminist, or gay.

gories: men, women, teenagers, senior citizens, African Americans, Japanese, teachers, programmers, soccer players, artists, and so on.

On the surface, categorization has obvious benefits. It allows us to deal efficiently and effectively with our world. We do not have to learn a new response to each item or object in a category; instead, we can act in a certain generalized way toward all members of the category. Categories allow us to economize on our behavior. Categorization is not just a simple filing system, however; it also leads us to develop *expectancies* based on category membership. Thus, we expect members of the bird category to fly and chirp, members of the plant category to be green and grow, and members of the comic book category to tell a story in pictures and words. We have expectancies about categories of people as well. We expect physicians, for example, to act in a professional manner, to be experts in their field, to be impersonal when examining us, to live in expensive homes, and so on.

Two major types of expectancies are relevant to constructing social reality: category-based expectancies and target-based expectancies. **Category-based expectancies** lead us to assume that members of a particular category of people (physicians, real-estate agents, people with disabilities, fifth graders) will behave in similar and consistent ways. Like categories themselves, category-based expectancies serve an important function: Consistent with our cognitive miser impulses, they help us to economize on our thought processes and behavior. However, there is a cost: They may be wrong. There is no guarantee that a person identified with a category will fit with our expectancies for that category. Category-based expectancies may not only be incorrect; they may blind us to a person's real nature.

Target-based expectancies are expectancies about a specific individual based on information about that person. For example, suppose you are considering an applicant for a job. As part of her application she took a battery of tests, and the results indicate that she is outgoing, intelligent, and highly motivated. These characteristics lead you to form a set of expectancies about her: She is probably going to be, in your estimation, a hardworking, conscientious employee. Your expectancies, in this instance, focus on a particular person (the job applicant) rather than a category of people (women, college graduates, Filipinos).

category-based expectancies
Expectancies that lead us to assume that members of a particular category of people will behave in similar and consistent ways.

target-based expectancies
Expectancies about a specific individual based on information about that person.

Our expectancies about people can be helpful, but they can also be resistant to change, even when we are faced with concrete evidence that they are wrong. Generally, target-based expectancies are more resistant to change than category-based expectancies with respect to a specific individual.

Carolyn Weisz and Edward Jones (1993) showed that we react differently to disconfirmation of category- versus target-based expectancies. In their study, one group of subjects was told that *an individual boy* they were going to evaluate was nonaggressive—a target-based expectancy. A second group of subjects was told that *a group of boys* they were going to evaluate was likewise nonaggressive—a category-based expectancy. All the subjects then heard an audiotape of a boy whose aggressive behavior obviously violated the expectancies of both the category-based and the target-based group of subjects. Weisz and Jones focused on how subjects reacted to the fact that the boy acted aggressively, not passively, disconfirming their expectancies.

The researchers found that the target-based subjects held to their expectancies—believing that the boy was nonaggressive—more strongly than did the category-based subjects. Target-based subjects rated the boy as more cooperative and friendly, confirming their expectancy, than did category-based subjects. Category-based subjects, however, dropped their expectancy about the boy quickly when confronted with his aggressive behavior. However, this did not change their expectancy about the group of boys as a whole, which they continued to view as passive. They simply discarded the expectancy about the individual boy, deciding that he was an exception to the rule.

These results suggest that when we have expectancies about a group and are confronted with a member of the group who doesn't fulfill those expectancies, we may modify our behaviors toward the individual but still maintain our general expectancies about the group. This has relevance for our interactions with members of ethnic or other groups about which we have certain expectancies. We may very well change our opinion of a particular person who disconfirms our expectancies, but the disconfirmation may have no effect on our original expectations of all other members of the groups.

Modifying a target-based expectancy seems to be more difficult than modifying a category-based expectancy, perhaps because it involves changing an entire impression of a person. Perceivers tend to resist such an overwhelming change in their social reality. Note, however, the power of expectancies: Perceivers in both situations strongly *wanted* to hold on to what they originally thought would occur.

Why do you think expectancies are so resistant to change? Can you think of situations in which your expectancies about an individual were contradicted by his or her behavior but it took you a long time to see those inconsistencies? How do you think others' expectancies about you affect what they think you really believe or feel?

What happens if our expectancies are wrong? Do we make corrections if what we perceive provides a *disconfirmation* of our expectancies? The answer to this question is complex, but it seems to depend to some extent on whether our expectancies are category-based or target-based. To begin to understand some of the factors involved in people's responses to discrepancies, take a look at the featured discussion "The Power of Expectancies."

Prototypes and Exemplars

How do people form and clarify the categories they use to organize their social environment? How do they go about categorizing items? Some situations, items, and objects are easily classified, but others are more ambiguous. *Game* is an example of a category with fuzzy boundaries (Fiske & Taylor, 1991). Clearly, baseball, chess, and poker are all games, but what about betting on a horse race? Teasing the neighbor's dog? "Playing the field"? Are these games too? What attributes are considered when items are classified?

One approach to categorization is to imagine a **prototype**—an abstract representation or model of the typical qualities of members of the category. What are the typical qualities of birds, for example? Birds have wings, they have feathers, and most of them fly. The prototype of a bird would include these qualities. Prototypes are characterized by a central concept (e.g., feathers, wings, and flight) against which other potential members of the category are evaluated.

Prototype models assume that for each category (birds, physicians, leaders), a prototype exists that includes all the typical attributes of that category (Medin, 1989). You might believe that the "proto-typical leader" is tall, forceful, and male. The prototype tells you what to expect from a leader, although it may not be very helpful when you meet a leader who is short, accommodating, and female (Schneider, 1991). As discussed in Chapter 5, prototypes play an important role in the expectancies we develop about members of social groups.

Exemplars help us form and clarify the categories we use to organize our social environment. If we wanted an exemplar of an elite track star, we could think of Jackie Joyner Kersee, who is sometimes described as "the fastest woman alive."

prototype An abstract representation or model of the typical qualities of the members of a category. Often used in making social judgments about groups.

exemplar A real-life specific example of a category. Often used in making social judgments about individuals.

Sometimes, instead of a prototype we use an **exemplar**—a specific example—to clarify a category. A robin is an exemplar of the category *birds*. Where a prototype is an average representation of a category, an exemplar is a real-life example of the category (Smith, 1988).

People often use exemplars in making social judgments. For instance, one study found that when professional scouts had to judge the likelihood that a college football player would do well in professional football, they used examples from the past to make that judgment (Gilovich, 1981). If a quarterback came from the hometown of a former great professional quarterback, the scouts were likely to predict success for that athlete. The scouts used an exemplar, a real live old-time star, to make a judgment, rather than a prototype, which would be a model of the average abilities of people who now play quarterback in professional football.

It is likely that people use a combination of prototypes and exemplars when constructing social reality. Prototypes tell us the various attributes that are common to members of a category; exemplars provide a concrete example (Cantor & Kihlstrom, 1987). The prototype of an elite track athlete might include the qualities strong, fast, and dedicated; the exemplar might be Jackie Joyner Kersee. Generally, we use prototypes when classifying groups—relying on a range of characteristics—and exemplars when classifying individuals (Smith, 1990).

Schemas

People know more about their social world than they gain from categorizing. The aim of social perception is to gain enough information to make relatively accurate judgments about people and social situations. We need ways of organizing the information we do have. Perceivers have strategies that help them know what to expect from others and how to respond. For example, when a father hears his infant daughter crying, he does not have to make elaborate inferences about what's wrong. He has in place an organized set of cognitions—related bits of information—about why babies cry and what to do about it. Psychologists call this set of organized cognitions a **schema.** As explained in Chapter 2, schemas contain prior knowledge of events that helps us interpret situations and guides our behavior. A schema concerning "crying babies" might include cognitions about dirty diapers, empty stomachs, pain, or anger.

Schemas influence what we remember and how we evaluate new information. When a physician hears her patient describe tightness in the chest during exercise, pain in the left arm, and an occasional pain along the neck and jawline, she can interpret the symptoms quickly. She links these symptoms and others, some seemingly unrelated, and knows what tests to order, what drugs to prescribe, and how to evaluate the course of the illness. Without a schema it would be impossible for someone to make these kinds of decisive interpretations (Fiske & Taylor, 1991).

Just as a self-schema is a set of ideas about the self, a schema about a situation or a person is a loose theory about how things work and how we and others should behave. When the crew of the *Vincennes* shot down the Iranian airbus, they were using a schema that included propositions about what happens when a hostile aircraft starts descending toward a ship in a war zone. Their decisions were driven by this schema rather than by data provided by the situation itself. The schema led them to believe that an attack was imminent; they then interpreted the incoming data to match that preconception.

Despite the possibility of such errors, schemas are an efficient way of organizing our experiences and telling us what to expect next. They help make the world a more understandable and predictable place, allowing us to make quick, seemingly effortless decisions about social situations. They help us construct social reality while expending the least amount of energy possible.

Origins of Schemas   Where do schemas come from? They develop from information about some social category or event or from experience with it. You can gain knowledge about sororities, for example, by hearing other people talk about them, by interacting with people who are in them, by reading about them, or by joining one. The more experience you have with sororities, the richer and more involved your schema will be. Similarly, the more

schema An organized set of related bits of information about persons, groups, events, and so on. Schemas provide an efficient way of organizing and understanding our experiences and predicting what will happen next.

experience the physician has with heart disease, the more elaborate her schema will be.

When we are initially organizing a schema, we place the most obvious features of an event or a category in memory first. If it's a schema about a person or a group of people, we begin with physical characteristics that we can see: gender, age, physical attractiveness, race or ethnicity, and so on. The physician's schema about heart disease might have initially focused on chest pain. As the schema developed, she would have placed other, more subtle symptoms in memory. Perhaps she would have remembered a patient who complained of a toothache but was actually having cardiac problems.

Types of Schemas   We have different types of schemas for various social situations (Gilovich, 1991). As noted in Chapter 2, we have self-schemas, which help us organize our knowledge about our own traits and personal qualities. *Person schemas* help us organize the characteristics of people and store them in our memory. For example, we may have a schema about people who are physically attractive. We may assume that they are confident and secure. A person schema is essentially the prototype for a given group of people.

Not only do we have schemas about ourselves and other people, but we also have schemas about social roles and social events. *Role schemas* are expectations about how people who fulfill certain roles should act. We expect store clerks to answer questions about merchandise, accept our money, and be reasonably courteous. *Event schemas,* or *scripts,* help us organize our experience and expectations about events, such as going to an expensive restaurant, picking someone up at the airport, or attending a funeral. In the latter case, our schema tells us that people will be solemn and perhaps tearful, that eulogies will praise the deceased, that people will wear dark clothing, and that no one will laugh.

The crew of the *Vincennes* was guided in their actions by an event schema. They "knew" what ought to happen. In training and in imagination, they played out that scenario many times over. In the end, the schema was confirmed.

The Relationship Between Schemas and Behavior   As happened with the crew of the *Vincennes*, schemas sometimes lead us to act in ways that serve to confirm them. In one study, for example, researchers convinced subjects that they were going to interact with someone who was hostile (Snyder & Swann, 1978). When the subjects did interact with that "hostile" person—who really had no hostile intentions—they behaved so aggressively that the other person was provoked to respond in a hostile way. Thus, the expectations of the subjects were confirmed, an outcome referred to as a **self-fulfilling prophecy** (Jussim, 1986; Rosenthal & Jacobson, 1968).

The notion of self-fulfilling prophecies suggests that we often create our own realities through our expectations. If we are interacting with members of a group we believe to be hostile and dangerous, for example, our actions may provoke the very behavior we are trying to avoid.

self-fulfilling prophecy The tendency to confirm our expectations of people by behaving toward them in ways that provoke them to act consistently with those expectations.

This does not mean that we inhabit a make-believe world in which there is no reality to what we think and believe. It does mean, however, that our expectations can alter the nature of social reality. Consider the effect of a teacher's expectations on students. How important are these expectations in affecting how students perform? In one study, involving almost 100 sixth-grade math teachers and nearly 1,800 students, researchers found that about 20% of the results on the math tests were due to the teachers' expectations (Jussim & Eccles, 1992). Twenty percent is not inconsiderable; it can certainly make the difference between an A and a B or a passing and a failing grade. The researchers also found that teachers showed definite gender biases. They rated boys as having better math skills and girls as trying harder. Neither of these findings appeared to have been correct in this study. But it showed why girls got better grades in math. The teachers incorrectly thought that girls tried harder and therefore rewarded them with higher grades because of the girls' presumed greater effort.

The other side of the self-fulfilling prophecy is *behavioral confirmation* (Snyder, 1992). This phenomenon occurs when perceivers behave as if their expectations are correct and the targets then respond in ways that confirm the perceivers' beliefs. Although behavioral confirmation is similar to the self-fulfilling prophecy, there is a subtle distinction. When we talk about a self-fulfilling prophecy, we are focusing on the behavior of the perceiver in eliciting expected behavior from the target. When we talk about behavioral confirmation, we are looking at the role of the target's behavior in confirming the perceiver's beliefs. In behavioral confirmation, the social perceiver uses the target's behavior (which is partly shaped by the perceiver's expectations) as evidence that the expectations are correct. The notion of behavioral confirmation emphasizes that both perceivers and targets have goals in social interactions. Whether a target confirms a perceiver's expectations depends on what they both want out of the interaction.

As an example, imagine that you start talking to a stranger at a party. Unbeknown to you, she has already sized you up and decided you're likely to be uninteresting. She keeps looking around the room as she talks to you, asks you few questions about yourself, and doesn't seem to hear some of the things you say. Soon you start to withdraw from the interaction, growing more and more aloof. As the conversation dies, she slips away, thinking, "What a bore!"

You turn and find another stranger smiling at you. She's decided you look very interesting. You strike up a conversation and find you have a lot in common. She's interested in what you say, looks at you when you're speaking, and laughs at your humorous comments. Soon you're talking in a relaxed, poised way, feeling and acting both confident and interesting. In each case, your behavior tends to confirm the perceiver's expectancies. Because someone shows interest in you, you become interesting. When someone thinks you're unattractive or uninteresting, you respond in kind, confirming the perceiver's expectations (Snyder, Tanke, & Berscheid, 1977). Figure 3-1 illustrates how we tend to confirm another individual's expectations.

The process of behavioral confirmation involves several steps (Snyder, 1993). First, the perceiver accepts preconceived beliefs about the target

FIGURE 3-1 *If someone appears to find us unattractive or boring, our self-esteem plummets and we feel like disappearing into the woodwork (left). If someone seems to find us fascinating, our self-esteem soars and our conversation sparkles (right). In either case, our behavior confirms the preconceptions of the other individual.*

(you are a bore, in the previous example). Second, the perceiver behaves as if these preconceptions are accurate. Third, the target responds to the perceiver by adapting behavior so that it conforms to the perceiver's expectations. Finally, the perceiver interprets the target's behavior as a direct confirmation of the perceiver's preconceived expectations.

Why does behavioral confirmation occur? What would motivate a target to confirm the expectations of a perceiver, especially if those expectations were negative? Two different motives come into play in these situations. The first is the need for stable and predictable interactions. This is more likely to apply when the main concern is an untroubled interaction, such as when chatting with a stranger at a party. In such a situation, behavioral confirmation is more probable because it adds to the predictability of the interaction (Fiske, 1992).

The second motive is the need for accuracy. Sometimes it's important to form an accurate impression of someone. For example, suppose you and another student whom you don't know very well must do a task for which you will get a joint grade. You will need to know what skills and abilities the other person has. You are motivated to respond to your partner as an individual and lay aside preconceived ideas. Your partner is also motivated to make sure you have no misconceptions. Behavioral confirmation is less likely under these circumstances.

As can be seen, whether the perceiver gets to confirm her preconceptions depends on what the target makes of the situation. To predict the likelihood of behavioral confirmation, we have to look at social interaction from the target's point of view. If the goal of the interaction from the target's viewpoint is simply to socialize with the other person, behavioral confirmation is likely. If the goal is more important—if the target needs to get to know the perceiver or if the perceiver's expectations threaten the target's self-concept—then behavioral disconfirmation is likely (Snyder, 1993). Note that the decision to confirm or disconfirm someone's expectations is by no means always a conscious one.

Assimilating New Information into a Schema   Schemas have some disadvantages because people tend to accept information that fits their schemas and reject that which doesn't fit. This reduces uncertainty and ambiguity, but it also increases errors. Early in the formation of a schema of persons, groups, or events, we are more likely to pay attention to information that is inconsistent with our initial conceptions because we do not have much information (Bargh & Thein, 1985). Anything that doesn't fit the schema surprises us and makes us take notice. However, once the schema is well formed, we tend to remember information that is consistent with that schema. Remembering schema-consistent evidence is another example of the cognitive miser at work: Humans prefer the least effortful method of processing and assimilating information. It helps make a complex world simpler (Fiske, 1993).

But while people may be cognitive misers, they are not cognitive idiots. If new information continually and strongly suggests that a schema is wrong, the perceiver will change it. Much of the time we are uncomfortable with schema-inconsistent information. Often we reinterpret the information to fit with our schema. But sometimes we change the schema because we see that it is wrong.

Stories

People often organize information in a form with which they feel most comfortable. There is evidence that people tend to integrate information by "packaging" their reasons for believing something in a form that is most persuasive and reasonable to both themselves and others. According to the *story model* approach to constructing social reality (Pennington & Hastie, 1986, 1988, 1992), we impose a structure on complex information by creating a coherent "story" and using it to connect facts and feelings about events.

A *story* is a schema that organizes information according to certain rules. That is, there is a beginning, a middle, and an end. There are characters—good guys and bad guys—and there are motives and reasons for behavior. All of these aspects of the story—motives, characters, and themes—are woven together into a narrative. A story is like an elaborate schema constructed to make sense of different pieces of information. Often the sensory impressions and pieces of evidence we get from our social world are disjointed and confusing; stories help us make sense of them.

For example, imagine that you are a juror on a complex murder trial. Over the course of a week, many witnesses testify. Each witness provides evidence concerning various aspects of the crime. Some evidence makes you think that the defendant is guilty, whereas other evidence makes you think he is innocent. How do you make sense out of such diverse information?

Jurors typically make sense of evidence in a trial by forming it into a coherent narrative story. As the trial progresses, they tend to incorporate evidence that fits into their story and discard evidence that doesn't. For this reason, lawyers are more successful when they outline a convincing story for the jury at the beginning of the trial.

Studies have shown that in a complex murder case, jurors spontaneously devise a story narrative that helps them explain the evidence (Pennington & Hastie, 1986, 1988, 1992). They start to form a story fairly early. They place this story in memory; it then guides the subsequent interpretation of the evidence. In other words, the juror actively searches for evidence that fits the preferred story. The story helps the juror understand and organize incoming information. Evidence that fits the story is remembered and incorporated, and evidence that does not fit the story is forgotten (ForsterLee, Horowitz, & Bourgeois, 1993). Where the story has gaps, the jurors fill those gaps with their own interpretations and beliefs to make it more plausible. To see how the lack of a coherent story hurts a lawyer's attempt to persuade a jury, refer to "The Importance of a 'Story': The Case of the Black Panthers."

IMPRESSION FORMATION

Dealing with our social world involves more than categorizing people, forming expectations about them, and developing schemas and stories to help us make sense out of their actions. The ultimate purpose of all of these methods of organizing social information is to be able to make accurate judgments about the motives and behavior of other people. It is important that we do this because the ability to predict how others will act helps us achieve our goals. The process by which we make these judgments about others is called **impression formation.**

We are primed by our culture to form impressions of people—Western culture emphasizes the individual, the importance of "what is inside the person" as the cause of behavior (Jones, 1990). We may also be programmed biologically to form impressions of those who might help or hurt. It's conceivable that those early humans who were better at making accurate inferences about others would have had superior survival chances (Flohr, 1987) and passed those abilities down to us.

impression formation The process by which we make judgments about the motives and behavior of other people.

In the late 1960s, members of the Black Panthers, a group of self-proclaimed revolutionaries, were put on trial for conspiring to bomb public buildings. The heart of the prosecution was that the Panthers had the motivation to commit the bombings. The prosecutor showed that the group met regularly and had had the opportunity to discuss committing the bombings. Undercover agents testified to the violence of the Panthers' rhetoric: They talked a lot about "offing the pigs" and rich whites. The prosecution clearly demonstrated that the Panthers could be very dangerous people.

But a persuasive case should have a number of interconnected elements; that is, it should tell a coherent story. The prosecutor showed that these "bad guys" had the motivation, but there's more to a crime than that. How were they going to blow up buildings? Did they have dynamite, bombs, incendiary equipment, or even firecrackers? Apparently not—or at least the prosecutor didn't mention any. The only hard evidence that the Panthers were a "revolutionary army" was that on the eve of a "major attack" on the "establishment," a large contingent of Panthers had been dispatched from New York to Baltimore to obtain *one* gun.

The defense strategy was not to look a gift horse in the mouth. Why present your version, your story, when the prosecutor's story does not meet the minimal criteria for a coherent narrative? The defendants' lawyer agreed that the Panthers were hellfire and brimstone revolutionaries, but then he simply asked where "the meat" of the case was. How were the Panthers going to carry out the conspiracy without bombs or guns?

A total of 156 counts had been brought in the indictment: The primarily white jury acquitted the Panthers on every one (Bennett, 1978). A case without a coherent story is not persuasive.

If you were giving advice to a trial lawyer, what might you tell her about how to arrange the evidence to present to the jury? What kinds of evidence should she leave out, and what kinds should she include? What cognitive needs are served by organizing material into a story format?

The Significance of First Impressions

How many times have you met someone about whom you formed an immediate negative (or positive) impression? How did that first impression influence your subsequent interactions with that person? First impressions can be powerful influences on our perceptions of others. Researchers have consistently demonstrated a **primacy effect** in the impression-formation process, which is the tendency of early information to play a powerful role in our eventual impression of an individual.

Further, first impressions can, in turn, bias the interpretation of later information. This was shown in a study in which individuals watched a person take an examination (Jones, Rock, Shaver, Goethals, & Ward, 1968). Some of the observers saw the test-taker do very well at the start and then get worse as the test continued. Other observers saw the test-taker do poorly at the beginning and then improve. Although both test-takers wound up with the same score, the test-taker who did well in the beginning was rated as more intelligent than the test-taker who did well at the end (Figure 3-2). In other words, the initial impression persisted even when later information began to contradict it.

primacy effect The tendency of early information to play a powerful role in our eventual impression of an individual.

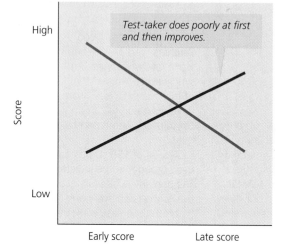

ACTUAL SCORES

High

Score

Low

Test-taker does poorly at first and then improves.

Early score   Late score

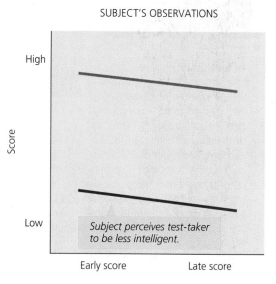

SUBJECT'S OBSERVATIONS

High

Score

Low

Subject perceives test-taker to be less intelligent.

Early score   Late score

FIGURE 3-2 *Actual and "observed" scores of two test-takers who performed better at the beginning and worse at the end, or vice-versa, on an examination. The experiment demonstrated the primacy effect—the importance of first impressions.* From Jones, Rock, Shaver, Goethals, and Ward, 1968.

TABLE 3-1

TRAIT LISTS USED BY ASCH

Trait List 1	Trait List 2
Intelligent	Intelligent
Skillful	Skillful
Industrious	Industrious
Warm	*Cold*
Practical	Practical
Determined	Determined
Cautious	Cautious

From Asch, 1946.

This *belief perseverance*, the tendency for initial impressions to persist despite later conflicting information, accounts for much of the power of first impressions. A second reason that initial impressions wear well and long is that people often reinterpret incoming information in light of the initial impression. Social perceivers try to organize information about other people into a coherent impression. Later information that is inconsistent with the first impression is often, though not always, reinterpreted to fit the initial belief about that person. If your first impression of a person is that she is friendly, you may dismiss a later encounter in which she is curt and abrupt as an aberration—"she's just having a bad day." We can see that our person schemas are influenced by the primacy effect.

Impression Formation Based on Limited Information   In the course of everyday affairs we encounter many people, and quite often our knowledge of their characteristics is very limited. This is especially true when we make our first impressions of someone. Solomon Asch (1946) showed that people devise a unified impression of individuals that makes sense to the perceiver even when the information is very limited. Asch presented subjects with one of the two lists of traits shown in Table 3-1 and asked them about their impressions of the person described by the list of traits. Notice that the two lists are identical except that the first includes the trait "warm" and the second includes the trait "cold."

Asch found that people constructed quite different impressions of people who differed with respect to that one trait (warm or cold). Someone described as cold and intelligent, for example, was perceived as calculating; someone described as warm and intelligent was perceived as wise and humane. Asch argued that all other traits on the list would be modified by whether they were paired with warm or cold. For Asch, the warm–cold dimension served as a *central trait*, or a trait dimension that influences how other traits are interpreted.

When you only have a few minutes, you have to shine! Research indicates that first impressions play an extremely powerful role in our eventual evaluation of another person. Even when subsequent information contradicts our initial impression, we tend to cling to our early beliefs.

But a central trait is not the only determinant of that first impression. Asch also suggested that we perceive another person as a whole, as a single psychological unit. Every trait possessed by the person is interpreted in the context of the whole cluster of traits that make up his or her personality. Consider the warm–cold dimension. Although it is certainly probable that we will like a warm person better than a cold person, much depends on the person's other traits, the entire context. For example, think of a warm person who is also unreliable and vain. Warm has an entirely different meaning in the context of unreliable and vain. In other words, the traits in each list actually conveyed different meanings depending on the context.

People often have a theory—known as an **implicit personality theory**—about what kinds of personality traits go together. "Intellectual," for example, is often linked to "cold," and "strong" and "adventurous" are often thought to go together (Higgins & Stangor, 1988). An implicit personality theory may help us make a quick impression of someone, but there is no guarantee that our initial impression will be correct.

Integrating Contradictory Information Sometimes people present us with contradictory traits that make a unified impression difficult to establish. The contradictions we encounter involve conflicts between what we expect of individuals we know (our friends, lovers, spouses) and the expectancies associated with their social category or role. When people act in unexpected ways that disconfirm our impressions of them, we—the social perceivers—are uncomfortable.

How do we integrate contradictory information about people? Asch would say that we try to make a coherent impression out of what we know. In one study designed to address this question (Kunda, Miller, & Claire, 1990), researchers asked subjects to describe some people who belonged to only one category, such as Harvard-educated, or carpenter, or businessman. They then asked these same subjects to describe some people who belonged to two conflicting (or at least more unexpected) categories, such as

implicit personality theory A theory people have about what kinds of personality traits go together.

Social norms help us form coherent impressions of others. During World War II, the image of "Rosie the Riveter" was used by the U.S. government to establish that it was "normal" for wives and mothers to work outside the home (left). In the 1950s the image of the fulfilled homemaker—embodied in television characters Donna Reed, Harriet Nelson, and June Cleaver—was promoted to encourage a woman to stay at home to nurture her husband and children (center). In the 1990s, the image of the successful career woman who might also choose to be a single parent was represented by television's Murphy Brown (right). In each case, norms and images pulled together new or potentially contradictory information about women's social roles, helping people form unified impressions of others.

gay construction worker, Harvard-educated carpenter, or leftist business-man. They found that when conflicting information came in, people were initially surprised and puzzled. It just didn't fit, for example, that a Harvard-educated person would occupy a low-status job. But all the subjects were able to resolve the incongruities and form a unified impression of the people they described. Here's how one subject described the Harvard-educated carpenter: "Someone who has inherited a lot of money and is working at what he enjoys, rather than where the money is. A nice person, rather than money-grubbing" (p. 557). Notice how the subject combined information in an imaginative way and devised a plausible story about the person.

Social norms sometimes help us make sense of contradictory information. During World War II, for example, many women took over the jobs that men left when they went to war. With the newly expanding factories making weapons of war, women who had been housewives were now machinists and riveters, bus drivers and lumberjacks, police officers and stevedores. The image of women in the war effort was best captured by "Rosie the Riveter." Rosie was not only a riveter but also a wife and a mother. Her image helped Americans reconcile these seemingly contradictory roles. The government promoted this image because women were essential not only to the war effort but to the running of wartime society as well.

After the war, with men back on the job, there was no longer a need for women in business and industry, nor was it necessary to reconcile contradictory roles for women. IBM and other major companies reinstated their prewar policy against hiring married women. After 5 years of keeping the war production lines going, American women were told that the work was "too heavy" for them (Hymowitz & Weissman, 1978).

Mechanisms of Impression Formation: Automatic and Controlled Processing

Much of our social perception involves **automatic processing**—forming impressions without much thought or attention (Logan, 1989). Thinking that is conscious and requires effort is referred to as **controlled processing.**

Automatic Processing Automatic processing is thinking that occurs primarily outside consciousness (Fiske & Taylor, 1991). It is effortless in the sense that it does not require us to use any of our conscious cognitive capacity (Bargh, 1989). We automatically interpret an upturned mouth as a smile, and we automatically infer that the smiling person is pleased or happy (Fiske & Taylor, 1991). Such interpretations and inferences, which may be built into our genetic makeup, are beyond our conscious control.

Automatic processing is the preferred method of the cognitive miser. Automatic thinking is at work in most of the cognitive processes described in this chapter, such as categorizing and forming first impressions. This is not to say that there is a clear line between automatic processing and controlled processing. Rather, they exist on a continuum, ranging from totally automatic (unconscious) to totally controlled (conscious), with degrees of more and less automatic thinking in between.

For instance, we may become aware of being in a good mood yet not be aware of how our mood is affecting our interpretation of information. Similarly, the captain of the *Vincennes* knew that he was under stress and that he was patrolling the Gulf aggressively. But he probably was not aware of how his mood and attitude might affect his understanding of events.

Sometimes we can be aware of what we are thinking and how those thoughts are affecting us, but still not know how the process started or how we may end it. For example, have you ever gotten a jingle stuck in your mind? You can't say why the jingle started, nor can you get it out of your mind, no matter how hard you try. You think of other things, and each of these distractors works for a while. But soon the jingle pops up again, more insistent than ever. Suppressing an unwanted thought seems only to make it stronger.

This phenomenon was vividly demonstrated in an experiment in which subjects were told not to think of a white bear for 5 minutes (Wegner, 1989). Whenever the thought of a white bear popped into mind, subjects were to ring a bell. During the 5-minute period, subjects rang the bell often. More interesting, however, was the discovery that once the 5 minutes were up, the white bears really took over, in a kind of "rebound" effect. Subjects who had tried to suppress thoughts of white bears could think of little else after the 5 minutes expired. The study demonstrates that even if we successfully fend off an unwanted thought for a while, it may soon return to our minds with a vengeance.

Because of this strong rebound effect, suppressed thoughts may pop up when we least want them. A bigot who tries very hard to hide his prejudice when he is with members of a particular ethnic group will, much to his

automatic processing The formation of impressions without much thought or attention. Much of our social perception involves automatic processing.

controlled processing The formation of impressions with conscious awareness, attention to the thinking process, and effort.

If you were to study a photo-graph of the crowd waiting for President Reagan to leave the Washington Hilton Hotel after de-livering a speech in 1981, would anything pop out at you? Yes, indeed: the one angry face of would-be assassin John Hinckley, Jr. in that otherwise happy crowd. A. Treisman and J. Souther (1985) have shown that people will auto-matically shift attention to a stim-ulus that differs sharply from surrounding stimuli—for exam-ple, a circle embedded in an array of squares. This appears to occur rather effortlessly, suggesting an automatic process, in which the distinct stimulus "pops out" at the observer.

What do circles and squares have to do with making infer-ences about social behavior? Let us replace the circles and squares with faces of people. Hinckley (the angry face) is the circle in the array of squares (happy faces). The perception of faces plays a critical role in the interpretation of emotion. Facial expressions are the most salient system conveying the emotional state of a person (Zajonc, 1985). Therefore, we ought to identify inconsistent, dis-cordant faces very efficiently. They

should pop out at us because there is something arresting, un-usual, and dramatic about some-one who is angry among happy people.

Hansen and Hansen (1988) tested the notion that an angry face in an array of happy faces—as well as a happy face in an array of angry faces—would be auto-matically and therefore quickly identified. They found that angry faces were identified in an array of happy faces more quickly than happy faces in an array of angry ones. Hansen and Hansen also found that adding distractors con-siderably slowed the rate at which a particular happy face was identi-fied in the angry array. However, distractors did not affect the iden-tification of angry faces in happy crowds. This supports the evi-dence that picking out a danger-ous, angry face in a sea of happy faces is an automatic process.

You might ask why the Secret Service agents did not pick out Hinckley's angry face in the sea of

happy faces. Of course, we really don't know why, but we could speculate that the agents had some expectations about the situ-ation that worked against even a casual survey of the crowd. They took President Reagan out a side door to avoid the crowds gath-ered at the main exit of the hotel. It was drizzling, which worked to keep the crowd down, and there was only a small group by the back entrance. Given these condi-tions—the quick exit out the back door, the rain, and the small group of people gathered at that back exit—the situation height-ened the agents' expectations that nothing was likely to occur.

If perceptual systems are set up to automatically pick out danger-ous people, what characteristics other than facial expressions do you think we pay attention to? Do you think perceptions of danger-ous expressions might differ from culture to culture? Do you think that what we often call our "gut" feeling about someone is really a reflection of some hard-wired "in-stinct" that tells us the person is "trouble"?

---

surprise, say something stupidly bigoted and wonder why he could not sup-press the thought (Wegner, 1993). This is especially likely to happen when people are under pressure. Automatic processing takes over, reducing the ability to control thinking.

Automatic processing is also likely to occur when we face a negative or dangerous situation. In fact, human beings display **automatic vigilance** with respect to events that could cause us harm. When a threat occurs, in-dividuals automatically turn their attention from a task and toward that threat (Pratto & John, 1991). We also tend to weigh negative information about others more heavily than positive information. It is not surprising, therefore, that we are very good at spotting unusual or threatening faces in

automatic vigilance A type of processing in which people automatically turn their atten-tion to a negative or dangerous stimulus.

crowds. To better understand how this natural human tendency operates in everyday life, refer to the featured discussion "Automatic Processing: Faces in a Crowd."

Controlled Processing   As mentioned earlier, controlled processing involves conscious awareness, attention to the thinking process, and effort. It is defined by several factors: First, we know we are thinking about something; second, we are aware of the goals of the thought process; and third, we know what choices we are making. For example, if you meet someone, you may be aware of thinking that you need to really pay attention to what this person is saying. Therefore, you are aware of your thinking process. You will also know that you are doing this because you expect to be dealing with this person in the future. You may want to make a good impression on the person, or you may need to make an accurate assessment. Third, you may be aware that by focusing on this one person you are giving up the opportunity to meet other people.

People are motivated to use controlled processing—that is, to allocate more of their cognitive energy to perceiving and interpreting—for a variety of reasons. They may have goals they want to achieve in the interaction, for example, or they may be disturbed by information that doesn't fit their expectancies. Processing becomes more controlled when thoughts and behavior are *intended* (Wegner & Pennebaker, 1993).

One study explored how thinking becomes more controlled and intentional when expectancies are violated (Hilton, Klein, & von Hippel, 1991). Researchers looked at how evaluators responded to the performance of a child when there was an inconsistency between the child's perceived ability and actual performance on a mental task. In general, evaluators spent more time assessing the child when performance violated expectations (the initial categorization). Inconsistency led to an increase in attention, especially when the evaluators expected the child to do well on mental tasks and the child performed poorly (Figure 3-3).

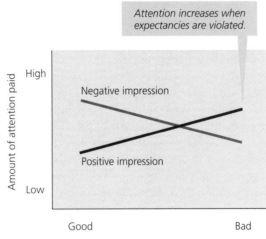

Attention increases when expectancies are violated.

High — Negative impression

Amount of attention paid

Low — Positive impression

Good   Bad

Initial performance of test-taker

FIGURE 3-3 *The effect of inconsistencies between an evaluator's expectation of a student's performance on a mental task and the student's actual performance on that task. Evaluators analyze the performance of a good student who does badly on an exam and also a bad student who does well more than they analyze the performance of a student whose performance matches the evaluator's expectancies.   From Hilton, Klein, and von Hippel, 1991.*

Accuracy in Impression Formation

We have seen that people are adept at forming impressions of others, even when incoming information is complex and contradictory. We have also seen that automatic processing is the preferred method of forming impressions, although people are willing to exert effort when necessary. Another set of questions now arises: How accurate are those impressions? Under what circumstances are people's impressions more accurate? Under what circumstances are they less accurate?

Accuracy and the Perceiver's Goals   As mentioned earlier, our interest in being accurate in our judgments of people and events varies according to the situation. When accuracy is important to us, we use controlled processing, paying close attention and setting aside our preconceptions. When accuracy is less important, we use automatic processing, paying less attention and forming more general impressions.

When accuracy is important, we often "tune" our perceptual processes to focus on certain characteristics. If we're interviewing someone for a job, we might tune in to good judgment, orientation to details, or other specific skills in a job applicant. This kind of focused perception has been referred to as *cognitive tuning* (Zajonc, 1960). We are particularly likely to use this kind of perception when we have to evaluate a person and pass on a unified impression to someone else. When we merely have to receive information without having to judge it carefully, we form a more fragmented and disorganized impression.

In situations where we must interact with another person to achieve a goal—as when two students have to work together for a grade—cognitive tuning is also extremely powerful. In one study, subjects were led to believe that they were going to interact with someone who was a former patient in a mental hospital (Neuberg & Fiske, 1987). Some subjects were told that they and the former patient would be part of a team competing with other pairs of students and patients to win money. Other subjects were told that only individual performance would count toward the prize. In the first instance, students and former patients were dependent on each other for a favorable outcome ("outcome-dependent" condition). In the second instance, the student's outcome was not dependent on the partner ("non-outcome-dependent condition").

In the outcome-dependent condition, students tended to ignore category-based information about mental patients (beliefs that most people have about mental patients) and paid much more attention to information given to them about the attributes of the specific person with whom they were paired. Because their goal was to win the prize, it was important to them to get to know their partner. As shown in Figure 3-4, students in the outcome-dependent condition spent more time examining the attributes of their partner than did students in the non-outcome-dependent condition. They also liked their partner more, presumably because closer attention made the partner more "human." Students in the non-outcome-dependent

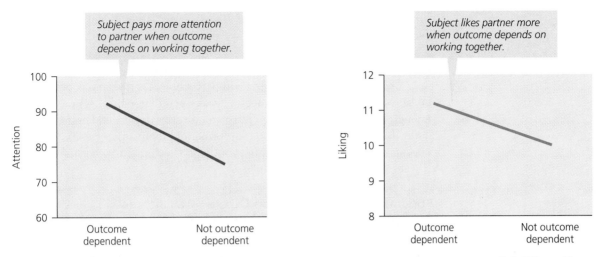

FIGURE 3-4 *Effects of "outcome dependency" on attention paid to the partner. Subjects spent more time getting to know their partner, and liked their partner more, when they had to work together to win a prize.* Adapted from Neuberg and Fiske, 1987.

condition were satisfied with category-based information about "former mental patients" and paid little heed to the individual traits of their partner.

When accuracy in assessing another person is important, people will allocate enough attention and resources to do the job (Hilton & Darley, 1991). When serving on a committee charged with hiring the best person for a job, or when serving as a juror deciding a defendant's fate, the perceiver must be very careful in making evaluations. When this is the case, impressions are normally at their highest levels of accuracy (Hilton & Darley, 1991; Neuberg, 1989).

Global and Circumscribed Accuracy   Sometimes our impression of someone is accurate but only for a limited aspect of the person's life. Let's say your friend Priya takes a psychological test that shows she is quiet and introverted. In your interactions with Priya, you know her to be just the opposite. In fact, you would call Priya an extravert. Are your impressions accurate, or is the test accurate?

The test is probably more accurate in a general sense, but you are equally accurate for the specific kinds of interactions you have with your friend (Schneider, 1991; Swann, 1984). Most of the time, Priya is at school or at work, where she is quiet and reserved. You see her socially, at parties, aerobics classes, and other gatherings with friends. In this context, she is friendly and outgoing. In a sense, there is no absolute standard against which Priya's behavior can be measured (Hastie & Rasinski, 1988).

Two kinds of accuracy in social perception have been described (Swann, 1984). One is *circumscribed accuracy*—accuracy restricted to social knowledge about a person in a confined situation. You know how Priya acts at parties and probably could predict how she would act in similar situations. Another kind of accuracy, *global accuracy,* is more wide-ranging (Swann, 1984). Global accuracy means that you have a generalized belief about the person's stable personality characteristics and can predict how the person would act in many different situations. If you knew that one of

Priya's basic traits was shyness and that she was outgoing only with people she knew well, then you would have global accuracy in predicting her behavior in many different situations. Priya's personality test has global accuracy; your impression of her has circumscribed accuracy.

What we see is that accuracy in perceiving other people is not perfect or absolute. Circumscribed accuracy is "good-enough" accuracy. Good enough for what? Good enough to serve our everyday goals. Perceivers generally, but not always, get enough information about other people to make reasonable, pragmatic judgments about who they are and what they will do (Fiske, 1993; Swann, 1984).

The Impression We Make on Others   We have looked at how we form impressions of other people and when we are likely to be more and less accurate in our perceptions. Impression formation has two sides, however; the other side is the impression we make on others. How accurate are we in assessing the impression we convey?

In general, most people seem to have a good sense of the impression they make on others. In one study designed to look at this question, subjects interacted with partners whom they had not previously met (DePaulo, Kenny, Hoover, Webb, & Oliver, 1987). After each interaction with their partners, subjects had to report on the impressions they had conveyed to the partner. The researchers found that the subjects were generally accurate in reporting the kind of impression their behavior communicated. They were also aware of how their behavior changed over time during the interaction and how it changed over time with different partners.

Another study also found that people are fairly accurate in identifying how they come across to others (Kenny & Albright, 1987). They also consistently communicate the same impression over time (Colvin & Funder, 1991). People do tend to overestimate how favorably they are viewed by other people, however. When they err, it is on the side of believing that they have made a better impression than they actually have.

Although most people seem to have a good sense of the impression they make on other people, some do not. In fact, some people never figure out that they are creating a bad impression. In a study designed to look at why some people do not seem to pick up on the cues that they are making a bad impression, individuals were observed interacting with people who had continually made either good or bad impressions (Swann, Stein-Seroussi, & McNulty, 1992). Swann and his co-workers found that subjects *said* basically the same generally positive things to both types of individuals. However, they *acted* differently toward the two types of individuals. They directed less approving nonverbal cues (such as turning away while saying nice things) at negative-impression individuals than at those who made positive impressions.

The researchers concluded that there are two reasons why people who continually make bad impressions do not learn to change. First, we live in a "white lie" society in which people are generally polite even to someone who acts like a fool. Second, the cues that people use to indicate displeasure may be too subtle for some people to pick up.

PERCEPTUAL ERRORS, BIASES, AND SHORTCUTS IN CONSTRUCTING SOCIAL REALITY

As a rule, the mind is structured so that automatic processes occur first, followed by conscious (controlled) corrections if required (Gilbert, 1991). With such a system, many of our social perceptions and impressions will be accurate enough for our purposes. However, some errors in social perception and impression formation inevitably occur. These errors occur as a consequence of the strategies we adopt as cognitive misers and the motivations that drive us as we try to understand the social world.

Common Errors in Reading Situations and People

Three related errors are common when we are trying to make sense of our social world (Ross & Nisbett, 1991). The first is failing to recognize the active role we play in constructing reality out of the words and actions of other people. Our private needs and motivations—as well as our social and cultural environment—transform our view of reality. Many Americans, for example, saw the *Vincennes* incident as a tragic but understandable accident. The Iranians, viewing the incident from their own perspective, saw it as a deliberate and despicable act of war.

The first error often leads to the second—failing to recognize fully that others construct versions of social reality that are different from our own. As with Captain Rogers, Commander Carlson, and the Iranians, each person constructs his or her own, individual (and somewhat different) version of social reality. This helps explain why eyewitnesses to a crime give different—sometimes drastically different—descriptions of the crime. Each witness may focus on a different aspect of the crime, based on his or her perceptual biases. Each person's social reality is constructed from the information he or she selects and processes.

This first error leads us to assume that others see things as we do, a phenomenon referred to as the **egocentric bias.** In an experiment demonstrating this second error (Newton, 1990), some subjects were asked to tap out a tune they were humming in their heads and other subjects were asked to identify the tune on the basis of the taps. The tappers were also asked to guess the probability that the listener could correctly identify the tune and to estimate the likelihood that most other people would be able to make a correct identification. The results demonstrated the egocentric bias at work. Tappers guessed that anywhere from 10% to 90% of listeners and others would correctly identify the tapped tune. However, only 2.5%—3 people out of 120—were able to correctly identify it.

To fully understand these findings, we need to consider how both the tapper and the listener construct their own reality (Griffin & Ross, 1991). The tapper "hears" a tune in her head ("Rock Around the Clock"), complete with vocals, guitar, drums, and keyboard, and taps it out. The listener hears only a series of irregular taps on a table. The tapper fails to distinguish her own construction of reality—she knows the tune, she hears the band—

egocentric bias The assumption that other people see things as we do.

Calvin and Hobbes

by Bill Watterson

Other people have their own points of view and their own versions of social reality, often drastically different from our own. The egocentric bias leads us to assume that everyone else sees the world the same way we do, often with unfortunate results.

from the true nature of her tappings (Griffin & Ross, 1991). Of course, once the listener is told what the tune is, the identification rate increases. The tapper and the listener then share the same reality.

The third error in reading situations and people is failing to consider the role of the situation. We have a tendency to base our understanding of people on their behavior while omitting the importance of the context or situation in which that behavior occurs. Commander Carlson of the *Sides* stated that the crew of the *Vincennes* were itching for an opportunity to show their stuff. By attributing the incident to the characteristics of the crew, Carlson failed to fully consider the situational context within which the incident occurred. The heightened tension aboard the *Vincennes* caused by the recent encounter with Iranian naval vessels and the weeks of having been on patrol in dangerous waters was downplayed.

Failing to consider the situation is a systematic bias in the way we perceive the world. When we observe someone's behavior, we tend to overlook or ignore the importance of the situation and exaggerate the influence of the individual's characteristics and personality in causing the observed behavior. This important process is explored more fully in Chapter 4.

The Illusion of Control

Individuals often believe that they can control events that are, in reality, beyond their control. This *illusion of control* will be instantly familiar to those who play poker. If the dealer inadvertently deals a card out of turn, other players are quick to say, "Misdeal, misdeal!" Each player "knows" that the misdealt card is the one he or she needs to fill that inside straight. Each player holds the erroneous belief that the individual has some causal role in the draw of the cards—an event that is purely random.

Much research has shown that people believe they have some control over random events. One reason for this belief may be that people often tend to *behave* as though they have control over an outcome that is actually random (Fleming & Darley, 1990) in what is referred to as a *purposeful action sequence*.

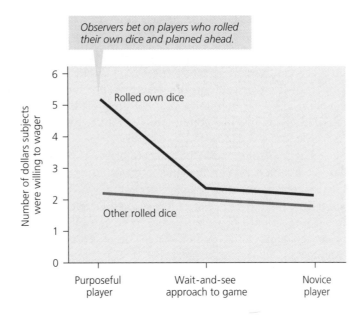

Observers bet on players who rolled their own dice and planned ahead.

Rolled own dice

Other rolled dice

Number of dollars subjects were willing to wager

Purposeful player — Wait-and-see approach to game — Novice player

FIGURE 3-5 *Number of dollars subjects are willing to wager as a function of player's strategy and dice-rolling condition. Observers put their money on players who rolled their own dice and who acted confident, despite the fact that these behaviors cannot affect the outcome. Observers succumbed to the illusion of control.* Fleming and Darley, 1990.

Consider the following situation. You are observing a backgammon game. There are three players: One player takes a purposeful approach, planning her moves in advance; a second player does not plan, but takes a wait-and-see posture; a third player is new to the game. Some players roll their own dice; other players have the dice rolled for them by someone else. When the "purposeful" player gets to roll the dice, she takes a confident stance, blowing on the dice, and so on. How would you wager on the ability of these players to throw the dice to get a winning outcome?

As shown in Figure 3-5, when this situation was set up experimentally, observers bet the most money on the purposeful player who rolled his own dice. Now keep in mind, blowing on the dice and looking confident do not impress or affect the dice. Yet, when observers saw the player performing this "purposeful action sequence," they inferred that the player had some way of affecting the outcome. Typically, people act in a purposeful way when they *do* have control over an outcome, but in this case, the outcome was determined by chance. No matter how purposefully the player acted, the dice were unaffected. The illusion of control was in the eyes of the perceiver (Fleming & Darley, 1990). And like the subjects in this experiment, we often believe we have control over events, and act as if we do, when such control is an illusion.

Shortcuts to Reality: Heuristics

As cognitive misers, we have a grab bag of tools that help us organize our perceptions effortlessly. These shortcuts—handy rules of thumb that are part of our cognitive arsenal—are called **heuristics.** Like illusions, heuristics help us make sense of the social world, but, also like illusions, they can lead us astray.

heuristics Rules of thumb that help us make sense of the social world but only in a superficial way.

The Availability Heuristic   If you are asked how many of your friends know people with AIDS, or have AIDS themselves, you will quickly think of those who do. The *availability heuristic* is defined as a shortcut used to estimate the frequency or likelihood of an event based on how quickly examples of it come to mind (Tversky & Kahneman, 1973). If AIDS is uncommon in your community, you will underestimate the overall incidence of AIDS; if you live in a community with many cases, you will overestimate its incidence.

The availability heuristic tends to bias our interpretations because the ease with which we can imagine an event affects our estimate of how frequently that event occurs. Television and newspapers, for example, tend to cover only the most visible, violent events. People therefore tend to overestimate the amount of violence and crime as well as the number of deaths from accidents and murder, since these events are most memorable (Kahneman, Slovic, & Tversky, 1982). For a critical analysis of this phenomenon, see the featured discussion "The Availability Heuristic at Work: Public Perception of Crime." As with all cognitive shortcuts, a biased judg-

THE AVAILABILITY HEURISTIC AT WORK: PUBLIC PERCEPTION OF CRIME

Tourists are shot and killed by thieves as they drive from Florida airports. A 12-year-old girl is abducted from her home in California and strangled. Two white men pour gasoline on a black man and set him on fire. These and many other brutal crimes were reported in the media in the past year. Such reports fuel our perception that violent crime in our society is spiraling out of control. According to a recent news article,

> the climate of fear that persists among the public is spawned by a widespread perception that crime is getting worse and that no one is safe at home or in the workplace. These growing fears appear to reflect a number of disturbing trends, including increasing reports of violent crimes committed against strangers, continuing media coverage of shocking incidents of wanton brutality, and a sense that the threat of prison has lost its meaning for many young offenders. (Hess, 1994, p. 6A)

How accurate is the perception that crime is increasing in our society? Despite our sense of chaos,

> the official crime statistics, though registering sharp increases in incidents of violent crime in certain urban neighborhoods, mostly black, show that crime rates generally are lower than they have been in years.

Although assaults have increased slightly, the homicide rate is down. And crimes against property in the suburbs, where much of the pressure for tougher anti-crime measures arises, are way down. Burglaries, for instance, are half what they were 20 years ago—from 88 per 1,000 homes in 1973 to 44 in 1991.

"Everything we know about crime now is that it is not getting

worse," said Michael Tonry of the University of Minnesota law school, "yet we also know that everybody believes it's getting worse." Most Americans, Tonry said, are quite safe. (Hess, p. 6A)

What accounts for this misperception on the part of the American public? Tonry says he blames the "disingenuous use of crime by politicians" and "sensationalist news media." In his opinion, "The politicians can't expose themselves politically to an opponent who'll take cheap shots and say they are soft on crime and unconcerned about victims" (Hess, p. 6A). According to criminologists,

> the fear over crime's supposed new pervasiveness is largely a result of politicians and the news media cashing in on the emotional issue. "What's happened is that a rational public discussion of crime is not occurring," said Frank Curran at the University of Cincinnati's Department of Criminal Justice.

ment occurs because the sample of people and events that we remember is unlikely to be fair and full. The crew and captain of the *Vincennes* undoubtedly had the recent example of the *Stark* in mind when they had to make a quick decision about the Iranian airbus.

The Representativeness Heuristic Sometimes we make judgments about the probability of an event or a person falling into a category based on how representative it (or the person) is of the category (Kahneman & Tversky, 1982). When we make such judgments, we are using the *representativeness heuristic*. This heuristic gives us something very much like a prototype (an image of the most typical member of a category).

To get an idea of how this heuristic works, consider "Steve," a person who is described to you as ambitious, argumentative, and very smart. Now, if you are told that Steve is either a lawyer or a dairy farmer, what would you guess his occupation to be (Figure 3-6)? Chances are, you would guess that he is a lawyer. Steve seems more representative of the lawyer category than of the dairy farmer category. Are there no ambitious and argumentative

"At every level, from Congress to the state legislatures, there are lots of punitive policies being proposed without any—I mean, any—consideration as to whether they can work or not. It's irresponsible, but no political leader now, in this climate, can risk standing up to it." (Hess, p. 6A)

Criminologists say that tougher crime-prevention measures, such as mandatory minimum sentences and longer terms, have little effect on crime rates and are a waste of money. But if get-tough legislation and harsher punishments are not effective in deterring criminals and reducing crime, what accounts for the recent decrease in crime rates? The answer appears to be demographic:

Experts say that 20 years of efforts by presidents, Congress, and state legislatures to attack crime have achieved less than one simple demographic development: the huge baby boomer generation is moving out of the age range in which people most often commit crimes.

Albert Altschuler, a criminal-law expert at the University of Chicago law school, said crime rates are driven mainly by demographics. If the population has a larger proportion of young males, 16 to 23 years old, the rate goes up; if not, it declines.

"Crime went up in the 1960s and '70s with the coming of age of the baby boomers," Altschuler said, "and started down in the mid-'80s as the percentage of 16- to 23-year-olds went down."

He predicted that rates would start to increase again around the turn of the century as the children of the late-phase baby boomers reach that critical age bracket. (Hess, p. 6A)

From the media, then, as well as from the overabundance of crime and police shows on TV, the public gains the impression that violent crime is increasing. Public opinion creates pressure on politi-

cians and elected officials to respond with some action. Any action, even if ineffective, creates a better impression than no action. Public officials and private citizens alike want to believe they have some control over what happens in their lives.

⎯⎯⎯⎯

The availability heuristic leads us to think that violent crime is much more common than it really is. What other misperceptions does the public have about crime and crime prevention? What role might categorization, schemas, automatic processing, and motivated inferences play in these misperceptions? What role does the cognitive miser play?

FIGURE 3-6 *If you're told that Steve is ambitious, argumentative, and very smart, would you say that he is a lawyer or a farmer? Using the representativeness heuristic, we assume that someone with these characteristics is more likely to be a lawyer than a farmer. We use this cognitive shortcut even when the odds are against its being accurate.*

dairy farmers? Indeed there are. But a heuristic is a shortcut to a decision, a "best guess."

Let's look at Steve again. Imagine now that Steve—still ambitious and argumentative—is 1 of 100 men; 70 of these men are dairy farmers, and 30 are lawyers. What would you guess his occupation to be under these conditions? The study that set up these problems and posed these questions found that most people still guess that Steve is a lawyer (Kahneman & Tversky, 1982). Despite the odds, they are misled by the powerful representativeness heuristic.

The subjects who made this mistake failed to use base-rate data, information about the population as opposed to information about just the individual (Steve). They knew that 70 of the 100 men in the group were farmers. Therefore, there was a 7 out of 10 chance that Steve was a farmer, no matter what his personal characteristics. This tendency to underuse base-rate data and to rely on the special characteristics of the person or situation is known as the *base-rate fallacy*.

The Simulation Heuristic   Imagine that you have picked a number in a lottery and have the chance to win millions if your number is chosen. You have to pick six separate numbers, anything from 1 to 49. To get your number, you picked the month and day of your birthday, the chapter and verse of your favorite Bible passage, and your sister's and mother's ages. On the night of the drawing you sit glued to the television set as the little balls pop up to select the winning number. You get the first number, and your hopes increase. You get the second number, and you start to get excited. The third and fourth numbers are correct, and you are now clawing at the ceiling. Two more and you win! Alas, life deals you a bad hand: The fifth number isn't even close to your sister's age. But it is exactly your brother's age! Just out of curiosity you keep watching. To your chagrin, you hit the sixth number! *If only* you had chosen your brother's age!

The *simulation heuristic* takes the verbal form "if only": "If only I had picked 8 instead of 4, I would be a millionaire right now." When using the simulation heuristic, people evaluate why something happened by running a "thought experiment" in their minds in which the cause of the event is undone to see whether it would still have occurred.

The "if only" mode affects the individual's evaluation of an event. People evaluate outcomes not only in terms of what they expected before the event but also in terms of what they think might have been. For example, when our lottery player correctly picked five out of six numbers in the lottery, she won a nice sum of money. But the alternative—the "what if" simulation—kept running through her mind. Even though she never expected to win anything, she now evaluates her winnings against what she thinks she might have won—millions. A sense of disappointment, although fleeting, arises from the contrast between what happened and what might have been (Miller, Turnbull, & McFarland, 1989, 1990).

Counterfactual Thinking The tendency to run scenarios in our head—to create positive alternatives to what actually happened—is most likely to occur when we can easily imagine a different and more positive outcome. For example, let's say you leave your house a bit later than you had planned on your way to the airport and miss your plane. Does it make a difference whether you miss it by 5 minutes or 30 minutes? Yes—the 5-minute miss causes you more distress, because you can easily imagine how you could have made up those 5 minutes and now been on your way to Acapulco. Any event that has a negative outcome but allows for a different, and easily imagined, outcome is vulnerable to **counterfactual thinking,** an imagined scenario that runs opposite to what really happened.

As another example, imagine that you took a new route home from school one day because you were tired of the same old drive. As you drive this unfamiliar route, you are involved in an accident. It's likely that you will think, "If only I had stuck to my usual route, none of this would have happened!" You play out a positive alternative scenario (no accident) that contrasts with what occurred. The inclination of people to do these counterfactual mental simulations is widespread, particularly when dramatic events occur (Wells & Gavanski, 1989).

Generally, we are most likely to use the simulation heuristic and counterfactual thinking if we perceive events to be mutable (changeable) (Miller et al., 1989). As a rule, we perceive dramatic or exceptional events (taking a new route home) as more mutable than unexceptional ones (taking your normal route). Various studies have found that it is the mutability of the event—the event that "didn't have to be"—that affects the perception of causality (Gavanski & Wells, 1989; Kahneman & Tversky, 1982). People's reactions to their own misfortunes and those of others may be determined, in great part, by the counterfactual alternatives evoked by those misfortunes (Miller et al., 1989).

Consider how tragic the fate of school teacher Christa McAuliffe was perceived to be. As a volunteer on the 1986 *Challenger* space shuttle flight, she was the only nonprofessional astronaut on board when the shuttle

counterfactual thinking The tendency to create positive alternatives to the negative outcome that actually occurred. This type of thinking is most likely to occur when we can easily imagine a different and more positive outcome.

Counterfactual thinking led many people to imagine alternative outcomes for the crew of the space shuttle Challenger, *which exploded a few seconds after launching in 1986. Observers found the fate of teacher Christa McAuliffe (second from left, top row) particularly tragic because, as the only nonprofessional astronaut on board, her presence was perceived as unusual, something that "didn't have to be."*

exploded and all seven crew members were killed. The public perceived her death in that context as more abnormal, more dramatic, and more mutable than the deaths of the six professional astronauts. We couldn't help but think she need not have been on that flight. We could easily imagine her in her normal routine, back in the classroom or at home. If only she hadn't been interested in going into space—if only she hadn't been selected from among the teachers who had applied—she would be alive today. It was less easy to imagine alternatives for the six others, because they were doing their appointed jobs. Just as we imagined alternative scenarios for Christa McAuliffe, we can be sure that the crew of the *Vincennes* imagined endless "what if" scenarios after the shooting of the airbus.

Accentuating the Positive: Motivated Errors in Perception

To say that we prefer positive outcomes to negative ones is to state the obvious. When bad things happen, we would like to rearrange reality, even if only in our minds. We also wish to organize and interpret social information in ways that maintain or increase our status or self-esteem. It seems that our cognitive strategies are biased toward constructing positive outcomes. This **self-serving bias** often leads us to make **motivated inferences**—interpretations of events that put the best face on reality and tilt it in our favor. Research indicates that people tend to organize and evaluate evidence so that it serves their best interests (Kunda, 1987, 1990).

Consider, for example, a young man who is thinking about getting married. He probably considers his chances of having a successful marriage

self-serving bias The tendency to bias our cognitive strategies toward constructing positive outcomes.

motivated inferences Interpretations of events that put the best face on reality and tilt it in our favor.

The self-serving bias can lead people to make motivated inferences—assumptions that cast their actions in a more positive light than is realistically warranted. When President Bill Clinton nominated Zoe Baird for attorney general in 1993, he didn't anticipate the public outcry that would occur about her having hired illegal aliens as household workers and not having paid Social Security taxes on their wages. In his zeal to fill his cabinet and to include women, Clinton apparently misjudged the public's feelings about individuals perceived as flaunting the law—especially tax law.

to be quite good, despite the high divorce rate among present-day American marriages. He can probably generate theories about why he will not get divorced despite the statistics. It is easy to do this because people have the capacity to construct a theory that will link almost any attribute they have to a positive outcome. If he has had many romantic relationships, he might argue that his wide-ranging experience will help make him more successful in marriage than other people. If he has had few such relationships, he might argue that his lack of emotional baggage from unhappy past relationships will help make him more successful than other people. No matter what people's experiences and characteristics are, it is possible for them to believe that they will contribute to a positive outcome (Kunda, 1990).

Do people process information in a self-serving way? To answer this question, Ziva Kunda (1990) instructed subjects to read a description of a target person who had one of two opposite sets of attributes, such as having an employed mother or having an unemployed mother. Subjects then had to rate the attributes in terms of how much each contributed to the success or failure of the target person's marriage. Finally, subjects had to rate themselves on the same list of attributes.

Kunda analyzed the differences between the ratings of the attributes when the subjects had the same characteristics as the target person (attributes matched) compared to when the subject differed from the target person (attributes did not match). Table 3-2 shows the ratings given to the attributes by subjects who did or did not match the target person. The higher the rating, the more the subject associated the attribute with a

TABLE 3-2

MOTIVATED INFERENCES AS A FUNCTION OF WHETHER THE SUBJECT DID OR DID NOT MATCH THE TARGET

Target's Attribute	Subject Matched Target	Subject Did Not Match Target
Employed mother	5.53*	4.40
Unemployed mother	4.96*	4.48
Introvert	3.65	4.37
Extravert	5.70*	5.30
Independent	4.50*	2.25
Dependent	4.92	5.03
Nonreligious	4.80*	4.12
Religious	6.81*	6.33
Liberal	4.81*	4.74
Conservative	4.89	5.73
Early relationship	6.47*	5.75
No early relationship	4.43*	3.57

* Higher ratings—usually given when the subject matched the target—indicate the subject thought the attribute predicted a happy marriage.

Following Kunda, 1987.

happy marriage. The lower the rating, the more the subject associated the attribute with divorce. As can be seen in the table, in 9 out of 12 cases (indicated by an asterisk), subjects whose attributes matched those of the target person inferred that having that attribute was a positive indicator for a happy marriage.

For example, if both the subject and the target person had an employed mother (a match), the subject rated that attribute as favorably related to a good marriage (5.53). If the target person did not have an employed mother and the subject did, the subject thought that having that attribute (an employed mother) would be likely to lead to divorce (4.40). Those who had an unemployed mother and matched the target person inferred that having an unemployed mother was a positive attribute (4.96). Those who did not have an unemployed mother thought that having that attribute was more likely to lead to divorce (4.48).

Kunda found that these motivated (self-serving) inferences occurred in a variety of situations. If subjects drank a lot of coffee, they tended to think that caffeine was not particularly unhealthy; if they didn't drink coffee, they thought caffeine was unhealthy. If subjects had attributes they thought predicted success in graduate school, they inferred that those attributes were important. If they did not have those attributes, they tended to downgrade the importance of these attributes.

Kunda's findings show that people spontaneously create self-serving causal theories that link their own characteristics to positive results and minimize any link between their attributes and unfavorable outcomes. Our inferences about the world are motivated by a need to believe that good things will happen to us (after all, many of our attributes are associated with good outcomes) and that bad things can be avoided (even if we have attributes associated with bad outcomes). Perhaps this is the only way we can deal with a risky and unpredictable world.

THE *VINCENNES* INCIDENT REVISITED

The captain and crew of the *Vincennes* took a great deal of criticism from the press and others for their actions in the Persian Gulf. We can see now that it would have taken a superhuman effort, or the implementation of new training procedures, for them to have acted otherwise. Their behavior was schema driven: The image they held of the enemy, along with their training, primed them to act in specific ways when under threat. The possibility of another interpretation of events required a leap of imagination they were unable to make.

We know that it takes effort to overcome our human tendency to process information in the most efficient and least effortful way possible. What can be done to prevent incidents like this from happening again? Training programs that alert combat crews to the possibility of multiple interpretations of situations may be one route to this goal.

LOOKING AHEAD

In this chapter we have explored the processes and strategies of social perception and impression management. We saw that each of us constructs our own, slightly skewed, version of social reality, based on our previous experiences, our expectations, our needs and goals. We saw that in processing social information we unconsciously take the least effortful route to an understanding of a situation. And we saw that this approach—the approach of the cognitive miser—leads us into a number of predictable errors.

In the next chapter we look more closely at a narrower range of social perception—the process of causal attribution, or deciding why people behave as they do. The chapter addresses a fundamental question of social perception: What motivates other people's behavior? We see that our responses range from automatic categorization to careful, reasoned, controlled processing. And again, we see that our cognitive processes incline us to apply a number of biases, which in turn lead us into predictable mistakes.

CHAPTER REVIEW

1. *How do we come to comprehend the motives and behavior of other people and make sense of the world?*
   We construct social reality—our own interpretation or version of events around us—through the processes of *social perception*. In creating this understanding we tend to be **cognitive misers,** preferring the easiest, least effortful means of processing social information.

2. *What are the methods and strategies of social perception?*
   The fundamental tool of social perception is **categorization.** Our initial response to new people and events is to decide, rather effortlessly, what category they belong to, and we respond to them as if they are representative members of that category. We may have either **category-based expectancies** about individuals, based on assumptions about the category to which they belong, or **target-based expectancies,** based on information about them as individuals. We also categorize by using **prototypes,** a representation of the average qualities of members of the category, and **exemplars,** a specific example of that category. In addition, we use **schemas,** organized sets of ideas about events or people. Relying on schemas without taking new information into account can lead to **self-fulfilling prophecies.** And sometimes we plug the gaps in the categorization process by devising stories, more involved constructions that guide us as we gather information and impose coherence on events. In addition, we tend to devise theories to help us organize information about others. One such theory, known as an **implicit personality theory,** is our attempt to predict what kinds of personality traits go together. "Intellectual," for example, is often linked to "cold," and "strong" and "adventurous" are often thought to go together.

3. *What is the importance of first impressions?*
   The process by which we make judgments about other people is called **impression formation.** First impressions can be powerful influences on our perceptions of others. Researchers have consistently demonstrated a **primacy effect** in impression formation, the tendency of early information to play a powerful role in our eventual impression of an individual. First impressions can also bias the interpretation of later information. If this information is inconsistent with the first impression, it is often, though not always, reinterpreted to fit the initial belief.

4. *What are the principal mechanisms of social perception?*
   Much social perception involves **automatic processing**—categorizing and forming impressions without much thought or attention. Automatic processing is thinking that is effortless and that occurs primarily outside consciousness. It is the preferred method of the cognitive miser. Automatic processing is also likely to occur when we face a negative or dangerous situation. In fact, human beings display **automatic vigilance** with respect to events that could cause them harm and automatically turn their attention from a task when a threat occurs.

   More conscious and effortful thinking is called **controlled processing.** We are motivated to use controlled processing—that is, to allocate more of our cognitive energy to perceiving and interpreting—when we have goals we want to achieve in social interaction or when we are disturbed by information that doesn't fit our expectancies.

5. *Are people accurate social perceivers?*
   The social perceiver can be accurate in forming impressions of others when motivated by the wish to attain some goal. If we have to accurately assess others, we do so in a careful and effortful way. If not, our

strategy is to use the least effortful, most automatic, way of forming impressions. We do not simply observe other people, however; we interact with them. The goals we have for the interaction affect our perception of others.

6. *What systematic errors does the social perceiver tend to make?*
   Social perceivers are vulnerable to several systematic errors in the service of the cognitive miser strategy. We often fail to recognize that we play an active role in constructing reality, that others construct versions of reality which differ from ours, and that others may not see things as we do (the **egocentric bias**). We tend to underestimate the importance of the situation in determining behavior and overestimate the role of internal characteristics. We often believe we can control events over which we actually have no control. We also tend to use **heuristics**—simple rules of thumb—to organize our perceptions effortlessly, and they can lead us to inaccurate impressions. Sometimes we overestimate the frequency of an event based on how quickly examples come to mind (the availability heuristic). Sometimes we make incorrect judgments about the probability of an event or person falling into a category based on how representative it is of the category (the representativeness heuristic). The simulation heuristic leads us to act as if we can undo an event that has occurred. **Counterfactual thinking** is the imagining of scenarios that run opposite to what really happened. **Motivated inferences** are interpretations of events that tilt reality in our favor, an example of the working of the **self-serving bias.**

SUGGESTIONS FOR FURTHER READING

Gilovich, T. (1991). *How we know what isn't so: The fallibility of human reason in everyday life*. New York: Free Press.
   A well-written overview of the flaws all social perceivers exhibit. Interesting and insightful analysis by one of the leading thinkers in the area.

Rachlin, T. (1994). *Behavior and the mind*. Oxford University Press.
   An expert in the field shows how mental mechanisms relate to human behavior.

Wegner, D., Ember, R., & Zanakos, S. (1993). Ironic process in the mental control of mood and mood-related thought. *Journal of Personality and Social Psychology, 65*, 6, 1093–1104.
   An interesting study, one in a series, that shows how perverse our cognitive processes can be. This research indicates that when we have a high mental load (for example, when we're under stress or time pressure), our attempts to control our thoughts will produce what Wagner calls ironic effects—the opposite of the desired effect.

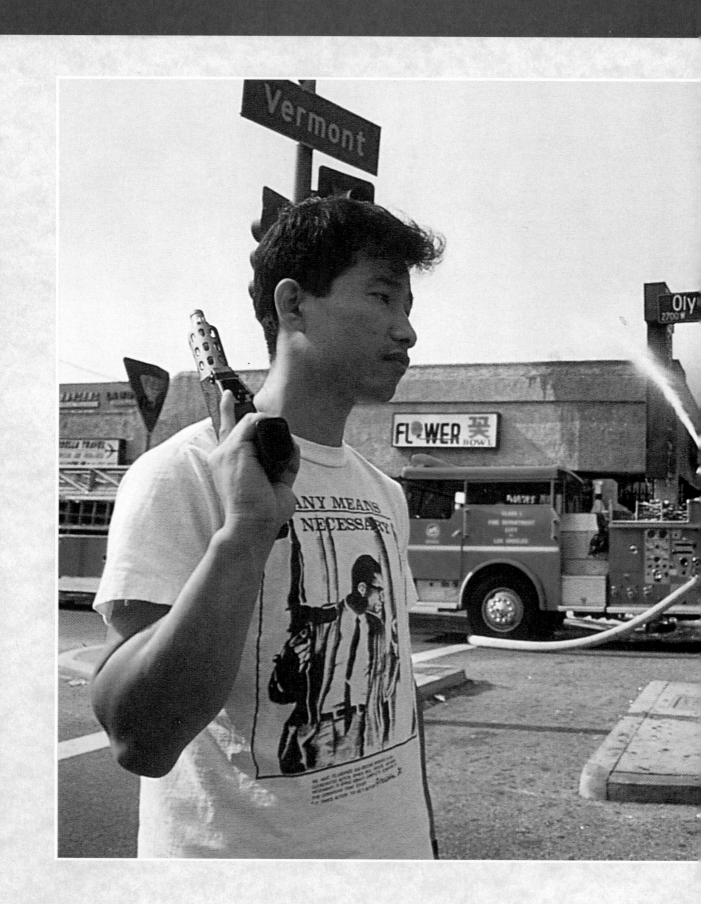

Chapter 4
Attribution

On September 3, 1974, John Dean—34 years old, a graduate of a prestigious law school, former counsel to President Richard M. Nixon—was fingerprinted, searched, photographed for mug shots, and sent to jail. Dean had served as special counsel to the president for 3 years; now he had to serve 1 to 4 years in a federal prison. Although Dean knew full well why he had been convicted, he found it hard to truly comprehend how he wound up staring at "sixteen feet of greenish iron bars" (Dean, 1977, p. 366).

Within weeks of taking his prestigious White House job, Dean had found himself in the middle of a conspiracy. During the 1972 presidential campaign, several assistants to the president, members of the Committee to Reelect the President (CREEP), had been involved in some political "dirty tricks." These included soliciting illegal campaign funds in violation of a newly passed campaign finance law. "Contributors" would bring one or two hundred thousand dollars (all in small denominations) in attaché cases to the White House. The money was put into a vault and used for whatever purposes CREEP wanted.

One "dirty trick" funded by CREEP was a burglary of the offices of the Democratic Party National Headquarters at the Watergate apartment complex. The former government agents who placed an electronic "bug" there were arrested before they got out of the building. The Watergate scandal—which would lead to Richard Nixon's resignation of the presidency—had begun.

Dean had the job of containing the spreading public knowledge of the illegal activities. Soon he had some serious problems with potential legal overtones. The actual Watergate burglars were in jail, threatening to "talk" because the money promised to them if things went wrong wasn't forthcoming. Two reporters at the *Washington Post* began to get information about the illegal activities at the White House from a source who was code-named "Deep Throat."

Soon a federal prosecutor began to investigate; the president told everybody to "stonewall it"—deny everything—when called to testify (Dean, 1977). According to his own account, Dean told the president that he, Nixon, ought to come clean with the American people and confess his wrongdoings. If the president did this, Dean felt sure, the public would forgive if not forget the scandal.

The president instead suggested that John Dean confess to everything, letting everyone else off the hook. Dean said no thank you, sir, and got a lawyer.

Dean testified before a Senate investigating committee and then became the star witness for the special prosecutor, who indicted several other presidential assistants. Dean had an encyclopedic, if not photographic, memory, and he was cool. He had the facts and no one could shake him. Dean's recall of events and conversations was remarkable. He made occasional errors, but he got most of it right (Neisser, 1981).

There was no proof other than Dean's statements until "the tapes." The president, to preserve his place in history, had tape-recorded everything that happened in the Oval Office. Few people knew this. A White House technician let it slip. Eventually, the U.S. Supreme Court ordered the president to surrender the tapes. The substance of Dean's testimony was verified.

If you were to read about the Watergate scandal in the newspaper today, you probably would ask yourself about the motives of those involved. What kind of person was John Dean? Was he coerced by men more powerful than he to cover up the White House's illegal actions? Or was he an independent actor, doing what he did because he believed that it was right?

In Chapter 3, we noted that individuals are primed by their culture and their biology to form impressions of other people. An important part of impression formation involves deciding *why* people behave as they do. Encountering people and events in their world, human beings always look for reasons, for causes, for explanations. Why did my neighbor look right through me as we passed on the street? Why did I do poorly on the midterm? Why hasn't my friend called me? Why is my roommate taking drugs? Why are my brother and his wife talking about getting a divorce? Social psychologists call the process of assigning causes for behavior causal **attribution.** Only by assigning causes can we make sense out of other people's behavior as well as our own.

In this chapter we consider how people think about situations like Watergate and people like John Dean. Did he believe illegal activities were justified for political reasons? Or did he succumb to pressures to act against his better judgment? What models and theories have been proposed to explain how we answer questions like these? What are the consequences, both for how we feel and how we act, that follow from these attributions? And what systematic errors do we make when we try to understand behavior, both our own and others'? These are some of the questions addressed in the pages that follow.

attribution The process of assigning causes for behavior.

THE ATTRIBUTION PROCESS: DECIDING WHY PEOPLE ACT AS THEY DO

Each of the theories developed to explain the process of attribution provides an important piece of the puzzle of how we assign causes and understand behavior. The aim of all these theories is to illuminate how people decide what caused a particular behavior. The theories are not concerned with finding the *actual* causes of someone's behavior. Instead, they are concerned with determining how we, in our everyday lives, think and make judgments about the *perceived* causes of behaviors and events.

In this section, five influential attribution theories or models are introduced:

- Correspondent inference theory
- Covariation theory
- Abnormal conditions theory
- Probabilistic contrast model
- Two-step and three-step models

The first two—correspondent inference theory and covariation theory—are the oldest and most general attempts to describe the attribution process. The other three represent more recent and less formal approaches to analyzing attribution.

Heider's Early Work on Attribution

The first social psychologist to systematically study causal attribution was Fritz Heider. He assumed that individuals trying to make sense out of the social world follow simple rules of causality. The individual, or "perceiver," operates as a kind of "naive scientist," applying a set of rudimentary scientific rules (Heider, 1958). Attribution theories are an attempt to discover exactly what those rules are.

Heider made a distinction between **internal attribution**—assigning causality to something about the person—and **external attribution**—assigning causality to something about the situation. He believed that decisions about whether an observed behavior has an *internal* (personal) or *external* (situational) source emerge from our attempt to analyze why others act as they do (*causal analysis*). Internal sources involve things about the individual—character, personality, motives, dispositions, beliefs, and so on. External sources involve things about the situation—other people, various environmental stimuli, social pressure, coercion, and so on. Our impression of John Dean depends a great deal on whether we see him as the type of person who would willingly and knowingly break the law (an internal attribution) or as a "regular" person who broke the law in response to enormous outside pressures (an external attribution). If we believe Dean was responsible for his behavior, we see him as purposely initiating the behavior and exercising control over it thereafter. If we believe he wasn't responsible, we see him as involved in a situation in which powerful others controlled and directed his actions. Heider (1944, 1958) examined questions about the role of internal and external sources as perceived

internal attribution The process of assigning causality to something about the person—character, personality, beliefs, and so on.

external attribution The process of assigning causality to something about the situation—other people, environmental stimuli, social pressure, and so on.

causes of behavior. His work defined the basic questions that future attribution theorists would confront. We turn now to the two theories that built directly on Heider's work.

Correspondent Inference Theory

Most observers made an internal attribution for John Dean's actions. They held him responsible for what he did. Assigning causes for behavior also means assigning responsibility. Of course, it is possible to believe that someone *caused* something to happen yet not consider the individual *responsible* for that action. A 5-year-old who is left in an automobile with the engine running and who gets behind the wheel and steers the car through the frozen-food section of Joe's convenience store *caused* the event but certainly is not *responsible* for it, psychologically or legally. Similarly, if we find that John Dean played a role in covering up illegal activities but did so because he believed that his superiors must be covering up for good reasons, we might not hold him completely responsible for his actions.

Nevertheless, social perceivers have a strong tendency to assign responsibility to the individual who has done the deed, the actor. A jury certainly decided that Dean had considerable responsibility for his actions. Consider another instance: Let's say your brakes fail, you are unable to stop at a red light, and you plow into the side of another car. Are you responsible for those impersonal brakes failing to stop your car? Well, it depends, doesn't it? Under what circumstances would you be held responsible, and when would you not? How do observers make such inferences? What sources of information do people use when they decide someone is responsible for an action?

In 1965, Edward Jones and Keith Davis proposed a theory they called *correspondent inference theory* to explain the processes used in making internal attributions about others, particularly when the observed behavior is ambiguous—that is, when the perceiver is not sure how to interpret the actor's behavior. We make a **correspondent inference** when we conclude that a person's overt behavior is caused by, or corresponds to, the person's internal characteristics or beliefs. We might believe, for example, that a person who writes an essay in favor of a tax increase really believes that taxes should be raised. What factors influence us to make correspondent inferences?

Choice and Intent According to correspondent inference theory, two major factors lead us to make a correspondent inference:

- We perceive that the person *freely chose* the behavior.
- We perceive that the person *intended to do* what he or she did.

Early in the Persian Gulf War of 1991, several U.S.-coalition aircraft were shot down over Iraq. A few days later some captured pilots appeared in front of cameras and denounced the war against Iraq. From the images we could see that it was likely they had been beaten. Consequently, it was obvious that they did not freely choose to say what they did. Under these conditions, we do not make a correspondent inference. We assume that the behavior tells us little or nothing about the true feelings of the person. Statements from

correspondent inference
The inference that occurs when we conclude that a person's behavior is caused by, or corresponds to, the person's internal characteristics or beliefs.

Does he really mean it? Few Americans believed Mike Durant's statements denouncing U.S. actions after his plane was shot down and he was captured in Somalia. We do not make a correspondent inference when we perceive that someone has not freely chosen his actions.

prisoners or hostages are always regarded with skepticism for this reason. The perception that someone has been coerced to do or say something makes an internal attribution less likely.

The second factor contributing to an internal attribution is intent. If we conclude that a person's behavior was intentional rather than accidental, we are likely to make an internal attribution for that behavior. To say that a person intended to do something suggests that the individual wanted the behavior in question to occur. To say that someone did not intend an action, or did not realize what the consequences would be, is to suggest that the actor is less responsible for the outcome.

American criminal law emphasizes intent. For example, when John Hinckley, Jr., fired a gun at President Ronald Reagan and his party as they emerged from the Washington Hilton Hotel on March 30, 1981, he grievously wounded several people, including the president and his press secretary, James Brady. At Hinckley's trial, his lawyers did not dispute the facts; the behavior was not at issue. What was at issue was intent. Hinckley's lawyers maintained that the defendant did not intend to shoot the president. They presented evidence to suggest that Hinckley lived in a fantasy world, divorced from reality, and that the president and his aides were nothing more than toys, cardboard figures, to him. Yes, the defense said, Hinckley did pull the trigger, but he did not understand that doing so would cause injury. Indeed, one defense psychiatrist reported in court that Hinckley was stunned to see Brady lying on the sidewalk, bleeding from the head wound that would put him in a wheelchair for the rest of his life.

The substance of the defense was that Hinckley had such a defect of mental capacity that he didn't know what he was doing when he acted. The

TABLE 4-1

Correspondent and Noncorrespondent Inferences

Behavior	Correspondent Inference	Noncorrespondent Inference
He ordered escargot.	He likes escargot.	He's trying to impress his date.
She's wind surfing.	She likes wind surfing.	She's showing off.
He says I'm smart.	He thinks I'm smart.	He's flattering me to get something.
She disagrees with her boss.	She's not afraid to stand up to her boss when she thinks he's wrong.	She's just trying to show the workers she's one of them.
Oliver North lied about Iran-Contras.	Oliver North is a liar.	Oliver North was pressured by his superiors to lie.
She got an A on the math test.	She's good at math.	She was lucky.
He spilled wine on the tablecloth.	He was mad at his wife and wanted to damage her best tablecloth.	It was an accident.
She admitted that what she had done was wrong.	She believed that what she had done was wrong.	She was trying to avoid punishment.

Adapted from Jones, 1990.

jury returned a verdict of not guilty by reason of insanity. Jury members decided that although Hinckley caused harm, he had not *intended* harm. In other words, because the outcome was unintended, the jury refused to make a correspondent inference.

A correspondent inference, then, is usually made when it is evident that the person freely chose to do something and intended the outcome to happen. Examples of both correspondent and noncorrespondent inferences are shown in Table 4-1.

Although choice and intention are the major factors determining whether we make a correspondent inference, we may also consider two other kinds of information:

- Common and noncommon effects
- Social desirability

We often use evidence about these two dimensions when we make judgments about the meaning of people's behavior.

Common and Noncommon Effects   Correspondent inference theory also suggests that we consider the *effects* of a behavior when making inferences about an individual's personality and motives for behavior. Imagine, for example, that a friend of yours is considering jobs offered to her by three different companies. Any decision she makes will have consequences, or effects, as shown in Figure 4-1. All the jobs offer good benefits and strong possibilities for advancement. In the terminology of correspondent inference theory, these are *common effects* of your friend's action—they are the same (Jones & Davis, 1965). No matter which job your friend chooses, she will have a job offering good benefits and good possibilities for advancement. Common effects tell the observer little about the motives of the person, because the outcomes are all the same.

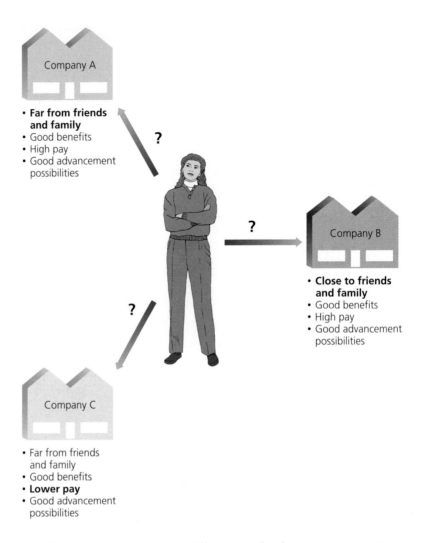

FIGURE 4-1 *Common and noncommon effects. We can tell quite a bit about a person's real motives by looking at the effects of her choices and behaviors that are different from the effects of other choices.*

Company A

- **Far from friends and family**
- Good benefits
- High pay
- Good advancement possibilities

Company B

- **Close to friends and family**
- Good benefits
- High pay
- Good advancement possibilities

Company C

- Far from friends and family
- Good benefits
- **Lower pay**
- Good advancement possibilities

There are also things that differ across the three companies. Company B is located close to your friend's family, and Company C has lower pay. These are *noncommon effects*—they differ from the outcomes of other alternatives. Generally, noncommon effects are more informative about a person's inner dispositions and motives. If your friend chooses Company A, she will have a good job but be far from her family. We can infer that family is less important to her. If she chooses Company B, she will have a good job and be close to her family. We can infer that family probably is important to her. The noncommon effect gave us some insight into her motives and personality.

Social Desirability   Generally, the choices we make have multiple effects (just like the effects of your friend's job decision). Some of these effects are *socially desirable*—generally approved by other people—whereas others are undesirable (Jones & Davis, 1965). Socially desirable behaviors tell us little about the motives of the person because everyone tends to behave that way. But if a person acts in a way that is not socially desirable, we gain some important information about that person. For example, if you are quiet at a funeral—the

Many people were astonished when Egyptian president Anwar Sadat (left) traveled to Jerusalem in 1977 to discuss peace with Israeli prime minister Menachem Begin (right). Sadat's move required great personal courage and vision because it ran so counter to prevailing attitudes among Arab nations. According to correspondent inference theory, when individuals act in socially undesirable or disapproved ways, we usually infer that they truly believe in what they are doing.

socially desirable way to act—it tells us little about how you really felt about the deceased. You may be sad or you may simply not want to behave in a way that lets others know what you really thought of the old cad. But if you break out in hysterical laughter when the deceased is described as a boon to humankind, we learn a lot more about how you truly feel. If we want to understand your (socially undesirable) behavior, we probably will infer that the cause is a deep and true feeling of distaste for this individual.

Let's consider a historical example of social desirability. In 1977 Anwar Sadat, the late president of Egypt, traveled to Israel to make peace with his long-time enemy. Now, Sadat was not the only Arab leader whose country was on hostile terms with Israel. Jordan, Syria, and Libya were all technically in a state of war with Israel. In this instance the socially desirable behavior for Sadat was to stick with his fellow Arab leaders. However, Sadat acted in a socially undesirable manner (with respect to the other Arab leaders) and started a process of negotiating peace with Israel. Sadat, along with Israeli prime minister Menachem Begin, won a Nobel Prize for his efforts to gain peace.

Social desirability alone may not provide us with enough information to make a correspondent inference. However, when social desirability is combined with noncommon effects, we have two of the most critical pieces of information needed to make correspondent inferences (Jones & Davis, 1965). We most easily make correspondent inferences from a person's behavior when noncommon effects exist *and* a person behaves in a socially undesirable way. Anwar Sadat's behavior violated both the common effects in the Middle East (war rather than peace) and the behavior toward Israel the other Arab leaders

Oskar Schindler was a member of the Nazi party and a war profiteer. He was also a rescuer of 1,200 Jews from near-certain death in the concentration camps of Eastern Europe. Many people have asked why he acted as he did. The answer may always remain an enigma.

Schindler was born in 1908 in Moravia, then a part of the Austrian Empire but to become in 1918 a part of the newly formed nation of Czechoslovakia. His family was Catholic, but Oskar was a negligent practitioner. His father owned a farm machinery plant and cared little about politics. Oskar's passion as a young man was motorcycles, and for a while he seemed to be headed for a career as a motorcycle racer. But marriage intervened, along with the Depression of the 1930s, and Oskar got a job as sales manager of a local company.

Though politically unsophisticated, Oskar was intelligent, charming, convivial, gregarious. He gained a reputation as a womanizer and a man who could hold his liquor. He had a gift for salesmanship and quickly developed good business contacts. When opportunities opened up in Poland after Germany invaded in 1939, he was ready to take advantage of them. He came to Cracow and began operating a factory with Jewish slave labor. Things went well for him, even as life deteriorated for the Jews of Poland.

Oskar woke up to the realities of Nazi intentions for the Jews on the day he watched the liquidation of the Cracow ghetto. From a nearby hilltop he saw soldiers driving the Jews from their homes, machine-gunning men, women,

and children at random, and sending them off to the camps. According to Thomas Keneally, author of *Schindler's List* (1982), Oskar "lay special weight on this day" (p. 133). Whereas he had seen earlier actions as temporary lunacies, he now realized that these events had official sanction.

> "Beyond this day," he would claim, "no thinking person could fail to see what would happen. I was now resolved to do everything in my power to defeat the system." (Keneally, p. 133)

Oskar Schindler in 1962.

Oskar ended up risking his life and spending every cent of his fortune to buy the lives of his factory workers from the Nazis. At the end of the war he was penniless, but, protected by the Jews he had saved, he emigrated to Brazil. He returned to Germany in 1958, eventually giving himself up to bankruptcy and alcoholism.

Why did he do it? Schindler never explained his actions. To

some he said simply, "There was no choice." To others he posed the question, "If you saw a dog going to be crushed under a car, wouldn't you help him?" (Miller, 1993, p. 118).

Some people have speculated that perhaps it was the thrill of danger, of risk taking, that lured Schindler on. Just as he was attracted to the dangers of dealing in the black market, perhaps he was attracted to taking risks with the Nazis. But this reasoning doesn't account for the many small gestures, the decency, and the caring quality of his behavior, nor can it fully explain the extent of his actions.

Others have wondered if Schindler had an "altruistic personality" and was the kind of person who habitually behaved in a helping way. But Schindler's widow, Emilie, once remarked that her husband "had done nothing astounding before the war and had been unexceptional since" (Keneally, pp. 396–397).

No matter what his motives, Schindler has come to symbolize the hidden—and mysterious— goodness in the human heart. Keneally concludes, "He was fortunate . . . that in that short fierce era between 1939 and 1945 he had met people who summoned forth his deeper talents" (p. 397).

Oskar Schindler responded to an extraordinary time with extraordinary actions. Do you think he had inner motivations that drove him to rescue those in need? Or were there other reasons for his actions? What evidence and what theories can you use to explain his behavior?

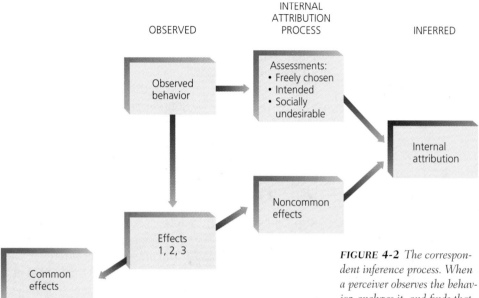

FIGURE 4-2 *The correspondent inference process. When a perceiver observes the behavior, analyzes it, and finds that it fulfills these requirements, he or she then makes an internal attribution.*

considered socially desirable. This made it more probable that the Israelis would believe that Sadat was sincere in his peacemaking efforts. For a look at another individual whose actions were socially disapproved, see the featured discussion "Interpreting Behavior: The Case of Oskar Schindler."

According to correspondent inference theory, people will make accurate attributions if they judge behavior according to these rules. But people often persist in believing that the cause of a behavior is internal to a person even when all the information suggests that the cause is external. This is called the **correspondence bias** (Jones & Harris, 1967). Remember the cognitive miser: Human beings take the least effortful way of thinking about the social world. We have a distinct bias for internal as opposed to external attributions. When we observe someone doing or saying something, we tend to assume that the behavior corresponds to the person's internal characteristics rather than considering the external context, the outside reasons that may have caused the behavior. Correspondence bias is discussed in greater detail later in this chapter, along with other kinds of biases.

In sum, then, correspondent inference theory proposes that a perceiver will make a correspondent inference (an internal attribution) if it appears that the actor freely chose an action and intended to do it. People also make correspondent inferences when the behavior involves noncommon effects—consequences that are unusual and therefore informative about the actor's motives—and when the behavior goes against what is socially desired or expected (Figure 4-2).

Correspondent inference theory focuses on the process by which we infer internal causes for an individual's behavior. But we do not always make internal attributions about behavior. Sometimes we look to the social situation for the causes of behavior. In the next section we explore an attribution theory that looks at the process of causal attribution more broadly and that includes the social situation in the attribution process.

correspondence bias People's tendency to persist in believing that the cause of a behavior is internal to a person even when all the information suggests that the cause is really external.

Covariation Theory

Attribution — the process of assigning cause for a behavior

Whereas correspondent inference theory focuses on the process of making internal attributions, covariation theory, proposed by Harold Kelley (1967, 1971), looks at external attributions—how we make sense of the situation, the factors outside the person that may be causing the behavior in question (Jones, 1990). The attribution possibilities that covariation theory lays out are similar to those that correspondent inference theory proposes. What is referred to as an internal attribution in correspondent inference theory is referred to as a *person attribution* in covariation theory. What is called an external attribution in correspondent inference theory is called a *situational attribution* in covariation theory.

The Covariation Principle   Like Heider, Kelley (1967, 1971) viewed the attribution process as an attempt to apply some rudimentary scientific principles to causal analysis. In correspondent inference theory, in contrast, the perceiver is seen in the role of a moral or legal judge of the actor. Perceivers look at intent and choice, the same factors that judges and jurors look at when assigning responsibility. Kelley's perceiver is more of a scientist: just the facts, ma'am.

According to Kelley, the basic rule applied to causal analysis is the **covariation principle,** which states that if a response is present when a situation (person, object, event) is present and absent when that same situation is absent, then that situation is the cause of the response (Kelley, 1971). In other words, people decide that the most likely cause of any behavior is the factor that covaries—occurs at the same time—most often with the appearance of that behavior.

As an example, let's say your friend Keisha saw the movie *Jurassic Park* and raved about it. You're trying to decide whether you would like it too and whether you should go see it. The question you have to answer is, What is the cause of Keisha's reaction? Why did she like this movie? Is it something about the movie? Or is it something about Keisha?

In order to make an attribution in this case, you need information. There are three sources or kinds of relevant information available to us:

- Consensus information
- Distinctiveness information
- Consistency information

Consensus information is information about how other people reacted to the same event or situation. You might ask, How did my other friends like *Jurassic Park*? How are the reviews? How did other people in general react to this stimulus or situation? If you find high consensus—everybody liked it—well, then, it's probably a good movie. In causal attribution terms, it's the movie that caused Keisha's behavior. High consensus leads to a situational attribution.

Now, what if Keisha liked the movie but nobody else did? Then it must be Keisha and not the movie: Keisha always has strange tastes in movies. Low consensus leads to a person attribution (nobody but Keisha

covariation principle The rule that if a response is present when a situation (person, object, event) is present and absent when that same situation is absent, then that situation is presumed to be the cause of the response.

likes it, so it must be Keisha). Notice that consensus information has similarities with the notion of social desirability in correspondent inference theory: If everyone behaves the same way, including the person, the perceiver learns little about that person.

The second source/kind of information we use to make attributions is *distinctiveness information.* We ask if there is something unique or distinctive about the situation that could have caused the behavior. If the behavior occurs when there is nothing distinctive or unusual about the situation (low distinctiveness), then we make a person attribution. If Keisha likes all movies, then we have low distinctiveness: There's nothing special about *Jurassic Park.* It must be Keisha. If there is something distinctive about the situation, then we make a situational attribution. If this is the only movie Keisha has ever liked, we have high distinctiveness, and there must be something special about the movie.

Low distinctiveness leads us to a person attribution; high distinctiveness leads us to a situational attribution. If the situation is unique—very high in distinctiveness—then the behavior probably was caused by the situation and not by something about the person. The combination of high consensus and high distinctiveness always leads to a situational attribution. The combination of low consensus and low distinctiveness always leads to a person attribution.

The third source/kind of information is *consistency information.* This is information about whether the action occurs over time and situations (Chen, Yates, & McGinnies, 1988). We ask, Is this a one-time behavior (low consistency), or is it repeated over time (high consistency)? In other words, is this behavior stable or unstable? Consistency is a factor that correspondent inference theory fails to take into account.

What do we learn from knowing how people act over time? If, for example, the next time we saw Keisha, she again raved about *Jurassic Park,* we would have evidence of consistency over time (Jones, 1990). We would have less confidence in her evaluation of the movie if she told us she now thought the movie wasn't very good (low consistency). We might think that perhaps Keisha was just in a good mood that night and that her mood affected her evaluation of the movie. Consistency has to do with whether the behavior is a reliable indicator of its cause.

The three sources of information used in making attributions are shown in Figures 4-3 and 4-4. Figure 4-3 shows the combination of information—high consensus, high consistency, and high distinctiveness—that leads us to make a situational attribution. Go see the movie: Everybody likes it (high consensus); Keisha, who likes few if any movies, likes it as well (high distinctiveness of this movie); and Keisha has always liked it (high consistency of behavior).

Figure 4-4 shows the combination of information—low consensus, high consistency, and low distinctiveness—that leads us to a person attribution. None of our friends likes the movie (low consensus); Keisha likes the movie, but she likes all movies, even *The Thing That Ate Newark* (low distinctiveness); and Keisha has always liked this movie (high consistency). Maybe we ought to watch TV tonight.

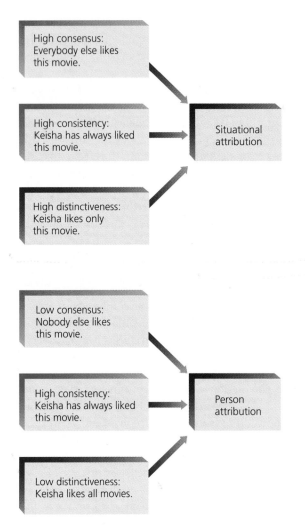

FIGURE 4-3 *Making a situational attribution. The combination of factors shown here leads us to place causality in the situation.*

High consensus: Everybody else likes this movie.

High consistency: Keisha has always liked this movie.

High distinctiveness: Keisha likes only this movie.

Situational attribution

FIGURE 4-4 *Making a person attribution. The combination of factors shown here leads us to place causality in the person.*

Low consensus: Nobody else likes this movie.

High consistency: Keisha has always liked this movie.

Low distinctiveness: Keisha likes all movies.

Person attribution

Not surprisingly, research on covariation theory shows that people prefer to make attributions to the person as opposed to the situation (McArthur, 1972). This conforms with the correspondence bias finding in correspondence inference theory and highlights again the tendency toward overemphasizing the person in causal analysis. It also fits with our tendency to be cognitive misers and take the easy route to making causal attributions.

Combining Information in a Social Context   When we are in real-life situations, we usually do not have access to information from all three informational dimensions (Schneider, 1991). Even if we do, we often ignore or underuse certain kinds of data. Generally, we underuse consensus information (Major, 1980). In other words, we do not usually have information concerning how everyone else behaves in a given situation. Often, we substitute how *we* feel *we* would behave in that situation and use that as consensus information. The theory, then, is an ideal: If perceivers followed the model exactly, then it would lead them to accurate attributions. Unfortunately, people don't always have full information, nor do they always follow the model.

What happens when we can't assign the cause strictly to one area or the other? Sometimes, perhaps much of the time, cause resides in some combination of person and situation. Consider, for example, a high-consensus and low-distinctiveness combination. Everybody likes this movie, and Keisha, who likes most movies, also likes this movie. Do we conclude that it's a good movie, or could it be that Keisha is just making her usual unqualified positive judgment? Probably it's a combination of both.

Or, if few people like this movie (low consensus), and Keisha likes very few movies but she likes this one (high distinctiveness), we again are unsure what to conclude. Probably there is an interaction between the movie and Keisha—something about it really impressed her. Now your attribution will depend on what you know about Keisha. In this case, the kind of attribution you make depends on what you know about the context of the social situation and your expectations about the person (McGill, 1989). In fact, in part, that's what consensus and distinctiveness information provide: knowledge about the social context. But consensus and distinctiveness information may not tell us all we need to know to make an accurate attribution. Sometimes we need specific information unrelated to consensus or distinctiveness.

The Discounting and Augmentation Principles   As noted, perceivers rarely have full information about consensus, distinctiveness, and consistency. People apply two principles that allow for attributions under conditions of limited information. The first is the **discounting principle,** which suggests that a perceiver will reject any potential cause for an event to the extent that other reasonable causes are available. If, for example, you see that I am grouchy (potentially a personality or internal cause) and you also know that I am facing a difficult family problem (a situational or external cause), you will be less likely to make a person attribution than if you did not know about my family problem.

The discounting principle is closely related to some mechanisms operating with correspondent inferences. In correspondent inference, we make internal attributions only when the effects of behavior are individualizing (Jones, 1990). For example, when a person behaves consistently within a role or in a socially desirable way, discounting is likely to occur. You think, quite reasonably, that it was the requirements of the role or the job that made the person act the way he or she did. The firefighter who helps put out a blaze is doing it because that's part of the job, not (necessarily) because of bravery or selflessness. We discount other potential causes (bravery) because the most obvious cause is that it's part of the role or the job.

The other side of discounting is the **augmentation principle.** Here, instead of discounting the importance of a factor in the attribution mix, the perceiver augments (increases) the importance of a factor. Suppose a person acts a certain way even though it has negative or undesirable effects for that person. Recall the act of Anwar Sadat in offering peace to Israel. He

discounting principle A rule applied by perceivers under conditions of limited information that leads them to decrease the importance of a potential cause of an event if other reasonable causes are present.

augmentation principle A rule applied by perceivers under conditions of limited information that leads them to increase the importance of a potential cause of an event.

Archbishop Oscar Romero lost his life for speaking out against El Salvador's ruling military junta and the right-wing death squads that terrorized the country in the 1980s. Because his actions placed him in great danger, we attribute them to deep personal convictions. According to covariation theory's augmentation principle, the greater the number of negative effects that result from a behavior, the more sincere that behavior is perceived to be.

risked not only the displeasure of many of his compatriots but assassination as well. In fact, Sadat did die of an assassin's bullet some years after his peace overture. In the correspondent inference model, these are noncommon effects (danger for Sadat as well as the disapproval of the other Arab leaders). In the covariation model, the inference made about noncommon behavior is explained by the augmentation principle. According to this principle, the greater the number of negative effects that can flow from a behavior, the more diagnostic (useful) that behavior is for making attributions. If the behavior occurs despite the presence of these factors, then the perceiver is likely to make a person attribution. We conclude that Sadat's motive was a sincere desire for peace.

To what extent is covariation theory—or any of the attribution theories discussed here—bound up with cultural norms? Some researchers have investigated the attribution process as it occurs in other cultures of the world. For a look at these investigations, see the featured discussion "Are Attribution Theories Culture-Bound?"

The concepts and research findings underlying attribution theory are derived from American and Western ideas and experiments. Do people in different cultures analyze causality the same way? Is attribution theory an accurate description of universal causal analysis—the way human beings assign causality—or is it limited to specific cultural settings and ways of knowing?

The answer seems to be that attribution theory in its various forms is generally accurate, across cultures, in explaining how people assign causality. There are, however, differences in emphasis. In one study, for example, Joan Miller (1984) compared the attributions of American and Hindu subjects. When Miller asked her subjects to give reasons for why a friend did good or bad things, she found that about half of the American subjects gave internal (person) explanations. They said the person was skillful or wrongheaded rather than, say, lucky or coerced. The first two adjectives are person attributions, while the latter two are situational. Miller's Hindu subjects were less likely to use person explanations and more likely to resort to situational reasons to explain behavior. They preferred situational explanations over personal ones in a ratio of about 9 to 1.

It may be that situational factors do play a more important role in Eastern cultures than they do in the West (Ross & Nisbett, 1991). That is, more behavior may be situationally determined in the collectivist societies of the East than in the individualistic societies of the West (Triandis, 1989). This orientation or world view would lead people in Eastern cultures to interpret the world somewhat differently than Westerners. The burden of causal analysis would fall more on external factors and less on internal ones.

In another study, Stipek, Weiner, and Kexing (1989) investigated the causal attribution process among people in the People's Republic of China. They expected to find differences between American and Chinese attributions because the Chinese have historically believed that achievement is due more to hard work than to ability. Chinese society deemphasizes the individual and glorifies the group. Therefore, one would not expect the kind of attributions to individual causes that are typical in Western cultures.

Accordingly, Stipek and his colleagues expected that Chinese students would not make internal, stable attributions for success or external, unstable explanations for failure as do American students. However, the study revealed that the Chinese students did indeed explain their successes and failures much as their American counterparts did. There was no evidence that the Chinese attributed success to effort (an internal, unstable attribution) over aptitude (an internal, stable attribution). Nor were the Chinese any less concerned with individual achievement than were the American students. These findings support the generality of attribution principles across the two cultures. Of course, both groups of subjects were college students; it could be that other subsets of the two populations, such as farmers or mechanics, would not display such congruence.

What about the three informational dimensions of covariation theory? Do they hold up across cultures? Do all people search for consensus, distinctiveness, and consistency information? Although research is limited, a study of Korean subjects suggests that the three dimensions are used the same way by these individuals as by Americans (Cha & Nam, 1985). There are some differences in emphasis: The Korean subjects were slightly more likely to make external attributions than were Americans. No other discernible differences were found between the two groups. It seems, then, that the attribution theories developed in the West apply generally to all human beings, regardless of cultural differences.

Why do you think there is some relative similarity in the kinds of attributions people make across cultures? Do you think people in various cultures define some important attributional concepts—effort, motivation—in the same way? Do you think we would find that people in different historical epochs would make attributions that are similar to our own?

Abnormal Conditions Theory

One aspect of causal analysis common to both correspondent inference and covariation theory is that unusual behaviors are likely to lead to causal attributions. People need to explain unusual or abnormal conditions more than any other types of situations. We do not, for example, say someone died because she stopped breathing (Jones, 1990). Rather, we say that the person died of cancer. Of course, the person did stop breathing, but everyone stops breathing at some point. Not everyone dies of cancer—that is the unusual or abnormal condition.

The **abnormal conditions theory** offers a description of the attribution process that is less formal than either correspondent inference or covariation theory (Hilton & Slugoski, 1986). It emphasizes the fact that people search for causal explanations when there are big gaps between what they expected and what actually occurred. This fits with the notion of the cognitive miser who questions her social constructions only when her expectations are clearly violated. Abnormal conditions theory also suggests that we are drawn to anything abnormal in the situation as an explanation.

The abnormal conditions model assumes that our attributions are influenced by our cultural knowledge—our conceptions of what kinds of behavior are expected in certain situations (Hilton, 1990). The movie *Stand and Deliver* illustrates this point very well. Latino students in Los Angeles high schools were not expected to score higher than almost everybody else in the country on a standardized calculus test. When they did, test officials attributed their success to cheating. Notice that this is an external or situational attribution, focusing on circumstances in the testing situation, rather than a person or internal attribution, which would focus on the students' math skills.

Only when the students did very well on a second calculus examination did the judges reconsider their attributions of the test scores. The calculus teacher, Jaime Escalante (portrayed by Edward James Olmos in the movie), had been able to improve the students' performance through his inspired teaching and the force of his faith in their abilities. The students' consistent success led to a shift in attributions for their success, from situational to personal.

The abnormal conditions theory suggests that we are more likely to want to find out what caused a behavior when there is a difference between what we expect and what actually happens. The idea that we are drawn to factors that are unusual or abnormal as the causes of behavior is very likely accurate, but it is not the only reason that we choose one causal factor over another (Jones, 1990).

The Probabilistic Contrast Model

The question of how we choose one cause over another, especially when we have limited information, is addressed in a theory that attempts to broaden the covariation model. According to the *probabilistic contrast model,* we make causal inferences about an event by identifying a *focal set* of possible

abnormal conditions theory
The theory that suggests people are more likely to want to find out what caused a behavior when there is a difference between what they expected and what happened.

Angel (left, played by Lou Diamond Phillips) struggles with a question asked by teacher Jaime Escalante (Edward James Olmos) in the 1988 movie Stand and Deliver. *Because Latino students were not expected to excel on standardized calculus tests, officials noticed their success and wrongly attributed it to cheating. According to abnormal conditions theory, we have a strong need to explain situations where there is a gap between what we expected and what actually occurs.*

causes and assigning probabilities to each one (Cheng & Novick, 1990, 1991, 1992).

For example, consider the fires that devastated areas of southern California in the fall of 1993. Several conditions are necessary for such a fire to start: some form of ignition (lightning, a careless person, an arsonist), appropriate conditions (dry brush, high winds, low humidity), the presence of oxygen in the atmosphere, and so on. Together, these factors comprise the focal set of potential causes that are likely to determine the outcome (the fire).

As we look at the focal set, we make distinctions among the factors. First, a factor can be a *cause* of the outcome when that outcome occurs regularly in the factor's presence and infrequently in its absence. Lightning is an example of a causal factor in a brush-fire situation. Second, a factor can be an **enabling condition**—any potential cause that allows the event to occur. In the California fires, for example, dry conditions, the presence of the Santa Ana winds, and the presence of oxygen are enabling conditions. Alone, these conditions do not cause a fire. However, combined with a cause (such as an arsonist), they increase the probability that a fire will occur. Consider another example: People who make excuses for an alcoholic spouse are called enablers. They are not the cause of the alcoholism, but they permit it to continue by ignoring or accepting it. Enabling conditions increase the probability that a causal factor will result in the outcome. Finally, a factor can be irrelevant to the outcome. For example, the number of squirrels in the forest is not a potential cause of fire.

Once we have distinguished the various kinds of factors in our focal set, according to the probabilistic contrast model, we begin to assign probabilities to each one. We ask what the likelihood is that each factor could have caused the event.

What are plausible rules to use to estimate the probabilities that a factor was the likely cause of an event? First, if a factor is *always* present when an event occurs, it cannot be considered a causal factor. Oxygen is

enabling condition Any potential cause that allows an event to occur.

always present when there is a forest fire, but it is certainly not the cause, just as cessation of breathing is not the "cause" of death. Instead, oxygen is an enabling condition. So there must be some variability with respect to the presence of a factor and an outcome to allow for probabilistic contrast (Cheng & Novick, 1992). Lightning is present much of the time when there is a fire (fires may be caused by factors other than lightning, as Smokey the Bear tells us). Lightning is a potential cause of fire.

The probabilistic contrast model proposes a different inference process than that proposed by earlier theories. It suggests that people search for strong contrasts among the focal set. They may not follow the rules of causal analysis defined by the covariation and correspondent inference models, especially when there is incomplete information (on consensus, distinctiveness, and consistency) or when the information is unclear. Research has borne out this assertion. People tend to assign probabilities to factors that seem likely to have been a cause of the event in question and then contrast those probabilities. Strong contrasts determine the attribution. During a thunderstorm, lightning is given a high probability as a causal factor and a camper dropping a lighted cigarette is assigned a low probability. The contrast tells us to bet on the lightning. Cheng and Novick argue that it is this less formal and simplified reasoning process that people use to assign causes to human behavior.

Two-Step and Three-Step Models

We have emphasized that people are cognitive misers, using the least effortful strategy available. But, as noted earlier, they are not cognitive fools (Fiske, 1992). We know that although impression formation is mainly automatic, sometimes it is not. People tend to make attributions in an automatic way, but there are times when they need to make careful and reasoned attributions.

Yaacov Trope (1986) has proposed a theory of attribution that specifically considers when people make effortful and reasoned analyses of the causes of behavior. Trope assumes, as do other theorists, that the first step in our attributional appraisal is an automatic categorization of the observed behavior followed by more careful and deliberate inferences about the person (Trope, Cohen, & Alfieri, 1991). Once the behavior is categorized ("John Dean broke the law") (step 1), inferences are made about Dean's personality ("John Dean is a devious person") (step 2). Note here that our very act of identifying the individual's behavior as negative governs the inferences made about him: He broke the law (categorization); therefore, he is a devious person (inference).

The first step, in which the behavior is identified, often happens quickly, automatically, and with little thought. The attribution made at this first step, however, may be adjusted in the second step. During this second step you may check the situation to see if John Dean's behavior was induced or controlled by something external to him. If you concluded that he was just a young aide to the president and had to obey the president's orders, then you might hold him less (internally) responsible for the Watergate cover-up. In such instances, an *inferential adjustment* is made (Trope et al., 1991).

What information does the perceiver use to make these attributions? Trope plausibly argues that perceivers look at the behavior, the situation in

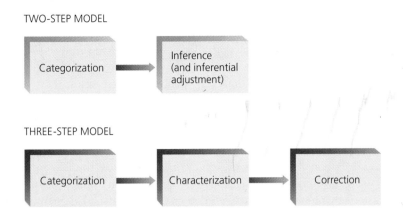

TWO-STEP MODEL

Categorization → Inference (and inferential adjustment)

THREE-STEP MODEL

Categorization → Characterization → Correction

FIGURE 4-5 *Trope's two-step model and Gilbert's three-step model. In both models, the first step is automatic characterization of a behavior. The second step in Trope's model is inference, that is, attribution, usually to the person. If the situation seems to be an important determinant of the behavior, an inferential adjustment may be made during this step. The second step in Gilbert's model is characterization, again, an internal attribution. The third step is correction, or adjustment to account for situational influences. Correction is the same as inferential adjustment.*

which the behavior occurs, and prior information about the actor. Our knowledge about situations helps us understand behavior even when we know nothing about the person. When someone cries at a wedding, we make a different inference about the cause of that behavior than we would if the person cried at a wake. Our prior knowledge about the person may lead us to adjust our initial impression of the person's behavior. If, for example, we knew that John Dean was a very open person (prior information), we would be more likely to attribute his deceptions to factors external to him, such as pressure from the president's senior aides.

A slightly different model has been developed by Daniel Gilbert and his colleagues (1989, 1991). Influenced by Trope's two-step model, they propose a model with three distinct stages. The first stage is the familiar automatic categorization of the behavior; the second, characterization, involves making an internal attribution; and the third, correction, consists of adjusting that attribution based on situational factors. Gilbert essentially divides Trope's first step, the identification process, into two parts, categorization and characterization. The third step is the same as Trope's inferential-adjustment second step.

For example, if you say "good to see you" to your boss, the statement may be categorized as friendly, the speaker may be characterized as someone who likes the other person, and, finally, this last inference may be corrected because the statement is directed at someone with power over the speaker (Gilbert, McNulty, Guiliano, & Benson, 1992). The correction is based on the inference that you had better be friendly to your boss. Gilbert suggests that categorization and internal characterization are relatively effortless, automatic processes, requiring little attention, whereas the correction, based on situational factors, is deliberate, conscious, controlled, and effortful (Gilbert & Krull, 1988).

Figure 4-5 portrays Trope's two-step model and Gilbert's three-step model. As you can see, the primary difference between the two is that Gilbert's model suggests that there is a separate (and perhaps more deliberate) second stage during which the perceiver decides if the initial categorization is correct. If it's not, a correction is made in the third step. Trope's two-step model combines inference about the initial characterization and the correction (inference adjustment) if necessary.

We move into the correction stage when there is an obvious conflict between our initial impression and new, incoming information. This conflict interrupts the automatic categorization. Gilbert and his co-workers have found that anything that disrupts automatic processing lessens the likelihood of making biased person attributions. For example, in one study, they gave subjects the task of making judgments about people. While making these evaluations, some subjects had to do other tasks, like counting the number of roman numerals flashing on different parts of a screen. These additional tasks seem to disrupt the automatic processes: These subjects do not show the person bias in attributions (Gilbert et al., 1992). In other words, the bias we have toward making attributions to the person is automatic and only a disruption of that automatic process leads to a correction, or inferential adjustment.

Attribution Theories: A Summary

At this point we have examined five influential theories about the attribution process. All of them owe much to the original insights of Fritz Heider (1958), and all have many ideas in common, particularly the notion that perceivers are cognitive misers.

Correspondent inference and covariation theories are the most general attempts to describe the attribution process. Research has generally shown that people do make correspondent inferences as suggested by this theory. A correspondent inference occurs when we conclude that a person's overt behavior matches his or her internal characteristics or beliefs. Covariation theory suggests that people attribute the cause of behavior to the factor that covaries (occurs most often) with the behavior. To make causal analyses, perceivers rely on information about the actor, the situation, and the stability of the behavior.

The abnormal conditions theory focuses on one aspect of the first two theories, that people need to explain unusual or abnormal conditions more than any other type of situation. This theory says that people are less formal in their causal analyses than the earlier theories suggested. The probabilistic contrast model, an attempt to update covariation theory, argues that people make intuitive, commonsense distinctions between causes and conditions. Rather than using complicated logic, people simply compare the probabilities that an event occurred because of one of several possible causes. The two-step model recognizes that the initial step in assigning causality is an automatic categorization of behavior; a second step may lead to a readjustment of that initial categorization, especially when the behavior or the situation is ambiguous. The three-step model considers further how and when people readjust their initial inferences.

EMOTIONAL AND BEHAVIORAL CONSEQUENCES OF MAKING ATTRIBUTIONS

The attributions we make about behavior (our own and that of others) are not just thoughts, existing solely in our mind. They also influence our emotional and behavioral responses. If, for example, you infer hostile intent be-

Our explanations for things that happen to us—whether based in fact or fantasy—have a profound effect on how we react. © 1994, The Washington Post Writers Group. Reprinted with permission.

hind a statement someone makes toward you, you are likely to feel dislike for that person and perhaps behave aggressively in return. If, on the other hand, you did not read hostile intent into what was said, your emotional and behavioral responses may be quite different.

Our evaluation of another person's behavior depends, of course, on how it affects us. For example, let's say your grade on an exam depends on a group project in which each member is responsible for researching certain information. One person fails to do her part, so you don't have all the information you need for the exam. Your first response might be anger: How could she be so irresponsible? What was she doing that was so important? Was she at the beach while you were slaving away in the library? Obviously, she's a jerk!

If you learn, however, that a family emergency prevented her from doing her part, you moderate your judgments, your attributions, and your emotional responses. You will also be less angry, and will make less angry attributions, if you can easily make up for the part she failed to do or if the information she was responsible for was not on the test. Our appraisal of a situation and how it affects us determines our emotional reaction to it and affects the attributions we make about it (Smith, Haynes, Lazarus, & Pope, 1993).

Consider the case of fallen TV evangelists. When their indiscretions or even criminal acts are exposed, one might expect their followers to be disillusioned and to take their loyalties elsewhere. According to one observer, this is not necessarily the case (Morgan, quoted in Lemann, 1994, p. 13):

> To those outside the fold, the adultery of Jim Bakker, the peccadilloes of [Jimmy] Swaggart, the financial difficulties of [Oral] Roberts, and [Pat] Robertson's political self-destruction seemed bizarre and outlandish. But for those within the fold, it was part of a natural cycle in which God cut down to size those who had lost track of their place and their mission. Periodic public displays of the Devil knocking the powerful off their high horses were a kind of rite, an essential sacrament reminding all, once again, that Satan was Lord of the world—an enemy who could raise his flag in the very center of the earthly kingdom. Witnessing the fall of Swaggart was like having the Lord at one's elbow saying quietly, "You see, you see."

When traumatic events happen to us, such as a robbery or a sexual assault, we inevitably look for explanations. Why did the event occur? Could something have been done so that it wouldn't have happened? Will it happen again? The broader issues underlying these questions are the assignment of causality by trauma victims and the emotional and behavioral consequences of those attributions.

Early research on this issue suggested that adjustment to trauma was enhanced if the victim of the trauma accepted some of the blame for the event (Bulman & Wortman, 1977). For example, paralyzed victims of "freak accidents" were found to cope better if they engaged in a degree of self-blame. Social psychologist Ronnie Janoff-Bulman (1979) has suggested that self-blame—that is, making an internal attribution for the traumatic event—may be therapeutic because it gives the victim the idea that she can control her fate.

The issue of self-blame is not necessarily simple, however.

Janoff-Bulman distinguishes two types of self-blame, differing in focus. *Characterological self-blame* is blame that is attached to one's relatively enduring personality and behavioral characteristics. So, for example, if a rape victim concludes that she was too trusting and stupid to have avoided the rape, she is engaging in characterological self-blame. The other type of self-blame is *behavioral self-blame,* which involves focusing self-blame on a set of behaviors relevant to the event. A rape victim may blame herself for failing to lock her car doors at the shopping mall or not being cautious enough. Theoretically, behavioral self-blame can help a rape victim think of ways to avoid *future* attacks, something that might contribute to positive adjustment.

The distinction between these two forms of self-blame is important because different outcomes

result from them. Characterological self-blame may hinder short-term or long-term adjustment because the attribution is being made to an internal, stable, uncontrollable factor: one's basic personality makeup. Behavioral self-blame, on the other hand, may contribute to positive adjustment because the attribution is to an internal, unstable, controllable factor: amount of effort expended to avoid the negative event.

Do victims of trauma engage in self-blame? The answer is a definite yes, at least among rape victims. Janoff-Bulman sent questionnaires to rape counselors at 48 rape crisis centers asking about the amount of self-blame among rape victims. The response indicated that self-blame was quite common. Overall, 74% of the rape victims blamed themselves, at least in part, for the rape. Sixty-nine percent of the victims reported behavioral self-blame, whereas 19% reported characterological self-blame. The relatively high incidence of self-blame among rape victims has been confirmed in other research (Myer &

When such incidents are interpreted as cosmic examples rather than personal betrayals, people are more likely to respond with tolerance than with indignation.

One area in which attribution patterns have a particularly powerful effect on emotions and behavior is rape. Not only do outsiders tend to assign some responsibility to survivors of rape (and of other traumas, for that matter), but the survivors tend to blame themselves. For a closer look at this disturbing pattern, see the featured discussions "Attribution Patterns and Recovery from Trauma" and "Attributions About Rape: Blaming the Victim."

In this section we explore the implications of some of the attributions we make about others and ourselves. First we consider how attributions

Taylor, 1986). However, there is also evidence that even among victims who assign some self-blame, victims are more likely to blame the rapist (Frazier, 1990).

What is the relationship between self-blame and adjustment? As mentioned, Janoff-Bulman suggested that behavioral self-blame may contribute to a positive adjustment after a rape. In fact, she provided some evidence for this in a simulation experiment in which subjects read and reacted to an account of a rape (Janoff-Bulman, 1982). However, research studying *actual* rape victims does not support Janoff-Bulman's results.

Generally, rape victims who engage in self-blame are more prone to postrape depression (Frazier, 1991). What about the differential effects of characterological self-blame versus behavioral self-blame? In their research, Julie Hill and Alex Zautra (1989) found the strongest relationship between postrape demoralization and characterological self-blame, a finding that supports Janoff-Bulman's hypothesis. However,

Janoff-Bulman's beliefs about perceived control were not borne out. Hill and Zautra found that a victim's ability to change something about the causes of rape (whether characterological or behavioral) did not relate to the amount of demoralization she felt.

In another study, Patricia Frazier (1990) administered a wide range of tests to rape victims. Frazier found, like Janoff-Bulman, that rape victims do engage in self-blame. However, both behavioral and characterological self-blame were associated with depression after the rape. This finding was supported in another questionnaire study of rape victims (Myer & Taylor, 1986) (although it may be due more to the victims' not making a clear distinction between the two kinds of self-blame). Frazier also reports that behavioral self-blame was associated only with thoughts of how the past event could have been avoided, but not with how future events could be avoided.

*S*elf-blame involves attribution to internal factors, such as one's carelessness or naiveté. What do you think the effect would be—in terms of both emotional reaction and behavioral adaptation—if attribution were made wholly to external factors, such as the deranged mind of the assailant, the social conditions that cause people to rob, or just plain bad luck? Considering that people in general have a tendency to attribute bad things that happen to them to external factors (the self-serving bias), who do you think rape victim stend to blame themselves? If you worked as a therapist, what kind of attributions would you try to counsel a rape victim to make?

about our own successes and failures influence our behavior. Then we examine the emotional and behavioral effects of attributions made in close relationships.

Attributions About Ourselves: Success and Failure

We know that we make attributions not only about others but also about our own behavior. We often find ourselves in the position of deciding how to account for our own successes and failures in achievement contexts. The attributions we make in these situations have important implications for our emotional well-being and future behavior. Social psychologist Bernard Weiner (1986) has devised a very influential theory of attribution that

Clifford Babcock and Claudia Cooper Van Luvender met in a bar on June 3, 1976, and left the bar together. Later that night, Babcock raped Van Luvender. After his arrest, Babcock took and failed a polygraph test. Later he admitted that he had raped the woman and pled guilty to rape.

In January of the following year, Babcock stood before Judge Charles M. Egan awaiting the judge's sentencing decision. To the shock and dismay of the rape victim and spectators, Judge Egan handed down a suspended sentence and put Babcock on probation. The judge remarked that the presentencing investigation led him to believe that the victim may have "contributed to the climate" that led to the rape (*New York Times,* January 22, 1977).

In this case, and in several others, an officer of the court stated that the behavior of the victim of a rape can contribute to the commission of the crime. In essence, the judge suggested that a victim's behavior can be an en-

abling event for a rape. The implication is that the victim bears some responsibility for the crime. Please understand that victims in criminal law do not bear responsibility for a crime. That is the law. So, is this an isolated decision of a particular judge? Or is there a more widespread trend toward attributing responsibility (at least in part) to victims of rape? Recall that a prime concern of attribution is to assign responsibility. Is there a conflict between people's attributional psychology and the law?

In fact, there is evidence to suggest that observers (a juror or a judge) may attribute at least partial responsibility to a rape victim (Bridges & McGrail, 1989; Brownmiller, 1975; Jones & Aronson, 1973). Studies show more responsibility is attributed to the

rape victim when she is somewhat acquainted with the rapist (e.g., they work in the same building) before the rape (Bolt & Caswell, 1981; Smith, Keating, Hester, & Mitchell, 1976). But if the victim and the rapist know each other more closely before the rape, or are dating, greater responsibility is attributed to the victim (Kanekar, Shaherwalla, Franco, Kunju, & Pinto, 1991; Bridges & McGrail, 1989).

A second factor is the victim's behavior before the rape. In one infamous case, Judge Archie Simonson (who was later removed from the bench for this decision) justified his lenient sentence for a youthful rape defendant by pointing to the supposedly provocative nature of female clothing in our society (among other societal ills). According to Simonson's logic, society as a whole is permissive and a 15-year-old boy should not be punished for reacting "normally" to that permissiveness. In this case, as in the previous case, the judge is

explicitly accounts for the motivational effects of causal analysis. As noted earlier, emotion plays a very important part in the attributional process. Weiner's theory addresses the role of emotion in the attribution process. It shows how attributions made about our performances affect our self-esteem and our future success or failure.

Weiner suggests that people explain their own failures and successes by considering three kinds of information:

- Locus of causation
- Controllability
- Stability

Locus of causation refers to the now familiar internal–external dimension: whether success or failure was due to internal characteristics, such as ability, effort, or something else about the person, or to external factors, such as luck, the time of day, or something else about the situation. In the case of the Hispanic students who did so well on the calculus test, officials clearly

suggesting an external attribution for a rapist's behavior. This time, however, the judge is pointing to the victim's behavior and manner of dress as enabling conditions for the rape. There is ample evidence that Judge Simonson's logic is widespread: More responsibility is assigned to rape victims who act in sexually provocative ways (Kanekar & Maharukh, 1980, 1981) and dress in sexually provocative ways (Edmonds & Cahoon, 1986; Lewis & Johnson, 1989).

Finally, observers also consider the behavior of the victim before the rape. More responsibility is attributed to a rape victim whose behavior is perceived as contributing in some way to the rape. For example, a woman tends to be blamed more if she was walking to her car after having a drink at a bar than if she was walking to her car after work (Krahe, 1988). Further, people believe that a woman who walks alone through a wooded park at 11:30 p.m. is more responsible for

her rape than a woman walking to her car in a parking lot at 5:00 p.m. This is an example of a kind of *defensive attribution*: This wouldn't happen to me because I would protect myself by not walking in such a dangerous place.

There is a gender difference in attribution of responsibility to rape victims. Males tend to attribute more responsibility to rape victims than do females (Bridges & McGrail, 1989; Jenkins & Dambrot, 1987). However, both males and females who subscribe to the "rape myth"—the idea that rape victims enjoy being raped and suffer few ill consequences (Burt, 1980)—are more likely to attribute responsibility to the victim than males and females who subscribe less to it (Jenkins & Dambrot, 1987; Krahe, 1988). Males are also less likely to define a "date rape" or "acquaintance rape" as actual rape and are more likely than females to believe that the victim of date rape wanted to have sex (Jenkins & Dambrot, 1987).

For the victim, the emotional and behavioral consequences of being held even partially responsible for rape are profound. These consequences are complicated by the prevalence of self-blame. There is another consequence as well: Once the victim is blamed, there is a decreased likelihood that the rapist will be convicted of the crime (Kanekar & Maharukh, 1981; Kanekar et al., 1991).

---

*D*o you think Judge Egan was surprised by the reaction to his decision? If not, what attribution bias would account for his surprise? If he wasn't surprised, what attributions do you think he had made about his critics? Both Judge Egan and Judge Simonson rendered their sentences based on some attributions about personal responsibility of rapists and rape victims. How widespread do you think those assumptions are in your generation?

---

attributed their success to external factors. They placed the locus of causation outside the students, in the situation.

Controllability refers to the degree to which the individual can control outcomes. The amount of effort you put into studying for an exam is controllable—you can choose to put in very little or a great deal of time. Luck, or chance, on the other hand, is uncontrollable. *Stability* refers to consistency. Stable characteristics (such as a belief that you are intelligent) endure over time and across situations, whereas unstable ones fluctuate.

Implications of Attributions for Future Behavior Attributions have consequences for how people act in the future. Let's say, for example, that you fail an exam. You need to explain the cause of that behavior to yourself. If you attribute your failure to a lack of motivation, then you can resolve to work harder in the future in order to do better. But if you attribute your failure to lack of aptitude, you probably will feel there isn't anything you can do to raise your grade.

These attributions are both internal, but one is unstable and the other is stable. You can always increase or decrease your effort, but you probably can't improve your innate aptitude. An attribution to an internal/unstable cause may lead you to work harder. An attribution to an internal/stable cause may lead you to give up.

External attributions have implications for motivation as well. You may attribute failure to the fact that the exam was too hard (an external but unstable cause); in this case, you might tell yourself that the next test could be easier. Or you may attribute failure to something about the teacher, an external and stable cause. The teacher won't change, but you still might do better in other courses or in this course with another teacher. In either case, your failure is not likely to lead you to give up all hope of ever passing another exam.

Of course, there are events over which you have no control. For example, the quality of the test—that is, whether it's a hard or easy test—is an uncontrollable event (at least by you). You might not study, walk in and take an easy test, and get a passing grade. You then might decide that you are just a lucky person, but no doubt one of these days fate would not be so kind and a test would be very hard—and then you could conclude that your luck had run out.

Clearly, then, the attributions we make about our own successes and failures evoke strong emotional responses and have an impact on our future performance. Table 4-2 shows how the three dimensions interact when we make causal attributions for our own success or failure.

Weiner's attribution theory predicts that our attribution patterns influence our expectations about future performance. Consider a student who is not doing well in a course. If the student perceives that the factors responsible for failure are internal (lack of ability), stable (consistent over time), and uncontrollable (nothing I do helps), the student will have an expectation of future failure and will not make any effort to change.

Another student, however, may attribute failure to bad luck or lack of effort, both unstable causes. Luck is external and unstable; it could change. Of course, people who believe luck controls their fate are not likely to study harder. Lack of effort is internal and unstable. Next time I'll work harder. In this instance, expectations for future performance are not affected that much. Attributions to unstable causes have less impact on our expectations than attributions to stable causes (Weiner, 1986).

Excuses for Failure   Weiner observes that people often deal with failure by making excuses for their performance. In one study, excuses for failure were found to serve three general purposes (Weiner, Figueroa-Munoz, & Kakihara, 1991):

- Preserving self-esteem
- Changing the expectancies of other people about the test-takers' future performance
- Lessening anger

TABLE 4-2

ATTRIBUTION IN AN ACHIEVEMENT CONTEXT

	Internal	
	Stable	*Unstable*
Controllable	Typical effort (I always/never study hard.)	Situational effort (I did/did not study for this test.)
Uncontrollable	Aptitude (I'm smart/I'm not smart.)	Mood (I was anxious/excited.)

	External	
	Stable	*Unstable*
Controllable	Teacher (The teacher liked me—I participated in class discussions./The teacher didn't like me—I cut class.)	Help from others (I should have joined the study group./I'm glad I joined the study group.)
Uncontrollable	Quality of test (The test was hard/easy.)	Luck (The test was on the one thing I didn't study./The test was on the one thing I studied.)

Adapted from Trenholm, 1989.

In this study, most excuses were external, uncontrollable, and unstable attributions. People said they failed because they had "other work to do and could not study," or they "felt sick," or they "did not wake up on time." These excuses are ways of presenting oneself so as to maintain self-esteem. Making excuses is not quite the same as self-handicapping, which involves putting an excuse in place before the fact. But the effect of the two may be the same, and both have similar advantages and disadvantages. If you don't do well on the exam because you slept late or didn't study, you might not be called dumb but you might be thought irresponsible.

Although externalizing failures may produce increases in self-esteem in the short run, they may also begin a cycle of failure. If the individual does not recognize that there are also internal causes for failure, he or she will not take steps to correct the true causes for failure. If this pattern of externalizing failure is changed and people begin to attribute failure to internal, *controllable,* and *stable* characteristics, their performance improves. In one study, college students who were not doing well in introductory psychology saw one of two interviews with another "student" who had also been failing (Noel, Forsyth, & Kelley, 1987). One group of subjects (the attribution group) saw a videotape in which the student indicated that he used to blame just about anything but himself for failure, but then realized

TABLE 4-3

GRADES OF STUDENTS WHO SAW ATTRIBUTION FILM COMPARED WITH GRADES OF THOSE WHO DIDN'T

Measure	Attribution Group	Control Group
Exam 3	76	64
Exam 4	65	57
Final exam	83	64
Final grade	75	62

From Noel, Forsyth, and Kelley, 1987.

that it was his lack of effort and hard work that had caused the failure. Another group of subjects (the control group) saw essentially the same tape, but no mention was made of a shift in attributional style. The subsequent grades of the students in the two groups were then compared. Those in the attribution group got higher marks on exams and had higher final grades in the course than those in the control group (Table 4-3).

The Effects of Attributions in Close Relationships

The attributions we make about our successes and failures are important to our future motivation and performance, and the attributions we make about friends' and strangers' behavior in everyday life are important to our accurate understanding of our social world. Similarly, the attributions we make about our partners in close interpersonal relationships are crucial to the future success of those relationships. We are constantly assigning causes to our partner's comments and actions, deciding why he or she didn't take out the garbage, clean up the bathroom, or remember our anniversary. What kinds of attribution patterns are seen in unhappy versus happy relationships?

Research indicates that unhappy couples spend a great deal of time thinking about negative events. That is, the greatest amount of attributional activity concerns bad things in the relationship. Unhappy couples spend little time explaining the causes of positive events to themselves (Holtzworth-Monroe & Jacobson, 1985). This is not surprising: Unhappy relationships probably have more bad events than good ones to explain. That's why they are distressed.

As with personal success and failure, partners may make attributions that are internal or external, controllable or uncontrollable, stable or unstable. A slightly different dimension is whether the attribution implies that the behavior is something the person "always" does—a global attribution—or something the person has done in this specific situation.

Let's consider one situation as an example: a wife working late and her husband waiting at home, wondering what's going on (Bradbury & Fincham, 1990). Several different attributions are possible. For one, he may think, "She's having a really busy day and needs to stay late to catch up." When she calls to explain why she is late, he offers the attribution, "Another hard day."

The attributions that partners make about each other's behavior have powerful implications for their relationship. This couple will be in the most trouble if their attributions are internal, stable, and global—in other words, if each believes the other's negative acts flow from stable, permanent personality traits: "You're a selfish, inconsiderate person and you never think of me!"

She replies, "Yes, sorry I didn't call sooner." This probably ends the exchange.

Note that the mate makes an external and unstable attribution, although the phrase "another hard day" suggests that this may have happened a few times before. The general sense of the attribution, however, is positive: "Okay, my wife has to work late (a negative event), but it is because of the press of circumstances (an external cause), it doesn't happen too often (an unstable cause), and it's limited to a specific situation.

Alternatively, the wife may call to say she'll be late, but before she can get a word out, the husband says, "You're late and you didn't call. Where have you been?" She replies, "I was stuck in a traffic jam in downtown Toledo." He challenges this: "You're lying! There is no traffic in downtown Toledo. You were just messing around with your new computer!" These attributions are internal (she chose to stay and play with the computer), unstable (this doesn't happen every day, just when she has a new electronic toy), and specific to this situation (she got a new computer).

In a third scenario, *he* calls her: "Late again! Don't you ever worry about anyone but yourself?" "Look," she says, "I had to finish some work." "Sure," he replies in an accusing tone, "you *always* have to finish work! And you're always attacking me because I wonder where you *really* are!" Here the attributions are internal (she's an inconsiderate person), stable (she's always been an inconsiderate person), and global (this behavior shows up in many situations).

This last scenario represents the most damaging attributions a partner can make—internal, stable, and global. The spouse does those nasty things because it's in her nature to do them, it always has been, and it always will be. The behavior is also seen as controllable—she could have come home on time, but she stayed late even though she knew her spouse would be upset and worried. She is perceived as intentionally behaving in a negative way.

Compared to happy couples, unhappy couples engage in causal reasoning that exaggerates the weight of negative events and diminishes the effect of positive events (Baucom, Sayers, & Duhe, 1989). That is, unhappy couples appear to spend a great deal of time blaming each other (Fincham &

Bradbury, 1988). The opposite dynamic plays out in abusive relationships. Women who stay in unhealthy marriages concentrate on the few positive aspects, a focus that helps keep them chained to the relationship (Herbert, Silver, & Ellard, 1991).

When couples obtain psychological counseling for marital difficulties—the most common reason people seek counseling (Bradbury & Fincham, 1990)—their attribution patterns often emerge as a source of significant discord. Couples in counseling can learn to focus more on the positive events in their marriage and to change the habitual ways they interpret their partner's motives and behavior. (Although much of the research on attribution in relationships has involved married couples, the findings are probably applicable to all close, committed relationships.)

ATTRIBUTION BIASES

We saw in Chapter 3 that individuals are not always accurate in determining what other people are really like. People make inaccurate attributions as well. They deviate from the rules that a "pure scientist" would apply as outlined in the correspondent inference and especially the covariation models. These deviations are *attribution biases*. Note, however, that some theories, particularly the probabilistic contrast model, argue that these biases are a consequence of the fact that people use a somewhat different attribution model than earlier theorists had assumed. In other words, according to the probabilistic contrast model, there are no "biases" in the sense that people do something wrong in the way they make attributions. People just don't use the models the way the earlier theorists thought they did.

Whether they are biases or not, there is a tendency for people to make attributions that do deviate from the classic attribution theories. A classic example of how our attributions may be misdirected is described in the featured discussion "A Case of Misattribution: The Schachter Experiments."

One bias found in all the attributional theories is the correspondence bias, the tendency to attribute causes to people more readily than to situations. This bias is so common it is generally referred to as the **fundamental attribution error.** Other typical attribution errors are the confirmation bias, the actor–observer bias, the false consensus bias, and the self-serving bias. Let's take a look at each of these in turn.

The Correspondence Bias, or the Fundamental Attribution Error

fundamental attribution error The tendency to attribute causes to people more readily than to situations. (The common name for the correspondence bias.)

As mentioned, the correspondence bias is the tendency to underestimate situational factors and to attribute the causes of behavior to the character or personality of the individual (Figure 4-6). This bias was demonstrated in a classic experiment in which subjects read essays that were either in favor of Fidel Castro, the Cuban leader, or opposed to him (Jones & Harris, 1967). The subjects knew that the essays they read had been part of an examination and that the writer either had a choice or had no choice about whether

In a classic experiment, Stanley Schachter and Jerome E. Singer (1962) demonstrated that two conditions are required for the production of an emotional response: physiological arousal and cognitions that label the arousal and therefore identify the emotion for the person experiencing it. Schachter and Singer injected subjects with epinephrine, a hormone that produces all the symptoms of physiological arousal: rapid breathing, increased heart rate, palpitations, and so on. Half of these subjects were informed that the injection would create a state of arousal. The other half were misinformed about the injection. A control group of subjects were not given any drug.

Subjects were then placed in a room to await another part of the experiment. Some subjects were in a room with a confederate of the experimenters who acted in a happy, excited, even euphoric manner, laughing, rolling up paper into balls, and shooting the balls into the wastebasket. Others encountered a confederate who was angry and threw things around the room. All subjects thought that the confederate was just another subject.

Schachter and Singer argued that the physiological arousal caused by the injection was open to different interpretations. The subjects who had been misinformed about the true effects of the injection had no reasonable explanation for their increase in arousal. The most obvious stimulus was the behavior of the confederate. Results showed that aroused subjects who were in a room with an angry person behaved in an angry way; those who were in a room with a happy confederate behaved in a euphoric way.

What about the subjects in the group who got the injection and were told what it was? These informed subjects had a full explanation for their arousal, so they simply thought that the confederate was strange and waited quietly.

The research shows how easily our emotional state can be manipulated. When we do not have readily available explanations for a state of arousal, we will search the environment to find a probable cause. If the cues we find point us toward anger or aggression, that is how we will behave. If the cues suggest joy or happiness, then our behavior will conform to those signals. It is true, of course, that this experiment involved a temporary and not very involving situation for the subjects. It is probable that people are less likely to make misattributions about their emotions when they are more motivated to understand the causes of their feelings and when they have a more familiar context for them.

How might misattribution of arousal work in everyday life? Do you think it occurs relatively often? Under what circumstances might misattribution lead to anger or violence? Does misattribution of arousal ever lead to positive social behaviors?

---

to write a pro- or anti-Castro essay. Subjects had to make an attribution about the *true* attitude of the writer.

When subjects knew that the writer had a choice in deciding which side to take, they assumed that the essay reflected how the writer really felt. Writers who had a choice and wrote pro-Castro essays were assigned a pro-Castro attitude, and those who freely chose to write an anti-Castro essay were quite plausibly thought to be anti-Castro. This is in line with correspondent inference theory. However, even when subjects knew that the essayist did *not* freely choose the topic, they *still* made an internal attribution. That is, they assigned pro-Castro attitudes to the authors of the pro-Castro essays and anti-Castro attitudes to the authors of the anti-Castro essays, no matter how much choice the essayist had.

Now why would subjects fail to consider the obvious fact that some essayists wrote answers that probably did not reflect their real opinions?

FIGURE 4-6 *When an acquaintance fails to say hello, our first impulse is to assume we're being snubbed rather than to look for something in the situation that diverted the person's attention from us. This tendency to locate the causes of behavior in people rather than in situations—the fundamental attribution error—distorts our view of social reality.*

Why did they make a correspondent inference? Similarly, why would some observers blame the captured American pilots for reading a statement their captors forced on them?

We have seen that people often use heuristics—shortcuts—when a situation gets too complicated. We also know that people are cognitive misers. In this study, the subjects were not sure about the writers' true beliefs. The least effortful strategy is to assume the writer really believed what she wrote. Using the terminology of the probabilistic contrast model, we could say that the subjects examined the focal set and assigned the highest probability to believing that the essayist meant what she wrote. The subjects might have thought, yes, we know the writer had to take a position, but how do we know he or she doesn't really believe this position? People usually say what they mean. It may be that this person did not, but my best bet is that she did mean it.

The fact that people make correspondent inferences when they shouldn't does not mean that correspondent inference theory is incorrect. It means that the theory represents the rules that perceivers would follow if they had full information and time to consider all of it. It is also possible that people calculate causes a bit differently than the formal rules of attribution dictate, as the probabilistic contrast model suggests.

As mentioned earlier, the correspondence bias, the tendency to underestimate the role of situational factors in explaining the behavior of others, is more commonly known as the *fundamental attribution error* (Ross et al., 1977). When we automatically attribute the causes for another person's behavior to internal forces and discount situational forces, we are committing this error. For a look at the fundamental attribution error in action, see the featured discussion "The Quiz Show Phenomenon."

If you have ever watched the television game show *Jeopardy*, you probably have seen the following scenario played out in various guises: A nervous contestant selects "Russian History" for $500. The answer is: "He was known as the 'Mad Monk.' " The contestant rings in and says, "Who was Molotov?" Alex Trebek, the host, replies, "Ah, noooo, the correct question is 'Who was Rasputin?' " As the show continues, certain things become evident. The contestants, despite knowing a lot of trivial and not so trivial information, do not appear to be as smart as Alex Trebek. Trebek appears to be very intelligent and very well informed.

Sometimes we make attributions about people without paying enough attention to the roles they are playing. Of course Alex Trebek looks smart (he may be smart); he has all the answers in front of him. Unfortunately, this last fact is sometimes lost on us. This so-called quiz show phenomenon was vividly shown in an experiment in which researchers simulated a TV game show for college students (Ross, Amabile, & Steinmetz, 1977). A few subjects were picked to be the questioners, not because they had any special skill or information but by pure chance. They had to devise a few fairly difficult but common-knowledge questions. A control group of questioners asked questions formulated by others. Members of both groups played out a simulation quiz game. After the quiz session, all subjects rated their own knowledge levels as well as the knowledge levels of their partners.

Now, all of us can think of some questions that might be hard for others to answer. Who was the Dodgers' third baseman in the 1947 World Series? Where is Boca Grande? When did Emma Bovary live? Clearly, the questioners had a distinct advantage. They could rummage around in their storehouse of knowledge, trivial and profound, and find some nuggets that others would not know.

When asked to rate the knowledge levels of the questioners as opposed to the contestants, *both* the questioners and the contestants rated the questioners as more knowledgeable, especially in the experimental group, where the questioners devised their own questions. Only a single contestant rated herself superior in knowledge to the questioner.

The fundamental attribution error can clearly be seen in this experiment: People attribute behavior to internal factors even when they have information indicating situational factors are at work. Because the questioners appeared to know more than the contestants, subjects thought the questioners were smarter. Everyone failed to account for the situation.

The quiz show phenomenon occurs in many social situations.

The relationship between doctor and patient and between teacher and student can be understood via this effect. When we deal with people in positions of high status or authority, who appear to have all the answers (such as doctors and teachers), we attribute their behavior to positive internal characteristics such as knowledge and intelligence. Such an attribution enhances their power over us. To dispel this myth, try asking one of your teachers or your doctor a question outside his or her narrow domain of knowledge. You may be surprised!

While much of the focus of the quiz show phenomenon is on how the audience reacts to the Alex Trebeks of the world, perhaps more interesting is how it affects the "quiz show hosts." Self-esteem across cultures is invariably tied to the prestige of your job, and the more prestige the job has the more likely you have the resources to get "all the answers" (Smith & Bond, 1994). How do you think being a "quiz show host" in real life (that is, a medical doctor, a judge, a professor, a teacher, a corporate executive) affects the individual in the nonprofessional parts of life? Does the quiz show phenomenon tell us something about why actors or billionaires try to enter politics? What about radio talk show hosts? Do they really believe after a while that they have all the answers?

Predicting the Future: How Good Are We? We have seen that perceivers underuse situational information in many circumstances. People tend to take behavior at face value and not consider situational factors, such as the role the person occupies.

Let's look at this issue in a slightly different way. What if I asked you to predict how your best friends would act in various situations in the future? Now, you might think that people would be good predictors about the behavior of their closest friends. After all, they have so much information about them. It turns out, however, that we make the fundamental attribution error when making predictions about the future behavior of both our best friends and ourselves. That is, we tend not to consider the role of the situation.

In one study, first-year undergraduates were asked to make predictions about their own future behavior in the coming year and about the future behavior of their roommates (Vallone, Griffin, Lin, & Ross, 1991). They had to answer questions about whether the subject would drop any courses, attend the "big game," break up with his or her girl- or boyfriend, become close friends with his or her roommate, pledge a sorority or fraternity, and so on. Subjects also had to indicate how confident they were about these predictions.

The overall accuracy of the predictions, along with the confidence expressed in the predictions, is shown in Figure 4-7. We can see that people were consistently overconfident in their predictions about others as well as about themselves.

Why the big gap? If we know so much about ourselves, why can't we be better at predicting what we will do in the future? The answer, of course, is that we cannot anticipate the influence of the situation, the effect of other people, the demands and opportunities of new situations, and the effects of chance on our future. The predictors simply do not allow for that uncertainty. As emphasized in Chapter 2, we like to believe we have control

FIGURE 4-7 Predicting the future: accuracy and confidence. Subjects were more confident about their predictions for the future than was warranted. People usually fail to take the effect of the situation and other unknowns into account when thinking about the future. From Vallone, Griffin, Lin, and Ross, 1991.

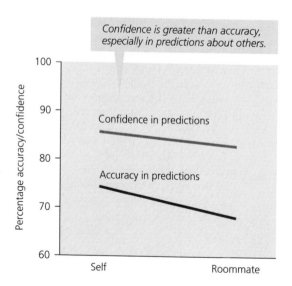

over ourselves, our lives, and our social world. In general, we don't like it when we have to admit, as Humphrey Bogart did in *Casablanca*, that "destiny has taken a hand."

Why We Make the Fundamental Attribution Error   Why do we err in favor of internal attributions? Several explanations have been offered for the fundamental attribution error, but two seem to be most useful: a focus on personal responsibility and the salience of behavior.

Western culture emphasizes the importance of individual personal responsibility. That is, we expect individuals to take responsibility for their behavior. We expect to be in control of our fates, our behavior, and we expect others to have control as well. We tend to look down on those who make excuses for their behavior. It is not surprising, therefore, that we perceive internal rather than external causes as primary to explaining behavior (Forgas, Furnham, & Frey, 1990).

Our expectation that people should be in control of their own fates sometimes leads us to blame individuals for forces over which they have little control. For example, there is a tendency to blame poor people for their own poverty (Forgas et al., 1990). After all, so the reasoning goes, if they wanted to break the cycle of poverty, they could do so by getting jobs, going to school, and bettering their lives. This logic denies the myriad of cultural, social, and economic factors (not under control of the individual) that make such a scenario unlikely. In cultures that place a lesser premium on individuality and personal responsibility, the fundamental attribution error is less common (Miller, 1984).

The second reason for the prevalence of the fundamental attribution error is the salience of

The fundamental attribution error leads us to make internal attributions in situations where it is unwarranted. We often blame homeless people for their own plight, despite our knowledge that homelessness is a complex societal problem and that families like this one may be homeless through no fault of their own. What other psychological functions might be served by blaming the victim?

behavior. In social situations, as in all perception situations, our senses and attention are directed outward. The "actor" becomes the focus of our attention. His or her behavior is more prominent than the less commanding background or environment. The actor becomes the "figure" (object in the foreground) and the situation the "ground" (the total background) in a complex figure–ground relationship. A well-established maxim of perceptual psychology is that the figure stands out against the ground and thus commands our attention.

The salience of an event has causal properties for a perceiver. Anything that has saliency (stands out) will seem to be the causal factor in a situation (Fiske & Taylor, 1991) and will be seen to covary with the behavior. If a person is in an automobile accident and then finds out she has cancer, for example, she will tend to attribute the cancer to the automobile accident.

The perceiver tends to be engulfed by the behavior, not the surrounding circumstances (Heider, 1958). If a person is behaving maliciously, we conclude he is a nasty person. The other factors that might have brought on this nastiness are not easily available or accessible to us. It is easy, even natural, to disregard or slight these external factors. Thus, we readily fall into the fundamental attribution error.

Correcting the Fundamental Attribution Error   So, are human beings helpless to resist this common misattribution of causality? Not at all. As you probably already know from your own experience, the fundamental attribution error does not always occur. There are circumstances that increase or decrease the chances of making this mistake. For example, you are less likely to make the error if you become more aware of (or attend to) information external to another person that is relevant to explaining the causes for his or her behavior. However, even under these circumstances, the error does not disappear; it simply becomes weaker. Thus, although the error is strong and occurs in many situations, it can be lessened when you have full information about a person's reason for doing something and are motivated to make a careful analysis.

Another related condition that influences the strength of the fundamental attribution error is the degree to which we must justify our attributions to others. When people are aware that they must publicly justify their attributions about others, the strength of the error is reduced (Tetlock, 1985). People then tend to be more careful and fashion a more complex appraisal of the actor's behavior. Recall that Trope's two-stage model suggests that while the first step in the attribution process is an automatic categorization, the observer may adjust in the second stage. In fact, the fundamental attribution error may occur when there is insufficient adjustment to the importance of the situation (Quattrone, 1982).

The existence of the first two conditions raises an interesting possibility: You may be less likely to make the fundamental attribution error about individuals whom you know well than about individuals whom you know less well. Generally, we tend to know more about people who are close to us (for example, close friends) than those who are not close to us. We may also have to justify our attributions more often to people who are close to us. Generally, research supports this third condition: We are less likely to make the fundamental attribution error about individuals we know well, compared to individuals whom we do not know as well (Ross & Nisbett, 1991).

Interestingly, the mere passage of time may influence our predisposition to make the fundamental attribution error. We *sometimes* switch from a personal perspective to a situational one as time passes. We make this switch when we have to think about the event—when we have to move from an automatic categorization of the event to a more careful consideration (Burger, 1991; Gilbert, Pelham, & Krull, 1988). When people discuss the end of a romantic relationship, something they have thought about, a shift from a dispositional perspective (it was your fault/my fault) to a situational view (we had too many things working against us) occurs (Koltai & Burger, 1989).

The Confirmation Bias

When we try to determine the cause or causes of an event, we usually have some hypothesis in mind. Say your college football team has not lived up to expectations, or you are asked to explain why American students lag behind others in standardized tests. When faced with these problems, we may begin by putting forth a tentative explanation. We may hypothesize that our football team has done poorly because the coach is incompetent. Or we may hypothesize that the cause of American students' poor performance is that they watch too much TV. How do we go about testing these hypotheses in everyday life?

When we make attributions about the causes of events, we routinely overestimate the strength of our hypothesis (Sanbonmatsu, Akimoto, & Biggs, 1993). We do this by the way we search for information concerning our hypothesis. Typically we tend to engage in a search strategy that confirms our hypothesis rather than disconfirms it. This is known as the **confirmation bias.**

One researcher asked subjects to try to discover the rule used to present a series of three numbers, such as 2, 4, 6. The question was, What rule is the experimenter using? What's your hypothesis? Let's say the hypothesis is consecutive even numbers. Subjects could test their hypothesis about the rule by presenting a set of three numbers to see if it fit the rule. The experimenter would tell them if their set fit the rule, and then they would tell the experimenter what they hypothesized the rule was.

How would you test your hypothesis? Most individuals would present a set such as 8, 10, 12. Notice the set is aimed at confirming the hypothesis, not disconfirming it. The experimenter would say, yes, 8, 10, 12 fits the rule. What is the rule? You say, any three ascending *even* numbers. The experimenter says that is *not* the rule. What happened? You were certain you were right.

The rule could have been any three ascending numbers. If you had tried to disconfirm your hypothesis, you would have gained much more diagnostic information than simply trying to confirm it. If you said 1, 3, 4 and were told it fit the rule, you could throw out your hypothesis about even numbers. We tend to generate narrow hypotheses that do not take into account a variety of alternative explanations.

In everyday life we tend to make attributions to causes that have importance for us. If you hate the football coach, you are much more likely to find evidence for his incompetence rather than note that injuries to various players affected the team's performance. Similarly, we may attribute the cause of American students' poor performance to be their TV watching habits rather than search for evidence that parents do not motivate their children or that academic performance is not valued among the students' peers.

All of us are prone to the confirmation bias. Scientists tend to confirm their pet theories, and teachers are likely to confirm their hypotheses about which students are smart and which are not. Politicians succumb to the

confirmation bias The tendency to seek information that verifies existing explanations for the cause of an event.

same error. George Bush believed that the electorate would keep him in office in 1992, despite indications that they would not. He discounted public dissatisfaction with the state of the economy, thinking people would ultimately come around to his camp. "Until the very last day," wrote one observer, "he could not quite believe that George Herbert Walker Bush, Leader of the Free World, Hero of the Persian Gulf, was going to lose to a slick Arkansas cracker, even one buffed up at Oxford. . . . Bush's blind spot about Clinton's political skill was shared by many Washington pundits who wrote off the Democratic challenger last winter and spring" (McDaniel, 1992, p. 12).

We saw earlier in this chapter that, according to the probabilistic contrast model, people tend to identify a focal set of possible causes for an event (Cheng & Novick, 1992). To avoid the confirmation bias we need to consider more than a narrow focal set. The confirmation bias is lessened when we are encouraged to come up with alternative explanations.

Given the fact that individuals make the fundamental attribution error, it is not surprising that people do not take all possible causal factors into account. The fundamental attribution error may be an example of a wider tendency to overlook alternative explanations in testing hypotheses (Sanbonmatsu et al., 1993).

The Actor–Observer Bias

John Dean believed that he and his co-workers in the White House were not at fault for much of the Watergate scandal. Outside observers thought otherwise. These observers attributed the scandal to a conspiracy hatched among the president's men. The actors, Dean and his colleagues, made external attributions, whereas the observers made internal attributions. This is the **actor–observer bias:** Actors prefer external attributions for their own behavior, especially if the outcomes are bad, whereas observers tend to make internal attributions for the same behavior. The actor–observer bias is especially strong when we are trying to explain negative behaviors (our own or others'). This bias alerts us to the importance of perspective when considering attributional errors. Differing perspectives affect the different constructions of reality that people produce.

A simple experiment you can do yourself will demonstrate the prevalence of the actor–observer bias (Fiske & Taylor, 1984). Using Figure 4-8, rate a friend on the adjectives listed, and then rate yourself. Ignoring the plus and minus signs, go back and add up all the numbers in both columns. If you are like most people, you will have given your friend higher ratings than you gave yourself.

Why these results? It is likely that you see your friend's behavior as relatively consistent across situations, whereas you see your own behavior as more variable. You probably were more likely to choose the zero category for yourself, showing that sometimes you see yourself as aggressive, thoughtful, or warm, and other times not. It depends on the situation. Other people's behavior is seen as more stable and less dependent on situational factors.

actor–observer bias The tendency for actors to prefer external attributions for their own behavior, especially if the outcomes are bad, whereas observers tend to make internal attributions for the same behavior.

First, rate a friend on the following characteristics using the scale that follows. Then go back and do the same for yourself.

Rating Scale

-2 Definitely does not describe
-1 Usually does not describe
 0 Sometimes describes, sometimes not
+1 Usually describes
+2 Definitely describes

	Friend	Self
Aggressive	_____	_____
Introverted	_____	_____
Thoughtful	_____	_____
Warm	_____	_____
Outgoing	_____	_____
Hard driving	_____	_____
Ambitious	_____	_____
Friendly	_____	_____
Total	_____	Total _____

Now, go back, ignore the pluses and minuses, and find the total of each column.

FIGURE 4-8 *Rating scale to test the actor–observer bias: Who has a more stable personality?* From Fiske and Taylor, 1984.

Again, the salience of the behavior plays a causal role in the attribution process (Figure 4-9). For the observer, the behavior of the other person is most salient. For the actor, the situational forces confronting her are most salient. The observer makes internal attributions. The actor, at least in part, subscribes to external attributions.

The crucial role of perspective in social perception situations can be seen in a creative experiment in which the perspectives of both observer and actor were altered (Storms, 1973). Using videotape equipment, the researcher had the actor view his own behavior from the perspective of an observer. That is, he showed the actor a videotape of himself as seen by somebody else (an observer). He also had the observer take the actor's perspective by showing the observer a videotape of how the world looked from the point of view of the actor. That is, the observer saw a videotape of herself as seen by the actor, the person she was watching.

When both observers and actors took these new perspectives, their attributional analyses changed. Observers who took the visual perspective of the actor made fewer person attributions and more situational ones. They began to see the world as the actor saw it. When the actor took the perspective of the observer, he began to make fewer situational attributions and more personal ones. Both observers and actors got to see themselves as

FIGURE 4-9 *Stopped for driving through a stop sign, we think of all the extenuating circumstances responsible for our negligence—a rough day at the office, thoughts about dinner, and those confusing traffic signs. The police officer sees it differently—normal road conditions, a careless driver! The actor–observer bias leads us to make external attributions and the police officer to make internal attributions.*

others see them—always an instructive, if precarious, exercise. In this case, it provided insight into the process of causal analysis.

Can we ever really understand the psychological perspective of others—that is, without carrying a camcorder around all the time? Or are we locked into the actor–observer bias? There are, in fact, conditions under which we do read people more carefully. In one study, subjects were asked to read essays that took a pro-life or pro-choice position on abortion and display either delight or disappointment as they spoke (Fleming & Darley, 1989). Half the speakers had clearly chosen their own speech, while the other half did not have a choice. This experiment was based on the original study of correspondence bias in which subjects listened to pro-Castro or anti-Castro speeches and had to decide what the speakers really believed (Jones & Harris, 1967).

In this study, researchers found that when the speaker did not have a choice, observers used facial expressions to evaluate the speaker's attitudes. When a speaker showed disappointment while making a pro-choice speech, and the observers knew that the speaker had to read that essay, the speaker was judged not to agree with the content of the theme. Facial expressions did not affect the observers' evaluation if the essay was freely chosen. This study indicates that correspondent inferences do not occur when the context of the behavior suggests that the speaker had to take that position or did not intend to say what she said. Notice, however, that only if the speaker literally has a gun to his or her head will we be persuaded not to make a correspondent inference.

The False Consensus Bias

When we analyze the behavior of others we often find ourselves asking, What would I have done? This is our search for consensus information

(what do other people do?) when we lack such information. In doing this, we often overestimate the frequency (and popularity) of our own views of the world (Ross, Greene, & House, 1977). The **false consensus bias** is simply the tendency to believe that everyone else shares our own feelings and behavior (Harvey & Weary, 1981). We tend to believe that others hold similar political opinions, find the same movies amusing, and think that baseball is the distinctive American game.

The false consensus bias may be an attempt to protect our self-esteem by assuming that our opinions are correct and are shared by most others (Zuckerman, Mann, & Bernieri, 1982). That is, the attribution that other people share our opinions serves as an affirmation and a confirmation of the correctness of our views. However, this overestimation of the trust-worthiness of our own ideas can be a significant hindrance to rational thinking. One may think that there is plenty of support "out there" for all kinds of opinions. And if people operate under the false assumption that their beliefs are widely held, the false consensus bias can serve as a justification for imposing one's beliefs on others (Fiske & Taylor, 1991).

Nancy Kerrigan (right) expected to win the gold medal in women's figure skating in the 1994 winter Olympics, but she came in second to Oksana Bayul (center). A person in this situation might attribute this outcome to external factors, such as bias on the part of the judges or the idiosyncracies of the scoring system. A person who wins, on the other hand, would no doubt attribute the outcome to his or her own hard work and talent. Thus does the self-serving bias help preserve self-esteem.

The Self-Serving Bias

In Garrison Keillor's mythical Minnesota town of Lake Woebegon, all the women are strong, all the men are good-looking, and all the children are above average. In thinking so well of themselves, the residents of Lake Woebegon are demonstrating the **self-serving bias,** which leads people to attribute positive outcomes to internal, dispositional factors and negative results to situational forces. A person typically thinks, I do well on examinations because I'm smart; I failed because it was an unfair examination. We take credit for success and deny responsibility for failure (Mullen & Riordan, 1988).

false consensus bias The tendency to believe that everyone else shares our own feelings, opinions, and behavior.

self-serving bias The tendency for individuals to take credit for success and deny responsibility for failure.

There is actually more evidence that people will take credit for success than the converse (that they will avoid responsibility for failure). They are willing to take "responsibility" for failure when it can be assigned to factors that are not stable in the attribution calculus (Mullen & Riordan, 1988). As Weiner (1986) reported, the explanations we assign to success and failure are critical for future expectations.

There is a long-standing controversy about why the self-serving bias occurs in the attribution process (Tetlock & Levi, 1982). One proposal, the motivational strategy, assumes that people need to protect self-esteem and therefore take credit for successes (Fiske & Taylor, 1984). We saw in Chapter 2 that protecting and enhancing self-esteem is a natural function of the self, which filters and shapes information in self-serving ways. A second approach emphasizes information-processing strategies. When people expect to do well, success fits their expectations; when success occurs, it makes sense, and they take credit for it. Then an internal attribution for success ("I'm terrific") is nothing more than the covariation principle at work (Miller & Ross, 1975). An objective observer may know that you were just lucky, but based on the way you have always made causal attributions, it is reasonable for you to connect your effort with a successful outcome.

THE CASE OF JOHN DEAN REVISITED: ATTRIBUTION BIASES IN THE WATERGATE SCANDAL

Let's reconsider the case of John Dean and Watergate. If we take a closer look at what the president and his men were saying in 1972 and 1973, we find several attribution biases at work. Certainly, we can see evidence of the actor–observer bias. The Watergate actors took an external perspective on events, whereas outside observers, the media, took an internal view. The actors' view was that they reacted to external events; observers believed that the fault could be found in the men involved.

President Nixon displayed the false consensus bias in two ways. First, he justified the administration's illegal actions by assuming that everyone was doing bad things, including those in previous administrations (some of this was fact). Second, he assumed that the public would support these illegal actions if they knew the full truth.

These assumptions led to the **group-serving bias,** which is like the self-serving bias but applies to groups. This phenomenon occurs when group members think that all the good things the group does are due to internal factors and all the bad things that happen to them are due to external causes. If other, competing groups do good things, it's because of external causes (luck, accident), and if they do bad things, it's due to internal factors (they are bad people) (Fletcher & Ward, 1988). In other words, groups take credit for the good and orphan the bad and do the opposite for competing groups. The group-serving bias led to the view by the president's men that they could illegally wiretap and burglarize their opponents: "They are bad, unpatriotic people, and furthermore, they would do it to us if they had our power."

group-serving bias The tendency for groups to take credit for success and deny responsibility for failure, and to do the opposite for competing groups.

The fundamental attribution error is evident as well. All opponents were characterized as bad people, without merit or honor (internal attributions). Anyone who disagreed with the administration was perceived as an enemy and placed on the "enemies list." Opposition, according to the White House view in 1972–73, could be motivated only by unpatriotic and selfish motives.

The president and his aides displayed the confirmation bias repeatedly. When the president was presented with his briefing book every morning, his staff managed to find newspaper stories that backed his views. The president never understood that the public overwhelmingly disapproved of the administration's actions, especially in the final days of his tenure in office.

The Watergate case also provides examples of the self-serving bias, or taking credit for success and denying responsibility for failure, which protects one's ego. The president, when summing up his career in the White House on the eve of his departure after his resignation, spoke almost exclusively of successes. The failures were, in his view, nothing but exaggerations by opponents of minor events.

What about Dean himself? During his many days of testifying before the Senate Watergate investigating committee, Dean displayed few of the attribution biases that are now familiar to us. A close look at the hearing transcripts gives us little to chew on: no fundamental attribution error, no actor–observer divergence, few self-serving attributions, and no sign of false consensus.

Perhaps public scrutiny forces us to forgo using these attribution biases (Tetlock, 1985). We have to be more rigorous in our analysis for fear of embarrassment. There is also another possibility. This public testimony could be the equivalent of the experiment in which the perspectives of the actor and the observer were reversed (Storms, 1973). When the actor took the observer's point of view, she tended to see the world as the observer did, and when the observer took the perspective of the actor, he, in turn, saw events just as the actor did. We might speculate that in the act of writing his 245-page statement, John Dean essentially put himself in the place of the actor-turned-observer. Therefore, the kind of attribution biases displayed by an actor would not occur in Dean's testimony.

Over time, people remember events from an observer's perspective rather than from their original point of view as a participant (Frank & Gilovich, 1989). In other words, when you recall an event, you look at it as if you had been an observer rather than a participant. John Dean assumed much more blame for events in his statement than one might expect. This excessive shouldering of blame probably was due in part to his adoption of a different perspective as he remembered events.

Another reason we did not see the self-serving bias is that Dean had tough-minded lawyers who carefully examined his testimony. In his book, Dean relates the following exchange after one of his lawyers read his statement:

"This is your testimony, I understand that," he [the lawyer] began, . . . "and I think it's good. In fact, it's a great statement of what happened, but you are asking for trouble in some places."

"What do you mean?"

"I mean that goddam self-serving crap you've got in there."

"I don't think that the statement is self-serving, Charlie. I confess a lot in there," I replied defensively.

"Well, generally that's true, but you've got a self-serving twist here and there," he persisted. "And listen, you're not going up there [to the Senate] to make any friends or win a popularity contest."

We worked through the statement. . . . (Dean, 1977, pp. 305–306)

Dean's statement "benefited" both from the observer's perspective he had to assume and from the advice of observers.

LOOKING AHEAD

In this chapter we saw that people are constantly seeking explanations for events in their social world. We also saw that the process of interpreting other people's behavior is complex and that several different models have been developed to explain it. We saw again that people automatically choose the easiest, most direct route to understanding and that this strategy has its flaws and costs.

In Chapter 5 we look at another aspect of social cognition—the development of prejudice and the formation of stereotypes. We see that such basic processes as categorization and in-group, out-group thinking lie behind prejudice and stereotypes. We also see that prejudice involves more than cognitive response; there are also biological, personality, and cultural factors involved. The chapter ends by showing how it is possible to alter the ways we think and the ways we structure social groups in order to short-circuit prejudice.

CHAPTER REVIEW

1. *What is causal attribution?*
   Causal **attribution** is the process of assigning causes to people's behavior, including our own. It involves making inferences about people's motives. Human beings want to understand why people act as they do, so they always look for reasons and explanations for behavior. When social psychologists study attribution, they are looking not at the actual causes of behavior but at the processes by which people interpret behavior. When we decide that someone acted a certain way because of some internal, dispositional characteristic—because the person wanted to act that way and believed in what he or she did—we are making an **internal attribution.** When we decide that someone acted a certain way because of circumstances and situational factors, we are making an **external attribution.**

2. *What are the principal theories or models for describing the attribution process?*
   The early models owe much to the original insights of Fritz Heider, who be-

lieved that people make attributions by following a certain set of rules. Later theorists tried to discover exactly what those rules are.

The correspondent inference and covariation models are the most general attempts to describe the attribution process. The former tries to explain attribution when perceivers are faced with ambiguous information. If we perceive that a person intended the behavior and freely chose it, we are likely to focus on the characteristics of the person and make an internal attribution, or **correspondent inference.** We also look closely at noncommon effects—outcomes that differ from the outcomes of other alternatives—and social desirability—general approval of the outcomes by society—in making correspondent inferences. Research confirms that we as perceivers have a strong tendency to make correspondent inferences even when the evidence doesn't support them, a tendency known as the **correspondence bias.**

Covariation theory suggests that people make attributions based on the **covariation principle.** According to this principle, people decide that the most likely cause of any behavior is the factor that covaries—occurs at the same time—most often with the behavior. The model emphasizes that people rely on three kinds of information—consensus information, distinctiveness information, and consistency information—to apply the covariation principle. When they don't have full information, they may apply the **discounting principle**—giving less weight to some causes—and the **augmentation principle**—giving more weight to some causes.

The abnormal conditions model highlights the importance of one of the aspects of the first two models, that people need to explain unusual or abnormal conditions more than any other types of situation. Causes are determined by looking for factors that occur regularly in the presence of the outcome and do not occur in its absence. Perceivers also examine **enabling conditions,** which are any potential cause that allows for the event to occur. Anything that is unusual or abnormal demands an attribution. In addition, the probabilistic contrast model suggests that causal analysis is based on the fact that perceivers assign different probabilities to the potential causes of events. They then contrast these probabilities and choose the factor that has the highest probability as the real cause. Trope's two-step model recognizes that the initial stage of assigning causality is an automatic categorization of behavior. A second stage may lead to an inferential adjustment. Gilbert's three-step model expands the first stage into two stages—categorization and characterization. The third stage, correction, is like the inferential adjustment stage of Trope's model.

3. *What emotional and behavioral consequences flow from the attributions we make?*
Attributions are not just analytic tools; they also have implications for emotional responses and for behavior. For example, rape victims are often viewed as contributing to the crime committed against them; in other words, their own behavior becomes a potential cause of the rape. When jury members blame the victim, they are less likely to convict the rapist.

The attributions we make about our own behavior, especially our successes and failures, also affect our future actions. We consider three kinds of information—locus of causation (internal or external), controllability, and stability—in examining these events. The best outcomes occur when we attribute success to internal and stable factors and failure to external and unstable factors.

Attributions made in close relationships are important to the future success or failure of those relationships. The most damaging attributions partners can make are internal, stable, and global (that is, suggest that this is something the partner always does). Unhappy couples tend to make attributions that emphasize negative events and motives and spend a lot of time blaming each other. Counseling can sometimes help couples change their attribution patterns.

4. *What cognitive biases affect the attribution process, and what predictable errors do we tend to make?*
The most common error is making a correspondent inference without supporting evidence. This error—attributing causes to people more readily than to situations—is so common that it is called the **fundamental attribution error.** Research indicates that this error occurs in a variety of circumstances, including predicting our own and our friends' future behavior. People are less likely to make this error when their automatic cognitive functioning is disrupted and they are forced to use controlled processing.

Related to the fundamental attribution error is the **confirmation bias,** which causes us to search for evidence in support of our preexisting hypotheses about situations. Also related to the fundamental attribution error is the **actor–observer bias,** whereby actors focus on external attributions and observers focus on internal attributions. This bias seems to occur because of differences in perspective. When we observe other people, the most obvious things are what they do. When we try to decide why we did something, the most obvious things are elements of the situation.

People also tend to believe that others think and feel the same way they do, a tendency known as the **false consensus bias,** and that positive outcomes are the result of their own efforts and negative outcomes are due to external factors, known as the **self-serving bias.** When the self-serving bias is applied to the groups people belong to, it is known as the **group-serving bias.** All of these biases can be found in the way various actors thought about and behaved in the Watergate conspiracy.

Suggestions for Further Reading

Jones, E. E. (1990). *Interpersonal perception.* New York: W. H. Freeman. Clearly written and logically presented, this volume is Jones's summary of his 30 years of work studying how we perceive ourselves and others.
Medvec, V. D., Made, S. A., & Gilovich, T. (in press). When more is less: Counterfactual thinking and satisfaction among Olympic gold medalists.

A study that shows there is some truth to the saying that second place, even in the Olympics, is "nowhere."

Weiner, B. (1993). On sin versus sickness. *American Psychologist, 48,* 957–963.
A leading exponent of attribution theory considers how we assign causes for illness; the stigma associated with illness; and the association of illness and sin.

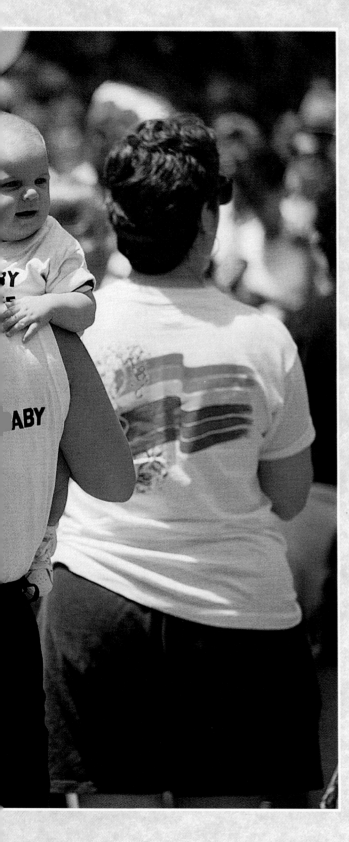

Chapter 5

Prejudice and Stereotypes

*V*incent Chin, a Chinese American, was in a topless bar one warm night in June of 1982 in Detroit, Michigan. He was celebrating his forthcoming marriage. Mr. Chin was happy this night; he was excited about his bride and thankful for his job as a draftsman. The pleasant mood of this rather unremarkable night was soon to be shattered by violence.

Two auto workers, frustrated and angry at the loss of jobs during the sharp economic recession of the early 1980s, spotted Mr. Chin as he walked past the bar. The two men assumed that Mr. Chin was Japanese, and they blamed Japan for the economic difficulties experienced by the auto industry in "Motown." They vented their frustration by killing Mr. Chin with baseball bats.

As one of them beat Mr. Chin to death, he screamed, "It's because of you we're out of work" (*Time,* Nov. 1, 1983, p. 46).

Judge Charles Kaufman gave the two confessed murderers, Ronald Ebens, a foreman at Chrysler, and his stepson, Michael Nitz, 3 years probation and fines of $3,780 each. The judge offered the opinion that these were not the kind of men you send to prison. After all, they had no prior criminal record (*Time,* Nov. 14, 1983). Lily Chin, Vincent's mother, expressed her disbelief at the incident and the sentence. She said, "I love America; how could things like this happen in America?"

Indeed, how could things like this happen in America? The very foundations of American society—equality, tolerance, justice—would seem to rule out such incidents as the racially motivated murder of Vincent Chin. But in fact, incidents like this have occurred throughout the history of the United States, and they continue to occur to this day. If anything, there has been a rise in the early 1990s in the amount of prejudice and hostility directed toward different racial and ethnic groups in this country.

Even a casual survey of expressions of abuse toward different groups on college campuses shows an increase in hate crimes. For example, a black female student at the University of Delaware saw a black doll "lynched" in the dorm room of another student. That image evoked images of real lynchings of African Americans in this country, crimes that occurred over the course of hundreds of years (Youngstrom, 1991). On one eastern campus, swastikas were painted on a Jewish student campus center, a gay man was chased and beaten, and drunken fraternity members hurled beer cans at women participating in a "Take Back the Night" rally against rape on the campus. The university, in response to the hostile atmosphere on campus, commissioned a survey to gauge the extent of hate on campus. The results were astonishing for the sheer volume of hatred. Women were the most abused of all groups, suffering both physical and verbal abuse. Of other groups, 40% of all gay men and lesbians, 33% of African Americans, 25% of Hispanics, and 20% of Asian Americans also suffered verbal or physical abuse. Only 5% of white males were assaulted during the previous academic year (Youngstrom, 1991).

Acts of hate were on the rise in 1993 and 1994 off campus as well. A survey conducted by the Anti-Defamation League reported the highest level of anti-Jewish acts in the past 15 years. These included vandalism of synagogues, harassments, threats, and physical assaults (*New York Times,* March 2, 1993). And, as the economy of the United States continued to slide in 1992 and 1993, there was an increase in the number of hostile acts (threatening telephone calls, bomb threats, physical violence) directed against Japanese Americans, whom some people blamed for the state of the economy.

Of course, incidents like these and the attitudes that allow them to occur are not new to the United States. In fact, such incidents and attitudes have a rich tradition that includes slavery, lynchings of blacks, the near extermination of native Americans, and the persecution of Irish, Asian, Jewish, Mormon, and other Americans.

In this chapter we take a close look at prejudice, stereotypes, and discrimination. We look for the underlying causes of incidents like Vincent Chin's murder. We ask, How did the auto workers come to hold their views? Was it something about their personalities that led them to murder? Or do the causes lie more in their social situation? What cognitive processes led them to hold negative attitudes toward those they perceived to be different from themselves? How pervasive and unalterable are those processes in human beings? And what can we do to reduce prejudice and bring our society closer to its ideals? These are some of the questions we address in the pages that follow.

THE DYNAMICS OF PREJUDICE, STEREOTYPING, AND DISCRIMINATION

On college campuses across the country, students from different groups are often the recipients of racial, gender, or ethnic prejudice, despite the fact that college is supposedly a bastion of enlightened discourse. Why does this occur? What leads to "Japanese bashing" or "gay bashing"? One answer to these questions lies in the prejudiced attitudes we form about members of different groups. From prejudiced attitudes often flow stereotypes, and from stereotypes, all too often, comes discrimination.

Prejudice

The term **prejudice** refers to a biased, often negative, attitude formed about a group of people. Prejudicial attitudes include belief structures, containing information about a group of people, as well as a set of expectations concerning the behavior of members of that group. When prejudice is directed toward a group, it leads to prejudgment of the individual members of that group.

Of course, prejudice can be either positive or negative. Fans of a particular sports team, for example, are typically prejudiced in favor of their own team. They often see calls made against their team as unfair, even when the referees are being impartial. Social psychologists, however, have been more interested in prejudice that involves a negative bias—that is, in cases where one group assumes the worst about another group and may base negative behaviors on these assumptions. It is this latter form of prejudice that is the subject of this chapter.

Prejudice comes in a variety of forms. The most visible are racism and sexism. **Racism** is the negative evaluation of others because of their apparent membership in a particular racial group. It can also be viewed as the belief that one racial group is inherently superior to another. Racial prejudice is based primarily on skin color. **Sexism** is the negative evaluation of others because of their membership in a particular gender category (Lips, 1993). Of course other forms of prejudice exist, such as religious and ethnic prejudice and heterosexism (fear and hatred of gay men and lesbians), but racism and sexism are the two most widespread prejudices in our society.

An important note should be added here about the concept of *race*. Throughout U.S. history, racial categories have been used to distinguish groups of human beings from one another. However, biologically speaking, race is an elusive—and problematic—concept. A person's "race" is not something inherited as a package from his or her parents, nor are biological characteristics, such as skin color, hair texture, eye shape, facial features, and so on, valid indicators of one's ethnic or cultural background. Consider, for example, an individual whose mother is Japanese and whose father is African American, or a blond, blue-eyed person who is listed by the U.S. Census Bureau as Native American because her maternal grandmother was Cherokee. To define these individuals by their "race" is simply inaccurate and inappropriate. Many scientists maintain that race does not exist as a biological concept.

Race does exist, however, as a social construct. People perceive and categorize others as members of racial groups and, often, act toward them accordingly. In this social sense, race—and racism—are very real, and important, factors in human relations. When we refer to *race* in this book, as when we discuss "race-related violence," it is this socially constructed concept, with its historical, societal, and cultural significance, that we mean.

prejudice A biased, often negative, attitude formed about a group of people.

racism The negative evaluation of others because of their apparent membership in a particular racial group.

sexism The negative evaluation of others because of their membership in a particular gender category.

Stereotypes

Prejudicial feelings do not stem from perceived physical differences among people, such as skin color or gender. Rather, prejudice relates more directly to

The natural human impulse to categorize leads us to group people together on the basis of perceived commonalities. If we make judgments and assumptions about individuals as members of that group, we are stereotyping. Stereotypes are often misleading: These gay men may be as dissimilar from each other in personality, occupation, interests, and so on, as any two people.

the characteristics we assume members of a different racial, ethnic, or other group to have. In other words, it relates to the way we think about others.

Recall from Chapter 3 that people have a strong tendency to categorize objects based on perceptual features or uses. We categorize chairs, tables, desks, and lamps as "furniture." We categorize love, hate, fear, and jealousy as "emotions." And we categorize people on the basis of their race, gender, nationality, and other obvious features. Of course, categorization is adaptive in the sense that it allows us to direct similar behaviors toward an entire class of objects or people. We do not have to choose a new response each time we encounter a categorized object.

Categorization is not necessarily the same as prejudice, although the first process powerfully influences the second. We sometimes take our predisposition to categorize too far, developing rigid and overgeneralized images of groups. This rigid categorization—this set of beliefs, positive or negative, about the characteristics or attributes of a group—is a **stereotype** (Judd & Park, 1993; Stangor & Lange, 1994). For example, we may believe that all lawyers are smart, a positive stereotype, or we may believe that all lawyers are devious, a negative stereotype. The political journalist Walter Lippmann (1922) aptly called stereotypes "pictures in our heads." When we encounter someone new who has a clear membership in one or another group, we reach back into our memory banks of stereotypes, find the appropriate picture, and fit the person to it.

In general, stereotyping is simply part of the way we do business cognitively every day. It is part of our cognitive "toolbox" (Gilbert & Hixon, 1991). We all have made judgments about individuals (Boy Scouts leader, police officer, college student, feminist) based solely on their group membership. Stereotyping is a time saver; we look in our "toolbox," find the appropriate utensil, and characterize the "college student." It certainly takes less time and energy than trying to get to know that person (individuation) (Macrae, Milne, & Bodenhausen, 1994). Again, this is an example of the "cognitive miser" at work. Of course, this means we will make some very unfair, even destructive judgments of individuals. All of us recoil at the idea that *we* are being judged solely on the basis of some notion that the evaluator has of group membership.

stereotype A set of rigid beliefs, positive or negative, about the characteristics or attributes of a group.

Discrimination

When prejudicial feelings are turned into overt behavior, the result is **discrimination.** Like stereotyping, discrimination is a normal part of our cognitive activity. It is one way our mental apparatus deals with the world. When you stop at a red light and go at a green light, you are discriminating. Discrimination becomes problematic when it is directed toward people simply because they are presumed to be members of a particular group.

As we saw in Chapters 2, 3, and 4, social perceivers make predictable errors as a consequence of their cognitive strategies. For example, we often fail to realize that our behavior affects the behavior of others and that our expectations affect the way people respond to us. We also tend to overemphasize internal factors and underemphasize external factors when seeking an explanation for other people's behavior. These and other errors and biases contribute to the problems associated with certain cognitive strategies.

The concepts of prejudice and discrimination, although closely tied, are different and can be independent of one another. An individual may have prejudiced thoughts about a group—such as that they are all of low intelligence—yet not overtly discriminate against members of that group (Tetlock, 1986). And just because a person does not discriminate, it does not necessarily mean that he or she is not prejudiced.

It is also worth noting that discrimination can occur without any underlying prejudice. Discrimination can emerge from institutional policies that have nothing to do with hatred of members of a particular group. For example, a company may use a screening test that is culturally biased, leading to the systematic exclusion of members of a certain racial group. Even though there may be no racist intent, the discrimination still occurs.

The Persistence and Recurrence of Stereotypes

Throughout history, members of "majority" groups (those in power) have held stereotypical images of members of "minority" groups (those not in power). These images supported prejudicial feelings, discriminatory behavior, and even widescale violence directed against minority-group members. History teaches us that stereotypes and prejudicial feelings are quite enduring. For example, some stereotypes of Jews and Africans are hundreds of years old. However, stereotypes and feelings may change, albeit slowly, as the context of our feelings toward other groups changes. Let's look at the history of feelings of Americans toward the Japanese (and vice versa) as an example of how images and feelings change—and change back—along with social context.

During World War II, Japan and the United States were enemies for four brutal years, 1941–45. For roughly the next 40 years, the two countries were at peace and had a harmonious relationship. The American occupation of Japan (1945–51) was benign. The Americans helped the Japanese rebuild their war-shattered factories, and the Japanese began to compete in world markets. But in the difficult economic times of the 1990s, many of the beliefs that characterized Japanese–American relations

discrimination Overt behavior directed toward people simply because they are presumed to be members of a particular group.

War propaganda typically makes use of stereotypes that dehumanize or ridicule the enemy. During World War II, the Japanese were portrayed as cruel, fanatical, and ambitious (left). These caricatures had a negative impact on real human beings—American citizens of Japanese descent, who were placed in internment camps for the duration of the war. The tearful mother and children on the right were photographed as they awaited transport to a camp.

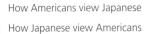

■ How Americans view Japanese
■ How Japanese view Americans

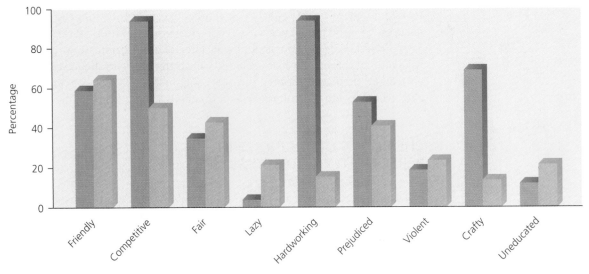

FIGURE 5-1 How Japanese and Americans view each other. Based on data from a Time/CNN poll, 1992, in Hillenbrand, 1992.

during World War II have reemerged, although in somewhat modified form. Figure 5-1 shows the results of a *Time*/CNN poll taken in January 1992. The two bars for each characteristic show how Americans view the Japanese and how the Japanese view Americans. Compared to how Japanese view Americans, Americans tend to see the Japanese as more competitive, hard-working, prejudiced, and crafty. The Japanese have a slight tendency to see Americans as undereducated, lazy, and not terribly hard-working.

Other evidence indicates that Americans see the Japanese as unfair, arrogant, and overdisciplined. They tend to see them as grinds who do nothing but work hard because of their conformity to group values (Weisman, 1991). The Japanese, for their part, see Americans as arrogant and lacking in "racial purity," morality, and dedication (Weisman, 1991). The stereotypes on both sides have been altered and transformed by the passage of time, but, like short skirts and wide ties, they tend to recycle. The periodicity of stereotypes suggests that they are based more on external factors such as economics and competition than on any stable characteristics of the group being categorized. The fate of Vincent Chin had much to do with the impact of hard economic times, which activated racial stereotypes.

Of course, the Japanese aren't the only group to experience prejudice and stereotyping in the United States. Have you ever wondered why so many Mormons settled in Utah? There is a simple answer to this: They were driven there as a result of religious intolerance and political and economic fears (Arrington & Bitton, 1980). The trail of persecution followed by the Mormons was marked by one incident after another. On March 14, 1832, for example, in Hiram, Ohio, Joseph Smith, the Mormon leader, was awakened from a sound sleep and taken outside by a mob, where he was stripped naked except for his shirt collar and covered with tar. Such incidents followed the Mormons wherever they went. In fact, in 1838 the governor of Missouri signed the following order: "The Mormons must be treated as enemies, and must be exterminated or driven from the State if necessary, for the public peace" (cited in Arrington & Bitton, 1980).

Prejudice, then, appears to be an integral part of human existence. It has endured throughout history and is still strong today. In the next sections we explore the causes of prejudice, focusing first on its roots in personality and social life and then on its roots in human cognitive functioning.

THE ROOTS OF PREJUDICE IN PERSONALITY AND SOCIAL LIFE

What are the causes of prejudice? In addressing this question, social psychologists have looked not only at our mental apparatus—our inclination to categorize—but at personality characteristics that might contribute to prejudicial feelings. They have pointed to one important personality dimension that seems to contribute to prejudice and discrimination: *authoritarianism*.

The Authoritarian Personality

Think of Archie Bunker, the patriarch of the Bunker family in the 1970s television show "All in the Family." While denying that he was prejudiced, Archie constantly spouted bigoted sentiments against various groups. In the late 1940s, T. W. Adorno and other psychologists at the University of California at Berkeley studied people who might have been the prototypes of Archie Bunker—individuals who wanted different ethnic groups to be suppressed and degraded, preferably by an all-powerful government or state. Archie Bunker embodies many of the characteristics of the **authoritarian personality** (Adorno, Frenkel-Brunswik, Levinson, & Sanford, 1950), which is characterized by submissive feelings toward authority, by rigid, unchangeable beliefs, and by racism and sexism.

Motivated by the tragedy of the murder of millions of Jews and other Eastern Europeans by the Nazis, Adorno and his colleagues conducted a massive study of the relationship between the authoritarian personality and the Nazi policy of genocide, the killing of an entire race or group of people. They speculated that the individuals who carried out the policy of mass murder were of a personality type that predisposed them to do whatever an authority figure ordered, no matter how vicious or monstrous.

The massive study produced by the Berkeley researchers, known as *The Authoritarian Personality*, was driven by the notion that there was a relationship, an interconnectedness, between the way a person was reared and various prejudices he or she later came to hold. Prejudiced people were highly *ethnocentric*; that is, they believed in the superiority of their own group or race (Dunbar, 1987). The Berkeley researchers argued that individuals who were ethnocentric were likely to be prejudiced against a whole range of ethnic, racial, and religious groups in their culture. They found that such people were indeed prejudiced against many or all groups that were different from themselves. A person who was "anti-colored" tended to be anti-Semitic (anti-Jewish) as well. These people seemed to embody a prejudiced personality type, the authoritarian personality.

The Berkeley researchers discovered that authoritarians had a particularly rigid and punishing upbringing. They were raised in homes in which children were not allowed to express any feelings or opinions except those considered correct by their parents and other authority figures. People in authority were not to be questioned and were, in fact, idolized. The child handled pent-up feelings of hostility toward these suppressive parents by becoming a kind of island, walling these feelings off by inventing very strict categories and standards. The child became impatient with uncertainty and ambiguity and came to prefer clear-cut and simple answers. Authoritarians had very firm categories: This was good, that was bad. Any groups that violated their notions of right and wrong were rejected.

This rigid upbringing engendered frustration and a strong concealed rage, which could be expressed only against those less powerful. The child learned that those in authority had the power to do as they wished. If the authoritarian obtained power over someone else, the suppressed rage came out in full fury. Authoritarians were at the feet of those in power and at the throats of those less powerful. The suppressed rage was usually expressed against a *scapegoat,* a relatively powerless person or group, such as Vincent Chin. This tended to occur most often during times of frustration, such as when economic times were bad.

The authoritarian personality, the individual who is prejudiced against all groups perceived to be different, may gravitate to hate groups. In 1992 police in Sacramento, California, arrested a teenager on charges of fire-bombing five targets—a synagogue, a local office of the National

authoritarian personality A personality type characterized by submissive feelings toward authority, by rigid, unchangeable beliefs, and by racism and sexism.

Association for the Advancement of Colored People, an office of the Japanese-American Citizens League, the home of an Asian American City Councilman, and a state office that handles discrimination claims. The teenager was characterized as a "believer in white supremacist groups." After the last fire, the Aryan Liberation Front claimed responsibility for the string of bombings and vowed to continue their armed struggle to change American society.

The early research on prejudice, then, emphasized the role of irrational emotions and thoughts that were part and parcel of the prejudiced personality. These irrational emotions, simmered in a pot of suppressed rage, were the stuff of prejudice, discrimination, and eventually intergroup violence. The violence was usually set off by frustration, particularly when resources, like jobs, got scarce.

The Social Roots of Prejudice: The Case of Racism

The research on the authoritarian personality provides an important piece of the puzzle of prejudice and discrimination. However, it is only one piece. Prejudice and discrimination are far too complex and prevalent to be explained by a single, personality-based cause. Prejudice occurs in a social context, and another piece of the puzzle can be found in the evolution of the feelings that form the basis of relations between dominant and other groups in a particular society.

To explore the social roots of prejudice, let's consider the situation of African Americans in the United States. In Chapter 1 we looked briefly at the history of slavery in this country. We saw that black slaves were considered the property of white slave owners, that this arrangement was justified by the notion that blacks were in some way less human than whites, and that their degraded condition was used as proof of their inferiority.

In 1863, in the middle of the Civil War, President Lincoln issued the Emancipation Proclamation, setting the slaves free. But abolition did little to end prejudice and negative attitudes toward blacks. The Massachusetts 54th regiment, for example, was an all-black Union Army unit—led by an all-white officer corps. Blacks were said to lack the ability to lead. Members of the 54th were also paid less than their white counterparts in other regiments.

Despite prejudice, some blacks did rise to positions of prominence. Frederick Douglass, who escaped from slavery and became a leader and spokesperson for African Americans, was instrumental in convincing President Lincoln to issue the Emancipation Proclamation and to allow black troops to fight in the Civil War. Toward the end of the war, over 100,000 black troops were fighting for the North. Some historians maintain that without these troops, the Civil War may have turned out differently.

Over the course of the next hundred years, African Americans made strides in improving their economic and social status, but most changes met with intense resistance from the majority community. Then in 1954 the U.S. Supreme Court ruled in *Brown v. Board of Education* that segregated ("separate but equal") schools violated the Constitution and mandated that

schools and other public facilities be integrated. Since then, the feelings of white Americans toward African Americans have become more positive (Goleman, 1991). This change in attitudes and behavior reflects the importance of *social norms* in influencing and regulating the expression of feelings and beliefs.

Yet there is a curious nature to these feelings. White Americans almost unanimously endorse such general principles as integration and equality, but they are generally opposed to steps designed to actualize these principles, such as mandatory busing or affirmative action (Katz, Wackenhut, & Hass, 1986). It may be that white Americans pay "lip service" to the principle of racial equality. They perceive African Americans as being *both* disadvantaged by the system *and* deviant. In other words, while white Americans are aware that African Americans may have gotten a raw deal, they also see them as responsible for their own plight (Katz et al., 1986). Remember, the human tendency to attribute behavior to internal rather than external causes makes it more likely that people will find the reasons for achievement or lack of it in the character of an individual or a group.

Although we may no longer have tarring and feathering of members of different groups, prejudice still exists in more subtle forms. If acquired early enough, it seems to become part of one's deepest feelings (Pettigrew, 1986, p. 20):

> Many southerners have confessed to me, for instance, that even though in their minds they no longer feel prejudice towards African Americans, they still feel squeamish when they shake hands with an African American. These feelings are left over from what they learned in their families as children.

Given American history and the importance of things racial in that history, and given the way people process information in a categorical and automatic way, some observers assume that racist feelings are the rule for Americans (Gaertner & Dovidio, 1986).

Over 100,000 African American troops fought for the North in the Civil War. The Emancipation Proclamation ended slavery and allowed African Americans to join the army, but it did not end prejudice and discrimination. Pictured here is Company E, Fourth Colored Infantry, at Fort Lincoln, photographed in 1865.

Incidents from daily life seem to bear out this conclusion. In 1992, for example, the owner of the Cincinnati Reds baseball team, Marge Schott, drew fire for her use of offensive epithets (*Time*, December 7, 1992). Her supporters claimed she wasn't a bigot or a hatemonger but just "from the old school."

In 1993 an AT&T company magazine published a drawing in which humans were shown talking on the telephone on several continents. But in Africa, a monkey was shown using the phone. AT&T issued an apology to its workers and to the NAACP, who called it "truly offensive." An AT&T spokesperson said he couldn't imagine how the drawing had gotten past the magazine's editors and proofreaders (*Wall Street Journal*, September 17, 1993).

Presidential candidate Ross Perot ran into trouble in 1992 when addressing the NAACP. He used the phrases "you people" and "your people" when talking about who would suffer the most from economic problems and runaway crime. Critics said the phrase reflected how out of touch he was with his audience. He also offended many listeners with his description of his father's generosity toward African Americans in the South: "The only words I ever heard him say were, 'Son, these are people too, and they have to live.'" Joseph H. Duff, president of the Los Angeles chapter of the NAACP, commented, "When he tried to tell us we're people, he made a big mistake. We know we're people" (*New York Times*, July 12, 1992, p. 22). Perot himself was baffled by his listeners' response. He commented that if he offended anyone, he was sorry.

Modern Racism At the same time that we acknowledge the persistence of racist beliefs, we see, in survey after survey, that negative stereotypes about African Americans in the United States are apparently lessening (Table 5-1). Why this contradiction? Since the study of the authoritarian personality was published several decades ago, it has become more difficult, socially and legally, to express prejudice against individuals from particular racial groups. Just recently, for example, a U.S. government official was removed from his job because he made a statement that could have been interpreted as anti–African American. The official denied that that was his intent, but even the appearance of prejudice in someone in an official position is unacceptable today.

Some social psychologists believe that many white Americans today are aversive racists, people who truly believe they are unprejudiced, who want to do the "right thing," but in fact feel very uneasy and uncomfortable in the presence of someone from a different racial group (Gaertner & Dovidio, 1986). When they are with members of other groups, they smile too much, are overly friendly, and are sometimes very fearful. These feelings do not lead the aversive racist to behave in a negative way toward members of other groups; rather, they lead him or her to avoid them.

This more subtle prejudice is marked by an uncertainty in feeling and action toward people from different racial groups. J. G. McConahay (1986) has referred to this configuration of feelings and beliefs as **modern racism**

modern racism A newer, more subtle prejudice marked by an uncertainty in feeling and action toward minorities. Modern racists express racism but in a less open manner than was formerly common.

TABLE 5-1

THE CHANGING FACE OF STEREOTYPES

	Percentage of Subjects Selecting Trait			
Trait	1932	1950	1967	1982
Attributed to African Americans				
Superstitious	84	41	13	6
Lazy	75	31	26	13
Happy-go-lucky	38	17	27	15
Ignorant	38	24	11	10
Musical	26	33	47	29
Attributed to White Americans				
Industrious	48	30	23	21
Intelligent	47	32	20	10
Materialistic	33	37	67	65
Ambitious	33	21	42	35
Progressive	27	5	17	9

From Rajecki, 1990.

(also called *symbolic racism* by other authors on the subject). Modern racists moderate their responses to individuals from different racial groups to avoid showing obvious prejudice; they express racism but in a less open manner than was formerly common. Modern racists would say that yes, racism is a bad thing and a thing of the past; still, it is a fact that African Americans "are pushing too hard, too fast, and into places where they are not wanted" (McConahay, 1986, p. 93).

McConahay has devised a scale to measure modern racism. Items from that scale are shown in Table 5-2, along with items from previous scales that measured what McConahay calls "old-fashioned racism." As can be seen, the older scale (old-fashioned racism) presents items in a rather uncomplicated, racist manner. According to McConahay, modern racists would show up as nonprejudiced on those scales. McConahay has found that the modern racist scale is sensitive enough to pick up more subtle differences in people's feelings and behavior about racial issues. The questions asked on this scale reveal a more elusive and indirect kind of prejudice.

In one of McConahay's experiments, participants (all of whom were white) were asked to play the role of a personnel director of a major company. All participants had taken a version of the modern racism scale. The "personnel director" received a résumé of a graduating college senior who was a very ordinary job candidate. The race of the candidate was manipulated: For half of the subjects a photograph of an African American was attached, and for the other half a photograph of a white person was attached.

Another variable was added to the experiment in addition to the race of the applicant. Half of each group of subjects were told that there were no other qualified candidates for the job. This was called the "no anchor"

TABLE 5-2

MODERN AND OLD-FASHIONED RACISM SCALES

Modern Racism	Old-Fashioned Racism
Over the past few years, African Americans have gotten more, economically, than they deserve. (Strongly agree = 5)	If an African American family with about the same income and education as you, moved next door, would you mind it a lot, a little, or not at all? (A lot = 4)
Over the past few years, the government and the news media have shown more respect for African Americans than they deserve. (Strongly agree = 5)	How strongly would you object if a member of your family had a friendship with an African American—strongly, somewhat, slightly, not at all? (Strongly object = 4)
It is easy to understand the anger of African American people in America. (Strongly disagree = 5)	How do you feel about the open housing law here in _____ which allows more racial integration? Do you strongly favor, somewhat favor, somewhat oppose, strongly oppose this law? (Strongly oppose = 5)
How many people here in _____ do you think miss out on good housing because white owners won't rent or sell to them—many, some, only a few, none at all? (None = 4)	Generally speaking, do you favor full racial integration, integration of some areas of life, or full separation of the races? (Full separation = 3)
African Americans are getting too demanding in their push for equal rights. (Strongly agree = 5)	In principle, do you think it is a good idea or a bad idea for children to go to schools that have about the same proportion of the races? (Full separation = 3)
How many African American people in _____ do you think miss out on jobs or promotions because of racial discrimination—many, some, only a few, none at all? (None = 4)	Generally, do you feel African Americans are smarter than, not as smart as, or about as smart as whites? (Not as smart = 3)

From McConahay, 1986.

condition, because the personnel directors had no basis for judgment, no other candidate against which to evaluate the ordinary candidate. The other half of each group saw the résumés of two other candidates, both white, who were far superior to the ordinary candidate, white or African American. This was called the "anchor" condition, because the personnel directors now had a basis for comparison.

Personnel directors in all four groups were asked to make a decision on the candidate on a scale ranging from "definitely would hire" to "definitely would not hire." McConahay's findings are shown in Figure 5-2. As shown on the graph, individuals who have high scores on the modern

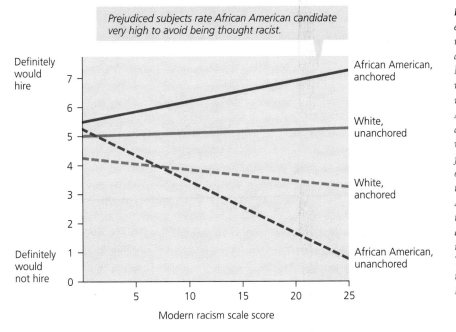

Prejudiced subjects rate African American candidate very high to avoid being thought racist.

African American, anchored

White, unanchored

White, anchored

African American, unanchored

Definitely would hire

Definitely would not hire

Modern racism scale score

FIGURE 5-2 *Hiring preferences as a function of modern racism scale scores, race of candidate, and decision context. Nonprejudiced subjects—those who scored near zero on the modern racism scale—rated African American candidates about the same, whether there was another candidate for the job (the "anchored" condition) or not. Prejudiced subjects gave the lowest rating to the African American candidate when there were no other candidates and the highest rating when there were other candidates. These subjects did not want to appear prejudiced.* From McConahay, 1986.

racism scale (indicating that they are prejudiced) do not treat white candidates any differently than their nonprejudiced counterparts. Whether they score 0 or 25 or somewhere in between on the scale, all subjects rated the white candidates, in both the anchor and the no-anchor condition, in a similar way. Subjects with low scores (near 0) rated white candidates about the same, whereas high scorers (closer to 25) rated the white no-anchor candidate a little higher than the white anchor candidate.

More interesting are the ratings of African American candidates. For nonprejudiced subjects, African Americans, anchored or not, are rated precisely the same. But look at the very large differences between candidates for the prejudiced subjects. An unanchored African American candidate is absolutely dismissed, whereas the anchored African American candidate— that is, compared to more qualified whites—is given the highest rating.

Why these differences? Recall that modern racists are rather uncertain about how to feel or act in situations with members of different racial or ethnic groups. They particularly do not want to discriminate when others will find out about it and can label what they did racist (Donnerstein & Donnerstein, 1973). To reject a very ordinary African American candidate when there were no other candidates probably would not be seen as prejudiced. After all, this was an ordinary candidate, not really very good. Note how much more favorably the modern racist judges the white candidate in the same anchor circumstances.

But when there is a chance that her behavior might be termed racist, the modern racist overvalues African Americans. This is seen when there are qualified white candidates (anchor condition). The modern racist goes out of her way to appear unprejudiced and therefore gives the ordinary

Despite the obstacles of racism, many African Americans have overcome prejudice and discrimination to excel in their fields. Maya Angelou inspired many Americans with her poem "On the Pulse of the Morning," read at President Clinton's 1993 inauguration. Angelou's role in this historic event reflected changing social norms; it will also help shape the norms of the future.

African American candidate the highest rating. Subjects who score low on the modern racism scale feel confident about how to feel and act in racial situations. People from different racial groups do not make them uncomfortable; they "call it like they see it" (Hass, Katz, Rizzo, Bailey, & Eisenstadt, 1991).

Criticisms of Modern Racism   The concept of modern racism is not without its critics. Some critics suggest that it is illogical to equate opposition to an African American candidate or affirmative action programs with racism (Sykes, 1992). Other critics point out that modern-racism researchers have not adequately defined and measured modern racism (Tetlock, 1986). They also point out that high correlations exist (ranging from about $r = .6$ to $.7$) between old-fashioned racism and modern racism. That is, if a person is a modern racist, he or she is also likely to be an old-fashioned racist. According to these critics, there simply may not be two forms of racism.

The fact is that race is a complex issue and contains many facets. In the past, according to public opinion surveys, whites were essentially either favorable or unfavorable to the cause of African Americans. But racial feelings are more subtle now. Someone might be against busing of school children but not opposed to having an African American neighbor (Sniderman & Piazza, 1994). Additionally, a person's racial attitudes are often affected by his or her politics. Individuals who have favorable attitudes toward

African Americans but who perceive affirmative action policies to be unfair may come to dislike African Americans as a consequence (Sniderman & Piazza, 1994).

Changing Social Norms   What accounts for the changes we see in the expression of racist sentiments and for the appearance of modern racism? Our society, primarily through its laws, has made the obvious expression of racism undesirable. Over the past 30 years, social norms have increasingly dictated the acceptance of members of different racial and ethnic groups into mainstream society. Overt racism has become socially unacceptable. But for many individuals, deeply held racist sentiments remain unchanged. Their racism has been driven underground by society's expectations and standards.

Because of changed social norms, charges of prejudice and discrimination are taken seriously by those against whom they are made. In 1993 the Denny's restaurant chain was charged with discriminating against black customers. In one incident, a group of black high school students in San Jose, California, were allegedly told they had to pay in advance for their late-night meal. In another, six black Secret Service officers in Maryland complained that they waited for service while a nearby table of white officers ordered, were served, ate their meal, and left. As other, similar incidents came to light, it began to seem that discrimination against African Americans was a company policy at Denny's (*Newsweek,* July 19, 1993, p. 36).

Denny's parent company, Flagstar Cos., launched a public relations campaign to defuse the charges. Television ads pledged that everyone who came to Denny's would be treated with respect and that any departures from that policy were unintentional. Nevertheless, business at Denny's declined, as did the price of Flagstar's stock. Consumer research indicated that the public was well aware of the incidents. The head of Flagstar expressed regret that he had not paid enough attention to running a corporation in an increasingly culturally diverse society. Only one of the 378 Denny's franchises, for example, was owned by an African American. The corporation had to suffer the consequences of his neglect: In 1994, Denny's was ordered to pay $46 million to customers who had been treated unfairly by the restaurant. The settlement was the largest ever awarded in a discrimination case involving public facilities (Herhold, 1994).

Despite such consequences, some people believe that our society's norms have been altered in the past few years, allowing racial and ethnic animosities to be more easily and safely expressed. Contributing to this atmosphere are political candidates like David Duke who express direct or indirect racist opinions and political advertisements that pit one group against another. The expression of racist feelings lessens the power of antiracist norms to moderate people's behavior. When we observe an increase in direct racial hatred, we can be sure that social norms are changing once again.

On the other hand, there is evidence that attitudes, although not necessarily behavior, toward specific groups have become more positive. For example, gender stereotypes seem to have lessened recently, at least among college students, if not among older individuals (Swim, 1994). In this case, social norms in favor of greater equality seem to be holding.

THE COGNITIVE ROOTS OF PREJUDICE

What, then, has happened to the prejudiced personality? It appears that it remains with us. Only the form of expression seems to have changed. The irrational forces that drive prejudice have not been seriously affected by historical or social change. In fact, cognitive social psychologists have argued that while prejudice may have personality and social causes, it also exists because of the mental strategies people use to structure their social worlds.

From Categories to Stereotypes

Cognitive social psychologists believe that one of the best ways to understand how stereotypes form and persist is to look at how humans process information. As we saw in Chapters 2 and 3, human beings tend to be cognitive misers, preferring the least effortful means of processing social information (Taylor, 1981). We have a limited capacity to deal with social information and therefore can deal with only relatively small amounts at any one time (Fiske & Taylor, 1991).

Given these limitations, people try to simplify problems by using shortcuts, primarily involving category-based processes (Bodenhausen & Wyer, 1985; Brewer, 1988). In other words, it is easier to pay attention to the group to which someone belongs than to the individual traits of the person. It takes less effort and less time for the person to use category-based (group-based) information than to try to deal with people on an individual basis (Macrae et al., 1994). Vincent Chin's attackers, for example, categorized him as "Japanese" because his features matched what they thought a Japanese person should look like.

The workings of the cognitive miser have been demonstrated in a variety of research studies. One finding is that when people's ability or motivation to process information is diminished, they tend to fall back on available stereotypes. In one series of experiments, Galen Bodenhausen and Meryl Lichtenstein (1987) found that when a juror's task was complex, he or she recalled more negative things about a defendant if the defendant was Hispanic than if the defendant did not belong to an identifiable group. When the jurors' task was simple, no differences in judgment were found between a Hispanic and a non-Hispanic defendant. When the situation gets more complicated, individuals tend to rely on these stereotypes.

In another experiment, Bodenhausen (1990) investigated how people made judgments when they were not at the height of their abilities. He tested subjects to determine if they were "night people"—individuals who function better in the evening and at night—or "day people"—individuals who function better in the morning. He then had subjects make judgments about a student's misconduct. Sometimes the student was described in

TABLE 5-3

RATINGS OF PERCEIVED GUILT OF A STUDENT AS A FUNCTION OF TIME OF DAY, PERSONALITY TYPE, AND STEREOTYPE ACTIVATION

	Time of Day		
	9 a.m.	3 p.m.	8 p.m.
Morning Types			
stereotype	4.92	6.67	6.50
no stereotype	5.39	5.61	5.79
Evening Types			
stereotype	6.79	5.13	5.60
no stereotype	5.05	5.67	6.45

Note: Higher scores mean more guilt.
From Bodenhausen, 1990.

nonstereotypic terms (his name was "Robert Garner"), and in other situations he was portrayed as Hispanic ("Roberto Garcia"), as African American, or as an athlete.

The experiment showed that when people are not at their peak (morning people at night or night people in the morning), they tend to solve problems by using stereotypes. As shown in Table 5-3, morning types relied on the stereotype to judge the student when presented with the case in the evening; evening types fell back on stereotypes in the morning. These findings suggest that category-based judgments take place when we do not have the capacity, the motivation, or the energy to pay attention to the target.

The strategies of the cognitive miser, and particularly the tendency to categorize, lead human beings into a variety of cognitive misconceptions and errors. These include the in-group bias, the illusory correlation, the fundamental attribution error, the confirmation bias, and the out-group homogeneity bias. We look at each of these next.

The In-Group Bias

One of the principal cognitive processes common to all human beings seems to be the tendency to identify with and prefer one's own group—the in-group—and at the same time to identify "different" others as belonging to a less favored out-group. Henri Tajfel, a social psychologist whose work we examined in Chapter 1, studied the phenomenon of in-group favoritism as a way of exploring out-group hostility. He was preoccupied with the issue of genocide—the systematic killing of an entire national or ethnic group. As a survivor of the Nazi genocidal attack on European Jews, 1939–45, Tajfel had a personal as well as a professional interest in this issue (Brown, 1986).

Unlike the earlier researchers who emphasized the irrational thoughts and emotions of the prejudiced personality as the source of intergroup violence, Tajfel thought that cognitive processes were involved. He believed that the process of categorizing people into different groups led to loyalty to the in-group, which includes those people one perceives to be similar to oneself in meaningful ways. Inevitably, as in-group solidarity forms, those who are perceived to be different are identified as members of the out-group (Allport, 1954; Billig, 1992).

As you recall from Chapter 1, Tajfel was searching for the minimal social conditions needed for prejudice to emerge (see the featured coverage of his work in Chapter 1). In his experiments with British school boys, he found that there was no situation so minimal that some form of in-group solidarity did not take shape. He concluded that the need to favor the in-group, known as the **in-group bias,** was a basic component of human nature. What are the reasons for this powerful bias?

As noted in Chapter 2, we derive important aspects of our self-concepts from our membership in groups (Turner, 1987). These memberships help us establish a sense of positive social identity. Think of what appears to be a fairly inconsequential case of group membership—being a fan of a sports team. When "your team" wins a big game, you experience a boost, however temporary, to your sense of well-being. Recall from Chapter 2 the concept of BIRGing—Basking in Reflected Glory. You don't just root for the team—you become part of the team. You say, "*We* beat the heck out of *them.*" Think for a moment about the celebrations that have taken place in Detroit, New York, Boston, and elsewhere after home teams won professional sports championships. It's almost as if it wasn't the Tigers or the Mets or the Celtics who won, but the fans themselves.

When your team loses the big game, on the other hand, you feel terrible. You're tempted to "jump ship." It's hard to read the newspapers or listen to sportscasts the next day. When your team wins, you say, "We won." When your team loses, you say, "They lost" (Cialdini, 1988). It appears that both BIRGing and jumping ship serve to protect the individual fan's self-esteem. The team becomes part of the person's social identity.

This Oakland A's fan takes in-group bias to an extreme. When "his team" wins, his self-esteem is enhanced. Belonging to the group known as "A's fans" is an important part of his social identity.

in-group bias The powerful tendency that humans have to favor the in-group, the group to which they belong, over out-groups.

Social Identity Theory Tajfel's (1982) *social identity theory* assumes that human beings are motivated to positively evaluate their own groups—and value them over other groups—in order to maintain and enhance self-esteem. The group confers on the individual a social identity—that part of a person's self-concept that comes from her membership in social groups and from her emotional connection with those groups (Tajfel, 1981).

Fundamental to social identity theory is the notion of categorizing the other groups, pigeonholing them, by the use of stereotypes—the general beliefs that most people have about members of particular social groups

FIGURE 5-3 *Even if national rivalries are unimportant to us, we root for our own team during the Olympics. According to social identity theory, in-group bias increases whenever group identity becomes a more prominent feature of the social landscape.*

(Turner, 1987). People are motivated to hold less than positive stereotypes of out-groups; by doing so they can maintain the superiority of their own groups and thereby maintain their positive social (and self) identity.

Generally, any threat to the in-group, whether economic, military, or social, tends to heighten in-group bias. Additionally, anything that makes a person's membership in a group more salient, more noticeable, will increase in-group favoritism. One series of experiments showed that when people were alone, they were likely to judge an out-group member on an individual basis, but when they were made aware of their in-group membership by the presence of other members of their group, they were likely to judge the out-group person solely on the basis of stereotypes of the out-group (Wilder & Shapiro, 1984, 1991). The increase of in-group feelings promoted judgments of other people on the basis of social stereotypes. When group membership gets "switched on"—as it does, for example when you are watching the Olympics or voting for a political candidate—then group values and social stereotypes play a larger role in how you react (Figure 5-3).

When Your Group Is Less Valued What about membership in a group that does *not* confer a positive social identity? Not all social groups have the same social status and perceived value. What can you do when your group is stigmatized, oppressed, or less valued than other groups? The logic is pretty simple: You have to raise its value, first by convincing group members of their own self-worth, and then by convincing the rest of society of the worth of the group. The function of all "consciousness raising" efforts and positive in-group slogans is to persuade the members of scorned or less valued in-groups that they are beautiful or smart or worthy or competent. This first step—maintaining and increasing self-esteem—can be approached in at least two ways (Crocker & Major, 1989; Crocker, Voelkl, Testa, & Major, 1991): attributing negative events to prejudice of the majority and comparing oneself to members of one's own group.

The first way that self-esteem can be maintained by minority members is to attribute any negative things that happen to a member of the group to the prejudice of the majority. If, for example, an African American woman is denied a job or a promotion, she can better maintain her self-esteem if she attributes this outcome to the prejudice of the person evaluating her. Of course, people are usually uncertain about the true motives of other people in situations like this. Although a rejection by a majority group member can be attributed to the evaluator's prejudice, the effects on the self-esteem of the minority person are complex.

Some of these effects were investigated in a study in which African American subjects were evaluated by white evaluators (Crocker & Major, 1989). When subjects thought that evaluators were unaware of their race, positive evaluations increased their self esteem. But when subjects knew that evaluators *were* aware of their race, positive evaluations *decreased* their self-esteem. Compared to whites, African Americans were more likely to attribute *both* positive and negative evaluations to prejudice. Any judgment, positive or negative, that the recipient thought was based on racism led to a decrease in self-esteem (Crocker et al., 1991).

Uncertainty about such evaluations thus has important consequences for self-esteem. In our society, African Americans are often evaluated primarily by whites, which suggests that they may always feel uncertain about their evaluators' motives (Crocker et al., 1991). This uncertainty may be exacerbated for African American females who are evaluated by white males (Coleman, Jussim, & Isaac, 1991).

The second way that members of less favored groups can maintain self-esteem is to compare themselves with members of their own group rather than with members of the more favored or fortunate groups. In-group comparisons may be less painful and more rewarding for members of stigmatized groups. Research supports this hypothesis in a number of areas, including pay, abilities, and physical attractiveness (Crocker & Major, 1989). Once group members have raised their value in their own eyes, the group is better placed to assert itself in society.

As the feelings of cohesiveness and belonging of the in-group increase, there is often an escalation in hostility directed toward the out-group (Allport, 1954). History teaches us that identifying with an in-group and identifying others with an out-group underlie many instances of prejudice and intergroup hostility. For a look at the patterns of discrimination that accompany many of these instances of stereotyping, see the featured discussion "Persecution of Out-Groups: A Fact of Life?"

A Biological Perspective on In-Group Bias Tajfel's research has shown us that the formation of an in-group bias serves basic social and self needs, primarily by maintaining personal self-esteem. Some scientists—specifically, the sociobiologists, scientists who take a biological approach to social behavior—believe that ethnocentrism (the increased valuation of the in-group and the devaluation of out-groups) has a foundation in human biological evolution. They point out that for the longest part of their history, humans lived in small groups ranging from 40 to 100 members (Flohr, 1987). People had to rely on the in-group and gain acceptance by its members. It was the only way to survive. It would make sense, then, that a strong group orientation would be part of our human heritage: Those who lacked this orientation would not have survived to pass their traits on to us.

Sociobiologists also point out that people in all cultures seem to show a naturally occurring *xenophobia,* or fear of strangers. This fear too may be part of our genetic heritage. Because early populations were isolated from each other (Irwin, 1987), people may have used similar physical appearance as a marker of blood relationship (Tonnesmann, 1987). Clearly, there was always the possibility that people who looked different could be a threat to the food supply or other necessities of survival. Sociobiologists argue that it's reasonable to expect that people would be willing to cooperate only with humans of similar appearance and biological heritage and that they would distrust strangers (Barkow, 1980).

In modern times, as Tajfel has shown, we still derive much of our identity from group membership. We fear being excluded from groups (Baumeister & Tice, 1990). High respect for our own groups often means a devaluing of other groups. This is not necessarily a big problem until groups have to compete for resources. Since the world does not appear to offer a surplus of resources, competition among groups is inevitable.

Of particular interest to sociobiologists is a study by Tajfel (1982) and his co-workers in which it was demonstrated that children show a preference for their own national group long before they have a concept of country or nation. Children ranging in age from 6 to 12 years were shown photographs of young men and were asked how much they liked those men. Two weeks later, the children were shown the same photographs again. They were also told that some of the men belonged to their nation and others did not. The children had to decide which young men were "theirs" (belonged to their country) and which did not. The researchers found that the children were more likely to assign the photographs they liked to their own nation. Therefore, liking and in-group feelings go together at an age (6) when children cannot really comprehend fully the idea of a nation (Flohr, 1987).

In sum, those who offer a biological perspective on intergroup prejudice say that strong in-group identification can be understood as an evolutionary survival mechanism. We can find examples throughout human history of particular ethnic, racial, and religious groups that have strengthened in-group bonds in response to threats from the dominant group (Eitzen, 1973; Myrdal, 1962). Strengthening of these in-group bonds helps the group survive. Of course, this is only one way of looking at the in-group bias. Acceptance of this notion does not require us to neglect our social psychological theories; it simply gives us some idea of the complexity of the issue (Flohr, 1987).

The Role of Language in Maintaining Bias   Categorization, as we know, is generally an automatic process. It is the first step in the impression formation process. As mentioned earlier, it is not the same as stereotyping and prejudice, but it powerfully affects these other processes. One way in which categorizing can lead to prejudice is through language. The way we

History teaches us that in-group, out-group dynamics underlie many instances of prejudice and intergroup hostility. Any feature, be it physical, cognitive, or behavioral, may lead to an in-group, out-group mentality. In other words, whether the differences we perceive in others involve how they look, how they think, or how they act, these differences induce prejudice, discrimination, or worse.

Consider the Mormons. They were persecuted and driven from a variety of places in the United States during the 1800s. One basis for this discrimination was that Mormons held different religious and social beliefs than the mainstream population of the country at the time. However, this was true of other groups as well, such as the Quakers (Arrington & Bitton, 1980).

Another factor contributed to the negative, prejudiced feelings that developed toward the Mormons. The Mormons established themselves within Christian communities but remained isolated from the wider community. Within their enclaves they developed their own social and economic systems. For example, in Kirtland, Ohio, the Mormons established a community and issued their own bank notes to be used as currency. In Independence, Missouri, the non-Mormon population was initially excited about the influx of Mormons to the area. They saw the Mormons as new customers to support local businesses. The Mormons, however, established their community and then did the bulk of their business through a store owned by a member of the Mormon church (Arrington & Bitton, 1980). The Mormons eventually came to be seen as an economic and political threat as well as a religious threat.

Stereotyping and persecution dogged the Mormons as they headed west to Utah. The same pattern of persecution can be found in the history of other groups identified as out-groups.

D. Stanley Eitzen (1973) studied the treatment of two very different groups—the Jewish population of Poland and the Chinese population of the Philippines—and found that they were stereotyped and persecuted for remarkably similar reasons. Eitzen identified four areas of similarity—historical factors contributing to stereotyping and prejudice, stereotypes of the various groups held by the majority, reactions of the groups to discrimination, and reasons for persecution. Virtually all the factors within each of these areas applied to the situations of both the Jews and the Chinese. Many of them also apply to the Mormons in the United States, and we would undoubtedly see this same pattern if we analyzed the history of other persecuted groups, including African Americans and Native Americans. These findings support the notion that patterns of in-group, out-group antagonism are rooted not only in social and cultural contexts but in the workings of the human mind and in the processes of group relations.

sculpt our world via the words and labels we use to describe people connects the category to prejudice. Social psychologist Charles Perdue and his colleagues tested the hypothesis that the use of words describing in-groups and out-groups unconsciously forms our biases and stereotypes (Perdue, Dovidio, Gurtman, & Tyler, 1990).

Perdue suggested that the use of collective pronouns—*we, us, ours, they, them, theirs*—is very influential in how we think about people and groups. We use these terms to assign people to in-groups and out-groups. In one study, Perdue and his colleagues showed subjects a series of nonsense syllables (*xeh, yof, laj*) paired with pronouns designating in-group or out-group status (*we, they*). Subjects were then asked to rate each of the non-

SIMILARITIES BETWEEN THE JEWS OF POLAND AND THE CHINESE OF THE PHILIPPINES

	Jews	Chinese
Historical Factors		
Values different from majority	X	X
Common occupational patterns	X	X
Located in urban areas	X	X
Segregation (compulsory)	X	X
Victims of common patterns of discrimination	X	X
Minority Reactions to Discrimination		
Internal solidarity	X	X
Formation of business and community organizations for defense and welfare	X	X
Schools to promote cultural identity	X	X
Emphasis on intellectual pursuits	X	little
Competitiveness	X	X
Circumvention of restrictive laws	X	X
Stereotypes of the Minority		
Clannish	X	X
Control of business	X	X
Lack of loyalty to the government	X	X
Refusal to assimilate	X	X
Unethical in business	X	X
Clever	X	X
Adaptable	X	X
Ambitious	X	X
Industrious	X	X
Mercenary	X	X
Reasons for Persecution		
Economic	X	X
Nationalistic	X	X
Religious	X	not overt
The sanction of tradition	X	X

From Eitzen, 1973.

Prejudice and negative attitudes often arise between groups that live in close proximity to each other and that seem to share certain commonalities, sometimes even a common ancestry. Outside observers often perceive such groups—Swedes and Norwegians, for example, or Arabs and Israelis, or Indians and Pakistanis—to be more similar to each other than different. What mechanisms in social cognition lead to this outcome? Or do you think these groups are prone to exaggerate their differences? If so, what do you think the reasons for such exaggerations might be?

sense syllables they had just seen in terms of the pleasantness or unpleasantness of the feelings they evoked. As shown in Figure 5-4, nonsense words paired with in-group pronouns were rated much more favorably than the same nonsense words paired with out-group pronouns or with control stimuli. Out-group pronouns gave negative meaning to previously unencountered and neutral nonsense syllables.

In a second experiment, these investigators demonstrated that in-group and out-group pronouns bias the processing of information about those groups. Subjects saw a series of positive and negative trait words, such as *helpful, clever, competent, irresponsible, sloppy,* and *irritable.* Now, a positive trait ought to be positive under any circumstance, and the same

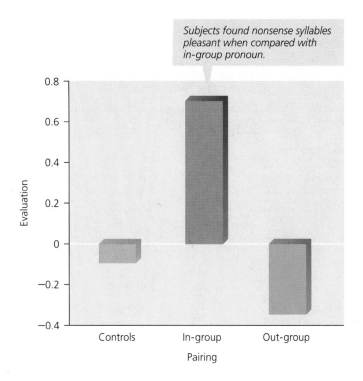

FIGURE 5-4 *Standardized ratings of target syllables as a function of pronoun pairing. Syllables paired with in-group pronouns (we, us) were judged to be pleasant. Syllables paired with out-group pronouns (they, them) were judged unpleasant. The in-group bias seems to be an automatic function.* From Perdue, Dovidio, Gurtman, and Tyler, 1990.

Subjects found nonsense syllables pleasant when compared with in-group pronoun.

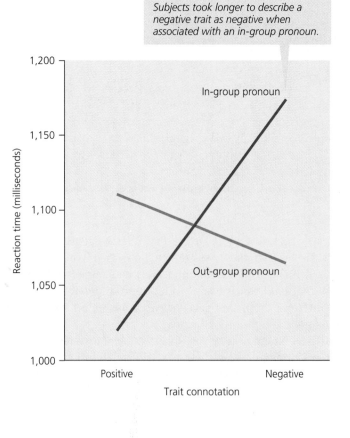

FIGURE 5-5 *Reaction times to positive and negative trait descriptors as a function of pronoun type (in-group pronoun versus out-group pronoun). It seems that information processing is biased by in-group, out-group thinking.* From Perdue, Dovidio, Gurtman, and Tyler, 1990.

Subjects took longer to describe a negative trait as negative when associated with an in-group pronoun.

should hold true for negative traits, wouldn't you agree? *Skillful* is generally positive, *sloppy* is generally negative. But as Figure 5-5 shows, it took subjects longer to describe a negative trait as negative when that trait had been associated with an in-group pronoun. Similarly, it took subjects longer to describe a positive trait as positive when it had been associated with an out-group pronoun. It took them little time to respond to a positive trait associated with an in-group pronoun and to a negative trait associated with an out-group pronoun.

These findings suggest that we have a nonconscious tendency (after all, the subjects were not aware of the associations) to connect in-group labels with positive attributes rather than negative ones and out-group labels with negative attributes rather than positive ones. These associations are so strong that they shape the way we process subsequent information. They also seem to be deep and long-lasting, a fact that may help explain why stereotypes remain so tenacious.

Illusory Correlations

The tendency to associate negative traits with out-groups is explained by one of the fundamental cognitive bases of stereotyping, the illusory correlation. An **illusory correlation** is an error in judgment about the relationship between two variables, or, in other words, a belief that two unrelated events covary (are systematically related) (Hamilton & Sherman, 1989). For example, a person may notice that each time he wears his old high school bowling shirt when he goes bowling, he bowls very well. He may come to believe that there is a connection between the two events. Similarly, if you think that members of a minority group are more likely than members of a majority group to have a negative trait, then you perceive a correlation between group membership and behavior (Schaller, 1991).

Sometimes this cognitive bias crops up even among trained professionals. For example, a physician had diagnosed a young, married African American woman with chronic pelvic inflammatory disease, an ailment related to a previous history of sexually transmitted disease (*Time,* June 1, 1992). This diagnosis was made despite the fact that there was no indication in her medical history that she had ever had such a disease. As it turned out, she actually had endometriosis, a condition unrelated to sexually transmitted diseases (*Time,* June 1, 1992). The physician's beliefs about young black women (that they are sexually promiscuous) led to a diagnosis consistent with those beliefs. Research supports this anecdote. For example, subjects have been found to ascribe different abilities to a girl depending on whether she is portrayed as having a lower or higher socioeconomic status background (Darley & Gross, 1983).

These examples illustrate the human tendency to overestimate the co-occurrence of pairs of distinctive stimuli (Sherman, Hamilton, & Roskos-Ewoldsen, 1989). In the case of the misdiagnosis, the presence of two distinctive stimuli—a young, black woman and a particular symptom

illusory correlation A belief that two unrelated events covary (are systematically related).

pattern—led the physician to conclude that the woman's disorder was related to her sexual history. The tendency to fall prey to this illusion has been verified in other experiments (Chapman & Chapman, 1967).

The illusory correlation helps explain how stereotypes form. The reasoning goes like this: Minority groups are distinctive because they are encountered relatively infrequently. Negative behavior is also distinctive because it is, in general, encountered less frequently than positive behavior. Because both are distinctive, there is a tendency for people to overestimate the frequency with which they occur together—that is, the frequency with which minority group members do undesirable things (Sherman et al., 1989).

Research shows that if people are presented with information about a majority group and a minority group and these groups are paired with either rare or common traits, people associate the smaller group with the rarer trait (Hamilton & Sherman, 1989). If both a minority and majority group have the same negative trait, say a tendency toward criminal behavior, the negative behavior will be more distinctive when paired with the minority as compared to the majority group. Our cognitive apparatus seems to lead us to make an automatic association between negative behavior and minority group membership.

Distinctive characteristics are also likely to play a critical role in the formation of category-based responses. In any gathering of people we pay more attention to those who appear to be different from others, such as a white in an otherwise all-black group or a man in an all-woman group. Skin color, gender, and ethnicity are salient characteristics. (For a look at a time when race was not a prime organizing factor for people, see the featured discussion "A Time Before Color Prejudice.")

Why are perceivers automatically drawn to salient characteristics? As discussed in Chapter 3, one function of automatic evaluation is to point to events that may endanger the perceiver (Pratto & John, 1991). Certainly, sociobiologists would agree with that notion. The human ability to recognize friend from foe, safety from danger, would have fundamental survival value (Ike, 1987). Recall the study described in Chapter 3 that showed how people automatically responded to an angry (salient) face in a happy crowd (Hansen & Hansen, 1988). An angry person among friends is dangerous. Another study demonstrated that individuals automatically turn their attention from a task to words, pictures, or events that might be threatening (Pratto & John, 1991). Subjects attended more rapidly to salient negative traits than to positive ones. This *automatic vigilance* may lead people to weight undesirable attributes in those around them differently than positive attributes.

When we encounter other groups, then, it's not surprising that we pay more attention to the bad things about them than the good. Negative social information grabs our attention. This greater attention to negative information may protect us from immediate harm, but it also helps perpetuate stereotypes and may contribute to conflict between groups (Pratto & John, 1991).

salient.— conspicuous

Few human features are as salient, as obvious, as skin color. Was there ever a time or a culture in which skin color was not used as a basic categorization feature? Some historians of the ancient Mediterranean suggest that there was a time before color prejudice. The initial encounter of black Africans and white Mediterraneans is the oldest chapter in the chronicle of black–white relations.

Frank M. Snowden, Jr. (1983) has traced the images of Africans as seen by Mediterraneans from Egyptian to Roman times. The first Africans encountered by Mediterraneans were soldiers or mercenaries. Mediterraneans knew that these black soldiers came from a powerful independent African state, Nubia, located in what today would be southern Egypt and northern Sudan. Nubians appear to have played an important role in the formation of Egyptian civilization (Wilford, 1992). Positive images of Africans appear in the artwork and writings of ancient Mediterranean peoples (Snowden, 1983).

These first encounters between blacks and whites were encounters between equals. The Africans were respected for their military skill and their political and cultural sophistication. Slavery existed in the ancient world but was not tied to skin color; anyone captured in war might be enslaved, whether white or black (Snowden, 1983). Prejudice, stereotyping, and discrimination existed too. Athenians may not have cared about skin color, but they cared deeply about national origin. Foreigners were excluded from citizenship. Women were also restricted and excluded. Only males above a certain age could be citizens and participate fully in society.

It is not clear when color prejudice reared its ugly head. It may have been with the advent of the African–New World slave trade in the 16th century. Whenever it began, it is likely that race and prejudice were not linked until some real power or status differences arose between groups.

Although slavery in the ancient world was not based exclusively on skin color, slaves were almost always of different ethnic group, national origin, religion, or, at the least, political unit than their owners. What role do you think in-group, out-group dynamics played in this custom? What other cognitive processes are at work when one group enslaves another?

From Illusory Correlations to Negative Stereotypes via the Fundamental Attribution Error

The fact that a negative bit of information about a different group has grabbed our attention does not necessarily lead to discrimination against that group. There must be a link between the salience of negative information and prejudiced behavior. The fundamental attribution error—the tendency to overestimate internal attributes and underestimate the effect of the situation—supplies this link and plays a role in the formation of discriminatory stereotypes. This is particularly true when perceivers do not take into account the roles assigned to people. Recall the "quiz show" study described in Chapter 4, in which subjects thought that the quiz show questioners were smarter than the contestants (Ross, Amabile, & Steinmetz, 1977), even though roles had been randomly assigned.

This confusion between internal dispositions and external roles has led to punishing negative stereotypes of different groups. Let's consider just

Because moneylending was one of the few professions open to European Jews, Jews in general came to be seen, via the fundamental attribution error, as tightfisted, avaricious, and shrewd. Anyone who wears the distinctive Jewish garb—as these Hasidim still do—might be perceived as having these traits.

one example—the experience of the Jews in Europe over the past several hundred years (Ross & Nisbett, 1991). Historically, Jews had many restrictions imposed on them in the countries where they resided. They were prevented from owning land; they often had to live in certain designated areas; they could not enter politics; and many professions were closed to them.

This exclusion from the greater society left the Jews with two options: either convert to Christianity or maintain their own distinctive culture. Most Jews opted for the latter, living within the walls of the ghetto assigned to them by the Christian majority and having little to do with non-Jews. Exclusion and persecution strengthened their in-group ties and also led the majority to perceive them as clannish. However, one segment of the Jewish population was highly visible to the mainstream society—the moneylenders. Moneylending was a profession forbidden to Christians and open to Jews (Ross & Nisbett, 1991). Although it was held in contempt, it was an essential function in national and international business, especially as capitalism began to develop. Jewish moneylenders became important behind-the-scenes figures in the affairs of Europe. Thus, the most distinctive members of the group—distinctive for their visibility, their economic success, and their political importance—were invariably moneylenders.

The distinctive negative role of moneylending, although restricted to only a few Jews, began to be correlated with Jews in general. Jews were also seen as distinctive because of their minority status, their way of life, their unique dress, and their in-group solidarity. All of these characteristics were a function of the situation and roles thrust on the Jews by the majority, but they came to be seen, via the fundamental attribution error, as inherent traits of Jewish people in general. These traits were then used as a justification for discrimination, based on the rationale that Jews were different, clannish, and money-grubbing.

Do these stereotypes still crop up today in "enlightened" American communities? Movie director Steven Spielberg grew up in New Jersey and

Arizona but never experienced anti-Semitism until his family moved to Saratoga, California, during his senior year in high school. "He encountered kids who would cough the word Jew in their hands when they passed him, beat him up, and throw pennies at him in study hall. 'It was my six months of personal horror. And to this day I haven't gotten over it nor have I forgiven any of them'" (*Newsweek,* December 20, 1993, p. 115).

Historically, Jews were not the only group to suffer from majority exclusion and the fundamental attribution error (Ross & Nisbett, 1991). The Armenians in Turkey, the Indians in Uganda, and the Vietnamese "boat people" were all money middlemen who took on that role because no other positions were open to them. All of these groups suffered terrible fates.

The Confirmation Bias

People dealing with Jews in the 18th century in Europe or with Armenians in Turkey at the turn of the 20th century found it easy to confirm their expectancies about these groups. Perceivers could recall the moneylenders, the strange dress, the different customs. Stereotypes are both self-confirming and resistant to change.

Numerous studies have shown that stereotypes can influence social interactions in ways that lead to their confirmation. In one study, some subjects were told that a person with whom they would soon talk was in psychotherapy; other subjects were told nothing about the person (Sibicky & Dovidio, 1986). In actuality, the individuals they talked to were randomly chosen students from basic psychology courses; none were in therapy. After the interviews, subjects were asked to evaluate the person with whom they had interacted. Those individuals identified as "therapy clients" were rated as less confident, less attractive, and less likable than the individuals not described as being in therapy.

We can see from this study that once people have a stereotype, they evaluate information within the context of that stereotype. After all, none of the people being interviewed in the experiment were in fact in therapy. The differences between the ratings had to be due to the participants' stereotypical view of what "somebody in therapy" must be like. Describing a person as being in therapy seems to lead to a negative perception of that person.

As we saw in Chapter 4, there is a self-confirming quality to expectations about others. People who hold negative stereotypes about certain groups may behave so that group members act in a way that confirms the stereotype (Crocker & Major, 1989). This is the confirmation bias, which contributes in many instances to self-fulfilling prophecies. If you expect a person to be hostile, your very expectation and the manner in which you behave may bring on that hostility. In the study just described, participants who thought that they were interacting with someone in therapy probably held a stereotypical view of "all people with psychological problems." It's likely that they behaved in a way that made those individuals uneasy and act in a less confident manner.

Because of the out-group ho-mogeneity bias, we often find members of groups to which we do not belong virtually in-distinguishable from one an-other: "They all look alike." Members of our own group, on the other hand, seem quite distinctive. How distinctive do you find the young women in each of these two groups? What relation do your percep-tions have to your own group membership?

The Out-Group Homogeneity Bias

An initial effect of categorization is that members of the category are seen as being more similar to each other than is the case when people are viewed as individuals. Because we have a fair amount of information about the members of our own group (the in-group), we are able to differentiate among them. But we tend to view members of other groups (out-groups) as being very similar to each other (Wilder, 1986)—"We are quite different from each other, but they are all alike" (Hamilton & Trolier, 1986). This phenomenon of perceiving members of the out-group as "all alike" is called the **out-group homogeneity bias** (Linville, Fischer, & Salovey, 1989).

The out-group homogeneity hypothesis was tested in one study involv-ing students from Princeton and Rutgers universities (Quattrone & Jones, 1980). Subjects, who were either Rutgers or Princeton students, saw a videotape of a student supposedly from the other school. The videotaped person had to decide whether he wanted to wait alone or with other people before being a subject in a psychological experiment. The actual subject then had to predict what the average student at the target university (Rutgers for Princeton students and Princeton for Rutgers students) would do in a similar situation.

Would the subjects see students at the other university as similar to the student they had viewed? Would they predict that most Princeton stu-dents (or Rutgers students) would make the same choice as the Princeton student (or Rutgers student) in the film clip? These questions get at the is-sue of whether people see out-group members as more similar to each other than in-group members. In fact, this is pretty much what the study showed, although there was a greater tendency to stereotype Princeton students than Rutgers students. That seems logical, since it is probably easier to con-jure up a stereotype of a Princeton student. In general, however, results supported the notion that the out-group homogeneity bias leads us to think that members of out-groups are more similar to each other than members of in-groups.

A second outcome of the out-group homogeneity bias is the assump-tion that any behavior of an out-group member reflects the characteristics

out-group homogeneity bias
The phenomenon of perceiving members of the out-group as "all alike."

of all group members. If a member of an out-group does something bad, we tend to conclude, "That's the way those people are." In contrast, when an in-group member does something equally negative, we tend to make a dispositional attribution, blaming the person rather than our own in-group for the negative behavior. This has been referred to as the **ultimate attribution error:** We are more likely to give in-group members the benefit of the doubt than out-group members (Pettigrew, 1979).

Once we construct our categories, we tend to hold on to them tenaciously. The tenacity may be both innocent and destructive. It is innocent because the process is likely to be automatic and nonconscious. It is destructive because stereotypes are inaccurate and often damaging; individuals cannot be adequately described by reference to the groups to which they belong.

Are Stereotypes Ever Accurate?

In general, social psychologists have not made a consistent attempt to determine the accuracy of stereotypes. Much of the early research on stereotypes assumed that stereotypes were inaccurate by definition. Recently, the issue of stereotype accuracy has been addressed by Charles Judd and Bernadette Park (1993). They have suggested several technical standards against which the accuracy of a stereotype can be measured. For example, consider the notion that Germans are efficient. One standard that Judd and Park suggest to measure the accuracy of that stereotype is to find data that answers the questions: Are Germans in reality more or less efficient than the stereotype? Is the group attribute (efficiency) exaggerated?

Of course, to apply these standards we need some objective data about groups. We need to know how groups truly behave with respect to various characteristics. For some attributes, say, kindness or sensitivity, it is probably impossible to obtain such information. For others, there may be readily available data.

In a study of the accuracy of stereotypes, white subjects' estimates of certain attributes of the African American population were compared with public records (MaCauley & Stitt, 1978, cited in Judd & Park, 1993). The attributes estimated were percentage of high school graduates, number of crime victims, and number of people on the welfare rolls. This study showed that whites underestimated the differences between African Americans and themselves with respect to these attributes. In other words, whites thought more African Americans graduated from high school than was true and they thought fewer African Americans were victims of crime than the data showed.

Is it important to know if a stereotype is accurate? Technically it is, because many of the (earlier) definitions of stereotypes assume that inaccuracy is part of the definition of the concept (Stangor & Lange, 1994). Most stereotypes are unjustified generalizations; that is, they are not accurate. But, even if they are accurate, stereotypes still have a damaging effect on our perception of others. None of us would wish to be judged as an individual by the worst examples of the group(s) to which we belong.

ultimate attribution error We are more likely to give in-group members the benefit of the doubt than out-group members.

groups. Low-prejudiced individuals hold practically the same stereotypes as prejudiced people, but they believe these stereotypes are wrong. They feel guilty and self-critical if they express prejudiced thoughts and feelings (Devine, Monteith, Zuwerink, & Elliot, 1991).

GENDER STEREOTYPING AND PREJUDICE: SEXISM

Most negatively stereotyped groups are minorities, numerically speaking, with one exception: women. Women constitute a majority in our society and yet experience the same kind of prejudice, stereotyping, and discrimination typically reserved for minority groups. In fact, as noted at the beginning of this chapter, women suffer more physical and verbal abuse on college campuses than any other group (Youngstrom, 1991). Prejudice and negative feelings toward either sex are referred to as sexism.

As mentioned earlier in this chapter, the study of the prejudiced personality suggests that a racist is also a sexist. Indeed, the struggles for civil rights for African Americans and women are historically linked (Oskamp, 1991). The abolitionist movement of the 19th century was supported by many early feminists. It was no accident that the novel that had the greatest impact on the perception of slavery in the North, *Uncle Tom's Cabin,* was written by a woman, Harriet Beecher Stowe. Abraham Lincoln is said to have once referred to her as the woman who started the Civil War.

But, as with prejudice in general, sexism cannot be explained merely by looking at the authoritarian personality. Instead, sexism has roots both in our social, cultural, and historical traditions and in the cognitive processes we have just been discussing.

Social and Historical Roots of Sexism

Many attitudes pervasive in our society today, including racist and sexist beliefs, are embedded in our history. Others are embedded in biological differences that become elaborated into rigid cultural distinctions between males and females. We consider here both of these roots of sexism.

Historical Roots of Sexism Let's consider here just one example of the historical embeddedness of sexism—the role of science in the maintenance of sexist beliefs. In the 19th century, women were thought to be intellectually inferior beings because they had smaller brains. Women were excluded from education because it was "scientifically" demonstrated that education would make women unable to bear children (Gould, 1985). Other pseudoscientific theories abounded, all indicating female inferiority. Poor blood, watery muscles, and a generally hysterical frame of mind all conspired to keep women where they belonged, according to 19th-century science. Women were deemed unsuitable both as professional scientists and as subjects of study.

This antifemale bias can still be seen in science today. Women are underrepresented in the sciences and engineering (Brush, 1991), as are other "minority" groups. When women do break into a scientific or engineering field, they are typically paid less than their male counterparts (Brush, 1991), with the disparities being quite large. Underlying these disparities are such factors as a male bias in portrayals of scientists in textbooks, inadequate preparation and lack of encouragement in math and science for women, and biased college entrance tests.

Women are also underrepresented in scientific research. Until recently, there were virtually no medical studies on disease that involved female subjects. Our knowledge about many diseases is derived from research using males as subjects. We do not know if the findings are applicable to females (*New York Times,* June 16, 1990). In one massive study on the effect of cholesterol on heart disease, all 4,000 subjects were males. In another, the effects of taking aspirin on heart disease were examined in 22,000 medical doctors, all male. Not only are females excluded from the subject samples, but diseases that primarily affect females, including ovarian cancer, osteoporosis, and even breast cancer, receive less research funding than other diseases.

Why do these disparities persist? For one thing, most scientific researchers are males. Perhaps like Freud—for whom women were a "dark continent"—they don't want to "complicate" their research and make it more expensive by using both male and female subjects. Of course, if males are the norm, then researchers may simply assume that any findings "probably" would apply to females as well.

The Social Context of Sexism: Gender Roles and Stereotypes We can also look at sexist beliefs from the point of view of real differences between males and females. Obviously, there are physical differences between men and women. There are also some measurable average differences in cognitive abilities and personality characteristics, such as aggressiveness. However, research shows that most of these differences are relatively small (Swim, 1994). Carol Tavris (1990) has suggested that in "their needs, capabilities and values, men and women are not as different as the moral majority or cultural feminists believe."

Children become aware of differences between males and females and of their own gender identity at about age 2 (Schaffer, 1981). This **gender identity,** which refers to a person's awareness of belonging to one of the two sexes, is encouraged by parents from the moment little girls are wrapped in pink blankets and little boys in blue. The awareness of gender leads to the understanding of **gender roles,** which consist of observable behavior that, according to society, marks the person as male or female (Schaffer, 1981). Gender roles are not unique to our society; every society makes assumptions about what activities, abilities, and social roles are appropriate for males and females. What does vary from one society to another is the content of those roles.

The existence of gender roles leads to **gender role stereotypes,** rigid ideas about how males and females act and must act. Gender role stereo-

gender identity A person's awareness of belonging to one of the two sexes.

gender role Observable behavior that, according to society, marks a person as male or female.

gender role stereotypes Rigid ideas about how males and females should act.

Carol Tavris and Alice Baumgardner (1986) asked 2,000 children, grades 3 to 12, "If you woke up tomorrow and discovered that you were a (boy/girl), how would your life be different?" The results of this study cast a bright light on the sexism endemic in our culture.

Elementary school boys described their answers as "The Great Disaster" and "The Fatal Dream." What would happen if these boys suddenly found themselves to be girls? A sample of some answers:

"People would all be better than me."

"I'd kill myself."

"I would hope that it was a dream."

The girls, on the other hand, wrote:

"People would take me seriously."

"My life would be easier."

"My daddy would love me now and have more time for me."

The boys were concerned about how they would look as girls. Would they be attractive or beautiful? Appearances counted for everything for girls because, as one boy said, "No one would care about my personality." Girls did not seem to be concerned about being "handsome," but they did allow that it would be nice not to have to spend all that time getting ready for school.

Boys were hostile about doing female activities because "girls cannot get to do anything that's fun." Girls thought it would be wonderful to do all the things they couldn't do as girls. For example, they could "run for president" or "take math and science courses" or "Dad would let me go to college."

Girls thought that life would simply be better if they were boys. They would be treated better and they would not have to carry the fear of rape with them. Boys worried about their safety if they were girls. Responses of both boys and girls may be said to reflect a fundamental contempt for females in our society by both sexes.

---

*R*igid gender role stereotypes lead everyone, men and women alike, to live within constraining limitations. In-group, out-group thinking is certainly one of the processes at work in the creation and maintenance of these stereotypes. What other processes and cognitive errors to you think contribute to gender role stereotypes? What conditions might lead to the sort of controlled processing that enables people to overcome sexist thinking?

types in our society have been consistent over the years (Spence, 1985). Men are commonly viewed as aggressive, independent, and ambitious. Women are viewed as affectionate, gentle, and sensitive (Oskamp, 1991). Notice that males are seen as having traits that are instrumental, useful for getting tasks done, whereas women are stereotyped as having expressive characteristics, helpful in relationships. These stereotypes have profound effects on the self-concepts of boys and girls; see the featured discussion "The Effects of Gender Role Stereotyping on Children."

The presumed masculine traits of self-confidence and assertiveness may be involved in the somewhat puzzling finding that girls, much more than boys, attribute failure to low ability rather than low motivation. Recall from Chapter 4 that attribution for failure to a stable cause (low ability) has long-term negative consequences. There is also evidence that girls respond to the threat of failure by decreasing their motivation (Ross & Nisbett, 1991). This is the case despite the fact that girls tend to be more highly praised by their teachers and receive less criticism than boys in elementary school (Dweck & Goetz, 1978).

Gender role stereotypes tell us that women cannot operate a power saw or build a house. Competent individuals like this woman belie gender stereotypes.

In fact, however, the positive feedback given to girls is more likely to relate to nonintellectual behaviors such as neatness, whereas boys were more likely to receive reinforcement for academic behaviors (Dweck, 1975; Dweck, Davidson, Nelson, & Enna, 1978). It seems clear that some subtle and other not so subtle cues reinforce boys for assertive academic behavior whereas girls are rewarded for "proper" behavior.

Gender role stereotypes can be positive as well as negative. For example, women have sometimes been characterized as more peace loving, moral, empathic, cooperative, and willing to live in harmony with others. Carol Tavris (1990) disabuses us of those notions: There is no empirical evidence that women are "naturally more pacifistic, empathic or earth loving than men." By their very nature, stereotypes, whether positive or negative, oversimplify.

Cognitive Roots of Sexism

We have seen that gender is one of the most salient characteristics, if not *the* most salient characteristic, human beings possess. It is therefore one of our most basic human categories. To realize how basic this distinction is, you need only be in the presence of a person whose gender is unclear. You are likely to experience a profound sense of confusion and discomfort.

As we have seen, human beings move naturally from categories to stereotypes and then on to other predictable assumptions. These assumptions are embedded in the context of our social lives and in the gender role stereotypes described earlier. What cognitive processes are at work here?

The Male Norm Because males are dominant, they are perceived as the "majority" even though they are a slight minority in terms of numbers. In their more powerful social roles, they have control over society's information, values, and forms of expression. They can thus imply, in both intentional and unintentional ways, that males are the standard against which all human beings are legitimately evaluated and judged. Let's consider how the male norm is expressed in two areas: psychological characterizations and stereotypes of nationalities.

Carol Tavris (1990) suggests that when psychological and social differences between women and men are described, women are implicitly compared to a male standard or norm. Women are seen as having "problems" when they differ from this male norm. A typical psychological profile might read, "Women have lower self-esteem than men do; women do not value their efforts as much as men do; women have more difficulty developing a separate sense of self." Tavris points out that if women had been considered the norm, the results might have read like this: "Men are more conceited than women; men are not as realistic as women in assessing their abilities; men have more difficulty in forming and maintaining attachments." Both of these sets of "conclusions" are biased, but we can easily see the bias in the description of men based on women's norms. The bias is not so clear when women are characterized in terms of male standards. This is a characterization with which we are familiar.

Other evidence suggests that people tend, consciously or not, to use the male as the standard for evaluating behavior. The stereotype of a mature and competent adult is much more similar to that of a mature and competent male than to a mature and competent female (Broverman, Vogel, Broverman, Clarkson, & Rosenkranz, 1972). In one study, Alice Eagly and Mary Kite (1987) asked subjects to describe people of various nationalities. The traits subjects mentioned were (stereo)typical of males of those nationalities rather than females. For example, Japanese people were described as industrious, competitive, proud, and ambitious, as were Japanese men (Table 5-4). The traits used to describe Japanese women—conservative, kind, devoted to others, and so on—were different from the attributes used

TABLE 5-4

TRAITS ASSIGNED TO JAPANESE NATIONALS, MEN, AND WOMEN

Japanese Nationality		Japanese Men		Japanese Women	
Trait	Percent	Trait	Percent	Trait	Percent
Family oriented	75.1	Traditional	80.4	Family oriented	78.4
Industrious	73.9	Industrious	80.1	Traditional	77.6
Traditional	72.6	Efficient	76.6	Honest	74.2
Intelligent	71.6	Proud	76.2	Conservative	73.4
Competitive	71.5	Family oriented	74.8	Efficient	71.2
Proud	70.4	Never give up	74.6	Conforming	70.8
Efficient	68.0	Competitive	74.4	Kind	68.0
Ambitious	67.3	Intelligent	73.2	Religious	67.9
		Ambitious	72.7	Devoted to others	67.7
				Understanding	67.1

Adapted from Eagly and Kite, 1987.

to portray the nationality. This pattern was found to be generally true for the 28 countries in this study.

Eagly and Kite attribute this tendency to equate the traits of men with the stereotypes of their nationalities to the higher status and power of men. Their higher status means that men will influence the events by which their country and its citizens are perceived. This perception leads people to equate males with "all people."

Social Roles Theory   In her *social roles theory*, Eagly (1987) argued that the relatively small differences existing between the sexes are exaggerated by the different roles the men and women occupy in society. She also argues that these real and imagined differences between the sexes become intensified because we assume that the nature of men and the nature of women are reflected by the social roles that history, biology, and chance have given them. Here we see the fundamental attribution error at work—we attribute qualities to people's internal natures more readily than to circumstances, situations, or the roles they play. When we perceive women as less powerful and more submissive than men, we assume it is because they are inherently weak and inferior. We overlook the fact that they are acting out the roles society has given them.

Eagly and Johnson (1990) reviewed the research on leadership roles of men and women in groups. Researchers had long assumed that women would lead in a more interpersonal way and that men would lead in a task-oriented way. This stereotype did not hold up under closer scrutiny. Eagly and Johnson found that both sexes lead in precisely the same way when they occupy powerful positions in organizations.

REDUCING PREJUDICE

A rather gloomy conclusion that may be drawn from the research on the cognitive processing of social information is that normal cognitive functioning leads inevitably to the development and maintenance of social stereotypes (Mackie, Allison, Worth, & Asunción, 1992). Social psychologists have investigated the strategies that people can use to reduce prejudice and intergroup hostility. In the following sections we explore some of these actions.

Contact Between Groups

In his book *The Nature of Prejudice* (1954), Gordon Allport proposed the **contact hypothesis.** According to this hypothesis, contact between groups will reduce hostility when the participants have *equal status* and a *mutual goal*. However, the contact hypothesis has not been strongly supported by research evidence (Miller & Brewer, 1984). Even if there is friendly contact, people still manage to defend their stereotypes. Friendly interaction between individual members of different racial groups may have little effect on their prejudices because the person they are interacting with may be

contact hypothesis The hypothesis that contact between groups will reduce hostility when the participants have equal status and a mutual goal.

seen as exceptional and not representative of the out-group (Horwitz & Rabbie, 1989).

In one study, two groups of boys at a summer camp were made to be competitive and then hostile toward each other (Sherif, Harvey, White, Hood, & Sherif, 1961). At the end of the camp experience, when the researchers tried to reduce the intergroup hostility, they found that contact between the groups and among the boys was not sufficient to reduce hostility. In fact, contact only made the situation worse. It was only when the groups had to work together in pulling a vehicle out of the mud so that they could continue on a long awaited trip that hostility was reduced. This cooperation on a goal that was important to both groups is called a *superordinate goal,* which is essentially the same as Allport's notion of a mutual goal.

Further evidence that under certain circumstances contact does lead to a positive change in the image of an out-group member comes from more recent research. College students were asked to interact with another student described as a former patient at a mental hospital (Desforges et al., 1991). Students were led to expect that the former patient would behave in a manner similar to a typical mental patient. Some of the subjects were initially prejudiced toward mental patients and others were not. After working with the former mental patient in a 1-hour-long cooperative task, the initially prejudiced subjects did show a positive change in their feelings about the former patient.

As shown in Figure 5-6, subjects experienced a three-stage alteration. At first they formed a category-based impression: "This is a former mental patient, and this is the way mental patients behave." But equal status and the necessity for cooperation (Allport's two conditions) compelled the subjects to make an adjustment in their initial, automatically formed impression (Fiske & Neuberg, 1990). This is the second stage. Finally, once the adjustment was made, subjects generalized the change in feelings to other mental patients (although they might have concluded, as tends to be more common, that *this* patient was different from other former mental patients). Note that the readjustment of the subjects' feelings toward the former mental patient was driven by paying attention to the personal characteristics of that individual.

In another setting (a school room), Eliot Aronson found that the use of tasks that require each person to solve some part of the whole problem reduces prejudice among school children (Aronson, Blaney, Stephan, Sikes, & Snapp, 1978). This approach, called the *jigsaw classroom,* requires that

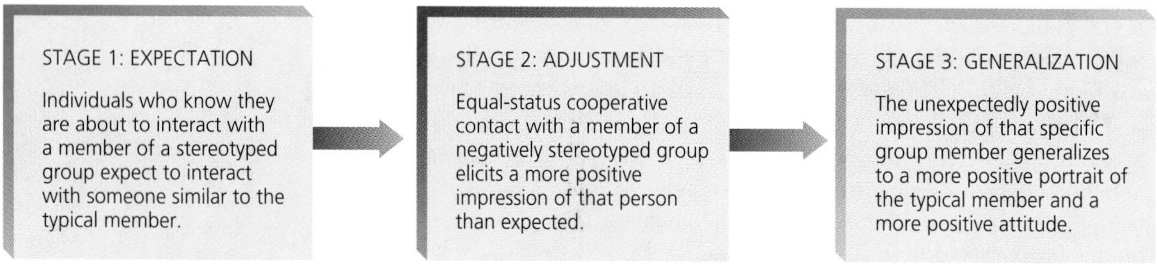

FIGURE 5-6 *Postulated three stages in the alteration of characteristics attributed to the typical group member and general attitudes toward the group through structured cooperative contact with a group member.*
From Desforges et al., 1991

STAGE 1: EXPECTATION	STAGE 2: ADJUSTMENT	STAGE 3: GENERALIZATION
Individuals who know they are about to interact with a member of a stereotyped group expect to interact with someone similar to the typical member.	Equal-status cooperative contact with a member of a negatively stereotyped group elicits a more positive impression of that person than expected.	The unexpectedly positive impression of that specific group member generalizes to a more positive portrait of the typical member and a more positive attitude.

each group member be assigned responsibility for a part of the problem. Group members then share their knowledge with everyone else. The concept works because the problem cannot be solved without the efforts of all members; thus, each person is valued. This technique also tends to increase the self-esteem of members of different ethnic groups because their efforts are valued.

Does the contact hypothesis work? Yes, but with very definite limits. It seems that both parties have to have a goal they both want and cannot achieve without the other. This superordinate goal also has to compel both to attend to each other's individual characteristics. It also seems to be important that they be successful in obtaining that goal.

Even when all of these conditions are met, individuals may revert to their prior beliefs when they leave the interaction. Palestinians and Israelis meeting in Egypt to resolve differences and conclude peace may find their stereotypes of the other side lessening as they engage in face-to-face, equal, and (perhaps) mutually rewarding contact. But when they go home, the pressure from other members of their groups may compel them to take up their prior beliefs again.

Personalizing Out-Group Members

According to Henri Tajfel (1982), the Nazis attempted to deny Jews and others their individuality, their identity, by defining them as outside the category of human beings, as *Untermenschen*, subhumans. This dehumanizing made it easy for even "humane" individuals to brutalize and kill because they did not "see" the individual men, women, and children who were their victims (Horwitz & Rabbie, 1989).

If dehumanizing people makes it easier to be prejudiced, even to carry out the worst atrocities, then perhaps humanizing people, *personalizing* them, can reduce stereotyping and prejudice. People are less likely to use gender stereotypes, for example, when they have the time to process information that tells them about the distinctive traits of individual males and females (Pratto & Bargh, 1991). Humanizing members of a group does not necessarily mean that we must know or understand each individual in that group (Bodenhausen, 1993). It means we understand that we and they have a shared humanity and that we all feel the same joys and pains. Overall, although personalization is not always successful, especially if the individual is disliked, it does make it more difficult for people to act in a prejudiced manner (Fiske & Neuberg, 1990).

In the movie *Schindler's List* (1993), an event occurs that illustrates the notion of humanizing the other group. Schindler has managed to save 1,200 Jews otherwise destined for the gas chambers by employing them in his factory. Schindler knows that the German guards have orders to kill all the Jews should the war end.

When news comes that the war is over, the guards stand on a balcony overlooking the factory floor, their weapons pointed at the workers. But these Germans have had contact with the Jews; they have seen Schindler treat them humanely, and they have heard them praying and celebrating the

Sabbath. Schindler, desperate to save his charges, challenges the Germans: "Do you want to go home as men or as murderers?" The guards hesitate and then slowly leave. Did the Germans put up their weapons out of a sense of shared humanity, or were they simply tired of killing people? In any event, the Jews survived.

Reducing the Expression of Prejudice Through Social Norms

In the spring of 1989, four African American students at Smith College received anonymous notes containing racial slurs. The incident led to campus-wide protests. It also inspired an experiment designed to determine the most effective way to deter such expressions of hatred (Blanchard, Lilly, & Vaughn, 1991). The answer? Attack the behaviors, the acts of hatred themselves, not people's feelings about racial issues.

In one experiment, students were asked how they felt the college should respond to these anonymous notes. Some subjects then "overheard" a confederate of the experimenters express the opinion that the letter writer, if discovered, should be expelled. Other subjects "overheard" the confederate justify the letters by saying the African American students probably did something to deserve it. The study showed that clear antiracist statements (the person should be expelled) set a tone for other students that discouraged the expression of racial sentiment. Because, as we have seen, racial stereotypes are automatically activated and resistant to change, the best way to discourage racial behavior is through the strong expression of social norms—disapproval from students, campus leaders, and the whole college community (Cook, 1984).

Another kind of hatred—homophobia—has been deflected in recent years by appeal to social norms as well as by the threat of social sanctions. The Gay and Lesbian Alliance Against Defamation (GLAAD), increasingly supported by public opinion, has targeted pop musicians who sing antigay lyrics and make antigay statements. Facing the cancellation of concerts and TV appearances, targeted musicians such as reggae star Shabba Ranks and rap singer Marky Mark have apologized and promised to refrain from spouting hate lyrics (Farber, 1993).

Is it realistically possible to reduce racist, sexist, homophobic, and ethnic hate acts? Strengthening social norms may be our best hope in approaching this problem. We turn now to one success story—the U.S. Army. Granted, it is a special case, and not all the lessons learned are applicable to other situations. But even in this case, things seemed hopeless at one point. The Army began to attack its problems only when it was about to disintegrate because of racial hatred.

A Success Story: The Disarming of Racism in the U.S. Army

During the Vietnam War, race relations in the U.S. Army were abysmal (Moskos, 1991). Fights between white and African American soldiers were

Racist animosity is particularly noxious when individuals have to be able to rely on one another. Partly because of this need for solidarity, the U.S. Army has made a concerted effort to eliminate racism within its ranks. Their strategies include equal-status interaction, a focus on superordinate goals, and a strict no discrimination policy.

commonplace in Army life in the 1970s. By the early 1980s the Army was making an organized and determined effort to eliminate racial prejudice and animosities. It appears to have succeeded admirably. Many of the strategies the Army used are based on principles discussed in this chapter. Let's consider what they were.

One important strategy used by the Army was the *level playing field* (Moskos, 1990, 1991). This means that from basic training onward, everyone is treated the same—the same haircuts, the same uniforms, the same rules and regulations. This helps to reduce advantages and handicaps and to make everyone equal. The Army also has a basic remedial education program that is beneficial for those with leadership qualities but deficits in schooling.

A second factor is a rigid *no discrimination policy*. Any expression of racist sentiments results in an unfavorable rating and an end to a military career. This is not to say that officers are free of racist sentiments; it merely means that officers jeopardize their careers if they express or act on such sentiments. A racial insult can lead to a charge of incitement to riot and is punishable by time in the brig. The Army uses social scientists to monitor the state of racial relations. It also runs training programs for "equal opportunity instructors," whose function is to see that the playing field remains level.

The Army's ability to enforce a nonracist environment is supported enormously by the *hierarchy* that exists both in the officer corps and among the noncommissioned officers. The social barriers that exist in the Army reflect rank rather than race. A sergeant must have a stronger identification with his or her peer sergeants than with members of the same race in lower ranks.

Finally, the Army's nondiscriminatory environment is visible in its *leadership*. Many African Americans have leadership roles in the Army, including General Colin Powell, the former chairman of the Joint Chiefs of Staff.

What lessons can we learn from the Army's experience? First, a fair implementation of the contact hypothesis is a good beginning point for reducing prejudice. Equal-status interaction and clear mutual goals, even superordinate goals, are essential ingredients of effective contact. Clear and forceful support of the program by leadership is another ingredient. Anyone who violates the policy suffers. At the same time, positive action is taken to level prior inequalities. The Army's special programs ensure that everyone has an equal chance.

Some of these lessons cannot be transferred out of the Army setting. Civilian society does not have the Army's strict hierarchy, its control over its members, or its system of rewards and punishments. But the fundamental lesson may be that race relations can best be served by strengthening positive social norms. When social norms are very clear, and when there is a clear commitment to nondiscrimination by leadership—employers, politicians, and national leaders—individual members of society have the opportunity to transcend their prejudices and act on their shared humanity.

THE MURDER OF VINCENT CHIN REVISITED

Perhaps we can begin to understand now why Vincent Chin was brutally murdered. Two men, driven by a vicious stereotype, by economic hard times, and by a social climate that blamed others (the Japanese) for our own troubles, took out their frustrations on an innocent victim. It's an old story, repeated ad nauseam.

But understanding is not the same as condoning or forgiving. We all hold cultural stereotypes, but we are responsible for expressing or not expressing them. As research shows, many of us do not wish to act on our worst prejudices and fears; we try to inhibit that side of ourselves. Not only are we responsible for our actions, but the leaders of our society are responsible for theirs. When leadership lays down a nondiscrimination policy and backs it up, it works.

LOOKING AHEAD

In this chapter we saw how categorization, as well as the various cognitive biases that are part of our mental apparatus, plays a basic role in the formation of prejudicial attitudes and discriminatory behavior. We saw that prejudice is an automatic response and that nonprejudiced thinking requires a more effortful strategy. We also continued to see how social and biological factors, along with cognitive influences, affect the way we structure the world.

While Chapter 5 looked at prejudiced attitudes, Chapter 6 looks at attitudes more broadly. We will see that attitudes are one more mechanism for making sense out of our social world. They organize information for us, summarize our thoughts, feelings, and intentions about specific issues, and guide our behavior. Like other emotional and cognitive constructs, attitudes help define us, both to ourselves and to others.

CHAPTER REVIEW

1. *What is the relationship among prejudice, stereotypes, and discrimination?*
   Prejudice (negative feelings directed at members of a group), **stereotypes** (rigid, internalized images held about members of a group), and **discrimination** (negative behaviors directed against members of a group) are related phenomena that help us understand why we treat members of certain groups with hostility. Prejudice (or prejudicial feelings) comes in a variety of forms, with **sexism** (negative feelings based on gender category) and **racism** (negative feelings based on apparent racial category) being most common. Stereotyped beliefs about members of a group often give rise to prejudicial feelings, which may give rise to discriminatory behavior.

2. *What evidence is there for the prevalence of these three concepts from a historical perspective?*
   History tells us that stereotyping, prejudice, and discrimination have been with human beings for a long time. Once formed, stereotypes and prejudices endure over time. Stereotyped views of Japanese by Americans (and vice versa) have endured from the World War II era through the present. Prejudicial feelings have also led to religious persecution in the United States against groups like the Mormons.

3. *What are the individual/personality and social roots of prejudice?*
   One personality dimension identified with prejudice is the **authoritarian personality.** Authoritarian individuals tend to feel submissive toward authority figures and hostile toward different ethnic groups. They have rigid beliefs and tend to be racist and sexist. Social psychologists have also explored how members of different groups, such as whites and African Americans, perceive each other. The United States has a long history of racist feelings and behavior. White Americans today may acknowledge that African Americans have received a raw deal, but they may still blame them, at least partially, for their problems. Although few whites today admit to overt prejudice, they may be aversive racists, professing unprejudiced attitudes but still feeling uncomfortable around African Americans. Another form taken by prejudice is **modern racism,** a less open form of racism in which racist sentiments come out only under certain circumstances.

4. *What are the cognitive roots of prejudice?*
   Cognitive social psychologists have focused on stereotypes and intergroup perceptions when attempting to understand prejudice. As humans we have a strong predisposition to categorize people into groups. We do this even when we have only the most minimal basis on which to make categorizations. We classify ourselves and those we perceive to be like us in the in-group, and others whom we perceive to be different

from us we classify in the out-group. As a result of this categorization we tend to display an **in-group bias:** favoring members of the in-group over members of the out-group.

Henri Tajfel proposed his social identity theory to help explain in-group bias. According to this theory we are motivated to maintain a positive self-concept, part of which comes from membership in groups. Identification with the in-group confers a social identity on us. Categorizing dissimilar others in the out-group is another aspect of the social identity process. When we feel threatened, in-group bias increases, thereby enhancing our self-concept.

The in-group bias may also have biological roots. We have a very strong wariness of the unfamiliar—xenophobia—which sociobiologists think is a natural part of our genetic heritage. It may have helped us survive as a species. It is biologically adaptive, for example, for a child to be wary of potentially dangerous strangers. The in-group bias may serve a similar purpose. Throughout history there are examples of various groups increasing solidarity in response to hostility from the dominant group in order to survive as a group. Prejudice, then, may be seen as an unfortunate by-product of natural, biologically based behavior patterns.

Because it is easier to deal with a person based on group-based stereotypes than to find out about that individual person, categorizing people using stereotypes helps us economize on cognitive processing effort. Quick categorization of individuals via stereotypes contributes to prejudicial feelings and discrimination. Automatic language associations, by which we link positive words with the in-group and negative words with the out-group, contribute to these negative feelings. Other cognitive biases and errors that lead to prejudice include the **illusory correlation,** the fundamental attribution error, the confirmation bias, the **out-group homogeneity bias,** and the **ultimate attribution error.**

5. *What are the cognitive roots of sexism?*
Carol Tavris suggests that when psychological and social differences between women and men are described, women are implicitly compared to a male standard or norm. Women are seen as having "problems" when they differ from this male norm. Social roles theory proposes that the relatively small differences that exist between the sexes are exaggerated by the different roles they occupy in society. These real and imagined differences between the sexes become intensified because we assume that the nature of men and women is reflected by the social roles that history, biology, and chance have given them.

6. *What can be done about prejudice?*
Although prejudice has plagued humans throughout their history, there may be ways to reduce it. The **contact hypothesis** suggests that increased contact between groups should increase positive feelings. However, mere contact may not be enough. Positive feelings are en-

hanced when there is a superordinate goal toward which groups work cooperatively. Another strategy is to personalize out-group members; this prevents falling back on stereotypes. It is also beneficial to increase the frequency of antiracist statements that people hear, a form of strengthening social norms. The strong expression of social norms—disapproval of prejudice in all of its variations—is probably the best way to discourage and reduce prejudiced acts.

SUGGESTIONS FOR FURTHER READING

Fiske, S. T. (1993). Controlling other people. *American Psychologist, 48,* 621–628.
   One of the leading social cognitivists examines the relationship between stereotyping and power. Fiske demonstrates that stereotyping is a way of maintaining the status quo for the powerful.

Levin, J., & McDevitt, J. (1993). *Hate crimes: The rising tide of bigotry and bloodshed.* New York: Plenum Publishing Company.
   A thoughtful and thorough examination of the distressing increase in prejudice-driven violence. The authors examine the origins of hate crimes and ask whether such crimes are part of our mainstream culture.

Sniderman, P. M., & Piazza, T. (1994). *The scar of race.* Cambridge, MA: Harvard University Press.
   An examination of current public attitudes on race, showing their complexities and subtleties.

Sykes, C. J. (1992). *A nation of victims.* New York: St. Martin's Press.
   An examination of how fragmented American society has become. Sykes shows that almost every group in the United States claims that it has been victimized and therefore should be compensated in some form.

Wilford, J. N. (1992, February 11). Nubian treasures reflect black influence on Egypt. *New York Times,* p. 29.
   An interesting report on a time before racial prejudice in the Mediterranean region.

Chapter 6

Attitudes

*I*da Tarbell is not a name most of us recognize. A history of American women doesn't give her even a single line (Hymowitz & Weissman, 1984). Yet she was at the center of American life for the first three decades of the 20th century. Teddy Roosevelt hurled the mocking epithet "muckraker" at her. It was a name she eventually wore proudly, for she, perhaps more than anyone else, told the American people about the corruption, conspiracies, strong-armed tactics, and enormous greed that went into "business as usual" at the turn of the century (Fleming, 1986).

Tarbell grew up in Titusville, Pennsylvania. Titusville no longer exists, but in the last decades of the 19th century it was the center of the booming oil industry. It was also the town that would make Standard Oil Company, and its founder, John D. Rockefeller, richer than anyone could imagine.

Tarbell grew up among derricks and oil drums, in oil-cloaked fields under oil-flecked skies. In 1872 her father's business was threatened by a scheme devised by Rockefeller and his partners that would allow them to ship their oil via the railroads at a much cheaper fare than any other producer, thus driving their competition out of business. Frank Tarbell and the others fought this scheme and forced the railroads to treat everyone fairly, at least temporarily. Ida was well informed about the conspiracy and, possessing her father's strong sense of justice, was outraged. She vowed that if she were given the chance, she would make people aware of the greed and dishonesty she had witnessed. At this time she was 15 years old (Weinberg & Weinberg, 1961).

Tarbell decided that she would have to understand the nature of oil. She determined to go to college, become a scientist, and never marry. Now, in the 19th century women simply did not go to college. Most people thought that too much education would endanger a woman's health and, worse, affect her chances of marriage. But Tarbell had made up her mind, and her parents were not deterred by prevailing attitudes. She enrolled at Allegheny College in Pennsylvania in the science curriculum.

In college, Tarbell was a free spirit. She became friends with whomever she wanted, ignored all the unwritten social rules, learned to be critical and disciplined in her work, and graduated with a degree in natural science. After working as a school teacher, she went off to Paris to become a writer. For years she wrote articles and biographies, but in 1900 she started to write about oil. She began to form an idea about a series of articles on the Standard Oil Company, which supplied almost all the oil that was used to light American homes (in the days before electricity).

Although Standard Oil had been investigated on charges of bribery and other illegal tactics by authorities for almost the entire 30 years of its existence, very little evidence existed in the public domain. Tarbell got around that by getting to know one of the company's vice presidents, Henry Rogers, who let her have access to private records. Rogers was unapologetic about his role. He cheerfully admitted that Rockefeller lied, cheated, double-dealt, and used violence, or the threat of it, to build an enormously successful, powerful, and efficient company (Fleming, 1986).

Tarbell's book, *The History of the Standard Oil Company* (1904), appeared in monthly installments in *McClure's* magazine. It was a sensation. It read like a suspense story, and readers couldn't wait until the next month's issue. The book had a readymade villain: John D. Rockefeller. He was portrayed as a money-hungry rogue without a shred of humanity. That's the way he has come down to us 100 years later. After the book came out, he tried to restore his image by giving some $35 million to charity. At the time, he was estimated to be worth over $900 million, a sum equivalent to several billion dollars in today's currency.

Tarbell's work had a tremendous impact on the nation. It led not only to a number of lawsuits against the oil industry for their monopolistic practices but also to federal antitrust laws that dismantled the original Standard Oil Company. Today we have a number of independent Standard Oil companies (Ohio, New Jersey, etc.) as a result of Tarbell's work.

Tarbell completed the Standard Oil articles in 1904, but for the next 30 years she was an important voice in economic and international issues. She never married, continued to write, did what she wanted, supported herself, and in fact became quite wealthy. She remained tough and inquisitive; above all, she maintained her exquisite sense of justice.

Even more remarkable than what Ida Tarbell did was the way she did it. She was entirely skeptical of all the common beliefs of her time. She did not believe in the theory of the inferiority of women, prevalent in the early years of her life, nor did she believe in the turn-of-the-century theory that women were morally superior and evolutionarily more advanced. She joined no organizations or social reform movements. Yet she took on the most powerful men in the country and became a formidable adversary (Fleming, 1986).

What made Ida Tarbell the way she was? To some degree she was no doubt born a fighter. By temperament she was determined, controlled, and unafraid. But her attitudes and behavior were also shaped and informed by her experiences. She grew up in a family that supported her in her independent ways and encouraged her to do what she thought right. She was powerfully influenced by her father, in whom she saw a strong sense of justice. Events that occurred during her formative years motivated and inspired her—and forever altered the way she viewed the world.

The attitudes that Ida Tarbell held played a fundamental role in the way she perceived the world around her. Like other mechanisms of social cognition, they organized her experiences for her, directed her behavior, and helped define who she was. In Chapter 5 we looked at prejudiced attitudes; in this chapter we look at attitudes more broadly. We begin by exploring what attitudes are and what role they play in the life of a person like Ida Tarbell. What are the elements that go into attitudes? How do they flow from and express our deepest values? What are the processes by which we acquire or develop attitudes? And what is the relationship between attitudes and behavior in our day-to-day life? How do attitudes express the relationship among what we think, what we feel, what we intend to do, and what we actually do?

WHAT ARE ATTITUDES?

The study of attitudes has been of fundamental concern to social psychologists throughout the history of the field. Other issues may come and go, dictated by fashion in theory and research and influenced by current events, but interest in attitudes remains. This preoccupation with attitudes is easy to understand. The concept of attitudes is central to explaining our thoughts, feelings, and actions with regard to other people, situations, and ideas.

In this section we explore the basic concept of attitudes. First we look at and elaborate upon a classic definition of the term. Then we consider how attitudes relate to values, what functions attitudes serve, and how attitudes can be measured.

Allport's Definition of Attitudes

The word *attitude* crops up often in our everyday conversation. We speak of having an attitude about someone or something. In this usage, *attitude* usually implies feelings that are either positive or negative. We also speak of someone who has a "bad attitude." In the TV show "Roseanne," the outspoken title character is often told by her bosses that she has an "attitude problem." In this usage, *attitude* implies some personality characteristic or behavior pattern that offends us.

Social psychologists use the term *attitude* differently than this. In order to study and measure attitudes, they need a clear and careful definition of the term. Gordon Allport, an early attitude theorist, formulated the following definition: "An **attitude** is a mental and neural state of readiness, organized through experience, exerting a directive or dynamic influence upon the individual's response to all objects and situations with which it is related" (1935). This is a rich and comprehensive definition, and although

attitude "A mental and neural state of readiness, organized through experience, exerting a directive and dynamic influence upon the individual's response to all objects and situations with which it is related" (Allport, 1935).

What are your attitudes toward . . . Anita Hill, Hillary Rodham Clinton, Jack Kevorkian, Rush Limbaugh? Where do these attitudes come from? What do they do for you?

there have been many redefinitions over the years, Allport's definition still captures much that is essential about attitudes. Consequently, we adopt it here as our central definition. The definition can be broken into several parts, each with some important implications (Rajecki, 1990) (Figure 6-1).

First, since attitudes are "mental or neural states of readiness," they are necessarily private. Scientists who study attitudes cannot measure them directly in the way that, for example, medical doctors can measure blood pressure. Only the person who holds an attitude is capable of having direct access to it. The social psychological measures of an attitude must be indirect.

Attitude:

A mental state of readiness,

organized through experience,

exerting a directive influence on a person's responses to related objects and situations.

Second, if attitudes are "organized through experience," they are presumably formed through learning from a variety of experiences and influences. Our attitudes about, say, appropriate roles for men and women are shaped by the attitudes passed on by our culture, especially by parents, friends, and other agents of socialization such as schools and television. Recall that even though the wider society was not supportive of women in nontraditional roles in Ida Tarbell's time, her parents were very supportive. The notion that our attitudes arise only from experience is too limiting, however. There is increasing evidence that some attitudes also have a genetic element (Tesser, 1993).

Finally, since attitudes exert "a directive or dynamic" influence upon the person's response to objects, people, and situations, then attitudes are directly related to our actions or behavior. The attitudes we hold predispose us to act in positive or negative ways toward the objects of those attitudes. Tarbell's early experience with Standard Oil clearly affected her later behavior.

Attitude Structures

An attitude is made up of four interconnected components:

- Cognitions
- Affective responses
- Behavioral intentions
- Behaviors

To understand this interconnectedness, let's consider the attitude of someone opposed to gun-control legislation. Her attitude can be stated as: "I am opposed to laws in any way controlling the ownership of guns."

This attitude would be supported by cognitions, or thoughts, about laws and gun ownership. For example, she might think that unrestricted gun ownership is a basic right guaranteed by the Second Amendment to the Constitution. The attitude would also be supported by affective responses, or feelings. She might feel strongly about her right to do what she wants to do without government interference, or she might feel strongly about protecting her family from intruders.

The attitude, and the cognitions and feelings that support it, can result in behavioral intentions and behaviors. Our hypothetical person might intend to send money to the National Rifle Association or to call her repre-

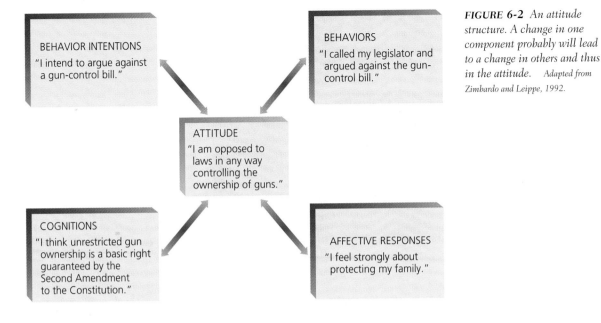

FIGURE 6-2 *An attitude structure. A change in one component probably will lead to a change in others and thus in the attitude.* Adapted from *Zimbardo and Leippe, 1992.*

sentative to argue against a gun-control bill. Finally, she might turn that intention into some real action and send the money or call her legislator.

An attitude is really a summary of an **attitude structure,** which consists of these interconnected components (Zimbardo & Leippe, 1992). Thus, the attitude "I am opposed to laws in any way controlling the ownership of guns" summarizes a series of interrelated thoughts, feelings, and intentions; this attitude structure is shown in Figure 6-2.

As can be seen from the figure, a change in one component of an attitude structure might very well lead to changes in the others (Zimbardo & Leippe, 1992). An attitude structure is dynamic, with each component influencing the others. For example, if a friend's child were injured playing with a loaded gun he found in the house, our gun-control opponent might have a change in her feelings. That neat structure displayed in Figure 6-2 would now be in turmoil. New feelings about guns might lead to new thoughts; intentions might change and, with them, behaviors.

Generally, the affective component dominates the attitude (Breckler & Wiggins, 1989). When we think of a particular object or person, our initial response is usually some expression of affect, as in, "I feel women will make good political candidates." We do not simply have attitudes about war, or the president, or baseball: We like these things or we do not. When an attitude is evoked, it is always with positive or negative feeling, although, to be sure, the feeling varies in intensity. It is likely that our most intensely held attitudes in particular are primarily affective in nature (Ajzen, 1989). Thus, you might think of an attitude as primarily a response emphasizing how you *feel* about someone or something, as primarily an evaluation of the person or object. But keep in mind also that this evaluation is based on all the thoughts and intentions and behaviors that go into the structure of the attitude (Zanna & Rempel, 1988).

attitude structure The interconnected components that make up an attitude. These include thoughts, feelings, behavioral intentions, and behaviors related to the object of the attitude.

Individuals with opposing attitudes toward an issue often have similar underlying values. These women on two sides of the abortion issue may both value life, love, freedom, and human rights but apply these values in different ways.

Attitudes as an Expression of Values

Our attitudes flow from and express our values (Ball-Rokeach, Rokeach, & Grube, 1984). A **value** is a conception of what is desirable; it is a guideline for a person's actions, a standard for behavior. Thus, for example, the attitude that more women and members of different ethnic groups should be elected to office might flow from the value of equality. The attitude that public officials who lie or cheat should be severely punished might flow from the value of honesty. The attitude that individuals in a relationship should share exactly what they think or feel about the other might also flow from the value of honesty. Ida Tarbell placed a high value on fairness and justice and was outraged by the actions of Standard Oil Company.

Notice that whereas attitudes are directed at objects, values are broad, abstract notions. Because values are more general than attitudes, there are few values but many attitudes. Just as an attitude can be seen as a system of cognitive, affective, and behavioral components, so a value can be seen as "containing" many interrelated attitudes. The value of equality could give rise not only to the attitude that more women and members of different ethnic groups should hold office but also to countless other attitudes, relating to the innumerable people, objects, issues, and ideas toward which one might direct thoughts, feelings, and behaviors.

Milton Rokeach, a social psychologist who spent most of his professional life studying how people organize their value systems, argued that there are two distinct categories of values (1973, 1979). He called one category terminal values. These are preferred end states, such as freedom, equality, and happiness. The other category he called instrumental values. These are preferred ways of doing things. Honesty and ambition are instrumental values.

According to Rokeach, two fundamental terminal values—equality and freedom—are especially predictive of a whole range of attitudes. Attitudes about the role of government, for example, can often be predicted by knowing how someone ranks these two values. A person who values

value A conception of what is desirable; a guideline for a person's actions; a standard for behavior.

TABLE 6-1

RATINGS OF VALUES BY PEOPLE WITH PRO AND ANTI ATTITUDES ON ABORTION

Rank	Oppose Abortion	Support Abortion
1	freedom	freedom
2	inner harmony	inner harmony
3	equality	equality
4	self-respect	happiness
5	mature love	self-respect
6	happiness	family security
7	wisdom	mature love
8	family security	comfortable life
9	true friendship	wisdom
10	salvation	pleasure
11	comfortable life	true friendship
12	pleasure	exciting life
13	social recognition	social recognition
14	world of beauty	sense of accomplishment
15	sense of accomplishment	salvation
16	exciting life	world of beauty
17	world at peace	world at peace
18	national security	national security

Adapted from Kristiansen and Zanna, 1988.

equality more highly probably would want the government to take an active role in education, health, and other social welfare issues. A person who values freedom more highly probably would prefer that government stay out of the way and let everyone fend for him- or herself.

Consider a person who rates equality higher than freedom. How might this affect her attitudes on specific issues? A high value placed on equality implies that the individual is more concerned with the common good rather than individual freedoms (although freedom might still be ranked relatively high by that person). This individual might be in favor of "sin taxes" (such as high tobacco and alcohol taxes) to raise money for national health care and might also be in favor of stronger gun-control laws. A person who considers freedom to be more desirable than equality probably would be against sin taxes ("it's none of the government's business if people want to kill themselves") and would also be against government regulation of gun ownership.

When asked, do people account for their attitudes by referring to specific values? And do people on opposing sides of an issue hold opposing values? In one study, researchers measured subjects' attitudes toward two issues—abortion and nuclear weapons (Kristiansen & Zanna, 1988). Next, subjects were asked to rank the (personal) importance of 18 values, such as freedom, equality, an exciting life, family security, and so on, and then relate each value to their attitudes on these two issues.

As Table 6-1 shows, people with different attitudes consider different values important. People who oppose the right to abortion, for example, give a higher ranking to the values "mature love," "wisdom," "true friendship," "salvation," and "a world of beauty" than do people who support the right to abortion. Those who support the right to abortion give a higher ranking to "happiness," "family security," "a comfortable life," "pleasure," "an exciting life," and "a sense of accomplishment" than do those who oppose the right to abortion.

At the same time, both groups shared many values. Both ranked "freedom," "inner harmony," and "equality" as the values most important to their attitude. And differences in the rankings of other values were slight. The results also suggest that people on either side of volatile issues might be much closer in their values than they realize.

What Do Attitudes Do for Us? The Function of Attitudes

Attitudes serve several important functions. First, they *define* us. The person who opposes gun control is telling us something important about herself. Her attitude has a kind of **badge value;** that is, it is an upfront statement about who she is or would like others to think she is (Abelson & Prentice, 1989).

Second, attitudes *direct* our future feelings and thoughts about the objects of those feelings and thoughts. In other words, a negative attitude toward gun control would lead the person holding it to search out and remember information that confirms the attitude. Certainly, Ida Tarbell's attitudes about greedy oil men affected her later action in a very clear way. Like schemas and stories, discussed in Chapters 2 and 3, attitudes are cognitive structures that guide perception and help us fill the gaps when information is lacking.

Finally, attitudes *summarize* our feelings, thoughts, intentions, and behavior for the cognitive miser. When a topic comes up, especially one with which you have some experience and familiarity, your attitude helps you respond. You don't have to diagram the whole attitude structure; the cognitive miser has neither the time nor the inclination to conjure up all the relevant feelings and thoughts. You simply express the attitude. Oh, yes, you say, I would vote for a woman for president, or I support gun control, or I think the government should increase funding of AIDS research. In essence, then, our attitudes help us operate efficiently in our social world.

Several specific functions of attitudes have been identified. Attitudes can serve a *utilitarian,* or adaptive, function when they lead us to value objects that help us reach our goals. Attitudes serve a *knowledge* function, helping us to make sense out of the world by categorizing objects and people. By expressing our values, attitudes can serve a *value-expressive* function. Finally, attitudes serve an *ego-defensive* function when they protect us against our fears and anxieties (Katz, 1960; McGuire, 1989).

Let's consider how racially prejudiced attitudes might serve all four functions. Someone might be prejudiced because if another group is kept down, there are more jobs for her group (utilitarian function). Prejudice

badge value An upfront statement about who a person is or would like others to think he or she is.

might also make life simpler for her, allowing her to categorize people simply by virtue of their membership in a group (knowledge function). If her life feels unsatisfactory and her job and her place in the world seem insecure, her prejudice might enable her to shift her resulting feelings of hostility to others (ego-defensive function). Finally, her prejudice might be expressive of basic values, such as a sense that people of different races are inherently unequal (value-expressive function).

The implications of the functions of attitudes were shown in a study that looked at people's hostile attitudes toward co-workers with AIDS (Pryor, Reeder, & McManus, 1991). Could this hostility be reduced by supplying co-workers with accurate information? Workers viewed a film that showed that working with a person who had AIDS was not dangerous. Workers whose negative attitude had a utilitarian function—they were worried about the possibility of contagion—were influenced by the information in the film. Other workers, however, had strong feelings against gay men; people with AIDS symbolized values they rejected. This was true even when the co-workers had contracted AIDS through a blood transfusion, not through any sexual activity. The workers' negative attitude, in other words, had a value-expressive function. This group of workers was not influenced by the information in the film. In short, attitudes that serve an instrumental function may be influenced by information and reason; attitudes that serve a value-expressive function are more difficult to change.

How Are Attitudes Measured?

What happens when investigators want to learn about people's attitudes on a particular issue, such as affirmative action, illegal aliens, or capital punishment? As pointed out earlier in this chapter, attitudes are private; we can't know what a person's attitudes are just by looking at her or him. For this reason, social psychologists use a variety of techniques to discover and measure people's attitudes. Some of these techniques rely on direct responses, whereas others are more indirect.

The Attitude Survey   The most commonly used techniques for measuring attitudes are attitude surveys. In an **attitude survey,** the researcher mails a questionnaire to a potential respondent or asks a series of questions on the telephone. Because respondents report on their own attitudes, an attitude survey is a self-report measure. A respondent indicates his or her attitude by answering a series of questions.

There may be several types of questions on an attitude survey. *Open-ended* questions allow subjects to provide an answer in their own words (Oskamp, 1991). For example, subjects might be asked: "What qualifications do you think are necessary in a president of the United States?" Although this type of question yields rich, in-depth information, the answers can be difficult to analyze. Consequently, most of the questions on an attitude survey are *close ended,* or restricted, questions like the following:

attitude survey A self-report measure in which a respondent indicates his or her attitude by answering a series of questions on a questionnaire or over the phone.

Are women qualified to be president of the United States?

_____ Yes

_____ No

_____ Maybe

_____ Don't know

Notice that this type of question forces subjects into making one of a limited number of choices.

Another kind of attitude survey is the *rating scale,* in which respondents indicate the extent to which they agree or disagree with a statement by circling a number on a scale. One of the most popular of these methods is Likert Scaling. Likert items ask the person to agree or disagree with attitude statements on a five-point scale; for example:

I believe women are qualified to serve in national office.

1	2	3	4	5
Strongly disagree		Neutral		Strongly agree

Likert's technique is a *summated rating scale,* so called because individuals are given an attitude score based on the sum of their responses.

Because attitudes are mental states, social scientists have to ask questions to discover what they are. This researcher is conducting an attitude survey, perhaps to find out how people feel about a new product, a community project, or a political candidate.

In evaluating election preferences or other attitudes, social psychologists usually are interested in the attitudes of a large group. Since it is not possible to survey every member of the group, researchers conducting an attitude survey select a *sample,* or a small subgroup of individuals, from the larger group, or population. Don't think that you need a huge sample to have a valid survey. In fact, most nationwide surveys use a sample of only about 1,500 individuals.

Although a sample need not be large, it must be representative. As you recall from Chapter 1, a *representative sample* is one that resembles the population in all important respects. Thus, for any category that is relevant to the attitude being measured (e.g., race and ethnicity, socioeconomic class, gender, age), the sample would contain the same proportion of people from each group within the category (e.g., from each race and ethnic group) as does the population whose attitudes are being measured. A representative sample contrasts with a biased sample, which is skewed toward some characteristic or characteristics and does not adequately represent the larger population.

Potential Biases in Attitude Surveys Presidential candidate Ross Perot commissioned a survey in March 1993 that included the following question: "Should laws be passed to eliminate all possibilities of special interests giving huge sums of money to candidates?" Ninety-nine percent of the people who responded to the survey said "yes." A second survey done by an independent polling firm asked the same question in a different way: "Do groups have the right to contribute to the candidate they support?" In response to this question, only 40% favored *limits* on contributions. Ninety-nine percent on one poll and 40% on another poll favored limits on spending. This is a textbook example of how the wording of the question can influence polling data (Goleman, 1993b).

Phrasing is important, but so also are the specific words used in a question. For example, in one survey commissioned some years ago by the American Stock Exchange, respondents were asked how much stock they owned. Much to everyone's surprise the highest stock ownership was found in the Southwest. It seems that the respondents were thinking of stock of the four-legged kind, not the Wall Street type. The moral is that you must consider the meaning of the words from the point of view of the people answering the questions.

Another potential bias is that individuals give opinions on subjects they know nothing about. In one classic study, for example, respondents were asked to rate how they felt about a number of national groups including fictitious groups such as Danerians and Pirenians and Wallonians. Respondents "liked" the first two but were prejudiced against "Wallonians" (Hartley, 1946).

Finally, respondents may lie or, to put it somewhat differently, they may not remember what they actually did or thought. Kipling Williams (1994) and his students asked voters whether they had voted in a very recent election. Almost all said they had. Williams was able to check the actual rolls of those who did vote (not how they voted) and found that only about 65% of his respondents had voted. Now, some may have forgotten, but many simply did not want to admit they had not done something that was the socially desirable thing to do, vote in an election (Paulhus & Reid, 1991).

Behavioral Measures   Because of the problems associated with self-report techniques, social psychologists have developed behavioral techniques of measuring attitudes. These techniques, in one way or another, avoid relying on responses to questions.

Unobtrusive measures assess attitudes by indirect means; the individuals whose attitudes are being measured are simply never aware of it. For example, in one study investigators measured voting preferences by tallying the number of bumper stickers for a particular candidate on cars in a parking lot (Wrightsman, 1969). Other researchers have measured attitudes toward competing brands of cola by searching through garbage cans. Still others have attempted to determine the most popular exhibit at a museum by measuring the amount of wear and tear on various parts of the carpet (Webb, Campbell, Schwartz, Sechrist, & Grove, 1981).

Another example of unobtrusive measurement of attitudes is the lost-letter technique (Milgram, Mann, & Hartner, 1965). If a researcher wants to measure a community's attitudes toward, say, its foreign residents, she might not get honest answers on a Likert-type questionnaire. But, if she has some stamps and envelopes, she can try the lost-letter technique.

This is what the researcher does: She addresses an envelope to someone with a foreign-sounding name at a local address. She puts a stamp on the envelope and then drops it on a crowded street near the post office so that it can easily be found and mailed. As her baseline control, she drops a stamped envelope addressed to someone whose name doesn't sound foreign. She repeats the procedure enough times to get a large enough sample. Then all she has to do is count the envelopes that turn up in the mail and compare the number with names that sound foreign to the number with names that don't. This is her measure of attitudes toward foreigners.

Attitudes can also be studied by measuring subjects' physiological responses when answering questions about their attitudes. *Psychophysiological measurements* of attitudes again involve questions about attitudes, as in surveys, but the focus is not so much on the verbal reply as on the accompanying physiological arousal. Can you, in truth, measure people's bodily responses to attitude issues and get an accurate reading of their real attitudes? John Cacioppo and Richard Petty (1983), who have wrought a revolution in how we study and measure attitudes, make a strong case for it. They point out that any production of emotion by attitudes must be reflected in responses by the sympathetic nervous system, the part of the nervous system that is involved in arousing the body to respond to stress-related situations. For example, the facial muscles, particularly those around the eyes and mouth, appear to react quickly to emotional stimuli.

At the same time, Cacioppo and Petty are very careful about their claims for psychophysiological measurements of attitudes. This caution is especially in order because any physiological response may have several different causes. For example, a researcher trying to assess the degree of emotion some issue aroused in a person might measure the amount of electricity the skin conducts. An increase in skin conductance means greater emotional response. But the greater emotional response can be caused by such factors as stress or the novelty of the situation, not just by the attitude object (Cacioppo & Petty, 1983). The researcher would know there was a physiological response but could not be entirely sure of its cause.

As noted, facial muscle movements seem to be especially promising as physiological indicators of feelings about attitudes (Cacioppo, Petty, & Tassinary, 1989). Depending on the results of research along these and similar lines, the relatively undeveloped field of psychophysiological measurement could make an important contribution to our ability to measure attitudes objectively.

HOW ARE ATTITUDES FORMED?

Attitudes affect how we think, feel, and behave toward a wide range of people, objects, and ideas that we encounter. Where do our attitudes come from? Are they developed, as Allport suggested, through experience? If so, just how do our attitudes develop through experience? And are there other ways in which we acquire our attitudes?

The term *attitude formation* refers to the movement we make from having no attitude toward an object to having some positive or negative attitude toward that object (Oskamp, 1991). How you acquire an attitude plays a very important role in how you use it and how often you use it. In this section we explore a range of mechanisms for attitude formation. Most of these mechanisms—mere exposure, direct personal experience, operant and classical conditioning, and observational learning—are based on experience and learning. However, the last mechanism we will look at is based on genetics.

Mere Exposure

Some attitudes may be formed and shaped by what Robert Zajonc (1968) called **mere exposure,** which means that simply being exposed to an object increases our feelings, usually positive, toward that object. The mere-exposure effect has been demonstrated with a wide range of stimuli, including foods, photographs, words, and advertising slogans (Bornstein, 1989).

In one study, researchers placed ads containing nonsense words like "NANSOMA" in college newspapers (Zajonc & Rajecki, 1969). Later, they gave students lists of words, which included "NANSOMA," to rate. Mere exposure to a nonsense word such as "NANSOMA" was enough to give it a positive rating. In another study, subjects were exposed to nonsense syllables and to Chinese characters (Zajonc, 1968). Repeated exposure increased the positive evaluations of both the nonsense syllables and the Chinese characters.

Generally, this means that familiarity may not, as the old saw goes, breed contempt. Familiar faces, ideas, and slogans become comfortable old friends. Think of the silly commercial jingle you sometimes find yourself humming almost against your will.

In fact, repeated exposures often work very well in advertising. The "Marlboro man," invented to convince male smokers that taking a drag on a filtered cigarette would enhance their manhood, has lasted through a generation of smokers. (The ad has lasted, the original model hasn't. He died of lung cancer.) When we walk down the aisle to buy a product, be it cigarettes or soap suds, the familiar name brand stands out and says, "Buy me." And we do.

Now, there are limits to this effect, at least in the experimental studies. A review of the mere-exposure research concluded that the effect is most powerful when it occurs randomly over time and that too many exposures will actually decrease the effect (Bornstein, 1989). A constant bombardment does not work very well.

Repeated exposures increase liking when the stimuli are neutral or positive to begin with. What happens when the stimuli are negative? It seems that continual exposure to some object that was initially disliked increases that negative emotion (Bornstein, 1989; Perlman & Oskamp, 1971). Say, for example, a person grew up disliking a different ethnic group because of comments she heard her parents make. Then, on repeated encounters with members of that group, she might react with distaste and increasing negativity. Over time, these negative emotions are likely to produce hostile beliefs about the group (Krosnick, Betz, Jussim, & Lynn, 1992). Thus, negative feelings of which a person might be hardly aware can lead, with repeated exposure to the object of those feelings, to increased negative emotions and ultimately to a system of beliefs that support those emotions. Stimuli, ideas, and values to which we are exposed shape us in ways that are not always obvious to us.

mere exposure The phenomenon in which simply being exposed to an object increases our feelings, usually positive, toward that object.

Direct Personal Experience

A second way we form attitudes is through direct personal experience. If we get mugged one Saturday night coming home from a movie, for example, we may change our attitudes toward criminals, the police, personal safety, and a range of other concerns. Or if we have a flat tire and someone stops to help, we may change our attitudes about the value of going out of our way to assist others. If our father's business were put in peril because of the dirty tactics of a large corporation like that of Ida Tarbell's, we would resent such organizations for the rest of our lives. Direct personal experience has the power to create and change attitudes.

Consider the story of Kate Michelman, executive director of the National Abortion Rights Action League (NARAL). Raised as a Catholic, she married at age 20 and dreamed of having six children. She and her husband did not use birth control, in keeping with Catholic teachings. When she had three children, ages 5, 4, and 3, her husband, a graduate student in archeology, abruptly told her he was leaving. She soon found she was pregnant with their fourth child. She realized that she could not care for another baby and still take care of the children she already had. As a devout Catholic, she did not believe in abortion, but she finally decided it was her only option.

At the time—1970—abortion was illegal in Pennsylvania. Michelman had to appear before a panel of four male physicians to appeal for the procedure on the grounds of psychiatric necessity. After a grueling question-and-answer session to gain their approval, she still had to get her husband's written permission. The experience provided her with an epiphany about women's reproductive rights. She realized that unless women had control over how many children they had, they did not have control over their own lives. She also realized that this lack of control threatened women's ability to protect their children and manage their families.

As a single mother, Michelman fought for child support from her ex-husband and struggled to raise her three daughters. She decided she wanted to work with troubled children and became involved, first, in programs designed to assist single mothers and their small children, and then in family planning programs. From there she took on the directorship of NARAL. Clearly, her attitudes about women's reproductive rights—as well as her life's work—were shaped by direct personal experience.

Attitudes acquired this way are likely to be strongly held and to affect behavior. People are also more likely to search for information to support such attitudes. For example, people who had experience with flu shots gathered further information about the shots and were more likely to get vaccinated each flu season (Davison, Yantis, Norwood, & Montano, 1985). People are also less likely to be vulnerable to someone trying to persuade them to abandon the attitude. If, for example, your attitude that the environment needs preserving was formed because you lived near a river and observed directly the impact of pollution, you will be less likely to be persuaded even by powerful counter-arguments (Wood, 1982). For two different examples of attitudes formed through personal experience, see the featured discussions "Forming Political Attitudes: The Case of Lyndon Baines Johnson" and "Forming Political Attitudes: The Case of Janet Reno."

Direct experience continues to form and shape our attitudes throughout life. One study examined the effects of direct experience with government agencies on younger and older individuals' attitudes toward government (Tyler & Schuller, 1991). The experiences involved, for example, getting a job, job training, unemployment compensation, and medical and hospital care. The older people changed their attitudes following a positive or negative experience as much as, if not more than, the younger people. This finding argues against the *impressionable years model*, which assumes that young people are more open to forming new attitudes, and supports the *lifelong openness model*, which emphasizes that people can form new attitudes throughout their life. We should note here that in later years Ida Tarbell came to know John D. Rockefeller's successor, Judge Gary, and wrote a much more favorable second edition to *The History of the Standard Oil Company*.

Learning

Most social psychologists would agree that the bulk of our attitudes are learned. That is, attitudes result from our experiences, not our genetic inheritance. Through socialization, individuals learn the attitudes, values, and behaviors of their culture. Important influences in the process include parents, peers, schools, and the mass media.

As an example, let's look at the formation of attitudes about politics. The formation of some of these attitudes begins early, perhaps at age six or seven. In one study, grade-school students thought that the American system was the

From beginning to end, the presidency of Lyndon Baines Johnson was dramatic. Johnson became president in 1963 when President John Kennedy was assassinated. He left office in a swirl of controversy at the height of the Vietnam War. Much of the drama of Johnson's presidency came from the fact that he had very definite political attitudes and behaved accordingly. An examination of LBJ's life leaves us with no doubt that these political attitudes were formed as a result of experiences early in his life.

Lyndon Johnson was born to an ambitious political father, who failed financially, and a doting mother, whom he perceived as his only true friend. The major theme of LBJ's life was to redeem his father's failure and to meet his mother's expectations (Caro, 1982). At age eight he spoke of his ambition in simple, stark terms: "I'm gonna be President."

As an adult he would pursue that ambition relentlessly. Desperately poor, shamed by his father's failure, haunted by poverty, defensive about his teachers college education, he lusted for power (Goodwin, 1976).

From his father's career, Lyndon Johnson developed the attitude that politics and political power were of paramount importance. Sam Johnson was a well-respected member of the Texas legislature; he represented a district from the state's hill country. Lyndon watched his father at work, observing from a very early age the stuff of politics. From his father's financial ruin, Lyndon developed the attitude that nobody was to be trusted. When Sam

Johnson went broke, everyone turned against him, even the many people for whom he had arranged pensions and to whom he had made loans (Dallek, 1991). During his long political career, LBJ earned a reputation as not trusting anyone. He saw what happened to his father, and much like Ida Tarbell's encounter with Standard Oil Company when she was 15, the experience was seared in his memory.

One of Johnson's hallmarks as a politician was his concern for the poor and oppressed. Johnson felt the federal government had a responsibility to the poor. These political attitudes were shaped by his early experiences with poor farmers in the hill country of Texas during the Depression. During a year's leave from San Marcos Teachers College, Johnson taught poor Latinos in the small town of Cotulla, Texas. He also worked hard to bring electricity and

best and that "America is the best country in the world" (Hess & Torney, 1967). When children are young, parents exert a major influence on their political attitudes, but later peers and the mass media have a greater impact. In fact, by the time young adults are seniors in high school there is a fairly low correlation between the political attitudes of children and those of their parents (Oskamp, 1991). Parents and children may identify with the same political party, but their attitudes about politics are likely to differ.

Instrumental and Classical Conditioning   During the course of socialization, a person's attitudes may be formed through instrumental and classical conditioning, two well-known learning processes. In **instrumental conditioning,** the individual's behavior is strengthened or weakened by means of reward or punishment. Parents may, for example, reward their daughter with praise when she expresses the attitude that doing math is fun. Each time the child is rewarded, the attitude becomes stronger. Or, parents may punish their son with a verbal rebuke when he expresses that same attitude. In these examples, instrumental conditioning serves to impart attitudes.

instrumental conditioning
A learning process in which the individual's behavior is strengthened or weakened by means of reward or punishment.

health care to the poor people in the area. For the rest of his life, he remembered the grinding poverty of the hill country. As president, he proposed civil rights and antipoverty measures that became part of his Great Society program. These policies and actions were shaped by his early experiences working with the poor.

Johnson's attitudes toward education were forged by his college experience. He believed education was the way out of poverty and despair. LBJ's first job out of college was as a public speaking teacher at Sam Houston High School. He threw himself into the job with his usual ferocity. To get students to feel comfortable in front of people, he had them stand up and make noises, any noises at all. " 'Ow, ow, ow' or 'Roaw, roaw, roaw,' " the young teacher yelped, according to the recollections of a former student (Caro, 1982, p. 206). " 'Every-

body's going to do it, so don't worry about it—just have fun,' " Caro recalls Johnson saying. "And we did . . . I have a memory of an enormous number of assignments, and he was terribly strict about them. And then came the heckling, no kidding, heckling. If the heckling was not fierce enough, the teacher would join in. The idea was to learn to keep your head" (Caro, 1982, p. 207). When Johnson later became a power in the Senate, he was a strong advocate of federal support for education. And his attitude toward hard work was shown, much to the dismay of his staff who had to keep up with him, by working 16 hours a day, 7 days a week.

This complicated and fascinating man was molded by his early experiences. Caro concludes:

All the traits of personality which the nation would witness decades

later—all the traits which affected the course of history—can be seen at San Marcos naked and glaring and raw. The Lyndon Johnson of college years was the Lyndon Johnson who would become President. He had arrived at college that Lyndon Johnson. He came out of the Hill Country formed, shaped—into a shape so hard that it would never change. (p. 287)

Why do you think Lyndon Johnson's attitudes about politics and people were forged so early and so powerfully? Under what circumstances have you formed personal attitudes that might match the intensity of those experienced by Johnson?

Simply rewarding people for expressing an attitude can affect what they believe. In one study, subjects took part in a debate and were randomly assigned to one or the other side of an issue (Scott, 1957). Those debaters who were told, again randomly, that they "won" were more likely to change their attitudes in the direction of their side of the topic than those who were told that they "lost."

In **classical conditioning,** a stimulus comes to evoke a response it previously did not call up. Classical conditioning occurs by repeatedly pairing this stimulus (the conditioned stimulus) with a stimulus that does have the power to evoke the response (the unconditioned stimulus).

How might attitudes be learned through classical conditioning? In one experiment, when an attitude object (a person) was paired with positive or negative stimuli, subjects came to associate the person with the positive or negative emotions (Krosnick et al., 1992). Subjects were shown nine different slides in which a "target" person was engaged in various activities such as walking on a street or getting into a car. Immediately before each slide there were very short exposures (13 milliseconds) of positive slides

classical conditioning A learning process in which a neutral stimulus is paired with a stimulus that causes a reflex response so that the neutral stimulus comes to evoke that response on its own.

When a reporter for *Time* magazine asked U.S. Attorney General Janet Reno if she had been urged to tone down her remarks during her confirmation hearings, Reno answered, "A lot of people had different advice on how I should handle confirmation hearings, and I said basically that I had to be myself. I talked about the things I cared about" (Gibbs, 1993, p.24).

Reno's independent spirit, her honesty and courage, made her something of a hero—and an anomaly—when she came to Washington in February 1993. She has been characterized as outspoken (if not blunt), earnest, and irrepressible. She has also become known for her unimpeachable integrity, her devotion to duty, and her inner strength. Reno herself remains unpretentious. She describes herself as an "awkward old maid with a sensible name and big, sensible shoes."

How did this woman come to have the traits that qualified her to be attorney general of the United States? What experiences shaped the attitudes that have made her one of the most respected women in America? Her background offers clues.

Reno grew up in Florida, the oldest of four children. Her mother, Jane Reno, was her deepest inspiration, instilling in her "a rare sense of confidence and a drive to succeed" (*Current Biography,* 1993, p. 48). An investigative reporter for the *Miami News,* Jane Reno told her children, "Good, better, best. Don't ever rest until good is better and better is best" (*Current Biography,* p. 48). Her mother built the house the family lived in, laying the bricks and putting in the plumbing. She was said to be equally adept at wrestling alligators and reciting poetry. The rather eccentric household included an assortment of wild and domestic beasts, including macaws, raccoons, goats, pigs, and skunks. There was no television, so young Janet Reno spent much of her time out-of-doors, and she quickly developed a passion for camping and canoeing. . . . As a girl Janet dreamed of becoming a baseball pitcher, a doctor, or possibly a marine biologist, but she eventually decided to become a lawyer because, by her own account, she "didn't want anybody telling me what to do." (*Current Biography,* p. 49)

Reno's family held out many inspiring models of female independence. Her maternal grandmother instilled in her children and grandchildren a passionate commitment to duty and family. In World War II, daughter Daisy became a nurse, landing with General Patton's army in North Africa and marching on Italy. Another, Janet's Aunt Winnie, joined the Women's Air Force Service Pilots, an elite corps of civilian flyers who tested combat aircraft, towed targets for ground artillery practice, and trained male pilots.

(e.g., newlyweds, a pair of kittens) or negative slides (e.g., a face on fire, a bloody shark). The subjects then reported their impressions of the person. Generally, subjects who had seen the person paired with warm, positive stimuli rated the person as having a better personality and as more physically attractive than did those who had seen the person paired with violent, negative stimuli.

Observational Learning   Although we often learn attitudes by getting rewarded, we can also learn simply by observing. One often hears parents, shocked by the aggressive attitudes and behavior of their child, ask, "Now, where could she have gotten that from?" Research has shown that children may learn to act aggressively by watching violent movies or by seeing their friends fight (Bandura, 1977). Observational learning occurs when we watch what people do and then "model," or imitate, that behavior. For ex-

Toward the end of the war, when the WASPS were disbanded, Winnie came back to Miami with some fellow pilots, a glamorous, tanned, confident crowd who lived in a group house and gave flying lessons. "I thought, 'I can do that, I can do anything I put my mind to,'" Janet recalled, "because those ladies went out and flew planes." (Gibbs, p. 23)

As state attorney of Dade County, Florida, Janet Reno became an advocate of children's rights, prosecuting child abuse cases and pursuing fathers who were delinquent on child support. During these years,

Reno saw firsthand the link between a miserable child and a vicious adult. She fought for better children's services, from health care to day care to preschool education, all on the grounds of crime prevention. (Gibbs, p. 25)

She also experimented with sending nonviolent, first-time offenders into counseling rather than to jail. Her program appears to have been successful.

As U.S. attorney general, Reno has focused on two linked issues she cares deeply about—children's services and a crime policy that focuses on prevention and rehabilitation rather than solely on punishment. Reno argues that prisons are necessary for violent criminals but that nonviolent criminals, particularly drug addicts, need treatment and rehabilitation. She wants to make America a child-centered society, a place where children can grow up in safety. On the subject of punishment versus prevention, Reno has said,

"You can't build enough prisons to house all the people who commit crimes for as long as you want to house them. So you have to keep prisons for people who are mean and bad people—you've got to keep *them* off the streets. But . . . most of the people we send to prison are coming back to the community. . . . Far better that you integrate them into the community in a sensible way and give them half a chance to succeed." (quoted in *Current Biography,* p. 50)

Reno has been criticized for being out of synch with President Clinton, who wants to fight crime with more prisons, more police, and harsher sentences for more crimes. The president's approach in fact reflects the mood of the country more than Reno's does. But it seems unlikely that Reno will change her views—or hold her tongue. She does what she thinks is right, based on profound personal convictions.

---

*J*anet Reno has strongly held opinions and attitudes about many issues. What are the origins of some of her attitudes? By what processes do you think she acquired them? Given that Reno and Clinton come from rather similar backgrounds, why do you think their attitudes toward crime and punishment are so different?

ample, a child who hears her mother say, "We should keep those kind of people out of our schools," will very likely express a version of that attitude.

Observational learning does not depend on rewards, but rewards can strengthen the learning. In the preceding example, when the child expresses the attitude she has imitated, the mother might reward her with an approving smile. Further, people are more likely to imitate behavior that is rewarded. Thus, if aggressive behavior seems to be rewarded—if children observe that those who use violence seem to get what they want—it is more likely to be imitated.

When there are discrepancies between what people say and what they do, children tend to imitate the behavior. A parent may verbally instruct a child that violence is a bad way of solving conflicts with other children. However, if the child observes the parent intimidate the newspaper carrier into bringing the paper to the front door rather than dropping it on the

Social learning theory suggests that we learn many of our attitudes through observational learning—watching what people do and modeling our behavior and thinking on theirs. What attitudes do you think this boy is developing?

driveway, the child has noticed the truth of the matter. The parent thinks she is imparting one attitude toward violence but in fact is conveying another.

The Effect of Television   The mass media play a dominant role in our society. For example, media heroes tend to be a very important influence in the development of our attitudes toward all manner of things: race, gender, violence, crime, love, and sex. AIDS became a national media focus when Magic Johnson announced that he had contracted the disease. Television is an especially pervasive medium. Research suggests that watching television is the main occupation of children and some adults in the United States. Many people spend more time in front of the tube than they do interacting with other human beings (Liebert & Sprafkin, 1988). Some children watch as much as 8 hours per day.

What do they see during those hours? Most get a constant fare of violence. This violence affects the attitudes of at least some children in their interactions with peers. The more violence they see, the more aggressive their interaction style. This effect is strongest for children in neighborhoods where violence is commonplace; the TV violence evidently serves as reinforcement.

In addition to providing aggressive models, TV programs emphasize situations that are linked to violence. After all, most of the characters on television are police officers, or lawyers who deal with police officers, or doctors who deal with police officers. People who watch a lot of TV are likely to overestimate, by far, the amount of violence and crime that occurs in the world (Jowett & O'Donnell, 1992). As a result, they are more likely to anticipate violence in their own lives. In other words, by emphasizing some events and ignoring others, television, along with other mass media, defines reality for us. It directly affects how many of us think and feel *about the world.*

The Effect of Textbooks   Did you find your elementary and high school textbooks dull? Textbooks, especially for areas outside the sciences, can sometimes be bland because it is in their interest to avoid controversy. They also have an interest in presenting the accepted, conventional views held by most people in the society in order to socialize students to prevailing social norms.

In an unusual look at history textbooks in the 20th century, Frances Fitzgerald contends that American history books and courses in grade school and high school neither make students good citizens nor "leave them with very much information about the American government" (1979). Fitzgerald makes a strong argument that the fury of many American college students during the 1960s came in part from their feeling that officials, teachers, and textbooks had hidden the truth about American history and politics, such as how European settlers treated native Americans, how involved the United States was in overthrowing other governments, and so on.

The way in which textbooks treat issues can have serious consequences for the formation of attitudes. Do you recall your history book's unit on the American Civil War? There was probably a section on "Billy Yank" and "Johnny Reb." Here is a version of the common portrayal of Johnny Reb:

> Johnny Reb had always known slaves. They were as much a part of his life as eating and sleeping. Johnny liked the black slaves. He believed that he treated them well. They had rocked him to sleep when he was little. He had played with them as a boy. He probably had worked with them in the fields. But he still wanted to keep the Blacks as slaves. (From *The United States of America* [p. 234] by J. Allen and A. Howland, 1974, Prentice-Hall)

This bit of history is historically inaccurate, since most Confederate soldiers did not own slaves. In fact, in 1862, the second year of the Civil War, the Confederate Congress passed a law exempting all slave owners who held more than 20 slaves from military service. The ordinary Southern soldier began to speak of "a rich man's war, a poor man's fight."

Accuracy aside, what does a passage like this convey? How might it influence attitudes about the Civil War and race? In the passage, Johnny Reb's owning slaves is presented as if it were just a quirk or a bad habit, nothing to get all excited about. Yet the fundamental fact of the American Civil War was slavery. No other civilized country in the world in 1860 had slavery. This is what unleashed the furies of the war, a war whose effects are still felt. Frances Fitzgerald wondered how anyone could learn to deal with issues of slavery and race if attitudes formed in childhood are based on misinformation.

Textbooks can also affect our attitudes, albeit in a more generalized, less obvious way, through their selective coverage. For example, especially in older texts, the role of women, blacks, Asians, and other groups in shaping American history is minimized because little is said. We noted earlier that Ida Tarbell seems to be virtually unknown even in books specifically about women in American history. Texts that present a one-sided picture of history contribute to one-sided attitudes.

Attitudes are formed, then, through a variety of socializing forces, including families, schools, the media, TV, and textbooks. But some attitudes may be rooted at least partially in our biology. We turn to this topic next.

The Heritability Factor

Most theories about the formation of attitudes are based on the idea that attitudes are formed primarily through experience. However, some research suggests that attitudes—and other complex social behaviors—may have a genetic component (Plomin, 1989).

When studying the genetic origins of a trait or behavior, geneticists try to calculate what proportion of it may be determined by heredity rather than by learning or other environmental influences. **Heritability** refers to the extent to which genetics accounts for differences among people in a given characteristic or behavior. For example, eye color is entirely determined by genetics; there are no environmental or learning influences. The heritability of eye color is 100%. If the heritability of a characteristic is less than 100%, then other influences are involved. Height, for example, is about 90% heritable; nutrition also plays a determining role.

Eye color and height are clearly based in one's heredity. But how can complex social structures such as attitudes have a genetic basis? The answer is that genetics may have an indirect effect on our attitudes. That is, characteristics that are biologically based might predispose us to certain behaviors and attitudes. For example, genetic differences in sensory structures such as hearing and taste could affect our preferences for certain kinds of music and foods (Tesser, 1993). As another example, consider aggressiveness, which, as research has shown, has a genetic component. Level of aggressiveness can affect a whole range of attitudes and behaviors, from watching violent TV shows and movies, to hostility toward women or members of other groups, to attitudes toward capital punishment (Oskamp, 1991). In this case, a biologically based characteristic is affecting how one thinks, feel, and acts.

Robert Plomin and his colleagues (1990) were interested in children's attitudes and behaviors related to television viewing. Learning—particularly the influence of parents and friends—certainly plays a role in the formation of TV-viewing attitudes and behaviors. Is it possible that genetics could also play a role? If so, how could we know this? To answer these questions, Plomin studied the TV viewing of adopted children, comparing it to the TV-viewing habits of the children's biological parents and adoptive parents. The question was, Would the child's behavior more closely resemble that of the biological parents or that of the adoptive parents? A close resemblance to the habits of the biological parents would argue for a biological interpretation. The biological parents did not share the same environment with the child. A close resemblance to the habits of the adoptive parents, on the other hand, would argue for an environmental interpretation. Thus, the study of adoptive children makes it possible to calculate the extent to which TV viewing is determined, indirectly, by genetics.

heritability The extent to which genetics accounts for differences among people in a given characteristic or behavior.

Plomin's findings were surprising. There was a very high resemblance between the TV viewing of the children and that of the biological parents. Although shared environment did influence the amount of viewing, the genetic component was much higher. This doesn't mean that children whose biological parents watch a lot of TV are doomed to be glued to the TV for the rest of their days. It simply suggests that there is something in our genetic makeup that may incline us to certain behaviors and attitudes.

Attitudes that have a high heritability factor might be expected to differ in certain ways from those that are primarily learned. Specifically, they might be expected to be more strongly held. Is this in fact the case? There are at least two indicators of attitude strength: A person responds quickly on encountering the object of that attitude, and the person is unlikely to give in to pressure to change the attitude. Evidence suggests that both of these indicators are indeed present with attitudes that have a high heritability factor (Tesser, 1993).

ATTITUDES AND BEHAVIOR

Intuitively, it makes sense that if we know something about a person's attitudes we should be able to predict his or her behavior. In Allport's definition of attitude, given at the beginning of this chapter, attitudes exert a directive influence on the individual's behavior.

There is a rationality bias in all of this—a belief that people will act in a manner consistent with their innermost feelings and ideas. Do we, in fact, behave in accord with our attitudes? Early researchers assumed that a close link did exist between attitudes and behavior. However, a review of attitude–behavior research revealed quite a different picture: Attitudes appeared to be, at best, only weak predictors of behavior (Wicker, 1969).

We begin this section by looking at one early study that appeared to show little correlation between attitudes and behavior. Social psychologists eventually concluded that a relationship exists but is more complex than they suspected. We look at their attempts to unravel the complexities and to thereby show that attitudes can predict behavior. More recently, other social psychologists have argued that our behavior often is nonrational and has nothing to do with our attitudes. We conclude the section by seeing how the rational and nonrational approaches can be reconciled.

An Early Study of Attitudes and Behavior

In one well-known study from the 1930s, a young sociologist traveled around the United States with a young Chinese couple (LaPiere, 1934). They traveled 10,000 miles and visited over 200 places (Oskamp, 1991). The 1930s were a time of relatively overt expression of prejudice against many groups, including Asians. What did LaPiere and the Chinese couple encounter? Interestingly, in their entire trip they were refused service by only one business.

Several months after the trip, LaPiere wrote to every establishment he and his friends had visited and asked the owners if they would object to serving a Chinese couple. About half of the establishments answered; of these, only nine said they would offer service, and only under certain conditions.

The visits measured the behavior of the business owners. The follow-up question about offering service was a measure of attitudes. Clearly, the expressed attitudes (primarily negative) and the behavior (primarily positive) were not consistent. This kind of finding led to a great deal of pessimism among attitude researchers concerning the link between attitudes and behavior.

But let's consider the inconsistency more closely. Our behavior is determined by many attitudes, not just one. LaPiere measured the owners' attitudes about Asians. He did not measure their attitudes about losing money or creating difficulties for themselves by turning away customers. Further, it is much easier to express a negative attitude when you are not face-to-face with the object of that attitude. Think of how easy it is to tell the aluminum-siding salesperson over the phone that you never want to hear about aluminum siding again as long as you live. Yet when the person shows up at your door you are probably less blunt and might even listen to the sales pitch. In the case of LaPiere's study, being prejudiced is easy by letter, harder in person.

To summarize, LaPiere's findings did not mean there is little relationship between attitudes and behavior. They just indicated that the presence of the attitude object (in this case, the Chinese couple) is not always enough to trigger the expression of the attitude. Other factors can come into play.

Reasoned Action

Closer scrutiny of the attitude–behavior research showed that it was when investigators tried to link general attitudes and specific behaviors that the relationship between attitudes and behaviors appeared very weak. When researchers looked at a specific attitude, they were often able to find a very good relationship between that attitude and behavior. However, when researchers asked people about a general attitude, such as their religious beliefs, and assessed a specific behavior related to that attitude, such as praying before meals, they found only a weak correlation (Eagly, 1992).

Martin Fishbein and Icek Ajzen (1975), in their theory of reasoned action, stated that people were relatively thoughtful creatures and were aware of their attitudes and behavior. But they may demonstrate the link between their attitudes and behavior in ways that differ from those expected by social psychologists. A person with strong religious attitudes may go to church only occasionally. However, this does not mean that the person is not committed to her religious attitude system. It simply means that the social psychologist has to measure a number of behaviors that are reasonably related to the attitudes. Strong religious attitudes should be related not only to going to religious services but also to doing charitable work, sending children for religious instruction, expressing interest in theology, and many other behaviors. Fishbein and Ajzen said that if we measure the aggregate, the entire mix of behaviors that are related to the attitude, we will find that attitudes and behavior are in fact related. In other words, to get at the true relationship between general attitudes and behavior, it is necessary to look at many different kinds of behavior, all plausibly related to the attitude.

Theory of Planned Behavior

Continuing their work on attitudes and behavior, Ajzen and Fishbein (1980) proposed the theory of planned behavior. This theory sensibly assumes that the best predictor of how we will behave is the strength of our intentions (Ajzen, 1987). As shown in Figure 6-3, the theory is essentially a three-step process to the prediction of behavior. The likelihood that individuals will carry out a behavior consistent with an attitude they hold depends on the strength of their intention, which is in turn influenced by three factors. By measuring these factors, we can determine the strength of intention, which enables us to predict the likelihood of the behavior.

The first factor that influences behavioral intention is *attitude toward the behavior*. Be careful here: We are talking about the attitude toward the behavior, not the object. For example, you might have a positive attitude about exercise because you believe that it reduces tension. Exercise is the object of the attitude. But you might not like to sweat. In fact, you hate to sweat. Will you exercise? The theory says that the attitude toward the behavior, which includes sweating, is a better predictor of your actions (than your attitude about exercise) because it affects your *intentions*.

The second factor, *subjective norms,* refers to how you think your friends and family will evaluate your behavior. For example, you might think, "All my friends exercise, and they will think that it is appropriate that I do the same." In this case, you may exercise despite your distaste for it. Your friends' behavior defines exercise as normative, the standard. "Wellness" programs that attempt to change dietary and exercise habits rely

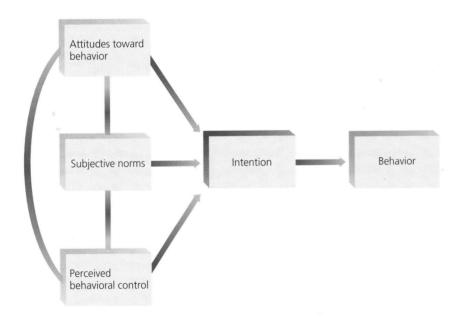

FIGURE 6-3 *A theory of planned behavior proposed by Martin Fishbein and Icek Ajzen (1980). The important determinant of whether or not someone will behave in a particular way is the individual's intention to act. Intention is determined by three factors: the person's attitudes toward the behavior, the norms of her friends and family, and the person's perceived ability to control the behavior.* Based on Ajzen, 1991.

heavily on normative forces. By getting people into groups, they encourage them to perceive healthy lifestyles as normative (everyone else is involved!).

Perceived behavioral control, the third factor, refers to the person's belief that the behavior they are considering is easy or hard to accomplish. For example, you will be more likely to engage in health-related preventive behaviors such as dental hygiene or breast self-examination if you believe that they can be easily done (Ronis & Kaiser, 1989).

In summary, the theory of planned behavior emphasizes that behavior follows from attitudes in a reasoned way. If the person thinks that a particular behavior associated with an attitude will lead to positive outcomes, that other people would approve, and that the behavior can be done readily, then the person will engage in the behavior (Eagly, 1992). People essentially ask themselves if they can reasonably expect that the behavior will achieve their individual and social needs.

Let's use the theory of planned behavior to analyze voting behavior. Assume you have a positive attitude about voting (the object). Will you actually vote? Let's say you think that it is the duty of every citizen to vote. Further, your friends are going to vote and you believe they'll think badly of you if you don't (subjective norms). Finally, you feel that you will be able to easily rearrange your schedule on election day (perceived behavioral control). If we know all of this about you, we can conclude you have a strong intention to vote and can make a pretty confident prediction that, in keeping with your attitude, you are likely to vote.

The accuracy of behavioral intentions in predicting behavior is evident in Gallup Polls. The Gallup organization has been conducting voting surveys since 1936, the year Franklin Delano Roosevelt ran against Alf Landon, governor of Kansas. The record of the Gallup Poll in national elections from 1936 to 1992 is shown in Table 6-2. In general, the polls are quite accurate. Yes, there have been a few exceptions over the past 57 years. They certainly got it wrong in 1948: The data indicated that Harry Truman did not have much of a chance to win. But nowhere in our history books do we hear mention of President Dewey, the governor of New York who ran against Truman and who was projected as the winner. In this case, the pollsters were wrong primarily because they stopped polling a little too early. They had not yet learned that people have other things on their minds than elections and may not start to pay serious attention to the campaign until a week or so before the actual vote. Pollsters will not make that error again.

Although the question "For whom will you vote, candidate X or candidate Y?" might appear to be a measure of attitude, it is really a measure of behavioral intention. Voting is a single act and can be measured by a single direct question. These are the circumstances in which consistency between attitude and behavior is likely to be the highest. Pollsters often try to determine the strength of these intentions by asking such questions as "How strongly do you feel about your preferred candidate?" and "How intense are your feelings?" Although refinements like these may add to the accuracy of voting surveys in the future, what is needed is a concrete way of measuring behavioral intentions.

TABLE 6-2

GALLUP POLL DATA 1936–1992

Year	Gallup Data		Actual Election Results		Error
1992	41.8%	Clinton	43.0%	Clinton	+1.2%
1988	56.0	Bush	54.0	Bush	+2.0
1984	59.0	Reagan	59.2	Reagan	−0.02
1980	47.0	Reagan	50.8	Reagan	−3.8
1976	48.0	Carter	50.0	Carter	−2.0
1972	62.0	Nixon	61.8	Nixon	+0.02
1968	43.0	Nixon	43.5	Nixon	−0.05
1964	64.0	Johnson	61.3	Johnson	+2.7
1960	51.0	Kennedy	50.1	Kennedy	+0.9
1956	59.5	Eisenhower	57.8	Eisenhower	+1.7
1952	51.0	Eisenhower	55.4	Eisenhower	−4.4
1948	44.5	Truman	49.9	Truman	−5.4
1944	51.5	Roosevelt	53.3	Roosevelt	−1.8
1940	52.0	Roosevelt	55.0	Roosevelt	+3.2
1936	55.7	Roosevelt	62.5	Roosevelt	−6.8

Note: Average error −0.45.

The Importance of Conviction

Some of our attitudes are important to us; others are much less important. One reason researchers underestimated the attitude–behavior link is that they did not focus on attitudes that are important to people (Abelson, 1988).

Attitudes held with *conviction* are those central to the person holding them. Examples include attitudes of racial and gender equality, racism and sexism, patriotism, religious fundamentalism, and occultism. Attitudes held with conviction are like possessions (Abelson, 1988). Recall that one function of an attitude is that it defines us; it tells people who we are. The person "owns" her attitudes, proudly displaying them to those who would appreciate them and defending them against those who would try to take them away. For example, someone deeply committed to one side or the other of the abortion issue will likely defend his view against the other side and show his solidarity with those on the same side. Such attitudes will be hard to change, as a change would mean a major alteration in the way the person sees the world.

Because attitudes to which people are strongly committed are hard to manipulate in a laboratory experiment, researchers have tended to stay away from them. As a result, social psychologists overestimated the ease with which attitudes might be changed and underestimated the relationship between attitudes and behavior. If an attitude is important to people, they expect that behavior in agreement with that attitude will help them get

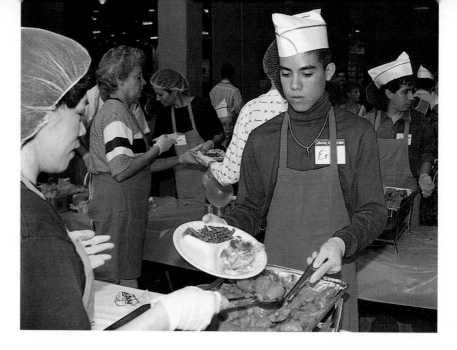

Attitudes held with conviction are closely linked with behavior. This young man would probably not be doing volunteer work if his attitudes toward service and community were not an important part of his self-concept.

what they want. Thus, important attitudes and behavior should tend to be closely linked.

An attitude held with conviction is easily *accessible*. This means that if you ask someone about a subject they feel strongly about, they respond quickly and have a lot of ideas about it. Moreover, attitude accessibility, the ease with which one can bring a particular attitude to mind, is increased by constant use and application of that attitude (Doll & Ajzen, 1992). In one study, researchers measured latencies (speed of response) with respect to questions about women's rights, abortion, and racial integration (Krosnick, 1989). Whatever the issue, people who considered an attitude important responded more quickly than those who considered it unimportant. Important attitudes are more available in memory and are more likely to correspond to behavior. If your stand on abortion or women's rights or gun ownership, or the Dallas Cowboys, is important, you are more likely to act in a manner consistent with that attitude.

You can get a sense of how accessible an attitude is for you by noting how long it takes you to recall it. For example, see how long it takes you to recall your attitude toward the following: living wills, parent–teacher associations, the death penalty, aisle seats, snakes, water filters, political action committees, the clergy, daylight-saving time, baseball. Some of these notions brought feelings and thoughts to mind quite quickly; others probably did not.

If attitude accessibility indicates strength of conviction, we might expect attitudes high in accessibility to be better predictors of behavior than attitudes lower in accessibility. Russell Fazio, who has extensively studied attitude accessibility, investigated this issue in connection with the 1984 presidential election (Fazio & Williams, 1986). The summer before the election, potential voters were asked whether or not they agreed with each of the following two statements: "A good president for the next 4 years would be Walter Mondale" and "A good president for the next 4 years would be Ronald Reagan." The respondents had to indicate how strongly they agreed or disagreed by pressing one of five buttons: "strongly agree," "agree," "don't care," "disagree," "strongly disagree."

The researchers measured the time that passed before respondents pressed the button. The delay interval between the moment you are confronted with an object and the moment you realize your attitude is called the *latency* (Rajecki, 1990). The longer respondents took to hit the button, the longer the latency and the less accessible the attitude. Not only were the researchers able to get a reading of the attitude toward the candidates, but they were able to get a measure of accessibility as well.

Then, the day after the election, respondents were asked whether they had voted and, if so, for whom they had voted. Was there a relationship between latency times and voting behavior? That is, did attitude accessibility predict behavior?

The answer is, it did. Attitude accessibility measured in June and July 1984 accurately predicted voting behavior in November. Those who had responded quickly for Reagan were more likely to vote for him than those who had taken longer to respond. The same relationship held, although not quite as strongly, for Mondale supporters.

The Nonrational Actor

The theories and ideas about attitudes and behavior discussed so far tend to assume a rational, almost calculated approach to behavior. In the theory of planned behavior, if you can get measures of people's attitude toward a behavior, their perception of how important others might approve or disapprove of what they do, and their sense of control over that behavior, then you can predict their intentions and therefore their likely behavior. If there is a significant criticism of the theory of planned behavior, it is that when you ask people to tell you about the components of their intentions, they know that their answers should be logical. If you reported that you voted but you had no interest in the candidates and you thought all candidates were crooks, this hardly makes you look like a logical individual.

Some theorists have taken the opposite approach: They assume that human beings are nonrational actors (Ronis & Kaiser, 1989). Our attitudes may often be totally irrelevant to our behavior. Cigarette smoking, for example, is so habitual as to be automatic, totally divorced from any attitude or behavioral intention the smoker may have. Most of our behaviors are like that (Ronis & Kaiser, 1989). We do them over and over without thought (Gilbert, 1991). You floss your teeth, but your attitude and intentions about dental hygiene are activated only when you run out of floss. Even though you believe flossing is important, and even though you remember that sign in your dentist's office that reads, "No, you don't have to floss all of your teeth—only the ones you want to keep," you now have to act on your attitude. Are you willing to get in the car at 11 p.m. and drive to the store to buy more dental floss? Similarly, if your regular aerobics class becomes inconvenient, is your attitude about the importance of exercise strong enough that you'll rearrange your whole schedule?

Have you ever arrived home after work or school and not been able to recall a single thing about how you got there? In everyday life we often run on a kind of automatic pilot. Our behavior becomes so routine and automatic that we are hardly aware of what we are doing. We are in a state of mind that Ellen Langer (1989) has termed *mindlessness,* one that involves reduced attention and a loss of active control in everyday activities. Mindlessness occurs when we're engaging in behaviors that have been "overlearned" and routinized. In this state we carry out the behaviors rigidly, according to a preconceived pattern and without thought or appraisal.

Mindlessness is fairly common in our everyday interactions. The cashier at a restaurant asks you: "How was everything?" You say that your steak was overcooked, your potato was cold, and the service was terrible. The cashier replies, "Here's your change, have a nice day." In this example, the cashier's question and response were automatic; she really didn't care how you enjoyed your meal.

Langer was interested in studying this state of mind (Langer, Blank, & Chanowitz, 1978). She had a researcher approach people waiting to use a copy machine in a library and ask to use it first. The request was phrased in one of several ways:

> "Excuse me, I have 5 pages to copy. May I use the machine because I am in a rush?"
>
> "Excuse me, I have 5 pages to copy. May I use the machine?"
>
> "Excuse me, I have 5 pages to copy. May I use the machine because I have to make copies?

The researcher also asked to make 20 copies in these three different ways.

Request 2 offers no reason for using the copier first, and request 3 offers a mindless reason ("because I have to make copies"); only request 1 provides a minimally acceptable reason ("because I am in a rush"). If the subjects in this situation were dealing with the request in a mindless fashion, they would fail to distinguish between legitimate and illegitimate (or ridiculous) reasons. As it turns out, any kind of excuse works as long as the request is small. When the request was to make 5 copies, people apparently did not appraise the quality of the excuse as long as one was offered: Having to make copies was just as good as being in a rush.

People snapped out of their mindless state, however, when the request was to make 20 copies. It is clear that when the behavior (the request) had a significant impact, people paid more attention to the difference between bad and good excuses. Although we usually pay close attention to good and bad reasons for people's behavior, it may be that the request to copy 5 pages isn't worth the effort. When the ante is raised to 20 pages, then we are more mindful.

What behaviors do you do each day that fit Langer's definition of mindlessness? Are you aware when you switch from a mindless to a mindful mode? Do you think we are aware when we are acting mindlessly? Would we all function better if we were mindful most if not all of the time?

In sum, people usually behave habitually, unthinkingly, even mindlessly. (For an example of this kind of mindless functioning, see the featured discussion "Mindless Behavior in Everyday Life.") They make active decisions only when they face new situations. Thus, there is a good chance of inconsistencies between our attitudes and our behavior.

The fact that we hold a number of attitudes without really thinking about them means there can be some interesting consequences once we are forced to think about them. Thinking about our attitudes and the reasons we hold them can sometimes be disruptive and confusing (Wilson, Dunn, Kraft, & Lisle, 1989). More generally, the process of introspecting—of looking into our own mind, rather than just behaving—can have this effect.

Timothy Wilson's work has shown that thinking about the reasons for our attitudes can often lead us to behave in ways that seem inconsistent with those attitudes (Wilson et al., 1989). For example, if you are forced to think about why you like your romantic partner, you might wind up ending the relationship in the near future. Much depends on the strength of the relationship. If the relationship is not strong, thinking about reasons might weaken it. If it is pretty strong, then reasoning might further strengthen it. The stronger our attitude or belief, the more likely that thinking about it will increase the consistency between it and our behavior (Fazio, 1986).

Why should thinking about reasons for our attitudes sometimes lead to inconsistency between our attitudes and behavior? The basic answer is that if we have never really thought about an attitude before, then thinking about it may cause us to change it (Wilson et al., 1989). If you are forced to count the ways you love your current partner and it takes you a lot of time to use all the fingers on one hand, you've gotten some insight into how you really think about the relationship.

This explanation was supported by a study in which people were asked their attitudes about social issues, such as the death penalty, abortion, and national health insurance, in two separate telephone surveys conducted a month apart (Wilson & Kraft, 1988). In the first survey, some people were asked to give their reasons for their opinions while others were just asked their opinions. A month later, those people who had been asked to give reasons proved more likely to have changed their opinion. So thinking about reasons seems to lead to change. Why?

The full explanation might lie in the biased sample hypothesis, proposed by Wilson and colleagues (1989). It goes like this: If you ask people why they believe something, they are not likely to say, "I don't know." Instead, they will conjure up reasons that seem plausible but may be wrong or incomplete. That is, since people often do not know their true reasons, they sample only part of those reasons. Thus, they present a biased sample of their reasons. People then assume the reasons in the biased sample are their true reasons for holding the belief. If these reasons don't seem compelling, thinking about them may persuade people to change their belief (Figure 6-4).

FIGURE 6-4 *Individuals often have inconsistent attitudes and beliefs that they have never really thought about. Being forced to think through some of these ideas — such as in response to an opinion survey — may very well lead to attitude change.*

The Rational and Nonrational Actors: A Resolution

Sometimes we are rational actors, sometimes we are nonrational actors. Sometimes our behavior is "coupled" to our attitudes, sometimes it is "uncoupled" from them. Isn't this where we began? Let's see if we can now resolve the apparent conflict. It makes sense to see attitudes and behavior as ordinarily linked, with uncoupling occurring primarily under two kinds of circumstances.

The first circumstance is when an attitude is not particularly important to you. You may not have thought about the attitude object much or have expressed the attitude very often. So in this case you don't really know what you think. True, capital punishment and national health care are important issues. But many of us may not have thought them through. When you are forced to consider these issues, you may be surprised by what you say. This may make you reconsider your attitude.

The second circumstance is slightly more complicated. Essentially, it is when you don't have a clear sense of your goals and needs. Let's go back to the theory of planned action for a moment. The theory says if you expect that a behavior can help you achieve your goals and social needs, you will do it. But people are often not clear about their goals and needs (Hixon & Swann, 1993). When you are not clear about what you want to accomplish, then your behavior will be relatively unpredictable and might well be uncoupled from your attitudes.

For example we exercise, but only sporadically, because we're mainly concerned about looking good in front of our health-obsessed friends. Our reasons are weak, not clear to us, and therefore our exercising behavior is infrequent and unpredictable. But if we or a friend the same age has a heart attack, we develop a much stronger attitude toward exercise. We now know that our reasons for exercising are to improve cardiovascular function, to enhance our sense of well-being, and, in short, to save our lives. Now we change our schedule around to exercise every day, subscribe to *Runner's World* magazine, invest in better exercise shoes, and so on.

In sum, then, our behavior is more likely to be consistent with our attitudes when the attitudes concern an area that is important to us and when the behavior helps us achieve clear and strong social needs. Attitudes we hold with conviction are not vulnerable to uncoupling because we have expressed those attitudes in a variety of situations and have thought deeply about them.

IDA TARBELL REVISITED

Today, Ida Tarbell is not a well-known historical figure. But she held her attitudes with conviction and expressed them courageously. Although she didn't like being called a muckraker at first, she realized that there was a lot of "muck" in American life that needed to be raked. President Roosevelt and the American public came to agree.

Tarbell followed her beliefs with a powerful sense of purpose. Her early experiences, her family's support, and her own strong education and temperament combined to produce a woman whose attitudes and behavior were consistently in accord. No doubt this is an unusual situation. Ida was a rational actor; the coupling of her attitudes and her life's work was fierce and unshakable.

LOOKING AHEAD

In the last five chapters we have considered how we construct our social world. This included how we categorize people and how we reduce uncertainty by using schemas and stories to fill the gaps and make our world more understandable and predictable. We discovered how we use social information to determine why people behave as they do (attribution). We learned that much of what we do is automatic because, as cognitive misers, we are concerned with the most efficient way of handling large amounts of social information. We found that our cognitive miser strategy can lead to stereotyping and prejudice. We also found that our prejudicial tendencies are affected as well by social and personality factors. Finally, we saw how one of the basic mechanisms for making sense out our social world, attitudes, are formed and expressed.

This chapter has focused on the fundamentals of attitudes: how we define them, how we acquire them, how we measure them, and if and when attitudes are linked to, and therefore help determine, our behavior. These are not the only issues concerning attitudes that psychologists, and others, find interesting. Advertisers, politicians, parents, educators, clergy, and dictators have no doubt that attitudes determine behavior. All of these people try to change, alter, and manipulate our attitudes. The broad process by which other people attempt to change our thinking or behavior is called *social influence,* and it is the topic of Part Two of this book.

CHAPTER REVIEW

1. *What are attitudes?*
   Gordon Allport, an early attitude theorist, formulated the following definition: "An **attitude** is a mental and neural state of readiness, organized through experience, exerting a directive or dynamic influence upon the individual's response to all objects and situations with which it is related" (1935).

2. *What components make up an attitude?*
   Attitudes are constructed of thoughts about the object of the attitude (cognitions), feelings (affect), behavioral intentions, and behaviors related to the object of the attitude. An attitude is really a summary of an **attitude structure,** which consists of these interconnected components.

3. *What is the relationship of attitudes to values?*
   Our attitudes flow from and express our values. A **value** is a conception of what is desirable; it is a guideline for a person's actions, a standard for behavior.

4. *What function do attitudes serve in day-to-day life?*
   First, attitudes *define* us. The person who opposes gun control is telling us something important about herself. Her attitude has a kind of **badge value.** Second, attitudes *direct* our future feelings and thoughts about the objects

of those feelings and thoughts. Attitudes *summarize* our feelings, thoughts, intentions, and behavior for the cognitive miser. When a topic comes up, especially one with which we have some experience and familiarity, our attitude helps us respond.

5. *How are attitudes measured?*
Social psychologists measure attitudes through self-report techniques, such as taking **attitude surveys;** through behavioral means, such as counting bumper stickers; and through psychophysiological measures, such as measuring facial muscle movements.

6. *What are the problems with attitude measurement?*
The phrasing and wording of questions on attitude questionnaires has a definite effect on how people report their attitudes. In addition, repondents often do not know or cannot recall what their behavior or attitudes actually were, so their reports are often wrong. Occasionally, repondents do not tell the truth because they want to be seen as doing the positive, socially desirable thing.

7. *How are attitudes formed?*
Some attitudes may be formed and shaped by **mere exposure,** which occurs when we are repeatedly in the physical presence of a stimulus; other attitudes may be formed through direct personal experience. During the course of socialization, attitudes may be formed through instrumental and classical conditioning, two well-known learning processes. In **instrumental conditioning,** the individual's behavior is strengthened or weakened by reward or punishment. In **classical conditioning,** a stimulus comes to evoke a response it previously did not call up. Although learning may account for most of attitude formation, recent research suggests that there may be some **heritability**—that is, that attitudes and other complex social behaviors may have a genetic component.

8. *What is the relationship between attitudes and behavior?*
The strength of the relationship depends on whether the attitude is strongly held, with conviction, or is weakly held. Research shows that strongly held attitudes tend to be firmly tied to behavior and are accessible. However, attitudes may be uncoupled from behavior, usually if the attitude object is not important to the person and if the person is unclear about his or her social goals and needs.

Suggestions for Further Reading

Dalleck, R. (1991). *Lone star rising: Lyndon Johnson and his times, 1908–1960.* New York: Oxford University Press.
This fascinating portrait of a larger-than-life man is a study of attitudes in the making.
Goleman, D. (1993, September 7). Pollsters enlist psychologists in quest for unbiased results. *New York Times,* p. 28.
How social psychologists can make public opinion polling more reliable.
Kaminer, W. (1992). Crashing the locker room. *The Atlantic, 270,* 58–71.
An engaging examination of sexism in journalism and elsewhere.

Part Two

SOCIAL INFLUENCE

We human beings not only think about one another; we also influence and are influenced by each other. Social influence is another area of great interest to social psychologists. How and why do we conform to social norms? To social pressure? How do people convince us to vote for them, buy their product, send them money? Under what circumstances do we mindlessly do what we're told, even if it goes against our values? When do we resist? What changes occur in our individual thinking and behavior when we become part of a group?

Part Two considers the various forms social influence can take. It begins with persuasion—the arguments and strategies we use to get others to change their attitudes or behavior. The discussion then turns to conformity and compliance, exploring the predictable ways we respond to and use social pressure, both subtle and not so subtle. This leads to a consideration of obedience, particularly destructive obedience, which occurs when people obey rules and laws that are immoral or inhumane. Finally, the last chapter of this part explores how the influence of others is heightened by the dynamics of a group situation. As in Part One, a focus of these chapters is how we can increase our awareness of social pressures and processes in order to become more conscious social actors.

Chapter 7

The Persuasion Process

*C*hicago, 1924: Jacob Franks, a wealthy businessman, answered the telephone and listened as a young but cultivated voice told him that his 14-year-old son, Bobby, had been kidnapped and could be ransomed for $10,000. The next morning, while Mr. Franks arranged for the ransom, he was notified that the nude and bloody body of his son had been found in a culvert on Chicago's South Side. Franks was sure that the boy in the morgue was not Bobby because the kidnappers had assured him that this was simply a business proposition. He sent his brother to the morgue to clear up the misidentification. Unfortunately, the body was that of his son. Bobby's head had been split open by a blow from a blunt instrument.

The case was solved quickly. The police found a pair of eyeglasses near the body and traced them to Nathan Leopold, Jr., the 20-year-old son of a prominent local entrepreneur. Leopold denied any connection to the murder, claiming he had

spent the day with his friend, Richard Loeb, the son of a vice president of Sears, Roebuck, and Company. However, both men soon confessed. Loeb, it seemed, had always dreamed of committing the "perfect crime." He had enlisted Leopold, and together they had gone to their old school playground and followed several different boys around. They finally settled on Bobby Franks and pushed him into their car. Loeb hit Bobby over the head with a chisel, and then he and Leopold drove in a leisurely fashion to the culvert, stopping along the way for a bite to eat.

The trial was a media circus. The Leopold and Loeb families hired the most famous trial lawyer of that time, Clarence Darrow, to plead for their sons. The men had already confessed, so the issue was not whether they were guilty. It was whether they would spend the rest of their lives in prison—or hang. The prosecution argued for hanging the murderers. Darrow pleaded for mercy.

Darrow had a tough fight; he needed all his persuasive skills to convince Judge Caverly of his point of view (a jury was not required). He spoke for 12 hours, trying to provide the judge with a rationale for sentencing the men to life imprisonment. He argued that life sentences would serve a better, more humane purpose than bowing to public opinion and hanging those two "mentally diseased boys." Darrow also claimed disinterest in the fates of his clients, an interesting ploy for a lawyer who spoke from morning to night on their behalf. In fact, he suggested that life in prison would be a worse fate than death. At the end of Darrow's oration, the judge was in tears, as were many spectators.

Darrow's arguments hit the mark. Judge Caverly sentenced Leopold and Loeb to life imprisonment for murder and 99 years for kidnapping. Darrow's impassioned, eloquent arguments persuaded the judge to spare his clients' lives (Weinberg, 1957).

Clarence Darrow's task was to convince the judge that his clients' lives should be spared. He knew that the judge favored the death penalty, as did almost all of the American public. If Darrow couldn't change the judge's attitude, he had to convince him that his attitude should not be *applied* in this case—that is, that he should *behave* contrary to his beliefs.

Darrow used all of his powers of persuasion to influence the judge. **Persuasion** is the application of rational and/or emotional arguments to convince others to change their attitudes or behavior. It is a form of social influence used not just in the courtroom but in every part of daily social life. The persuasion process goes on in the classroom, in church, in the political arena, in the media. Persuasive messages are so much a part of our lives that we are often oblivious of the bombardment from billboards, TV, radio, newspapers, parents, peers, and public figures.

Persuasion, then, is a pervasive form of social influence. We are all *agents* of social influence when we try to convince others to change their attitudes or behavior. We are also *targets* of social influence when others try to persuade or coerce us to do what they want us to do.

In this chapter we explore the process of persuasion, looking at the strategies communicators use to change people's attitudes or behavior. We consider the techniques of persuasion used by a brilliant trial lawyer like Clarence Darrow. How was Darrow able to be so effective? He was a famous trial lawyer, highly regarded and highly credible. Was his persuasiveness a function of something about him? Or was it something about the argument he made? What role did his audience—Judge Caverly—play in the persuasiveness of the argument? In what ways might the judge have taken an active role in persuading himself of the validity of Darrow's case? And how does persuasion—both interpersonal persuasion and mass persuasion—affect all of us every day as we go about our lives? These are some of the questions addressed in this chapter.

THE YALE COMMUNICATION MODEL

What is the best way to communicate your ideas to others and persuade them to accept your point of view? An early view suggested that the most

persuasion The application of rational and/or emotional arguments to convince others to change their attitudes or behavior.

TABLE 7-1

PRIMARY COMMUNICATION VARIABLES IN THE YALE COMMUNICATION MODEL

Communicator	Message	Audience
Credibility	Argument type	General persuasibility
Expertise	Rational versus emotional	Knowledge and prior beliefs
Trustworthiness	Positive versus negative	Demographic characteristics
Attractiveness	Message style	Age
Familiarity	Delivery	Gender
Likability	Language	Socioeconomic status
Similarity	Presentation	Personality characteristics
Power	Implicit versus explicit conclusions	Self-esteem
Resource control	One-sided versus two-sided arguments	Effects of active participation
Desire for compliance	Ordering of arguments	
Surveillance	Amount of material	
	Length	
	Use of repetition	
	Extremity of position	

Adapted from McGuire, 1985.

effective approach to persuasion was to present logical arguments that showed people how they would benefit from changing their attitudes. This view was formulated by Carl Hovland, who had worked for the U.S. government in its propaganda efforts during World War II. After the war he returned to Yale University, where he gathered a team of thirty co-workers and began to systematically study the process of persuasion. Out of their efforts came the **Yale communication model** (Hovland, Janis, & Kelley, 1953).

According to the Yale model, the most important factors comprising the communication process are expressed by the question "Who says what to whom by what means?" This question suggests that there are four factors involved in persuasion. The "who" refers to the *communicator,* the person making the persuasive argument. The "what" refers to the persuasive *message,* its organization and content. The "whom" is the target of the persuasive message, the *audience.* Finally, the "means" points to the importance of the *channel* or medium through which the message is conveyed, such as television, radio, or interpersonal, face-to-face communication. For each factor, there are several variables that can potentially influence the persuasion process. Shown in Table 7-1 are the variables that affect the most thoroughly researched factors (the communicator, the message, and the audience).

These four factors are not independent of each other; they interact to create a persuasive effect. In practice, the content and presentation of the message depend on the communicator, the audience, and the channel. Darrow carefully chose his messages according to what arguments best suited the judge, the public, the trial setting, and his own preferences. We turn now to a discussion of the four factors, considering selected variables within each component. We also look at how the factors interact with each other.

Yale communication model
A model used to investigate the effects of four factors on the persuasiveness of a communication. These factors are: (1) the communicator, (2) the persuasive message, (3) the audience, (4) the channel, or medium.

Credibility is the most important element affecting a communicator's ability to persuade. How credible—that is, trustworthy and knowledgeable—do you think this audience of press corps members finds President Clinton?

The Communicator

Have you ever seen a late-night "infomercial" on TV? These half-hour commercials usually push a "miracle" product, such as the car wax that can supposedly withstand a direct hit from a hydrogen bomb. The car is vaporized but the wax survives. There is an "expert" (usually the inventor) who touts the product's virtues. Do you believe what this person tells you? Many people must, given the large amounts of money made from infomercials. However, many people clearly are not convinced. If you are not persuaded, one thing you may focus on is the communicator. You may find yourself questioning this fellow's integrity (since he will profit by persuading you to buy the atomic car wax) and consequently disbelieving his claims. In other words, you question his credibility.

Credibility: Expertise and Trustworthiness   Clarence Darrow knew the importance of **credibility**—the power to inspire belief. During his final arguments in the Leopold and Loeb case, Darrow continually tried to undermine the prosecution's credibility and to increase his own credibility in the eyes of the judge. For example, Darrow said of his opponent:

> I have heard in the last six weeks nothing but the cry for blood. I have heard from the office of the state's attorney only ugly hate. I have seen a court urged . . . to hang two boys, in the face of science, in the face of philosophy, in the face of the better and more humane thought. (Weinberg, 1957, p. 134)

Although other variables are important, including a communicator's perceived attractiveness and power, credibility is the most critical variable affecting the ability to persuade. Credibility has two components: expertise and trustworthiness. Expertise refers to a communicator's credentials and

credibility The believability of a communicator; the most critical factor affecting a communicator's ability to persuade.

stems from the person's training and knowledge. Trustworthiness refers to the audience's assessment of the communicator's character as well as his or her motives for delivering the message. We ask, "Why is this person trying to convince us?" Trustworthiness may be diminished when we perceive that the communicator has something to gain from persuading us.

Expertise and trustworthiness do not always go together. A communicator may be high in one but low in the other. A research physician speaking about a new drug to treat AIDS may have expertise and derive credibility from that expert knowledge. But if we discover that the physician stands to gain something from sales of the drug, we probably will question her trustworthiness. We wonder about her character and motives and may no longer consider her a credible source.

A political figure with the unfortunate mix of high expertise, low trustworthiness was President Richard Nixon. He was highly knowledgeable on matters of state but was not perceived as very trustworthy. During his period of political prominence, a poster appeared that depicted him looking particularly shifty and asked, "Would you buy a used car from this man?" Even before that—in fact, from the beginning of his political career—he was known as "tricky Dick." In contrast, a source can be highly trustworthy but low in expertise. This was the case with President Ronald Reagan. During speeches he often used unsubstantiated statistics, sending his aides scrambling for sources. However, the public generally saw him as trustworthy. People *wanted* to believe him. Public opinion surveys showed again and again that a majority of the public viewed President Reagan as personally attractive and likable, and these qualities prime us to accept a persuader's message (Roskos-Ewoldsen & Fazio, 1992).

Trustworthiness is, in part, a judgment about the motives of the communicator. If someone is trying very hard to persuade us, we are likely to question his or her motives (Eagly, Wood, & Chaiken, 1978). We may be more convinced by the communicator's arguments if we don't think he or she is trying to persuade us (Walster (Hatfield) & Festinger, 1962). This is the theory behind the "hidden camera" technique used by television advertisers. Presumably, a person touting the virtues of a fabric softener on hidden camera must be telling the truth. The communicator is not trying to convince us; he or she is giving an unbiased testimonial.

A communicator who appears to argue against his or her own best interest is more persuasive than a communicator who takes an expected stance (Eagly et al., 1978). This was the case when newly-appointed U.S. Attorney General Janet Reno took responsibility for the 1993 attack by federal agents on David Koresh's Branch Davidian headquarters in Waco, Texas. The attack, subsequently acknowledged by the government as ill planned, led to a fiery holocaust in which most of the cult members, including many children, died. At a time when everyone connected with the attack was denying responsibility for it, Reno publicly assumed the responsibility for ordering the assault. Although her statement was not in her own best interest, it enhanced the public's sense of her character and credibility.

Clarence Darrow also seemed to be arguing against his own best interest when he suggested to the judge that he did not care about the fate of his clients. Instead, he maintained, he was strongly interested in what the verdict meant for the future of humanity:

> I am pleading for the future; I am pleading for a time when hatred and cruelty will not control the hearts of men, when . . . all life is worth saving, and that mercy is the highest attribute of man.
> (Weinberg, 1957, p. 139)

Darrow tried to increase his credibility by saying he was not acting out of self-interest or concern for the fate of Leopold and Loeb; he was fighting for a moral cause. Of course, Darrow did not mention that his fee was one of the highest ever paid to an attorney. For a closer look at the role of credibility in effective speech making, see the featured discussion "Persuasive Speaking: Changing Votes in the Senate."

Limits on Credibility: The Sleeper Effect Does a credible communicator have an advantage over a noncredible one in the long run? Apparently not. Research has shown that there are limits to a credible communicator's influence. The Yale group found that although the credibility of the communicator has a strong effect on attitude change, over time people forget who said what, so the effects of credibility wear off. Initially, people believe the credible source. But 6 weeks later, they are about as likely to show attitude change from a noncredible source as from a credible source. So, if you read an article in the *National Enquirer*, it probably would have little effect on you right away. But after a few weeks, you might show some change despite the source's low credibility. The phenomenon of a message having more impact on attitude change after a long delay than when it is first heard is known as the **sleeper effect.**

One possible cause of the sleeper effect may be that the communicator's credibility does not increase the listener's understanding of the message (Kelman & Hovland, 1953). In other words, people understand messages from credible and noncredible communicators equally well. As the effects of credibility wear off over time, listeners are left with two equally understood (or misunderstood) messages (Gruder et al., 1979).

Three factors make it more likely that the sleeper effect will occur (Rajecki, 1990):

1. There is a strong persuasive argument.
2. There is a *discounting cue,* something that makes the receiver doubt the accuracy of the message, such as lack of communicator credibility or new information that contradicts the original message.
3. Enough time passes that the discounting cue and the message become disassociated, and people forget which source said what.

Studies show that the sleeper effect occurs most reliably when the receivers get the discounting cue *after* they hear the message rather than before (Pratkanis, Greenwald, Leippe, & Baumgardner, 1988). If the discounting cue comes before the message, the receiver doubts the message before it is even conveyed. But if the discounting cue comes after the message, and if the argument is strong, the receiver probably has already

sleeper effect The phenomenon of a message from a noncredible source having more impact on attitude change after a long delay than when it is first heard.

Members of Congress usually do not change their votes as a result of the speeches they hear, but two exceptions occurred in 1993. In both cases, communicator credibility enhanced the persuasive effect of the speech.

One debate centered on a crime bill with a controversial amendment, proposed by Senator Dianne Feinstein of California, banning semiautomatic assault weapons. Arguing for the bill, Feinstein had referred to a 1984 mass killing in a McDonald's restaurant in which a gunman had killed 21 people with—according to Feinstein—an Uzi. Senator Larry Craig of Idaho countered that the gunman had used a shotgun, adding derisively, "So, the gentlelady from California needs to become a little bit more familiar with firearms and their deadly characteristics." (The gunman had in fact used both an Uzi and a shotgun.) Craig's comments provoked Feinstein to a dramatic response:

> I am quite familiar with firearms. I became mayor as a product of assassination. I found my assassinated colleague [San Francisco Supervisor Harvey Milk] and put a finger through a bullet hole trying to get a pulse. I proposed gun control legislation in San Francisco. . . . I was trained in the shooting of a firearm when I had terrorist attacks . . . at my house, when my husband was dying, when I had windows shot out. Senator, I know something about what firearms can do. (Lochhead, 1993, pp. A1, A17)

The Senate was stunned into silence by Feinstein's statement. The amendment passed, 51 to

49, despite intense opposition from the gun lobby.

A similar situation occurred when Senator Jesse Helms of North Carolina proposed an amendment renewing a design patent containing a representation of the Confederate flag for the United Daughters of the Confederacy, a group of "mostly elderly ladies" who did "good works." Helms attached the amendment to a national service bill and expected it to pass as a matter of course. However, Senator Carol Moseley Braun of Illinois, an African American member of the Senate, objected, quietly at first and then more indignantly. There was no reason why the women could not do their volunteer work with or without a logo, she said, but the U.S. Congress should not approve a symbol of the Confederacy and of slavery:

> [T]he United Daughters of the Confederacy have every right to honor their ancestors and to choose the Confederate flag as their symbol if they like. However, those of us whose ancestors fought on a different side in the Civil War, or who were held, frankly, as human chattel under the Confederate flag, are duty bound to honor our ancestors as well by asking whether such recognition by the U.S. Senate is appropriate. . . .
>
> The emblems of the Confederacy have meaning to Americans even 100 years after the end of the Civil War. Everybody knows what the Confederacy stands for. Everybody knows what the insignia means. . . . [T]he Confederate effort was around preserving the institution of slavery. . . . [T]he battle was fought to . . . keep the States from separating themselves over the issue of whether or not my ancestors could be held as property, as chattel, as objects of commerce and trade in this country. . . .
>
> [O]n this issue there can be no consensus. It is an outrage. It is an insult. It is absolutely unacceptable to me and to millions of Americans, black or white, that we would put the imprimatur of the United States Senate on a symbol of this kind of idea. . . .
>
> [F]ollowing the Civil War, . . . that peculiar institution [slavery] was put to rest for once and all. . . . And the people of this country do not want to see a day in which flags like that are underwritten, underscored, adopted, approved by this U.S. Senate. (*Congressional Record*—Senate, 1993, pp. S9253, S9254, S9258)

After listening to Senator Moseley Braun's statements, 27 senators changed their votes (Clymer, 1993). The amendment was defeated, 75 to 25.

Both Feinstein and Moseley Braun cited personal experience and history in support of their positions. Do you think this added to their credibility? To what extent did they appeal to their listeners' sense of morality? Of fairness? Of justice? What other qualities, either of the message, of the speakers, or of the audience, made these statements persuasive?

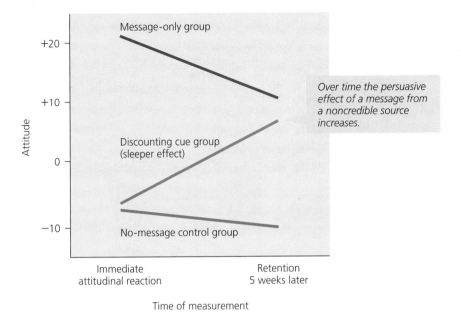

Attitude

+20 — Message-only group

+10 —

0 — Discounting cue group
(sleeper effect)

−10 — No-message control group

Over time the persuasive effect of a message from a noncredible source increases.

Immediate attitudinal reaction   Retention 5 weeks later

Time of measurement

FIGURE 7-1 *The sleeper effect in persuasive communication. At the time a persuasive message is delivered, the reaction to a credible source (line labeled "message-only group") is much more positive than the reaction to a noncredible source (line labeled "discounting cue group"). In fact, the persuasive effect of the message delivered by a noncredible source is no better than no message at all (line labeled "no-message control group"). But after 5 weeks, the persuasive power of the original credible speaker has declined and that of the noncredible speaker has increased.* After Gruder et al., 1979.

been persuaded. Over time, the memory of the discounting cue "decays" faster than the memory of the persuasive message (Pratkanis et al., 1988). Since the message is stored before the discounting cue is received, the message is less likely to be weakened. After a long period has elapsed, all the receiver remembers is the original persuasive message (Figure 7-1).

What can we say happens to a persuasive message after several weeks? When the discounting cue occurs before the message, the effect of the message diminishes. When the discounting cue occurs after the message, the power of the message is reinforced. The lesson for persuaders, then, is that they should attack their adversary before he or she makes a case or conveys a rebuttal.

The Message and the Audience

Thus far we have seen that the characteristics of the communicator can influence the degree to which we modify our attitudes in response to a persuasive message. But what about the message itself? What characteristics of messages make them more or less persuasive, and how do these elements interact with the characteristics of the audience? We address these questions next.

What Kind of Message Is Most Effective? The Power of Fear
An important quality of the message is whether it is based on rational or emotional appeals. Early research showed that appeal to one emotion in particular—fear—can make a message more effective than can appeal to reason or logic. Psychologists found at first that an appeal containing a mild threat and evoking a low level of fear was more effective than an appeal eliciting very high levels of fear (Hovland et al., 1953). Then research suggested that moderate levels of fear may be most effective (Leventhal,

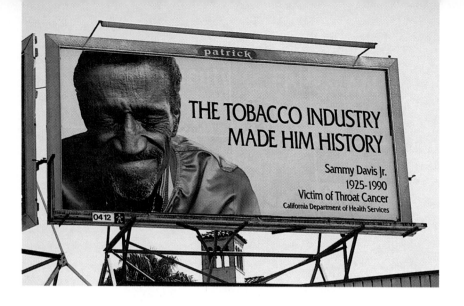

1970). That is, you need enough fear to grab people's attention but not so much you send them running for their lives. If the message is boring, people do not pay attention. If it is too ferocious, they are repelled.

However, persuaders need to do more than make the audience fearful; they need to provide a possible solution. If the message is that smoking cigarettes results in major health risks, and if the communicator does not offer a method for smokers to quit, then little attitude or behavior change will occur. The smoker will be motivated to change behavior if effective ways of dealing with the threat are offered. This principle is in keeping with the Yale group's notion that people will accept arguments that benefit them.

Of course, individuals often avoid messages that make them uncomfortable. This simple fact must be taken into account when determining a persuasion strategy. For example, a strong fear appeal on the television is not very effective. The message is there only by our consent; we can always change the channel. This is why the American Cancer Society's most effective antismoking commercial involved a cartoon character named "Johnny Smoke," a long, tall cowboy cigarette. He was repeatedly asked, as he blew smoke away from his gun: "Johnny Smoke, how many men did you shoot today?" That was it: no direct threat, no explicit conclusion about the harm of smoking. It was low-key, and the audience was allowed to draw their own conclusions.

Despite evidence that high fear messages tend to repulse people, fear appeals are certainly used heavily in health education, politics, and advertising. The assumption is that making people afraid persuades them to stop smoking or to vote for a certain candidate or to buy a particular product (Gleicher & Petty, 1992). Does fear work? Sometimes it does. As we see later in the chapter, "dirty politics" emphasizing fear appeals have worked quite well.

In one study of the effect of low versus high fear, Faith Gleicher and Richard Petty (1992) had students at Ohio State University listen to one of four different simulated radio news stories about crime on campus. The broadcasts were either moderate in fear (crime was presented as a serious problem) or only mildly fearful (crime was not presented as a serious prob-

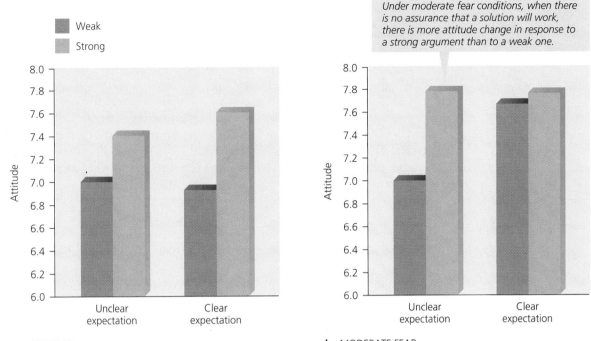

Weak

Strong

a. LOW FEAR

b. MODERATE FEAR

lem). Besides manipulating fear, the researchers varied whether the appeals had a clear assurance that something could be done about crime (a crimewatch program) or that little could be done (that is, the crimewatch programs do not work).

The researchers also varied the strength of the arguments; some subjects heard strong arguments, and others heard weak ones. In other words, some subjects heard powerful arguments in favor of the crimewatch program while others heard powerful arguments that showed crimewatch did not work. In the weak argument condition, some subjects heard not very good arguments in favor of crimewatch while others heard equally weak arguments against the effectiveness of crimewatch. In all of these variations of the persuasive message, the speaker was the same person with the same highly credible background.

The researchers found that under low fear conditions, strong persuasive arguments produced more attitude change than weak arguments, whether or not the programs were expected to be effective (Figure 7-2). In other words, if crime did not appear to be a crisis situation, students were not overly upset about the message or the possible outcome (effectiveness of the crimewatch program) and were simply persuaded by the strength of the arguments.

However, people who heard moderately fearful broadcasts focused on solutions to the crime problem. When there was a clear expectation that something could be done about crime on campus, weak and strong arguments were equally persuasive. If students were confident of a favorable outcome, they worried no further and did not thoroughly analyze the

FIGURE 7-2 Attitude toward a crimewatch program, as a function of fear, expectation of program effectiveness, and argument quality. Under low fear conditions (a), the strength of the arguments determines the amount of attitude change shown by the subjects. When the arguments are strong, individuals are more convinced than when the arguments are weak. This suggests that the subjects are processing effortfully. Under moderate fear conditions (b), there is a difference in attitude change only when there is no clear expectation that the crimewatch program will work. That is, strong arguments are more convincing than weak arguments, indicating that moderate fear leads to effortful processing. When subjects are assured that the crimewatch programs will work, then any argument—strong or weak—will convince them. From Gleicher and Petty, 1992.

messages. But when the effectiveness of crime-fighting programs was in question, students did discriminate between strong and weak arguments. In other words, when there was no clear assurance that something effective could be done, fear motivated the subjects to carefully examine the messages, so they tended to be persuaded by strong arguments. Again, concern for the outcome made them evaluate the messages carefully.

What we know from the Petty and Gleicher study is that fear initially motivates us to find some easily available, reassuring remedy. We'll accept an answer uncritically if it promises us that everything will be okay. But if no such promise is there, then we have to start to think for ourselves. So fear in combination with the lack of a clear and effective solution (a program to fight crime, in this case) leads us to analyze possible solutions carefully.

Note that Petty and Gleicher were not dealing with really high fear. Ethical considerations prevent researchers from creating such a situation in the laboratory. It may be that very high fear shuts off all critical thinking for most of us.

What do we know, then, about the effectiveness of using fear to persuade? The first point is that if we do scare people, it's a good idea to give them some reassurance that they can protect themselves from the threat we've presented. The *protection-motivation* explanation of how fear appeals work argues that intimidation motivates us to think about ways to protect ourselves (Rogers, 1983). We are willing to make the effort to evaluate arguments carefully. But, in keeping with the cognitive miser strategy, if we don't need to analyze the arguments, we won't.

The Importance of Timing: Primacy Versus Recency The effectiveness of any persuasive attempt hinges on the use of an effective strategy, including the timing of the message's delivery. When is it best to deliver your message? If you were given the option of presenting your message before or after your opponent in a debate, which should you choose? Generally, persuasive situations like these are governed by a *law of primacy* (Lawson, 1969). That is, the message presented first has more impact than the message presented second.

However, the law of primacy does not always hold true. It depends on the structure of the situation. A primacy effect occurs when the two messages follow one another closely and there is a delay between the second message and the audience response or assessment. In this situation, the first message has the greater impact. But when there is a delay between the two messages and a response or assessment is made soon after the second message, we see a *recency effect*—the second message has a greater impact (Figure 7-3).

The primacy and recency effects apply most clearly under certain conditions—when both sides have equally strong arguments and when listeners are reasonably motivated to understand them. If one side has a much stronger argument than the other side, listeners are likely to be persuaded by the strong argument whether it is presented first or last (Haugtvedt & Wegener, 1993). When listeners are *very* motivated, very interested in the

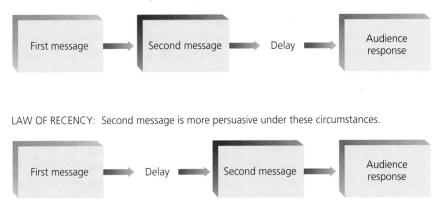

LAW OF PRIMACY: First message is more persuasive under these circumstances.

First message → Second message → Delay → Audience response

LAW OF RECENCY: Second message is more persuasive under these circumstances.

First message → Delay → Second message → Audience response

FIGURE 7-3 *The effect of timing on persuasiveness. When the second message closely follows the first and there is a delay before the audience responds, the law of primacy applies. When there is a delay between the two messages and no delay before the audience responds, the law of recency applies.*

issue, they are more likely to be influenced by the first argument (the primacy effect) than by those they hear later on (Haugtvedt & Wegener, 1993).

Fitting the Message to the Audience   The Yale group was also interested in the construction and presentation of persuasive messages. One of their findings was that messages have to be presented differently to different audiences. For example, an educated or highly involved audience requires a different type of persuasive message than an uneducated or uninvolved audience. Rational arguments are effective with educated or analytical audiences (Cacioppo, Petty, & Morris, 1983). Emotional appeals work better with less educated or less analytical groups.

One-Sided Versus Two-Sided Messages   The nature of the audience also influences how a message is structured. For less educated, uninformed audiences a *one-sided* message works best. In a one-sided message you present only your side of the issue and draw conclusions for the audience. For a well-educated, well-informed audience, a *two-sided* message works best. The more educated audience probably is already aware of the other side of the argument. If you attempt to persuade them with a one-sided argument, they may question your motives. Also, well-educated audience members can draw their own conclusions. They probably would resent your drawing conclusions for them. Thus, a more educated audience will be more persuaded by a two-sided argument (Hovland, Janis, & Kelley, 1953).

One-sided and two-sided appeals also have different effects depending on the initial attitudes of the audience. Generally, a one-sided message is effective when the audience already agrees with your position. If the audience is against your position, a two-sided message works best. You need to consider both the initial position of audience members and their education level when deciding on an approach. A two-sided appeal is best when your audience is educated, regardless of their initial position. A one-sided appeal works best on an uneducated audience that already agrees with you.

FIGURE 7-4 *The inoculation effect. A persuasive attack on the cultural truism "Tooth-brushing is beneficial" caused a considerable decrease in belief in the truism. Subjects were a bit more able to resist the attack when they were first persuaded with arguments that supported the truism (supportive defense). But far more resistance to the attack occurred when subjects were first inoculated by hearing a minor attack that they could easily refute.* Data from McGuire and Papageorgis, 1961.

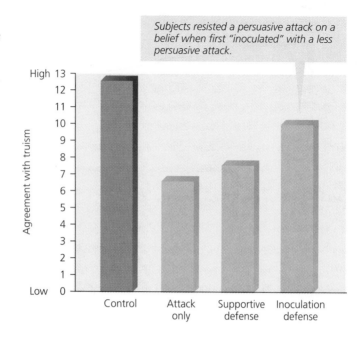

Subjects resisted a persuasive attack on a belief when first "inoculated" with a less persuasive attack.

Inoculating the Audience When presenting a two-sided message, you don't want to accidentally persuade the audience of the other side. Therefore, the best approach is to present that side in a weakened form to "inoculate" the audience against it (McGuire, 1985). When you present a weakened message, listeners will devise their own counterarguments: "Well, *that's* obviously not true! Any fool can see through that argument! Who do they think they're kidding?" The listeners convince themselves the argument is wrong. **Inoculation theory** is based on the medical model of inoculation. People are given a weakened version of a bacterium or a virus so that they can develop the antibodies to fight the disease on their own. Similarly, in attempting to persuade people of your side, you give them a weakened version of the opposing argument and let them develop their own defenses against it.

In a study of the inoculation effect, McGuire and Papageorgis (1961) exposed subjects to an attack on their belief that brushing their teeth prevented tooth decay. Obviously, everybody believes that brushing your teeth is beneficial. This is a cultural truism, something we all accept without thinking or questioning. Therefore, we may not have any defenses in place if someone challenges those truisms.

Subjects in one group heard an attack on the tooth-brushing truism. A second group received a supportive defense that reinforced the concept that brushing your teeth is good for you. A third group was "inoculated," first hearing a mild attack on the truism and then hearing a defense of tooth-brushing. A fourth group, the control group, received no messages. Of the three groups who heard a message, the "inoculated" group was most likely to believe tooth-brushing was beneficial (Figure 7-4). In fact, people in the "inoculated" group, who were given a mild rebuttal of the truism,

inoculation theory The theory that if a communicator exposes an audience to a weakened version of the opposing argument, the audience will devise counterarguments to that weakened version.

were *more likely* to believe in the benefits of tooth-brushing than were the people who heard only a supportive defense of the truism.

This study highlights the fact that the inoculation defense is the best protection against an attack. It motivates people to generate their own counterarguments and makes them more likely to believe the persuader's side of the issue. In this case, forewarned is truly forearmed.

The Role of Discrepancy Another aspect of the audience a persuader has to consider is their preexisting attitudes in relation to the message he or she wants to convey. For instance, imagine you are going to deliver a pro-choice message to a room full of people with strong attitudes against abortion. Obviously, your message will be very different from the preexisting attitudes of your audience. This is a *high-discrepancy* situation. On the other hand, if you are trying to convince a room full of pro-choice individuals, your message will not be very different from preexisting attitudes. This is an example of *low discrepancy*. In either of these cases, you would not expect much persuasion. In the first case, your message is too discrepant from the one your audience already holds; they will reject your message without giving it much thought. In the second case, you are basically saying what your audience already believes, so there won't be much persuasive effect or attitude change. Generally, a moderate amount of discrepancy produces the greatest amount of change.

Discrepancy interacts with the characteristics of the communicator. A highly credible communicator can induce change even when a highly discrepant message, one we ordinarily would reject or that contradicts a stereotype, is delivered. In one study, researchers found that Scottish subjects had definite stereotypes of male hairdressers and of "skinheads" (Macrae, Shepherd, & Milne, 1992). Male hairdressers were perceived as meek, and skinheads were perceived as aggressive. However, a report from a psychiatrist that stated the contrary—that a particular hairdresser was aggressive or a skinhead was meek—altered the subjects' opinions of those two groups.

Of course, a credible communicator cannot say just anything and expect people to believe it. An effective communicator must be aware of the audience's likely perception of the message. Clarence Darrow carefully staked out a position he knew the judge would not reject. He didn't argue that the death penalty should be abolished because he knew that the judge would not accept that position. Rather, he argued that the penalty was not appropriate in this specific case because of the defendants' ages and their mental state:

> And, I submit, Your Honor, that by every law of humanity, by every law of justice, . . . Your Honor should say that because of the condition of these boys' minds, it would be monstrous to visit upon them the vengeance that is asked by the State. (Weinberg, 1957, p. 163)

In other words, even highly credible communicators have to keep in mind how discrepant their message is from the audience's views. For communicators with lower credibility, a moderate amount of discrepancy works best.

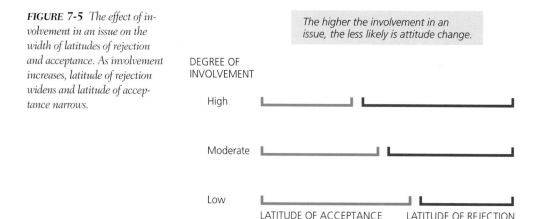

FIGURE 7-5 *The effect of involvement in an issue on the width of latitudes of rejection and acceptance. As involvement increases, latitude of rejection widens and latitude of acceptance narrows.*

The higher the involvement in an issue, the less likely is attitude change.

DEGREE OF INVOLVEMENT

High

Moderate

Low

LATITUDE OF ACCEPTANCE   LATITUDE OF REJECTION

Social Judgment Theory How does discrepancy work? Muzafer Sherif suggested that the audience makes social judgments about the difference between the communicator's position and their own attitude on an issue (Sherif & Hovland, 1961; Sherif, Sherif, & Nebergall, 1965). This *social judgment theory* argues that the degree of personal involvement in an issue determines how the target will evaluate an attempt at persuasion.

Sherif suggested that an individual's perception of a message falls into one of three judgment categories, or latitudes. The *latitude of acceptance* is the set of positions the audience would find acceptable. The *latitude of rejection* is the set of arguments the person would not accept. The *latitude of noncommitment* is a neutral zone falling between the other two and including positions the person does not accept or reject but will consider.

The breadth of the latitudes is affected by how strongly the person feels about the issue, how "ego-involved" he or she is. As involvement increases, the latitudes of acceptance and noncommitment narrow, but the latitude of rejection increases (Eagly & Telaak, 1972) (Figure 7-5). In other words, the more important an issue is, the less likely you are to accept a persuasive message unless it is similar to your position. Only messages that fall within your latitude of acceptance, or perhaps in your latitude of noncommitment, will have a chance of persuading you. As importance of an issue increases, the number of acceptable arguments decreases.

Sherif measured the attitudes of Republicans and Democrats in a presidential election and found that very committed Republicans and very committed Democrats rejected almost all of the other side's arguments (Sherif, Sherif, & Nebergall, 1965). However, voters who were less extreme in their commitment were open to persuasion. Moderates of both parties usually accepted as many arguments from the opposition as they rejected. Therefore, as Darrow knew, a persuasive message must fall at least within the audience's latitude of noncommitment to be accepted.

The Problem of Multiple Audiences In many circumstances, a communicator must persuade multiple audiences with diverse attitudes, education levels, levels of involvement, latitudes of acceptance, and so forth. Clarence Darrow's primary audience was the judge, but he also had to keep the pub-

During the Persian Gulf War, many observers were puzzled by Saddam Hussein's seemingly boastful and exaggerated claims to victory. Some of their confusion stemmed from differences between European American and Middle Eastern communication styles, but some was also due to the fact that Hussein had to address multiple audiences—his own people and the rest of the world.

lic in mind. Similarly, a prisoner of war forced to make statements contrary to his beliefs has to convince his captors he's sincere but let his comrades know he's lying. And politicians often wish to appeal to one group without offending another. The same message must mean different things to different audiences. This is the **multiple audience problem**—how to send different meanings in the same message to diverse audiences (Fleming, Darley, Hilton, & Kojetin, 1990).

How do people manage these difficult situations? Researchers interested in this question had communicators send messages to audiences composed of friends and strangers (Fleming et al., 1990). The communicators were motivated to send a message that would convey the truth to their friends but deceive the strangers. Subjects in this experiment were quite accurate at figuring out when their friends were lying. Strangers were not so accurate. Recall the fundamental attribution error and the correspondence bias from Chapter 4: We tend to believe that people mean what they say. In general we are not very good at detecting lies (Ekman, 1985).

Friends were also able to pick up on the communicator's hidden message because they shared some common knowledge. For example, one communicator said she was going to go to Wales, a country her friends knew she loved, and was going to do her shopping for the trip in a department store her friends knew she hated. The message was clear to those in the know: She's lying. The department store reference was a private code or key that close friends understood.

This is the way communicators can convey different meanings in the same message: They use special, private keys that only one audience understands. We often see private keys used in political ads, especially those ads aimed at evoking stereotypes and emotional responses. Consider the 1991 gubernatorial race in Mississippi. Incumbent Governor Ray Mabus, a Democrat campaigning on a plan to improve the state's education system, was in a tight race with Republican Kirk Fordice, a businessman.

Fordice's campaign emphasized the bad economic times. It also became clear that Fordice was aiming exclusively at the white vote. His cam-

multiple audience problem
The problem that occurs when a communicator must send different meanings in the same message to diverse audiences.

paign ran several ads against welfare, including one that showed a photo of an African American woman holding a baby. It also showed a middle-class African American woman pushing a shopping cart (Jamieson, 1992). The presence of two African Americans, one "good" (middle class) and one "not so good" (lower class) protected Fordice from a direct attack that the ad was racist. However, the ad's intended audience (whites) knew the private keys: "Blacks are the welfare problem in Mississippi, and Fordice will take care of it." Fordice won the race by getting almost none of the African American vote and a large majority of the white vote.

THE COGNITIVE APPROACH TO PERSUASION

You may have noted that, in the Yale model of persuasion, the audience seems to be nothing more than a target for messages. People just sit there and take it, accepting the message or not. Cognitive response approaches, on the other hand, emphasize the active participation of the audience (Greenwald, 1968). The cognitive approach looks at *why* people react to a message the way they do, why they say that a message is interesting or that a communicator is biased.

Cognitively oriented social psychologists emphasize that a persuasive communication may trigger a number of related experiences, memories, feelings, and thoughts that individuals use to process the message. Therefore, both what a person thinks about when she hears the persuasive message and how the person applies those thoughts, feelings, and memories to analyzing the message are critical. We now turn to the individual's cognitive response to the persuasive message.

The Elaboration Likelihood Model

One well-known cognitive response model is the **elaboration likelihood model (ELM).** This model, first proposed by Richard Petty and John Cacioppo (1986a), makes clear that audiences are not just passive receptacles but are actively involved in the persuasion process. Their attention, involvement, distraction, motivation, self-esteem, education, and intelligence determine the success of persuasive appeals. ELM owes a lot to the Yale model, incorporating much of the Yale research on the important roles of communicator and message. But its primary emphasis is on the role of the audience, especially their emotions and motivations.

According to ELM, two routes to persuasion exist: a central processing route and a peripheral processing route. Persuasion may be achieved via either of these routes.

Central Route Processing **Central route processing** involves *elaboration* of the message by the listener. This type of processing usually occurs when the person finds the message personally relevant and has preexisting ideas and beliefs about the topic. The individual uses these ideas and beliefs to create a context for the message, expanding and elaborating on the

elaboration likelihood model (ELM) A cognitive model of persuasion suggesting that the success of a persuasive message depends on how actively involved the listener becomes in processing it.

central route processing A form of information processing in which the listener relies on the information itself to make a decision, using preexisting ideas and beliefs to create a context for the message.

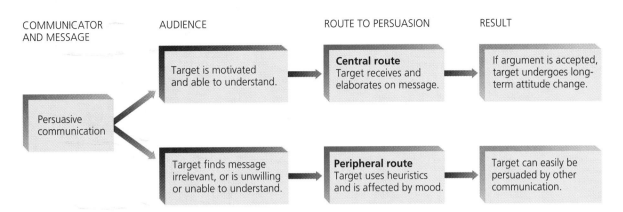

COMMUNICATOR AND MESSAGE	AUDIENCE	ROUTE TO PERSUASION	RESULT

Persuasive communication

Target is motivated and able to understand. → **Central route** Target receives and elaborates on message. → If argument is accepted, target undergoes long-term attitude change.

Target finds message irrelevant, or is unwilling or unable to understand. → **Peripheral route** Target uses heuristics and is affected by mood. → Target can easily be persuaded by other communication.

new information. Because the message is relevant, the person is motivated to listen to it carefully and process it in an effortful manner (Figure 7-6).

A juror listening to evidence that she understands and finds interesting, for example, will generate a number of ideas and responses. As she assimilates the message, she will compare it to what she already knows and believes. In the Leopold and Loeb trial, Judge Caverly may have elaborated on Darrow's argument for life imprisonment by recalling that in the Chicago courts, no one had been sentenced to death after voluntarily entering a guilty plea, and no one as young as the defendants had ever been hanged.

Elaboration of a message does not always lead to acceptance, however. If the message does not make sense or does not fit the person's knowledge and beliefs, elaboration may lead to rejection. For example, Judge Caverly might have focused on the brutal and indifferent attitude that Leopold and Loeb displayed toward Bobby Franks. If Darrow had not put together a coherent argument that fit the evidence, the judge probably would have rejected his argument. But the story Darrow told *was* coherent. By emphasizing the "diseased minds" of his clients, enhanced by the suggestion that they probably were born "twisted," he explained the unexplainable: why they killed Bobby Franks. At the same time, he made Leopold and Loeb seem less responsible. Thus, Darrow presented the judge with credible explanations on which he could expand to reach a verdict.

Central route processors elaborate on the message by filling in the "gaps" with their own knowledge and beliefs. Messages processed this way are more firmly tied to other attitudes and are therefore more resistant to change. Attitude change that results from central route processing is stable, long-lasting, and difficult to reverse.

Peripheral Route Processing What if the listener is not motivated, or is not able to understand the message, or simply does not like to deal with new or complex information? In this case, the listener takes another route to persuasion, a peripheral route. In **peripheral route processing,** listeners rely on something other than the message to make their decisions; they are persuaded by cues peripheral or marginal to the message. A juror may be favorably influenced by the appearance of the defendant, for example.

FIGURE 7-6 *Two routes to persuasion in the elaboration likelihood model. Whether or not an individual processes a message centrally or peripherally depends primarily on the person's motivation and ability to comprehend the message. Anything that detracts from these factors, such as a very complex or a very boring message, will lead to peripheral processing.* Adapted from Petty and Cacioppo, 1986a.

peripheral route processing
A form of information processing in which the listener relies on irrelevant or marginal cues to make a decision.

"*Surely not guilty. Next case.*"

Or perhaps she remembers when her uncle was in a similar predicament and thinks, "He wasn't guilty either."

Emotional cues are very effective in persuading peripheral route processors (Petty & Cacioppo, 1986a). Recall the experiment on the effects of fear appeals in campus crime newscasts: A strong emotional appeal offering a reassuring solution was accepted whether the argument itself was strong or weak. Subjects were not processing centrally; they paid no attention to the quality of the argument. They simply wanted reassurance, and the existence of a possible solution acted as a peripheral cue, convincing them the argument must be valid. High or moderate fear makes us accept whatever reassuring solution is presented to us.

Peripheral route processing often leads to attitude change, but, because the listener has not elaborated on the message, the change is not very stable and is vulnerable to counterpressures (Kassin, Reddy, & Tulloch, 1990). A juror who processes centrally will be firm in his or her conclusions about the evidence, but the peripheral route juror will be an easy target for the next persuader in the courtroom (ForsterLee, Horowitz, & Bourgeois, 1993).

Though we have distinguished between the central and peripheral routes, message processing is not an either/or proposition. In fact, you may

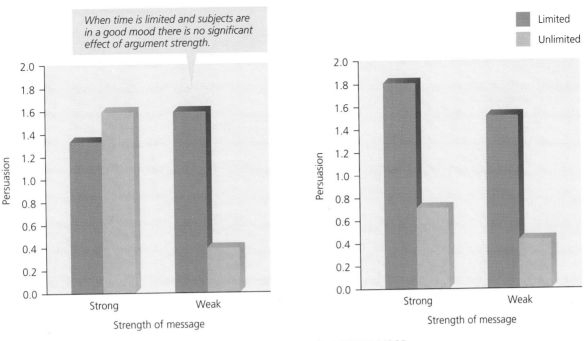

When time is limited and subjects are in a good mood there is no significant effect of argument strength.

Limited
Unlimited

a. POSITIVE MOOD

b. NEUTRAL MOOD

process some parts of a message centrally, others peripherally. For example, a juror may be interested in and understand the scientific evidence presented at trial and process that information centrally. However, when an economist takes the stand, the juror may be bored or may think that people in bow ties are untrustworthy, and then process that testimony peripherally.

The Effect of Mood on Processing Many speakers try to put their audience in a good mood before making their case. They tell a joke or an amusing story, or they say something designed to make listeners feel positive. Is this a good strategy? Does it make an argument more persuasive? It depends.

When people are in a good mood, they tend to be distracted. Good moods bring out many related pleasant feelings and memories. Everything seems rosy. People in good moods cannot concentrate very well on messages; they cannot process information centrally. In one study on the influence of mood, people were put in either a good or a neutral mood and were given either an unlimited or very limited amount of time to listen to a message (Mackie & Worth, 1989). The strength of the persuasive messages also varied: One message contained strong arguments; the other, only weak arguments. The researchers reasoned that for the subjects in good moods, strong and weak arguments would be equally effective. As shown in Figure 7-7, this was found to be the case, but only when there was a limited amount of time to study the messages. People in good moods did not distinguish between strong and weak arguments because they were not processing centrally.

FIGURE 7-7 The effects of mood on the persuasiveness of a message. A good mood seems to hinder central processing (a): When people are feeling good and have limited time to understand the message, there is no significant effect of argument strength. Only when subjects in good moods have unlimited time can they energize and bring to bear all of their cognitive resources—that is, only then can they process centrally, distinguishing stronger arguments from weaker ones. When subjects are in a neutral mood (b), strong arguments are more convincing more often than weaker ones in both limited and unlimited time conditions.
Adapted from Mackie and Worth, 1989.

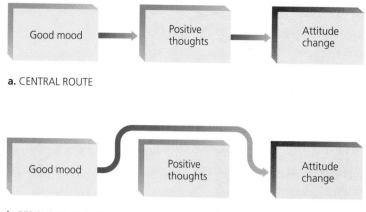

FIGURE 7-8 *The effects of a good mood on central and peripheral route processes. When an individual is using central route processing (a), a good mood leads to positive thoughts about the message and then to attitude change. When an individual is using peripheral route processing (b), a good mood leads directly to an unthinking attitude change.* Adapted from Petty, Schumann, Richman, and Strathman, 1993.

a. CENTRAL ROUTE

b. PERIPHERAL ROUTE

Good feelings do not, however, always prevent central processing. If people in good moods are motivated to carefully evaluate and elaborate on a message, and if they have enough time, they will process centrally. A good mood will not have a direct effect on their attitudes, but it may make them think more positive thoughts about the message (if it is a strong one and they have time to consider it) (Petty, Schumann, Richman, & Strathman, 1993). The good thoughts then lead to positive attitude change. For those using peripheral route processing, good moods don't lead to more positive thoughts and then to positive attitude change. They aren't thinking about the message at all and are not elaborating on it. Instead, for them, good mood leads directly to attitude change. Figure 7-8 shows how good mood affects central and peripheral processors differently.

So, is it a good idea to put your audience in a good mood? Obviously it is if you have a weak argument. Generally, mood is a peripheral cue (Schwarz, Bless, & Bohner, 1992). Therefore, attitude change based on mood is rather fragile, and the next communicator could very well convince the audience of something completely contrary.

The Effect of Personal Relevance on Processing Another factor affecting central versus peripheral route processing is personal relevance. If an issue is important to us and affects our well-being, we are more likely to pay attention to the quality of the message. In one study, college students were told that the university chancellor wanted to have all seniors pass a comprehensive examination before they could graduate (Petty, Cacioppo, & Goldman, 1981). Subjects hearing the *high-relevance version* of this message were told the policy would go into effect the following year and so would affect them. Subjects hearing the *low-relevance version* were informed that the policy wouldn't be implemented for several years and so would not affect them.

The researchers also varied the quality of the arguments and the expertise of the communicator. Half the subjects heard persuasive arguments, and the other half heard weaker arguments. Half were told that the plan was based on a report by a local high school class (low communicator ex-

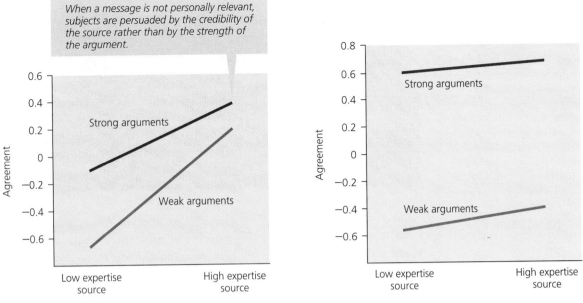

When a message is not personally relevant, subjects are persuaded by the credibility of the source rather than by the strength of the argument.

a. LOW RELEVANCE

b. HIGH RELEVANCE

FIGURE 7-9 Central or peripheral route processing as a function of message relevance. When a message has low personal relevance (a), attitudes are affected by the expertise of the communicator, indicating that peripheral processing is going on. When a message has high personal relevance (b), attitudes are affected by the quality of the argument, suggesting the occurrence of central processing.
Data from Petty, Cacioppo, and Goldman, 1981.

pertise), and the other half was told the source was the Carnegie Commission on Higher Education (high expertise).

Results indicated that relevance did influence the type of processing subjects used (Figure 7-9). Students who thought the change would affect them were persuaded by the strong argument and not by the weak one. In other words, they carefully examined the arguments, using central processing. Students who thought the change wouldn't affect them simply relied on the expertise of the communicator. They were persuaded when they thought the plan was based on the Carnegie Commission report, whether the arguments were strong or weak. Low relevance, in other words, enhances the influence of communicator credibility and increases the likelihood that listeners will use peripheral processing.

Does high relevance mean that you will always be persuaded by strong and rational arguments? Not at all. An issue may be highly relevant to you because it involves an important personal *value*. In this case, even a very persuasive argument probably won't change your opinion. In the current abortion debate, for example, an extreme position on either side is based on fundamental values relating to privacy, coercion, and the nature of life. The issue is certainly relevant to individuals with extreme views, but they are unlikely to be persuaded to change their opinions by any argument.

If, however, an issue is highly relevant because of a particular *outcome*, rather than a value, then a strong, persuasive argument might work (Johnson & Eagly, 1989). If you are strongly opposed to taking a senior comprehensive exam, a persuasive message about outcome, such as the possibility that passing such an exam would increase your chances of getting into graduate school, might well convince you.

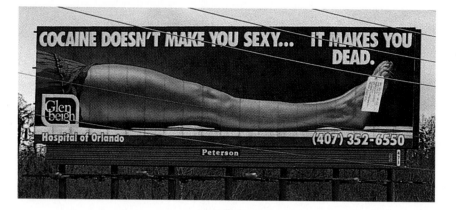

Does vividness add to the persuasive effect of a message? This billboard's use of emotionally charged language and a shocking image forces us to pay more attention than we otherwise would. But it may be convincing primarily among people for whom the issue is not personally relevant—those who don't use cocaine—and therefore have little reason to consider it further. Vividness does not necessarily make a message more persuasive for those who are motivated to think it through.

Personal relevance has been an issue for many people concerned about funding for AIDS research. Because this disease was originally associated with certain groups—gay men and injecting drug users—public officials were inclined to give it less attention—and allocate less research money—than diseases that more commonly struck the majority of the population. AIDS activists struggled with the issue of how to make people realize that the disease is a problem for the entire society. One person, Mary Fisher, spoke persuasively about AIDS before the Republican National Convention in 1992. She attempted to establish a connection between people with AIDS and members of the audience by invoking their common humanity:

> Though I am white, and a mother, I am one with a black infant struggling with tubes in a Philadelphia hospital. Though I am female, and contracted this disease in marriage, . . . I am one with the lonely gay man sheltering a flickering candle from the cold wind of his family's rejection. . . . We may take refuge in our stereotypes, but we cannot hide there long. Because HIV asks only one thing of those it attacks: Are you human? And this is the right question: Are you human? (quoted in Osborn & Osborn, 1994, p. B20)

Those who hear this question—Are you human?—must admit that in this sense, at least, AIDS is personally relevant for them.

Does Vivid Language Persuade? What about the effect of vivid language on persuasiveness? Does it make a difference in our attitudes or behavior? Advertisers and other persuaders certainly believe that vivid messages, presented in eye- or ear-catching terms, are persuasive. Social psychologists interested in this issue stated, "Everybody knows that vividly presented information is impactful and persuasive" (Taylor & Thompson, 1982, p. 155). However, when these researchers surveyed the literature on vividness, they found very weak support for the persuasive power of vivid materials.

In one study of the "vividness effect," people were given vivid and nonvivid versions of crime stories in the news (Collins, Taylor, Wood, &

Thompson, 1988). The vivid versions used colorful language and provided bizarre details. People listened to a vivid or nonvivid story and then rated its quality in terms of emotion, imagery, interest, and so forth as well as its persuasiveness. In a second study, people also had to predict how others would respond to the stories.

The studies found no evidence of a vividness effect; vivid messages had about the same persuasive effect as nonvivid messages. However, people *did* believe that vivid messages affected other people. What influenced the subjects if vividness did not? Interest: If the message involved a topic that interested them, people felt the message was more effective. Remember the effects of personal relevance in the elaboration likelihood model of persuasion.

On the other hand, some messages—such as political ads—do appear to benefit from vividness. Perhaps they work because they interest people and force them to pay more attention than they normally might have. One study examined the effects of vivid language in a trial (Wilson, Northcraft, & Neale, 1989). The trial concerned a dispute between a contractor and a subcontractor on a building project. People playing the role of jurors watched different videotapes of the trial. One version had vivid phrasing; the other, nonvivid language (p. 135):

1. There was a <u>spiderweb</u> of cracks through the slab. (vivid)
   There was a <u>network</u> of cracks through the slab. (nonvivid)
2. The slab was <u>jagged</u> and had to be sanded. (vivid)
   The slab was <u>rough</u> and had to be sanded. (nonvivid)

The "jurors" tended to award the plaintiff more money when they heard vivid phrases.

So, is there a vividness effect or not? Based on the evidence, it seems that vivid messages have an initial effect, especially if there is little else to compete with them. In the trial situation, vivid information had a strong impact when the jurors were presented with a lot of evidence that was not directly important for their decision, such as a history of the building project and pictures of the construction site. Then the jurors heard the vivid language ("a spiderweb of cracks through the slab"). Given the background of irrelevant information, they were influenced by the one or two vivid messages they heard.

In a longer trial, or in a situation where much information has already been made available, or when the audience is particularly interested in the issue, one vivid message may not have a significant impact. However, when people are not particularly interested, a vivid message may have significant impact. In other words, vividness is a peripheral cue. When individuals find the message interesting and personally relevant, they process centrally, and vividness has little effect. But when the cognitive miser is at work, a vivid message may have a definite influence on attitudes.

Need for Cognition: Some Like to Do It the Hard Way Some people prefer central route processing no matter what the situation or how complex the evidence. These people have a high **need for cognition (NC)**

need for cognition (NC) A characteristic of the individual relating to the need to deal with the content of a message in an effortful way. A person can have either a high NC or a low NC.

(Cacioppo, Petty, & Morris, 1983). High NC people like to deal with difficult and effortful problems. On a scale assessing this cognitive characteristic, they agree with such statements as "I really enjoy a task that involves coming up with new solutions to problems," and they disagree with such statements as "I only think as hard as I have to."

High NC people are concerned with the validity of the messages they receive, which suggests that they rely mainly on central route processing (Cacioppo et al., 1983). High NC individuals also organize information in a way that allows them to remember messages and use them later (Lassiter, Briggs, & Bowman, 1991). Those low in cognitive need tend to pay more attention to the physical characteristics of the speaker, indicating peripheral processing (Petty & Cacioppo, 1986a).

ELM research has shown that people who have a need to process information centrally—high NC people—accept and resist persuasive arguments in a different way than those low in need for cognition. Since they're processing centrally, they elaborate on the messages they hear. They are influenced by the qualities of the argument or the product advertised rather than by peripheral cues (Haugtvedt, Petty, & Cacioppo, in press), and they tend to hold newly formed attitudes longer and are more resistant to counterpersuasion (Haugtvedt & Petty, 1992).

The Heuristic Model of Persuasion

A second cognitive model of persuasion is the **heuristic and systematic information processing model (HSM).** Proposed by Shelley Chaiken (1987), HSM has much in common with ELM. As in ELM, there are two routes for information processing: the systematic and the heuristic. Systematic processing in HSM is essentially the same as central processing in ELM, and heuristic processing is the same as peripheral processing. Heuristics, as you recall from Chapter 3, are simple guides or shortcuts that people use to make decisions when something gets too complicated or when they are just too lazy to process systematically.

The main difference between the two theories lies in the claim of HSM that reliance on heuristics is much more common than is usually thought (Chaiken, Liberman, & Eagly, 1989). If motivation and ability to comprehend are not high, individuals rely on heuristics most of the time. Some of these heuristics might be, "Experts can be trusted," or "The majority must be right," or "She's from the Midwest; she must be trustworthy," or "If it was on the evening news, it must be true."

Heuristic processing can be compared to scanning newspaper headlines. The information you receive is minimal, and the truth or relevance of the headline will be determined by those simple rules. "Congress Cannot Agree on a Budget," reads the headline. Your response would be to quickly check the available heuristics that might "explain" the headline. Here it is: "Politicians are incompetent." Next headline, please. HSM suggests that people are more likely to agree with communicators who are expert and with messages with which most people agree. Again we see the cognitive miser at work.

heuristic and systematic information processing model (HSM) A cognitive model of persuasion suggesting that listeners rely on heuristics or peripheral cues most of the time.

Cognitive dissonance occurs when we notice an inconsistency between our attitudes and our behavior. We may, for example, believe in animal rights but buy cosmetics tested on animals or food produced by factory farming. If an organization like People for the Ethical Treatment of Animals, or one of its supporters like singer k.d. lang, succeeds in raising our consciousness to the level of discomfort, we will probably change either our attitude or our behavior.

MODELS OF SELF-PERSUASION

Direct persuasion by a communicator is not the only route to attitude or behavior change. Attitude change may also occur if we find our existing attitudes in conflict with new information, or if our behavior is inconsistent with our beliefs. Leon Festinger (as mentioned in Chapter 6, one of the most influential theorists in the history of social psychology) observed that people try to appear consistent. When we act counter to what we believe or think, we must justify the inconsistency. In other words, if we say one thing and do something else, we need a good reason. Usually, we persuade ourselves that we have a good reason, even if it means changing our previous attitudes. Inconsistency is thus one of the principal motivations for attitude change.

Cognitive Dissonance Theory

Festinger's *cognitive dissonance theory* proposes that if inconsistency exists among our attitudes, or between our attitudes and our behavior, we experience an unpleasant state of arousal called **cognitive dissonance** (Festinger, 1957). The arousal of dissonance motivates us to change something—our attitudes or our behavior—to reduce or eliminate the unpleasant arousal. Reducing the tension helps us achieve *consonance*, a state of psychological balance.

Cognitive dissonance theory is like *homeostatic theory* in biology. Consider what happens when you are hungry: Your brain detects an imbalance in your blood sugar levels, causing a physiological state of hunger. You are motivated to reduce this unpleasant state of arousal by finding and consuming food. Similarly, when cognitive consonance is disrupted, you feel tension and are motivated to reduce it.

The five key assumptions of cognitive dissonance theory can be summarized as follows:

1. Attitudes and behavior can stand in a consonant (consistent) or a dissonant (inconsistent) relationship with one another.

cognitive dissonance An unpleasant state of arousal resulting from conflicts among a person's attitudes or between attitudes and behavior.

2. Inconsistency between attitudes and behavior gives rise to a negative motivational state known as cognitive dissonance.
3. Because cognitive dissonance is an uncomfortable state, people are motivated to reduce the dissonance.
4. The greater the amount of dissonance, the stronger the motivation to reduce it.
5. Dissonance may be reduced by rationalizing away the inconsistency or by changing an attitude or a behavior.

How Does Cognitive Dissonance Lead to Attitude Change? Exactly how does cognitive dissonance change attitudes? To find out, imagine that you have volunteered to be a subject in a social psychological experiment. You are instructed to sit in front of a tray of objects and repeatedly empty and refill the tray for the next hour. Then, to add more excitement to your day, you are asked to turn pegs in holes a little at a time. When it's over, you are asked to tell the next subject how interesting and delightful the tasks were. For doing this, you are paid the grand sum of $1. Unbeknown to you, other subjects go through the same experience and are also asked to tell an incoming subject how interesting the tasks are, but each is paid $20.

When this classic experiment was done in 1959 (Festinger & Carlsmith, 1959), almost all the subjects agreed to misrepresent how much fun the experiment was. Several weeks later, the subjects were contacted by a third party and asked whether or not they had enjoyed the study. Their responses turned out to depend on how much money they had been paid. You might predict that the subjects who had gotten $20 said that they had enjoyed their experience more than those who had gotten only $1. Well, that's not what happened. Subjects paid $20 said the tasks were boring, and those paid $1 said they had enjoyed the tasks. A third group, the control subjects, were given no reward and were not told that anyone else had received one. Like the $20 group, they said the tasks were boring.

Cognitive dissonance theory argues that change occurs when people experience dissonance. Where is the dissonance in this experiment? Being paid $1, a trifling sum even in 1959, was surely insufficient justification for lying. If a dollar-subject analyzed the situation logically, it would look like this: "I lied to someone because the experimenter asked me to, and I got paid only a buck." Conclusion: "Either I am a liar or I am stupid." Neither conclusion fits with what we generally think of ourselves. The dissonance is between what we want to think of ourselves and how we have behaved. So, how does the subject resolve the dissonance? The behavior can't be undone, so the subject engages in self-persuasion: "I'm not a liar or stupid, so I must have meant what I said. I enjoyed the experiment." The $20-group has an easily available, if not very flattering, justification for the lie: "I needed the money."

The Reverse-Incentive Effect The implications of this study and many more that have replicated the effect over the years are intriguing. One concept that came from the original study is the **reverse-incentive effect:** When people are given a large payment for doing something, they infer that the activity must be difficult or tedious or risky (Freedman, Cunningham, & Krismer, 1992). Thus,

reverse-incentive effect The phenomenon of an activity being perceived as less desirable the more highly it is rewarded.

professional athletes who once played the game just for fun may now moan about playing the game for $5 million a year. People seem to get suspicious when they are paid large sums for doing something they enjoyed doing in the first place. They feel a little apprehensive and develop a less positive view of the activity (Crano & Sivacek, 1984).

Dissonance theory argues, then, that the *less* the reward or the *less* the threatened punishment used to make people behave counter to their attitudes, the *more* people have to provide their own justifications for their behavior. The more they have to persuade themselves of the rightness of the behavior, the more their attitude is likely to change.

The Importance of Free Choice We have seen that an important condition in the arousal of dissonance is whether behavior is freely chosen or coerced. In another study of cognitive dissonance, subjects were asked to write an essay arguing a position that ran counter to their real beliefs (Elkin & Leippe, 1986). Further, they did this attitude-inconsistent act when they felt they had freely chosen it. Dissonance theorists call this situation *induced compliance*. The researchers found that when subjects wrote an essay counter to their beliefs, they showed greater physiological arousal than if they had written an essay consistent with their beliefs. This finding is compatible with predictions from cognitive dissonance theory, specifically that dissonance increases feelings of tension (physiological arousal).

This study reinforced the finding that people do not experience dissonance if they do not choose the inconsistent behavior (Brehm & Cohen, 1962). If they are forced to do something, the coercion is justification enough for the discrepant actions. If they don't have to justify their behavior to themselves, there is no self-persuasion. Attitudes are always the weak link in the dissonance equation. You can't change your behavior after the fact; your only resort is to change your attitudes.

Professional athletes often find they're making more money but enjoying it less. When people are paid to do something they once did for fun, they tend to develop a negative attitude toward the activity—an example of the reverse-incentive effect.

Responsibility: Another View of Cognitive Dissonance Another, more recent view suggests that cognitive dissonance occurs only when our actions produce negative consequences (Cooper & Scher, 1992). According to this view, it's not the inconsistency that causes dissonance so much as our feelings of personal responsibility when bad things happen (Cooper & Fazio, 1984).

Let's say, for example, that you wrote a very good essay in favor of something you believed in, like not raising tuition at your school. You knew that the essay could be presented to the school's board of trustees, the body that determines tuition rates. You then learned that your essay was actually used to convince the board to raise tuition. Or perhaps you were asked to write an essay taking a position you did not believe in, like raising tuition. You then learned that the essay convinced the board to raise tuition. How would you feel?

According to this view, simply doing something counter to your beliefs will not produce dissonance unless there are negative results. If you are opposed to tuition hikes and write an essay in favor of them, but there are no hikes as a result, you do not experience dissonance.

In several similar studies, people were asked to write essays advocating a position—raising tuition—that conflicted with their beliefs. When rates were increased and essayists felt responsible for the outcome, they resolved the dissonance by changing their attitude in the direction of the outcome. That is, they began to say they were more in favor of a fee increase than before they wrote the essay. When students wrote essays in favor of a fee increase and fees were not increased, they did not experience dissonance and did not change their attitudes. When there is no tension, there is no attitude change.

So, what creates dissonance—inconsistency or a sense of responsibility? There have been hundreds, perhaps thousands, of experiments that support the basic ideas of cognitive dissonance theory, namely, that inconsistency leads to attitude change. That there are valid alternatives simply means the theory may have to incorporate those ideas and continue to be revised.

Lessons of Cognitive Dissonance Theory   What can we learn about persuasive techniques from cognitive dissonance theory? The first lesson is that cognitive inconsistency often leads to change. Therefore, one persuasive technique is to point out to people how their behavior runs counter to their beliefs. Presumably, if people are aware of their inconsistencies, they will change. Persuasion may also occur if individuals are made aware that their behavior may produce a negative outcome (Cooper & Scher, 1992).

A second lesson is that any time you can induce someone to become publicly committed to a behavior that is counter to their beliefs, attitude change is a likely outcome. One reason for the change is that people use their public behavior as a kind of heuristic, a rule that says people stand by their public acts and bear personal responsibility for them (Baumeister & Tice, 1984; Zimbardo & Leippe, 1992). In other words, the rule is, "If I did it, I mean it."

Cognitive dissonance plays an important role in the formation and maintenance of cults. Once people make a public commitment to a leader and a movement, it is hard for them to acknowledge their doubts or misgivings. Instead, they have to throw more and more of their resources into maintaining their commitment, even when it becomes obvious to others that the loyalty is misplaced. This phenomenon has occurred many times in human history. It happened in 1978 in Guyana, in Jonestown, the "utopian" community of the Reverend Jim Jones. On his orders, his followers committed mass suicide by drinking Kool Aid laced with cyanide. It happened again in 1993 in Waco, Texas. For a closer look at the tragedy that occurred there, see the featured discussion "The Lure of Cults: Persuasion Among the Branch Davidians."

Alternatives to Cognitive Dissonance Theory

Not all social psychologists believe cognitive dissonance theory is the best way to explain what happens when cognitive inconsistencies occur. Other theories have been proposed to explain how people deal with these discrepancies.

David Koresh used his charismatic personality to attract followers to the Branch Davidians. He also took advantage of cognitive dynamics, including the psychological tension that results from cognitive dissonance, to keep people committed to his cult.

Self-Perception Theory   Daryl Bem, a student of the great behaviorist psychologist, B. F. Skinner, challenged cognitive dissonance theory because, he asserted, he could explain people's behavior without looking at their inner motives. Bem (1972) proposed **self-perception theory,** which explains discrepant behavior by simply assuming that people are not self-conscious processors of information. People observe their own behavior and assume that their attitudes must be consistent with that behavior. If you eat a big dinner, you assume that you must have been hungry. If you take a public stand on an issue, the rule of self-perception theory is, "I said it, so I must have meant it." We don't look at our motives; we just process the information and conclude that there is no inconsistency.

Bem has supported his theory with some interesting experiments. In one, he trained people to tell the truth whenever a "truth" (green) light was lit and to lie whenever a "lie" (red) light was lit. When the green light was on, people had to say something about themselves that was true. When the red light was on, people had to lie about themselves. Bem then asked the subjects to make further statements that were either true or false under both truth and lie lights. Subjects who told lies when the truth light was on came to believe that those false statements were true. Likewise, subjects who made true statements when the lie light was on reported that they lied.

The point of self-perception theory is that we make inferences about our behavior in much the same way an outside observer might. If you were observing the experiment, you would infer, quite reasonably, that whatever anyone said when the light was red was a lie and anything said under the green light was true. The subjects assumed the same thing. According to self-perception theory, something does not have to happen "inside" the

self-perception theory The theory that people draw conclusions about their attitudes and motives by simply observing their own behavior.

In March 1993, a religious cult known as the Branch Davidians came to national attention when a stand-off began with the Bureau of Alcohol, Tobacco and Firearms (ATF) in Waco, Texas. The cult was led by David Koresh, who claimed to receive orders from God. Koresh created the group's social reality. He separated cult members from the rest of the world, both physically and psychologically. He told them that he was Jesus and that "others" would deny the fact and try to destroy the cult. The Davidians stocked arms, food, and ammunition to prepare for apocalypse and confrontation with the outside world. Koresh's predictions seemed to come true when ATF agents came to seize the cult's automatic weapons. Guns blazed on both sides, leaving several agents dead and wounded.

A siege of the compound began that lasted close to 2 months. Federal authorities grew increasingly concerned about the welfare of the many children inside and about the lack of progress in the negotiations with Koresh. Finally, assured by experts that the Davidians would not commit mass

suicide if threatened, agents pumped tear gas into the compound to force them outside. However, fires erupted inside the buildings, apparently started by the cult. Eighty-six cult members—including 23 children—were incinerated. Apparently, the Davidians chose self-destruction rather than destruction of their reality. Why were members so persuaded by Koresh's outrageous claims? How did they become so committed to the cult?

All cults have many characteristics in common. The primary feature is a charismatic leader. He or she takes on a supernatural aura and persuades group members to devote their lives and fortunes to the cult. Koresh was such a charismatic individual, able to convince large groups of people through clever arguments and persuasive appeals. For example, he refuted doubters by claiming to possess sole understanding of the Scriptures and changed inter-

pretations often to keep cult members constantly uncertain and reliant on him. Koresh used charm and authority to gain control of followers' lives. However, charisma alone is not enough to account for the mindsets of the Davidians. We must also look at the cognitive dynamics of the individual members to see how they became so committed to Koresh and his ideals.

Joining the cult was no easy feat. At first, few demands were made, but after a while, members had to give more. In fact, members routinely turned over all of their possessions, including houses, insurance policies, and money. Once in the group, life was quite harsh. Koresh enforced strict (and changeable) rules on every aspect of members' lives, including personally rationing all their food, imposing celibacy on the men while taking women as his wives and concubines, and inflicting physical abuse. In short, residents of the compound had to expend quite a bit of effort to be members.

All the requirements for membership relate directly to what we know about attitudes and behav-

person for inconsistencies to be resolved. No tension, no motivation to reconcile attitudes and behavior—just information processing.

Rationalization and Self-Affirmation Theory The fact that millions of people smoke is proof that dissonance does not always lead to behavior change. Everyone knows that smoking leads to lung cancer, heart disease, and other problems, including the strong and occasionally aggressive disapproval of nonsmokers. People have to reduce the dissonance between smoking and the knowledge that smoking causes such serious harm. The solution is to rationalize: "Nothing will happen to me," or "I'll stop when I'm 40," or "My grandfather lived until 80, and he smoked like a chimney." Rationalizations are important in maintaining a coherent self-concept, as the following interchange from the movie *The Big Chill* shows:

ior from dissonance theory. For example, dissonance research shows that the harder people have to work to get into a group, the more they value that group (Aronson & Mills, 1959). By turning over all of their possessions, members were making an irreversible commitment to the cult. Once such a commitment is made, people are unlikely to abandon positive attitudes toward the group (Festinger, Riecken, & Schachter, 1982). After expending so much effort, questioning commitment would create cognitive dissonance (Osherow, 1988). It is inconsistent to prove devotion to a belief by donating all of your possessions and then to abandon those beliefs. In other words, to a large extent, cult members persuade themselves. Dissonance theory predicts that the Davidians would come to value the group highly and be disinclined to question Koresh. This is in fact what happened.

Interestingly, cult members do not lose faith when the situation begins to sour. In fact, there is sometimes an *increase* in the strength of their commitment. One study investigated a "dooms-day" society, a group that predicts the end of the world (Festinger et al., 1982). The study found that when a prophecy failed, members became *more* committed to the group. There are five conditions that must be met before this effect will occur:

1. The belief must be held with deep conviction and must be reflected in the believer's overt behavior.
2. The believer must be strongly committed to the beliefs and must have taken some step toward commitment that is difficult to reverse (for example, giving all of his or her money to the group).
3. The belief must be specific and related enough to real world events that it can be disconfirmed, or proven false (for example, the prediction that the world will end on a specified day).
4. There must be undeniable evidence that the belief is false (the world doesn't end).
5. The individual believer must have social support for the belief after disconfirmation.

Most—perhaps all—of these five conditions were present in the Waco tragedy. Members were committed to their beliefs and gave everything they had to Koresh. There was evidence that the situation was unstable; several members had left the cult, and some were even talking to federal officials. And when it started to become obvious that Koresh was not invincible, members had each other to turn to for social support. As negotiations deteriorated, Koresh altered his rhetoric to emphasize apocalyptic visions, rationalizing the cult's destruction and self-sacrifice. Cult members probably came to believe it was their destiny to die if necessary. The power of persuasion can be seen in the tragic results.

———

In what ways does the Yale communication model apply to the Branch Davidian case? The elaboration likelihood model? What kinds of information do you think cult members would have been likely to process centrally? Peripherally? What other persuasive tactics and effects do you recognize in the incident at Waco?

Sam: Why is it what you just said strikes me as a mass of rationalizations?

Michael: Don't knock rationalization. Where would we be without it? I don't know anyone who could get through a day without two or three rationalizations. They're more important than sex.

Sam: Ah, come on. Nothing's more important than sex.

Michael: Oh yeah? You ever gone a week without a rationalization?

Dissonance may threaten a person's self-concept with negative implications, making the person appear stupid or unethical or lazy (Steele, 1988). Nonsmokers probably view smokers as all three. Then why don't people in dissonant situations alter their behavior? In the case of cigarette smoking, a large part of the answer is the highly addictive nature of nicotine. Many people try to quit and fail, or they can't face the prospect of never having another cigarette. So they're stuck with the dissonance. **Self-affirmation theory** suggests that people may not try to reduce dissonance if they can maintain (affirm) their self-concept by proving that they are adequate in other ways: "Yes, I may be a smoker, but I'm also a good mother, a respected professional, and an active citizen in my community." These self-affirmations remove the sting inherent in a dissonance situation (Zimbardo & Leippe, 1992). People cope with a threat to one aspect of the self by affirming an unrelated part of the self (Steele, 1988).

Psychological Reactance   Psychological tension can be reduced in several ways. Sometimes when people realize they have been coerced into doing or buying something against their wishes, they try to regain or reassert their freedom. This response is called **psychological reactance** (Brehm & Brehm, 1981). The theory of psychological reactance, an offshoot of cognitive dissonance theory, suggests that when some part of our freedom is threatened, we become aroused and motivated to restore that freedom.

The Coca-Cola Company found this out in 1985 when they tried to replace the old Coke formula with "New Coke." They conducted an in-depth marketing study of the new product that included 200,000 taste tests. The tests showed that people really liked New Coke. The company went ahead with plans to retire the old formula and to put New Coke in its place.

However, the issue was not taste; it was perceived choice. People resented having a choice taken away and reacted by buying the traditional Coke as if it were manna from heaven, never to be seen again. Some people even formed Old Coke clubs. The company got over 1,500 angry calls and letters every day (Gelman, Wang, Powell, & Smith, 1985). Coca-Cola had to change its marketing plans, and "Classic Coke" still holds an honored place on the grocery shelves (Oskamp, 1991). Whether consumers liked New Coke did not matter. Their emotional ties to old Coke did matter, as did their freedom to buy it. New Coke just wasn't it for these folks.

MASS PERSUASION

self-affirmation theory The theory that people may not try to reduce dissonance if they can maintain (affirm) their self-concept by proving that they are competent in other ways.

psychological reactance A counteracting response to an action perceived as coercive or threatening to one's freedom.

Throughout the chapter, the social psychology of persuasion has been discussed primarily in interpersonal terms. That is, much of what we have discussed deals with individuals constructing strategies and arguments to persuade people one-on-one or speaking directly to an audience. However, in today's society, persuasion often takes place on a larger scale, through mass media or in situations where the audience cannot interact with the persuader. Examples of mass persuasion abound: political candidates trying to obtain our vote, magazines telling us what the latest fads are, and endless advertisers vying for our money. In this section we explore a sample of persuasion situations and techniques that occur on a mass level.

Persuading people to change their sexual behavior is more difficult than persuading them to make other lifestyle changes. The AIDS education campaign must be credible, creative, and relentless if it is to reach young people. How does this billboard attempt to persuade? Is it effective?

Public Health Campaigns: Educating People About AIDS

No single health issue has dominated public consciousness in the past 15 years as much as acquired immunodeficiency syndrome, or AIDS. This disease is currently the ninth leading cause of death in the United States and the nation's number one health priority. Nearly 300,000 Americans have been diagnosed with AIDS, and more than a million are believed to be infected with the human immunodeficiency virus (HIV), the virus that causes the disease. The Centers for Disease Control and Prevention estimate that over 25,000 American college students probably are already infected (Insel & Roth, 1994, p. 465).

Although there is no cure for AIDS, a tremendous amount of information about it is available. This includes information about how the virus is transmitted and about the horrors of the disease itself. The focus of government and public health campaigns is on prevention through education. Messages about AIDS are aimed at persuading people to alter their sexual behaviors in order to minimize risk (Weisse, Nesselhof-Kendall, Fleck-Kandath, & Baum, 1990).

Changing Sexual Attitudes and Behavior Although educational efforts have been effective among some populations at risk for HIV infection, they have been far from successful among others. Behavior change has been greatest among members of the gay community, where the rate of infection has dropped sharply. However, evidence suggests that many gay and bisexual men still engage in high-risk behaviors (Weisse et al., 1990). Less change is apparent among other at-risk populations, including injecting drug users, the poor and homeless, and prostitutes. The rate of infection is increasing most rapidly among women and children (who contract it during birth from infected mothers). Clearly, information is not enough to persuade people to change behaviors that could kill them (Gerrard, Gibbons, Warner, & Smith, 1993).

One reason people are not persuaded by information about AIDS or other threats is that they simply believe bad things will not happen to them. This phenomenon has been called the **illusion of unique invulnerability** (Perloff, 1987). We know that bad things happen—cars are stolen, unwanted pregnancies occur, people get lung cancer—but we think they happen only to others, not to us. Therefore, despite the evidence, we act as if we're invulnerable and resist precautions.

A survey of the sexual risk-taking behaviors and attitudes of college students and of an older, noncollege group—members of a health club—showed that almost everyone (96%) had extensive and tolerably accurate knowledge about the importance of using condoms to prevent HIV transmission and the dangers of having unprotected anal intercourse (Cronin & Rosa, 1990). However, knowledge and behavior were unrelated; people knew the dangers and still engaged in risky behavior. Moreover, amount of education did not affect sexual behavior: People who had attended graduate school did not behave differently than college students or high school graduates.

The survey revealed that less than 23% of the subjects always used condoms, even though over 50% of the health club members had over 10 sexual partners in their lifetime (Table 7-2). Most of the participants simply did not think they were at risk: Only about 10% thought HIV infection could be a possibility for them. Besides, many of the subjects—nearly 90%—rationalized that a cure would be found for AIDS.

Persuading Adolescents to Practice Safe Sex   Given the resistance of individuals to changing their sexual behavior, how can public health offi-

TABLE 7-2

PERCENTAGE OF PEOPLE WHO HAVE ALWAYS PRACTICED SAFE SEX

No. of Partners	College Campus (52 people)		Health Clubs (90 people)	
	Yes	No	Yes	No
1	0%	100%	0%	100%
2–5	12	88	14	86
6–10	25	75	7	93
11–25	17	83	18	82
26–50	0	0	20	80
50+	0	0	14	86
Total	14	86	13	87

Adapted from Cronin and Rosa, 1990.

illusion of unique invulnerability The false belief that bad things happen only to other people.

cials get people to stop killing themselves? If the facts about AIDS aren't persuasive enough, how can people be convinced to stop putting themselves at risk?

Let's look at one group that is particularly vulnerable to HIV infection—adolescents. Although young people in their teens and twenties tend not to have high rates of HIV infection, it's likely that rates will increase soon because these groups always have been vulnerable to sexually transmitted diseases (Weisse et al., 1990). One important factor in targeting young people is that the image of "impressionable years" has some truth. It doesn't mean that older people do not change; they do. But susceptibility to attitude and behavior change is strongest during adolescence and early adulthood (Krosnick & Alwin, 1989). If adolescents can be motivated to pay attention to safe-sex messages, they may listen to the evidence and analyze it in order to make an informed decision. As you recall from the elaboration likelihood model, when individuals use central processing, they elaborate on the message and, as a result, experience long-term attitude change. In other words, if individuals form strong attitudes about safe sex practices during adolescence, those attitudes are likely to stick.

How can health officials reach adolescents with persuasive messages about protecting themselves from AIDS? First of all, credible communicators are particularly important for this audience (Krosnick & Alwin, 1989). We have seen that the more credible the communicator, the more effective the persuasive message is. This is especially true with people whose attitudes are not well formed yet, specifically adolescents. Magic Johnson, as a much admired sports figure and a hero to aspiring youth, had the credibility to speak effectively about AIDS.

Second, the message must be credible, in both form and content. The message that teenagers should abstain from sex, for example, is unrealistic and therefore unconvincing. The message should contain enough interest and fear to get the audience's attention but not so much that they will reject the message as noncredible. AIDS messages that focus on safer sex practices, especially the use of condoms, are likely to have the most effect.

How often should a persuasive message be shown to an audience? What is the effect of frequent exposure? One study showed that repetition of a message was effective up to a point, and then listeners became weary of it (Cacioppo & Petty, 1979). In this study, the magic number was three exposures. Televised messages usually run longer than this, of course, and it may take a long time before a message loses its power to influence. Other studies have looked at the strength of the message as a variable in effectiveness. Results indicate that frequently repeated weak messages get negative reactions but that frequently repeated strong messages get positive reactions (Petty & Cacioppo, 1986a).

Finally, the channel for the message must be accessible and appealing. Television, video, and rock music are all channels that are familiar and credible for an adolescent audience. Madonna's "Like a Prayer" is a good example of an effective format for persuading adolescents. It included advice and information about AIDS and risk reduction. The communicator was credible, particularly because she had nothing tangible to gain from conveying this message.

FIGURE 7-10 *A message has more persuasive effect if the communicator is trustworthy, if the message itself is credible and realistic, and if the channel is an accessible one. This is especially true when the message is about such a private and emotionally charged area as sexual behavior.*

The message was strong without being threatening, and the channel (tape, CD) was familiar and accessible (Figure 7-10).

What about self-persuasion? Jeff Stone and his colleagues (1994) applied a new twist on cognitive dissonance theory to the prevention of HIV transmission among sexually active young adults. Stone asked subjects to develop a speech about using condoms for the prevention of HIV transmission and to deliver it in front of a TV camera. These individuals were then systematically reminded of the fact that they had admitted to not using condoms in the past. Cognitive dissonance theory predicts that a conflict like this between public statements and private behavior leads to a change in behavior. Results showed that subjects who were made aware of this inconsistency, this "hypocrisy," were much more likely than other subjects to purchase condoms in the future.

The Limits of Persuasion However, we should not overstate the odds that persuasion efforts will work. There is limited empirical evidence that educating or informing people about the risk of HIV transmission increases precautionary behavior (Gerrard, Gibbons, Warner, & Smith, 1993). This is not true for other health risks. You can persuade people to use seat belts or to stop smoking or to change their eating habits. What's different about AIDS? Sex. Sexual relationships are central to our personal identities (Gerrard et al., 1993). We are resistant to making changes recommended by others in something we perceive as so basic and so private. We would rather take risks than surrender our values or intimate "freedoms." Or we would rather delude ourselves into thinking we are not really at risk.

Political Campaigning: The Art of Dirty Politics

We see another form of mass persuasion in political campaigning. How do candidates get voters to elect them to office? Do they try to inform the electorate about their plans and programs? Do they try to convey their values and aspirations for the country? Or do they focus on their opponents, trying to muddy their names? The last strategy, though unsavory, has been a common one throughout American history. Dirty politics, also known as **attack campaigning,** involves trying to destroy the credibility of an opponent by any means, fair if possible but foul if necessary (Jamieson, 1992). Clarence Darrow believed in attack campaigning and never missed a chance to characterize the prosecution as cold-hearted and bloody-minded.

If you think current politics are dirty, consider the following example. When Thomas Jefferson first ran for the presidency of the United States, the president of Yale University, Reverend Timothy Dwight, warned that if Jefferson won, the Bible would be burned, churchgoers would be compelled to sing the French national anthem, and men might see their "wives and daughters the victims of legal prostitution; soberly dishonored; speciously polluted" (Jamieson, 1992).

Modern political ads are more visual and sophisticated than such assaults, but they are just as nasty. Consider the case of the Willie Horton ads in the 1988 presidential campaign. When Michael Dukakis took office as governor of Massachusetts, a furlough program was in place that had been started by his Republican predecessor. According to the plan, certain convicts were allowed furloughs, or passes, to leave prison over the weekend. It was an attempt, modeled on a federal program, to reduce prison overcrowding and to ease convicts back into society. During Dukakis's two terms as governor, 11,497 convicts had been furloughed a total of 67,378 times. Of those convicts, 268 were "late" in returning from their furloughs, and five committed crimes while on leave. Four were white, one a former police officer, and the fifth was an African American man named William ("Willie") Horton.

While on furlough, Horton raped a white woman and assaulted her husband. During the 1988 presidential campaign, the Republicans aired ads about Horton as a way of accusing Dukakis of being soft on crime. The ads not only described Horton's crimes but also falsely accused him of torturing and murdering the rape survivor's husband (Jamieson, 1992).

What were the ads all about? Figure 7–11 shows two still photos from one of the ads. You first see the rather forbidding photograph of Willie Horton, then prisoners going in and out of prison via the revolving door, which emphasizes the claim that Michael Dukakis allowed convicted murderers, particularly the dangerous and—not coincidentally—African American Willie Horton to kidnap, stab, and rape. In fact, of the 268 escaped criminals, only 4 were convicted murderers (Jamieson, 1992). Unfortunately for Dukakis, Willie Horton was one of them. Dukakis was unable to detach himself from the image of Horton for the duration of the campaign.

Why was the ad so effective? Certainly, it was made more accessible to the public because it created a furor and was played repeatedly on news programs (somewhat like the Rodney King videotape). We also know from the

attack campaigning An approach to political persuasion that focuses on destroying an opponent's credibility rather than on conveying one's own plans and programs.

FIGURE 7-11 *The Willie Horton ad campaign. This ad, put together by a conservative political action committee, propelled the image of a convicted murderer onto TV screens in 1988 and linked him irrevocably with Democratic presidential candidate Michael Dukakis. Attack campaigning is unsavory but apparently effective. Once it's made, a negative impression carries more weight than any perceived strengths or positive information about a candidate.*

elaboration likelihood model that fear may lower our tendency or ability to process information via the central route. Fear appeals such as the Horton ads tend to drain our ability to analyze them carefully (Jamieson, 1992). Further, a rational presentation of the facts does not seem to work as a response to a fear appeal. All the voting public knew was that 268 Willie Hortons escaped. They were not inclined to listen to a rational rebuttal.

Do negative ads work? For example, do they affect voting behavior? We have no definitive evidence that they do. People did remember the Horton ads. However, recalling vivid ads and being affected by them are not necessarily the same thing. Negative, vivid ads are heuristics people use when they do not follow the issues and, therefore, do not process centrally.

Jill Klein (1991) examined the influence of negative information as compared to positive information on the impressions voters form of candidates for office. She found evidence for a **negativity effect:** Negative information weighed more heavily and was more predictive of the overall impression of a candidate than positive information. Therefore, a perceived character weakness is more critical than any perceived strengths a candidate may project. This result certainly suggests that negative campaigning can work.

Appealing to the Unconscious: Subliminal Persuasion

Dirty tricks are not limited to politics. In Chapter 6 we discussed *subliminal influence,* the influence of stimuli presented below the level of conscious awareness. The assumption underlying subliminal influence attempts is that a stimulus can be presented so quickly that while the recipient may not consciously see or recognize it, the message will nevertheless affect the individual's attitudes and behavior. Thus, flashing "Buy U.S. Savings Bonds" on a movie screen below the level of conscious awareness will make us run out and buy bonds.

negativity effect The phenomenon whereby negative information about a political candidate has more impact than positive information.

In Chapter 6 we saw from experiments that subliminal stimuli did influence people, although the effects were not very strong or long-lasting. In one study, a photograph of a person was flashed subliminally to subjects (Bornstein, Leone, & Galley, 1987). Later, subjects tended to agree with the positions advocated by the person in the photograph. Thus, there is some evidence that subliminal influence extends to short-term, simple behaviors in a laboratory setting (Zimbardo & Leippe, 1992). What happens when we leave the laboratory?

Clearly, many important people think subliminal influence is a real threat. The National Association of Broadcasters does not permit subliminal advertising, nor do the governments of Britain and Australia (Pratkanis & Aronson, 1992). In 1990 subliminal messages became the subject of a lawsuit when two families sued the rock group "Judas Priest." Two young men had committed suicide after listening to one of the band's records. Their families alleged that Judas Priest put a subliminal message ("do it") on one of the tracks and so provoked the young men to kill themselves. Social psychologist Anthony Pratkanis was an important witness for the defendants (Judas Priest). He testified that there is no clear evidence that subliminal messages affect individuals' behavior. He convinced the court that the band could not have subliminally persuaded the men to commit suicide.

Pratkanis cited several relevant studies. One researched the effectiveness of audiotapes containing subliminal messages (Greenwald, Spangenberg, Pratkanis, & Eskenazi, 1991). These "self-help" tapes claimed that by using subliminal messages they could increase listeners' self-esteem or vocabulary or help them to stop smoking. Greenwald tested the effectiveness of these tapes by asking interested people to listen to them for 5 weeks. Unbeknown to the volunteers, the experimenters mislabeled the tapes. A tape containing a self-esteem message was labeled a memory-improvement tape, and a memory-improvement tape was labeled a self-esteem tape. Other subjects received accurately labeled tapes. Everybody took memory and self-esteem tests before beginning the experiment.

Five weeks later, subjects who listened to a mislabeled "memory-improvement" tape thought that their memories had improved, and those who listened to a falsely labeled "self-esteem" tape thought they now had better self-esteem. Subjects took memory and self-esteem tests again, and their scores showed *no improvement* in memory or self-esteem. As the researchers noted, "what people expect is what they believe, but not necessarily what [they] get" (Pratkanis & Aronson, 1992, p. 203). Thus, except for some short-term behavior changes in laboratory studies, subliminal messages do not seem to persuade.

Propaganda

When the setting for persuasion takes place on a mass scale, we often use the term *propaganda*. Most theorists suggest that persuasion involves an interaction among people in which attitude change is voluntary. By contrast, propaganda takes advantage of people's emotions and tries to circumvent or prevent critical thinking about issues (Pratkanis & Aronson, 1992). The line between persuasion and propaganda is thin. Propaganda is an attempt to manipulate and control the way people feel as well as the way they act.

Propaganda Techniques   The techniques used by propagandists may vary from case to case. However, the goal is the same: Persuade the masses. Common propaganda techniques include the following (Brown, 1967):

- *Use of stereotypes:* Propagandists often take advantage of our natural tendency to stereotype people. Propaganda can eventually lead us to think of a group of people in terms of the stereotype rather than as individual human beings.
- *Substitution of names:* Propagandists often use derogatory names to refer to disliked groups. Victims of propaganda become dehumanized, and it becomes easier to persecute them.
- *Selection of facts:* Propagandists do not present a balanced view of events. They select specific facts that support their point of view.
- *Downright lying:* Falsehoods are used to persuade others.
- *Repetition:* The same message is repeated over and over. Repeated exposure eventually leads to acceptance of the message.
- *Assertion:* Propagandists are not interested in debating. Instead, they assert their point forcefully.
- *Pinpointing an enemy:* Propaganda is most effective if an enemy can be identified who poses a threat to all. This directs aggression or blame away from the propagandists and strengthens in-group feelings of unity and solidarity. This technique plays on the "us versus them" mentality.
- *Appeals to higher authority:* Propagandists will try to closely align their leaders with a higher power (religious, political, ideological) to legitimize their views and behavior.

Many of these propaganda techniques were used by Serbian president Slobodan Milosevic in his 1992 bid for reelection against prime minister Milan Panic. Nicknamed the "butcher of the Balkans," Milosevic had been elected president in 1989 by enflaming ethnic enmities among the Serbs, Croats, and Muslims, who had managed to live together peaceably in communist Yugoslavia. Playing on their fears, hatreds, and memories of past injustices at the hands of the Croats and Muslims, Milosevic told the Serbs, "No one will ever beat you again" (Walsh, 1993, p. 45). Milosevic pursued a policy of aggressive territorial conquest and "ethnic cleansing" that led the United Nations to impose economic sanctions on the country.

In the 1992 campaign, Serbs were encouraged to believe that if Milosevic lost, "outside forces" might impose Muslim rule on the country. Serbian women could end up in harems (Morrow, 1992, p. 38), or Serbians might all be placed in concentration camps (Nelan, 1993, p. 49). Milosevic claimed that only a victory by his party would end the U.N. sanctions; voting for the opposition, he suggested, would extend the sanctions and the suffering of the Serbian people (Landay, 1993). He also assured the people that sanctions had had little effect, even though, in reality, production was down dramatically, shelves were empty, and unemployment and inflation were soaring.

Milosevic relied on state-run radio and television to support his candidacy and to distort and suppress that of his opponent. Virtually all the information available to the Serbian people was filtered through the strictly controlled media. Whereas Milosevic's appearances and policies were covered nightly on the news, information about Panic and his views was censored, watered down, or not shown at all. The media also waged a campaign against Panic, labeling him a traitor and an agent of the C.I.A. (Rosenberger, 1993, p. 22). Perhaps not wanting to trust everything to propaganda, however, Milosevic "by all accounts" also resorted to rigging the election (Walsh, 1993, p. 46). Official results gave him 56% of the vote.

A Case Study: The American Revolution Propaganda is not a 20th-century invention, although the growth of mass media such as newspapers and television has made propaganda more pervasive and effective. However, we can learn much about propaganda by taking a look at how it was used in the American Revolution (1776–83). This was a war of propaganda. It had to be: Most people had substantial doubts about resisting the British. After all, the American colonists thought of themselves as English. George Washington's army was never very large, and he always had trouble getting supplies and pay for his troops. Most colonists wished, quite sensibly, to be left alone to conduct their lives.

The Revolution was, first and foremost, a war of ideas. The revolutionary idea, new and dangerous, was an independent United States of America. People had to be persuaded to fight for this radical concept. Keep in mind that the colonists were experiencing the greatest economic boom in their history. Many saw no reason to separate from prosperous England.

By 1770 the revolutionaries were waging a propaganda war against the British. British troops were quartered in Boston, and some locals put out the story that they were continually drunk and committing "outrage" (Morrison, 1965). Apparently none of these stories were true, but the propaganda took its toll. British soldiers were mugged on the streets and made to feel generally unwelcome, despite their policy of being friendly.

In March 1770, when tensions were high because of labor disputes, a group described by John Adams as "Negroes and mulattoes, Irish teagues (toughs) and outlandish jack-tars (sailors)" began throwing snowballs at the British (Morrison, 1965, p. 200). The British responded to this provocation by calling out about 20 soldiers, who confronted a clamoring mob of several hundred. Taunted by the mob and pelted by stones, one soldier lost his discipline and fired his musket into the crowd. Other muskets joined in. Three colonists were killed, and two others eventually died from their wounds.

Led by Massachusetts legislator Samuel Adams, the revolutionaries quickly turned the event into a call to arms. Adams milked what he called the "Boston Massacre" for everything it was worth, combining images and emotion in an exaggerated brew of half-truths. This is essentially how propaganda works.

Paul Revere's engraving of the Boston Massacre is an eighteenth-century example of propaganda. Revere manipulated colonial sentiment by depicting the British as cold-blooded murderers carrying out a planned military maneuver and the Bostonians as respectable citizens innocently going about their business.

Paul Revere made an engraving of the event in which he showed the British in battle formation, taking deliberate aim at 20 civilians. In the engraving, Revere also increased the number of men killed, depicted the British as butchers, and portrayed Crispus Attucks, a black man killed by the British, as white. This engraving was seen throughout the colonies. Essentially, it was a political cartoon. In fact, when the soldiers were tried for murder, their attorney, John Adams, warned jurors not to pay attention to Revere's engraving (Jowett & O'Donnell, 1992). A colonial jury returned a not guilty verdict in favor of the British troops. Nevertheless, Sam Adams turned the date of the massacre into a national holiday of anger. The Sons of Liberty staged a march on that date, followed by overblown speeches and displays of "relics" from the massacre.

In perhaps their most effective use of propaganda, the revolutionaries immediately gave local newspapers their version of the story. Newspapers of that time did not aspire to objectivity and were already anti-British. Since newspapers and personal letters were the main means of communication, control of the newspapers was essential. Conveniently, Sam Adams worked for the *Boston Gazette*. He formed a propaganda team, the Committee of Correspondence, who gathered news and reported back to him. Adams then sent out his version of the news to other papers (Jowett & O'Donnell, 1986).

Although Adams was often considered a rabble-rouser, greedy for power, he had a clear view of his cause and the means to achieve it. He believed the British were trying to control the colonies by taxing imported goods and by keeping officials (such as governors) on the British payroll (Morrison, 1965). However, most colonists were not overly concerned with these issues. Sam Adams needed a more inflammatory appeal, and he turned the Boston Massacre into that issue.

Adams invented five rules of propaganda in making his case. These rules are as valid a description of propaganda today as they were then:

1. The aims of the cause must be justified.
2. The advantages of victory must be made clear and known.
3. The people need to be aroused to action by instilling hatred of the enemy.
4. Logical arguments of the enemy need to be negated.
5. All issues must be stated in clear-cut, black-and-white terms. (Jowett & O'Donnell, 1986)

Sam Adams never took a social psychology course, but he anticipated a number of facts we now know about persuasion. He knew the importance of credible communicators. Patrick Henry, Thomas Jefferson, and Richard Henry Lee were early converts to the cause. They helped provide rousing speeches, most containing fear appeals that suggested what would happen if the colonists did not resist the British. Later, the chorus was joined by George Washington and Benjamin Franklin, both well-respected men of great reputation—and skilled propagandists.

Adams understood that the colonists had to know exactly why a revolution was the only reasonable course. He controlled the channels of communication and delivered his message skillfully and often. He was a shrewd judge of his audience and knew how to appeal to the common worker. Adams allowed the people to hear only weakened or falsified versions of communications from the British king, in effect inoculating the colonists and making them immune to British appeals to reason. The rest, as they say, is history.

THE LEOPOLD AND LOEB CASE REVISITED

Clarence Darrow used all his powers of persuasion to save his clients, Leopold and Loeb, from execution. As a skilled communicator, he knew how important it was to establish and maintain his credibility. Many of his arguments aimed, sometimes subtly, sometimes not, at destroying his opponent's credibility and enhancing his own.

Darrow also understood that a communicator who seems disinterested in persuading his audience is usually more successful than one who is clearly trying to persuade. He took the high moral ground, arguing that it would be inhumane to execute two young men who weren't entirely responsible for their actions.

Darrow did not neglect his audiences, the trial judge and the public. He carefully structured and presented his arguments in order to have the greatest effect on them. Darrow knew that arguments too far from the judge's "latitude of acceptance" would not succeed. He didn't argue against capital punishment (although he personally opposed it), just capital punishment in this particular case. He knew Judge Caverly was listening carefully to his arguments, elaborating on them and placing them in the context of American criminal justice. He knew the world was listening too. The Leopold and Loeb "thrill murder" case became one of the most infamous incidents in U.S. history, for Americans were shocked at the spectacle of two wealthy young men who killed "just to see what it would feel like."

In his long career, Clarence Darrow used his persuasive skills to defend over 50 other accused murderers, only one of whom was executed. His most famous defense, however, was of William Scopes, a school teacher charged with teaching Darwin's theory of evolution—a crime in Tennessee in 1925. Darrow lost the case to the impassioned—and persuasive—eloquence of William Jennings Bryan, but the Tennessee state supreme court later overturned Scopes's conviction.

As for Leopold and Loeb, Judge Caverly handed down his decision on September 10, 1924. They were sentenced to life imprisonment for murder and 99 years for kidnapping. Loeb died in 1936 in a prison fight; a model prisoner, Leopold was released at the age of 70 and spent the rest of his life in Puerto Rico helping the poor.

LOOKING AHEAD

In this chapter we have examined various models of persuasion—explanations for how and why people modify their attitudes or behavior in response to persuasive arguments. We have also looked at a number of examples of mass persuasion and considered the factors that contribute to their effectiveness.

Although persuasion is a pervasive form of social influence in our society, it is not the only form. People often modify their attitudes or behavior in response to less explicit influences, such as social conventions and norms. They also make and respond to direct requests. In Chapter 8 we turn to an examination of two related forms of social influence, conformity and compliance.

CHAPTER REVIEW

1. *What is persuasion?*
    Persuasion is a form of social influence whereby a communicator uses rational and/or emotional arguments to convince others to change their attitudes or their behavior.

2. *What is the Yale communication model?*
    The **Yale communication model** is a theoretical model that guides persuasion tactics. It is based on the assumption that persuasion will occur if a persuader presents a logical argument that makes clear how attitude change is beneficial. The Yale model focuses on the **credibility** of the communicator, an important determinant of the likelihood that persuasion will occur. The components of credibility are expertise and trustworthiness. Although an important factor in the persuasiveness of a message, communicator credibility may not have long-lasting effects. Over time, a message from a noncredible source may be as persuasive as one from a credible source, a phenomenon known as the **sleeper effect.** This is more likely to

occur if there is a strong persuasive argument; if a discounting cue is given; and if sufficient time passes that people forget who said what.

Other variables in the Yale model are the message, the audience, and the channel. Messages that include a mild to moderate appeal to fear seem to be more persuasive than others, provided they offer a solution to the fear-producing situation. The timing of the message is another factor in its persuasiveness, as is the structure of the message and the extent to which the communicator attempts to fit the message to the audience. Research supports **inoculation theory,** which holds that giving people a weakened version of an opposing argument is an effective approach to persuasion. Good communicators also know their audience well enough not to deliver a highly discrepant message. When this cannot be avoided, as when there is a **multiple audience problem,** communicators use hidden messages and private keys and codes to get their point across.

3. *What are the cognitive response approaches to persuasion?*
   Cognitive response models focus on the active role of the audience. They assert that people respond to persuasive messages by connecting them with their own knowledge, feelings, and thoughts related to the topic of the message. The **elaboration likelihood model (ELM),** which examines how individuals respond to the persuasive message, proposes two routes to persuasion. The first, **central route processing,** is used when people have the capacity and motivation to understand the message and analyze it in a critical and effortful manner. Central route processors elaborate on the message by connecting it to their knowledge and feelings. Sometimes this elaboration will persuade the recipient, depending on the strength of the message. Central route processors tend to experience more durable attitude changes.

   The second avenue to persuasion is **peripheral route processing.** This occurs when individuals do not have the motivation or interest to process effortfully. Instead, they rely on cues other than the merits of the message, such as the attractiveness of the communicator. Whether a person uses central or peripheral route processing depends on a number of factors, including mood, personal relevance, and use of language. Some people, those with a high **need for cognition (NC),** prefer to use central processing all the time.

   A related model, the **heuristic and systematic information processing model (HSM),** focuses more heavily on the importance of heuristics or peripheral cues. This model notes that often issues are too complex or too numerous for effortful, systematic processing to be practical.

4. *What are the models of self-persuasion?*
   Cognitive dissonance theory proposes that people feel an uncomfortable tension when their attitudes, or attitude and behavior, are inconsistent. This psychological discomfort is known as **cognitive dissonance.** According to the theory, people are motivated to reduce this tension, and attitude change is a likely outcome. Dissonance theory suggests that the less reward people receive for a behavior, the more compelled they feel to provide their own justification for it, especially if they believe they have freely chosen it.

Similarly, the more they are rewarded, the more they infer that the behavior is suspect. The latter is known as the **reverse-incentive effect.**

Another, more recent view suggests that cognitive dissonance results not so much from inconsistency as from the feeling of personal responsibility that occurs when inconsistent actions produce negative consequences.

One alternative to cognitive dissonance theory is **self-perception theory,** which argues that behavior and attitude change can be explained without assuming that people are motivated to reduce the tension supposedly produced by inconsistency. Instead, self-perception assumes that people are not self-conscious processors of information. They simply observe their own behavior and assume that their attitudes must be consistent with that behavior.

Another alternative to cognitive dissonance, **self-affirmation theory,** explains how people deal with the tension that dissonant thoughts or behaviors provoke. Self-affirmation theory suggests that people may not try to reduce dissonance if they can maintain their self-concept by proving that they are adequate in other ways, that is, by affirming an unrelated and positive part of the self.

Individuals may reduce psychological tension in another way as well. When people realize they have been coerced into doing or buying something against their will, they sometimes try to regain or reassert their freedom. This response is called **psychological reactance.**

5. *How are the tactics of persuasion used on a mass scale?*
The same persuasive tactics that operate in interpersonal settings can be and are used in mass communication. One example is the public health campaign to persuade people to change their sexual practices in order to protect themselves from HIV infection. Although these efforts have been effective among some populations, they have been far from successful among others. One reason people are not persuaded by information about AIDS or other serious threats is that they simply believe bad things will not happen to them. This phenomenon has been called the **illusion of unique invulnerability.** Efforts to change people's sexual behaviors must be very persuasive, using credible communicators, familiar channels, and a moderate appeal to fear that includes a solution to the problem (e.g., the use of condoms).

A second example of mass persuasion occurs in the political arena. Many political campaigns throughout American history have emphasized **attack campaigning,** aimed at destroying the character and credibility of the opponent. There is no definitive evidence that negative campaigning works, but negative information does weigh more heavily and is more predictive of the overall impression of a candidate than positive information. This **negativity effect** means that a perceived character weakness is more critical than any perceived strengths a candidate may project.

Subliminal influence is another example of mass persuasion. However, experimental research has shown that, except for some short-term behavior changes in laboratory studies, subliminal messages do not seem to persuade.

6. *What is propaganda?*
Propaganda is an attempt, on a mass scale, to manipulate and control the

way people feel as well as the way they act. Propaganda typically tries to circumvent critical thinking. Although we tend to think of propaganda as a 20th-century phenomenon, it has been used throughout history. It was, for example, widely used during the American Revolution to persuade colonists to support the revolutionary cause.

SUGGESTIONS FOR FURTHER READING

Jamieson, K. H. (1992). *Dirty politics: Distraction, deception, & democracy.* New York: Oxford University Press.
  The dean of the Annenberg School of Communication has given us an insightful and lively examination of not only the most recent elections but also the use of persuasion tactics in politics throughout American history.
Pratkanis, A. R., & Aronson, E. (1992). *The age of propaganda.* New York: W. H. Freeman.
  A well-written nontechnical examination of the application of the social psychology of persuasion to everyday events by two of the leading researchers in the area of persuasion and social influence.
Spence, G. (1990). *With justice for none.* New York: Penguin Books.
  A personal examination of the legal system by a successful trial lawyer who knows all the tricks of persuasion.

Chapter 8

Conformity and Compliance

The jury had been empaneled to hear the case *State v. LeRoy Reed*. Reed, a paroled felon, had been arrested for possessing a gun. Frank, a firefighter, sat in the jury box, carefully listening and watching.

The prosecuting attorney argued that the defendant should be found guilty of violating his parole despite any sympathy that might be felt for him. The defense attorney argued that even though Reed had bought a gun, he should *not* be found guilty. According to the defense, Reed bought the gun because he believed that it was required for a mail-order detective course in which he had enrolled. Reed wanted to better his life, and he thought that becoming a private detective was just the ticket. He admired real-life detectives very much. He had told a police detective at the County Courthouse that he was learning to be a detective and had bought a gun. The detective was incredulous and told Reed to go home and get it. Reed did

so and was promptly arrested. Possessing a gun is a criminal offense for felons. Evidence also showed that Reed was able to read at only a fifth-grade level and probably did not understand that he was violating his parole by purchasing a weapon.

The judge told the jury that according to the law, they must find Reed guilty if he possessed a gun and knew that he possessed a gun. As he went into the jury room, Frank was convinced that Reed was guilty. After all, the prosecutor had presented sufficient evidence concerning the points of law that, according to the judge, must be fulfilled for conviction. Reed had bought a gun and certainly knew that he possessed that gun.

As the deliberations began, however, it became obvious that not all jurors agreed with Frank. The results of a first-ballot vote taken by the foreperson showed that nine jurors favored acquittal and only three, including Frank, favored conviction. After further discussion, two of the jurors favoring conviction changed their votes. Frank alone held firm to his belief in the defendant's guilt.

As the deliberations progressed, the other jurors tried to convince Frank that a not-guilty verdict was the fairest verdict. This pressure made Frank very anxious and upset. He continually put his face in both hands and closed his eyes. Continued efforts to persuade Frank to change his verdict failed. After a while, however, Frank, still unconvinced, decided to change his verdict. He told the other jury members that he would change his verdict to not guilty but that he "would just never feel right about it."

Why did Frank change his verdict, even though he did not agree with his fellow jurors? This case, vividly brought to life in the PBS film "Inside the Jury Room," forces us not just to look at Frank's behavior but also to speculate about our own. Would each of us be as willing to compromise our beliefs in the face of a unanimous majority who think differently? Under what conditions can our behavior be modified by others? These questions are at the very core of what distinguishes social psychology from other areas of psychology: the influence of others on our behavior.

In Chapter 7 we saw how persuasive arguments from others can influence our behavior. Frank was certainly exposed to such arguments. However, he did not accept them as a basis for changing his verdict. Rather, Frank modified his verdict in response to the knowledge that 11 of his fellow jurors believed that LeRoy Reed should be found not guilty. Thus, as Frank's case illustrates, sometimes we modify behavior based on perceived pressure from others rather than through a process of accepting what they say.

Like Frank, we are often influenced by what those around us do. For example, when you are seated in a classroom, you will note that most people are behaving similarly: They are taking notes and listening to the professor. In social situations, such as the classroom, the behavior of others often defines the range of appropriate behavior. This is especially true when the situation is new or ambiguous. What if, for example, the fire alarm rang while you were sitting in class? Would you immediately get up and leave? Or would you look around to see what others do? Most people insist that they would get up and leave. However, experience teaches us otherwise. If your classmates were just sitting in their seats calmly, you probably would do the same. The social influence processes that operate on you in the classroom situation can also be applied to understanding situations like Frank's changing his verdict.

In this chapter we explore two types of social influence: conformity and compliance. We ask, How does social influence sometimes cause us to do or say things that we don't necessarily believe in, as was the case with Frank? Why was Frank able to hold out when there were others on his side but finally gave in when he was the only one for conviction? What other factors and types of situations make us more or less likely to conform? When we conform, do we always conform with the majority, or can a minority sometimes lead us to conform to their point of view? And what factors affect our tendency to comply—to agree to a direct request? These are some of the questions addressed in this chapter.

CONFORMITY: GOING ALONG WITH THE CROWD

As a juror, Frank was placed in an uncertain position because he was receiving conflicting input about the situation. From the judge and the prosecution he received a message about the law that convinced him that Reed was guilty and that his responsibility as a juror was to convict him of violating his parole. From his fellow jurors, on the other hand, he received a different message, a message that made him doubt this conclusion. The other jurors told him that in their opinion, Reed should be found not guilty despite the evidence. They believed that extenuating circumstances, including Reed's lack of intent to commit a crime, made a not guilty verdict appropriate. Additionally, Frank was well aware that he was the only juror holding out for conviction. The force brought to bear by the social situation eventually caused Frank to change his verdict, although privately he did not agree with most of his fellow jurors. Frank was the "victim" of social influence.

If Frank had had to decide Reed's fate on his own, he would have convicted him. But once he was in a social context, he had to reconsider his personal views in light of the views of others. He yielded to group pressure even though he felt the group was wrong. Frank's behavior is illustrative of what social psychologists call conformity. **Conformity** occurs when we modify our behavior in response to real or imagined pressure from others. Notice that nobody directly asked or ordered Frank to change his verdict. Instead, he responded to the subtle and not-so-subtle pressures his fellow jurors applied.

Informational and Normative Social Influence

What is it about the social situation that can cause us to change our opinion, even if we privately feel such an opinion shift is wrong? To adequately address this question we need to make a distinction between two kinds of social influence: informational social influence and normative social influence (Deutsch & Gerrard, 1955).

Sometimes we modify our behavior in response to information that we receive from others. This is known as **informational social influence.** In many social situations, other people provide important information through their actions and words. Imagine yourself in the place of one of Frank's fellow jurors, say, the jury foreperson. You think the defendant is guilty, but nine of your fellow jurors think the opposite. They try to convince you of the defendant's innocence by sharing their perceptions of the evidence with you. One juror may remind you of an important piece of information that you had forgotten; another may share an interpretation of the defendant's behavior that had not occurred to you. If you modify your opinion based on such new or reinterpreted information, you are responding to informational social influence.

This is in fact what happened to the foreperson in the LeRoy Reed case. Initially he was among the three jurors who were voting to convict. But after hearing the group discuss the issues and the evidence, he came to see the crime and the surrounding circumstances in a different way. Based on his reinterpretation of the evidence, he decided to change his verdict. He did so in direct response to what was said and how other jurors said it.

Generally, we are subject to informational social influence because we want to be accurate in our judgments. We use other people's opinions as a source of information by which to test the validity of our own judgments.

conformity A change in behavior that occurs in response to real or imagined pressure from others.

informational social influence The type of social influence in which a person changes behavior in response to information others provide.

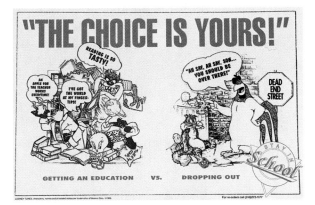

We conform because we perceive that others have correct information (Campbell & Fairey, 1989). Shifts in opinion based on informational social influence result from the sharing of arguments and factual information (Kaplan & Miller, 1987). Essentially, opinion and behavior change come about via the kind of persuasion processes discussed in Chapter 7.

Conformity also comes about as a result of **normative social influence.** In this type of social influence situation, we modify our behavior in response to a **norm,** an unwritten social rule, that suggests what constitutes appropriate behavior in a particular situation. Our behavior is guided not only by rational consideration of the issue at hand but also by the discomfort that we experience when we are in disagreement with others. We are motivated to conform to norms, and to the implicit expectations of others, in order to gain social acceptance and to avoid appearing different or being rejected (Campbell & Fairey, 1989).

In the case of LeRoy Reed, Frank was not influenced directly by the informational content of the jury deliberations. Instead, the fact that others disagreed with him became crucial. The arguments and opinions expressed by the other jurors suggested to him that the operational norm was that the law didn't apply in this case; Reed ought to be acquitted despite evidence pointing to his guilt. Frank changed his verdict in order to conform to this norm.

In a normative social influence situation at least two factors are relevant. First, the input we obtain from others serves as a clue to the nature of the norm in effect at any given time (Kaplan & Miller, 1987). Frank was surprised to discover what the norm was in the jury room. Second, the size and unanimity of the majority convey information about the strength of the norm in effect. As we see later in this chapter, these two variables are important in determining the likelihood and amount of behavior change in a social influence situation.

Although both informational and normative social influence can exert powerful control over our behavior, their effects are different. The changes caused by informational social influence tend to be stronger and more enduring than those caused by normative social influence (Burnstein & Sentis, 1981). This is because changes caused by new information or a new interpretation of existing information may be persuasive and convincing. As

When we modify our behavior in response to arguments and facts—even if presented in cartoon form, as on the left— we are responding to informational social influence. We conform because we see that others have correct information, in this case about the benefits of staying in school versus dropping out. When we modify our behavior in response to unwritten social rules about appropriate behavior in certain situations, we are responding to normative social influence. The boys on the right are conforming— in what they wear, what they talk about, how they sit, how they wear their hair—because they want to be accepted and fit in.

normative social influence
The type of social influence in which a person changes behavior in response to a norm.

norm An unwritten social rule that guides or regulates acceptable or appropriate behavior in a particular situation.

we saw in Chapter 7, the opinion changes that result from persuasion are usually based on our accepting information, elaborating on it, and altering our attitudes and behavior accordingly. This type of information processing tends to produce rather stable, long-lasting change.

For normative social influence to occur we need not be convinced that our opinion is incorrect. We respond to our perception of what we believe others want us to do. Consequently, a change in opinion, attitude, or behavior brought about by normative pressure is often fragile. Once normative pressure eases up, we are likely to go back to our previous opinions. Frank went along with the other members of the jury, but he did not really believe they were right.

Because norms play such an important role in our behavior, and because normative social influence is so critical an element in conformity and other forms of social influence, we turn now to a more detailed discussion of these important forces.

Social Norms: The Key to Conformity

Norms play an important role in our everyday lives. These unwritten rules guide much of our social behavior. Humans seem to be predisposed to form norms—and conform to them—even in the most minimal situations. Norms exist on many levels, ranging from broad cultural norms to smaller-scale, situation-specific norms. We have cultural norms for how close we stand to another person when talking, for how men and women interact in business settings, and for the clothing we wear. We have situation-specific norms for how to behave in class or in the courtroom.

Violating norms makes us uncomfortable. We are embarrassed if we show up at a wedding reception in casual dress and find everyone else dressed formally, or if we go to tennis camp in tennis whites only to discover everyone else wearing the camp T-shirt. In general, standing out from the crowd—being the only different one—is something human beings don't like.

To get a better idea of how norms develop and how normative social influence works, imagine that you are taking part in an experiment. You are sitting in a totally dark room waiting for a point of light to appear on the wall across from where you are sitting. After the light is shone, you are asked to judge how far the light moved (in inches). In fact, unknown to you, the light is stationary and only appears to move (this phenomenon is called the autokinetic effect). If asked to make successive judgments of the amount of movement that you perceive, what will occur? Will your judgments vary widely, or will they show some consistency? If you have to do the same task with two others, will your judgments remain independent or blend with those of the others?

These questions were asked by Muzafer Sherif (1936, 1972) in his classic studies on norm formation. When subjects did the task alone, Sherif found that their judgments eventually reflected some internalized standard

THE FAR SIDE   By GARY LARSON

Suddenly, Professor Liebowitz realizes he has
come to the seminar without his duck.

that put a limit on their estimates of how far the light moved. That is, rather than being haphazard, individual subjects showed evidence of establishing a range and norm to guide their judgments. When these subjects were then placed within a group context, the individualized ranges and norms blended into a single group norm. Some of Sherif's results are shown in Figure 8-1.

The left side of the figure shows the results from three individual subjects who first did the task alone. Notice that individual judgments covered quite a range (from about 1 inch to 7½ inches). But after three sessions in which the individuals judged the distance in groups, their judgments converged, producing a funnel-shaped graph. According to Sherif, this convergence shows that the group, without specific instructions to do so, developed a group norm. Interestingly, this group norm was found to persist even when the subjects were brought back to do the task again a year later!

In a similar manner, the jury in the LeRoy Reed case developed a norm as deliberations progressed. Initially, some of the jurors followed the "norm" imposed by the judge: Follow the law and convict Reed if the necessary criteria were met. As the jury deliberated, a new norm began to emerge which suggested that the jurors need not follow the law so closely or that they could reinterpret the law in the light of Reed's situation. One by one those jurors who initially wanted to follow the letter of the law converged on the group norm. Frank was the last to move to this new norm.

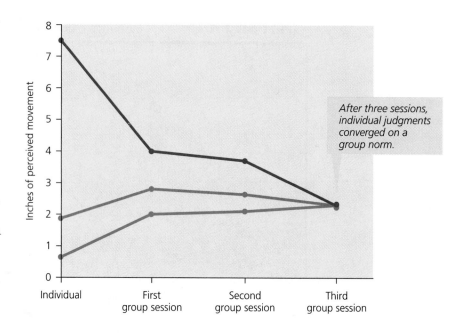

FIGURE 8-1 *The formation of group norms. In attempting to judge the distance moved by a (stationary) point of light, three subjects doing the task alone showed a range of over 6 inches. When placed in a group, these same individuals gradually converged on an agreed-upon distance of a little over 2 inches. Similarly, individuals operating in a group gradually come to hold the same opinions and attitudes—that is, a group norm emerges.* Adapted from Sherif, 1936.

After three sessions, individual judgments converged on a group norm.

Classic Studies in Conformity

The convergence of judgments shown in Sherif's study should not be surprising. The autokinetic effect is misleading, so the task was ambiguous, depending on subjective estimates of the distance traveled by a light. Individual judgments eventually converged on a group norm, demonstrating conformity. But what happens if the task is less ambiguous? Do subjects still conform to a group norm? Or do they maintain their independence? These are some of the questions Solomon Asch addressed in a now-classic series of experiments (1951, 1955, 1956).

The Asch Paradigm   Imagine that you have signed up for an experiment investigating perceptual judgments. When you arrive at the lab, you find that several other subjects are already present. You take the only remaining seat. You are told that the experiment involves judging the length of lines presented on a card at the front of the room. You are to look at each of three lines and decide which one matches a standard presented to the left (Figure 8-2). The experimenter tells you that each of you will give your judgment orally one after another. Because you are in the last chair you will give your judgment last.

The experiment begins uneventfully. Each member of the group gives what you consider the correct response, and then you give your response. But soon the others begin to give answers you believe to be incorrect, and you must decide what to do. Should you give the correct answer (which is obvious) or go along with the majority, who are wrong?

Before we see what happened, let's take a closer look at the Asch paradigm. The "other subjects" were not really subjects at all. They were confederates of the experimenter who were instructed to give incorrect answers

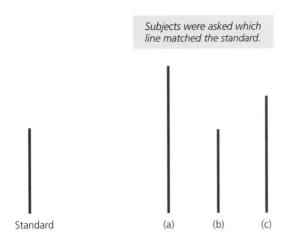

Subjects were asked which line matched the standard.

Standard   (a)   (b)   (c)

FIGURE 8-2 *Lines like those used in Asch's conformity experiment. Subjects were asked to state which of the three lines on the right matched the standard line. When all the other participants in the experiment agreed on an incorrect answer, subjects conformed with the incorrect majority 33% of the time.*

on several "critical trials." Misinformation provided by the incorrect majority places the real subject in a dilemma. On the one hand, the subject has the evidence of his own senses that tells him what the correct answer is. On the other hand, the subject has information from the majority concerning what is correct. The subject is placed in a situation where he must decide between these two competing sources of information. From these competing sources of information, pressure on the subject arises.

Now, when you are faced with a situation like the one created in the Asch experiments, there are two ways you can test reality to determine which line really matches the standard. You can jump up, whip out your pocket measuring tape, rush to the front of the room, and measure the lines. This is directly testing your perceptions against reality. However, you probably won't do this because it will violate your sense of the operative social norm—how you should act in this situation. The other way is to test the accuracy of your perceptions against those of others through a *social comparison* process (Festinger, 1954). Asch's paradigm strongly favors doing the latter. Given that subjects in these experiments probably will not measure the lines, what do they do about the conflict between information from their own senses and information from the majority?

Conformity in the Asch Experiments Asch's experimental paradigm placed the subject's own perceptions into conflict with the opinions of a unanimous majority advocating a clearly incorrect judgment. When confronted with the incorrect majority, Asch's subjects made errors in the direction of the incorrect majority on over 33% of the critical trials. Therefore, Asch showed a conformity rate of 33% on his line-judgment task. Almost all subjects knew the correct answer. When they did the same task alone, the error rate (mismatching the line with the standard) was 7.4%, one fourth the error rate when other subjects were present. Yet many changed their opinions to be in conformity with the group judgment.

Now, you might be thinking that conformity occurred *only* one third of the time. Although it might not sound like much, bear in mind that the task was easy; on any given trial the correct answer was clear. Remember too, as just mentioned, that almost everybody knew the right answer.

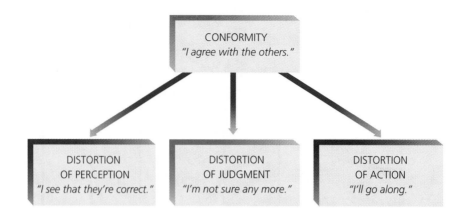

FIGURE 8-3 *Asch identified different paths to conformity among the yielding subjects in his experiments. Some subjects experienced distorted perception, some distorted judgment, and some distorted action.*

Paths to Conformity, Paths to Independence   Based on his results and interviews with subjects, Asch classified subjects as either yielding (conforming) or independent (nonconforming) (Asch, 1951). Of the yielding subjects, some (but relatively few) gave in completely to the majority. These subjects suffered from "distortion of perception" and "saw" the majority judgments as correct. They appeared to believe that the incorrect line was actually the correct one. The largest group of yielding subjects displayed "distortion of judgment." These subjects yielded because they lacked confidence in their own judgments—"I'm not sure any more." Without such confidence, subjects were not able to stick with their own perceptions and remain independent. Finally, some yielding subjects experienced "distortion of action." Here, subjects knew that the majority was wrong but conformed so that they did not appear different to the other subjects—"I'll go along" (Figure 8-3). This is what happened to Frank. Interestingly, there was a remarkable consistency among yielding subjects. Once bound to the majority, they stayed on the path of conformity.

Of the independent subjects, about 25% remained totally independent, never agreeing with the incorrect majority (Asch, 1955). These subjects had a great deal of confidence in their own judgments and withstood the pressure from the majority completely. Other independent subjects remained so because they felt a great need to remain self-reliant; still others remained independent because they wanted to do well on the task.

Asch's interviews tell us that there are many paths to conformity or independence. Some subjects remain independent because they trust their own senses, whereas others remain independent because they feel a great need to do so. These latter subjects appear to remain independent because of *psychological reactance*. As described in Chapter 7, psychological reactance occurs when individuals feel that their freedom of choice or action is threatened because other people are forcing them to do or say things (Brehm & Brehm, 1981). To reestablish independence, they reject the majority's pressure and go their own way. Even when individuals choose to remain independent, however, they still feel the pressure the incorrect majority exerts. Resisting the pressure of the majority is not easy. Independent subjects can withstand that pressure and stick with their own perceptions.

Social pressure is a powerful force for conformity. These striking workers are applying a kind of pressure to strike breakers that many people would find unbearable.

How Does Social Influence Bring About Conformity?

What is it about social influence situations that causes conformity? When your opinion is different from that of a unanimous majority, you are faced with a dilemma. On the one hand, your senses (or belief system) suggest one thing; on the other, the social situation (the majority) suggests something quite different. Placed in such a situation you experience conflict, which is psychologically uncomfortable (Moscovici, 1985). When you grapple with this conflict, your tendency is to pay attention to the views of the majority. Once the majority influence is removed, however, attention is focused back on the stimulus (for example, the judgment of lines in the Asch studies). Once majority influence is removed, you will return to your previous judgments (Moscovici, 1985).

The effects of dividing attention between the majority and the stimulus were demonstrated in a study in which subjects were asked to judge how similar two noises were in volume (Tesser, Campbell, & Mickler, 1983). Subjects performed this task under conditions of high social pressure, when three members of a majority disagreed with the subject's evaluation of the noise, or under conditions of low social pressure, when only one person disagreed. Under high social pressure, subjects responded by either attending very little *or* attending a great deal to the stimulus to be judged. Under low social pressure, subjects paid a moderate amount of attention to the stimulus.

Researchers speculated that high social pressure would lead to high levels of arousal. This arousal is due to the competing tendencies to pay attention to the stimulus and to pay attention to the source of social influence, other people. The net result is that a person will "default" to his or her dominant way of behaving. Those who have a strong tendency to conform may resolve the conflict by adopting the view of the majority. Others, less prone to the effects of social influence, may increase their attention to the stimulus as a way to resolve the conflict. By focusing on the stimulus, they take their minds off the social pressure. Like Frank in the jury room, some subjects in the Asch studies actually put their hands over their ears or eyes so that they did not hear or see what other people said. This was the only way they could resist conforming.

Factors That Affect Conformity

We have established that the opinions of others can alter our behavior. However, we have not yet explored how variables such as the nature of the task, the size of the majority, and the effect of one other person in agreement work to alter behavior. To address this issue, we explore several variables relating to the amount of conformity observed in social influence situations.

The Nature of the Task The first variable that can affect the amount of conformity observed is the nature of the task. As the task facing the individual becomes more ambiguous, the amount of conformity increases (Crutchfield, 1955). Asch's task was a simple one, involving the judgment of the length of lines, and produced a conformity rate of about 33%. Conformity research conducted with more ambiguous stimuli shows even higher levels of conformity. For example, Sherif's (1936) experiment on norm formation using the autokinetic effect (an extremely ambiguous task) found conformity rates of about 70%.

Other research involving attitudinal issues with no clear right or wrong answer produced conformity rates similar to Sherif's. In one study, highly independent professionals such as army officers or expert engineers were led to believe that other professionals had answered an opinion item differently than they had (Crutchfield, 1955). For example, colonels in the army were told that other colonels had agreed with the item "I often doubt that I would make a good leader." Now, this is blasphemy for army officers, who are trained to lead. Yet when faced with a false majority, 70% of the officers said they agreed with that item. Privately, they disagreed, strongly.

The type of task faced by a group may also determine the *type* of social influence (informational or normative) that comes into play. For example, informational social influence should be strongest when subjects face an "intellective issue," where they can use factual information to arrive at a clearly correct answer (Kaplan & Miller, 1987). Normative social influence should be more crucial on a "judgmental issue." A judgmental issue is based on moral or ethical principles, where there are no clear-cut right or wrong answers. Therefore, resolution of the issue depends on opinion, not fact.

In a jury simulation study investigating the use of informational and normative social influence, Martin Kaplan and Charles Miller (1987) empaneled six-person juries to judge a civil lawsuit. The juries were required to award the plaintiff compensatory damages and punitive damages. Compensatory damages are awarded to reimburse the plaintiff for suffering and losses due to the defendant's behavior. Generally, awarding compensatory damages is a fact-based "intellective task." If, for example, your lawn mower blows up because the No Pain, No Gain Lawn Mower Company put the gas tank in the wrong place, it is easy for the jury to add up the cost of the mower plus whatever medical costs were incurred. Punitive damages, on the other hand, are awarded to deter the defendant from repeating such actions in the future. The issue of punitive damages is a "judgmental task." How much should you punish the manufacturer so that they cease making mowers that blow up?

The results of the study indicated that juries doing an intellective task (awarding compensatory damages) were more likely to use informational social influence than normative social influence. When the task has a clear standard, then it is the information that majority members can bring forth that convinces other jurors. Juries doing a judgmental task, on the other hand, were more likely to use normative influence. Where there is no clear-cut answer, the jurors in the majority try to convince the minority to agree by pressuring them to conform to the group (majority) decision.

Think back to Frank's jury experience in the LeRoy Reed case. Some of the forces that produced Frank's conformity may be clearer now. Essentially, the task facing the jury could have been defined either as intellective (focusing on the facts presented at the trial relating to Reed's guilt or innocence) or as judgmental (focusing on the broader ethical/moral issues of convicting Reed, who was not very bright and thought he needed a gun as part of his new career as a private detective). A majority of jurors, right from the outset of the deliberations, favored the judgmental route. Frank's initial opinion conflicted with the norm that developed. But, as a result of normative social influence, he eventually changed his verdict.

The Size of the Majority Research has shown that as the size of the majority increases, so does conformity, up to a point (Asch, 1951, 1956; Milgram, Bickman, & Berkowitz, 1969). Generally, as shown in Figure 8-4, there is a "nonlinear" relationship between the size of the majority and conformity. That is, majority influence significantly increases until some critical majority size is reached. After that, the addition of more majority members does not significantly increase conformity. For example, Milgram and colleagues (1969) found that increasing the number of individuals (confederates of the experimenter) on a sidewalk who looked upward toward the sky increased conformity (the percentage of passersby looking upward) up to a majority size of five, and then leveled off (see Figure 8-4).

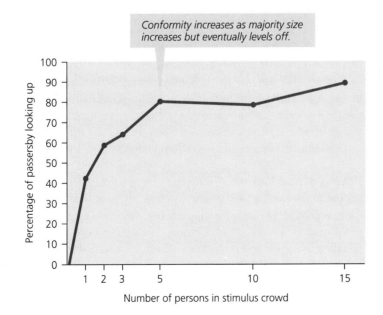

Conformity increases as majority size increases but eventually levels off.

Percentage of passersby looking up

Number of persons in stimulus crowd

FIGURE 8-4 *The effect of majority size on conformity. Social influence increases up to some critical majority size and then levels off. After that, adding more people to a majority does not increase conformity.*
Adapted from Milgram, Bickman, and Berkowitz, 1969.

There is no one absolute critical size of a majority after which addition of majority members does not significantly increase conformity. Milgram and colleagues found that conformity leveled off after a majority size of five. Asch (1951), using his line-judgment task, found that conformity leveled off after a majority size of three. Regardless of the critical size of the majority, the general nonlinear relationship between majority size and conformity is firmly established.

Why does conformity level off after some critical majority size? Two explanations have been suggested (Baron, Kerr, & Miller, 1992). First, as majority members are added beyond the critical point, the individual in the conformity situation might suspect that the additional majority members are going along to avoid making trouble in the group. If the individual conformer perceives this to be the motive for joining the majority, the power of the additional majority members is reduced. Second, as the size of the majority grows, each new majority member is probably noticed less. That is, the individual is more likely to notice a third person added to a majority of two than to notice a tenth person added to a majority of nine.

Increases in the size of a majority are most likely to produce increased conformity in normative social influence situations, when the situation causes us to question our perceptions and judgments (Campbell & Fairey, 1989). When a majority is arrayed against us and we cannot obtain adequate information about the stimuli that we are to judge, we conform. This is exactly what happened in Asch's experiment.

Normative social influence also produces conformity when a judgment is easy and the individual is sure the group is wrong but cannot resist the pressure of the majority. This is what happened in the jury room. Informational influence was nil. The other jurors could not offer any information that Frank did not have already. They did not dispute the evidence. They made the judgment that the law, not the evidence, was wrong. The jurors wanted Frank to conform to this norm. Eventually, as we know, he did.

When you know you're right and the rest of the group is wrong, more conformity results when the majority comprises three members than if it comprises only one (Campbell & Fairey, 1989). This makes sense because it is normative influence that is operating in this situation. But what if you are not certain whether the majority is right or wrong? In this case you search for information that could inform your decision, information that will help you make the right choice. It's informational influence that counts here. Just a few people, perhaps even one, can convince you through informational social influence if their information is persuasive (Campbell & Fairey, 1989).

Having a True Partner   Often the changes caused by the forces producing conformity are fragile and easily disrupted. This is the case when we find that there is another person who supports our perceptions and actions in a given social situation. Imagine, for example, that you've been invited to a "black tie" wedding reception at a posh country club on a Saturday night. When an invitation specifies "black tie," the norm is for men to wear tuxedos and women to wear formal dresses. Now, suppose that you don't want to dress so formally but feel you should because everyone else will (normative social influence). But then suppose that you speak to a friend who is also attending and who also doesn't want to wear a tuxedo or a formal dress. The two of you agree to wear less formal attire, and you feel comfortable with your decision. The next weekend, you are invited to another "black tie" party, but this time your friend is not attending. What will you do this time? You decide to dress formally.

This example illustrates an important social psychological phenomenon. The **true partner effect** occurs when we perceive that there is someone who supports our position; we are then less likely to conform than if we are alone facing a unanimous majority. This effect was first demonstrated empirically by Asch (1951). In one variation of his experiment, Asch had a "true partner" emerge at some point during his conformity experiment. On a given trial, the true partner would break with the incorrect majority and support the real subject's judgments. The results of this manipulation were striking: Conformity was cut by nearly 80%! As in the example of the "black tie" parties, when we have a true partner we are better able to withstand the strong forces of normative social influence.

Why does this occur? There are many possible explanations. For example, when we violate a norm by ourselves, we draw attention to ourselves as deviant. Recall that some of Asch's subjects conformed because they did not want to appear different. Apparently, it makes us very uncomfortable to be perceived by others as different. When we have a true partner, we can diffuse the pressure by convincing ourselves that we are "not the only ones" breaking a norm.

Another explanation for the true partner effect draws on the social comparison process (Festinger, 1954; Kruglanski & Mayseless, 1990). As discussed in Chapter 2, social comparison theory proposes that we compare our thoughts, beliefs, and actions with those of others to find out if we are in agreement. When we find that we agree, we feel validated; it is rewarding when we receive such confirmation. Our confidence in our beliefs increases because they are shared with others.

Think back to the second "black tie" party. Without a true partner, you bring your behavior into line with the norm in effect: wearing formal attire. Asch (1951) found the very same thing when he had the true partner withdraw his support of the subject. When the subject was abandoned, his conformity went back up to its previous level.

The true partner effect applies in jury deliberations; we saw that Frank experienced great distress when he was the only one holding out for conviction. Earlier in the deliberations, Frank had other jurors (true partners) who supported his view. When those jurors changed their votes, their support for Frank disappeared. Now Frank faced not only a unanimous majority but also one that included two former true partners. Would things have turned out differently if one other juror had stuck with Frank? Perhaps. The courts have acknowledged that conformity pressures are greater when a person is the single advocate of a particular point of view. For a closer look at this phenomenon, see the featured discussion "When 10:2 Is Not the Same as 5:1."

true partner effect The phenomenon whereby an individual's tendency to conform with a majority position is lessened if there is one other person who supports that individual's position.

In 1970 the U.S. Supreme Court decided a case that involved the reduction of the size of a jury from twelve to six (*Williams v. Florida*, 1970). In that ruling the court addressed the issue of conformity pressures within the larger and smaller juries. The court acknowledged the fact that the larger jury was more representative of the population and was, consequently, more likely to have more jurors who deviated from the majority. However, they reasoned, incorrectly, that a 10:2 (guilty:not guilty) split in the larger jury was equivalent to a 5:1 split in the smaller jury. The court focused its attention on the size of the majority, not the ratio.

Mathematically, the court's logic cannot be argued. However, in the larger jury the two-person bloc is more likely to withstand conformity pressure than the single juror in the six-person jury. In a twelve-person jury, the odds of a holdout, a dissenter, finding one or more true partner(s) are statistically much greater than in a six-person jury (Saks & Hastie, 1978). Based on what Asch (1951) found, we would expect the minority of two to be more able to hold out against the majority than the minority of one. This is exactly what happens. A twelve-person jury is twice as likely to hang (be unable to reach a unanimous verdict) than a six-person jury (Horowitz & Willging, 1984; Kalven & Zeisel, 1966).

Ironically, in a later decision (*Ballew v. Georgia*, 1978), the Supreme Court acknowledged its earlier misreading of the conformity pressure issue. However, it did not see fit to reverse the *Williams* decision. The Court did, however, decide that a jury consisting of six members was just too small. The line has been drawn.

———

When evaluating the Supreme Court's misinterpretation of how conformity pressures work within groups, can you think of some reasons why it made such an error? Why do you think a juror can hold out against a majority better when a true partner is present? If you were the lone juror standing against a unanimous majority, do you think you could hold out and hang the jury? If so, why do you think you would be different from most individuals in that position? Why do you think the Supreme Court drew the line at a jury size of six?

Are There Gender Differences in Conformity? Besides investigating situational forces that affect conformity, social psychologists have investigated how individual characteristics affect conformity. For the most part this research has failed to produce any consistent findings. One possible exception is the relationship between conformity and gender.

Early research suggested that women were more likely to conform than men (Eagly & Carli, 1981). For example, 43% of the studies published before 1970 reported this phenomenon, in contrast to only 21% published after 1970. Did changes in the cultural climate make women less likely to conform? Or did early conformity studies have a male bias, as expressed in "male-oriented" tasks and a predominantly male environment? Research indicates that the nature of the task was not important in producing the observed gender differences, but the gender of the experimenter was. Generally, larger gender differences are found when a man runs the conformity experiment. No gender differences are found when a woman runs the experiment (Eagly & Carli, 1981).

An analysis of the research also shows that there are conditions under which women are more likely to conform than men, and others under which men are more likely to conform than women (Eagly & Chrvala, 1986). For example, women are more likely to conform than men in group pressure situations—that is, under conditions of normative social influence—as compared to persuasion situations, where informational social influence is being applied (Eagly, 1978; Eagly & Carli, 1981).

Two explanations have been proposed for gender differences in conformity (Eagly, 1987). First, gender may serve as a status variable in newly formed groups. Traditionally, the female gender role is seen as weaker than the male role. In everyday life, males are more likely to hold positions of high status and power than women. Men are more likely to be in the position of "influencer" and women in the position of "influencee." The lower status of the female role may contribute to a greater predisposition to conform on the part of women, especially in group pressure situations. Second, women tend to be more sensitive than men to conformity pressures when their behavior is under surveillance—that is, when they have to state their opinions publicly (Eagly, Wood, & Fishbaugh, 1981). When women must make their opinions public, they are more likely than men to conform. In the Asch paradigm, subjects were required to state their opinions publicly. This favors women conforming more than men.

In a study conducted to evaluate these two explanations for the observed gender differences in conformity, male and female subjects participated in a two-session experiment (Eagly & Chrvala, 1986). During the first session the subjects completed a questionnaire on campus issues. The questions were read aloud, and subjects indicated agreement or disagreement with opinion issues on 15-point scales. Three weeks later subjects returned to the laboratory and were told that they would discuss the previously rated issues in five-person groups. Subjects were told that they would each receive a copy of the responses given during the first session and then would give their impression of the other group members. The responses from session 1 were, of course, bogus and controlled by the experimenters.

Four variables were evaluated in this experiment. First, researchers manipulated the type of impression subjects formed of the other subjects. Subjects rated others on either likability or expertise. Second, surveillance was manipulated by telling some subjects that they would have to read their opinions aloud (surveillance) or that they would not have to read their opinions aloud (no surveillance). Third, researchers recorded the subjects' age and categorized them as either older (19 years or older) or younger (under age 19). Finally, the gender of the subject was recorded.

Researchers found no evidence for a general relationship between gender and conformity. That is, females as a group were no more likely than males to conform. Age, however, did relate significantly to conformity, with younger subjects conforming more than older subjects. Additionally, surveillance yielded more conformity than nonsurveillance conditions.

A closer look at the results of this study shows a more complex pattern. The most interesting finding was the relationship among gender, age, and surveillance. When there was no surveillance, age and gender did not significantly relate to conformity. However, under surveillance conditions,

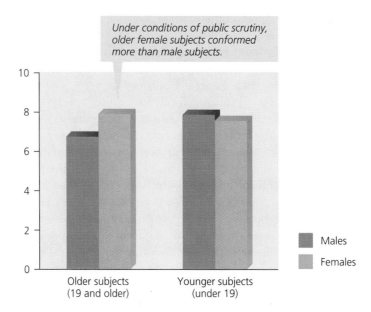

FIGURE 8-5 *The effects of age and gender on conformity under surveillance conditions. Among older subjects, females were more conforming than males when they thought they were going to have to read their opinions aloud (surveillance conditions). Among younger subjects, there were no significant differences between males and females under these conditions. When there was no surveillance in this experiment, there were no significant differences in conformity between males and females in either age group.* Data from Eagly and Chrvala, 1986.

Under conditions of public scrutiny, older female subjects conformed more than male subjects.

Males
Females

Older subjects
(19 and older)

Younger subjects
(under 19)

age and gender differences emerged. As shown in Figure 8-5, among "older" subjects, women conformed more than men. However, no gender difference was evident for younger subjects. Researchers explain this finding by speculating that as college students progress through their academic careers, a setting in which men hold most of the positions of status, they become more sensitized to hierarchical relationships (Eagly & Chrvala, 1986). In short, as women progress through college, they increasingly adopt gender role expectations (that is, they become more conforming).

The interaction between gender and conformity is clearly complex. Because of gender role socialization, women may show greater conformity than men in certain situations, especially those in which men hold positions of status or power. But these gender differences are small (Eagly & Carli, 1981). Therefore, a general statement about differences in conformity between men and women would be inaccurate (Deaux & Major, 1987; Eagly & Johnson, 1990).

Are There Historical and Cultural Differences in Conformity? Asch conducted his classic experiment on conformity during the 1950s in the United States. The sociocultural climate that existed at the time favored conformity. The country was still under the stifling influence of "McCarthyism," which vilified those who failed to conform to "normal" American ideals. This climate may have contributed in significant ways to the levels of conformity Asch observed (Larsen, 1982; Perrin & Spencer, 1981). Researchers working in England failed to obtain conformity effects as strong as those Asch had obtained (Perrin & Spencer, 1981). This raised a question: Were the Asch findings limited to a particular time and culture?

Unfortunately, this question has no simple answer. Evidence suggests that within the United States, rates of conformity vary with the sociopolitical climate (Larsen, 1974, 1982). The conformity rate in the early 1970s

Senator Joseph McCarthy, shown testifying in a Senate hearing room in 1954 (top), came to symbolize the spirit of conformity that permeated American society in the 1950s. Those whose lives failed to meet rigorous standards of "normalcy" were in danger of losing their reputations and their jobs. Times had changed by the late 1960s and early 1970s (left), when nonconformity became a value and people had more freedom to make divergent lifestyle choices. Conformity studies are probably influenced by attitudes toward conformity in the broader culture at the time.

was 62.5% (that is, 62.5% of subjects conformed at least once in an Asch-type experiment), compared to a rate of 78.9% during the early 1980s (Larsen, 1982). Compare this to Asch's (1956) rate of 76.5%. Results like these suggest that conformity rates may be tied to the cultural climate in force at the time of a study.

The evidence for cross-cultural influences is less clear. A host of studies suggest that conformity is a fairly general phenomenon across cultures. Conformity has been demonstrated in European countries such as Belgium, Holland, and Norway (Doms & Van Avermaet, 1980; Milgram, 1961; Vlaander & van Rooijen, 1985) as well as in non-Western countries such as Japan, China, and some South American countries (Huang & Harris, 1973; Matsuda, 1985; Sistrunk & Clement, 1970). Additionally, some research suggests that there may be cross-cultural differences in conformity when North Americans are compared to non–North Americans (see

In Twelve Angry Men, *Henry Fonda plays a juror who convinces the other eleven jurors that the defendant is innocent. Minority influence of this sort is very unusual. It would be much more common in a real trial for the lone juror to give in to majority influence.*

Furnham, 1984, for a review) and across other non–North American cultures (Milgram, 1961).

What is the bottom line? It is safe to say that the Asch conformity effect is fairly general across cultures. However, some cultural groups may conform at different levels than others. Conformity also appears to fluctuate in size across time within a culture.

MINORITY INFLUENCE

In the classic film *Twelve Angry Men,* Henry Fonda portrayed a juror who was firmly convinced that a criminal defendant was not guilty. The only problem was that the other 11 jurors believed the defendant was guilty. As the jurors began to deliberate, Fonda held fast to his belief in the defendant's innocence. As the film progressed, Fonda convinced each of the other 11 jurors that the defendant was innocent. The jury finally returned a verdict of not guilty.

In this fictional portrayal of a group at work, a single unwavering individual not only was able to resist conformity pressure but also convinced the majority that they were wrong. Such an occurrence would be extremely rare in a real trial (Kalven & Zeisel, 1966). With an 11 to 1 split the jury would almost always go in the direction of the majority (Isenberg, 1986; Kalven & Zeisel, 1966). The film does, however, raise an interesting question: Can a steadfast minority bring about change in the majority? For almost 35 years after Sherif's original experiments on norm formation, this question went unanswered. It was not until 1969 that social psychologists began to investigate the influence of the minority on the majority. This line of investigation has been pursued more by European social psychologists than American.

Can a Minority Influence the Majority?

In the first published experiment on minority influence, researchers devised an Asch-like conformity situation. Subjects were led to believe that they were taking part in a study on color perception (Moscovici, Lage, & Naffrechoux, 1969). Subjects were shown a series of slides and asked to say the color of the slide aloud. Unbeknown to the real subjects (four, making up the majority), two confederates (comprising the minority) had been instructed to make an error on certain trials, by calling a blue slide green, for example. Researchers found that 8.42% of the judgments made by the real subjects were in the direction of the minority, compared to only .025% of the judgments in a control condition in which there was no incorrect minority. In fact, 32% of the subjects conformed to the incorrect minority. Thus, a minority can have a surprisingly powerful effect on the majority.

In this experiment, the minority subjects were consistent in their judgments. Researchers theorized that consistency of behavior is a strong determinant of the social influence a minority can exert on a majority (Moscovici et al., 1969). An individual in a minority who expresses a deviant opinion consistently may be seen as having a high degree of confidence in his or her judgments. In the color perception experiment, majority subjects rated minority members as more confident in their judgments than themselves. The consistent minority caused the majority to call into question the validity of their own judgments.

What is it about consistency that contributes to the power of a minority to influence a majority? Differing perceptions and attributions made about consistent and inconsistent minorities are important factors. A consistent minority is usually perceived as being more confident and less willing to compromise than an inconsistent minority (Wolf, 1979). A consistent minority may also be perceived as having high levels of competence, especially if it's a relatively large minority (Nemeth, 1986). Generally, we assume that if a number of people share a point of view, it must be correct. As the size of the minority increases, so does perceived competence (Nemeth, 1986).

Although research shows that consistency increases the power of a minority to influence a majority, consistency must be carefully defined. Will a minority that adopts a particular view and remains intransigent be as persuasive as one that is more flexible? Two styles of consistency have been distinguished: rigid and negotiating (Mugny, 1975). In the rigid style, the minority advocates a position that is counter to the norm adopted by the majority but is unwilling to show flexibility. In the negotiating style, the minority, while remaining consistent, shows a willingness to be flexible. Each of these styles contributes to the minority's image in the eyes of the majority (Mugny, 1975). The rigid minority is perceived in a less positive way than a negotiating minority, perhaps leading to perceptions that the rigid minority's goal is to block the majority. Conversely, the negotiating minority may be perceived as having compromise as its goal.

Generally, research suggests that a more flexible minority has more power to influence the majority than a rigid one, as long as the perception of minority consistency remains (Mugny, 1975; Nemeth, Swedlund, & Kanki, 1974). The perception of the minority is also partially dependent on the degree to which it is willing to modify its position in response to new information. A minority that adapts to new information is more influential than a minority that holds a position irrespective of any additional information (Nemeth et al., 1974).

As the political and social climate of a society changes, minority views can become majority positions. In the 1960s, the times were right for the emergence of the civil rights movement (top) and the spread of its principles throughout society. The 1990s brought different attitudes to the surface, such as those embodied by former Ku Klux Klan leader David Duke (bottom).

A minority will also have an easier time influencing a majority if the minority's view fits with the general cultural "zeitgeist" (the moral, cultural, or intellectual spirit of an era) than if it flies in the face of that zeitgeist (Maass & Clark, 1984). For example, Geneviève Paicheler (1979) found that an individual with a minority opinion had a greater influence on a majority if that opinion was in line with an existing norm than if the minority opinion opposed that norm. Even when the zeitgeist is right, it may take time for a minority to show a significant effect on a majority. Laboratory research, for example, shows that a minority has a greater effect on the majority during later experimental trials than during earlier ones (Nemeth et al., 1974).

These findings may help explain why fringe political groups can go for long periods of time with little influence and then suddenly have a surge of popularity. For example, during the 1920s in Germany, the Nazi party was small and had no significant effect on German politics. However, as the economic and political climate within Germany changed, and along with it the zeitgeist, the Nazis' power grew and they became more and more influential.

More recently in the United States, we have seen some minority positions influence majority opinion, although on a smaller scale. Environmental concerns, formerly confined to groups like Greenpeace and Citizens for a Better Environment, have moved into public consciousness. Antismoking sentiments, once restricted to physicians and a small number of "extremist" individuals, are now the norm in many parts of the country. The movement toward more restrictive gun-control legislation became a majority position with the passage of the Brady bill in 1994.

Less promising changes can also be seen. For many years the zeitgeist in the United States was favorable for civil rights and more equitable treatment of different ethnic groups. However, changes in this climate have occurred so that there is now less tolerance for such groups, as shown by an increase in acts of violence against certain racial and religious groups and by the enhanced status of right-wing political parties. For example, during the 1990 senatorial race in Louisiana, David Duke, a former Ku Klux Klan Grand Wizard, was nearly elected to the United States Senate. Changes in the political zeitgeist make extreme positions

seem plausible and legitimate. Once legitimized, the opinions of the minority can exert a greater influence on the opinions of the majority.

Majority and Minority Influence: Two Processes or One?

Social influence, as we have seen, operates in two directions: from majority to minority and from minority to majority. The discovery of minority influence raised an issue concerning the underlying social psychological processes controlling majority and minority influence. Do two different processes control majority and minority influence, or is there a single process controlling both?

The Two-Process Model Judgments expressed by a minority may be more likely to make people think about the arguments raised (Moscovici, 1980). This suggests that two different processes operate: majority influence, which occurs almost exclusively on a public level, and minority influence, which seems to operate on a private level. Majority influence, according to the two-process approach, operates through the application of pressure. People agree with a majority because of public pressure, but often they really don't accept the majority's view on a private level. The fact that the majority exerts great psychological pressure is reflected in the finding that people feel very anxious when they find themselves in disagreement with the majority (Asch, 1956; Nemeth, 1986). However, as soon as majority pressure is removed, people return to their original beliefs. Majority influence, in this model, is like normative influence—it does not necessarily have a lasting effect. For example, Frank, in the LeRoy Reed case, changed his verdict in response to group pressure. However, he probably went home still believing, deep down, that Reed should have been convicted.

Minority influence, according to the two-process approach, operates by making people think more deeply about the minority's position (Nemeth, 1986). In doing so, they evaluate all the aspects of the minority view. The majority decides to agree with the minority because they are converted to its position (Nemeth, 1992). Minority influence is like informational influence. The character played by Henry Fonda in *Twelve Angry Men* convinced the majority members to change their votes through informational social influence. Thus, unlike the majority influencing Frank in the Reed case through normative pressure, Fonda changed the minds of the other jurors by applying persuasive, informational arguments.

A Single-Process Model: Social Impact Theory The dual process model suggests that there are *different* psychological processes underlying majority and minority influence. A competing view, the single-process approach to social influence, suggests that one psychological process accounts for both majority and minority influence. The first theory designed to explain majority and minority influence with a single underlying process was proposed by

FIGURE 8-6 *A model of Latané's social impact theory. The amount of social influence experienced by a target is a product of the strength of the sources of influence (S), their immediacy (I), and their number (N). Social impact theory proposes that a single psychological process underlies both majority and minority influence. In other words, this model can explain how a majority influences a minority and how a minority influences a majority.* From Latané, 1981.

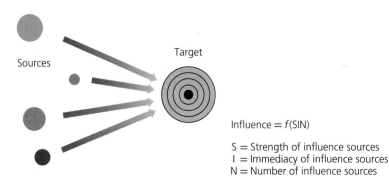

Influence = f(SIN)

S = Strength of influence sources
I = Immediacy of influence sources
N = Number of influence sources

Bibb Latané (Latané, 1981; Latané & Wolf, 1981). Latané's **social impact theory** suggests that social influence processes can be summed up by the formula

Influence = f(SIN)

where S represents the strength of the source of the influence, I represents the immediacy (or closeness) of the source of influence, and N represents the number of influence sources.

Latané (1981) suggested an analogy between the effect of social influence and the effect of light bulbs. If, for example, you have a bulb of a certain strength (for example, 50 watts) and place it 10 feet from a wall, it will cast light of a given intensity against the wall. If you move the bulb closer to the wall (immediacy), the intensity of the light on the wall increases. Moving it farther from the wall decreases the intensity. Increasing or decreasing the wattage of the bulb (the strength of the source) also changes the intensity of the light cast on the wall. Finally, if you add a second bulb (number), the intensity of light will increase.

Similarly, the amount of social influence increases if the strength of a source of influence is increased (for example, if the source's credibility is enhanced), if the source's immediacy is increased, or if the number of influence sources is increased. This general model is illustrated in Figure 8-6.

Let's return to Frank's dilemma to see how this model would apply to a real-world influence situation. During the deliberation process, information came out about the backgrounds of the jurors involved in the case. Some of the jurors were professionals (e.g., a school psychologist, an English professor, and a physician). Frank attributed higher status to these jurors because of their professions, which in turn enhanced their credibility in his eyes. In the model, this amounts to an increase in source strength. Immediacy and numbers were also relevant. The jury deliberated in one, relatively small room, making the majority "immediate" with respect to Frank. Finally, Frank faced a large number of influence sources—initially 9, but eventually 11. Given this mix of S, I, and N, it is not surprising that Frank eventually gave in.

Latané also suggested that there is a nonlinear relationship between the number of sources and the amount of influence. According to Latané, adding a second influence source to a solitary source will have greater impact than adding the 101st source to 100 sources. Social impact theory pre-

social impact theory A single-process theory of majority and minority influence suggesting that social influence is a function of the strength, immediacy, and number of influence sources.

dicts that influence increases rapidly between zero and three sources and then diminishes beyond that point, which is consistent with the research on the effects of majority size.

Social impact theory can be used to account for both minority and majority influence processes. In a minority influence situation, social influence forces operate on both the minority and majority, pulling each other toward the other's position (Latané, 1981). Latané suggests that minority influence will depend on the strength, immediacy, and number of influence sources in the minority, just as in majority influence. Thus, a minority of two should have greater influence on the majority than a minority of one, a prediction that has received empirical support (Arbuthnot & Wayner, 1982; Moscovici & Lage, 1976).

Another Single-Process Model: The Social Influence Model In general, social psychologists have accepted Latané's social impact theory (Nowak, Szamrej, & Latané, 1990). However, the theory is not without its critics. Sarah Tanford and Steven Penrod, for example, have pointed out a discrepancy between Latané's prediction that the greatest increase in social influence will occur between zero and one and what really happens in social influence situations (Tanford & Penrod, 1984). They have proposed an alternative to Latané's social impact theory, which they call the **social influence model** (SIM). Much like Latané's social impact theory, the social influence model attempts to explain the dynamics of majority and minority influence with respect to the relative size of each. Through a series of computer simulations, Tanford and Penrod developed a set of *growth function curves* that relate the amount of social influence to the relative sizes of the majority and minority. Tanford and Penrod show that the predictions about the relationship between majority size and amount of conformity made by the social influence model more closely match actual findings in social influence research. Generally, the social influence model provides a closer match with empirical data and can better handle minority influence situations than Latané's theory.

Both the social impact model and SIM suggest that both majority and minority influence can be explained by one principle. At this point, however, it is not clear whether this is in fact the case or whether there are two different processes at work. More research is needed to answer this question.

COMPLIANCE: RESPONDING TO A DIRECT REQUEST

In 1973 Arthur Walker retired from the United States Navy's submarine service. In 1975 he and his brother John started a small company called Walker Enterprises, specializing in installing stereos in new automobiles. For the most part the company was Arthur's. John's major contribution was putting up the capital.

Walker Enterprises was not very successful, and soon the brothers had to liquidate it. John agreed to take care of most of the debts incurred by the company. After Walker Enterprises folded, Arthur took a job with VSE

social influence model A single-process explanation for majority and minority influence that relates the amount of social influence to the relative sizes of the majority and minority.

Corporation, a defense contractor. His job was to evaluate U.S. Navy ships and advise the company on what repairs were needed while the ships were in the Navy yard at Norfolk, Virginia. Many classified U.S. government documents were kept at VSE; Arthur had access to some of them.

Things went smoothly for Arthur for a while. One day, however, his brother John asked him if he could gain access to some documents for him. Unbeknown to Arthur, John was a spy selling secrets to the Russians. John paid Arthur $6,000 for the unclassified documents, a very large sum of money for unclassified material. Arthur felt guilty about taking the money because John was paying the debts from Walker Enterprises, so he gave John $2,000 back.

A few days later John asked Arthur for some more documents. He provided a camera so that Arthur could photograph the documents. Arthur obtained some more unclassified documents containing the general plans for an amphibious assault ship. As it turned out, the Russians were then developing a similar ship, so the documents proved extremely valuable.

After a while, John asked Arthur if he could obtain some classified documents. Arthur said he thought he could get his hands on some classified technical manuals. He requested the "damage control book" for the USS *Blue Ridge* from the VSE security office. This document was classified *confidential,* the lowest level of classification. Arthur told the security office that he needed the book to evaluate where the ship should be overhauled. The *Blue Ridge* was the flagship for the Pacific fleet and carried the fleet commander and his staff. The damage control book clearly showed the ship's weaknesses and vulnerabilities. Arthur removed several pages. Later that night he went to John's office and photographed the pages, then returned them the next day.

At this point Arthur was hooked. John pressured Arthur to try to get a new job at VSE that would give him more access to classified documents. However, it was not to be. On May 20, 1985, FBI agents went to Arthur's house and informed him that his brother had been arrested for espionage. Arthur feigned shock. But after several days of questioning, Arthur confessed to being a spy himself. He was eventually sentenced to life in prison.

Reflecting on what happened to him, Arthur noted that his brother never directly asked him to be a spy. Spying, he said, was like sinning: "Once you start sinning you either stop sinning or you just keep going and going and carry this guilt around" (Early, 1988, p. 210). It was hard to say no to his brother, he explained, once he had him hooked.

Arthur Walker's entanglement in the world of espionage provides an example of how you can be induced into doing something against your will or your better judgment. Throughout his time as a spy Arthur Walker knew that he was doing something wrong, and he felt guilty about it. However, once he started down the path of espionage, he could not turn back.

Although you've probably never been a spy, you most likely have been in situations where you did something and then asked yourself why. Perhaps it was donating to a charity you weren't particularly interested in, or maybe it was buying a car. In many situations like these, the "pitches" we are exposed to are not made in a haphazard way. In fact, the "pitches" used by solicitors for charities and by salespersons are based on well-known principles of social psychology.

In this section we discuss techniques used to gain **compliance**—the modification of behavior in response to a direct request—as well as the social psychological forces that produce compliance. In compliance situations, the person making the request has no power to force you to do as he or she asks. For example, your neighbor can ask that you move your car so that she can back a truck into her driveway. However, assuming your car is legally parked, she has no legal power to force you to move your car. If you go out and move your car, you have (voluntarily) complied with her request.

The Dynamics of Compliance

Let's take a moment to analyze how Arthur Walker became a spy. His brother approached him and made a relatively small request: Obtain some unclassified documents. Since the initial documents Arthur obtained were unclassified, no laws were broken. However, it was Arthur's first step toward becoming a spy. Remember that Arthur was paid a large sum of money for the initial documents and that he was already indebted to his brother for paying off some debts. By providing the first set of documents Arthur started to commit himself to that course of action. After a while John Walker "upped the ante" and asked Arthur to get some classified documents. Again Arthur complied.

How did John get his brother to provide classified documents? Notice that the first request was a small one: Get the unclassified documents. Once the first request was fulfilled, John made a larger request: Get some classified documents. Arthur was eased into his role as a spy through a series of graded steps, starting with a small request and then moving to a larger one. This technique is fairly typical of how the Russians recruited U.S. citizens to provide classified information. They started out with a small request (perhaps to provide a list of employees of a company) and gradually increased the size of the request. Few, if any, people will reverse themselves after they have been hooked. The tactics used by the Russians, and by John Walker, are grounded in principles of compliance that are used every day.

In the sections that follow we explore four commonly used compliance tactics: the foot-in-the-door technique, the door-in-the-face technique, lowballing, and the that's-not-all technique. As we go through each one, try to think of situations in which you have experienced it and how you reacted to it. By understanding how these techniques are applied, you may be better able to resist high-pressure "sales pitches."

The Foot-in-the-Door Technique   Imagine that you are doing some shopping in a mall and a person approaches you. She asks you to sign a petition condemning drunk driving. Now, most people would be happy to sign such a petition. After all, it is for a cause that most people support, and it takes a minimal amount of effort. Imagine further that you agree to this initial request and sign the petition. After you sign the petition, the solicitor then asks you for a $5 donation to PADD (People Against Drunk Driving). You find yourself digging into your wallet for a $5 bill to contribute.

Consider another scenario. You are again in the mall doing some shopping when a person from PADD approaches you and asks you for a $5 dona-

compliance The modification of behavior in response to a direct request, even though the person making the request has no power to enforce compliance.

By Scott Adams

HERE'S YOUR EMPLOYEE LOCATOR DEVICE.

SENSORS IN THE BUILDING WILL BE ABLE TO TRACK YOU AT ALL TIMES.

WE'LL KNOW HOW MANY TIMES YOU USE THE RESTROOM AND HOW LONG.

IT'S A DOG COLLAR... THE FINAL HUMILIATION.

ONCE YOU GOT USED TO WORKING IN CUBICLES, LIKE GERBILS, WE KNEW ANYTHING WAS POSSIBLE.

MY CONFORMANCE RATIONALIZATION MECHANISMS ARE KICKING IN.

IT'S NOT SO BAD. A COLLAR IS SIMPLY AN EFFICIENT DESIGN. EVERYONE IS DOING IT.

IT'S NOT SO BAD.

IT'S POWERED BY THIS SIX FOOT LONG EXTENSION CORD.

Once the foot is in the door (or the worker in the cubicle, or the collar around the neck), subsequent requests don't seem so outrageous. DILBERT *reprinted by permission of UFS, Inc.*

foot-in-the-door technique
A compliance technique in which a small request is made first and is then followed by a larger one.

tion to help fight drunk driving. This time, instead of digging out your wallet, you tell the solicitor to hit the road and you go back to your shopping.

These two scenarios illustrate a common compliance effect: the **foot-in-the-door technique** (FITD). You were first asked to do something small and effortless: signing a petition. Next, you were asked for a donation, a request that was a bit more costly than simply signing a petition. Essentially, in the first scenario you are in a position similar to the one in which Arthur Walker found himself. Once you agreed to the first, smaller request, you were more inclined to agree to the second, larger request. This is the essence of the FITD technique. When people agree to a small request before a larger one is made, they are more likely to agree to the larger request than if the larger request was made alone.

In the experiment that first demonstrated the FITD technique (Freedman & Fraser, 1966), subjects were contacted in their homes by a representative of a fictitious marketing research company under four separate conditions: (1) Some subjects were asked if they would be willing to answer a few simple questions about the soap products used in their households (a request to which most subjects agreed). The questions were asked only if the subject agreed. This was called the "performance" condition. (2) Other subjects were also asked if they would be willing to answer a few simple questions, but when they agreed, they were told that the company was simply lining up subjects for a survey and that they would be contacted later. This was called the

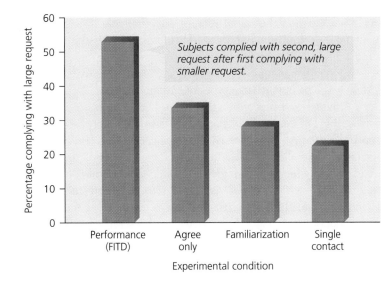

FIGURE 8-7 *The foot-in-the-door (FITD) technique. Subjects who first complied with a small request were much more likely to comply with a second, larger request later on. The other groups in the study consisted of subjects who agreed to comply but didn't have to do anything; subjects who were simply familiarized with the request; and subjects who received only the second, large request. As shown, each of these techniques was progressively less effective than the FITD technique.* Data from Freedman and Fraser, 1966.

"agree-only" condition. (3) Still other subjects were contacted, told of the questionnaire, and told that the call was merely to familiarize people with the marketing company. This was the "familiarization" condition. (4) A final group of subjects were contacted only once. This was the "single-contact" (control) condition.

Subjects in the first three conditions were called again a few days later. This time a larger request was made. The subjects were asked if they would allow a team of five or six people to come into their homes for 2 hours and do an inventory of soap products. In the single-contact condition, subjects received only this request. The results of the experiment, shown in Figure 8-7, were striking. Notice that over 50% of the subjects in the "performance" condition (which is the FITD technique) agreed to the second, larger request, compared to only about 22% of the subjects in the "single-contact" group. Notice also that simply agreeing to the smaller request or being familiarized with the company was not sufficient to significantly increase compliance with the larger request. The FITD effect occurs only if the smaller task is actually performed.

Since this seminal experiment, conducted in 1966, many other studies have verified the FITD effect. Researchers quickly turned their attention to investigating the underlying *causes* for the effect.

Why It Works: Three Hypotheses One explanation for the FITD effect is provided by *self-perception theory* (Bem, 1972). Recall from Chapter 7 that we sometimes learn about ourselves from observing our own behavior and making inferences about the causes for that behavior. According to the **self-perception hypothesis,** the FITD works because agreeing to the first request causes changes in our perceptions of ourselves. Once we agree to the smaller, original request, we perceive ourselves as the type of person who gives help in that particular situation, and thus we are more likely to give similar help in the future. Generally, research has supported this idea (DeJong, 1979; Goldman, Seever, & Seever, 1982; Snyder & Cunningham, 1975).

Originally it was believed that merely agreeing to any initial request was sufficient to produce the FITD effect. However, we now know differently.

self-perception hypothesis
An explanation for the foot-in-the-door technique suggesting that after agreeing to the smaller request, the person comes to see himself or herself as someone who helps in that particular situation.

FITD works when the initial request is sufficiently large to elicit a commitment from an individual and the individual attributes the commitment to internal, dispositional factors. That is, the person reasons, "I am the type of person who cooperates with people doing a market survey" (or contributes to PADD, or helps in particular types of situations).

Although self-perception theory has been widely accepted as an explanation for FITD, another explanation has also been proposed. This is the **perceptual contrast hypothesis,** which suggests that the FITD effect occurs because the smaller, initial request acts as an "anchor" (a standard of reference) against which other requests are judged (Cantrill & Seibold, 1986). The later request can be either assimilated to or contrasted with the anchor. Theoretically, in the FITD situation, the second, larger request is assimilated to the anchor (the smaller, first request) and is seen as less burdensome than if it were presented alone. That is, the second and larger request is seen as more reasonable because of the first request with which the person has already agreed. Although this hypothesis has generated some interest, there is not as much support for it as there is for the self-perception explanation.

Another explanation for the effectiveness of the FITD effect focuses on the thought processes of its recipients. It has been suggested that information about the solicitor's and recipient's behavior affects compliance in the FITD effect (Tybout, Sternthal, & Calder, 1983). According to this view, targets of the FITD technique undergo changes in attitudes and cognitions about the requested behavior. Compliance on a second request depends, in part, on the information available in the subject's memory that relates to the issue (Hornik, 1988).

This hypothesis was put to test in a field experiment involving requests for contributions to the Israeli Cancer Society (ICA) (Hornik, 1988). Subjects were first asked to fulfill a small request: to distribute ICA pamphlets. Subjects agreeing to this request were given a sticker to display on their doors. One version of the sticker touted the subject's continuing involvement in the ICA campaign. A second version suggested that subjects had fulfilled their obligation completely. Ten days later subjects were contacted again and asked to donate money to the ICA. Additionally, the control group of subjects were contacted for the first time.

The results of this study confirmed the power of the FITD technique to produce compliance (compared to the control group). Those subjects who received the sticker implying continued commitment to the ICA showed greater compliance with the later request than did either those who had received the sticker showing that an obligation was fulfilled or those in the control group. Subjects in the continued commitment group most likely held attitudes about themselves, had information available, and had self-perceptions suggesting continued commitment. This translated into greater compliance.

Limits of the Technique As you can see, the FITD technique is a very powerful tool for gaining compliance. Although the effect has been replicated over and over, there is evidence that it has its limits. One important limitation of the FITD technique is that the requests being made must be

perceptual contrast hypothesis An explanation for the foot-in-the-door technique suggesting that the smaller, initial request acts as a standard of reference against which other requests are judged.

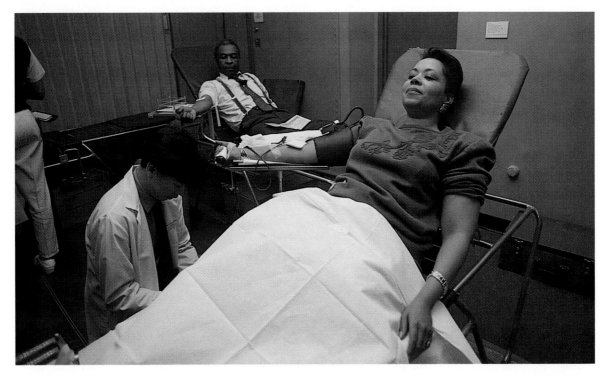

socially acceptable (Dillard, Hunter, & Burgoon, 1984). People do not comply with requests they find objectionable.

Another limitation to the FITD technique is the cost of the behavior called for. When a high-cost behavior is called for (e.g., donating blood), the FITD technique does not work very well (Cialdini & Ascani, 1976; Foss & Dempsey, 1979). Does this mean that the FITD technique cannot be used to increase socially desirable but high-cost behaviors like blood donation? Not necessarily. A small modification in the technique may prove effective: adding a moderately strong request between the initial small and final large requests. Adding such an intermediate request increases the power of the FITD technique (Goldman, Creason, & McCall, 1981). A gradually increasing, graded series of requests may alter the potential donor's self-perceptions, which are strongly associated with increased compliance in the FITD paradigm. This is essentially what happened to Arthur Walker. He was seduced into being a spy by such a variation of the FITD technique. His brother used a graded and gradual series of requests until Arthur found that he was in too deep to climb out.

Interestingly, although the FITD technique does not increase blood donations significantly, it can be used to induce people to become organ donors (Carducci & Deuser, 1984). Why the difference between these two donation behaviors? It may be that the two behaviors involve differing levels of commitment. Blood donation takes time and involves some pain and discomfort. Organ donation, which takes place after death, does not. Blood

The foot-in-the-door technique—making a small request and following it with a larger one—does not work very well with high-cost behaviors, such as giving blood. Compliance can be increased by making a moderate request between the small and large requests. What kind of request would induce you to donate blood?

FIGURE 8-8 *The door-in-the-face compliance technique may activate the norm of reciprocity: When we think the solicitor has made a concession and is offering a compromise, we feel compelled to respond in kind. This technique probably also plays on our fear of looking small-minded and cheap.*

donation requires action; organ donation requires only agreement. It appears that blood donation is seen as a higher-cost behavior than organ donation. Under such high-cost conditions the FITD technique, in its original form, does not work very well.

The Door-in-the-Face Technique   Imagine that you are sitting at home reading a book when the telephone rings. The caller turns out to be a solicitor for a charity that provides food baskets for needy families at Thanksgiving. The caller describes the charity program and asks if you would be willing to donate $250 to feed a family of 10. To this request you react as many people do: "*What!* I can't possibly give that much!" In response the caller offers you several other alternatives, each requiring a smaller and smaller donation (for example, $100, $50, $25, and $10). Each time the caller asks about an alternative you feel more and more like Ebenezer Scrooge, and finally you agree to provide a $25 food basket.

Notice the tactic used by the solicitor. You were first hit with a large request, which you found unreasonable, and then a smaller one, which you agreed to. The technique the solicitor used was just the opposite of what would take place in the FITD technique (a small request followed by a larger one). In this example you have fallen prey to the **door-in-the-face technique** (DITF; Figure 8-8).

After being induced into buying a candy bar from a Boy Scout who used the DITF technique, one researcher decided to investigate the power of this technique to induce compliance (Cialdini, 1988). Subjects were approached and asked if they would be willing to escort a group of "juvenile delinquents" to a local zoo (Cialdini et al., 1975). Not surprisingly, most subjects refused this request. But in the DITF condition this request was preceded by an even larger one, to spend 2 hours per week as a counselor for juvenile delinquents for at least 2 years! It's even less surprising that this request was turned down. However, when the request to escort delinquents to the zoo followed the larger request, commitments for the zoo trip increased dramatically (Figure 8-9). Subsequent studies verified the power of

door-in-the-face technique
A compliance technique in which a large request is made first and is then followed by a smaller one.

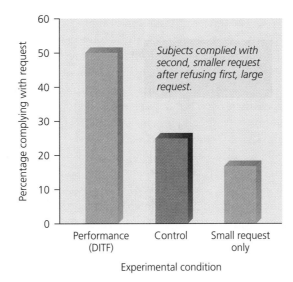

FIGURE 8-9 *The door-in-the-face (DITF) technique. Subjects who were first approached with a large request, which they turned down, and then asked for something smaller were more likely to comply than subjects who received only the smaller request. This technique may activate the norm of reciprocity, an unspoken rule about making concessions to others when they make concessions to us. Research indicates that the DITF technique is more effective at inducing compliance than the FITD technique.* Data from Cial-dini et al., 1975

[Chart labels: Y-axis "Percentage complying with request" 0, 10, 20, 30, 40, 50, 60. X-axis "Experimental condition" Performance (DITF), Control, Small request only. Text box: "Subjects complied with second, smaller request after refusing first, large request."]

the DITF technique to induce compliance (for example, Cialdini & Ascani, 1976; Williams & Williams, 1989).

Why It Works: The Norm of Reciprocity   Some researchers have suggested that the DITF technique works because the target of the influence attempt feels compelled to match the concession (from the first, larger request to the smaller, second request) made by the solicitor (Cialdini et al., 1975). The social psychological mechanism operating here is the **norm of reciprocity** (Gouldner, 1960). The norm of reciprocity states that we should help those who help us. Remember Aesop's fable about the mouse who came across a lion with a thorn in its foot? Despite the obvious danger to itself, the mouse helped the lion by removing the thorn. Later, when the lion came upon the mouse in need of help, the lion reciprocated by helping the mouse. This is an illustration of the norm of reciprocity. The norm of reciprocity is apparently a very powerful force in our social lives (Cialdini, 1988).

Implied in this original statement of the norm is the idea that we may feel compelled to reciprocate when we perceive that another person is making a concession to us. This norm helps explain the DITF effect. It goes something like this: When a solicitor first makes a large request and then immediately backs off when we refuse and comes back with a smaller request, we perceive that the solicitor is making a concession. We feel pressure to reciprocate by also making a concession. Our concession is to agree to the smaller request, because refusing the smaller request would threaten our sense of well-being tied to the norm of reciprocity. In the DITF technique, then, our attention becomes focused on the behavior of the solicitor, who appears to have made a concession (Williams & Williams, 1989). If we don't reciprocate, we may later feel guilty or fear that we will appear unreasonable and cheap in the light of the concession the solicitor made.

norm of reciprocity A powerful social norm suggesting that people should help those who help them.

The power of the norm of reciprocity has been shown in empirical research. For example, one study found that more subjects agreed to buy raffle tickets from someone who had previously done them a favor (bought the subject a soft drink) than from someone who had not done them a favor (Regan, 1971). In this study the norm of reciprocity exerted a greater influence than overall liking for the solicitor. Research has also shown that the norm of reciprocity is central to the DITF effect (Cialdini, 1988; Cialdini et al., 1975; Goldman & Creason, 1981). If a solicitor makes more than one concession (when a solicitor reads a list of smaller and smaller requests), compliance is higher than if the solicitor makes only one concession (Goldman & Creason, 1981). This is especially true if the intermediate request is moderate (Goldman, Creason, & McCall, 1981).

Other Explanations   Although there is support for the role of reciprocity in the DITF effect, some researchers have questioned its validity and have suggested alternative explanations for these situations. One such alternative is the perceptual contrast hypothesis. As discussed earlier, this hypothesis focuses on the contrast in size between the first and second requests. Applied to the DITF effect, the perceptual contrast hypothesis suggests that subjects agree to the second (small) request because it appears more reasonable in the light of the first (large) request. The subject may perceive that the second request is less costly than the first. Although there is some evidence against this view (Shanab & Isonio, 1982), there is also evidence to support it (Miller, Seligman, Clark, & Bush, 1976; Shanab & O'Neill, 1979).

A second possible explanation for the DITF effect is the **worthy person hypothesis** (Foehl & Goldman, 1983). In most DITF studies, the solicitation is made for a worthy cause (Foehl & Goldman, 1983). Refusing the second, smaller request in a DITF experiment may make subjects feel guilty because they have rejected a worthy request.

Finally, there is evidence that our fear of appearing cheap may be an important factor in falling prey to solicitations. The number of people contributing to the American Cancer Society was increased by simply tacking on the statement "Even a penny would help" to a neutral solicitation pitch (Cialdini & Schroeder, 1976). Adding the "even a penny" statement makes even a paltry contribution legitimate and may make the individual feel cheap or guilty for not giving (Cialdini & Schroeder, 1976). The "even a penny" statement did not affect the *amount* of money contributed. Apparently, once we get over the hump of deciding to give, we give as much as we would have anyway.

The Low-Ball Technique   Yet another technique for inducing compliance is the **low-ball technique** (also known as low-balling). In low-balling, a solicitor (usually a salesperson) makes you an offer that seems too good to be true. For example, a car salesperson may quote you an extremely low price for a car. The catch, of course, is that she must have it approved by the sales manager. She leaves for some time, leaving you to "stew." During this stewing period you probably are convincing yourself that this is the car you want (Cialdini, 1988).

worthy person hypothesis An explanation for the door-in-the-face technique suggesting that because most DITF situations involve worthy causes, refusing the second (smaller) request induces guilt and thus leads to compliance.

low-ball technique A compliance technique in which an unreasonably low offer is made and, when commitment is elicited, replaced with a higher offer on the pretense that the lower one could not be honored.

Low-balling is a common sales technique. The salesperson offers an unbelievably low price, leaves to check the figures or do some paperwork, then returns apologetically with a higher price. Since you have used your time alone to commit yourself to the purchase, you are likely to buy the product anyway, at the higher price.

When she returns, she informs you that the manager couldn't possibly sell the car for such a low price or that there was some error made in calculating the price (for example, forgetting to add in the price of rustproofing). She makes a new offer that is higher than the original offer. If you find yourself buying the car for the higher price, you have fallen prey to low-balling.

Low-balling, much like the FITD and DITF techniques, is a two-step process. First, an initial commitment is obtained from the target. Car salespersons often try to get you to give them a check to "show good faith" and sign a form with your "offer" (the low price). The second step is to reveal the higher price, either through a hidden cost (dealer preparation, for example) or through management's refusal of the low offer.

Like the other compliance strategies, low-balling does induce compliance. For example, in one study, subjects were asked to be in an experiment that began at 7:00 a.m. Under these conditions, only 31% of those asked said they would be willing to participate. However, if they were "low-balled"—told about the starting time only after they had agreed to participate—56% of those asked agreed (Cialdini, Cacioppo, Bassett, & Miller, 1978).

The two principal psychological mechanisms operating in the low-ball technique are *commitment* and *consistency* (Cialdini, 1988). Commitment occurs when you take significant steps toward a particular course of action (Kiesler, 1971). For example, once you decide to make an offer on a car and give a deposit, you are taking significant steps toward buying that car. Once you make this initial commitment to the salesperson, you are likely to follow through on it (Burger & Petty, 1981). There is evidence that commitment to a *person* (e.g., a salesperson) is more important than commitment to the *behavior* (e.g., buying a car) in compliance (Burger & Petty, 1981). So you may not

Every few years or so, many Americans catch the bug to buy a new car. What happens when they enter the auto showroom? Let's follow a potential buyer—let's call her Jackie—as she moves through this process. As soon as she walks through the door, she becomes an object of interest to a salesperson—let's call him Jim. To sell Jackie a car, Jim will apply a carefully planned program of social influence. The figure outlines the steps in this "buyer commitment process" as developed and used by one midwestern auto dealership.

The process begins (at the bottom of the pyramid) with three steps designed to "build trust" between the customer and the salesperson. During this phase, Jim probably will do just about anything for Jackie: get her a cup of coffee, let her use the phone, perhaps even watch her kids while she peruses the showroom. All of these little favors add up, not only to a feeling of trust but to a feeling of obligation as well.

Next comes the hard sell, during which the salesperson presents the car and "builds value." This stage includes a "demo ride." Getting Jackie to take the

demo ride is a first, small step in gaining a commitment from her to buy the car. Jim now has his foot in the door! He may even tell Jackie she can take the car home for the night or the weekend. Is he being altruistic because he likes her? Don't bet on it! He's still building obligation. Remember the *norm of reciprocity*? If Jim (whom Jackie now trusts) does something nice for her (lets her take the car home), she may feel obligated to do something nice in return (buy the car).

Next comes "buyer commitment." Jim doesn't want Jackie to walk out the door without buying. He may elicit a verbal commitment on her part, which will be difficult for her to go back on later. He may even get her to buy a car that day if a price can be agreed on. They enter the stage of negotiation. Having gone through a rite of passage during which the norm of reciprocity was energized, Jackie is unlikely to back out now. At this point she

may give a deposit. This does more than just hold the car for her. It is an overt behavior that deeply commits her to the purchase.

But Jackie's not done yet! Next comes the appointment with the business manager—Jason—who, Jim explains, will "do the paperwork and arrange the loan." But Jason does something else as well: He tries to sell Jackie all kinds of "add ons." He urges her to purchase an extended service agreement, something he personally wouldn't want to live without. When she balks, he "spontaneously" offers to throw in rustproofing at no extra charge. It's a deal no one in her right mind would pass up!

Jackie eventually gets her new car, and Jim and Jason get their sales commission. Like most salespersons, Jim and Jason are trained in social influence techniques, and they use them. They understand that these techniques are deeply manipulative and that people find them very hard to resist. Jackie is really under no obligation to buy the car even if she has a cup of coffee, uses the phone, goes for a demo ride, and takes the car home for the weekend. But

be as inclined to buy the car if you negotiate first with the salesperson and then with the sales manager than if you had continued negotiating with the original salesperson.

Commitment affects our behavior in two ways. First, we typically look for reasons to justify a commitment after making it (Cialdini, 1988). This is consistent with cognitive dissonance theory, as discussed in Chapter 7. Typically, we devise justifications that support our decision to buy the car. Second, we also have a desire to maintain consistency between our thoughts and actions and among our actions (Cialdini, 1988; Festinger, 1957). When the salesperson returns with a higher offer, we may be inclined to accept the

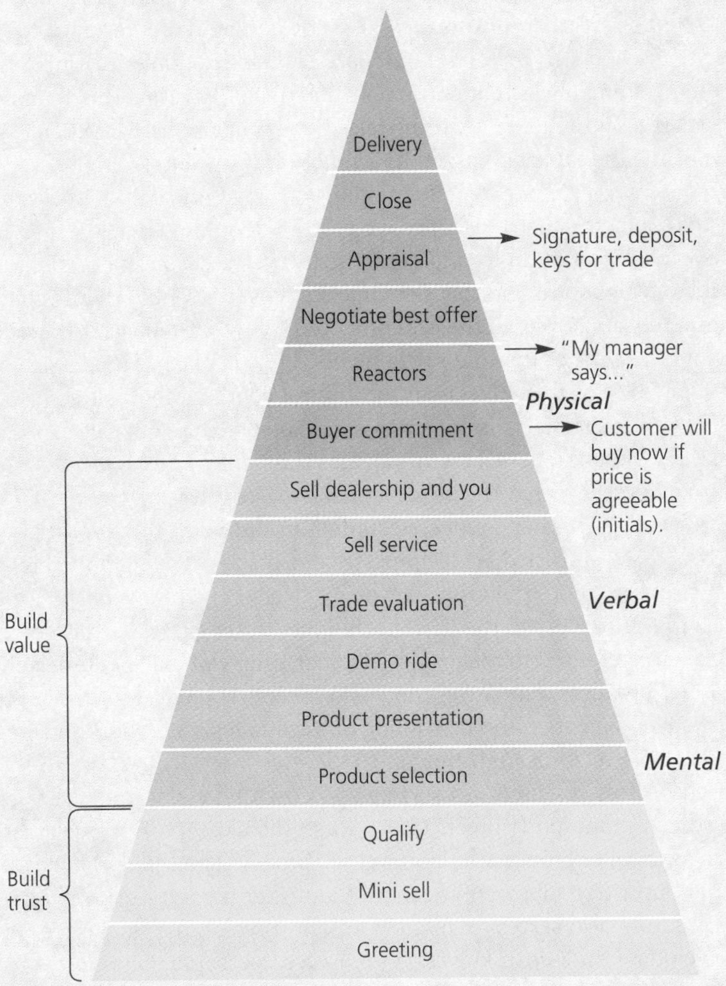
Delivery
Close
Appraisal
Signature, deposit, keys for trade
Negotiate best offer
Reactors
"My manager says..."
Physical
Buyer commitment
Customer will buy now if price is agreeable (initials).
Sell dealership and you
Sell service
Trade evaluation
Verbal
Demo ride
Product presentation
Product selection
Mental
Qualify
Mini sell
Greeting
Build value
Build trust

BUYER COMMITMENT PROCESS

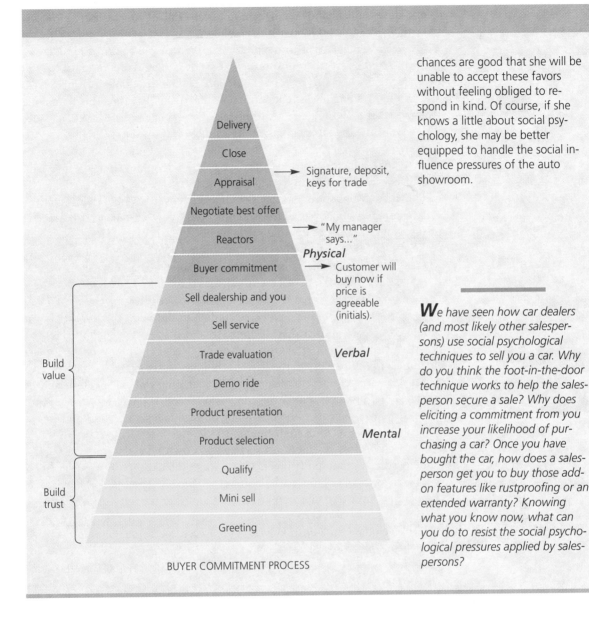

chances are good that she will be unable to accept these favors without feeling obliged to respond in kind. Of course, if she knows a little about social psychology, she may be better equipped to handle the social influence pressures of the auto showroom.

We have seen how car dealers (and most likely other salespersons) use social psychological techniques to sell you a car. Why do you think the foot-in-the-door technique works to help the salesperson secure a sale? Why does eliciting a commitment from you increase your likelihood of purchasing a car? Once you have bought the car, how does a salesperson get you to buy those add-on features like rustproofing or an extended warranty? Knowing what you know now, what can you do to resist the social psychological pressures applied by salespersons?

offer because refusal would be dissonant with all the cognitions and justifications we developed during the stewing period.

The That's-Not-All Technique Another technique used by solicitors/salespersons is to get you to commit to a purchase by throwing in all kinds of extras. You see this often on late-night television commercials for various products. For example, an advertisement for a set of cookware (for the unbelievably low price of only $29.95) first touts the features of the cookware (nonstick, lifetime warranty, etc.), trying to convince you that the cookware is a real deal. Next, you get the "that's-not-all" pitch: If you "order now," you get a set of

Ginsu knives and a handy-dandy orange juicer—all, of course, for the low-low price of $29.95 (plus shipping and handling).

Advertisements that throw in items to induce you to buy a product are using the **that's-not-all technique** (TNA). By adding more and more to the deal, they induce you to make the purchase. A field experiment using a bake sale as the experimental situation demonstrated the power of this technique (Burger, 1986). On the table were cupcakes with no price listed. When a subject approached the table and asked how much the cupcakes were, one of two answers was given. In one condition, the person at the table (the experimenter) told subjects that the cupcakes cost 75 cents but that the price included two cookies (control condition). In the second condition (the TNA condition), subjects were told that the cupcakes cost 75 cents. Then a confederate whispered something to the experimenter. A few seconds later the experimenter told the subject that the price included two cookies. The results were striking: Only 40% of the subjects in the control condition bought a cupcake, whereas 73% of the subjects in the TNA condition bought a cupcake.

The TNA technique seems to operate through a process of reciprocation. You may perceive that the seller is making a concession by offering you more merchandise for your money. According to the norm of reciprocity, you should then feel compelled to reciprocate and make a concession (buy the product). However, more than this may be involved. Perceptions of the "seller" are critical to the success of the TNA technique. If, for example, you perceive that the seller is required to make an additional offer, you may be less likely to buy his or her products than if the concession seems voluntary (Burger, 1986). When the seller appears to be bargaining or negotiating with you, the concession is likely to be reciprocated (Burger, 1986).

Based on this research, a two-stage process underlying the TNA technique has been proposed (Burger, 1986). First, the appearance of negotiating on price by the seller arouses the norm of reciprocity. The seller's concessions compel the buyer to reciprocate. Second, the higher price (or original offer of only one product) also serves as an anchor against which the final price (or final deal including the Ginsu knives) is compared (perceptual contrast). Thus, through the processes of reciprocity and perceptual contrast we may be induced to buy more readily than if this compliance technique were not employed.

Compliance Techniques: Summing Up

We have described and analyzed four different compliance techniques. Are they all equally effective, or are some more effective than others? Research indicates that the DITF technique elicits more compliance than the FITD technique (Brownstein & Katzev, 1985; Cialdini & Ascani, 1976). There is also evidence that a combined FITD/DITF strategy elicits greater compliance than either of the techniques alone (Goldman, 1986). However, low-balling may be more effective for gaining compliance than either the FITD or the DITF techniques (Brownstein & Katzev, 1985). In one experiment, subjects were stopped and asked to donate money to a museum fund drive. The request was made under FITD, DITF, low-ball, or a control condition. The average amount

that's-not-all technique A compliance technique in which extras are added to an initial offer, often as apparently spontaneous gestures of generosity.

of money donated was highest under the low-ball conditions, compared to the FITD, DITF, and control conditions (which did not differ significantly from one another). For a look at how these techniques are used in combination with each other in real-life situations, see the featured discussion "Buying a Car: An Exercise in Social Influence."

All of these compliance techniques have been and will be used to induce people to buy products (some of which they may want and some of which they may not want). The psychological mechanisms of reciprocity, commitment, consistency, and perceptual contrast operate to varying degrees to produce compliance. Because we all share these mechanisms, we all find ourselves on occasion doing something we don't really want to do. Sellers of all types use compliance techniques to sell their products (Cialdini, 1988). The best way to guard ourselves against these techniques is to recognize and understand them when they're used.

THE JURY ROOM REVISITED

In the LeRoy Reed case, Frank tried to stand up to 11 other jurors. He held out for a guilty verdict as long as he could. Eventually he gave in and changed his vote. Frank was exposed to both informational and normative social influence. He was unconvinced by the persuasive arguments of the other jurors but was finally swayed by the pressure to conform.

Frank was placed in the unenviable position of being a minority of one. The research on conformity tells us that he stood little chance of standing his ground. If he had had a "true partner" who stood with him, he might have been able to hold out. He and his partner might even have been able to sway the other jurors to vote guilty, through the process of minority influence. But such was not the case. Frank ended up conforming—he changed his vote even though he had not changed his mind.

LOOKING AHEAD

Conformity and compliance are two important social influence mechanisms that affect our social behavior, sometimes below the level of conscious awareness. We conform to a dress code a group of friends establishes because we don't want to look different. We comply with a salesperson's request because we are vulnerable to the compliance techniques the person uses.

But social influence does not stop with persuasion, conformity, and compliance. We often find ourselves in the position of receiving a command from someone in authority, such as our supervisor at work. If we do what we are told, we are operating within the parameters of yet another form of social influence: obedience. Obedience and disobedience are the subjects of Chapter 9. In other cases we find ourselves belonging to a group that must make a decision, whether at work, at school, or in the community. Social influence is at work here too; in these situations, group processes become relevant. Group processes are addressed in Chapter 10.

CHAPTER REVIEW

1. *What is conformity?*

   Conformity is one type of social influence. It occurs when we modify our behavior in response to real or imagined pressure from others. Frank, the man cast into the role of juror in a criminal trial, entered the jury deliberations convinced that the defendant was guilty. Throughout the deliberations, Frank maintained his view based on the information he had heard during the trial. However, in the end, Frank changed his verdict. He did this because of the perceived pressure from the other 11 jurors, not because he was convinced by the evidence that the defendant was innocent. Frank's dilemma, pitting his own internal beliefs against the beliefs of others, is a common occurrence in our lives. We often find ourselves in situations where we must modify our behavior based on what others do or say.

2. *What is the source of the pressures that lead to conformity?*

   The "pressure" can arise from two sources. We may modify our behavior because we are convinced by information provided by others, which is **informational social influence.** Or we may modify our behavior because we perceive that a **norm,** an unwritten social rule, must be followed. This is **normative social influence.** In the latter case, information provided by others defines the norm we then follow. Norms play a central role in our social lives. The classic research by Sherif (1936, 1972) making use of the autokinetic effect showed how a norm forms.

3. *What research evidence is there for conformity?*

   Solomon Asch (1951, 1955, 1956) conducted a series of now-classic experiments that showed conformity effects with a relatively clear, simple perceptual line judgment task. He found that subjects conformed to an incorrect majority on 33% of the critical trials where a majority (composed of confederates) made obviously incorrect judgments. In postexperimental interviews, Asch found that there were a variety of reasons why a subject would conform (yield) or not conform (remain independent).

4. *What factors influence conformity?*

   Research by Asch and others found several factors that influence conformity. Conformity is more likely to occur when the task is ambiguous than if the task is clear-cut. Additionally, conformity increases as the size of the majority increases up to a majority size of three. After a majority size of three, conformity does not increase significantly with the addition of more majority members. Finally, Asch found that conformity levels go down if you have another person who stands with you against the majority. This is the **true partner effect.**

5. *Do women conform more than men?*

   Although early research suggested that women conformed more than men, later research revealed no such simple relationship. Research indicates that the nature of the task was not important in producing the observed sex differences. However, women are more likely to conform when the experimenter is a man. No gender differences are found when a woman runs the experiment. Also, women are more likely to conform than men under conditions of normative social influence than under informational social influence conditions. Two explanations have been offered for gender differences in conformity. First, gender may serve as a status variable in newly formed groups, with men cast in the higher-status roles and women in the lower-status roles. Second, women tend to be more sensitive than men to conformity pressures when they have to state their opinions publicly.

6. *Can the minority ever influence the majority?*
Generally, American social psychologists have focused their attention on the influence of a majority on the minority. However, in Europe social psychologists have focused on how minorities can influence majorities. A firm, consistent minority has been found capable of causing change in majority opinion. Generally, a minority that is consistent but flexible and adheres to opinions that fit with the current "spirit of the times" has a good chance of changing majority opinion.

7. *How does minority influence work?*
Currently, a debate is under way concerning the underlying mechanisms controlling majority and minority influence. Some theorists contend that majority and minority influence represent two distinct processes, with majority influence being primarily normative and minority influence primarily informational. However, other theorists argue that a single process can account for both majority and minority influence situations. According to Latané's **social impact theory,** social influence is related to the interaction between the strength of the influence source, the immediacy of the influence source, and the number of influence sources. Tanford and Penrod's **social influence model** was derived based on a series of computer simulations and appears to provide a better explanation for social influence than social impact theory. To date, neither the two- nor the single-process approach can explain all aspects of minority, or majority, influence.

8. *Why do we sometimes end up doing things we would rather not do?*
Sometimes we modify our behavior in response to a direct request from someone else. This is known as **compliance.** Sometimes, such as in the case of Arthur Walker, who was recruited to be a spy for the former Soviet Union, we are eased into behaviors on a step-by-step basis that we would ordinarily avoid. Social psychologists have uncovered four main techniques that can induce compliance.

9. *What are these techniques, and why do they work?*
In the **foot-in-the-door technique,** a small request is followed by a larger one. Agreeing to the second, larger request is more likely after agreeing to the first, smaller request. This technique appears to work for three reasons. First, according to the **self-perception hypothesis,** agreeing to the first request may result in shifts in one's self-perception. After agreeing to the smaller request, you come to see yourself as the "type of person" who helps. Second, the **perceptual contrast hypothesis** suggests that the second,

larger request seems less involved following the smaller, first request. Third, our thought processes may undergo a change after agreeing to the first request. The likelihood of agreeing to the second request depends on the thoughts we developed based on information about the first request.

The **door-in-the-face technique** reverses the foot-in-the-door strategy: A large (seemingly unreasonable) request is followed by a smaller one. Agreement to the second, smaller request is more likely if it follows the larger request than if it is presented alone. The door-in-the-face technique works because the **norm of reciprocity** is energized when the person making the request makes a "concession." The door-in-the-face technique may also work because we do not want to seem cheap, through perceptual contrast, and our desire not to be perceived as someone who refuses a worthy cause. This latter explanation is the **worthy person hypothesis.**

The **low-ball technique** is another two-stage process. A product is offered at a very low price and then, after a commitment is made, the price is raised. Commitment and consistency are the principal forces that make low-balling work. The commitment occurs when you take significant steps toward buying the product. Once the commitment is made we then strive to maintain consistency between our thoughts and our actions. Refusal of the higher price would be inconsistent with all the positive thoughts we developed about the product.

Finally, the **that's-not-all technique** involves "throwing in" something at no additional cost. This technique appears to work via the norm of reciprocity. When the salesperson throws something in, she is doing you a "favor." You may feel compelled to do something nice in return (buy the product).

SUGGESTIONS FOR FURTHER READING

Cialdini, R. B. (1993). *Influence: Science and practice* (3rd ed.). Glenview, IL: Scott Foresman.

This fascinating and easy-to-read book takes you inside the world of social influence. Cialdini, having had experience going undercover as a salesperson, gives a unique perspective on social influence. You will come away a bit wiser from this book!

Early, P. (1988). *Family of spies: Inside the John Walker spy ring.* New York: Bantam Books.

This book chronicles the Walker spy scandal. It gives some excellent insights into how one might be recruited into being a spy.

Latané, B. (1981). The psychology of social impact. *American Psychologist, 36,* 343–356.

This article is an excellent introduction to Latané's social impact theory.

Maas, A., & Clark, R. D. (1984). Hidden impact of minorities: Fifteen years of minority influence research. *Psychological Bulletin, 95,* 428–450.

This article reviews the critical issues addressed in the research on minority influence. Discussions of minority style, normative context, and different types of minorities are included.

Paicheler, G. (1979). Polarization of attitudes in homogeneous and heterogeneous groups. *European Journal of Social Psychology, 9*, 85–96.

This article covers several interesting topics concerning the impact of a minority on majority opinion. The role of normative context (zeitgeist) and the gender of the minority are evaluated experimentally in this study.

Chapter 9

Obedience and Disobedience

*T*he day began as any other. There was no reason to suspect that anything out of the ordinary was going to happen. Outside the village, the American soldiers gathered. The officer in command told his men that the order of the day was to "clear the village." When he gave the signal, the soldiers rounded up the villagers, about 350 of them, mainly women and children.

Some of the people huddled together in the center of the village, guarded by a soldier. The soldier assumed that the villagers would be moved out of the village before it was burned down. The commanding officer came up to the soldier and said, "You know what to do with them, don't you?" The soldier replied that he did, thinking his commander meant to watch them carefully. The commanding officer returned about 10 minutes later and asked, "How come you

ain't killed them yet?" The soldier replied that he thought that he was just supposed to guard them. The commanding officer told the soldier that he wanted the villagers dead.

At that point the slaughter began. The soldiers pushed the villagers into a ravine and shot them. As the soldiers moved out of the village, their mission accomplished, over 300 unarmed women, children, and babies lay dead.

The events in that Vietnamese village, My Lai, were recounted by journalist Seymour Hersh (1970). The platoon of American soldiers was commanded by Lt. William Calley. When these events were publicized, Calley was put on trial. He pleaded that he not be held responsible for the soldiers' actions. They had been acting on his orders, but he too, he argued, had been carrying out orders issued by his superiors.

Whether Calley had been given direct orders to murder the villagers has never been established. Calley was tried by court martial, found guilty, and sentenced to house arrest. He went home to Georgia and became a real estate salesman. The soldiers he commanded were found innocent.

Nothing in William Calley's personal history would have suggested that he was capable of ordering and taking part in mass murder. Calley seemed to be a remarkably commonplace individual. Similarly, the soldiers under

Wearing clothes in public is a convention with which most people willingly conform. When someone breaks with this convention—as "the Naked Guy" did in Berkeley in 1992—society often responds with more compelling measures. In this case, a law forbidding public nudity was passed to bring the nonconformist into line.

his command were ordinary men. Each probably had his own thoughts and feelings about systematically killing unarmed women and children. Each of them was most likely a decent individual. Despite all of this, they carried out their orders, as they were trained to do. Such is the nature of **obedience,** the process by which we modify our behavior in response to a command from someone in authority.

In this chapter we consider a number of issues related to obedience. We ask, How is it that ordinarily "normal" individuals can abandon their usual restraints against such monstrous behavior? Are those who commit acts like those committed in My Lai driven to such behavior by antisocial tendencies? Or are they victims of circumstance, reacting to external pressures? Under what conditions might we expect people to behave like Calley and his men? And when might we expect people to refuse to carry out such orders? These are some of the questions addressed in this chapter.

CONFORMITY AND OBEDIENCE: PERSONAL CHOICE OR HUMAN NATURE?

Living in society requires certain compromises. As an example, consider the convention of wearing clothes. Even if it's very hot, even if we would be more comfortable unclothed, we wear clothes whenever we are in public. It's conventional to do so; there are customs that constrain us to be clothed in public. In 1992 a student at the University of California at Berkeley broke with this convention. He began appearing on the street, on campus, and in class wearing only sandals. He became known as "the Naked Guy." He wasn't breaking any laws—just conventions. To deal with this unconventional individual, the university instituted a policy forbidding public

obedience The social influence process by which a person changes his or her behavior in response to a direct order from someone in authority.

nudity and the city of Berkeley passed a law to the same effect. Until then, policies and laws had been unnecessary, since most people are not interested in appearing nude in public. Conventional behaviors like these make social life easier and more predictable. Pressure to do these customary acts is subtle, probably below conscious awareness, and not usually burdensome.

Conformity

As we saw in Chapter 8, there is also more overt pressure placed upon us, such as when others wish us to conform to their point of view or position. Groups, particularly groups we value, can greatly influence us. Even groups made up of people we do not know have the power to make us doubt the evidence of our senses. Recall, from Chapter 8, Solomon Asch's experiment (1951) in which subjects agreed with a clearly incorrect group estimate of the length of lines. No one told them to misjudge the lines. And although some denied it, they knew they were wrong; nevertheless, they conformed to the erroneous group judgment.

Sometimes the pressure to conform is more direct and insistent, and the risks of resisting are greater. Consider, for example, the case of Benjamin O. Davis, Jr. Davis was the first African American cadet to graduate from the United States Military Academy at West Point in the 20th century. Early in Davis's first year, 1928, some upperclassmen decided to get rid of him because he was African American. They used what was known as "silencing." Other cadets were forbidden to speak to Davis, except in the line of duty. For the remaining 4 years of Davis's West Point career, no one spoke to him except out of professional necessity. He lived alone, without a roommate, without friends, without social contact with his classmates.

Few people could have survived such treatment, but Davis did. He went on to become a three-star general and was much decorated for his service. What about the hundreds of cadets who conformed to a norm that some of them must have felt was inhumane and immoral? Not one resisted the pressure of the group. We do not know if any of the cadets considered befriending Davis, but if they had, they would have been putting their future careers in jeopardy. Such was the power of that group.

Several of Davis's classmates later denied that he had been "silenced" or that they had participated in it. In his autobiography, Davis (1991) wrote:

> It also amazed me that in later years many officers stated publicly that I had not been silenced during my stay at the Academy. In 1973, I received a note from Gen. William ("Bozo") McKee, . . . in which he referred to a newspaper report alleging that I had been silenced at West Point. "I just don't believe this," he wrote. "If this is an outright lie, I don't think you should let it go by." I never answered General McKee's note. (p. 28)

On their own, perhaps many of Davis's classmates would have treated him as just another cadet. But under the power of the group's influence, they went along like sheep.

Obedience

Certainly no group, no society could exist very long if it couldn't make its members obey laws, rules, and customs. Generally, obedience is not a bad thing. But when the rules and norms people are made to obey are negative, obedience is one of the blights of society. This kind of obedience is called **destructive obedience.** Destructive obedience occurs when a person obeys an authority figure and behaves in ways that are counter to accepted standards of moral behavior, ways that conflict with the demands of conscience. The behavior of Lt. Calley and his men is an example of destructive obedience.

Unfortunately, destructive obedience—the form of obedience we are most concerned with in this chapter—is a recurring theme in human history. Calley's men were not the first, nor the last, to carry out orders that resulted in harm or death to others. At the Nuremberg trials following World War II, many Nazi leaders responsible for murdering millions of people fell back on the explanation that they were following orders. More recently, in the ethnic violence between Serbs and Bosnians in the former Yugoslavia, Serbian soldiers allegedly received orders to rape Muslim women in captured towns or villages. Islamic tradition condemns women who have been raped or who become pregnant outside marriage; these orders are intended to destroy the fabric of Muslim family life. Like Calley's men, the Serbian soldiers have been ordered to engage in blatantly immoral and illegal behavior.

The Banality of Evil: Eichmann's Fallacy

It would be a relief to believe that Calley, the Nazis, and the Serbian soldiers are deviant individuals predisposed to antisocial behavior. Unfortunately, history tells us that those who perpetrate evil are often quite ordinary. William Calley was ordinary before and after My Lai. So was Adolph Eichmann, one of the architects of the Holocaust and the Nazi officer responsible for the delivery of European Jews to concentration camps in World War II.

Eichmann's job was to ensure that the death camps had a steady flow of victims. He secured the railroad cattle cars needed to transport the human cargo. His job was managerial, bureaucratic; often he had to fight with competing German interests to get enough boxcars. When the war was over, Eichmann, a most-wanted war criminal, escaped to Argentina. From 1945 to 1961, he worked as a laborer outside Buenos Aires. His uneventful existence ended in 1961 when he was captured by Israeli secret agents, who spirited him back to Israel. There he stood trial for crimes against humanity. After a long trial, Eichmann was found guilty and was later hanged.

The Israelis constructed a special clear, bulletproof witness box for Eichmann to appear in during the trial. They were afraid that someone in Israel might decide to mete out some personal justice. What did the man in the glass booth look like? Eichmann was a short, bald man whose glasses slipped down his nose now and then. You could walk past him a hundred times on the street and never notice him. During the trial, Eichmann

destructive obedience The type of obedience that leads people to behave in ways that are counter to accepted standards of moral behavior.

Adolph Eichmann stands in a bulletproof witness box during his 1962 trial in Israel for crimes against humanity during World War II. Eichmann claimed he should be found innocent because he was an ordinary person who was "only following orders." But in accordance with principles established at the Nuremburg trials following the war, he was judged to be responsible for his actions and was found guilty.

portrayed himself as a man anxious to please his superiors, ambitious for advancement. Killing people was a distasteful but necessary part of his job. Personally, he had no real hatred of the Jews. He was just following orders.

Philosopher and social critic Hannah Arendt observed Eichmann in the dock. She was struck by the wide gap between the ordinariness of the man and the brutal deeds for which he was on trial. In her book *Eichmann in Jerusalem: A Report on the Banality of Evil* (1963), Arendt essentially accepted Eichmann's defense. Her analysis of Eichmann suggested that evil is often very commonplace. Those who carry out acts of destructive obedience are often ordinary people, rather like you and me.

People were shocked by Eichmann and by Arendt's analysis. They had expected a Nazi war criminal to be the epitome of evil. There was a prevailing belief that evil deeds are done by evil people, a belief referred to as **Eichmann's fallacy** (Brown, 1986). This is really the question we would like to answer: Do evil deeds always lead us back to an evil person? Although it might make us feel better if the answer to this question were "yes," we shall see in this chapter that things are not, unfortunately, so simple.

Ultimately, Who's Responsible for Evil Deeds?

After World War II the Allies tried many of the high-ranking Nazis who, like Eichmann, claimed innocence. Their principal defense was to shift responsibility to their superiors: They were "only following orders." More recently, a former East German border guard, Ingo Heinrich, was brought to trial for his role in preventing East German citizens from escaping to the West during the height of the cold war. Heinrich, along with his fellow border guards, had orders to shoot to kill anyone attempting to escape over the Berlin Wall. Heinrich did just that. But some of his comrades, under the

Eichmann's fallacy The false belief that evil deeds must be done by evil people.

When the Berlin Wall came down in 1989, the question arose, Should East German border guards who shot citizens escaping to the West be tried for murder? Or should they be absolved of responsibility because they were obeying orders? At least one guard was convicted and sent to prison.

same orders, shot over the heads of escapees. After the fall of the Berlin Wall and the reunification of Germany, Heinrich was arrested and charged with murder. He was eventually convicted and sentenced to 3½ years in prison.

The cases of Eichmann and Heinrich raise some important issues about responsibility. Is "I was only following orders" a valid defense? Does it erase personal responsibility? Or should individuals be held accountable for their behavior, even if they were following orders? On the surface it would appear that Eichmann and Heinrich were personally responsible for their behavior. However, a deeper examination of authority and its effects on behavior suggests a more complex picture, a picture with many aspects. These issues and questions served as the catalyst for what are probably the most famous experiments in social psychology, the obedience experiments designed and conducted by Stanley Milgram.

THE NATURE OF OBEDIENCE

Stanley Milgram was a student of Solomon Asch. In his conformity experiments, Asch used a simple experimental model to examine an important social issue: the effect of groups on individual conforming behavior. Milgram could see that some variation of that model could be used to study the disturbing issues raised by Arendt and others about the nature of obedience. He felt that an empirical investigation of destructive obedience was necessary (Aron & Aron, 1989). Direct experimental tests of the degree to which, and under what conditions, people would obey a malevolent authority had not yet been made. Such a test promised to help clarify the debate and also be good science.

Milgram's Experiments on Obedience

How does one test destructive obedience in a laboratory setting? Milgram devised a simple yet powerful situation. Before we look at it, let's consider the sociohistorical "climate" in the United States. The year was 1962. Vietnam was but a blip on the back pages of the newspapers. The Kennedy assassinations had not yet occurred, nor had the murder of Martin Luther King, Jr., Watergate, or the riots in the streets of Newark, Detroit, and Watts. This was America before the real '60s began, still holding on to some of the innocence, however illusory, of the '50s. This context is important to consider because it may have influenced how people behaved in Milgram's experiments.

The Subject's Perspective   Let's begin by considering what these experiments looked like from a subject's perspective (Elms, 1972). Imagine you are living in New Haven, Connecticut. One day you notice an ad in the paper asking for volunteers for an experiment on learning and memory at nearby Yale University. The researchers are clearly seeking a good representation of the general population (Figure 9-1). The ad piques your curiosity,

FIGURE 9-1 Milgram's original newspaper advertisement calling for subjects for his obedience experiment. Notice that the ad portrays the experiment as "a scientific study of memory and learning."   From Elms, 1972.

Public Announcement

WE WILL PAY YOU $4.00 FOR ONE HOUR OF YOUR TIME

Persons Needed for a Study of Memory

*We will pay five hundred New Haven men to help us complete a scientific study of memory and learning. The study is being done at Yale University.

*Each person who participates will be paid $4.00 (plus 50¢ carfare) for approximately 1 hour's time. We need you for only one hour: there are no further obligations. You may choose the time you would like to come (evenings, weekdays, or weekends).

*No special training, education, or experience is needed. We want:

Factory workers	Businessmen	Construction workers
City employees	Clerks	Salespeople
Laborers	Professional people	White-collar workers
Barbers	Telephone workers	Others

All persons must be between the ages of 20 and 50. High school and college students cannot be used.

*If you meet these qualifications, fill out the coupon below and mail it now to Professor Stanley Milgram, Department of Psychology, Yale University, New Haven. You will be notified later of the specific time and place of the study. We reserve the right to decline any application.

*You will be paid $4.00 (plus 50¢ carfare) as soon as you arrive at the laboratory.

and you decide to answer it. You drive over to the campus, find the ivy-covered building, and wander down the hall searching for the laboratory. Soon you see a man also searching. You and he join forces, find the lab, and learn that you are both subjects in this experiment.

First, a young man, Mr. Williams, Dr. Milgram's associate, writes out a check to each of you for $4.50. Williams tells you that little is known about the impact of punishment on learning, and that is what this experiment is about. You become a bit concerned when Williams says that one of you will be a learner and the other will be a teacher. Your fears about getting punished soon evaporate when you draw lots to see who will be the learner and you draw the role of the teacher.

Preliminaries out of the way, Williams leads you both into a room past an ominous-looking piece of equipment labeled "Shock Generator, Thorpe ZLB, . . . Output 15 volts–450 volts" (Milgram, 1974). The learner, Mr. Wallace, is told to sit in a straight-backed metal chair. Williams coolly tells you to help strap Wallace's arms down to prevent "excessive movement" during the experiment, which you do. Williams then applies a white paste to Wallace's arms, which he says is electrode paste, "to avoid blisters and burns." Wallace is now worried, and he asks if there is any danger. Williams says, "Although the shocks can be extremely painful, they cause no permanent tissue damage" (Elms, p. 114).

In front of the learner is a row of switches that he will use to respond to your questions. Williams tells you that a light panel in the other room will register the learner's responses. If his answers are correct, you, the teacher, tell him so. If incorrect, you deliver an electric shock from the shock generator.

It's time to start the experiment. You leave Wallace strapped to the shock generator and follow Williams into the next room. He places you before a control panel that has 30 levers, each with a little red light and a big purple light above. The lights have signs above them reading 15 volts, 30 volts, 45 volts, and so on, up to 450 volts. There are also printed

On the left is the elaborate piece of equipment Stanley Milgram's subjects used to shock a "learner" when he made mistakes. On the right, one of the researchers (foreground) and a subject strap electrodes to the learner's wrists. The learner was actually a professional actor and no shocks were ever administered, but the subjects believed they were causing pain—in some cases, life-threatening pain—to another human being.

descriptions of the shock levels above the labels, reading Slight Shock, Moderate Shock, Strong Shock, Intense Shock, Extreme Intense Shock, and finally, over the last few switches, in red, Danger: Severe Shock XXXXX. At this point, you hope that Wallace is brighter than he looks (Elms, 1972).

Before you begin the experiment, Williams gives you a sample shock of 45 volts, which gives you a little jolt. Next, you are told that your task is to teach Wallace several lists of word pairs, such as blue–box, nice–day, wild–duck. You read the entire list of word pairs and then test him, one pair at a time, by providing the first word from each pair.

At first the test is uneventful; Wallace makes no errors. Then he makes his first mistake, and you are required to give him a 15-volt shock. Williams tells you that for every error after that, you are to increase the shock by 15 volts. On subsequent trials Wallace makes frequent errors. When you get to 105 volts, you hear Wallace yell through the wall, "Hey, this really hurts!"

Williams, cool as ever, doesn't seem to notice. You certainly do. At 150 volts, the moaning Wallace yells, "Experimenter, get me out of here! I won't be in the experiment any more. I refuse to go on!" (Elms, p. 115). You look at Williams. He says softly but firmly, "Continue."

Williams brings you more word-pair lists. You begin to wonder what you and Wallace have gotten into for $4.50. You are now at 255 volts, Intense Shock. Wallace screams after every shock. Whenever you ask Williams if you can quit, he tells you to continue. At 300 volts you wonder if Wallace is going to die. "But," you think, "they wouldn't let that happen at Yale . . . or would they?"

"Hey, Mr. Williams," you say, "whose responsibility is this? What if he dies or is seriously hurt?" Williams does not bat an eye: "It's my responsibility, not yours. Just continue with the experiment." He reminds you that, as he told you before, the labels apply to small animals, not humans.

Finally it's over. There are no more shock switches to throw. You're sweaty, uneasy. Wallace comes in from the other room. He's alive and seems okay. You apologize. He tells you to forget it, he'd have done the same if he had been in your shoes. He smiles and rubs his sore wrists, everybody shakes hands, and you and Wallace walk out together.

Predicted Behavior and Results in the Milgram Experiment   How do you think you would behave in Milgram's experiment? Most people think they would refuse to obey the experimenter's orders. Milgram was interested in this question, so he asked a wide range of individuals, both expert (psychiatrists) and nonexpert (college students and noncollege adults), how they thought subjects would behave in this situation. They all predicted that the subjects would break off the experiment, defying the experimenter. The psychiatrists predicted that subjects would break off when the learner began to protest, at the 150-volt level. So, if you believe that you would defy the experimenter and refuse to inflict pain on another person, you are not alone.

The underlying assumption of these predictions is that individual principles will be more powerful determinants of behavior than situational factors. The predictions reflect the notion that moral knowledge predicts moral behavior; in other words, if you know what's right, you'll do it.

However, the results of Milgram's first "baseline" experiment (in which there was no feedback from the victim) don't support these rosy predictions. A majority of subjects (65%) went all the way to 450 volts. In fact, the average shock level delivered by the subjects in this first experiment was 405 volts! We can infer from this result that, under the right circumstances, most of us probably also would go all the way to 450 volts.

Of course, no electric shock was ever given to Wallace, who was, in fact, a professional actor, playing out a script. However, Milgram's subjects did not know that the entire situation was contrived. For a closer look at the implications of this deception, see the featured discussion "The Ethics of the Obedience Experiments."

Situational Determinants of Obedience

Milgram himself was surprised at the levels of obedience observed in his first experiment. He and others conducted several additional experiments investigating the situational factors that influence levels of obedience. In the following sections we explore some of these situational factors.

Proximity of the Victim   In his first series of experiments, Milgram tested the limits of obedience by varying the proximity, or closeness, between the teacher and the learner (victim). The conditions were:

1. *Remote victim.* The teacher and the learner were in separate rooms. There was no feedback from the victim to the teacher. That is, Wallace didn't speak, moan, or scream.
2. *Voice feedback.* The teacher and the learner were in separate rooms, but Wallace began to protest the shocks as they became more intense. This is the experiment just described. In one version of the voice-feedback condition, Wallace makes it clear that he has a heart condition. After receiving 330 volts he screams, "Let me out of here. Let me out of here. My heart is bothering me" (Milgram, 1974, p. 55).
3. *Proximity.* The teacher and the learner were in the same room, sitting only a few feet apart.
4. *Touch proximity.* The teacher and the learner were in the same room, but the learner received the shock only if his hand was placed on a shock plate. At one point the learner refused to keep his hand on the plate. The teacher was told to hold the learner's hand down while delivering the shock. The teacher often had to hand-wrestle the victim to be sure the hand was properly placed on the shock plate.

These four conditions decrease the physical distance between the teacher and the learner. Milgram found that reducing the distance between the teacher and the learner affected the level of obedience (Figure 9-2). In the remote-victim condition, 65% of the subjects obeyed the experimenter and went all the way to 450 volts (the average shock intensity was 405 volts). As you can see from Figure 9-2, obedience was not substantially reduced in the voice-feedback condition. In this condition, obedience dropped only 2.5% to 62.5%, with an average shock intensity of 368 volts.

Stanley Milgram explored the dimensions of obedience in 21 experiments over a 12-year period. More than a thousand subjects participated in these experimental variations. In the first basic experiment (1963), 26 out of the 40 male subjects shocked the learner to the limit: 450 volts. The "teachers" took their role seriously. Clearly, most of them wished they didn't have to shock the person in the next room, but the pressure of the experimenter seemed to give them no way out.

Of course, no shock was ever given to the learner, but subjects didn't know this. Because they were engaging in behavior that went against accepted moral standards, they were put through the "emotional wringer." Some subjects had very unpleasant experiences. They would "sweat, tremble, stutter, bite their lips, groan, dig their fingernails into their flesh" (Milgram, 1963, p. 375). A few had "full-blown uncontrollable seizures" (p. 375). No one enjoyed it.

Milgram's experiment, and its effects on the persons who participated, raises an interesting question about the ethics of research. Should we put people through such experiences in the name of science? Was the subjects' anguish "worth it"?

Several observers, including Diana Baumrind (1964), criticized

Milgram for continuing the research when he saw its effect on his subjects. After all, the critics argued, the subjects agreed to take part only in an experiment on memory and learning, not in one on destructive obedience and the limits of people's willingness to hurt others.

But Milgram never doubted the value of his work. He believed it was important to find the conditions that foster destructive obedience. He further believed that his subjects learned a great deal from their participation; he knew this because they told him so. Milgram went to great lengths to make sure the teachers knew that Wallace was not harmed and that he held no hard feelings. He also had a psychiatrist interview the subjects a year or so after their participation; the psychiatrist reported that no long-term harm had been done (Aron & Aron, 1989).

The current rules for using subjects in psychological experiments would make it exceedingly difficult for anyone in the United States to carry out an experiment like Milgram's. All universities require that research proposals be

evaluated by institutional review boards (IRBs), which decide if subjects might be harmed by the research. A researcher must show the IRB that benefits of research to science or humankind outweigh any adverse effects on the subjects. If a researcher were allowed to do an experiment like Milgram's, he or she would be required to ensure that the welfare of the subjects was protected. In all likelihood, however, we will not see such research again.

In Chapter 1 we reviewed the code of ethics of the American Psychological Association (APA). As we noted in this featured discussion, Milgram's research has been criticized for possible ethical violations. Do you think Milgram's experiments were unethical? Why or why not? Which of the APA ethical principles did Milgram violate? Should we evaluate Milgram's research (conducted in the early 1960s) against present-day ethical requirements? Would Milgram have found the same things had he adhered strictly to present-day ethical codes? Are Milgram's findings important enough to permit some relaxing of ethical requirements? What do you think a present-day IRB would say if you wanted to do an experiment like Milgram's?

Thus, verbal feedback from the learner, even when he indicates his heart is bothering him, is not terribly effective in reducing obedience.

Significant drops in the rates of obedience were observed when the distance between the teacher and the learner was decreased further. In the proximity condition, where the teacher and the learner were in the same room and only a few feet apart, 40% of the subjects went to 450 volts (with an average shock intensity of 312 volts). Finally, when the teacher was re-

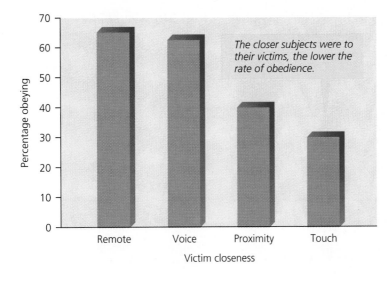

The closer subjects were to their victims, the lower the rate of obedience.

FIGURE 9-2 *The effect of victim proximity on obedience. The closer subjects were to their victims in Milgram's experiments, the less likely they were to obey commands to harm them. Obedience was highest (65% of the subjects obeyed) when the victim was in the next room and provided no vocal feedback, and lowest (30% of the subjects obeyed) when the subject had to hold the victim's hand on the shock plate. It seems that when victims are remote—whether out of sight and hearing or "dehumanized" in some way—it is easier for human beings to inflict harm on them. Conversely, the closer they are, the harder it is to harm them.* Data from Milgram, 1974.

quired to hold the learner's hand on the shock plate in the touch-proximity condition, only 30% obeyed and went to 450 volts (the average shock intensity was 269 volts).

Why does decreasing the distance between the teacher and the learner affect obedience so dramatically? Milgram offered several explanations (1974). First, decreasing the distance between the teacher and the learner increases **empathic cues** from the learner, cues about his suffering, such as screaming or banging on the wall. In the remote-victim condition, the teacher receives no feedback from the learner. There is no way for the teacher to assess the level of suffering of the learner, making it easier on the teacher's conscience to inflict harm. In the feedback conditions, however, the suffering of the learner is undeniable. The teacher has a greater opportunity to observe the learner in voice-feedback, proximity, and touch conditions than in the remote-victim condition. It is interesting to note, however, that even in the touch-proximity condition a sizable percentage of subjects (39%) were willing to fully obey the experimenter. It is apparent that there are some among us who are willing to discount empathic cues and continue to do harm to others in a "face-to-face," intimate-contact situation. For example, there was no shortage of Nazis willing to shoot Jews at close range during the early stages of the Holocaust.

Milgram also suggested that in the remote-victim condition a "narrowing of the cognitive field," or **cognitive narrowing,** occurs. That is, the teacher can put the learner out of mind and focus on the learning task instead. As the victim becomes more observable, such narrowing becomes more difficult and obedience is reduced. These results suggest that it is more difficult to inflict harm on someone you can see, hear, or touch. This is why it's probably easier to drop bombs on a city of 500,000 from 30,000 feet than to strangle one person with your bare hands.

The Power of the Institution   A second variable Milgram investigated was the nature of the institution behind the authority. The original studies

empathic cues Cues provided by a victim in an obedience situation about his or her suffering, such as screaming or banging on the wall.

cognitive narrowing A strategy used by subjects in Milgram's experiments in which they ignore the screams of the victim and focus attention on the task of pulling the switches, allowing for the reduction of tension inherent in the obedience situation.

The more remote the victim, the easier it is to inflict harm. Real human beings were injured and killed in the 1991 bombing of Baghdad, but bomber pilots had little connection with that reality. Even more distance separated the victims from the millions of television viewers who watched the bombing from the comfort of their living rooms.

were conducted at Yale University. To test the possibility that subjects were intimidated by the school's power and prestige, Milgram rented a loft in downtown Bridgeport, Connecticut, and conducted the experiment under the name "Research Associates of Bridgeport." He also had the experimenter represent himself as a high school biology teacher. Under these conditions, obedience fell to 47.5%, down from 65% in the original, baseline study. Although this difference of 17.5% does not meet conventional levels of statistical significance, it does suggest that removing some of the trappings of legitimacy from an authority source reduces obedience somewhat.

The Presence and Legitimacy of the Authority Figure   What if the authority figure was physically removed from the obedience situation? In another variation on his original experiment, Milgram had the experimenter give orders by telephone, which varied the immediacy of the authority figure, as opposed to varying the immediacy of the victim. He found that when the experimenter is absent or tries to "phone" in his instructions to give shock, obedience levels drop sharply, to as little as 20%. The closer the authority figure, the greater the obedience.

After Milgram's original research was publicized, other researchers became interested in the aspects of authority that might influence obedience levels. One line of research pursued the perceived legitimacy of the authority figure. Two different studies examined the effect of a uniform on obedience (Bickman, 1974; Geffner & Gross, 1984). In one (Geffner & Gross, 1984), experimenters approached subjects who were about to cross a street and requested that they cross at another crosswalk. Half the time the experimenter was uniformed as a public works employee, and half the time the experimenter was not in uniform. The researchers found that subjects were more likely to obey uniformed than nonuniformed individuals (Figure 9-3).

FIGURE 9-3 *The trappings of authority have an effect on obedience and disobedience. When subjects in one study were told to use a different crosswalk, they were more likely to obey someone in a public works uniform than someone in street clothing.*

Conflicting Messages About Obedience Milgram also investigated the impact of receiving conflicting orders. In two variations, subjects receive such conflicting messages. In one, the conflicting messages come from the learner and the experimenter. The learner demands that the subject continue delivering shocks while the experimenter advocates stopping the experiment. In the second variation, two authority figures deliver the conflicting messages. One urges the subject to continue while the other urges the subject to stop.

When such a conflict arises, subjects choose the path that leads to a positive outcome: termination of harm to the learner. When there was conflict between authority sources, or between the learner and the authority source, not one subject went all the way to 450 volts.

Group Effects A fourth variation involved groups of teachers, rather than a single teacher. In this variation, a real subject was led to believe that two others would act as co-teachers. (These other two were confederates of the experimenter.) When the learner begins to protest, at 150 volts, one confederate decides not to continue. Defying the experimenter's instructions, he walks away and sits in a chair across the room. At 210 volts the second confederate follows.

Milgram's results showed that having the two confederates defy the experimenter reduced obedience markedly. Only 10% of the subjects obeyed to 450 volts (mean shock intensity = 305 volts). Thirty-three percent of the subjects broke off after the first confederate defied the experimenter but before the second confederate. An additional 33% broke off at the 210-volt level after the second confederate defied the experimenter. Thus, two thirds of the subjects who disobeyed the experimenter did so immediately after the confederates defied the experimenter.

Why does seeing two others disobey the experimenter significantly reduce the subject's obedience? One explanation centers on a phenomenon called diffusion of responsibility. **Diffusion of responsibility** occurs when an individual spreads responsibility for his or her action to other individuals present. In the obedience situation where there are two other teachers delivering shocks, the subject could tell himself that he was not solely responsible for inflicting pain on the learner. However, when the two confederates break off, he is left holding the bag; he is now solely responsible for delivering shocks. Generally, when people are in a position where they can diffuse responsibility for harming another person, obedience is higher than if they have to deliver the harm entirely on their own and cannot diffuse responsibility (Kilham & Mann, 1974). In short, having two people defy the experimenter placed the subject in a position of conflict about who was responsible for harming the learner.

There is another explanation for the group effects Milgram observed. When the two confederates break off from the experiment, a new norm begins to form: disobedience. The old norm of obedience to the experimenter is placed into conflict with the new norm of disobedience. The norm of disobedience is more "positive" than the norm of obedience with respect to the harm to the learner. Remember that when subjects were given the choice between a positive and a negative command, most chose the positive. The lone subjects in the original studies, however, had no such opposing norms and so were more inclined to respond to the norm of obedience. Evidently, having role models who defy authority with impunity emboldens us against authority. Once new norms develop, disobedience to oppressive authority becomes a more viable possibility.

Summing Up: Situational Determinants of Obedience Milgram's program of research produced a wealth of information about the factors that influence obedience. Some of his findings are summarized in Table 9-1. What can we conclude from the classic obedience experiments? First, proximity is a factor. The closer the victim or the farther away the authority, the lower the obedience levels. Authority is another factor. The more prestigious and powerful the authority, the higher the obedience. The more legitimate an authority appears (for example, by wearing a uniform), the more likely it is that subjects will obey. However, even a person with quite moderate authority trappings can compel people to obey.

We also know that most people are inclined to be humane but still may not be able to resist authority. Given conflicting orders from different authority sources, for example, subjects tend to obey the authority who urges stopping the experiment instead of the one who urges continuing. And when subjects have a disobedient model, they are more likely to disobey themselves. It is as if a disobedient model opens another possibility, another channel, which most people had not considered. It seems that people want to do the right thing but have no language of disobedience readily available. The disobedient models and the benevolent authority (who says to stop) supply that language.

diffusion of responsibility The phenomenon that occurs when an individual spreads responsibility for his or her action to other individuals present.

TABLE 9-1

Summary of Milgram's Results

Condition	Mean Maximum Shock Level[a]	Percent Obedience[b]
Baseline	405	65
Change of personnel	333	50
Experimenter absent	272.25	20.5
Female subjects	370.95	65
Downtown office	314.25	47.5
Subject chooses shock	82.5	2.5
Learner demands shock	150	0
Ordinary man as authority	243.75	20
Subject as bystander	373.5	68.8
Authority figure as victim	150	0
Contradictory authorities	150	0
Two peers rebel	246.75	10
Peer administers shock	429.75	92.5

[a] Average maximum shock delivered in volts.
[b] Percent of subjects who "went all the way" to 450 volts.

Based on data from Milgram, 1974.

The Role of Gender in Obedience

In Milgram's original research, only male subjects were used. In a later replication, Milgram also included female subjects. He found that males and females obeyed at the same levels. However, some later research showed that there is a gender difference in obedience. In an experiment conducted in Australia, Wesley Kilham and Leon Mann (1974) found that males conformed more than females. In another study conducted in the United States, Robert Geffner and Madeleine Gross (1984) found that males obeyed a uniformed authority more than females did.

Another way to approach the issue of gender effects in obedience is to determine if male or female authority figures are more effective in producing obedience. In Geffner and Gross's (1984) experiment, the effects of experimenter gender, subject gender, and subject age on obedience were investigated. The results showed no simple effect of experimenter gender on obedience. Instead, experimenter gender and subject age interacted, as shown in Figure 9-4. Notice that there was no difference between older and younger subjects ("younger" subjects being under age 30, and "older" subjects being over age 50) when the experimenter was female. However, when the experimenter was male, younger subjects obeyed the male experimenter more than older subjects did.

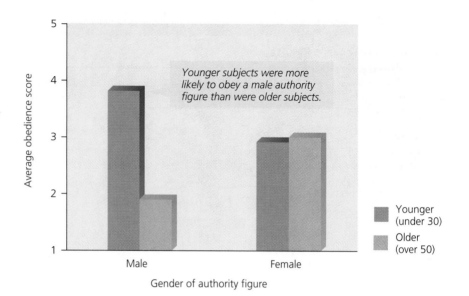

FIGURE 9-4 *The effects of authority-figure gender and subject age on obedience. In this experiment, when the authority figure was female, older and younger subjects did not differ significantly on obedience scores. When the authority figure was male, younger subjects were more obedient than older subjects.* Data from Geffner and Gross, 1984.

Obedience or Aggression?

Milgram's experiment used an aggressive response as the index of obedience. Could it be that subjects were displaying aggression toward the learner, which had little to do with obedience? Such an interpretation appears unlikely. In situations where subjects are allowed to choose the level of shock to deliver to the learner, the average shock delivered was 82.5 volts, with 2.5% of subjects obeying completely. This is quite a drop from the 405 volts with 65% obeying completely in the baseline condition (Milgram, 1974).

These results were supported by a replication of Milgram's experiment by other researchers (Mantell, 1971). In one condition of this experiment, subjects were allowed to set the level of shock delivered to the learner. Compared to 85% of subjects who used the highest level of shock in a replication of Milgram's baseline experiment (no feedback from the learner), only 7% of the subjects in the "self-decision" condition did so. These results and others (Kilham & Mann, 1974; Meeus & Raaijmakers, 1986; Shanab & Yahya, 1978) lead us to the conclusion that subjects were displaying obedience to the experimenter rather than their own aggressive impulses.

Obedience Behavior Across Cultures and Situations

Milgram's original experiments were conducted in the United States, using a particular research technique. Would his results hold up across cultures and across experimental situations?

Some critics of Milgram's study, Dutch researchers Meeus and Raaijmakers (1986), argued that the type of obedience required in Milgram's experiment—physically hurting another person—was not realistic. Such behavior is rare in everyday life. They argued that people are more often asked to hurt others in more subtle ways. For example, your employer might

When faced with an authority figure like the Ayatollah Khomeini, are some groups of people more or less likely to obey than others? Studies indicate that although obedience varies somewhat across cultures, it is a universal feature of human social behavior.

ask you to do something that makes another employee look bad. Would you obey?

Meeus and Raaijmakers studied a different form of obedience: "administrative obedience." Dutch subjects were told that the psychology department of a university was commissioned to screen applicants for various state and civic positions and that the department was using this opportunity to test the effects of stress on test achievement. According to instructions, subjects made a series of disparaging statements about a person taking a test for a state job. Fifteen statements, each more disruptive than the previous, were used. The "mildest" statement was "Your answer to question 9 was wrong" (p. 323); a "moderate" statement was "If you continue like this, you will fail the test" (p. 323); and the "strongest" statement was "According to the test, it would be better for you to apply for lower functions" (p. 323). Understandably, job applicants became increasingly upset with each comment.

Most of the Dutch subjects obeyed; 90% read all 15 statements. This resembles the Milgram experiment in which subjects had to increase shock in 15 stages as the victim became more upset. In Milgram's terms, they gave the full 450 volts. When questioned about it, they attributed responsibility for the harassment to the experimenter.

In another variation on Milgram's experiment, Australian subjects assumed the role of either transmitter of the experimenter's instructions or executor (Kilham & Mann, 1974). In the transmitter condition, subjects relayed orders to continue shocking a learner to a confederate of the experimenter who delivered the shocks. In the executor condition, subjects received orders indirectly from the experimenter through a confederate of the experimenter. The hypothesis was that there would be greater obedience when the subject was the transmitter of orders, rather than the executor of orders, presumably because the subject is not directly responsible for inflicting harm upon the victim. Results supported this hypothesis. Subjects in the transmitter role showed higher levels of obedience than those in the executor role.

Milgram's obedience effect has been supported by other cross-cultural research. For example, obedience among Jordanian adults was found to be 62.5%—comparable to the 65% rate found by Milgram among

Americans—and among Jordanian children, 73% (Shanab & Yahya, 1977). The highest rates of obedience are reported among subjects in Germany. In a replication of Milgram's original baseline experiment, 85% of German men obeyed the experimenter (Mantell, 1971). Overall, it appears that obedience is an integral part of human social behavior.

Critiques of Milgram's Research

There were aspects of Milgram's experiments, and others like them, which were never precisely defined but probably influenced levels of obedience. Consider, for example, the gradual, stepwise demands made on the subject. Each 15-volt increment may have "hooked" the subjects a little more. This is in keeping with the foot-in-the-door technique, discussed in Chapter 8. Obeying a small, harmless order (deliver 15 volts) made it likely that they would more easily obey the next small step, and the next, and so on (Gilbert, 1981). Each step made the next step seem not so bad. Imagine if the subject was asked to give 450 volts at the very start. It is likely that many more people would have defied the experimenter.

What about the protests made by many subjects? Very few subjects went from beginning to end without asking if they should continue or voicing some concern for the victim. But they were always told, "You must continue; you have no choice." Perhaps, as some observers suggest, the experiments are as much a study of "ineffectual, and indecisive, disobedience" as of destructive obedience (Ross & Nisbett, 1991). When subjects saw others disobey, they suddenly knew how to disobey too, and many of them did so.

There is another, even more subtle factor involved here. The experiments have a kind of unreal, "Alice-in-Wonderland" quality (Ross & Nisbett, 1991). Events do not "add up." The subject's job is to give increasing levels of electric shock to a learner in order to study "the effects of punishment on learning." The shocks increase as the learner makes errors. Then (in some variations), the learner stops answering. He can't be learning anything now. Why continue to give shocks? Further, the experimenter clearly does not care that the victim is no longer learning.

Some observers suggest that since the situation does not really make sense from the subject's perspective, the subject becomes confused (Ross & Nisbett, 1991). The subject acts indecisively, unwilling or unable to challenge authority. Not knowing what to do, the subject continues, with great anxiety, to act out the role that the experimenter has prescribed.

This analysis suggests that Milgram's experiments were not as much about slavish obedience to authority as they were about the capacity of situational forces to overwhelm people's more positive tendencies. This may, however, be a futile distinction. Either way, the victim would have been hurt if the shock had been real.

WHY DO PEOPLE OBEY?

Thus far, we have seen that individuals in a variety of obedience situations will obey an authority figure and act in ways that would harm another per-

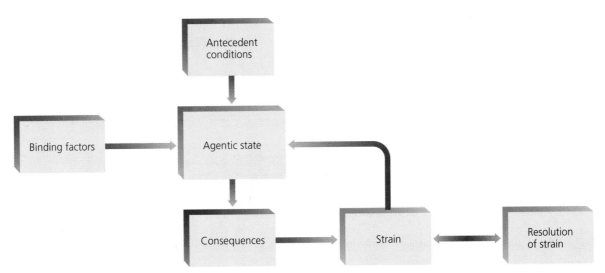

son. Why does this occur? Milgram (1974) devoted a great deal of effort to explaining obedience behavior. He developed a model suggesting that there are three main factors contributing to obedience: the agentic state, binding factors, and antecedent conditions. In this section we look at Milgram's model, illustrated in Figure 9-5, and explore each of these factors.

The Agentic State

There is a critical point during the Milgram experiments when the subject must decide whether to act on his or her own moral principles or to go along with the experimenter. Subjects usually asked the experimenter whether they should continue when the victim began to protest. Many subjects expressed concern over who was responsible for the victim. The experimenter made several responses but eventually said that it was "my" (the experimenter's) responsibility. Once the subjects in Milgram's experiment feel that they bear no responsibility for the outcome, they are willing to act as *agents* of the experimenter. They enter what Milgram called an **agentic state.**

Milgram suggested that entry into the agentic state is crucial for obedience to occur. In the agentic state, the individual becomes focused on the source of authority, tuning in to instructions and turning away from the suffering of the victim. This happens because the victim has no power and the authority does. The authority, in effect, redefines the social situation as one in which he or she takes on all responsibility for the consequences of the subject's actions.

Binding Factors

Milgram suggested that once in the agentic state, the subject becomes bound to the authority figure through **binding factors.** A subject who has inflicted high levels of shock, and who has tried to stop the experiment and failed, may be appalled by his own behavior. Some soldiers at My Lai were sickened by the act of shooting mothers with babies in their arms; they

FIGURE 9-5 *Milgram's model of factors contributing to obedience. For destructive obedience to occur, individuals must enter an agentic state, in which they see themselves as mere agents of an authority figure who assumes responsibility for their actions. Antecedent conditions—personality characteristics that predispose individuals to be obedient—contribute to a person's tendency to enter the agentic state. Binding factors, such as respect for the authority figure, fear of the consequences of disobedience, and the need to justify negative actions already taken, also contribute to the agentic state and hold people in it. Strain occurs when people see the consequences of their actions and question their roles. Strain may be resolved by several tactics, such as denial, cognitive narrowing, or disobedience. From Milgram, 1974.*

agentic state A psychological state an individual enters when he or she feels no responsibility for any outcome of an obedience situation, thus becoming an agent of the authority figure.

binding factors Factors that bind an individual to an authority figure in an obedience situation.

THE BASES OF SOCIAL POWER

Power is an important asset for an authority. It typically consists of a set of resources that the authority may use to make people comply with commands. Several categories or sources of social power have been identified by researchers in social psychology (French & Raven, 1968; Raven & Kruglanski, 1970; Raven & Rubin, 1983).

1. *Reward power.* This source of power resides in the authority's ability to provide and control reinforcers. A parent, for example, may attempt to control the behavior of a child by offering a reward for desired behavior. Implied in reward power, of course, is the ability of the authority figure to withhold rewards if desired behavior does not occur.
2. *Coercive power.* Authorities often have the power to punish. Since people want to avoid punishment and pain, this is a powerful resource. Both reward and coercive power have a major draw-

back, however: The authority must keep his or her eye on the subordinate at all times. Without such surveillance, the subordinate may not obey. Recall, for example, that when the experimenter in the Milgram variation left the room, obedience dropped sharply. An authority who uses reward power is better liked than one who punishes.

3. *Expert power.* If the authority has knowledge and ability, people can be influenced by the belief that the authority knows what is right. The basis of power from an expert source is respect rather than fear of what that authority can do for, or to, a subordinate. Many professionals have access to this source of power.
4. *Referent power.* This power derives from the willingness or

the desire of people to identify with the authority. Members of groups have referent power as well. People may like and identify with their fellow group members and consequently do what they do.
5. *Legitimate power.* This type of power flows from the acceptance of rules that order relationships. Elected officials have legitimate power because a majority of the population voted for them.

These bases for social power can be seen mixing in different ways for individuals in positions of leadership. What type or types of power does the president of the United States have? How about a dictator like Iraqi president Saddam Hussein? Can you think of anyone you know who has a great deal of expert power? If you can, identify the basis for that power. Can you think of any drawbacks to a leader's relying heavily on coercive power?

continue to suffer nightmares about their acts to this very day. Nevertheless, in the heat of the moment, they could not bring themselves to disobey orders. There was some bond (perhaps respect) with the authority figure that kept them from acting as independent moral beings. (For a closer look at other ways authority figures can compel people to obey them, see the featured discussion "The Bases of Social Power.")

The individual in an obedience situation is bound to the authority figure through successive, recurrent acts of obedience (Milgram, 1974). Each time the subject gave a shock, or each time the S.S. guard forced people into the gas chambers, or each time the soldier shot a child at My Lai, he had to justify his act. Milgram suggested that one form of justification is to carry out the obedience to its conclusion. Otherwise, the individual would have had to admit that the victims did not deserve this treatment and that he had done something horrible. It's easier just to finish the job.

A second reason the agent is bound to the authority is that disobedience requires breaking the rules. In the Milgram situation, subjects were paid *before* the experiment began. More important, the subject has made a commitment to the experimenter (Milgram, 1974). According to Milgram, the individual's commitment to the authority figure is not taken lightly and is difficult to break. If $4.50 was enough to get a subject committed, imagine the degree of commitment felt by Lt. Calley's men on that fateful day at My Lai.

Antecedent Conditions

Since not all people obey as readily as others, is it fair to assume that those who obey and those who do not somehow differ? Some definite personal characteristics distinguish those who obeyed from those who didn't. Milgram referred to these characteristics as **antecedent conditions.** For example, better educated people were more likely to defy the experimenter, as were those in "moral" professions—medicine, teaching, and law. People in more technical fields, such as engineering and the physical sciences, were more likely to obey (Elms, 1972). Catholics obeyed more than Protestants, and enlisted military men more than officers. Of course, these were general patterns; individual exceptions always occur.

Profession and religion are not core personality traits, however. In a thorough review of the research on the role of individual differences in response to authority, Thomas Blass (1991) argues that a willingness to *trust* authority was crucial to entering what Milgram called the agentic state. One personality measure that should tap trust in authority is **authoritarian submission,** defined as a "submissive, uncritical attitude toward idealized moral authorities of the in-group" (Adorno, Frenkel-Brunswick, Levinson, & Sanford, 1950). The California F Scale, so called because it was developed at the University of California, Berkeley, by Theodor Adorno and his colleagues, includes several items that measure authoritarian submission. For example, agreement with the following items would suggest such a submissive tendency:

1. What this country needs most, more than laws and political programs, is a few courageous, tireless, devoted leaders in whom the people can put their faith.
2. There is hardly anything lower than a person who does not feel a great love, gratitude and respect for his parents. (Adorno et al., 1950)

People who obey the experimenter in the Milgram variations tend to be significantly more authoritarian than those who defy (Elms & Milgram, 1966). Obedient subjects show more trust in the benign purposes of the authority (Blass, 1991). In the Milgram model, this means that they think no great harm will befall the victim because, as they believe, the authority is benevolent.

Adorno and his colleagues argued that high authoritarians behave consistently when they feel afraid or threatened. In these conditions, they want strong leaders to protect them. Their admiration for power increases, as does their contempt for weakness. They become cynical, superstitious, and intolerant of other groups (Sales, 1972).

We have, then, some sense of the "obedient personality." But researchers have yet to use these personality concepts to adequately predict who will and will not obey (Blass, 1991). Milgram, for example, was sure that individual

antecedent conditions Personality and other background factors that increase the likelihood that a person will obey the orders of an authority figure.

authoritarian submission A personality measure of trust in authority.

personality characteristics mattered in the situation he created. However, he admitted he couldn't discover or identify them. He finally concluded that "the disposition a person brings to the experiment is probably less important a cause of his behavior than most readers think. For the social psychology of this century reveals a major lesson: often it is not so much the kind of person a man is as the kind of situation he finds himself in that determines how he will act" (Milgram, 1974, p. 205). Milgram's experiments showed how situational pressures make it difficult for people to use their moral knowledge to guide their own actions (Blass, 1991).

For many people, this is an uncomfortable conclusion. Taken to its logical end, it implies that almost any of us, placed in the same situation as Eichmann, the soldiers at My Lai, or the Serbs in Bosnia, could have behaved the same way they did. Not all of us, mind you, since some people did disobey in the Milgram studies, and some soldiers at My Lai did not fire or shot up in the air.

Becoming an Agent of Authority

The most infamous example of destructive obedience is the extermination of close to 12 million people by the Nazis. Those who were directly responsible for the mass murders were members of the S.S., the elite guard of Hitler's army. S.S. soldiers were carefully chosen and cultivated to fulfill their duties; in other words, they were socialized into the Nazi belief system.

Socialized to Obey　The Nazis understood the importance of socializing individuals to obey. They began early, training children to conform and fol-

In the 1930s German children were taught to idolize Hitler, hate Jews, and follow orders. Because of this socialization, they were less likely to question the Nazi belief system as they got older. Individuals usually become agents of authority through such a process of gradual indoctrination.

The education of German children under the Nazis (1933–45) has been chronicled by G. A. Ziemer (1972) in his book *Education for Death*. Schools were concerned not so much with teaching academic skills as with indoctrinating children into Nazi philosophy and screening candidates for future service in the S.S. This is true of most societies that are more concerned with obedience than with education.

The Nazis encouraged women to have as many children as possible and to give some of them up to the state. By the early 1940s there were many orphans in German schools. A similar policy was employed both in Romania under Nicolae Ceausescu and in Iran under the late shah. The secret police of both countries came to be filled with state-raised orphans.

For children in the Nazi education system, including those turned over to the state and those living with their parents, indoctrination began at an early age. Children under the age of 4 were socialized into the Nazi belief system in special preschools. Ziemer encountered one young boy who said, "We will become soldiers. I want to shoot a Frenchman." Simply put, children born in Nazi Germany belonged to Hitler.

At age 6, the German boy was given a uniform that included heavy black shoes, brown shorts and shirt, a swastika armband, and a cap. Development, both physical and academic, was carefully watched. At 10, children had to pass a set of rigorous tests before they could move on to the next educational level, the *Jungvolk* ("young folk"). Here, children were further prepared for a life devoted to the Nazis and Hitler. They were expected now to be willing to die for the Führer.

Children were screened again at 14. Those ready to move on graduated into the Hitler Youth, where indoctrination continued. Only the strongest and most devoted got this far. Eventually, the children who came up through the ranks entered the army and took the following oath (Ziemer, 1972):

> I swear by God this holy oath, that I will unconditionally obey the Führer of the German Reich and the German People, Adolph Hitler, Commander in Chief of the Army, as a brave soldier. I will forever defend this oath at the cost of my own life. (p. 169)

Of those going through the Nazi education system, Ziemer wrote:

> Hitler is making Nazis who are eager for action, eager for conquest, ready to die for him and his ideals. They respect authority and are not afraid to work. They would dig their own graves if he asked them to. (p. 193)

Of course, the war was over before many of these young men could take their place in the S.S. But some—those 15 years old or even younger—were pressed into military service at the end of the war to defend Berlin from the Allies. Many of these youths died in battle before they were old enough to think for themselves.

Ziemer's work raises questions about the role of educational institutions in the socialization of obedience: What long-term effects do you think the Nazis' education for death had on the children exposed to it? What influence would such an indoctrination have on these children as adults, long after Hitler's Germany perished in the flames of World War II? Do you think obedience is socialized in U.S. schools? If so, how? Do U.S. schools indoctrinate students with values in addition to teaching students basic knowledge? What is the long-term effect of teaching values in schools?

low orders and rewarding those individuals who showed the most promise. For a closer look at this process, see the featured discussion "Indoctrination into the Nazi System: Education for Death."

The Nazis also understood that it was important to socialize adults, to lead them gradually into actions they might otherwise resist. Journalist Gitta Sereny (1974) conducted an in-depth interview with Franz Stangl, the commandant of one of the most infamous Nazi death camps, Treblinka.

Stangl reported that before Treblinka, his assignments involved killing people systematically. One such assignment was to "Tiergartenstrasse 4," where the Nazis carried out euthanasia (mercy killing) of mentally and physically handicapped Germans. At first Stangl, by his own report, was revolted by this idea. Gradually, however, he adjusted to the mercy killings. By the time he reached Treblinka, he had been socialized into mass killings.

A similar process was used in Greece to train torturers for the secret police (EAT-ESA) between 1967 and 1974, when Greece was ruled by a military junta (Haritos-Fatouros, 1988). Greek army recruits were screened to identify those with appropriate political beliefs and hostile attitudes toward other groups. These attitudes were reinforced through daily lectures by officers at the training camp. As with the members of the Nazi S.S., future members of the EAT-ESA had preexisting prejudices that were strengthened by indoctrination.

Greek soldiers who made it through the "first cut" were subjected to a second screening after 3 months of military training. Candidates were selected based on their ability to endure severe physical beatings and to exercise to exhaustion; their obedience to the demands of authority; and their willingness to go through the special training necessary to become a torturer. A third screening identified those recruits who were motivated to use the instruments of torture. By this time, only 1.5% of the original group of recruits remained (Haritos-Fatouros, 1988). The gradual, step-by-step nature of this process smoothed the transition from army recruit to torturer.

As suggested earlier, socialization may also have played a role in Milgram's laboratory research on obedience. By giving graded shocks, subjects were "socialized" into destructive obedience in much the same way that Franz Stangl was socialized into his role of commandant of Treblinka and selected Greek soldiers were socialized into the role of torturer. In Milgram's experiment, no single step seemed shockingly inhumane, and yet with each one, subjects became more committed to the overall course of action and its outcome.

How Destructive Obedience Is Maintained It is one thing to train or socialize people to obey authority. Milgram suggested that primary factors in obedience were entering an agentic state and being bound to the authority. But Milgram dealt with obedience only in short-term situations, the hour or so that subjects were in his experiment. How is destructive obedience maintained in long-term situations and in larger organizations? Herbert Kelman and Lee Hamilton (1989) have suggested that three important factors are involved in the development and maintenance of destructive obedience: authorization, routinization, and dehumanization.

Authorization occurs when an individual abandons the moral guidelines that ordinarily influence human behavior in favor of guidelines set forth by an authority figure. According to Kelman and Hamilton, acts of destructive obedience sanctioned by authority are automatically justified. The individual no longer needs to think about his or her behavior or to make decisions. When the Milgram experimenter took responsibility for any harm that might occur, many subjects shocked the victim to the maximum. Of

authorization The abandonment by an individual of normal moral guidelines in favor of guidelines set forth by an authority figure; a factor in destructive obedience.

course, individuals vary in their willingness or predisposition to accept authority (Kelman & Hamilton, 1989). Evidence suggests that even in Nazi Germany, there was significant resistance to the Nazis (Peukert, 1987).

A second factor that fosters obedience is **routinization.** This is a particularly important factor in long-term situations. After taking the first step, authorization, the individual has entered a psychological situation that makes obedience likely to continue (Kelman & Hamilton, 1989). Routinization occurs when obedience becomes a habit, part of the daily routine of the individual. Routinization simplifies decisions about how to act; it encourages obedient behavior by focusing the individual's attention on his or her job rather than on the implications and meanings of the behavior. This is very much like Milgram's notion of binding.

Routinization was a common feature of the obedience shown by those who ran the Nazi death camps during World War II. Franz Stangl reported that even though he did not always agree with what was occurring in Treblinka, he carried out his duty (Sereny, 1974). For Stangl, killing became routinized. He would "go to work" and do his "job," then go home at night, like any other "worker." The moral implications of his work—exterminating human life—were subordinated by his duty to follow orders.

Routinization also played a role in training torturers for the Greek secret police (Gibson & Haritos-Fatouros, 1986). Recruits were desensitized to acts of torture through gradual exposure to such acts. Eventually, those acts came to be regarded as routine even though they conflicted with the recruits' existing moral standards (Gibson & Haritos-Fatouros, 1986).

Authorization and routinization set the stage. However, destructive obedience can occur only when the victims have been stripped (in the eyes of the obeyer) of those qualities that make them human. This process has been called **dehumanization** (Kelman & Hamilton, 1989). Just as dehumanization makes it easier to express prejudice toward members of a group (as discussed in Chapter 5), it also makes it easier to engage in destructive obedience.

Dehumanization is an important part of military training. For example, during World War II the Germans became "krauts," and the Japanese "nips." In Germany the Nazis portrayed Jews and other eastern Europeans as "vermin" and "Untermenschen" (or subhuman). Dehumanization was also evident in the process of training torturers for the Greek secret police (Gibson & Haritos-Fatouros, 1986). During early training sessions, recruits were subjected to indoctrination lectures against Communists and other enemies of the Greek state. Later, in more advanced training sessions, it was drummed into the recruits' heads that their victims were "worms" who must be crushed (Gibson & Haritos-Fatouros, 1986). The process of dehumanization, for the Nazis and Greek torturers, makes it easier to harm the

Although dehumanization of the enemy is seen more often in military training, it can also be used against economic "enemies." The perception of an economic rival as an enemy—as in this portrayal of a Japanese businessman as a money-hungry imperialist— increases in-group solidarity, boosts self-esteem, and makes it easier to think of the outgroup in simplistic and stereotypical terms.

routinization The reduction of obedient actions to habitual, routine behaviors; a factor in destructive obedience.

dehumanization The stripping away of perceived human qualities from a victim by an obeyer; a factor in destructive obedience.

When one person disobeys, it can provide a model for others—a new social norm—and even inspire an entire social movement. This was the case when Rosa Parks refused to give up her seat on a bus to a white man in segregated Montgomery, Alabama. Here, Parks is shown sitting in the front of a bus after the U.S. Supreme Court ruled that segregated public transit was unconstitutional.

victim. After all, it is easier to squash an "insect" than it is to murder another human being.

Dehumanization also occurred in Milgram's experiment. Recall that the highest levels of obedience occurred when the victim was remote. The absence of cues from the victim made it easier for the subject to forget that he was a living, and suffering, human being. As the victim became more immediate, and therefore more human, to the subject, obedience was reduced. Dehumanization played a role in the killings at My Lai, too. Some soldiers did not see women and babies. They saw "gooks," the enemy. This further reduced the soldiers' feelings of responsibility because they were not "wasting" humans.

DISOBEDIENCE

Although history shows us that obedience can and has become an important norm guiding human behavior, there are also times when disobedience occurs. In 1955, for example, a black seamstress named Rosa Parks refused to give up her seat on a Montgomery, Alabama, bus to a white passenger. Her action was in violation of a law that existed at the time. Parks was arrested, convicted, and fined $10 for her refusal.

Parks's disobedience served as a catalyst for events that shaped the civil rights movement. Within 2 days of her arrest, leaflets were distributed in the African American community calling for a 1-day strike against the bus line. Her cause was taken up by Martin Luther King, Jr., and other African American leaders. The bus strike that was supposed to last only a day lasted for a year. Eventually, laws requiring African Americans to sit at the back of a bus, or to surrender a seat to a white passenger, were changed. From Rosa Parks's initial act of disobedience flowed a social movement, along with major social change.

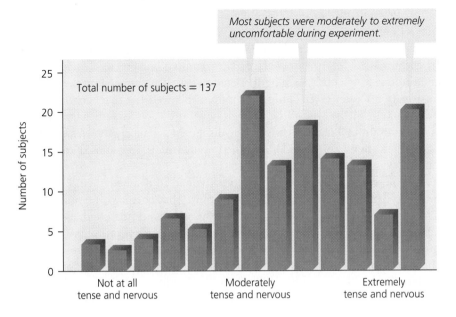

FIGURE 9-6 *Role strain in Milgram's experiments. Most subjects experienced moderate to extreme levels of tension and anxiety, indicating role strain. Subjects were clearly uncomfortable inflicting pain on another person, even when they were assured it was not their responsibility.* From Milgram, 1974.

Role Strain: Breaking the Agentic State

What enables a person to break free of her or his bonds to authority and disobey? Milgram argued that obedience is fostered when an individual enters an agentic state with an authority. The person must find a way to break the agentic state if disobedience is to occur. This can be a difficult process. However, there are factors that can weaken the agentic bond between an individual and an authority.

In an obedience situation, the limits of the role we play are defined for us by the authority source. As long as we are comfortable with—or at least can tolerate—that role, obedience continues. However, if we begin to seriously question the legitimacy of that role, we begin to experience what Milgram (1974) called **role strain.**

In this situation, the individual in the agentic state begins to feel tension, anxiety, and discomfort over his or her role in the obedience situation. In Milgram's experiment, subjects showed considerable signs of role strain in response to the authority figure's behavior (Milgram, 1974). As shown in Figure 9-6, very few subjects were "not at all tense and nervous." Most showed moderate or extreme levels of tension and nervousness.

Milgram (1974) suggested that this tension arose from several sources:

- The cries of pain from the victim, which can lead the agent to question his behavior.
- The inflicting of harm on another person, which involves violating established moral and social values.
- Potential retaliation from the victim.
- Confusion that arises when the learner screams for the teacher to stop while the authority demands that he continue.
- Harmful behavior, when this behavior contradicts one's self-image.

role strain Psychological tension, anxiety, and discomfort experienced as a result of one's role in an obedience situation; a factor that can weaken the agentic bond to an authority figure.

How can the tension be reduced? Subjects tried to deny the consequences of their actions by not paying attention to the victim's screams, by dealing only with the task of flipping switches. As mentioned earlier, Milgram called this method of coping cognitive narrowing. Teachers also tried to cheat by subtly helping the learner—that is, by reading the correct answer in a louder voice. These techniques allowed the teacher to tolerate doing harm that he wished he did not have to do. Other subjects resolved the role strain by breaking the role, by disobeying. This choice was difficult; people felt they had "ruined" the experiment, which they considered legitimate.

Role strain can, of course, eventually lead to disobedience. However, real-world obedience situations, such as those that occur within military organizations, often involve significant pressures to continue obedience. Nazi soldiers who made up the squads that carried out mass murders (Einsatzgruppen) were socialized into obedience and closely allied themselves with their authority sources. When role strain is felt by people in this type of situation, disobedience is difficult, perhaps impossible.

However, this does not necessarily mean that the role strain is ignored. Creative psychological mechanisms may develop to cope with it. A fair number of members of the Einsatzgruppen experienced role strain. In his study of Nazi doctors, Robert Lifton (1986) found that many soldiers who murdered Jews firsthand experienced immediate psychological reactions, such as physical symptoms and anxiety. For example, General Erich von dem Bach-Zelewski (one of the Nazis' premier Einsatzgruppen generals) was hospitalized for severe stomach problems, "psychic exhaustion," and hallucinations tied to the shooting of Jews (Lifton, 1986). The conflict soldiers felt was severe: They couldn't disobey, and they couldn't continue. As a result, they removed themselves from the obedience situation by developing psychological problems.

Psychological Factors: Reassessing the Legitimacy of the Authority

In their book *Crimes of Obedience,* Herbert Kelman and Lee Hamilton (1989) point out that authority is more often challenged when the individual considers the authority source illegitimate. Recall that when Milgram conducted his experiment in downtown Bridgeport instead of at Yale University, he found a decrease in obedience. When an authority source loses credibility, disobedience becomes possible.

Kelman and Hamilton suggest that two kinds of psychological factors precede disobedience. The first consists of cognitive factors—the way we think about obedience. In order to disobey, the individual involved in an obedience situation must be aware of alternatives to obedience. For example, Calley's men were not aware that a soldier may disobey what he has good reason to believe is an illegal order, one that violates the rules of war.

Disobedience is also preceded by motivational factors. An individual in the obedience situation must be willing to buck the existing social order (whether in the real world or in the laboratory) *and* accept the consequences. The importance of this motivation to disobey is supported by Milgram's find-

thrown only after major changes in the political system of the Soviet Union that had controlled Eastern Europe since 1945, the end of World War II. Eventually, that climate caught up to the Soviet Union, which disintegrated completely in 1991.

Rebellion against authority may also occur within social climates that do not fully support such rebellion. The resistance movements in France during World War II, for example, helped undermine the German occupation forces—despite the fact that most of France was ruled with an iron fist by the Germans. Within Germany itself there was some resistance to the Nazi regime (Peukert, 1987). Even the ill-fated student uprising in Tiananmen Square took place within a climate of liberalization that had evolved over several years before the uprising. Unfortunately, the climate reversed rapidly.

MY LAI REVISITED

It was a group of ordinary individuals who descended on My Lai that fateful day and massacred innocent civilians. The research on obedience leaves us with the inescapable conclusion that, placed in the right situation, many of us could do the same—obey blindly, even if it meant killing people. Eichmann's fallacy, the idea that evil is often done by ordinary individuals, rings true.

The situational forces operating on the soldiers at My Lai were overwhelming. They had served in a war for a prolonged period of time. They had received extensive military training, which emphasizes obedience to authority, binds individuals closely to authority figures, and authorizes and routinizes killing. And they had been exposed to military propaganda that dehumanized the Vietnamese. To disobey Lt. Calley's orders, they would have had to recognize disobedience as a viable option, which was exceedingly unlikely. They also would have had to accept the consequences of disobeying a superior officer under combat conditions, which could mean facing a court martial.

The 1969 massacre at My Lai shocked and outraged people all over the world. At home, it reinforced the growing disillusion with the war and mobilized public sentiment for withdrawal from Vietnam. Like other cases of destructive obedience, the incident had wide-ranging repercussions. It served not only as a reminder of the fragile and tentative nature of the bonds that join people together in human society but also as a catalyst for change.

LOOKING AHEAD

In this chapter we continued the discussion of social influence processes begun in Chapter 7. Persuasion, conformity, compliance, and obedience are important examples of social influence, but there are other forms as well. Whenever we work in a group with others, we also are subjected to social influence. In Chapter 10, we take a look at group dynamics. You will see how groups form, how individual behavior is influenced by being in a group, how groups make decisions, and how social influence pressures arise in groups.

CHAPTER REVIEW

1. *What do social psychologists mean by the term* obedience?
   Obedience is the social influence process by which a person changes his or her behavior in response to a direct order from someone in authority. The authority figure has the power, which can stem from several sources, to enforce the orders. Generally, obedience is not always bad. Obedience to laws and rules is necessary for the smooth functioning of society. However, sometimes obedience is taken to an extreme and causes harm to others. This is called **destructive obedience.**

2. *Are evil deeds done by evil persons?*
   We might like to think that those who carry out orders to harm others are inhuman monsters. However, Hannah Arendt's analysis of Adolph Eichmann, a Nazi responsible for deporting millions of Jews to death camps, suggests that evil is often very commonplace. Those who carry out acts of destructive obedience are often very ordinary people. The false idea that evil deeds can be done only by evil people is referred to as **Eichmann's fallacy.**

3. *What research has been done to study obedience?*
   Recurring questions about destructive obedience led Stanley Milgram (1963, 1974) to conduct a series of ingenious laboratory experiments on obedience. Subjects believed that they were taking part in a learning experiment. They were to deliver increasingly strong electric shocks to a "learner" each time he made an error. When the subject protested that the shocks were getting too strong, the experimenter ordered the subject to continue the experiment. In the original experiment, where there was no feedback from the learner to the subject, 65% of the subjects obeyed the experimenter, going all the way to 450 volts.

4. *What factors influence obedience?*
   In variations on his original experiment, Milgram uncovered several factors that influenced the level of obedience to the experimenter—such as moving the "learner" closer to the subject. Explanations for the proximity effect include increasing **empathic cues** from the learner to the subject and **cognitive narrowing,** which is focusing attention on the obedience task at hand, not on the suffering of the victim. Moving the experiment from prestigious Yale University to a downtown storefront resulted in a modest (but not statistically significant) decrease in obedience as well. Research after Milgram's suggests that the perceived legitimacy of authority is influential. We are more likely to respond to an order from someone in uniform than from someone who is not in uniform. Additionally, if the authority figure is physically removed from the laboratory and gives orders by phone, obedience drops.

   Conflicting sources of authority also can disrupt obedience. Given the choice between obeying an authority figure who says to continue harming the learner and obeying one who says to stop, subjects are more likely to side with the one who says to stop. Seeing a peer disobey the experimenter is highly effective in reducing obedience. Two explanations have been offered for this effect. The first explanation is **diffusion of responsibility:** When others are involved in the obedience situation, the subject may spread around the responsibility for doing harm to the learner. The second explanation centers on the development of a new antiobedience norm when one's peers refuse to go along with the experimenter. If an antiobedience norm develops among disobedient confederates, subjects are likely to disobey the authority figure.

5. *Are there gender differences in obedience?*
   Although Milgram's original research suggested that there is no difference in levels of obedience between male and female subjects, two later studies suggest that males obey more than females and that among younger individuals there is more obedience to male than female sources of authority.

6. *Do Milgram's results apply to other cultures?*
   Milgram's basic findings hold up quite well across cultures and situations. Cross-cultural research done in Australia, Jordan, Holland, and Germany has produced obedience levels that support Milgram's findings, even when the obedience tasks diverge from Milgram's original paradigm.

7. *What criticisms of Milgram's experiments have been offered?*
   Milgram's research paradigm has come under close scrutiny. Some observers question the ethics of his situation. After all, subjects were placed in a highly stressful situation and were deceived about the true nature of the research. However, Milgram was sensitive to these concerns and took steps to head off any ill effects of participating in his experiment. Other critiques of Milgram's research suggested that using the graded shock intensities made it easier for subjects to obey. The foot-in-the-door effect may have been operating.

   Another criticism of Milgram's research was that the whole situation had an unreal quality to it. That is, the situation confuses the subject, causing him to act indecisively. Thus, Milgram's experiments may be more about how a situation can overwhelm the normal positive aspects of behavior rather than about slavish obedience to authority.

8. *How can obedience to authority be explained?*
   Milgram suggested that in an obedience situation individuals enter an **agentic state,** in which the individual becomes an agent of the authority figure. This state is influenced by **binding factors** (for example, performing successive acts of obedience) and **antecedent conditions,** or personal characteristics of the obeyer. One such personal characteristic is **authoritarian submission,** which is a submissive, uncritical attitude toward in-group authority. Although Milgram considered the role of personality in obedience, he believed that situational forces are much more important.

   Obedience to authority also may be brought about through a socialization process. The obedient individual often is eased, or socialized, into the agentic state, step by step. Additionally, Kelman and Hamilton suggest that obedience is mediated by **authorization** (when normal moral guidelines are abandoned in favor of new ones defined by authority), **routinization** (obedience becoming a habit), and **dehumanization** (seeing victims as subhuman).

9. *How does disobedience occur?*

Historically, acts of disobedience have had profound consequences for the direction society takes. When Rosa Parks refused to give up her bus seat, she set a social movement on course. Disobedience has played an important role in the development of social movements and social change.

Disobedience may occur when role strain builds to a point where a person will break the agentic state. If a person in an obedience situation begins to question his or her obedience, **role strain** (tension and anxiety about the obedience situation) may arise. If this is not dealt with by the individual, he or she may break the agentic state. One way people handle role strain is through cognitive narrowing. Disobedience is likely to occur if an individual is strong enough to break with authority, has the resources to do so, and is willing to accept the consequences. Finally, research on disobedience suggests that there is strength in numbers. When several people challenge authority, disobedience becomes likely.

Suggestions for Further Reading

Blass, T. (1991). Understanding behavior in the Milgram obedience experiment: The role of personality, situations, and their interactions. *Journal of Personality and Social Psychology, 60,* 398–413.

An excellent article presenting the evidence for personality and situational variables in determining obedience. The article also presents an interactionist perspective on obedience.

Gibson, J. T., & Haritos-Fatouros, M. (1986, November). The education of a torturer. *Psychology Today,* pp. 50–58.

This article provides a highly readable overview of the research on the education of Greek recruits to be torturers. The article ties the methods used by the Greek secret police to elements of Milgram's (1974) model of obedience.

Heck, A. (1985). *A child of Hitler: Germany in the days when God wore a swastika.* Frederick, CO: Renaissance House.

Alphons Heck has written an autobiographical account of his experiences as a member of the Hitler Youth in Nazi Germany. He describes how he idolized Adolph Hitler, joined the Hitler Youth, and fought in World War II for the Nazis. This book may help answer some of the questions raised in the featured discussion "Indoctrination into the Nazi System: Education for Death."

Kelman, H., & Hamilton, L. (1989). *Crimes of obedience: Toward a social psychology of authority and responsibility.* New Haven, CT: Yale University Press.

This book provides a readable excursion into the problem that obedience has caused historically. It also provides an overview of the conditions that favor disobedience.

Milgram, S. (1974). *Obedience to authority*. New York: Harper & Row.

An excellent overview of Milgram's research and writings on obedience. Milgram's ideas about the causes for obedience, as well as numerical data, are presented.

Sereny, G. (1974). *Into that darkness: An examination of conscience*. New York: Vintage Press.

Gitta Sereny, a journalist, conducted interviews with Franz Stangl, the commandant of the Treblinka death camp run by the Nazis. Stangl describes how he gradually was socialized into the role of a killer.

Chapter 10

Group Processes

uring the presidential election campaign of 1960, candidate John F. Kennedy made a promise to thousands of Cuban exiles living in the United States: If elected, he would return them to a "free Havana" and overthrow Fidel Castro, the Cuban dictator. Soon after his election Kennedy acted on his campaign promise. He and his closest advisors considered a plan inherited from the Eisenhower administration. The plan, conceived by Eisenhower's vice president, Richard Nixon, and developed by the Central Intelligence Agency (CIA), involved secretly arming and training a brigade of Cuban exiles and putting them ashore on the Cuban coast at a beach known as the Bay of Pigs (Wyden, 1979).

A scant 2 days after his inauguration, Kennedy and his top advisors met in closed sessions to consider the invasion plan. Kennedy had recruited "the best and the brightest" for his advisory group—distinguished members of American business and academic circles. Robert McNamara was Kennedy's secretary of defense and the man the president regarded as the smartest and most efficient member of his cabinet. McNamara had been recruited from his position as president of Ford Motor Company. Robert Kennedy, the president's brother and attorney general, was another trusted advisor. Many people found him abrasive, even arrogant, and certainly outspoken. Dean Rusk, secretary of state, a former Rhodes scholar, had served the government in several different policy-making positions and at the time of his appointment to the cabinet was head of the Rockefeller Foundation.

Allen Dulles, head of the CIA, was a legendary spy, a man admired and respected by the newcomers to the government. McGeorge Bundy, special assistant for National Security Affairs, had been recruited from Harvard University, where he was dean of Arts and Sciences. Harvard historian Arthur Schlesinger, Jr., attended the meetings on the invasion plan at the president's invitation. And there were others, all with successful careers behind them, all shrewd thinkers accustomed to speaking their minds.

The advisors met to discuss the plan many times over the next 2 months, getting briefed by Dulles and members of the Joint Chiefs of Staff, who appeared in full military regalia. Never really questioning the advisability of the plan, the group decided to give the CIA the green light. The invasion was on.

Kennedy's group made several assumptions about the invasion. They assumed that the Cuban military was too weak and disorganized to put up any serious resistance to the 1,500-man brigade of exiles. They also assumed that the invasion could be kept a secret, that the invasion force, if defeated, could escape to the mountains (which were separated from the beach by 80 miles of swampland), and that the Cuban people would rise against the dictator once they knew of the invasion. All of these assumptions proved to be fatally incorrect (Janis, 1972).

The exiles' brigade was met by a force of over 100,000 well-trained, well-equipped Cuban soldiers supported by state-of-the-art Russian jet fighters. American warships stood by, forbidden to lend tactical support. The exiles fought bravely but after 2 days were defeated. Some died, but 1,200 of them were captured. Castro ransomed the captives to the United States for $53 million in food, medical supplies, and spare auto parts.

How did the Bay of Pigs fiasco happen? How did these highly intelligent, independent-minded individuals manage to agree to and recommend a half-baked plan that resulted in military failure and political disgrace? Chosen for their ability to solve problems and make quality decisions, they sought out little information, called in few outside experts, believed everything the military chiefs said to them, discussed no alternatives, and rendered a decision that led to disaster (Wyden, 1979). In their memoirs and later statements, many of these men said they had significant doubts about the wisdom of the decision, yet they said nothing (Schlesinger, 1965).

The trouble with the Bay of Pigs decision was that these experts were not asked their opinions individually. Instead, they had to work in a group setting. And clearly, participation in the advisory group changed their behavior significantly. We saw in Chapters 8 (on conformity) and 9 (on obedience) that individuals are strongly influenced by the presence of others. In social settings people may doubt their own perceptions, suppress their reservations, withhold their opinions, be swayed by social pressures. These effects can be even stronger in true groups.

In this chapter we explore the effects of groups on individuals. We ask, What special characteristics distinguish a group like Kennedy's advisory committee from a simple gathering of individuals? What forces arise within such groups that change individual behavior? Do groups offer significant advantages over individuals operating on their own? For example, would President Kennedy have been better off making a decision by himself rather than assembling and relying on an advisory group? And what are the group dynamics that can lead to such faulty, disastrous decisions? These are some of the questions addressed in this chapter.

FIGURE 10-1 *People standing around near each other constitute an aggregate. Individuals interacting with and influencing each other constitute a group.*

WHAT IS A GROUP?

Groups are critical to our everyday existence. We are born into a group, we play in groups, we work and learn in groups. As we saw in Chapters 3 and 5, we gain much of our self-identity and self-esteem from our group memberships. But what is a *group*? Is it simply a collection of individuals who happen to be at the same place at the same time? If this were the case, the people standing on a street corner waiting for a bus would be a group. Your social psychology class has many people in it, some of whom may know one another. Some people interact, some do not. Is it a group? Well, it is certainly an *aggregate*, a gathering of people, but it probably does not feel to you like a group.

Groups have special social and psychological characteristics that set them apart from collections or aggregates of individuals. Two major features distinguish groups:

- In a group, members interact with each other.
- Group members influence each other through this social interaction.

By this definition, the collection of people at the bus stop would not qualify as a group. Although they may influence one another on a basic level (if one person looked up to the sky, others probably would follow suit), they do not truly interact. A true **group** has two or more individuals who mutually influence one another through social interaction (Forsyth, 1990) (Figure 10-1). That is, the influence arises out of the information (verbal and nonverbal) that members exchange. Kennedy's decision-making group certainly fit this definition. The group members interacted during committee meetings, and they clearly influenced one another.

This definition of a group may seem broad and ambiguous, and in fact, it is often difficult to determine whether an aggregate of individuals qualifies as a group. To refine our definition and to get a closer look at groups, we turn now to a closer look at their characteristics.

group Two or more individuals who interact with each other and who mutually influence each other.

In addition to interacting with and influencing each other, members of groups share group norms, have emotional ties to one another, and need each other to meet group goals. Which of these characteristics do you see in the groups pictured here?

Characteristics of Groups

Interaction and mutual influence among people in the group are only two of a number of attributes that characterize a group. What are the others?

First of all, a group typically has a purpose, a reason for existing. Groups serve many functions, but a general distinction can be made between instrumental groups and affiliative groups. *Instrumental groups* exist to perform some task or reach some specific goal. President Kennedy's task force was an instrumental group, as are most decision-making groups. A jury is also an instrumental group. Its sole purpose is to find the truth of the claims presented in a courtroom and reach a verdict. Once this goal is reached, the jury disperses.

Affiliative groups exist for more general, and often more social, reasons. For example, you might join a fraternity or a sorority simply because you want to be a part of that group—to affiliate with people you would like to be with. You may identify closely with the values and ideals of such a group. You derive pleasure, self-esteem, and perhaps even prestige by affiliating with the group.

A second characteristic of a group is that group members share perceptions of how group members are to behave. From these shared perceptions emerge **group norms,** or expectations about what is acceptable behavior. As pointed out in Chapter 8, norms can greatly influence individual behavior. For example, the parents of the children on a soccer team might develop into a group on the sidelines of the playing fields. Over the course of the season or several seasons, they learn what kinds of comments they can make to the coach, how much and what kind of interaction is expected among the parents, how to cheer and support the players, what they can call out during the game, what to wear, what to bring for snacks, and so on. A parent who argued with a referee or coach or who used abusive language would quickly be made to realize he or she was not conforming to group norms.

Third, within a true group, each member has a particular job or role to play in the accomplishment of the group's goals. Sometimes these roles are formally defined; for example, a chairperson of a committee has specific duties. However, roles may also be informal (DeLamater, 1974). Even when no one has been officially appointed leader, for example, one or two people usually emerge to take command or gently guide the group along. Among the soccer parents, one person might gradually take on additional responsibilities, such as organizing carpools or distributing information from the coach, and thus come to take on the role of leader.

Fourth, members of a group have affective (emotional) ties to others in the group. These ties are influenced by how well various members live up to group norms and how much other group members like them (DeLamater, 1974). President Kennedy's advisory group was formed with an instrumental purpose in mind, but it turned into an affiliative group in which members were more concerned about status and feelings than problem solving.

Finally, group members are interdependent. That is, they need each other to meet the group's needs and goals. For example, a fraternity or a sorority will fall apart if members do not follow the rules and adhere to the norms so that members can be comfortable with each other. Members of Kennedy's policy-making group depended on the group's acceptance of their behavior in order to stay in the group and have a voice in the decision-making process.

What Holds a Group Together?

Once a group is formed, what forces hold it together? Group **cohesiveness**—the strength of the relationships that link the members of the group (Forsyth, 1990)—is essentially what keeps people in the group. Cohesiveness is influenced by several factors:

- *Group members' mutual attraction.* Groups may be cohesive because the members find each other attractive or friendly. Whatever causes people to like each other more increases group cohesiveness (Levine & Moreland, 1990).

group norms Expectations that group members share about what is acceptable behavior.

cohesiveness The strength of the relationships that link the members of a group.

- *Members' propinquity (physical closeness, as when they live or work near each other).* Sometimes simply being around people regularly is enough to make people feel that they belong to a group. The various departments in an insurance company—marketing, research, sales, and so on—may think of themselves as groups.
- *Their adherence to group norms.* When members live up to group norms without resistance, the group is more cohesive than when one or two members deviate a lot or when many members deviate a little.
- *The group's success at moving toward its goals.* Groups that succeed at reaching their goals are obviously more satisfying for their members and therefore more cohesive than those that fail. If groups do not achieve what the members wish for the group, they cease to exist or at the very least are reorganized.

Groups vary with respect to the commitment and togetherness that members feel toward one another. When cohesiveness is strong, members feel tightly bound to one another, remain in the group, follow group norms, and work to achieve group goals. An example of a cohesive group that developed extremely powerful group norms is the pool of test pilots from which the first U.S. astronauts were selected. Tom Wolfe (1979) has described the mystique that developed around these group norms:

> A young man might go into military flight training believing that he was entering some sort of technical school in which he was simply going to acquire a certain set of skills. Instead, he found himself all at once enclosed in a fraternity. . . .
>
> The idea . . . seemed to be that a man should have the ability to go up in a hurtling piece of machinery and put his hide on the line and then have the moxie, the reflexes, the experience, the coolness, to pull it back in the last yawning moment—and then to go up again *the next day,* and the next day, and every next day. . . . The idea was to prove at every foot of the way up that you were one of the elected and anointed ones who had *the right stuff.* . . . (pp. 18–19)

When group cohesiveness is weak, on the other hand, individuals feel less bound to the group and are more likely to leave. Those who remain are less likely to obey group norms than members of highly cohesive groups. Those employees who have survived the "downsizing" of large U.S. companies are often less loyal to the organization even though they kept their jobs. They realize they too can be "downsized," and they begin to look for other options. These surviving employees also tend to be less productive in the sense that they refuse to try anything unusual or innovative. Everybody who survives tends to "hunker down" (*Business Week,* January 10, 1994). The cohesiveness of the group has been diminished.

HOW AND WHY DO GROUPS FORM?

We know that humans have existed in groups since before the dawn of history. Clearly, then, groups have survival value. Groups form because they meet needs that we cannot satisfy on our own. Let's take a closer look at what these needs are.

Meeting Basic Needs

Groups help us meet a variety of needs. In many cases, these needs—whether biological, psychological, or social—cannot be separated from each other. There are obvious advantages to group membership. The sociobiologists, who believe that there is a biological basis for all social behavior, suggest that early humans had a better chance of survival when they banded together in groups (Wilson, 1975). Couched in terms of natural selection, evolution would have favored those who preferred groups to those who preferred to live in isolation. We would have inherited this preference from our ancient predecessors.

But groups meet more than biological needs. They also meet psychological needs. Our first experiences occur within the context of the family group. Some people believe that our adult reactions to groups stem from our feelings about our family. That is, we react toward group leaders with much the same feelings we hold toward our fathers or mothers (Schutz, 1983). Many recruits to religious cults that demand extreme devotion are searching for a surrogate family (McCauley & Segal, 1987). We saw in Chapter 7 that the Branch Davidians sacrificed everything for their leader, David Koresh. Even after fire killed most of the members of the cult, the survivors venerated Koresh. When several of the survivors went on trial in 1994 for the murder of four federal agents, they refused to allow their lawyers to lay the blame on Koresh, a move that would have reduced the likelihood of conviction and therefore been in their own best interest. The need to honor their leader and father figure outweighed all other considerations.

Groups also satisfy a variety of social needs, such as social support—the comfort and advice of others—and protection from loneliness. Groups make it easier for people to deal with anxiety and stress. Human beings are social beings; we don't do very well when we're isolated. In fact, research shows that social isolation, the absence of meaningful social contact, is as strongly associated with death as is cigarette smoking or lack of exercise (Brannon & Feist, 1992).

Groups also satisfy the human need for *social comparison*. We compare our feelings, opinions, and behaviors with those of other people, particularly when we are unsure about how to act or think (Festinger, 1954). We compare ourselves to others who are similar to us to get accurate information about what to do. Those in the groups we affiliate with often suggest to us the books we read, the movies we see, the clothes we wear.

Social comparison also helps us obtain comforting information (Taylor & Brown, 1988). Students, for example, may be better able to protect their self-esteem when they know that others in the class also did poorly on the exam. B students compare themselves favorably with C students, and D students compare themselves with those who failed. We humans are relieved to find out that some others did even worse than we did. This is *downward comparison,* the process of comparing our standing with that of those less fortunate.

As noted earlier, groups play a large role in influencing individual self-esteem. In fact, individuals craft their self-concept from all the groups with which they identify and in which they hold membership, whether the group is a softball team or a sorority or a street gang.

Marilyn Brewer (1993) suggests that individuals join small groups such as teams or sororities to resolve two conflicting needs: the need to differentiate oneself from others and the need to blend into, and identify with, groups. Brewer's *optimal distinctiveness theory* suggests that individuals try to balance these competing needs. When one need is satisfied (merging into a group), then the second need (individual distinctiveness) is activated.

Individuals obtain much of their self-esteem by comparing their group to other groups (Sleek, 1993). If their group does well in comparison to other groups, then individual self-esteem is increased. Our self-esteem is also affected when we compare ourselves with other group members. Brewer (1993) has shown that when we observe a member of our group performing in a praiseworthy manner, it increases our own self-esteem. But, if the group member blunders, then our own self-esteem decreases.

Of course, groups are also a practical social invention. Group members can pool their resources, draw on the experience of others, and solve problems that they may not be able to solve on their own. Some groups, such as families, form an economic and social whole that functions as a unit in the larger society.

Why Do People Join?

Some groups are readymade—the family, the neighborhood, the parents of the children in a class or on a team. Other groups we actively join. What motivates an individual to join a group? Why do some prefer to join groups rather than operate on their own?

People join a group, first of all, because it promises to fulfill some need they have. A person wishing to be a better speaker, for example, might join a Toastmasters club. Someone who wanted to meet other people, get some exercise, and have fun might join a ballroom dancing class. An individual trying to overcome a drinking problem might join Alcoholics Anonymous.

Much of what impels people to join groups, then, is a need to enhance themselves. Groups provide feelings of well-being and self-esteem (Tajfel, 1982). Although joining a new group has its costs—time, effort, getting to know new people in unfamiliar situations—people often believe that the self-enhancement they will experience as a member of the group will outweigh those costs (Brinthaupt, Moreland, & Levine, 1991). Though Kennedy's advisors were all successful, they had a strong need to increase their prestige and self-esteem by being affiliated with the powerful members of this group (Janis, 1972). This need to impress other members of a group is especially true when members are "newcomers" and need to establish their status.

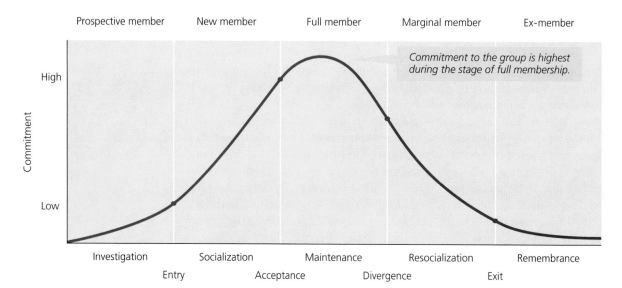

Prospective member   New member   Full member   Marginal member   Ex-member

Commitment to the group is highest during the stage of full membership.

Commitment — High / Low

Investigation   Socialization   Maintenance   Resocialization   Remembrance

Entry   Acceptance   Divergence   Exit

FIGURE 10-2 *The life cycle of group membership. Members go through a predictable series of stages over time, from investigating the group, through full membership, to departure and remembrance. Stars indicate the points of entry, acceptance, divergence, and exit.* From Moreland and Levine, 1982.

The Life Cycle of Group Membership

Members of groups seem to go through an ordered set of stages in the life cycle of their membership. Figure 10-2 shows a model of the socialization of group members over time (Moreland & Levine, 1982). This cycle does not apply to everyone who joins a group but is a general description of what most people go through.

As shown in the figure, there are five ordered stages of a member's experience in a small group. The first involves a set of *investigation* activities, in which groups and potential members of those groups look one another over. If the person decides to enter the group, a *socialization* process occurs, in which the new recruit and the established members find a way of accommodating one another. The newcomer gets the knowledge needed to function in her new group and is encouraged to obey group norms (Moreland & Levine, 1989).

In the third stage of the life cycle of membership, the recruit is fully accepted and no longer has to be watched to make sure she is worthy of membership. In this *maintenance* stage, the group plays a central role in the life of the member (Moreland, 1987). The member might now take a leadership role or do something else that will advance the group's well-being.

At this point, the member's passage through the group is on its downward arc. She may begin to find that the group no longer meets her goals or that she is no longer perceived as a valued member. This is when members show divergence from group norms. If the person is a high-status member, the group will be less likely to make an issue of this. In any event, the other members of the group will try to bring the deviate back into line—to *resocialize* her back into the mainstream of the group. These attempts may involve trying to meet the member's need to keep her in the group. For example, if a valued member of an industrial team searches for another job, her colleagues might urge the company to offer her more money or a change in her work role to try to keep her.

These efforts are also preparations to prepare both the group and the member for the eventual *exit* of that person. Exit from the group generally happens gradually rather than abruptly. The attempt to resocialize a member helps her feel wanted and probably helps to relieve guilt other members may feel over her departure. Once the person has left the group, a period of *remembrance* occurs. This may continue for a very short time, or it may persist for the rest of the departed member's life. This is when the person becomes an "old-timer." Every summer, Major League baseball teams hold reunions for their former players, who play an old-timers' game.

Roles in Groups

Not all members are expected to do the same things or obey precisely the same norms. The group often has different expectations for different group members. These shared expectations help to define individual roles, such as team captain, a formal role, or newcomer, an informal role (Levine & Moreland, 1990).

Newcomers Group members can play different roles in accordance with their seniority. Newcomers are expected to obey the group's rules and standards of behavior (its norms) and show that they are committed to being good members (Moreland & Levine, 1989). More senior members have "idiosyncratic" credit and can occasionally stray from group norms (Hollander, 1985). They have proven their worth to the group and have "banked" that credit. Every now and then it's all right for them to depart from acceptable behavior (norms) and spend that credit. New members have no such credit. The best chance new members have of being accepted by a group is to behave in a passive and anxious way.

Recall that many of Kennedy's advisors were barely settled in the new government when they were asked to evaluate the Bay of Pigs plan. It was their first major foreign policy decision. They were presented with a plan formulated and recommended by military and intelligence experts, people who were "old-timers." The newcomers responded with passive, anxious behavior.

Deviates What happens when the new members find that the group does not meet their hopes or the senior members feel the recruit has not met the group's expectations? The group may try to take some corrective action by putting pressure on the member to conform. Groups will spend much time trying to convince someone who does not live up to group norms to change (Schachter, 1951). If the deviate does not come around, the group then disowns her. The deviate, however, usually bows to group pressure and conforms to group norms (Levine, 1989).

Deviates are rejected most when they interfere with the functioning of the group (Kruglanski & Webster, 1991). Imagine an advisor to President Kennedy objecting to the Cuban invasion after the decision had been made. No matter how persuasive the person's objection to the invasion, it is very likely that the deviate would have been told to be silent; he would have been interfering with the group's ability to get the job done. Experimental research has verified that when a group member dissents from a group decision close to the group's deadline for solving a problem, the rejector is more likely to be condemned than if the objection is stated earlier (Kruglanski & Webster, 1991).

Groups that require extreme devotion recognize the need in many of their members for a family. They discourage deviates from leaving by—among other tactics—serving as a surrogate family, as suggested earlier (McCauley & Segal, 1987). The fear of being rejected by your family strikes at the core of your identity. After all, even if you wish you had another family, you realize the one you have is the only one you are likely to have. It is no accident that many religious cults require their members to give up family and friends, renounce their past, and become devoted to the sect.

HOW DO GROUPS INFLUENCE THE BEHAVIOR OF INDIVIDUALS?

We have considered why people join groups, what the life cycle of group membership is, and what roles individuals play in groups. Now let's consider another question: What effect does being in a group have on individual behavior and performance? Does group membership lead to self-enhancement, as people who join groups seem to believe? Does it have other effects? Some social psychologists have been particularly interested in investigating this question. They have looked not just at the effects of membership in true groups but also at the effects of being evaluated by an audience, of being in an audience, and of being in a crowd.

Recall that groups affect the way we think and act even when we only imagine how they are going to respond to us. If you practice a speech, just imagining that large audience in front of you is enough to make you nervous. The actual presence of an audience affects us even more. But how? Let's take a look.

The Effects of an Audience on Performance

Does an audience make you perform better? Or does it make you "choke"? The answer seems to depend, at least in part, on how good you are at what you're doing. The presence of others seems to help when the performer is doing something he or she does well: when the performance is a *dominant*, well-learned skill, a behavior that is easy or familiar (Zajonc, 1965). If you are a class A tennis player, for example, your serve may be better when people are watching you. The performance-enhancing effect of an audience on your behavior is known as **social facilitation.** If, however, you are performing a nondominant skill, one that is not very well learned, then the presence of an audience detracts from your performance. This effect is known as **social inhibition.**

The social facilitation effect, the strengthening of a dominant response due to the presence of other people, has been demonstrated in a

social facilitation The performance-enhancing effect of an audience on behavior.

social inhibition The performance-detracting effect of an audience on behavior.

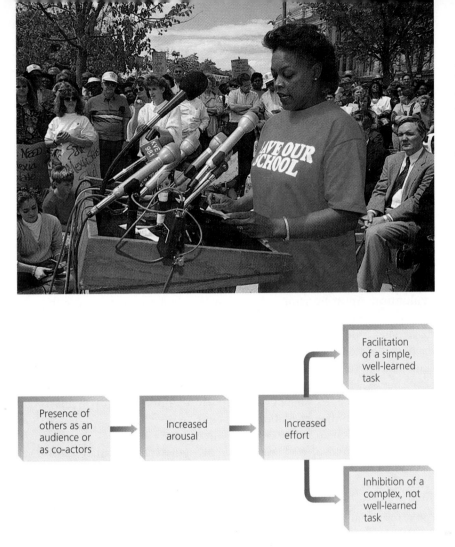

If public speaking is something at which this woman excels, the presence of an audience will probably enhance her performance—an effect known as social facilitation. If she isn't prepared or lacks self-confidence, the audience may impair her performance—an effect known as social inhibition. Most researchers agree that both of these effects involve increased arousal due to the presence of others.

FIGURE 10-3 *The arousal theory of social facilitation. According to this view, the presence of an audience creates increased arousal in a performer, which in turn increases effort. If the task involves a dominant, well-learned behavior, performance is enhanced. If the task involves a less well learned behavior, performance is impaired.*

wide range of species, including roaches, ants, chicks, and humans (Zajonc, Heingartner, & Herman, 1969). Humans doing a simple task perform better in the presence of others. On a more difficult task, the presence of others inhibits performance.

Why does this happen? How does an audience cause us to perform better or worse than we do when no one is watching? Psychologists have several alternative explanations.

Increased Arousal Robert Zajonc (1965) has argued that a performer's effort always increases in the presence of others due to increased arousal. Increased arousal increases effort; the consequent increased effort improves performance when the behavior is dominant and impairs performance when the behavior is nondominant. If you are good at tennis, then increased arousal and therefore increased effort make you play better. If you are not a good tennis player, the increased arousal and increased effort probably will inhibit your performance (Figure 10-3).

FIGURE 10-4 The evaluation apprehension theory of social facilitation. According to this view, the presence of an audience increases anxiety about being judged, or evaluation apprehension. This kind of arousal leads to enhanced performance if the task involves a dominant skill or to impaired performance if the task involves a less familiar skill.

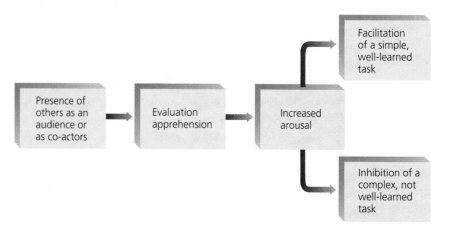

Evaluation Apprehension An alternative explanation for the effects of an audience on performance centers not so much on the increased effort that comes from arousal but on the judgments we perceive others to be making about our performance. A theater audience, for example, does not simply receive a play passively. Instead, audience members sit in judgment of the actors, even if they are only armchair critics. The kind of arousal this situation produces is known as **evaluation apprehension.** Some social scientists believe that evaluation apprehension is what causes differences in performance when an audience is present (Figure 10-4).

Those who favor evaluation apprehension as an explanation of social facilitation and social inhibition suggest that the presence of others will cause arousal only when they can reward or punish the performer (Geen, 1989). The mere presence of others does not seem to be sufficient to account for social facilitation and social inhibition (Cottrell, 1972). In one experiment, when the audience was made up of blindfolded or inattentive persons, social facilitation of performance did not occur. That is, if the audience could not see the performance, or did not care about it, then evaluation apprehension did not occur, nor did social facilitation or social inhibition (Cottrell, Wack, Sekerak, & Rittle, 1968).

The Distraction-Conflict Effect Another explanation of the presence-of-others effect is **distraction-conflict theory** (Baron, 1986). According to this theory, arousal results from a conflict between demands for attention from the task and demands for attention from the audience. There are three main points to the theory. First, the presence of other people distracts attention from the task. Our tennis player gets all kinds of attention-demanding cues—rewards and punishments—from those watching him play. He may be aware of his parents, his ex-girlfriend, his tennis coach, an attractive stranger, and his annoying little brother out there in the crowd. This plays havoc with a mediocre serve. Second, distraction leads to conflicts in his attention. Our tennis player has just so much attentional capacity. All of this capacity ought to be focused on throwing the ball in the air and hitting it across the net. But his attention is also focused on those he knows in the crowd. Third, the conflict between these two claims for his or her attention stresses the performer and raises the arousal level (Figure 10-5).

evaluation apprehension An explanation for social facilitation suggesting that arousal is caused by apprehension over being evaluated by others.

distraction-conflict theory A theory of social facilitation suggesting that arousal stems from conflict between paying attention to demands from a task and demands from others present.

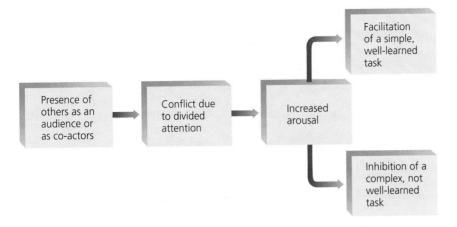

FIGURE 10-5 *The distraction-conflict theory of social facilitation. According to this view, the presence of an audience creates a conflict for attention, distracting the performer from the task and increasing arousal. Again, if the task is something the performer can do very well, this increased arousal enhances performance. But if the task is something the performer is less skilled at, performance suffers.*

One type of situation in which a distraction-conflict effect is particularly noticeable is professional sporting events with enormously high stakes. During the regular baseball season, for example, the "home field advantage" prevails—teams win more games when they play on their home fields, probably because they know the crowd is behind them and has positive expectations (Sanna & Shotland, 1990). But when the stakes increase—as during the final games of the World Series—the home field advantage may turn into a disadvantage. Roy Baumeister (1984) examined baseball records to investigate the effects of supportive and nonsupportive crowds on the performance of professional athletes during the World Series. He found that home teams won about 60% of the first two games, but they lost the final game 60% of the time. He concluded that the players experienced added pressure from the fans' expectations that the team would win because they were playing at home and from their awareness of the enormous disappointment that would occur if they lost. This attentional conflict increased their arousal levels to the extent that even well-learned, dominant responses (hitting and throwing a baseball) suffered (Mullen & Baumeister, 1987).

The Effects of Group Participation on Performance

We have seen that being watched affects how we perform. Let's take this a step further and examine how being a member of a group affects our performance.

We noted earlier that people who join groups do so largely for self-enhancement: they believe that group membership will improve them in some way. They will become better speakers, better citizens, better soccer players, better dancers or singers; they will meet people and expand their social circle; they will make a contribution to a cause, a political candidate, or society. Does group membership actually lead to improved performance? Or does it detract from individual effort and achievement, giving people the opportunity to "goof off"? Both effects have been documented, depending on a number of factors.

These cyclists probably make somewhat better time when they're riding together than when they're alone. Being in a group often has a positive effect on individual performance.

Enhanced Performance   Imagine that you are a bicycling enthusiast. Three times a week you ride 20 miles, which takes you a little over an hour. One day you happen to come upon a group of cyclists and decide to ride along with them. When you look at your time for the 20 miles, you find that your time is under 1 hour, and a full 10 minutes under your best previous time. How can you account for your increased speed? Did the other riders simply act as a wind shield for you, allowing you to exert less effort and ride faster? Or is there more to this situation than aerodynamics? Could it be that the mere presence of others somehow affected your behavior?

This question was asked by Norman Triplett, one of the early figures in social psychology (1898). Triplett, a cycling enthusiast, decided to test a theory that the presence of other people was sufficient to increase performance. He used a laboratory in which alternative explanations for the improvement in cycling time (for example, other riders being a wind shield) could be eliminated. He also conducted what is perhaps the first social psychological experiment. He had children engage in a simulated race on a miniature track. Ribbons were attached to fishing reels. By winding the reels the children could drag ribbons around a miniature race track. Triplett had the children perform the task either alone or in pairs. He found that the children who played the game in the presence of another child completed the task more quickly than children who played the game alone. The improved performance of the children and the cyclists when they participate in a group setting rather than alone gives us some evidence that groups do enhance individual performance.

Social Loafing and Free Rides   Is it true that the presence of others is *always* arousing and that participating in a group always leads to enhanced individual performance? Perhaps not. In fact, the opposite may occur. Sometimes when we are in a group situation, we relax our efforts and rely on others to take up the slack. This effect is called **social loafing.**

Max Ringelmann, a French agricultural engineer living at the turn of the century, was interested in improving productivity (Kravitz & Martin, 1986). He wondered how best to plow a field or turn a mill. Are four horses twice as productive as two? Would four men turn a crank twice as fast as two men? Ringelmann (1913) conducted experiments to address these

social loafing The effect that sometimes occurs when, in a group situation, individuals relax their efforts and rely on others to take up the slack.

questions. He used a rope-pulling task—a tug-of-war—and found that as he increased the number of men on each team, the group became less productive. Individuals seemed to pull less hard on the rope as other team members were added.

Why does this occur? Perhaps there are losses related to coordination difficulties: Several people have more trouble coordinating their efforts than only a few people (Steiner, 1972). A second possibility is that some people were simply loafing, not working to their full capacity.

More recent research has supported the latter possibility. Sometimes, people are not more effortful in the presence of others; they in fact may loaf when working with others in groups (Harkins & Szymanski, 1987; Latané, Williams, & Harkins, 1979; Williams & Karau, 1991). In one experiment, participants were informed that they had to shout as loudly as they could to test the effects of "sensory feedback on the ability of groups to produce sound." The researchers compared the noise produced by individuals who thought they were shouting or clapping alone to the noise they made when they thought they were in a group. If groups did as well as individuals, then the group production would at least equal the sum of the individual production. But the research findings showed that groups did not produce as much noise as the combined amount of noise individuals made (Latané et al., 1979). Some group members did not do as much as they were capable of doing as individuals: They loafed. In some instances, then, participation of others in the task (for example, in a tug-of-war game) lowers individual motivation and reduces performance on the task. Simply put, people sometimes exert less effort when working on a task in a group context (Harkins & Petty, 1982).

Why should the group reduce individual performance in some cases and enhance it in others? The nature of the task may encourage social loafing. In a game of tug-of-war, if you do not pull the rope as hard as you can, who will know or care? If you don't shout as loud as you can, what difference does it make? You cannot accurately assess your own contribution, nor can other people evaluate how well you are performing. Social loafing occurs across a variety of tasks, ranging from the trivial to the moderately important (Karau & Williams, 1993). Social loafing tends *not* to occur in very important tasks. However, many of our everyday tasks are repetitive and dull and are vulnerable to social loafing (Karau & Williams, 1993).

Regardless of the task, some individuals work harder than others in groups (Kerr, 1983). **Free riders** do not do their share of the work. Why not? They are cynical about the other members; they think others may be holding back, so they hold back also. People do not want to be "suckers," doing more than their share while others take it easy. Even if they know that their co-workers are doing their share and are competent, individuals may look for a free ride (Williams & Karau, 1991).

The larger the group, the more common social loafing and free riding. It is harder to determine individual efforts and contributions in big groups. People are likely to feel more responsible for the outcome in smaller groups (Kerr, 1989). Of course, not everyone loafs in groups, nor do people loaf in all group situations.

free riders Group members who do not do their share of the work.

What decreases the likelihood of social loafing? It is less likely to occur if individuals feel that it is important to compensate for other, weaker group members (Williams & Karau, 1991). When the task is important and motivation to perform is high, then **social compensation**—working harder to make up for the weakness of others—seems to overcome the tendency toward social loafing and free riding.

Social loafing is also less likely when individual contributions can be clearly identified. Generally, when individuals can be identified and cannot simply "blend in" with the background of other workers, they are less likely to loaf (Williams, Harkins, & Latané, 1981). The members of an automobile manufacturing team, for example, are more careful about their tasks and less willing to pass on defective work if they have to sign for each piece they do. If responsibility for defects is clear, if positive effort and contribution are rewarded, and if management punishes free riders, then social loafing will be further diminished (Shepperd, 1993).

Social loafing is a phenomenon that is very robust and occurs in a variety of situations and cultures (Karau & Williams, 1993). It has been found to be more common among men than among women and among members of Eastern as opposed to Western cultures. These cultural and gender differences seem to be related to values. Many women and many individuals in Eastern cultures attach more importance to group harmony and group success and satisfaction. Many men, especially men in Western cultures, attach more value to individual advancement and rewards and to other people's evaluations. Groups tend to mask individual differences. For this reason, Western men may have less inclination to perform well in group situations. The result is social loafing (Karau & Williams, 1993).

Deindividuation and Anonymity: The Effect of Groups on Identity and Responsibility

We have seen that when certain individuals feel they can't be identified by their actions or achievements, they tend to loaf. This is a common group effect. A decline in individual identity seems to mean a decline in a person's sense of responsibility. Anonymity can alter people's ethical and moral behavior.

The Negative Side of Anonymity   Observers of group behavior have long known that certain kinds of groups have the potential for great mischief. Groups at sporting events have engaged in murder and mayhem when their soccer teams have lost. One element present in such groups is that the individuals are not easily identifiable. People get lost in the mass and seem to lose their self-identity and self-awareness. Social psychologists have called this loss of inhibition while engulfed in a group **deindividuation** (Zimbardo, 1969).

People who are deindividuated seem to become less aware of their own moral standards and are much more likely to respond to violent or aggressive cues (Prentice-Dunn & Rogers, 1989). In fact, deindividuated people are quick to respond to any cues. Research suggests that when people

social compensation The tendency to work harder to make up for the weakness of others in the group when the task is important and motivation to perform is high.

deindividuation The loss of self-identity and self-awareness that can occur when people are in large groups.

Being part of a group can lead to deindividuation—a loss of self-identity and self-awareness. Group members surrender their sense of personal responsibility and give themselves over to group goals. Uniforms and disguises, like the robes and hoods of the Ku Klux Klan, enhance the sense of anonymity that results from deindividuation.

are submerged in a group, they become impulsive, aroused, and wrapped up in the cues of the moment (Spivey & Prentice-Dunn, 1990). Their action is determined by whatever the group does.

Groups and organizations whose primary purpose involves violence often attempt to deindividuate their members. Certainly, the white sheets covering the members of the Ku Klux Klan are a prime example of this. So, too, are the training methods of most military organizations. Uniforms serve to lower a sense of self-awareness and make it easier to respond to aggressive cues.

There is some evidence that the larger the group, the more likely it is that individual group members will deindividuate. Differences have been found in the behavior of larger and smaller crowds that gather when a troubled person is threatening to leap from a building or bridge (Mann, 1981). Out of 21 such cases examined, in 10 the crowds baited the victim to jump, whereas in the remaining 11 the victim was not taunted and was often rescued. What was the difference between these two sorts of cases?

The baiting crowds tended to be larger—over 300 people. The baiting episodes were more likely to take place after dark, and the victim was usually situated higher up, typically above the 12th floor. Additionally, the longer the episode continued, the more likely was the taunting. All of these factors—the large size of the crowd, the distance between that crowd and the victim, the anonymity lent by darkness—contributed to the deindividuation of the members of the crowd. And the longer these deindividuated people waited, the more irritable they became. Another study found that when a crowd is bent on violence, the larger the crowd, the more vicious the behavior (Mullen, 1986). Larger crowds and smaller numbers of victims can lead to atrocities such as hangings, torture, and rape.

A vivid portrait of the transformation of dissatisfied individuals into an angry, anonymous mob is provided by Sattareh Farman Farmaian (1992), describing riots that occurred in Tehran, Iran, in 1963:

> The news that the government had arrested a venerated mullah . . . raced through the bazar like a brushfire. Within hours, mullahs, theology students, and guild leaders had plastered the walls with his

picture and organized thousands of tradesmen, craftsmen, vendors, and others to march in a demonstration and shout anti-government slogans. . . . The army, under orders to shoot to kill, mowed them down.

Not only tradesmen, peddlers, and young seminarians but teachers, factory workers, office clerks, university students, and National Front activists . . . poured into the streets to hurl sticks and stones at the police and soldiers. They attacked government buildings and desecrated the Armenian cemetery. . . . The central city was a battle zone. Nobody knew how many were being injured or killed. (p. 252)

The Positive Side of Anonymity There is, however, a less well known aspect of deindividuation. If the group decides to do something positive, members may follow along. Deindividuation makes us vulnerable to the group's strong cues—positive as well as negative. Group members who lose their sense of self-awareness may put themselves in great danger to help other people. Soldiers who rescue their comrades on the field of battle show a complete lack of self-awareness.

In one study, it was shown that anonymity can have positive as well as negative consequences (Gergen, Gergen, & Barton, 1973). Researchers had subjects enter a small, totally dark room. Only a pinpoint of red light over the door broke the darkness (so people could find their way out). There were a total of eight people—four males and four females—in the room, none of whom knew or could see each other. Infrared cameras recorded events. Subjects were told, "There are no rules . . . as to what you should do . . . at the end you will be escorted alone from the room and there will be no opportunity to meet the other individuals." The researchers were interested in the nature and effects of group norms, which control much of our behavior. Here there were no group norms, no rules, and no possibility of being identified. What would people do?

At first, most people were disoriented. They sat down and kept quiet. Then they began to touch other people. They moved around. Some people left, others came in. One subject later said, "People sat in smaller groups, and . . . were silent. . . . The darkness no longer bothered me. The last group of us sat closely together, touching, feeling a sense of friendship and loss as a group member left. I felt that it was fun and nice. In fact I missed them." Many kissed, and most felt sexual tension.

The researchers also ran this experiment in a lighted room. Whereas individuals in the darkened room had touched, hugged, moved around, and were sexually aroused, those in the lighted room stayed still, did not touch, and talked a lot.

Subjects in the darkened room enjoyed their experience and volunteered to return without payment. They had become aware of a yearning for closeness and had experienced an intimacy that was unavailable in the lighted room. In this instance, anonymity was liberating (Gergen et al., 1973). As in situations in which anonymity has negative consequences, individuals had lost some of their sense of personal awareness, and this had increased their emotional arousal. This kind of arousal apparently can lead to socially destructive or socially positive experiences, depending on the situation.

We turn now to a final set of questions: How do groups operate to solve problems, make decisions, and reach group goals?

GROUP DECISION MAKING AND GROUP PRODUCTIVITY

Early in the chapter we distinguished between groups with an instrumental purpose and groups with an affiliative purpose. Many, if not most, groups are formed for the purpose of making decisions—a clearly instrumental purpose. This was President Kennedy's purpose in assembling his advisory group on the Cuban invasion. We form decision-making groups because we believe that combining the talents of individuals will increase the effectiveness of decision making and thus the productivity of our endeavor. We extend the old saying "Two heads are better than one" to groups of "heads." Let's see if the truisms are true.

Individual Decisions Versus Group Decisions

First of all, let's consider whether group decisions are in fact better than individual decisions. Is it better to have a team of medical personnel decide whether our CAT scan indicates we need surgery, or is that decision better left to a single surgeon? Did Kennedy benefit from the workings of his group, or would he have been wiser to think through the situation on his own?

Does a Group Do Better Than the Average Person? In general, research shows that groups do outperform individuals—at least the *average* individual—on many jobs and tasks (Stasser, Kerr, & Davis, 1989). Three reasons have been proposed for the observed superiority of groups over the average person. First of all, groups do a better job than the average person because they *recognize truth*—accept the right answer—more quickly. Second, groups are better able to *reject error*—reject incorrect or implausible answers (Laughlin, 1980; Laughlin, VanderStoep, & Hollingshead, 1991; Lorge & Solomon, 1955). Third, groups have a better, more efficient memory system than do individuals. This permits them to process information more effectively.

Groups may possess what has been called **transactive memory systems**—sets of individual memories (Wegner, 1986). Group members learn about each other's expertise and assign memory tasks on that basis. This not only leaves others to concentrate on the memory tasks they do best, it also provides the group with memory aids. Someone in the group may be good in math, for example, so that person is assigned the task of remembering math-related information. When the group wants to recall that information, they go to this expert and use her as an external memory aid. Memory thus becomes a transaction, a social event in the group. For some or all of these

transactive memory systems
Sets of individual memories that groups possess and make use of in processing information and making group decisions.

Which decisions are better—those made by an individual or those made by a group? This businesswoman may make excellent decisions on her own. Research shows that groups can outperform the average person but not the brightest member of the group.

reasons, groups seem to outperform the average person on many decision-related tasks.

Does a Group Do Better Than Its Best Member?

We noted that research has shown that groups outperform the average person. But what about the smartest person, the "best and brightest" member of the group?

To test the hypothesis that groups can find correct responses better than individuals, college students were asked to try to discover an arbitrary rule for separating a deck of cards into those that did and did not fit the rule (Laughlin, VanderStoep, & Hollingshead, 1991). If the rule was "hearts," for example, then all cards of the hearts suit would fit the rule and all others would not. Subjects had to guess the rule and then test it by playing a card. The feedback from the experimenter gave them information on which to base their next guess. The researchers also varied the amount of information that subjects had to deal with. They presented some subjects with only two arrays of cards, others with three, and others with four. The more arrays, the more difficult the task.

The performance of four-person groups was then compared to the performance of each of the four group members, who had to do a similar task individually. Figure 10-6 shows the proportion of correct responses produced by the group in comparison with the correct responses of the individuals in the group who performed best alone, second-best, third-best, and worst.

As can be seen, the best individual was able to generate more correct guesses than the group or than any other individual member. The group's performance was equal to its second-best member. The third- and fourth-best members were inferior to the group. As the task became more difficult—as the arrays increased to four, which made much more information available—the performance of both the best individual and the group fell. The researchers also compared the abilities of groups and their individual

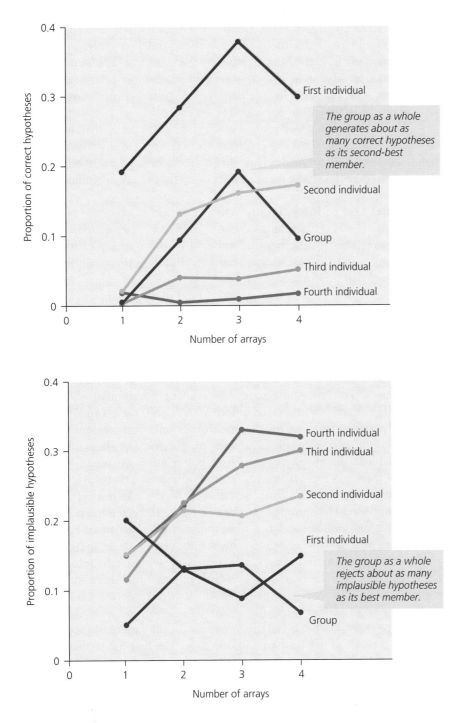

FIGURE 10-6 *The performance of a group in comparison with the performances of its individual members, as measured by the proportion of correct responses generated. The individual who gave the highest proportion of correct responses did better than the group as a whole, but the group did better than the third-best and fourth-best individuals. In other words, when performance is evaluated in terms of proportion of correct responses, groups do reasonably well, about as well as their second-best member.* From Laughlin, VanderStoep, and Hollingshead, 1991.

The group as a whole generates about as many correct hypotheses as its second-best member.

FIGURE 10-7 *The performance of a group in comparison with the performances of its individual members, as measured by proportion of implausible hypotheses rejected. The group as a whole and the best individual performed about the same in this measure.* From Laughlin, VanderStoep, and Hollingshead, 1991.

The group as a whole rejects about as many implausible hypotheses as its best member.

members in rejecting implausible hypotheses. The fewer implausible ideas subjects or groups raised, the better they did with respect to rejecting false leads. As Figure 10-7 shows, groups and the best individual were better at rejecting false leads than were the second-, third-, and fourth-best individuals.

This research suggests that groups in general perform as well as their best or second-best individual member working independently. You might ask, Why not just have the best member do the task? But keep in mind that it is often not possible to identify the group's best member prior to completing the task. This finding tells us that groups tend to perform competently, particularly when the information load is not overwhelming.

We have seen how well groups perform with respect to the abilities of their members. Let's take a closer look at the workings—the dynamics—of how those decisions are made. How do groups gather and use the information possessed by individual members? How do they reach decisions?

The Group's Use of Information   One advantage groups have over individual decision makers is that a variety of individuals can usually bring to the discussion a great deal more information than can one person. This is usually seen as the great advantage of groups. But does the group make adequate use of that information?

Research shows that group members tend to discuss information that they share in common and avoid discussing information that only one person has. Individuals also avoid discussing or disclosing information that goes counter to the group's preferred decision (Stasser, Taylor, & Hanna, 1989): There is a pronounced tendency to avoid conflict.

In one experiment, each member of a committee received common information about three candidates for student government (Stasser & Titus, 1987). Each also received information about each candidate that none of the others received (unshared information). The committee members met in four-person groups to rank the candidates. The sheer number of facts available to the members varied from one group to the next. When the number of facts was high, the raters ignored information that was unshared. That is, they rated the candidates based solely on the information that they held in common. The information they chose to share tended to support the group decision. They did not share information that would have conflicted with the decision. Because the results of this study indicate that group members try to avoid conflict by selectively withholding information, the researchers concluded that face-to-face, unstructured discussion is not a good way to inform group members of unshared information (Stasser, 1992).

There appear to be at least two reasons for the failure of face-to-face groups to report and use unshared information. The first has to do with the way people think. Whatever is most salient (the shared information) tends to overwhelm that which recedes into the background (the unshared information). In other words, group members hear the shared information and simply neglect to bring up or take into account the unshared information. The second reason, as suggested earlier, is that individuals may be motivated to ignore or forget information (unshared) that they think may cause conflict.

The nature of a group's task may also affect how the group searches for information and uses shared and unshared facts. To investigate this possibility, experimenters hypothesized that groups would be more likely to share all information if they knew that the problem had a definitively correct answer than if the task called only for a judgment (Stasser & Stewart, 1992). Subjects in this study were given information about a crime. In some groups, all the information was given to all the members. In other groups, some information was given only to individual members. In other words, in the latter groups, some members had unshared information. In addition, half of the groups were told that there was enough evidence to solve the crime, while others were informed that since the evidence was less than full, the group would have to make a judgment call.

The results showed that groups given the task with the correct answer were much more likely to search for the unshared information and get the right answer than groups given a judgment problem. What differed was the expectation that there was or was not a correct answer (Stasser & Stewart, 1992). When the group members think or know that the task has a definite answer, they are more forthright in bringing up anything (unshared) that could help the group. The group strategy changes. People want to search for any information that helps them be successful.

What other factors besides the nature of the task might induce groups to search for and use hidden or unshared information? One is the character of the discussion process. When the discussion occurs in such a way that each member is strongly encouraged to share his or her unique knowledge with the group, it be possible to overcome the group's reluctance to consider this information (Wright, Luus, & Christie, 1990). When information loads are kept low, unshared information is also less likely to be ignored (Stasser, 1992). Otherwise, there may simply be too large a mass of information for the group to consider.

Kennedy's advisory group was often overloaded with information, and anyone who did bring up unshared facts was ignored or even ostracized. In such an atmosphere, people are very strongly inclined to concentrate only on information they all have in common.

In sum, then, a definite advantage of groups is that they have access to more information than any single individual might have. But groups are more likely to actually make use of this information if

- the problem they're considering has a definitive answer;
- they are primed to search for and use all the information that individual members may have; and
- the amount of information they are given is kept manageable.

How Do Groups Blend Individual Choices into Group Decisions?

Once a decision-making group is using the information its members possess, it still has to reach a decision. To do this, some decision rules have to be made. A **decision rule** is a rule about how many members must agree before the group can reach a decision. Decision rules set the criteria for how individual choices will be blended into a group product or decision (Pritchard & Watson, 1992). Two common decision rules are majority rule (the winning alternative must receive more than half the votes) and unanimity rule (consensus—all members must agree).

decision rule A rule about how many members must agree before the group can reach a decision.

Groups will find a decision rule that leads to good decisions and stick with that rule throughout the life cycle of the group (Miller, 1989). The majority rule is used in most groups (Davis, 1980). The majority dominates both through informational social influence—controlling the information the group uses (Stasser, Kerr, & Davis, 1989)—and through normative social influence—exerting the group's will through conformity pressure. We saw in Chapter 8 how difficult it is to resist normative influence, particularly when the majority is large and the minority is small.

A unanimity rule, or consensus, forces the group to consider the views of the minority more carefully than a majority rule. Group members tend to be more satisfied by a unanimity rule, especially those in the minority, who feel that the majority paid attention and considered their point of view (Hastie, Penrod, & Pennington, 1983).

The decision rule used by a group may depend on what kind of task the group is working on. When the group deals with intellective tasks—problems for which there is a definitive correct answer, such as the solution to an equation—the decision rule is that *truth wins.* In other words, when one member of the group solves the problem, all members (who have mathematical knowledge) recognize the truth of the answer. If the problem has a less definitively correct answer, such as, say, the solution to a word puzzle, then the decision rule is that *truth supported wins.* When one member comes up with an answer that the others support, that answer wins (Kerr, 1992).

When the group deals with judgmental tasks—tasks that do not have a demonstrably correct answer, such as a jury decision in a complex case—then the decision rule is *majority wins* (Laughlin & Ellis, 1986). That is, whether the formal decision rule (the one the judge gives to the jury) is unanimity or a 9 out of 12 majority (a rule common in some states), a decision is usually made once the majority rule has been satisfied. Even if the formal rule is unanimity, unpersuaded jurors tend to go along with the majority once 9 or 10 of the 12 jurors agree.

What Factors Affect the Decision-Making Ability of a Group?

What makes a good decision-making group? Is there a particular size that works best? A particular composition? What other factors have an impact on the abilities and effectiveness of a group? Consider President Kennedy's advisory group. It was fairly large—perhaps 12 or more people attended each session. And group members were similar in temperament, background, and education. Is that a good recipe for a decision-making group?

Group Composition Several group investigators emphasize the composition of a group as its most fundamental attribute (Levine & Moreland, 1990). Questions often arise about how to best constitute groups, especially decision-making groups. For example, some people have asked whether random selection of citizens is the best way to put together a jury, especially for a complex trial (Horowitz & Willging, 1991).

Some researchers have investigated whether groups with high-ability members perform better than groups composed of individuals of lesser abilities. In one study, the composition of three-person battle tank crews was varied (Tziner & Eden, 1985). Some crews had all high-ability members, some had mixtures of high- and low-ability members, and others had all low-ability members. Their results showed that the abilities of the members interacted in unanticipated ways. Tank groups composed of all high-ability individuals performed more effectively than expected from the sum of their individual talents. And groups composed of all low-ability members did worse than expected.

Psychologist Robert Sternberg believes that every group has its own intelligence level, or "group I.Q." (Williams & Sternberg, 1988). The group's I.Q. is not simply the sum of each member's I.Q. Rather, it is the blending of their intellectual abilities with their personalities and social competence.

In one study, Sternberg asked volunteers who had been tested on their intelligence and social skills to devise a marketing plan for a new product, an artificial sweetener (Williams & Sternberg, 1988). Other groups had similar tasks, all of which required creative solutions. The decision-making groups that produced the most creative solutions were those that contained at least one person with a high I.Q. and others who were socially skillful, or practical, or creative. In other words, the successful groups had a good mix of people with different talents who brought different points of view to the problem.

This research highlights the fact that everybody in the group must have the skills to make a contribution. If one member of the group is extremely persuasive or extremely good at the task, the other members may not be able to use their abilities to the best effect. According to one study, successful leaders should have I.Q. scores no more than 10 points higher than the average I.Q. score of the group (Simonton, 1985). This minimizes the possibility that the most talented person will dominate the group. If this person is more extraordinary, then the collective effort will be hurt by his or her presence (Simonton, 1985).

The gender of group members also influences problem-solving ability (Levine & Moreland, 1990). One study showed that although groups composed of all males were generally more effective than all-female groups, the success of the groups really depended on the kind of problem they had to solve. Male groups do better when they have to fulfill a specific task, whereas female groups do better at communal activities that involve friendship and social support (Wood, 1987).

Group Size Conventional wisdom tells us that two heads are better than one. If this is so, then why wouldn't three be better than two, four better than three, and so on? Does increasing a group's size also increase its ability to arrive at correct answers, make good decisions, and reach productivity goals?

Increasing the number of members of a group does increase the resources available to the group and therefore the group's potential productivity (Steiner, 1972). On the other hand, increasing group size also leads to

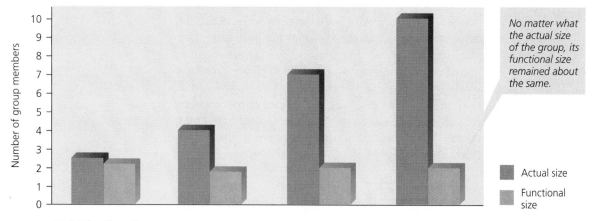

No matter what the actual size of the group, its functional size remained about the same.

Actual size

Functional size

FIGURE 10-8 *The effects of group size on group member participation in problem solving. As actual group size increased, the number of group members who spoke up—the functional size of the group—did not increase. A group of ten people has only as many active participants as a group of three or four.* From Bray, Kerr, and Atkin, 1978.

more **process loss** (Steiner, 1972). In other words, the increase in resources due to more group members is counterbalanced by the increased difficulty in arriving at a decision. Large groups generally take more time to reach a decision than small groups (Davis, 1969).

Another problem facing larger groups is unequal participation of members. This was clearly a problem for the Bay of Pigs advisors. The lower-status members and the "newcomers" tended to say very little. In order for increased resources to increase productivity, those resources must be made available to the group. However, in larger groups all members do not contribute equally to the discussion. As shown in Figure 10-8, in larger groups (of six to ten members), two or three people dominate the discussion. Some members may be uncomfortable speaking up in this size group, so their resources are lost to the group. In smaller groups (of three or four members), participation is more even. Thus the *functional size* of the group (i.e., the number of members actually contributing their resources) falls short of the actual size of the group as the actual size increases (Bray, Kerr, & Atkin, 1978).

Yet smaller is not always better. We often misperceive the effect of group size on performance. Researchers interested in testing the common belief that small groups are more effective than large groups gave a number of groups the task of solving social dilemmas, problems that require individuals to sacrifice some of their own gains so that the entire group benefits (such as conserving water during a drought) (Kerr, 1989).

Those who participated in the study thought that the size of their group was an important determinant of their ability to satisfactorily resolve social dilemmas. People in larger groups felt there was very little they could do to influence the decisions of the group. They tended to be less active and less aware of what was going on than comparable members of smaller groups. They believed that smaller groups would more effectively solve social dilemmas than larger groups, mainly by cooperating.

But in fact there was no difference in effectiveness between the small and large groups in solving social dilemmas. People did enjoy small groups more than large ones, but the product and the quality of the decisions of

process loss The increased difficulty in arriving at a decision that results from increasing group size.

These students would probably be able to generate more good ideas on their own than in a group. Research indicates that brainstorming is not a very effective approach to collaboration: People tend to lose their ideas while others are talking. The larger the group, the more loss there is.

both sizes of groups were much the same. Thus, small groups offer only an **illusion of efficacy.** That is, they think they are more effective than larger groups, but the evidence suggests they may not be, based on their actual productivity.

Another popular group process—brainstorming—may also provide only an illusion of efficacy. In brainstorming, members are encouraged to just let their ideas flow without being critical of those ideas. Members of brainstorming groups think that they produce more interesting and creative ideas in an interactive group than when alone. But, according to research, groups that brainstorm are really not any more productive in coming up with good ideas than are individuals. It seems that when one person is talking, other members block their own ideas and responses and therefore lose them. This is another example of process loss. Increasing group size serves only to increase blocking (Diehl & Stroebe, 1991; Kerr, 1992; Paulus, Dzindolet, Poletes, & Camacho, 1993).

One situation in which blocking seems not to occur is when brainstorming is done electronically, that is, when people interact over a computer network. In one study (Dennis, Valacich, & Nunamaker, 1990), groups of varying sizes (three, nine, and eighteen members) worked on an idea-generation problem, with each person working on a computer. In this case, larger groups produced more ideas of higher quality than smaller groups. Electronic communication may have prevented the blocking effect observed in face-to-face brainstorming, because individuals could transmit their ideas any time without worrying about what others were saying at that moment.

Does this mean that direct social interaction—one of the fundamental features of a group—may actually hinder the kind of productivity that depends on such creative processes as brainstorming? It depends. Notice that the electronic group members still need to "hear" other people's ideas, because their own ideas were stimulated by the ideas of others. But when an individual is on a creative roll and ideas are coming fast and furious, interruptions by others are counterproductive. In this sense, direct social interaction may sometimes be an obstacle to reaching group goals. Recall that

illusion of efficacy The illusion that small groups are more effective than large groups.

much the same result was found in the study of how groups deal with un-shared information (Stasser, 1992): Face-to-face unstructured discussion did not turn out to be an effective way for individuals to share information.

One difference between a face-to-face group and a computer network is the greater cohesiveness of the face-to-face group. Does cohesiveness affect group productivity or decision-making ability?

Group Cohesiveness   Does a cohesive group outperform a noncohesive group? When we consider decision-making or problem-solving groups, two types of cohesiveness become important: *task-based cohesiveness* and *interpersonal cohesiveness* (Zaccaro & Lowe, 1988). Groups may be cohesive because the members respect each other's abilities to help obtain the group's goals; this is task-based cohesiveness. Other groups are cohesive because the members find each other to be likable; this is interpersonal cohesiveness.

Each type of cohesiveness influences group performance in a some-what different way, depending on the type of task facing the group. When a task does not require much interaction among members, task-based cohesiveness increases group productivity, but interpersonal cohesiveness does not (Zaccaro & McCoy, 1988). For example, if a group is working on writing a paper and each member is responsible for different parts of that paper, then productivity is increased to the extent that the members are committed to doing a good job for the group. The group members do not have to like each other to do the job well.

Now, it is true that when members of the group like each other, their cohesiveness increases the amount of commitment to a task and increases group interaction as well (Zaccaro & Lowe, 1988). But the time they spend interacting may take away from their individual time on the task, thus offsetting the productivity that results from task-based cohesiveness.

Some tasks require interaction, such as President Kennedy's advisory group. On these tasks groups that have high levels of both task-based and interactive cohesiveness perform better than groups that are high on one type but low on the other or that are low on both (Zaccaro & McCoy, 1988).

Cohesiveness can also detract from the successful completion of a task when group members become too concerned with protecting each other's feelings and do not allot enough attention to the actual task. Groups that are highly cohesive have members who are very concerned with one another. This may lead group members to stifle criticism of group decisions. This in fact is what happened in Kennedy's advisory group, according to the participants' memoirs and statements. People were afraid to say what they really thought of the plan to invade Cuba with a brigade of ill-trained exiles (Janis, 1972).

Members of strongly cohesive groups are less likely to disagree with each other than are members of less cohesive groups, especially if they are under time pressure to come up with a solution. Ultimately, then, very high cohesiveness may prevent a group from reaching a high-quality decision (Courtwright, 1978). Cohesiveness is a double-edged sword: It can help or hurt a group depending on the demands of the task.

Leadership Style   In what way is group decision-making ability or productivity affected by the style of its leader? In most groups, one person assumes a leadership role. Leadership may be formally conferred on a group member, or the leader may emerge, unappointed, because he or she has some special skills or knowledge, a "strong personality," or an interest in leading the group. The group leader, whether formally appointed or tacitly acknowledged, can exert a strong influence on the group.

Just as there are task-oriented (instrumental) groups and person-oriented (affiliative) groups, so there are task-oriented leaders and morale- (person-) oriented leaders. The success of these leadership styles may depend on the situation the leader encounters (Fiedler, 1967). Some situations favor a task-oriented leader; others favor a person-oriented leader. Personality and situations may interact to determine leadership effectiveness. This theory is known as the **contingency model** of leadership because good leadership is deemed contingent, or dependent, on the leader's personality characteristics *and* the qualities of the group situation (Fiedler, 1967).

The contingency model suggests that an effective leadership style must fit the situation. The same individual probably is not capable of leading in all circumstances. For example, placing a task-oriented leader into a situation that requires someone more sensitive to the morale of the group members is a recipe for failure. President Kennedy seemed to naturally express a task-oriented style. However, during the Bay of Pigs crisis, a situation that called for a task-oriented leader, one who would carefully examine information and alternatives, Kennedy may have been reluctant to assume that role.

For a somewhat different view of leadership, see the featured discussion "U.S. Presidents and Leadership Styles."

Are there gender-based differences in leadership style? The common wisdom is that women are person-oriented leaders and men are task-oriented leaders. But a review of the research on leadership roles of men and women reveals that both women and men lead in precisely the same way—both are task oriented—when they occupy powerful positions in organizations (Eagly & Johnson, 1990). It seems that organizational forces

contingency model A theory of leadership suggesting that effective leadership is dependent on the interaction between the leader's personality characteristics and the qualities of the group situation.

Is leadership a matter of being the right person, or is it more a matter of being in the right place at the right time? Abraham Lincoln, for example, is considered a great leader. Is it because he was a man of high intelligence and extraordinary foresight, or was the mantle of greatness laid upon him by the conditions that existed during his presidency?

Dean Simonton (1988) analyzed the biographies of the first 39 U.S. presidents. Although the political, economic, and social circumstances of any era play a profound role in the events that occur, Simonton found that the presidents could be reliably categorized by their leadership style. Some presidents demonstrated more than one style. The styles are as follows:

- *The interpersonal leader*. This style characterizes presidents who allowed their advisors independence, who were courteous and considerate, and who were willing to compromise. George Washington, Millard Fillmore (yes, he was a president), Gerald Ford, and Lincoln are in this group.
- *The charismatic leader*. This president has a flair for the dramatic, works on his self-image, deals skillfully with the press, and enjoys the ceremo-

nial part of his job. Andrew Jackson was charismatic, as were Franklin Roosevelt, John Kennedy, Teddy Roosevelt, Lyndon Johnson, and Ronald Reagan. These presidents influenced people by the sheer power of their personality.
- *The deliberative leader*. This leader comprehends his decisions, sees alternatives, is informed, weighs long-term consequences, and is cautious in action. Washington, John Adams, John Quincy Adams, and Thomas Jefferson are the prime examples of this style.
- *The creative leader*. This category includes presidents who initiated new programs and were innovative as president. Franklin Roosevelt, Jefferson, Kennedy, Johnson, and Nixon all fall into this group.
- *The neurotic leader*. The neurotic leader is more concerned with political success than with effective leadership. He tends to experience health problems in office, especially when under stress. He is a complicated and occasionally devious leader. Grant, Johnson, and

Nixon are prime examples of this style.

To what extent does the success of each of these leadership styles depend on the circumstances the leader encounters? Simonton's approach emphasizes the individual personalities of presidents as determinants of their success or failure. We, of course, have no way of knowing whether Teddy Roosevelt would have been a more or less successful president had he been president in another era. The lesson of social psychology is that leadership success or failure is a fortuitous combination of individual characteristics and situational factors.

---

*S*imonton's concept of leadership places a great deal of emphasis on the president's personality. How does this approach match Fiedler's contingency-model concept of leadership? Can you think of some other social behaviors that emphasize individual characteristics at the expense of situational ones? What about the individuals who have been president in your lifetime? Has their success or failure been determined more by the force of their personalities or by the events of the times?

minimize the tendency for men and women to manage in stereotypical ways. This finding underlines the importance of considering the environment in which leadership occurs.

Some other gender differences in leadership style do seem to exist. In a leaderless group, men tend to emerge as leaders (generally defined) more often than do women (Eagly & Karau, 1991). However, men are most likely to arise as leaders when the group has a short-term mission and when complex social interactions are not needed (Eagly & Karau, 1991). Generally, men are most likely to emerge as leaders in a task-oriented environment,

According to Fred Fiedler, the best way to decide whether a leader is task oriented or morale oriented is to have him or her rank co-workers, particularly the least preferred co-worker. In one such experiment, task-oriented leaders rated their least preferred co-worker (LPC) much lower than did morale-oriented leaders (Fiedler, 1967). That finding seems reasonable, since morale-oriented leaders try to maintain the positive feelings of the group. Rejecting one member would hurt group morale.

To find out what kind of leader you are, think of a person you find difficult to work with. You don't necessarily dislike this person; you simply find it very hard to get a job done when working with him or her. Now rank this person on the following traits by circling a number between 1 and 8 for each pair of adjectives.

Do you think that an individual's rating of the least preferred co-worker is the best way to measure leadership style? If not, what would you replace it with? Do you think this LPC scale fairly reflects your leadership style?

Pleasant	8	7	6	5	4	3	2	1	Unpleasant
Friendly	8	7	6	5	4	3	2	1	Unfriendly
Rejecting	1	2	3	4	5	6	7	8	Accepting
Tense	1	2	3	4	5	6	7	8	Relaxed
Distant	1	2	3	4	5	6	7	8	Close
Cold	1	2	3	4	5	6	7	8	Warm
Supportive	8	7	6	5	4	3	2	1	Hostile
Boring	1	2	3	4	5	6	7	8	Interesting
Quarrelsome	1	2	3	4	5	6	7	8	Harmonious
Gloomy	1	2	3	4	5	6	7	8	Cheerful
Open	8	7	6	5	4	3	2	1	Guarded
Backbiting	1	2	3	4	5	6	7	8	Loyal
Untrustworthy	1	2	3	4	5	6	7	8	Trustworthy
Considerate	8	7	6	5	4	3	2	1	Inconsiderate
Nasty	1	2	3	4	5	6	7	8	Nice
Agreeable	8	7	6	5	4	3	2	1	Disagreeable
Insincere	1	2	3	4	5	6	7	8	Sincere
Kind	8	7	6	5	4	3	2	1	Unkind

To calculate your score, add up the numbers you have circled for each of the adjective pairs. If your score is 56 or less, you tend to be a task-oriented (low LPC) leader. If your score is 63 or above, you tend to be a morale-oriented (high LPC) leader. If your score is between 57 and 62, you don't fall distinctly into either category; you may have some qualities of both types.

and women are slightly more likely than men to take command when social leadership is needed.

That men often emerge as group leaders may not relate solely to stereotypes. Men and women behave differently in groups. Men tend to make more task-oriented contributions than women do. It should not be surprising, then, that men emerge as leaders more often than women in a task-oriented group environment.

Every individual probably is inclined to be more task oriented or more person oriented when it comes to leadership. To find out what kind of leader *you* tend to be, complete the scale included in the featured discussion "What Kind of Leader Are You? The Least Preferred Co-worker (LPC) Scale."

THE DYNAMICS OF GROUP DECISION MAKING: GROUP POLARIZATION AND GROUPTHINK

Now that we have considered various aspects of group decision making, let's consider how the decision-making process works. Although we empower groups to make many important decisions for us, they do not always make good decisions. As we have seen, even a high-powered group of advisors to the president of the United States can make unfortunate decisions. We turn now to a consideration of two important and related aspects of group interaction and decision making: group polarization and groupthink.

Group Polarization

Earlier in this chapter we saw how membership in a group can enhance or diminish individual performance on a task. Groups can also exert an influence on individuals' opinions and attitudes.

The Risky Shift The first research on the impact of groups on individual opinions was conducted in the early 1960s. Researchers were interested in testing the common wisdom that groups make more conservative decisions than individuals do (Stoner, 1961). In one study, management students worked both individually and then in groups of six to solve dilemmas that involved deciding how much risk to take. Here is an example of one of these dilemmas:

> Mr. A, an electrical engineer, who is married and has one child, has been working for a large electronics corporation since graduating from college 5 years ago. He is assured of a lifetime job with a modest, though adequate, salary and liberal pension benefits upon retirement. On the other hand, it is very unlikely that his salary will increase much before he retires. While attending a convention, Mr. A is offered a job with a small, newly founded company that has a highly uncertain future. The new job would pay more to start and would offer the possibility of a share in the ownership if the company survived the competition of the larger firms.
>
> Imagine that you are advising Mr. A. Listed below are the several probabilities or odds of the new company proving financially sound. Please check the *lowest* probability that you would consider acceptable to make it worthwhile for Mr. A to take the new job.

The choices were 1 in 10, 3 in 10, 5 in 10, 7 in 10, 9 in 10, and "under no circumstances." The groups had to make a decision under a unanimity decision rule (consensus). Contrary to expectations, groups tended to recommend significantly riskier alternatives than did individuals. This difference between the individual and the group decisions is called the shift to risk, or the **risky shift effect.** Specifically, the risky shift occurs when the group decision (say, 3 in 10) is riskier than the average of the individual decisions (say, 7 in 10).

risky shift effect The tendency for a group to recommend riskier alternatives than individual group members would recommend on their own.

FIGURE 10-9 *The phenomenon of group polarization: Individual decision tendencies become more extreme after group discussion.*

In subsequent studies, the risky shift effect was found to vary in degree according to the nature of the problem. Generally, business and career decisions led groups to take greater risks than individuals took, and personal and romantic decisions led groups to become more cautious and to take fewer risks than individuals took (the cautious shift) (Turner, Wetherell, & Hogg, 1989).

As this line of research progressed, it became clear that the risky and cautious shifts were part of a more general phenomenon now known as **group polarization** (Moscovici & Zavalloni, 1969; Myers & Lamm, 1976). Group polarization occurs when the initial decision tendency of the group becomes more extreme following group discussion (Figure 10-9). For example, researchers asked French students about their attitudes toward Americans, which, prior to group discussion, had been negative (Moscovici & Zavalloni, 1969). After group discussion, researchers measured attitudes again and found that group discussion tended to "polarize," or pull the attitude to a more extreme position. The initial negative attitudes became even more negative after discussion.

group polarization The phenomenon that occurs when the initial decision tendency of the group becomes more extreme following group discussion.

In another study, researchers found that if a jury was initially leaning in the direction of innocence, group discussion led to a "shift to leniency." If, on the other hand, the jury was initially leaning in the direction of guilt, there was a "shift to severity" (Myers & Lamm, 1976). Group polarization can also be recognized in some of the uglier events in the real world. Groups of terrorists become more extreme, more violent, over time (McCauley & Segal, 1987). Extremity shifts, as we have seen, appear to be a normal aspect of group decision making (Blascovich & Ginsburg, 1974).

Why Does Group Polarization Occur? Following the original findings about the risky shift, group polarization theory generated increasing interest on the part of social psychologists. The search began for an underlying cause for the findings. Something that takes place during the group's discussion causes the shift. What is it?

Researchers focused on two processes in group discussion: social comparison and persuasive arguments. Group discussion, as we have seen, provides opportunities for social comparison. We can now compare how we think with how everyone else thinks. We might have thought that our private decision was a risky one, but then we find that other people have taken even riskier stands. This causes us to redefine our idea of riskiness and shift our opinion toward more extreme choices.

The second cause of the group polarization is persuasive arguments (Burnstein, 1982; Burnstein & Vinokur, 1977). We already have seen that people tend to share information they hold in common. This means that the arguments put forth and supported are those the majority of group members support. The majority can often persuade others to accept those arguments (Myers & Lamm, 1975). For example, most people in Kennedy's advisory group spoke in favor of a military response to Cuba and persuaded doubters of their wisdom.

Research has supported the idea that discussion polarizes groups. In one early study on the risky shift, group meetings were set up under several conditions (Wallach & Kogan, 1965). In some groups, members merely exchanged information about their views by passing notes; there was no discussion, just information exchange. In others, individuals discussed their views face-to-face. In some of the discussion groups, members were required to reach consensus; in others they were not. The researchers found that group discussion, with or without reaching consensus, was the only necessary and sufficient condition required to produce the risky shift. The mere exchange of information without discussion was not enough, and forcing consensus was not necessary (Wallach & Kogan, 1965).

Tajfel's social identity theory, discussed in Chapter 5, provides another explanation for group polarization. Briefly, this theory suggests that as we identify ourselves with a group, an in-group bias takes root. We perceive ourselves to be similar to other members of the in-group. According to this view, identification with a group reinforces our agreement with current opinions of the other members of the group and therefore leads to group polarization (Mackie & Cooper, 1984; Turner, Wetherell, & Hogg, 1989).

Groupthink

The finding that group decisions tend to be more extreme than the decisions of individuals is an important one. It offers some insight into how it is that groups composed of competent, intelligent individuals can reach poor decisions, including the decision to launch the Bay of Pigs invasion. In fact, the disastrous outcome of that decision led to a new area of study called *groupthink*.

The late Irving Janis (1972, 1982) carried out several post hoc (after the fact) analyses of what he terms historical fiascos. Janis found common threads running through these decision failures. He called this phenomenon *groupthink*, "a mode of thinking that people engage in when they are deeply involved in a cohesive in-group, when the members' striving for unanimity overrides their motivation to realistically appraise alternative courses of actions" (Janis, 1982, p. 9). **Groupthink** is a breakdown in the rational decision-making abilities of members of a cohesive group. As we have seen, members of a highly cohesive group become motivated to reach unanimity and protect the feelings of other group members and are less concerned with reaching the best decision.

In examining poor decisions and fiascos, we do have to acknowledge the benefits we gain from hindsight. From our privileged point of view here in the present, we can see what we believe to be the fatal flaws of many decisions of the past, especially those with disastrous outcomes. This is obviously dangerous from a scientific perspective (a danger that Janis recognized). It can lead us to overstate the power of groupthink-like processes. What would have happened, for example, if the invasion of Cuba had been a rousing success and a democratic government installed there? The decisions that we now view as disastrous would have been cheered, not jeered. How many historical decisions had all the markings of groupthink but led to good outcomes? It is important to keep a sense of perspective as we apply concepts like groupthink to both historical and contemporary events.

Conditions That Favor Groupthink   The crux of Janis's groupthink concept involved pressures toward uniformity that hinder the complete evaluation of the available courses of action and dangers. Janis suggested that this tendency was directly related to three factors:

1. *The cohesiveness of the group.* Generally, the more cohesive the decision-making group, the greater the risk that it will fall victim to groupthink.

2. *Stress.* The more stress, the greater the group's susceptibility to groupthink. Indeed, groups under stress do show a decrease in performance (Worchel & Shackelford, 1991).

3. *The persuasive strength of its leader.* A leader who is strong and highly directive (that is, makes his or her views known and pushes the group in that direction) sets a tone that favors the emergence of groupthink.

groupthink A breakdown in the rational decision-making abilities of members of a cohesive group when desire for unanimity overrides the concern for reaching a good decision.

Social psychologist Clark McCauley has provided a slightly different analysis. McCauley (1989) identified three conditions that he believed are always involved when groupthink occurs:

1. *Group insulation.* The decision-making group does not seek analysis and information from sources outside the group.
2. *Promotional leadership.* The leader presents his or her preferred solution to the problem before the group can evaluate all the evidence.
3. *Group homogeneity.* Groups that are made up of people of similar background and opinions are prone to have similar views.

These three antecedents, according to McCauley, lead the group to a premature consensus.

Symptoms of Groupthink   Groups that suffer from groupthink show a fairly predictable set of "symptoms." Unlike the antecedent conditions just discussed, which increase the likelihood of groupthink, the symptoms protect the group against negative feelings and anxieties during the decision process. Janis (1972) defined several major symptoms of groupthink:

1. *The illusion of invulnerability.* Group members believe that nothing can hurt them. For example, prior to the Japanese attack on Pearl Harbor in 1941, advisors to the U.S. commander believed that Pearl Harbor was invincible. Typically, this illusion leads to excessive optimism: The group believes that anything it does will turn out for the better.
2. *Rationalization.* Group members tend not to realistically evaluate information presented to them. Instead, they engage in collective efforts to rationalize away damaging information. For example, when the space shuttle *Challenger* exploded in 1986, officials apparently rationalized away information about the O-rings, whose failure caused the explosion. Negative information about the O-rings dating back as far as 1985 was available but ignored. Six months before the disaster, a NASA budget analyst had warned that the O-rings were a serious problem. His warning was labeled an "overstatement."
3. *A stereotyped view of the enemy.* If a group sees the enemy as too weak, evil, or stupid to do anything about the group's decision, they are displaying a stereotyped view of that enemy. The Bay of Pigs advisory group believed that the Cuban military was too weak and inept to withstand an invasion by 1,500 lightly armed Cuban refugees with antiquated aircraft. Instead, the invading force was met by a huge, well-trained, well-equipped Cuban army supported by advanced Soviet fighter jets.
4. *Conformity pressures.* In Chapter 8 we saw that majority influences can operate within a group to change the opinions of dissenting members. Strong conformity pressures are at work when groupthink emerges. That is, group members who raise objections are pressured to change their views. One of the engineers involved in the *Challenger* launching was initially opposed to the launch. Under extreme pressure from others, he changed his vote.

5. *Self-censorship.* Once it appears that anyone who disagrees with the group's view will be pressured to conform, members of the group who have dissenting opinions do not speak up because of the consequences. This leads to self-censorship. After the initial opposition to the *Challenger* launching was rejected rather harshly, for example, other engineers were less likely to express doubts.

6. *The illusion of unanimity.* Because of the strong atmosphere of conformity and the self-censorship of those members who have doubts about the group decision, the group harbors the illusion that everyone is in agreement.

7. *Mindguarding.* Just as a person who fears physical harm may take on a bodyguard, groups suffering from groupthink want protection from potentially damaging information. A mindguard is a group member who takes it upon him- or herself to protect the group from such information. According to Janis, these members assume their role spontaneously. They are not specifically appointed or told to protect the group. In the Bay of Pigs discussion, Robert Kennedy, the president's brother, apparently took it upon himself to be a mindguard. He told an advisor who had begun to express misgivings about the invasion plans that he might be right but it was best not to upset the president.

Preventing Groupthink What changes can leaders and groups make to minimize groupthink? Based on changes President Kennedy initiated after the Bay of Pigs, Janis has identified the following eight measures (1972):

1. The leader of the group should assign each member the role of critical evaluator. This person is to give a high priority to expressing doubts and raising questions.

2. The leader of the group should not make his or her views known to the group and should remain impartial. This prevents the leader from biasing the group with his or her views.

3. The group should be broken up into smaller subgroups, each with its own leader, to work on specific aspects of a problem. After working on parts of the problem, the subgroups should meet together as a whole group and work on the problem further.

4. Each member of the group should be encouraged to discuss the group's solutions with trusted aides or advisors outside the group.

5. Outside experts should be brought in, even if they do not agree with what the group's solution to the problem might be.

6. At each meeting one member should be appointed to play the role of "devil's advocate" to argue against the group.

7. If the decision affects another party, some of the group's discussion should focus on the potential reaction of that party.

8. After the decision has been made, the group should meet again for a "second chance" at evaluating the decision.

Groupthink Reconsidered: Group Dynamics for the 1990s The groupthink hypothesis attempts to explain historical fiascos by pointing to certain flaws and failures in group dynamics. This hypothesis has stood the test of time, gaining wide acceptance and stimulating much thought about decision-making groups. But, as with almost any theory, new information and ideas have led researchers to continue probing the original issues. Some social scientists have begun to look for factors other than those outlined by Janis that might lead groups to make bad decisions.

Glen Whyte (1989) suggests that group polarization, risk taking, and the possibility of fiasco all increase when a group "frames" a decision in terms of potential failure. As an example, consider the *Challenger* situation: If the spaceship wasn't launched, those in charge would be accused of failure and funding for the space program might be cut off. It seemed to make more sense to the decision makers to risk the launch than to cancel it. If the O-rings failed, the launching entailed a very big risk. But, after all, the O-rings had not failed in the past, and they would fail only in cold weather. No problem—the launch site was in Florida. Unfortunately, on the morning of the launch, the temperature fell to freezing. A disaster resulted. The way the group "framed" the decision—both alternatives, to go or not to go, carried risks—led them to make a bad choice.

Elements of groupthink have been identified in decisions leading up to the loss of the space shuttle Challenger, shown here as it explodes over Florida waters. These elements included conformity pressures, rationalization of damaging information, and self-censorship among those with dissenting views.

Whyte argues that if group members see all of their choices as having potentially negative outcomes, they are more likely to favor the risky decisions over the more cautious ones. The risk involved in the Bay of Pigs invasion, for example, had to be balanced against the negative consequences of doing nothing. Similarly, when NASA officials decided to launch the *Challenger*, they had to balance the potential for disaster against the negative outcomes of "no go," such as falling behind on launch schedules and having funds cut.

Whyte believes that groups that have made disastrous decisions were working in an environment that actually favored a risky decision over more cautious choices. In such situations, the group is likely to become polarized around a risky decision; group members will adopt attitudes that are more extreme once they have entered into group discussion. In other words, the manner in which a group frames a problem with respect to risk may be as important as faulty group dynamics in leading to bad decisions (Whyte, 1989).

Other researchers have examined some of Janis's other conclusions. Their work suggests that group cohesiveness may not be as crucial for the emergence of groupthink as Janis believed (Courtwright, 1978; Flowers, 1977), although directive leadership may be (Flowers, 1977). Recent research by Philip Tetlock and associates (1992) indicates that very cohesive groups may not be any more prone to groupthink than less cohesive groups. Tetlock also failed to find evidence that increasing stress levels makes groupthink more likely. What he did find was that groupthink could be best predicted by faulty decision-making structures and procedures. The second best predictor was **consensus seeking,** which leads groups to become more concerned with maintaining morale and getting everybody to agree than with the quality of the group decision (Tetlock, Peterson, McGuire, Chang, & Feld, 1992).

In other words, a leader who does not let group members speak freely and who controls the discussion is likely to foster a bad decision. A group that is more concerned with feelings than with quality decision making is also a prime candidate for groupthink. Groups that allow people to disagree, that promote critical analysis, and that have decision-making rules that help people contribute to the discussion are the least likely to fall prey to groupthink (Tetlock et al., 1992). In sum, then, this research indicates that the two most powerful factors involved in groupthink—and defective decision making—are procedural faults and consensus seeking.

Regardless of exactly what conditions and qualities lead to groupthink, we know that poor decisions, whether in government, business, schools, the community, or the family, can have a powerful effect on people's lives. When a poor decision is made and the outcome is disastrous, many observers rush to assign blame. It is far harder—but far more worthwhile—to try to understand the processes that underlie how groups work and make decisions. When we do that, we have the opportunity to improve decision making—and avoid disaster—in the future.

THE BAY OF PIGS REVISITED

President Kennedy continued to use the counsel of the men who advised him on the Bay of Pigs, but he never allowed the same group dynamics to prevail. His subsequent successful handling of the Cuban missile crisis reflected his ability to defuse groupthink and make effective use of expert advice. However, the same lessons apparently went unnoted by later presidents. Lyndon Johnson allowed himself to become mired in the Vietnam War by relying on the counsel of select policy advisors and ignoring warnings from other experts. And Richard Nixon found himself out of office after surrounding himself with advisors who assured him the public supported him on Watergate.

LOOKING AHEAD

In the four chapters of Part Two we have examined various forms of social influence. We considered the processes involved in persuasion, the forces at work in conformity and compliance, and the factors that contribute to

consensus seeking A tendency that leads groups to become more concerned with maintaining morale and getting everybody to agree than with the quality of the group decision.

obedience and disobedience. In this chapter we have looked at how individuals are affected by their participation and membership in groups. We shift our focus now to another aspect of social interaction—how we relate to others in our social world. Part Three, Social Relations, considers the forces at work when we form, maintain, and dissolve close relationships; when we behave aggressively, intentionally hurting others; and when we behave altruistically, going out of our way to help others.

CHAPTER REVIEW

1. *What is a group?*

A **group** is an assemblage of two or more individuals who influence one another through social interaction. Group members share perceptions of what constitutes appropriate behavior (**group norms**), and they have formal and informal roles. Group members are interdependent; that is, they depend on each other to meet group goals and they have emotional (affective) ties with each other. Groups can be either instrumental (existing to perform a task or reach a goal) or affiliative (existing for more general, usually social, reasons).

Groups vary in **cohesiveness,** the strength of the relationships that link the members of the group. Groups may be cohesive because the members like one another (interpersonal cohesiveness); because they are physically close to one another (propinquity); because they adhere to group norms; or because they help each other do a good job and therefore attain group goals (task-based cohesiveness).

2. *Why do people join groups?*

Groups help people meet their biological, psychological, and social needs. Groups were certainly useful in the evolutionary history of humans, aiding the species in its survival. Among the basic needs groups meet are social support; protection from loneliness; and social comparison, the process by which we compare our feelings, opinions, and behaviors with those of others in order to get accurate information about ourselves. People join groups to fulfill these needs and to enhance themselves.

3. *What is involved in the process of becoming a group member?*

Members of groups go through an ordered set of stages in the life cycle of membership. First they investigate a potential group to see if it will satisfy their needs. If they decide to join, they become socialized into the group, learning the group norms they must obey if they are to be worthy group members. Following this period of socialization, they become valued members, the maintenance stage of membership. At some point, as their needs change, they begin to wonder if the group is still meeting their needs and may begin to deviate from group norms. The group tries to retain them by resocializing them, but eventually they may exit the group and search for others that better meet their needs.

4. *What effect does an audience have on performance?*
The presence of other people or audiences may enhance our performance, a process known as **social facilitation.** Other times, the presence of a critical audience or an audience with high expectations decreases performance ("choking"). Research has shown that the presence of others helps when people perform a dominant, well-learned response but diminishes performance when they perform a skill not very well learned or novel (**social inhibition**). This may be due to increased effort as a result of increased arousal; or it may be due to anxiety about being judged (**evaluation apprehension**), which increases arousal; or, according to **distraction-conflict theory,** it may be due to conflicts for attention.

5. *How does being in a group affect performance and other behavior?*
Sometimes being in a group enhances performance. Other times, individuals performing in groups display **social loafing,** a tendency not to perform to capacity. This seems to occur when the task is not that important or when individual output cannot be evaluated. When people become **free riders,** others often work harder to make up for their lack of effort, a process known as **social compensation.**

When members of a crowd cannot be identified individually and therefore feel they have become anonymous, they may experience **deindividuation,** a loss of self-identity. Their sense of personal responsibility diminishes, and they tend to lose their inhibitions. This is more likely to happen if the crowd is large or if they are physically distant from a victim. Deindividuation can be a factor in mob violence. Loss of personal identity can also be positive, such as when group members act without thinking to save others' lives.

6. *When it comes to decision making, are groups better than individuals, or are individuals better than groups?*
Groups are better than the average group member in recognizing the truth of a solution and in rejecting poor solutions. Groups are also more effective in processing information, perhaps because they use **transactive memory systems.** Memory of information becomes a transaction among group members rather than an individual process. Groups do not perform better than their very best individual member.

Decision-making groups need to make good use of the available information, but it seems that face-to-face, unstructured discussion is not a very good way to inform group members of unshared information (data that only one or a few members have). The larger the group becomes, the more likely it is that participants will ignore information known to only a few of its members.

7. *How do groups reach decisions?*
Decision-making groups need to develop **decision rules**—rules about how many people must agree—in order to blend individual choices into a group outcome. Two common decision rules are majority and unanimity (consensus). Generally, the majority wins is the dominant

decision rule, but the selection of a decision rule often depends on the group task.

8. *What factors affect the decision-making ability and effectiveness of a group?*

Group composition is important to the decision-making ability of a group. Groups of high-ability individuals seem to perform better than groups of low-ability individuals, but members' abilities blend and mix in unexpected ways to produce a "group I.Q." Groups seem to perform better when members have complementary skills but when no single member is much more talented than the others.

Group size also affects group productivity. Although increasing group size increases the resources available to the group, there is also more **process loss;** that is, it becomes harder to reach a decision. And as more people are added to the group, the number of people who actually make a contribution—the group's functional size—does not increase.

Some groups and group processes offer an **illusion of efficacy**—people think they are more effective than they are. This is true of small groups, which many people erroneously think are better at solving social dilemmas than larger groups, and it is true of brainstorming, which many people think is a better way of producing ideas than individual efforts.

Another factor in group effectiveness is group cohesiveness. When a task does not require much interaction among members, task-based cohesiveness—cohesiveness based on respect for each other's abilities—increases group productivity, but interpersonal cohesiveness—cohesiveness based on liking for each other—does not. Sometimes interpersonal cohesiveness can impede the decision-making abilities of the group, because people are afraid of hurting each other's feelings.

Leadership is also a factor in group effectiveness. According to the **contingency model** of leadership, good leadership depends on the personal characteristics of the individual leader in combination with the characteristics of the situation.

9. *What is group polarization?*

Group decision making often results in **group polarization**—that is, the initial decision tendency of the group becomes more extreme following group discussion. Groups tend to make decisions that are riskier than the decisions their members would make as individuals, a difference called the **risky shift effect.** It seems that the group discussion pulls the members' attitudes toward more extreme positions, as a result both of social comparison and of persuasive arguments.

10. *What is groupthink?*

Groups often make bad decisions when they become more concerned with keeping up their members' morale rather than with reaching a realistic decision. This lack of critical thinking can lead to **groupthink,** a breakdown in the rational decision-making abilities of members of a cohesive group. The group becomes driven by **consensus seeking;**

members do not want to "rock the boat." This was what appeared to happen to Kennedy's advisors during the Bay of Pigs fiasco.

Groupthink is favored by group cohesiveness, stress, and the persuasive strength of the leader. It is also more likely to occur when a group is insulated and homogeneous and has a leader who promotes a particular point of view. Several measures can be taken to prevent groupthink, including encouraging a critical attitude among members, discussing group solutions with people outside the group, and bringing in outside experts who don't agree with the group's solution.

Another approach suggests that group polarization, risk taking, and the possibility of a disastrous decision being reached all increase when a decision is framed in terms of potential failure. If all outcomes are seen as potentially negative, according to this view, group members will tend to favor the riskier ones over the more cautious ones. Finally, groupthink has been found to occur more often when the group process doesn't allow everyone to speak freely and fully and when group leaders become obsessed with maintaining morale.

SUGGESTIONS FOR FURTHER READING

Dennis, A. R., & Valacich, J. S. (1993). Computer brainstorms: More heads are better than one. *Journal of Applied Psychology, 78,* 531–537.
  While research with face-to-face groups has shown that brainstorming is not an efficient way of producing new ideas, this study shows that use of electronic computer-mail techniques can improve the exchange of ideas.
Feinstein, J. (1989). *Forever's team.* New York: Simon & Schuster.
  An extraordinary look at how membership in a group—a college basketball team—changed the lives of its members.
Hogg, M. A., & Abrams, D. (Eds.). (1993). *Group motivation.* London: Harvester/Wheatsheaf.
  Enlightening and readable coverage of how groups form and function.
Janis, I. L. (1982). *Groupthink* (2nd ed.). Boston: Houghton Mifflin.
  The classic study of why group decisions in diplomacy and war can go wrong.

Part Three
SOCIAL RELATIONS

Perhaps even more basic to human social life than how we think about one another and how we influence one another is how we interact with one another. Social interaction is the third broad area of interest to social psychologists. Why are we attracted to some people and repelled by others? What forces keep us in relationships, and what dynamics lead to their decline? Why do we sometimes lash out at those around us, seeking to inflict pain or injury on other human beings? What is going on when we offer help to those in need, and why do we sometimes ignore them, thinking only of our own lives?

Part Three considers the dynamics of social relations. It begins with interpersonal attraction, considering why we human beings establish relationships with each other, how relationships change over time, and how passion, intimacy, and commitment mix in loving and "liking" relationships. The discussion then moves on to interpersonal aggression, exploring the various models that have been proposed to explain this darker side of human nature. The last chapter of this part examines altruism and helping behavior, focusing particularly on the conditions that make it more likely that people will help those in need. In all these explorations, although we find the predictable and the explainable, we also encounter the mystery of the human heart, as it manifests in contradictory gestures of love and avoidance, of frustration and hostility, of empathy, egoism, and pure selflessness.

Chapter 11
Interpersonal Attraction and Close Relationships

*B*oth had been born in California and had lived in the San Francisco Bay Area. Both eventually left the United States to live in Paris. The first meeting of these two people, who would be lifelong friends and lovers, did not begin very well. They had become acquainted the previous night at a Paris restaurant and had arranged an appointment for the next afternoon at Gertrude's apartment. Gertrude was in a rage when Alice was a half-hour late, perhaps in anticipation of the meeting. Gertrude met her guest at the door like a "vengeful goddess," informing her that she was "not accustomed to wait."

But Gertrude soon recovered her good humor, and they went walking in the streets of Paris. They found that they both loved walking, and they began to share their thoughts and feelings as they strolled. They stopped for ices and cakes in a lit-

tle shop that Gertrude liked because it reminded her of San Francisco. The day went so well that Gertrude suggested dinner at her apartment the following evening. Thus began a relationship that would last for nearly 40 years.

Alice B. Toklas was small and dark. Gertrude Stein was large, weighing over 200 pounds, with short hair and a striking roman face. Neither was attractive in the conventional sense. Both loved art and literature and opera. They were in the right place. Paris in the early years of this century was home to great painters like Pablo Picasso and Henri Matisse and to enormously talented writers like Ernest Hemingway and F. Scott Fitzgerald. Gertrude knew them all. They flocked to her home to talk, listen, and bask in Gertrude's presence.

Alice moved into Gertrude's apartment, for it was Gertrude who had a steady supply of money. Gertrude, who had dropped out of medical school in her final year, had decided to write novels. As the two women grew closer, their walks grew longer and their talks more intimate. They traveled to Italy, and it was there, outside Florence, that Gertrude proposed that they "marry." Although of course they couldn't formally marry, they shared each other's lives fully.

Then, in 1946, Gertrude, now 70, displayed the first signs of the cancer that would soon kill her. Gertrude handled this crisis in character, forcefully refusing any medical treatment. Not even her lifelong companion could convince her to do otherwise.

When, several months later, Gertrude collapsed, she was rushed to a hospital in Paris. In her hospital room before the surgery, Gertrude grasped her companion's small hand and asked, "What is the answer?" Tears streamed down Alice's face as she replied, "I don't know, Lovey."

The hospital attendants put Gertrude Stein on a cot and rolled her toward the operating room. Alice murmured words of affection. Gertrude commanded the attendants to stop. Turning to Alice, she said, "If you don't know the answer, then what is the question?" Gertrude settled back on the cot and chuckled softly. It was the last time they saw each other (Burnett, 1972; Simon, 1977; Toklas, 1963).

We have briefly recounted what was perhaps the most famous literary friendship of this century, the relationship between Gertrude Stein and Alice B. Toklas. Stein and Toklas were not married. They did not flaunt their sexual relationship, for the times in which they lived were not particularly accommodating to what Stein called their "singular" preferences. Yet their partnership involved all the essential elements of a *close relationship*: intimacy, friendship, love, and sharing. Philosophers have commented that a friend multiplies one's joys and divides one's sorrows. This, too, was characteristic of their relationship.

In this chapter we explore the nature of close relationships. We ask such questions as, What draws two people together into a close relationship, whether a friendship or a more intimate love relationship? What influences attractiveness and attraction? How do close relationships develop and evolve, and how do they stand up to conflict and destructive impulses? What are the components of love relationships? And finally, what are friendships and how do they differ from love? These are some of the questions we address in this chapter.

THE ROOTS OF INTERPERSONAL ATTRACTION AND CLOSE RELATIONSHIPS

It is a basic human characteristic to be attracted to others, to build important relationships with friends and lovers. What are the roots of interpersonal attraction and close relationships? In this section we explore two needs that underlie attraction and relationships: the need for affiliation and the need for intimacy. Not everyone has the social skills or resources necessary to initiate and maintain close relationships. Therefore, we will also look at the emotions of social anxiety and loneliness.

FIGURE 11-1 *Some people have a higher need for affiliation than others. These individuals tend to seek out the company of friends and acquaintances and place themselves in settings where social interaction is likely, such as a common study room. People with a lower need for affiliation might choose a more solitary setting to read or study.*

Affiliation and Intimacy

Although each of us can endure, and perhaps even value, periods of solitude, for most of us extended solitude is aversive. After a time we begin to crave the company of others. People have a **need for affiliation,** a need to establish and maintain relationships with others (Wong & Csikzentmihalyi, 1991). Contact with friends and acquaintances provides us with emotional support, attention, and the opportunity to evaluate the appropriateness of our opinions and behavior through the process of social comparison. The need for affiliation is the fundamental factor underlying our interpersonal relationships.

People who are high in the need for affiliation wish to be with friends and others more than do people who are low in the need for affiliation, and they tend to act accordingly (Figure 11-1). For example, in one study, college men who had a high need for affiliation picked living situations that increased the chances for social interaction. They were more likely to have more housemates or to be willing to share a room than men with a lower need for affiliation (Switzer & Taylor, 1983). Men and women show some differences in the need for affiliation. Teenage girls, for example, have been found to spend more time with friends and less often wished to be alone than did teenage boys (Wong & Csikzentmihalyi, 1991). This is in keeping with other findings that women show a higher need for affiliation than do men.

But merely being with others is often not enough to satisfy our social needs. We also have a **need for intimacy,** a need for close and affectionate relationships (McAdams, 1982). Intimacy, with friends or lovers, involves sharing and disclosing personal information. Individuals with a high need for intimacy tend to be warm and affectionate and to show concern about other people. Women generally seem to display a much greater need for intimacy than men do (McAdams, 1989).

need for affiliation A need to establish and maintain relationships with others.

need for intimacy A need for close and affectionate relationships in which personal information is disclosed and sharing occurs.

Lonely or just alone? Human beings need some solitude, but they also need close relationships. People feel lonely when their relationships are not giving them the warmth and intimacy they feel they need.

The needs for affiliation and intimacy are positive social needs that motivate us to approach other people. They are the roots of interpersonal attraction, which is defined as the desire to start and maintain relationships with others. But there are also emotions that may stand in the way of our fulfilling these needs and forming relationships. We look at these emotions next.

Loneliness and Social Anxiety

Loneliness is a psychological state that results when we perceive an inadequacy in our relationships—a discrepancy between the way we want our relationships to be and the way they actually are (Peplau & Perlman, 1982). When we are lonely, we lack the high-quality intimate relationships that we need. Loneliness may occur within the framework of a relationship. For example, women often expect more intimacy in marriage than they get and that lack of intimacy can be a cause of loneliness in married women (Tornstam, 1992).

Loneliness is common during adolescence and young adulthood, times of life when old friendships fade and new ones must be formed. For example, consider an 18-year-old going off to college. As she watches her parents drive away, she is likely to feel, along with considerable excitement, a sense of loneliness or even abandonment. New college students often believe that they will not be able to form friendships and that no one at school cares about them. The friendships they make don't seem to match their high school friendships in intimacy. These students often don't realize that everybody else is pretty much in the same boat. Loneliness is often a significant factor when a student drops out of school.

Loneliness is a subjective experience and not dependent on the number of people we have surrounding us (Peplau & Perlman, 1982). We can be alone and yet not be lonely—sometimes we want and need solitude. On

loneliness A psychological state that results when we perceive an inadequacy in our relationships—a discrepancy between the way we want our relationships to be and the way they actually are.

the other hand, we can be surrounded by people and feel desperately lonely. Our feelings of loneliness are strongly influenced by how we evaluate our personal relationships (Peplau & Perlman, 1982). We need close relationships with a few people to buffer ourselves against feeling lonely.

As suggested earlier, loneliness can be associated with certain relationships or certain times of life. There are, however, individuals for whom loneliness is a lifelong experience. Such individuals have difficulty in forming relationships with others; consequently, they go through life with few or no close relationships. What is the source of their difficulty? The problem for at least some of these people may be that they lack the basic social skills needed to form and maintain relationships. Experiences of awkward social interactions exacerbate these individuals' uneasiness in social settings. Lacking confidence, they become increasingly anxious about their interactions with others.

Social anxiety arises from a person's expectation of negative encounters with others (Leary, 1983a, 1983b). Socially anxious people anticipate uncomfortable interactions and think that other people will not like them very much. When Alice Toklas met the literary and artistic notables in Gertrude Stein's circle, she often tried to make herself as inconspicuous as possible. One day Stein told Toklas that even Picasso was nervous at these gatherings. Toklas didn't believe this at first (Stein was quite capable of exaggeration), but whether it was true or not, Toklas soon gained confidence. People who suffer from social anxiety tend to display some of the following interrelated traits (Nichols, 1974):

- A sensitivity and fearfulness of disapproval and criticism.
- A strong tendency to perceive and respond to criticism that does not exist.

social anxiety A feeling of discomfort that arises from a person's expectation of negative encounters with others.

- Low self-evaluation.
- Rigid ideas about what constitutes "appropriate" social behavior.
- A tendency to foresee negative outcomes to anticipated social interactions, which arouses anxiety.
- An increased awareness and fear of being evaluated by others.
- Fear of situations in which withdrawal would be difficult or embarrassing.
- The tendency to overestimate one's reaction to social situations (for example, believing that you are blushing when you are not).
- An inordinate fear of the anxiety itself.
- A fear of being perceived as losing control.
- Progressive buildup of social difficulties.
- An unpredictability of the anxiety response.

Attachment and Close Relationships

The habits of the heart may be shaped by our earliest relationships. Developmental psychologists have noted that infants form attachments with their parents or primary caregivers based on the kinds of interactions they have (Ainsworth, 1992). These patterns of attachment, or *attachment styles,* evolve into **working models,** mental representations of what the individual expects to happen in close relationships (Shaver, Hazan, & Bradshaw, 1988). Attachment theory suggests that the attachment styles developed in early childhood govern the way individuals form and maintain close relationships in adulthood. Three attachment styles have been identified: secure, anxious/ambivalent, and avoidant. Statements describing each style are shown in Table 11-1.

According to research, people who identified their attachment style as secure characterized their lovers as happy, friendly, and trusting and said that they and their partner were tolerant of each other's faults (Shaver et al., 1988). Avoidant lovers were afraid of intimacy, experienced roller-coaster emotional swings, and were constantly jealous. Anxious/ambivalent lovers experienced extreme sexual attraction coupled with extreme jealousy. Love is very intense for anxious lovers because they strive to merge totally with their mate; anything less increases their anxiety. This experience of love for anxious lovers is a strong desire for union and a powerful intensity of sexual attraction and jealousy. It is no accident that anxious lovers, more than any other style, report love at first sight (Shaver et al., 1988).

Attachment theory is supported by evidence that securely attached individuals felt positively toward their early family relationships whereas avoidant adults reported painful separation from the mother and exhibited distrust of others (Feeney & Noller, 1990). Anxiously attached adults reported a lack of independence and a wish for a deep and strong love relationship.

In dating relationships, the secure style is associated with satisfaction and trust. One study of 144 dating couples found that the secure style was correlated with positive feelings about the relationship whereas anxious and avoidant styles were correlated with more negative emotions (Simpson, 1990). Of those couples who broke up, avoidant-style men were less upset by the dissolution of the relationship than anyone else. This, too, follows from attachment theory, since avoidant individuals are less emotionally involved in the first place.

working model A mental representation of what an individual expects to happen in a close relationship.

TABLE 11-1

ADULT ATTACHMENT STYLES, AS INDICATED BY RESPONSES TO THE QUESTION, WHICH OF THE FOLLOWING BEST DESCRIBES YOUR FEELINGS?

	Answers and Percentages	
	Newspaper Sample	University Sample
Secure I find it relatively easy to get close to others and am comfortable depending on them and having them depend on me. I don't worry about being abandoned or about someone getting too close to me.	56%	56%
Avoidant I am somewhat uncomfortable being close to others; I find it difficult to trust them completely, difficult to allow myself to depend on them. I am nervous when anyone gets too close, and often, love partners want me to be more intimate than I feel comfortable about.	25%	23%
Anxious/Ambivalent I find that others are reluctant to get as close as I would like. I often worry that my partner doesn't really love me or won't want to stay with me. I want to merge completely with another person, and this desire sometimes scares people away.	19%	20%

From Shaver, Hazan, and Bradshaw, 1988.

Are attachment styles a factor in long-term relationships? In a study of 322 young married couples, all under age 30, a tendency was found for those with similar attachment styles to marry one another (Senchak & Leonard, 1992). Attachment style is not destiny, however. This is shown by the observation that people may display different attachment styles in different relationships (Bartholomew & Horowitz, 1991). None of these findings, however, come from long-term studies on the effects of attachment styles beyond childhood. Longitudinal research that follows individuals from infancy at least until early adulthood would give us more definitive information about whether early attachment styles really influence the way we respond in adult love relationships.

DETERMINANTS OF INTERPERSONAL ATTRACTION

What determines why we are attracted to and seek to form relationships with some individuals but not others? Social psychologists have developed a number of models addressing this question. In this section we look at several of these models. We then look at some specific factors identified by these models that play a role in attraction: physical proximity, similarity, and physical attractiveness.

Models of Interpersonal Attraction

One obvious reason we are attracted to specific other people is that they provide rewards for us. This is the central idea behind **reward theory,** proposed by Theodore Newcomb (1961), who noted that the degree of attraction we feel toward another person varies according to the frequency with which that person rewards us. Attraction depends on mutually rewarding relations. (While reward theory emphasizes mutual reward, we are also attracted to people who do not feel the same about us. "Unrequited love" is discussed later in this chapter.)

Just how do others reward us? Newcomb noted several ways in which individuals may find others rewarding. First, simply being near people we like is rewarding *(physical proximity)*. Second, we are rewarded when others agree with our ideas *(similarity)*. Third, Newcomb suggested, we are rewarded when others fulfill our needs *(complementarity)*. Thus, for example, a dependent person would be attracted to someone who is nurturant and independent, and that person in turn would be attracted to the dependent person. As we shall see, ample evidence supports physical proximity and similarity. Complementarity is *not* very well supported, however (Rawlins, 1992).

Newcomb's idea that rewards influence attraction was developed further in **reinforcement-affect theory,** proposed by Donn Byrne and Gerald Clore (Byrne, 1971; Byrne & Clore, 1970). The theory builds on basic principles of learning. We associate positive affect with people and events that are rewarding to us and negative affect with people and events that are distasteful to us. Having a good time is rewarding to us; being uncomfortable is distasteful. Through a process of classical conditioning, a person we have met—initially a neutral stimulus—becomes associated with positive affect if we have a good time while with him or her or with negative affect if we feel uncomfortable in the person's presence. Thus, the individual takes on reinforcing qualities, and interpersonal attraction increases or decreases on further exposure to him or her.

A third model of interpersonal attraction, **balance theory,** proposed by Fritz Heider (1958), looks at relationships from the point of view of the individuals experiencing them. From the point of view of an individual, a *balanced relationship* occurs when that individual and another have the same interests and views. A balanced relationship is rewarding; an unbalanced relationship is not. Thus, as a rule, balance in a relationship increases attraction, whereas unbalance reduces attraction.

Think for a moment about a good friend of yours and how you would feel if you suddenly found out that she had a totally different opinion than you did on an important issue, such as abortion or human rights. Your relationship would be unbalanced and uncomfortable. You and your friend could balance the relationship either by one of you changing your opinion or by deciding not to talk about that issue. Good friends can sometimes tolerate imbalances on certain issues for the sake of the friendship. But

reward theory The theory that the degree of attraction we feel toward another person varies according to the frequency with which that person rewards us.

reinforcement-affect theory The theory that we associate positive affect with people (and events) that are rewarding to us and negative affect with people (and events) that are distasteful to us.

balance theory A theory that looks at relationships from the point of view of the individuals experiencing them. A balanced relationship, which is rewarding to both partners, occurs when one individual and another have the same interests and views.

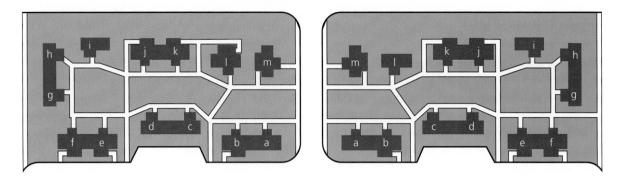

FIGURE 11-2 *Student residences in a study of physical proximity and the formation of friendships. Students in residences that faced the street (a and m) formed fewer friendships within the community than students in residences that faced the courtyard. Physical proximity is an important factor in interpersonal attraction.* From Festinger, Schachter, and Back, 1959.

well-balanced relationships are more comfortable and more rewarding than unbalanced ones.

Physical Proximity

How did you and your best friend first meet? Most likely, you met because you happened to be physically close to each other at some point in your life. For example, you might have been neighbors or sat next to each other in elementary school. Physical proximity, or physical immediacy, is an important determinant of attraction, especially at the beginning of a relationship.

The importance of physical proximity in the formation of friendships was shown by a study of the friendship patterns that developed among students living in on-campus residences for married students (Festinger, Schachter, & Back, 1959). In one of the residences studied, housing consisted of small units arranged around a courtyard. All the units except *a* and *m* faced the courtyard; *a* and *m* faced the street (see Figure 11-2). Students living in units *a* and *m* had fewer friends within the mini-community than did students living in units facing the courtyard. Moreover, as shown in Figure 11-3, as the physical distance between units *increased,* the number of friendships *decreased.* Students living close to one another were more likely to become friends than those living far apart.

Physical proximity is such a powerful determinant of attraction that it may even overshadow other, seemingly more important, factors. One study looked at friendship choices among police recruits in a police academy class (Segal, 1974). Recruits were assigned to seats alphabetically, and the single best predictor of interpersonal attraction turned out to be the letter that a person's last name started with. Simply put, those whose names were close in the alphabet and were thus seated near each other were more likely to become friends than those whose names were not close in the alphabet and were thus seated apart. The proximity effect proved more important than variables such as common interests and religion.

Why is proximity so important at the beginning stages of a friendship? The answer seems to have two parts: familiarity and the opportunity for interaction. To understand the role of familiarity, think about this common experience. You buy a new tape or compact disc, but when you first listen to it, you don't like it very much. However, after repeated listenings, it "grows on you." That is, exposure to the new music seems to increase your appreci-

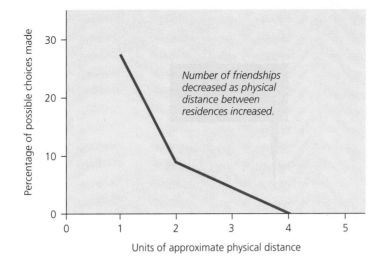

FIGURE 11-3 *Number of friendships made in relation to physical distance between residences. As the distance between residences increased, the number of friendships decreased. This measure provided further evidence that physical proximity and interpersonal attraction are strongly related.* From Festinger, Schachter, and Back, 1959.

ation of it. A similar effect occurs with people we encounter. Both are examples of the *mere exposure effect* (as described in Chapter 6), in which repeated exposure to a stimulus enhances one's positive feeling toward that stimulus. Since it was first identified in 1968 by Robert Zajonc, there have been over 200 studies of the mere exposure effect (Bornstein, 1989). These studies used a wide range of stimuli, and in virtually every instance, repeated exposure to a stimulus produced liking.

Physical proximity, in addition to exposing us to other people, also increases the chances that we will interact with them. That is, proximity also promotes liking because it gives us an opportunity to find out about each other. Physical proximity and the nature of the interaction combine to determine liking (Schiffenbauer & Schavio, 1976). If we discover that the other person has similar interests and attitudes, we will be encouraged to pursue the interaction.

There are, however, limits to the effects of physical proximity. Physical proximity can conflict with our need for *personal space*. We each define the immediate space around us as our own. We set up an invisible boundary, and when people cross it uninvited, we are annoyed and tend to react defensively (Sommer, 1969). Think about how you would feel if you were in an uncrowded theater and someone came and sat right next to you. You probably would look upon that person with suspicion and might respond by leaning away or even moving to another seat. In this case, physical proximity makes it less likely that you will be attracted to another person.

Similarity

The importance of similarity as a determinant of interpersonal attraction is suggested by all three models we looked at. Similarity in attitudes and beliefs, interests, personality, and even physical appearance strongly influences the likelihood of interpersonal attraction. And the more serious the relationship with another person, the more we search for similarity across a variety of areas.

One important element in interpersonal attraction is similarity—in attitudes, interests, lifestyles, even physical qualities like size and stamina. These partners share a spirit of adventure and are closely matched in physical appearance.

Clearly, there are many possible points of similarity between people. Attitude similarity, for example, might mean that two people are both Democrats, are both Catholics, and in addition to their political and religious beliefs, have similar views on a wide range of other issues. However, it's not the absolute *number* of similar attitudes between individuals that influences the likelihood and strength of attraction. Far more critical are the *proportion* and *importance* of similar attitudes. It does little good if someone agrees with you on everything except for the one attitude that is *central* to your life (Byrne & Nelson, 1965).

What about the notion that, in romantic relationships, opposites attract? This notion is essentially what Newcomb called *complementarity.* As already mentioned, researchers have found little evidence for complementarity (Duck, 1988). Instead, a **matching principle** seems to apply in romantic relationships. People tend to become involved with a partner with whom they are usually closely matched in terms of physical attributes or social status (Schoen & Wooldredge, 1989).

Different kinds of similarity may have different implications for attraction. If you and someone else are similar in *interests,* then liking results. Similarity in *attitudes,* on the other hand, leads to respect for the other person. In a study of college freshmen, similarity in *personality* was found to be the critical factor determining the degree of satisfaction in friendships (Carli, Ganley, & Pierce-Otay, 1991). This study found similarity in *physical attractiveness* to have some positive effect on friendships but not a large one.

Why does similarity promote attraction? Attitude similarity promotes attraction in part because of our need to verify the "correctness" of our beliefs. Through the process of *social comparison* we test the validity of our beliefs by comparing them to those of our friends and acquaintances (Hill, 1987). When we find that other people believe as we do, we can be more confident that our attitudes are valid. It is rewarding to know that someone we like thinks the way we do. It shows how smart we both are. Similarity

matching principle The tendency for people to become involved with a partner with whom they are closely matched in terms of physical attributes or social status.

may also promote attraction because we believe we can predict how a similar person will behave (Hatfield, Walster, & Traupmann, 1978).

Taking a somewhat different view of the effect of similarity, Milton Rosenbaum (1986) argued that it is not so much that we are attracted to similar others as that we are repulsed by people who are dissimilar. Further examination of this idea that *dissimilarity breeds repulsion* suggests that dissimilarity serves as an initial filter in the formation of relationships. Once a relationship begins to form, however, similarity becomes the fundamental determinant of attraction (Byrne, Clore, & Smeaton, 1986; Smeaton, Byrne, & Murnen, 1989). Thus the effect of similarity on attraction may be a two-stage process, with dissimilarity and other negative information leading us to make the initial "cuts," and similarity and other positive information then determining with whom we become close.

Physical Attractiveness

Physical attractiveness is an important factor in the early stages of a relationship. Research shows, not surprisingly, that we find physically attractive people more appealing than unattractive people, at least on initial contact (Eagly, Ashmore, Makhijani, & Longo, 1991). Moreover, as will be discussed, our society values physical attractiveness, so a relationship with an attractive person is socially rewarding to us.

In their now-classic study of the effects of physical attractiveness on dating, Elaine Hatfield and her colleagues led college students to believe that they had been paired at a dance based on their responses to a personality test, but in fact the researchers had paired the students randomly (Hatfield, Aronson, Abrahams, & Rottman, 1966). At the end of the evening, the couples evaluated each other and indicated how much they would like to date again. For both males and females, the desire to date again was best predicted by the physical attractiveness of the partner. This is not particularly surprising, perhaps, because after only one brief date the partners probably had little other information to go on.

Physical attractiveness affects not only our attitudes toward others but also our interactions with them. A study of couples who had recently met found that, regardless of gender, when one person was physically attractive, the other tried to intensify the interaction (Garcia, Stinson, Ickes, Bissonette, & Briggs, 1991). Men were eager to initiate and maintain a conversation no matter how little reinforcement they got. Women tried to quickly establish an intimate and exclusive relationship by finding things they had in common and by avoiding talk about other people.

There do, however, seem to be gender differences in the importance of physical attractiveness. Generally, women are less overwhelmed

Compared with average-looking people, physically attractive individuals like Kim Basinger and Alec Baldwin enjoy many advantages, including more attention, more opportunities, and more positive responses from others. Research indicates that the preference for attractive faces may have an innate component.

by attractive males than are men by attractive females (Buss, 1988a). Women are more likely than are men to report that attributes other than physical attractiveness, such as a sense of humor, are important to them.

Dimensions of Physical Attractiveness   What specific physical characteristics make someone attractive? Facial appearance has been shown to strongly affect our perceptions of attractiveness through much of our life span (McArthur, 1982; Zebrowitz, Olson, & Hoffman, 1993). Moreover, various aspects of facial appearance have specific effects. For example, facially attractive people are seen as more warm, honest, and sincere when their face has a babyish quality (Berry, 1991).

One group of researchers suspected that people find symmetrical faces more attractive than asymmetrical faces (Thornhill & Gangestad, 1994). They took photographs of males and females, fed those photos into a computer, created computer versions of the faces, and made precise measurements of the symmetry of the faces. They then asked subjects to rate the computer-generated images for attractiveness. They found that people do judge symmetrical faces to be more attractive than asymmetrical ones.

The researchers also asked the photographed students to fill out questionnaires about their sex and social lives. Those with symmetrical faces reported that they were sexually active earlier than others and had more friends and lovers. Why should symmetry and facial features in general be so important? The answer may lie more in our biology than in our psychology, an issue we explore later in the chapter.

Physique also profoundly affects our perceptions of attractiveness. Our society has widely shared notions of which bodily attributes are attractive. We have positive perceptions of people who fit these notions and negative perceptions of those who do not. We sometimes even display discriminatory behavior against those who deviate too far from cultural standards.

People can be categorized by body type into ectomorphs (thin, perhaps underweight), mesomorphs (athletic build), and endomorphs (overweight). Positive personality traits tend to be attributed to mesomorphs and negative ones to people with the other body types (Ryckman et al., 1991). There is some ambivalence about ectomorphs, especially as societal attitudes toward thinness seem to shift, influenced by such factors as an increasing health consciousness and an association of excessive thinness with acquired immunodeficiency syndrome (AIDS). Perceptions of endomorphs, in contrast, remain consistently negative. For a closer look at the implications of these negative perceptions, see the featured discussion "The Stigma of Obesity." Of course, some people are more intensely attuned to physical appearance than are others. It appears that those people who are most conscious of their own appearance are the most likely to stereotype others on the basis of physique.

Attractiveness judgments and stereotyping in everyday life may not be as strong as they are in some laboratory studies. In these studies we make "pure" attraction judgments: We see only a face or a physique. When we deal with people, we evaluate an entire package even if much of what we

Sharon Russell, who is now a successful nurse in a Florida hospital, was once thrown out of a nursing school program. She had fulfilled all the program requirements, and her grades were good, but she wasn't allowed to graduate. The reason? Russell weighed over 250 pounds.

Russell has frequent experiences with the social consequences of obesity, although they pale in comparison with this single act of discrimination. She states that "people make me feel like I'm in a circus on display" and that people initially assume that she is "lazy, stupid, and not motivated." Sharon's problems are shared to some degree by the 25–30% of Americans who are obese—that is, who are 25% or more above their ideal weight.

As Russell's remarks make clear, the problems lie largely in the attitudes of other people. Although ideas of beauty have changed over time, and although plumpness has sometimes been considered acceptable or even pleasing, obesity has always been condemned. In *The Canterbury Tales,* written in the 14th century, Chaucer refers to gluttony as sinful, "full of all wickedness." In more recent times we have Jabba the Hutt, a villain in the *Star Wars* movie trilogy, who is depicted as an obese and grotesque creature.

Research confirms that obese individuals are subject to negative stereotyping in our society. In one study (Harris, 1990), subjects judged a stimulus person who was depicted as either normal weight or (with the help of extra clothing) obese. They evaluated "Chris," the stimulus person, along several dimensions, includ-

ing the likelihood that Chris was dating or married, Chris's self-esteem, and Chris's ideal romantic partner. The results, almost without exception, reflected negative stereotyping of an obese Chris compared to a normal-weight Chris. Subjects judged that the obese Chris was less likely to be dating or married compared to the normal-weight Chris. They also rated the obese Chris as having lower self-esteem than the normal-weight Chris and felt that her ideal love partner should also be obese.

Studies also show the practical consequences of these attitudes. For example, it has been shown that overweight college students are less likely than other students to get financial help from home (Crandall, 1991). This effect was especially strong with respect to female students and was true regardless of the resources the student's family had, the number of children in the family, or other factors that could affect parents' willingness to provide financial help. The researchers suggest that the finding might be largely explained by parents' negative attitudes toward their overweight children and consequent lack of optimism about their future. In a related domain, there is evidence that businesspeople sacrifice $1,000 in annual salary for every pound they are overweight (Kolata, 1992).

One reason obese individuals are vilified is that we believe that

their weight problem stems from laziness and a lack of discipline. If we know that an individual's weight problem is the result of a biological disorder and thus beyond his or her control, we are less likely to make negative judgments of that individual (DeJong, 1980). What we fail to realize is that most obese people cannot control their weight. There is a genetic component in obesity, and this tendency can be exacerbated by social and cultural factors, such as lack of information and an unhealthy lifestyle.

Sharon Russell successfully sued the university that refused to let her graduate from its nursing program. The jury found the university in breach of contract: It had accepted Russell's money, she had gotten good grades and met all the requirements for graduation, but it had refused to grant her a degree. In this case, prejudice and negative stereotyping did not pay off; Russell won a $43,000 settlement from the school.

---

*O*ur reactions to obese individuals seem to involve a number of social psychological processes. For example, what role does the fundamental attribution error play in our perception of obese persons? What role does it play in our view of anyone who is stigmatized, including those who are mentally or physically challenged? What explanation accounts for the idea that Sharon Russell's ideal love partner would also be likely to be obese? How do you think evolutionary psychologists would explain our reactions to obese individuals?

Literature and film give us innumerable examples of the perceived connection between physical appearance and inner qualities. The Wicked Witch in the Wizard of Oz *is just one representation of this perception: The beautiful are good while ugliness equates with evil.*

see initially is only the wrapping. The entire package includes many attributes. A person may be overweight but may also have a mellifluous voice and a powerful personality. In a laboratory study in which subjects were exposed to a person's face and voice, the perception of the person's physical attractiveness was affected by judgments about that person's vocal attractiveness and vice versa (Zuckerman, Miyake, & Hodgins, 1991). Gertrude Stein was a woman many people found attractive even though she weighed over 200 pounds. Her striking face and her powerful personality were the main attributes that people remembered after meeting her.

Roots of the Physical Attractiveness Bias   Not only do we find attractive individuals more appealing physically, but we also confer on them a number of psychological and social advantages. Moreover, unattractive individuals may experience discrimination because of their appearance.

   Physical attractiveness, as we earlier noted, is a critical component of human mating. David Buss (1994) has observed that the importance of physical attractiveness has increased in the United States in every decade since the 1930s. This is true for both men and women, although men rate physical attractiveness as much more important than do women.

   What is the origin of the **physical attractiveness bias?** Much of the bias is probably learned. However, a number of distinctly different cultures seem to have the same biases. This doesn't necessarily mean that these biases aren't learned; various cultures may simply value the same characteristics. Studies comparing judgments of physical attractiveness in Korea and in the United States found agreement on whether a face was attractive and whether the face conveyed a sense of power. In both countries, for example, faces with broad chins, thin lips, and receding hairlines were judged to convey dominance (Triandis, 1994).

physical attractiveness bias
The tendency to confer on attractive individuals a number of psychological and social advantages.

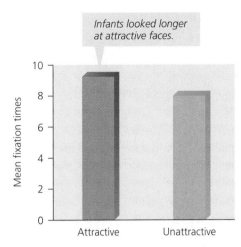

Infants looked longer at attractive faces.

Mean fixation times

Attractive   Unattractive

FIGURE 11-4 *Infant "fixation time" when looking at attractive and unattractive faces. Infants 2 or 3 months old looked longer at attractive faces than at unattractive faces, a behavior interpreted as a preference for the attractive faces. Because the infants in this study were so young, researchers have concluded that the physical attractiveness bias is innate, at least in part, rather than learned.* From *Langlois, Roggman, Casey, Riesner-Danner, and Jenkins, 1987.*

One cultural stereotype is that "what is beautiful is good." That is, we tend to believe that physically attractive individuals possess a wide range of desirable characteristics and that they are generally happier than unattractive individuals (Dion, Berscheid, & Walster, 1972). We also have the stereotype that "what is beautiful is glamorous" (Bassili, 1981). We think that good-looking people have energy, competence, and good social skills (Eagly et al., 1991).

It is obvious that we learn to associate attractiveness with positive virtues and unattractiveness with vice, even wickedness. Children's books and movies often portray the good characters as beautiful and the villains as ugly. In Walt Disney's *The Little Mermaid,* the slender, beautiful mermaid Ariel and the evil, obese sea witch are cases in point. Such portrayals are not limited to works for children. The hunchback of Notre Dame, the Phantom of the Opera, and Freddy Kruger are all physically unattractive evildoers.

However, there is some evidence that the attractiveness bias may have a biological component as well. In one experiment, infants 2 or 3 months old were exposed to pairs of adult faces and their preferences were recorded (Langlois, Roggman, Casey, Riesner-Danner, & Jenkins, 1987). Preference was inferred from a measure known as *fixation time,* or the amount of time spent looking at one face or the other. If the infant prefers one over the other, the infant should look at that face longer. As shown in Figure 11-4, when attractive faces were paired with unattractive faces, infants displayed a preference for the attractive faces.

It is unlikely that social learning could account for the preference shown by Langlois's subjects unless we are willing to believe that the attractiveness bias is learned very rapidly in the first 2 months. Nevertheless, it is not clear what biological advantage is gained by an innate preference for more attractive human faces. This is the issue we raised earlier: Other than an esthetic preference and an ego boost, what advantage does attractiveness offer a mate?

The evolutionary biologists suggest that perhaps beauty is more than skin deep. Recall the research on the attractiveness of symmetrical faces. It seems that not only do humans value symmetry but so do a variety of other species. For example, Watson and Thornhill (1994) have reported that female scorpion flies can detect and prefer as mates males with symmetrical wings. Male elks with the most symmetrical racks host the largest harems.

Evolutionary biologists believe that symmetry is reflective of underlying genetic quality. Lack of symmetry is thought to be caused by various stresses, such as poor maternal nutrition, late maternal age, attacks by predators, or disease, and may therefore reflect bad health or poor genetic quality. Thus, the preference for symmetry in potential mates, whether human or animal, may be instinctive (Watson & Thornhill, 1994).

DYNAMICS OF CLOSE RELATIONSHIPS

We have discussed why people form close relationships and why they form them with the people they do. We turn now to the dynamics of close relationships—how they develop, how they are maintained in the face of conflict, and how in some cases conflict can lead to their dissolution.

But what exactly are *close relationships?* What psychological factors define them? There appear to be three crucial factors, all of which we saw in the relationship between Gertrude Stein and Alice Toklas. The first factor is emotional involvement, feelings of love or warmth and fondness for the other person. The second is sharing, including sharing of feelings and experiences. The third is interdependence, which means that one's well-being is tied up with that of the other (Kelley et al., 1983). As is clear from this definition, a close relationship can be between husband and wife, lovers, or friends. Note that even when research focuses on one type of close relationship, it is usually also applicable to the others.

Relationship Development

Models of how relationships develop emphasize a predictable sequence of events. This is true of both models we examine in this section, the stage model of relationship development and social penetration theory. According to the *stage model of relationship development,* proposed by George Levinger and J. D. Snoek (1972), relationships evolve through the following stages:

Stage 0, no relationship. This is a person's status with respect to virtually all other people in the world.

Stage 1, awareness. We become conscious of another's presence and feel the beginning of interest. When Stein and Toklas first met in the company of friends, the conversation suggested to each of them that they might have much in common.

Stage 2, surface contact. Interaction begins but is limited to topics such as the weather, politics, and mutual likes and dislikes. Although the contact is superficial, each person is forming impressions of the other. Stein and Toklas moved into this stage the day after their first meeting and soon moved beyond it.

Stage 3, mutuality. The relationship moves, in substages, from lesser to greater interdependence. The first substage is that of involvement, which is characterized by a growing number of shared activities (Levinger, 1988). A subsequent substage is commitment, characterized by feelings of responsibility and obligation each to the other. Although not all close relationships involve commitment (Sternberg, 1988), those that have a serious long-term influence on one's life generally do. We noted how Stein and Toklas began by sharing activities, then feelings, and then an increasing commitment to each other.

A second model of relationship development, **social penetration theory,** developed by Irwin Altman and Dalmas Taylor (1973), centers on the idea that relationships change over time in both breadth—the range of topics people discuss and activities they engage in together—and depth—the extent to which they share their inner thoughts and feelings. Relationships progress in a predictable way from slight and superficial contact to greater and deeper involvement. First the breadth of a relationship increases. Then there is an increase in its depth, and breadth may actually decrease. Casual friends may talk about topics ranging from sports to the news to the latest rumors at work. But they will not, as will more intimate friends, talk about their feelings and hopes. Close friends allow each other to enter their lives—social penetration—and share on a deeper, more intimate level, even as the range of topics they discuss may decrease.

Evidence in support of social penetration theory comes from a study in which college students filled out questionnaires about their friendships several times over the course of a semester and then again 3 months later (Hays, 1985). Over 60% of the affiliations tracked in the study developed into close relationships by the end of the semester. More important, the interaction patterns changed as the relationships developed. As predicted by social penetration theory, interactions of individuals who eventually became close friends were characterized by an initial increase in breadth followed by a decrease in breadth and an increase in intimacy, or depth.

An important contributor to increasing social penetration—or to the mutuality stage of relationship development—is *self-disclosure,* the ability and willingness to share intimate areas of one's life. College students who kept diaries of their interactions with friends reported that casual friends provided as much fun and intellectual stimulation as close friends but that close friends provided more emotional support (Hays, 1988b). Relationship development is fostered by self-disclosure simply because we often respond to intimate revelations with self-disclosures of our own (Jourard, 1971).

Interestingly, self-disclosure may be more difficult in romantic relationships than in friendships, at least when it concerns dissatisfaction with the other person. Sternberg (1988) suggests that sometimes people have less to lose when self-disclosing to a friend and have more to lose when disclosing to a lover. Self-disclosing to a lover with whom you feel a certain discontent may be costly. Although some research has shown that people may actually reveal more about themselves to strangers than to lovers, these

social penetration theory A model of relationship development that centers on the idea that relationships change over time in both breadth—the range of topics people discuss and activities they engage in together—and depth—the extent to which they share their inner thoughts and feelings.

findings do not consider the nature of the disclosures (Morton, 1978). In general, some people find self-disclosure easier than others do; part of the reason may be related to differences in attachment styles, as described earlier in the chapter.

Evaluating Relationships

Periodically we evaluate the state of our relationships, especially when something is going wrong or some emotional episode occurs. Ellen Berscheid (1985) has observed that emotion occurs in a close relationship when there is an interruption in a well-learned sequence of behavior. Any long-term dating or marital relationship develops sequences of behavior—Berscheid calls these *interchain sequences*—that depend on the partners coordinating their actions. For example, couples develop hints and signals that show their interest in lovemaking. The couple's lovemaking becomes organized, and the response of one partner helps coordinate the response of the other. A change in the frequency or pattern of this behavior will bring about a reaction, positive or negative, from the partner. The more intertwined the couples are, the stronger are their interchain sequences; the more they depend on each other, the greater the impact of interruptions of these sequences.

Social Exchange Theory   One perspective on how we evaluate relationships is provided by **social exchange theory** (Thibaut & Kelley, 1979), which suggests that people make assessments according to rewards and costs, which correspond to all the positive and all the negative factors derived from a relationship. Generally, rewards are high if a person gets a great deal of gratification from the relationship, whereas costs are high if the person either must exert a great deal of effort to maintain the relationship or experiences anxiety about the relationship. According to this economic model of relationships, the outcome is decided by subtracting costs from rewards. If the rewards are greater than the costs, the outcome is positive; if the costs are greater than the rewards, the outcome is negative.

This doesn't necessarily mean that if the outcome is positive we will stay in the relationship or that if the outcome is negative we will leave it. We also evaluate outcomes against comparison levels. One type of comparison level is our expectation of what we will obtain from the relationship. That is, we compare the outcome with what we think the relationship should be giving us. A second type is a comparison level of alternatives, in which we compare the outcome of the relationship we are presently in with the expected outcomes of possible alternative relationships. If we judge that the alternative outcomes would be no better, or even worse, than the outcome of our present relationship, we will be less inclined to make a change. If, on the other hand, we perceive that an alternative relationship promises a better outcome, we are more likely to make a change.

Equity Theory   **Equity theory,** like social exchange theory, says that we evaluate our relationships based on their rewards and costs, but it also fo-

social exchange theory The theory that people evaluate a relationship according to rewards and costs, which correspond to all the positive and all the negative things derived from the relationship.

equity theory A theory that we evaluate our relationships based on their rewards and costs and on our perception of equity, or balance, within them.

cuses on our perception of equity, or balance, in relationships (Hatfield, Traupmann, Sprecher, Utne, & Hay, 1985). Equity in a relationship occurs when the following equation holds:

$$\frac{\text{Person A's Benefits [rewards} - \text{costs]}}{\text{A's Contributions}} = \frac{\text{Person B's Benefits [rewards} - \text{costs]}}{\text{B's Contributions}}$$

Rewards may include, but are not limited to, companionship, sex, and social support. Costs may include loss of independence and increases in financial obligations. The contributions made to the relationship include earning power or high social status. The rule of equity is simply that person A's benefits should equal person B's if their contributions are equal. However, fairness requires that if A's contributions are greater than B's, A's benefits should also be greater.

Thus, under equity theory, the way people judge the fairness of the benefits depends on their understanding of what each brings to the relationship. For example, the spouse who earns more may be perceived as bringing more to the marriage and therefore as entitled to higher benefits. The other spouse may, as a result, increase his costs, perhaps by taking on more of the household chores.

In actual relationships, of course, people differ, often vigorously, on what counts as contributions and on how specific contributions ought to be weighed. For example, in business settings, many individuals believe that race or gender should count as a contribution when hiring. Others disagree strongly with that position.

Has the fact that most women now work outside the home altered the relationship between wives and husbands as equity theory would predict? It appears, in keeping with equity theory, that the spouse who earns more, regardless of gender, often has fewer child-care responsibilities than the spouse who earns less (Steil & Weltman, 1991, 1992).

However, it also appears that cultural expectations lead to some inequity. Husbands tend to have more control over financial matters than wives do regardless of income (Biernat & Wortman, 1991). Moreover, a study of professional married couples (in which the partners earned relatively equal amounts) found that although the wives were satisfied with their husbands' participation in household chores and child rearing, in reality there was considerable inequity (Biernat & Wortman, 1991). Women were invariably the primary caregivers for the children. Men did spend time with their children and did many of the household chores, but they were not the primary caregivers. This may reflect a lack of equity in these relationships, or it may mean that women simply do not fully trust their husbands to do a competent job in taking care of the children.

What happens when people perceive inequity in a relationship? As a rule, they will attempt to correct the inequity and restore equity. If you realize that your partner is dissatisfied with the state of the relationship, you might try, for example, to pay more attention to your partner and in this way increase the rewards he or she experiences. If equity is not restored, your partner might become angry or withdraw from the relationship. Inequitable relationships are relationships in trouble.

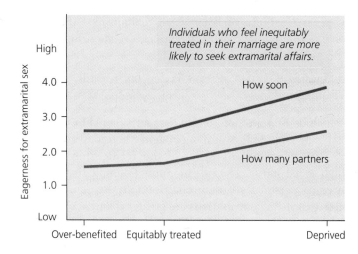

FIGURE 11-5 *Interest in having extramarital affairs as a function of equity in the marriage. Individuals who feel underbenefited, or deprived, in the relationship are more likely to want to have affairs. Those who feel fairly treated or overbenefited are less interested in having affairs. This measure supports equity theory, which focuses on partners' perceptions of justice and fairness in relationships.*

From Hatfield, Traupmann, and Walster, 1978.

In one study, researchers measured the level of perceived equity in relationships by means of the following question and scale (Hatfield, Walster, & Berscheid, 1978).

Comparing what you get out of this relationship with what your partner gets out of it, how would you say the relationship stacks up?

+3   I am getting a much better deal than my partner.
+2   I am getting a somewhat better deal.
+1   I am getting a slightly better deal.
 0   We are both getting an equally good . . . or bad . . . deal.
−1   My partner is getting a slightly better deal.
−2   My partner is getting a somewhat better deal.
−3   My partner is getting a much better deal than I am.

Respondents were grouped into three categories: those who felt that their relationship was equitable; those who felt that they got more out of the relationship than their partners and therefore were overbenefited; and those who felt that they got less than their partners and therefore were underbenefited.

The researchers then surveyed 2,000 people and found that, as expected, those individuals who felt underbenefited were much more likely to engage in extramarital sex than those who thought that their relationship was equitable or felt overbenefited (Hatfield, Walster, & Traupmann, 1978). Figure 11-5 shows how eager people are to engage in extramarital affairs based on their evaluation of the relationship. Note that those who feel deprived, that is, evaluate their status as underbenefited, have many extramarital partners and engage in affairs sooner than individuals who judge themselves to be equitably treated or are overbenefited in the relationship. Generally, couples who feel that they are in an equitable relationship are more likely to maintain the relationship than those who were less equitably matched (Hill, Rubin, & Peplau, 1976).

Although the research just reviewed suggests that people make rather cold-blooded, marketplace judgments about the quality of their relationships, it is likely that they also have other ways of evaluating relationships. For example, a distinction has been made between relationships governed by *exchange principles,* where, as we have seen, people benefit each other with the expectation of receiving a benefit in return, and relationships governed by *communal principles,* in which individuals benefit each other in response to the other's needs (Clark, 1986). In communal relationships, if one partner can put more into the relationship than the other, so be it. That is, people may deliberately underbenefit themselves for the sake of the relationship.

Love relationships are often governed by communal principles. As has been indicated, equity issues tend to become important when problems arise, especially when the relationship begins to decline.

Responses to Conflict

When relationships are deemed to be unfair, or inequitable, the result will almost inevitably be conflict. Conflict can also occur when a partner behaves badly—and everyone behaves badly at one time or another. The mere passage of time also makes conflict more likely. Couples are usually more affectionate and happier as newlyweds than they are 2 years later (Huston & Vangelisti, 1991). What happens, then, when conflicts arise? How do people in a relationship respond to conflicts?

The Role of Attribution We saw in Chapter 4 that people's perceptions of what caused conflicts and their responses (attributions) to the conflicts are crucial factors in the success or failure of relationships. Our perceptions of equity in our relationships have much to do with how we assign causes to our partner's comments and actions. Unhappy married couples tend to focus on the negative aspects of their relationship and to make negative attributions about each other's behavior. They spend little time thinking about positive marital events (Holtzworth-Munroe & Jacobson, 1985). Negative attribution patterns become part of the relationship, and conflict increases.

In a study of the relationship between married partners' causal attributions and their marital satisfaction over a year, researchers found making negative attributions *may be the cause* of lower marital satisfaction (Bradbury & Fincham, 1992). In other words, if you assume the worst when your partner works late for several days, then both of you become less satisfied with the relationship over time.

Accommodation Sometimes, instead of escalating the conflict, couples find ways to accommodate each other, even when one or both have acted in a negative or destructive manner (Rusbult, Verette, Whitney, Slovik, & Lipkus, 1991). Typically our initial impulse in response to a negative act such as our partner embarrassing us in front of other people is to be hurtful in return. That is, we tend toward the primitive response of returning the hurt in kind.

Then other factors come into play. That initial impulse gets moderated by second thoughts: If I react this way, I'm going to hurt the

(Heaton & Albrecht, 1991). If, however, there is another relationship handy or the marriage is perceived as intolerable, then exit becomes the choice (Felmlee, Sprecher, & Bassin, 1990).

Let's look at a case study to see why and how a particular marriage dissolves. Although the story of Susan and Bill is unique, it has much in common with the stories of many other troubled relationships.

From almost the very beginning, Susan knew that this relationship was not right for her. When she and Bill were dating, she sometimes felt uncomfortable, even when they made love. At some point, they progressed naturally from dating to marriage. On their wedding day, Bill was beaming but Susan felt somehow confused.

Over the years, the relationship seemed fine on the surface, as Susan and Bill pursued careers and had children. In her private world, however, the part she did not share with Bill, Susan slowly came to fully realize her dissatisfaction. Much of the time she was angry with Bill, sometimes just because he was there. Bill wondered why Susan was so upset, but then she had always been upset with him. He thought of the relationship as basically happy. Susan knew something had to be done. She thought that perhaps if Bill left his boring job he would "grow" and become the person she wanted him to be. Bill resisted changing jobs, and Susan got angrier.

Sociologist Diane Vaughn (1986) would say that Bill and Susan are typical of couples in relationships that are dissolving. The decay begins in secret, in one partner's unspoken unhappiness. The other partner, knowing nothing, is unable to do anything. Even if the unhappiness begins to surface, the partners conspire to cover it up. One partner doesn't want to hurt the other's feelings, and the other doesn't really want to know.

Susan began to leave the marriage years before it ended. She made plans and contemplated her future. In keeping with the *principle of least interest,* she, as the least interested or committed partner, had the most power to determine the direction of the relationship.

Susan met someone and fell in love. She had found a *transitional person,* someone who would help her leave her marriage and smooth the change to the new life. Although Susan still would not divorce Bill, she told him that she was extremely unhappy, that their sex life was terrible, and that they had nothing in common except the children. She hoped that she would goad him into leaving or that he would make a fatal mistake, that is, say or do something that would give her justifiable reason to leave. When nothing happened, Susan finally suggested a separation and Bill moved out. A year later Bill and Susan divorced.

Not surprisingly, Susan was better able to cope with the divorce than Bill. As the initiator, Susan had been preparing for the separation for quite a while. For Bill, the separation was abrupt, almost catastrophic. Researchers have found two factors associated with the ability to cope well with the end of a relationship: having relatively little invested in the relationship, and having the resources, such as money and education, to adjust financially (Kurdek, 1991).

Bill's main need after the divorce was to build up his self-esteem, to get over feeling rejected and worthless. He did so in part by blaming Susan, totally, for the breakup. Indeed, after a while he could not understand why he had married her in the first place. He started his own business and eventually remade his life. He resisted getting deeply into a new relationship until he felt he was ready. That was a good idea because affairs begun just after a dissolution tend to be based on a particular set of circumstances—loneliness, anxiety—that very likely will change. However, both Susan and Bill did remarry. The dissolution of a marriage tends to be followed, and often quickly, by another marriage: Roughly 80% of people who divorce remarry.

Overall, research suggests that there is general agreement on what makes relationships work and what contributes to their failure (Hatfield & Rapson, 1993; Notarius & Markman, 1993; Strong & DeVault, 1994). Much of the research has been done with married couples, but, as suggested earlier, it can be applied to any long-term relationships, heterosexual, gay, or lesbian.

LOVE AND FRIENDSHIP

In her work *A Vindication of the Rights of Women* (1792), Mary Wollstonecraft described love as "the common passion in which chance and sensation replace choice and reason" (p. 57). We can see that choice and reason were not operating for one young man who described how he felt when the woman he had been seeing for a year abruptly ended their relationship:

> I really didn't see it coming. She was so beautiful and I knew despite our difficulties that we would get married. During her last visit she said that this was the end. She had to follow her career and she won't be happy living here. She said that she didn't think that I needed her that much, anyway. I was stunned and then she was gone. I saw her a couple of times after that, once in a movie theater. I don't know whether she was with somebody or not, but seeing her, knowing she wasn't mine anymore, made me physically ill. I had to leave. I couldn't explain it to my friends. I suppose I'll get over this, but it's been a couple of years and I still think of her a lot. I still feel a lot of pain.

Some people never feel the pain of love; others have decided the pain is too much and say they will never love again (Thompson & Borrello, 1992). About 10% of the adult subjects in one study reported they had *never* been in love (Tennov, 1979).

For the rest of us, the general phenomenon of love encompasses romantic love, the love of a parent for a child and child for parent, the love of friends for each other, the love of one's country. Love is heterosexual, gay or lesbian, bisexual, and nonphysical as well. Love is apparently universal. An anthropological survey of 166 cultures across the world found clear evidence from oral and written records of the existence of romantic love in almost 90% of those cultures (Jankowiak & Fischer, 1992). Tales of romance

The many faces of love. This most precious of all human feelings comes in a variety of forms — love between parent and child, passionate love between romantic partners, the love of good friends for each other, the companionate love of long-time spouses.

are found in the ancient literatures throughout the world, from the Kama Sutra to the poems of Sappho (Fisher, 1992).

In many cultures examined by anthropologists, romantic love doesn't necessarily mean marriage. It is still an alien idea in most cultures that romance has anything to do with the choice of a spouse. Nor is romantic love exclusively heterosexual, by any means. But whatever the orientation of the partners, romance is everywhere.

Psychologists and other behavioral scientists have long thought that love was simply too mysterious a topic to study scientifically (Thompson &

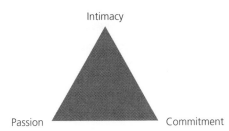

FIGURE 11-6 *Robert Stern-*
berg's triangular theory of love.
The theory proposes that the
three components of passion,
intimacy, and commitment are
present or absent in different
combinations in different
kinds of love. From Sternberg,
1986.

Borrello, 1992). Recently, however, psychologists have become more adventuresome, and love is now a topic of increasing interest (Hendrick & Hendrick, 1987). This is only right because love is among the most intense human emotions. People have lied and cheated and killed for it, yet no one quite knows what it is (Sternberg & Gracek, 1984).

Love's Triangle

Robert Sternberg (1986, 1988) has proposed a **triangular theory of love,** based on the idea that love has three components: passion, intimacy, and commitment. As shown in Figure 11-6, the theory represents love as a triangle, with each component defining a vertex.

Passion is the emotional component of love. The "aching" in the pit of your stomach when you think about your love partner is a manifestation of this component. Passion is "a state of intense longing for union with the other" (Hatfield & Walster, 1981). Passion tends to be strongest in the early stages of a romantic relationship. It is sexual desire that initially drives the relationship.

Intimacy is the component that includes self-disclosure—the sharing of our innermost thoughts—as well as shared activities. Intimate couples look out for each other's welfare, experience happiness by being in each other's company, are able to count on each other when times are tough, and give each other emotional support and understanding (Sternberg & Gracek, 1984).

The third vertex of the triangle is *commitment*—the long-term determination to maintain love over time. It is different from the decision people make, often in the heat of passion, that they are in love. Commitment does not necessarily go along with a couple's decision that they are in love.

According to Sternberg, the components of love need not occur in a fixed order. There is a tendency for passion to dominate at the start, for intimacy to follow as a result of self-disclosure prompted by passion, and for commitment to take the longest to fully develop. However, in an arranged marriage, for example, commitment occurs before intimacy, and passion may be the laggard.

Sternberg defined various kinds of love, based on the presence or absence of intimacy, passion, and commitment. Table 11-2 shows each of these kinds of love and the component or components it is associated with. Before we look at some of these types, however, we consider a view that tries to explain why passion, intimacy, and commitment may have evolved as components of human love.

triangular theory of love A theory that love has three components—passion, intimacy, and commitment—and that various kinds of love are defined by the presence or absence of these three components.

TABLE 11-2

	Love Component		
Kind of Love	Intimacy	Passion	Commitment
Non-love	No	No	No
Liking	Yes	No	No
Infatuated love	No	Yes	No
Empty love	No	No	Yes
Romantic love	Yes	Yes	No
Companionate love	Yes	No	Yes
Fatuous love	No	Yes	Yes
Consummate love	Yes	Yes	Yes

From Sternberg, 1986.

An Evolutionary Explanation of Love

Sociobiologists and evolutionary psychologists, who study the effect of biology on social behavior, view love as the result of three basic needs or instincts related to the propagation of the species: the need of the child for protection, the need of the parent to protect the child, and the sexual instinct.

According to Glenn Wilson (1981), men are biologically driven to pass on their genes to the largest possible number of children, and so they are naturally "harem builders." That is, they maximize their number of children if they engage in many short-term sexual encounters rather than being monogamous. Women are motivated to protect the children they bear, so they are less interested in numerous sex partners and more interested in a long-term, committed relationship.

Women may also seek and be rewarded by more casual sexual relations (Buss, 1994), but for different reasons. Infidelity in women typically occurs because they are dissatisfied with their current partner or they wish to have a partner, however temporarily, who will lavish resources on them that their current partner cannot. These resources are often things the women do not consider very important for their marriage or long-term relationships.

These differences have been borne out in current research. When unmarried college men and women were asked how many sex partners they would like to have within a number of time periods, ranging from the next hour to their entire lifetime, men responded with considerably higher numbers than women did (Buss & Schmitt, 1993). As shown in Figure 11-7, these unmarried college men wanted to have at least 18 sex partners in their lifetime; women wanted to have 4 or 5. Men, reflecting an optimism probably not grounded in experience, wished for 5 sex partners in the next year; women wished for only 1. In fact, on average, women expected to have only 0.8 partner in the next week.

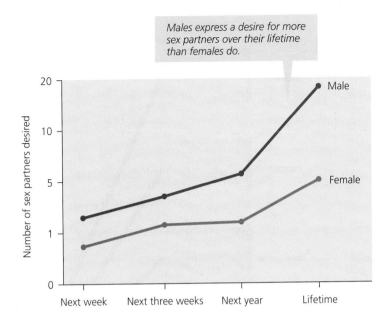

Males express a desire for more sex partners over their lifetime than females do.

Number of sex partners desired

20

10

5

1

0

Next week   Next three weeks   Next year   Lifetime

Male

Female

FIGURE 11-7 *Number of sex partners desired by unmarried college males and females in the future. Males indicated that they wanted more sex partners than females did. Sociobiologists believe the male desire for numerous sex partners comes from a biological drive to pass on their genes to as many offspring as possible. Females are motivated to protect the children they bear and so are more interested in long-term relationships. The sociobiological view suggests that all social behavior has biological underpinnings.* Data provided by David Buss at Colloquium, University of Toledo, 1994.

If these differences between males and females exist, then why do males form long-term, monogamous relationships? When and why do they opt for committed relationships? According to sociobiologists, long-term marriages ensure that other needs crucial to the propagation of the species are met, particularly the need of offspring for protection (Wilson, 1981). Thus, not only does passion serve a function, but so does commitment and, for that matter, intimacy, which helps preserve the commitment.

David Buss, a prominent evolutionary social psychologist, has studied the processes of attracting and keeping a mate. To find and retain a "reproductively valuable mate," humans engage in love acts—behaviors with near-term goals, such as display of resources the other sex finds enticing. The ultimate purpose of these acts is to increase reproductive success (Buss, 1988a, 1988b). Human sexual behavior can thus be viewed in much the same way as the sexual behavior of other animal species. Figure 11-8 shows different love acts and how they are associated with various near-term (proximate) goals and with the ultimate goal of successful reproduction.

The love acts in Figure 11-8 were identified in studies of college students. Subjects in one study (Buss, 1988b) listed some specific behaviors they used to keep their partner from getting involved with someone else. Buss found that males tended to use display of resources (money, cars, clothes, sometimes even brains), whereas females tried to look more attractive and threatened to be unfaithful if the males didn't shape up. Buss argued that these findings support an evolutionary interpretation of mate retention: The tactics of males focus on providing resources for the female, and the tactics of females focus on their value as a reproductive mate and on arousing the jealousy of the male who needs to ensure they are not impregnated by a rival.

Many of Buss's findings about human mating behavior are disturbing because both men and women, in pursuit of the sexual goals, cheat and

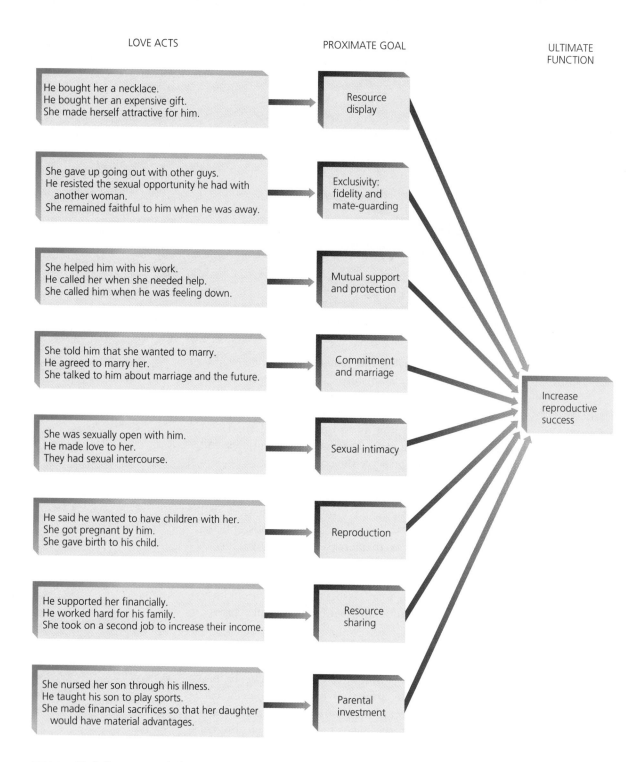

FIGURE 11-8 *Proximate and ultimate goals of love acts. According to the sociobiological view of love, individuals engage in various interpersonal behaviors designed to attract and keep mates ("love acts"). The ultimate goal of these behaviors is to increase reproductive success.* From Buss, 1988b.

Couples like these hikers may enjoy consummate love if they have sufficient quantities of affection, romance, trust, tolerance, and good will. According to Robert Sternberg, consummate love combines the three components of love—passion, intimacy, and commitment.

frustrate their mates and derogate their rivals. However, some of his findings are kinder to our species. For example, he points out that the most effective tactics for men who wish to keep their mates are to provide love and kindness, to show affection, and to tell their mates of their love. That sounds rather romantic.

Types of Love

What, then, are Sternberg's types of love? Probably the most fascinating type is *romantic love*, which involves passion and intimacy but not commitment. Romantic love is reflected in that electrifying yet conditional statement: "I am in love with you." Compare this with the expression reflecting consummate love: "I love you."

Romantic love can be found around the world and throughout history. Romantic love doesn't necessarily mean marriage, however, for two main reasons. First, whereas marriage is almost universally heterosexual, romantic love need not be. Second, as mentioned above, it is still an alien idea in most cultures that romance has anything to do with the choice of a spouse. Even in our own culture, the appeal of marrying for love seems to have increased among women in recent years, perhaps because women's roles have changed and they no longer have as great a need to find a "good provider" (Berscheid, Snyder, & Omoto, 1989).

The importance of passion in romantic love is clear. Romantic lovers live in a pool of emotions, both positive and negative—sexual desire, fear, exultation, anger—all experienced in a state of high arousal. Intense sexual desire and physical arousal are the prime forces driving romantic love (Berscheid, 1988). Passionate lovers soon begin to share their innermost thoughts and desires and thereby foster the second component of romantic love, intimacy.

Tennov (1979) distinguished a particular type of romantic love, which she called *limerence* and characterized as occurring when "you suddenly feel a sparkle (a lovely word) of interest in someone else, an interest fed by the image of returned feeling." Limerence is not driven solely or even primarily by sexual desire. It occurs when a person anxious for intimacy finds someone who seems able to fulfill all of his or her needs and desires and is driven by the hope that these needs and desires will be fulfilled. For limerent lovers, all the happiness one could ever hope for is embodied in the loved one. Indeed, one emotional consequence of limerent love is a terror that all hope will be lost if our lover leaves us (Brehm, 1988).

Consummate love combines all three vertices of love's triangle: passion, intimacy, and commitment. These couples have it all; they are able to maintain their passion and intimacy along with a commitment to a lifetime together. How do they do it? For lessons on maintaining consummate love, see the featured discussion "Keeping the Flame Alive."

Although we may fantasize about romantic love and view consummate love as a long-term ideal, other types of love can also bring happiness. Many couples are perfectly happy with *companionate love,* which has little or no passion but is infused with intimacy and commitment. Such partners are "friends for life" and generally have great trust in and tolerance for each other. Although they may regret the lack of passion, they are pragmatic and able to live happily within the rules or limits of the relationship (Duck, 1983).

Unrequited Love

A special and very painful kind of infatuated love is love that is unfulfilled. Unrequited love occurs when we fall deeply and passionately in love and that love is rejected. Almost all of us have had some experience of unrequited love. In one study, 98% of the subjects had been rejected by someone they loved intensely (Baumeister, Wotman, & Stillwell, 1993).

What makes unrequited love so painful is that both individuals feel victimized. Very often, unrequited love ostensibly starts as a platonic friendship, but then one of the individuals admits that it was never just friendship, that he (or she) was always secretly in love (Baumeister, Wotman, & Stillwell, 1993). In many cases, the object of the unrequited love is often unable to express lack of interest in terms that are sufficiently discouraging. The unrequited lover takes anything as encouragement, sustains hope, and then finds the final rejection devastating. The object of unwanted love, after the initial boost to the ego, feels bewildered, guilty, and angry.

Romance need not cease with the end of the honeymoon. Some couples are able to make it last throughout the life of their relationship. Nathaniel Branden (1988), who has studied couples in successful long-term relationships, found that these couples engage in the following behaviors:

- They express love verbally. Simply, they continually tell each other "I love you."
- They are physically affectionate. They hold hands and kiss and cuddle and, if need be, provide each other with warm comforters and hot chocolate.
- They are sexually active. Sex is a fundamental part of their relationship.
- They express their appreciation for each other. They tell each other, "You look nice in that suit," or "I loved the meal you made," or even, "I really like the way you mowed the lawn."
- They self-disclose. They are willing to tell each other their true intimate thoughts.
- They support each other emotionally and materially. When one is down or depressed the other provides support, and they share income and all other resources that they have.
- They put up with a lot. They forgive each other. They put up with the other's shortcomings and demands with tolerance and grace because, for these couples, the shortcomings and demands are a small price to pay for happiness.

———————

Do you think these relationship-maintaining tactics are consciously arrived at by the partners? Or are they simply the byproduct of a good relationship, one that makes kind and thoughtful acts easy to do? What evolutionary purpose do you think might be served by these actions? If consummate lovers do these things, what would a similar list for companionate lovers or romantic lovers consist of?

In a typical case of spurned love, a college woman took pity on a young man whom no one liked and one night invited him to join her and some friends in a game of Parcheesi. He thought the invitation signaled something more than she intended. Much to her horror, he began to follow her around and told her how much he loved her. She wanted this to stop, but she was unable to tell him how upset she was, because she was afraid of hurting his feelings. He interpreted her silence as encouragement and persisted (Baumeister, Wotman, & Stillwell, 1993).

Men are more likely than women to experience unrequited love (Baumeister, Wotman, & Stillwell, 1993). This is because, as observed earlier, men are more beguiled by physical attractiveness than are women. Men tend to "fall upward," in Roy Baumeister's words; that is, they tend to fall in love with someone more desirable than they are. Interestingly, people report that they have been the object of unrequited love twice as many times as they have been rejected by another. We would prefer to remember or believe that we have been loved in vain rather than having loved in vain.

Secret Love

If unrequited love is the most painful kind of love, then secret love may be the most interesting. Secrecy seems to increase the attraction of a relationship. Researchers have found that people continued to think more about past relationships that had been secret than about those that had been open (Wegner, Lane, & Dimitri, 1994). In fact, many individuals were still very much preoccupied with long past secret relationships. In a study of secrecy and attraction, subjects paired as couples were induced to play "footsie" under the table while they were involved in a card game with another couple (Wegner et al., 1994). The researchers found that when the under-the-table game was played in secret, participants reported greater attraction for the other person than when it was not played in secret.

Why does secrecy create this strong attraction? Perhaps it's because individuals involved in a secret relationship think constantly and obsessively about each other. After all, they have to expend a lot of energy in maintaining the relationship. They have to figure out how to meet, how to call each other so that others won't know, and how to act neutrally in public to disguise their true relationship. Secrecy creates strong bonds between individuals. Secrecy can also be the downfall of ongoing relationships. The sudden revelation of a secret infidelity will often crush an ongoing relationship and further enhance the secret one (Wegner et al., 1994).

Liking and Loving

According to Sternberg's definition, liking involves intimacy without passion or commitment. Given that liking involves intimacy, does liking lead to romantic loving? The answer to this question appears to be no. Liking evidently leads only to liking. It is as if the two states—liking and loving—are on different tracks (Berscheid, 1988). People may be fond of each other and may go out together for a long time without their affection ever quite ripening into romantic love. Can we say, then, that liking and loving are basically different?

Zick Rubin (1970, 1973) thought that liking and loving were indeed essentially different. He constructed two separate measures, a liking scale and a loving scale, to explore the issue systematically. He found that while both friends and lovers were rated high on the liking scale, only lovers were rated high on the loving scale. Moreover, separate observations revealed that dating couples who gave each other high scores on the loving scale tended more than others to engage in such loving actions as gazing into each other's eyes and holding hands. A follow-up study found that these couples were more likely to have maintained the relationship than were those whose ratings on the loving scale were lower. Therefore, according to Rubin, while we may like our lovers, we do not generally love those we like, at least with the passion we feel toward our lovers.

Friendships

The friendships that we form during our lives can be loving and intimate. The basis for friendship may be an ongoing interdependence between people (Hays, 1988a).

FIGURE 11-9 *Men tend to focus on activities with their friends, perhaps talking about personal concerns along the way. Women tend to get together with the primary goal of sharing personal news.*

Gender Differences in Friendships Female same-sex friendships and male same-sex friendships show somewhat different patterns (Brehm, 1985). Males tend to engage in activities together, whereas females tend to share their emotional lives. Richard and Don may play basketball twice a week, and while playing they may talk about their problems and feelings, but that is not their purpose in getting together. Karen and Terri may have lunch twice a week with the express purpose of sharing their problems and feelings (Figure 11-9). Men live their friendships side by side; women live them face to face (Hendrick, 1988; Wright, 1982).

The degree of this difference may be diminishing. In the last few decades there appears to have been a marked increase in the importance both men and women assign to personal intimacy as a source of fulfillment (McAdams, 1989). Some recent research suggests that men and women self-disclose with equal frequency and perhaps intensity (Prager, Fuller, & Gonzalez, 1989).

Men and women report having about the same number of close friends. Women tend to view their close friends as more important than men do, but men's close friendships may last longer than women's (Fiebert & Wright, 1989).

Men typically distinguish between same-sex and cross-sex friendships. For men, cross-sex bonds offer the opportunity for more self-disclosure and emotional attachment. Men, generally, obtain more acceptance and intimacy from their female friends than from their male friends (Duck, 1988). However, for heterosexual men, cross-sex relationships are often permeated with sexual tension (Rawlins, 1992).

Women, in comparison, do not sharply distinguish among their friendships with males and females. They also see differences in their feelings for the various men in their lives. Some of their relationships with men are full of sexual tension, whereas other men may be liked, even loved, but sexual tension may be absent in those relationships.

Greater levels of interaction with females are associated with fewer episodes of loneliness for both men and women. Why? Interactions with women are infused with disclosure, intimacy, and satisfaction, and all of these act as buffers against loneliness (Wheeler, Reis, & Nezlek, 1983). Women seem to make better friends than men do. It is telling that married men, when asked to name their best friend, are likely to name their wives. The expectations women have for friendship are often not satisfied by their spouse, and they tend to have at least one female friend in whom they confide (Oliker, 1989).

Friendships Over the Life Cycle Friendships are important throughout the life cycle. But they also change somewhat, in relation to the stage of the life cycle and to factors in the individual's life.

Sharing and intimacy begin to characterize friendships in early adolescence, as a result of an increasing ability to understand the thoughts and feelings of others. Girls have more intimate friendships in their early adolescent years than boys do, and this tends to remain true throughout life (Rawlins, 1992).

Why are boys less intimate than girls with same-sex friends? The reason might be that girls trust their friends more than boys do (Berndt, 1992). Girls tend to listen to their friends and protect their friends' feelings, whereas boys tend to tease or embarrass their friends when the opportunity arises.

The more intimate the adolescent friendships, the more loyal and supportive they are. However, disloyalty and lack of support can sometimes result from pressure to conform to the peer group. Of course, these issues are not unique to adolescent friendships. Conflicts between intimacy and social pressure simply take on different forms as people get older (Berndt, 1992).

As individuals move into early and middle adulthood, the end of a marriage or other long-term intimate relationship can profoundly affect the pattern of a couple's friendships. When a woman experiences the breakup of a relationship, her friends rally around and support her (Oliker, 1989). Often, the couple's close friends will have already guessed that the relationship was in trouble. When the breakup occurs, they tend to choose one partner or the other, or to simply drift away, unable to deal with the new situation.

In later adulthood, retirement affects our friendships. We no longer have daily contact with co-workers and thus lose a source of potential friends. With increasing age, new issues arise. The death of a spouse affects friendships perhaps as much as the breakup of a marriage. People who are recently widowed can often feel like "fifth wheels" (Rawlins, 1992). The physical problems often associated with old age can lead to a conflict between a need for independence and a need for help (Rawlins, 1992). As a result, older friends might have to renegotiate their relationships to ensure that both needs are met.

Whatever the problems, friendships among the elderly are often uplifting and vital. This is well illustrated by the following statement from a 79-year-old widower: "I don't know how anyone would ever live without friends, because to me, they're next to good health, and all your life depends on friendship" (quoted in Rawlins, 1992).

GERTRUDE STEIN AND ALICE TOKLAS REVISITED

Gertrude Stein and Alice Toklas were friends and lovers for 40 years. At the beginning of their relationship they both exemplified the needs for affiliation and intimacy that bring human beings together. They were instantly attracted to each other by similarities in their interests and attitudes. Alice claimed that when she encountered genius, a bell rang, and she heard this bell when she met Gertrude and began reading her work. She offered praise and admiration, and Gertrude responded with appreciation and love. With the arrival of Alice, a friend observed, "A new era opened up for Gertrude."

There was also a measure of complementarity in their relationship. While Gertrude presided over the gatherings of artists, writers, and personalities in her salon, Alice presided over the "wives" and perfected her skills as a legendary gourmet cook. A powerful personality in her own right, Alice served as critic, promoter, and muse to Gertrude, who developed into an innovative and influential writer and one of the most celebrated women of letters of the 20th century.

Gertrude and Alice worked together, played together, and loved together. In every way possible, their relationship exemplified Sternberg's concept of consummate love. A friend referred to their relationship as a "lifetime of complete understanding." After Gertrude died, Alice lived on in loneliness for 21 years. She died in 1967 at the age of 81 and was buried next to Gertrude.

LOOKING AHEAD

In this chapter we have examined some of the basics of interpersonal attraction and close relationships. We have considered why human beings are attracted to each other, how they develop and maintain relationships, and how elements of passion, intimacy, and commitment are combined in a broad range of liking and loving relationships.

In the next chapter we turn to a different human impulse: aggression. We examine the dynamics of interpersonal aggression, looking for its roots in biology, society, and culture. We see that people are motivated to act aggressively, even violently, toward each other in a variety of situations. We also see that, because human beings are guided by more than biological impulses, they are capable of controlling and minimizing aggression in their interactions and relationships.

CHAPTER REVIEW

1. *What is a close relationship?*
   The essence of a close relationship is intimacy, friendship, sharing, and love between two people.

2. *What are the roots of interpersonal attraction and close relationships?*
   Human beings possess positive social motives, the **need for affiliation**—the desire to establish and maintain rewarding interpersonal relationships—and the **need for intimacy**—the desire for close and affectionate relationships, which influence us to seek fulfilling relationships. There are, however, motives that may inhibit the formation of social relationships, particularly **loneliness** and **social anxiety,** which arise because of a person's expectation of negative encounters with, and evaluations from, others.

   Another important factor in interpersonal attraction and close relationships is our earliest interaction with our primary caregiver, which shapes our particular attachment style. Attachment styles are patterns of interacting and relating that influence how we develop affectional ties with others later in life. These styles evolve into **working models,** mental representations of what we as individuals expect to happen in a close relationship.

3. *What are the determinants of attraction?*
   Three models have been proposed to account for why we become attracted to certain others. **Reward theory** suggests that we are attracted to others if they provide rewards for us. This idea was extended by **reinforcement-affect theory,** which proposed that through a process of association (much like classical conditioning) we become attracted to individuals whom we associate with positive outcomes. **Balance theory** suggests that a balanced relationship occurs when two individuals have the same interests and views. A balanced relationship is rewarding; an unbalanced relationship is not. Thus, as a rule, balance in a relationship increases attraction, whereas unbalance reduces attraction.

   Several factors influence the development of interpersonal attraction. Physical proximity is an initially important determinant of potential attraction. The importance of proximity can be partly accounted for by the mere exposure effect, which suggests that repeated exposure to a person increases familiarity, which in turn increases attraction. Proximity is also important because it increases opportunities for interaction, which may increase liking.

   Another factor affecting attraction is similarity. We are attracted to those we perceive to be like us in interests, attitudes, personality, and physical attractiveness. We tend to seek out partners who are at the same level of attractiveness as we are (the **matching principle**). Matching becomes more important as a relationship progresses.

   We also tend to be more attracted to people who are physically attractive, which is a third factor in interpersonal attraction. Generally, males are more overwhelmed by physical attractiveness than females. Facial appearance, body appearance, and the quality of one's voice contribute to the perception of physical attractiveness. We tend to ascribe positive qualities to physically attractive people.

The down side to the **physical attractiveness bias** is that we tend to stigmatize those who are unattractive and ascribe negative qualities to them. In our society, obese people are particularly stigmatized and are portrayed negatively in art, literature, and films.

There is research evidence that the physical attractiveness bias is rooted in our biology: Even at 2 months, infants attend more to an attractive than an unattractive face. A new theory suggests that attractiveness, in the form of facial and body symmetry, may reflect genetic soundness. The physical attractiveness bias would thus have survival value for the species.

4. *How do close relationships form and evolve?*
   Most theories of relationship development emphasize an initial increase in shared activities followed by an increase in mutuality. That is, friends or lovers begin to share more intimate thoughts and feelings and become more and more interdependent.

   At some point, individuals begin to evaluate the status of their relationships according to the rewards and costs derived from them. According to **social exchange theory,** people evaluate a relationship against two comparison levels: what they think they should be getting out of a relationship and how the present relationship compares with potential alternatives. **Equity theory** maintains that people evaluate relationships according to the relative inputs and outcomes for each party in the relationship. If inequity exists, the relationship may be in trouble.

   How we interpret the behaviors of our partner in a close relationship is important in maintaining a relationship. Generally, unhappy couples spend much time thinking about negative events and make more negative attributions about each other's motives than happy couples do. More successful couples know how to maintain and enhance their relationship, often through an **accommodation process.** They work hard at handling conflict in a positive, constructive way.

5. *How do relationships end?*
   When a relationship begins to decline there are four possible responses, described as voice (seeking solutions), loyalty (waiting things out), neglect (withdrawing), and exit (leaving). Generally, the course of a flagging relationship is determined by the degree of commitment the partners feel toward each other and the perceived quality of the alternatives. Often the initial stages of the dissolution of a close relationship begin quietly, in secret, with one (or both) parties slowly disengaging.

6. *What are the components and dynamics of love?*
   In Sternberg's **triangular theory of love,** love has three components: passion, intimacy, and commitment. Different mixes of these three

components define different types of love. Romantic love, for example, has passion and intimacy; it involves strong emotion and sexual desire. Companionate love has intimacy and commitment; it is based more on mutual respect and caring than on strong emotion. Consummate love has all three components. Limerence is an exaggerated form of romantic love that occurs when a person anxious for intimacy finds someone who seems able to fulfill all his or her needs.

Unrequited love—love that is not returned—is the most painful kind of love. Secret love seems to have a special quality. Secrecy makes a partner more attractive and creates a bond between individuals.

7. *What is the evolutionary view of love?*
   Sociobiologists suggest that the three components may have evolved because of the need of human infants for protection, the need of parents to protect their child, and the sexual instinct. Passion, intimacy, and commitment are seen as important to the survival of the species. An implication of sociobiological theory is that males, seeking to reproduce their genes as widely as possible, will prefer many short-term sexual encounters or relationships and that females, seeking to protect the children they bear, will prefer long-term relationships. Ultimately, however, males do participate in long-term relationships, partly because such relationships have more survival value for the species.

8. *What is the nature of friendships?*
   According to Sternberg, friendships are characterized by liking and involve intimacy but not passion or commitment. Friendships are based on an ongoing interdependence between people. There are some gender differences in friendships, although these differences may have decreased in recent years. Both males and females need the intimacy offered by friendships. However, females still seem to view friends as more important than males do, and females make better friends. Interactions with females are more likely to be characterized by disclosure, intimacy, and satisfaction, all of which act as buffers against loneliness.

SUGGESTIONS FOR FURTHER READING

Austen, J. (1980). *Pride and prejudice.* New York: New American Library. (Originally published in 1813.)
   Jane Austen's intricate and wonderfully crafted novel of the relationship between two prideful and opinionated young people in early 19th-century England is a classic. It teaches much about character and relationships and the role of love and affection in an ordered and class-conscious society.

Buss, D. M. (1994). *The evolution of desire: Strategies of human mating.* New York: Basic Books.
   Everything you wanted to know about sex and love written with clarity, humor, and sensitivity by one of the foremost evolutionary psychologists. Buss is convincing in his argument that in order for us to truly understand love we must first understand our evolutionary past.

Sternberg, R. J. (1988). *The triangle of love*. New York: Basic Books.
An original look at love by a social psychologist. Sternberg presents in non-technical terms his triangle theory of love and the data he gathered to support the theory. An important work because it is one of the first systematic attempts by a psychologist to study love scientifically.

Chapter 12

Interpersonal Aggression

*T*he sign warns that weapons are not allowed in the building. Anyone entering the building must pass through a metal detector, it states, and bags and packages will be hand-searched. What building is this? The Pentagon? An international airport? No, it is Jefferson High School in Brooklyn, New York. Jefferson is located in a neighborhood where violence and poverty are everyday realities. Violence is no stranger to the students here. Over the past several years, scores of students have been killed or seriously injured in shooting and stabbing incidents. Despite the fact that the four-story, red brick building has security gates on the windows, steel-plated doors, and metal detectors to prevent students from bringing guns to school, the violence continues.

The sign and other security measures certainly didn't work one morning in March 1992. That day Khalil Sumpter, a 15-year-old student, entered the school with a .38 caliber revolver. The gun had two bullets, one intended for 16-year-old Tyrone Sinkler, the other for 17-year-old Ian Moore. Sumpter did not choose his targets randomly. He had an ongoing argument with his two fellow students, especially Tyrone Sinkler. He and Sinkler had taken part in a mugging that had gone sour, and they had been arguing about it for some time. The conflict between Sumpter and Sinkler was compounded by the fact that Sumpter believed that Sinkler was going to kill him. In fact, Sumpter testified at his trial that Sinkler had taken a shot at him the day before and threatened to kill his mother. He decided to strike first.

Sumpter arrived at school late. He waited in the hall, outside Sinkler's and Moore's classroom. When the bell rang, Sinkler and Moore came out of the room. Without saying a word, Sumpter approached his schoolmates, pulled out the gun, and fired both bullets. Moore was hit in the heart and died instantly. Sinkler was rushed to a local hospital, where he later died of head wounds. The cycle of violence that began with an argument had ended in death.

The killings at Jefferson High School, though shocking, represent only the tip of the iceberg. Aggression is acted out in New York City schools on a daily basis. Nor is the epidemic of violence limited to New York or even to cities; violent incidents occur nationwide and worldwide. In one such incident, for example, Melinda Loveless and three of her friends abducted 12-year-old Shanda Sharer. Loveless was jealous because Sharer was close to her lover. She and her friends tortured Sharer and burned her alive in a field. In another incident, dissimilar except for its violent nature, Baruch Goldstein, a Jewish extremist, entered a mosque in Israel where Palestinians were gathered. Using a military assault rifle he systematically murdered over 30 Palestinians and wounded scores of others as they prayed.

Although as humans we are capable of immense good, we are also capable of extreme brutality, as exemplified by the acts of Khalil Sumpter, Melinda Loveless, Baruch Goldstein, and many others like them. Aggression is an unfortunate and recurring theme in human history. It occurs both between individuals and between large groups and nations. These two forms of aggression appear to be controlled by somewhat different factors and so are discussed separately in this book (see Chapter 16 for a discussion of intergroup conflict and aggression).

In this chapter, we look at the underlying causes of aggression as it occurs on the interpersonal level. We ask such questions as, Why does a person like Khalil Sumpter go to school with a gun one day and shoot two schoolmates? Was he a disturbed individual, or was he a product of his environment? Was he angry, frustrated? Had he learned that this was a socially acceptable method of resolving a disagreement? What role did his family play in his attitudes and inclinations? What about the effect of the media on his behavior? Finally, what can be done to lessen the use of violence and aggression as a form of conflict resolution? What steps can we as individuals and as a society take to prevent this kind of tragic event from occurring again? These are some of the questions addressed in this chapter.

WHAT IS AGGRESSION?

What exactly is aggression? The term tends to generate a certain amount of confusion, because a layperson's concept of aggression differs somewhat from what social psychologists study. In day-to-day life we hear about the "aggressive" salesperson who will not take no for an answer and the "aggressive" businessperson who stops at nothing to win a promotion. The sense of the term in these usages is forceful, overbearing, or overly assertive.

Social psychologists, however, define **aggression** as any behavior that is intended to inflict harm (whether psychological or physical) on another organism or object. There are several important things to note about this definition. First, a crucial element of the definition is *intent*: A person must

aggression Any behavior that is intended to inflict harm (whether psychological or physical) on another organism or object.

Social psychologists define aggression as behavior intended to inflict harm on another organism or object. To what extent are the people pictured here—children throwing tires on a hijacked bus in Belfast, a teenage member of a Los Angeles girl gang, and armed Palestinians in a Gaza Strip refugee camp—displaying aggressive behavior?

have intended to harm in order for the act to be classified as aggressive. If someone deliberately hits a neighbor with a baseball bat during an argument, it is considered aggressive. If the person accidentally hits the neighbor with a baseball bat while playing ball in the yard, it is not considered aggressive.

Note too that the harm intended by an aggressive act need not be physical. A Navy commander who continually sexually harasses a female subordinate, causing stress, anxiety, and depression, may not be doing her any overt physical harm. However, he is causing her psychological harm. Finally, aggression is not limited to actions directed at living organisms. Aggression might also be directed at inanimate objects. A person might smash the window of a neighbor's car in retaliation for some real or imagined conflict with that neighbor.

This broad definition covers a great deal of ground, but it requires further elaboration. Using this definition, we would be tempted to liken the actions of a police officer who kills a murder suspect in the line of duty with those of a paid assassin who kills for profit. Because such a wide range of behavior can be called aggressive, psychologists have defined several different types of aggression. We look at these next.

Levels and Types of Aggression

Clearly, aggression exists on many different levels and is made up of several types of behavior. Not all aggression, for example, stems from the same underlying motives and intentions. Some aggression, referred to as **hostile aggression,** stems from anger and hostility (Feshbach, 1964). Its primary goal is to inflict injury on some person or object to satisfy angry or hostile impulses. For example, Khalil Sumpter was undoubtedly angry with Tyrone Sinkler over their roles in the failed mugging and over Sinkler's (perceived) intention to kill him. Acts of aggression that stem from such emotional states are examples of hostile aggression. Other aggression, referred to as **instrumental aggression,** stems from the desire to achieve a goal. Melinda Loveless, for example, used aggression to get rid of a rival.

Hostile aggression and instrumental aggression are not mutually exclusive. One can commit an aggressive act with *both* underlying motives. When Baruch Goldstein killed over 30 Palestinians in a mosque, he had two motives. For one, he was motivated by intense hatred of the Palestinians, whom he perceived as trying to take away land that rightfully belonged to Jews. For another, he may also have been motivated by the hope of derailing the fragile peace talks between the Palestine Liberation Organization and the Israeli government. His act thus had a hostile component (hatred) and an instrumental component (derailing the peace talks).

Some forms of aggression don't inflict physical harm. Instead, the victim is harmed verbally through gossip, character assassination, damage to her physical property (Moyer, 1987), or interference with her advancement toward a goal. This form of aggression is **symbolic aggression.** For example, if a person spreads rumors about a co-worker in order to keep her from getting promoted, the person has used symbolic aggression. Although no physical harm was done, the co-worker was blocked from achieving a goal.

Symbolic aggression can be either hostile or instrumental. The office worker may have spread the rumor because she was angry at her co-worker—a case of hostile aggression. Alternatively, she could have spread the rumor to secure the promotion for herself at her co-worker's expense—a case of instrumental aggression.

Yet another form of aggression is **sanctioned aggression.** A soldier taking aim and killing an enemy soldier in a battle setting is engaging in sanctioned aggression. Self-defense, which occurs when a person uses aggression to protect himself or others from harm, is another example of sanctioned aggression. Society declares that in certain situations, aggression is acceptable or even mandatory. A soldier who refuses to engage in aggressive behavior may be subject to disciplinary action or even have his or her military service abruptly ended. Typically, sanctioned aggression is instrumental in nature. Soldiers kill each another to save their own lives, to follow orders,

hostile aggression Aggression that stems from anger and hostility. Its primary goal is to inflict injury on some person or object to satisfy angry or hostile impulses.

instrumental aggression Aggression that stems from the desire to achieve a goal.

symbolic aggression Aggression that harms the victim verbally through gossip, character assassination, damage to physical property, or interference with advancement toward a goal.

sanctioned aggression Aggression that society finds acceptable or even mandatory, such as the aggressive behavior of a soldier at war.

to help win the war. There need not be anger between enemy soldiers for them to try to kill each other.

Gender Differences in Aggression

When we talk about aggression, one of the most striking features is the difference between males and females. Certainly, females can be aggressive (as was Melinda Loveless), but in general, males show higher levels of physical aggression than females (Archer, Pearson, & Westeman, 1988). This is true among humans (Eagly & Steffen, 1986) and among animals (Vallortigara, 1992). Interestingly, the difference between the sexes is larger among children than among adults (Hyde, 1984). Further, males tend to favor aggression (verbal or physical) as a method of conflict resolution (Reinisch & Sanders, 1986). They also are more likely to be the target of physical aggression (Archer et al., 1988).

Do males and females differ on all types of aggression? No, males are more physically aggressive than females, and females are more verbally aggressive than males (Archer et al., 1988; Eagly & Steffen, 1986). Females are also more likely to use indirect aggression (for example, manipulating social relationships); males tend to favor more direct (physical) forms of aggression (Lagerspetz, Bjorkqvist, & Peltonen, 1988).

There are further gender differences in the cognitive aspects of using aggression. Females report more guilt over using aggression than do males and are more concerned about the harm their aggression may inflict on others (Eagly & Steffen, 1986). This difference is especially pronounced when physical aggression is used.

Why do these differences exist? Possible causes fall into two major areas: biological factors and social factors. Biological factors include both brain mechanisms and hormones. Most of the research in this area has centered on the male hormone testosterone. Higher levels of this hormone are associated with heightened aggression in both humans and animals. We explore this topic more fully in the next section, "Biological Explanations for Aggression."

Despite hormonal differences between males and females, differences in aggression may relate more closely to gender roles than to biology (Eagly & Steffen, 1986). Both boys and girls are encouraged to engage in gender-typed activities, and the activities deemed appropriate for boys are more aggressive than those for girls (Lytton & Romney, 1991). For example, parents, especially fathers, encourage their sons to play with war toys like GI Joe figures and their daughters to play with dolls like Barbie. Socialization experiences probably further reinforce the inborn male "push" toward being more aggressive.

It is important to note that although social psychological research (both in the laboratory and in the field) shows a consistent difference between males and females in aggression, this difference is very small (Eagly & Steffen, 1986). Gender accounts for very little of the variability we see in aggression among people (Hyde, 1984). In other words, although males and females differ in lev-

One of the few measurable differences between males and females is in physical aggression. Most of this difference appears to be the result of socialization. This little girl has received many messages, both implicit and explicit, that it is acceptable for her to be tender and nurturant with a doll. Boys get very different messages about appropriate toys and play.

els of aggression, we should not conclude that gender is the only—or even a predominant—factor in aggression.

Nevertheless, we must also note that there are relatively large gender differences in aggression. Statistics for violent crimes show that males are far more likely to commit violent offenses than females, by a wide margin. According to statistics compiled by the U.S. Department of Justice for 1988, for example, males commit 90% of murders (including nonnegligent manslaughter), 94% of robberies, and 91% of aggravated assaults (Flanagan & Maguire, 1992). With respect to murder, the gap between males and females has widened over the years. In 1976 males committed 83.4% of murders compared to 16.6% for females, and in 1988 males committed 88% of murders compared to 12% for females (Flanagan & Maguire, 1992). So, even though the difference in measurable aggressiveness between the genders is small, in any specific real-world situation this difference is magnified and elaborated into a large discrepancy between the genders in aggressive acts.

Factors That Contribute to Aggression

If we analyze Khalil Sumpter's action, we probably can come up with a variety of potential explanations for his behavior. For example, was he responding to biological forces when he shot Sinkler? Young males have some of the highest rates of aggressive acts in our society. Was he angry or frustrated with Sinkler? Frustration is often cited as a cause of aggression. Did his belief that Sinkler intended to kill him lead to his decision to strike first? Attributions about intent may play a role in an aggressive response. How did he develop the world view, the social reality, that made such an act possible? Many believed that

Scenes of violence and death related to the use of guns are played out every day in the United States. For example, on April 24, 1994, Ken Flickinger stalked his estranged wife, Anne Flickinger. He caught up with her in a grocery store parking lot. After shooting and wounding Anne's parents, he turned his gun on Anne and, according to an eyewitness's report, shot her in the head at point-blank range. Ken Flickinger then fled the scene with the police in chase. When it was obvious that he was going to be caught, Ken Flickinger committed suicide.

Each year thousands of Americans are killed or injured by guns, some intentionally, some unintentionally. The United States ranks first among industrialized nations in violent-death rates, and deaths caused by firearms exceed in number the combined total of

those of the next 17 nations (Insel & Roth, 1994). Despite efforts to curb the availability of handguns, such as the 1994 enactment of a five-day waiting period to purchase handguns (formerly called the Brady Bill), handguns still proliferate and can be acquired easily by those who really want them.

Gun control is one of the most hotly debated issues in the United States. Proponents of gun control point to the terrible toll that guns are exacting on society. They point to the image of James Brady (former President Reagan's press secretary) lying on a Washington street from a gunshot to the head from a would-be presidential assassin. They point to incidents like

the Flickinger murder/suicide, to images of young victims of gun violence, like Tyrone Sinkler and Ian Moore, or to any of hundreds of minor confrontations escalated into deadly encounters because a loaded gun was available. Their argument is that guns instigate violence. Is there any validity to this assertion?

Leonard Berkowitz and Anthony LePage (1967) conducted a now-classic experiment on this issue. Subjects—some angered, some not—were given an opportunity to be aggressive by administering electric shocks to another person. In one condition, a shotgun and a handgun were left lying on a table in full view of the subjects. In a second condition, the items lying on the table were badminton racquets and shuttlecocks. Their results showed that the presence of the weapons increased aggression among an-

aggression, like all forms of social behavior, is learned. Finally, did easy access to a weapon have a role in Sumpter's violent act? For a closer look at this last possibility, see the featured discussion "Situational Cues and Aggression: The Weapon Effect."

We turn now to the broad question, What causes aggression? As suggested here, different factors have been found to contribute to aggressive behavior. Biological factors play a part, as do social factors. Additionally, research has shown that frustration often leads to aggression. These factors are the topics of the next section.

BIOLOGICAL EXPLANATIONS FOR AGGRESSION

Biological explanations for aggression occur on two levels, the "macro" and the "micro." On the macro level, aggression is considered for its evolutionary significance, its role in the survival of the species. On the micro level, aggression is investigated as a function of brain and hormonal activity. We consider here two theories that look at aggression on the macro level—the ethological approach

gered, but not nonangered, subjects. This phenomenon of the presence of weapons increasing aggression became known as *the weapon effect*.

Although Berkowitz and LePage provide compelling evidence that merely being in the presence of a weapon can increase aggression, other research sometimes fails to produce the weapon effect. For example, Buss, Booker, and Buss (1972), in a series of five experiments in which subjects actually fired a gun, failed to produce a consistent weapon effect. However, Buss and colleagues did not anger their subjects. Could this have accounted for the lack of a weapon effect?

A review of the literature generally confirms the existence of the weapon effect (Carlson, Marcus-Newhall, & Miller, 1990). Carlson and colleagues point out

that situational cues, such as the presence of a weapon, are most likely to have an effect on aggression if subjects are "already experiencing negative affect" (p. 623). In other words, the presence of a weapon may increase aggression only if a person is experiencing negative affect, such as anger.

In many of the incidents involving a person intentionally using a gun to kill others, anger or some other form of negative affect is present. For example, the Flickingers had gone through a bitter separation. Obviously, Ken Flickinger harbored a great deal of anger toward Anne Flickinger. Similarly, the disgruntled employee who goes on a shooting spree after being fired and Khalil Sumpter, who killed Tyrone Sinkler and Ian Moore after a long-running dispute, undoubtedly experienced negative affect on some level.

*I*n these, and similar incidents, the mix of negative affect and the presence of a weapon increases the likelihood that violence will occur. Would Ken Flickinger have killed his estranged wife if he had not had access to a gun? Would the level of violence have been different had another weapon been used (e.g., a knife)? What similarities do you see between Ken Flickinger's act and Khalil Sumpter's? Would outlawing guns prevent violent crime or at least significantly cut down on its occurrence? Or should we direct our attention at identifying and reducing the negative affect that contributes to the use of a gun?

and the approach of sociobiology—and then we consider the physiology of aggression.

Ethological Theory

Ethology is the study of the evolution and functions of animal behavior (Drickamer & Vessey, 1986). **Ethological theory** views behavior in the context of survival; it emphasizes the role of instincts and genetic forces in shaping how animals behave (Lorenz, 1963). From the ethological perspective, aggression is seen as a behavior that evolved to help a species adapt to its environment and evolve. Aggression is governed by innate, instinctual motivations and triggered by specific stimuli in the environment, according to ethologists. Aggressive behavior helps establish and maintain social organization within a species.

For example, many species mark and defend their territories, the space they need to hunt or forage. If they didn't do this, they wouldn't survive. Territorial defense occurs when one member of a species attacks another member for crossing territorial boundaries. The intruder is driven off by aggressive displays or overt physical attacks. Aggression is also used to establish

ethological theory The theory that views behavior in the context of survival; it emphasizes the role of instincts and genetic forces in shaping how animals behave.

The unfortunate consequences of aggression are death, loss, and grief. Guns and bombs allow humans to pursue aggressive goals against remote victims, unaware of any conciliatory gestures the victims may be making.

dominance hierarchies within groups of animals. Within a troop of baboons, for example, the dominant males enjoy special status. These males ascend to their positions of power by exercising physical aggression.

Although animals use aggression against each other, few species possess the power to kill a rival with a single blow (Lorenz, 1963). In most species, furthermore, there are biological inhibitions against killing another member of the species. When a combatant makes a conciliatory gesture, such as rolling over and exposing its neck, the aggressive impulse in the other animal is automatically checked. Thus, aggression may involve merely exchanging a few violent actions; the fight soon ends with no major harm done.

How does ethological theory relate to the human animal? First of all, humans display territorial behavior just as animals do. Konrad Lorenz, the foremost ethologist of the century, believed that aggression had little to do with murderous intent and a lot to do with territory (Lorenz, 1963). Ethologists, for example, might see aggressive behaviors among gang members as a matter of protecting one's turf. Members of urban street gangs have been known to physically attack members of rival gangs who cross territorial boundaries (Johnson, 1972).

Second, there is evidence that aggression plays a role in the organization of dominance hierarchies in human groups just as it does among animals. In one study, researchers organized first- and third-grade children into play groups and observed the development of dominance hierarchies within those groups (Pettit, Bakshi, Dodge, & Coie, 1986). Aggression was found to play a significant role in establishing dominance among both groups Interestingly, however, among the older children another variable emerged as important in establishing dominance: leadership skills. Leaders did not always have to use aggression to control the group.

Finally, ethological theory points out that humans still possess the instinct to fight. Unlike most animals, however, humans can make the first blow the last. Technology has given us the power to make a single-blow kill

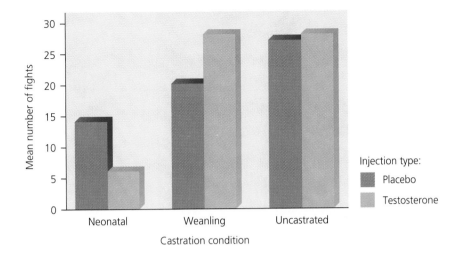

FIGURE 12-2 *Results of Conner and Levine's (1969) study of the effects of testosterone on aggression. The study showed that when there was no early testosterone exposure (neonatal castration), later exposure to testosterone did not lead to significantly more aggression than exposure to a placebo. When there was early testosterone exposure (weanling castration), later exposure to testosterone did increase aggressive behavior.* From Conner and Levine, 1969.

the male hormone. Their brains were normally masculinized and more receptive to the activation function of the testosterone injections received later in life. We can conclude that high testosterone levels will be effective in elevating levels of aggression only if there is normal exposure to male hormones early in life.

Another experiment demonstrated that hormonal influences interact with social influences to affect aggression. In this experiment, male rats were castrated and then implanted with a capsule (Albert, Petrovic, & Walsh, 1989a). For some rats the capsule was empty, for others it contained testosterone. These rats were then housed with another rat under one of two conditions. Half of the rats were housed with a single feeding tube, requiring the animals to compete for food. The other half were housed with two feeding tubes, so no competition was necessary. The treated rats were then tested for aggression. The results were striking. Testosterone increased aggression *only* if the rats competed for food. If the rats were not required to compete, the levels of aggression were quite low, about the same as those for the rats implanted with the empty capsule.

Female aggression may also be mediated by hormones. In another study, the ovaries were removed from some female rats but not from others (Albert, Petrovic, & Walsh, 1989b). The rats were then housed with a sterile yet sexually active male rat. Weekly, the male rat was removed and an unfamiliar female rat was introduced into the cage. Female rats whose ovaries had been removed displayed less aggression toward the unfamiliar female than those whose ovaries had not been removed, suggesting a role of female hormones in aggression among female rats.

The Physiology of Aggression: Summing Up What can we learn from this research on the physiological aspects of aggression in animals? How much of it can be applied to human beings? Not many people would attribute Khalil Sumpter's murderous behavior to an overabundance of testosterone or abnormal brain circuitry. Research with animals supports the

In the movie Falling Down, *Michael Douglas portrays a man on the edge. Overwhelmed by a series of petty annoyances—a traffic jam, a convenience store clerk who refuses to break a large bill, a fast-food employee who won't let him order breakfast—he "snaps" and goes on a rampage. Frustration plays a major role in the aggressive behavior of this character.*

general conclusion that aggression does have a physiological component. However, in humans, biological forces cannot account for all, or even most, of the instances in which aggression is displayed (Huesmann & Eron, 1984). The human being is a profoundly cultural animal. Although aggression is a basic human drive, the expression of that drive depends on forces operating in a particular society at a particular time. Khalil Sumpter's behavior was the product not only of his biology but also of his violent social world. Laws and social and cultural norms serve as powerful factors that can inhibit or facilitate aggressive behavior.

THE FRUSTRATION–AGGRESSION LINK

Imagine for a moment that you are standing in front of a soda machine, the kind that pours you a drink in a cup. You dig into your pocket and come up with your last 50 cents. You breathe a sigh of relief. You are very thirsty and have just enough money to get a soda. You put your money into the machine and press the button for a Diet Pepsi. You watch and wait for the cup to drop. But no cup appears. Instead, the soda begins to pour out, draining through the grate where the cup should have been. After the soda stops pouring, the cup finally comes down. You mutter a few choice words, kick the machine, and crumple the cup and throw it across the room.

Analysis of this incident gives us some insight into a factor that social psychologists believe instigates aggression. In the example a goal you wished to obtain—quenching your thirst—was blocked. This produced an emotional state that led to aggression. Your reaction to such a situation illustrates the general principles of a classic formulation known as the **frustration–aggression hypothesis** (Dollard, Doob, Miller, Mowrer, & Sears, 1939).

In its original form, the frustration–aggression hypothesis stated that "aggression is always a consequence of frustration . . . the occurrence of

frustration–aggression hypothesis The hypothesis that aggression is caused by frustration resulting from blocked goals.

aggressive behavior always presupposes the existence of frustration and, contrariwise, . . . the existence of frustration leads to some form of aggression" (Dollard et al., 1939, p. 1). In other words, according to the frustration–aggression hypothesis, when we are frustrated, we behave aggressively.

FIGURE 12-3 *The phenomenon of displaced aggression: When an individual is frustrated by a target against whom retaliation is unwise, he may "take it out" on an innocent victim.*

Components of the Frustration–Aggression Sequence

What are the components of the frustration–aggression sequence? An assumption of the frustration–aggression hypothesis is that emotional arousal occurs when goal-directed behavior is blocked. Frustration occurs, then, when two conditions are met. First, we expect to perform certain behaviors, and second, those behaviors are blocked (Dollard et al., 1939).

Frustration can vary in strength, depending on three factors (Dollard et al., 1939). The first is the strength of the original drive. If you are very thirsty, for example, and are deprived of a soda, your frustration will be greater than if you are only slightly thirsty. The second factor is the degree to which the goal-directed behavior is thwarted. If the machine filled your cup halfway, for example, you would be less frustrated than if you received no soda at all. The third factor is the number of frustrated responses. If your thwarted attempt to get a soda came on the heels of another frustrating event, your frustration would be greater.

Once we are frustrated, what do we choose as a target? Our first choice is the source of our frustration (Dollard et al., 1939)—the soda machine, in our example. But sometimes aggression against the source of frustration is not possible. The source may be a person in a position of power over us, such as our boss. When direct aggression against the source of aggression is blocked, we may choose to vent our frustration against another target, a safer one. If we have a bad day at work or school, we may take it out on an innocent roommate or family member when we get home. This process is called **displaced aggression** (Dollard et al., 1939) (Figure 12-3).

displaced aggression The redirection of aggression to a target that is not the source of the frustration.

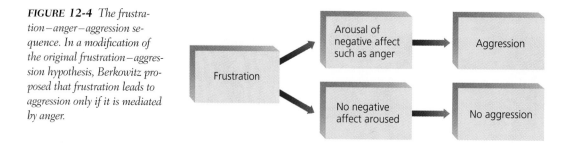

Although the original frustration–aggression hypothesis stated categorically that frustration always leads to aggression, acts of frustration-based aggression can be inhibited (Dollard et al., 1939). If there is a strong possibility that your aggressive behavior will be punished, you may not react aggressively to frustration. If a campus security guard were standing beside the soda machine, for example, you probably wouldn't kick it for fear of being arrested.

Factors Mediating the Frustration–Aggression Link

The frustration–aggression hypothesis stirred controversy from the moment it was proposed. Some theorists questioned whether frustration inevitably led to aggression (Miller, 1941). Others suggested that frustration leads to aggression only under specific circumstances, such as when the blocked response is important to the individual (Blanchard & Blanchard, 1984).

As criticisms of the original theory mounted, modifications were made. For example, Berkowitz (1989) proposed that frustration is connected to aggression by negative affect, such as anger. If, as shown in Figure 12-4, the frustration of goal-directed behavior leads to anger, then aggression will occur. If no anger is aroused, no aggression will result. If anger mediates frustration, we must specify which frustrating conditions lead to anger. Theoretically, if the blocking of goal-directed behavior does not arouse anger, then the frustrated individual should not behave aggressively. Let's consider other factors that mediate the frustration–aggression link.

Attributions About Intent An important link in the behavioral chain that led Khalil Sumpter to kill Tyrone Sinkler was his belief that Sinkler *intended* to kill him. Whether Sinkler actually intended to kill Sumpter has never been resolved (the only evidence for it was Sumpter's word). However, when deciding to act aggressively, we take into account a person's intent, more so than his or her actual behavior (Ohbuchi & Kambara, 1985).

Recall from Chapter 4 that we are always interpreting people's behavior, deciding that they did something because they meant it (an internal attribution) or because of some outside, situational factor (an external attribution). The type of attribution made about a source of frustration is one important factor contributing to aggression. If someone's behavior frus-

	No reversal	Reversal/No knowledge	Reversal/Knowledge
High attack selected by opponent	High attack intended. High attack delivered. Inferred intent of opponent: Deliver high attack.	High attack intended. Low attack delivered. Inferred intent of opponent: Deliver high attack since opponent did not know about miswiring.	Low attack intended. Low attack delivered. Inferred intent of opponent: Deliver low attack since opponent knew about miswiring. High attack selected knowing low attack would be delivered.
Low attack selected by opponent	Low attack intended. Low attack delivered. Inferred intent of opponent: Deliver low attack.	Low attack intended. High attack delivered. Inferred intent of opponent: Deliver low attack since opponent did not know about miswiring.	High attack intended. High attack delivered. Inferred intent of opponent: Deliver high attack since opponent knew about miswiring. Low attack selected knowing high attack would be delivered.

FIGURE 12-5 *Design of Ohbuchi and Kambara's (1985) study of the role of attributions about intent in aggression. In this complex experiment, subjects made inferences about the intentions of an opponent who delivered shocks under varying conditions.*

trates us and we make an internal attribution, we are more likely to respond with aggression than if we make an external attribution.

In one study on attribution of intent and aggression, female Japanese subjects were told they were participating in an experiment on how well people perform tasks under disturbing conditions—receiving an electric shock (Ohbuchi & Kambara, 1985). During the first session of the experiment, the subject attempted to solve several problems while her "opponent" (also a female) delivered electric shocks. The opponent could select either a "high attack" or a "low attack" (referring to shock intensity). The opponent's choice of attack level was displayed to the subject on a light panel.

Some subjects actually received the level of shock intended by the opponent. This was called the "no reversal" condition. Other subjects, in two "reversal conditions," were told that the shock machine had been miswired and that the shocks received were the opposite of what the opponent intended (and what was shown on the light panel). Thus, if a light came on indicating the opponent intended to deliver a high shock level, the shock actually delivered was low (and vice versa). In one reversal condition, subjects were led to believe that the opponent did not know of the miswiring problem (reversal/no knowledge). In the second reversal condition, subjects were led to believe that the opponent did know of the miswiring problem (reversal/knowledge). The design of this experiment is shown in Figure 12-5.

In a second session of the experiment, the subject and opponent exchanged roles, so the subject now delivered the electric shocks to the opponent. The main measure of aggression was the average shock intensity chosen by the subjects in retaliation for the shocks they had received.

Before we look at the results of this experiment, let's see what kinds of inferences the subject might have drawn. Imagine that you are a subject in the "high attack," "reversal/no knowledge" condition. Here you know that the opponent intended to select a high attack. However, a low attack was actually delivered. Further, you know that the opponent did not know about the miswiring, so the opponent did not know you were actually getting the low attack. What inference might you draw about your opponent's

FIGURE 12-6 *Results of Ohbuchi and Kambara's (1985) study of the role of attributions about intent in aggression. When subjects thought their opponents intended to give them a low shock but inadvertently gave them a high shock, they responded less aggressively than if they thought the opponent intended a high shock and delivered a low shock. Subjects thus responded more to the intent of the attacker than to the actual level of shock received.* From Ohbuchi and Kambara, 1985.

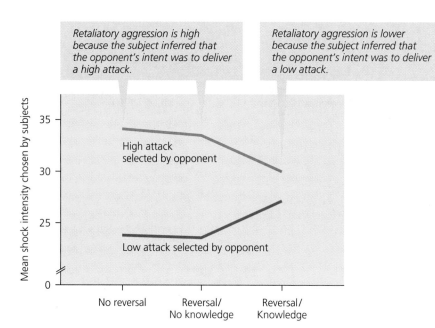

intentions? You probably would infer that she intended you to have the high attack, regardless of the level of attack delivered.

Contrast this with the "high attack," "reversal/knowledge" condition. Here, your opponent knows that you will receive a shock level opposite of the one she selects. So, in this case, the opponent intended to deliver a low shock and did so by selecting the high attack switch. You probably would infer that she intended to deliver the low attack all along.

The results of the experiment, illustrated in Figure 12-6, showed that in the no reversal condition (when subjects believed that the opponent was delivering the level of shock she intended), retaliatory aggression was more severe when the opponent chose a high level of shock than if the opponent chose a low level of shock. A similar pattern was evident in the reversal/no knowledge condition. When the opponent selected the high shock switch, not knowing a low shock was actually being delivered, the subject inferred negative intent and retaliated at a high level.

However, the subject did not infer the negative intent and did not retaliate when the opponent chose the low attack but unknowingly delivered the high attack. In the reversal/knowledge condition, where the opponent supposedly knew of the miswiring, the subject knew that the true intent of the opponent was to deliver the low attack. In this situation, retaliation is reduced. The opposite is true when the opponent selected the low attack switch, knowing that a high attack would be delivered. In this case retaliation increased.

This experiment demonstrated that the intent behind an aggressive act is more important in determining the degree of retaliation than the actual harm done. Those subjects who inferred a negative intent (as in the high attack, reversal/no knowledge condition) retaliated the most. The actual shock level delivered was not as important as the intent behind the opponent's act.

In Khalil Sumpter's case, if he actually perceived that Tyrone Sinkler was going to kill him (even if Sinkler never shot at Sumpter), Sumpter may have been incited to aggression based on what he perceived to be Sinkler's intent.

There is additional evidence about the importance of attributions for aggression. Research shows that if we are provided with a reasonable explanation for the behavior of someone who is frustrating us, we will react less aggressively than if no explanation is given (Johnson & Rule, 1986; Kremer & Stephens, 1983). Moreover, if we believe that aggression directed against us is "typical" for the situation in which it occurs, we are likely to attribute our attacker's actions to external factors. Thus, we will retaliate less than if we believe the attacker was choosing "atypical" levels of aggression (Dyck & Rule, 1978). In this case we would be more likely to attribute the attacker's aggression to internal forces and to retaliate in kind if given the opportunity.

Perceived Injustice and Inequity Another factor that can contribute to anger, and ultimately to aggression, is the perception that we have been treated unjustly. The following account of a violent sports incident illustrates the power of perceived injustice to incite aggression (Mark, Bryant, & Lehman, 1983, pp. 83–84):

> In November 1963 a riot occurred at Roosevelt Raceway, a harness racing track in the New York Metropolitan area. Several hundred fans swarmed onto the track. The crowd attacked the judges' booth, smashed the tote board, set fires in program booths, broke windows, and damaged cars parked in an adjacent lot. Several hundred police officers were called to the scene. Fifteen fans were arrested, fifteen others hospitalized.
>
> What incited this riot? The sixth race was the first half of a daily double, in which bettors attempt to select the winners of successive races, with potentially high payoffs. During the sixth race, six of the eight horses were involved in an accident and did not finish the race. In accordance with New York racing rules, the race was declared official. All wagers placed on the six non-finishing horses were lost, including the daily double bets. Many fans apparently felt that they were unjustly treated—that the race should have been declared "no contest."

This incident is not unique. Frequently we read about fans at a soccer match who riot over a "bad call" or fans at a football game who pelt officials with snowballs or beer cans following a call against a home team. In each case the fans are reacting to what they perceive to be an injustice done to the home team.

Aggression is often seen as a way of restoring justice and equity in a situation. Khalil Sumpter, in one respect, used violence to "even the score" with Tyrone Sinkler. The perceived inequity in a frustrating situation, as opposed to the frustration itself, leads to aggression (Sulthana, 1987). For example, a survey of female prison inmates who had committed aggravated assault or murder suggested that an important psychological cause for their

Richard Farley surrenders in February 1988 after stalking through a California office building where he once worked, shooting everyone he saw. Farley, who was fired for alleged sexual harassment, claimed to be seeking revenge for his dismissal and for his unrequited obsession with Laura Black, the woman who filed the complaint. Aggression is often used as a way to restore equity—to "get even"—especially among those with little power.

aggression was a sense of having been treated unjustly (Diaz, 1975). This perception, apparently rooted in an inmate's childhood, persisted into adulthood and resulted in aggressive acts.

Of course, not all perceived injustice leads to aggression. Not everyone rioted at the New York race track, and most sports fans do not assault referees for bad calls. There may be more of a tendency to use aggression to restore equity when the recipient of the inequity feels particularly powerless (Richardson, Vandenberg, & Humphries, 1986). In one study, subjects with lower status than their opponents chose higher shock levels than did subjects with equal or higher status than their opponents (Richardson et al., 1986). We can begin to understand, from these findings, why groups who believe themselves to be unjustly treated, who have low status, and who feel powerless resort to aggressive tactics, especially when frustrated, to remedy their situation. Riots and terrorism are often the weapons of choice among those with little power. For a discussion of the role of perceived injustice in large-scale rioting, see the featured discussion "From Newark to Los Angeles: Frustration and American Urban Race Riots."

THE SOCIAL LEARNING EXPLANATION FOR AGGRESSION

The frustration–aggression hypothesis focuses on the responses of individuals in particular, frustrating situations. But clearly, not all people respond in the same ways to frustrating stimuli. Some respond with aggression, while others respond with renewed determination to overcome their frustra-

In recent history, violent uprisings have occurred at regular intervals in many American cities. Urban riots have occurred in Newark, NJ (July 1967); Tampa, FL (June 1967); Cincinnati, OH (June 1967); Detroit, MI (July 1967); Miami, FL (1980, 1982, 1984, 1989); and Los Angeles, CA (1965, 1992). During the summer of 1967, urban riots were epidemic nationwide. What factors contribute to these uprisings?

The National Advisory Commission on Civil Disorders studied this question and issued a report (1968) analyzing the riots that had occurred through 1967. They concluded that the riots were caused by a combination of "issues and circumstances, social, economic, political, and psychological, which arise out of the historical pattern of Negro–white relations in America" (p. 203). The report cites the rising expectations of African Americans during the early years of the civil rights movement and the growing sense of disillusionment and disappointment that followed, as gains slowed and almost stopped in the face of increasing racism and changing economic conditions. Dashed expectations gave rise to frustration and feelings of injustice, which ultimately translated into rage.

Against such a background of frustration and perceived injustice, a specific event is often enough to precipitate violence. In the urban riots of the 1960s, as well as in the 1992 Los Angeles riot, an identifiable stimulus event triggered rioting. The Newark riot, for example, was touched off by rumors that an African American cab driver had been arrested and beaten by Newark police officers. The 1989 Miami riot was sparked by the fatal shooting of an African American motorcyclist by a police officer. And the 1992 Los Angeles rioting was touched off by what many viewed as an unjust verdict in the trial of the white police officers charged with beating African American motorist Rodney King.

Johnson (1972) suggests three theories to explain urban riots. The "riffraff theory" suggests that those who riot are somehow disturbed criminal types. The "rising expectations theory" maintains that not all groups of people have experienced the same rise in living standards. Finally, the "blocked opportunity theory" suggests that riots occur because racism and discrimination have blocked certain ethnic groups from attaining desired goals.

A study by Caplan and Paige (1968) found no support for the riffraff theory and only partial support for the rising expectations theory. Support was strongest for the blocked opportunity theory. The blocking of goals causes frustration, which eventually leads to aggression. Additionally, impoverished living conditions may give rise to an attribution pattern that increases the likelihood of aggression. This pattern involves attributing one's plight to factors that are external (whites and politicians are to blame for the problems some ethnic groups have), stable (things have always been like this), and uncontrollable (no matter what we do, we can't improve our living standard). A sense of powerlessness, which has been found among some members of ethnic groups, combines with perceived discrimination to increase frustration and anger (Ransford, 1970). Anger may be vented through violence when a high-profile event occurs.

Thus, the basic ideas behind the original frustration–aggression hypothesis and its recent updates can help us understand urban rioting in the United States. Blocked goals give rise to frustration; untenable living conditions foster anger; perceived injustices and attributions about intent add to the mix. The stage is set for aggression and violence if some critical event occurs. Many urban areas are thus accurately described as powder kegs waiting to be ignited.

The causes for the urban riots that have occurred in the United States are complex. However, the social psychological concepts developed in this chapter shed some light on such occurrences. How, for example, could you use the frustration–aggression hypothesis to help explain many of the urban riots? What mediating factors do you see operating in any link between frustration and the riots? How are the causes for the riots similar to and dissimilar to the factors that contributed to the riot at the New York race track? Given the social psychological underpinnings of urban riots, what do you suggest as solutions to the problem of these recurrent flare-ups?

tion. It appears that some people are more predisposed to aggression than others. How can we account for these differences?

Although there are genetically based, biological differences in aggressiveness among individuals, social psychologists are more interested in the role of socialization in the development of aggressive behavior (Huesmann, 1988; Huesmann & Malamuth, 1986). *Socialization,* as mentioned earlier, is the process by which children learn the behaviors, attitudes, and values of their culture. Socialization is the work of many agents, including parents, siblings, schools, churches, and the media. Through the socialization process children learn many of the behavior patterns, both good and bad, that will stay with them into adulthood.

Aggression is one behavior that is developed early in life via socialization and persists into adulthood (Huesmann, Eron, Lefkowitz, & Walder, 1984). In fact, a long-term study of aggressive behavior found that children who were rated by their peers as aggressive at age 8 were likely to be aggressive as adults, as measured by self-ratings, ratings by subjects' spouses, and citations for criminal and traffic offenses (Huesmann, Eron, Lefkowitz, & Walder, 1984).

The stability of aggression over time applies to both males and females (Pulkkinen & Pitkanen, 1993). However, the age at which early aggressiveness predicts later aggressive behavior differs for males and females. In one study, researchers investigated the relationship between Swedish children's aggressiveness (measured by teacher ratings) at two ages (10 and 13) and crime rates through age 26 (Stattin & Magnusson, 1989). For males, aggressiveness ratings at both age levels were significant predictors of serious crimes committed later in life. However, for females, only aggressiveness ratings at age 13 predicted later criminal behavior. For males and females, early aggressiveness was most closely related to crimes of the "acting out" type, such as violent crimes against property and other people, rather than drug offenses, traffic offenses, or crimes committed for personal gain (Stattin & Magnusson, 1989).

Taken together, these studies show a clear pattern of early aggression being significantly related to aggression later in life (as measured by crime statistics). Although there is some difference between males and females (at least in terms of the age at which the relationship between early aggression and later aggression begins), it is clear that the relationship between childhood aggression and adulthood aggression is true for both males and females.

What happens during these early years to increase aggression among some children? In the sections that follow we look at how socialization relates to the development of aggressive behavior patterns.

The Socialization of Aggression

social learning theory The theory that behavior is learned, primarily through observational learning.

Unlike the biological approaches to aggression, Albert Bandura's **social learning theory** (1973) maintains that aggression is learned, much like any other human behavior. Aggression can be learned through two general processes: (1) direct reinforcement and punishment and (2) observational learning. Khalil Sumpter, Tyrone Sinkler, and Ian Moore grew up in a neighborhood where violence was commonplace. They saw that aggression was a method of getting one's way. They probably even tried it for themselves and obtained some goal. If aggression pays off, one is then more likely to use aggressive behavior again, learning through the process of direct reinforcement. If the aggression fails, or one is punished for using aggression, aggression is less likely to be used in the future.

Observational Learning Although the processes of direct reinforcement and punishment are important, social learning theory maintains that the primary channel of learning is **observational learning,** or modeling. This occurs when, for example, a young Khalil Sumpter standing in a playground sees a person get money by beating up another person. People quickly learn that aggression can be effective. By watching others, they learn new behaviors, or they have already existing behaviors encouraged or inhibited.

Do video games foster aggression and violence? If these children see violent behavior in their social environment, and especially if they see it rewarded, then playing violent video games can reinforce the aggressive scripts they have acquired.

Bandura (1973) and his colleagues (Bandura, Ross, & Ross, 1963) provided powerful evidence in support of the transmission of aggression through observational learning. They showed that children who watch an aggressive model can learn new patterns of behavior and will display them when given the opportunity to do so. For a description of this research, see the featured discussion "Bobo Dolls and Learning Aggression Through Observation."

Aggressive Scripts: Why and How They Develop One mechanism believed to underlie the relationship between observation and aggression is the formation of **aggressive scripts** during the socialization process. Scripts are internalized representations of how an event should occur. Recall from Chapter 3 that another term for a script is *event schema.* You may, for example, have a script about what goes on at a college basketball game: You go to the arena, sit in your seat, and cheer for your team. Such scripts influence how people behave in a given social situation.

Exposing a child to aggressive models—parents, peers, television characters, video games—during socialization contributes to the development of aggressive scripts (Huesmann, 1986; Huesmann & Malamuth, 1986). These scripts, in turn, lead to increased aggression and a tendency to interpret social interactions aggressively. And they can persist, greatly influencing levels of aggression in adulthood.

Aggressive scripts develop through three phases (Huesmann & Malamuth, 1986). During the *acquisition and encoding phase,* the script is first learned and placed into the child's memory. Much like a camcorder, a child who sees violence—or is reinforced directly for violence—records the violent scenes into memory. A script will be most easily encoded into

observational learning Learning by watching others; the primary channel of learning in social learning theory. Also referred to as modeling.

aggressive script A form of script (an internalized representation of an event) that leads to increased aggression and a tendency to interpret social interactions aggressively.

According to Albert Bandura's (1973) social learning theory, children acquire aggressive behavior by watching others act aggressively. Bandura and his colleagues designed an ingenious experiment to test this central principle of social learning theory.

In this experiment, children were exposed to a model who behaved aggressively against a "bobo doll," a large, inflatable plastic punching doll. The model engaged in some specific behavior, such as kicking and punching the doll while screaming, "Sock him in the nose" (Bandura, Ross, & Ross, 1961). After the child observed the model engage in this behavior, he or she was taken to a room with several toys. After a few minutes the experimenter came in and told the child that he or she could not play with the toys because they were being saved for another child (this was to frustrate the child). The child was then taken to another room with several other toys, including the bobo doll.

Bandura did a number of variations on this basic situation. In one experiment, for example, the children saw the model being rewarded, being punished, or receiving no consequences for batting around the bobo doll (Bandura, 1965). In another, children observed a live model, a filmed model, or a cartoon model (Bandura, Ross, & Ross, 1963). In all the variations, the dependent variable was the same: the number of times the child imitated the aggressive behaviors the model displayed.

Bandura found that when the children saw aggression being rewarded, they showed more imitative responses than when it was punished. Live models evoked the most imitative responses, followed by film models and then cartoon models, but any aggressive model increased imitative responses over the nonaggressive or no model conditions (see the figure). Exposure to the aggressive model elicited other aggressive responses that the child had not seen the model do (Bandura et al., 1963). Apparently, an aggressive model can motivate a child to behave aggressively in new ways, not the modeled ways.

Bandura concluded that observational learning can have the following effects (1973). First, a child can learn totally new patterns of behavior. Second, a child's behavior can be inhibited—if the model is punished—or disinhibited—if the model is rewarded. *Disinhibition* in this context means that a child already knows how to perform a socially unacceptable behavior (such as hitting or kicking) but is not doing it for a reason. Seeing a model rewarded removes inhibitions against performing the behavior. Bandura calls this process *vicarious reinforcement*. And third, a socially desirable behavior can be en-

memory if the child believes the script-related behavior is socially acceptable (Huesmann, 1988). Growing up in a violent neighborhood, for example, exposed Khalil Sumpter to daily acts of violence. Undoubtedly, he acquired and encoded an aggressive script based on his experiences.

The stored script is strengthened and elaborated upon during the *maintenance phase.* Strengthening and elaboration occur each time a child thinks about an aggressive event, watches an aggressive television show, or plays aggressively (Huesmann, 1988; Huesmann & Malamuth, 1986). Prior to the fateful day at Jefferson High School, Khalil Sumpter had engaged in numerous aggressive acts. He had a criminal record for robbery and mugging. Each time he engaged in an aggressive act it helped maintain and strengthen the aggressive script he had developed earlier.

Finally, during the *retrieval and emission phase* the internalized script guides the child's behavior whenever a situation similar to the one in the script occurs. If the child has watched too many Clint Eastwood movies, for example, competition for a toy with another child may lead to a "make my day" scenario. The script may suggest to young Clint that competition is

hanced by observing models engaged in prosocial activities.

Bandura's findings have been observed across cultures. Eva McHan (1985) replicated Bandura's basic experiment in Lebanon. Children were exposed either to a film showing a child playing aggressively with a bobo doll or to a film showing the boy playing nonaggressively with some toys. McHan found that the children who were exposed to the aggressive film were more aggressive in a subsequent play situation. They also exhibited more novel aggressive behaviors than children who had seen the nonaggressive film. These results exactly replicate Bandura's original findings and offer additional support for the social learning approach to aggression.

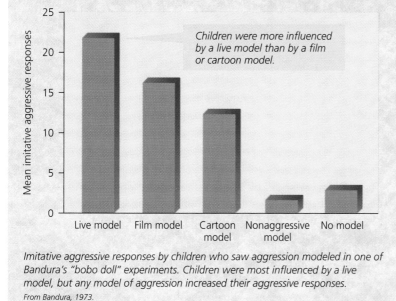

Children were more influenced by a live model than by a film or cartoon model.

Imitative aggressive responses by children who saw aggression modeled in one of Bandura's "bobo doll" experiments. Children were most influenced by a live model, but any model of aggression increased their aggressive responses.
From Bandura, 1973.

Bandura's research, as well as later confirming research, demonstrates the power of observational learning of aggression. How does vicarious reinforcement of aggression help explain incidents like Khalil Sumpter's murdering his schoolmates? How do Bandura, Ross, and Ross's findings apply to the problem of children learning aggressive behaviors from watching television? Do you think that toys linked to television shows for children augment the aggression seen on those shows? Given what we know about observational learning of aggression, how could observational learning be used to reduce aggression?

best resolved using aggression. Khalil Sumpter's behavior certainly fits with this model. Sumpter got to see real-life Clint Eastwood behavior every day. Recall that Sumpter felt that Sinkler was going to kill him. The competition and conflict between Sumpter and Sinkler was solved, once and for all, by the use of aggression. The aggressive script was played out to its bloody conclusion.

The Role of the Family in Developing Aggressive Behaviors

Although children are exposed to many models, the family provides the most immediate environment and is the most influential agent of socialization. It makes sense, then, that aggressive behavior is closely linked with family dynamics.

One developmental model proposed to explain the evolution of aggressive behavior is the **social-interactional model** (Patterson, DeBaryshe, & Ramsey, 1989). According to this model, antisocial behavior

social-interactional model A developmental model suggesting that antisocial behavior (such as aggression) arises early in life as a result of poor parenting.

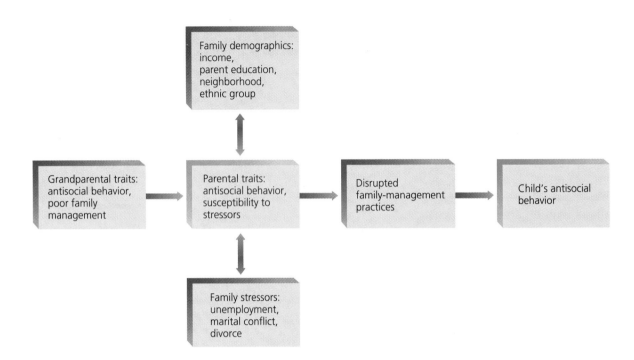

FIGURE 12-7 *The social-interactional model of antisocial behavior. Many factors are seen as interacting to produce aggression and antisocial behavior in children. They include the personality traits of the parents, the way the parents were raised by their parents, social and economic factors, and stresses in the family. When parents use harsh and aggressive child-rearing techniques—especially physical and verbal punishment—the child is likely to be aggressive too. From Patterson, DeBaryshe, and Ramsey, 1989.*

(such as aggression) arises early in life as a result of poor parenting, such as harsh, inconsistent discipline and poor monitoring of children. Poor parenting leads to behavior problems in the child, which in turn contribute to rejection by peers and academic problems in school. Such children often become associated with deviant peer groups in late childhood and adolescence. Ultimately, delinquency results.

Aggressive Parenting   Key to the social-interactional model is the disciplinary style adopted by parents and the parent–child interaction style that results. Some parents have an "antisocial" parenting style, according to the model. Several factors contribute to such behavior in parents. As shown in Figure 12-7, these factors include antisocial behavior and poor family management by their *own* parents, family demographics, and family stressors. Parents' antisocial behavior contributes to disruptions in their family management practices and ultimately to antisocial behavior in the child.

Parents who fall into a harmful cycle of parenting generally rely heavily on the use of power, or harsh measures designed to control the child's behavior. They also use physical and/or verbal punishment. Do these techniques encourage children to act aggressively themselves? The answer is a firm yes! Although parents use power assertion and punishment with their children to make them comply, research shows that it actually reduces children's compliance (Crockenberg & Litman, 1986). This noncompliance may, in turn, cause parents to adopt an even more coercive disciplinary style.

Murray Straus conducted a series of correlational studies (summarized in Straus, 1991) on the relationship between the use of physical punishment and aggressive behavior. Straus obtained information from adolescents and adults about the frequency with which they experienced physical punishment while they were children. Straus reported, first, that almost 90% of American parents of children aged 3 to 4 used some form of physical punishment. The rate of physical punishment declined slowly after age 4 but remained at a relatively high level—60% or above—until the child was 13 years old. Thus, physical punishment as a parenting technique is widespread in our society. Straus also found that as the frequency of physical punishment used during socialization increased, so did the rate of physical aggression used outside the family later on in adulthood. More ominously, as the frequency of physical punishment increased, so did homicide rates.

Physical punishment is not the only form of parental behavior associated with heightened aggression. Parents also subject their children to verbal and symbolic aggression, which can include these behaviors (Vissing, Straus, Gelles, & Harrop, 1991, p. 228):

- Insulting or swearing at the child
- Sulking or refusing to talk about a problem
- Stomping out of the room or house
- Doing or saying something to spite the child
- Threatening to throw something at or hit the child
- Throwing, smashing, hitting, or kicking something

Like physical aggression, verbal/symbolic aggression is commonly directed at children and can contribute to "problems with aggression, delinquency, and interpersonal relationships" on the part of the children (Vissing et al., 1991, p. 231). This relationship holds even when the effects of other variables—such as physical aggression, age and gender of the child, socioeconomic status, and psychosocial problems of the child—are held constant. Moreover, parents' use of verbal/symbolic aggression as part of their parenting style is more highly associated with aggression in children than is physical aggression.

Supporting evidence comes from a 22-year study of the relationship between the parental behaviors of rejection, punishment, and low identification with their children and aggression in children (Eron, Huesmann, & Zelli, 1991). This study suggests that parental rejection and punitiveness are significantly correlated with aggression in childhood and later in adulthood. Children whose parents rejected them at age 8, for example, showed a greater tendency toward aggression as adults than nonrejected children, and harsh parental punishment, particularly for girls, led to increased aggression. Generally, parental rejection and punitiveness were found to have their most enduring relationship with aggression if the rejection and punitiveness began before age 6.

The picture, however, is quite complex. For example, rejected children tend to behave in ways that lead parents to reject them (Eron et al., 1991). So parental rejection that is related to aggression later in life may be partly caused by the child's behavior—a vicious cycle.

Role Modeling of Aggressive Behavior   What is the link between parental aggression and child aggression? The most likely explanation is role modeling. Whenever parents use physical or verbal aggression, they are modeling that behavior for their children. This is a special case of observational learning. Children observe their parents behaving aggressively; they also see that the aggressive behavior works, since ultimately the children are controlled by it. Since the behavior is reinforced, both parents and children are more likely to use aggression again. The message sent to the child is loud and clear: You can get your way by using physical or verbal aggression. Through these processes of learning children develop aggressive scripts (Eron et al., 1991), which organize and direct their aggressive behavior, in childhood and in adulthood.

Child Abuse and Neglect   Parental discipline style is not the only family-related factor related to increases in aggression. Child abuse has also been linked to aggressive behavior later in life, especially among children who also have intrinsic vulnerabilities, such as cognitive, psychiatric, and neurological impairments (Lewis, Lovely, Yeager, & Della Femina, 1989). Research shows that being abused or witnessing abuse is strongly related to highly violent behavior patterns. But physical abuse is not the only kind of abuse that contributes to increased aggressive behavior. Abused *and neglected* children are more likely to be arrested for juvenile (26%) and adult (28.6%) violent criminal behavior, compared to a nonabused/nonneglected control group (16.8% and 21.1% arrest rates for juvenile and adult violent crime, respectively) (Widom, 1992). Children who were only neglected had a higher arrest rate for violent crime (12.5%) than nonneglected children had (7.9%).

Being the victim of child abuse has another pernicious effect. Exposure to abusive situations desensitizes one to the suffering of others. In one study (Main & George, 1985), for example, abused and nonabused children were exposed to a peer showing distress. Nonabused children showed concern and empathy for the distressed peer. Abused children showed a very different pattern. These children did not respond with concern or empathy, but rather with anger, including physical aggression. Thus, child abuse and neglect are major contributors not only to aggressive behavior later in life but also to an attitude of less caring for another person's (perhaps a crime victim's) suffering.

Family Disruption   Yet another family factor that contributes to aggressive behavior patterns is family disruption (for example, disruption caused by an acrimonious divorce). Research shows that disruption of the family is significantly related to higher rates of crime (Mednick, Baker, & Carothers, 1990; Sampson, 1987). One study investigated the relationship between several family variables, such as family income, male employment, and family disruption (defined as a female-headed household with children under age 18), and homicide and robbery rates among African Americans and whites (Sampson, 1987). The study found that the single best predictor of African American homicide was family disruption. A similar pattern emerged for African American and white robbery. Family disruption, which was strongly related to living under economically deprived conditions, was found to have its greatest effect on juvenile crime, as opposed to adult crime. It was found that, at least for robbery, the effects of family disruption cut across racial boundaries. Family disruption was equally harmful to African Americans and whites.

Another study looked at family disruption from a different perspective: the impact of divorce on children's criminal behavior (Mednick, Baker, & Carothers, 1990). The study examined Danish families that had divorced but were stable after the divorce (i.e., the divorce solved interpersonal problems between the parents), divorced but unstable after the divorce (i.e., the divorce failed to resolve interpersonal problems between the parents), and not divorced. The study showed the highest crime rates among adolescents and young adults who came from a disruptive family situation. The crime rate for those whose families divorced but still had significant conflict was substantially higher (65%) than for those whose families divorced but were stable afterward (42%) or families that did not divorce (28%).

The Role of the Family: Summing Up Clearly, an important contributor to aggression is the climate and structure of the family in which a child grows up. Inept parenting, in the forms of overreliance on physical or verbal punishment, increases aggression. Child abuse and neglect, as well as family disruption, also play a role in the development of aggressive behavior patterns. Children learn their aggressive behavior patterns early as a result of being in a family environment that supports aggression. And, as we have seen, these early aggressive behavior patterns are likely to continue into adolescence and adulthood.

The Role of Television in Teaching Aggression

Although parents play the major role in the socialization of children and probably contribute most heavily to the development of aggressive scripts, children are exposed to other models as well. Over the years, considerable attention has been focused on the role of television in socializing aggressive behaviors. Generally, most research on this topic suggests that there is a link (though not necessarily a causal link) between exposure to television violence and aggressive behavior (Huesmann, 1988; Huesmann, Lagerspetz, & Eron, 1984; Josephson, 1987).

Some of the early research in the area showed that males are more influenced than females by violent television (Liebert & Baron, 1972). However, more recent research suggests that gender may not be important in understanding the relationship between exposure to televised violence and aggression (Huesmann et al., 1984). The correlations between watching television violence and aggression are about the same for male and female children. However, one interesting gender difference exists. Children, especially males, who identify with television characters (that is, want to be like them) are most influenced by television violence.

Watching television violence may also have some subtle effects. People who watch a lot of violence on television tend to become desensitized to the suffering of others, as we saw was the case with abused children (Rule & Ferguson, 1986). Further, children who watch a lot of violent

Aggressive models abound in our culture, from movie actors like Arnold Schwarzenegger, shown here in Last Action Hero, *to sports "superheroes" like Shaquille O'Neal. Research indicates that children who watch a great deal of violence on television become desensitized to suffering and develop favorable attitudes toward aggression.*

television generally have a more favorable attitude toward aggressive behavior than children who watch less.

Even sanctioned aggression can increase the incidence of aggressive behavior among those who view it on television. The impact of well-publicized heavyweight championship fights on aggression has been documented (Phillips, 1983). Among adults, homicide rates were found to increase for 3 days after these boxing matches (Miller, Heath, Molcan, & Dugoni, 1991). When a white person loses the match, homicides of whites increase; when an African American loses the match, homicides of African Americans increase. A similar effect can be seen with suicide rates. The number of suicides increases during the month in which a suicide is reported in the media, compared to the month before the report appears (Phillips, 1986). Interestingly, the rate remains high (again compared to the month before the report) a month after the report.

Although most studies support the general conclusion that there is a relationship between watching media portrayals of violence and aggression, a few words of caution are appropriate (Freedman, 1984):

- The relationship may not be strong. Correlational studies report relatively low correlations between watching media violence and aggression, and experimental studies typically show weak effects.
- Although watching violence on television is associated with increased aggression, there is some evidence that watching television is also associated with "socially appropriate" behavior such as cooperative play or helping another child (Gadow & Sprafkin, 1987).
- Other variables, such as parental aggressiveness and socioeconomic status, also correlate significantly with aggression (Huesmann et al., 1984). One 3-year study conducted in the Netherlands found that the

small correlation between violent television viewing and aggression ($r = .23$ and $.29$ for boys and girls, respectively) virtually disappeared when children's preexisting levels of aggression and intelligence were taken into account (Wiegman, Kuttschreuter, & Baarda, 1992).

- Many studies of media violence and aggression are correlational and, as explained in Chapter 1, cannot be used to establish a causal relationship between these two variables. Other variables, such as parental aggressiveness, may contribute causally to both violent television viewing and aggression in children.

Exposure to media violence, then, is one among many factors that can contribute to aggression (Huesmann et al., 1984). Available research does show a consistent—but sometimes small—relationship between media violence and aggression. But interpersonal aggression probably can best be explained with a "multiprocess" model, one that includes media violence and a wide range of other influences (Huesmann et al., 1984). In all likelihood, media violence interacts with other variables in complex ways to produce aggression.

Viewing Sexual Violence: The Impact on Aggression

Television is not the only medium that has come under fire for depicting violence. Many groups have protested the depiction of violence against women in pornographic magazines and in movies. These groups claim that such sexually explicit materials influence the expression of violence, particularly sexual violence, against women in real life.

In the debate about pornographic materials, researchers have made a distinction between *sexually explicit* and *sexually violent* materials (Linz, Penrod, & Donnerstein, 1987). Sexually explicit materials are those specifically created to produce sexual arousal. A scene in a movie depicting two nude people engaging in various forms of consensual sex would be sexually explicit. Sexually violent material includes scenes of violence within a sexual context that are degrading to women. These scenes need not necessarily be sexually explicit (e.g., showing nudity). A rape scene (whether nudity is shown or not) would be sexually violent. Of course, materials can be both sexually explicit and sexually violent.

Sexual violence against women—most notably rape—has endured throughout history, despite the fact that virtually every society in history has had sanctions against it (Zillman, 1984). If anything, sexual violence against women, including against married women by their husbands, is on the rise (Finkelhor & Yllo, 1982; Zillman, 1984). Between 1970 and 1989, for example, the number of rapes in the United States increased from 26,888 to 78,411 (*Time Almanac,* 1992). This may be an underestimate because rape is an underreported crime. The United States consistently has one of the highest rates of sexual violence in the world.

Although the causes of rape are complex (Groth, 1979; Malamuth, 1986), some researchers and observers have focused on pornography as a factor that contributes to the social climate in which sexual violence against women is supported (e.g., Brownmiller, 1975; Burt, 1980; Donnerstein, Donnerstein, & Evans, 1975). Current research and thinking points to the conclusion that media portrayals of sexual violence against women may increase such violence and contribute to attitudes that allow, if not condone, sexual violence.

The Role of Exposure to Erotic Material in Aggression What research evidence is there for these conclusions? Some early research on the effects of media portrayals of sexual violence found that viewing erotic stimuli increased male aggression against females (Zillman, 1971). This was especially true if the subject was previously angered by the target of aggression (Donnerstein & Barrett, 1978). As the interest in this area of research grew, it became obvious that the effects of exposure to erotic stimuli were more complex than met the eye. For example, some studies showed an increase in male aggression against females after exposure (e.g., Donnerstein & Barrett, 1978), whereas others showed a decrease (e.g., Baron, 1974; Donnerstein, Donnerstein, & Evans, 1975).

As it turns out, not all erotic materials produce increases in male aggression against women. Mildly erotic stimuli, such as pictures from *Playboy* magazine or films depicting consenting couples engaging in sexual intercourse, actually decrease aggression (Donnerstein, 1980; Donnerstein et al., 1975). But erotica portraying sexual violence does increase aggression against women (Donnerstein, 1980; Donnerstein et al., 1975).

Does it make a difference whether the woman in a sexually aggressive film is shown reacting positively or negatively to the sexual violence? Apparently not. In both cases, male aggression against females increases (Donnerstein & Berkowitz, 1981). Male aggression against other males does not increase, however. And increases in such violence typically occur only after the subject has been angered (Donnerstein & Barrett, 1978; Donnerstein et al., 1975).

The Role of Sexual Arousal in Aggression It has been established that factors that increase arousal, in general, increase aggression as well, under the "right" circumstances. Sexual arousal is one form of arousal that has been linked to sexual aggression. One study showed that when male college students listened to a story depicting sexual violence, they became sexually aroused (Malamuth & Check, 1983). But not all males were equally aroused by the sexual violence. Other variables had an influence, including the woman's response to the sexual violence (arousal or disgust), whether the woman consented to the violent sex, and the subject's likelihood of raping (LR) a woman (assessed by a psychological test for this characteristic).

As shown in Figure 12-8, male arousal to depictions of sexual violence is quite complex. When the woman was portrayed as disgusted by the violence, Figure 12-8a, low LR men were aroused only if the woman consented to the sexual acts and high LR men were not much affected by whether the woman consented or not. When the woman was portrayed as being aroused by the sexual violence, Figure 12-8b, both low and high LR males were aroused. Low LR men were not much affected by whether the

excitation-transfer model A model suggesting that when two sources of arousal occur closely together in time, the arousal from one may be transferred to the other.

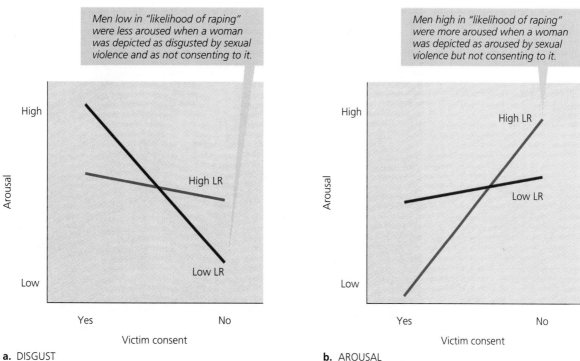

Men low in "likelihood of raping" were less aroused when a woman was depicted as disgusted by sexual violence and as not consenting to it.

Men high in "likelihood of raping" were more aroused when a woman was depicted as aroused by sexual violence but not consenting to it.

a. DISGUST

b. AROUSAL

woman consented or not, but high LR males were much more aroused when the woman was portrayed as not consenting.

These results, and the results from a similar study (Malamuth & Check, 1980), indicate that males are aroused by depictions of sexual violence and rape. This is especially true when the victim is depicted being aroused by or "enjoying" the sexual violence (Malamuth & Check, 1980). Thus, it is not just rapists, or those predisposed to rape, who are aroused by media portrayals of sexual violence.

How does the arousal experienced by males viewing sexual violence get translated into aggression? According to the **excitation-transfer model,** when two sources of arousal occur closely together in time, the arousal from one may be transferred to the other (Zillman, 1984). Recall that only angered males show increased violence toward females after exposure to sexually explicit materials. This is especially likely if the subject is angered after seeing the explicit material (Donnerstein et al., 1975). According to the excitation-transfer model, the arousal attached to the erotic material is transferred to the arousal associated with being angered. The anger-based arousal, now heightened by the transfer of sexual arousal, leads to increased aggression.

When a subject is angered before seeing erotic material, his response is influenced by whether the material is sexually explicit or not. Mild erotica decreases aggression, whereas explicit erotica increases aggression (Donnerstein et al., 1975). Here the mild erotica distracts the subject from the anger-based arousal. No transfer takes place. Rather, transfer may be inhibited and aggression reduced. Consequently, as mentioned earlier, mild

FIGURE 12-8 *Factors involved in men's responses to sexual violence (pornography). When a woman was depicted as disgusted by the violence (a), men low in "likelihood of raping" (LR) were aroused only if the woman consented; high LR men were somewhat aroused whether she consented or not. When a woman was depicted as aroused by the violence (b), it didn't make much difference to low LR men whether she consented or not, but high LR men were much more aroused when she did not consent. These results of Malamuth and Clark's experiment indicated that men in general are aroused by depictions of sexual violence, but men with certain psychological characteristics respond more than other men.* Adapted from Malamuth and Check, 1983.

Some people argue that pornography contributes to an atmosphere in which violence against women is perceived as acceptable. Violent pornography does seem to have this effect, but mild erotica tends to decrease sexual aggression against women.

forms of erotica, such as pictures from *Playboy* magazine or scenes of sex between consenting couples, may inhibit sexual violence against women (Donnerstein et al., 1975).

Of course, sexual arousal does not usually lead to aggression. Most males can easily control their sexual and aggressive impulses. A wide range of social norms, personal ethics, and moral beliefs act to moderate the expression of violence toward women, even when conditions exist that, according to research, lead to increased violence.

The Impact of Sexually Violent Material on Attitudes Besides increasing violence against women, exposure to sexually violent material has another damaging effect. It fosters attitudes, especially among males, that tacitly allow rape to continue. As described in Chapter 4, there is a pervasive rape myth in American society, which fosters such beliefs as "only bad girls get raped," "if a woman gets raped, she must have asked for it," "women 'cry rape' only when they've been jilted or have something to cover up," and "when a woman says no, she really means yes" (Burt, 1980, p. 217; Groth, 1979). Such beliefs are most common among men who believe in stereotyped sex roles, hold adversarial sexual beliefs, and find interpersonal aggression an acceptable form of behavior. Thus, the rape myth is integrally tied to a whole set of related attitudes (Burt, 1980).

Do media portrayals of sexual violence contribute to rape myths and attitudes? Research suggests that they do (Malamuth & Check, 1981, 1985). In these studies, viewing sexually explicit, violent films increased male subjects' (but not female subjects') acceptance of violence against women. Such portrayals also tended to reinforce rape myths. Media portrayals of a woman enjoying sexual violence had their strongest impact on males who were already predisposed to violence against women (high LR men) (Malamuth & Check, 1985). Higher scores on the LR scale were also associated with other beliefs that support the rape myth, such as a belief that rape is justified and the perception that the victim enjoyed the rape (Malamuth, Haber, & Feshbach, 1980).

Finally, we should note that increases in rape-myth acceptance do not relate solely to exposure to "X-rated" films with strong sexual and violent contents. "Softer" portrayals of violence against women (those lacking strong sexual and violent content) seen in mainstream movies and on television also have an effect on acceptance of the rape myth and violence toward women (Linz, Penrod, & Donnerstein, 1987; Malamuth & Check, 1981).

Neil Malamuth and James Check, for example, had some subjects watch films that were widely distributed in mainstream movie theaters that depicted sexual violence against women (e.g., *The Getaway*). In these films the sexual violence was portrayed as justified and having positive consequences. Other subjects watched films with no sexual violence (e.g., *Hooper*). After viewing the films, subjects (both male and female) completed measures of rape-myth acceptance and acceptance of interpersonal violence. The results showed that for male subjects, exposure to the films with sexual violence against women increased acceptance of the rape myth and acceptance of interpersonal violence against women. Female subjects showed no such increase in acceptance of the rape myth or violence against women. In fact, there was a slight trend in the opposite direction for female subjects.

These "softer" portrayals of sexual violence with unrealistic outcomes in films and on television (for example, the raped woman marrying her rapist) may have a more pernicious effect than hard-core pornography. Because they are widely available, many individuals see these materials and may be affected by them. The appetite for such films has not subsided since Malamuth and Check's 1981 experiment. Films depicting violence against women are still made and widely distributed.

Men Prone to Sexual Aggression: Psychological Characteristics We have seen that male college students are aroused by depictions of rape and can be instigated to aggression against women through exposure to sexually explicit, violent materials. Does this mean that all, or at least most, males have a great potential for sexual aggression, given the appropriate circumstances? No, apparently not. Psychological characteristics play a part in a man's inclination to express sexual aggression against women (Malamuth, 1986).

In one study, six variables were investigated to see how they related to self-reported sexual aggression. The six "predictor variables" were:

- dominance as a motive for sexual behavior
- hostility toward women
- accepting attitudes toward sexual aggression

- antisocial characteristics/psychoticism
- sexual experience
- physiological arousal to depictions of rape

Subjects' sexual aggression was assessed by a test that measured whether pressure, coercion, force, and so on were used in sexual relationships.

Positive correlations were found between five of the six predictor variables and sexual aggression directed against women. Psychoticism was the only variable that did not correlate significantly with aggression. However, the presence of any one predictor alone was not likely to result in sexual aggression. Instead, the predictor variables tended to interact to influence sexual aggression. For example, arousal to depictions of rape is not likely to translate into sexual aggression unless other variables are present. So, just because a man is aroused by depictions of rape, he will not necessarily be sexually violent with women. In other words, several variables interact to predispose a man toward sexual aggression.

Sexually Explicit Materials and Aggression: Summing Up   What do we know, then, about the effects of exposure to sexual violence on aggression? The research suggests the following conclusions:

- Exposure to mild forms of nonviolent erotica tends to decrease sexual aggression against women.
- Exposure to explicit or sexually violent erotica tends to increase sexual aggression against women but not against men.
- Individuals who are angry are more likely to be more aggressive after viewing sexually explicit or violent materials than individuals who are not angry.
- Male college students are aroused by depictions of rape. However, men who show a greater predisposition to rape are more aroused, especially if the woman is portrayed as being aroused.
- Exposure to media portrayals of sexual aggression against women increases acceptance of such acts and contributes to the rape myth. Thus, sexually explicit, violent materials contribute to a social climate that tolerates rape.
- No single psychological characteristic predisposes a man to sexual aggression. Instead, several characteristics interact to increase the likelihood that a man will be sexually aggressive toward women.

REDUCING AGGRESSION

We have seen that interpersonal aggression comes in many different forms, including murder, rioting, and sexual violence. We also have seen that many different factors can contribute to aggression, including innate biological impulses, situational factors like frustration, situational cues like the presence of weapons, and aggressive scripts internalized through the process of socialization. We turn now to a more practical question: What can be done to reduce aggression? Although aggression can be addressed on a societal level—such as through laws regulating violent television programming and pornography—the best approach is to undermine aggression in childhood, before it becomes a life script.

Undermining Aggression in the Family

According to the social-international model, described earlier in this chapter, antisocial behavior begins early in life and results from poor parenting. The time to target aggression, then, is during early childhood when the socialization process is just under way. Teachers, health workers, and police need to look for the signs of abuse and neglect and intervene as soon as possible (Widom, 1992). Waiting until an aggressive child is older is not the best course of action (Patterson et al., 1989). Intervention attempts with adolescents produce only temporary reductions in aggression, at best.

One way to counter the development of aggression is to give parents guidance and help with their parenting. Parents who show tendencies toward inept parenting can be identified, perhaps through child welfare agencies or schools, and offered training programs in productive parenting skills. Such training programs have been shown to be effective in reducing noncompliant and aggressive behavior in children (Forehand & Long, 1991). Children whose parents received training in productive parenting skills were also less likely to show aggressive behavior as adolescents.

What types of parenting techniques are most effective in minimizing aggression? Parents should avoid techniques that provide children with aggressive role models. Recommended techniques include positive reinforcement of desired behaviors and time-outs (separating a child from activities for a time) for undesired behaviors. Also, parenting that involves *inductive techniques,* or giving age-relevant explanations for discipline, is related to lowered levels of juvenile crime (Shaw & Scott, 1991). Parents can also encourage prosocial behaviors, behaviors that involve helping, cooperating, or sharing. It is a simple fact that prosocial behavior is incompatible with aggression. If a child learns to be empathic and altruistic in his or her social interactions, aggression is less likely to occur. To support the development of prosocial behaviors, parents can take several specific steps (Bee, 1992, pp. 331–443):

- Set clear rules and explain to children why certain behaviors are unacceptable. For example, tell a child that if she hits another child, that other child will be hurt.
- Provide children with age-appropriate opportunities to help others, such as setting the table, cooking dinner, and teaching younger siblings.
- Attribute prosocial behavior to the child's internal characteristics; for example, tell the child how helpful she is.
- Provide children with prosocial role models who model caring, empathy, helping, and other positive traits.

One approach to reducing aggression is cognitive intervention—teaching individuals that aggressive scripts can be replaced with more positive interpretations of their social environment. Programs like the one shown here use role playing to help teenagers learn new responses to potentially violent situations.

Reducing Aggression with Cognitive Intervention

Reducing aggression through better parenting is a long-term, global solution to the problem. Another, more direct approach to aggression in specific individuals makes use of *cognitive intervention*. We have seen that children who are exposed to violence develop aggressive scripts. These scripts increase the likelihood that a child will interpret social situations in an aggressive way. Kenneth Dodge (1986) suggests that aggression is mediated by the way we process information about our social world. According to this **social information processing view** of aggression, there are five important steps involved in instigating aggression (as well as other forms of social interaction). These are (as cited in Kendall, Ronan, & Epps, 1991):

1. We perceive and decode cues from our social environment.
2. We develop expectations of others' behavior based on our attribution of intent.
3. We look for possible responses.
4. We decide which response is most appropriate.
5. We carry out the chosen response.

An individual with aggressive tendencies sees her own feelings reflected in the world. She is likely to interpret and make attributions about the behaviors of others that center on aggressive intent. This leads her to

social information processing view A view of social interaction suggesting that our social behavior (including aggressive behavior) is mediated by how we process social information.

respond aggressively to the perceived threat. Generally, aggressive individuals interpret the world as a hostile place, choose aggression as a desired way to solve conflict, and enact those aggressive behaviors to solve problems (Kendall et al., 1991).

Programs to assess and treat aggressive children have been developed using cognitive intervention techniques. Some programs use behavior management strategies (teaching individuals to effectively manage their social behavior) to establish and enforce rules in a nonconfrontational way (Kendall et al., 1991). Aggressive children (and adults) can be exposed to positive role models and taught to consider nonaggressive solutions to problems.

Other programs focus more specifically on teaching aggressive individuals new information-processing and social skills that they can use to solve interpersonal problems (Pepler, King, & Byrd, 1991). Individuals are taught to listen to what others say and, more important, think about what they are saying. They are also taught how to correctly interpret others' behaviors, thoughts, and feelings, and how to select behaviors other than aggressive ones to solve interpersonal problems. These skills are practiced in role-playing sessions where various scenarios that could lead to aggression are acted out and analyzed. In essence, the aggressive child (or adult) is taught to reinterpret social situations in a less threatening, hostile way.

These cognitively based therapy techniques have produced some encouraging results. It appears that they can be effective in changing an individual's perceptions of social events and in reducing aggression. However, the jury is still out on these programs. It may be best to view them as just one technique among many to help reduce aggression.

JEFFERSON HIGH SCHOOL REVISITED

If we were to spend a day with Khalil Sumpter, we could identify many factors that led him to his deadly act of aggression against his fellow students at Jefferson High. Sumpter had an ongoing dispute with Tyrone Sinkler, a dispute that no doubt aroused frustration and anger, which we know can lead to aggression. Additionally, Sumpter believed that Sinkler intended to harm him and his family. We also know that people are likely to use retaliatory aggression when they attribute aggressive intentions to others. Sumpter felt an injustice had been done to him, and people often use aggression to restore equity in relationships and situations. Ready access to a gun, an aggressive cue, also contributed to Sumpter's act.

If we could walk down the street outside Jefferson High, we would see living conditions that contribute to an attitude that values aggression. Shootings, stabbings, and other acts of aggression were commonplace both inside the school and in the neighborhood. Living in such an environment fosters the development of aggressive scripts. Ordinary, everyday situations are then likely to be interpreted in an aggressive manner. Although we don't know if Sumpter experienced family disruption, we can be sure he was exposed to violent messages from television, video games, and movies. In all of these ways, Sumpter, like countless others in our society, learned that aggression was an acceptable way to solve interpersonal problems.

LOOKING AHEAD

In this chapter we have explored interpersonal aggression, an enduring behavior pattern that is part of the negative side of human social life. Humans, as we noted early in the chapter, are capable of horrendous acts of aggression against one another. However, this negative side is balanced by a more positive side. Humans have been known to put their lives on the line to save perfect strangers in life-threatening situations. So we are capable of immense good as well. In the next chapter we explore one aspect of the positive side of human nature: altruism and helping behavior. We see how humans often help others, even at their own expense and in the face of great danger.

CHAPTER REVIEW

1. *How do social psychologists define aggression?*
   For social psychologists the term **aggression** carries a very specific meaning, which differs from a layperson's definition. For social psychologists, aggression is any behavior intended to inflict harm (whether psychological or physical) on another organism or object. Key to this definition are the notions of intent and the fact that harm need not be limited to physical harm but can also include psychological harm.

2. *Is there only one type of aggression?*
   Social psychologists distinguish different types of aggression, including **hostile aggression** (aggression stemming from emotions such as anger or hatred) and **instrumental aggression** (aggression used to achieve a goal). Another type of aggression, **symbolic aggression,** involves doing things that block another person's goals. **Sanctioned aggression** is aggression that society approves, such as a soldier in war or a police officer shooting a suspect in the line of duty.

3. *Are there gender differences in aggression?*
   Research has established that there are, in fact, differences in aggression between males and females. One of the most reliable differences between males and females is the male's greater predisposition toward physical aggression, most evident among children. Males tend to favor physical aggression as a way to settle a dispute and are more likely than females to be the target of aggression. Females, however, tend to use verbal aggression more than males. Males and females also think differently about aggression. Females tend to feel guiltier than males about using aggression and show more concern for the harm done by aggres-

sion. The observed gender differences are most likely a result of the interaction between biological and social forces.

Laboratory research on gender differences in aggression suggest that the difference between males and females is reliable but quite small. However, crime statistics bear out the commonly held belief that males are more aggressive than females. Across three major categories of violent crime (murder, robbery, and assault), males commit far more violent crimes than females.

4. *How can we explain aggression?*
As is typical of most complex behaviors, aggression has multiple causes. Several explanations for aggression can be offered, including both biological and social factors.

5. *What are the biological explanations for aggression?*
Biological explanations include attempts by ethologists and sociobiologists to explain aggression as a behavior with survival value for individual and groups of organisms. **Ethological theory** suggests that aggression is related to the biological survival and evolution of an organism. This theory emphasizes the roles of instincts and genetics. **Sociobiology,** like ethology, looks at aggression as having survival value and resulting from competition among members of a species. Aggression is seen as one behavior biologically programmed into an organism.

The roles of brain mechanisms and hormonal influences in aggression have also been studied. Stimulation of certain parts of the brain elicits aggressive behavior. Interacting with social factors, these neurological factors increase or decrease the likelihood of aggression. The male hormone testosterone has also been linked to aggressive behavior. Higher concentrations of testosterone are associated with more aggression. Like brain mechanisms, hormonal influences interact with the social environment to influence aggression.

6. *What is the frustration–aggression hypothesis?*
The **frustration–aggression hypothesis** suggests that aggression is caused by frustration resulting from blocked goals. This hypothesis has raised much controversy. A modified version suggests that frustration does not lead to aggression unless negative affect like anger is aroused.

Once frustrated, we choose a target for aggression. Our first choice is the source of the frustration, but if the source is an inappropriate target, we may vent our frustration against another target. This is called **displaced aggression.**

Cognitive mediators, such as attributions about intent, have been found to play a role in the frustration–aggression link as well. If we believe that another person *intends* to harm us, we are more likely to react aggressively. If we are given a good reason for why we are being frustrated, we are less likely to react aggressively.

Another social psychological mechanism operating to cause aggression is perceived injustice. Aggression can be used to restore a sense of justice and equity in such situations. Research suggests that a perceived inequity in a frustrating situation is a stronger cause for aggression than the frustration itself.

7. *How does social learning theory explain aggression?*
According to **social learning theory,** aggression is learned, much like any other human behavior. The primary means of learning for social learning theorists is **observational learning,** or modeling. By watching others we learn new behaviors or have preexisting behaviors inhibited or disinhibited.

One mechanism believed to underlie the relationship between observation and aggression is the formation of **aggressive scripts** during the socialization process. These aggressive scripts lead a person to behave more aggressively and to interpret social situations in aggressive terms. During the socialization process, children develop aggressive scripts and behavior patterns because they are exposed to acts of aggression, both within the family and in the media.

8. *How does the family socialize a child into aggression?*
Research shows that aggressive behavior patterns develop early in life. Research also shows that there is continuity between childhood aggression and aggression later in life; that is, the aggressive child is likely to grow into an aggressive adult.

According to the **social-interactional model,** antisocial behavior, such as aggression, results from inept parenting. Parental use of physical or verbal aggression is related to heightened aggressiveness among children, with verbal aggression being particularly problematic. Parents who use physical and verbal aggression with their children provide them with aggressive role models.

Child abuse and neglect also have been found to lead to increases in aggression (as measured by violent crime). In addition, child abuse leads to a desensitization to the suffering of others. An abused child is likely to respond to an agemate in distress with anger and physical abuse, rather than concern or empathy (as would a nonabused child). Child abuse, then, leads to a callous attitude toward others as well as increases in aggression.

Finally, family disruption also relates to increases in aggression. Children from disrupted homes have been found to engage in more criminal behavior as adults than children from nondisrupted homes.

9. *What role do the media play in aggression?*
One important application of social learning theory to the problem of aggression is the relationship between media portrayals of aggression and aggressive behavior. Research suggests that children who watch aggressive television programs tend to be more aggressive. Although some early research suggested that males were more affected by television violence than females, more recent research suggests that there is no reliable, general difference between males and females. One gender difference that does emerge is that children, especially males, who

identify with television characters are most affected by television violence. Additionally, heavy doses of television violence desensitize individuals to violence.

Although many studies have established a link between watching media violence and aggression, the observed effects are small and some studies show just the opposite effect. We should be cautious about overplaying the role of media violence in aggressive behavior.

10. *Is there a link between sexual violence portrayed in the media and sexual aggression directed toward women?*
The research on the link between violent sexual media portrayals and violence directed at women leads to six conclusions: (1) Exposure to mild forms of erotica tends to decrease sexual violence against women. (2) Exposure to explicit or sexually violent erotica increases aggression against women but not against men. (3) Individuals who are angry are more likely to be more aggressive after viewing sexually explicit or violent materials than individuals who are not angry. (4) Male college students are aroused by depictions of rape. However, individuals who show a greater predisposition to rape are more aroused, especially if the victim is shown being aroused by sexual violence. (5) Exposure to media portrayals of sexual violence increases acceptance of violence against women and contributes to the rape myth. Thus, sexually explicit, violent pornography contributes to a social climate that tolerates rape. (6) There is no single psychological characteristic that predisposes a man to sexual violence. Instead, several characteristics interact to increase the likelihood that a man will be sexually violent.

Arousal appears to be an important factor contributing to the link between exposure to sexually violent material and sexual aggression. According to the **excitation-transfer model,** when two sources of arousal occur closely together in time, the arousal from one may be transferred to the other. This model suggests that the arousal attached to the erotic material is transferred to the arousal associated with being angered. The anger-based arousal, now heightened by the transfer of sexual arousal, leads to increased aggression.

Finally, research suggests that males with certain characteristics may be at particular risk for committing sexual violence against women. Men who show dominance as a motive for sexual behavior, display hostility toward women, have accepting attitudes toward sexual aggression, are sexually experienced, and show physiological arousal to depictions of rape are more likely to commit sexual violence against women. However, no one of these factors alone can reliably predict sexual violence against women.

11. *How can aggression be reduced?*
Many factors contribute to aggression, including biological predispositions, frustration, the presence of aggressive cues, the media, and family factors. The most fruitful approach to reducing aggression is to target family factors that contribute to aggression. Aggression can be

reduced if parents change inept parenting styles, don't abuse or neglect their children, and minimize family disruption. Parents should reduce or eliminate their use of physical and verbal aggression directed at children. Positive reinforcement for desired behavior and time-out techniques should be used more often. Socializing children to be altruistic and caring can also help reduce aggression.

According to the cognitive approach, children would be encouraged to reinterpret situations as nonaggressive. The **social information processing view** of aggression maintains that there are five important steps involved in the instigation to aggression: We perceive and decode cues from our social environment, we develop expectations of others' behavior based on our attribution of intent, we look for possible responses, we decide which response is most appropriate, and we carry out the chosen response. The cognitive approach suggests that aggressive individuals need to change their view of the world as a hostile place, to manage their aggressive impulses, and to learn new social skills for dealing with interpersonal problems.

SUGGESTIONS FOR FURTHER READING

Baron, R. A., & Richardson, D. R. (1994). *Human aggression* (2nd ed.). New York: Plenum.
This is an update of a classic book on human aggression that is clearly written and covers the latest research and theories. Further, it also examines aggression in natural settings, such as the effects of pornography on aggression, aggression in sport, and the effects of alcohol and drugs on aggression.

Berkowitz, L. (1989). Frustration–aggression hypothesis: Examination and reformation. *Psychological Bulletin, 106,* 59–73.
In this article, Leonard Berkowitz reviews the frustration–aggression hypothesis in its original form. He then goes on to develop the hypothesis further, suggesting that frustration will lead to aggression only if the frustration arouses negative affect, such as anger or fear. It provides a good, one-source overview of the frustration–aggression hypothesis.

Brewer, J. D. (1994). *The danger from strangers.* New York: Plenum.
James Brewer explores what makes an individual vulnerable to violent crime. The vividness of the interviews with victims lend power to the book. Brewer advises the reader on such matters as carrying weapons and precautions one should take to avoid violent confrontations.

Liebert, R. M., & Sprafkin, J. (1988). *The early window.* New York: Pergamon Press.
This book summarizes the issues concerning the effects of television on children. In addition to covering the issue of violence on television and its effects on children, it addresses more general issues surrounding the impact of television on children, including advertising and prosocial programs.

Lorenz, K. (1963). *On aggression.* London: Methuen.
In this classic work, Konrad Lorenz presents the ethological perspective

on aggression. The book reviews years of research with animals on aggression. It concludes with chapters that address the applicability of the animal-research findings to human aggression.

Rule, J. B. (1988). *Theories of civil violence.* Berkeley, CA: University of California Press.

In this book, James Rule explores the roots of civil unrest. The book includes chapters on the relationship between political ideology and civil unrest, as well as chapters centering on the social and psychological roots of civil unrest.

Chapter 13
Altruism

When Peter Still was 6 years old, he was kidnapped and taken into slavery in the South. For the next 40 years, Still remained a slave in Alabama, not knowing the fate of his parents and brothers and sisters. He never gave up hope that he would someday be free. Over a period of years he saved enough money to buy his freedom. He did not have enough money to buy the freedom of his wife and two sons, however. He decided to leave them in Alabama, travel to the North, and arrange to obtain their freedom after he arrived. He made his way back to Philadelphia and tried to find his parents and siblings. He contacted William Still, a prominent businessman and abolitionist, who, unknown to Peter, was his long-lost brother.

The *Pennsylvania Freeman,* a local newspaper, found Peter Still's story to have human interest and reported his plight. Seth Conklin, a white man, read about Still in the paper. He was so moved by the story that he felt it was his humanitarian duty to help Still recover the family he had left behind in Alabama. Conklin contacted Still and offered his help, asking nothing in return. At first Still refused Conklin's help. Instead, Still went to Alabama with the intention of buying his family's freedom. Unfortunately, he did not have enough money, and even if he had, strict Alabama laws concerning buying slaves into freedom may have prevented him.

Returning to Philadelphia, Still decided to take Seth Conklin up on his offer. Conklin laid out a plan to go to Alabama and bring back Still's family. Conklin's decision to help was very dangerous. At the time, black slaves were legally the property of their owners. Fugitive slave laws, newly passed by the U.S. Congress, made it a crime to help fleeing slaves. Those who helped slaves escape were commonly arrested, jailed, or even killed. Conklin was risking his life for a family of blacks he did not know.

Conklin set out for Alabama with a few articles of clothing and a small sum of money. Once he located Still's family, he befriended the slave master and then spirited the woman and children out of the state to freedom. His trip back to the North was difficult and dangerous. He found no help; there were no good Samaritans along the way. Quite the contrary. He wrote in a letter dated February 3, 1851, mailed from Eastport, Mississippi, that "the whole country for miles around is inhabited by 'Christian wolves.'" These "wolves" were church-going Christians who would abduct any unknown black and turn him or her in for a reward.

Because of the irregularity of the steamboat schedules, Conklin and his charges had to find alternative means of transportation. Often traveling at night over land and water, they made the slow, dangerous trip northward. Once, while traveling over water in a small rowboat, they came under gunfire from shore.

In March 1851, Conklin and Still's family arrived in Indiana. Conklin wrote to Still informing him of his arrival in Indiana and seeking to arrange a reunion within a few days. Unfortunately, no such reunion would occur. Conklin and Still's family were apprehended. Conklin tried to free Still's family via legal means, but his efforts were futile. Eventually, Conklin was arrested and, in chains, both he and Still's family were returned to Alabama. Not too long afterward a white man's body was found "drowned, with his hands and feet in chains, and his skull fractured" (Still, 1872/1968). The body was later positively identified as that of Seth Conklin.

What motivated Seth Conklin? Why would a man forgo his comfortable existence and risk all for people who had previously meant nothing to him? Why do we care about the fate of other people? Indeed, do we care at all? These are fundamental questions about human nature. Theologians, philosophers, evolutionary biologists, novelists have all suggested answers. Social psychologists have suggested answers too, contributing their empirical findings to the discussion.

Seth Conklin's behavior was clearly out of the ordinary. Not many whites left their firesides in the North to rescue the families of former slaves. The most notable aspect of Conklin's behavior was that he expected nothing in return, neither material nor psychological rewards. His actions were purely altruistic. So Conklin was an unusual human being—but not a unique one. Others have performed equally selfless acts.

In this chapter we consider why people help others, when they help, and what kinds of people help. We ask, What lies behind behavior like Seth Conklin's? Does it spring from compassion for our fellow human beings? Does it come from a need to be able to sleep at night, to live with ourselves? Or is there some other motivation? What circumstances led Conklin to offer the help he did, and what process did he go through to come to that decision? Or was his decision more a function of his character, his personal traits? Was he perhaps an example of an "altruistic personality"? And what about Peter Still? What was the effect on him of receiving Conklin's help? What factors determined how he responded to that help? These are some of the questions we address in this chapter.

WHY DO PEOPLE HELP?

There are two types of motives for behaviors such as Seth Conklin's. Sometimes we help because we want to relieve a person's suffering. This type of behavior—motivated by the desire to relieve a victim's suffering—is called **altruism.** Other times we help because we hope to gain something from it for ourselves. We may give to a charity to get a tax deduction, for example, or we may give because we think it makes us look good. Often, we experience personal satisfaction and increased self-esteem after helping. When we give help with an eye on the reward we'll get, our behavior is not really altruistic. It falls into the category of behaviors known simply as **helping behavior.**

Notice that the distinction between altruism and helping behavior lies in the *motivation* for performing the behavior, not the outcome. A person who is motivated purely by the need to relieve the suffering of the victim may receive a reward for her actions. However, she didn't perform the actions with the expectation of receiving that reward. This marks her behavior as altruistic.

The distinction between altruism and helping behavior may seem artificial, since the outcome in both cases is that someone in need receives help. Does it matter what motivates the behavior? Yes, it does. The *quality* of the help given may vary according to the motivation behind the behavior. For example, there were others besides Seth Conklin who helped slaves escape in pre–Civil War days, but some of them were paid for their efforts. The slaves who paid their helpers were not necessarily treated very well. In one case a ship captain agreed to ferry some escaped slaves to freedom. Once they reached the shores of freedom, the captain turned the slaves in

altruism A type of behavior that helps a person in need and is motivated purely by the desire to help the other person.

helping behavior A type of behavior that is at least partially motivated by the desire to relieve one's personal distress or to attain some reward rather than solely based on relieving the suffering of a victim.

and kept the money. Similarly, Christians in Nazi-occupied Europe who helped hide Jews for pay did not extend the same level of care as those who were not paid. Jews hidden by "paid helpers" were more likely to be mistreated, abused, and turned in than those hidden by the more altruistic "rescuers" (Tec, 1986).

The question posed by social psychologists about all of these acts is, What motivates people to help? Is there really any such thing as altruism, or are people always hoping for some personal reward when they help others? Researchers have proposed a number of hypotheses to answer this question.

Empathy: Helping in Order to Relieve Another's Suffering

Social psychologist C. Daniel Batson (1987, 1990a, 1990b) suggests that we may help others because we truly care about them and their suffering. This caring occurs because humans have strong feelings of **empathy,** compassionate understanding of how the person in need feels. Feelings of empathy encompass sympathy, pity, and sorrow (Eisenberg & Miller, 1987). If we read about the victims of civil war in Bosnia or Somalia and feel the anguish of those who suffered, we are feeling empathy. According to Batson's **empathy–altruism hypothesis,** empathy motivates people to help those in need.

Psychologists have never been comfortable with the idea that people may do selfless acts. The idea of a truly altruistic act runs contrary to the behavioristic tradition in psychology. According to this view, behavior is under control of overt reinforcers and punishers. Behavior develops and is maintained if it is reinforced. Thus, the very idea of a selfless, nonrewarded act seems farfetched.

Egoism: Helping in Order to Relieve Personal Distress

When we see or hear about someone in need, we often experience personal distress. Now, distress is an unpleasant emotion and we try to avoid it. After all, most of us do not like to see others suffer. Therefore, we may give help not out of feelings of empathy for the victims but in order to relieve our own personal distress. This motive for helping is called **egoism.** For example, if you saw the suffering in Bosnia or Somalia and thought, "If I don't do something, I'll feel terrible all day," you would be focused on your own distress rather than the distress of the victims. Generally, egoistic motives are more self-centered and selfish than empathic motives (Batson, Fultz, & Schoenrade, 1987). Thus, there are different paths to helping, one involving empathy and the other personal distress. These two competing explanations of helping are shown in Figure 13-1.

How can we know which of these two paths better explains helping behavior? Note that when the motivation is to reduce personal distress,

empathy Compassionate understanding of how a person in need feels.

empathy–altruism hypothesis An explanation for altruism suggesting that arousal of empathy motivates people to help those in need.

egoism The motive for helping that is based on relieving one's own personal distress.

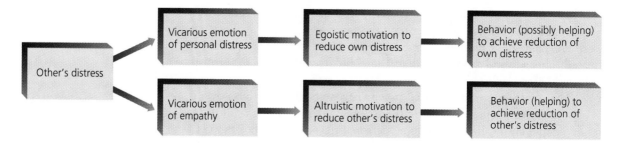

FIGURE 13-1 *Two paths to helping behavior. The empathy–altruism hypothesis proposes that helping behavior results from feelings of understanding and compassion for another person (lower route). The personal distress hypothesis proposes that helping behavior results from the desire to reduce one's own discomfort in the presence of another person's suffering (upper route). Research shows that, in at least some cases, helping behavior is motivated by pure altruism.* From Batson, Fultz, and Schoenrade, 1987.

helping is only one solution. Another is to remove ourselves from the situation. But when the motivation is altruistic, only one solution will be effective: helping the victim. The egoist, motivated by reducing personal distress, will be more likely to respond to someone in need by escaping the situation if possible. The altruist, motivated by empathy for the victim, will not.

Batson designed some experiments to test the relative merits of the personal distress versus the empathy–altruism explanations by varying the ease with which subjects could avoid contact with the person in need. In one study, subjects watched someone (apparently) experiencing pain in response to a series of electric shocks (Batson, 1990a). Some subjects were told that they would see more of the shock series—the difficult-escape condition. Others were told that they would see no more of the shock series, although the victim would still get shocked—the easy-escape condition.

As Table 13-1 shows, the personal distress reduction explanation predicts that everyone will behave the same in this situation. When escape is easy, everyone will avoid helping—we all want to relieve our feelings of personal distress. When escape is difficult, everyone will help—again, we all want to relieve our feelings of personal distress. The empathy–altruism explanation, on the other hand, predicts that people will behave differently, depending on their motivation. This will be particularly apparent when it is easy to escape. Under these conditions, those motivated by egoistic concerns will escape. Those motivated by empathy will help even though they could have easily escaped.

Batson's research confirmed the empathy hypothesis, which predicts that empathic feelings matter very much. Some people chose to help even when escape was easy, indicating that it was their caring about the victim, not their own discomfit, that drove their behavior (Figure 13-2). Other research has also shown that it is the helper's empathic feelings for the person in need that is the prime motivator for helping (Dovidio, Allen, & Schroeder, 1990).

Another question that has been addressed by social psychologists is whether there is a relationship between religion and altruism. Is it true, for example, that a person who is religious has more empathy for people in need of help than less religious people? Do religious people care more about others and help them more when they need help? For a closer look at these questions, see the featured discussion "Altruism and Religion."

TABLE 13-1

PREDICTIONS OF PERSONAL DISTRESS HYPOTHESIS VERSUS EMPATHY–ALTRUISM HYPOTHESIS: RATE OF HELPING IN ESCAPE EASE × EMPATHY EXPERIMENTS

	Empathy	
	Low	High
Personal Distress Reduction Explanation		
Escape Ease		
Easy	Low	Low
Difficult	High	High/very high
Empathy–Altruism Hypothesis		
Escape Ease		
Easy	Low	High
Difficult	High	High

Adapted from Batson, 1990a.

FIGURE 13-2 Some people help even when it is easy to escape the situation. Their behavior supports the idea that altruism is motivated more by empathy than by the desire to avoid personal distress or feelings of shame and guilt.

Maintaining Self-Esteem: Helping in Order to Avoid Guilt and Shame

Everett Sanderson was standing on a subway platform one day when a woman fell onto the tracks. Sanderson leapt down onto the tracks and pulled the woman to safety just moments before a train rushed into the

Charity is one of the central tenets of most organized religions. Religious institutions encourage members to donate food, clothing, and money for the less fortunate, and religious teachings stress helping and giving. One would expect, then, that dedication to religion would be positively related to altruistic behavior. Is this so? It turns out that the answer is more complex than one might think.

When people report on their own behavior, religion and altruism seem to be closely related. For example, one survey found that 58.7% of individuals who reported going to church at least once in the past 7 days said that they "almost always" took steps to help others, compared to only 31.4% of the individuals who had not attended church during that time period (Langford & Langford, 1974). Other self-report research supports this general idea (Benson et al., 1980).

But when we move from the realm of self-report to the realm of actual helping behavior, the relationship between religion and helping becomes less clear. In one experiment—described in detail in the text—John Darley and Daniel Batson (1973) led seminary students to believe that they had to hurry to another building to give a speech. Subjects who were in a hurry were less likely to stop and help a person slumped in a doorway than subjects who were not in a hurry. Darley and Batson looked at those who decided to help to see if their religious orientation was related to the type of help given.

By religious orientation, Darley and Batson meant the underlying reasons and motivation for embracing religious practice. Researchers (e.g., Batson & Gray, 1981; Batson, Oleson, Weeks, Healey, & Reeves, 1989; Darley & Batson, 1973) have identified three religious orientations: the *end orientation,* in which religion is viewed as an end in itself and is valued by the individual intrinsically; the *quest orientation,* in which religion is seen as a way to achieve self-awareness, reexamine values, and satisfy personal doubts; and the *means orientation,* in which religion is seen as a way to achieve a goal, such as higher social status. Batson and his co-workers developed a measure to quantify these orientations.

Darley and Batson found that subjects tending toward a quest orientation gave help that was "tentative and incomplete." That is, they were hesitant about helping. And when the victim said that he was okay, those with a quest orientation broke off attempts to help. Subjects who tended toward an end orientation were more persistent in their help. Even when the victim said he was okay, had taken his medicine, and preferred to be left alone, those with an end orientation persisted in their attempt to help.

In a later experiment, Batson and Rebecca Gray (1981) also investigated the relationship between religious orientation and helping. They found that those with an end orientation helped mainly based on their own need to be helpful rather than on the

station. When asked why he went to a stranger's aid, he replied that he would not have been able to live with himself had he not helped.

Perhaps a similar thought motivated Seth Conklin some 150 years ago. Perhaps people help because not helping would violate their view of themselves as moral and altruistic and would make them feel guilty. Or perhaps they are concerned with what others may think if they do not help, and they would experience shame. The notion that people may help because of the shame and guilt they will feel if they do not help—known as the **empathy–punishment hypothesis**—is another challenge to the empathy–altruism hypothesis.

Batson has accepted the challenge of this hypothesis. He thought that people who help to avoid guilt or shame should help less when provided with a good justification for not helping. After all, if you can plausibly justify

empathy–punishment hypothesis An explanation for altruism suggesting that people help because of the shame and guilt they feel if they do not.

needs of the person needing help. These individuals persisted in trying to help an individual, regardless of whether the victim wanted help or not. In contrast, those with a quest orientation tended to focus their help on the needs of the victim. Individuals with a quest orientation offered help, but only if the victim wanted help.

At first glance, those with an end orientation would appear to be more altruistic than those with a quest orientation. After all, they were more persistent in their attempts to give help. However, this behavior may be more indicative of an egoistic motive for helping than a truly altruistic motive. The logic seems to be: "If I don't help (even if a person doesn't want help), I'll feel bad and violate my view of myself as a religious, helping person." There is evidence for this. Individuals with an end orientation tend to have a great need to be helpful (Batson & Gray, 1981). Generally, those with an end orientation are operating on an egoistic motive (Batson et al., 1989). Those with a quest orientation appear to be operating more out of altruism and empathy. They focus on the needs of the victim rather than on their own need to be helpful (Batson, 1990b; Batson et al., 1989).

Other relationships between religion and altruism have been discovered as well. For example, religious individuals are more willing to volunteer for church-related helping activities than less religious individuals. However, these same religious individuals are less inclined to volunteer for non-church-related activities (Hunsberger & Platonow, 1986).

The way individuals interpret their religion may also make a difference in whether they behave altruistically or not. Research on Christians who rescued Jews from the Nazis during World War II has found a generally weak relationship between religion and rescuing (Tec, 1986). That is, just because a person attended church regularly did not mean that he or she would become a rescuer. Instead, rescuers tended to view their religion in a very special way, being highly independent in their interpretation of religious doctrines. Rescuers tended to adopt the religious doctrine that all people in need should be helped, regardless of religion or race (Tec, 1986).

In summary, one cannot say that being religious makes a person more altruistic. Instead, one's religious orientation, the nature of the help needed, and one's interpretation of religious doctrine combine to make the relationship between religion and altruism complex.

We have seen how religion and altruism relate in complex ways. In what situations, other than those mentioned here, would you expect a religious person to help more than a nonreligious person? Do you think that the situation or religious orientation is more important in influencing altruism? Why do you think that one's personal interpretation of religion is an important factor mediating the religion–altruism link? Can you think of people you know, or know of, who have the different religious orientations defined by Darley and Batson? If so, do they fit the patterns suggested by Darley and Batson's research?

---

not helping to other people (avoid shame) and to yourself (avoid guilt), then no punishment occurs. If, however, your motive for helping is purely altruistic, then reduction of the victim's distress is the issue, not good rationalizations for not helping.

Batson and his colleagues (1988) designed research to pit the empathy–altruism hypothesis against the empathy–punishment explanation. There were two variables in this experiment: the subject's level of empathy for the victim (high or low) and the strength of the justification for not helping (strong or weak). Subjects listened to a simulated news interview in which a college senior named Katie was interviewed about her parents' and sister's recent deaths in an automobile accident and her current role as sole supporter of her younger brother and sister. Empathy was manipulated by instructing subjects either to pay attention to the "technical

Researchers debate whether helping flows more from feelings of empathy for a victim or from a desire to reduce personal distress. When a person could easily avoid a painful situation, it seems likely that helping is empathic rather than egoistic. This woman has little to gain from caring for babies with AIDS beyond the joy of knowing she helped.

aspects" of the news program (low empathy) or to "try to imagine how the person who is being interviewed feels" (Batson et al., 1988, p. 61).

After hearing the news program, the subjects read two letters left by the professor in charge of the experiment. The first letter thanked the subjects for participating and indicated that it occurred to him that some subjects might want to help Katie. The second letter was from Katie herself, outlining ways that the subjects could help her (e.g., babysitting, helping around the house, helping with fundraising projects). Subjects indicated their willingness to help on a response form that was used for the justification manipulation. The response form had eight spaces for individuals to indicate whether they would help Katie. In all cases, seven of the eight spaces were already filled in with fictitious names. In the low justification for not helping condition, five of the seven individuals on the list had agreed to help Katie. In the high justification for not helping condition, only two of the seven agreed to help.

The empathy–punishment explanation predicts that when there is a strong justification for not helping, the amount of empathy aroused won't matter. The empathy–altruism hypothesis predicts that empathic motivation matters most when justification for not helping and empathy are high. Only when people fail to empathize with the person in need does high justification for not helping have an effect on helping. The results of the research support the empathy–altruism hypothesis (Batson, 1990a; Batson et al., 1988). If a person has empathic feelings and truly cares about the person in need, rationalizations, however strong, do not stop her from helping.

Where do we stand at the current time on these hypotheses about helping? Although the research of Batson and others supports the empathy–altruism hypothesis (Batson et al., 1988; Dovidio et al., 1990), other research has not supported it. For example, a strong relationship has been found between feeling sad and giving help, a finding that does not support the empathy–altruism hypothesis (Cialdini & Fultz, 1990). If we give help when we feel sad, it seems more likely that we are helping to relieve personal distress than out of pure altruism.

At this point it is probably best to adopt a position between the competing hypotheses. People may be motivated by empathic altruism, but they do seem to need to know that the victim benefited from their help (Smith, Keating, & Stotland, 1989). This allows them to experience "empathic joy" for helping the victim. Empathic joy simply means that the helper feels good about the fact that her efforts helped someone and that there was a positive outcome for that person. The helper gets a reward—the knowledge that someone she helped benefited.

Biological Explanations: Helping in Order to Preserve Our Own Genes

As mentioned earlier, some psychologists have been skeptical about the existence of purely altruistic behavior, because they believe behavior is shaped and regulated by rewards and punishments. But there is another reason psychologists have been skeptical about the existence of pure altruism, and that reason is biological: People or animals who carry altruism involving personal danger to its logical conclusion—as Seth Conklin did—die. Because self-preservation, or at least the preservation of one's genes (that is, one's children or relatives), is a fundamental rule of evolutionary biology, pure altruism stands on some shaky grounds (Wilson, 1978). Self-sacrificing behavior is very rare. When it occurs, we reward it extravagantly. The Medal of Honor, for example, is given for extraordinary bravery, behavior that goes beyond the call of duty.

Evolutionary biologists find altruistic behavior fascinating because it presents a biological paradox: In light of the principle of survival of the fittest, how can a behavior have evolved that puts the individual at risk and makes survival less likely (Wilson, 1975)? The principle of natural selection favors the success of selfish behavior. Those animals that take care of themselves and do not expend energy on helping others are more likely to survive and more likely to reproduce their genes. The basic measure of biological fitness is the relative number of an individual's offspring that survive and reproduce (Wilson, 1975).

The evolutionary biologist's answer to the paradox is to suggest that there are no examples of purely altruistic, totally selfless behavior in nature. Instead, there is behavior that may have the effect of helping others but also serves some selfish purpose. For example, consider the white-fronted bee eater, a bird living in eastern and southern Africa (Goleman, 1991). These birds live in complex colonies consisting of 15 to 25 extended families. Family units consist of about four overlapping generations. When breeding time arrives, some family members do not breed. Instead, they serve as "helpers" who devote themselves to constructing nests, feeding females, and defending the young. This helping is called *alloparenting*, or cooperative breeding.

How could such behavior have evolved? The bee eaters who do not breed lose the opportunity to pass on their genes to offspring. However, their behavior does help to ensure the survival of the whole colony and specifically of the family members with whom they share genes. This conclusion is supported by the fact that the bee eater helpers provide cooperative help only to their closest relatives. Birds that could have provided help but do not turn out to be "in-laws"—birds that have no genetic connection with the mating pairs. Although the helping behavior does not further the survival of the individual's genes, it does serve to preserve the individual's *gene pool*.

Do humans differ significantly from animals when it comes to altruism? According to sociobiologists, human social behavior is governed by the same rules that order all animal behavior. A central problem of sociobiology is to explain how altruism can exist even though such behavior endangers individual fitness and survival (Wilson, 1975, 1978). However, there is ample evidence that altruism among humans flourishes and endures.

One possible resolution to this apparent paradox lies in the idea that human survival, dating to the beginnings of human society, depended on cooperation. Human beings, being smaller, slower, and weaker than many other animal species, needed to form cooperative groups to survive. Cooperation and altruism (helping one another) would have been selected for, genetically, because they increased the survival of human beings (Hoffman, 1981). Unlike animals, humans do not restrict their helping to close genetic relatives. Instead, humans can maintain the gene pool by helping those who share common characteristics, even if they are not close kin (Glassman, Packel, & Brown, 1986). Helping non-kin may help one preserve one's distinguishing characteristics in the gene pool in a manner analogous to helping kin.

Social psychologists acknowledge that biology plays a role in altruistic behavior. Altruism does not occur as often or as naturally as aggression, but it does occur. However, social psychology also points out that altruistic behavior in humans is determined by more than the biological dimension of our nature.

Reprise: Why Do We Help?

Why did Seth Conklin go to such extraordinary lengths to help Peter Still and his family? Still was not his kin, so Conklin was not motivated by the urge to protect his gene pool. Nor was he motivated simply by a desire to reduce his own personal distress on reading about Still's predicament, although we can be sure that Conklin felt emotional pain. He could have relieved his distress by putting the paper down and going on about his life. He probably wasn't motivated by what his neighbors would say either, since most of them were able to live with Peter Still's story.

No, Seth Conklin must have been motivated by altruistic empathy, by compassionate understanding of how Still felt. Conklin simply knew that he had to help. Altruistic behavior, as noted earlier, does occur. But the extraordinary long-term helping exemplified by Seth Conklin needs further explanation. We return to this issue a bit later in this chapter.

Kitty Genovese screamed for help when she was attacked by a man with a knife in Queens, New York, in 1964. Thirty-eight people in nearby apartments heard her screams, but none responded. What characteristics of the situation and of the individuals involved do you think contributed to this outcome? How do you think you would have responded?

HELPING IN EMERGENCIES: A FIVE-STAGE DECISION MODEL

Seth Conklin's decision to help Peter Still's family is an example of one type of helping involving a long-term commitment to a course of action. We refer to this type of helping as *long-term helping*. Conklin's help involved a commitment that was extended over a period of months and required a great investment of effort and resources. However, there are many other situations that require quick action involving a short-term commitment to helping. For example, if you saw a child fall into a pond, you probably would rescue that child. We refer to this type of helping as *situation-specific helping*. This type of helping, which is most likely to be in response to an emergency, does not require a long-term investment of effort and resources.

Emergency situations in which bystanders give help occur quite often. But there are also many instances in which bystanders remain passive and do not intervene, even when a victim is in clear need of help. One such incident captured the attention not only of the public but also of social psychologists: the tragic death of Kitty Genovese on March 13, 1964.

Kitty Genovese, a 24-year-old waitress, was coming home from work in Queens, New York, late one night. As she walked to her apartment building, she was attacked by a man wielding a knife. She screamed for help. In response to her screams, 38 of her neighbors took notice from their apartments. One yelled for the man to stop. The attacker ran off, only to return when it was obvious that nobody was coming to her aid. He stabbed Genovese repeatedly, eventually killing her. The attack lasted 40 minutes. Once the police were called, they responded within 2 minutes.

The tragedy of Kitty Genovese, and similar incidents that occur all too frequently, raised many questions among the public and among social scientists. Dissatisfied with explanations that blamed life in the big city ("urban apathy"), social psychologists John Darley and Bibb Latané began to devise some explanations about why the witnesses to Kitty Genovese's murder did nothing to intervene. Darley and Latané sketched out a social psychological model to explain the bystanders' behavior.

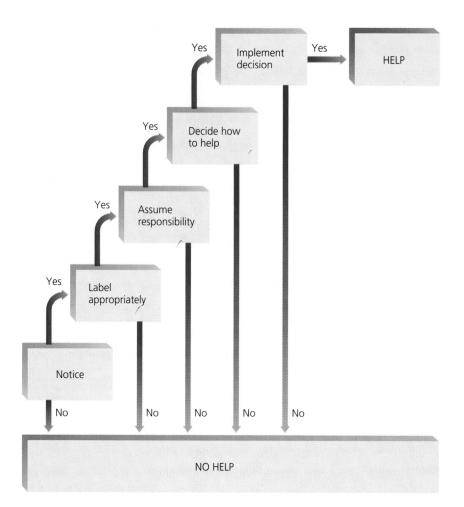

FIGURE 13-3 *Five stages in Darley and Latané's decision model of helping. According to the model, help will be provided only if the potential helper makes a "yes" decision at each stage.* Based on Darley and Latané, 1968; and Latané and Darley, 1968.

The model proposed that there are five stages a bystander must pass through, each representing an important decision, before he or she will help a person in need (Latané & Darley, 1968). In their original formulation of the model, Latané and Darley suggested that a bystander must notice the emergency situation, label the situation correctly as an emergency, and assume responsibility for helping. Darley and Latané (1968) proposed that there is even something beyond assuming responsibility: The individual must decide how to help. Help, according to these researchers, could take the form of direct intervention (like Seth Conklin's behavior) or indirect intervention (like calling the police). The general model proposed by Latané and Darley (1968) and Darley and Latané (1968), along with an additional stage, is shown in Figure 13-3.

At each stage of the model, the individual must assess the situation and make a "yes" or "no" decision. At any point in the decision process, a "no" decision will lead to failure to help. A "yes" decision itself does not guarantee intervention; it simply allows the person to move to the next stage of the model. According to the model, help will be given only if a "yes" decision is made at each stage. Let's consider now each of the five stages.

Noticing the Situation

Before we can expect a person to intervene in an emergency, that person must have noticed an emergency exists. In general, we are particularly likely to notice a stimulus that is brightly colored, noisy, or somehow stands out against a background. This is also true when noticing an emergency. Our chances of noticing an emergency are increased if it stands out against the background of everyday life. For example, we are more likely to notice an automobile accident if there is a loud crash than if there is little or no sound. Anything that makes the emergency more conspicuous will increase the probability that we will attend to it.

Labeling the Situation as an Emergency

If a person has noticed the emergency, the next step is to correctly label the situation as one that requires intervention. One very important factor in this stage is whether there is ambiguity, uncertainty, about what has happened. For example, imagine that you look out the window of your second-floor apartment one day and notice, immediately below the window, a car with its driver's side door open and a person lying half in and half out of the car. Has the person collapsed, perhaps of a heart attack or a stroke? Or is the person changing a fuse under the dashboard or fixing the radio? If you decide on the latter explanation, you will turn away and not give it another thought. You have made a "no" decision in the labeling stage of the model.

Emergencies can be highly ambiguous because there is often more than one interpretation for a situation. Is the person upstairs beating her child or merely disciplining her? Is the man staggering down the street sick or drunk? Is that person slumped in the doorway injured, or is he a drunken derelict? These questions must be resolved if we are to correctly label a situation as an emergency requiring our intervention.

When two 10-year-old boys abducted a 2-year-old from a shopping center in Liverpool in 1993 and subsequently killed him, they walked together 2½ miles along a busy road congested with traffic. Thirty-eight people remembered seeing the three children, and some said later that the toddler was being dragged or appeared to be crying. Apparently, the situation was ambiguous enough—were they his older brothers, trying to get him home for dinner?—that no one stopped. A driver of a dry-cleaning van said he saw one of the older boys aim a kick at the toddler, but it looked like a "persuading" kind of kick such as one might use on a 2-year-old (Morrison, 1994). The driver failed to label the situation correctly.

The Ambiguity of the Situation Research has confirmed that situational ambiguity is an important factor in whether people help (Figure 13-4). In one study, subjects were seated in a room and asked to fill out a questionnaire (Yakimovich & Salz, 1971). Outside the room, a confederate of the experimenter was washing windows. When the experimenter signaled, the confederate knocked over his ladder and pail, fell to the pavement, and grabbed his ankle. In one condition (the verbalization condition), the

FIGURE 13-4 *Is it an emergency or not? When a situation is ambiguous, people often fail to help because they label it incorrectly.*

confederate screamed and cried for help. In the other condition (the no-verbalization condition), the confederate moaned but didn't cry for help.

In both conditions, subjects jumped up and went to the window when they heard the sound of the crash. Therefore, all subjects noticed the emergency. In the verbalization condition, 81% (13 of 16) tried to help the victim. In the no-verbalization condition, however, only 29% (5 of 17) subjects tried to help. The clear cry for help, then, increased the probability that people would help. Without it, it wasn't clear that the man needed help.

Note also that the potential helpers had all seen the victim before his accident. He was a real person to them. Recall in the Kitty Genovese case that the witnesses had not seen her before she was stabbed. Given this fact and that the murder took place in the fog of the early morning hours, ambiguity must have existed, at least for some witnesses.

The Presence of Others The presence of other bystanders may also affect the labeling process. Reactions of other bystanders often determine the response to the situation. If bystanders show little concern over the emergency, individuals will be less likely to help. When we are placed in a social situation (especially an ambiguous one), we look around us to see what others are doing (the process of social comparison). If others are not concerned, we may not define the situation as an emergency and we probably will not offer to help.

In one study, increasing or decreasing the availability of cues from another bystander affected helping (Darley, Teger, & Lewis, 1973). Subjects were tested either alone or in groups of two. Those participating in groups were either facing each other across a table (face-to-face condition) or seated back-to-back (not-facing condition). An emergency was staged (a fall) while the subjects worked on their tasks. More subjects who were alone helped (90%) than subjects who were in groups. However, whether subjects were facing each other made a big difference. Subjects who were facing each other were significantly more likely to help (80%) than subjects not facing each other (20%). Consider what happens when you sit across from someone and you both hear a cry for help. You look at her, she looks at you. If she then goes back to her work, you probably will not define the situation as an emergency. If she says, "Did you hear that?" you are more likely to go investigate.

Generally, we rely on cues from other bystanders more and more as the ambiguity of the situation increases. Thus, in highly ambiguous emergencies we might expect the presence of others who are passive to suppress helping. The fact that the witnesses to Kitty Genovese's murder were in their separate apartments and did not know what others were doing and thinking operated to suppress intervention.

Assuming Responsibility to Help: The Bystander Effect

Noticing and correctly labeling a situation as an emergency are not enough to guarantee that a bystander will intervene. It is certain that the 38 witnesses to Kitty Genovese's murder noticed the incident and probably labeled it as an emergency. What they did not do is conclude that they had a responsibility to help. Darley and Latané (1968), puzzled by the lack of intervention on the part of the witnesses, thought that the presence of others might inhibit rather than increase helping. They designed a simple yet elegant experiment to test for the effects of multiple bystanders on helping. Their experiment demonstrated the power of the **bystander effect,** where a person in need of help is *less* likely to receive help as the number of bystanders increases.

Subjects in this experiment were told it was a study of interpersonal communication. They were asked to participate in a group discussion of their current problems. To ensure anonymity, the discussion would take place over intercoms. In reality, there was no group. The experimenter played a tape of a discussion to lead the subject to believe that other group members existed.

Darley and Latané varied the size of the group. In one condition, the subject was told that there was one other person in the group (so the group consisted of the subject and the victim); in a second condition, there were two other people (subject, victim, and one other); in the third condition, there were five other people (subject, victim, and four others). The discussion went along uneventfully until it was the victim's turn to speak. The actor who played the role of the victim on the tape simulated a seizure. Darley and Latané noted the number of subjects who tried to help and how long it took them to try to help.

The study produced two major findings. First, the size of the group had an effect on the percentage of subjects helping. When the subject believed that he or she was alone in the experiment with the victim, 85% of the subjects helped. The percentage of subjects offering help declined

bystander effect The finding that helping behavior is less likely to occur as the number of bystanders (witnesses to an emergency) increases.

THE FAR SIDE   By GARY LARSON

Crossing the village, Mowaka is overpowered by army ants. (Later, bystanders were all quoted as saying they were horrified, but "didn't want to get involved.")

when the subject believed there was only one other bystander (62%) or four other bystanders (31%). In other words, as the number of bystanders increased, the likelihood of the subject helping the victim decreased.

The second major finding was that the size of the group had an effect on time between the onset of the seizure and the offering of help. When the subject believed he or she was alone, help occurred more quickly than when the subject believed other bystanders were present. In essence, the subjects who believed they were members of a larger group became "frozen in time" by the presence of others. They had not decided to help or not to help. They were distressed but could not act.

Why Does the Bystander Effect Occur? The best explanation offered for the bystander effect is **diffusion of responsibility** (Darley & Latané, 1968). According to this explanation, each bystander assumes that another bystander will take action. If all the bystanders think that way, no help will be offered. This explanation fits quite well with Darley and Latané's findings where the bystanders could not see each other, as was the case in the Kitty Genovese killing. Under these conditions, it is easy to see how a bystander (unaware of how other bystanders are acting) might assume that someone else has already taken or will take action.

What about emergency situations in which bystanders *can* see one another? In this case the bystanders could actually see that others were not helping. Diffusion of responsibility under these conditions may not explain bystander inaction (Latané & Darley, 1968). Another explanation has been offered for the bystander effect that centers on **pluralistic ignorance,** which occurs when a group of individuals acts in the same manner despite

diffusion of responsibility An explanation for the bystander effect suggesting that each bystander assumes that another bystander will take responsibility to help.

pluralistic ignorance An explanation for the bystander effect. When bystanders to an emergency act as though no emergency exists, the situation is redefined as a nonemergency and helping drops.

the fact that each person has different perceptions of an event (Miller & McFarland, 1987). In the bystander effect, pluralistic ignorance operates when the bystanders in an ambiguous emergency situation look around and see each other doing nothing; they assume that the others are thinking that the situation is not an emergency (Miller & McFarland, 1987). In essence, the collective inaction of the bystanders leads to a redefinition of the situation as a nonemergency.

Latané and Darley (1968) provide evidence for this explanation. Subjects filled out a questionnaire alone in a room, with two passive bystanders (confederates of the experimenter), or with two other actual subjects. While the subjects were filling out the questionnaire, smoke was introduced into the room through a vent. The results showed that when subjects were alone in the room, 75% of the subjects reported the smoke, many within 2 minutes of first noticing it. In the condition where the subject was in the room with two passive bystanders, only 10% reported the smoke. In the last condition, where the subject was with two other subjects, 38% reported the smoke. Thus, the presence of bystanders once again suppressed helping. This despite the fact that subjects in the bystander conditions denied that the other people in the room had any effect on them (Latané & Darley, 1968).

In postexperimental interviews, Latané and Darley searched for the underlying cause for the observed results. They found that subjects who reported the smoke felt that the smoke was unusual enough to report, although they didn't feel that the smoke was dangerous. Subjects who failed to report the smoke, which was most likely to occur in the two-bystander conditions, developed a set of creative reasons why the smoke should not be reported. For example, some subjects believed that the smoke was smog piped into the room to simulate an urban environment, or that the smoke was truth gas designed to make them answer the questionnaire truthfully. Whatever reasons these subjects came up with, the situation was redefined as a nonemergency.

Exceptions to the Bystander Effect Increasing the number of bystanders does not always suppress helping; there are exceptions to the bystander effect. One group of researchers staged a rape on a college campus and measured how many subjects intervened (Harari, Harari, & White, 1985). The subjects had three options in the experimental situation: fleeing without helping, giving indirect help (alerting a police officer who is out of view of the rape), or giving direct help (intervening directly in the rape). Figure 13-5 shows the experimental situation and the various paths available to subjects.

Male subjects were tested as they walked either alone or in groups. (The groups in this experiment were simply subjects who happened to be walking together and not interacting with one another.) As the subjects approached a certain point (see Figure 13-5), two actors staged the rape. The woman screamed "Help! Help! Please help me! You bastard! Rape! Rape!" (Harari et al., 1985, p. 656). The results of this experiment did not support the bystander effect. Subjects walking in groups were more likely to help

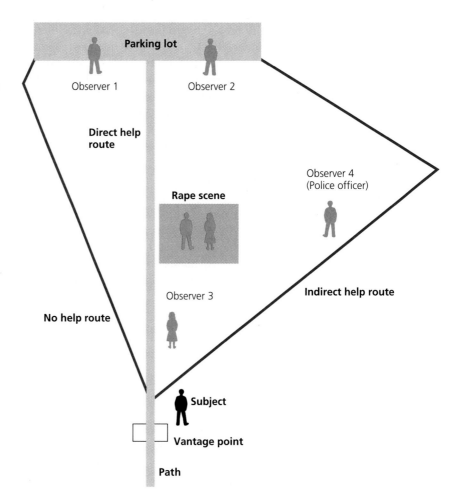

FIGURE 13-5 The setup of a staged rape scene on a college campus. Subjects walking either alone or in groups had a choice of three responses when they realized a "rape" was occurring—giving no help, giving indirect help by alerting a police officer, or giving direct help. In a reversal of the bystander effect, subjects in groups were more likely to provide direct help than lone subjects, probably because the situation was perceived as dangerous. From Harari, Harari, and White, 1985.

(85%) than subjects walking alone (65%). In this situation—a victim is clearly in need and the helping situation is dangerous—it seems that bystanders in groups are more likely to help than solitary bystanders (Clark & Word, 1974; Harari et al., 1985).

The bystander effect also seems to be influenced by the roles people take. In another study, some subjects were assigned to be the leaders of a group discussion and others to be "assistants" (Baumeister, Chesner, Senders, & Tice, 1988). When a seizure was staged, subjects assigned the role of leader were more likely to intervene (80%) than those assigned the role of assistant (35%). It appears that the responsibility inherent in the leadership role on a specific task generalizes to emergencies as well.

Deciding How to Help

The fourth stage of the five-stage model of helping is deciding how to help. In the staged rape study, for example, subjects had a choice of directly intervening to stop the rape or aiding the victim by notifying the police (Harari, Harari, & White, 1985). What influences decisions like this?

There is considerable support for the notion that people who feel competent, who have the necessary skills, are more likely to help than those who feel they lack such competence. In a study in which subjects were exposed to a staged arterial bleeding emergency, the likelihood of providing effective help was determined only by the expertise of the subjects (some had Red Cross training) (Shotland & Heinhold, 1985).

There are two reasons why greater competence may lead to more helping. First, feelings of competence increase confidence in one's ability to help and knowledge of what ought to be done (Cramer, McMaster, Bartell, & Dragna, 1988). Second, feelings of competence increase sensitivity to the needs of others and empathy toward victims (Barnett, Thompson, & Pfiefer, 1985). People who feel like leaders are probably also more likely to help because they feel more confident about being able to help successfully.

Many emergencies, however, do not require any special training or competence. Seth Conklin had no more competence in rescuing slave families than anyone else in Philadelphia. In the Kitty Genovese case, a simple telephone call to the police would have been all that was needed. Clearly, no special competence was required.

Implementing the Decision to Help

Having passed through these four stages, a person may still choose not to intervene. To understand why, imagine that as you drive to campus, you see a fellow student standing next to his obviously disabled car. Do you stop and offer to help? Perhaps you are late for your next class and you feel that you do not have the time. Perhaps you're not sure it's safe to stop on the side of the highway. Or perhaps the student strikes you as somehow undeserving of help (Bickman & Kamzan, 1973). These and other considerations influence your decision to help or not.

Assessing Rewards and Costs for Helping Social psychologists have found that people's evaluation of the rewards and costs involved in helping affect their decision to help or not. There are potential rewards for helping (e.g., gratitude from the victim, monetary reward, recognition by peers) and for not helping (e.g., avoiding potential danger, arriving for an appointment on time). Similarly, there are costs for helping (e.g., possible injury, embarrassment, inconvenience) and for not helping (e.g., loss of self-esteem). Generally, research indicates that the greater the cost of helping, the less likely people are to help (Batson, O'Quin, Fultz, & Vanderplas, 1983; Darley & Batson, 1973; Piliavin & Piliavin, 1972; Piliavin, Piliavin, & Rodin, 1975).

In a study of this relationship, Darley and Batson (1973) told seminarians taking part in an experiment at Princeton University that a high school

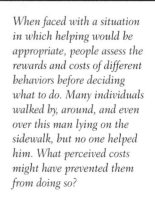

When faced with a situation in which helping would be appropriate, people assess the rewards and costs of different behaviors before deciding what to do. Many individuals walked by, around, and even over this man lying on the sidewalk, but no one helped him. What perceived costs might have prevented them from doing so?

group was visiting the campus and had requested a seminarian speaker. Half the subjects were told they had little time to get across campus to speak to the high school group, and the other half were told they had plenty of time. Additionally, some subjects were asked to speak on why they chose to enter the seminary, and others were asked to speak about the meaning of the parable of the good Samaritan. The seminarians then left the building to give their talk, and lo and behold, while walking down a narrow lane, they saw a young man collapse in front of them. What did they do?

Now, do you recall the story of the good Samaritan? A traveler is set upon by robbers and left by the side of the road. A priest and a Levite, people holding important positions in the clergy of the time, walked by swiftly without helping. But a Samaritan, passing along the same road, stopped and helped. We might say that, for whatever reasons, helping was too costly for the priest and the Levite but not too costly for the Samaritan.

What about the seminarians? The "costly" condition in this experiment was the tight schedule: Stopping to help would make them late for their talk. Was helping too costly for them? Yes, it was. Subjects who were in a hurry, even if they were thinking about the story of the good Samaritan, were less likely to stop and help than were subjects who were not in a hurry.

The Effect of Mood on Helping   Likelihood of helping can even be affected by the bystander's mood. The research of Alice Isen (1987) and her co-workers has shown that adults and children who are in a positive mood are more likely to help others than people who are not. People who had found a dime in a phone booth in a shopping mall were more likely to pick up papers dropped by a stranger than persons who had not found a coin. Students who had gotten free cookies in the library were more likely to volunteer to help someone and were less likely to volunteer to annoy somebody else when asked to do so as part of the experiment.

Although positive mood is related to an increase in helping, it does not lead to more helping if the person thinks that helping will destroy the good mood (Isen & Simmonds, 1978). Good moods seem to generate good thoughts about people, and this increases helping. People in good moods are also less concerned with themselves and more likely to be sensitive to other people, making them more aware of other people's needs and therefore more likely to help (Isen, 1987).

Characteristics of the Victim   A decision to help (or not to help) is also affected by the victim's characteristics. For example, males are more likely to help females than to help other males (Eagly & Crowley, 1986; West, Whitney, & Schnedler, 1975). Females, on the other hand, are equally likely to help male and female victims (Eagly & Crowley, 1986). Physically attractive people are more likely to receive help than unattractive people (Benson, Karabenick, & Lerner, 1976). In one study, a pregnant woman, whether alone or with another woman, received more help than a nonpregnant woman or a facially disfigured woman (Walton et al., 1988).

As a result of "just-world thinking," we often deny help to victims we perceive as in some way responsible for their own plight. This Vietnam veterans program directly confronts the notion that homeless people don't deserve help.

Potential helpers also make judgments about whether a victim deserves help. If we perceive that a person got into a situation through her own negligence and is therefore responsible for her own fate, we tend to generate "just-world" thinking (Lerner & Simmons, 1966). According to the **just-world hypothesis,** people get what they deserve and deserve what they get. This type of thinking often leads us to devalue a person whom we think caused her own misfortune (Lerner & Simmons, 1966). Generally, we give less help to victims we perceive to have contributed to their own fate than to those we perceive as needy through no fault of their own (Berkowitz, 1969; Schopler & Matthews, 1965).

However, we may relax this exacting standard if we perceive that the person in need is highly dependent on our help. In one experiment, subjects received telephone calls at home in which the caller mistook them for the owner of "Ralph's Garage" and told them that her car had broken down (Gruder, Romer, & Korth, 1978). The caller says either that she meant to have the car serviced but forgot (help needed due to victim's negligence) or that the car was just serviced (no negligence). In one condition, after the subject informs the caller that she has not reached Ralph's Garage, the caller says that she has no more change to make another call (high dependency). In another condition, no mention is made of being out of change. In all conditions the caller asks the subject to call Ralph's Garage for her. The researchers found that subjects were more likely to help the negligent victim who had no more change than the negligent victim who presumably had other ways to get help (Figure 13-6). It seems that high dependence mediates just-world thinking. Regardless of whether the victim deserves what she gets, we can't help but take pity on her.

Just-world thinking also comes into play when we consider the degree to which a victim contributed to his or her own predicament. If you, as a helper, attribute a victim's suffering to his or her own actions (i.e., make an internal attribution), you will be less likely to help than if you attribute the suffering to some external cause (Schmidt & Weiner, 1988). When making judgments about individuals in need of help, we take into account the

just-world hypothesis The hypothesis suggesting that individuals get what they deserve and deserve what they get.

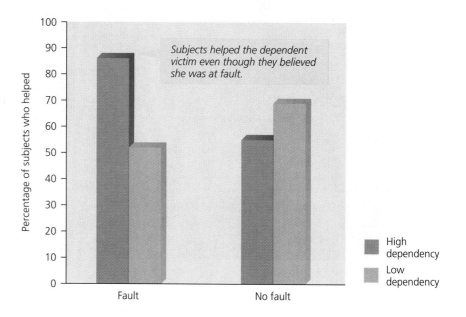

FIGURE 13-6 *The effect of high dependency on willingness to help. In Gruder's "Ralph's Garage" experiment, subjects were more likely to help a victim who had nowhere else to turn than victims who had other resources, even if the subject thought the victim's plight was due to her own negligence.* From data in Gruder, Romer, and Kroth, 1978.

Subjects helped the dependent victim even though they believed she was at fault.

Percentage of subjects who helped

High dependency

Low dependency

Fault   No fault

degree to which the victim had control over his or her fate (Schmidt & Weiner, 1988). For example, Greg Schmidt and Bernard Weiner (1988) found that subjects expressed less willingness to help a student in need of class notes if he needed the notes because he went to the beach instead of class (a controllable situation) than if he had medically related vision problems that prevented him from taking notes (uncontrollable situation).

Why do perceptions of controllability matter? Schmidt and Weiner report that the emotions aroused are important factors in one's reaction to a person in need. If a victim's situation arouses anger, as in the controllable situation, we are less likely to give help than if the victim's situation arouses sympathy (as in the uncontrollable situation). Apparently, we are quite harsh when it comes to a victim whom we perceive as having contributed to his or her own plight. We reserve our sympathy for those victims who had little or no control over their own fates.

In an interesting application of this effect, Bernard Weiner and his colleagues (Graham, Weiner, Giuliano, & Williams, 1993; Weiner, 1993; Weiner, Perry, & Magnusson, 1988) have applied this analysis to victims of various illnesses. Subjects tended to react with pity (and less anger) toward victims of conditions over which the victims had little control (e.g., Alzheimer's disease, cancer). Conversely, subjects tended to react with anger (and less pity) for victims of supposedly controllable conditions (e.g., AIDS, obesity) (Weiner, 1993; Weiner et al., 1988). The emotion tied to the victim's situation (pity versus anger) mediated willingness to help. Subjects indicated less willingness to help victims with controllable problems than those with uncontrollable problems (Weiner et al., 1988). Additionally, subjects assigned greater responsibility to a person with a disease (e.g., AIDS) if the victim's behavior was perceived to have contributed to his or her disease than if the victim's behavior was not perceived to have contributed. For example, if a person with AIDS contracted the disease via a blood transfusion, less responsibility is assigned to the victim than if the person contracted the disease via a sexual route (Graham et al., 1993).

Finally, there is evidence that characteristics of the helper may interact with perceived controllability in determining affective responses to victims and helping behavior (Zucker & Weiner, 1993). In an analysis of reactions to individuals living in poverty, Gail Zucker and Bernard Weiner found that politically conservative individuals were likely to blame the victim for being in poverty, attributing poverty to characteristics of the victim. Consequently, these individuals tend to react with anger and are less willing to help. On the other hand, more liberal individuals see poverty as driven by societal forces, not under control of the victim, and react with pity and are more willing to help.

Another characteristic of the victim investigated by social psychologists is race. Are African Americans more or less likely than whites to receive help when they need it? Research from this area is summarized in the featured discussion "Altruism and Helping Across Racial Categories."

Reprise: When Do We Help?

In a nutshell, the research on helping behavior in an emergency suggests the following:

- We help when we decide that an emergency exists, that it is our responsibility to help, when other bystanders provide clear cues that this is an emergency, and when we feel competent to help.
- We are more likely to help others when we are alone except if the situation is dangerous and we need the help of other bystanders.
- We are less likely to help when the costs of helping are high, but more likely to help when we occupy a leadership role. It is probable that feeling competent lowers the cost of helping.
- We are less likely to help when we believe that the victim contributed to or had control over his or her fate. The most likely reason for this is that victims whom we believe contributed to their own fate arouse negative emotions such as anger.

Increasing the Chances of Receiving Help

We have been looking at helping behavior from the point of view of the potential helper. But what about the person in need of help? Is there anything a victim can do to increase the chances of being helped? Given all the obstacles along the path of helping, it may seem a small miracle that anyone ever receives any help. If you are in a position of needing help, however, there are some things you can do.

First, make your plea for help as loud as possible. Yelling and waving your arms increase the likelihood that others will *notice* your plight. Make your plea as clear as possible. You do not want to leave any room for doubt that you need help. This will help bystanders correctly *label* the situation as an emergency.

If you only went by stories on television and in the newspapers, you might think that African Americans and whites in our society never help each other. But this is simply not true. Recall from Chapter 1 that many African Americans risked their lives to save whites during the Los Angeles riots in 1992. A group of black residents of South Central Los Angeles helped get Reginald Denny to the hospital, saving his life. Interracial helping does occur. What does the social psychological research say about this issue?

Numerous studies have been conducted to investigate aspects of interracial helping (Benson, Karabenick, & Lerner, 1976; Dovidio & Gaertner, 1981; Gaertner, Dovidio, & Johnson, 1982). In one, for example, white subjects, assessed as either high or low in prejudice, were given an opportunity to help an African American or a white victim (Gaertner et al., 1982). The subjects were either alone (subject and victim) or with four others (three bystanders and the victim). The researchers recorded the amount of time subjects took to give the victim aid.

Their results showed that white victims were helped more quickly than African American victims, especially by prejudiced subjects, when bystanders were present. African Americans and whites were helped equally quickly when no bystanders were present. Thus, the bystander effect is stronger for African American than white victims (Gaertner & Dovidio, 1977; Gaertner et al., 1982).

Given the opportunity to diffuse responsibility, bystanders will avail themselves of the opportunity more with African American than with white victims (Gaertner & Dovidio, 1977). This may occur because when multiple bystanders are present, an African American victim is seen as less severely injured than a white victim (Gaertner, 1975). When there is a single bystander, there is no such differential assessment of injury severity (Gaertner, 1975).

Other factors also influence the help given to African American versus white victims. In another study, white subjects were given an opportunity to help an African American or white male (Dovidio & Gaertner, 1981). This person was introduced as the subject's "supervisor" or "subordinate" and was said to be of either higher or lower cognitive ability than the subject. When given an opportunity to help, white subjects helped the African American subordinate (lower status) more than the African American supervisor (higher status), regardless of the ability level. However, African American subjects gave help based more on ability than on status. According to this study, status is relevant in whites' decision to help African Americans, with more help given to lower-status African Americans (Dovidio & Gaertner, 1981). Ability is more relevant in African Americans' decision to help whites, with more help given to high-ability than low-ability whites.

The relationship between race and helping behavior is complex and involves numerous situational factors as well as racial attitudes.

Next, you want to increase the chances that a bystander will *assume responsibility* for helping you. Don't count on this happening by itself. Anything you can do to increase a bystander's personal responsibility for helping will increase your chances of getting help. Making eye contact is one way to do this; making a direct request is another.

The effectiveness of the direct-request approach was graphically illustrated in a field experiment in which a confederate of the experimenter approached subjects on a beach (Moriarty, 1975). In one condition the confederate asked the subject to watch his "things" (a blanket and a radio) while the confederate went to the boardwalk for a minute (the subject is given responsibility for helping). In another condition the confederate simply asked the subject for a match (social contact, but no responsibility). A short time after the confederate left, a second confederate came along

A review of the literature by Crosby, Bromley, and Saxe (1980) found mixed results. These researchers drew three conclusions:

1. Bias exists against African American victims, but the bias is not extreme. Clear discrimination against African American victims was reported in 44% of the studies reviewed; 56% showed no discrimination or reverse discrimination,
2. Whites and African Americans discriminate against the opposite race at about the same level, and
3. Whites discriminate against African American victims much more under remote conditions (for example, over the telephone) than in face-to-face situations.

In a more recent study, researchers investigated race differences in the level of help given to elderly individuals who lived at home (Morrow-Howell, Lott, & Ozawa, 1990). They analyzed a program in which volunteers were assigned to help elderly clients shop and to provide them with transportation, counseling, and telephone social support. This study found very few differences between African American and white volunteers. For example, both African American and white volunteers attended training sessions at equal rates and were evaluated equally by their supervisors.

There was, however, one interesting difference between African American and white volunteers when the race of the client was considered. According to client reports, volunteers who were of a different race than the client spent less time with clients than volunteers of the same race. Additionally, when the volunteer and client were of the same race, the client reported that there were more home visits and that the volunteer was more helpful than if the volunteer and client differed in race.

A few cautions are in order here, however. There was no independent measure of the amount of time volunteers spent with clients or the quality of service rendered. The data on the volunteers' performance were based on client reports. It could be that same-race clients were simply more inclined to rate their volunteers positively than were different-race clients. Nevertheless, the study documented a program of helping in which altruistic tendencies transcended racial barriers.

Given the recent rise in tensions between different ethnic groups in the United States, the issue of inter-race altruism takes on increasing importance. Although inter-race altruism is observed, research suggests that race plays a role in the decision to give help. Why do you think a racial bias exists in altruism? Do you think it is easier to arouse empathy for a same-race than for a different-race victim? If so, why? In the light of the research reported here, what steps could be taken to increase inter-race helping? In the study of nursing-home clients, why might same-race volunteers be evaluated more favorably than different-race volunteers?

and took the radio and ran off. More subjects helped in the personal-responsibility condition (some actually ran the second confederate down) than in the nonresponsibility condition. Thus, making someone personally responsible for helping increases helping.

HELPING IN LONG-TERM SITUATIONS: SITUATIONAL AND PERSONALITY INFLUENCES

Much of the research on helping behavior that we have discussed suggests that whether people help depends on situational factors. For example, research has shown that the costs of helping, the degree of responsibility for helping, the assumed characteristics of the victim, and the dangerousness of the situation all affect helping behavior. None of these factors are under the control of the potential helper. They are part of the situation.

Situational factors seem to be crucial in situations that require spontaneous helping (Clary & Orenstein, 1991). The situations created in the laboratory, or for that matter in the field, are analogous to looking at a single frame in a motion picture. Recall the seminarians. They were in a hurry, and while thinking of the parable of the good Samaritan they practically leapt over the slumped body of a person in need of their help. Is this unexpected event a fair and representative sample of their behavior? It was for that particular situation. But, unless we look at what comes before and after, we cannot make judgments about how they would behave in other situations. Looking at these "single frame" glimpses of helping can lead us to overlook personality variables.

Although personality factors come into play in all forms of altruism, they may be more likely to come to the fore in long-term helping situations. Helping on a long-term basis, whether it involves volunteering at a hospital or Seth Conklin helping the Still family, requires a degree of planning. This planning might take place before the help begins, as was the case for Seth Conklin. Or it may occur after help begins. For example, rescuers of Jews in Nazi-occupied Europe often did not plan their initial helping acts (Tec, 1986). However, their continued helping required thought and planning. During planning, helpers assess risks, costs, and priorities, and they match personal morals and abilities with victims' needs. This is the kind of planned helping Seth Conklin had to do.

History teaches us that in times of great need, a select few individuals emerge to offer long-term help. What is it about these people that sets them apart from others who remain on the sidelines? Perhaps some individuals possess an **altruistic personality,** or a cluster of personality traits, including empathy, that predispose them to great acts of altruism. While there is evidence for the existence of such a personality cluster (Oliner & Oliner, 1988), we must also remain mindful that situational forces may still be important, even in long-term helping situations. In the sections that follow we explore how situational factors and personality factors combine to influence altruism. We begin by considering the factors that influenced a relatively small number of individuals to help rescue Jews from the Nazis during their World War II occupation of Europe.

Righteous Rescuers in Nazi-Occupied Europe

As Hitler's final solution (the systematic extermination of European Jews) progressed, life for Jews in Europe became harder and more dangerous. Although most of Eastern Europe's and many of Western Europe's Jews were murdered, some did survive. Some survived on their own by passing as Christians or leaving their homes ahead of the Nazis. Many, however, survived with the help of non-Jews who risked their lives to help them. The state of Israel recognizes a select group of those who helped Jews for their heroism and designates them **righteous rescuers** (Tec, 1986).

altruistic personality A cluster of personality traits, including empathy, that predispose a select few individuals to great acts of helping.

righteous rescuers The designation bestowed by the state of Israel on Christians who helped save Jews from the Nazis during World War II.

Individuals who worked to save Jews during World War II are recognized by Israel as "righteous rescuers." Oskar Schindler, portrayed here by Liam Neeson in the 1993 movie Schindler's List, *was one such person. What do you think motivates people who engage in long-term helping at the risk of their own lives?*

Sadly, not as many individuals emerged as rescuers as one might wish. The number of rescuers is estimated to have been between 50,000 and 500,000, a small percentage of those living under Nazi rule (Oliner & Oliner, 1988). In short, only a minority of people were willing to risk their lives to help others.

It should not be too surprising that the majority did not help the Jews. Those caught helping Jews, even in the smallest way, were subjected to punishment, death in an extermination camp, or summary execution. In other cases, especially in Poland, rescuing Jews amounted to flying in the face of centuries of anti-Semitic attitudes and religious doctrine that identified Jews as the killers of Jesus Christ (Oliner & Oliner, 1988; Tec, 1986). The special problems facing Polish rescuers are illustrated in the following quotation from a Polish rescuer (Tec, 1986):

> My husband hated Jews. . . . Anti-Semitism was ingrained in him. Not only was he willing to burn every Jew but even the earth on which they stood. Many Poles feel the way he did. I had to be careful of the Poles. (p. 54)

Because Polish rescuers violated such powerful social norms, some social psychologists have suggested that their behavior is an example of **autonomous altruism,** selfless help that society does not reinforce (Tec, 1986). In fact, such altruism may be *discouraged* by society. Rescuers in countries outside of Poland may have been operating from a different motive. Most rescuers in Western Europe, although acting out of empathy for the Jews, may have had a *normocentric* motivation for their first act of helping (Oliner & Oliner, 1988). A normocentric motivation for helping is oriented more toward a group (perhaps society) that an individual identifies with than toward the individual in need. In small towns in southern France, for example, rescuing Jews became normative, the accepted and expected thing to do. This type of altruism is known as **normative altruism,** altruism that society supports and encourages (Tec, 1986).

autonomous altruism A form of selfless altruism that society does not support and might even discourage.

normative altruism A form of altruism that society supports and encourages.

The Oliners and the Altruistic Personality Project

One family victimized by the Nazis in Poland was that of Samuel Oliner. One day in 1942, when Samuel was 12 years old and living in the village of Bobawa, he was roused by the sound of soldiers' boots cracking the predawn silence. He escaped to the roof and hid there in his pajamas until they left. When he dared to come down from his rooftop perch, the Jews of Bobawa lay buried in a mass grave. The village was empty.

Two years earlier, Samuel's entire family had been killed by the Nazis. Now he gathered some clothes and walked for 48 hours until he reached the farm of Balwina Piecuch, a peasant woman who had been friendly to his family in the past. The 12-year-old orphan knocked at her door. When Piecuch saw Samuel, she gathered him into her house. There she harbored him against the Nazis, teaching him what he needed to know of the Christian religion to pass as a Polish stable boy.

Samuel Oliner survived the war, immigrated to the United States, and went on to teach at Humboldt State University in Arcata, California. One of his courses was on the Holocaust. In it he examined the fate of the millions of Jews, Gypsies, and other Europeans who were systematically murdered by the Nazis between 1939 and 1945. In 1978 one of his students, a German woman, became distraught, saying she couldn't bear the guilt over what her people had done.

At this point Oliner realized that the history of the war, a story of murder, mayhem, and sadism, had left out a small but important aspect: the accomplishments of the many altruistic people who acted to help Jews and did so without expectation of external rewards (Goldman, 1988; Oliner & Oliner, 1988). Samuel Oliner and his wife, Pearl Oliner, established the Altruistic Personality Project to study the character and motivations of those altruists, whom the Oliners rightly call heroes.

Situational Factors Involved in Becoming a Rescuer

Oliner and Oliner (1988) and Nechama Tec (1986) investigated the *situational forces* that influence individuals to become rescuers. These situational factors can be captured in the five questions for which the Oliners wanted to find answers:

1. Did rescuers know more about the difficulties the Jews faced than nonrescuers?
2. Were rescuers better off financially and therefore better able to help?
3. Did rescuers have social support for their efforts?
4. Did rescuers adequately evaluate the risks, the costs of helping?
5. Were rescuers asked to help, or did they initiate helping on their own?

The Oliners interviewed rescuers and a matched sample of nonrescuers over the course of a 5-year study and compared the two groups. The Oliners used a 66-page questionnaire, translated into Polish, German, French, Dutch, Italian, and Norwegian, and used 28 bilingual interviewers. Results indicated that the situational differences between rescuers and nonrescuers were not as significant as expected. For example, rescuers were not wealthier then nonrescuers. Tec (1986) reports that the greatest number of Polish helpers came from the "peasant class," not the upper class of Poles. Additionally, rescuers and nonrescuers alike knew about the persecution of the Jews and knew the risks involved in going to their aid (Oliner & Oliner, 1988).

Only two situational variables are relevant to the decision to rescue. First, family support was important for the rescue effort (Tec, 1986). Sixty percent of the rescuers in Tec's sample reported that their families supported the rescue effort, compared to only 12% who said that their families opposed rescue efforts, a finding that was mirrored in Oliner and Oliner's study. Evidence suggests that rescue was made more likely by the rescuers' being affiliated with a group that supported the rescue effort (Baron, 1986). We can conclude that support from some outside agency, be it the family or another support group, made rescue more likely.

The second situational factor was how the rescuer first began his or her efforts. In most cases (68%), rescuers helped in response to a specific request to help; only 32% initiated help on their own (Oliner & Oliner, 1988). Tec (1986) reported a similar result. For most rescuers the first act of help was unplanned (Tec, 1986). But, once a rescuer agreed to help that first time, he or she was likely to help again. Help was refused in a minority of instances (about 15%), but such refusal was related to specific risks involved in giving help. Most rescuers (61%) helped for 6 months or more (Tec, 1986). And 90% of the people rescuers helped were strangers (Goldman, 1988).

These situational factors—the costs of helping, a request for help, and the support of other bystanders in a group of which the rescuer was a member—have also been identified in research as important in influencing the decision to help.

Personality Factors Involved in Becoming a Rescuer

The results of the work by Oliner and Oliner (1988) suggest that rescuers and nonrescuers differed from each other less by circumstances than by their upbringing and personalities. The Oliners found that rescuers exhibited a strong feeling of personal responsibility for the welfare of other people and a compelling need to act on that felt responsibility. They were moved by the pain of the innocent victims, by their sadness, helplessness, and desperation. Empathy for the victim was an important factor driving this form of altruism. Interestingly, rescuers and nonrescuers did not differ significantly on general measures of empathy. However, they did differ on a particular type of empathy called *emotional empathy,* which centers on one's sensitivity to the pain and suffering of others (Oliner & Oliner, 1988). According to the Oliners, this empathy, coupled with a sense of social responsibility, increased the likelihood that an individual would make and keep a commitment to help.

Beyond empathy, rescuers shared several other characteristics (Tec, 1986). First, they showed an inability to blend in with others in the environment. That is, they tended to be socially marginal, not fitting in very well with others. Second, rescuers exhibited a high level of independence and self-reliance. They were likely to pursue their personal goals even if those goals conflicted with social norms. Third, rescuers had an enduring commitment to helping those in need long before the war began. The war did not make these people altruists; rather, it allowed these individuals to remain altruists in a new situation.

Fourth, rescuers had (and still have) a matter-of-fact attitude about their rescue efforts. During and after the war, rescuers denied that they were heroes, instead saying that they did the only thing they could do. Finally, rescuers had a universalistic view of the needy. That is, rescuers were able to put aside the religion or other characteristics of those they helped. Interestingly, some rescuers harbored anti-Semitic attitudes (Tec, 1986). But they were able to put those prejudices aside and help a *person* in need. These characteristics, along with high levels of empathy, contributed to the rescuers' decisions to help the Jews.

The research on rescuers clearly shows that rescuers differed in significant ways from those who were nonrescuers (Oliner & Oliner, 1988) or paid helpers (Tec, 1986). How can we account for these differences? To answer this question we must look at the family environments in which rescuers were socialized.

Altruism as a Function of Child-Rearing Style   In Chapter 12 we established that inept parenting contributes to the development of antisocial behaviors like aggression. Oliner and Oliner found that the child-rearing styles used by parents of rescuers contributed to the development of prosocial attitudes and behaviors. The techniques used by parents of rescuers fostered empathy in the rescuers.

According to social learning theory, parents contribute to altruistic development by directly reinforcing their child's attitudes and behaviors. For example, if a child helps her little brother with a difficult puzzle the parent may reinforce the helper with praise or even a material reward. Although direct reinforcement occurs, much of the parents' influence on the child is subtle, taking place through the processes of modeling and imitation (Eisenberg & Mussen, 1989). When children see their parents behaving in a positive way, they are likely to imitate those behaviors. This effect is explored in greater detail in the featured discussion "Altruism and Social Learning Theory: Learning to Be Helpful."

Parents of rescuers provided role models for their children that allowed them to develop the positive qualities needed to become rescuers later in life. For example, rescuers (more than nonrescuers) came from families that stressed the universal similarity of all people, despite superficial differences among them (Oliner & Oliner, 1988). Families stressed the aspect of religion that encouraged caring for those in need. Additionally, families of rescuers did not discuss negative stereotypes of Jews, which was more common among families of nonrescuers. As children, then, rescuers were exposed to role models that instilled many positive qualities.

Social learning theory holds that children acquire many of their behaviors through observational learning, or modeling. Research has supported these ideas. Children who are exposed to aggressive models, for example, show more aggression than those exposed to nonaggressive models (Bandura, 1973). Does the same process work for helping behaviors? That is, can an individual (adult or child) learn to be helpful through exposure to helpful models? Is providing helpful models an important part of a child's prosocial socialization?

Several experiments confirm that exposure to a helpful model increases helping among children (Bryan & Walbek, 1970; Lipscomb, Larrieu, McAlister, & Bregman, 1982; Rice & Grusec, 1975). For example, Thomas Lipscomb and his colleagues had children from two grades (kindergarten or sixth grade) play a game with an experimenter. During the game both the child and the experimenter could win pennies. Children and the experimenter could deposit their pennies into a can for themselves and/or into a can for the March of Dimes. The experimenter, who served as the model, acted in either a charitable manner (donating some pennies to the March of Dimes), a neutral manner (leaving winnings on the table), or a selfish manner (keeping all winnings). The experimenters then counted the number of pennies the children donated. They found that the younger children (kindergartners) donated more pennies when exposed to the charitable model than to the neutral or the selfish model. The model's behavior had

no effect on the older children's behavior.

Research also shows that a model for behavior is a more powerful influence over children's helping than are verbal exhortations to be generous (Bryan & Walbek, 1970). When a model preaches charity, the model has less effect on a child's willingness to donate than if the model engages in charitable behavior (Bryan & Walbek, 1970). Additionally, verbal reinforcement has a different effect on children's helping, depending on whether a model behaves in a charitable or selfish manner (Midlarsky, Bryan, & Brickman, 1973). Verbal social approval from a selfish model does not increase children's donations. However, social approval from a charitable model does.

Another interesting question concerning the role of observational learning on helping is the influence of television. Recall from Chapter 12 that children can learn aggressive behaviors from watching television programs that have violent content. In a similar manner, children can learn prosocial, helping behaviors from watching television. In one study, children were exposed to either a prosocial show or a neutral show and then placed in a situation in which they could be helpful. This study found that children exposed to the prosocial show helped more than those exposed to the neutral show (Sprafkin, Liebert, & Poulos, 1975). Other research shows that

exposure to television programs like "Mister Rogers' Neighborhood" can also increase helping among children (Friedrich & Stein, 1975).

Finally, modeling effects also work for adults. For example, motorists on a Los Angeles freeway who saw a man changing a flat tire for a woman were more likely to stop to help another motorist down the road than drivers who had not seen the helpful model (Bryan & Test, 1967). The principle of a helpful model is well known. Next time you see a street musician, notice that his guitar case usually has several dollar bills in it. This is known as "salting." The presence of the bills suggests to you that other helpful passersby had already made a donation. The suggestion is likely to increase the probability that you will give too.

Models obviously have a powerful effect on both aggressive and prosocial behaviors. Why, however, do you think that a prosocial model has more effect on younger children than older children? What factors can you think of to explain the fact that a model's behavior is more important than what the model says? Based on what you know about the effect of prosocial models on children's altruism, if you were given the opportunity to design a television character to communicate prosocial ideals, what would that character be like? What would the character say and do to foster prosocial behavior in children? Similarly, what types of models should we be exposing adults to in order to increase helping?

It is not enough for parents simply to embrace altruistic values and provide positive role models, however (Staub, 1985); they must also exert firm control over their children. Parents who raise altruistic children coach them to be helpful and firmly teach them how to be helpful (Goleman, 1991; Staub, 1985). Parents who are warm and nurturant and use reasoning with the child as a discipline technique are more likely to produce an altruistic child than cold, uncaring, punitive parents (Eisenberg & Mussen, 1989). This was certainly true of families of rescuers. Parents of rescuers tended to avoid using physical punishment, in favor of an inductive style that focused on verbal reasoning and explanation.

As important as the family is in the socialization of altruism, it cannot alone account for how a child grows up to be an altruistic individual. The child's cognitive development, or his or her capacity to understand the world, also plays a role.

Altruism as a Function of Cognitive Development As children grow, their ability to think about and understand other people and the world changes. The cognitive perspective focuses on how altruistic behavior develops as a result of changes in the child's thinking skills. To study altruism from this perspective, Nancy Eisenberg presented children with several moral dilemmas that pit one person's welfare against another person's welfare. Here is one example:

> Bob, a young man who was very good at swimming, was asked to help young crippled children who could not walk to learn to swim so that they could strengthen their legs for walking. Bob was the only one in his town who could do this job well because only he had both life-saving and teaching experiences. But helping crippled children would take much of Bob's free time left after work and school, and Bob wanted to practice very hard as often as possible for a series of very important swimming contests coming up. If Bob did not practice swimming in all of his free time, his chances of winning the contests and for receiving a paid college education or sum of money, would be greatly lessened. (Eisenberg & Mussen, 1989, p. 124)

The dilemma pits Bob's needs against those of other people. The children in Eisenberg's study were asked several questions about what Bob should do. For example, "Should Bob agree to teach the crippled children? Why?" Based on their responses, they were classified according to Eisenberg's levels of prosocial reasoning. Eisenberg's findings show that as children get older they are more likely to understand the needs of other people and are less focused on their own selfish concerns. The research suggests that this is a continual process and that people's altruistic thinking and behavior can change throughout life.

The idea that the development of altruism is a lifelong process is supported by the fact that rescuers did not magically become caring and empathic at the outset of the war. Instead, the ethic of caring grew out of their personalities and interpersonal styles, which had developed over the course of their lives. Rescuers were altruistic long before the war (Huneke, 1986;

Swedish diplomat Raoul Wallenberg helped Hungarian Jews escape to Sweden during World War II. He began helping in response to a single request and then escalated his efforts as the need for more help became apparent. As a personality characteristic, altruism seems to "grow" in steps; with each helping act, the individual increasingly sees himself or herself as a person who helps.

Oliner & Oliner, 1988; Tec, 1986) and tended to remain more altruistic than nonrescuers after the war (Oliner & Oliner, 1988).

Becoming an Altruistic Person   Altruism requires something more than empathy and compassionate values (Staub, 1985). It requires the psychological and practical competence to carry those intentions into action (Goleman, 1991). Goodness, like evil, begins slowly, in small steps. Recall from Chapters 8 and 9 on social influence that we are often eased into behaviors in small steps (for example, through the foot-in-the-door technique). In a similar manner, many rescuers eased themselves into their roles as rescuers gradually. First, people responded to a request for help and hid someone for a day or two. Once they took that first step, they began to see themselves differently—as the kind of people who rescued the desperate. Altruistic actions changed their self-concept: Since I helped, I must be an altruistic person. As we saw in Chapter 2, one way we gain self-knowledge is through observation of our own behavior. We then apply that knowledge to our self-concept.

This is how Swedish diplomat Raoul Wallenberg got involved in rescuing Hungarian Jews during World War II (Staub, 1985). The first person he rescued was a business partner who happened to be a Hungarian Jew. Wallenberg then became more involved and more daring. He began to manufacture passes for Jews, saying that they were citizens of Sweden. He even handed out passes to Jews who were being put in the cattle cars that would take them to the death camps. Wallenberg disappeared soon after, and his fate is still unknown. Apparently, there is a unique type of person who is likely to take that very first step to help and to continue helping until the end (Goleman, 1991). Wallenberg, and the other rescuers, were such people.

A SYNTHESIS: SITUATIONAL AND PERSONALITY FACTORS IN ALTRUISM

We have seen that both situational factors and personality factors influence the development and course of altruism. How do these factors work

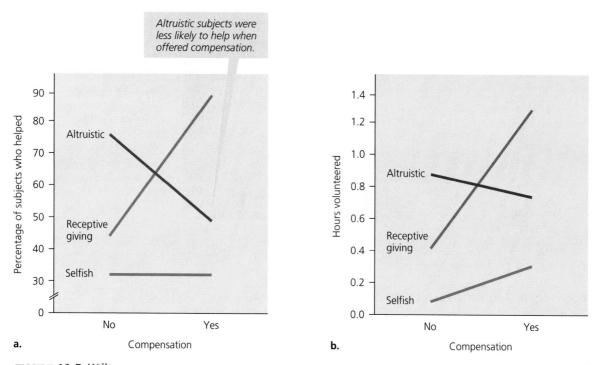

Altruistic subjects were less likely to help when offered compensation.

a. Compensation

b. Compensation

FIGURE 13-7 *Willingness to help as a function of orientation toward giving and receiving help. Subjects identified as "receptive giving" (oriented toward giving help in order to receive something in return) were more likely to help when they received compensation, but subjects identified as "altruistic" (oriented toward giving but not receiving) were less likely to help under these circumstances. Subjects identified as "selfish" (oriented toward receiving but not giving) were not much affected by compensation. These results supported Romer's interactionist view of altruism and helping behavior.* From Romer, Gruder, and Lizzadro, 1986.

interactionist view of altruism The view that an individual's internal motives (whether altruistic or selfish) interact with situational factors to determine whether he or she will help.

together to produce altruistic behavior? Two approaches provide some answers: the interactionist view and the application of the five-stage decision model to long-term helping situations.

The Interactionist View

The **interactionist view of altruism** argues that an individual's internal motives (whether altruistic or selfish) interact with situational factors to determine whether a person will help (Callero, 1986; Romer, Gruder, & Lizzadro, 1986). D. Romer and his colleagues identified four altruistic orientations based on the individual's degree of nurturance (the need to give help) and of succorance (the need to receive help):

1. Altruistic, those who are motivated to help others but not to receive help in return.
2. Receptive giving, those who help to obtain something in return.
3. Selfish, those who are primarily motivated to receive help but not give it.
4. Inner sustaining, those who are not motivated to give or receive help.

In their study, Romer and colleagues led people to believe that they would be compensated or not compensated for their help. On the basis of the four orientations just described, these researchers predicted that individuals with an altruistic orientation would help even if compensation was not expected; receptive givers would be willing to help only if they stood to gain something in return; selfish people would not be oriented toward helping, regardless of compensation; and those described as inner sustaining would neither give nor receive, no matter what the compensation.

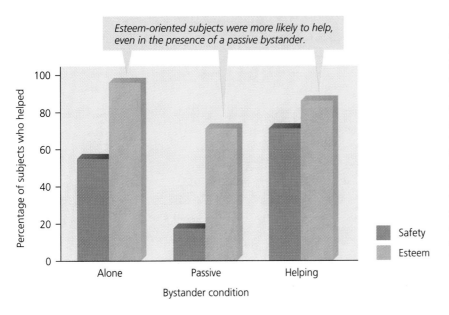

FIGURE 13-8 *The relationship between personality characteristics and likelihood of helping in different bystander conditions. Subjects categorized as "esteem oriented" were more likely to help in all situations than subjects categorized as "safety oriented." Notable in this study was the reversal of the bystander effect. Esteem-oriented subjects were very likely to help even in the presence of a passive bystander, a condition that usually reduces the likelihood of helping.* Based on data in Wilson, 1976.

Romer's results confirmed this hypothesis. Figure 13-7 shows the results on two indexes of helping: the percentage of subjects who agree to help and the number of hours volunteered. Notice that altruistic people were less likely to help when compensation was offered. This is in keeping with the reverse-incentive effect described in Chapter 7. When people are internally motivated to do something, giving them an external reward decreases their motivation and their liking for the activity.

There is also evidence that personality and the situation interact in a way that can reduce the bystander effect. In one study, researchers categorized subjects as either "esteem oriented" or "safety oriented" (Wilson, 1976). Esteem-oriented individuals are motivated by a "strong sense of personal competency" rather than what others do. Safety-oriented individuals are more dependent on what others do. Subjects were exposed to a staged emergency (a simulated explosion that supposedly hurt the experimenter), either while alone, in the presence of a passive bystander (who makes no effort to help), or in the presence of a helping bystander (who goes to the aid of the experimenter).

The study showed that esteem-oriented subjects were more likely to help than safety-oriented subjects in all cases (Figure 13-8). Of most interest, however, is the fact that the esteem-oriented subjects were more likely to help when a passive bystander was present than were the safety-oriented subjects. Thus, subjects who are motivated internally (esteem oriented) are not just more likely to help than those who are externally motivated (safety oriented); they are also less likely to fall prey to the influence of a passive bystander. This suggests that individuals who helped in the classic experiments on the bystander effect may possess personality characteristics that allow them to overcome the help-depressing effects of bystanders.

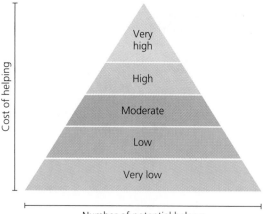

FIGURE 13-9 *The effect of personality on likelihood of helping. For situations in which helping has a very low cost, such as giving directions, many people will help. As the costs of helping increase, the number of people who will help decreases. For very high-cost helping, such as helping Jews escape the Nazis, perhaps only those individuals with altruistic personalities are able to help.*

We might also expect that the individual's personality will interact with the costs of giving help. Some individuals help even though the cost of helping is high. For example, some subjects in Batson's research described earlier in this chapter helped by offering to change places with someone receiving electric shocks even though they could have escaped the situation easily. And rescuers helped despite the fact that getting caught helping Jews meant death. In contrast, there are those who will not help even if helping requires minimal effort.

The degree to which the personality of the helper affects helping may depend on the perceived costs involved in giving aid. In relatively low-cost situations, personality will be less important than the situation. However, in high-cost situations, personality will be more important than the situation. As the perceived cost of helping increases, personality exerts a stronger effect on the decision to help. This is represented in Figure 13-9. The base of the triangle represents very low-cost behaviors. As you move up the triangle, the cost of helping increases. The relative size of each division of the triangle represents the number of people who would be willing to help another in distress.

An extremely low-cost request (for example, giving a stranger directions to the campus library) would result in most people helping. People's personalities matter little when it costs almost nothing to help. In fact, probably more effort is spent on saying no than directing the passerby to the library. When the cost of helping becomes high, even prohibitive, as in the case of rescuing Jews from the Nazis, fewer people help. However, there are those who successfully overcome the situational forces working against helping, perhaps due to their altruistic personalities, and offer help.

Applying the Five-Stage Decision Model to Long-Term Helping

Earlier in this chapter we described a five-stage decision model of helping. That model has been applied exclusively to the description and explanation of helping in spontaneous emergencies. Now that we have explored some other aspects of helping, we can consider whether that model may be applied to long-term and situation-specific spontaneous helping. Let's consider how each stage applies to the actions of those who rescued Jews from the Nazis.

Noticing the Situation   For many rescuers, seeing the Nazis taking Jews away provoked awareness. One rescuer, Irene Gut Opdyke, first became aware of the plight of the Jews when she happened to look through a hotel window and saw Jews being rounded up and taken away (Opdyke & Elliot, 1992). Oliner and Oliner (1988) reported that rescuers were motivated to action when they witnessed some external event like the one Opdyke had witnessed. Of course, however, many nonrescuers also saw the same events yet did not help.

Labeling the Situation as an Emergency   A critical factor in the decision to rescue Jews was to label the situation as one serious enough to require intervention. Here, the differences between rescuers and nonrescuers became important. Apparently, rescuers were more likely to see the persecution of the Jews as something serious that required intervention. The persecutions appeared to insult the sensibilities of the rescuers. Nonrescuers often decided that Jews must truly have done something to deserve their awful fate. They tended to blame the victim and by so doing relieved themselves of any responsibility for helping.

Rescuers also had social support to help because they belonged to groups that valued such action. This is consistent with the notion that encouragement from others may make it easier to label a situation as one requiring intervention (Dozier & Miceli, 1985).

Assuming Responsibility to Help   The next step in the process is for the rescuer to assume responsibility to help. For rescuers, the universalistic view of the needy, ethics of justice and caring, and generally high levels of empathy made assuming responsibility probable. In fact, many rescuers suggested that once they noticed the persecution of Jews they "had to do something." Their upbringing and view of the world made assumption of responsibility almost a given rather than a decision. The main difference between the rescuers and the nonrescuers who witnessed the same events was that the rescuers interpreted the events as a call to action (Oliner & Oliner, 1988). For the rescuers, the witnessed event connected with their principles of caring (Oliner & Oliner, 1988) and led them to assume responsibility.

Another factor may have come into play when the rescuers (or a bystander to an emergency situation) assumed responsibility. Witnessing maltreatment of the Jews may have activated the **norm of social responsibility** in these individuals. This norm involves the notion that we should help others without regard to receiving help or a reward in exchange (Berkowitz, 1972; Schwartz, 1975).

norm of social responsibility
The norm stating that we should help others in need without regard for future reward or help in return.

Deciding How to Help   Rescuers helped in a variety of ways (Oliner & Oliner, 1988). They had to assess the alternatives available and decide which was most appropriate. Alternatives included donating money to help Jews, providing false papers, and hiding Jews. It appears that, at least sometimes, perceived costs were not an issue. For example, Irene Gut Opdyke hid several Jews in the basement of a German major's house in which she was the housekeeper, even after she witnessed a Polish family and the family of Jews they were hiding hanged by the Nazis in the town marketplace.

Implementing the Decision to Help   The final stage, implementing the decision to help, includes assessing rewards and costs for helping and potential outcomes of helping versus not helping. When Everett Sanderson rescued someone who had fallen onto the subway tracks, he said he could not have lived with himself if he had not helped. This is an assessment of outcomes. For Sanderson, the cost for not helping outweighed the cost for helping, despite the risks.

It is quite probable that the altruistic personalities we have been studying made similar assessments. Because of their upbringing and the events of their lives that defined them as altruistic people, they decided that helping was less costly to them than not helping. Most of them engaged in long-term helping. This suggests that they assessed the outcome of their initial decision to help and decided that it was correct. This was certainly true of Seth Conklin and of Balwina Piecuch. It was also true of the Polish woman in the following example, which illustrates the interactionist nature of helping—the interplay of situational and personality factors and the combination of spontaneous and long-term events:

> A woman and her child were being led through Cracow, Poland with other Jews to a concentration station. The woman ran up to a bystander and pleaded, Please, please save my child. A Polish woman took the young boy to her apartment, where neighbors became suspicious of this sudden appearance of a child and called the police. The captain of the police department asked the woman if she knew the penalty for harboring a Jewish child. The young woman said, with some heat, "You call yourself a Pole . . . a gentleman . . . a man of the human race?" She continued her persuasive act, claiming that one of the police in the room had actually fathered the child "and stooped so low as to be willing to have the child killed." (Goldman, 1988)

Both the woman and the young boy survived the war.

ALTRUISTIC BEHAVIOR FROM THE PERSPECTIVE OF THE RECIPIENT

Our discussion of altruism up to this point has centered on the helper. But helping situations of course involve another person: the recipient of the help. Social psychologists have asked two broad questions that relate to the recipient of helping behavior: What influences an individual's decision to seek help? What reactions do individuals have to receiving help?

Many people in need actively seek help from others. These Haitians sought refuge from political violence in their homeland in 1991 and were taken by the U.S. Coast Guard to Guantanamo Bay Naval Base where they were housed in a temporary tent city. Like the decision to provide help, the decision to seek help can be seen as a process with several steps.

Seeking Help from Others

The earlier discussion of helping in emergencies may have suggested that helping behavior occurs when someone happens to stumble across a situation in which help is needed. Although this does happen, there are also many situations in which an individual actively seeks out help from another. Peter Still actively sought his brother William's help in rescuing his family from slavery. But he also refused Seth Conklin's initial offer of help, believing he could rescue his family on his own. Many Jews in Nazi-occupied Europe approached potential helpers and asked for help. And today, we see many examples of people seeking help: refugees seeking entrance to other countries, the homeless seeking shelter, the uninsured seeking health care.

Seeking help has both positive and negative aspects. On the positive side, the help a person needs will often be forthcoming. For example, medical care may be given for a life-threatening condition. On the negative side, a person may feel threatened or suffer loss of self-esteem by asking for help (Fisher, Nadler, & Whitcher-Algana, 1982). In our society a great premium is placed on being self-sufficient and taking care of oneself. There is a social stigma attached to seeking help, along with potential feelings of failure. Generally, seeking help generates costs (as does helping) (DePaulo & Fisher, 1980).

A Decision Model for Seeking Help   Allen Gross and Peg McMullen (1982) have suggested that a person deciding whether to seek help may go through a series of decisions, much like the helper does in Darley and Latané's five-stage decision model. According to Gross and McMullen, a person asks three questions before seeking help (Gross & McMullen, 1982, p. 308):

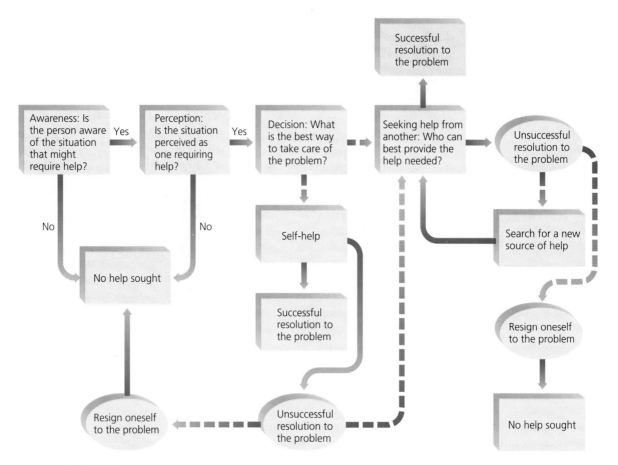

FIGURE 13-10 *A decision model for seeking help. The process includes awareness of a problem, perception that it requires help, a decision to seek help, and a decision about what kind of help to seek. According to the model, help will not be sought unless the individual makes a "yes" decision at each step.* Adapted from Gross and McMullen, 1982.

1. Do I have a problem that help will alleviate?
2. Should I seek help?
3. Who is most capable of providing the kind of help I need?

To describe the help-seeking process, Gross and McMullen developed a complex model, presented in simplified form in Figure 13-10. Let's see how this model works. Imagine that you have begun to have trouble falling asleep at night. Before you will seek help, you must first become aware that there is a problem. If you had trouble falling asleep only a few times, you probably will not identify it as a problem, and you will not seek help. But if you have trouble falling asleep for a few weeks, you may identify it as a problem and move to the next stage of help seeking.

Now you must decide if the situation is one that requires help. If you decide that it is not (the problem will go away by itself), you will not seek help. If you decide that it is, you move on to the next stage—deciding on the best way to alleviate the problem. Here you can opt for self-help (go to the drugstore and buy some over-the-counter drug) or help from an outside party (a psychologist). If you choose self-help and it is successful, the problem is solved and no further help is sought. If the self-help is unsuccessful, you could then seek help from others or resign yourself to the problem and seek no further help. If you opt for outside help, you must then decide who can best help you. No further help is sought if the outside help is successful and the problem is solved. When outside help is unsuccessful, you might seek out a different source of help or resign yourself to the problem and seek no further help.

The likelihood that you may ask for and receive help may also depend on the nature of the groups (and society) to which you belong. Members of groups often behave altruistically toward one another (Clark, Mills, & Powell, 1986) and are often governed by *communal relationships.* Members benefit each other in response to each other's needs (Williamson & Clark, 1989). These relationships are in contrast to *exchange relationships,* in which people benefit each other in response to, or with the expectation of, receiving a benefit in return. Communal relationships are characterized by helping even when people cannot reciprocate each other's help (Clark, Mills, & Powell, 1986).

Factors Influencing the Decision to Seek Help Clearly, the decision to seek help is just as complex as the decision to give help. What factors come into play when a person is deciding whether or not to seek help?

For one, individuals may be more likely to ask for help when their need is low than when it is high (Krishan, 1988). This could be related to the perceived "power" relationship between the helper and the recipient. When need is low, people may perceive themselves to be on more common footing with the helper. Additionally, when need is low there is less cost to the helper. People may be less likely to seek help if the cost to the helper is high (DePaulo & Fisher, 1980).

Another variable in this decision-making process is the person from whom the help is sought. Are people more willing to seek help from a friend or from a stranger? In one study, the relationship between the helper and the recipient (friends or strangers) and the cost to the helper (high or low) were manipulated (Shapiro, 1980). Generally, subjects were more likely to seek help from a friend than from a stranger (Figure 13-11). When help was sought from a friend, the potential cost to the helper was not important. When the helper was a stranger, subjects were reluctant to ask when the cost was high.

There are several possible reasons for this. First, people may feel more comfortable and less threatened asking a friend than a stranger for costly help. Second, the *norm of reciprocity* (see Chapter 8) may come into play in a more meaningful way with friends (Gouldner, 1960). People may reason that they would do it for their friends if they needed it. Thus, the expectation of reciprocity may make it easier to ask for high-cost help from a friend. Third, people may perceive that they will have more opportunities to reciprocate a friend's help. They may never see a stranger again.

A final variable that comes into play in deciding to seek help is the type of task on which the help is needed. If someone is doing something easy (but needs help), the person is less likely to seek help than if the task is hard (DePaulo & Fisher, 1980). And if the task is something in which the person has ego involvement, she is also less likely to seek help. So, for

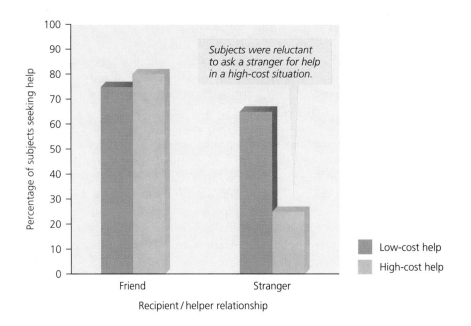

FIGURE 13-11 *Likelihood of seeking help from friends or strangers. People in general are more likely to seek help from friends than from strangers. This tendency is heightened when the cost of helping is high.* Based on data in Shapiro, 1980.

example, an accountant would be unlikely to seek help preparing her own taxes even if she needed the help.

Reacting to Help When It Is Given

Receiving help is thus a double-edged sword. On the one hand, people are grateful for receiving help. On the other hand, they may experience negative feelings when they are helped, feelings of guilt, lowered self-esteem, and indebtedness. Jews who were hidden by rescuers, for example, probably were concerned about the safety of their benefactors; they may also have been disturbed by the thought that they could never reciprocate the help they received.

Generally, there are four potentially negative outcomes of receiving help. First, an inequitable relationship may be created. Second, those who are helped may experience psychological reactance; that is, they may feel their freedom is threatened by receiving help. Third, those who receive help may make negative attributions about the intent of those who have helped them. Fourth, those who receive help may suffer a loss of self-esteem (Fisher et al., 1982). Let's look at two of these outcomes: inequity and threats to self-esteem.

The Creation of an Inequitable Relationship Recall from Chapter 11 that we strive to maintain equity in our relationships with others. When inequity occurs, we feel distress and are motivated to restore equity. Helping someone creates inequity in a relationship (Fisher et al., 1982), because the recipient feels indebted to the helper (Leventhal, Allen, & Kemelgor, 1969). The higher the cost to the helper, the greater the inequity and the greater the negative feelings (Gergen, 1974).

Those who give help often feel good about themselves, but those who receive it may have a negative reaction. Receiving help may create feelings of dependence and indebtedness that can lead to resentment, lowered self-esteem, and a sense of failure. To what extent do you think such a reaction is influenced by cultural values?

Inequity can be reversed when the help is reciprocated. Generally, a recipient reacts more negatively to that help and likes the helper less if he or she does not have the ability to reciprocate (Castro, 1974). Recipients are also less likely to seek help in the future when they have not been able to reciprocate, especially if the cost to the helper was high.

The relationship between degree of indebtedness and need to reciprocate is a complex one. For example, if someone helps you voluntarily, you will reciprocate more than if someone is obliged to help you as part of a job (Goranson & Berkowitz, 1966). You are also more likely to reciprocate when the cost to the donor is high, as opposed to low (Pruitt, 1968). Interestingly, the absolute amount of help given is less important than the cost incurred by the helper (Aikwa, 1990; Pruitt, 1968). For example, if a person who makes $100,000 per year gave you $1,000 (1% of the income), you would feel less indebted to that person than if you received the same $1,000 from someone who makes $10,000 per year (10% of the income).

Threats to Self-Esteem   Perhaps the strongest explanation for the negative impact of receiving help centers on threats to self-esteem. When people become dependent on others, especially in our society, their self-esteem and self-worth come into question (Fisher et al., 1982). Under these conditions, receiving help may be a threatening experience.

There is considerable support for the **threat to self-esteem model.** In one study, subjects who received aid on an analogy task showed greater decrements in situational self-esteem (self-esteem tied to a specific situation) than subjects not receiving help (Balls & Eisenberg, 1986). In another study, researchers artificially manipulated subjects' situational self-esteem by providing them with either positive or negative information about themselves (Nadler, Altman, & Fisher, 1979). The researchers then created a situation in which the individual received aid or no aid. Subjects who received self-enhancing information (positive self-information) showed more negative affect when aid was offered than when no aid was offered. Subjects who received negative self-information showed positive affect when they were helped.

threat to self-esteem model
A model suggesting that victims might refuse help because accepting help is a threat to their self-esteem.

Thus, subjects who had positive thoughts about themselves were more negatively affected by help than those who had negative thoughts about themselves. The offer of help was a greater threat to those with high self-esteem than to those with low self-esteem. In other words, not only does receiving help threaten self-esteem, but the higher a person's self-esteem is, the more threatened that person is by offers of help. For example, if you consider yourself the world's best brain surgeon, asking for assistance on a case would be more disturbing to you than if you saw yourself as an average brain surgeon.

When someone with high self-esteem fails at a task, that failure is inconsistent with his or her positive self-image (Nadler, Fisher, & Streufert, 1976). Help offered in this situation is perceived as threatening, especially if it comes from someone who is similar (Fisher & Nadler, 1974; Nadler et al., 1979). Receiving help from someone similar may be seen as a sign of relative inferiority and dependency (Nadler et al., 1979).

Conversely, when a person with high self-esteem receives help from a dissimilar person, he or she experiences an increase in situational self-esteem and self-confidence. When a person with low self-esteem receives help from a similar other, that help is more consistent with the individual's self-image. For these individuals, help from a similar other is seen as an expression of concern, and they respond positively (Nadler et al., 1979).

A model to explain the complex relationship between self-esteem and receiving help is shown in Figure 13-12 (Nadler, Fisher, & Ben Itchak, 1983). The model suggests that help from a friend is more "psychologically significant" than help from a stranger. This greater significance is translated into negative affect if failure occurs on something that is ego involving (for example, losing a job). Here, help from a friend is seen as a threat to one's self-esteem, and a negative reaction follows.

There are also gender differences in how people react to receiving help. In one study, males and females were paired with fictitious partners of comparable, superior, or inferior ability and were offered help by that partner (Balls & Eisenberg, 1986). Females paired with a partner of similar ability showed greater reductions in situational self-esteem than males paired with a similar partner. Thus, females perceived help as more threatening to self-esteem than did males. Females, however, were more satisfied than males with the help they received. Females were also more likely than males to express a need for help.

In sum, then, reactions to receiving help are influenced by several factors, including the ability to reciprocate, the similarity or dissimilarity of the helper, self-esteem, and gender. Other factors can play a role as well. For example, if the helper has positive attributes and is seen as having good motives, the person receiving help is more likely to feel positive about the experience. A positive outcome is also more likely if the help is offered rather than requested, if the help is given on an ego-relevant task, and if the help does not compromise the recipient's freedom (for example, with a very high obligation to repay the helper). Overall, we see that an individual's reaction to receiving help is influenced by an interaction between situational vari-

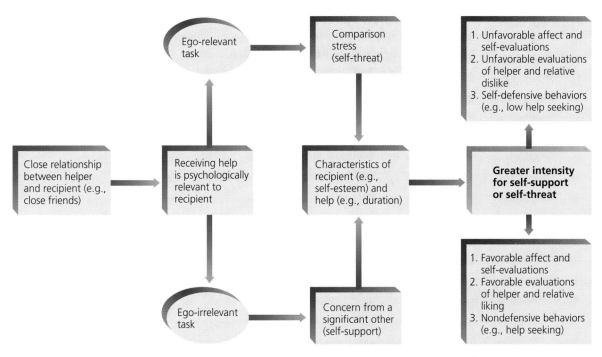

FIGURE 13-12 *The effect of various factors on reactions to receiving help from a friend or "psychologically significant" other. If the task is ego-relevant, and if the recipient has high self-esteem and the help lasts a long time, the recipient is likely to have a negative reaction to being helped. If the task is not ego-relevant, and if the recipient has lower self-esteem and the help doesn't last a long time, the recipient is likely to have a positive reaction to being helped. The model suggests that reactions to help are influenced by an interaction between situational variables and personality variables.* Adapted from Nadler, Fisher, and Itchak, 1983.

ables (for example, the helper's characteristics) and personality variables (Fisher et al., 1982).

SETH CONKLIN REVISITED

Seth Conklin offered help to perfect strangers and ultimately lost his life for his efforts. Conklin was undoubtedly an empathic person who felt the suffering of Peter Still's family. In deciding to help, he must have gone through a process similar to the one described in this chapter. He noticed the situation requiring help when he read about the Still family in the newspaper. He labeled the situation as one that required help, and he assumed responsibility for helping. He knew what he had to do to help: go south and bring the Still family north. Finally, he implemented his decision to help. Conklin's behavior fits quite well with the five-stage decision model of altruism.

Conklin's decision is also similar to the decisions made by hundreds of rescuers of Jews. In both types of situations, individuals put their lives on the line to save others. Although we do not know much about what kind of person Conklin was, we can safely assume that he had emotional empathy and a strong sense of social responsibility. Most likely, Conklin came from a family with characteristics similar to the characteristics of rescuers' families. Like the rescuers, Conklin left us with an inspiring example of an altruistic person who put the welfare of others above his own.

LOOKING AHEAD

This chapter brings to a close our coverage of social relations. We have seen how we come to be friends and lovers with others, how we are sometimes aggressive, and how we are at other times helpful. In the next chapter we begin an exploration of topics in applied social psychology. Chapter 14 introduces the work that social psychologists have done in the area of psychology and the law. We see in that chapter how many of the principles developed thus far in this text apply to aspects of the legal system, such as jury selection, eyewitness testimony, and jury decision making.

CHAPTER REVIEW

1. *What is altruism and how is it different from helping behavior? Why is the difference important?*

   Altruism is behavior that helps a person in need that is focused on the victim and is motivated purely by the desire to help the other person. Other, similar behaviors may be motivated by relieving one's personal distress or to gain some reward. These behaviors are categorized as **helping behavior.** The motivation underlying an act of help is important because it may affect the quality of the help given.

2. *What are empathy and egoism, and how do they relate to altruism?*

   Empathy refers to compassionate understanding of how a person in need feels. Some acts of helping are focused on and motivated by our desire to relieve the suffering of the victim, rather than our own discomfort. This is essentially what the **empathy–altruism hypothesis** proposes—that altruism is related to empathy for the victim. Although the empathy–altruism hypothesis has received research support, it remains a controversial hypothesis. In contrast, **egoism** refers to a motive for helping that is focused on relieving our own discomfort, rather than on relieving the victim's suffering.

3. *What about the idea that we may help to avoid guilt or shame?*

   This has been raised as a possibility in the **empathy–punishment hypothesis,** which states that people help to avoid the guilt and shame associated with not helping. Research pitting this hypothesis against the empathy–altruism hypothesis has fallen on the side of empathy–altruism. However, the book is still open on the validity of the empathy–altruism hypothesis.

4. *Does biology play any role in altruism?*

   There is evidence that helping has biological roots, as suggested by sociobiologists. According to this view, helping is biologically adaptive and helps a species survive. The focus of this explanation is on survival of the gene pool of a species rather than survival of any one member of a species. According to evolutionary biologists, animals are most likely to help members of their own family through alloparenting. For humans, a similar effect occurs: We are most likely to help others who are like us and who thus share genetic material with us.

Although this idea has some merit, it cannot account for the complexity of animal or human altruism. We might have predicted, based on the biological explanation, that Seth Conklin would not have been motivated to help Peter Still's family because he and Still were not closely related and were from different racial groups.

5. *How do social psychologists explain helping in emergency situations?*
To explain helping (or nonhelping) in emergencies, social psychologists John Darley and Bib Latané have developed a decision model with five stages: noticing the emergency, labeling the emergency correctly, assuming responsibility to help, knowing what to do, and implementing the decision to help. At each stage many variables influence an individual's decision to help.

At the noticing stage, anything that makes the emergency stand out increases the likelihood of help being offered. However, emergencies are often ambiguous and we may mislabel them, in which case we do not give help.

Next, we must assume personal responsibility for helping. This is less likely to occur when there are several other bystanders. This is known as the **bystander effect.** Two reasons for this failure to help when bystanders are present are **diffusion of responsibility** (assuming that someone else will help) and **pluralistic ignorance** (responding to the inaction of others). Although the bystander effect is a powerful, reliable phenomenon, there are exceptions to it. Research shows that when help requires dangerous intervention people are more likely to help when in groups than when alone.

Even if we assume responsibility we may not help because we do not know what to do or lack skills, or we may think that someone else is more qualified to help. Finally, we may fail to help because the costs of helping are seen as too high. Costs are increased when we might be injured or otherwise inconvenienced by stopping to help.

6. *What other factors affect the decision to help?*
Mood makes a difference. Bystanders who are in a positive (good) mood are more likely to help others. However, people may not help if they think helping will spoil their good mood. Characteristics of the victim also play a role. Females are more likely to be helped if the helper is male. Physically attractive people are more likely to be helped than unattractive people. We also take into account whether we feel that the victim deserves help. If we believe the victim contributed to his or her own problems, we are less likely to help than if we believe the victim did not contribute. This fits with the **just-world hypothesis,** the idea that people get what they deserve and deserve what they get. We may relax this standard if we believe the victim strongly needs our help.

7. *If I need help, how can I increase my chances of getting it?*
You need to help people come to the right decision at each stage of the decision model. To ensure that you get noticed, make any plea for help as loud and as clear as possible. This will also help bystanders correctly label your situation as an emergency. To get someone to assume

responsibility, make eye contact with a bystander. Better yet, make a direct request of a particular bystander for help. Research shows that making such a request increases a bystander's sense of responsibility for helping you and increases the likelihood of helping.

8. *How do personality characteristics influence helping?*
Although situational factors play an important role in helping, especially spontaneous helping, they may not give us a true picture of the helper and how he or she might behave across helping situations. Personality characteristics may become more relevant when nonspontaneous, long-term helping is considered. In this case, more planning and thought are required. Some individuals might possess an **altruistic personality,** or a cluster of traits, including empathy, that predispose a person to helping.

Research on rescuers of Jews in Nazi-occupied Europe—who have been designated **righteous rescuers** by the state of Israel—provides evidence for the existence of an altruistic personality. Rescuers from Eastern Europe (especially Poland) displayed **autonomous altruism,** altruism that is not supported by social norms. Rescuers from Western Europe were more likely to display **normative altruism,** altruism that society supports and recognizes.

9. *What situational and personality variables played a role in the decision to help Jews in Nazi-occupied Europe?*
Although situational factors did not exert as strong an influence on the decision to help as one might expect, two have been found to be significant: the presence of family or group support and the initiation of rescue efforts as a result of a specific request for help. Once rescuers began helping, they were likely to continue helping.

There were also personality variables that related to the decision to become a rescuer. Compared to nonrescuers, rescuers were higher in emotional empathy (sensitivity to the suffering of others) and had a strong sense of social responsibility. Other characteristics of rescuers included an inability to blend with others, a high level of independence and self-reliance, a commitment to helping before the war, a matter-of-fact attitude about their helping, and a universalistic view of the needy.

10. *What factors contribute to a person developing an altruistic personality?*
Oliner and Oliner found that families of rescuers of Jews in Nazi-occupied Europe and families of nonrescuers differed in their styles. Families of rescuers provided role models for helping and stressed the universal nature of all people. They emphasized aspects of religion that focus on caring for others, and they were less likely to discuss negative stereotypes of Jews. Parents of altruistic individuals tended to be warm and nurturing in their parenting style. Parents of rescuers used less physical punishment than parents of nonrescuers, relying instead on induction.

Cognitive development also contributes to the development of an altruistic personality. As children get older, they are more likely to understand the needs of others. This development is a lifelong process.

Rescuers did not magically become altruists when World War II broke out. Instead, they tended to be helpers long before the war. Becoming a rescuer involved a series of small steps. In many cases, rescuers started with a small act and then moved to larger ones.

11. *What is the interactionist view of altruism?*

According to the **interactionist view of altruism,** personality and situational factors interact to influence helping. Research has identified four altruistic orientations: altruistic (those who are motivated to help others but not to receive help in return), receptive giving (those who help to obtain something in return), selfish (those who are primarily motivated to receive help but not give it), and inner sustaining (those who are not motivated to give or receive help).

Research shows that individuals with an altruistic orientation are less likely to help if compensation is offered. There is also evidence that personality factors can help a person overcome the bystander effect. Esteem-oriented individuals (who are motivated internally) are more likely to help than safety-oriented individuals (who are externally motivated) when a passive bystander is present. Additionally, personality and cost of help might interact. For low-cost behaviors, we would expect personality factors to be less important than for high-cost behaviors.

12. *How does long-term helping relate to models of emergency helping?*

With slight modification, Latané and Darley's five-stage model applies to long-term helping. Noticing, labeling, accepting responsibility, deciding how to help, and implementing the decision to help are all relevant to acts of long-term help. Additionally, at the accepting-responsibility stage the **norm of social responsibility** may have been activated. This norm suggests that we should help those in need without regard for reward.

13. *What factors influence a person's likelihood of seeking and receiving help?*

Seeking help from others is a double-edged sword: The person in need is more likely to receive help but also incurs a cost. Helping also involves costs for the helper. A person in need of help weighs these costs when deciding whether to ask for help, progressing through a multi-stage process. A person is most likely to seek help when his or her needs are low and from a friend, especially if the cost to the helper is high. A person is less likely to seek help with something easy than with something hard.

Receiving help is also a double-edged sword. The help relieves the situation but leads to negative side-effects, including feelings of guilt, lowered self-esteem, and indebtedness to the helper. Generally, there are four negative reactions to receiving aid: the creation of inequity between the helper and the recipient, psychological reactance, negative attributions about the helper, and threats to one's self-esteem. There is considerable support for the **threat to self-esteem model** of reactions to receiving help. How much a person's self-esteem is threatened depends on several factors, including the type of task and the source of the help. Males and females differ in their responses to receiving help. Females react more negatively to receiving help but are more satisfied than males with the help they received.

SUGGESTIONS FOR FURTHER READING

Batson, C. D. (1990). How social an animal? The human capacity for caring. *American Psychologist, 45,* 336–346.

In this article, C. Daniel Batson presents an overview and arguments for the empathy–altruism hypothesis. A history of the concepts of egoism and altruism is offered along with a discussion of the importance and limitations of our capacity for empathy for others.

Dozier, J. B., & Miceli, M. P. (1985). Potential predictors of whistle-blowing: A prosocial behavior perspective. *Academy of Management Review, 10,* 823–836.

In this article, Darley and Latané's five-stage model of helping is adapted and applied to a specific example of long-term helping: whistle-blowing. Whistle-blowers are individuals who risk their jobs, and perhaps their lives, to bring to the public eye dangerous actions taken by businesses or government. Dozier and Miceli show how whistle-blowers go through the same stages when deciding to help as an individual facing an emergency.

Opdyke, I. G., & Elliot, J. M. (1992). *Into the flames: The life story of a righteous rescuer.* San Bernardino, CA: Borgo Press.

This book is an autobiography of Irene Gut Opdyke, a righteous rescuer. Opdyke describes how she came to hide a group of Jews in the basement of the house in which she worked as a housekeeper for a German major. In vivid detail she describes her first experience with the persecution of the Jews and why she decided to risk her life to help those persecuted by the Nazis. In an ironic twist of fate, Opdyke describes what happened after the major discovered her secret.

Tec, N. (1986). *When light pierced the darkness.* New York: Oxford University Press.

This book details Nechama Tec's study of Christian rescuers in Poland. In the first part of the book, Tec describes the social climate within Poland during World War II and how rescuers had to overcome centuries of anti-Semitic attitudes in order to be a rescuer. The study also compares rescuers with paid helpers and shows how the quality of the care Jews received was influenced by the underlying motives of the person helping (altruism or money).

Weiner, B. (1993). On sin versus sickness: A theory of perceived responsibility and social motivation. *American Psychologist, 48,* 957–965.

In this article Bernard Weiner gives an overview of his research on the relationship between attributions, affective responses to victims, and helping. A theory is developed suggesting that if we perceive that a victim had control over his or her fate, we experience negative affect (anger) and are less willing to help than if we perceive that a victim is in distress because of uncontrollable factors.

Part Four

APPLIED SOCIAL PSYCHOLOGY

*T*hroughout this book we have seen how social psychology can inform our views of the world and help us interpret complex social situations. The principles and concepts of social psychology apply to countless events that occur daily both in our personal lives and on the larger stages of community, nation, and world. As we have seen, these principles fall into the three broad areas of social cognition, social influence, and social relations.

Part Four considers how the principles of social psychology can be applied to the study of three areas, law, health, and international conflict. It begins with law, examining such questions as how group dynamics affect jury deliberations, how attorneys can be most persuasive, and how judges can best ensure fair trials. The discussion then turns to health, considering, for example, the social perceptions that help individuals cope with illness and the best ways of persuading people to adopt health-promoting behaviors. The final chapter discusses international conflict, considering the roots of conflict and the best approaches to conflict resolution. As in all the earlier chapters, we find that social psychology can be used to help human beings function more consciously and constructively in their social worlds.

Chapter 14

Social Psychology and Law

The report crackled over the police radio: An automobile was traveling down Ventura Boulevard at over 100 miles per hour. Patrol cars from the California Highway Patrol and the Los Angeles Police Department gave pursuit. The police officers managed to stop the car with its three occupants. The driver, an African American man, was ordered out of the vehicle and onto the ground. Rodney King's confrontation with Los Angeles police officers had begun.

King apparently failed to obey the officers' orders; he even physically attacked them. After the police officers finally subdued the struggling King, several officers began to beat him, using the "power strokes" they were taught in the police academy. They also shot him with a 50,000-volt Taser stun gun. Some of the officers thought King was on PCP, a drug that can make people violent and unpredictable. One of the officers, Laurence Powell, also guessed that King had spent time in prison. He came

to this conclusion through a series of inferences: He observed that King had a well-developed physique, which, he thought, could have come only from working out with weights, which, he further surmised, King could have had access to only in prison. The police officers continued beating King until he stopped moving, and then they beat him for a while longer. From the beating King suffered 11 skull fractures, a broken ankle, a crushed cheekbone, internal injuries, and brain damage.

A bystander watching from the window of a nearby apartment captured the entire event on his camcorder. The tape was shown on news shows all over the country, creating a furor about police brutality. But the controversy surrounding the videotape was nothing compared to what was to come. Four Los Angeles police officers—Stacey Koon, Laurence Powell, Timothy Wind, and Theodore Briseno—were arrested and charged with assaulting King with a deadly weapon and with violating their trust as police officers. The four officers were indicted and went to trial on the charges.

Although the beating took place in Los Angeles County, the defense convinced the judge that a fair trial for the officers was impossible in that county because of the emotional climate and publicity surrounding the case. A change of venue (trial locale) was granted. For convenience's sake, the trial was moved about 50 miles north of Los Angeles to Simi Valley, a conservative, predominantly white community of about 100,000 people with a large population of police officers and their families. The jury that would hear the case comprised ten whites (six men and four women), one Hispanic, and one Filipino. Of these twelve jurors, three were former security guards or patrol officers in the U.S. Armed Forces, three were members of the National Rifle Association, and one had a brother who was a retired Los Angeles police officer (*Time,* May 11, 1992).

The jurors heard witnesses and watched the famous videotape, frame by frame. They heard the police officers describe the situation from their perspective. They did not, however, hear from Rodney King. The prosecutor felt that putting King on the stand could harm the state's case against the officers. King's history of criminal activity, widely reported in the press, would certainly be entered into evidence at the trial through tough cross-examination. After many days of testimony and arguments, the jury finally retired to deliberate to a verdict. To the shock and dismay of many who had seen the videotape, the jury acquitted three of the four officers and could not arrive at a verdict on the fourth. The verdict precipitated some of the worst urban rioting ever seen in the United States.

What happened in this trial? This question, as well as many questions about the American judicial system, were raised following the verdict and the rioting. Some people felt the system had failed. Here were four police officers, caught on videotape beating a subdued man. How could the jury have found them not guilty? Was the verdict a product of racism, as some charged? In the spring of 1993, the same four officers faced another Los Angeles jury on federal charges of violating Rodney King's civil rights. This time, Officers Powell (who did most of the beating) and Koon (the supervising sergeant) were found guilty.

For several years now, social psychologists have been studying the American legal system and applying social psychological principles, theories, and methods to legal issues. After all, the law ultimately rests on assumptions about how people will behave. In fact, law and psychology are both concerned with the prediction and control of human behavior. Through its findings in such areas of inquiry as social perception, prejudice and stereotyping, attitudes, group processes and dynamics, persuasion, and conformity, social psychology can clarify some of the assumptions that the law routinely makes about human beings. A sampling of areas in which social psychological findings can be applied to the law is listed in Table 14-1.

In this chapter we consider how social psychology applies to the law and how it can help us understand events like the Rodney King trial. We ask such questions as, How are jury members selected in a case like the King trial? Do the characteristics of the jurors affect the outcome of a trial? In this case that means, Did it matter that the jury was mostly white?

TABLE 14-1

APPLICATION AREAS: SOCIAL PSYCHOLOGY AND THE LAW

	Application
Before the trial	Factors affecting the police officer's decision to arrest
	Factors affecting the prosecutor's decision to prosecute
	Factors affecting the judge's bail decision
	The insanity plea and defense
	Petitions concerning trial procedure
	Jury selection
	Characteristics of jurors
During the trial	The impact of opening and closing statements on jurors
	The interpretation and use of evidence by jurors
	The effect of witness and defendant characteristics on jurors
	Pretrial publicity
	The impact of eyewitness testimony on jurors
	Eyewitness accuracy
	Criminal and civil procedure: How the trial is conducted
	The impact of the judge's instructions on the jury
	The composition of the jury
After the trial	Jury deliberations
	Sentencing decisions

During the trial, how were the jurors persuaded by the attorneys' statements and by the testimony? Once they went behind the closed doors of the jury room, how did they function as a group? And what forces operated in the case to produce the verdicts handed down by the jury? These are just some of the issues addressed in the pages that follow.

THE ROLE OF THE TRIAL IN THE CRIMINAL JUSTICE SYSTEM

The criminal justice system has many facets and stages, including the arrest process, the filing of formal charges, pretrial hearings, the trial, and sentencing. Important decisions are made at various stages as a case progresses through the system. For example, a number of variables affect a police officer's decision to arrest a suspect, or a prosecutor's decision to press a case, or a judge's decision to release a defendant on bail. For a closer look at one of these stages, see the featured discussion "The Decision to Set Bail."

During the period between arrest and trial, a defendant may be allowed to remain free provided he or she posts *bail.* Typically, the court sets an amount of money that the defendant must pay to remain free and that serves as a guarantee the defendant will appear for trial. Bail allows the defendant to continue his or her normal activities (for example, going to work). It also allows the defendant to contribute more effectively to his or her defense (Sikes, 1975). Defendants who are free between arrest and trial are less likely to be convicted (Goldfarb, 1965).

How do judges decide how much bail to set? Research based on observations of bail-setting hearings of five judges indicates that they rely most heavily on the recommendations of the prosecuting and defense attorneys (Ebbesen & Konecni, 1982). None of the case-related variables (e.g., community ties, prior record, crime severity) had any *direct* effect on the judge's decision. However, these variables may have an *indirect* effect on the judge. Undoubtedly, the prosecuting and defense attorneys consider these factors when deciding what to recommend to the judge. Crime severity and community ties especially interact to determine the recommendations the attorneys make (Ebbesen & Konecni, 1982).

Legally irrelevant variables may influence a judge's decision concerning bail. Race may play a factor in the decision to hold a defendant prior to trial. For example, Schlesinger (1988), in a report on defendants from federal courts, found that whites were less likely to be detained before trial (18.5%) than nonwhites (42%— 19.1% were black and 22.9% fell into an "other" race category). Hispanics were more likely to be held (33.2%) than non-Hispanics (14.1%). Additionally, there appears to be a gender bias. The same report found that in 1985 nearly twice as many males (20.5%) as females (10.8%) were likely to be detained prior to trial. Also, Bernat (1984) found that female prostitutes were more likely to be released prior to arraignment than male prostitutes. Interestingly, males who had solicited prostitution were more likely to be released prior to arraignment (73.6%) than the women whom they had solicited (12.9% were released prior to arraignment).

Although characteristics of the defendant may bias a pretrial release decision, legal factors tend to interact with them (Schutt & Dannefer, 1988). Overall, the effects of defendant characteristics such as race, gender, and socioeconomic status are less important in pretrial release decisions than are legally relevant factors (Nagel, 1983).

Although bail is generally available to most defendants, it may not be available to all. The Bail Reform Act of 1984 allows for the detention of an arrestee if it can be shown that there are no release conditions that could "reasonably assure" the safety of other persons and the community. For example, in *United States v. Salerno* (1987), the Supreme Court upheld the use of the Bail Reform Act to deny bail to a "lethally dangerous" Mafia leader. The Court reasoned that such a defendant would commit other crimes while out on bail and that society's need for protection weighed more than the defendant's right to bail. In cases like this, preventive detention has been applied to both adults and juveniles (Ewing, 1991).

---

*B*ail is a system that allows the defendant to be free prior to his or her trial. Why do you think that a person on bail is less likely to be convicted than one who is held in jail prior to trial? What steps might the courts take to reduce the race and gender biases that appear to exist in the bail system? What changes in the bail system would you like to see, and why?

Surprisingly, most criminal cases do not go to trial. There are several resolutions possible before a trial occurs. In some cases, for example, prosecutors may decide there is not enough evidence to continue with the case and drop the charges. In other cases, where there is sufficient evidence, both sides may, and probably will, enter into *plea bargaining.* This is a process of negotiation between the defendant (that is, the defendant's attorney) and the prosecutor about what the crime is worth. The defendant may be willing to take a known sentence arrived at through plea bargaining rather than take a chance on a trial and an unknown and perhaps more severe sentence.

Even though the trial itself accounts for the resolution of perhaps only 10% of all cases, we focus on the trial process in this chapter. We do this because the trial is the engine that drives the system. For example, the two sides would not plea bargain if a trial didn't loom in the future. More than that, the jury trial is the cornerstone of the American criminal justice system. It has evolved over the course of 800 years from a seed planted in England's Magna Charta in 1215. The jury trial represents the basic idea that all citizens, no matter how low or high, are entitled to their day in court, to a fair hearing before an impartial jury of their peers drawn from their community. This is what is meant by *due process,* a concept found in both the Fifth and the Fourteenth Amendments to the U.S. Constitution.

A typical criminal trial is played out in three acts, each with a number of scenes. The first act involves selecting a jury. A panel of citizens, known as the *venire,* is drawn from the community. From the venire the jury is selected. The second act is the trial itself. During the trial the lawyers make opening and closing statements, witnesses are presented, and the judge issues instructions to the jurors. If there were eyewitnesses to the crime, they often form the centerpiece of this part of the process. The third and final act is played out behind closed doors. After hearing all the evidence and arguments, the jury retires to deliberate (discuss the evidence) and reach a verdict. The climax of act three is reached when the jury announces its verdict in open court. Of course, after this three-act play ends there is an encore: A guilty defendant must be sentenced. In the sections that follow we look more closely at each of these parts of the criminal trial.

JURY SELECTION

The first "scene" of any trial begins with the selection of a jury. In the original Rodney King trial, 10 of the 12 jurors were white and were probably sympathetic to the police defendants. Would it have mattered if there had been blacks on the jury? A majority of individuals polled after the trial believed this to be the case: Sixty-four percent of whites and 89% of blacks believed that the verdict would have been different if the jury had included black members (*Time,* May 11, 1992). This belief raises an important question concerning the composition of a jury: Can either side stack the cards in its favor by selecting certain types of jurors in terms of race, ethnicity, sex, age, religion, and other personal characteristics?

The Voir Dire

During jury selection, or **voir dire** (which roughly means "to speak the truth"), each side has the opportunity to question potential jurors and exercise challenges to have them removed. Technically, the goal of the voir dire

voir dire Roughly means "to speak the truth." A time during which the prosecution and the defense have the opportunity to question potential jurors and exercise challenges to have them removed.

During the voir dire, lawyers have the opportunity to question prospective jurors about their backgrounds, attitudes, and beliefs. An underlying—but questionable—assumption of this process is that certain characteristics predispose individuals to vote one way or the other.

is to select a fair, impartial jury. Prospective jurors who show clear prejudice during the voir dire are excused from service for "cause."

The voir dire is carried out by the attorneys, by the judge, or by both. As might be predicted, jurors do not always tell the truth during the voir dire questioning. Sometimes the truth is painful to admit in public, such as prejudice against a group—racial, ethnic, even gender—to which the defendant belongs. This may be especially true when jurors are questioned only or primarily by the judge (as is true in federal court as opposed to state courts). The judge seems to bring about conformity on the part of the jurors; they are less likely to admit uncomfortable truths (Narby, Cutler, & Moran, 1993). Lawyers may be more successful in getting jurors to be honest in their answers, although the evidence is not entirely clear on this point (Dexter, Cutler, & Moran, 1992; Hastie, 1991).

Making Use of the Voir Dire Attorneys use the voir dire not just to weed out unqualified jurors but also to select jurors that will be favorably disposed to their arguments. The prosecution wants jurors who will be receptive to the state's case, and the defense wants just the opposite. What evolves is a game between the prosecution and the defense to select a jury that is most sympathetic to its case. Each side is allowed to challenge (remove from consideration for service on that trial) a limited number of potential jurors without specifying the reasons. These are called *peremptory challenges*. The prosecutor in the King case, for example, might have used a peremptory challenge to excuse members of conservative political groups who might side with the police officer defendants. Peremptories must be used carefully; once they are expended, an attorney has no recourse if a particularly unacceptable juror comes up.

In the conventional method of jury selection, attorneys question the jurors, probing for biases. During this process they rely on intuition and apply their own theories of human behavior, developed through experience with juries. An alternative approach to jury selection makes use of the methods of social science. This is known as **scientific jury selection**

scientific jury selection A method of jury selection that makes use of the methods of social science.

Joan Little, an African American woman, was tried in Raleigh, North Carolina, for the murder of her white jailer. She killed him, she said, when he entered her cell demanding oral sex. The prosecutor argued that Little had lured the jailer into her cell, then killed him. In the Raleigh courtroom, potential jurors were asked, among others, the following questions (Couric, 1986):

> "Do you think male jailers take advantage of female prisoners?"
> "Do you think most women who have been raped may have encouraged the attack?"
> "Do you think President Nixon was treated unfairly during Watergate?"
> "What magazines do you subscribe to?"

A team of seven social scientists sat behind the defense counsel and scrutinized everything anyone said or did in the courtroom in hopes of finding a sympathetic jury. Apparently they succeeded. Little, who had stabbed her jailer 11 times with an ice pick, was acquitted. It is in cases such as this that scientific jury selection (SJS) made its formidable reputation.

Scientific jury selection is based on the assumption that a juror's biases are related to specific personal traits and demographic characteristics (age, sex, race, ethnic background, etc.). The first step in SJS is to survey the general population from which the jurors in the actual case will be drawn. People are asked their opinions about issues that are generally related to the case. Other parts of the questionnaire are designed to gather demographic and related information. Answers to opinion questions are then tabulated and correlated with the personal and demographic. This was the procedure used in the Little case.

The second step of the scientific method is to construct a set of juror profiles ranging from the most favorable type of juror (for your side) to the least favorable. For example, based on the responses to the questionnaire, a hypothetical best juror profile might look like this: female, between the ages of 19 and 29, high school graduate, reader of romance novels, unmarried, lower middle class. A worst juror profile might look like this: male, white, over 50, business or professional, married, college graduate. A number of different profiles, perhaps 10, ranging from the best to the worst, are constructed, and the lawyers use them to select jurors.

(SJS). Typically, the defense attorney hires a team of social scientists to help select the jury. For a closer look at how this works, see the featured discussion "Scientific Jury Selection: The Joan Little Trial."

Attorneys also use the voir dire to begin the process of persuading the jurors, even before the trial begins. About 80% of the statements made by attorneys during voir dire may be intended to indoctrinate jurors (Broeder, 1965).

The Role of Individual Characteristics   Attempting to select jurors who are favorable to one side or the other presumes a relationship between a juror's attitudes, personality, and how he or she will vote. Obviously, the prosecution wants to select jurors who will be predisposed to vote guilty, and the defense wants jurors who will be sympathetic with the defendant. Some of the differing goals and agendas of each side in a criminal trial are shown in Table 14-2. As the table suggests, attorneys believe they can predict how a juror might vote based on his or her individual characteristics. For example, note in the table that the prosecution and the defense have different agendas when it comes to the authoritarian–egalitarian dimension. In the-

Does the scientific method work? Steven Penrod (1990) thinks not. His research shows that predicting a juror's attitudes about a trial from demographics does not work very well. Other re-

Joan Little in 1975 in front of the Beaufort County Courthouse following a pretrial hearing.

search shows that the method may work in specific cases and with specific personality characteristics (Horowitz, 1980). If the judge allows an extended voir dire in which many questions may be asked to get at personality variables, the scientific method may be effective in predicting juror behavior (Cutler, Moran, & Narby, 1992). Most of the time, however, the judge simply wants to get on with the trial and will not permit an extended voir dire (Penrod, 1990). Imagine jurors being given a battery of personality tests before every trial. It just doesn't happen!

The scientific method of jury selection also tends to be expensive. Joan Little, who was impoverished, was able to avail herself of SJS because a large voluntary fund was raised to help her. This fund helped pay for the social scientists. It also helped pay for expensive lawyers. You may draw

your own conclusion about which was more important to the outcome.

Some critics have charged that using scientific jury selection is an attempt to "stack" a jury in the favor of the defense. Do you think that paying a social psychologist to help pick a jury amounts to "stacking" the jury? What would happen if the State (via the prosecutor) decided to use its vast resources to employ social scientists to pick juries favorable to the State's case? Does the cost factor mean that only those individuals who can afford to hire social scientists will benefit from this practice? Can you think of any alternatives to the current practice of scientific jury selection that would be better?

ory, the authoritarian individual—someone who is predisposed to look to authority, in the form of rules and laws, for stability and safety—should be more inclined to favor the prosecution's case than an egalitarian individual, someone who believes in equal political and civil rights for everyone. Is this assumption correct?

Generally, authoritarians are more likely to side with the prosecution than are nonauthoritarians (Berg & Vidmar, 1975; Boehm, 1968; Werner, Kagehiro, & Strube, 1982). Authoritarians recall more information about the defendant's character, whereas nonauthoritarians recall more about evidence presented (Berg & Vidmar, 1975). Additionally, authoritarians are more likely than nonauthoritarians to make use of inadmissible evidence, especially if it favors the prosecution (Werner et al., 1982). Recent analysis of this issue points to a reliable correlation between authoritarians and conviction of a defendant (Narby et al., 1993). Therefore, on a general level we can conclude that authoritarians do tend to favor the prosecution's cause.

However, there are exceptions to this general rule. It appears that authoritarians do not *always* side with the prosecution. Personality variables interact with the type of case being tried. In one study, for example,

TABLE 14-2

GOALS OF VOIR DIRE FOR PROSECUTION AND DEFENSE

Specific Means	Prosecution	Defense
Predisposition to side with authority	Select authoritarian jurors	Select egalitarian jurors
Susceptibility to conformity pressure	Attempt to maximize interjuror conformity	Select jurors who are prone to dissent
Openness of cognitive set	Select jurors with a closed cognitive set	Select jurors who are willing to consider conflicting information
Estimate of guilt	Convince jurors of high probability of guilt	Convince jurors of low probability of guilt
Criterion for conviction	Low threshold of reasonable doubt	High threshold of reasonable doubt

From Fried, Kaplan, and Klein, 1975.

subjects read a transcript of a trial that depicted a riot following a rock concert (Mitchell, 1979). During the riot, a confrontation between a police officer and a citizen resulted in one of them being killed. Half of the subjects were led to believe that the police officer was the victim; the other half were led to believe that the citizen was the victim. Sentiment toward the defendant was also manipulated by having a psychologist provide either flattering or unflattering testimony about the defendant. Subjects were told the defendant had been found guilty and were asked to decide on his punishment.

The study showed that egalitarian jurors were more lenient toward the citizen defendant than toward the police officer defendant (Figure 14-1), perhaps because they held the police officer to a higher standard of behavior. The reverse was true for the authoritarian jurors: They were more lenient when the police officer was the defendant. Some of the jurors in the original Rodney King trial appear to have fit the profile of authoritarian jurors, so this may have been a factor in the outcome of that trial. Authoritarians are also likely to be harsh with a defendant in a murder case and lenient with a defendant in a self-defense case (Becker & Barry, 1979). Both situations have to do, in some sense, with keeping order and avoiding chaos. Authoritarians would want to severely punish a person who murders but would forgive a person who kills when threatened by harm from someone else.

Even though a relationship exists between some personality variables and some types of cases (that is, authoritarians are very likely to convict in murder cases), there is no simple connection between a person's background or personality characteristics and how that person will vote in a trial. Rather, a complex interaction between individual and situational variables determines how a person will vote in any given trial. This would seem to argue against systematic attempts by hired experts to help select juries that will be favorable toward the defense (Saks, 1981).

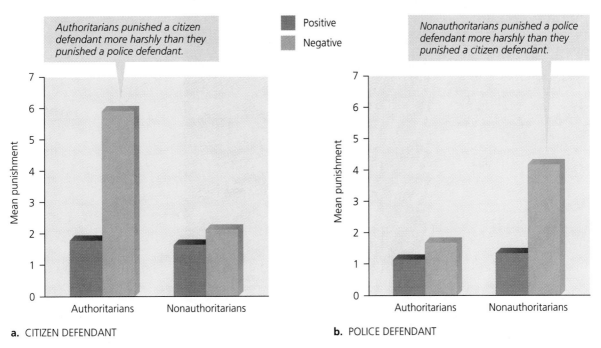

Authoritarians punished a citizen defendant more harshly than they punished a police defendant.

Positive
Negative

Nonauthoritarians punished a police defendant more harshly than they punished a citizen defendant.

a. CITIZEN DEFENDANT

b. POLICE DEFENDANT

When the Death Penalty Applies

Many states allow defendants to be sentenced to death for certain crimes. The U.S. Supreme Court has observed that the death penalty "is different from other punishments." Therefore, capital cases must be handled with special concern for a fair application of that ultimate punishment (Horowitz & Willging, 1984). In order to be sure that the death penalty is not imposed arbitrarily, laws have been written to permit the jury to consider both the guilt of the defendant and the punishment.

A capital trial uses a bifurcated procedure consisting of two separate phases, both before the same jury. In the first phase, the *guilt phase,* the jury determines the guilt or innocence of the defendant. The second, the *penalty phase,* occurs only if the defendant is found guilty. In this phase, the defense presents evidence about why a sentence other than death should be imposed. The prosecution, of course, presents countering testimony.

In cases where the death penalty can be imposed, a special jury is empaneled. This jury includes jurors who are willing to impose the death penalty. Anyone who admits during the voir dire that he or she is absolutely against the death penalty will be excluded, for cause, from the jury. Jurors falling in this category are called *excludables.* Only jurors who either are in favor of the death penalty or are "indifferent" to it, who have no strong feelings one way or the other, are allowed on the jury. These jurors are called *nonexcludables.* What results is a **death-qualified jury,** a jury that supports the state's interest in applying capital punishment.

Recall from Chapter 10 that the composition of any decision-making group affects the performance of that group. In a capital case an entire class of individuals—those who oppose capital punishment—is excluded

FIGURE 14-1 Punishments given to citizen versus police defendants by authoritarians and nonauthoritarians. (a) Authoritarians punished citizen defendants more harshly in a murder case than police defendants; nonauthoritarians punished police defendants more harshly than they punished citizen defendants (b). These findings indicate that authoritarians do not always side with the prosecution. They also indicate that personal characteristics, such as authoritarianism, do predict how a juror will vote in a trial. From data in Mitchell, 1979.

death-qualified jury A jury comprising members who are willing to impose the death penalty; this jury is considered to be conviction prone.

When a defendant is accused of a capital crime, individuals who are categorically opposed to the death penalty are excluded from the jury. Some observers believe that the exclusion of individuals like those shown here—protesting executions at San Quentin prison—results in juries biased in favor of the death penalty.

from the jury. Are nonexcludable jurors, in fact, somehow different from excludable jurors? If they are, does this result in a bias for or against the defendant? And, if a bias exists, what can be done about it? In this section we address these three questions. Before we do, however, let's briefly review the death-qualification process.

The Death-Qualification Process The death-qualification process involves lawyers and/or judges, depending on where the trial takes place, asking potential jurors during the voir dire about their opinion on the death penalty. If they admit that they are against it, the court will probe the juror to see if they are *really* against it. For example, a juror might be asked if she would still be against the death penalty if someone invaded her house, murdered her husband and her dog, and burned her house down. If she says that in that case she would be for the death penalty, she is considered to be *rehabilitated* and is eligible to serve. Of course, the defense attorney might use a peremptory challenge to remove this potential juror from the jury.

Note that potential jurors are asked about their attitudes toward the death penalty *before* they hear any evidence about the defendant's possible guilt or innocence. The very act of death qualification—excluding those jurors who say they are against the death penalty—has been shown to bias the jury to favor the prosecution (Haney, 1984). After all, a potential juror sitting in the courtroom who sees other jurors automatically removed for expressing doubts about the death penalty might reasonably conclude that the court frowns upon such opposition.

Differences Between Excludable and Nonexcludable Jurors Excludable and nonexcludable jurors differ in some meaningful, important ways. For example, nonexcludables tend to place less importance on due process than excludables. That is, nonexcludables place less emphasis on protecting the rights of the accused than they do on punishing criminals (Fitzgerald & Ellsworth, 1984). Overall, nonexcludables (compared to excludables) are more punitive and therefore more likely to favor harsh punishment to deter crime, more likely to favor strict law enforcement regardless of costs, more likely to trust the prosecutor, and less sensitive to constitutional guarantees (Fitzgerald & Ellsworth, 1984). The bottom line is that nonexcludables start out with an antidefense bias and are less willing to consider issues that the defense might bring up during the trial.

There appears to be a definite "profile" of excludable and nonexcludable jurors. For example, more blacks (25.5%) than whites (16.5%) are excludable, and more women (21%) than men (13.1%) are excludable. Lower-income jurors are more likely to be excluded than higher-income jurors. More Democrats (21.3%) than Republicans (10.1%) are excludable. And Jews, atheists, and agnostics are more likely to be excluded than Catholics and Protestants. Thus, the death-qualified jury is overrepresented by white, high-income, Republican males (Fitzgerald & Ellsworth, 1984; Moran & Comfort, 1986) who tend to be politically conservative and authoritarian (Moran & Comfort, 1986). The death-qualified jury, then, is not representative of the wider community.

Do these differences between excludables and nonexcludables mean that a jury composed of nonexcludables will be more likely to convict the defendant than a more balanced jury? The answer appears to be yes (Horowitz & Seguin, 1986; Jurow, 1971; Moran & Comfort, 1986; Narby et al., 1993). Such a jury is also more likely to sentence the defendant to death than a mixed jury (both excludables and nonexcludables) or a jury comprising only excludables (Horowitz & Seguin, 1986). This is most likely because nonexcludables tend to be more authoritarian than excludables, as noted earlier, and authoritarians tend to side with the prosecution.

Solutions to the Problem of Bias in Death-Qualified Juries   There are no easy solutions to the problem of the bias inherent in the death-qualification process. The Supreme Court has been reluctant to invalidate the death-qualification process, although it has acknowledged the problem (Thompson, 1989). Various suggestions for changes to the death-qualification process have been offered, but not implemented. For example, excludable jurors might be "rehabilitated" through a modified questioning procedure or through exposure to a series of crime descriptions that are increasingly brutal and vivid (Cox & Tanford, 1989). Rehabilitated excludables are more tolerant of ambiguity, less crime control oriented, and less punitive than nonexcludables (Cox & Tanford, 1989). Unfortunately, the modified questioning procedure may increase conviction proneness of death-qualified juries (Harasty & Horowitz, 1991). That is, once excludables are rehabilitated they may become more like nonexcludables and be therefore more likely to convict.

Another remedy for the death-qualification problem centers on the fact that not all excludables are alike. Excludables can be categorized as guilt nullifiers (jurors who would vote not guilty in any case in which the death penalty is possible), penalty nullifiers (jurors who would vote guilty but not impose the death penalty under any circumstances), or both (Thompson, 1989). One possible solution to the problem of bias in the death-qualification process is to allow penalty nullifiers to serve on the jury during the guilt phase but not during the penalty phase of a trial. During the penalty phase, only nonexcludables would consider whether or not to impose the death penalty. Theoretically, this might reduce the tendency of death-qualified juries to convict (because excludables are included during the guilt phase) yet retain the potential for having the death penalty imposed upon conviction (Horowitz & Seguin, 1986).

THE TRIAL

During the trial, each side presents witnesses who provide evidence intended to convince the jury that the defendant is guilty (for the prosecution) or innocent (for the defense). In the sections that follow we explore how social psychological variables come into play in the courtroom during a trial.

Opening Statements

After the judge makes some opening remarks defining the roles of the jurors and other participants, the trial is ready to get under way. The first thing that happens is that each side is given the opportunity to make an *opening statement* to the jury. Although the content of the opening statement may differ from jurisdiction to jurisdiction, in most cases opening statements consist of a preview and summary of the evidence that each side will present during the trial. During the opening statements, each side presents its theory about the defendant's guilt or innocence. Of course, the prosecution presents a theory showing that the defendant is guilty. The defense presents an alternative theory, casting doubt on the defendant's guilt.

Order of Presentation   Because the prosecution has the burden of proof in a criminal trial (that is, an individual is innocent unless proven guilty, so the prosecution must prove guilt), the prosecution presents its opening statement first. This gives the prosecution a slight edge over the defense. All other things being equal, the *law of primacy*, as described in Chapter 7, operates in this situation (Lawson, 1969)—that is, the side that presents its arguments first generally has an advantage over the side presenting second. However, the defense may offset this advantage by electing to make its opening statement *after* the prosecution has presented its entire case, especially if there is to be a recess between the prosecution's presentation and the defense's. When there is a delay between persuasive messages, the *law of recency*—the most recent persuasive argument has the greatest impact—may come into play and offset the prosecution's initial advantage.

Research indicates, however, that if the defense delays its opening statement, the defendant is more likely to be convicted than if the opening statement were presented immediately following the prosecutor's opening statement (Wells, Wrightsman, & Miene, 1985). Delaying the defense's opening state-

FIGURE 14-2 When an attorney previews the evidence in her opening statement, shaping it into a coherent story line, jurors often use that story to frame and make sense of everything that follows during the trial.

ment also reduces the influence of the defendant's testimony and of the defense attorney's closing statement. Generally, then, it is better if the defense attorney presents his or her opening statement immediately after the prosecutor rather than hope that a recency effect will occur with a delayed opening statement.

The Impact of Opening Statements The content of the opening statements presented to a jury is important. Opening statements can often predispose a jury to vote either for or against the defendant, in some cases even overriding the evidence presented at trial (Figure 14-2). How is it that opening statements can be so important?

Recall from Chapter 3 that jurors handle complex evidence presented during a trial by constructing a *story* about "what happened" (Pennington & Hastie, 1986, 1988, 1992). According to this *story model*, evidence that is presented during the trial is incorporated into the story that is developing in the juror's mind. An effective opening statement can lead a juror (and later a jury) to begin developing either a pro-prosecution or a pro-defense story. In essence, an effective opening statement can set the *theme* for the story. This theme then affects how jurors process and use the evidence presented during the trial (Wrightsman, 1991).

Evidence for the importance of an effective opening statement comes from several studies (Pyszczynski, Greenberg, Mack, & Wrightsman, 1981; Pyszczynski & Wrightsman, 1981; Wells et al., 1985). In one study, jurors' attitudes were evaluated 12 times during a mock trial and at the end of the trial. The extent of the opening statements was varied and the trial evidence itself held constant. Generally, the results showed that jurors begin to form impressions fairly early in the trial based on the opening statements. If the prosecution made an extensive opening statement (summarizing evidence), jurors began with a belief that the defendant was guilty and were unlikely to change that belief significantly as the trial progressed. This was true even if the defense made an extensive opening statement as well. The defense had the advantage only if it made an extensive opening statement and the prosecution made a superficial

A lawyer examines a witness—typically the centerpiece of the trial. Because jurors respond not just to facts but to peripheral cues as well, lawyers often try to undermine testimony by casting doubt on a witness's credibility.

one. In this latter condition, jurors began with a pro-defense tilt that was maintained throughout the trial. An extensive opening statement seemed to give jurors a firm context within which to interpret later evidence.

Promising and Not Delivering   By presenting a preview of the evidence, lawyers hope to establish a favorable context for their case. What happens if an attorney promises to produce a witness or a piece of evidence and then never delivers? In one experiment, mock jurors (subjects playing the role of jurors) were presented with one of two versions of an opening statement (Pyszczynski et al., 1981). In one version the defense attorney claimed that a witness would be presented providing an airtight alibi for the defendant. In a second version this claim was never made. During the mock trial itself the promised evidence was *never presented.* At the end of the trial the prosecutor's response to the claim made by the defense was also varied. In one condition the prosecutor pointed out that the defense never fulfilled its promise to produce the alibi witness, whereas in another condition the prosecutor did not point out the unfulfilled promise.

The results of this experiment were startling. If the jurors heard the unfulfilled promise but were not reminded of it by the prosecution, they were more likely to find the defendant innocent than if the promise were never made. Only when the prosecutor pointed out the unfulfilled promise did the jurors reject it. Thus, even an unfulfilled promise can become part of the story woven by jurors and affect the outcome of the trial.

The Evidence

Opening statements, as we have seen, are an important part of the persuasion process in trials. However, jurors do not base their entire decision on opening statements. As the trial progresses there are shifts, sometimes large and sometimes small, in jurors' attitudes that coincide with the evidence presented (Pyszczynski et al., 1981; Pyszczynski & Wrightsman, 1981; Weld & Danzig, 1940). The evidence itself is the most important information presented to jurors during the trial and is the most important determinant of the ultimate outcome of the trial (Visher, 1987).

Examination of Witnesses During a typical trial, each side presents witnesses who provide evidence to the jury. As with the opening statements, the prosecution presents its witnesses first and questions each one to elicit critical facts. This is known as *direct examination* of a witness. The defense has the opportunity to ask the witness questions as well, during *cross-examination*. Meanwhile, the jury looks on, trying to make sense out of the sometimes conflicting statements the witness makes during direct and cross-examination.

Through the presentation of evidence, each side hopes to persuade the jury of the defendant's guilt or innocence. How does this persuasion process take place? The *elaboration likelihood model,* described in Chapter 7, suggests that there are two routes to persuasion: a central route and a peripheral route. Information processed along the central route is attended to and evaluated carefully for its content. Information processed along the peripheral route is not so carefully processed. Instead, emotions and feelings come into play.

The elaboration likelihood model can help us understand how jurors make decisions based on trial evidence. When evidence is clear and relatively easy to understand, jurors are able to construct a coherent narrative (ForsterLee, Horowitz, & Bourgeois, 1993). In this situation, they are likely to use central route processing to understand the case. When evidence is complex, ambiguous, and difficult to understand, jurors find it harder to construct a coherent narrative. They are likely to default to the peripheral route and consider legally irrelevant information. Factors involved in these two processes are shown in Figure 14-3.

The side that can tell the most reasonable story and explains more of the facts usually wins. In the original Rodney King trial, for example, the defense offered this story: Rodney King was the prime cause of the beating. If he had complied with orders, the beating would have stopped immediately or it may never have occurred. The defense also contended that racial prejudice played no part in the policemen's behavior, except possibly in the case of Officer Laurence Powell. The police had no choice but to act as they did. They were simply doing their job.

Did the story have some holes? Yes. One of the four police officers testified that he knew the police had lost control. There were recorded racist comments by at least one of the officers. Further, King was still being beaten after he stopped resisting. Why the not-guilty verdicts? The jury found the defense account more persuasive than the one offered by the prosecuting attorney, who focused on the videotape. By focusing on that tape, the prosecutor forfeited the possibility of telling a good story, one with good guys and bad guys, motives and hatreds. The prosecutor could have focused on the racial statements made by some of the officers and the fact that at least one of the defendants had a history of being very tough on minority suspects.

"HAS THE MASS MEDIA REACHED A VERDICT?"

Pretrial publicity is a persistent problem facing the court system. The problem occurs when facts or other information about a case is published in newspapers and/or broadcast on television or radio prior to the trial. The U.S. Constitution guarantees a defendant a fair trial. It also guarantees freedom of the press. These two constitutional guarantees often come into conflict. The major issue is whether such publicity biases a jury against the defendant.

The Effects of Pretrial Publicity on the Jury

The Rodney King case was given massive and almost instantaneous publicity. Was it possible, after multiple TV showings of portions of the videotape, that there were 12 people in the country old enough to be jurors who had not formed an opinion on the case? The least the trial court could do, according to the judge, was to remove the case from Los Angeles County, where the event had occurred.

Similarly, in the William Kennedy Smith rape trial, the impact of pretrial publicity on a jury in southern Florida was an issue. In a pretrial hearing in the Smith case (televised on CNN), lawyers representing the news media suggested that the release of the information about the three previous rapes would not prejudice a jury against Smith. They cited a survey suggesting that all the publicity was generating interest in Smith's case but was not prejudicial.

Social psychological research, however, paints a different picture. In one study, two groups of simulated jurors read newspaper stories about a trial (Padawer-Singer, Singer, & Singer, 1977). The stories read by one group included "prejudicial information" (for example, information about the defendant's prior record and an alleged recanted confession). The clippings read by the second group did not include the prejudicial information.

pretrial publicity Information about a case that can influence jurors that is published in newspapers or broadcast on television or radio prior to a trial.

The study showed that the prejudicial information altered both the jurors' perceptions of the defendant and the ultimate outcome of the trial. For example, 42.9% of the jurors exposed to the prejudicial information saw the defendant as "untruthful," compared to 28.7% of those not exposed to the prejudicial information. The prejudicial information also had an impact on jury deliberations. The newspaper stories were more likely to be discussed during deliberations when they contained the prejudicial information than if they did not contain the prejudicial information. Finally, conviction was significantly more likely (80%) when the prejudicial information was given than when it wasn't (39%).

General pretrial publicity has less effect than pretrial publicity related directly to the charge against the defendant (Greene & Wade, 1987). However, publicity surrounding a crime committed by another person that is similar to the one on which a defendant is being tried may affect the outcome of that trial (Greene, 1990).

Remedies for Pretrial Publicity   Three remedies have been suggested for pretrial publicity effects (Kramer, Kerr, & Carroll, 1990). First, the judge can, and often does, instruct the jury not to allow pretrial publicity to affect its decision. Second, the effects of pretrial publicity may be reduced through jury deliberations. Finally, the judge can grant a continuance (a brief delay) between the appearance of the publicity and the trial date, giving things a chance to "settle down."

Which, if any, of these remedies are effective? One study investigated two types of pretrial publicity: informational and emotional (Kramer et al., 1990). Informational pretrial publicity consists of facts relating directly to the case being tried (for example, that the police had found incriminating evidence). Emotional pretrial publicity consists of information that inflames the emotions of the jurors (for example, information about the effects of the crime on the victim's family). In this study, some juries were exposed to informational publicity, others to emotional publicity, and still others to no publicity. In one remedy condition, juries were instructed to ignore the publicity; in another remedy condition, a continuance was granted.

Results showed that pretrial publicity does affect verdicts and the content of the jury's deliberations despite efforts to blunt it. Instructing a jury to ignore pretrial publicity did not significantly reduce its effects (a finding that is consistent with the general finding that judicial instructions are ineffective in reducing bias). Nor did jury deliberation reduce the impact of the pretrial publicity. The jury discussed both kinds of publicity, and the presence of pretrial publicity increased the number of pro-conviction statements made during deliberations. Granting a continuance significantly reduced the effects of pretrial publicity, but only of *informational* pretrial publicity. The effects of emotional pretrial publicity persisted even after the delay. Thus, of the three remedies, only one—granting a continuance—had any noticeable effect.

Another approach is also possible: extensive questioning of potential jurors during the voir dire to determine how influenced they have been by pretrial publicity. When a case has generated a lot of publicity, judges are more likely to allow lawyers to ask extensive, free-wheeling questions. The importance of this practice can be seen in high-profile trials in which defendants were acquitted, such as the original King trial and the Smith case. Here, jurors were not persuaded to convict despite strongly prejudicial pretrial publicity.

The effects of an extended voir dire as a remedy for bias due to pretrial publicity were examined in a study in which jurors were given special instructions during the voir dire (Dexter, Cutler, & Moran, 1992). Jurors were told that journalists who had published pretrial stories had different goals than the legal system and different criteria for proof. Jurors were also asked to hold fellow jurors accountable if they raised pretrial publicity in the jury deliberations, and they were reminded in various ways that only the evidence presented in court was to be considered in their decision. The attorney obtained a commitment from many of the jurors to base the verdict on the evidence presented in the court and to make sure other jurors did the same. Recall from Chapter 7 that accountability and commitment tend to make people live up to their pledges. Jurors subjected to an extensive voir dire in this study were less likely to find the defendant guilty than jurors who had participated in a minimal voir dire, without the lengthy inquiry and the lecture. These are the techniques, then, that attorneys and judges may want to use to minimize the effects of pretrial publicity.

THE EYEWITNESS

During the trial, many types of evidence can be presented. Police officers and expert witnesses may testify about details of the crime and crime scene. Expert witnesses may testify about the defendant's state of mind. The defendant may testify in his or her own defense. However, there is one type of evidence that is of paramount importance to the jury: the eyewitness. An **eyewitness** is a person who observed the crime and can relate the events to the jury in court. Eyewitnesses are crucial to the outcome of criminal trials (Loftus, 1979a). The presence of an eyewitness markedly increases conviction rates. Because of the eyewitness's crucial role and the fact that many social psychological variables influence perception, there is a vast body of research on the performance of eyewitnesses. Before we examine some of this research, let's see what it is like to be an eyewitness to a crime.

The Experience of Being an Eyewitness

Imagine that you make some extra spending money by working in a supermarket. One night, after the store has closed, you're sweeping the floor near the "out" door, which happens to still be unlocked. Suddenly a man opens the door and steps into the store. You look up and tell him the store is closed. He reaches under his coat and pulls out a gun, a revolver. He points it directly at you and tells you to back up. At first the gun doesn't look real to you—you're struck by how large and shiny it appears—but the bullets in the chamber convince you it is. You back up.

eyewitness A person who observed a crime and can relate the events to the jury in court.

It is unlikely that this victim of a violent attack in a Brooklyn, New York, park will be able to give an accurate or objective account of the incident. Trauma, stress, and fear are just some of the factors that distort perceptions at the scene of a crime, particularly a violent crime.

The man is wearing a camel-colored overcoat and a hat. His face is heavily made up with theatrical makeup. Two other men now appear behind him. One is wearing a black leather jacket and a clown mask. He stands by the door holding a small automatic pistol. The third man is also heavily made up.

Two of the men proceed to the bookkeeper's office and empty the contents of the safe. The first man continues to stand near the door, holding his gun pointed down at his side. You keep your eyes on the floor. Two thoughts go through your mind: "Please don't let him ask me for money" and "Just look at the floor, don't stare at him. If I see too much he might take me with him." Then the two men reappear and all three leave, telling you not to move or call the police.

Of course, you do move and call the police. You are questioned by the police at the scene and, a few days later, at the police station. You are shown a "mug book" and asked if you recognize anyone. You are also shown an assortment of weapons to help you identify the weapons used.

You have been an eyewitness to a crime. What was your experience like? Were your perceptions accurate, or were they clouded by fear? Did you pay attention to what was going on, or were you preoccupied with what might happen to you? Were you swayed by the presence of a gun? Could your descriptions be used to convict someone of the crime? These questions all relate to a special category of evidence that can often make or break a criminal case: eyewitness testimony. As we will discuss, several variables affect the accuracy of the eyewitness's perceptions of a crime.

Eyewitness Accuracy

When an eyewitness views a crime, several variables affect the accuracy of his or her perceptions. Consider your experience in the event just described. You were confronted by a disguised man brandishing a formidable-looking weapon. You spent most of the time looking at the floor and worrying about your own safety. The incident lasted just a few minutes. A few days intervened between when you witnessed the crime and when you

When a weapon is present, people instinctively focus on it rather than on other details of the situation. This terrorist at the Beirut Airport can be sure the hostages in the plane paid more attention to the guns aimed at them than to what the hijackers looked like.

made a formal statement to the police. Some or all of these factors may have influenced your recollection of the event.

Two classes of variables can influence the accuracy of an eyewitness: estimator variables and system variables (Wells, 1978). **Estimator variables** are related directly to the eyewitness and the conditions under which the eyewitness viewed the crime. They include lighting, exposure time, and personal biases of the eyewitness. **System variables** are variables that are under control of the criminal justice system. They include the time that elapses between the crime and the questioning of a witness, the manner in which a lineup is conducted, and the way that questions are asked of eyewitnesses. Both classes of variables influence the accuracy of eyewitness perceptions, memories, and reports. We turn now to some variables that affect eyewitness accuracy.

Weapon Focus Weapons command our attention and change our perceptual world. When a gun is pointed at us, we are less able to pay attention to other details of a situation. This phenomenon is called **weapon focus** (Loftus, 1979a). As you might expect, the presence of a weapon reduces eyewitness accuracy.

Weapon focus is a function of attention. When we view a scene, we don't pay equal attention to all details. Instead, we select out the most salient details, the features that stand out; these are the details we remember best later. In a study that demonstrated the importance of detail salience, subjects were shown a 2-minute-long movie depicting an automobile striking a pedestrian in a supermarket parking lot (Marshall, Marquis, & Oskamp, 1971). Prior to the experiment the film was pretested to determine the salience of the various details depicted. This was done by counting the number of times particular details were mentioned by subjects who had viewed the film. Some details were mentioned often (high salience) and others rarely (low salience). After viewing the film, the subjects were asked what they could recall about the film. Researchers measured two factors: the accuracy of their perceptions (proportion of details correctly reported) and the completeness of their perceptions (the proportion of details mentioned).

estimator variable A variable that is related directly to the eyewitness and the conditions under which the eyewitness viewed the crime.

system variable A variable affecting eyewitness accuracy that is under the control of the criminal justice system.

weapon focus The phenomenon that occurs when the presence of a gun causes an eyewitness to pay less attention to other details of the crime scene.

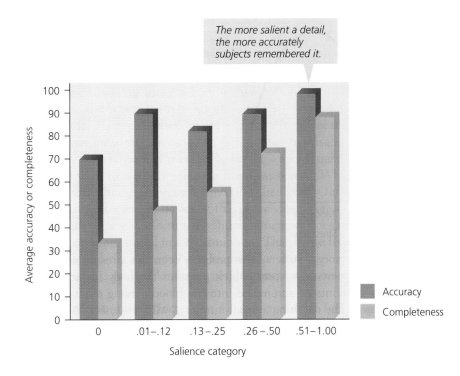

The more salient a detail, the more accurately subjects remembered it.

FIGURE 14-4 The effect of detail salience on eyewitness memory. The more a detail stood out, the more likely subjects were to remember it accurately and include it in their account of an incident. This study supported the phenomenon known as weapon focus: When a gun is present, witnesses notice and pay attention to it, giving less attention to other details of the crime scene. From data in Marshall, Marquis, and Oskamp, 1971.

As shown in Figure 14-4, high-salience details were more likely to be included than low-salience details. However, even very low-salience items were recalled quite accurately (an accuracy score of near 70 out of 100). Detail salience is most critical for the completeness of a witness's report. In this case, the higher the salience of an item, the more complete the report of that detail. Thus, details that stand out, such as a weapon, are most likely to be remembered and reported by an eyewitness to a crime.

A weapon is clearly a salient detail, as shown in research. Fewer subjects were able to correctly identify a suspect in a lineup when a weapon was used during a crime than when no weapon was used (Loftus, Loftus, & Messo, 1987). When a weapon was present, subjects tended to stare at it (measured via eye fixations to the weapon). Of course, while they were staring at the weapon, they were not looking at other details, such as the suspect's face and clothing. And when witnesses are asked to identify a suspect later on, they are less able to do so accurately when a weapon was present than when no weapon was present (Maass & Kohnken, 1989).

Violence of the Crime Another important variable that affects eyewitness accuracy is the violence of the crime. When a crime is violent, eyewitnesses are generally less accurate than when a crime is nonviolent (Clifford & Scott, 1978).

Why does this occur? You might recall the *Yerkes-Dodson law* from your introductory psychology course. This law, illustrated in Figure 14-5, suggests that there is an inverted U-shaped function relating stress and performance. Under conditions of high stress, performance—including

described the same suspect as "tall," the witness may blend the short with the tall and come to believe that the suspect was of "average height." This process is known as **compromise memory** (Loftus, 1979a).

Although the existence of the misinformation effect has been demonstrated quite frequently, some controversy exists over exactly what causes it. The debate raises age-old controversies about the nature of human memory. Some believe that conflictual postevent information actually alters the original memory trace and makes it unavailable to the eyewitness (Loftus, 1979a, 1979b). Others dispute the idea that the original memory trace is altered (McCloskey & Zaragoza, 1985).

At this point it is not possible to specify exactly the mechanism underlying the misinformation effect. It is safe, however, to conclude that if a witness is exposed to misleading postevent information, the witness's *report* of what was experienced may be influenced in the direction of the misleading information. Regardless of the reason for the distortion, the bottom line is that what the witness says may not be an accurate reflection of the original event he or she witnessed. Rather, it may contain elements of the original memory and new elements added based on exposure to postevent information.

In sum, then, eyewitness memory is prone to errors of both encoding and recall. When eyewitnesses take the stand, the testimony they give may be more a description of what they saw—or think they saw—than an accurate one-to-one recollection of the event. For a closer look at one approach to enhancing eyewitness memory, see the featured discussion "Hypnosis and the Eyewitness."

The Lineup

As a part of many criminal investigations, an eyewitness may be called to the police station to try to identify a suspect in a lineup, sometimes from a live lineup, sometimes from a photo array. In either case, the procedures used to conduct a lineup may influence whom the eyewitness picks.

In a typical lineup, a suspect is included along with others who resemble him or her, known as "foils" or "distractors." The purpose of these distractors is to make the recognition task more difficult for the eyewitness and to reduce false recognitions. Who should the distractors be? In most cases, police pick distractors who resemble the suspect in the lineup. That is, after the police make an arrest based on a description from a witness, they select distractors who resemble the arrested suspect.

Bias in the Lineup Eyewitnesses can apparently be influenced by the way a lineup is conducted. In one study, eyewitnesses attempted to identify a suspect from a photo array (Buckhout, 1974). Photos of various potential suspects were spread out on a table. In one condition, all the pictures were in the same orientation and all the suspects had similar facial expressions. In a second condition, one of the photographs was tilted and the person's facial expression was changed. Tilting a photograph and changing that person's expression increased the likelihood that eyewitnesses would identify

compromise memory Memory distortion that occurs when a person blends new information encountered after witnessing an event with information that is already in memory.

HYPNOSIS AND THE EYEWITNESS

Details of crimes are often forgotten or not reported by eyewitnesses. In some cases, hypnosis has been used to refresh the memories of these witnesses. Perhaps the most famous instance of hypnotically refreshed memory was in the case of the kidnapping of a school bus load of children in Chowchilla, California. The bus driver escaped and, under hypnosis, provided police with all but one digit of the license number of a pick-up truck involved in the incident. This helped the police to uncover more information and eventually solve the case.

If hypnosis can help police catch criminals and juries convict them, why don't we hear more about its use? Actually, many people misunderstand what hypnosis is. They get their ideas about hypnosis from theatrical performances, where a subject is hypnotized and then clucks like a chicken. Or they may have heard about individuals who, under hypnosis, regress to an early age and recall minute details of childhood events. Despite these stories, hypnosis is not really a mysterious process. It is simply a state of deep relaxation during which an individual is in a heightened state of suggestibility.

When hypnosis is used in criminal cases, several issues arise. A fundamental question, for example, is whether hypnosis *actually* increases one's ability to recall details of an event. Unfortunately, the news is not good. A considerable number of studies suggest that hypnosis is no better at increasing recall than other, nonhypnotic relaxation techniques (Smith, 1983) or simple recall (Spanos, Quigley, Gwynn, Glatt, & Perlini, 1991). Hypnotized subjects are more confident in their lineup identifications, whether they are correct or not (Spanos et al., 1991). Additionally, there is concern that hypnotized witnesses, especially highly suggestible ones, will generate pseudomemories (Spanos, Gwynn, Comer, Baltruweit, & de Groh, 1989). Although the evidence for this latter problem is mixed, it still remains a concern.

What does the jury make of hypnotically refreshed testimony provided in court? An experiment by Edith Greene, Leanne Wilson, and Elizabeth Loftus (1989) showed that jurors are skeptical of such testimony. Hypnotically refreshed evidence was not given as much weight by jurors as evidence produced by nonhypnotically induced immediate recall. Additionally, hypnosis was found to *reduce* the credibility of the witness (Greene, Wilson, & Loftus, 1989). During deliberations, jurors who had heard from a hypnotically refreshed witness were more likely to make negative comments about the witness's credibility than jurors who heard nonhypnotically refreshed testimony (Greene et al., 1989).

Because of these problems and concerns, hypnotically refreshed testimony is not widely used. In fact, only 13 states allow the introduction of such testimony in court (Wrightsman, 1987). In most of these states, the hypnosis must be carried out by a professional who is not a police officer and hypnosis sessions must be videotaped so that the procedures used can be reviewed by court officials to make sure that questioning was not suggestive (Wrightsman, 1987). These steps make it easier to evaluate the validity of the testimony produced.

---

*T*he use of hypnosis to refresh a witness's memory is controversial. Do you think the potential benefits of using hypnosis (e.g., enhanced memory) are worth the risks (e.g., false memories)? What steps might the police take to ensure that if hypnosis is used the memories recovered will be as accurate as possible? Do you think that judges should give juries special instructions concerning hypnotically refreshed testimony?

---

that person as the suspect. This most likely occurs because the witness's attention is drawn to the tilted photograph.

Another form of bias can occur when the police officer conducting a lineup knows which individual is the suspect. In a variation of the "clever Hans" effect (in which a horse trainer inadvertently sent cues to his performing horse, giving the impression that the horse could perform math),

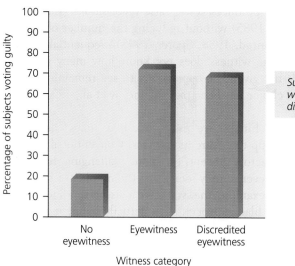

FIGURE 14-7 *The effect of discrediting an eyewitness. Eyewitnesses are so powerful that their testimony dramatically increases the conviction rate over conditions where there are no eyewitnesses. Even more striking is the finding that discrediting an eyewitness has little effect on conviction rate; jurors are still strongly swayed by eyewitness testimony.* From data in Loftus, 1979a.

Subjects voted guilty even when an eyewitness was discredited.

As shown in Figure 14-7, when no eyewitness was present, the conviction rate was very low (18%). With an eyewitness, the conviction rate jumped markedly (to 72%). Discrediting the eyewitness did not significantly reduce conviction rates (68%).

Interestingly, it doesn't take much to enhance the credibility of an eyewitness. If an eyewitness testifies that he or she remembers some trivial detail, unrelated to the crime itself, the witness's credibility and ability to persuade the jury are increased (Bell & Loftus, 1988, 1989).

Many of the problems associated with eyewitness testimony are increased when the event took place many years earlier. For a closer look at one example of this situation, see the featured discussion "The Case of Ivan the Terrible."

Children as Eyewitnesses

Eyewitness testimony is particularly problematic when the witness is a child. Generally, adults assume that younger children are less credible witnesses than older children and adults (Goodman, Golding, Helgeson, Haith, & Michelli, 1987). In most jurisdictions, the competence of child witnesses must be established before the child will be allowed to testify. The use of children as witnesses in court has a long, though uneven, history. Children were accorded almost mystical status during the infamous Salem witch trials during the 16th century. In those trials, children were the principal accusers and witnesses. Their testimony was used to send many alleged "witches" and "wizards" to their death. In later times, the courts looked on testimony from children with skepticism. Until 1895 a child was assumed to be an incompetent (Haugaard, Reppucci, Laird, & Nauful, 1991). In 1895 (*Wheeler v. United States*) the Supreme Court ruled that children could not automatically be deemed incompetent. Instead, the competence of a child witness must be determined on a case-by-case basis by the trial judge (Haugaard et al., 1991). Today, children once again play a central role in some criminal cases, especially those involving child sexual abuse. In these cases, a child may be the *only* witness to the crime.

The use of child witnesses in criminal cases raises three concerns: children's ability to accurately perceive an event, children's ability to accurately recall an event, and children's concept of the truth. In general, it is assumed that children will not be as accurate in their perceptions and memories of a criminal event as adults. Children are believed to be more susceptible to suggestion than adults, which can alter memories of events. How accurate are these assumptions?

Studies of Children's Perception and Memory   In one study of the relationship between a witness's age and his or her ability to correctly perceive and recall an event, subjects (adults, 6-year-olds, or 3-year-olds) interacted with an adult for 5 minutes (Goodman & Reed, 1986). Five days later subjects came back and were given three tests. On the first, they were asked a series of questions about the situation, some of which were suggestive (that is, relating to things that were not present or events that did not occur). On the second, they were asked to identify the adult from a photo lineup. On the third test, they were simply asked to tell what happened.

The adults and 6-year-olds performed equally in identifying the person from the photo lineup. The 3-year-olds did worse than the other groups. They tended to spend less time than the adults or 6-year-olds looking at the photographs. On the suggestive questions, adults were fooled less often than the children, with the 3-year-olds being most susceptible to suggestive questions (Goodman & Reed, 1986).

Although children are generally more suggestible than adults, they may not always be more suggestible. Children are especially prone to suggestibility when their memories are fuzzy to begin with; when the questioner is of high status (Goodman & Helgeson, 1988); and when the questioner is an adult rather than another child (Ceci, Ross, & Toglia, 1987). Interestingly, the child's suggestibility can be reduced if the child is forewarned that some of the questions might be confusing and that he or she should give an answer only if confident of it (Warren, Hulse-Trotter, & Tubbs, 1991).

Other researchers have investigated how accurate children of various ages (5–6 and 9–10) and adults were in recounting an actual incident that occurred to them (Leippe, Manion, & Romanczyk, 1992). Results showed that 5–6-year-old children were less accurate in their narrative descriptions of the event than 9–10-year-olds or adults (the latter age groups did not differ). The younger children gave shorter, less complete descriptions than the older children or the adults. The younger children were also perceived by adult observers as less credible than the older children or the adults.

Another difference between children and adults is that a child's memory for an event may not be as *enduring* as an adult's memory for the same event (Poole & White, 1992). Although children can be as accurate as adults in testifying about an event right after it happened, their memory fades over time much more than the memories of adults. And over time,

Ivan the Terrible was a beast. A guard at Treblinka, a notorious Nazi death camp where an estimated 850,000 Jews died during World War II, he was a person who enjoyed killing. He liked to humiliate his victims before he butchered them. He wasted neither bullets nor gas on babies; he simply flung them against stone walls, splattering their brains. After the war, the search for Ivan the Terrible went on for close to 35 years.

John Demjanjuk was living the quiet life of a retired auto worker in Cleveland, Ohio. Demjanjuk was an immigrant from the Ukraine, coming to the United States shortly after World War II. His troubles began when his name appeared on a list of suspected war criminals living in the United States. Demjanjuk was believed to be a guard at another camp, Sobibor (Sereny, 1992). Demjanjuk's picture was shown to several survivors of Sobibor, but they could not identify him as the guard. However, several survivors recognized Demjanjuk as Ivan the Terrible (Sereny, 1992). After years of legal maneuvering and increased communication between the

United States and the Soviet Union, John Demjanjuk was stripped of his United States citizenship in 1981. In 1986 he was extradited to Israel to stand trial as Ivan the Terrible.

The evidence against Demjanjuk appeared solid. The prosecution had documentary evidence—Treblinka identification cards and the like—suggesting that Demjanjuk was Ivan the Terrible. There were also Demjanjuk's conflicting statements about his whereabouts during the war and his role as a guard at Sobibor (Sereny, 1992). But the most critical aspect of the trial was the powerful, emotional testimony of eyewitnesses—the haunted survivors of Treblinka who had seen firsthand Ivan's evil deeds. Their testimony was gripping (Dafraniere, 1992):

"I recognized him at first sight with complete certainty."

"That's exactly what Ivan looked like."

There were 10 such eyewitnesses who, after 35 years, positively identified Demjanjuk as Ivan the Terrible. Were these witnesses correct, despite the passage of over 30 years? At first it appeared as though they were. Demjanjuk was convicted of being Ivan the Terrible and sentenced to death by hanging on April 25, 1988 (Sereny, 1992). He spent the next several years in an Israeli prison awaiting his fate. During that time appeals were filed and the evidence began to mount that Demjanjuk may not have been Ivan the Terrible. Eventually, the Israeli supreme court overturned Demjanjuk's conviction and he was released.

Demjanjuk's case illustrates some of the difficulties inherent in eyewitness testimony, especially when the events occurred so long ago. Despite the passage of time, the eyewitnesses were convinced that Demjanjuk was Ivan the Terrible. This fact did not escape the court, whose members apparently believed the witnesses. Elizabeth Loftus, who has questioned the accuracy of eyewitness testimony for over two decades, noted several problems with the identification of Demjanjuk as Ivan. The first, obviously, was the time lapse between the crimes and the iden-

children appear to embellish their memories with new information that was not part of their initial experience.

Conclusions About Children's Testimony What do we know, then, about children's testimony? First, under the right circumstances a child can remember just as much about an event as an adult. If the child and the adult are questioned in a structured manner (asked specific, direct, clear questions), they are about equal in accuracy. In a less structured situation (free recall), children are less accurate than adults (Goodman & Reed,

tification. The second problem was the photos that were initially presented to survivors who thought they could identify Ivan. Demjanjuk's photos were shown with those of seven other suspects who did not even remotely resemble him. To make matters worse, Demjanjuk's photograph was larger than those of the other suspects, and he was shown in a different pose from the others. The third problem was that the Israeli police advertised to find death camp survivors who could identify Ivan. The ad gave Demjanjuk's name as a suspect before the witnesses were ever interviewed (Dafraniere, 1992).

Was Demjanjuk Ivan the Terrible? Do the problems with the eyewitness testimony prove that he was not Ivan? Was another person, Ivan Marchenko, who was a guard at Treblinka, actually Ivan the Terrible? (Compare the photographs of Marchenko and Demjanjuk.) Other documentary evidence may yet settle the issue.

John Demjanjuk (left) and Ivan Marchenko (right) during World War II. Demjanjuk was positively identified by eyewitnesses as Nazi killer "Ivan the Terrible" 35 years after the end of the war. Demjanjuk's lawyers were able to create enough doubt in judges' minds to gain a reversal, partly by claiming that the real Ivan the Terrible was Marchenko. Given the passage of time, do you think the judges were justified in discounting the eyewitness testimony?

The general point that Elizabeth Loftus makes is that people do get prosecuted and convicted on the basis of eyewitness testimony alone. Those who question the accuracy of identification by eyewitnesses, no matter how compelling the testimony, believe that innocent people may be convicted in the absence of material evidence that supports the eyewitness. Do you think that this was what happened in Demjanjuk's case? Could 10 eyewitnesses all have misidentified him? If they did, why do you think that the Israeli court believed their testimony? Do you think that an eyewitness can be accurate after the passage of long periods of time, as happened in Demjanjuk's case? What could have been done to ensure that the eyewitnesses in Demjanjuk's case were more accurate?

1986). Second, children and adults are similar in their ability to pick someone out of a lineup (Goodman & Reed, 1986). However, children are more likely than adults to make a choice when confronted with a lineup, perhaps indicating that children have more lax standards about making a selection (Parker & Carranza, 1989).

Third, children are more open to suggestion and leading questions than adults. It is easier to plant an idea in the mind of a child than in that of an adult. Later this may come out as a "fact" during a trial. Fourth, the younger the child witness, the more inaccurate he or she is likely to be.

Older children are less prone to errors than younger children (Goodman & Reed, 1986; Warren, Hulse-Trotter, & Tubbs, 1991). However, even children as young as ages 5 or 6 do not "misremember" events (recall events that did *not* occur) a short time after they are experienced (Leippe, Romanczyk, & Manion, 1991).

Finally, although younger children (under age 7) have poorer memories than older eyewitnesses, their memories may be poor only for incidents that were relatively brief (Leippe et al., 1991). Children who have been abused by the same person over a long period of time may not be any less accurate than anybody else.

Concern about children's testimony centers around three issues: the child's ability to perceive an event accurately, her ability to recall an event accurately, and her concept of the truth. In the past, children's accounts, particularly of sexual abuse, were often ignored or discounted. In recent years, children have been shown to be generally credible.

Educating Jurors About Eyewitness Testimony

We have seen that jurors tend to be woefully ignorant of the potential flaws of eyewitness identifications and testimony (Cutler, Penrod, & Stuve, 1988). It is estimated that about one half of the wrongful convictions per year result from jurors putting too much stock in faulty eyewitness testimony (Rattner, 1988).

One solution to this problem is to have a social psychologist provide expert testimony about the potential pitfalls of eyewitness testimony. The expert can "educate" the jurors about such issues as the weapon focus and other variables that influence perception and memory of a crime. In fact, such expert testimony has been allowed and used in criminal trials. However, not all social psychologists agree with this practice (McCloskey & Egeth, 1983). Two major issues arise when considering the role of expert witnesses: First, are jurors already aware of the problems associated with eyewitness testimony? Second, will an expert make jurors overly skeptical and lead them to reject all eyewitness testimony?

Research indicates that an expert can make jurors more sensitive to the factors that affect eyewitness identification (Cutler, Penrod, & Dexter, 1989). For example, jurors are not generally aware of the weapon focus, and an expert can increase juror knowledge in this area (Cutler, Penrod, & Dexter, 1989). In general, an expert increases jurors' knowledge of the factors that can affect eyewitness identification, reduces the juror's reliance on the confidence of the eyewitness, and helps the juror make correct inferences about the credibility of an eyewitness (Cutler, Penrod, & Dexter, 1989). Research also indicates that expert witnesses raise a juror's knowledge and sensitivity without significantly increasing skepticism (Cutler, Dexter, & Penrod, 1989; Cutler, Penrod, & Dexter, 1989). Overall, the benefits gained by having an expert present outweigh any potential negative side-effects.

Sometimes lawyers call on an expert to explain the factors that can affect eyewitness testimony. Jurors are less likely to believe everything a witness says if they learn about such phenomena as the weapon effect or the distortion of perceptions that occurs when violence is used.

JURY DELIBERATIONS

Once the jury is selected, jury members sit as individuals and hear all the evidence in the case. They are not permitted to discuss the case with each other or anyone else. After the evidence is presented, the judge instructs the jury about the law applicable to the case. Jury members then retire to a jury room and by their own devices deliberate and come to a verdict.

Once the jury members retire to the jury room, they become a group. They must discuss the case and arrive at a verdict. How do the individual opinions of jurors get forged into a jury decision? What social psychological variables affect the jury's decision? And how do group dynamics affect the whole process?

Jury Size

In 1970, in the case of *Williams v. Florida,* the Supreme Court ruled that six-person juries were constitutional (see the featured discussion of this case in Chapter 8). Now, six- (or eight- or nine-) person juries are used in almost all jurisdictions for certain types of trials, such as trials for misdemeanors and minor felonies. The advantage of a six-person jury is that it is less costly in terms of time and money. Implied in this decision is the belief that the quality of the decision made by the six-person jury is the same as that made by a twelve-person jury.

The Decision-Making Process and Jury Size Are six-person juries fundamentally the same as twelve-person juries? Yes and no. The actual size of the jury seems to affect the outcome of a trial less than social psychologists first anticipated. It now seems likely that there are no significant differences with respect to whether the jury finds the defendant guilty or innocent (Hastie, Penrod, & Pennington, 1983). However, as we noted in Chapter 8, hung juries are more common with twelve-person than with six-person juries.

But the outcome of a trial is not the only measurement of jury performance. The *process* of reaching a verdict—how the jury deliberates and the fairness of that deliberation—is also important. To complicate matters, at about the same time the Supreme Court made its ruling about jury size it also altered the decision rules that guide juries. In *Johnson v. Louisiana* (1972) and related cases, the Supreme Court allowed for nonunanimous rulings (nine out of twelve, for example) in criminal cases.

A question then arises: If a jury of twelve needs only nine people to reach a verdict, will an initial vote of nine to three end the deliberations before they get started? What if the three have the truth? Without deliberation, the majority will never have the benefit of their opinions and insights. In response to this objection, the Supreme Court argued that the "conscientious juror" will not let this occur. That juror will stay and listen to all points of view whether or not the decision rule has been met.

Another question is, If the verdict is the same whether the evidence is fully discussed or not and whether a unanimous or a majority decision rule is in place, what difference does it make how much the jury deliberates? Most citizens would say it matters very much. People want a "fair" jury, a jury that will correctly distinguish the guilty from the not guilty (McCoun & Tyler, 1988; Tyler, 1988, 1990). Citizens want juries to *thoroughly* evaluate the evidence and to put aside personal biases. Despite the Supreme Court's assurances, it seems likely that smaller juries will not discuss evidence as thoroughly as larger juries.

Citizens also want the composition of the jury to fairly reflect the community's population as a whole, and six-person juries are less representative simply because they are smaller. Both smaller juries and decision rules requiring less than unanimity seem to violate citizens' expectations. Part of the upheaval that followed the original King verdict was due to the notion that some principles of procedural fairness had been violated. Many people in Los Angeles felt that the composition of the King jury had not been representative of the community.

Conformity Pressure as a Function of Jury Size   As we saw in Chapter 8, pressure is exerted on jurors to accept the majority view. A major side-effect of the shift from twelve-person to six-person juries is the potential for different conformity effects.

Because fewer people are involved, minorities are less likely to be represented on a small jury. Now, minority in this sense does not refer only to race, sex, or ethnic origin. It also refers to dissenting opinions. In a six-person jury the odds are that there will be only one juror with a dissenting opinion, whereas in the twelve-person jury two minority views are more likely. Thus, in the six-person jury there will be a 5:1 split and in the twelve-person jury a 10:2 split.

As described in Chapter 8, the Supreme Court reasoned in *Williams v. Florida* that the 5:1 split was equivalent to the 10:2 split. But two social psychological findings argue against this logic (Asch, 1951). First, a person with a "true partner" is more likely to hold out against the majority than a lone dissenter. Thus, the two-member minority is in a better position to withstand conformity pressure than the one-member minority in the six-person group. Second, there is a nonlinear relationship between majority size and conformity. Conformity increases up to a group size of about four. Therefore, it does not really matter if there are five or ten members of the majority. The conformity pressure exerted by these disparate majorities will not differ significantly. Five against one, however, is more powerful than ten against two because the one has no social support.

Arriving at a Decision

During the **deliberation** process, the decisions of the individual jurors must be blended into a single, unanimous (in most cases) group decision. Generally, the predeliberation distribution of individual verdicts is a good predictor of the final verdict of the jury (Kalven & Zeisel, 1966; Tanford & Penrod, 1986). That is, if there is an 11:1 (guilty:not guilty) predeliberation distribution, the jury will convict in 99% of the cases (Kalven & Zeisel, 1966). A reversal such as the one depicted in the film *Twelve Angry Men,* in which the character played by Henry Fonda systematically convinces the other eleven jurors to vote not guilty, is extremely rare.

As the majority:minority split becomes more even, the probability of conviction (or acquittal) drops accordingly (Kalven & Zeisel, 1966; Tanford & Penrod, 1986). It appears that juries operate under a simple decision rule: If there is a two-thirds majority, the likelihood is that the jury will find in the direction of the majority. If the majority is less than two thirds, but more than one half, then the likelihood is that the jury will hang (Davis, Kerr, Atkin, Holt, & Meek, 1975). In cases where the split is even or almost even, juries often default to acquittal (Tanford & Penrod, 1986).

Social Influence in the Jury Room Individual decisions translate into a final verdict via two social psychological mechanisms: informational social influence and normative social influence (Tanford & Penrod, 1986). Recall from Chapter 8 that informational social influence involves a person changing his or her view based on the content of the deliberations and that normative social influence involves a person changing based on perceived pressure to conform.

Individual verdicts influence the verdict indirectly, working through the deliberation process (Tanford & Penrod, 1986). One could say that each juror contributes information to the deliberation that is consistent with his or her judgment of guilt. When this information is made known to the other jurors, opinion change takes place. Normative social influence is a function of the initial distribution of verdicts within the jury and has a direct effect on the final verdict (Tanford & Penrod, 1986). For example, if the jury takes a predeliberation ballot and there is an 11:1 split for conviction, social pressure is exerted on the deviant member to conform to the group, and the jury is very likely to convict. It is unlikely that this one person will hold out for acquittal, even if he or she holds a strong belief that the defendant should be found not guilty.

deliberation The final phase of a trial, in which the jurors discuss the evidence as a group and reach a unanimous (in most cases) decision.

The Effect of Deliberation on Individual Opinion We know that individual juror sentiments are pretty good predictors of the final jury decision. What seems to happen is that juries (about 90% of them) wind up in the direction they were going in the first place (Myers & Kaplan, 1976). Jury deliberation seems to polarize the jury. That is, the jury's initial direction is enhanced or intensified by deliberation, as in any decision-making group (i.e., group polarization occurs), as discussed in Chapter 10. If nine out of twelve jurors vote initially for conviction, the group is polarized in that direction. Through the group processes of persuasion and conformity, the minority three will likely, although not always, come to agree with the majority nine.

Jury Nullification: An Alternative Role for the Jury

The official role of the jury in the American legal system is to listen to the evidence and then apply the law, as handed down by the judge, to that evidence to reach a verdict. But what if the jury doesn't think the law is fair or doesn't feel that the defendant, even if guilty, ought to be punished? In fact, the jury can do whatever it wishes. It may return an acquittal even though the law and the facts demand a guilty verdict. It is possible that the original Rodney King jury, in spite of the damning videotape, felt that police officers should not be punished even if they were too zealous in apprehending a suspect. A decision that goes against the law and the facts pertaining to a case is known as **jury nullification,** and it is a controversial point in the legal system.

Jury nullification has an honorable place in American history and has played an important role in the evolution of law. For example, during the pre–Civil War era, juries were reluctant to apply the fugitive slave laws, which set harsh penalties for helping slaves escape from the South. Similarly, during the 1960s, juries were unwilling to apply harsh drug laws to cases involving small amounts of marijuana. In both cases, laws were changed based on juries' unwillingness to convict despite clear evidence for conviction. Jury nullification allows a jury to apply its own beliefs, values, attitudes, and sentiments to the law. In theory, the jury represents the wider community. Thus, the jury that nullifies is expressing the opinion of the entire community.

Now, every jury has the power to nullify, but they may not have the right. Saying that a jury has the "power" to nullify means that juries in the American legal system can do whatever they please: They can acquit an obviously guilty person or convict an obviously innocent person. The catch is that juries are not routinely told by the judge that they have this power. Some jurists believe that instructing the jury about nullification would result in runaway juries that ignore the law, leading to anarchy. There is little evidence to support this belief. In the states that allow juries to be instructed on nullification (Maryland, Indiana, and West Virginia), anarchy has not broken out. If the unwritten power of juries to nullify were written into law, they would then have the "right," in addition to the power, to nullify.

jury nullification A jury's decision that consciously goes against the law and the facts pertaining to a case.

Even if the jury is not explicitly given the right to nullify, defense attorneys can (during the closing statement, for example) ask jury members to rely on their conscience. That is, the jury can acquit in the face of overwhelming evidence for guilt without fear of reprisals. However, in almost all states the jury is not overtly told that it can nullify.

Do juries nullify the law? Certainly, they do not routinely do so. Juries generally follow the evidence and the law (Visher, 1987). That is, they do what they are paid to do. Sometimes, however, when faced with unpopular laws or very sympathetic defendants, juries simply decide that although the defendant may be legally guilty, he or she is not morally guilty, and they acquit no matter what the evidence (Horowitz, 1985, 1988).

SENTENCING DECISIONS

After a jury has convicted a defendant, or the defendant has pleaded guilty (via plea bargaining or nonbargained pleas), a punishment is meted out. This punishment may take the form of probation (no incarceration) or incarceration (a specific prison sentence). It is the judge's duty to pronounce sentence on a convicted defendant.

The Judge's Decision

How do judges make a decision about an appropriate sentence? Immediately after conviction in court (or a guilty plea), the judge orders a *presentencing investigation,* usually carried out by the probation department. During this investigation a probation officer probes the defendant's background and prepares a report for the judge. In most cases the final section of the report contains the probation officer's summary and recommendations. The judge will read this report and eventually decide on a sentence to impose.

On the day of the sentencing hearing, the judge makes his or her decision known. In federal courts, there are mandated (prescribed) sentences for various crimes, so the judge has limited options. However, most criminal trials take place in state courts, and here the judge has wide latitude in assigning punishment.

On what factors does a judge base a sentencing decision? An intensive investigation revealed that the single most important variable influencing judges' decisions is the recommendation the probation officer makes in the presentencing investigation (Konecni & Ebbesen, 1982). In a vast majority of cases, the judge imposes the recommended sentence. Thus, what looks like a complex decision on the part of the judge, taking into account many factors, may really be a relatively simple one.

The Impact of Race on Sentencing Decisions

Since judges are typically given considerable discretion in sentencing, there exists the possibility for unequal application of punishment to different

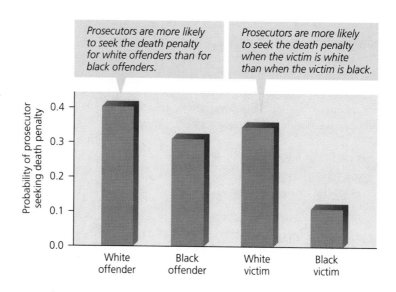

FIGURE 14-8 *Likelihood of a prosecutor's seeking the death penalty as a function of race. When an offender is white, prosecutors are more likely to seek the death penalty than when the offender is black. Prosecutors are also more likely to seek the death penalty if the victim is white than if the victim is black.*

From data in Jacoby and Paternoster, 1982.

Prosecutors are more likely to seek the death penalty for white offenders than for black offenders.

Prosecutors are more likely to seek the death penalty when the victim is white than when the victim is black.

defendants. The same crime may be "worth" different punishments depending on the judge and on the jurisdiction (the county or the state) in which the crime occurred.

One aspect of sentencing that has received close scrutiny is the impact of race on the length of prison terms. One group of researchers analyzed sentences from six separate jurisdictions across the country and found little evidence for systematic racial bias *for those defendants convicted via a trial* (Welch, Spohn, & Gruhl, 1985). They did find some bias when *all sentences* were considered (trials and guilty pleas). In this analysis, they found that black defendants were more likely to be incarcerated than white defendants when they pleaded guilty. This may be due to bias that occurs prior to sentencing, perhaps during the preparation of the presentencing report, usually prepared by the probation department, that the judge uses when making a sentencing decision.

As it turns out, blacks are less likely than whites to plead guilty (Welch et al., 1985) and thus more likely to go to trial. Sentences tend to be harsher when defendants are found guilty in a trial than when they plead guilty. It may be that blacks are offered less desirable plea bargains; therefore, they plead guilty less often and consequently receive more severe sentences—following trial convictions—than whites (Welch et al., 1985).

Is race a factor in cases involving the death penalty? It depends on several interacting variables. First, research shows that prosecutors are more likely to seek the death penalty for white offenders than for black offenders (Jacoby & Paternoster, 1982; Paternoster & Kazyaka, 1988), as indicated in Figure 14-8. Second, the race of the *victim* is also important. As shown in Figure 14-8, prosecutors are also more likely to seek the death penalty when the victim was white (45%) as opposed to black (20%). Finally, the "mix" of the race of the offender and the victim is also important. Prosecutors appear to be least likely to seek the death penalty when a black kills another black (Paternoster & Kazyaka, 1988), as shown in Figure 14-9.

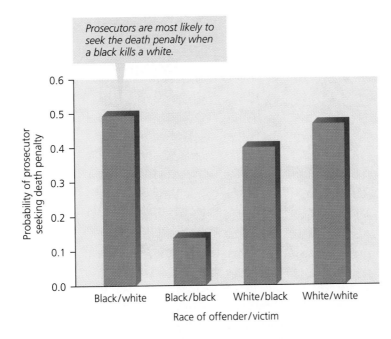

Prosecutors are most likely to seek the death penalty when a black kills a white.

FIGURE 14-9 *Likelihood of a prosecutor's seeking the death penalty as a function of offender/victim race. Prosecutors are most likely to seek the death penalty when the victim is white, whether the offender is black or white. They are less likely to seek the death penalty when the victim is black and least likely to seek it when both the offender and the victim are black.* From data in Paternoster and Kazyaka, 1988.

When we look at cases in which defendants actually received a death sentence, a different picture emerges (Paternoster & Kazyaka, 1988; Radelet, 1981). White defendants are equally likely to be sentenced to death as black defendants, and in some cases they are more likely. In fact, there are more whites than blacks on death row (Gest, 1986), and more whites than blacks were executed between 1977 and 1983 (Jolly & Sagarin, 1984).

Does this mean that racial bias does not exist (or is reversed) at the sentencing stage? Not really. Race comes into play in the imposition of the death penalty when the *race of the victim* is considered. Research shows that regardless of race, a defendant is more likely to receive the death penalty if he kills a white than if he kills a black (Jacoby & Paternoster, 1982; Radelet, 1981).

Why does this racial disparity exist? Robert Bohm (1994) investigated racial bias in the death penalty in 2 Georgia districts. Bohm found that the race of the victim related to death penalty decisions: Regardless of the defendant's race, the death penalty was sought more often when the victim was white. Interestingly, Bohm investigated potential causes for the race bias observed in death penalty cases. He found that white prosecutors were more likely to remove black jurors (78%) than white jurors (21%) from capital cases. Thus, in most capital cases juries were predominantly white. Bohm suggests that the practice of excluding black jurors, combined with the overwhelming predominance of white justice system personnel (that is, prosecutors and judges) contributes to an atmosphere that supports racial disparities in the application of the death penalty.

In 1977 Warren McCleskey killed a police officer in Atlanta while robbing a furniture store. In the 7-year period prior to McCleskey's crime, some 16 cases involving the murder of a police officer had occurred.

Does the U.S. judicial system treat offenders differently depending on the race of their victim? Apparently so. Analysis of sentencing records shows that when the victim of a homicide is African American, the prosecution seeks a milder punishment than when the victim is white. These citizens are protesting the treatment given to the police officer who killed Earl Black in New York City in 1992, allegedly by using excessive force.

McCleskey, who is black, was the only perpetrator to draw the death penalty. McCleskey appealed his death sentence.

McCleskey argued in his appeal (*McCleskey v. Kemp,* 1987) that evidence provided by University of Iowa law professor David Baldus showed conclusively that black defendants who kill whites are more likely to be executed in Georgia than are killers of blacks. The statistical evidence was that the death-sentencing rate for "white victim" cases was 11 times that of "black victim" cases. Even taking into consideration that 230 other variables could have accounted for this result, such as the possibility that white victims may have been killed in a more vicious way than blacks, the Baldus data still showed that blacks who killed whites were four times more likely to receive the death penalty than any other class of murderers.

The Supreme Court ruled in a 5–4 decision that while the statistical evidence was valid, such a discrepancy did not prove unconstitutional discrimination unless McCleskey could prove that *he* received the death penalty because he was black. McCleskey, whose case and 13 appeals strongly influenced death penalty law, was denied a final reprieve when the Supreme Court limited the number of new appeals death row inmates may submit. He was executed in 1991, 13 years after his conviction.

In sum, then, prosecutors are more likely to seek the death penalty for white than for black offenders. They are also more likely to seek the death penalty if the victim was white than if the victim was black. However, whites are more likely to *receive* the death penalty than blacks. But race still comes into play here. A defendant is more likely to *receive* the death penalty if the victim was white, regardless of his or her own race. Clearly, the relationship between race and the death penalty is complex.

THE RODNEY KING TRIAL REVISITED

The first Rodney King trial provided us with an excellent example of how various aspects of social psychological research apply to the law. The crime was caught on videotape and played hundreds of times prior to the trial. Because of the pretrial publicity, the judge granted a motion to move the case from Los Angeles to nearby Simi Valley. There, the jury was drawn from a population that was highly likely, based on their personal characteristics and attitudes, to side with a police officer defendant.

During the King trial a jury was selected through the voir dire process, witnesses were presented, and the jury deliberated to a verdict. Although most of us were not in the courtroom or the jury room, we can make an educated guess about the psychological processes that occurred there. The jurors listened to the evidence, formed individual opinions, and entered the deliberations with those opinions. Perhaps a predeliberation vote was taken, which laid each juror's verdict preference on the table. Of course, predeliberation verdicts do not directly influence the final outcome. Instead, the jurors' views operate through the deliberation process. If the jury was split on a decision, we can be sure that social influence—perhaps both informational and normative—was applied to any dissenting jurors. In the end, these processes brought the King jury to a verdict that many Americans saw as unfair and that precipitated violence. Only a second trial—this time, on federal charges of violating King's civil rights—was able to mitigate, to some extent, the effects of the original not-guilty verdict.

LOOKING AHEAD

Although social psychology and the law has become a major area of interest for social psychologists over the past 20 years or so, it is not the only applied area that has captured the interest of social psychologists. Some social psychologists dedicate their research to understanding the interface between psychology and health. Social psychologists have studied such questions as, What impact does stress have on a person's tendency to become sick? What methods do people use to cope with stress, illness, and trauma? And how does a person's lifestyle affect his or her health? These questions are addressed in the next chapter, Social Psychology and Health.

CHAPTER REVIEW

1. *Even though the criminal trial is the cornerstone of the criminal justice system, is it true that many cases never get to trial?*

   Only a small percentage of cases (about 10%) reach the stage of going to trial. Most cases are resolved in some way prior to the trial. One way a case can be resolved is for the prosecutor to drop charges if there is insufficient evidence against the defendant. Another method is through plea bargaining, which is a process of negotiation between the prosecution and the defense. In exchange for a guilty plea, the defendant receives a reduced charge and sentence.

2. *What is the voir dire?*

   The first "scene" of a trial is **voir dire,** or jury selection. Potential jurors are questioned and may be challenged (for cause or with a peremptory challenge) by the trial attorneys. Recently, social psychologists have been hired by the defense to help select juries that will be sympathetic to the defendant. This is called **scientific jury selection.** Although the official purpose of the voir dire is to select jurors, relatively little time is spent on this function. Instead, attorneys use voir dire as their first opportunity to persuade the jury. Eighty percent of the statements made during voir dire are intended to indoctrinate jurors rather than to discover bias.

3. *Is there a relationship between a juror's characteristics and how he or she will vote?*

   Attempting to select jurors who are favorable to one side or another presumes a relationship between a juror's attitudes and personality and how he or she will vote. Research shows that individuals who are authoritarian are more likely to side with the prosecution than are nonauthoritarian individuals. However, there are cases in which authoritarians may side with the defense, such as when the defendant is a police officer or when the defendant is charged with killing in self-defense. There is no simple relationship between a juror's personality and his or her verdict.

4. *What happens in cases in which the defendant faces the death penalty?*

   In cases involving the death penalty, a special jury selection method is used: death qualification. Jurors are asked about their attitudes toward the death penalty. Those who oppose it or could not impose it on someone are excluded from the jury. These "excludable" jurors differ in meaningful ways from nonexcludables who will serve on the jury. The jury that ultimately is selected comprises individuals who favor the death penalty or would at least consider it. This jury is called a **death-qualified jury.** Critics have charged that this results in a jury biased against the defendant, a charge that has received research support. Death-qualified juries are more conviction prone than non-death-qualified juries. Various remedies for the death-qualification bias have been proposed, such as rehabilitating excludables so that they would qualify for service on a death-qualified jury.

5. *What happens when the trial begins?*
   When the trial itself gets under way, jurors then become the target of persuasive arguments from both the prosecution and the defense. The opening statements made by each side may affect jurors' decisions, with the prosecution having the greatest advantage because it goes first (a law of primacy holds in courtroom persuasion). Opening statements influence jurors by providing them with a theme for a story of how a crime occurred. This theme influences how jurors process subsequent information presented during the trial. Although opening statements may be effective, an attorney can shoot him- or herself in the foot if a promise is made that cannot be delivered (especially if the other side reminds the jury of the unfulfilled promise).

   During direct examination a witness is questioned by a "friendly" attorney. Testimony is elicited from the witness through careful questioning. However, during cross-examination the witness faces an attorney who will try to shake the testimony given during direct examination. One tactic used during cross-examination is the use of innuendo. Witnesses will be asked presumptuous questions, a technique that has been found to reduce the effectiveness of witnesses.

   By far the most important factor affecting a juror's decision is the evidence. Jurors process the evidence presented during the trial along either the central or the peripheral processing route. Jurors appear to construct a coherent story narrative to account for the evidence that is presented. If the evidence is easy to understand and clear, it can be processed along the central route. If it is complex and ambiguous, story construction is more difficult and peripheral processing may occur.

6. *Why is pretrial publicity a problem, and what can be done to remedy it?*
   Social psychological research has shown that **pretrial publicity** can affect the outcome of a trial. Negative publicity appears to bias the jury against the defendant. However, there are limits to the effects of publicity. General pretrial publicity has less impact on the jury than publicity related directly to the case being tried. To reduce the effect of pretrial publicity, the judge can, and often does, instruct a jury to disregard it, or he or she can grant a continuance (a delay) so that the effects of pretrial publicity will "die down." Jury deliberations may also attenuate the impact of pretrial publicity. Research suggests that the judge's instructions are not effective in reducing publicity effects. Granting a continuance does reduce the effects of factual pretrial publicity but not emotional pretrial publicity.

7. *What is an eyewitness, and what factors affect eyewitness accuracy?*
   Perhaps the most important type of evidence presented at a trial comes from an **eyewitness,** someone who has seen the crime firsthand. Much social psychological research has been conducted on the accuracy of the eyewitness. This research shows that eyewitness accuracy is influenced by two classes of variables: **estimator variables** (witness variables that are not under control of the criminal justice system) and **system variables** (variables under control of the criminal justice system).

One variable affecting the accuracy of an eyewitness is the presence of a weapon. If a weapon is present, witnesses tend to focus attention on it. This is called **weapon focus.** Perception and memory for other details is poorer when a weapon is present than if no weapon is present. The violence of the crime witnessed may also influence eyewitness accuracy. And if the witness must make a cross-race identification, more errors are likely to occur than if a same-race identification is required.

8. *Humans have pretty good memory abilities. How can an eyewitness's memory be inaccurate?*
   Contrary to what many people think, human memory does not work like a videotape recorder. Instead, we encode fragments of an event into memory, and when we have to recall that event we put those fragments back together into a coherent narrative. This is known as **reconstructive memory.** The dynamic nature of human memory opens the door for memory distortions.

   Research shows that misleading information, encountered either before or after an event, can distort an eyewitness's memory. This is the **misinformation effect.** Another memory distortion occurs when new information is encountered after witnessing an event that conflicts with what is already in memory. In this case a person may blend the new information with the old to form a **compromise memory.** A memory distortion can involve a specific piece of information about a specific memory or a more general attribution about the responsibility of those involved in the event. Unfortunately, we do not know exactly how misleading information affects memory.

9. *How can a biased lineup affect an eyewitness?*
   Biased lineups lead to misidentifications. The lineup may be biased if the others in the lineup (the distractors) do not resemble the suspect or if the police officer knows who the suspect is and subtly communicates this to the witness. The size of the lineup has also been studied. The lineup should be large enough so that the suspect will not be picked by chance, but simply increasing size will not reduce bias. The absolute size of the lineup is less important than its **functional size,** which refers to the number of distractors who resemble the suspect. Bias can be reduced if the functional size of the lineup is increased.

10. *How much is the jury influenced by an eyewitness?*
    An eyewitness can have a tremendous influence on the jury. The jury may use eyewitness testimony even if the eyewitness is discredited or if objective evidence is presented to counter the eyewitness's testimony. Jurors tend to believe eyewitnesses, especially if they are confident on the stand. Unfortunately, there is virtually no relationship between a witness's confidence and his or her actual accuracy. Jurors are impressed by, and will attach high credibility to, an eyewitness who remembers many trivial details of the crime scene, even if those details are not related to the crime itself.

11. *What about cases in which a child is an eyewitness?*
When the eyewitness testifying in court is a child, special problems arise. Young children (3-year-olds) have been found to be less accurate as eyewitnesses than older children or adults. Young children are also more susceptible to suggestive questions than older children or adults. Children tend to give less complete answers than adults, and their memories may be more susceptible to inaccuracy over long periods of time.

12. *How do the courts handle the problems associated with eyewitnesses?*
Because of some of the problems associated with eyewitness accuracy and overbelief of eyewitnesses by jurors, social psychologists are sometimes called into court as expert witnesses to testify to the jury about the research that has been conducted on eyewitness identifications. Such expert testimony can make jurors more critical of eyewitness testimony without making them overly skeptical. Such expert testimony can help a jury evaluate eyewitness testimony more accurately.

13. *What happens during the jury's deliberations?*
Jury **deliberation** marks the final phase of a trial. During deliberation the jurors retire to discuss the evidence as a group. Some controversy exists over the size of the jury. In *Williams v. Florida* (1976), the Supreme Court allowed for the use of six-person juries in some cases. Although the smaller jury may not differ from the larger jury in some ways (e.g., verdicts reached), it does differ in some important ways, especially if a nonunanimous decision rule is allowed. Under these conditions the smaller jury may not discuss the evidence as thoroughly as a larger jury. Additionally, six-person juries are less representative of the community. Consequently, it is less likely that the six-person jury will have more than one dissenting member than the twelve-person jury. Conformity research shows that a minority of one is less likely to hold out against the majority than a minority of two. Thus, the six-person jury is less likely than the twelve-person jury to hang.
   During jury deliberations the individual verdicts of jurors must be blended into a single, unified verdict. Generally, the distribution of pre-deliberation individual verdicts is a good predictor of the final verdict. So, for example, with an 11:1 split for conviction, the jury is likely to convict. However, as the split becomes more even, arriving at a single verdict becomes more difficult. In such cases, informational and normative social influence operate during the deliberation process. Dissenting jurors may change their votes based on facts presented during deliberation (informational influence) or as the result of conformity pressure (normative influence). Research on the jury as a group also shows that through group polarization processes an individual juror's attitudes undergo changes as a result of deliberation.

14. *Is the jury allowed to interpret law, or must it always follow the law?*
The role of a jury has changed markedly over time. At one time, juries were allowed to apply the law based on their own values and concepts

of the law. Today, however, we restrict the jury to rendering a verdict based solely on the evidence presented at a trial. However, the jury retains an unofficial power to apply its own standards to the law. In some cases the jury may choose to acquit a defendant even if the evidence clearly points to conviction. This is known as **jury nullification.** Nullification has played an important role historically. For example, pre–Civil War juries effectively nullified the unpopular fugitive slave laws. Although juries tend to follow the evidence and the law given by the court, there are cases where the jury does nullify.

15. *What factors affect the sentence the defendant receives?*
   If a defendant is found guilty (either at trial or through a guilty plea), the judge must decide on an appropriate sentence. Routinely, the judge orders a presentencing investigation, carried out by the probation department. Despite all the pomp and circumstance surrounding the sentencing hearing, the judge tends to follow the recommendation made in the presentencing investigation.

   The judge is given wide discretionary powers when it comes to sentencing. Race has been found to influence a judge's decision when imposing a sentence. Blacks as a group tend to receive harsher sentences than whites (when convictions via trial and pleas are considered). Racial bias has also been found when the death penalty is considered, although the relationship between race and the death penalty may be quite complex. Overall, prosecutors are more likely to seek the death penalty for white offenders than for black offenders. They are also more likely to seek the death penalty if the *victim* was white than if the victim was black. Prosecutors appear to be least likely to seek the death penalty when a black kills another black.

SUGGESTIONS FOR FURTHER READING

American Psychologist (1993), Volume 48.
   In this issue are several excellent articles reviewing the literature in eyewitness identification. Two articles in particular address the issue of what we know (Wells, 1993) and do not know (Egeth, 1993) about eyewitness identification and testimony.
Doris, J. (1991). *The suggestibility of children's recollections.* Washington, DC: American Psychological Association.
   This is an excellent, one-source introduction to the issue of the suggestibility of children's memories. Chapters are included on the susceptibility of children's memories to misleading information, the implications of children's suggestibility for sexual-abuse investigations, and studies of interviewing children.
Kalven, H., & Zeisel, H. (1966). *The American jury.* Boston: Little, Brown.
   This classic, monumental work stands as the most comprehensive study of the American jury system ever conducted. Kalven and Zeisel systematically compare judge and jury decisions and provide data concerning the role of the defendant, deliberations, and eyewitnesses (as well as a wealth of other topics) in jury decisions.

Wrightsman, L. S., Nietzel, M. T., & Fortune, W. H. (1994). *Psychology and the legal system* (3rd ed.). Pacific Grove, CA: Brooks/Cole.

This is a textbook on the field of psychology and the law. It provides an overview of the field including information on the roles of lawyers and psychologists in the legal system, theories of crime, police investigations, eyewitness identification, jury selection, the trial process, and sentencing (among other topics). This is an excellent one-stop source for an overview of psychology and the law.

Chapter 15

Social Psychology and Health

Sy was a classic "couch potato." He was overweight and overwrought. He had a stressful job, full of deadlines and impossible demands. He was paid very well but was often very angry about the pressure he was under at work.

Sy didn't have much of a social life; he was divorced and socially isolated. His job gave him little time to develop friendships. When it came to a choice between spending time with a friend or "catching up" on work, it was no contest: Sy felt compelled to work.

Sy didn't pay much attention to what he ate, but he loved fatty foods. His favorite food was a hot dog wrapped in bacon. When he wasn't eating, he had a cigarette in his hand. His physician and friend, Bill, told Sy he needed to lose weight, get more exercise, quit smoking, and reduce the stress in his life or he could expect, before long, to "wake up dead."

One day Sy saw an advertisement for a liquid diet concoction that promised safe, easy weight loss. The photo of a well-known sports personality appeared in the ad with the words, "If I can do it, so can you." Sy was inspired. He bought the drink and began to lose weight. Then he began to exercise. He started to run, and he bought the newest, most fashionable exercise clothes. When he saw Bill again, he was proud of his new condition. Bill was pleased too but suggested that Sy have a stress test to make sure exercising was safe for him. He asked Sy if he had experienced any shortness of breath or chest pain while running.

Sy's answer—"No, not really"—concerned Bill, so he did some blood work on his friend and set up an appointment for him to take an exercise stress test at a local hospital. The results of the blood tests suggested that Sy was *probably* healthy but ought to have the stress test anyway. Sy called the day before he was to take the stress test, saying he had to go to New Mexico on business and would reschedule when he got back. Bill cautioned Sy not to push himself and to be sure to reschedule.

Several months later, Sy returned to Bill's office for further testing. Bill was pleased with the results of these blood tests. He told Sy that although he could not give him a blanket assurance that he had nothing to worry about, he thought Sy was probably healthy. But suddenly, after months of avoiding tests, Sy asked for rigorous treatment. Bill was surprised, but he quickly scheduled a stress test. It was too late. Before the scheduled stress test, in the early hours of a promising spring morning,

Sy felt a crushing pain in the center of his chest. It felt like someone had dropped a concrete block on top of him.

It turned out that Sy had experienced symptoms for months — chest pain, some numbness in his hand, an odd tingling in his left arm, pain along his jaw line and neck. He asked his friends if they had ever experienced those sensations. Some said yes. Sy was reassured, thinking that if others had the same symptoms, they probably weren't too serious. He had also read an article in *Runner's World* suggesting that runners are at low risk for heart disease. Besides, Sy "knew" that only "old fat guys" had heart attacks.

When Sy began to feel the crushing pain in the center of his chest, along with waves of nausea, feelings of dread, and a sense of certainty that he was about to die, he still denied that he was having a heart attack. A co-worker rushed to call the paramedics, but Sy stopped him. He wanted to prove that he was really all right, so he did 30 pushups. Then he passed out. He died in the hospital 3 days later of a second massive heart attack. He was 43 years old.

Although Sy's premature death from heart disease was not entirely his fault, he did have control over some of what happened to him. What aspects of his life might he have changed? He could have taken steps to reduce his stress levels at work. He could have eaten healthier foods and lost weight earlier in life, and he could have quit smoking. He also could have followed his physician's advice and gotten the stress test.

Sy's case is not particularly unusual. Stress, denial of symptoms, lack of adherence to medical advice, and the inability to change an unhealthy lifestyle all contribute to a variety of diseases. Conditions that have been shown to be affected by such factors include heart disease, cancer, gastrointestinal disorders, hypertension (high blood pressure), obesity (defined as being 20% or more above the upper limit for weight on a height–weight table), and a number of other physical disorders (Spacapan, 1988a).

Unmanaged stress and other lifestyle factors also have an effect on the immune system, as verified by substantial scientific evidence. Studies have shown that negative moods and feelings, such as depression, anxiety, fear, and anger, are associated with a decline in immune functioning, at least temporarily. The connections take place through a complex communication system involving the brain, the endocrine system (glands and hormones), and the immune system. The immune system is the body's first line of defense against illness. When it breaks down, the body becomes vulnerable to disease and death.

It is probable that roughly half of all modern diseases have a significant preventable component. Smoking cigarettes, for example, contributes heavily to lung cancer and heart disease. It has been estimated that changes in behavior, as well as early detection and treatment, would prevent 45% of deaths from heart attacks and strokes, 23% of deaths from cancer, and 50% of deaths from diabetes (Fanning, 1990).

The *social psychology of health* is concerned with the relationships among the biological, psychological, and social factors that influence health and illness (Gatchel, Baum, & Krantz, 1989). The related field of *behavioral medicine* is concerned with the application of the scientific findings of health psychology to the prevention of behaviors harmful to health (Gatchel et al., 1989).

In this chapter we focus on three areas of social psychology and health—stress, lifestyle factors in disease, and strategies to prevent disease and injuries. We ask, What is stress, and how does it affect the health of a person like Sy? Why did he deal with his symptoms the way he did? What lifestyle factors played a role in his heart disease, and why was he unable to change them? Indeed, how can people be persuaded to make any changes in their lives? And what are the best approaches to improving people's health, on both an individual level and a societal level? These are some of the questions addressed in this chapter.

THE NATURE OF STRESS

There are several ways of defining and thinking about stress (Bishop, 1994). One way, referred to as the *stimulus* definition of stress, focuses on the stimuli that produce stress. Stress is defined in terms of what is happening in the environment. According to this way of looking at stress, different people respond pretty much the same way to given events. Any individual who experienced a great deal of work-related stress, for example, would probably become ill, in this view.

A second way of defining stress, the *response* definition of stress, focuses on how people react, both physiologically and psychologically, when they are in stressful situations. The response of the body in stressful situations has been studied extensively by Hans Selye (1976), a pioneer in the area of stress and physiology. Selye proposed a three-step model called the *general adaptation syndrome* describing the reaction of the body to a stressor—any event or situation that requires that a person make an adjustment (Figure 15-1). Stage 1 of this model is the *alarm* stage, in which the body reacts to the stressor with an instinctive, automatic response. A branch of the autonomic nervous system (a part of the nervous system that operates independently of conscious thought) releases hormones into the bloodstream that prepare the body for "fight or flight." Heart rate accelerates,

FIGURE 15-1 Selye's general adaptation syndrome (GAS). This predictable pattern of physical responses to a stressor consists of three stages: alarm, resistance, and exhaustion. GAS is a biological mechanism designed to help people survive in life-or-death situations. In the modern world, where life-threatening situations are relatively rare, the response itself can pose a threat to the health and life of the organism. Adapted from Selye, 1982.

| Stressor | → | Stage 1 ALARM Body prepares for action with increased arousal. | → | Stage 2 RESISTANCE Body attempts to return to normal. | → | Stage 3 EXHAUSTION Body can no longer resist stressor; physiological breakdown begins. |

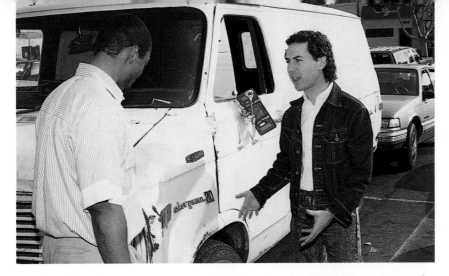

bronchi dilate to allow more air into the lungs, the liver releases sugar for extra energy, digestion halts, perspiration increases to cool the skin, hearing and vision become more acute, and endorphins are released to provide pain relief in case of injury (Insel & Roth, 1994).

The body resists such dramatic change, however, and as soon as possible it initiates the adjustments needed to restore balance. Stage 2 is the *resistance* stage, in which the alarm reaction is halted and the body attempts to restore normal functioning. However, if the stressful situation persists, or if there is a series of such events, the organism has difficulty returning to normal. Both the alarm reaction and the resistance stage require a considerable amount of energy. If these stages go on for too long, reserve stores of energy are depleted and the third stage, *exhaustion,* sets in. This is not the everyday kind of exhaustion; rather, it is a profound, life-threatening physiological exhaustion that may be accompanied by such symptoms as distorted thinking and perceptions (Insel & Roth, 1994). At this point the person becomes vulnerable to disease or death (Spacapan, 1988a).

A third definition of stress, the one used in social psychology, focuses on the observation that stress is a *transaction* between the individual and the environment. In this perspective, the most critical aspect of stress is the way in which the individual perceives and responds to the stressful event (Bishop, 1994). The experience of stress is mediated by the individual's judgment of the situation and her ability to cope with that situation. Implied in this definition is the idea that the experience of stress is subjective. Stress is in the eye of the beholder. If individuals perceive that the demands made of them exceed their ability to cope with those demands, then the situation is stressful for them (Cohen, Tyrrell, & Smith, 1993). If individual resources exceed the demands of the situation, however great those demands may be, then the situation will not be perceived or experienced as stressful.

Life Stressors and Illness

In the early 1960s, two physicians working at the naval air base in San Diego began to notice that many of the sailors who visited the infirmary had undergone stressful life events in the previous few months (Holmes &

TABLE 15-1

SELECTED ITEMS FROM THE SOCIAL READJUSTMENT RATING SCALE

Rank	Life Event	Stress Value
1	Death of a spouse	100
2	Divorce	73
3	Marital separation	65
4	Jail term	63
5	Death of a close family member	63
6	Personal injury or illness	53
7	Marriage	50
8	Fired from job	47
9	Marital reconciliation	45
10	Retirement	45
11	Change in health of a family member	44
12	Pregnancy	40
13	Sexual difficulties	39
14	Gain of new family member	38
15	Change in financial status	37
16	Death of a close friend	36
17	New line of work	35
18	Change in the number of arguments with spouse	35
23	Son or daughter leaving home	29
25	Outstanding personal achievement	28
27	Begin or end school	26
30	Trouble with boss	23
33	Change in schools	20
38	Change in sleeping habits	16
41	Vacation	13
42	Christmas	12

Adapted from Holmes and Rahe, 1967.

Rahe, 1967). The two doctors began to keep track of the events—they called them **life stressors**—that appeared to affect the health of the sailors. Many of these stressors were marital and sexual problems, but others were successes, such as promotions; failures, such as being passed over for a promotion; worries over mortgages and rents; parking tickets; and other stuff of daily life.

To study the relationship between stress and health, the two physicians devised a questionnaire called the Schedule of Recent Events, which was later modified and published as the *Social Readjustment Rating Scale* (SRRS) (Holmes & Rahe, 1967). An adapted version of this scale is shown in Table 15-1. Holmes and Rahe told their subjects to use marriage as their base and to assume that it was worth 50 (stress) points. They then asked subjects to rate the other life events on the list in comparison to marriage. They found that the more points sailors accumulated in one year, the more likely they were to get sick. Accumulating 300 points or more, a really bad year, was virtually a guarantee of illness.

life stressors Positive or negative events that an individual perceives as stressful and that apparently have a cumulative effect on health.

Now, there are two things to note about the list of life events. First, both good and bad events are considered stressful; getting married is almost as stressful as going to jail. Second, it may not be that the stressful event causes illness; a person may already be getting sick and therefore be experiencing some of these difficulties. People who do not feel well may be more likely to have sexual problems, for example, or to get low grades in school, or to experience problems at work. Therefore, although there may not always be a causal relationship between stressful life events and disease, it is not surprising that scores on the SRRS correlate with subsequent illness.

Sources of Stress

Sources of stress tend to be cumulative. They build until they reach a level that may overwhelm the individual's ability to cope. And, as we have seen in the work of Holmes and Rahe, there are many potential sources of stress. Let's consider just two sources: everyday hassles and on-the-job stress.

Everyday Hassles   There are indications that everyday hassles are excellent predictors of susceptibility to disease. These include such frustrating and irritating daily events as worrying about one's weight, not having enough time to get homework done, standing in line, and arguing with roommates or family members (Lazarus & Folkmann, 1984).

One group of researchers devised a "hassle scale" that organizes hassles into categories (Delongis, Folkman, & Lazarus, 1988):

- Household hassles, such as preparing meals
- Health hassles, such as getting the flu
- Financial hassles, such as bouncing a check
- Work hassles, such as being dissatisfied on the job
- Personal hassles, such as being lonely or overweight
- Time-pressure hassles, such as not having enough time to do everything you want or need to
- Environmental hassles, such as worrying about crime and personal safety

As it turns out, scores on the hassle scale are highly related to health problems.

Many of the daily hassles we experience are actually self-produced. Consequently, the stress associated with them is self-produced. Such hassles as having a quarrel with a landlord or contracting a sexually transmitted disease can be blamed, at least in part, on the individual experiencing them. Other hassles are not self-produced, such as the death of a close friend or relative. Most of the total stress we face is of the first kind, events that we have a hand in producing (Epstein & Katz, 1992). This means that we have some control over these sources of stress. How we deal with various situations in life is thus critical to our health.

Job Stress   No matter what job you have, or will get in the future, you can count on some stress associated with it. In a 1979 survey by the American

STRESSED OUT ON THE JOB

John Taylor worked as a letter carrier with the U.S. Postal Service. His job was one that many would "kill" for, a civil service position with good pay and job security. But one day in August 1989, Taylor entered the post office in Escondido, California, carrying a rifle instead of his letter bag. He proceeded to go on a shooting rampage, killing two of his fellow postal workers and his wife. He eventually turned the rifle on himself, committing suicide.

John Taylor's shooting spree was not unique in post office history, nor was it the worst. Similar scenarios have been played out over the past several years. In Michigan, a fired postal worker went on a rampage like Taylor's, killing several postal workers. In New Orleans, a postal worker killed his supervisor by shooting him in the face and then wounded three others. In Boston, an angry postal worker strafed the city from a stolen helicopter with an AK-47 assault rifle. And on May 6, 1993, two unhappy postal workers—one in southern California, another in Dearborn, Michigan—both harboring grievances, killed and wounded fellow postal workers. Between 1983 and 1993, 34 postal workers and supervisors were shot to death by fellow employees on the job. In fact, up to December 1989, there had been 355 attacks of postal employees on their supervisors and 183 attacks by supervisors on the workers (*Time*, December 1989).

While violent events occur in many different work settings, the postal service seems especially vulnerable to violence. Why? Apparently, the seemingly serene post office is a hotbed of job stress and poor labor–management relations. For example, in ever-increasing attempts to speed up the mail, the postal service has installed new optical sorting machines. These machines pass up to 30,000 pieces of mail *per hour* by the eyes of postal workers. The worker must code the first three digits of the ZIP code into the machine as the letter passes. The worker has about a second to read the code and key it into the machine. The machine is relentless, and supervisors are not tolerant of errors. In fact, an inquiry found that postal supervisors often use an overly harsh style of management.

Behind the scenes at the post office is a cauldron of seething emotions, job stress, draconian management practices, and violence. An enormous number of grievances are filed by postal workers every year (sometimes 150,000 per year), and disciplinary actions are common (*Time*, December 1989). The oppressive atmosphere sometimes creates unbearable job stress and leads to explosions of violence like John Taylor's rampage.

---

*I*f stress is a transaction between the individual and the situation, what personality factors and what situational factors would account for these violent events? Why do you think the perpetrators are always males and never females? How could these kinds of events be prevented?

Academy of Family Physicians, 80% of business executives, 66% of teachers and secretaries, 44% of garment workers, and 38% of farmers reported that they "usually" or "always" work under stress (Veninga & Spradley, 1982). Respondents reported four kinds of stressors: pressure from supervisors, work overload, deadlines, and low salaries. Jobs do vary in the amount of stress associated with them, of course. Police officers and firefighters, for example, who face the prospect of being injured on the job, are likely to experience more stress than computer programmers. Sometimes working conditions make a job unbearable. For a closer look at what can happen in this case, see the featured discussion "Stressed Out on the Job."

Job stress manifests itself in a variety of ways. A worker experiencing job stress may have more health problems and a higher rate of absenteeism

Women are more likely than men to experience the stress of multiple social roles and obligations. This woman has to concern herself not just with her career but also with her child's development, the quality of his day care, and what to do with him when he's sick.

than one not experiencing job stress. If left unchecked, job stress may lead to a phenomenon known as **burnout,** a psychological condition in which energy and motivation are sapped (Veninga & Spradley, 1982). Burnout means that people have depleted energy reserves, lowered resistance to illness, increased dissatisfaction and pessimism, and increased absenteeism and inefficiency at work.

But job stress does not always lead to illness and burnout. An individual's personality characteristics may determine how well job stress is handled. Richard Lawrence (1984) suggested that reactions to job stress are a function of three factors: personality factors (e.g., aggressiveness, defensiveness), stressors (e.g., danger, problems with supervisors), and behavioral responses (e.g., coping mechanisms, denial). Lawrence conducted a study to investigate his *personality-stress response model* using 104 police officers. Each officer took a battery of tests including a standard personality measure and the Police Stress Inventory. The Police Stress Inventory indicated that there are four main stressors inherent in police work: court procedures/decisions, administration, equipment, and community relations (Lawrence, 1984, p. 256). Lawrence found that response to a stressor depended on the individual officer's personality. For example, officers who were "suspicious and threat-sensitive" were most upset when they had to appear in court and were disturbed by the decisions made by the courts. Officers who were "controlled and compulsive, outgoing, and easily upset" were most bothered by faulty equipment, such as radios that didn't work or squad cars that broke down.

Another variable that interacts with job stress is gender. Women experience certain job stresses that men don't (Gutek, 1990). Women have a variety of roles and obligations, often both at work and at home. A satisfying job may help a woman deal with the stresses of home life, but difficulties in both the home and the work place make for very high stress levels (Gutek, 1990).

Other significant sources of job stress for women are pay inequalities and sexual harassment. Research shows that at least 10% of working women have experienced sexual harassment at work (Gutek, 1990).

burnout A psychological condition in which energy and motivation are sapped.

Women who complain about harassment may find promotion blocked, experience less job satisfaction, and have to deal with serious emotional problems that stem from the incidents, thus adding to whatever "normal" levels of job stress exist.

Both men and women bring work stress home. Men, however, are more likely to let stress at home affect their work. Women's traditional abilities to deal with socioemotional problems help them cope with problems at home more effectively than men. In fact, many working women protect their working husbands from the demands of home life. This may be why marriage correlates with improved emotional adjustment for men but not for women (Gutek, 1990). In fact, unmarried women appear to show more positive psychological adjustment than do married women (Bishop, 1994).

COPING WITH STRESS

Although stress has been associated with many physical and psychological disorders, not everyone who experiences stress is afflicted. Some people develop effective mechanisms to cope with the stress that they experience. These **coping mechanisms** help individuals lessen and manage both the causes and the effects of stress (Baum, Grunberg, & Singer, 1982). In this section we look at the mechanisms people use to cope with stress. In the next two sections we consider how people cope with trauma and with illness.

Perceived Control and Self-Efficacy Beliefs

A person's ability to cope with stress depends to a large extent on the degree of control the individual thinks he or she has over the stress-producing events. **Perceived control** is important to any coping response; it indicates that the person believes she has power over what happens in her life. When the life events on the Holmes and Rahe scale are broken down into "controllable" and "uncontrollable," only the uncontrollable events correlate highly with future illness (Thompson, Cheek, & Graham, 1988). Even the trivial everyday hassles that drive us crazy are those that have an uncontrollable quality to them, such as the painter who says he will be at your house on Tuesday at 9 a.m. and doesn't show up until Wednesday at noon.

coping mechanisms Mechanisms that help individuals lessen and manage both the causes and the effects of stress.

perceived control An individual's perception that he or she has some control over what happens in life.

self-efficacy The notion that one can be effective in dealing with events, including those that are stressful or threatening.

People who believe that they have some degree of control over what happens to them also feel that they can effectively cope with stressful or threatening events (Affleck, Tennen, Pfeiffer, & Fifield, 1987). These individuals usually express feelings of **self-efficacy,** the notion that one can do what one sets out to do (Bandura, 1986). People who have strong feelings of self-efficacy are likely to respond to stress by throwing more effort and resources into coping with the threat.

One study found that 27% of the individuals who felt at risk for AIDS had thoughts about suicide (Schneider, Taylor, Hammen, Kemeny, & Dudley, 1991). These thoughts had little to do with their actual physical condition but were an attempt to cope with the probability that they would

Perceived control and self-efficacy beliefs have important consequences for both physical and mental health. Flowers and family pictures help these two nursing home residents individualize their room and maintain a sense of control over their own lives.

soon develop and subsequently die of AIDS. As we saw in Chapter 2, suicide and suicidal thoughts can be seen as an attempt to exercise some control over the future. By thinking that they had an "out" if they had to experience pain and suffering, they were actually increasing their sense of control over their lives.

Another study of the effects of perceived control and self-efficacy beliefs on health status was conducted with patients in a nursing home as subjects (Langer & Rodin, 1976). Typically, when people enter nursing homes, they are expected to allow the home's staff to run their lives. Meals are planned and scheduled, as are visiting hours. All rooms are furnished exactly alike. In fact, families expect that when they place a relative in a nursing home, all the person's needs will be met.

In this study, patients on one floor of a high-quality nursing home were given a modest increase in control over their lives. They were told they could arrange their rooms the way they liked, choose how to spend their spare time, and decide when or if they watched TV, listened to the radio, or engaged in other activities. This was the experimental group. Patients on the other floors of the nursing home—the control groups—were told that the staff would arrange for all their needs. Since patients were randomly assigned to different floors, there was no reason to believe that any floor had healthier or unhealthier individuals.

Eighteen months later, the mortality rates of the two groups were compared. The researchers found that 15% of the patients on the experimental floor had died and 30% of the patients on the other floors had died. Why the difference? The researchers suggest that those patients who perceived that they had some control over their environment were more positive, more sociable, and generally happier than other patients. This translated into better health and lower mortality rates.

The Effects of Positive Mood

Positive moods also affect the way both sick and healthy people deal with stress. In one study, researchers made groups of ill or healthy subjects feel sad, happy, or neutral (Salovey & Birnbaum, 1989). Subjects who were sad reported more general aches and pain than did happy subjects. A positive mood increased the subjects' belief that they could lessen their symptoms and cope so that they could carry on daily activities. Mood may also influence the course of illness (Salovey & Birnbaum, 1989). A sad, depressed mood often leads to feelings of fatigue and weakness. People may tend to interpret these symptoms as part of their "physical" illness. Such a misinterpretation of symptoms may slow recovery.

Some researchers argue that there is a "disease-prone" personality, in which a persistent depressed mood plays an important role (Friedman & Booth-Kewley, 1987). There is even some evidence linking food allergies with depression (Marshall, 1993). However, allergy and depression are probably connected by some underlying neurochemical disorder that is aggravated by psychological stress. There is no evidence that food allergies cause depression.

A good mood is often expressed in laughter. The German philosopher Friedrich Nietzsche observed about humans that "the most acutely suffering animal on earth invented laughter." Research shows that laughter may play a role in altering the course of some types of illnesses. In one study, researchers looked at the effects of laughter and relaxation on the ability of subjects to withstand the discomfort produced by the inflation of a blood-pressure cuff (Cogan, Cogan, Waltz, & McCue, 1987). Subjects listened to one of three audiotapes: a humorous tape that induced laughter, a relaxation tape, or an "informative narrative." A fourth group, the control group, did not hear a tape. Subjects who heard a humorous tape were able to withstand the most discomfort, followed by the relaxation group. The other two groups were able to withstand the least discomfort.

Much of the research into the effects of positive mood on health was inspired by former magazine publisher Norman Cousins (1979, 1989). Cousins was stricken with a severe inflammation of the spine and joints, and his physicians told him that the disorder would leave him disabled. Cousins would not accept this prognosis. Day after day he watched Marx brothers movies from his hospital bed. He found that 10 minutes of solid laughter gave him 2 hours of pain-free sleep. Cousins eventually left the hospital free of pain and other symptoms.

Although laughter was good medicine, Cousins and the scientists who support his ideas do not claim that you can actually laugh your way out of serious disease. Cousins used laughter as a metaphor, a figure of speech, for all those emotions involved in hope, faith, and determination that may affect people's perception of stress and of their ability to cope (Cassilth, Lusk, Miller, & Miller, 1985). Note that the technique Cousins used permitted him to feel he had control over his illness and could be effective in doing something about it.

Cousins's account of his use of laughter in his recovery has led to some interesting developments. Some hospitals have equipped the rooms of cancer patients with TVs and stereos so that they see or hear their own equivalent of the Marx brothers. The Duke University Comprehensive Cancer Center uses humor, art, music, literature, and anything related to

Women tend to have higher levels of social support—an important factor in good health—than men. These women may share very personal information with each other and in return receive validation of their experiences and support for their choices.

the patient's interests as part of the treatment, including a "laugh wagon" stocked with humorous tapes and books, which is as important as the "pill wagon" in the treatment scheme (Cousins, 1989).

Social Support

It is interesting that loss of a spouse is related to disease and death in men but not in women. The explanation for this finding may be that women have higher levels of social support, have more friends, belong to more organizations, and have better coping strategies than men (Adler, 1990). *Social support* is a network of social relationships with people who provide help (psychological, social, financial) during crises. Social support appears to act as a psychological buffer that absorbs, cushions, and thus diminishes the stress brought on by severe threat.

Social support is vital to health. In a study of heart patients completed at a major medical school, individuals who lacked a spouse or a confidant were three times as likely to die within 5 years as those who were married or had a close friend (Brody, 1992). Having someone to talk to is potent medicine. However, as you might suspect, talking to just anyone will not do. In a study of the reactions of students to taking a medical-school entrance examination, test-takers who had more "companionate" contacts—interactions with friends and neighbors in leisure activities—were best able to cope (Bolger & Eckenrode, 1991) (Figure 15-2). These contacts were discretionary; obligatory contacts appeared to increase stress. The one "ob ligated" contact that did help buffer stress was the contact married students had with their spouses.

Just as social support enhances health, *social isolation*—the lack of close social contact—endangers it. In an international study of the effects of isolation and loneliness on health, more than 37,000 people in three countries were evaluated by researchers (House, Landis, & Umberson, 1988). Socially isolated individuals—those who said that they had no one to confide in or who had less than one close contact with another person

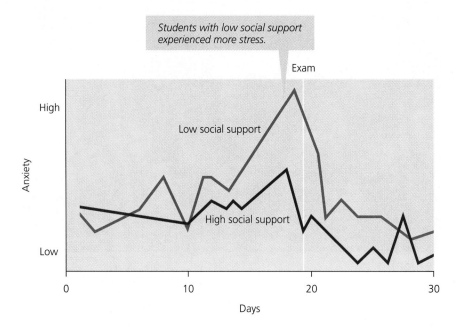

FIGURE 15-2 *The effect of high and low social support on anxiety caused by taking a medical-school entrance exam. Students with better social support experienced less stress when under pressure.*
From Bolger and Eckenrode, 1991.

each week—were found to be at greater risk for ill health than nonisolated individuals.

Social isolation actually poses a greater mortality risk than smoking (Gatchel et al., 1989). People with weak social ties have been found to be twice as likely to die as those with strong relationships. Recall that Sy was a social isolate at the time of his death. His isolation may have been a factor in his fate. Social isolation is more deadly to men than to women. This is probably because even when women have few social contacts, these ties are of a higher quality than those men have. Social support is not limited to interaction with other humans. For a closer look at another form of support, see the featured discussion "Pets as Stress Moderators."

Personality Factors

We have seen that there is a relationship between stress and illness. We have also seen that the stressfulness of an event often depends on how the individual perceives and interprets that event. Some people are very vulnerable to stress—they are prone to interpret events in a way that makes them more stressful—and others are less vulnerable. What is it that buffers some individuals from stress?

Researchers have looked at personality factors as variables in the stress–disease connection. Psychologist Suzanne Kobasa has suggested that there is a combination of characteristics that protects individuals from stress-related illness (Kobasa, Maddi, Puccetti, & Zola, 1985). She refers to this combination as *hardiness.* People with hardy personalities see events in terms of commitment, challenge, and control. They are actively involved in family, job, and community and thus have a sense of purpose, or commitment. They see change as a challenge rather than a problem. And they feel that they have control over their lives and can influence the course of

Science seems to have recently supported what (almost) every pet owner knows: Pets may play a role in buffering people from stress and illness. Research has shown that pet owners who are elderly visit the doctor less often than elderly individuals who don't own pets. In fact, pets seem to play a role in helping patients with coronary heart disease survive longer. Exactly how pets function to buffer stress has only recently been investigated.

Karen Allen, Jim Blascovich, Joe Tomaka, and Robert Kelsey (1991) asked 45 women who owned dogs to take part in a study designed to determine exactly what effects the animals had on the ability of their owners to cope with stress. The women were asked to perform a stressful mental arithmetic task in the presence of a friend or their pet or neither. The presence of their pets resulted in a lowered physiological reaction to the task. That is, when the women performed the arithmetic task with only their pet present, their pulse rate, blood pressure, and skin conductance showed less arousal than when in the presence of a friend or by themselves.

Why this reaction? Pets are comforting and nonevaluative. They don't care whether you get the right answer. Some of the subjects in this study, especially the divorced women, commented that whereas husbands may come and go, and children may grow up and leave, "a dog is forever." These women told the experimenters that the pets "never withhold their love, never get angry and leave, and they never go out looking for new owners" (Allen et al., 1991, p. 588).

If pets serve to reduce stress, what other events or interactions might serve the same purpose? How would you determine if having a pet is stress reducing or if people who own pets are the type of individuals who know how to reduce stress?

events (Funk & Houston, 1987). In short, hardy individuals can recast potentially negative incidents to make them less stressful (Wiebe, 1991).

Kobasa (1979) developed a hardiness scale that combined measures of commitment, challenge, and control. Using responses to this scale, she was able to distinguish between hardy and nonhardy individuals. She then found that scores on the hardiness scale accurately predicted current and future health problems (Kobasa, Maddi, & Courington, 1981). Hardy individuals appear to be better at resisting stress than nonhardy individuals. One reason for this seems to be that they can tolerate frustration better than nonhardy individuals (Hull, Van Treuren, & Virnelli, 1987; Hull, Van Treuren, & Propson, 1988). They evaluate a threatening task as less stressful than do less hardy people. They also appraise potentially stressful events both more rationally and more optimistically than others.

A test measuring hardiness developed by Kobasa (1984) is presented in Figure 15-3. You might like to score yourself and see how you rate on the hardiness dimension.

Optimism Versus Pessimism

Hardy individuals are optimists. We have also seen that laughter and good moods appear to help hospitalized patients cope with their illnesses. Is it possible that a generally optimistic view of life is an effective coping strategy? Optimism is the inclination to anticipate the most favorable outcomes

FIGURE 15-3 *The Hardiness Scale, a measuring device that distinguishes between hardy individuals, who cope well with stress, and nonhardy individuals, who are adversely affected by stress.* From Kobasa, 1984.

Write down how much you agree or disagree with each statement by placing a number in the blank before it. Use the following scale:

0 = strongly disagree
1 = mildly disagree
2 = mildly agree
3 = strongly agree

___ A. Trying my best at work makes a difference.
___ B. Trusting to fate is sometimes all I can do in a relationship.
___ C. I often wake up eager to start on the day's projects.
___ D. Thinking of myself as a free person leads to great frustration and difficulty.
___ E. I would be willing to sacrifice financial security in my work if something really challenging came along.
___ F. It bothers me when I have to deviate from the routine or schedule I've set for myself.
___ G. An average citizen can have an impact on politics.
___ H. Without the right breaks, it is hard to be successful in my field.
___ I. I know why I am doing what I'm doing at work.
___ J. Getting close to people puts me at risk of being obligated to them.
___ K. Encountering new situations is an important priority in my life.
___ L. I really don't mind when I have nothing to do.

To score yourself:
These questions measure control, commitment, and challenge. For half the questions, a high score (like 3 "strongly agree") indicates hardiness; for the other half, a low score (disagreement) does.

To get your scores on control, commitment, and challenge, first write in the number of your answer—0, 1, 2, or 3—next to the letter of each question on the score sheet. Then add and subtract. To get your score on "control," for example, add your answers to questions A and G; add your answers to B and H; and then subtract the second number from the first.

Add your scores on control, commitment, and challenge together to get a score for total hardiness.

A total score of 10–18 shows a hardy personality; 0–9: moderate hardiness; below 0: low hardiness.

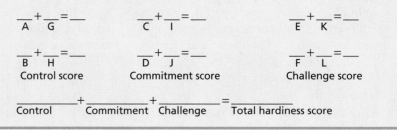

for events. The idea that optimism can positively affect health is not a new one. However, the idea has been systematically explored only recently.

In a study of coping styles, college students were interviewed about how they dealt with stress during the tension-filled final weeks of a semester (Scheier & Carver, 1987). **Coping style** reflects the characteristic manner in which a person tries to minimize the psychological and physical pain associated with disease and negative life events (Snyder, Ford, & Harris, 1987). While it may be possible to train yourself to use an optimistic style, it is probably more accurate to say that optimism or pessimism is a personality trait that is enduring. Students with an optimistic coping style reported far fewer physical symptoms than students with less optimism. Similar find-

coping style The characteristic manner in which a person tries to minimize the psychological and physical pain associated with disease and negative life events.

ings have been reported with groups of hospitalized and nonhospitalized elderly patients. Optimists reported fewer physical symptoms than pessimists and were in better condition emotionally and physically.

An optimistic coping style also appears to help individuals recover more rapidly and more effectively from coronary bypass surgery. Research has demonstrated that optimistic bypass patients had fewer problems after surgery than pessimistic patients (Scheir et al., 1986). The optimists reported more positive family, sexual, recreational, and health-related activities than pessimistic patients following their surgery.

Many individuals react to threatening events by developing **positive illusions,** beliefs that include unrealistically optimistic notions about their ability to handle the threat and create a positive outcome (Taylor, 1989). These positive illusions are adaptive in the sense that people who are optimistic will be persistent and creative in their attempts to cope with the psychological and physical threat of disease. Having positive illusions is an important determinant of good mental health (Taylor et al., 1992). The use of these positive illusions is not limited to individuals coping with disease. One way most of us construct an optimistic outlook on our lives is to convince ourselves that the future looks promising.

The tendency to display positive illusions has been shown in individuals who have tested positive for the human immunodeficiency virus (HIV, the virus that causes AIDS) but have not yet displayed any symptoms of AIDS (Taylor, Kemeny, Aspinwall, & Schneider, 1992). These individuals often expressed the belief that they had developed an immunity to the virus and that they could "flush" the virus from their systems. They acted on this belief by paying close attention to nutrition and physical fitness.

Interestingly, people who had tested negative for HIV were actually more pessimistic about developing AIDS symptoms than those who had tested positive. Illusions are clearly more important when people are already facing the actual threat. It seems that knowledge of being HIV-positive is necessary for positive illusions to form.

Why Does the Optimistic Style Work? Positive illusions may develop because they help the threatened person successfully cope with severe threats (Taylor, 1989). Optimistic people who have had heart surgery seem to take control of their postoperative life. Optimists plan, set goals, and, perhaps most important, do not dwell on the negative and depressive aspects of the situation (Figure 15-4) (Scheir & Carver, 1987). It is likely that the relative absence of negative thoughts is the crucial key to recovery.

Optimistic cancer patients do not deny the reality of their illness, but they still manage to believe they will survive, and they do all they can to make that wish come true. They often use *parallel processing*—thinking about the disease on two separate tracks—to deal with their situation (Taylor et al., 1992). The first track is emotional and semirational; the person thinks positively about managing the disease—"It's not that bad, I can beat it"—and envisions the best possible outcome. The second track is a rational, direct coping process in which the patient realistically deals with the day-to-day aspects of treatment, such as getting to the hospital for

positive illusions An individual's beliefs that include unrealistically optimistic notions about his or her ability to handle a threatening event and create a positive outcome.

FIGURE 15-4 *Optimistic people seem to take control of their lives after surgery or severe illness, sometimes developing "positive illusions" that help them cope.*

chemotherapy treatments. Optimistic patients, in other words, do not simply believe they are invulnerable. They know that they must carry out a rational course of action—maintaining a proper diet, exercising, getting enough rest—to positively affect their illness.

Be Happy, Don't Worry: The Secret to Long Life?

Optimism and cheerfulness apparently are positive traits. If optimism helps us deal with a current health crisis, does it also help us live longer? Maybe not. Sy was harried and stressed out, but he was always cheerful. He thought that life would turn around for him someday. He was never prudent or careful. He believed life was to be lived to the hilt.

As it turns out, the voice of restraint may win this one. According to a 60-year study of more than 1,000 men and women, being cautious and somewhat gloomy may be the real key to a long life. In the early 1920s, Lewis Terman began a study of over 1,000 boys and girls (average age 11) who had high I.Q.'s. Other scientists continued to study this group throughout their lives. Scientists not only studied the intellectual performance of these individuals but also tracked their personalities, measuring such aspects as their sociability, self-esteem and confidence, activity level, and cheerfulness—a combination of sense of humor and optimism (Goleman, 1993c).

Some striking findings have been reported based on these data (Friedman et al., 1993). First, individuals who were cautious and conscientious were 30% less likely to die in any given year than their "live to the hilt" peers. Those who were cheerful and outgoing as children were 6% more likely to die in any given year than their gloomy peers. Cheerfulness predicted a shorter lifespan (Friedman et al., 1993). These differences were not, as you might think, due to more accidents among the less conscientious. The less prudent individuals did not have a significantly higher accidental death rate than the more prudent (Goleman, 1993c).

How can we explain the seemingly contradictory findings that optimism helps us deal with a medical crisis and yet predicts a shorter lifespan? The contradiction may be more apparent than real. Many of the studies reporting that an optimistic coping style is beneficial to recovery from medical trauma tend to define optimism as a sense of control over the events of life (Goleman, 1993c). Remember that those who do best after a heart attack are the individuals who take control over their diet, exercise, and other aspects of their lifestyle.

The prudent and the dour know that life can go wrong. The youngster who always locks up her bike, does her homework, and practices her jump shot until it gets dark becomes the adult who plans carefully, drinks and smokes little if at all, takes only prudent risks, and plans for the worst. When the worst comes, she is ready. Such individuals may live longer largely because they have developed ways to cope with stress, illness, and trauma. Individuals who are not conscientious do things now and worry about the consequences after. They are more impulsive than conscientious individuals, less organized, and more willing to take risks to have fun (Goleman, 1993c).

Behavioral Factors: Exercise

A number of behavioral, lifestyle factors contribute to people's ability to handle stress. One is doing relaxation exercises, such as meditation, progressive relaxation techniques, or visualization. Another is doing regular aerobic exercise. Research has shown that physically fit individuals are less vulnerable to the effects of stress than those less fit. In a study of 110 men and women tested for life stress, fitness, and mental health, findings suggested that fitness acts as a stress buffer, a kind of shock absorber, in two ways (Brown, 1991).

First, physical fitness gives people a sense of mastery (self-efficacy) and control over their lives. As we saw earlier, individuals who feel they have control over events generally have a less intense reaction to stress than those who perceive they have little control. Second, fitness activities divert attention from stressful events, at least temporarily. When people are running or playing tennis, their attention focuses on the activity and gives them a temporary respite from the day's stresses. For example, individuals report that exercise tends to overcome sad moods and makes them have more positive thoughts (Erber & Therriault, 1993).

Of course, exercise also has physical effects, including improved functioning of body systems, favorable changes in body chemistry, higher energy levels, and greater mental alertness. As these changes occur, individuals often gain even more of a sense of control over their lives, which again helps them handle stressful events as they occur.

Exercise is an effective antidote to stress and an essential component of a healthy lifestyle. These members of a step aerobics class can expect several health benefits from regular workouts, including stronger muscles, improved cardiovascular health, a better emotional state, and a sense of mastery and control over their lives.

The Social Context of Illness

In considering the variables that influence how people cope with stress and illness, we have so far looked at cognitive factors (such as how people think about stress), personal factors (such as optimistic coping style), and behavioral factors (such as exercising). But equally or even more important than these individual factors are the social variables that determine a person's place in the social structure. These include such variables as age, socioeconomic status (SES), sex, race, and marital status (Pennebaker, 1989).

Age, of course, is related to the frequency of illness. Older adults experience more symptoms and take more medication than younger adults (Bishop, 1994). Studies have also shown that women report more illness than men, although this may be because women recall symptoms more accurately than men do (Bishop, 1994).

Marital status and living arrangements are also related to the experience of illness. Research has consistently shown that married people report fewer symptoms, take less medication, and think of themselves as being in better health than their unmarried counterparts. Individuals living with one to three others claim to be in the best health (Bishop, 1994).

SES is another potent factor in determining health status. People with high SES report fewer symptoms, take less medication, and have a more positive sense of personal health than those with lower SES (Insel & Roth, 1994). High SES means that the individual has greater resources and time to gather health-related information, obtain the best medical care, and purchase the right foods. The modest "fitness boom" that has been going on for the past 10 years or so has been largely an upper-middle-class phenomenon.

COPING WITH TRAUMA

The coping methods and styles discussed so far are those people use to deal with everyday stresses. But some stresses are so severe that they leave deep emotional and/or physical scars. People typically don't want to talk about these events and prefer to deny or repress them. These severe stresses, or **traumas,** require special coping techniques.

The Nature of Traumatic Experiences

What kind of events are we talking about? Two descriptions from the research of James W. Pennebaker (1989) will serve as examples. One is the experience of a student at a private university who, when she was 10 years old, was told to clean up her room in anticipation of a visit from her frail grandmother. She forgot about her task, as 10-year-olds are wont to do. While visiting, her grandmother stepped on one of the girl's toys, fell down the stairs, broke her hip, was taken to the hospital, and died shortly thereafter.

trauma A severe stress that leaves deep emotional and/or physical scars and that requires special coping techniques.

The second example is the story of a 68-year-old concentration camp survivor, recounting the last days of the Lodz ghetto, in Poland, in 1942 (Pennebaker, 1989):

> They were throwing babies from the second floor window of the orphanage. I can still see the pools of blood [and hear] the screams, the thuds of their bodies. I just stood there afraid to move. The Nazi soldiers faced us, with their grins. (p. 212)

For further discussion of how people manage to cope in even the most inhumane, unbearable circumstances, see the featured discussion "Enduring the Unendurable."

A striking aspect of the traumas reported by the student subjects in Pennebaker's (1989) research was the extent of tragedy and shock experienced by young people, not yet 21, who seemed immensely privileged and who were attending a prestigious private university. Trauma and tragedy seem to know no social boundaries. The traumas experienced by the Holocaust survivors in the study were unspeakable. Clearly, many participants had experienced terrible psychological traumas—and had been repressing them for a long time.

The Effects of Repressing Traumatic Memories

Although people want to "forget" traumatic events, there has long been a popular idea in psychology that holding back one's strong emotional reactions to these events has a negative effect on the body and the mind. The work of Pennebaker (1989) has been aimed at discovering the effects of such repression. Pennebaker has used a variety of participants in his research. As just suggested, they range from students at a private university to survivors of the Nazi concentration camps.

Pennebaker's work starts with the assumption that an important means of coping with stress is talking about it. He hypothesized that people who have experienced trauma and do not confide in others are much more likely to have health problems. To test this hypothesis, he examined the number of times individuals visited a physician in a 6-month period after the occurrence of the trauma (Pennebaker, Colder, & Sharp, 1988). Those who did not talk about their trauma had many more medical appointments than those who did (Figure 15-5). Other research has confirmed

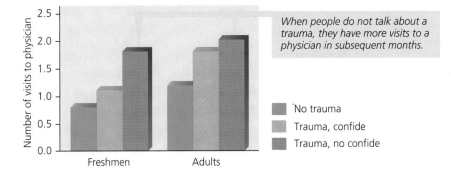

When people do not talk about a trauma, they have more visits to a physician in subsequent months.

No trauma
Trauma, confide
Trauma, no confide

FIGURE 15-5 *Effect of confiding about trauma on number of medical appointments. When people do not talk about a traumatic experience, they tend to have more visits to a physician in the 6 months following the trauma. Those who do talk about their experience have fewer visits.* From Pennebaker, 1989.

Throughout history, humans have found unimaginably cruel ways to treat other humans. Such experiences stretch—and break—the endurance of many victims. Others somehow find the resources to cope with the trauma. They are the survivors.

The African slave trade was one such barbarous endeavor. People were kidnapped, put in chains, and packed into the holds of ships for an ocean voyage of many thousands of miles. After a few days the cargo hold was fouled with the smell of human waste, vomit, blood, and death. Many of the "cargo" never made it. Those who did survive found themselves in an alien world surrounded by people who looked different from anyone they had ever seen before.

Of all the experiences these Africans endured, the physical abuse and discomfort were probably the least traumatic. Far worse was being torn from a familiar existence within a social support network that included family, friends, and fellow villagers and being thrust into a totally alien existence (Huggins, 1977).

The Nazi death camps were a similarly traumatic experience for the Jews during World War II. Much like the Africans of earlier centuries, Jews were subjected to unendurable trauma: physical abuse, degradation, and, most important, being thrust into a new and hellish existence. It began with the trip to the camp. Hundreds of Jews were packed into railroad boxcars for the journey to obscure places like Auschwitz, Poland. Inside the railroad cars, the temperature became oppressive and the air filled with the odor of human excrement and vomit. In this environment the human cargo "lived" for several days. Arrival at the camp gave little relief. Inmates were forced to live under conditions not terribly different from conditions in the boxcars. How could anyone possibly survive?

Terrence Des Pres (1976) did an extensive study of life inside the barbed wire fences of the death camps. He was able to identify the conditions under which inmates lived and those under which they died. Des Pres reports that survival, for the few, involved two steps. The first step was an initial collapse under the weight of the oppressive conditions. From the time people stepped off the train, they were subjected to humiliation (they were stripped naked, their heads were shaved), physical abuse (they were beaten), and emotional trauma (they saw bodies strewn about the camp and roads) (Des Pres, 1976). These experiences led to a total collapse of the ability to cope.

However, a second phase of adjustment then ensued, in which there was a reintegration and a reestablishment of a sense of the self (Des Pres, 1976). Much like waking from a bad dream, survivors "went from withdrawal to

Pennebaker's thesis that disclosing past traumas results in fewer physical symptoms of ill health (Greenberg & Stone, 1992).

Participants in Pennebaker's research were asked to write or talk about the "most upsetting or traumatic experience of your entire life" (Pennebaker, 1989). The subjects wrote version after version of these accounts over several days. The technique proved very powerful. People felt sad; they felt depressed; they cried. They told stories of deceit and adversity, misery and tragedy. Their handwriting reflected the emotional turmoil they were feeling as they related and relived their experiences. However, as they continued to write, their handwriting changed, becoming less controlled, less legible, more free form. As suggested by the samples shown in

engagement, from passivity to resistance" (Des Pres, 1976, p. 77). In short, inmates woke up to the

Elie Wiesel survived Nazi death camps and went on to speak eloquently for all survivors. Some combinations of traits, skills, attitudes, and luck allowed certain individuals not only to survive but to transcend the horrors of the Holocaust.

reality of what was needed for long-term survival.

Of course, not all inmates were "survivors." Many of those coming to the camps died very quickly. Unable to cope with the death of loved ones or with the filth, degradation, and humiliation in their new lives, these individuals simply gave up and died (Des Pres, 1976). Other nonsurvivors did not die so quickly. Some inmates remained in a state of shock and apathy for a long period of time; the situation was simply too overwhelming for them. These unfortunate souls were referred to as *Muselmanner*—the "walking dead." Eventually, they starved to death or found themselves in situations that led to a quick death (Des Pres, 1976). Individuals in these two categories never made it to the second stage of survival. Those who had a strong constitution and a strong will to live became the survivors of the Nazi version of hell.

Whether the experience is slavery, or living in a death camp, or

some other highly traumatic experience such as being in a prisoner-of-war camp, there are those who die quickly, those who are slowly worn down, and those who survive. Survivors overcome all the odds and emerge as strong, defiant individuals. Frederick Douglass escaped from slavery and became a powerful voice for freedom. Elie Wiesel survived the death camps and later hunted down Nazi war criminals. They endured the unendurable—and transcended it.

Some people manage to survive horrendous experiences. How do you think they do it? What factors—cognitive, social, personality, situational—from the study of health psychology might help to explain why some people survive and others don't?

Figure 15-6, these individuals were allowing their repressed memories loose.

The Effects of Confronting Traumatic Memories

When Pennebaker measured the effects of this kind of disclosure, he found that subjects who fully revealed their feelings about terrible events showed improved immunological functioning and lowered skin-conductance rates. This latter measure reflects the fact that when there is a reduction in autonomic nervous system activity (that is, stress-related reactions),

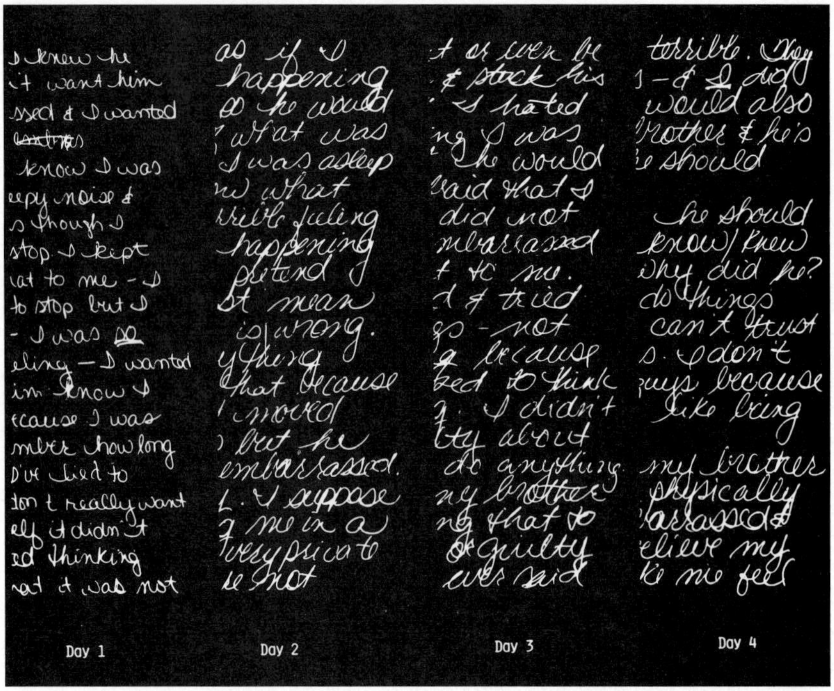

FIGURE 15-6 *Change in handwriting of a female writing about the same traumatic incident over 4 days. The more she disclosed about the incident, and the more she relived the experience emotionally, the more relaxed and open her handwriting became. Changes in handwriting in this study were taken as evidence that subjects who disclosed their feelings were reducing the amount of psychological and physiological tension they held about the event.* From Pennebaker, 1989.

skin-conductance readings go down. The lower readings indicate a lessening of psychological tension. Subjects were "letting go" as they expressed their feelings about the long-suppressed trauma. Those who could not let go of the trauma and had trouble revealing important thoughts about the event showed heightened skin-conductance rates.

The body uses a great deal of energy to continually repress memories of negative events and all the thoughts and emotions intertwined with those memories. Confronting the trauma requires that we recall the event and experience the buried emotions associated with it. This act offers release from the prison of repression. Pennebaker's work shows that confiding in someone protects the body from the stressful, energy-draining effects of holding on to traumatic memories.

Sometimes victims of terrible events deliberately rehearse and repeat their story so many times that they strip it of all emotion (Wegner, 1988). Holocaust survivors have been heard to explain, in clinical detail and without a trace of emotion, how the Nazis carried out their tortures. This is not "letting go." Talking alone is not the same as "confronting," which involves experiencing the emotions associated with the event.

In an experiment designed to investigate this distinction, subjects saw a movie that vividly reenacted woodworking accidents (Mendolia & Kleck, 1993). Some subjects were encouraged to report their emotions as they saw the film; others were asked to just recount the facts. The "emotion" subjects were more physically upset than the "facts" subjects when they initially talked about the film. But 2 days later, the subjects were shown the movie again, and this time the "emotion" subjects were less upset than the "facts" subjects. For the "emotions" subjects, arousal decreased over time, but a

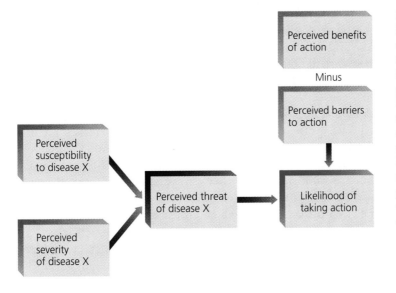

FIGURE 15-7 *The health belief model. According to this model, the likelihood of a person changing a health-related behavior is determined by the perceived threat of a particular disease in combination with the perceived benefits of change and the manageability of making the change. The health belief model is often (but not always) accurate in predicting when people will make health-promoting behavior changes.*

plain how individuals (patients) decide which health-promoting behaviors they will adopt. The health belief model suggests that the likelihood of an individual adopting a health-promoting behavior (exercise, low-fat diet, etc.) depends on the perceived threat of the disease in question. As Figure 15-7 shows, that perceived threat is determined by the individual's realization that she is susceptible to the disease *and* the individual's perception of the severity of that disease.

According to the model, the likelihood that Sy would have adopted certain health-promoting behaviors would have initially depended on whether he thought he was susceptible to heart disease. Certainly he knew that heart disease was serious. But he also thought that he was not susceptible. Or at least he said he wasn't susceptible. Remember Sy said that "only fat old guys have heart attacks."

The likelihood of Sy taking action was low. If Dr. Bill could have convinced Sy that he was in danger, then the likelihood of Sy taking preventive action would have been much higher.

Figure 15-7 also suggests that the likelihood of Sy adopting health-promoting actions depended on whether he thought the behavior had benefits and whether or not the obstacles to that behavior were manageable. It wasn't until Sy read an article about the health-promotion benefits of exercise that he considered running. But Sy did not begin to run until he became convinced that the benefits gained outweighed the obstacles (time, pain, giving up a drink with the boys after work).

This health belief model has been used to predict when individuals will adopt health-promoting behavior. But its success has been mixed (Taylor, 1990a). One reason may be that when patients think the disease that is threatening them is very serious, they may not think that anything will work. Did Sy really think only old fat guys had heart attacks? Probably not—he was too smart for that. Just before his fatal attack, Sy admitted that he was "scared silly" that he had heart disease and did everything to deny it. In fact, there is evidence that diabetics are more likely to adhere to their very difficult health regimen if they perceive a *low threat* of disease (Bond, Aiken, & Somerville, 1992).

On the other hand, some patients become so anxious about their symptoms that they become *hypervigilant* (Janis, 1984). Rather than rationally accept their diagnosis, or deny that they are sick at all, they overreact to their symptoms. They become consumed with their illness and read everything remotely related to it. If the prescribed medication does not seem to work right away, they try something else, usually something they read about in a magazine or hear about from a friend. They want a "magic bullet," a treatment that will cure their disease immediately. It appears that hypervigilant patients simply do not trust their physicians.

In fact, the principal reason patients do not comply with a prescribed course of treatment is probably lack of trust in the physician (Stone, 1979). This lack of trust, in turn, often develops from communication difficulties (Taylor, 1986). Patients' noncompliance with medical recommendations may be due to the unsatisfactory nature of patient–physician communication and interaction (Ditto & Hilton, 1990). Physicians are frequently poor at communicating with their patients. One reason for this is that they cannot afford to spend much time explaining medical issues to their patients. They get paid for performing procedures and running tests, not for talking with their patients.

Norman Cousins, whose work on the power of laughter was described earlier in this chapter and who served on the faculty of UCLA Medical School, catalogued many stories of poor communication and insensitivity on the part of physicians. He quotes a young female professor who questioned her physician about his diagnosis. She says the physician told her

> not to bother my head about such things, that he was the doctor and knew what to do. When I remonstrated with him and told him I wanted to discuss with him some things I had looked up in the medical literature, he seemed insulted by my persistence and told me that if I did not trust him I should go elsewhere. I told him that I did not distrust him but I wanted to have the kind of partnership with him you had with your doctor. He said that if I wanted a partner I should go into business, and that he had spent ten years of his life studying how to take care of patients, not how to be a good partner. (Cousins, 1989, pp. 45–46)

As this incident shows, the "fit" between patient and physician can be very important in determining the quality of the relationship. Problems may stem not just from differences in communication style but also from differences in the type of relationship each party wants. The young professor was intelligent and independent; she wanted a kind of egalitarian alliance with her doctor. Other patients would be more comfortable with a more submissive posture, one in which the doctor is perceived as an all-knowing author-

Although the basics of a healthy lifestyle are fairly well known, many people have not been exposed to this information. If these young men make a regular habit of eating high-fat, high-cholesterol junk food, they are increasing their risk of heart disease later in life.

ity figure who makes decisions and explains little. Research confirms that when physicians and patients are matched on communication style, the patients like the physician and are more likely to comply with medical advice (Kalish, Hilton, & Ditto, 1988).

Why Don't Patients Adhere to Doctor's Orders?   Psychologists and physicians do not have a clear understanding as to why so many patients fail to obtain the full benefit of their treatment by adhering to medical instructions. Physicians are not very good at predicting which of their patients will or will not follow instructions. Psychologists have found that neither the patients' personality nor socioeconomic class reliably predicts who will adhere (Kaplan et al., 1993). However, there is some evidence that those in the highest socioeconomic class are somewhat more likely to adhere to the recommended medical regimen (Taylor, 1990).

What may matter most is the patients' assessment of what benefits are likely to occur if they follow the medical advice. If they think the benefits outweigh the costs, they will follow it. If not, the pills go into the disposal. More research is needed with respect to how people decide whether or not to follow medical advice (Kaplan et al., 1993).

LIFESTYLE AND HEALTH

We have looked at some of the social psychological factors involved in how people cope with stress, trauma, and illness. We turn now to a related topic: how people live their lives in ways that promote or undermine their health. As we have noted, many diseases that kill us—most notably, cardiovascular disease (diseases of the heart and blood vessels) and cancer—are to some extent preventable. Cardiovascular disease, the leading cause of death in the United States, kills about 930,000 Americans every year, more than the

- *Take responsibility for your own health status.*
- *Learn to manage stress in effective ways.*
- *Get enough sleep.*
- *Maintain high self-esteem.*
- *Cultivate satisfying and close relationships with other people.*
- *Avoid tobacco and other drugs.*
- *Use alcohol in moderation, if at all.*
- *Eat well and maintain normal weight.*
- *Exercise regularly.*
- *Understand your sexuality and practice safe sex.*
- *Know the facts about cardiovascular disease, cancer, infections, sexually transmitted diseases, and injuries. Use your knowledge to protect yourself.*
- *Know your own personal and family health history, and protect yourself against diseases or conditions for which you are at risk.*
- *Understand how environmental factors affect your health, and protect yourself from environmental hazards.*

next seven leading causes of death combined (Insel & Roth, 1994). Cancer claims over 500,000 lives each year, and over 1,000,000 people are diagnosed with cancer in the United States each year. More than half of these are cured, but about 44% die (Insel & Roth, 1994). Together, heart disease and cancer account for 60% of all the deaths in the United States (Zimbardo & Leippe, 1992).

Eating, drinking, and smoking behaviors all play a role in heart disease and cancer. The basic principles of a healthful lifestyle have been well known for quite a while and include eating properly, exercising, managing stress effectively, maintaining normal weight, and getting enough sleep. For a more detailed outline of a healthy lifestyle, see Figure 15-8. Obvious examples of behaviors that don't promote health or that are even self-destructive include smoking, abusing alcohol and other drugs, overeating, not wearing seat belts, and not practicing safe sex.

If the basics of a wellness lifestyle are commonly known, why is it that so many people don't follow them? What factors contribute to their "noncompliance" with this prescription for healthful behavior? A number of factors are probably involved, including personality, psychological, and cognitive factors. For example, some people exhibit *sensation-seeking* behavior. These individuals seem to have a strong need for excitement and adventure. Depending on what is available to them, they may rock climb, hang glide, sky dive, or bungee jump. Most of all, they drive fast and are involved in many more fatal automobile crashes than people who drive more conservatively (Zuckerman, 1990).

Cognitive factors also play a role: The way we think about health issues can lead us to make poor decisions and behave in self-destructive

FIGURE 15-9 *From which man do you think this woman would be most likely to contract a sexually-transmitted disease? People often use implicit personality theories—assumptions about characteristics that "go together"—in assessing the risk of contracting a sexually-transmitted disease from a sexual partner.*

ways. The cognitive errors and biases with which we are so familiar may blind us to risks in certain situations. An obvious example is how we assess the risk of contracting AIDS from a sexual partner. A study showed that college students use *implicit personality theories* in judging this risk (Williams et al., 1992). Students rated partners they knew and liked as posing less risk than partners they didn't know. They held the belief that you needed to use a condom at the beginning of a relationship, but "once you get to know the person . . . as soon as you begin trusting the person . . . you really don't have to use a condom" (p. 926). On the other hand, students judged a partner to be risky if he or she was provocatively dressed, was first met in a bar, was older, came from a large city, or was overly anxious for sex (Figure 15-9).

As you recall from Chapter 3, implicit personality theory—the idea that certain characteristics, such as conservative dress and a clean bill of health, always go together—is not a good way to judge people. How long you've known a person is also not a reliable predictor of who is HIV-positive. By relying on an implicit personality theory, the students in the Williams and colleagues study were jeopardizing their lives.

Obesity

Obesity poses a health challenge primarily because it increases the individual's vulnerability to heart disease, hypertension, diabetes, and numerous other debilitating conditions. Because our society values slenderness, obesity also strikes at people's self-esteem and self-image. Worrying about one's weight is a very common—and stress-inducing—"everyday hassle" (Lazarus & Folkman, 1984). It has been estimated that two out of three women in the United States are on a diet at any one time (Chaiken & Pliner, 1987). One indicator of "weight worry" in our society is the abundance of weight-loss and diet books on the best-seller list.

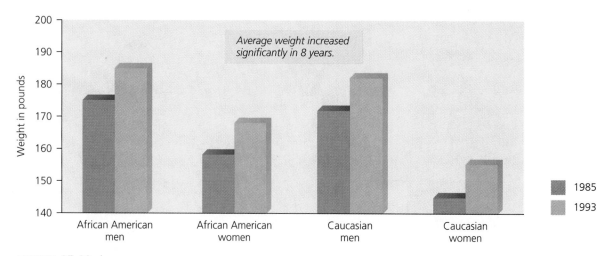

FIGURE 15-10 *Average weight of African American and Caucasian men and women, aged 25–30, 1985 and 1993. Despite the increasing emphasis on slenderness and fitness in our society, the average weight of young adults has increased by a significant amount.* From data supplied by Cora E. Lewis, University of Alabama, Birmingham.

Concern about being overweight is an issue for Western societies in which food is plentiful. In other parts of the world, most people are more concerned about getting enough to eat. A Chinese student, new to the United States, once complimented her professor for being so fat. After all, the Chinese equivalent of "Hi, how are you?" is "Did you eat yet?" Obesity to this young student was a mark of robust good health, character, and even attractiveness. Not so in North American culture!

Despite concern about being overweight, the average weight of North American adults 25 to 30 years of age rose 10 pounds between 1985 and 1993 (Lewis & Bild, 1994). In 1993 the average weight of young adults was 171 pounds compared to 161 pounds in 1985 (Figure 15-10). This was true for both men and women and for both Caucasians and African Americans. The average current weight is 184 pounds for men and 158 pounds for women.

Obesity is a complex phenomenon with biological, social psychological, and cultural components. Although the parts have not yet been untangled, let's look at them separately here.

Biological Factors Research indicates that some human beings may have an innate tendency to become obese. For example, infants differ in their preference for sugar water: Some love it, and some hate it (Rodin, 1974). This preference is neither psychological nor cultural. There is also evidence that some people are born with more fat cells than others. The number of fat cells seems to be laid down during late childhood. Once these fat cells are present it is very difficult to reduce the number of them (Brownell, 1984). It is possible, however, to reduce the size of the cells. When a person gains weight, these cells grow in volume, and when the person loses weight, they shrink. A person generally stops losing weight when fat cells reach normal size (Kaplan et al., 1993). There is some evidence to suggest that we may have a hardwired "set point" weight that is ideal for each of us and which is difficult to alter or modify.

People also differ in their metabolic rates, the rate at which the body uses energy and nutrients to maintain its functions. People with more body fat tend to have lower metabolic rates, meaning that they need less food to maintain their weight than do those with higher metabolic rates. Research also indicates that metabolic rates may change in response to recurrent cycles of dieting. When people lose weight and then gain it back, their metabolism may become more efficient, making it harder for them to lose weight the next time. The pitiless fact is that when someone diets, the body "thinks" it is starving and takes precautionary measures by slowing down metabolism—permanently.

Overeating   Biological and genetic factors are largely beyond our control, but other contributors to obesity can be controlled. Overeating is one of them. Although research does not indicate conclusively that obese people eat more than nonobese people, many obese people engage in episodes of binge eating. During these episodes they eat uncontrollably, consuming large amounts of food. As we saw in Chapter 2, they "shut down" on the inhibitions that keep them from overeating and focus narrowly on the immediate sensations of eating and drinking.

How much *should* people eat? Research with rats suggests that the healthiest course of action is to eat less—perhaps as much as 60% less than what would be freely chosen (Walford, 1986). Rats who eat a restricted diet live about 50% longer than rats who eat freely; they also remain relatively free of disease. Curiously, rats fed the restricted diets become compulsive and frenetic exercisers after about 2 months on the diet. They run miles and miles on a treadmill and do not slack off as they get older (Walford, 1986).

Is it the reduced calories or the exercise that increases the rats' lifespan? Not enough generations of rats have been tested to provide a definitive answer to this question. In any event, eating for humans is different from eating for rats. For humans, eating is a social activity and has social implications.

External Cues and Social Influence   Part of the reason for binge eating among obese people may be that they are more attuned to external cues than normal-weight people are. Their eating is less related to internal states, such as hunger pangs, than to such cues as the sight and smell of food. If the food looks and smells good, they will eat whether they are hungry or not.

Stanley Schachter was the first to pose this *externality hypothesis* to account for the differences between normal-weight and obese individuals. His work (Nisbett, 1968; Schachter, 1973), as well as the work of Judith Rodin (1974), indicated that obese individuals are more attentive not only to food-related cues but also to any type of external signs. One study showed that obese subjects who were solving problems were more easily distracted from their tasks by external cues such as noise than were subjects of normal weight (Rodin, 1974). Not all obese individuals are externally oriented, however, and not all nonobese people are internally directed.

External sensitivity is likely to be present in all weight classes (Rodin, 1981). One task for researchers is to determine how normal-weight people who are externally oriented manage to maintain optimal weight.

Other researchers have looked at the effect of eating alone versus eating with others. One study revealed that overweight people buy more food in a cafeteria setting when they eat by themselves than when they anticipate eating with others (Edelman, Engell, Bronstein, & Hirsch, 1986; Krantz, 1979). In contrast, nonobese individuals choose more food when accompanied by others than when alone (Van Velsor, 1990).

Another experiment explored the role of external cues and social influence in a dining situation. To get a sense of this study, imagine that you are at a fine French restaurant. You have done well: You ate the sole, light on the sauce, a touch of bread and salad, a sip of the Chateau Rothschild. Alas, you are now subjected to one of four dessert conditions: (1) The waiter hands you a dessert menu (the control condition); or (2) the waiter carries a dessert as he hands you the menu (the visual cues condition); or (3) the waiter strongly recommends a dessert as he hands you the menu (the social influence condition); or (4) the waiter strongly recommends one dessert while carrying another as he hands you the menu (the competition condition).

When this experiment was conducted, obese diners were found to be more responsive to visual cues—that is, they were more likely to order a dessert in condition 2—than were diners of normal weight (Herman, Olmstead, & Polivy, 1983). The obese diners were also vulnerable to social influence and were very likely to order the recommended dessert in condition 3. They were no more likely to order dessert in the control condition or in the competition condition than were their normal-weight counterparts. The blend of visual food cues and social influence, then, creates a situation in which the tendency to overeat is intensified.

Cognitive Factors What role do thinking patterns have on obesity? Some researchers have looked at how people on diets think about food, eating, and themselves. One study found that dieters differed in their eating behavior depending on what they thought they had already consumed. When dieters were told they had just had a high-calorie appetizer, they were more likely to binge when presented with additional food than were similar subjects who thought they had just eaten a low-calorie snack (Polivy & Herman, 1983).

These results support the notion that dieters have constructed a narrow self-schema that emphasizes thoughts about food, eating, appearance, and weight. When they stay on their diet, they see themselves as good people. When they go off the diet, they are bad people. They expend so much effort in curbing eating that when inhibition fails, they lose control. Their behavior is of an all-or-none variety—either they diet or they "pig out." There is no rational middle ground (Crandall, 1988).

There is some variation among dieters, however. Dieters who have high self-esteem do not lose control when a lot of food is available

(Heatherton, Herman, & Polivy, 1991). Dieters who have lower self-esteem are more likely to "lose it." This fits with the idea that unrestrained eating occurs when dieters confront anxieties that threaten their self-esteem (Heatherton & Baumeister, 1991). As discussed in Chapter 2, threats to self-esteem can motivate people to "escape the self" by thinking only about what is happening now. They forget about their long-term goals and think only about how good a pizza would taste right now: "I did poorly on my GREs, there's no hope for me anyway, I might as well enjoy myself. Heavy on the pepperoni, please."

Coronary Heart Disease

Another common health problem with behavioral determinants is coronary heart disease (CHD). In this condition, the arteries supplying blood to the heart become clogged with fatty deposits that prevent blood from reaching the heart muscle. If the coronary arteries become completely blocked, a heart attack occurs. In some cases, the muscle sustains damage but is able to continue functioning; in many other cases, the damage is fatal.

Research shows that certain risk factors make CHD more probable. These factors include, but are not limited to, high blood pressure, smoking, unhealthy cholesterol levels, obesity, and a sedentary lifestyle. In addition, certain personality and behavioral tendencies incline individuals toward heart disease. These tendencies have been labeled the **Type A behavior pattern** (TABP). People identified as Type A are more than twice as likely to get coronary heart disease than others and to get it prematurely, before their sixties (Suls & Sanders, 1989; Williams & Barefoot, 1988).

The Type A Behavior Pattern   What came to be known as TABP was first identified when two California cardiologists, Dr. Meyer Friedman and Dr. Ray Rosenman, began to notice that most of their cardiac patients had fairly similar "personality" traits. Their first clue had come from the upholsterer who was refitting the waiting room. He pointed out that the edge of the arms of all the chairs had been rubbed away. These patients were wound as tight as springs (Friedman & Rosenman, 1974).

Type A has come to be defined as a behavioral–emotional complex that involves: (1) general behaviors such as ambitiousness, competitiveness, aggressiveness, and impatience, (2) specific behaviors such as musculature tenseness, alertness, a rapid and forceful style of speech, and rapid actions of all kinds, and (3) emotions such as hostility, anger, irritability, and cynicism (Rosenman, Swan, & Carmelli, 1988). As we see below, the third element—hostility—has been identified as the critical component of TABP contributing to heart disease.

What kind of people are Type A's? Most of them are male, although an increasing number of females are beginning to exhibit this pattern, especially those who work outside the home (Lynch & Schaffer, 1989). Type A's are people who have a strong need to achieve but who may set unrealistic,

Type A behavior pattern A combination of behaviors and emotions that are characteristic of individuals who have high levels of hostility, competitiveness, and time urgency.

unreachable goals (Ward & Eisler, 1987). They are impatient; they hate waiting. It means wasting time. Many Type A's have a constant, almost insatiable need for recognition and approval. Finally, and most important, Type A's are characterized by strong aggressive and hostile feelings.

Another complex of personality and behavior traits has been labeled Type B. Type B's are as ambitious and probably as competitive as Type A's, but they simply don't feel the rage or anger that A's seem to experience. Type A's are more insecure about their status; B's are more secure and do not set impossible goals. Type B's do not respond to stress with the anger and impatience typical of Type A's. It has been estimated that about 45% of the population fall into the Type A pattern and another 45% into the Type B pattern. The remaining 10% seem to fall somewhere in between.

It seems that Type A behavior is not limited to humans. Studies indicate that the same kind of behavior in monkeys can lead to CHD (Cohen, Kaplan, Cunnick, Manuck, & Rabin, 1992). Monkeys are good subjects to study because they develop CHD very much as humans do. They are also competitive and aggressive, two behavior patterns associated with CHD. Monkeys live in a social system that emphasizes hierarchical rankings; some monkeys are dominant, others are subordinate. Dominant monkeys living in unstable, and therefore stressful, environments are more likely to develop CHD than dominant monkeys living in a stable and less stressful world. These monkeys express a great deal of hostility and aggression. They do not have higher blood pressure or higher scores on other risk factors than monkeys under less stress. What distinguishes them is the expression of hostility.

The Role of Hostility   Of all the components associated with TABP, hostility is the one factor that most clearly distinguishes those individuals who have CHD from those who do not (Williams & Barefoot, 1988). These people are cynical and mistrustful of people. They openly express anger and contempt for others. The evidence shows that hostile individuals have more extensive blockage in the coronary arteries than nonhostile individuals (Suls & Sanders, 1989). They are also more likely to die of CHD than those with less hostility. Of course, hostility cannot be pinpointed as the sole cause, or even as a cause, of CHD. The differences between hostile and nonhostile individuals in rates of CHD are probably the result of a combination of factors, possibly including physiological differences between people. In other words, some other factors may cause people both to express hostility and to develop CHD.

Two other variables in this mix are gender and amount of social support. There is evidence that males are more hostile than females. In one 4-year study, researchers charted the expression of hostility in male and female teenagers as well as the social support they received from their families (Woodall & Mathews, 1993). Over the 4 years, males were consistently more hostile than females; additionally, their hostility increased as they got older. The researchers observed the greatest amount of hostility in males who had low social support from their family. These males with a lot of ex-

Researchers originally thought that the person with the driving aggressive, competitive approach to life—the type A personality—was at higher risk for heart disease than more relaxed individuals. Further study has indicated that anger and hostility are probably the critical factors. If these two people habitually respond to others in angry, confrontational ways, they may well be risking their lives.

pressed hostility and little family support were at risk for CHD at an early age, even before age 21. Although social support is especially important to the hostile Type A person, research suggests that Type A's have more marital or dating problems and are less likely to confide in their friends (Suls & Sanders, 1989).

PREVENTING ILLNESS AND INJURY

We have seen that many modern diseases—as exemplified by obesity and coronary heart disease—have a relatively large behavioral component. We can infer from this that preventing and treating these conditions involves, to a large extent, making changes in behavior. Although this is good news, there is a downside. As we saw in Chapter 7, persuading people to modify their behavior, even when their lives are at stake, is not an easy task.

Two levels of dealing with preventable diseases have been identified. The first, *primary prevention,* aims at stopping the behaviors that cause the problem or the disease before they get started. Examples of primary prevention are educating adolescents about the dangers of smoking; teaching people how to drive safely; providing prenatal care to pregnant women; immunizing infants against communicable diseases; and avoiding cancer-causing agents in the environment. The second level, *secondary prevention,* is concerned with modifying behavior once the problem has already started or after the person is already at risk (Taylor, 1986). Examples of secondary prevention are treating a low-birthweight infant to prevent later problems;

treating cancers quickly to prevent their spread; and providing victims of trauma with counseling to prevent depression or suicide.

Two different approaches to primary and secondary prevention have been used. Health psychology emphasizes that individuals need to assume active responsibility for their own health (Taylor, 1990b). They need to exercise, change their eating habits, quit smoking, or modify other behaviors. If they don't take an active role in changing their behavior, they may not continue to enjoy good health. This approach, derived from the health belief model discussed earlier, suggests that the best way to prevent major illnesses like CHD and AIDS is to identify individuals who are at risk, target them by testing and screening, and then give them the information they need to change their behavior.

Although the health belief model makes good sense, it assumes that people are fairly rational decision makers. But we have seen that this is not the case. Do you recall what people do when they get negative information? They deny, minimize, and misremember. The flaw in the health belief model is that giving people accurate information is no guarantee that they will make productive or rational use of it.

A second approach to primary and secondary prevention is provided by the **public health model.** According to this model, the most effective way to prevent or alter high-risk behaviors is to devise methods that automatically prevent people from engaging in them. The individual remains essentially passive and is not required to take an active, responsible role.

Let's consider now how each of these models works. We look at the health belief model as it is applied to modifying Type A behavior. We then explore the public health model as it is applied to injury control and prevention.

The Health Belief Model: Modifying Type A Behavior

Many tactics have been used to try to modify Type A behavior in individuals who either have had a heart attack or have been identified as at high risk for heart disease (O'Rourke, Houston, Harris, & Snyder, 1988). An underlying assumption of most of these programs is that Type A is not so much a personality trait (as the originators of the concept tended to think) as a coping style, a set of reactions that certain individuals have when facing stressful situations (Carmelli, Dame, Swan, & Rosenman, 1991). Obviously, coping reactions are easier to modify than personality traits.

Most programs involve some kind of cognitive restructuring. Type A's are taught new ways of looking at the world. They learn that they need not try to gain total control over the world, because it is impossible and unnecessary to do so. They are taught how to modify unreasonable or unattainable goals, and they are taught relaxation and coping techniques. This approach seems to be successful (O'Rourke et al., 1988). Even if, as some evidence indicates, part of the TABP is hardwired—that is, some people have a physiological reactivity pattern that tends to overheat quickly and

public health model An approach to illness and injury prevention stating that the most effective way to prevent or alter high-risk behaviors is to devise methods that automatically prevent people from engaging in those behaviors.

The health belief model is based on the idea that once people have the information they need, they will give up risky behaviors and adopt healthier ones. Mass media campaigns to educate the public about issues like smoking and AIDS are based on this assumption. How does this billboard attempt to inform? To persuade? How effective do you think it is?

there is little they can do about it—these individuals can release tension through aerobic exercise.

In his books *The Trusting Heart* and *Anger Kills,* Redford Williams (1989, 1993), a leading proponent of the hostility–CHD link, has described many ways people can change the way they see and respond to the world. For a closer look at his prescription, see the featured discussion "Modifying Hostile Behavior to Protect Your Heart."

It is interesting to note that TABP is a risk factor for heart disease but not for other diseases. Type A's are driving, ambitious, pragmatic people. In many ways, they are the kind of people that Kobasa (1979) described as being hardy. It seems that the hardy person is buffered against most illnesses except CHD (Contrada, 1989). How might the Type A buffer himself or herself against CHD? It would be necessary to make cognitive and behavioral changes so that while continuing to be committed and challenged by work, the person avoids anger, cynicism, and hostility (Brown, 1986).

Another approach to preventing heart disease is to focus more on secondary prevention. As with AIDS (see Chapter 7), mass media campaigns have been used to try to modify the behaviors that contribute to heart disease. One campaign was carried out by the Stanford Heart Disease Prevention Program (Meyer, Nash, McAlister, Maccoby, & Farquhar, 1980). The plan was to try to influence the population in several towns in California to lower their risk of CHD by changing behaviors such as smoking and not exercising. Town 1 was given a standard mass media campaign, consisting of ads encouraging behavioral change. Town 2 was given a much more intensive, 24-month campaign that blanketed the town with messages about changing high-risk behavior. Town 3 received the same treatment as

Town 2, but in addition, a large group of people were recruited from Town 3 for special educational sessions. All the recruited subjects were, because of poor habits, at very high risk for CHD. They were given films and lectures about how to "eat right." They were also trained in techniques to help them quit smoking and lose weight.

The behavior of all subjects in the three towns was followed for 3 years (the 2 years of the experiment and 1 following year). As shown in Figure 15-11, both Towns 2 and 3 displayed significant changes in high-risk behavior, especially as compared with Town 1. The most impressive result was that Town 3, which had the combination of intense media messages and "hands-on" workshops, displayed the greatest amount of change, sharply lowering risk-related behaviors. The study showed that if enough resources are available, and if the population is not too large, it is possible to

they are saying, and never interrupt. Every time you start thinking about yourself, turn your attention back to what the other person is saying. Avoid being judgmental or giving advice.

9. *Practice trusting others.* Look for safe opportunities to trust others. Don't feel you always have to take charge. Learning to trust reduces cynicism.

10. *Take on community service.* Reduce isolation and alienation by donating your time to a good cause. Doing so helps reinforce your sense of connectedness with others.

11. *Increase your empathy.* When you feel yourself getting angry with someone, try putting yourself in that person's shoes. When you see things from another perspective, your empathy will probably increase. And empathy and anger simply don't mix.

12. *Be tolerant.* Disapproving of others increases angry thoughts and heightens alienation. Learn to accept other people as they are, not as you would like them to be.

13. *Forgive.* Rather than blame those who have harmed you, release your anger by forgiving them. Realize that you can consciously choose to forgive people.

14. *Have a confidant.* Cultivate at least one intimate relationship, and spend a lot of time with that person, whether a spouse, a lover, or a friend. As you deepen the bonds of mutual support, try sharing and disclosing more of your most personal thoughts and feelings.

15. *Laugh at yourself.* Find the humor in situations and in your own reactions. You can use self-directed humor to combat hostile feelings.

16. *Become more religious.* Joining a religious community can help you achieve a more positive philosophical outlook. It can also provide a strong social support system.

17. *Pretend today is your last.* If you have trouble reducing hostility, imagine that you have a fatal illness and are going to die soon. Coming face to face with your own mortality may help you see the wisdom of "walking away from anger."

Making changes like those outlined by Williams can improve an individual's quality of life even if that person is not at risk for heart disease. How likely do you think it is that someone who doesn't feel threatened by heart disease would make such behavioral and attitudinal changes? According to the health belief model, what would have to happen before that person would start making changes? Are you considering trying any of Williams' strategies? If so, why?

mount a campaign that significantly reduces high-risk behavior (Zimbardo & Leippe, 1992).

Both primary and secondary prevention were used in this influence campaign. Some people probably were convinced to modify their behavior fairly early in life (primary prevention). Others, such as the high-risk volunteers of Town 3, were persuaded to change established behaviors (secondary prevention).

The Public Health Model: Preventing Injuries

The second approach to primary and secondary prevention is the public health model. In this model, people do not have to take primary responsibility for changing their behavior; others take action or make decisions, and

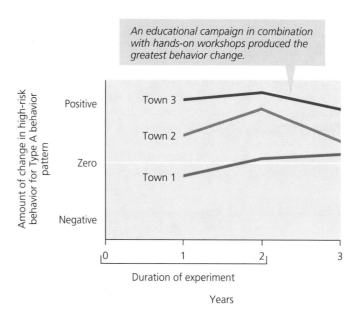

FIGURE 15-11 *Effects of influence techniques in three California towns in the Stanford Heart Disease Prevention Program. At the end of 3 years, high-risk behavior had been reduced the most in Town 3, which received an intensive media campaign and hands-on workshops. This combination of strategies was more effective than an intensive media campaign alone (Town 2) or a standard media campaign (Town 1).* From Bolger and Eckenrode, 1991.

individuals must comply with them. For example, parents do not decide whether or not their children get certain vaccinations. Children *must* be vaccinated before they may attend school (Singer & Krantz, 1982). The intervention to prevent certain communicable childhood diseases is automatic and determined by the public health system. Similarly, laws requiring that motorcyclists and bicyclists wear helmets take the decision out of the individual's hands.

The public health model can be seen most clearly in current approaches to serious injuries, formerly referred to as accidents. Safety experts are trying to phase out the term *accidents* because it suggests that such events are "accidental"—beyond human control. On the contrary, most injuries are the predictable outcomes of factors that can be controlled, such as human behavior (drinking and driving) or faulty equipment. In a recent attempt to get this idea across, a National Safety Council Ad showed a picture of a tree-lined road with the caption "They don't hit you" (Williams & Lund, 1992). Experts distinguish between unintentional injuries, which occur when no harm is intended, and intentional injuries, which are purposely inflicted, as in the case of homicide and suicide (Insel & Roth, 1994).

Injuries are the fourth leading cause of death in the United States and the *leading* cause of death for Americans under age 45 (Rosenberg & Finley, 1992). The single largest cause of injury is automobile crashes. Consequently, numerous interventions have been proposed to reduce the number of motor vehicle–related injuries and deaths. Some proposals, based on the health belief model, have been aimed at getting individuals to play an active role. Campaigns have been launched to discourage drinking and driving, to support the "designated driver" concept, and to encourage people to "buckle up."

However, many of these attempts have not worked. The seat belt is a case in point. Using seat belts has been shown to be the most effective action drivers can do to survive crashes. In fact, the failure to use a seat belt puts the nonwearer at higher risk for early death than smoking, alcohol abuse, or obesity (Sleet, 1987). Many people don't understand that the seat belt provides protection at the time of the "second collision," which occurs when the occupant of the car hits something inside the car. Seat belts also spread the force of the collision over the whole body, and they prevent people from being thrown from cars. Despite these facts, public information and education campaigns have been unable to persuade the general public to use their seat belts. Ad campaigns designed to increase seat belt use have been remarkably ineffective (Frank, Bouman, Cain, & Watts, 1992).

Changes made in accordance with the public health model have been more successful. For example, safety features have been added to American cars. As required by law, all new cars are being made with center high-mounted brake lights, which have been shown to decrease rear-end crashes by over 17%, particularly in the daytime (Williams & Lund, 1992). Many cars also have automatic seat belts, which move into position when the car is started or the door is closed. They are considered passive restraints because the individual doesn't have to take any action to engage them. Air bags are becoming standard equipment on many cars as well. However, they offer limited benefits, since they provide protection only in front-end collisions and deflate immediately after inflating. They are most effective when used in combination with seat belts.

A good part of the motivation for automatic and passive injury-prevention methods comes from the fact that other attempts have failed. As the costs of unhealthful lifestyles increase, we can expect that the public health model will become more popular. A society faced with mounting health care costs may be forced to prevent people from harming themselves, especially when the public ends up paying for it.

SY'S HEART ATTACK REVISITED

It's easy to see in retrospect how Sy might have changed his life. He could have lost weight, changed his diet, and learned to balance his working life with a less isolated social life. Whether it was possible for him to change, however, is another question. He habitually denied the possibility of bad things happening to him. He thought that people who ate and drank in moderation and who lived prudently were dull and boring. And he didn't confront his symptoms until it was too late.

If Sy had been more prudent about his lifestyle, more realistic about his symptoms, and less compulsive about work, he might be alive today. The sad thing was that he had begun to change. He just couldn't overcome all those years of neglecting his health, both physically and emotionally.

LOOKING AHEAD

In this chapter we have seen how the principles and research findings of social cognition, in conjunction with the application of other social and personality variables, can inform our understanding of stress and illness. In the next and final chapter we explore the social psychological roots of international conflict. We again see that basic research in social cognition, particularly with respect to stereotypes, gives us insight into human behavior and interaction. Principles of social perception and intergroup relationships also inform us about why international conflicts begin and what might be done to control them.

CHAPTER REVIEW

1. *What role does social psychology play in enhancing our understanding of health and illness?*
   Many modern diseases have a preventable component. People's lifestyles and health-related behaviors play a critical role in whether or not they get sick. Social psychology can help us understand the dynamics of people's behavioral responses to stress, trauma, illness, and lifestyle change.

2. *What is stress?*
   Stress can be thought about in different ways. The stimulus definition of stress focuses on the stimuli in the environment that produce stress. The response definition of stress focuses on people's physiological and psychological responses to stressful situations. This approach has been extensively studied by Hans Selye, who has proposed the general adaptation syndrome to describe the body's response to stress. In the first stage, alarm, the body reacts with a "fight or flight" hormonal response. In the second stage, resistance, the body attempts to return to normal functioning. If the first and second stages last for long or indefinite periods of time, a stage of life-threatening exhaustion may ensue. All the stages place great demands on the body.
   Social psychology views stress as a transaction between the individual and the environment. It emphasizes the importance of how people perceive and respond to events. When people perceive an event or a situation as exceeding their ability to cope with it, it is stressful for them. If they do not perceive it as exceeding that ability, it is not stressful for them.

3. *What is the relationship between stress and illness?*
   The inability to cope with stress is an important psychological cause of illness. **Life stressors** are positive or negative events that individuals perceive as stressful, and they apparently have a cumulative effect on health. The assessment tool known as the Social Readjustment Rating Scale assigns scores to various life events and can be used to predict the likelihood of future illness. Two important sources of stress are

everyday hassles, such as difficulties encountered in the household or concerns about personal appearance and weight, and job stress, such as having too much work or impossible deadlines. If left unchecked, job stress may lead to a phenomenon known as **burnout**, a psychological condition in which energy and motivation are sapped. Since many of these sources of stress have a self-produced component, developing effective coping mechanisms can reduce stress and the likelihood of illness.

4. *What mechanisms do people use to deal with stress?*
   Many people devise effective **coping mechanisms** that are aimed at lessening and managing both the causes and the effects of stress. Generally, people who feel they have some control over events (**perceived control**) and believe they can be effective in dealing with these events (**self-efficacy**) devise more effective coping styles. One very effective **coping style** involves maintaining a positive mood and an optimistic view of life. When faced with threat, many optimists develop **positive illusions**, beliefs that include unrealistic hopefulness about their ability to handle the threat and create a positive outcome. Nevertheless, it appears that these positive illusions are adaptive in the sense that people who are optimistic will be persistent and creative in their attempts to cope with the psychological and physical threat of disease or other stressful events.

   Also important in handling stress are a network of social support, personality factors such as the trait complex labeled hardiness, and behavioral factors such as exercising. Finally, the social context—including factors such as age, race, and socioeconomic status—plays a role in how people handle stress and illness.

5. *What do people do to deal with extreme stress?*
   More severe stresses, known as **traumas**, require special coping techniques. People tend to respond to trauma by repressing the terrible emotions. But it appears that such repression takes so much energy that it makes the person vulnerable to illness. The best method of dealing with the trauma is to confide in someone about it, to talk out all the pain and anguish. When this occurs, the immune system resumes its normal functioning levels.

6. *How do individuals deal with medical diagnoses?*
   When we receive the news that we may be ill, there is a tendency to deny the reality of that diagnosis and to downplay its seriousness. This is known as the **minimization effect.** Perhaps people need time to marshall their resources to deal with this new threat. People especially tend to minimize diseases that are common, such as high blood pressure. They seem to conclude that if others have this, it can't be too serious. People also protect themselves against a health threat by **downward comparison,** the process of comparing themselves with someone who is in a worse predicament. An uncertain diagnosis seems to be hardest for people to deal with. They are unable to generate

positive illusions when they have no symptoms and no certainty that they are ill.

Very often, people fail to comply with their physician's advice. Instead, they engage in such psychological processes as denial and minimization. This is especially true when they don't trust their physician, a condition that results most often from communication problems.

7. *What is the role of lifestyle in maintaining health?*
Since many modern diseases have a preventable component, how people live their lives can either promote or damage their health. Two modern diseases—obesity and coronary heart disease (CHD)—have a number of behavioral components. Obesity is a complex phenomenon affected by heredity, behavioral factors, social influence, and cognitive factors. Overeating is one factor over which people have some control. A combination of external cues and social influence seem to create situations in which the tendency to overeat is intensified. Dieters often lose all inhibitions about eating when their self-esteem is threatened. They may overeat to "escape the self" and reduce their anxiety about how they feel about themselves.

Coronary heart disease also has a strong lifestyle component. Risk factors for CHD include high blood pressure, smoking, unhealthy cholesterol levels, obesity, a sedentary lifestyle, and the complex of traits and behavior known as the **Type A behavior pattern.** Type A's are ambitious, competitive, aggressive, and hostile. The last component seems to be the critical risk factor for CHD. Anger and hostility damage the cardiovascular system, especially in the absence of a strong social support system.

8. *What methods do people use to prevent illness and injuries?*
Many of the techniques applied in illness- and injury-prevention programs emphasize the responsibility of the individual to make changes in his or her behavior. This approach reflects the **health belief model.** An alternative, the **public health model,** argues that the most effective way of preventing or altering high-risk behaviors is to devise methods that operate automatically, without the need for people to take primary responsibility. Although some prevention is achieved through the health belief model (by educating people about what constitutes a healthful lifestyle and how to change their behavior), the public health model seems to be more effective, especially in reducing injuries.

Suggestions for Further Reading

Shilts, R. (1987). *And the band played on: Politics, people, and the AIDS epidemic.* New York: St. Martin's Press.
The late journalist Randy Shilts describes in moving terms the political, medical, and human aspects of AIDS.

Skelton, J. A., & Croyle, R. T. (1991). *Mental representations in health and illness.* New York: Springer.

This book explores how we think about illness and how these mental representations affect our health.

Taylor, S. E. (1990). Health psychology: The science and the field. *American Psychologist, 45,* 4–50.

Shelley Taylor, a leading researcher in health psychology, discusses the issues facing the field and suggests an agenda for the future.

Weiner, B. (1993). On sin and sickness. *American Psychologist, 48,* 957–965.

A leading attribution theorist explores how our notions of sin are related to our conceptions of illness.

Chapter 16

Social Psychology, Conflict, and Conflict Resolution

*S*ince May 1948, when the state of Israel was created, there have been four major wars between Israel and the Arab nations, in 1948, 1956, 1967, and 1973. Although a de facto peace—defined as the absence of war—exists in the region, smaller-scale conflicts between the Israelis and the Arabs, especially the Palestinians, continue on an almost daily basis. Numerous attempts have been made to negotiate peace in the region, including the 1978 Camp David Accord and the 1994 agreement between the Israelis and the Palestine Liberation Organization. But tension and hostility continue, and the violence rages on.

This conflict, which has its roots in history, has proven to be one of the world's most intractable, defying efforts to solve it in a peaceful manner. What lies behind the Arab–Israeli conflict?

Events of the past several thousand years all played a role in setting the stage for

the current situation. In 587 B.C., the Jews were expelled from the area by Babylonia, an event known as the Diaspora. In A.D. 70 the Jews were again dispersed throughout the world, this time following a failed revolt against Roman rule. Since ancient times, a dream of the Jews has been to reestablish a homeland in Palestine, a land that many Jews believed God had promised to them. This was, and still is, the basis for Zionism, the Jewish nationalist movement. In the late 19th century, Zionism became a worldwide political movement, and Jews began moving to Palestine in increasing numbers.

Palestine, home to many peoples and a region of fervent nationalism, has existed under foreign domination for millennia. Under Roman and then Byzantine rule, the people of Palestine became overwhelmingly Christian. In the 7th century A.D., the area was conquered by Arabs and came under the sway of Islam. From the 16th century until World War I, the region was part of the Turkish Ottoman Empire, and toward the end of World War I, it was conquered and occupied by Britain.

On November 2, 1917, British Foreign Secretary Arthur Balfour sent a letter to Lord Rothschild, the head of the British Zionist Federation, stating that Britain would support a national homeland for the Jews in Palestine as long as it did not "prejudice the rights" of the non-Jews already living in the region. This letter, known as the Balfour Declaration, was incorporated into the official British Mandate, approved by the League of Nations, and took effect in 1922. As Jewish immigration increased, the

British quickly learned that they could not satisfy the needs of both sides: It was not possible to establish a new state without prejudicing the rights of individuals already living in Palestine.

World War II brought the next wave of Jewish immigration into Palestine, fueled by wartime persecutions of the Jews, the Holocaust, and a postwar desire of many European Jews to leave Europe. Despite British attempts to curb this immigration, the Jewish population in Palestine grew. In 1947 the newly-formed United Nations, which included no Arab nations as members, voted to partition Palestine into two nations, one Jewish and one Palestinian. Soon after, the British, who were coming under increasing attack from militant Jews, decided to leave the Middle East. On May 14, 1948, the Jews of Palestine declared their independence and created the state of Israel.

Tensions immediately rose, and Egypt, Syria, Jordan, and Lebanon attacked the newly formed Jewish state. As a result of this first large-scale war, the Israelis captured territory that had been mandated as the Palestinian state by the United Nations. Hundreds of thousands of Palestinians fled to other Arab nations, where many still reside in refugee camps. A generation of Palestinians has grown up in these camps, with only one wish: to reclaim the territory they see as their homeland and establish a Palestinian state in Palestine. As noted earlier, four major wars have followed the creation of Israel, and thousands have died in what they see as a holy cause, "with God on their side." Although there have been steps toward peace, the conflict continues.

As the events of the past century in the Middle East graphically illustrate, aggression and violence readily escalate into full-fledged wars. But the Middle East is not the only area of tension and violence in the world. Brutal conflicts are occurring among the Serbs, Croats, and Muslims in the former Yugoslavia; the peoples of Armenia and Azerbaijan (former republics of the Soviet Union) have been at each other's throats for years; recently, government troops, the Hutus, and the Tutsis in Rwanda rekindled hostilities; and there is still conflict between rival clans in Somalia. Throughout human history, ethnic and other forms of conflicts have flared and raged, defying rational attempts to solve them and often leading to war.

Conflict and war have been an integral part of human existence for thousands of years. It has been estimated that in the past 3,700 years there have been only 270 years of peace (Train, 1983). Josef Goebbels, Adolph Hitler's minister of propaganda, once called war "the simplest affirmation of life." Trying to suppress war, he said, would be like trying to suppress the processes of nature.

TABLE 16-1

NUMBER OF WARS IN THE 20TH CENTURY

	Duration of War in Years				
Cause of War	<1	1–5	5–10	>10	Ongoing
Civil war	4	7	2	6	10
Territorial	5	4	1	0	1
Ethnic/political	11	4	2	0	3
Independence	2	7	2	1	0
Total number of wars	22	22	7	7	14

In this century alone, over 80 million people have died as a direct result of war, 50 million of them during World War II. There have been at least 72 separate wars in this century, ranging from major world wars to isolated civil wars. That amounts, on the average, to a war about every year or so.

A content analysis of 20th-century wars reveals that most wars are civil wars (Table 16-1). In general, civil wars occur when rival political factions in the same nation come into overt conflict. Other causes for war are political/ethnic disputes, border/territorial disputes, and wars of independence. Quite a few of these wars lasted less than a year, but others lasted up to 10 years or are still going on.

Whether war is an inevitable part of human nature is a question beyond the scope of this chapter. Nevertheless, war has been a constant fact of human existence for several thousand years (McNeill, 1981). What is within the scope of this chapter are the underlying factors that contribute to the international conflict that so often results in war.

In this chapter we explore some of the underlying social psychological processes that come into play in international conflict. We also explore how these processes operate in conflict reduction and resolution. We ask, What forces contribute to international conflicts like the one between the Arabs and the Israelis or the one between the United States and Iraq that culminated in the 1991 Gulf War? What role is played by competition for scarce resources (such as land and oil) and by seemingly incompatible aspirations (such as territorial expansion and national sovereignty)? What about unequal power—how does it factor into conflict and violence between groups or nations? And what is the role of those cognitive biases we've found to be so prevalent in social interactions, such as stereotyping and in-group—out-group thinking?

Turning to conflict resolution, we also ask, How can cooperation be fostered in place of competition? How can parties to a conflict learn to see each other's points of view? And how can negotiation and third-party intervention best be used to support conflict resolution? These are some of the questions this chapter addresses.

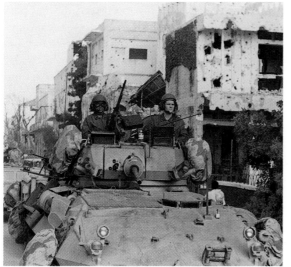

Images of war: An Assyrian war chariot with charioteer, a bas-relief from the palace of Assurbanipal in Nineveh, 7th century B.C.; U.S. Marines escorting a warlord to the signing of a peace agreement in Mogadishu, Somalia, December 1992; a Bosnian woman grieves at the grave of her son, killed in Sarajevo, October 1992.

THE NATURE OF CONFLICT

Although it is interesting to look at the number and duration of wars, such an analysis does not tell us much about underlying causes. War is usually the culmination of an escalating **conflict** between nations. On the most basic level, a conflict is simply a disagreement. It can be over social issues, beliefs and teachings (ideologies), or specific behaviors (Smith, 1987). More specifically, a conflict occurs when the aspirations and goals of two parties—in this case, nations—are incompatible or when two (or more) parties have divergent interests regarding a particular issue (Pruitt & Carnevale, 1982).

More often than not, a resolution to a conflict that satisfies one party does not satisfy the other. For example, the aspirations of the Jews to establish a homeland in Palestine clashed with the aspirations of the Palestinians already living in the region. The aspirations of the Jews were met (at least partially) when the United Nations voted to partition Palestine. Unfortunately, the aspirations of the Palestinians were subordinated. The friction that resulted led to a cycle of escalating conflict and war.

Many of the same principles that underlie interpersonal hostility and aggression (discussed in earlier chapters) apply to intergroup and

conflict A disagreement over social issues, beliefs and teachings (ideologies), or specific behaviors that occurs when the aspirations of two parties are incompatible or when two (or more) parties have divergent interests concerning the same issue.

international conflict. In-group–out-group thinking, stereotyping, and cognitive biases, for example, are at work in any of these situations. Racial tensions and violence in the United States have elements in common with ethnic conflict in other parts of the world. Because they have similar roots, they are also subject to similar remedies. In other words, the approaches to international conflict resolution described in this chapter may also be applied to domestic and smaller-scale situations.

But to focus only on the psychological underpinnings of conflict would not provide the full picture. Large-scale international conflicts arise from a combination of historical, cultural, and psychological forces. The Arab/Palestinian–Israeli conflict is rooted not only in current mutual perceptions and misperceptions but also in historical events. These events have shaped the attitudes, opinions, and behaviors of the conflicting parties.

The same is true of other long-lasting conflicts with deep historical roots. The conflict in Northern Ireland dates back to the 13th century, when Britain invaded and took over its smaller neighbor. Conflicts in the former Yugoslavia are rooted in differences among the Serbs, Muslims, and Croats who inhabit the area. Their history of conflict dates back almost a thousand years. Under Communist rule from the end of World War II to the early 1990s, these ethnic groups lived together quietly, sometimes even harmoniously, for 46 years. The Communist regime controlled ethnic conflict and violence with terror. When the Yugoslav "nation" broke up in the early 1990s, the ancient and terrible history of that region reasserted itself and a bloody civil war broke out.

Even though international conflict takes place on a wide stage, we shouldn't lose sight of its effect on individuals. Innocent citizens are nearly always victimized by large-scale violence and war. The citizens of Somalia, for example, were caught between warring political factions who prevented food from reaching starving people in the interior sections of the country. To gain some insight into how an individual's life might be disrupted by conflict and war, see the featured discussion "When War Becomes Personal." It is the story of a college student who put her career in journalism on hold to become a sniper in a conflict she never wanted.

THE ROOTS OF INTERNATIONAL CONFLICT

As noted earlier, international conflict has many causes—historical, economic, cultural, and ethnic. It also has social roots, involving how groups relate to one another, and cognitive roots, involving how people think about events in their social world. In this section we explore the social and cognitive roots of international conflict.

The Social Roots of Conflict: Competition Among Groups

One of the most common and enduring causes of conflict is competition among groups for limited resources, whether land, water, oil, or other nat-

"**S**trijela" is a sniper for Bosnian forces in Sarajevo. Her name means "Arrow" in English, and she is a 20-year-old former journalism student at Sarajevo University. Like just about all other college students, she never imagined that her future would include toting a high-powered rifle in an elite sniper corps. "I never thought that something like this could happen to me," says Arrow. "I never thought I could do what I'm doing" (Associated Press, July 1, 1992). However, something intervened to interrupt her chosen career: Her city of Sarajevo in Bosnia (formerly Yugoslavia) came under siege by Serbian troops.

After the disintegration of the Soviet Union, beginning in 1989 with the fall of the Berlin Wall, the "iron curtain" countries of Eastern Europe—those countries within the Soviet sphere of influence—began to experience a rise in nationalism. In Yugoslavia, nationalistic conflicts among Serbs, Bosnians, and Croats erupted into civil war. Initially, Arrow limited her war activities to participating in protests and marches. One day,

however, she witnessed a man jump from behind a building and fire on a group of unarmed protesters. At that moment she decided that she had to do something more.

That something was to volunteer to help defend her city. Arrow's father was a police officer, so she had grown up around guns. She had taken up target shooting as a hobby and become quite proficient with a rifle. Before the war began, she was hoping to compete on her national shooting team. Her shooting skills eventually landed her in the elite sniper unit as its only woman member.

In her role as sniper, Arrow has killed many enemy soldiers. She sometimes spends up to 12 hours choosing a target—usually a sniper for the other side. Arrow says she has lost count of the number of enemy soldiers she has killed, although she admits that

it's quite a few. Her commander, a 40-year-old businessman, reports that her kills are second only to his 67 kills.

Although she is good at her job, Arrow has mixed feelings about what she is doing. On the one hand, she sees defending her city as important. On the other hand, she is bothered by killing. She is unsure how it will affect her in years to come. She, along with her colleagues in the sniper corps, fears the emotional toll that their activities will have on them. But for the moment, they don't feel they have any choice.

Strijela is a "normal" woman who found herself in an insane circumstance. She abandoned, at least temporarily, her goal to become a journalist to defend her home. How do you think you would react if your home was threatened by an enemy? Would you do as Strijela did and become a sniper or fight in another way? What short-term and long-term effects do you think becoming a sniper would have on you?

ural resources. Whenever competition between groups arises, conflict is not far behind. Competition involves two or more groups striving for the same goal. In the course of competition, more often than not, the attainment of the goal by one group means the frustration of the other group's goals. Out of the dangerous mix of fulfillment of one group's goals at the expense of the other group's comes intensified hostility and ultimately conflict.

This was demonstrated dramatically in the 1991 conflict between Kuwait and Iraq. Iraq's goal was to control the oil fields on the Iraq–Kuwait border. Kuwait's goal was to continue pumping oil from those same fields. These goals were obviously incompatible. Iraq attempted to resolve the problem by invading and annexing Kuwait, satisfying its own goals but blocking Kuwait's. The continuing conflict soon escalated into violence and war.

The Robbers Cave Experiment   The relationship between competition and conflict was demonstrated in a classic study conducted by Muzafir Sherif and his co-workers (Sherif, Harvey, White, Hood, & Sherif, 1961). For this experiment, the researchers took two groups of 11- and 12-year-old boys who did not know one another to a summer camp in Oklahoma dubbed "Robbers Cave."

When the groups got to camp, phase 1 of the experiment began. The groups took up quarters far enough away from each other so that each was unaware of the other's existence. During phase 1 (the first week) of this naturalistic experiment, the boys, 11 in each group, did all the things that work to build group identity: wilderness tasks, pitching tents, group activities, and the like. Each group quickly built up a group identity. One group called themselves the "Rattlers"; they thought of themselves as pretty tough guys who knew a thing or two about fighting and using four-letter words. The second group, the "Eagles," were made of more sensitive stuff. They tended not to use four-letter words and instead enjoyed nude swimming.

At the end of the first week, both Rattlers and Eagles became aware that another group was on the campgrounds, and phase 2 of the experiment began. When Rattlers or Eagles knew that some other group had used the baseball field or the swimming hole, they were heard saying, "They better not be there when we get there."

Sherif and his colleagues then began a 5-day-long tournament for prizes between the stalwart Rattlers and the sensitive Eagles. The competition, which consisted of ball games, tugs of war, races, and other games, was ferocious. And as happens at sports events, particularly hockey games, fights broke out. The counselors had their hands full. At the end, the Eagles won the tournament. They received a much desired trophy, which was promptly stolen in a raid by the never-say-die Rattlers. The Eagles, who had no doubt learned a thing or two from the Rattlers, returned the favor with a commando raid of their own. This time weapons—sticks and bats—were part of the arsenal of combat.

In essence, Sherif created a conflict analogous to those we see in the world every day. Strong feelings of in-group solidarity were generated, and strong out-group hostility flowed as a natural consequence. Interestingly, as we see below, Sherif was also able to undo the conflict that he had created.

Elements of Conflict in the Robbers Cave Experiment   All the elements that usually lead to intergroup hostility were present by the end of the second week of the Robbers Cave experiment (Brown, 1986). First of all, *stereotypes* quickly emerged. Both groups thought of themselves as brave and tough, but the Eagles saw the Rattlers as "rotten cussers," and the Rattlers thought the Eagles were "smart alecks and crybabies."

Second, *ethnocentrism*—prizing the in-group much more than the out-group—develops in situations such as the Robbers Cave experiment. Sherif and Sherif (1973) conducted another study at a summer camp in Massachusetts. This study was a little different from the Robbers Cave study. During stage 1, the boys were all housed together and were allowed to make friends as they wished. For stage 2, the boys were divided into two

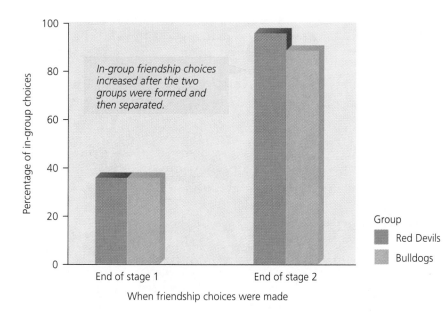

FIGURE 16-1 *In-group friendship choices for two groups in Sherif and Sherif's (1973) experiment. There were more in-group friendship choices at the end of stage 2 than at the end of stage 1. The researchers concluded that positive feelings toward the in-group and negative feelings toward the out-group developed, a hallmark of ethnocentrism.* Based on data from Sherif and Sherif, 1973.

groups (the Red Devils and the Bulldogs) and housed separately. Sherif and Sherif charted the friendship choices of boys at the end of stage 1 and stage 2. As shown in Figure 16-1, the percentage of friendships that came from the in-group was relatively low at the end of stage 1. (Note that these percentages represent choices of eventual in-group members because the two groups were not formed until after stage 1.) At the end of stage 2, after the separate groups were formed, friendship choices came almost exclusively from the in-group. Here we have an example of the development of in-group cohesiveness and the avoidance of out-group individuals, which is a central feature of ethnocentrism.

Third, the *perceived unfair distribution of rewards* or resources, a fundamental cause of group hostility, became a factor as soon as the Eagles won the trophy. Since both groups were engaging in in-group thinking and thus saw themselves as the better group, any distribution of rewards would be viewed as unfair by one group or the other. The thinking is, "If the trophy goes to another group, it must be unfair, since we're better, we're number one." In cases like this, the problem is not so much that one group doesn't get enough. It's that another group, a less deserving group, gets more. This perception of not doing well, or not getting one's share of the rewards, in comparison to others with whom you are in direct competition is called **relative deprivation.** The idea that competition for rewards leads to intergroup conflict is the central thesis of **realistic conflict theory.**

Does Competition Always Lead to Conflict? Although Sherif's research is widely cited as an example of how intergroup competition leads to conflict, there is evidence that such competition does not inevitably lead to conflict. Many groups compete with one another without significant hostility or conflict. Tyerman and Spencer (1983) conducted a study that was similar in many ways to Sherif's Robbers Cave study. Their study was

relative deprivation The perception of members of a group that they are not doing well in comparison with others with whom they are in direct competition.

realistic conflict theory A theory suggesting that intergroup conflict arises from competition for rewards.

Intergroup conflict can be exacerbated by a previous history of hostility and violence. When Yugoslavia unraveled, its ethnic populations brought out their memories, real and imagined, of past abuses at the hands of their neighbors. These Serbian soldiers, shown at a cafe in Sarajevo, represent just one of the warring groups.

conducted at a camp for scout troops. A major difference between the two studies was that Sherif's subjects did not know one another before the study and Tyerman and Spencer's subjects did know each other and were all members of scout troops.

Unlike Sherif, Tyerman and Spencer found that intergroup competition did not arouse significant hostility and conflict. This finding suggests that one factor affecting intergroup conflict is the prior relationship among the groups involved. Groups that have a positive prior relationship may be less likely to end up in conflict, and even if conflict does emerge, it may be easier to resolve.

Of course, if groups have a negative prior relationship, conflict may be inevitable and bloody when groups compete. This is what happened in the former Yugoslavia. When the "nation" broke up in the early 1990s, the Serbs, Muslims, and Croats all remembered bitter events from the past, such as ethnic violence during and after World War II. Each group had different and competing territorial aspirations. Each strongly distrusted the others; each was certain that the other groups were fierce, untrustworthy, and violent. When faced with the competing goals, aspirations, and perceptions of their neighbors, none of the ethnic groups could imagine cooperating with each other.

Social Traps When groups establish a competitive relationship, whether they are boys at camp or whole ethnic populations, they often get locked into a conflictual mode of dealing with each other that is difficult to escape. There are innumerable historical examples of this process, including the Israeli-Palestinian conflict. When groups find themselves in such a position, they have fallen into a **social trap** (Platt, 1973). A social trap occurs when "organizations or whole societies get themselves started in some di-

social trap A situation that occurs when groups (or individuals) in a competitive relationship get locked into a conflictual mode of dealing with each other that is difficult to escape.

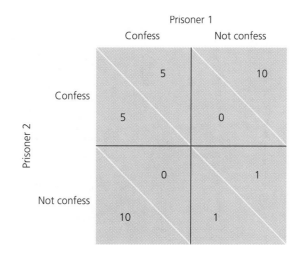

Prisoner 1

Confess   Not confess

Prisoner 2

Confess

5   10

5   0

Not confess

0   1

10   1

FIGURE 16-2 *The payoff matrix for a prisoner's dilemma game. The outcome of the game is influenced by whether players take a competitive approach—in which case one gets 10 years and the other gets off—or a cooperative approach—in which case both get either 5 years or 1 year. Once players begin the game with a particular approach, they tend to get locked in to that mode of thinking and find it difficult to change.*

rection or set of relations that later prove to be unpleasant or lethal and they see no easy way to back out of or avoid" (Platt, 1973, p. 641).

One form of social trap is the **prisoner's dilemma,** in which two parties can end up cooperating or competing with each other, depending on early moves in the scenario. A typical prisoner's dilemma scenario goes something like this: You and a friend commit a crime and are caught. Once in prison you are housed in separate cells. After a while you are offered a deal to turn state's evidence against your friend. You are told that you will be given a reduced sentence if you confess. However, your payoff depends on whether you alone confess or if both you and your friend confess. If you confess and your friend does not, you receive a suspended sentence (0 years in prison) and your friend receives a 10-year sentence. If you don't confess and your friend does, the outcome is reversed—you get 10 years, your friend gets off. If you both confess, you both receive the same sentence of 5 years. Finally, if neither of you confesses, you each receive a year. This typical *payoff matrix* for a prisoner's dilemma is shown in Figure 16-2.

What would you do in this situation? If you decide to confess, you can certainly cut your losses. At worst you end up with a 5-year sentence, and at best you go free. However, you may also condemn your friend to a 10-year sentence. On the other hand, if you remain silent and your friend confesses, you run the risk of ending up with a 10-year sentence.

In most cases, people react to situations like the prisoner's dilemma by getting locked into either a cooperative mode or a competitive mode (Platt, 1973). If the initial moves (during early trials in a prisoner's dilemma experiment) are cooperative, then individuals are likely to fall into the cooperative mode. But if the initial moves are contentious or uncooperative, the parties fall into the uncooperative mode (Platt, 1973). Once the parties in the game get locked into a particular mode, it is difficult to break out of it, not unlike the civil war in Bosnia or the behavior of the United States and the former Soviet Union in the early days of the nuclear arms race. In this latter example, both parties entered a competitive mode, attempting to build more missiles than the other side. Once locked into an uncooperative

prisoner's dilemma A form of social trap in which two parties or individuals may get locked into cooperation or competition depending on early moves in the scenario.

In their approach to resources, human beings tend to think of short-term personal gain rather than the long-term good of whole populations. The result is a degraded environment that threatens the viability of the entire planet. More responsible approaches stress cooperation rather than competition.

mode, the two parties were unlikely to become cooperative with each other later.

To understand another kind of social trap, imagine this scenario: You are living in a small rural town back in the 1700s. In the center of town there is a commons, a large grassy pasture of a fixed size that you and other farmers use to graze your herds. All of you share the resources provided by the commons. Because your livelihood depends on how many cattle you can raise, you graze as many cattle as possible. The other farmers also need to make a living, so, like you, they graze as many cattle as possible. After a while, you begin to notice that the commons is getting worn out, the grass thin and the soil depleted. The commons is overpopulated; it simply cannot support that many cattle. Although you and the other farmers thought you were improving your lot, you all lose in the end.

This scenario is known as the **commons dilemma** (Hardin, 1968). In a situation where individuals or groups compete for limited resources, two conflicting needs must be balanced. Each individual farmer wants to maximize his outcomes by grazing as many cattle as possible. However, steps taken to maximize individual gains often come at the expense of the good of the larger group. As each individual or group falls deeper and deeper into protecting his or her self-interest, conflict becomes more likely and cooperation less likely.

This effect is also illustrated in the nuts game, a simple game that simulates the commons dilemma (Edney, 1979). In this game, subjects sit around a large plastic bowl. An experimenter places 10 nuts (the kind you get at a hardware store) in the bowl and explains that the point is to end up with as many nuts as possible at the end of the game. Any person can take as many nuts as he or she wishes at any time during a trial. The catch is that the experimenter will double the number of nuts in the bowl every 10 seconds. Subjects can maximize the number of nuts they end up with by waiting until the number has doubled several times. So cooperation—waiting until the number has doubled—maximizes the rewards each player

commons dilemma A social trap in which individuals or groups compete for limited resources and two conflicting needs must be balanced: the needs of each individual to maximize his or her outcomes and the good of the larger group.

gets, and competition—taking nuts sooner—leads to lower individual reward. What did subjects do? Sixty-five percent of the groups tested in this study never reached the first doubling. Instead, subjects grabbed as many nuts as possible as soon as the game began.

Platt's theory of social traps focuses on the role of reinforcement and punishment for various types of behavior. There are, of course, reinforcers for short-term, personal goal-directed behavior. For example, you may benefit by adding cattle to your herd or by grabbing as many nuts as you can. The cost of this behavior is that resources will be depleted and all will suffer (Brewer & Kramer, 1986). There are also reinforcers for longer-term, group-oriented behaviors. Although individuals may not gain as much in the short term, resources will be maintained and all will ultimately benefit.

Social traps often occur when long-term and short-term reinforcements come into conflict. Resources, such as grass in the commons, nuts in the bowl, oil, water, clean air, and access to public lands, become depleted when individual or group needs are placed above the needs of the larger population. Unfortunately, people commonly place short-term, personal gains ahead of long-term, group-oriented gains (Platt, 1973).

Both the prisoner's dilemma and the commons dilemma represent models of conflict situations. People or groups have a choice of acting competitively or cooperatively, of thinking of their own needs or the needs of the larger population, of acting for short-term gain or long-term benefit. Once individuals or groups become competitive and focused on short-term gains, it is difficult for them to change directions and spontaneously become cooperative. Instead, they get locked into mutually destructive social traps.

Many conflicts in the world arise over the apportionment of resources among populations. As we saw in the models just described, parties in a conflict over limited resources rarely cooperate to maximize resources across groups. Whenever humans compete for limited resources, they tend to try to get as much as possible for themselves, regardless of how it affects others. For example, there is a great deal of friction between the "haves" and the "have-nots" (with respect to oil resources) in the Middle East. Currently, there is an unequal apportionment scheme operating. Those countries that sit atop large oil reserves, such as Kuwait and Saudi Arabia, have become tremendously wealthy. Countries not sitting on large oil reserves, like Jordan, become poorer and poorer. Few tears were shed by the have-nots in the Middle East when Iraq invaded Kuwait in 1990. Some analysts have suggested an equal apportionment of oil revenues among all Arab peoples as a way of reducing tensions in the area.

The Role of Power in Conflict Situations The distribution of wealth is not the only factor that influences conflict. In many instances, conflict is maintained because one side has more power than the other. That side can force its will on the other. We see this in the Israeli–Palestinian conflict, where the Israelis have far more military power than the Palestinians; we also see it in Northern Ireland, where the British have more power than the Irish.

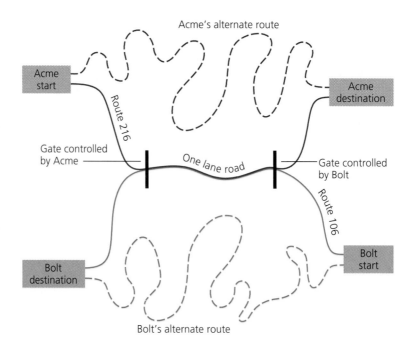

FIGURE 16-3 *Routes available to players in the trucking-company game. Players could use their own long, circuitous routes unimpeded but had to take turns using the direct central route. In different conditions, one or the other player had a gate with which to control this route, or both had gates, or neither had gates. Researchers were interested in which condition promoted the most cooperation and resulted in the most profits for the players.* From Deutsch and Krauss, 1960.

The importance of power in conflict situations was shown in a classic study involving a power game (Deutsch & Krauss, 1960). Each subject was in control of a trucking company. The goal of the game was to make as much money as possible within a specific period of time by trucking goods. To move goods, the trucks could use one of two routes (Figure 16-3). Each trucking company had available a route that it could use unimpeded. This route was long, however, and using it cost money. There was also a direct route (the central route shown in Figure 16-3) that took less time. But this route could be used by only one truck at a time.

The power relationship between the players was manipulated by providing one side, both sides, or neither side with a gate that could be closed to block the direct route. If only one player had a gate, that player could prevent the other from using the direct route, but the second player could not do the same. If both had gates, both could cut off access to the direct route.

The principal measure of cooperation/conflict was the amount of money made by each side. The researchers found that cooperation was most likely to occur when neither side was provided with a gate (Figure 16-4). When only one side was provided with a gate, that player tended to use the gate to his or her advantage (and to the disadvantage of the other). When both sides had a gate, cooperation was least likely—and profits were lowest.

We can say, by extension, that two comparably armed nations will be least likely to cooperate. For example, during the nearly 50-year-long "cold war" between the United States and the former Soviet Union, cooperation was minimal between the two nations on many issues, because they both had huge nuclear arsenals (analogous to the gates used in the study just de-

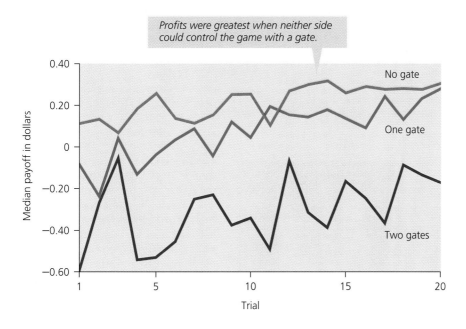

Profits were greatest when neither side could control the game with a gate.

FIGURE 16-4 *Profits in the trucking-company game. Cooperation and profits were greatest when neither side had the option of controlling the route with a gate. Cooperation and profits were lowest when both sides had a gate. These results support the idea that mutual disarmament is most likely to lead to cooperation.* From Deutsch and Krauss, 1962.

scribed). We can also say that not having a weapon may be a good thing, especially if the other side lacks one as well. Perhaps one way to deal with serious international conflict is to disarm both sides, which may encourage cooperation rather than conflict.

Conflicting Aspirations and International Conflict Groups may have more than conflicting needs for resources like land and water. They may also have conflicting aspirations, goals, and ideals. For example, one way to understand how the Israeli–Palestinian conflict started and how it is maintained is to look at the differing aspirations and interests of the parties involved. According to a model developed by Pruitt and Rubin (1986), conflict occurs when the parties involved perceive that their interests are widely divergent or mutually exclusive. In this case, both the Israelis and the Palestinians want to control the same 8,000-square-mile patch of land—two mutually exclusive aspirations.

An important variable influencing conflict situations is the *rigidity* of each party's aspirations (Pruitt & Rubin, 1986). When the aspirations of the parties involved are very rigid and unchangeable, the resulting conflict will be difficult to resolve. According to Pruitt and Rubin, there are two major sources of rigidity, both having to do with the values underlying the aspirations. One is the importance of the values, their centrality to the group's belief system. In the Middle East, underlying values include religious beliefs and a strongly felt need for security, both of which are very important to the contending sides. The other is a perception of the underlying values in terms of "either-or" categories. Either-or perceptions mean that each side sees the struggle as a **zero-sum game,** in which what one side wins, the other loses, and vice versa. The Israelis, for example, have tended to see the

zero-sum game A type of game or conflict in which a win for one side means a loss for the other.

The conflict in the Middle East involves two cultures whose deeply rooted religious and cultural beliefs make compromise difficult, if not impossible. But surprisingly, the two sides have some remarkable similarities. Both groups have incidents of martyrdom at the center of their tradition, and both have developed a kind of siege mentality in relation to the rest of the world. Both groups see themselves as downtrodden victims as well as protectors of holy traditions. The psyche and culture of both groups, nurtured and reinforced over hundreds of years, make it hard for each side to understand the other. Instead, high levels of mistrust, hostility, and tension are maintained and reinforced.

The Jewish psyche is permanently imprinted with images of persecution and martyrdom. In the first century A.D., for example, 1,000 Jewish Zealots held out against Roman legions for three years at Masada, a mountaintop fortress. When they saw that capture was inevitable, they took their own lives rather than surrender. In this century, 56,000 lightly armed Jews held off Nazi troops for 3 months before the Warsaw Ghetto was liquidated during World War II. Twenty thousand

Masada, the mountaintop fortress where 1,000 Jewish Zealots held out against the Romans for 3 years. The Zealots' martyrdom is imprinted on the psyche of Jews.

Jews were killed in street fighting, and 36,000 were captured and sent to their death in the gas chambers.

But the Jews aren't the only group with a siege mentality. The Shias, who make up about 11% of Muslims living in Arab nations, have a world view that presupposes unjust persecution as a cos-

mological given. The Shias perceive themselves as an elite sect unto themselves. They see themselves as the party of opposition and the defenders of the oppressed. They see the Israelis as invaders requiring a defensive response. This world view fueled the 8-year Iran–Iraq war of the 1980s. It also helps maintain the Arab–Israeli conflict, and it makes Iran (which is over 90% Shia) identify with underdog causes in the Middle East and around the world (such as in Bosnia).

The Shia world view dates back to the seventh century A.D., to events that occurred soon after the prophet Muhammad's death in A.D. 632. The first four caliphs (leaders) to succeed Muhammad arose from among his close companions. Many felt that the fourth caliph, Ali, the prophet's son-in-law, should have directly succeeded the prophet. However, that position was taken by Yazid, from the clan of the Ummayads. A growing number of disenchanted Muslims began viewing Yazid and the other Ummayad as usurpers, and they encouraged Hussain, Ali's son and the prophet's grandson, to challenge Yazid. Hussain, seeing his support growing, publicly declared himself a contender for caliph and came

security of their nation as an either-or proposition: Israel could be secure only if the Palestinians were denied a homeland on the West Bank. The establishment of a Palestinian homeland there was seen as undermining that value.

If we consider the Palestinian–Israeli conflict, we see that both sides have extremely rigid aspirations, based on highly important values. Israelis believe their nation must remain a Jewish homeland and haven. Palestinians believe they have the right to a Palestinian state on the same land claimed by Israel. The Jews were offered the possibility of a Jewish state in Uganda in the 1930s, and they turned it down. Similarly, the

into direct conflict with Yazid, who dispatched an army to stop him.

The forces of Hussain and Yazid met on the plains of Kerbala, Iraq, in A.D. 680. Most of Hussain's initial supporters, on seeing Yazid's well-equipped army, quickly abandoned him and his cause, and his remaining followers died violent deaths on the battlefield. Yazid then delivered an ultimatum to Hussain, ordering him to disclaim the leadership of Islam. Hussain refused, preferring to die for his cause and the protection of his people. The accompanying painting shows Hussain's final days, his body riddled with arrows, when most of his followers had died and the remaining women and children were about to be enslaved and dragged to Yazid's prison in Damascus.

The confrontation between Yazid and Hussain gave rise to a schism that persists to this day in Islam between the Shias and the Sunnis. Hussain's advocates (shown as masked figures at the top of the painting and decapitated bodies at the bottom) have come to be known as Shias; those who backed Yazid (shown at the top left in the painting) came to be known as Sunnis. The Shias believe that Hussain, in choosing

confrontation against numerical, tactical, and military odds, did so for ideological reasons centering on the idea that "to compromise with evil is to perpetrate it."

A painting depicting the martyrdom of the Imam Hussain. Hussain's martyrdom is an integral part of the Shia Muslim psyche.

The Shia psyche has been shaped by Hussain's unjust and violent death. To this day, passion plays are presented in Shia communities on the anniversary of Hussain's death, vividly reenacting his last valiant battle, the massacre of his relatives, and the enslavement of his women and children. The images associated with Hussain and their meaning make the Shias stoic in their belief that they must defend Islam from such infidel invaders as the Israelis.

Because of their belief systems, neither side in the Arab–Israeli conflict is likely to compromise

significantly. Shia Arabs may never come to accept Israel's right to exist, even if a Palestinian homeland is established. Similarly, ultranationalistic Jews may never come to accept a Palestinian homeland on land they see as part of greater Israel. And even if extremists on both sides are in a minority, it takes but one, or a handful, of these individuals to add fuel to the conflict, as did Baruch Goldstein in his 1994 attack on Muslims worshiping in a mosque. The volatile mix of religious, cultural, and nationalistic fervor feeds intransigence and makes prospects for peace in the region dim at best.

---

*B*oth the Israelis and the Arabs have a siege mentality rooted in important historical and religious events that shape each group's view of the world. Can you think of how similar roots of intransigence apply to other conflicts occurring around the world? How could a conflict based on such grounds be dealt with effectively? Do you think that it would be possible to change the siege mentality of parties to conflicts? If so, how?

We would like to thank Dr. Mohammed Fazel for contributing most of this material.

Palestinians cannot accept a Palestine on any land other than Palestine itself (Fazel, 1991). The homeland, then, for both sides, must be in Palestine.

For both sides, too, the aspirations are based on either-or values. If there is an Israeli state, there cannot be a Palestinian state, and if there is a Palestinian state, there cannot be an Israeli state. When aspirations are couched in these terms, a "win" for one side (having one's aspirations met) means a "loss" (not having one's aspirations met) for the other. For a closer look at this conflict, see the featured discussion "The Dynamics of Intransigence."

The Cognitive and Perceptual Roots of International Conflict

Negative stereotypes—one important cognitive mediator of intergroup conflict—tend to be "invisible" until brought to conscious awareness. The Walt Disney Company was surprised when some Arab American groups complained that the film Aladdin *was racist and offensive. In response, Disney edited the lyrics of the song "Arabian Nights" (although the word "barbaric" was retained). What other stereotypes do you recognize in a character like Jaafar?*

Although the social forces underlying conflict are powerful, they do not give us a complete picture of why conflicts begin and how they are maintained. To get a more complete understanding of conflict, we must consider how cognitive and perceptual factors operate to support conflict. We have seen throughout this book that the way we think about our social world profoundly affects how we feel and behave in response. We have also seen that, as powerful as our minds our, we are naturally disposed to a number of serious biases and errors. In this section we consider how these errors come into play in international conflict.

Stereotyping the Enemy   One important cognitive mediator of conflict is stereotyping. Recall from Chapter 5 that a stereotype is a rigid categorization, an oversimplified, internalized image, of a group of people. Stereotyping individuals involves ascribing characteristics to them based on our notions about the group to which they belong. Stereotypes have a powerful influence on how we perceive, judge, and behave toward others.

Generally, the beliefs and stereotypes that groups hold about each other play an important part in intergroup conflict. Beliefs may be held with varying amounts of confidence, of course, but some beliefs can be imbued with so much confidence that they come to be held as factual (Bar-Tal & Geva, 1986). So, if the parties in an international conflict have strong beliefs about each other, those beliefs may take on the value of fact, even if they are based largely on inferences.

There is no doubt that Arabs and Jews living in the Middle East hold negative stereotypes of each other (Shipler, 1986). Israeli Jews see Arabs as fearsome warriors who are capable of bold actions; as violent, unpredictable, and untrustworthy; and, paradoxically, as cowardly. Arabs see Jews in much the same terms. Jews are perceived as brutal, violent, aggressive, and remorseless. Most of the stereotypes are developed and supported by a network of rumor as well as by publications for both children and adults (Shipler, 1986). They persist despite (or because of) the fact that most Arabs and Jews who hold them have never had real contact with members of the other group. Some of these notions are so deeply ingrained that the stereotypical Arab and Jew play roles in the nightmares of the other group (Bilu, 1989).

cognitive discrepancy A condition that occurs when each group develops totally opposite explanations for the causes of a conflict.

Cognitive Discrepancy   Another cognitive factor in international conflict is **cognitive discrepancy** (Bar-Tal & Geva, 1986). Cognitive discrepancy occurs when each group develops totally opposite explanations for the causes of the conflict. The Israelis believe that the Arabs are responsible for the Arab–Israeli conflict and develop a whole set of cognitions in support of that belief (land is needed to guarantee security, the Arabs attacked Israel several times, and so on).

For their part, the Arabs perceive that the Israelis are responsible for the conflict and generate a set of cognitions to support that perception (the Israelis took Arab land, the Israelis violate the human rights of Palestinians, and so on). These discrepant cognitions help maintain the conflict at high levels. The net result of discrepancy is that each side accepts only its set of beliefs as valid, while completely rejecting the beliefs of the other side (Bar-Tal & Geva, 1986).

Misperception in Conflict Situations   Often, misperception is at the heart of intergroup conflict. Ralph White (1968), for example, points out that mutual misperceptions were key factors in World Wars I and II and the Vietnam War. White has identified six forms of misperception that can contribute to the escalation of conflict into wars:

1. *The diabolical-enemy image.* Each side sees the other as having dubious character, as being, in fact, diabolical.
2. *The virile self-image.* Each side sees "backing down" as an affront to its own power and honor, so it must take a "firm stand" against the other side.
3. *The moral self-image.* Each side sees itself as morally upright, while the other side is evil. This is the converse of the diabolical-enemy image. Often, both sides believe that God is on their side.
4. *Selective inattention.* Each side in a conflict selectively ignores important aspects of the conflict, perhaps paying attention to a single potential outcome.
5. *Absence of empathy.* In the throes of conflict, each side ignores the perspectives and needs of the other side. The parties to the conflict cannot see things from the other side's point of view.
6. *Military overconfidence.* In the midst of conflict the fear generated may give rise to overconfidence in one's ability to "teach the other side a lesson" (White, 1968, p. 11). Assumptions made based on this misperception may lead to excessive risk taking and escalation of conflict.

These misperceptions clearly occurred during the 1991 Gulf War between Iraq and the U.S.-led coalition of nations. Each side characterized the other as the embodiment of evil. President Bush even proclaimed Hussein a worse despot than Adolph Hitler (a gross exaggeration). Each side placed great value in not backing down. We heard catch phrases like "we are drawing a line in the sand" and "this aggression will not stand." Of course, each side invoked God to justify its actions. And neither side was particularly good at stopping and evaluating the escalating conflict from the other side's point of view.

Eventually, according to White, such misperceptions lead to escalation and large-scale military conflicts. Beyond the six misperceptions

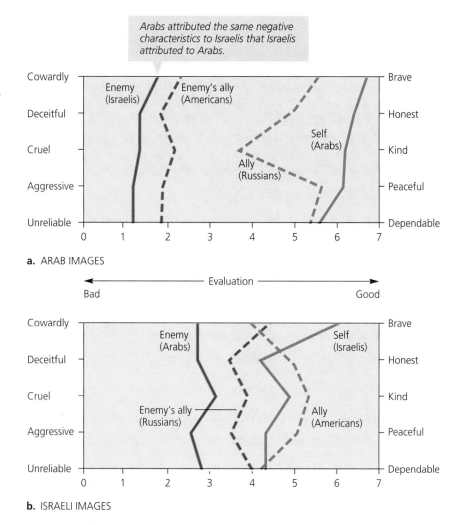

FIGURE 16-5 *Mirror-image perceptions of Israelis and Arabs. Both groups saw their adversaries and themselves in similar terms, although the Arabs had more intensely negative views of the Israelis than the Israelis had of the Arabs.*

From Haque and Lawson, 1980.

Arabs attributed the same negative characteristics to Israelis that Israelis attributed to Arabs.

a. ARAB IMAGES

Evaluation
Bad ← → Good

b. ISRAELI IMAGES

described by White, another harmful misperception helps maintain and escalate conflict—mirror-image perceptions. We consider this special type of misperception next.

Mirror-Image Perceptions The mutual perceptions of conflicting parties are often **mirror-image perceptions** of each other. That is, each side sees the other in essentially the same negative ways. In one study, 50 Arabs (who were direct parties to the Arab–Israeli conflict) and 50 Israelis were asked to rate themselves and members of the out-group on several dimensions (for example, cowardly–brave, deceitful–honest) (Haque & Lawson, 1980). They found that both Arabs and Israelis rated their own groups on the positive ends of the bipolar dimensions. For example, as shown in Figure 16-5, Arabs saw themselves as brave, honest, and kind and Israelis as cowardly, deceitful, and cruel. The opposite pattern emerged for Israelis; they saw themselves as brave and kind and the Arabs as cowardly and deceitful. Each side saw the other as having the same objectionable qualities, although Arab perceptions were stronger than Israeli perceptions. As Figure

mirror-image perceptions A mode of perception in which each side sees the other in essentially the same negative way.

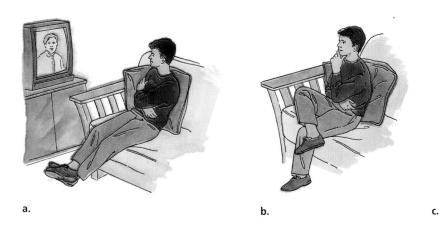

a.   b.   c.

16-5 shows, the Arabs rated the Israelis considerably more harshly than the Israelis rated the Arabs.

The Freezing of Perceptions The inflexible stance of the two sides in a conflict can be understood in the light of these cognitive aspects of conflict: accepting one's beliefs as factual, cognitive discrepancy, general patterns of misperception, and mirror imaging. Each group accepts its own beliefs as true and unchanging while rejecting the other group's beliefs and assuming that members of the out-group have objectionable qualities. Perceptions and beliefs thus become frozen (Bar-Tal & Geva, 1986).

Three consequences flow from the freezing of beliefs (Bar-Tal & Geva, 1986). First, through **biased selection of information,** each group has the tendency to pay attention to only those facts that are consistent with their belief structure, which further reinforces the belief structure. One-sided news reporting is an example of biased selection. Second, members of each group distort facts through a process of **biased interpretation.** Members of each group interpret events and facts in a manner consistent with their own beliefs. They see aggression committed by their group as more justified than aggression committed by members of the out-group (Crabb, 1989). Israelis may bomb guerrilla camps to prevent random violence against Israeli citizens; Arabs attack Israelis to stop further bombing raids. The cycle is repeated endlessly.

Third, through **biased elaboration,** the highly selected and distorted information is incorporated into an existing cognitive framework. Additional assumptions about the other group may arise out of such a process, and these are eventually elevated to the status of fact (Figure 16-6) (Bar-Tal & Geva, 1986).

CONFLICT RESOLUTION

Clearly, intergroup (or international) conflict is a complex phenomenon. Given its complexity, we cannot expect to arrive at a single prescription that

FIGURE 16-6 *Once beliefs become frozen, group members pay attention only to facts consistent with their existing belief structures — biased selection of information (a). Group members distort facts to make them conform to their belief structures — biased interpretation (b). And they incorporate this selected and distorted information into their existing cognitive framework — biased elaboration (c).*

biased selection of information A freezing of perception in which each group pays attention to only those facts that are consistent with their belief structure, further reinforcing that belief structure.

biased interpretation A mode of thinking in which members of each group interpret events and facts in a manner consistent with their own beliefs and see aggression committed by their group as more justified than aggression committed by members of the other group.

biased elaboration A cognitive mechanism in which group members carefully select and distort information so that it can be easily incorporated into an existing cognitive framework.

would be effective in resolving all conflicts. Instead, we can begin to understand the dynamics of conflict resolution by looking back at the underlying causes of a given conflict and targeting those forces that support and maintain the conflict. In this section we consider, one by one, the factors discussed in the previous section that contribute to conflict in the first place, and we show some ways each of those factors can be addressed to reduce the likelihood that conflict will continue and escalate.

Intergroup Cooperation

Competition, as we have seen, can be a powerful determinant of intergroup conflict. It makes sense, then, that if we can bring conflicting groups together in a cooperative effort, conflict can be reduced. After all, nothing unites people like a common crisis.

There is evidence that intergroup cooperation can foster positive feelings between conflicting groups. In the third phase of the Robbers Cave study, Sherif investigated the impact on intergroup conflict of a **superordinate goal,** the attainment of which is mutually beneficial to groups in conflict. Sherif and his colleagues created a series of "crises" that the Eagles and Rattlers had to work together to solve. One crisis involved a threat to the camp's water supply. The boys were told that the camp's water supply came from a single water tank and that a problem had developed somewhere in the water system. The boys had to find the source of the problem so that it could be repaired. Sherif found that providing such superordinate goals led to a reduction in intergroup hostility, providing evidence for the cooperation–conflict reduction link.

Although cooperation may be effective in reducing conflict in some situations, however, it is certainly not a magic solution. Sherif (1958) reported that the cooperation had only a temporary diminishing effect on the hostile feelings generated by the intergroup conflict. Once the crisis was solved and the boys returned to their normal day-to-day routine, the conflict returned. Once again, we have a parallel to the Israeli–Palestinian conflict. Despite the fact that an agreement was reached in 1994 between Yitzak Rabin, the Israeli prime minister, and Yasser Arafat, leader of the Palestine Liberation Organization, hostilities continued between Israelis and Palestinians on the West Bank and the Gaza Strip. Negotiations and a handshake cannot undo years of enmity between groups.

Further, the outcome of a cooperative effort is important. If there is a successful outcome, then cooperation may breed intergroup liking. However, if the cooperative effort fails, conflict may increase, as each group begins to attribute blame to the other side. The conflict not only persists but may become even stronger, because negative stereotypes of the out-group have been reinforced. When peace talks fail, even bloodier conflicts may ensue.

Power Restoration

superordinate goal A goal that is mutually beneficial to groups in conflict.

Power relationships have been found to play an important role in escalating conflict (recall the "trucking company" experiment). Conflict often arises

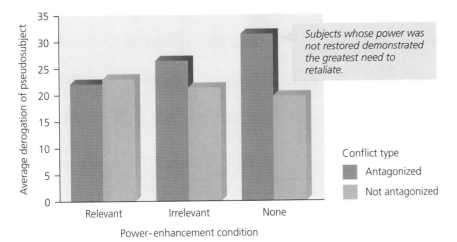

FIGURE 16-7 *The effect of power restoration on conflict. When subjects had their power reduced by antagonistic comments and then had it restored in a relevant manner, they were less inclined to lash out at their supposed antagonist when given the opportunity. Subjects were most likely to retaliate when there was no power restoration.* From data in Fagenson and Cooper, 1987.

because one party feels that its power has been diminished or threatened by the other side (Fagenson & Cooper, 1987). The Palestinians, for example, undoubtedly feel relatively impotent in the face of Israeli military power. According to the **power-restoration theory** (Fagenson & Cooper, 1987; Worchel, 1961), power reduction leads to conflict and aggression. The side whose power is reduced feels that it is under siege by the other side. The theory suggests that if power can be restored, conflict will be reduced.

In an experiment to test the ability of power restoration to reduce conflict, subjects were either antagonized by another "subject" or not antagonized (Fagenson & Cooper, 1987). The other subject was actually a "pseudosubject" whose criticism of the real subject's work was prerecorded. The criticism represented power reduction. After the antagonization manipulation, subjects were subjected to one of three power-restoration schemes: relevant power restoration (restoring the subject's power relative to the pseudosubject), no power restoration, or irrelevant power restoration. The main measure in this experiment was the degree to which the real subject downgraded work supposedly produced by the pseudosubject.

As shown in Figure 16-7, the results of this experiment generally support the power-restoration theory. Antagonization was not crucial when subjects were subjected to relevant power restoration. Having their power restored removed the subjects' need to belittle the pseudosubject. On the other hand, when no power restoration was experienced, subjects degraded the pseudosubject in an attempt to restore their own power.

Understanding Aspirations: The Dual-Concern Model

We saw earlier that conflicting aspirations are often a factor in intergroup conflict. Pruitt and Rubin (1986) have proposed the **dual-concern model** to identify the forces that maintain conflict and those that can lead to the resolution of conflict. According to this model, each side in a conflict has concerns that it feels are important (Pruitt & Rubin, 1986). If one side attempts to resolve a conflict while thinking only of its own concerns, that

power-restoration theory A theory suggesting that power reduction leads to conflict and aggression, and that restoring the balance of power between parties can reduce conflict.

dual-concern model A model that identifies the forces that maintain conflict and those that can lead to the resolution of conflict. According to this model, each side in a conflict has concerns that it feels are important and that must be considered in any attempt at conflict resolution.

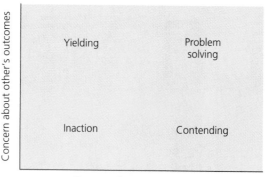

FIGURE 16-8 *The four responses to conflict described by the dual-concern model. The responses result from varying levels of concern about one's own outcome and the outcome for the other party. High concern for the outcome of both parties leads to problem solving, which is the most desirable approach.* From Pruitt and Rubin, 1986.

side is said to be *contending,* adhering to its own aspirations while trying to get the other side to yield (Pruitt & Rubin, 1986). When each side takes into account the other's aspirations, the sides are said to be *problem solving.* Problem solving is the preferred approach because it is more likely to produce a solution that is acceptable to both sides.

The dual-concern model also identifies two other responses to conflict: inaction and yielding. When the parties to a conflict do nothing, they have chosen *inaction.* Of course, this does nothing to resolve the conflict because neither side is taking any steps to deal with it. Ultimately, inaction is detrimental to both sides. A conflict can also be dealt with by *yielding.* That is, one or both sides in a conflict can give in. If one side gives in—its aspirations are totally ignored—and the other does not—its aspirations are completely satisfied—then there is the potential for future conflict. The party that gave in under pressure (political and/or military, for example) will feel that it received the short end of the stick and be dissatisfied. Yielding is usually difficult for either side because each side has invested so much time and energy in the conflict (Pruitt & Rubin, 1986). The relationships between the concerns of each party in a conflict and the four responses are shown in Figure 16-8.

Problem Solving and Achieving Integrative Solutions The preferred approach to conflict resolution, according to the dual-concern model, is problem solving. Let's take a closer look at this process.

According to Pruitt and Rubin, problem solving has three potential outcomes. When each side agrees to give a little and accepts that all of its aspirations cannot be met, *compromise* occurs. Each side settles for a little less than it hoped for originally. Although compromise sounds like a reasonable solution, it may leave residual resentments, especially if one side or the other has had to compromise its values.

A second outcome of problem solving is *agreement on a procedure for deciding who will win.* This outcome involves both parties sitting down and deciding which side will have its aspirations met and which side will not. This type of problem solving may follow armed conflict when one side has "defeated" the other. After the Gulf War, for example, the U.S.-led coalition sat down with the defeated Iraqis to settle on conditions to officially end

The United Nations met in 1990 to try to resolve the Persian Gulf crisis before it escalated into an armed conflict, but a diplomatic solution could not be reached. Later, the U.N. imposed harsh cease-fire conditions on Iraq. Integrative solutions are difficult to achieve when the atmosphere is confrontational, as it was before the war, or punitive, as it was afterwards.

the war. This form of problem solving amounted to little more than a statement of terms that the Iraqis had to accept. Later, the United Nations formalized these terms in a set of harsh conditions that had to be met before a permanent cease fire could go into effect. Iraq reluctantly accepted all those conditions. Although this strategy may have produced a settlement, the seeds of conflict are still there, ready to germinate again when and if Iraq regains its military power.

The third and most desirable outcome of problem solving is an **integrative solution** to a conflict. In this kind of solution, the aspirations of both sides are reconciled and blended to produce a result that integrates the needs of both sides and produces joint benefits (Pruitt & Carnevale, 1982). In some cases it is possible to reach completely integrative solutions, where the aspirations of both sides are met. In many other cases, however, only a partially integrative solution is possible, leaving each side with a little less than it hoped for, or a compromise.

Real-world conflicts are hard to resolve. Too often the parties become rigid, contentious, and hostile—a combination more likely to lead to escalation than to resolution. But there are systematic ways to approach conflict resolution. Pruitt and Rubin (1986) suggest the following four steps as a way to move toward problem solving:

Step 1. The sides should determine if there is actually a conflict of concerns and aspirations. Mutual misperceptions and misbeliefs may lead to the illusion that there is greater conflict than actually exists.

Step 2. Each side should analyze its own aspirations and interests and set them at a reasonably high level. The parties should be prepared to stick to those aspirations. This strategy will be most effective in conflicts that are low or moderate in intensity.

Step 3. The sides should search for an integrative solution that will reconcile their aspirations.

Step 4. If an agreement cannot be reached based on the aspiration levels set in Step 2 and problem-solving attempts in Step 3, each side should be prepared to lower its aspirations and concede some (lower priority) issues.

integrative solution The most desirable solution to a conflict in which the aspirations of both parties are reconciled and blended to produce a result that integrates the needs of both sides and produces joint benefits.

Pruitt and Rubin maintain that conflicting groups should strongly consider problem solving as a way to resolve the conflict. Problem solving is desirable for several reasons. First, in conflicts where each side has strong aspirations based on deeply held values (such as in the Palestinian–Israeli conflict), neither side is likely to yield. For example, despite the peace talks between the Israelis and the Palestine Liberation Organization, the Israelis, operating from a position of military strength, are still reluctant to withdraw completely from the West Bank. On the other hand, the Palestinians (despite being at a disadvantage) have shown an equally strong unwillingness to yield to the Israelis. They see any early gains in the area of self-rule as a step toward an eventual Palestinian homeland in the West Bank and the Gaza Strip. In this situation the only way out of the conflict is to find a solution that takes into account the concerns and aspirations of both parties. One potential solution some have suggested would be for Palestinians to control all internal functions of the disputed territories (police functions, schools, etc.) while Israel, at least for, say, 5 years, controls external affairs.

Second, integrative solutions, because they are mutually agreed on and benefit both sides, tend to be more stable than those based on a one-sided strategy such as yielding. Third, integrative solutions can strengthen positive feelings through the cooperative efforts needed to reach an integrative solution. Finally, problem solving leads to wider benefits for the entire community. There may be a "peace benefit," for example; that is, resources previously spent on the tools of conflict (tanks, planes, guns) are redirected to supporting social programs (food, housing, education).

Pruitt and Carnevale (1982) suggest that integrative solutions often involve each side giving up the idea that it will get *exactly* what it wants. For example, the Palestinians may have to give up on the idea of an independent homeland covering the entire West Bank, while the Israelis may have to give up on the idea of making the West Bank a permanent part of greater Israel. Additionally, achieving an integrative solution may involve working within the framework of any alternatives already proposed. For example, the Israelis and the Palestinians might be wise to follow the framework for an agreement worked out by Rabin and Arafat. However, they should be careful not to become overly focused on existing alternatives, as this could cause them to become locked into a single mode of thought, lose perspective, and miss potentially creative solutions. If existing frameworks are not adequate, then new alternatives may have to be developed and considered (Pruitt & Carnevale, 1982).

Types of Integrative Solutions   Pruitt and Carnevale (1982) have identified four types of integrative solutions. The first type involves *cost cutting*. A solution is found that cuts the losses of the party on the short end of the stick. In many instances, one party (party A) gets more out of a solution than another (party B). By cutting B's losses, while maintaining A's needs, an integrative solution becomes more likely. Party B may express several concerns over such a solution: It may feel that it is setting a precedent of weakness for future negotiations, or it may think the solution weakens its

The meeting of Anwar Sadat, Jimmy Carter, and Menachem Begin at Camp David in 1978 provides an example of the integrative solution known as bridging. Once security concerns were identified as primary issues for both the Egyptians and the Israelis, the United States bridged the concern by guaranteeing the security of both sides.

image. Pruitt and Carnevale suggest that for the problem of precedent setting, any solutions should be decoupled from future actions. That is, it should be made clear that any concessions are a one-shot deal. For the problem of image, Pruitt and Carnevale suggest several strategies, including issuing disclaimers, diminishing the significance of the concessions, or pointing out that the solution was involuntary.

A second type of integrative solution involves one side offering the other *compensation* for any losses. For example, Israel has expressed an interest in keeping the Golan Heights, captured from Syria during the 1967 war. Syria has demanded the return of the Golan Heights. One possible integrative solution is for Israel to offer compensation to the Syrians for any part of the Golan Heights retained. This is an example of specific compensation because the compensation is relevant to the central issues of a dispute. Other forms of compensation are *homologous indirect compensation* and *substitute compensation* (Pruitt & Carnevale, 1982). In homologous indirect compensation, offers are made that are not related directly to the dispute. For example, Israel could offer to destroy some of its weapons of mass destruction in return for keeping the Golan Heights. Substitute compensation involves decoupling elements of the dispute from the compensation. For example, the United States could offer Syria economic aid in exchange for giving up the Golan Heights. Regardless of the compensation scheme adopted, trust is an important commodity. Each side must trust the other to carry out its ends of the compensation agreement.

The third type of integrative solution is *bridging*, in which a new alternative is proposed that meets the needs of both parties. For bridging to work, the core issue of a conflict must be identified. Once this has been done, a solution can be offered that satisfies both parties' needs in that area. A good example of bridging occurred during the Camp David peace talks between President Jimmy Carter, President Anwar Sadat of Egypt, and Prime Minister Menachem Begin of Israel. A prime concern to both sides was security. The United States bridged this concern by offering security guarantees to both sides.

The fourth type of integrative solution is *logrolling*. In most cases, conflicts involve multiple issues. Each party may not be willing to make concessions on all issues. In logrolling, one party makes a concession on one issue and the other party makes a concession on another.

Although these four integrative solutions can be clearly described, it is not easy to implement them in real conflict situations. In many conflicts, issues become intertwined or linked with each other or with outside issues or concerns (Pruitt & Carnevale, 1982). For example, the Israelis' claim to the West Bank is rooted not just in a desire for more living space but also in their reverence for that parcel of land as the center of their religion and the fact that portions of the West Bank have large underground water supplies. Of course, the Palestinians have similar feelings about the same land. In order to reach an integrative solution, issues must be unlinked from each other and from other issues and clearly identified. Unfortunately, in the real world, this is often nearly impossible to accomplish.

Solving Conflicts with Negotiation

In order to implement any steps toward problem solving, the parties involved in a conflict must begin some process of working together. Often this involves some kind of formal **negotiation.** During negotiation sessions, information is exchanged, views are laid on the table, positions are clarified, and solutions are proposed. Each side presents its demands or proposals for evaluation by the other side, which in turn presents counterdemands or counterproposals. Negotiation is thus a sequential process (Rubin & Brown, 1975).

Getting the Parties to Negotiate Although negotiation is commonly believed to be a good way to deal with conflict, several issues must be dealt with before it can occur. For example, how do you get the parties together to negotiate? Should the parties negotiate directly, or should a third party intervene?

History tells us that when parties are involved in a highly intense conflict, it may be difficult to even get them to sit down together to negotiate. Often, each side sets preconditions that must be met before any negotiations can take place. For example, in the months leading up to the Gulf War, the United States and Iraq could not even agree on a date for a meeting to try to head off the war. The United States and North Vietnam argued for a year over the shape of the table to be placed in the negotiation room.

Although these preconditions may seem trivial, they have critical meaning. The argument over the shape of the table had to do with who would be present at the negotiations. The arguing of the Israelis and the Arabs was equally crucial. Israelis wanted face-to-face negotiations with individual Arab nations because such an arrangement would signify that the opposing side "recognizes" the state of Israel. Arab nations have been unwilling to make this diplomatic gesture for the past 45 years. The Arabs wanted a large, joint conference because they believed the strength of their

negotiation A method of conflict resolution in which parties meet to exchange information, give views, clarify positions, and propose solutions.

Seemingly insoluble conflicts can sometimes be resolved through the actions of an epistemic authority, a person who breaks through frozen perceptions and offers people a new vision of how things might be. Sadat was such a figure in the Middle East, as Gandhi was in India. By offering a new model—nonviolence—Gandhi inspired and powered India's movement for independence from Great Britain. Gandhi is shown here in 1946 with his eventual successor, Jawaharlal Nehru.

numbers would force Israel to make concessions that Israel would not agree to in individual negotiations.

All is not lost, however. A deadlock may be broken by the emergence of an *epistemic authority,* an individual who can influence others to modify their beliefs and perceptions (Bar-Tal & Geva, 1986). Such an authority figure can actually force others to unfreeze their counterproductive beliefs and perceptions about the other party. We might consider the late Egyptian leader Anwar Sadat such an authority figure. At a time of seemingly insoluble conflict between Egypt and Israel, Sadat made a bold move: He offered to go to Israel to meet with Israeli leaders in an effort to resolve the conflict. Through his actions, more so than his words, he forced Israelis and Egyptians to change the way they viewed each other. Of course, President Sadat was assassinated by Arabs who did not wish to resolve the conflict with Israel this way.

The Role of Communication One of the functions of negotiation is to get the parties to communicate. We might assume that if the parties to a conflict can just start talking, they will be able to work out a solution. However, both history and social psychological research show us that communication by itself may not be enough to ensure successful conflict resolution. Research has shown clearly that merely allowing conflicting parties to communicate does not help resolve conflict (Deutsch & Krauss, 1962). In fact, it may even heighten conflict. If both parties enter into the communicative effort with the same old misperceptions and ideas about each other, any communication attempt may break down into a blustering display of mutual blame.

This was graphically illustrated in a Cable News Network (CNN) roundtable discussion involving two Israeli government officials and two

Palestinian representatives. The "discussion" eventually broke down into finger pointing and defensive posturing. It ended with the "moderator" saying she was glad she would not be involved in real negotiations with the two sides. Of course, real negotiations take place in private; these Israeli and Arab representatives may have felt compelled to strongly defend their side on television.

For communication between disputants to be beneficial, the message must be worded carefully and presented repeatedly. Research has shown that a message stressing the interdependence and mutual interests of parties in conflict (in a prisoner's dilemma game) can effectively reduce hostile feelings and lead to productive interpersonal behavior (Lindskold, Han, & Betz, 1986). A message that repeats old negative themes, such as blaming and hostility, is counterproductive. Rephrasing and repeating a conciliatory message increases the perceived credibility and trustworthiness of the individual giving the message and shifts the emphasis of the disputants from an individualistic orientation (gain as much as possible) to a more cooperative one (Lindskold et al., 1986).

Communication may also be beneficial if it is directed by a third party. Research shows that when conflicting parties are given instructions on how to effectively communicate by a third party, communication effectively decreases conflict (Deutsch & Krauss, 1960). Third-party intervention is discussed in detail later in this chapter.

GRIT: Graduated and Reciprocal Initiatives in Tension Reduction

Although negotiation and communication are important techniques in reducing conflict, sometimes a conciliatory gesture by one side can be an effective impetus to conflict resolution (Lindskold et al., 1986). If one side makes a unilateral move, the other side often reciprocates. As you recall from Chapter 8, the norm of reciprocity is a powerful determinant of social behavior: If you do something nice for me, I feel compelled to reciprocate by doing something nice for you. This norm forms the basis for a conflict-resolution technique known as **graduated and reciprocal initiatives in tension reduction,** or GRIT (Osgood, 1962).

The first step in the GRIT program is a unilateral move of conciliation by one side. In an arms race situation, for example, one side might make a unilateral decision to reduce its arsenal. A unilateral move is made with no preconditions and with no prior negotiation (Lindskold, 1986). This is basically what former President Gorbachev of the Soviet Union did in 1989 when he announced a unilateral withdrawal of Soviet forces from Eastern Europe. The side making the conciliatory move hopes that the other side will reciprocate and begin a cycle of conflict de-escalation.

Although GRIT sounds simple (make a concession and wait for reciprocation), certain conditions must be met for the tactic to work. GRIT begins with one side announcing its intention to begin reducing tensions and presenting a statement of the benefits for the other side. Each unilateral step is announced in advance and identified as part of a general strategy.

graduated and reciprocal initiatives in tension reduction (GRIT) A conflict-reduction technique that involves one side making a unilateral concession and hoping that the other side will reciprocate; it uses the norm of reciprocity as its basis.

Lindskold (1986) has outlined ten important points relating to the GRIT conflict resolution strategy; they are summarized here:

1. To establish a conciliatory atmosphere, one party should announce that it will take unilateral steps to reduce tension. The statement should point out the advantages to the other party of reciprocating the opening move.
2. Each unilateral step should be announced in advance and clearly identified as a step in the general tension-reduction strategy.
3. Each step should be accompanied by a statement urging the other party to reciprocate.
4. Each announced step should be carried out, regardless of reciprocity from the other party.
5. Steps taken to reduce tension should be continued for a long period of time, even if not reciprocated. This keeps the pressure on the other party to reciprocate.
6. Each step taken should be clear and easily verified.
7. Each unilateral step should involve some risk, but no steps should be so risky that they hamper the party's ability to retaliate for an attack by the other side.
8. The party making the unilateral moves must be willing to retaliate for any attack from the opponent.
9. Successive steps taken should involve increasing risk. That is, when the other party reciprocates, the side initiating GRIT should make the next step riskier than the one before.
10. Unilateral moves should be tailored to specific aspects of the conflict. For example, a promise of medical supplies might be tied to withdrawal of forces from some specified military installation. Other moves could be targeted at other concessions from the other side.

Points 1 through 3 in the GRIT strategy help to enlist international support for the unilateral moves and put pressure on the other side to reciprocate. Points 4 through 6 establish the credibility of the initiator of GRIT by showing the general public that it is willing to follow through on a creative initiative. Establishing credibility is essential, especially in a conflict where there is mutual mistrust. For example, the reaction of the United States to the initial announcements of the Soviets was one of suspicion. Gorbachev's moves were at first perceived as a propaganda ploy to drive a wedge among NATO allies.

The final four points establish that the parties are willing to take action in case of a violation of the unwritten GRIT agreement to de-escalate. This ensures the security of each side.

The goal of GRIT is to modify the behavior of the disputants involved in a conflict. Each side is rewarded through reciprocated conciliatory gestures (Lindskold, 1986). Failure to reciprocate is met with punishment in the form of withdrawal of the conciliatory offer. Through a process of reinforcement and punishment, GRIT brings about behavior change.

On the surface, the GRIT strategy sounds like a good idea. But does it work? A review of three sources of evidence—real-world uses of GRIT, laboratory simulation studies of GRIT, and experimental games using GRIT—indicated that in general, GRIT can be an effective strategy for reducing conflict (Lindskold, 1986). It is effective especially if the conflicting parties are of relatively equal strength so that each side has the power to reinforce or punish the other side for positive or negative responses to GRIT moves. However, a strategy involving repeating and rephrasing a conciliatory message within a GRIT strategic framework proves superior to GRIT alone (Lindskold, Han, & Betz, 1986). In other words, if parties send conciliatory messages frequently and in different forms, conflict resolution is enhanced.

Third-Party Intervention

In many conflict situations, especially intense ones, the disputants often cannot find a way to settle their differences, even if they truly want to (Pruitt & Rubin, 1986). In an atmosphere of high tensions, unilateral moves such as those called for in GRIT are unlikely. Note that Soviet gestures toward the United States did not occur at the height of cold war tensions with the United States. Instead, they took place during a time of de-escalating conflict and decreasing tension. GRIT is also unlikely to be used in a conflict where one side is much stronger than the other, as in the Israeli–Palestinian conflict. The stronger side has no reason to make a unilateral move. The weaker side, if it makes a conciliatory gesture, may be seen as weakened further by the gesture.

When the parties to a conflict cannot work out their differences through straight negotiation, **third-party intervention** can sometimes help resolve a conflict. In third-party intervention, an individual not involved in the conflict (e.g., a diplomat) agrees to act as a "go-between" for the conflicting parties. The agreement between the Israelis and Yasser Arafat was mediated by such a third party, a diplomat from Norway. The third party is likely to change the relationship between the conflicting parties for the better by helping to break unproductive, negative cycles of mutually hostile behavior.

A third party can serve in any number of roles (Pruitt & Rubin, 1986). He or she can play an informal role by acting as an *intermediary* between conflicting parties. An intermediary serves as a conduit, a neutral line, for the exchange of ideas early in the conflict-resolution process. A third party can also serve a more formal role by acting as a *mediator* or an *arbitrator*. A mediator, like an intermediary, fosters communication between the conflicting parties. In this formal role, however, the mediator may actually make proposals and urge the parties to the dispute to consider compromise. However, the mediator has no power to impose a solution. In contrast, an arbitrator has the power to impose a solution. Typically, the arbitrator listens to both sides and then arrives at a binding decision.

Different kinds of third parties seem to be preferred in different situations (Heuer & Penrod, 1986). In cases of intense conflict, disputants seem to prefer a third party who will play a directive role but still leave some control with them (Heuer & Penrod, 1986). When the conflicting parties are locked into a situation where neither side can make reciprocal concessions,

third-party intervention A conflict-resolution technique in which an individual not involved in the conflict agrees to act as a go-between for the conflicting parties.

the disputants seem to prefer arbitration (where the third party has the power to impose a solution). However, when the conflicting parties see that compromise is possible, they prefer mediation. Finally, when an integrative solution to the conflict is possible, negotiation (no third party) is preferred.

A third party can affect the outcome of conflict resolution either prior to intervention or during intervention (Johnson & Tullar, 1972). We consider these two effects next.

Anticipated Third-Party Intervention   Does the prospect of third-party intervention move groups in conflict toward a solution? The answer to this question is complex. Some research shows that when faced with the prospect of arbitration—intervention in which a solution will be imposed—disputants are more likely to settle their differences on their own (Johnson & Pruitt, 1972). But other research has found that anticipated arbitration lengthens the conflict-resolution process and leads to more deadlocks than anticipated mediation does (Breaugh, Klimoski, & Shapiro, 1980). The prospect of arbitration may cause each side to "dig in its heels" and establish a firm position in preparation for the intervention process.

Anticipation of third-party intervention can also cause the disputants considerable anxiety, especially if they have a strong need to "save face." They are going to have to believe or show that they have gained many of their objectives in negotiation or else they will lose credibility with their groups. Indeed, in some parts of the world, losing credibility means that someone may kill you. It has often been speculated that the reluctance of Yasser Arafat to enter into negotiations for many years stems from the very real threat of assassination by his own side if he were to do so. This is another way that anticipation of intervention may have a counterproductive rather than a productive effect.

Actual Third-Party Intervention   Researchers have identified three possible ways in which third-party intervention can influence the course of conflict resolution: by modifying the physical/social setting, by modifying the issue structure, and by modifying the disputants' motivation to reach an agreement (Pruitt & Rubin, 1986).

Modifying the Physical/Social Setting   A third party can structure the negotiation situation in such a way that conflict resolution becomes easier. For example, the third party can help by structuring communication between the disputants (Pruitt & Rubin, 1986). Open communication is essential to conflict resolution, but it must be handled correctly. Recall that simply allowing conflicting parties to communicate will not reduce conflict (Deutsch & Krauss, 1960). In cases of intense conflict the third party can separate the disputants, not allowing direct communication, and serve as a conduit for ideas and proposals. In addition, the third party can educate each side on effective ways of communicating (Pruitt & Rubin, 1986).

A third party can also affect negotiations by modifying two other important aspects of the negotiation situation: site openness and the time frame for negotiations (Pruitt & Rubin, 1986). *Site openness* refers to the degree to which the negotiations will be public. The best strategy may be to have the site closed during the early stages of conflict resolution when proposals and counterproposals are being made (Pruitt & Rubin, 1986). The disputants can then put out their proposals without making a public commitment to them. Once a public commitment is made, it is difficult to back away from a proposal without losing face. Later, when agreement has been reached, the site can be opened.

Imposing time limits may help the conflicting parties to move toward settlement (Pruitt & Johnson, 1970). However, time pressure can be a double-edged sword. If the disputants enter the negotiations with a strong individualistic orientation, that is, with the intention of gaining as much as possible for their own side, time pressure reduces the chances of finding an integrative solution to the conflict (Carnevale & Lawler, 1986). Conversely, if the disputants enter negotiations with a more cooperative attitude, time pressure may increase cooperation and foster integrative solutions (Carnevale & Lawler, 1986). Third parties would do well to analyze the aspirations of both sides, along with their motives, before applying time pressure.

Finally, a third party can structure the social setting by providing additional resources for the disputants (Pruitt & Rubin, 1986). The third party can use his or her resources to compensate each of the parties for any concessions made or to reward each of the parties for concessions. For example, former President Jimmy Carter promised both Israel and Egypt military and economic aid, as well as a guarantee of security, for concessions made at Camp David.

Modifying the Issue Structure Third parties can also determine how issues will be discussed. For example, issues might be handled separately and sequentially. In the case of the Israelis and the Arabs, they could try first to settle border disputes, then discuss arms control, and so on, until all issues have been settled. Another way to structure the issues is by considering all issues together as a package. Generally, considering issues together as a package produces better solutions than considering them separately, unless the conflict is very intense. In this case, issues may have to be separated (Pruitt & Rubin, 1986). The third party can also break issues into more manageable clusters and introduce subordinate goals for the disputants to consider (Pruitt & Rubin, 1986).

Modifying the Disputants' Motivation to Reach an Agreement A third party can increase the disputants' motivation to reach a settlement by encouraging concessions within an atmosphere that prevents either side from losing face. The third party can "take responsibility" for concessions. In effect, the disputants can emerge from negotiations by pointing to the third party as a source of compromise, thus saving face. At the same time, the third party can foster trust between the disputants by having each side make a small concession that is irreversible (Pruitt & Rubin, 1986). Often a small initial concession made by one party leads to a reciprocal concession made by the other party.

Can there be peace in the Middle East? The courageous acts of Rabin and Arafat, like those of Sadat and Begin before them, offered hope that the complex and difficult conflict between Israelis and Arabs would some day be resolved.

Third-Party Intervention: Summing Up   A review of the literature suggests that three broad generalizations can be made about third-party interventions (Rubin, 1980):

1. A third party can bring about concessions without the conflicting parties losing face. This leads to a faster, more effective solution to the conflict.
2. Third-party intervention is most effective when the intensity of the conflict is low. When the conflict is very intense, third-party intervention may not be effective and may even impede progress toward conflict resolution.
3. In some cases, conflicting parties want to—and can—work out their own problems and see third parties as intrusive and unwelcomed.

THE ISRAELI–PALESTINIAN CONFLICT REVISITED

The ongoing conflict between the Israelis and the Palestinians is the quintessential intergroup conflict. It has all the ingredients that make conflicts so difficult to resolve. Although the sides have much in common, social and cognitive forces conspired to keep them from living in peace.

The two groups, first of all, are in competition for the same small plot of land. The aspirations of the Israelis for a homeland have been met, but those of the Palestinians have been thwarted. The Israelis see a Palestinian homeland on the West Bank and the Gaza Strip as a threat to their security. Both sides have become ensnared in a classic social trap.

The unequal power relationship between the two sides has also contributed to the continuation of the conflict. The Israelis prevail in confrontation after confrontation because of their superior military, but the Palestinians battle on with the passion of the underdog. Historically, the Israelis have had little motivation to make significant concessions to the Palestinians. Even the most recent peace overtures turn a very small portion of the occupied territories over to Palestinian rule.

Although the two sides in this conflict have been engaged in negotiations, they have not been able to work out their problems on their own. The few successful moves toward peace have come about as the result of third-party intervention. In 1977 U.S. President Jimmy Carter helped formalize the agreement between Egypt and Israel that was initiated by Egyptian President Anwar Sadat, resulting in the Camp David Accord. In 1994 a Norwegian diplomat brought Israel and the Palestine Liberation Organization together, and the agreement was again formalized with U.S. help.

It would appear that a comprehensive settlement in the Middle East is going to be very difficult to achieve. Given the religious and cultural beliefs of the two groups, the best we may be able to hope for is a reduction of tension over time and a gradual acceptance by both sides of the benefits of cooperation.

CHAPTER REVIEW

1. *What is conflict?*
   On a basic level, a **conflict** is a disagreement among parties. On a deeper level, a conflict occurs when two parties are competing for resources, when the aspirations and goals of two parties are incompatible, or when two (or more) parties have divergent interests regarding a particular issue. Conflict between nations often escalates into war. In the 20th century alone there have been at least 72 wars (about one every year).

2. *What are some of the social factors that lead to conflict?*
   Social psychologists have investigated the factors that contribute to large-scale international conflict. Key among the causes is competition among groups. When one group's aspirations are met, and another's are not, conflict is likely to occur. The classic Robbers Cave experiments conducted by Sherif and his colleagues point out how easily competition can lead to conflict. In such situations stereotypes emerge, "ethnocentrism" develops, and groups begin to evaluate their own gains against the gains of the "enemy." When members of one group perceive that they are receiving fewer rewards than they deserve relative to another group, they experience **relative deprivation.** The general idea

that competition for rewards underlies intergroup conflict is the central thesis of **realistic conflict theory.**

However, intergroup competition does not always lead to conflict. If members of different groups have a positive relationship prior to competition, then competition does not necessarily lead to conflict. Of course, if there is an initially negative relationship between groups, then conflict is likely.

3. *What is a social trap?*
   A **social trap** occurs when two (or more) parties get started in some direction that proves to be unpleasant or lethal and cannot easily avoid or back out of that course of action. Simulation games like the **prisoner's dilemma** game illustrate how starting on a competitive course leads to conflict. Another social trap, the **commons dilemma,** shows that conflict can arise when parties compete for limited resources.

4. *What role does power play in conflict?*
   Conflict can be exacerbated when power is misused in the conflict. Classic research shows that stalemates often occur when both parties in a conflict have the power to control each other's outcomes.

5. *What role do conflicting aspirations play in conflicts?*
   Conflicting aspirations often underlie conflicts between groups. When one group's aspirations can be met only by depriving another group of reaching its aspirations, conflict is likely. This either-or situation is known as a **zero-sum game,** where the gains of one side mean that the other side loses. Conflicts become particularly difficult when the aspirations of the parties are rigid. This is precisely the case in the relationship between the Israelis and the Palestinians.

6. *What are some of the cognitive underpinnings of international conflict?*
   Several cognitive factors contribute to the maintenance of international conflicts. First, there is a tendency to stereotype the enemy in a conflict situation. These stereotypes have a powerful influence on how the other side is perceived and judged. Second, **cognitive discrepancy** occurs when each group develops totally opposite explanations for the causes of the conflict. Each side blames the other for the conflict and develops a whole set of cognitions to support its view of the conflict.

   A host of perceptual distortions also occur in conflict situations. These include the diabolical-enemy image, the virile self-image, the moral self-image, selective inattention, absence of empathy, and military overconfidence. Enemies often have **mirror-image perceptions** of each other. Each side sees the other in essentially the same, negative ways.

   Another perceptual phenomenon that occurs in conflict situations is the freezing of perceptions. Each side comes to accept its version as factual; perceptions become frozen and resistant to change. Three consequences flow from the freezing of perceptions and beliefs: **biased selection of information** (each group pays attention to only those facts that are consistent with their belief structure, further reinforcing the belief structure), **biased interpretation** of events (each group interprets events and facts in a manner consistent with their own beliefs), and **biased elaboration** (highly selected and distorted information is incorporated into an existing cognitive framework).

7. *How can conflicts be reduced through intergroup cooperation?*
Fostering cooperation among groups reduces tension and conflict. If the parties in a conflict have a **superordinate goal** that they can both work toward, conflict will be reduced. This was demonstrated in Sherif's Robbers Cave experiment. Unfortunately, the goodwill between groups was short lived. Once the emergency was resolved, the conflict returned. The outcome of the joint effort is important. A successful outcome is more likely to reduce conflict than a failed outcome.

8. *What can be done in conflicts where there is an imbalance of power?*
When one side has power and the other does not, conflict is likely to continue. One approach to this aspect of conflict is **power-restoration theory,** which suggests that power reduction leads to conflict and aggression. The side whose power is reduced feels that it is under siege by the other side. If power can be restored, conflict will be reduced. Generally, there is research evidence that power restoration helps reduce conflict.

9. *What about the problem of competing aspirations?*
According to the **dual-concern model,** each side in a conflict has concerns and aspirations that it feels are important. According to this model, conflict reduction depends on how the two sides respond to each other's concerns. If one side tries to solve the conflict without considering the other side's concerns, it is contending. On the other hand, when each side takes into account the other side's concerns and aspirations, the sides are using problem solving, which is preferred over contending because it is more likely to lead to a solution agreeable to both sides. Two other responses to conflict within this model are inaction and yielding, neither of which is an effective way to resolve conflict.

According to the dual-concern model, problem solving is the preferred method of conflict resolution because it is most likely to lead to an **integrative solution,** which involves reconciling and blending aspirations to produce a result that integrates the needs of both sides and produces joint benefits. This outcome of problem solving will lead to a lasting solution because the aspirations of each side have been addressed and met. Two other outcomes of problem solving are *compromise,* which occurs when each side agrees to give a little and accepts that not all aspirations can be met, and *agreement on a procedure for deciding who will win.* This outcome involves both parties sitting down and deciding which side will have its aspirations met and which side will not.

10. *What kinds of integrative solutions have been identified?*
Four types of integrative solutions have been identified. First, cost cutting involves finding a solution that cuts the losses of the weaker party, making an integrative solution more likely. Second, one side can offer

the other compensation for its losses. Third, bridging involves proposing a new alternative that meets the needs of both parties. For bridging to work, the core issue of a conflict must be identified so that an integrative solution can be found. Fourth, logrolling can be used when a conflict involves multiple issues. One party makes a concession on one issue, and the other party makes a concession on another. Unfortunately, these four types of integrative solutions have proven difficult to apply in real-life conflict situations.

11. *Can't conflicting parties work out their own problems through negotiation?*
Negotiation is a popular method for resolving conflicts. Negotiation occurs when the parties sit down and exchange information, lay views on the table, clarify positions, and offer solutions. Unfortunately, as history teaches us, it is difficult to even get conflicting parties to the negotiating table. Once at the table the parties begin to communicate. However, just sitting down and talking is usually not effective and may even increase conflict. This is true if the parties stick to old misperceptions and ideas about each other. For communication between disputants to be beneficial, the message must be worded carefully and presented repeatedly. Research has shown that a message stressing the interdependence and mutual interests of parties in conflict can effectively reduce hostile feelings and lead to productive interpersonal behavior.

12. *What is the GRIT strategy?*
GRIT is a conflict-reduction technique that is based on the norm of reciprocity. It involves several steps, beginning with one party making a clear, unambiguous unilateral concession with no preconditions. The other side is encouraged to reciprocate. After the initial move and reciprocal move by the opponent, more concessions are made. Tensions are reduced gradually in a stepwise fashion. Generally, GRIT has been found (in laboratory simulations) to be an effective way to reduce conflict.

13. *How can an outside party help resolve a conflict?*
In some conflict situations, especially intense ones, the parties may not be able to work out a solution on their own. In this case, **third-party intervention** can be helpful. A third party can serve as an *intermediary* (a conduit for information and ideas), a *mediator* (who serves as a conduit for information and ideas, but also proposes solutions and urges the parties to consider compromise), or an *arbitrator* (who has the power to impose a solution). The nature of the dispute may influence the type of third-party intervention preferred by disputants, with arbitration favored when the disputants are unable or unwilling to make reciprocal concessions. The mere anticipation of third-party intervention may affect the likelihood of a settlement being found. However, it is not clear whether it will increase or decrease the likelihood of a settlement. Third parties can help disputants reach a settlement by modifying the physical/social setting, regulating site openness, setting a time frame for negotiations, modifying the structure of the issue, and increasing motivations for reaching a settlement.

SUGGESTIONS FOR FURTHER READING

Cole, J. R. I., & Keddie, N. R. (Eds.). (1986). *Shi'ism and social protest.* New Haven, CT: Yale University Press.

This book provides an excellent overview of the role of Shi'ism in world politics and conflict. In addition to a presentation of the history of Shi'ism presented, the role of the Shias in current world events is also covered. Sections of the book speak directly to the Israeli–Arab conflict.

Edney, J. J. (1979). The nuts game: A concise commons dilemma analog. *Environmental Psychology and Nonverbal Behavior, 3,* 252–254.

In this short article, Edney describes the "nuts game," which simulates the commons dilemma. The nuts game is easy to execute, and it might be fun to try out the game for yourself and relate your results to principles discussed in this chapter. You might want to try variations on Edney's game. For example, have groups play the game with one person designated as the "nut taker," and see what happens.

Shipler, D. K. (1986). *Arab and Jew: Wounded spirits in a promised land.* New York: Times Books.

This is an excellent, highly readable source concerning the history of the Israeli–Arab conflict. Shipler explores the social, cognitive, and perceptual factors that underlie the conflict between the Arabs and the Israelis.

Worchel, S., & Austin, W. G. (1986). *Psychology of intergroup relations.* Chicago: Nelson Hall.

This edited text provides a wide range of chapters written by experts in their respective fields. Chapters cover the forces that underlie and maintain conflict, as well as ideas on how conflict can be reduced.

Glossary

abnormal conditions theory The theory that suggests people are more likely to want to find out what caused a behavior when there is a difference between what they expected and what actually happened.

accommodation process The process of interacting in such a way that, despite conflict, the relationship is maintained and enhanced.

actor–observer bias The tendency for actors to prefer external attributions for their own behavior, especially if the outcomes are bad, whereas observers tend to make internal attributions for the same behavior of others.

agentic state A psychological state an individual enters when he or she feels no responsibility for any outcome of an obedience situation, thus becoming an agent of the authority figure.

aggression Any behavior that is intended to inflict harm (whether psychological or physical) on another organism or object.

aggressive script A form of script (an internalized representation of an event) that leads to increased aggression and a tendency to interpret social interactions aggressively.

altruism A type of behavior that helps a person in need and is motivated purely by the desire to help the other person.

altruistic personality A cluster of personality traits, including empathy, that predisposes a select few individuals to great acts of helping.

antecedent conditions Personality and other background factors that increase the likelihood that a person will obey the orders of an authority figure.

attack campaigning An approach to political persuasion that focuses on destroying an opponent's credibility rather than on conveying one's own plans and programs.

attitude "A mental and neural state of readiness, organized through experience, exerting a directive and dynamic influence upon the individual's response to all objects and situations with which it is related."

attitude structure The interconnected components that make up an attitude. These include thoughts, feelings, behavioral intentions, and behaviors related to the object of the attitude.

attitude survey A self-report measure in which a respondent indicates his or her attitude by answering a series of questions on a questionnaire or over the phone.

attribution The process of assigning causes for behavior.

augmentation principle A rule applied by perceivers under conditions of limited information that leads them to increase the importance of a potential cause of an event.

authoritarian personality A personality type characterized by submissive feelings toward authority, by rigid, unchangeable beliefs, and by racism and sexism.

authoritarian submission A personality measure of trust in authority.

authorization The abandonment by an individual of normal moral guidelines in favor of guidelines set forth by an authority figure; a factor in destructive obedience.

autobiographical memory Memory for information relating to the self.

automatic processing The formation of impressions without much thought or attention. Much of our social perception involves automatic processing.

automatic vigilance A type of processing in which people automatically turn their attention to a negative or dangerous stimulus.

autonomous altruism A form of selfless altruism that society does not support and might even discourage.

badge value An upfront statement about who a person is or would like others to think he or she is.

balance theory A theory that looks at relationships from the point of view of the individuals experiencing them. A balanced relationship, which is rewarding to both partners, occurs when one individual and another have the same interests and views.

biased elaboration A cognitive mechanism in which group members carefully select and distort information so that it can be easily incorporated into an existing cognitive framework.

biased interpretation A mode of thinking in which members of each group interpret events and facts in a manner consistent with their own beliefs and see aggression committed by their group as more justified than aggression committed by members of the other group.

biased selection of information A freezing of perception in which each group pays attention to only those facts that are consistent with their belief structure, further reinforcing that belief structure.

binding factors   Factors that bind an individual to an authority figure in an obedience situation.

burnout   A psychological condition in which energy and motivation are sapped.

bystander effect   The finding that helping behavior is less likely to occur as the number of bystanders (witnesses to an emergency) increases.

categorization   The process by which we classify items, objects, or concepts, placing them together in groupings on the basis of their similarities with each other.

category-based expectancies   Expectancies that lead us to assume that members of a particular category of people will behave in similar and consistent ways.

central route processing   A form of information processing in which the listener relies on the information itself to make a decision, using preexisting ideas and beliefs to create a context for the message.

classical conditioning   A learning process in which a neutral stimulus is paired with a stimulus that causes a reflex response so that the neutral stimulus comes to evoke that response on its own.

cognitive discrepancy   A condition that occurs when each group develops totally opposite explanations for the causes of a conflict.

cognitive dissonance   An unpleasant state of arousal resulting from conflicts among a person's attitudes or between attitudes and behavior.

cognitive miser   This label can be applied when a person uses the least effortful means of processing social information.

cognitive narrowing   A strategy used by subjects in Milgram's experiments in which they ignore the screams of the victim and focus attention on the task of pulling the switches, allowing for the reduction of tension inherent in the obedience situation.

cohesiveness   The strength of the relationships that link the members of a group.

compliance   The modification of behavior in response to a direct request even though the person making the request has no power to enforce compliance.

compromise memory   Memory distortion that occurs when a person blends new information encountered after witnessing an event with information that is already in memory.

confirmation bias   The tendency to seek information that verifies existing explanations for the cause of an event.

conformity   A change in behavior that occurs in response to real or imagined pressure from others.

consensus seeking   A tendency that leads groups to become more concerned with maintaining morale and getting everybody to agree than with the quality of the group decision.

contact hypothesis   The hypothesis that contact between groups will reduce hostility when the participants have equal status and a mutual goal.

contingency model   A theory of leadership suggesting effective leadership is dependent on the interaction between the leader's personality characteristics and the qualities of the group situation.

control group   The group of subjects in an experiment that does *not* receive the experimental treatment.

controlled processing   The formation of impressions with conscious awareness, attention to the thinking process, and effort.

coping mechanisms   Mechanisms that help individuals lessen and manage both the causes and the effects of stress.

coping style   The characteristic manner in which a person tries to minimize the psychological and physical pain associated with disease and negative life events.

correlational research   Research in which two or more variables are measured to see if there is a relationship between them.

correspondence bias   People's tendency to persist in believing that the cause of a behavior is internal to a person.

correspondent inference   The inference that occurs when we conclude that a person's behavior is caused by, or corresponds to, the person's internal characteristics or beliefs.

counterfactual thinking   The tendency to create positive alternatives to the negative outcome that actually occurred. This type of thinking is most likely to occur when we can easily imagine a different and more positive outcome.

counterproductive strategies   Self-destructive behavior in which a person seeks positive outcomes but uses ineffective (counterproductive) strategies to achieve them.

covariation principle   The rule that if a response is present when a situation (person, object, event) is present and absent when that same situation is absent, then that situation is presumed to be the cause of the response.

credibility   The believability of a communicator; the most critical factor affecting a communicator's ability to persuade.

death-qualified jury   A jury comprising members who are willing to impose the death penalty, making the jury conviction prone.

decision rule   A rule about how many members must agree before the group can reach a decision.

dehumanization   The stripping away of perceived human qualities from a victim by an obeyer; a factor in destructive obedience.

deindividuation The loss of self-identity and self-awareness that can occur when people are in large groups.

deliberation The final phase of a trial, in which the jurors discuss the evidence as a group and reach a unanimous (in most cases) decision.

dependent variable The variable the researcher measures to determine the influence of the independent variable on the subject's behavior.

destructive obedience The type of obedience that leads people to behave in ways that are counter to accepted standards of moral behavior.

diffusion of responsibility An explanation for the bystander effect stating that witnesses to an emergency assume that someone else will take action.

discounting principle A rule applied by perceivers under conditions of limited information that leads them to decrease the importance of a potential cause of an event if other reasonable causes are present.

discrimination Overt behavior directed toward people simply because they are presumed to be members of a particular group.

displaced aggression The redirection of aggression to a target that is not the source of the frustration.

distraction-conflict theory A theory of social facilitation suggesting that arousal stems from conflict between paying attention to demands from a task and demands from others present.

door-in-the-face technique A compliance technique in which a large request is made first and is then followed by a smaller one.

downward comparison A way people protect themselves against a health threat by comparing themselves with someone who is in a worse predicament.

dual-concern model A model that identifies the forces that maintain conflict and those that can lead to the resolution of conflict. According to this model, each side in a conflict has concerns that it feels are important and that must be considered in any attempt at conflict resolution.

egocentric bias The assumption that other people see things as we do.

egoism The motive for helping that is based on relieving one's own personal distress.

egotistical bias The tendency of people to present themselves as responsible for success whether they are or not.

Eichmann's fallacy The belief that evil deeds must be done by evil people.

elaboration likelihood model (ELM) A cognitive model of persuasion suggesting that the success of a persuasive message depends on how actively involved the listener becomes in processing it.

empathic cues Cues provided by a victim in an obedience situation about his or her suffering (e.g., banging on a wall, screaming).

empathy Compassionate understanding of how a person in need feels.

empathy–altruism hypothesis An explanation for altruism suggesting that arousal of empathy motivates people to help those in need.

empathy–punishment hypothesis An explanation for altruism suggesting that people help because of the shame and guilt they feel if they do not.

enabling condition In the probabalistic contrast theory of attribution, any condition that increases the likelihood that an event or behavior will occur.

equity theory A theory that we evaluate our relationships based on their rewards and costs and on our perception of equity, or balance, within them.

estimator variable A variable affecting eyewitness accuracy, not under control of the criminal justice system, related to the eyewitness and the conditions under which the eyewitness viewed a crime.

ethological theory The theory that views behavior in the context of survival; it emphasizes the role of instincts and genetic forces in shaping how animals behave.

evaluation apprehension An explanation for social facilitation suggesting that arousal is caused by apprehension over being evaluated by others.

excitation-transfer model A model suggesting that when two sources of arousal occur closely together in time, the arousal from one may be transferred to the other.

exemplar A real-life specific example of a category. Often used in making social judgments about individuals.

experimental group The group of subjects in an experiment that receives the experimental treatment.

experimental research Research that involves changing the value of a variable suspected of influencing behavior and seeing whether and how much that change affects behavior. Results allow researchers to discover causal relationships among variables.

external attribution The process of assigning causality to something about the situation—other people, environmental stimuli, social pressure, and so on.

eyewitness A person who observed a crime and can relate the events to the jury in court.

false consensus bias The tendency to believe that everyone else shares our own feelings, opinions, and behavior.

field experiment A type of field research in which the researcher manipulates independent variables and collects measures of the dependent variables (the subject's behavior) in the subject's natural environment rather than in a laboratory.

field study A type of field research in which the researcher makes unobtrusive observations of the subjects without making direct contact or interfering in any way.

field survey A type of field research in which the researcher directly approaches subjects and asks them questions.

foot-in-the-door technique A compliance technique in which a small request is made first and is then followed by a larger one.

free riders Group members who do not do their share of the work.

frustration–aggression hypothesis The hypothesis that aggression is caused by frustration resulting from blocked goals.

functional size In a lineup, the number of individuals who resemble the suspect.

fundamental attribution error The tendency to attribute a person's behavior to internal rather than external factors.

gender identity A person's awareness of belonging to one of the two sexes.

gender role Observable behavior that, according to society, marks a person as male or female.

gender role stereotypes Rigid ideas about how males and females should act.

graduated and reciprocal initiatives in tension reduction (GRIT) A conflict-reduction technique that involves one side making a unilateral concession and hoping that the other side will reciprocate; it uses the norm of reciprocity as its basis.

group Two or more individuals who interact with each other and who mutually influence each other.

group norms Expectations that group members share about what is acceptable behavior.

group polarization The phenomenon that occurs when the initial decision tendency of the group becomes more extreme following group discussion.

group-serving bias The tendency for groups to take credit for success and deny responsibility for failure, and to do the opposite for competing groups.

groupthink A breakdown in the rational decision-making abilities of members of a cohesive group when desire for unanimity overrides the concern for reaching a good decision.

health belief model An approach to illness and injury prevention that emphasizes the responsibility of the individual to make changes in his or her behavior.

helping behavior A type of behavior that is at least partially motivated by the desire to relieve one's personal distress or to attain some reward rather than solely based on relieving the suffering of a victim.

heritability The extent to which genetics accounts for differences among people in a given characteristic or behavior.

heuristic and systematic information processing model (HSM) A cognitive model of persuasion suggesting that listeners rely on heuristics or peripheral cues most of the time.

heuristics Rules of thumb that help us make sense of the social world but only in a superficial way.

hindsight bias The tendency to regard the results of research to be obvious only *after* one has found out what the results are.

hostile aggression Aggression that stems from anger and hostility. Its primary goal is to inflict injury on some person or object to satisfy angry or hostile impulses.

illusion of efficacy The illusion that small groups are more effective than large groups.

illusion of unique invulnerability The false belief that bad things happen only to other people.

illusory correlation A belief that two unrelated events covary (are systematically related).

implicit personality theory The idea that if a person has a certain personality characteristic, he or she will also have certain others.

impression formation The process by which we make judgments about the motives and behavior of other people.

impression management The process of presenting ourselves in certain ways in order to control the impressions that others form of us.

independent variable The variable manipulated by a researcher in an experiment.

informational social influence The type of social influence in which a person changes behavior in response to information others provide.

informed consent The ethical research principle stating that subjects must be fully informed about the nature of the research in which they are participating.

in-group bias The powerful tendency that humans have to favor the in-group, the group to which they belong, over out-groups.

inoculation theory The theory that if a communicator exposes an audience to a weakened version of the opposing argument, the audience will devise counterarguments to that weakened version.

instrumental aggression Aggression that stems from the desire to achieve a goal.

instrumental conditioning A learning process in which the individual's behavior is strengthened or weakened by means of reward or punishment.

integrative solution The most desirable solution to a conflict in which the aspirations of both parties are reconciled and blended to produce a result that integrates the needs of both sides and produces joint benefits.

interactionist view of altruism The view that an individual's internal motives (whether altruistic or selfish) interact with situational factors to determine whether he or she will help.

internal attribution The process of assigning the cause for behavior to something about the person—character, personality, beliefs, and so on.

jury nullification A jury's decision that consciously goes against the law and the facts pertaining to a case.

just-world hypothesis The hypothesis suggesting that individuals get what they deserve and deserve what they get.

life stressors Positive or negative events that an individual perceives as stressful and that apparently have a cumulative effect on health.

loneliness A psychological state that results when we perceive an inadequacy in our relationships—a discrepancy between the way we want our relationships to be and the way they actually are.

low-ball technique A compliance technique in which an unreasonably low offer is made and, when commitment is elicited, replaced with a higher offer on the pretense that the lower one could not be honored.

matching principle The tendency for people to become involved with a partner with whom they are closely matched in terms of physical attributes or social status.

mere exposure The phenomenon in which simply being exposed to an object increases our feelings, usually positive, toward that object.

minimization effect The tendency to deny the reality of bad news, such as about one's health, and to downplay its seriousness.

mirror-image perceptions A mode of perception in which each side sees the other in essentially the same negative way.

misinformation effect Memory distortion that occurs when a piece of information that was not part of the original event becomes part of a witness's memory of the event.

modern racism A newer, more subtle prejudice marked by an uncertainty in feeling and action toward minorities. Modern racists express racism but in a less open manner than was formerly common.

motivated inferences Interpretations of events that put the best face on reality and tilt it in our favor.

multiple audience problem The problem that occurs when a communicator must send different meanings in the same message to diverse audiences.

need for affiliation A need to establish and maintain relationships with others.

need for cognition (NC) A characteristic of the individual relating to the need to deal with the content of a message in an effortful way. A person can be either high or low on the need for cognition.

need for intimacy A need for close and affectionate relationships in which personal information is disclosed and sharing occurs.

negative correlation The relationship between two variables when their values change in opposite directions, one increasing and the other decreasing.

negativity effect The phenomenon whereby negative information about a political candidate has more impact than positive information.

negotiation A method of conflict resolution in which parties meet to exchange information, give views, clarify positions, and propose solutions.

norm An unwritten social rule that guides or regulates acceptable or appropriate behavior in a particular situation.

normative altruism A form of altruism that society supports and encourages.

normative social influence The type of social influence in which a person changes behavior in response to pressure to conform a norm.

norm of reciprocity A powerful social norm suggesting that people should help those who help them.

norm of social responsibility The norm stating that we should help others in need without regard for future reward or help in return.

obedience The social influence process by which a person changes his or her behavior in response to a direct order from someone in authority.

observational learning Learning by watching others; the primary channel of learning in social learning theory. Also referred to as modeling.

out-group homogeneity bias The phenomenon of perceiving members of the out-group as "all alike."

perceived control An individual's perception that he or she has some control over what happens in life.

perceptual contrast hypothesis An explanation for the foot-in-the-door technique suggesting that the smaller, initial request acts as a standard of reference against which other requests are judged.

peripheral route processing A form of information processing in which the listener relies on irrelevant or marginal cues to make a decision.

persuasion The application of rational and/or emotional arguments to convince others to change their attitudes or behavior.

physical attractiveness bias The tendency to confer on attractive individuals a number of psychological and social advantages.

pluralistic ignorance An explanation for the bystander effect in helping. When bystanders act as though no emergency exists, the situation is redefined as a nonemergency and helping drops.

positive correlation The relationship between two variables when their values change in the same direction, increasing or decreasing.

positive illusions An individual's beliefs that include unrealistically optimistic notions about his or her ability to handle a threatening event and create a positive outcome.

possible selves Selves we would like to attain and those we want to avoid or are afraid of becoming.

power-restoration theory A theory suggesting that power reduction leads to conflict and aggression, and that restoring the balance of power between parties can reduce conflict.

prejudice A biased, often negative, attitude formed about a group of people.

pretrial publicity Information about a case that can influence jurors that is published in newspapers or broadcast on television or radio prior to a trial.

primacy effect The tendency of early information to play a powerful role in our eventual impression of an individual.

primary self-destruction Self-destructive behavior involving actions that are harmful because the person foresees and desires the pain.

process loss The increased difficulty in arriving at a decision that results from increasing group size.

prototype An abstract representation or model of the typical qualities of the members of a category. Often used in making social judgments about groups.

psychological reactance A counteracting response to an action perceived as coercive or threatening to one's freedom.

public health model An approach to illness and injury prevention stating that the most effective way to prevent or alter high-risk behaviors is to devise methods that automatically prevent people from engaging in those behaviors.

racism The negative evaluation of others because of their apparent membership in a particular racial group.

random assignment The method of assigning subjects to groups in an experiment so that each subject has an equal chance of being assigned to the experimental or control group.

reconstructive memory The process by which we reconstruct an event during recall, putting together details of the event that we had stored in memory.

reflected appraisals Our view of how other people react to us.

reinforcement-affect theory The theory that we associate positive affect with people (and events) that

are rewarding to us and negative affect with people (and events) that are distasteful to us.

reverse-incentive effect The phenomenon of an activity being perceived as less desirable the more highly it is rewarded.

reward theory The theory that the degree of attraction we feel toward another person varies according to the frequency with which that person rewards us.

righteous rescuers The designation bestowed by the state of Israel on Christians who helped save Jews from the Nazis during World War II.

risky shift effect The tendency for a group to recommend riskier alternatives than individual group members would recommend on their own.

role strain Psychological tension, anxiety, and discomfort experienced as a result of one's role in an obedience situation; a factor that can weaken obedience.

routinization The reduction of obedient actions to habitual, routine behaviors; a factor in destructive obedience.

sanctioned aggression Aggression that society finds acceptable or even mandatory, such as the aggressive behavior of a soldier at war.

schema An organized set of related bits of information about persons, groups, events, and so on. Schemas provide an efficient way of organizing and understanding our experiences and predicting what will happen next.

scientific jury selection A method of jury selection that makes use of the methods of social science.

scientific method A method for developing explanations of behavior that involves four steps: (1) identifying a phenomenon to study, (2) developing a testable tentative statement about the relationship between variables, (3) designing a research study, and (4) carrying out the research study.

self-affirmation theory The theory that people may not try to reduce dissonance if they can maintain (affirm) their self-concept by proving that they are competent in other ways.

self-concept All the ideas, thoughts, and information we have about ourselves.

self-efficacy The notion that one can be effective in dealing with events, including those that are stressful or threatening.

self-esteem A component of the self that consists of a person's positive and negative self-evaluations.

self-focus The extent to which the individual monitors his or her own behavior and is more concerned with self than with others.

self-fulfilling prophecy The tendency to confirm our expectations of people by behaving toward them in ways that provoke them to act consistently with those expectations.

self-handicapping When, prior to doing something important (like taking an exam), a person provides himself or herself with a ready excuse in case of failure.

self-monitoring Focusing on one's own behavior in a given social situation. The degree, ranging from low to high, to which individuals self-monitor reflects their need to manage and control the impressions they make on others.

self-perception hypothesis An explanation for the foot-in-the-door technique suggesting that after agreeing to the smaller request, the person comes to see himself or herself as someone who helps in that particular situation.

self-perception theory The theory that people draw conclusions about their attitudes and motives by observing their own behavior.

self-schema An arrangement of information, thoughts, and feelings that we believe to be true about ourselves. Self-schemas organize our experiences, help us interpret situations, and guide our behavior.

self-serving bias The tendency to bias our cognitive strategies toward constructing positive outcomes. In other words, the tendency for individuals to take credit for success and deny responsibility for failure.

self-verification Confirmation of our self-concept from others—we tend to behave in ways that lead others to see us as we see ourselves.

sexism The negative evaluation of others because of their membership in a particular gender category.

sleeper effect The phenomenon of a message that has been delivered by a negative source having more impact on attitude change after a long delay than when it is first heard.

social anxiety A feeling of discomfort that arises from a person's expectation of negative encounters with others.

social cognition The processes we use to think about and interpret our own behavior and that of others.

social comparison The process by which we compare our reactions, abilities, and attributes to those of others.

social compensation The tendency to work harder to make up for the weakness of others in the group when the task is important and motivation to perform is high.

social exchange theory The theory that people evaluate a relationship according to rewards and costs; which correspond to all the positive and all the negative things derived from the relationship.

social facilitation The performance-enhancing effect of an audience on behavior.

social impact theory A single-process theory of majority and minority influence suggesting that social in-

fluence is a function of the strength, immediacy, and number of influence sources.

social influence model A single-process explanation for majority and minority influence that relates the amount of social influence to the relative sizes of the majority and minority.

social information processing view A view of social interaction suggesting that our social behavior (including aggressive behavior) is mediated by how we process social information.

social inhibition The performance-detracting effect of an audience on behavior.

social-interactional model A developmental model suggesting that antisocial behavior (such as aggression) arises early in life as a result of poor parenting.

social learning theory The theory that behavior is learned, primarily through observational learning.

social loafing The effect that sometimes occurs when, in a group situation, individuals relax their efforts and rely on others to take up the slack.

social penetration theory A model of relationship development that centers on the idea that relationships change over time in both breadth—the range of topics people discuss and activities they engage in together—and depth—the extent to which they share their inner thoughts and feelings.

social perception The process by which we make sense out of people's behavior; it involves inferring motives and attributing causes.

social psychology The scientific study of how individuals think and feel about, interact with, and influence each other, individually and in groups.

sociobiology The study of the biological basis for social behavior.

sociohistorical perspective A framework for understanding social psychological principles, research, and theory that emphasizes the importance of social, cultural, and historical context and the relevance of social psychology to current and historical events.

stereotype A set of rigid beliefs, positive or negative, about the characteristics or attributes of a group.

superordinate goal A goal that is mutually beneficial to groups in conflict.

symbolic aggression Aggression that harms the victim verbally through gossip, character assassination, damage to physical property, or interference with advancement toward a goal.

system variable A variable affecting eyewitness accuracy that is under the control of the criminal justice system.

target-based expectancies Expectancies about a specific individual based on information about that person.

that's-not-all technique A compliance technique in

which extras are added to an initial offer, often as apparently spontaneous gestures of generosity.

theory A set of interrelated statements or propositions about the causes of a particular phenomenon that help organize research results, make predictions about how certain variables influence social behavior, and give direction to future research.

third-party intervention A conflict-resolution technique in which an individual not involved in the conflict agrees to act as a go-between for the conflicting parties.

threat to self-esteem model A model suggesting that victims might refuse help because accepting help is a threat to their self-esteem.

transactive memory systems Sets of individual memories that groups possess and make use of in processing information and making group decisions.

trauma A severe stress that leaves deep emotional and/or physical scars and that requires special coping techniques.

triangular theory of love A theory that love has three components—passion, intimacy, and commitment—and that various kinds of love are defined by the presence or absence of these three components.

true partner effect The phenomenon whereby an individual's tendency to conform with a majority position is lessened if there is one other person who supports that individual's position.

type A behavior pattern A combination of behaviors and emotions that are characteristic of individuals who have high levels of hostility, competitiveness, and time urgency.

ultimate attribution error We are more likely to give in-group members the benefit of the doubt than out-group members.

value A conception of what is desirable; a guideline for a person's actions; a standard for behavior.

voir dire Roughly means "to speak the truth." A time during which the prosecution and the defense have the opportunity to question potential jurors and exercise challenges to have them removed.

weapon focus The phenomenon that occurs when the presence of a gun causes an eyewitness to pay less attention to other details of the crime scene.

working model A mental representation of what an individual expects to happen in a close relationship.

worthy person hypothesis An explanation for the door-in-the-face technique suggesting that because most DITF situations involve worthy causes, refusing the second (smaller) request induces guilt and thus leads to compliance.

Yale communication model A model used to investigate the effects of four factors on the persuasiveness of a communication. These factors are (1) the communicator, (2) the persuasive message, (3) the audience, and (4) the channel, or medium.

References

Abelson, R. (1986). Beliefs are like our possessions. *Journal for the Theory of Social Behavior, 16,* 223–250.

Abelson, R. (1988). Conviction. *American Psychologist, 43,* 267–275.

Abelson, R. P., & Prentice, D. A. (1989). Beliefs as possessions: A functionalized perspective. In A. Pratkanis, S. Breckler, & A. G. Greenwald (Eds.), *Attitude structure and function.* Hillsdale, NJ: Erlbaum.

Adler, T. (1990, January). Happiness-health link remains questionable. *APA Monitor,* p. 9.

Adorno, T. W., Frenkel-Brunswik, E., Levinson, D. J., & Sanford, R. N. (1950). *The authoritarian personality.* New York: Harper.

Affleck, G., Tennen, H., Pfeiffer, C., & Fifield, J. (1987). Appraisals of control and predictability in adapting to a chronic disease. *Journal of Personality and Social Psychology, 53,* 273–279.

Aikwa, A. (1990). Determinants of the magnitude of indebtedness in Japan: A comparison of relative weight of the recipient's benefits and the donor's costs. *Journal of Psychology, 124,* 523–533.

Ainsworth, M. D. S. (1992). Epilogue. In D. Cicchetti, M. M. Greenberg, & M. Cummings (Eds.), *Attachment in the preschool years.* Chicago: University of Chicago Press.

Ajzen, I. (1985). From actions to intentions: A theory of planned behavior. In J. Kuhl & J. Beckman (Eds.), *Action control: From Cognition to Behavior.* New York: Springer-Verlag.

Ajzen, I. (1987). Attitudes, traits, and actions: Dispositional prediction of behavior in personality and social psychology. In L. Berkowitz (Ed.), *Advances in experimental social psychology* (Vol. 20). San Diego, CA: Academic Press.

Ajzen, I. (1989). Attitude structure and behavior. In A. R. Pratkanis, S. J. Breckler, & A. G. Greenwald (Eds.), *Attitude structure and function.* Hillsdale, NJ: Erlbaum.

Ajzen, I. (1991). The theory of planned behavior. *Organizational Behavior and Human Decision Processes, 50,* 179–211.

Ajzen, I., & Fishbein, M. (1980). *Understanding attitudes and predicting human behavior.* Englewood Cliffs, NJ: Prentice-Hall.

Albert, D. J., Petrovic, D. M., & Walsh, M. L. (1989a). Competitive experience activates testosterone-dependent social aggression toward unfamiliar males. *Physiology and Behavior, 45,* 723–727.

Albert, D. J., Petrovic, D. M., & Walsh, M. L. (1989b). Ovariectomy attenuates aggression by female rats cohabiting with sexually active sterile males. *Physiology and Behavior, 45,* 225–228.

Allen, J., & Howland, A. (1974). *The United States of America.* New York: Prentice-Hall.

Allen, K. M., Blascovich, J., Tomaka, J., & Kelsey, R. M. (1991). Presence of human friends and pet dogs as moderators of autonomic responses to stress in women. *Journal of Personality and Social Psychology, 61,* 582–589.

Allport, G. W. (1935). Attitudes. In C. Murchison (Ed.), *Handbook of social psychology.* Worcester, MA: Clark University Press.

Allport, G. (1954). *The nature of prejudice.* Reading, MA: Addison-Wesley.

Altman, I., & Taylor, D. A. (1973). *Social penetration: The development of interpersonal relationships.* New York: Holt, Rinehart, & Winston.

American Psychological Association. (1992). Ethical principles of psychologists and code of conduct. *American Psychologist, 47,* 1597–1611.

Arbuthnot, J., & Wayner, M. (1982). Minority influence: Effects of size, conversion and sex. *Journal of Psychology, 111,* 285–295.

Archer, J., Pearson, N. A., & Westeman, K. E. (1988). Aggressive behaviour of children aged 6–11: Gender differences and their magnitude. *British Journal of Social Psychology, 27,* 371–384.

Arendt, H. (1963). *Eichmann in Jerusalem: A report on the banality of evil.* New York: Viking Press.

Arkin, R. M., & Baumgardner, A. H. (1986). Self-presentation and self-evaluation. In R. F. Baumeister (Ed.), *Public self and private self.* New York: Springer-Verlag.

Aron, A., & Aron, E. N. (1989). *The heart of social psychology* (2nd ed.). Lexington, MA: Lexington Books.

Aronson, E., Blaney, N., Stephan, C., Sikes, J., & Snapp, M. (1978). *The jigsaw classroom.* Beverly Hills, CA: Sage.

Aronson, E., & Mills, J. (1959). The effects of severity of initiation on liking for a group. *Journal of Abnormal and Social Psychology, 59,* 177–181.

Arrington, L. J., & Bitton, D. (1980). *The Mormon experience.* New York: Vintage Books.

Asch, S. E. (1946). Forming impressions of personality. *Journal of Abnormal and Social Psychology, 41,* 1230–1240.

Asch, S. (1951). Effects of group pressure upon the modification and distortion of judgment. In H. Guetzgow (Ed.), *Groups, leadership and men.* Pittsburgh: Carnegie Press.

Asch, S. E. (1955). Opinions and social pressures. *Scientific American, 193,* 31–35.

Asch, S. E. (1956). Studies of independence and conformity: A minority of one against a unanimous majority. *Psychological Monographs, 70.*

AT&T apologizes for racist drawing in worker magazine. (1993). *Wall Street Journal,* September 17, p. B6.

Averill, J. R. (1985). The social construction of emotion: With special reference to love. In K. J. Gergen & K. E. Davis (Eds.), *The social construction of the person.* New York: Springer-Verlag.

Ball-Rokeach, S., Rokeach, M., & Grube, J. W. (1984). *The great American values test.* New York: Free Press.

Balls, P., & Eisenberg, N. (1986). Sex differences in recipient's reactions to aid. *Sex Roles, 14,* 69–79.

Banaji, M. R., & Steele, C. M. (1989). The social cognition of alcohol use. *Social Cognition, 7,* 137–151.

Bandura, A. (1965). Influence of models' reinforcement contingencies on the acquisition of imitative responses. *Journal of Personality and Social Psychology, 1,* 589–595.

Bandura, A. (1973). *Aggression: A social learning analysis.* Englewood Cliffs, NJ: Prentice-Hall.

Bandura, A. (1977). *Social learning theory.* Englewood Cliffs, NJ: Prentice-Hall.

Bandura, A. (1986). *Social foundations of thought and action: A social cognitive theory.* Englewood Cliffs, NJ: Prentice-Hall.

Bandura, A., & Jourden, F. J. (1991). Self-regulatory mechanisms governing the impact of social comparison on complex decision making. *Journal of Personality and Social Psychology, 60,* 941–951.

Bandura, A., Ross, D., & Ross, S. A. (1961). Transmission of aggression through imitation of aggressive models. *Journal of Abnormal and Social Psychology, 63,* 575–582.

Bandura, A., Ross, D., & Ross, S. A. (1963). Imitation of film-mediated aggressive models. *Journal of Abnormal and Social Psychology, 67,* 601–607.

Bargh, J. (1989). Conditional automaticity: Varieties of automatic influences in social perception and cognition. In J. S. Uleman & J. A. Bargh (Eds.), *Unintended thought.* New York: Guilford Press.

Bargh, J. A., & Thein, R. D. (1985). Individual construct accessibility, person memory, and recall-judgment link: The case of information overload. *Journal of Personality and Social Psychology, 49,* 1129–1146.

Barkow, J. H. (1980). Sociobiology. In A. Montagu (Ed.), *Sociobiology examined.* Oxford, England: Oxford University Press.

Barnett, M. A., Thompson, M., & Pfiefer, J. R. (1985). Perceived competence to help and the arousal of empathy. *Journal of Social Psychology, 125,* 679–680.

Barnett, R., & Marshall, N. (1990, November). *Job satisfaction as a buffer against stress.* Paper presented at conference on Work and Well-being: An Agenda for the '90's.

Baron, L. (1986). The Holocaust and human decency: A review of research on the rescue of Jews in Nazi-occupied Europe. *Humboldt Journal of Social Relations, 13,* 237–251.

Baron, R. A. (1974). The aggression-inhibiting influence of heightened sexual arousal. *Journal of Personality and Social Psychology, 30,* 318–322.

Baron, R. S. (1986). Distraction-conflict theory: Progress and problems. In L. Berkowitz, *Advances in experimental social psychology* (Vol. 19). Orlando, FL: Academic Press.

Baron, R. S., Kerr, N. L., & Miller, N. (1992). *Group process, group decision, group action.* Pacific Grove, CA: Brooks/Cole.

Bar-Tal, D., & Geva, N. (1986). A cognitive basis of international conflicts. In S. Worchel & W. G. Austin (Eds.), *Psychology of intergroup relations.* Chicago: Nelson Hall.

Bartholomew, K., & Horowitz, L. M. (1991). Attachment styles among young adults: A test of a four-category model. *Journal of Personality and Social Psychology, 61,* 226–244.

Bartlett, F. (1932). *Remembering: A study in experimental and social psychology.* Cambridge, England: The University Press.

Bassili, J. N. (1981). The attractiveness stereotype: Goodness or glamour? *Basic and Applied Social Psychology, 2,* 235–252.

Batson, C. D. (1987). Prosocial motivation: Is it ever truly altruistic? In L. Berkowitz (Ed.), *Advances in experimental social psychology* (Vol. 20). New York: Academic Press.

Batson, C. D. (1990a). How social an animal: The human capacity for caring. *American Psychologist, 45,* 336–346.

Batson, C. D. (1990b). Good Samaritans—or priests and Levites? *Personality and Social Psychology Bulletin, 16,* 758–768.

Batson, C. D. (1990c). Goal-relevant cognitions associated with helping by individuals high on intrinsic, end religion. *Journal for the Scientific Study of Religion, 29,* 346–360.

Batson, C. D., Dyck, J. L., Brandt, J. R., Batson, J. G., Powell, A. L., McMaster, M. R., & Griffitt, C. (1988). Five studies testing two egoistic alternatives to the empathy-altruism hypothesis. *Journal of Personality and Social Psychology, 55,* 52–77.

Batson, C. D., Fultz, J., & Schoenrade, P. A. (1987). Distress and empathy: Two qualitatively distinct vicarious emotions with different motivational consequences. *Journal of Personality, 55,* 19–39.

Batson, C. D., & Gray, R. A. (1981). Religious orientation and helping behavior: Responding to one's own pain or to the victim's needs. *Journal of Personality and Social Psychology, 40,* 511–520.

Batson, C. D., Oleson, K. C., Weeks, J. L., Healy, S. P., & Reeves, P. J. (1989). Religious prosocial motivation: Is it altruistic or egoistic? *Journal of Personality and Social Psychology, 57,* 873–884.

Batson, C. D., O'Quin, K., Fultz, J., & Vanderplas, M. (1983). Influence of self-reported distress and empathy on egoistic versus altruistic motivation to help. *Journal of Personality and Social Psychology, 45,* 706–718.

Baucom, D. H., Sayers, S. L., & Duhe, A. (1989). Attributional style and attributional patterns among married couples. *Journal of Personality and Social Psychology, 56,* 596–616.

Baum, A., Grunberg, N. E., & Singer, J. E. (1982). The use of psychological and neuroendocrinological measurements in the study of stress. *Health Psychology, 1,* 217–236.

Baum, A., & Nesselhof-Kendall, S. (1988). Psychological research and the prevention, etiology, and treatment of AIDS. *American Psychologist, 43,* 900–908.

Baumeister, R. F. (1984). Choking under pressure: Self-consciousness and paradoxical effects of incentives on skillful performance. *Journal of Personality and Social Psychology, 46,* 610–620.

Baumeister, R. F. (1986). *Identity.* New York: Oxford University Press.

Baumeister, R. F. (1987). How the self became a problem: A psychological review of historical research. *Journal of Personality and Social Psychology, 52,* 163–176.

Baumeister, R. F. (1988). Masochism as escape from the self. *Journal of Sex Research, 25,* 28–59.

Baumeister, R. F. (1990). Suicide as escape from the self. *Psychological Review, 97,* 90–113.

Baumeister, R. F., Chesner, S. P., Senders, P. S., & Tice, D. M. (1988). Who's in charge here: Group leaders do lend help in emergencies. *Personality and Social Psychology Bulletin, 14,* 17–22.

Baumeister, R. F., & Scher, S. J. (1988). Self-defeating behavior patterns among normal individuals: Review and analysis of common self-destructive tendencies. *Psychological Bulletin, 104,* 2–22.

Baumeister, R. F., & Tice, D. M. (1984). Role of self-presentation and choice in cognitive dissonance under forced compliance: Necessary or sufficient causes? *Journal of Personality and Social Psychology, 46,* 5–13.

Baumeister, R. F., & Tice, D. M. (1990). Anxiety and social exclusion. *Journal of Social and Clinical Psychology, 9,* 165–195.

Baumeister, R. F., Wotman, S. R., & Stillwell, A. M. (1993). Unrequited love: On heartbreak, anger, guilt, scriptlessness, and humiliation. *Journal of Personality and Social Psychology, 64,* 377–394.

Baumgardner, A. H. (1990). To know oneself is to like oneself: Self-certainty and self-affect. *Journal of Personality and Social Psychology, 58,* 1062–1072.

Baumgardner, A. H., Kaufman, C. M., & Crawford, J. A. (1990). To be noticed favorably: Links between the private self and the public self. *Personality and Social Psychology Bulletin, 16,* 705–716.

Baumrind, D. (1964). Some thoughts on ethics of research: After reading Milgram's "behavioral study of obedience." *American Psychologist, 19,* 421–423.

Bazerman, M. H. (1986, June). Why negotiations go wrong. *Psychology Today,* pp. 54–58.

Becker, L. A., & Barry, T. H. (1979). *Self-defense murder and the bleeding heart authoritarian.* Paper presented at the annual meeting of the Midwestern Psychological Association, Chicago.

Bee, H. (1992). *The Developing Child* (6th ed.). Glenview, IL: Harper Collins.

Bell, B. E., & Loftus, E. F. (1988). Degree of detail of eyewitness testimony and mock juror judgments. *Journal of Applied Social Psychology, 18,* 1171–1192.

Bell, B. E., & Loftus, E. F. (1989). Trivial persuasion in the courtroom: The power of (a few) minor details. *Journal of Personality and Social Psychology, 56,* 669–679.

Bem, D. J. (1966). Inducing belief in false confessions. *Journal of Personality and Social Psychology, 3,* 707–710.

Bem, D. J. (1967). Self-perception: An alternative interpretation of cognitive dissonance phenomena. *Psychological Review, 74,* 183–200.

Bem, D. J. (1972). Self-perception theory. In L. Berkowitz (Ed.), *Advances in experimental social psychology* (Vol. 6). San Diego, CA: Academic Press.

Bennett, W. L. (1978). Storytelling in criminal trials: A model for social judgment. *Quarterly Journal of Speech, 64,* 1–22.

Bennett, W. L., & Feldman, M. (1978). *Reconstructing reality in the courtroom.* New Brunswick, NJ: Rutgers University Press.

Benson, P. L., Dehority, J., Garman, L., Hanson, E., Hochswender, M., Lebold, C., Rohr, R., & Sullivan, J. (1980). Intrapersonal correlates of nonspontaneous helping behavior. *Journal of Social Psychology, 110,* 87–95.

Benson, P. L., Karabenick, S. A., & Lerner, R. M. (1976). Pretty pleases: The effects of physical attractiveness, race and sex on receiving help. *Journal of Experimental Social Psychology, 12,* 409–415.

Berg, K. S., & Vidmar, N. (1975). Authoritarianism and recall of evidence about criminal behavior. *Journal of Research in Personality, 9,* 147–157.

Berglas, S., & Jones, E. E. (1978). Drug choice as a self-handicapping strategy in response to noncontingent success. *Journal of Personality and Social Psychology, 36,* 405–417.

Berkowitz, L. (1969). Resistance to improper dependency relationships. *Journal of Experimental Social Psychology, 5,* 283–294.

Berkowitz, L. (1972). Social norms, feelings and other factors affecting altruism. In L. Berkowitz (Ed.), *Advances in experimental social psychology.* New York: Academic Press.

Berkowitz, L. (1978). Whatever happened to the frustration-aggression hypothesis? *American Behavioral Scientist, 21,* 691–708.

Berkowitz, L. (1988). Introduction. In L. Berkowitz (Ed.), *Advances in experimental social psychology* (Vol. 21). San Diego, CA: Academic Press.

Berkowitz, L. (1989). Frustration-aggression hypothesis: Examination and reformation. *Psychological Bulletin, 106,* 59–73.

Berkowitz, L., & LePage, A. (1967). Weapons as aggression-eliciting stimuli. *Journal of Personality and Social Psychology, 7,* 202–207.

Bernat, F. P. (1984). Gender disparity in setting of bail: Prostitution offenses in Buffalo, NY 1977–1979. *Journal of Offender Counseling, Services and Rehabilitation, 9,* 21–47.

Berndt, T. J. (1992). Friendship and friends' influence in adolescence. *Current Directions in Psychological Sciences, 1,* 156–159.

Berry, D. (1991). Attractive faces are not all created equal: Joint effects of facial babyishness and attractiveness on social perception. *Personality and Social Psychology Bulletin, 17,* 523–528.

Berscheid, E. (1985). Compatibility, interdependence, and emotion. In W. Ickes (Ed.), *Compatible and incompatible relationships.* New York: Springer-Verlag.

Berscheid, E. (1988). Some comments on the anatomy of love: Or whatever happened to old-fashioned lust? In R. J. Sternberg & M. L. Barnes (Eds.), *The psychology of love.* New Haven, CT: Yale University Press.

Berscheid, E., Snyder, M., & Omoto, A. M. (1989). The relationship closeness inventory; assessing the closeness of interpersonal relationships. *Journal of Personality and Social Psychology, 57,* 792–807.

Berscheid, E., & Walster, E. (1974). A little bit about love. In T. L. Huston (Ed.), *Foundations of interpersonal attraction.* New York: Academic Press.

Berscheid, E., & Walster, E. H. (1978). *Interpersonal attraction* (2nd ed.). Reading, MA: Addison-Wesley.

Bettelheim, B., & Janowitz, I. (1950). *The dynamics of prejudice.* New York: Harper.

Bickman, L. (1974). The social power of a uniform. *Journal of Applied Social Psychology, 4,* 47–61.

Bickman, L., & Kamzan, M. (1973). The effect of race and need on helping behavior. *Journal of Social Psychology, 89,* 73–77.

Biernat, M., & Wortman, C. (1991). Sharing of home responsibilities between professionally employed women and their husbands. *Journal of Personality and Social Psychology, 60,* 844–860.

Billig, M. (1992, January 27). The baseline of intergroup prejudice. *Current Contents,* p. 12.

Bilu, Y. (1989). The other as a nightmare: The Israeli–Arab encounter as reflected in children's dreams in Israel and the West Bank. *Political Psychology, 10,* 365–389.

Bishop, G. D. (1994). *Health psychology.* Boston: Allyn & Bacon.

Blanchard, D. C., & Blanchard, R. J. (1984). Affect and aggression: An animal model applied to human behavior. In R. J. Blanchard & D. C. Blanchard (Eds.), *Advances in the study of aggression* (Vol. 1). New York: Academic Press.

Blanchard, F. A., Lilly, T., & Vaughn, L. A. (1991). Reducing the expression of racial prejudice. *Psychological Science, 2,* 101–105.

Blascovich, J., Ernst, J. M., Tomaka, J., Kelsey, R. M., Salomon, K. L., & Fazio, R. H. (1993). Attitude accessibility as a moderator of autonomic reactivity during decision making. *Journal of Personality and Social Psychology, 64,* 165–176.

Blascovich, J., & Ginsburg, G. P. (1974). Emergent norms and choice shifts involving risks. *Sociometry, 37,* 274–276.

Blass, T. (1991). Understanding behavior in the Milgram obedience experiment: The role of personality, situations, and their interactions. *Journal of Personality and Social Psychology, 60,* 398–413.

Bodenhausen, G. V. (1990). Stereotypes as judgmental heuristics: Evidence of circadian variations in discrimination. *Psychological Science, 1,* 319–322.

Bodenhausen, G. V. (1993). Emotion, arousal, and stereotypic judgment: A heuristic model of affect and stereotyping. In D. Mackie & D. Hamilton (Eds.), *Affect, cognition, and stereotyping: Interactive processes in group perception.* San Diego, CA: Academic Press.

Bodenhausen, G. V., & Lichtenstein, M. (1987). Social stereotypes and information-processing strategies: The impact of task complexity. *Journal of Personality and Social Psychology, 52,* 871–880.

Bodenhausen, G. V., & Wyer, R. S. (1985). Effects of stereotypes on decision making and information processing strategies: The impact of task complexity. *Journal of Personality and Social Psychology, 48,* 267–282.

Boehm, V. (1968). Mr. prejudice, Miss sympathy and the authoritarian personality: An application of psychological measuring techniques to the problem of jury bias. *Wisconsin Law Review,* 734–750.

Bohm, R. M. (1994). Capital punishment in two judicial circuits in Georgia: A description of the key actors and the decision-making process. *Law and Human Behavior, 18,* 319–338.

Bolger, N., & Eckenrode, J. (1991). Social relationships, personality, and anxiety during a major stressful event. *Journal of Personality and Social Psychology, 61,* 440–449.

Bolt, M., & Caswell, J. (1981). Attribution of responsibility to a rape victim. *Journal of Social Psychology, 114,* 137–138.

Bond, G. G., Aiken, L. S., & Somerville, S. C. (1992). The health belief model and adolescents with insulin-dependent diabetes mellitus. *Health Psychology, 11,* 190–198.

Bordens, K. S., & Abbott, B. B. (1991). *Research design and methods: A process approach* (2nd ed.). Mountain View, CA: Mayfield.

Bornstein, R. F. (1989). Exposure and affect: Overview and meta-analysis of research, 1968–1987. *Psychological Bulletin, 106,* 265–289.

Bornstein, R. F., Leone, D. R., & Galley, D. J. (1987). The generalizability of subliminal mere exposure effects: Influence of stimuli perceived without awareness on social behavior. *Journal of Personality and Social Psychology, 53,* 1070–1079.

Bothwell, R. K., Brigham, J. C., & Malpass, R. S. (1989). Cross-racial identification. *Personality and Social Psychology Bulletin, 15,* 19–25.

Bradbury, T. N., & Fincham, F. D. (1990). Attributions in marriage: review and critique. *Psychological Bulletin, 107,* 3–33.

Bradbury, T. N., & Fincham, F. D. (1992). Attributions and behavior in marital interaction. *Journal of Personality and Social Psychology, 63,* 613–628.

Branden, N. (1988). A vision of romantic love. In R. J. Sternberg & M. L. Barnes (Eds.), *The psychology of love.* New Haven, CT: Yale University Press.

Brannon, J., & Feist, J. (1992). *Health psychology* (2nd ed.). Belmont, CA: Wadsworth.

Bray, R. M., Kerr, N. L., & Atkin, R. S. (1978). The effect of group size, problem difficulty, and sex on group performance. *Journal of Personality and Social Psychology, 36,* 1224–1240.

Breaugh, J. A., Klimoski, R. J., & Shapiro, M. B. (1980). Third-party characteristics and intergroup conflict resolution. *Psychological Reports, 47,* 447–451.

Breckler, S. J., & Wiggins, E. C. (1989). On defining attitude and attitude theory: Once more with feeling. In A. R. Pratkanis, S. J. Breckler, & A. G. Greenwald (Eds.), *Attitude structure and function.* Hillsdale, NJ: Erlbaum.

Brehm, J., & Cohen, A. R. (1962). *Explorations in cognitive dissonance.* New York: John Wiley & Sons.

Brehm, S. (1985). *Intimate relations.* New York: Random House.

Brehm, S. (1988). Passionate love. In R. J. Sternberg & M. L. Barnes (Eds.), *The psychology of love.* New Haven, CT: Yale University Press.

Brehm, S. S., & Brehm, J. W. (1981). *Psychological reactance: A theory of freedom and control.* New York: Academic Press.

Brewer, M. B. (1988). A dual process model of impression formation. In T. K. Srull & R. S. Wyer (Eds.), *Advances in social cognition* (Vol. 1). Hillsdale, NJ: Erlbaum.

Brewer, M. (1993, August). *The social self, inclusion and distinctiveness.* Address to the American Psychological Convention, Toronto.

Brewer, M. B., & Kramer, R. M. (1986). Choice behavior in social dilemmas: Effects of social identity, group size and decision framing. *Journal of Personality and Social Psychology, 50,* 543–549.

Bridges, J. S., & McGrail, C. A. (1989). Attributions of responsibility for date and stranger rape. *Sex Roles, 21,* 273–286.

Brigham, J. C. (1986). Race and eyewitness identifications. In S. Worchel and W. G. Austin (Eds.), *Psychology of intergroup relations.* Chicago: Nelson-Hall.

Brinthaupt, T. M., Moreland, R. L., & Levine, J. M. (1991). Sources of optimism among prospective group members. *Personality and Social Psychology Bulletin, 17,* 36–45.

Brody, J. E. (1992, February 25). Maintaining friendships for the sake of good health. *New York Times,* p. B8.

Broeder, D. W. (1965). Voir dire examinations: An empirical study. *Southern California Law Review, 38,* 503–527.

Broverman, I. K., Vogel, S. R., Broverman, D. M., Clarkson, F. E., & Rosenkrantz, P. S. (1972). Sex role stereotypes: A current appraisal. *Journal of Social Issues, 28,* 59–78.

Brown, J. D. (1991). Staying fit and staying well: Physical fitness as a moderator of life stress. *Journal of Personality and Social Psychology, 60,* 555–561.

Brown, J. A. C. (1967). *Techniques of persuasion: From propaganda to brainwashing.* New York: Pelican Books.

Brown, R. (1986). *Social Psychology* (2nd ed.). New York: Free Press.

Brownell, K. D. (1984). The addictive disorders. *Annual Review of Behavior Therapy, Theory, and Behavior, 9,* 211–258.

Brownmiller, S. (1975). *Against our will: Men, women, and rape.* New York: Simon & Schuster.

Brownstein, R. J., & Katzev, R. D. (1985). The relative effectiveness of three compliance techniques in eliciting donations to a cultural organization. *Journal of Applied Social Psychology, 15,* 564–574.

Brunner, H. H., Nelon, M., Breakefield, X. O., Ropers, H. H., & van Oost, B. A. (1993). Abnormal behavior associated with a point mutation in the structural gene for monomamine oxidase A. *Science, 262,* 578–580.

Brush, S. G. (1991). Women in engineering and science. *American Scientist, 79,* 404–419.

Bryan, J. H., & Test, M. (1967). Models and helping: Naturalistic studies in aiding behavior. *Journal of Personality and Social Psychology, 6,* 400–407.

Bryan, J. H., & Walbek, N. (1970). Preaching and practicing self-sacrifice: Children's actions and reactions. *Child Development, 41,* 329–353.

Buckhout, R. (1974). Eyewitness testimony. *Scientific American, 231,* 23–31.

Bulman, R., & Wortman, C. (1977). Attributions of blame and coping in the "real world": Severe accident victims react to their lot. *Journal of Personality and Social Psychology, 35,* 351–383.

Burger, J. M. (1986). Increasing compliance by improving the deal: The that's-not-all technique. *Journal of Personality and Social Psychology, 51,* 277–283.

Burger, J. M. (1991). Changes in attribution over time: The ephemeral fundamental attribution error. *Social Cognition, 9,* 182–193.

Burger, J. M., & Petty, R. E. (1981). The low-ball compliance technique: Task or person commitment? *Journal of Personality and Social Psychology, 40,* 492–500.

Burnett, A. (1972). *Gertrude Stein.* New York: Atheneum.

Burnstein, E. (1982). Persuasion as argument processing. In H. Brandstatter, J. H. Davis, & G. Stocker-Kreichgauer (Eds.), *Group decision making.* London: Academic Press.

Burnstein, E., & Sentis, K. (1981). Attitude polarization in groups. In R. E. Petty, T. M. Ostrom, & T. C. Brock (Eds.), *Cognitive responses in persuasion.* Hillsdale, NJ: Erlbaum.

Burnstein, E., & Vinokur, A. (1977). Persuasive argumentation and social comparison as determinants of attitude polarization. *Journal of Experimental Social Psychology, 13,* 315–332.

Burt, M. (1980). Cultural myths and supports for rape. *Journal of Personality and Social Psychology, 38,* 217–230.

Bushman, B. J., & Cooper, H. M. (1990). Effects of alcohol on human aggression: An integrative research review. *Psychological Bulletin, 107,* 341–354.

Buss, A., Booker, A., & Buss, E. (1972). Firing a weapon and aggression. *Journal of Personality and Social Psychology, 22,* 296–302.

Buss, D. M. (1988a). Love acts: The evolutionary biology of love. In R. J. Sternberg & M. L. Barnes, *The psychology of love.* New Haven, CT: Yale University Press.

Buss, D. M. (1988b). From vigilance to violence: Tactics of mate retention in American undergraduates. *Ethology and Sociobiology, 9,* 291–317.

Buss, D. M. (1994). *The evolution of desire: Strategies of human mating.* New York: Basic Books.

Buss, D. M., & Schmitt, D. P. (1993). Sexual strategies theory: An evolutionary perspective on human mating. *Psychological Review, 100,* 204–232.

Byrne, D. (1971). *The attraction paradigm.* New York: Academic Press.

Byrne, D., & Clore, G. L. (1970). A reinforcement model of evaluative processes. *Personality: An International Journal, 1,* 103–128.

Byrne, D., Clore, G. L., & Smeaton, G. (1986). The attraction hypothesis: Do similar attitudes affect anything? *Journal of Personality and Social Psychology, 51,* 1167–1170.

Byrne, D., & Nelson, D. (1965). Attraction as a linear function of proportion of positive reinforcements. *Journal of Personality and Social Psychology, 1,* 659–663.

Cacioppo, J. T., Andersen, B. L., Turnquist, D. C., & Tassinary, L. G. (1989). Psychophysiological comparison theory: On the experience, description, and assessment of signs and symptoms. *Patient Education and Counseling, 14,* 177–196.

Cacioppo, J. T., & Petty, R. E. (1979). Effects of message repetition and position on cognitive response, recall, and persuasion. *Journal of Personality and Social Psychology, 37,* 97–109.

Cacioppo, J. T., & Petty, R. E. (1983). *Psychophysiology: A sourcebook.* New York: Guilford Press.

Cacioppo, J. T., Petty, R. E., & Morris, K. (1983). Effects of need for cognition on message evaluation, recall, and persuasion. *Journal of Personality and Social Psychology, 45,* 805–818.

Cacioppo, J. T., Petty, R. E., & Tassinary, L. G. (1989). Sociophysiology: A new look. In L. Berkowitz (Ed.), *Advances in experimental social psychology* (Vol. 22). San Diego, CA: Academic Press.

Cacioppo, J. T., Uchino, B. N., Crites, S. L., Snydersmith, M. A., Smith, G., Berman, G. G., & Lang, P. J. (1992). Relationship between facial expressiveness and sympathetic activation in emotion: A critical review, with emphasis on modeling underlying mechanisms and individual differences. *Journal of Personality and Social Psychology, 62,* 110–128.

Callero, P. L. (1986). Putting the social in prosocial behavior: An interactionist approach to altruism. *Humboldt Journal of Social Relations, 13,* 15–32.

Campbell, J. D., & Fairey, P. J. (1989). Informational and normative routes to conformity: The effect of faction size as a function of norm extremity and attention to the stimulus. *Journal of Personality and Social Psychology, 57,* 457–468.

Cantor, N., & Kihlstrom, J. F. (1987). *Personality and social intelligence.* Englewood Cliffs, NJ: Prentice-Hall.

Cantrill, J. G., & Seibold, D. R. (1986). The perceptual contrast explanation of sequential request strategy effectiveness. *Human Communication Research, 13,* 253–267.

Caplan, N. S., & Paige, J. M. (1968). A study of ghetto rioters. *Scientific American, 219,* 15–21.

Carducci, B. J., & Deuser, P. S. (1984). The foot-in-the-door technique: Initial request and organ donation. *Basic and Applied Social Psychology, 5,* 75–82.

Carli, L. L., Ganley, R., & Pierce-Otay, A. (1991). Similarity and satisfaction in roommate relationships. *Personality and Social Psychology Bulletin, 17,* 419–427.

Carlson, M., Marcus-Newhall, A., & Miller, N. (1990). Effects of situational aggression cues: A quantitative review. *Journal of Personality and Social Psychology, 58,* 622–633.

Carlson, N. R. (1991). *Physiology of behavior* (4th ed.). Boston: Allyn & Bacon.

Carmelli, D., Dame, A., Swan, G., & Rosenman, R. (1991). Long-term changes in Type A behavior: A 27-year follow-up of the Western Collaborative Group Study. *Journal of Behavioral Medicine, 14,* 593–606.

Carnevale, P. J. D., & Lawler, E. J. (1986). Time pressure and the development of integrative agreements in bilateral negotiations. *Journal of Conflict Resolution, 30,* 636–659.

Caro, R. (1982). *The years of Lyndon Johnson: The path to power.* New York: Knopf.

Carver, C. S. (1975). Physical aggression as a function of objective self-awareness and attitudes toward punishment. *Journal of Personality and Social Psychology, 11,* 510–519.

Cassilth, B. R., Lusk, E. J., Miller, D. S., & Miller, C. (1985). Psychosocial correlates of survival in advanced malignant disease. *New England Journal of Medicine, 312,* 368–373.

Castro, M. A. C. (1974). Reactions to receiving aid as a function of cost to donor and opportunity to aid. *Journal of Applied Social Psychology, 4,* 194–209.

Ceci, S. J., Ross, D. R., & Toglia, M. P. (1987). Suggestibility of children's memory: Psycholegal implications. *Journal of Experimental Psychology: General, 116,* 38–49.

Cha, J. H., & Nam, K. D. (1985). A test of Kelley's cube theory of attribution: A cross-cultural replication of McArthur's study. *Korean Social Science Journal, 12,* 151–180.

Chaiken, S. (1987). The heuristic model of persuasion. In M. P. Zanna, J. M. Olson, & C. P. Herman (Eds.), *Social influence: The Ontario symposium* (Vol. 5). Hillsdale, NJ: Erlbaum.

Chaiken, S., Liberman, A., & Eagly, A. (1989). Heuristic versus systematic information processing within and beyond the persuasion context. In J. S. Uleman & J. A. Bargh (Eds.), *Unintended thought* (pp. 212–252). New York: Guilford Press.

Chaiken, S., & Pliner, P. (1987). Women, but not men, are what they eat: The effect of meal size and gender on perceived femininity and masculinity. *Personality and Social Psychology Bulletin, 13,* 166–176.

Chaiken, S., & Stangor, C. (1987). Attitudes and attitude change. *Annual Review of Psychology, 38,* 575–630.

Chamberlin, H. (1972). *A minority of members: Women in the U.S. Congress.* New York: Praeger.

Chapman, L. L., & Chapman, J. (1967). Genesis of popular but erroneous psychodiagnostic observations. *Journal of Abnormal Psychology, 72,* 193–204.

Chen, H., Yates, B. T., & McGinnies, E. (1988). Effects of involvement on observers' estimates of consensus, distinctiveness, and consistency. *Personality and Social Psychology Bulletin, 14,* 468–478.

Cheng, P. W., & Novick, L. R. (1990). A probabilistic contrast model of causal induction. *Journal of Personality and Social Psychology, 58,* 545–567.

Cheng, P. W., & Novick, L. R. (1991). Causes versus enabling conditions. *Cognition, 40,* 83–120.

Cheng, P. W., & Novick, L. R. (1992). Covariation in natural causal induction. *Psychological Review, 99,* 365–382.

Christiansen, K., & Knussmann, R. (1987). Androgen levels and components of aggressive behavior in men. *Hormones and Behavior, 21,* 170–180.

Christianson, S. A. (1992). Emotional stress and eyewitness memory: A critical review. *Psychological Bulletin, 112,* 284–309.

Cialdini, R. B. (1988). *Influence: Science and practice* (2nd ed.). Glenview, IL: Scott, Foresman.

Cialdini, R. B., & Ascani, K. (1976). Test of a concession procedure for inducing verbal, behavioral, and further compliance with a request to give blood. *Journal of Applied Psychology, 61,* 295–300.

Cialdini, R. B., Borden, R. J., Thorne, A., Walker, M. R., Freeman, S., & Sloan, L. R. (1976). Basking in reflected glory: Three football (field) studies. *Journal of Personality and Social Psychology, 39,* 406–415.

Cialdini, R. B., Cacioppo, J. T., Bassett, R., & Miller, J. A. (1978). Low-ball procedure for producing compliance: Commitment then cost. *Journal of Personality and Social Psychology, 36,* 463–476.

Cialdini, R. B., & Fultz, J. (1990). Interpreting the negative mood-helping literature via "mega"-analysis: A contrary view. *Psychological Bulletin, 107,* 210–214.

Cialdini, R. B., & Schroeder, D. A. (1976). Increasing compliance by legitimizing paltry contributions: Even a penny will help. *Journal of Personality and Social Psychology, 34,* 599–604.

Cialdini, R. B., Vincent, J. E., Lewis, S. K., Catalan, J., Wheeler, D., & Darby, B. L. (1975). Reciprocal concessions procedure for inducing the door-in-the-face technique. *Journal of Personality and Social Psychology, 31,* 206–215.

Cioffi, D. (1991). Asymmetry of doubt in medical diagnosis: The ambiguity of "uncertain wellness." *Journal of Personality and Social Psychology, 61,* 969–980.

Clark, M. S. (1986). Evidence for the effectiveness of manipulations of desire for communal versus exchange relationships. *Personality and Social Psychology Bulletin, 12,* 414–425.

Clark, M. S., Mills, J., & Powell, M. C. (1986). Keeping track of needs in exchange and communal relationships. *Journal of Personality and Social Psychology, 51,* 333–338.

Clark, R. D., & Word, L. E. (1974). What is the apathetic bystander? Situational characteristics of the emergency. *Journal of Personality and Social Psychology, 29,* 279–287.

Clary, E. G., & Orenstein, L. (1991). The amount and effectiveness of help: The relationship of motives and abilities to helping behavior. *Personality and Social Psychology Bulletin, 17,* 58–64.

Clifford, B. R., & Scott, J. (1978). Individual and situational factors in eyewitness testimony. *Journal of Applied Psychology, 63,* 352–359.

Clymer, A. (1993, July 12). Daughter of slavery hushes Senate. *New York Times.*

Cogan, R., Cogan, D., Waltz, W., & McCue, M. (1987). Effects of laughter and relaxation on discomfit thresholds. *Journal of Personality and Social Psychology, 45,* 1313–1324.

Cohen, S., Kaplan, J. R., Cunnick, J. E., Manuck, S. B., & Rabin, B. S. (1992). Chronic social stress, affiliation, and cellular immune response in nonhuman primates. *Psychological Science, 3,* 301–304.

Cohen, S., Tyrrell, D. A. J., & Smith, A. P. (1993). Negative life events, perceived stress, and susceptibility to the common cold. *Journal of Personality and Social Psychology, 64,* 131–140.

Cohen, S., & Williamson, G. M. (1991). Stress and infectious disease in humans. *Psychological Bulletin, 109,* 5–24.

Coleman, L. T., Jussim, L., & Isaac, J. L. (1991). Black students' reactions to feedback conveyed by white and black teachers. *Journal of Applied Social Psychology, 21,* 460–481.

Collins, R. L., Taylor, S. E., Wood, J. V., & Thompson, S. C. (1988). The vividness effect: Elusive or illusory? *Journal of Experimental Social Psychology, 24,* 1–18.

Colvin, C. R., & Funder, D. C. (1991). Predicting personality and behavior: A boundary acquaintance effect. *Journal of Personality and Social Psychology, 60,* 884–894.

Congressional Record—Senate. (1993, July 22). Pp. S9253–S9264.

Conner, R. L., & Levine, S. (1969). Hormonal influences on aggressive behavior. In S. Garattini & E. B. Sigg (Eds.), *Aggressive behavior.* New York: John Wiley.

Contrada, R. J. (1989). Type A behavior, personality, hardiness, and cardiovascular responses to stress. *Journal of Personality and Social Psychology, 57,* 895–903.

Cook, S. W. (1984). Cooperative interaction in multiethnic contexts. In N. Miller & M. B. Brewer (Eds.), *Groups in contact: The psychology of desegregation.* Orlando, FL: Academic Press.

Cooley, C. H. (1902). *Human nature and the social order.* New York: Scribner.

Cooper, J., & Scher, S. J. (1992). Actions and attitudes: The role of responsibility and aversive consequences in persuasion. In T. Brock & S. Shavitt (Eds.), *The psychology of persuasion.* San Francisco: W. H. Freeman.

Cooper, L., & Fazio, R. H. (1984). A new look at cognitive dissonance theory. In L. Berkowitz (Ed.), *Advances in experimental social psychology* (Vol. 17). San Diego, CA: Academic Press.

Cottrell, N. B. (1972). Social facilitation. In C. G. McClintock (Ed.), *Experimental social psychology.* New York: Holt, Rinehart and Winston.

Cottrell, N. B., Wack, D. L., Sekerak, G. J., & Rittle, R. M. (1968). Social facilitation of dominant responses by the presence of an audience and the mere presence of others. *Journal of Personality and Social Psychology, 9,* 245–250.

Couric, E. (1986). Jury sleuths: In search of a perfect panel. *National Law Journal, 8,* 1.

Courtwright, J. (1978). A laboratory investigation of groupthink. *Communications Monographs, 45,* 229–245.

Cousins, N. (1979). *Anatomy of an illness.* New York: W. W. Norton.

Cousins, N. (1989). *Head first: The biology of hope.* New York: E. P. Dutton.

Cousins, S. D. (1989). Culture and self-perception in Japan and the U.S. *Journal of Personality and Social Psychology, 56,* 124–131.

Cox, M., & Tanford, S. L. (1989). An alternative method of capital jury selection. *Law and Human Behavior, 13,* 167–184.

Crabb, P. B. (1989). When aggression seems justified: Judging intergroup conflict from a distance. *Aggressive Behavior, 15,* 345–352.

Cramer, R. E., McMaster, M. R., Bartell, P. A., & Dragna, M. (1988). Subject competence and minimization of the bystander effect. *Journal of Applied Social Psychology, 18,* 1133–1148.

Crandall, C. S. (1988). Social contagion of binge eating. *Journal of Personality and Social Psychology, 55,* 588–598.

Crandall, C. S. (1991). Do heavy weight students have more difficulty paying for college? *Personality and Social Psychology Bulletin, 17,* 606–611.

Crano, W. D., & Sivacek, J. (1984). The influence of incentive-aroused ambivalence on overjustification effects in attitude change. *Journal of Experimental Social Psychology, 20,* 137–158.

Crockenberg, S., & Litman, C. (1986). Autonomy as competence in 2-year-olds: Maternal correlates of child defiance, compliance and self-assertion. *Developmental Psychology, 26,* 961–971.

Crocker, J., & Major, B. (1989). Social stigma and self-esteem: The self-protective properties of stigma. *Psychological Review, 96,* 608–630.

Crocker, J., Voelkl, K., Testa, M., & Major, B. (1991). Social stigma: The affective consequences of attributional ambiguity. *Journal of Personality and Social Psychology, 60,* 218–228.

Crohan, S. E. (1992). Marital happiness and spousal consensus on beliefs about marital conflict: A longitudinal investigation. *Journal of Social and Personal Relationships, 9,* 89–102.

Cronin, P., & Rosa, J. (1990, May). *The effects of age differences on sexual risk-taking behaviors, attitudes and justifications.* Paper presented at Midwestern Psychological Association Meetings, Chicago.

Crosby, F., Bromley, S., & Saxe, L. (1980). Recent unobtrusive studies of black and white discrimination and prejudice: A literature review. *Psychological Bulletin, 87,* 546–563.

Croyle, R. T., & Ditto, P. H. (1990). Illness cognition and behavior: An experimental approach. *Journal of Behavioral Medicine, 13,* 31–52.

Croyle, R. T., & Hunt, J. R. (1991). Coping with health threat: Social influence processes in reactions to medical test results. *Journal of Personality and Social Psychology, 60,* 382–389.

Croyle, R. T., & Williams, K. D. (1991). Reactions to medical diagnosis: The role of stereotypes. *Basic & Applied Psychology, 12,* 227–236.

Crutchfield, R. S. (1955). Conformity and character. *American Psychologist, 10,* 191–198.

Csikszentmihalyi, M. (1990). *Flow: The psychology of optimal experience.* New York: Harper & Row.

Current Biography (1993, September). Reno, Janet, pp. 48–52.

Cutler, B. L., Moran, G. P., & Narby, D. J. (1992). Jury selection in insanity defense cases. *Journal of Research in Personality, 26,* 165–182.

Cutler, B. L., Dexter, H. R., & Penrod, S. D. (1989). Expert testimony and jury decision making: An empirical analysis. *Behavioral Sciences and the Law, 7,* 215–225.

Cutler, B. L., & Penrod, S. D. (1988). Improving the reliability of eyewitness identifications: Lineup construction and presentation. *Journal of Applied Psychology, 73,* 281–290.

Cutler, B. L., Penrod, S. D., & Dexter, H. R. (1989). The eyewitness, the expert psychologist, and the jury. *Law and Human Behavior, 13,* 311–332.

Cutler, B. L., Penrod, S., & Stuve, T. E. (1988). Juror decision making in eyewitness identification cases. *Law and Human Behavior, 12,* 41–56.

Dafraniere, S. (1992, August 12). Identifying Ivan: Does memory mislead? *The Washington Post,* p. A29.

Dallek, R. (1991). *Lone Star rising: Lyndon Johnson and his times, 1908–1960.* New York: Oxford University Press.

Darley, J. M., & Batson, C. D. (1973). "From Jerusalem to Jericho": A study of situational and dispositional variables in helping behavior. *Journal of Personality and Social Psychology, 27,* 100–108.

Darley, J. M., & Gross, P. H. (1983). A hypothesis confirming bias in labelling effects. *Journal of Personality and Social Psychology, 44,* 20–33.

Darley, J. M., & Latané, B. (1968). Bystander intervention in emergencies: Diffusion of responsibility. *Journal of Personality and Social Psychology, 8,* 377–383.

Darley, J. M., Teger, A. I., & Lewis, L. D. (1973). Do groups always inhibit individuals' response to potential emergencies? *Journal of Personality and Social Psychology, 26,* 395–399.

Davis, B. O., Jr. (1991). *American.* Washington, DC: Smithsonian Institution Press.

Davis, J. H. (1969). *Group performance.* New York: Addison-Wesley.

Davis, J. H. (1973). Group decision and social interaction: A theory of social decision schemes. *Psychological Review, 80,* 97–125.

Davis, J. H. (1980). Group decision and procedural justice. In M. Fishbein (Ed.), *Progress in social psychology* (Vol. 1). Hillsdale, NJ: Erlbaum.

Davis, J. H., Kerr, N. L., Atkin, R. S., Holt, R., & Meek, D. (1975). The decision process of 6- and 12-person mock juries assigned unanimous and two-thirds majority rules. *Journal of Personality and Social Psychology, 32,* 1–14.

Davison, A. R., Yantis, S., Norwood, M., & Montano, D. E. (1985). Amount of information about the attitude object and attitude-behavior consistency. *Journal of Personality and Social Psychology, 49,* 1184–1198.

Dean, J. W. (1977). *Blind Ambition.* New York: Pocket Books.

Deaux, K., & Major, B. (1987). Putting gender into context: An interactive model of gender-related behavior. *Psychological Review, 94,* 369–389.

Deffenbacher, K. (1980). Eyewitness accuracy and confidence: Can we infer anything about their relationship? *Law and Human Behavior, 4,* 243–260.

DeJong, M. (1980). The stigma of obesity: The consequence of naive assumptions concerning the causes of physical deviance. *Journal of Health and Social Behavior, 21,* 75–87.

DeJong, W. (1979). An examination of self-perception mediation of the foot-in-the-door effect. *Journal of Personality and Social Psychology, 37,* 2171–2180.

DeLamater, J. (1974). A definition of "group." *Small Group Behavior, 5,* 30–44.

Delgado, J. M. R. (1969). Offensive-defensive behaviour in free monkeys and chimpanzees induced by radio stimulation of the brain. In S. Garattini & E. B. Sigg (Eds.), *Aggressive behavior.* New York: John Wiley.

Delongis, A., Folkman, S., & Lazarus, R. S. (1988). The impact of daily stress on health and mood: Psychological and social resources as mediators. *Journal of Personality and Social Psychology, 54,* 486–495.

Dennis, A. R., Valacich, J. S., & Nunamaker, J. F. (1990). An experimental investigation of the effects of group size in an electronic meeting environment. *IEEE Transactions on Systems, Man, and Cybernetics, 25,* 1049–1057.

DePaulo, B. M., & Fisher, J. D. (1980). The costs of asking for help. *Basic and Applied Social Psychology, 1,* 23–35.

DePaulo, B. M., Kenny, D. A., Hoover, C., Webb, W., & Oliver, P. V. (1987). Accuracy of person perception: Do people know what kinds of impressions they convey? *Journal of Personality and Social Psychology, 52,* 303–315.

Derlega, V. J., Winstead, B. A., & Jones, W. H. (1991). *Personality: Contemporary theory and research.* Chicago: Nelson-Hall.

Desforges, D., Lord, C. G., Ramsey, S. L., Mason, J. A., Van Leeuwen, J. G., West, S. C., & Lepper, M. R. (1991). Effects of structured cooperative contact on changing negative attitudes towards stigmatized social groups. *Journal of Personality and Social Psychology, 60,* 531–544.

Des Pres, T. (1976). *The survivor.* New York: Oxford University Press.

Deutsch, M., & Gerrard, H. B. (1955). A study of normative and informational social influence upon individual judgment. *Journal of Abnormal and Social Psychology, 51,* 629–636.

Deutsch, M., & Krauss, R. M. (1960). The effect of threat on interpersonal bargaining. *Journal of Abnormal and Social Psychology, 61,* 181–189.

Deutsch, M., & Krauss, R. M. (1962). Studies of interpersonal bargaining. *Journal of Conflict Resolution, 6,* 52–76.

Devine, P. G. (1989). Stereotypes and prejudice: Their automatic and controlled components. *Journal of Personality and Social Psychology, 56,* 5–18.

Devine, P. G., Monteith, M. J., Zuwerink, J. R., & Elliot, A. J. (1991). Prejudice without compunction. *Journal of Personality and Social Psychology, 60,* 817–830.

Dexter, H. R., Cutler, B. L., & Moran, G. (1992). A test of voir dire as a remedy for the prejudicial effects of pretrial publicity. *Journal of Applied Social Psychology, 22,* 819–832.

Diaz, C. R. (1975). The feeling of injustice as a cause of homicidal passion. *Revista de Psicologia–Universidad de Monterrey, 4,* 41–49. English Abstract.

Diehl, M., & Stroebe, W. (1987). Productivity loss in brainstorming groups. *Journal of Personality and Social Psychology, 53,* 497–509.

Diehl, M., & Stroebe, W. (1991). Productivity loss in idea-generating groups: Tracking down the blocking effect. *Journal of Personality and Social Psychology, 61,* 392–403.

Dillard, J. P., Hunter, J. E., & Burgoon, M. (1984). Sequential-request persuasive strategies: Meta analysis of foot-in-the-door and door-in-the-face. *Human Communication Research, 10,* 461–488.

Dion, K. K., Berscheid, E., & Walster, E. (1972). What is beautiful is good. *Journal of Personality and Social Psychology, 24,* 285–290.

Dion, K. L., & Dion, K. K. (1988). Romantic love: Individual and cultural perspectives. In R. J. Sternberg & M. L. Barnes (Eds.), *The psychology of love.* New Haven, CT: Yale University Press.

Ditto, P. H., & Hilton, J. L. (1990). Expectancy processes in the health care interaction sequence. *Journal of Social Issues, 46,* 97–124.

Ditto, P. H., & Jemmott, J. B. (1989). From rarity to evaluative extremity: Effects of prevalence information on the evaluation of positive and negative characteristics. *Journal of Personality and Social Psychology, 57,* 16–26.

Dodge, K. A. (1986). A social information processing model of social competence in children. In M. Perlmutter (Ed.), *Minnesota Symposium on Child Psychology* (Vol. 18). Hillsdale, NJ: Erlbaum.

Dodson, C., & Reisberg, D. (1991). Indirect testing of eyewitness memory: The (non)effect of misinformation. *Bulletin of the Psychonomic Society, 29,* 333–336.

Doll, J., & Ajzen, I. (1992). Accessibility and stability of predictors in the Theory of Planned Behavior. *Journal of Personality and Social Psychology, 63,* 754–765.

Dollard, J., Doob, L., Miller, N., Mowrer, O., & Sears, R. (1939). *Frustration and aggression.* New Haven, CT: Yale University Press.

Doms, M., & Van Avermaet, E. (1980). Majority influence and conversion behavior: A replication. *Journal of Experimental Social Psychology, 16,* 283–292.

Donnerstein, E. (1980). Aggressive erotica and violence against women. *Journal of Personality and Social Psychology, 39,* 269–277.

Donnerstein, E., & Barrett, G. (1978). Effects of erotic stimuli on male aggression toward females. *Journal of Personality and Social Psychology, 36,* 180–188.

Donnerstein, E., & Berkowitz, L. (1981). Victim reactions in aggressive erotic films as a factor in violence against women. *Journal of Personality and Social Psychology, 41,* 710–724.

Donnerstein, E., & Donnerstein, M. (1973). Variables in interracial aggression: Potential in-group censure. *Journal of Personality and Social Psychology, 27,* 143–150.

Donnerstein, E., Donnerstein, M., & Evans, R. (1975). Erotic stimuli and aggression: Facilitation or inhibition. *Journal of Personality and Social Psychology, 32,* 237–244.

Dovidio, J. F., Allen, J. L., & Schroeder, D. A. (1990). Specificity of empathy-induced helping: Evidence for altruistic motivation. *Journal of Personality and Social Psychology, 59,* 249–260.

Dovidio, J. F., & Gaertner, S. L. (1981). The effects of race, status, and ability on helping behavior. *Social Psychology Quarterly, 44,* 192–203.

Dower, J. W. (1986). *War without mercy.* New York: Pantheon Books.

Doyle, J. A. (1985). *Sex and gender.* Dubuque, IA: Wm. C. Brown.

Doyle, J. A., & Paludi, M. A. (1991). *Sex and gender* (2nd ed.). Dubuque, IA: Wm. C. Brown.

Dozier, J. B., & Miceli, M. P. (1985). Potential predictors of whistle-blowing: A prosocial perspective. *Academy of Management Review, 10,* 823–836.

Drickamer, L. C., & Vessey, S. H. (1986). *Animal behavior: Concepts, processes and methods* (2nd ed.). Boston: Prindle, Weber, & Schmidt.

Duck, S. W. (1982). A topography of relationship disengagement and dissolution. In S. W. Duck (Ed.), *Personal relationships: Vol. 4. Dissolving personal relationships.* New York: Academic Press.

Duck, S. W. (1983). *Friends for life.* Brighton: Harvester.

Duck, S. W. (1988). *Handbook of personal relationships.* New York: John Wiley.

Dunbar, R. I. M. (1987). Sociobiological explanations and the evolution of ethnocentrism. In V. Reynolds, V. Falger, & I. Vine (Eds.), *The sociobiology of ethnocentrism.* Athens: University of Georgia Press.

Dunning, D., Griffin, D. W., Milojkovic, J. D., & Ross, L. (1990). The overconfidence effect in social prediction. *Journal of Personality and Social Psychology, 58,* 568–581.

Dweck, C. (1975). The role of expectations and attributions in the alleviation of learned helplessness. *Journal of Personality and Social Psychology, 31,* 674–685.

Dweck, C., Davidson, W., Nelson, S., & Enna, B. (1978). Sex differences in learned helplessness: II. The contingencies or evaluative feedback in the classroom and III. An experimental analysis. *Developmental Psychology, 14,* 268–276.

Dweck, C., & Goetz, T. E. (1978). Attributions and learned helplessness. In J. Harvey, W. Ickes, & R. F. Kidd (Eds.), *New directions in attribution theory* (Vol. 2). Hillsdale, NJ: Erlbaum.

Dyck, R. J., & Rule, B. G. (1978). Effect on retaliation of causal attributions concerning attack. *Journal of Personality and Social Psychology, 36,* 521–529.

Eagly, A. H. (1978). Sex differences in influenceability. *Psychological Bulletin, 85,* 86–116.

Eagly, A. (1987). *Sex differences in social behavior: A social role interpretation.* Hillsdale, NJ: Erlbaum.

Eagly, A. H. (1992). Uneven progress: Social psychology and the study of attitudes. *Journal of Personality and Social Psychology, 63,* 693–710.

Eagly, A. H., Ashmore, R. D., Makhijani, M. G., & Longo, L. C. (1991). What is beautiful is good, but . . . : A meta-analytic review of research on the physical attractiveness stereotype. *Psychological Bulletin, 110,* 109–128.

Eagly, A. H., & Carli, L. L. (1981). Sex of researchers and sex-typed communications as determinants of sex differences in influenceability: A meta-analysis of social influence studies. *Psychological Bulletin, 90,* 1–20.

Eagly, A. H., & Chrvala, C. (1986). Sex differences in conformity: Status and gender role interpretations. *Psychology of Women Quarterly, 10,* 203–220.

Eagly, A. H., & Crowley, M. (1986). Gender and helping behavior: A meta-analytic review of the social psychological literature. *Psychological Bulletin, 100,* 309–330.

Eagly, A. H., & Johnson, B. T. (1990). Gender and leadership style: A meta-analysis. *Psychological Bulletin, 108,* 233–256.

Eagly, A. H., & Karau, S. J. (1991). Gender and the emergence of leaders: A meta-analysis. *Journal of Personality and Social Psychology, 60,* 685–710.

Eagly, A. H., & Kite, M. E. (1987). Are stereotypes of nationalities applied to both women and men? *Journal of Personality and Social Psychology, 53,* 451–462.

Eagly, A. H., & Steffen, V. J. (1986). Gender and aggressive behavior: A meta-analytic review of the social psychological literature. *Psychological Bulletin, 100,* 309–330.

Eagly, A. H., & Telaak, K. (1972). Width of the latitude of acceptance as a determinant of attitude change. *Journal of Personality and Social Psychology, 23,* 388–397.

Eagly, A. H., Wood, W., & Chaiken, S. (1978). Causal inferences about communicators and their effect on opinion change. *Journal of Personality and Social Psychology, 36,* 424–435.

Eagly, A. H., Wood, W., & Fishbaugh, L. (1981). Sex differences in conformity: Surveillance by the group as a determinant of male conformity. *Journal of Personality and Social Psychology, 40,* 384–394.

Early, P. (1988). *Family of spies: Inside the John Walker spy ring.* New York: Bantam Books.

Ebbesen, E. B., & Konecni, V. J. (1982). An analysis of the bail system. In V. J. Konecni & E. B. Ebbesen (Eds.), *The criminal justice system: A social-psychological analysis.* San Francisco: W. H. Freeman.

Edelman, B., Engell, D., Bronstein, P., & Hirsch, E. (1986). Environmental effects of the intake of overweight and normal weight men. *Appetite, 7,* 71–83.

Edmonds, E. M., & Cahoon, D. D. (1986). Attitudes concerning crimes related to clothing worn by female victims. *Bulletin of the Psychonomic Society, 24,* 444–446.

Edney, J. J. (1979). The nuts game: A concise commons dilemma analog. *Environmental Psychology and Nonverbal Behavior, 3,* 252–254.

Edwards, S. B., & Flynn, J. P. (1972). Corticospinal control of striking in centrally elicited attack behavior. *Brain Research, 41,* 51–65.

Eisenberg, N., Fabes, R. A., Miller, P. A., Fultz, J., Shell, R., Mathy, R. M., & Reno, R. R. (1989). Relation of sympathy and personal distress to prosocial behavior: A multimethod study. *Journal of Personality and Social Psychology, 57,* 55–66.

Eisenberg, N., & Miller, P. A. (1987). The relation of empathy to prosocial and related behaviors. *Psychological Bulletin, 101,* 91–119.

Eisenberg, N., & Mussen, P. (1989). *The roots of prosocial behavior in children.* Cambridge: Cambridge University Press.

Eitzen, D. S. (1973). Two minorities: The Jews of Poland and the Chinese of the Philippines. In D. E. Gelfand & R. D. Lee (Eds.), *Ethnic conflicts and power: A cross-national perspective.* New York: John Wiley and Sons.

Ekman, P. (1985). *Telling lies: Clues to deceit in the marketplace, politics, and marriage.* New York: Norton.

Elkin, R. A., & Leippe, M. R. (1986). Physiological arousal, dissonance, and attitude change: Evidence for a dissonance-arousal link and a "don't remind me" effect. *Journal of Personality and Social Psychology, 51,* 55–65.

Ellison, K. W., & Buckhout, R. (1981). *Psychology and criminal justice.* New York: Harper & Row.

Elms, A. (1972). *Social psychology and social relevance.* Boston: Little, Brown.

Elms, A., & Milgram, S. (1966). Personality characteristics associated with obedience and defiance toward authoritative command. *Journal of Experimental Research in Personality, 1,* 282–289.

Epstein, S., & Katz, L. (1992). Coping ability, stress, productive load, and symptoms. *Journal of Personality and Social Psychology, 62,* 813–825.

Erber, R., & Therriault, N. (1993, October). *Sweating to the oldies: The mood-absorbing qualities of exercise.* Paper presented at the annual meeting of the Society for Experimental Social Psychology, San Diego.

Erdley, C. A., & D'Agostino, P. R. (1988). Cognitive and affective components of automatic priming effects. *Journal of Personality and Social Psychology, 54,* 741–747.

Eron, L. D., Huesmann, L. R., Lefkowitz, M. M., & Walder, L. O. (1972). Does television violence cause aggression? *American Psychologist, 27,* 253–263.

Eron, L. D., Huesmann, L. R., & Zelli, A. (1991). The role of parental variables in the learning of aggression. In D. J. Pepler & K. H. Rubin (Eds.), *The development and treatment of childhood aggression.* Hillsdale, NJ: Erlbaum.

Ewing, C. P. (1991). Preventive detention and execution: The constitutionality of punishing future crimes. *Law and Human Behavior, 15,* 139–164.

Fagenson, E. A., & Cooper, J. (1987). When push comes to power: A test of power restoration theory's explanation for conflict escalation. *Basic and Applied Social Psychology, 8,* 273–293.

Fanning, D. (1990, March 18). Humiliating time for a boss who smokes. *New York Times,* p. B8.

Farber, J. (1993). We're not gonna take it. *Rolling Stone,* May 13, p. 21.

Farmaian, S. F. (1992). *Daughter of Persia.* New York: Doubleday.

Fazel, M. (1991). Personal communication.

Fazio, R. H. (1986). How do attitudes guide behavior? In R. M. Sorrentino & E. T. Higgins (Eds.), *Handbook of motivation and cognition: Foundations of social behavior.* New York: Guilford Press.

Fazio, R. H. (1988). On the power and functionality of attitudes: The role of attitude accessibility. In A. R. Pratkanis, S. J. Breckler, & A. G. Greenwald (Eds.), *Attitude structure and function.* Hillsdale, NJ: Erlbaum.

Fazio, R. H., Chen, J., McDonel, E., & Sherman, S. J. (1982). Attitude accessibility, attitude-behavior consistency, and the strength of the object-evaluation association. *Journal of Experimental Social Psychology, 18,* 339–357.

Fazio, R. H., & Williams, C. J. (1986). Attitude accessibility as a moderator of the attitude-perception and attitude-behavior relationships. *Journal of Personality and Social Psychology, 51,* 505–514.

Feeney, J. A., & Noller, P. (1990). Attachment style as a predictor of adult romantic relationships. *Journal of Personality and Social Psychology, 58,* 281–291.

Felmlee, D., Sprecher, S., & Bassin, E. (1990). The dissolution of intimate relationships: A hazard model. *Social Psychology Quarterly, 53,* 13–30.

Felner, R. D., Rowlinson, R. T., & Terre, L. (1986). Unraveling the Gordian Knot in life exchange events. In S. M. Auebach & A. L. Stolberg (Eds.), *Children's life crises events: Prevention strategies.* New York: McGraw-Hill.

Feshbach, S. (1964). The function of aggression and the regulation of aggressive drive. *Psychological Bulletin, 71,* 257–272.

Festinger, L. (1954). A theory of social comparison processes. *Human Relations, 7,* 117–140.

Festinger, L. (1957). *A theory of cognitive dissonance.* Stanford, CA: Stanford University Press.

Festinger, L., & Carlsmith, J. M. (1959). Cognitive consequences of forced compliance. *Journal of Abnormal and Social Psychology, 58,* 203–210.

Festinger, L., Riecken, H. W., & Schachter, S. (1982). When prophecy fails. In A. Pines & C. Maslach (Eds.), *Experiencing social psychology: Readings and projects.* New York: Knopf.

Festinger, L., Schachter, S., & Back, K. W. (1959). *Social pressures in informal groups: A study of human factors in housing.* New York: Harper & Row.

Fiebert, M. S., & Wright, K. S. (1989). Midlife friendships in an American faculty sample. *Psychological Reports, 64,* 1127–1130.

Fiedler, F. W. (1967). *A theory of leadership effectiveness.* New York: McGraw-Hill.

Fincham, F. D., & Bradbury, T. N. (1988). The impact of attributions in marriage: An experimental analysis. *Journal of Social and Clinical Psychology, 7,* 147–162.

Fincham, F., & Bradbury, T. N. (1993). Marital satisfaction, depression, and attributions: A longitudinal analysis. *Journal of Personality and Social Psychology, 64,* 442–452.

Finkelhor, D., & Yllo, K. (1982). Forced sex in marriage: A preliminary research report. *Crime and Delinquency, 28,* 459–478.

Fishbein, M., & Ajzen, I. (1975). *Belief, attitude, intention, and behavior: An introduction to theory and research.* Reading, MA: Addison-Wesley.

Fisher, H. (1992). *Anatomy of love.* New York: Norton.

Fisher, J. D., & Nadler, A. (1974). The effect of similarity between donor and recipient on recipient's reactions to aid. *Journal of Experimental Social Psychology, 4,* 230–243.

Fisher, J. D., Nadler, A., & Whitcher-Algana, S. (1982). Recipient reactions to aid. *Psychological Bulletin, 91,* 27–54.

Fiske, S. T. (1982). Schema-triggered affect: Applications to social perception. In M. S. Clark & S. T. Fiske (Eds.), *Affect and cognition: The 17th Annual Carnegie Symposium on Cognition.* Hillsdale, NJ: Erlbaum.

Fiske, S. T. (1992). Thinking is for doing: Portraits of social cognition from Daguerreotype to Laserphoto. *Journal of Personality and Social Psychology, 63,* 877–889.

Fiske, S. T. (1993). Social cognition and social perception. In M. R. Rosenzweig & L. W. Porter (Eds.), *Annual Review of Psychology, 44,* 155–194.

Fiske, S. T., & Neuberg, S. L. (1990). A continuum of impression formation, from category-based to individuating processes: Influence of information and motivation attention and interpretation. In M. Zanna (Ed.), *Advances in experimental social psychology* (Vol. 23). San Diego, CA: Academic Press.

Fiske, S. T., & Taylor, S. E. (1984). *Social cognition.* Reading, MA: Addison-Wesley.

Fiske, S. T., & Taylor, S. E. (1991). *Social cognition* (2nd ed.). New York: McGraw-Hill.

Fitzgerald, F. (1979). *America revised: History textbooks in the twentieth century.* Boston: Little, Brown.

Fitzgerald, F. S. (1925). *The great Gatsby.* New York: Collier Books.

Fitzgerald, L. F., Shullman, S., Bailey, N., Richards, M., Swecker, J., Gold, Y., Ormerod, M., & Weitzman, L. (1988). The incidence and dimensions of sexual harassment in the workplace. *Journal of Vocational Behavior, 32,* 152–175.

Fitzgerald, R., & Ellsworth, P. C. (1984). Due process vs. crime control: Death qualification and jury attitudes. *Law and Human Behavior, 8,* 31–51.

Flanagan, T. J., & Maguire, K. (1992). *Bureau of Justice statistics: Sourcebook of criminal justice statistics–1991.* Albany, NY: Hindelang Criminal Justice Center.

Fleming, A. (1976). *Ida Tarbell: First of the muckrakers.* New York: Thomas Y. Crowell.

Fleming, A. (1986). *Ida Tarbell.* New York: Bantam Books.

Fleming, J. H., & Darley, J. M. (1989). Perceiving choice and constraint. The effects of contextual and behavioral cues on attitude attribution. *Journal of Personality and Social Psychology, 56,* 27–40.

Fleming, J. H., & Darley, J. M. (1990). The purposeful-action sequence and the illusion of control. *Personality and Social Psychology Bulletin, 16,* 346–357.

Fleming, J. H., & Darley, J. M. (1991). Mixed messages: The multiple audience problem and strategic communication. *Social Cognition, 9,* 25–46.

Fleming, J. H., Darley, J. M., Hilton, J. L., & Kojetin, B. A. (1990). Multiple audience problem: A strategic communication perspective on social perception. *Journal of Personality and Social Psychology, 58,* 593–609.

Fletcher, G. J. O., & Ward, C. (1988). Attribution theory and processes: A cross-cultural perspective. In M. H. Bond (Ed.), *The cross-cultural challenge to social psychology.* Newbury Park, CA: Sage Publications.

Flohr, H. (1987). Biological bases of social prejudices. In V. Reynolds, V. Falger, & I. Vine (Eds.), *The sociobiology of ethnocentrism.* Athens: University of Georgia Press.

Flowers, M. (1977). A laboratory test of some implications of Janis' groupthink hypothesis. *Journal of Personality and Social Psychology, 35,* 888–896.

Foehl, J. C., & Goldman, M. (1983). Increasing altruistic behavior by using compliance techniques. *Journal of Social Psychology, 119,* 21–29.

Forehand, R., & Long, N. (1991). Prevention of aggression and other behavior problems in the early adolescent years. In D. J. Pepler & K. H. Rubin (Eds.), *The development and treatment of childhood aggression.* Hillsdale, NJ: Erlbaum.

Forgas, J. P., Furnham, A., & Frey, D. (1990). Cross-national differences in attributions of wealth and economic success. *Journal of Social Psychology, 129,* 643–657.

ForsterLee, L., Horowitz, I. A., & Bourgeois, M. J. (1993). Juror competence in civil trials: The effects of preinstruction and evidence technicality. *Journal of Applied Psychology, 78,* 14–21.

Forsyth, D. R. (1990). *Group dynamics* (2nd ed.). Pacific Grove, CA: Brooks/Cole.

Foss, R. D., & Dempsey, C. B. (1979). Blood donation and the foot-in-the-door technique. *Journal of Personality and Social Psychology, 37,* 580–590.

Frank, M. G., & Gilovich, T. (1989). Effect of memory perspective on retrospective causal attribution. *Journal of Personality and Social Psychology, 57,* 399–403.

Frank, R. G., Bouman, D. E., Cain, K., & Watts, C. (1992). Primary prevention of catastrophic injury. *American Psychologist, 47,* 1045–1049.

Frazier, P. A. (1990). Victim attributions and post-rape trauma. *Journal of Personality and Social Psychology, 59,* 298–304.

Frazier, P. A. (1991). Self-blame as a mediator of post-rape depressive symptoms. *Journal of Social and Clinical Psychology, 10,* 47–57.

Freedman, J. L. (1984). Effect of television violence on aggressiveness. *Psychological Bulletin, 96,* 227–246.

Freedman, J. L. (1986). Television violence and aggression: A rejoinder. *Psychological Bulletin, 3,* 372–378.

Freedman, J. L., Cunningham, J. A., & Krismer, K. (1992). Inferred values and the reverse-incentive effect in induced compliance. *Journal of Personality and Social Psychology, 62,* 357–368.

Freedman, J. L., & Fraser, S. C. (1966). Compliance without pressure: The foot-in-the-door technique. *Journal of Personality and Social Psychology, 4,* 195–202.

French, J. R. P., Jr., & Raven, B. H. (1968). The bases of social power. In D. Cartwright & A. Zander (Eds.), *Group dynamics: Research and theory.* New York: Harper & Row.

Fried, M., Kaplan, K. J., & Klein, K. W. (1975). Juror selection: An analysis of voir dire. In R. J. Simon (Ed.), *The jury system in America.* Beverly Hills, CA: Sage Publications.

Friedman, H. S., & Booth-Kewley, S. (1987). Validity of the Type A construct: A reprise. *Psychological Bulletin, 104,* 381–384.

Friedman, H. S., Tucker, J. S., Tomlinson-Keasey, C., Schwartz, J. E., Wingard, D. L., & Criqui, M. H. (1993). Does childhood personality predict longevity? *Journal of Personality and Social Psychology, 65,* 176–185.

Friedman, L. M. (1985). *A history of American law* (2nd ed.). New York: Simon & Schuster.

Friedman, M., & Rosenman, R. H. (1974). *Type A behavior and your heart.* New York: Knopf.

Friedrich, L. K., & Stein, A. H. (1975). Prosocial television and young children: The effects of verbal labeling and role playing on learning and behavior. *Child Development, 46,* 27–38.

Funk, S. C., & Houston, B. K. (1987). A critical analysis of the Hardiness Scale's validity and utility. *Journal of Personality and Social Psychology, 53,* 572–578.

Furnham, A. (1984). Studies of cross-cultural conformity: A brief critical review. *Psychologia: An International Journal of Psychology, 27,* 65–72.

Gadow, K. D., & Sprafkin, J. (1987). Effects of viewing high versus low aggression cartoons on emotionally disturbed children. *Journal of Pediatric Psychology, 12,* 413–427.

Gaertner, S. L. (1975). The role of racial attitudes in helping behavior. *Journal of Social Psychology, 97,* 95–101.

Gaertner, S. L., & Dovidio, J. F. (1977). The subtlety of white racism, arousal, and helping behavior. *Journal of Personality and Social Psychology, 35,* 691–707.

Gaertner, S. L., & Dovidio, J. F. (1986). The aversive form of racism. In J. F. Dovidio & S. L. Gaertner (Eds.), *Prejudice, discrimination, & racism.* San Diego, CA: Academic Press.

Gaertner, S. L., Dovidio, J. F., & Johnson, G. (1982). Race of victim, nonresponsive bystander, and helping behavior. *Journal of Social Psychology, 117,* 69–77.

Gamson, W. A., Fireman, B., & Rytina, S. (1982). *Encounters with unjust authority.* Homewood, IL: Dorsey Press.

Garcia, S., Stinson, L., Ickes, W., Bissonette, V., & Briggs, S. R. (1991). Shyness and physical attractiveness in mixed-sex dyads. *Journal of Personality and Social Psychology, 61,* 35–49.

Garrison, J. (1992, June 21). The mother of the abortion rights movement. *Image,* pp. 6–11, 28–29.

Gatchel, R. J., Baum, A., & Krantz, D. S. (1989). *An introduction to health psychology.* New York: McGraw-Hill.

Gavanski, I., & Wells, G. L. (1989). Counterfactual processing of normal and exceptional events. *Journal of Experimental Social Psychology, 25,* 314–325.

Geen, R. G. (1989). Alternative conceptions of social facilitation. In P. B. Paulus (Ed.), *Psychology of group influence* (2nd ed.). Hillsdale, NJ: Erlbaum.

Geen, R. G., & Quanty, M. (1977). The catharsis of aggression: An evaluation of a hypothesis. In L. Berkowitz (Ed.), *Advances in experimental social psychology* (Vol. 10). New York: Academic Press.

Geffner, R., & Gross, M. M. (1984). Sex role behavior and obedience to authority: A field study. *Sex Roles, 10,* 973–985.

Gelman, E., Wang, P., Powell, B., & Smith, V. E. (1985, July 22). Hey America, Coke are it. *Newsweek,* pp. 40–43.

Gergen, K. J. (1974). Toward a psychology of receiving help. *Journal of Applied Social Psychology, 4,* 187–193.

Gergen, K. J., Gergen, M., & Barton, H. (1973, October). Deviance in the dark. *Psychology Today,* pp. 129–130.

Gerrard, M., Gibbons, F. X., Warner, T. D., & Smith, G. E. (1993). Perceived vulnerability to HIV infection and AIDS preventive behavior: A critical review of the evidence. In J. B. Pryor & G. D. Reeder (Eds.), *The social psychology of HIV infection.* Hillsdale, NJ: Erlbaum.

Gest, T. (1986, October 20). Black and white issue? *U.S. News and World Report,* pp. 24–25.

Gibbons, F. X. (1990). Self-attention and behavior: A review and theoretical update. In M. P. Zanna (Ed.), *Advances in experimental social psychology* (Vol. 23). San Diego, CA: Academic Press.

Gibbs, N. (1993, July 12). Truth, justice and the Reno way. *Time,* pp. 20–27.

Gibson, J. T., & Haritos-Fatouros, M. (1986, November). The education of a torturer. *Psychology Today,* pp. 50–58.

Gilbert, D. T. (1989). Thinking lightly about others: Automatic components of the social inference process. In J. Uleman & J. A. Bargh (Eds.), *Unintended thought.* New York: Guilford Press.

Gilbert, D. T. (1991). How mental systems believe. *American Psychologist, 46,* 107–119.

Gilbert, D. T., & Hixon, J. G. (1991). The trouble of thinking: Activation and application of stereotypic beliefs. *Journal of Personality and Social Psychology, 60,* 509–517.

Gilbert, D. T., & Krull, D. S. (1988). Seeing less is knowing more: The benefits of perceptual ignorance. *Journal of Personality and Social Psychology, 54,* 193–202.

Gilbert, D. T., McNulty, S. E., Guiliano, T. A., & Benson, J. E. (1992). Blurry words and fuzzy deeds: The attribution of obscure behavior. *Journal of Personality and Social Psychology, 62,* 18–25.

Gilbert, D. T., Pelham, B. W., & Krull, D. S. (1988). On cognitive busyness: When person perceivers meet persons perceived. *Journal of Personality and Social Psychology, 54,* 733–740.

Gilbert, S. J. (1981). Another look at the Milgram obedience studies: The role of the graduated series of shocks. *Personality and Social Psychology Bulletin, 7,* 600–695.

Gilovich, T. (1981). Seeing the past in the present: The effects of associations to familiar events on judgments and decisions. *Journal of Personality and Social Psychology, 40,* 797–808.

Gilovich, T. (1991). *How we know what isn't so: The fallibility of human reason in everyday life.* New York: Free Press.

Glassman, R. B., Packel, E. W., & Brown, D. L. (1986). Greenbeards and kindred spirits: A preliminary mathematical model of altruism toward nonkin who bear similarities to the giver. *Ethology and Sociobiology, 7,* 107–115.

Gleicher, F., & Petty, R. E. (1992). Expectations of reassurance influence the nature of fear-stimulated attitude change. *Journal of Experimental Social Psychology, 28,* 86–100.

Gold, P. E. (1987). Sweet memories. *American Scientist, 75,* 151–155.

Goldfarb, R. L. (1965). *Ransom.* New York: Harper & Row.

Goldman, M. (1986). Compliance employing a combined foot-in-the-door and door-in-the-face procedure. *Journal of Social Psychology, 126,* 111–116.

Goldman, M. (1988). The fate of Europe's Jews under Nazi rule. *Toledo Jewish News,* pp. 6–14.

Goldman, M., & Creason, C. R. (1981). Inducing compliance by a two-door-in-the-face procedure and a self-determination request. *Journal of Social Psychology, 114,* 229–235.

Goldman, M., Creason, C. R., & McCall, C. G. (1981). Compliance employing a two-feet-in-the-door procedure. *Journal of Social Psychology, 114,* 259–265.

Goldman, M., Seever, M., & Seever, M. (1982). Social labeling and the foot-in-the-door effect. *Journal of Social Psychology, 117,* 19–23.

Goleman, D. (1991). *Psychology updates.* New York, Harper-Collins.

Goleman, D. (1993a). Poets know how spurned lovers suffer; science finds pain on the other side, too. *New York Times,* February 9, B1.

Goleman, D. (1993b). Pollsters enlist psychologists in quest for unbiased results. *New York Times,* September 7, p. 28.

Goleman, D. (1993c). The secret of long life? Be dour and dependable. *New York Times,* November 9, B8.

Goodman, G. S., Golding, J. M., Helgeson, V., Haith, M. M., & Michelli, J. (1987). When a child takes the stand: Jurors' perceptions of children's eyewitness testimony. *Law and Human Behavior, 11,* 27–40.

Goodman, G. S., & Helgeson, V. (1988). Children as eyewitnesses: What do they remember? In L. E. Aurbach-Walker (Ed.), *Handbook of sexual abuse of children: Assessment and treatment issues.* New York: Springer Publishing Company.

Goodman, G. S., Levine, M., Melton, G. B., & Ogden, D. W. (1991). Child witnesses and the confrontation clause: The American Psychological Association brief in *Maryland v. Craig, 15,* 13–30.

Goodman, G. S., & Reed, R. S. (1986). Age differences in eyewitness testimony. *Law and Human Behavior, 10,* 317–332.

Goodwin, D. K. (1976). *Lyndon Johnson and the American dream.* New York: Harper and Row.

Goranson, R. E., & Berkowitz, L. (1966). Reciprocity and responsibility reactions to prior help. *Journal of Personality and Social Psychology, 3,* 227–232.

Goranson, R. E., & Berkowitz, L. (1974). Reciprocity and responsibility reactions to prior help. *Journal of Personality and Social Psychology, 3,* 227–232.

Gottman, J. M., & Levenson, R. W. (1986). Assessing the role of emotion in marriage. *Behavioral Assessment, 8,* 31–48.

Gould, S. J. (1985). *The mismeasure of man.* New York: W. W. Norton.

Gouldner, A. W. (1960). The norm of reciprocity: A preliminary statement. *American Sociological Review, 25,* 161–178.

Graham, S., Weiner, B., Giuliano, T., & Williams, E. (1993). An attributional analysis of reactions to Magic Johnson. *Journal of Applied Social Psychology, 23,* 996–1010.

Greenberg, M. A., & Stone, A. A. (1992). Emotional disclosure about traumas and its relation to health: Effects of previous disclosure and trauma severity. *Journal of Personality and Social Psychology, 63,* 75–84.

Greene, E. (1990). Media effects on jurors. *Law and Human Behavior, 14,* 439–450.

Greene, E., & Wade, R. (1987). Of private talk and public print: General pretrial publicity and juror decision making. *Applied Cognitive Psychology, 2,* 123–135.

Greene, E., Wilson, L., & Loftus, E. F. (1989). Impact of hypnotic testimony on the jury. *Law and Human Behavior, 13,* 61–78.

Greenwald, A. G. (1968). Cognitive learning, cognitive response to persuasion, and attitude change. In A. G. Greenwald, T. C. Brock, & T. M. Ostrom (Eds.), *Psychological foundations of attitudes.* New York: Academic Press.

Greenwald, A. G. (1980). The totalitarian ego: Fabrication and revision of personal history. *American Psychologist, 35,* 603–612.

Greenwald, A. G. (1989). Self-knowledge and self-deception. In J. S. Lockard & D. L. Paulhus (Eds.), *Self-deception: An adaptive mechanism.* New York: Prentice-Hall.

Greenwald, A. G., & Banaji, M. R. (1989). The self as a memory system: Powerful but ordinary. *Journal of Personality and Social Psychology, 57,* 41–54.

Greenwald, A. G., & Pratkanis, A. R. (1984). The self. In R. S. Wyer & T. K. Srull (Eds.), *Handbook of social cognition.* Hillsdale, NJ: Erlbaum.

Greenwald, A. G., Spangerberg, E. R., Pratkanis, A. R., & Eskenazi, J. (1991). Double-blind tests of self-help audiotapes. *Psychological Science, 2,* 119–122.

Griffin, D. W., & Ross, L. (1991). Subjective construal, social inference, and human misunderstanding. In M. P. Zanna (Ed.), *Advances in experimental social psychology* (Vol. 24). San Diego, CA: Academic Press.

Gross, A. E., & McMullen, P. A. (1982). The help-seeking process. In V. J. Derlaga & J. Grezlak (Eds.), *Cooperation and helping behavior: Theories and research.* New York: Academic Press.

Groth, A. N. (1979). *Men who rape: The psychology of the offender.* New York: Plenum Press.

Gruder, C. L., Cook, T. D., Hennigan, K. M., Flay, B. R., Alessis, C., & Halamaji, J. (1979). Empirical tests of the absolute sleeper effect predicted from the discounting cue hypothesis. *Journal of Personality and Social Psychology, 36,* 1061–1074.

Gruder, C. L., Romer, D., & Korth, B. (1978). Dependency and fault as determinants of helping. *Journal of Experimental Social Psychology, 14,* 227–235.

Gutek, B. (1990, November). *A survey of sexual harassment on the job.* Paper presented at conference on work and well-being: An agenda for the '90's.

Haddon, W. H., Jr., & Baker, S. P. (1987). Injury control. In D. W. Clark & B. MacMahon (Eds.), *Preventive and community medicine* (2nd ed.). Boston: Little, Brown.

Hamilton, D. L., & Sherman, S. J. (1989). Illusory correlations: Implications for stereotype theory. In D. Bar-Tal, C. F. Graumann, A. W. Kruglanski, & W. Stroebe (Eds.), *Stereotypes and prejudice.* New York: Springer-Verlag.

Hamilton, D. L., & Trolier, T. K. (1986). Stereotypes and stereotyping: An overview of the cognitive approach. In J. Dovidio & S. L. Gaertner (Eds.), *Prejudice, discrimination, & racism.* Orlando, FL: Academic Press.

Haney, C. (1984). On the selection of capital juries: The biasing effects of the death-qualification process. *Law and Human Behavior, 8,* 121–132.

Hansen, C. H., & Hansen, R. D. (1988). Finding the face in the crowd: An anger superiority effect. *Journal of Personality and Social Psychology, 54,* 917–924.

Haque, A., & Lawson, E. D. (1980). The mirror image phenomenon in the context of the Arab–Israeli conflict. *International Journal of Intercultural Relations, 4,* 107–115.

Harari, H., Harari, O., & White, R. V. (1985). The reaction to rape by American male bystanders. *Journal of Social Psychology, 125,* 653–668.

Harasty, A., & Horowitz, I. A. (1991). *An experimental investigation of alternatives to death qualification.* Unpublished paper, University of Toledo, Ohio.

Hardin, G. (1968). The tragedy of the commons. *Science, 166,* 1103–1107.

Haritos-Fatouros, M. (1988). The official torturer: A learning model of obedience to the authority of violence. *Journal of Applied Social Psychology, 18,* 1107–1120.

Harkins, S. G., & Petty, R. E. (1982). Effects of task difficulty and task uniqueness on social loafing. *Journal of Personality and Social Psychology, 43,* 1214–1229.

Harkins, S. G., & Szymanski, K. (1987). Social loafing and social facilitation: New wine in old bottles. In C. Hendrick (Ed.), *Review of personality and social psychology* (Vol. 9). Newbury Park, CA: Sage.

Harris, M. B. (1990). Is love seen as different for the obese? *Journal of Applied Social Psychology, 20,* 1209–1224.

Hartley, E. L. (1946). *Attitudes and prejudice.* New York: Crown Point Press.

Harvey, J. H., & Weary, G. (1981). *Perspectives on attributional processes.* Dubuque, IA: W. C. Brown.

Harvey, J. H., & Weary, G. (1984). Current issues in attribution theory and research. *Annual Review of Psychology, 35,* 427–459.

Hass, R. G., Katz, I., Rizzo, N., Bailey, J., & Eisenstadt, D. (1991). Cross-racial appraisals as related to attitude ambivalence and cognitive complexity. *Personality and Social Psychology Bulletin, 17,* 83–92.

Hastie, R. (1991). Is attorney-conducted voir dire an effective procedure for the selection of impartial juries? *American University Law Review, 40,* 703–726.

Hastie, R., Penrod, S., & Pennington, N. (1983). *Inside the jury.* Cambridge, MA: Harvard University Press.

Hastie, R., & Rasinski, K. A. (1988). The concept of accuracy in social judgment. In D. Bar-Tal & E. Kruglanski (Eds.), *The social psychology of knowledge.* Cambridge, England: Cambridge University Press.

Hatfield, E. (1988). Passionate and companionate love. In R. J. Sternberg & M. L. Barnes (Eds.), *The psychology of love.* New Haven, CT: Yale University Press.

Hatfield, E. (Walster), Aronson, V., Abrahams, D., & Rottman, L. (1966). Importance of physical attractiveness in dating behavior. *Journal of Personality and Social Psychology, 4,* 508–516.

Hatfield, E., & Rapson, R. I. (1993). *Love, sex, and intimacy: Their psychology, biology and history.* New York: Harper-Collins.

Hatfield, E., Traupmann, J., Sprecher, S., Utne, M., & Hay, J. (1985). Equity and intimate relationships: Recent research. In W. Ickes (Ed.), *Compatible and incompatible relationships.* New York: Springer-Verlag.

Hatfield, E., & Walster, G. W. (1981). *A new look at love.* Reading, MA: Addison-Wesley.

Hatfield, E. H., Walster, G. W., & Berscheid, E. (1978). *Equity theory and research.* Boston: Allyn & Bacon.

Hatfield, E. H., Walster, G. W., & Traupmann, J. (1978). Equity and premarital sex. *Journal of Personality and Social Psychology, 36,* 82–92.

Haugaard, J. J., Reppucci, N. D., Laird, J., & Nauful, T. (1991). Children's definitions of the truth and their competency as witnesses in legal proceedings. *Law and Human Behavior, 15,* 253–272.

Haugtvedt, C. P., & Petty, R. E. (1992). Personality and persuasion: Need for cognition moderates the persistence and resistance of attitude change. *Journal of Personality and Social Psychology, 63,* 308–319.

Haugtvedt, C. P., Petty, R. E., & Cacioppo, J. T. (in press). Need for cognition and advertising: Understanding the role of personality in consumer behavior. *Journal of Consumer Psychology.*

Haugtvedt, C. P., & Wegener, D. T. (1993, May 1). *Need for cognition and message order effects in persuasion.* Paper presented at the sixty-fifth annual meeting of the Midwestern Psychological Association, Chicago.

Hays, R. B. (1985). A longitudinal study of friendship development. *Journal of Personality and Social Psychology, 48,* 909–924.

Hays, R. B. (1988a). Friendship. In S. Duck (Ed.), *Handbook of personal relationships.* New York: John Wiley.

Hays, R. B. (1988b). The day-to-day functioning of casual versus close friendships. *Journal of Social and Personal Relationships, 5,* 261–273.

Heatherton, T. F., & Baumeister, R. F. (1991). Binge eating as an escape from self-awareness. *Psychological Bulletin, 110,* 86–108.

Heatherton, T. F., Herman, C. P., & Polivy, J. (1991). Effects of physical threat and ego threat on eating behavior. *Journal of Personality and Social Psychology, 60,* 138–143.

Heaton, A. W., & Sigall, H. (1991). Self-consciousness, self-presentation, and performance: Who chokes, and when? *Journal of Applied Social Psychology, 21,* 175–188.

Heaton, T. B., & Albrecht, S. L. (1991). Stable unhappy marriages. *Journal of Marriage and the Family, 53,* 747–758.

Hebb, D. O., & Thompson, W. R. (1968). The social significance of minimal studies. In G. Lindzey & E. Aronson (Eds.), *The handbook of social psychology* (2nd. Ed., Vol. 2). Reading, MA: Addison-Wesley.

Heider, F. (1944). Social perception and phenomenal causality. *Psychological Review, 51,* 258–374.

Heider, F. (1958). *The psychology of interpersonal relations.* New York: Wiley.

Hendrick, C. (1988). Roles and gender in relationships. In S. Duck (Ed.), *Handbook of personal relationships.* New York: Wiley.

Hendrick, C., & Hendrick, S. S. (1989). Research on love: Does it measure up? *Journal of Personality and Social Psychology, 56,* 784–794.

Hendrick, S. S., & Hendrick, C. (1987). Love and sex attitudes: A close relationship. In W. H. Jones & D. Perlman (Eds.), *Advances in personal relationships* (Vol. 1). Greenwich, CT: JAI Press.

Herbert, T. B., Silver, R. C., & Ellard, J. H. (1991). Coping with an abusive relationship: How and why women stay. *Journal of Marriage and the Family, 53,* 311–326.

Herek, G. M., & Glunt, E. K. (1988). An epidemic of stigma: Public reactions to AIDS. *American Psychologist, 43,* 886–891.

Herhold, S. (1994, May 24). Denny's settles bias case for $46 million. *San Jose Mercury News,* p. 1 & 16a.

Herman, C. P., Olmstead, M. P., & Polivy, J. (1983). Obesity, externality, and susceptibility to social influence: An integrated analysis. *Journal of Personality and Social Psychology, 45,* 926–934.

Hersh, S. (1970). *My Lai 4: A report on the massacre and its aftermath.* New York: Vintage Books.

Hess, D. (1994, January 27). Angst is up, but crime rate is down. *San Jose Mercury News,* pp. 1A, 6A.

Hess, R. D., & Torney, J. V. (1967). *The development of political attitudes in children.* Chicago: Aldine.

Heuer, L. B., & Penrod, S. (1986). Procedural preference as a function of conflict intensity. *Journal of Personality and Social Psychology, 51,* 700–710.

Hewstone, M., Hantzi, A., & Johnston, L. (1991). Social categorization and person memory: The pervasiveness of race as an organizing principle. *European Journal of Social Psychology, 21,* 517–528.

Higgins, E. T. (1989). Self-discrepancy theory: What patterns of self-beliefs cause people to suffer? In L. Berkowitz, *Advances in experimental social psychology* (Vol. 22). San Diego, CA: Academic Press.

Higgins, E. T., & Bargh, J. A. (1987). Knowledge accessibility and activation: Subjectivity and social perception. *Annual Review of Psychology, 38,* 59–69.

Higgins, E. T., & Stangor, C. (1988). Context-driven social judgment and memory when "behavior engulfs the field" in reconstructive memory. In D. Bar-Tal & A. W. Kruglanski (Eds.), *The social psychology of knowledge.* Cambridge, England: Cambridge University Press.

Higgins, E. T., & Tykocinsky, O. (1992). Self-discrepancies and biographical memory: Personality and cognition at the level of psychological situation. *Personality and Social Psychological Bulletin, 18,* 527–535.

Hill, C. A. (1987). Affiliation motivation: People who need people . . . but in different ways. *Journal of Personality and Social Psychology, 52,* 1008–1018.

Hill, C. T., Rubin, Z., & Peplau, L. A. (1976). Breakups before marriage: The end of 103 affairs. *Journal of Social Issues, 32,* 147–168.

Hill, J. L., & Zautra, A. J. (1989). Self-blame attributions and unique vulnerability as predictors of post-rape demoralization. *Journal of Social and Clinical Psychology, 8,* 368–375.

Hillenbrand, B. (1992, February 10). America in the Mind of Japan. *Time,* 20–23.

Hilton, D. J. (1990). Conversational processes and causal explanation. *Psychological Review, 107,* 65–81.

Hilton, D. J., & Slugoski, B. R. (1986). Knowledge-based causal attribution: The abnormal conditions focus model. *Psychological Review, 93,* 75–88.

Hilton, J. L., & Darley, J. M. (1991). The effects of interaction goals on person perception. In M. P. Zanna (Ed.), *Advances in experimental social psychology* (Vol. 24). San Diego, CA: Academic Press.

Hilton, J. L., Klein, J. G., & von Hippel, W. (1991). Attention allocation and impression formation. *Personality and Social Psychology Bulletin, 17,* 548–559.

Hixon, J. G., & Swann, W. B., Jr. (1993). When does introspection bear fruit? Self-reflection, self-insight, and interpersonal choice. *Journal of Personality and Social Psychology, 64,* 35–43.

Hoffman, M. L. (1981). Is altruism part of human nature? *Journal of Personality and Social Psychology, 40,* 121–137.

Hollander, E. P. (1985). Leadership and power. In G. Lindzey & E. Aronson (Eds.), *Handbook of social psychology* (Vol. 2). New York: Random House.

Holmes, T. H., & Rahe, R. H. (1967). The Social Readjustment Rating Scale. *Journal of Psychosomatic Medicine, 11,* 213–218.

Holtzworth-Monroe, A., & Jacobson, N. S. (1985). Causal attributions of married couples: When do they search for causes? What do they conclude? *Journal of Personality and Social Psychology, 48,* 1398–1412.

Hornik, J. (1988). Cognitive thoughts mediating compliance in multiple request situations. *Journal of Economic Psychology, 9,* 69–79.

Horowitz, I. A. (1980). Juror selection: A comparison of two methods in several criminal cases. *Journal of Applied Social Psychology, 10,* 86–99.

Horowitz, I. A. (1985). The effect of jury nullification instructions on verdicts and jury functioning in criminal trials. *Law and Human Behavior, 9,* 25–36.

Horowitz, I. A. (1988). Jury nullification: The impact of judicial instructions, arguments, and challenges on jury decision making. *Law and Human Behavior, 12,* 439–454.

Horowitz, I. A., & Bordens, K. S. (1990). An experimental investigation of procedural issues in toxic tort trials. *Law and Human Behavior, 14,* 269–286.

Horowitz, I. A., & Seguin, D. (1986). The effects of bifurcation and death qualification on the guilt determination process. *Journal of Applied Social Psychology, 16,* 165–185.

Horowitz, I. A., & Willging, T. E. (1984). *The psychology of law: Integrations and applications.* Boston: Little, Brown.

Horowitz, I. A., & Willging, T. E. (1991). Changing views of jury power: The nullification debate 1787–1988. *Law and Human Behavior, 15,* 165–182.

Horwitz, M., & Rabbie, J. M. (1989). Stereotype of groups, group members, and individuals in categories: A differential analysis. In D. Bar-Tal, C. F. Graumann, A. W. Kruglanski, & W. Stroebe (Eds.), *Stereotyping and prejudice.* New York: Springer-Verlag.

House, J. S., Landis, K. R., & Umberson, D. (1988). Social relationships and health. *Science, 241,* 540–545.

Houston, B. K. (1988). Cardiovascular and neuroendocrine reactivity, global type A, and the components of type A behavior. In B. K. Houston & C. R. Snyder (Eds.), *Type A behavior pattern.* New York: Plenum.

Hovland, C. I., Harvey, O. J., & Sherif, M. (1957). Assimilation and contrast effects in reactions to communication and attitude change. *Journal of Abnormal and Social Psychology, 55,* 244–252.

Hovland, C. I., Janis, I. L., & Kelley, H. H. (1953). *Persuasion and communication.* New Haven, CT: Yale University Press.

Huang, L., & Harris, M. (1973). Conformity in Chinese and Americans: A field experiment. *Journal of Cross-Cultural Psychology, 4,* 427–434.

Huesmann, L. R. (1986). Psychological processes promoting the relationship between exposure to media violence and aggressive behavior by the viewer. *Journal of Social Issues, 42,* 125–139.

Huesmann, L. R. (1988). An information processing model for the development of aggression. *Aggressive Behavior, 14,* 13–24.

Huesmann, L. R., & Eron, L. D. (1984). Cognitive processes and the persistence of aggressive behavior. *Aggressive Behavior, 10,* 243–251.

Huesmann, L. R., Eron, L. D., Lefkowitz, M. M., & Walder, L. O. (1984). Stability of aggression over time and generations. *Developmental Psychology, 20,* 1120–1134.

Huesmann, L. R., Lagerspetz, K., & Eron, L. D. (1984). Intervening variables in the TV violence-aggression relation: Evidence from two countries. *Developmental Psychology, 20,* 746–775.

Huesmann, L. R., & Malamuth, N. M. (1986). Media violence and antisocial behavior: An overview. *Journal of Social Issues, 42,* 1–6.

Huggins, N. I. (1977). *Black odyssey: The Afro-American ordeal in slavery.* New York: Pantheon Books.

Hull, J. G., Van Treuren, R. R., & Propson, P. M. (1988).

Attributional style and the components of hardiness. *Personality and Social Psychology Bulletin, 14*, 505–513.

Hull, J. G., Van Treuren, R. R., & Virnelli, S. (1987). Hardiness and health: A critique and alternative approach. *Journal of Personality and Social Psychology, 53*, 518–530.

Huneke, D. K. (1986). The lessons of Herman Graebe's life: The origins of a moral person. *Humboldt Journal of Social Relations, 13*, 320–332.

Hunsberger, B., & Platonow, E. (1986). Religion and helping charitable causes. *Journal of Psychology, 120*, 517–528.

Huston, T. L., & Vangelisti, A. L. (1991). Socioemotional behavior and satisfaction in marital relationships: A longitudinal study. *Journal of Personality and Social Psychology, 61*, 721–733.

Hyde, J. S. (1984). How large are gender differences in aggression? A developmental meta-analysis. *Developmental Psychology, 20*, 722–736.

Hymowitz, C., & Weissman, M. (1984). *A history of women in America.* New York: Bantam Books.

Ike, B. W. (1987). Man's limited sympathy as a consequence of his evolution in small kin groups. In V. Reynolds, V. Falger, & I. Vine (Eds.), *The sociobiology of ethnocentrism.* Athens: University of Georgia Press.

Insel, P. M., & Roth, W. T. (1994). *Core concepts in health* (7th ed.). Mountain View, CA: Mayfield.

Irwin, C. J. (1987). A study in the evolution of ethnocentrism. In V. Reynolds, V. Falger, & I. Vine (Eds.), *The sociobiology of ethnocentrism.* Athens: University of Georgia Press.

Isen, A. M. (1987). Positive affect, cognitive processes and social behavior. In L. Berkowitz (Ed.), *Advances in social psychology* (Vol. 20). New York: Academic Press.

Isen, A. M., & Simmonds, S. F. (1978). The effect of feeling good on helping: Cookies and kindness. *Social Psychology, 41*, 346–349.

Isenberg, D. J. (1986). Group polarization: A critical review and meta-analysis. *Journal of Personality and Social Psychology, 50*, 1141–1151.

Jacoby, J. E., & Paternoster, R. (1982). Sentencing disparity and jury packing: Further challenges to the death penalty. *Journal of Criminal Law and Criminology, 73*, 379–387.

James, W. (1890). *The principles of psychology.* New York: Dover.

Jamieson, K. H. (1992). *Dirty politics: Distraction, deception, & democracy.* New York: Oxford University Press.

Janis, I. L. (1972). *Victims of groupthink.* Boston: Houghton Mifflin.

Janis, I. L. (1982). *Groupthink* (2nd ed.). Boston: Houghton Mifflin.

Janis, I. L. (1984). Improving adherence to medical recommendations: Prescriptive hypotheses derived from recent research in social psychology. In A. Baum, S. E. Taylor, & J. E. Singer (Eds.), *Handbook of psychology and health* (Vol. 4). Hillsdale, NJ: Erlbaum.

Jankowiak, J., & Fischer, E. (1992). A cross-cultural study of romantic love. *Ethology, 24*, 121–129.

Janoff-Bulman, R. (1979). Characterological versus behavioral self-blame: Inquiries into depression and rape. *Journal of Personality and Social Psychology, 37*, 1798–1809.

Janoff-Bulman, R. (1982). Esteem and control bases of blame: "Adaptive" strategies for victims versus observers. *Journal of Personality, 50*, 180–192.

Jemmott, J. B., Croyle, R. T., & Ditto, P. H. (1988). Commonsense epidemiology: Self-based judgments from laypersons and physicians. *Health Psychology, 7*, 55–73.

Jemmott, J. B., Ditto, P. H., & Croyle, R. T. (1986). Judging health status: Effects of perceived prevalence and personal relevance. *Journal of Personality and Social Psychology, 50*, 899–905.

Jenkins, M. J., & Dambrot, F. H. (1987). The attribution of date rape: Observers' attitudes and sexual experiences and the dating situation. *Journal of Applied Social Psychology, 17*, 875–895.

Johnson, B. T., & Eagly, A. H. (1989). Effects of involvement on persuasion: A meta-analysis. *Psychological Bulletin, 106*, 290–314.

Johnson, D. F., & Pruitt, D. G. (1972). Preintervention effects of mediation versus arbitration. *Journal of Applied Psychology, 56*, 1–10.

Johnson, D. F., & Tullar, W. L. (1972). Style of third-party intervention, face-saving, and bargaining behavior. *Journal of Experimental Social Psychology, 8*, 319–330.

Johnson, R. N. (1972). *Aggression in man and animals.* Philadelphia: W. B. Saunders.

Johnson, T. E., & Rule, B. G. (1986). Mitigating circumstances, information, censure, and aggression. *Journal of Personality and Social Psychology, 50*, 537–542.

Jolly, R. W., & Sagarin, E. (1984). The first eight after Furman: Who was executed with the return of the death penalty? *Crime and Delinquency, 30*, 610–623.

Jones, C., & Aronson, E. (1973). Attribution of fault of a rape victim as a function of respectability of the victim. *Journal of Personality and Social Psychology, 26*, 415–419.

Jones, E. E. (1990). *Interpersonal perception.* New York: W. H. Freeman.

Jones, E. E., & Davis, K. E. (1965). From acts to dispositions: The attribution process in person perception. In L. Berkowitz (Ed.), *Advances in experimental social psychology* (Vol. 2). New York: Academic Press.

Jones, E. E., & Gerard, H. B. (1967). *Foundations of social psychology.* New York: Wiley.

Jones, E. E., & Harris, V. A. (1967). The attribution of attitudes. *Journal of Experimental Social Psychology, 3*, 1–24.

Jones, E. E., Rock, L., Shaver, K. G., Goethals, G. R., & Ward, L. M. (1968). Pattern of performance and ability attribution: An unexpected primacy effect. *Journal of Personality and Social Psychology, 10*, 317–340.

Josephson, W. L. (1987). Television violence and children's aggression: Testing the priming, social script, and disinhibition predictions. *Journal of Personality and Social Psychology, 53*, 882–890.

Jourard, S. M. (1971). *Self-disclosure: An experimental analysis of the transparent self.* New York: John Wiley.

Jowett, G. S., & O'Donnell, V. (1986). *Persuasion and propaganda.* Beverly Hills, CA: Sage.

Jowett, G. S., & O'Donnell, V. (1992). *Propaganda and persuasion* (2nd ed.). Beverly Hills, CA: Sage.

Judd, C. M., Drake, R. A., Downing, J. W., & Krosnick, J. A. (1991). Some dynamic properties of attitude structures: Context-induced response facilitation and polarization. *Journal of Personality and Social Psychology, 60*, 195–202.

Judd, C. M., & Park, B. (1993). Definition and assessment of accuracy in social stereotypes. *Psychological Review, 100*, 109–128.

Jurow, G. Y. (1971). New data on the effect of a death-qualified jury on the guilt determination process. *Harvard Law Review, 84*, 567–611.

Jussim, L. (1986). Self-fulfilling prophecies: A theoretical and integrative review. *Psychological Review, 93*, 429–445.

Jussim, L. (1991). Social perception and social reality: A reflection-construction model. *Psychological Review, 98*, 54–73.

Jussim, L., & Eccles, J. S. (1992). Teacher expectations II: Construction and reflection of student achievement. *Journal of Personality and Social Psychology, 63*, 947–961.

Kahneman, D., Slovic, P., & Tversky, A. (1982). *Judgment under uncertainty: Heuristics and biases.* New York: Cambridge University Press.

Kahneman, D., & Tversky, A. (1982). The simulation heuristic. In D. Kahneman, P. Slovic, & A. Tversky (Eds.), *Judgment under uncertainty: Heuristics and biases.* New York: Cambridge University Press.

Kalish, J., Hilton, J. L., & Ditto, P. H. (1988). The effects of patients' expectations and physicians' communication styles on doctor–patient interactions. Unpublished manuscript, University of Michigan, Ann Arbor.

Kalven, H., & Zeisel, H. (1966). *The American jury.* Boston: Little, Brown.

Kaminer, W. (1992). Crashing the locker room. *The Atlantic, 270,* 58–71.

Kanekar, S., & Maharukh, B. K. (1980). Responsibility of a rape victim in relation to her respectability, attractiveness, and provocativeness. *Journal of Social Psychology, 112,* 153–154.

Kanekar, S., & Maharukh, B. K. (1981). Factors affecting responsibility attributed to a rape victim. *Journal of Social Psychology, 113,* 285–286.

Kanekar, S., Shaherwalla, A., Franco, B., Kunju, T., & Pinto, A. J. (1991). The acquaintance predicament of a rape victim. *Journal of Applied Social Psychology, 21,* 1524–1544.

Kaplan, M. F., & Miller, C. E. (1977). Judgments and group discussion: Effect of presentation and memory factors on polarization. *Sociometry, 40,* 337–343.

Kaplan, M. F., & Miller, C. E. (1987). Group decision making and normative and informational social influence: Effects of type of issue and assigned decision rule. *Journal of Personality and Social Psychology, 53,* 306–313.

Kaplan, R., Sallis, J. F., Patterson, T. L. (1993). *Health and human behavior.* New York: McGraw Hill.

Karau, S. J., & Williams, K. D. (1993). Social loafing: A meta-analytic review and theoretical integration. *Journal of Personality and Social Psychology, 65,* 681–706.

Kassin, S. M. (1983). Deposition testimony and the surrogate witness: Evidence for a "messenger effect" in persuasion. *Law and Human Behavior, 9,* 281–288.

Kassin, S. M., Reddy, M. E., & Tulloch, W. F. (1990). Juror interpretations of ambiguous evidence: The need for cognition, presentation order, and persuasion. *Law and Human Behavior, 14,* 1, 43–56.

Kassin, S. M., Williams, L. N., & Saunders, C. L. (1990). Dirty tricks of cross examination: The influence of conjectural evidence on the jury. *Law and Human Behavior, 14,* 373–384.

Katz, D. (1960). The functional approach to the study of attitudes. *Public Opinion Quarterly, 24,* 163–204.

Katz, I., & Hass, R. G. (1988). Racial ambivalence and American value conflict: Correlational and priming studies of dual cognition structures. *Journal of Personality and Social Psychology, 55,* 893–905.

Katz, I., Wakenhut, J., & Hass, R. G. (1986). Racial ambivalence, value duality, and behavior. In J. F. Dovidio & S. L. Gaertner (Eds.), *Prejudice, discrimination, and racism.* Orlando, FL: Academic Press.

Kelley, H. H. (1967). Attribution theory in social psychology. *Nebraska Symposium on Motivation, 14,* 192–241.

Kelley, H. H. (1971). Attribution theory in social interaction. In E. E. Jones, D. Kanouse, H. H. Kelley, et al., *Attribution: Perceiving the causes of behavior.* Morristown, NJ: General Learning Press.

Kelley, H. H., Berscheid, E., Christensen, A., Harvey, J. H., Huston, T. L., Levinger, G., McClintock, E., Peplau, L. A., & Peterson, D. R. (1983). *Close relationships.* New York: Freeman.

Kelman, H. C., & Hamilton, L. (1989). *Crimes of obedience:*

Toward a social psychology of authority and responsibility. New Haven, CT: Yale University Press.

Kelman, H. C., & Hovland, C. I. (1953). "Reinstatement" of the communicator in delayed measurement of opinion change. *Journal of Abnormal and Social Psychology, 48,* 327–335.

Kendall, P. C., Ronan, K. R., & Epps, J. (1991). Aggression in children/adolescents: Cognitive-behavioral treatment perspectives. In D. J. Pepler & K. H. Rubin (Eds.), *The development and treatment of childhood aggression.* Hillsdale, NJ: Erlbaum.

Keneally, T. (1982). *Schindler's list.* New York: Simon & Schuster.

Kennedy, P. H. (1987). *The rise and fall of the great powers: Economic change and military conflict from 1500 to 2000.* New York: Random House.

Kenny, D., & Albright, L. (1987). Accuracy in interpersonal perception: A social relations analysis. *Psychological Bulletin, 102,* 390–402.

Kerr, N. L. (1983). Motivation losses in small groups: A social dilemma analysis. *Journal of Personality and Social Psychology, 45,* 819–828.

Kerr, N. L. (1989). Illusions of efficacy: The effects of group size on perceived efficacy in social dilemmas. *Journal of Experimental Social Psychology, 25,* 287–313.

Kerr, N. L. (1992). Issue importance and group decision making. In S. Worchel, W. Wood, & J. A. Simpson (Eds.), *Group process and productivity.* Newbury Park, CA: Sage.

Kiesler, C. A. (1971). *The psychology of commitment: Experiments linking behavior to the belief.* New York: Academic Press.

Kihlstrom, J. F., & Cantor, N. (1984). Mental representations of the self. In L. Berkowitz (Ed.), *Advances in experimental social psychology* (Vol. 17). San Diego, CA: Academic Press.

Kilham, W., & Mann, L. (1974). Level of destructive obedience as a function of transmitter and executive roles in the Milgram obedience paradigm. *Journal of Personality and Social Psychology, 29,* 696–702.

Klein, J. G. (1991). Negativity effects in impression formation: A test in the political arena. *Personality and Social Psychology Bulletin, 17,* 412–418.

Klein, S. B., Loftus, J., & Plog, A. (1992). Trait judgments about the self: Evidence from encoding specificity paradigm. *Personality and Social Psychology Bulletin, 18,* 730–735.

Kobasa, S. C. (1979). Stressful life events, personality, and health: An inquiry into hardiness. *Journal of Personality and Social Psychology, 37,* 1–11.

Kobasa, S. C. (1984, September). How much stress can you survive? *American Health Magazine,* pp. 64–77.

Kobasa, S. C., Maddi, S. R., & Courington, S. (1981). Personality and constitution as mediators in the stress–illness relationship. *Journal of Health and Social Behavior, 22,* 368–379.

Kobasa, S. C., Maddi, S. R., Puccetti, M. C., & Zola, M. A. (1985). Effectiveness of hardiness, exercise and social support as resources against illness. *Journal of Psychosomatic Research, 29,* 525–533.

Kobasa, S. C., Maddi, S. R., & Zola, M. A. (1983). Type A and hardiness. *Journal of Behavioral Medicine, 6,* 41–51.

Kobasa, S. C., & Puccetti, M. C. (1983). Personality and social resources in stress resistance. *Journal of Personality & Social Psychology, 45,* 839–850.

Kohnken, G., & Brockman, C. (1987). Unspecific postevent information, attribution of responsibility, and eyewitness performance. *Applied Cognitive Psychology, 1,* 197–207.

Kolata, G. (1992, November 24). After kinship and marriage,

anthropology discovers love. *New York Times,* p. B9.

Koltai, D. C., & Burger, J. M. (1989). *The effects of time on attributions for relationship dissolutions.* Paper presented at the annual meetings of the Western Psychological Association, Reno, NV.

Konecni, V. J., & Ebbesen, E. B. (1982). An analysis of the sentencing system. In V. J. Konecni & E. B. Ebbesen (Eds.), *The criminal justice system: A social-psychological analysis.* San Francisco: W. H. Freeman.

Krahe, B. (1988). Victim and observer characteristics as determinants of responsibility attributions of victims of rape. *Journal of Applied Social Psychology, 18,* 50–58.

Kramer, G. P., Kerr, N. L., & Carroll, J. S. (1990). Pretrial publicity, judicial remedies, and jury bias. *Law and Human Behavior, 14,* 409–438.

Krantz, D. S. (1979). A naturalistic study of social influences on meal size among moderately obese and nonobese subjects. *Psychosomatic Medicine, 41,* 19–27.

Kravitz, D. A., & Martin, B. (1986). Ringelmann rediscovered: The original article. *Journal of Personality and Social Psychology, 50,* 936–941.

Kremer, J. F., & Stephens, L. (1983). Attributions and arousal as mediators of mitigation's effect on retaliation. *Journal of Personality and Social Psychology, 45,* 335–343.

Kreutzer, J. S., Schneider, H. G., & Myatt, C. R. (1984). Alcohol, aggression, and assertiveness in men: Dosage and expectancy effects. *Journal of Studies on Alcohol, 45,* 275–278.

Krishan, L. (1988). Recipient need and anticipation of reciprocity in prosocial exchange. *Journal of Social Psychology, 128,* 223–231.

Kristiansen, C. M., & Zanna, M. P. (1988). Justifying attitudes by appealing to values: A functional perspective. *British Journal of Social Psychology, 27,* 247–256.

Krosnick, J. (1989). Attitude importance and attitude accessibility. *Personality and Social Psychology Bulletin, 15,* 297–308.

Krosnick, J. A., & Alwin, D. F. (1989). Aging and susceptibility to attitude change. *Journal of Personality and Social Psychology, 57,* 416–425.

Krosnick, J. A., Betz, A. L., Jussim, L. J., & Lynn, A. R. (1992). Subliminal conditioning of attitudes. *Personality and Social Psychology Bulletin, 18,* 152–163.

Kruglanski, A. W. (1977). The place of naive contents in a theory of attribution; reflections on Calder's and Zuckerman's critiques of the endogenous-exogenous partition. *Personality and Social Psychology Bulletin, 3,* 592–605.

Kruglanski, A. W., & Mayseless, O. (1990). Classic and current comparison research: Expanding the perspective. *Psychological Bulletin, 108,* 195–208.

Kruglanski, A. W., & Webster, D. M. (1991). Group members' reactions to opinion deviates and conformists at varying degrees of proximity to decision deadline and of environmental noise. *Journal of Personality and Social Psychology, 61,* 212–225.

Kunda, Z. (1987). Motivation and inference: Self-serving generation and evaluation of evidence. *Journal of Personality and Social Psychology, 53,* 636–647.

Kunda, Z. (1990). The case for motivated reasoning. *Psychological Bulletin, 108,* 480–498.

Kunda, Z., Miller, D. T., & Claire, T. (1990). Combining social concepts: The role of causal reasoning. *Cognitive Science, 14,* 551–557.

Kurdek, L. A. (1991). The dissolution of gay and lesbian couples. *Journal of Social and Personal Relationships, 8,* 265–278.

Lagerspetz, K. M., Bjorkqvist, K., & Peltonen, T. (1988). Is indirect aggression typical of females? Gender differences in aggressiveness in 11- to 12-year-old children. *Aggressive Behavior, 14,* 403–414.

Landay, J. S. (1993). Tuning in to "Slobovision." *Christian Science Monitor,* November 10, 9.

Lang, A. R., Goeckner, D. J., Adesso, V. J., & Marlatt, G. A. (1975). Effects of alcohol on aggression in male social drinkers. *Journal of Abnormal Psychology, 84,* 508–518.

Langer, E. (1989). *Mindfulness.* Reading, MA: Addison-Wesley.

Langer, E., Blank, A., & Chanowitz, B. (1978). The mindlessness of ostensibly thoughtful action: The role of placebic information in interpersonal interaction. *Journal of Personality and Social Psychology, 36,* 886–893.

Langer, E., & Rodin, J. (1976). The effects of choice and enhanced personal responsibility for the aged: A field experiment in an institutional setting. *Journal of Personality and Social Psychology, 34,* 191–198.

Langford, B. J., & Langford, C. C. (1974). Church attendance and self-perceived altruism. *Journal for the Scientific Study of Religion, 13,* 221–222.

Langlois, J. H. (1986). From the eye of the beholder to behavioral reality: The development of social behaviors and social relations as a function of physical attractiveness. In C. P. Herman, M. P. Zanna, & E. T. Higgins (Eds.), *Physical appearance, stigma, and social behavior: The Ontario symposium* (Vol. 3). Hillsdale, NJ: Erlbaum.

Langlois, J. H., Roggman, L. A., Casey, R. J., Riesner-Danner, L. A., & Jenkins, V. Y. (1987). Infant preferences for attractive faces: Rudiments of a stereotype? *Developmental Psychology, 23,* 363–369.

LaPiere, R. T. (1934). Attitudes vs. actions. *Social Forces, 13,* 230–237.

LaPiere, R. T. (1936). Type-rationalizations of group apathy. *Social Forces, 15,* 232–237.

Larsen, K. (1974). Conformity in the Asch experiment. *Journal of Social Psychology, 94,* 303–304.

Larsen, K. (1982). Cultural conditions and conformity: The Asch effect. *Bulletin of the British Psychological Society, 35,* 347.

Larsen, R. J., & Ketelaar, T. (1991). Personality and susceptibility to positive and negative emotional states. *Journal of Personality and Social Psychology, 61,* 132–140.

Lassiter, G. D., Briggs, M. A., & Bowman, R. E. (1991). Need for cognition and the perception of ongoing behavior. *Personality and Social Psychology Bulletin, 17,* 156–160.

Latané, B. (1981). The psychology of social impact. *American Psychologist, 36,* 343–356.

Latané, B., & Darley, J. M. (1968). Group inhibition of bystander intervention in emergencies. *Journal of Personality and Social Psychology, 10,* 215–221.

Latané, B., Williams, K. D., & Harkins, S. G. (1979). Many hands make light the work: The causes and consequences of social loafing. *Journal of Personality and Social Psychology, 37,* 822–832.

Latané, B., & Wolf, S. (1981). The social impact of majorities and minorities. *Psychological Review, 88,* 438–453.

Laughlin, P. R. (1980). Social combination processes of cooperative problem solving groups on verbal intellective tasks. In M. Fishbein (Ed.), *Progress in social psychology* (Vol. 1). Hillsdale, NJ: Erlbaum.

Laughlin, P. R., & Ellis, A. L. (1986). Demonstrability and social combination processes on mathematical intellective tasks. *Journal of Experimental Social Psychology, 22,* 177–189.

Laughlin, P. R., VanderStoep, S. W., & Hollingshead, A. D. (1991). Collective versus individual induction: Recognition of truth, rejection of error, and collective information processing. *Journal of Personality and Social Psychology, 61,* 50–67.

Lawrence, R. A. (1984). Police stress and personality factors: A conceptual model. *Journal of Criminal Justice, 12,* 247–263.

Lawson, R. G. (1969). The law of primacy in the criminal courtroom. *Journal of Social Psychology, 77,* 121–131.

Lazarus, R. S., & Folkman, S. (1984). *Stress, appraisal, and coping.* New York: Springer.

Leary, M. R. (1983a). *Understanding social anxiety: Social, personality, and clinical perspectives: Volume 153. Sage library of social research.* Beverly Hills, CA: Sage.

Leary, M. R. (1983b). Social anxiousness: The construct and its measurement. *Journal of Personality Assessment, 47,* 66–75.

Leary, M., & Kowalski, R. M. (1990). Impression management: A literature review and the two-component model. *Psychological Bulletin, 107,* 34–47.

Lefkowitz, M. (1991). *Women's life in Greece and Rome.* Baltimore, MD: Johns Hopkins University Press.

Leippe, M. R., Manion, A. P., & Romanczyk, A. (1992). Eyewitness persuasion: How and how well do fact finders judge the accuracy of adults' and children's memory reports? *Journal of Personality and Social Psychology, 63,* 181–197.

Leippe, M. R., Romanczyk, A., & Manion, A. P. (1991). Eyewitness memory for a touching experience: Accuracy differences between child and adult witnesses. *Journal of Applied Psychology, 76,* 367–379.

Lemann, N. (1994). Mysteries of the middle class, review of *Rising in the West: The true story of an 'Okie' family from the Great Depression through the Reagan years,* by Dan Morgan. *The New York Review of Books,* February 3, pp. 9–13.

Lerner, M. J., & Simmons, C. H. (1966). Observers' reactions to the "innocent victim": Compassion or rejection? *Journal of Personality and Social Psychology, 4,* 203–210.

Levenson, R. W., & Gottman, J. M. (1983). Marital interaction: Physiological linkage and affective exchange. *Journal of Personality and Social Psychology, 45,* 587–597.

Leventhal, G. S., Allen, J., & Kemelgor, B. (1969). Reducing inequity by reallocating rewards. *Psychonomic Science, 14,* 295–296.

Leventhal, H. (1970). Findings and theory in the study of fear communication. In L. Berkowitz (Ed.), *Advances in experimental social psychology* (Vol. 5). San Diego, CA: Academic Press.

Levine, J. M. (1989). Reaction to opinion deviance in small groups. In P. Paulus (Ed.), *The psychology of group influence* (2nd ed.). Hillsdale, NJ: Erlbaum.

Levine, J. M., & Moreland, R. L. (1990). Progress in small group research. *Annual Review of Psychology, 41,* 585–634.

Levinger, G. (1988). Can we picture "love"? In R. J. Sternberg & M. L. Barnes (Eds.), *The psychology of love.* New Haven, CT: Yale University Press.

Levinger, G., & Snoek, J. D. (1972). *Attraction in relationships: A new look at interpersonal attraction.* Morristown, NJ: General Learning Press.

Lewin, K. (1936). *A dynamic theory of personality.* New York: McGraw-Hill.

Lewis, C. E., & Bild, D. (1994, March). *Weight changes in young adults 1985–1993.* Paper presented to the convention of the American Heart Association, Tampa.

Lewis, D. O., Lovely, R., Yeager, C., & Della Femina, D. (1989). Toward a theory of the genesis of violence: A follow-up study of delinquents. *Journal of the American Academy of Child and Adolescent Psychiatry, 28,* 431–437.

Lewis, L. (1932). *Sherman, fighting prophet.* New York: Harcourt, Brace and Company.

Lewis, L., & Johnson, K. K. (1989). Effect of dress, cosmetics, sex of subject, and causal inference on attribution of victim responsibility. *Clothing and Textiles Research Journal, 8,* 22–27.

Liebert, R. M., & Baron, R. A. (1972). Some immediate effects of televised violence on children's behavior. *Developmental Psychology, 6,* 469–475.

Liebert, R. M., & Sprafkin, J. (1988). *The early window: The effects of television on children and youth* (3rd ed.). New York: Pergamon.

Lifton, R. J. (1986). *The Nazi doctors: Medical killing and the psychology of genocide.* New York: Basic Books.

Likert, R. (1932). A technique for the measurement of attitudes. *Archives of Psychology, 140.*

Lindsay, D. S., Jack, P. C., & Christian, M. A. (1991). Other-race face perception. *Journal of Applied Psychology, 76,* 587–589.

Lindsay, D. S., & Johnson, M. K. (1989). The reversed eyewitness suggestibility effect. *Bulletin of the Psychonomic Society, 27,* 111–113.

Lindsay, R. C. L., Lea, J. A., & Fulford, J. A. (1991). Sequential lineup presentation: Technique matters. *Journal of Applied Psychology, 76,* 741–745.

Lindsay, R. C. L., & Wells, G. L. (1985). Improving eyewitness identifications from lineups: Simultaneous versus sequential lineup procedures. *Journal of Applied Psychology, 70,* 556–564.

Lindsay, R. C. L., Wells, G. L., & O'Conner, F. J. (1989). Mock-juror belief of accurate and inaccurate eyewitnesses: A replication and extension. *Law and Human Behavior, 13,* 333–340.

Lindskold, S. (1986). GRIT: Reducing distrust through carefully introduced conciliation. In S. Worchel & W. G. Austin (Eds.), *Psychology of intergroup relations.* Chicago: Nelson Hall.

Lindskold, S., Han, G., & Betz, B. (1986). The essential elements of communication in the GRIT strategy. *Personality and Social Psychology Bulletin, 12,* 179–186.

Linville, P. W. (1985). Self-complexity and affective extremity. Don't put all your eggs in one cognitive basket. *Social Cognition, 3,* 92–120.

Linville, P. W. (1987). Self-complexity as a cognitive buffer against stress-related illnesses and depression. *Journal of Personality and Social Psychology, 52,* 663–676.

Linville, P. W., Fischer, G. W., & Salovey, P. (1989). Perceived distributions of the characteristics of in-group and out-group members: Empirical evidence and computer simulation. *Journal of Personality and Social Psychology, 57,* 165–188.

Linz, D., Penrod, S., & Donnerstein, E. (1987, Fall). The attorney general's commission on pornography: The gaps between "findings" and facts. *American Bar Foundation Research Journal,* pp. 713–736.

Lippmann, W. (1922). *Public opinion.* New York: Harcourt, Brace & World.

Lips, H. (1993). *Sex and gender.* Mountain View, CA: Mayfield.

Lipscomb, T. J., Larrieu, J. A., McAlister, H. A., & Bregman, N. J. (1982). Modeling and children's generosity: A developmental perspective. *Merrill Palmer Quarterly, 28,* 275–282.

Lochhead, C. (1993, November 12). Feinstein's retort stuns Senate. *San Francisco Chronicle,* pp. A1, A17.

Locke, K. D., & Horowitz, L. M. (1990). Satisfaction in interpersonal interactions as a function of similarity in level of dysphoria. *Journal of Personality and Social Psychology, 58,* 823–831.

Loftus, E. F. (1979a). *Eyewitness testimony.* Cambridge, MA: Harvard University Press.

Loftus, E. F. (1979b). The malleability of human memory. *American Scientist, 67,* 312–320.

Loftus, E. F., Loftus, G. R., & Messo, J. (1987). Some facts about "weapon focus." *Law and Human Behavior, 11,* 55–62.

Loftus, E. F., Schooler, J. W., & Wagenaar, W. A. (1985). The fate of memory: Comment on McCloskey and Zaragoza. *Journal of Experimental Psychology: General, 114,* 375–380.

Logan, G. A. (1989). Automaticity and cognitive control. In J. S. Uleman & J. A. Bargh (Eds.), *Unintended thought.* New York: Guilford Press.

Lorenz, K. (1963). *On aggression.* London: Methuen.

Lorge, I., & Solomon, H. (1955). Two models of group behavior in the solution of Eureka-type problems. *Psychometrika, 20,* 139–148.

Luginbuhl, J., & Palmer, T. (1991). Impression management aspects of self-handicapping: Positive and negative effects. *Personality and Social Psychology Bulletin, 17,* 655–662.

Luus, C. A. E., & Wells, G. L. (1991). Eyewitness identification and the selection of distractors for lineups. *Law and Human Behavior, 15,* 43–58.

Lydon, J. E., Jamieson, D. W., & Zanna, M. (1988). Interpersonal similarity and the social and intellectual dimensions of first impressions. *Social Cognition, 6,* 269–286.

Lydon, J. E., & Zanna, M. P. (1990). Commitment in the face of adversity: A value affirmation approach. *Journal of Personality and Social Psychology, 58,* 1040–1168.

Lynch, D. J., & Schaffer, K. S. (1989). Type A and social support. *Behavioral Medicine, 15,* 72–74.

Lytton, H., & Romney, D. M. (1991). Parents' differential socialization of boys and girls: A meta-analysis. *Psychological Bulletin, 109,* 267–296.

Maass, A., & Kohnken, G. (1989). Eyewitness identification: Simulating the "weapon effect." *Law and Human Behavior, 13,* 397–408.

Maass, A., & Clark, R. D. (1984). Hidden impact of minorities: Fifteen years of minority influence research. *Psychological Bulletin, 95,* 428–450.

Maass, A., West, S. G., & Cialdini, R. B. (1987). Minority influence and conversion. In C. Hendrick (Ed.), *Review of Personality and Social Psychology* (Vol. 8). Newbury Park, CA: Sage.

MaCauley, C., & Stitt, C. L. (1978). An individual and quantitative measure of stereotypes. *Journal of Personality and Social Psychology, 36,* 929–940.

Mackie, D. M. (1986). Social identification effects in group polarization. *Journal of Personality and Social Psychology, 50,* 720–728.

Mackie, D. M., Allison, S. T., Worth, L. T., & Asunción, A. G. (1992). The impact of outcome biases on counterstereotypic inferences about groups. *Personality and Social Psychology Bulletin, 18,* 44–51.

Mackie, D. M., & Cooper, J. (1984). Attitude polarization: Effects of group membership. *Journal of Personality and Social Psychology, 46,* 575–585.

Mackie, D. M., & Worth, L. T. (1989). Processing deficits and the mediation of positive affect in persuasion. *Journal of Personality and Social Psychology, 57,* 27–40.

MacMurray, V. D., & Cunningham, P. D. (1973). Mormons and gentiles: A study in conflict and persistence. In D. E. Gelfand & R. D. Lee (Eds.), *Ethnic conflicts and power: A cross-national perspective.* New York: John Wiley and Sons.

Macrae, C. N., Milne, A. B., & Bodenhausen, G. V. (1994). Stereotypes as energy saving devices: A peek inside the cognitive tool box. *Journal of Personality and Social Psychology, 66,* 37–47.

Macrae, C. N., Shepherd, J. W., & Milne, A. B. (1992). The effects of source credibility on the dilution of stereotype-based judgments. *Personality and Social Psychology Bulletin, 18,* 765–775.

Main, M., & George, C. (1985). Responses of abused and disadvantaged toddlers to distress in agemates: A study in the day care setting. *Developmental Psychology, 21,* 407–412.

Major, B. (1980). Information acquisition and attribution processes. *Journal of Personality and Social Psychology, 39,* 1010–1024.

Malamuth, N. M. (1986). Predictors of naturalistic sexual aggression. *Journal of Personality and Social Psychology, 50,* 953–962.

Malamuth, N. M., & Check, J. V. P. (1980). Sexual arousal to rape and consenting depictions: The importance of the woman's arousal. *Journal of Abnormal Psychology, 89,* 763–766.

Malamuth, N. M., & Check, J. V. P. (1981). The effects of mass media exposure on acceptance of violence against women: A field experiment. *Journal of Research in Personality, 15,* 436–446.

Malamuth, N. M., & Check, J. V. P. (1983). Sexual arousal to rape depictions: Individual differences. *Journal of Abnormal Psychology, 92,* 55–67.

Malamuth, N. M., & Check, J. V. P. (1985). The effects of aggressive pornography on beliefs in rape myths: Individual differences. *Journal of Research in Personality, 19,* 299–320.

Malamuth, N. M., Haber, S., & Feshbach, S. (1980). Testing hypotheses regarding rape: Exposure to sexual violence, sex differences and the "normality" of rapists. *Journal of Research in Personality, 14,* 121–137.

Malloy, T. E., & Albright, L. (1990). Interpersonal perception in a social context. *Journal of Personality and Social Psychology, 58,* 419–428.

Malpass, R. S., & Devine, P. G. (1981). Eyewitness identification: Lineup instructions and the absence of the offender. *Journal of Applied Psychology, 66,* 482–489.

Malpass, R. S., & Kravitz, D. A. (1969). Recognition for faces of own and other race. *Journal of Personality and Social Psychology, 13,* 330–334.

Mann, L. (1981). The baiting crowd in episodes of threatened suicides. *Journal of Personality and Social Psychology, 41,* 703–709.

Mantell, D. M. (1971). The potential for violence in Germany. *Journal of Social Issues, 27*(4), 101–112.

Mark, M. M., Bryant, F. B., & Lehman, D. R. (1983). Perceived injustice and sports violence. In J. G. Goldstein (Ed.), *Sports violence.* New York: Springer-Verlag.

Marks, G., Graham, J. W., & Hansen, W. B. (1992). Social projection and social conformity in adolescent alcohol use: A longitudinal analysis. *Personality and Social Psychology Bulletin, 18,* 96–101.

Markus, H. (1977). Self schemata and processing information about the self. *Journal of Personality and Social Psychology, 35,* 63–78.

Markus, H., & Kitayama, S. (1991). Culture and self: Implications for cognition, emotion, and motivation. *Psychological Review, 98,* 224–253.

Markus, H., & Kitayama, S. (in press). Cultural variation in the self-concept: Implications for cognition, emotion, and motivation. In G. R. Goethals & J. Strauss (Eds.), *Multidisciplinary perspectives on the self.* New York: Springer-Verlag.

Markus, H., & Kunda, Z. (1986). Stability and malleability of the self-concept. *Journal of Personality and Social Psychology, 51,* 858–866.

Markus, H., & Nurius, P. (1986). Possible selves. *American Psychologist, 41,* 954–969.

Markus, H., & Wurf, E. (1987). The dynamic self-concept: A social psychological perspective. *Annual Review of Psychology, 38,* 299–337.

Markus, H., & Zajonc, R. B. (1985). The cognitive perspective in social psychology. In G. Lindzey & E. Aronson (Eds.), *The handbook of social psychology: Vol. 1. Theory and methods.* New York: Random House.

Marshall, J., Marquis, K. H., & Oskamp, S. (1971). Effects of kind of question and atmosphere of interrogation on accuracy and completeness of testimony. *Harvard Law Review, 84,* 1620–1643.

Marshall, P. S. (1993). Allergy and depression: A neurochemical threshold model of the relation between the illnesses. *Psychological Bulletin, 113,* 23–43.

Matsuda, N. (1985). Strong, quasi- and weak conformity among Japanese in the modified Asch procedure. *Journal of Cross-Cultural Psychology, 16,* 83–97.

McAdams, D. P. (1982). Intimacy motivation. In A. J. Stewart (Ed.), *Motivation and society.* San Francisco: Jossey-Bass.

McAdams, D. P. (1989). *Intimacy.* New York: Doubleday.

McArthur, L. Z. (1972). The how and what of why: Some determinants and consequences of causal attribution. *Journal of Personality and Social Psychology, 22,* 171–193.

McArthur, L. Z. (1982). Judging a book by its cover: A cognitive analysis of the relationship between physical appearance and stereotyping. In A. Hastorf & A. Isen (Eds.), *Cognitive social psychology.* New York: Elsevier/North Holland.

McAuley, E., Wraith, S., & Duncan, T. E. (1991). Self-efficacy, perceptions of success, and intrinsic motivation for exercise. *Journal of Applied Social Psychology, 21,* 139–155.

McCauley, C. (1989). The nature of social influence in groupthink: Compliance and internalization. *Journal of Personality and Social Psychology, 57,* 250–260.

McCauley, C., & Segal, M. E. (1987). Social psychology of terrorist groups. In C. Hendrick (Ed.), *Group processes and intergroup relations: Review of personality and social psychology* (Vol. 9). Newbury Park, CA: Sage.

McCloskey, M., & Egeth, H. (1983). What can a psychologist tell a jury? *American Psychologist, 38,* 550–563.

McCloskey, M., & Zaragoza, M. (1985). Misleading postevent information and memory for events: Arguments and evidence against memory impairment hypothesis. *Journal of Experimental Psychology: General, 114,* 1–16.

McConahay, J. G. (1986). Modern racism, ambivalence, and the modern racist scale. In J. F. Dovidio & S. L. Gaertner (Eds.), *Prejudice, discrimination, and racism.* San Diego, CA: Academic Press.

McCoun, R. J., & Tyler, T. R. (1988). The basis of citizens' perceptions of the criminal jury: Procedural fairness, accuracy and efficiency. *Law and Human Behavior, 12,* 333–352.

McDaniel, A. (1992, November/December). Exit on the high road. *Newsweek,* p. 12.

McGill, A. L. (1989). Context effects in judgments of causation. *Journal of Personality and Social Psychology, 57,* 189–200.

McGuire, W. J. (1969). The nature of attitudes and attitude change. In G. Lindzey & E. Aronson (Eds.), *The handbook of social psychology* (2nd ed., Vol. 3). San Diego, CA: Academic Press.

McGuire, W. J. (1985). Attitudes and attitude change. In G. Lindzey & E. Aronson (Eds.), *The handbook of social psychology* (3rd ed., Vol. 2). New York: Random House.

McGuire, W. J. (1989). The structure of individual attitudes. In A. Pratkanis, S. Breckler, & A. G. Greenwald (Eds.), *Attitude structure and function.* Hillsdale, NJ: Erlbaum.

McGuire, W. J., & McGuire, C. V. (1988). Content and process in the experience of self. In L. Berkowitz (Ed.), *Advances in experimental social psychology* (Vol. 21). San Diego, CA: Academic Press.

McGuire, W. J., & Papageorgis, D. (1961). The relative efficacy of various types of prior belief-defense in producing immunity against persuasion. *Journal of Abnormal and Social Psychology, 62,* 327–337.

McHan, E. (1985). Imitation of aggression by Lebanese children. *Journal of Social Psychology, 125,* 613–617.

McLean, A. A. (1979). *Work stress.* Reading, MA: Addison-Wesley.

McNeill, W. H. (1981). *The pursuit of power.* Chicago: University of Chicago Press.

McNeill, W. H. (1982). *The pursuit of power: Technology, armed force, and society since A.D. 1000.* Chicago: University of Chicago Press.

Medin, D. L. (1989). Concepts and conceptual structure. *American Psychologist, 44,* 1469–1481.

Mednick, B. R., Baker, R. L., & Carothers, L. E. (1990). Patterns of family disruption and crime: The association of timing of the family's disruption with subsequent adolescent and young adult criminality. *Journal of Youth and Violence, 19,* 201–220.

Meeus, W., & Raaijmakers, Q. (1986). Administrative obedience: Carrying out orders to use psychological-administrative violence. *European Journal of Social Psychology, 16,* 311–324.

Mendolia, M., & Kleck, R. E. (1993). Effects of talking about a stressful event on arousal: Does what we talk about make a difference? *Journal of Personality and Social Psychology, 64,* 283–292.

Meyer, A. J., Nash, J. D., McAlister, A. L., Maccoby, N., & Farquhar, J. W. (1980). Skills training in a cardiovascular health education campaign. *Journal of Consulting and Clinical Psychology, 48,* 129–142.

Midlarsky, E., Bryan, J. H., & Brickman, P. (1973). Aversive approval: Interactive effects of modeling and reinforcement on altruistic behavior. *Child Development, 44,* 321–328.

Miell, D. E., & Duck, S. W. (1986). Strategies in developing friendships. In V. J. Derlega & B. A Winstead (Eds.), *Friendship and social interaction.* New York: Springer-Verlag.

Milgram, S. (1961). Nationality and conformity. *Scientific American, 205,* 45–51.

Milgram, S. (1963). Behavioral study of obedience. *Journal of Abnormal Psychology, 67,* 371–378.

Milgram, S. (1974). *Obedience to authority.* New York: Harper Colophon Books.

Milgram, S., Bickman, L., & Berkowitz, L. (1969). Note on the drawing power of crowds of different size. *Journal of Personality and Social Psychology, 13,* 79–82.

Milgram, S. L., Mann, L., & Harter, S. (1965). The lost letter technique: A tool of social science research. *Public Opinion Quarterly, 29,* 437–438.

Miller, C. E. (1989). The social psychological effects of group decision rules. In P. Paulus (Ed.), *Psychology of group influence* (2nd ed.). Hillsdale, NJ: Erlbaum.

Miller, D. T., & McFarland, C. (1987). Pluralistic ignorance: When similarity is interpreted as dissimilarity. *Journal of Personality and Social Psychology, 53,* 298–305.

Miller, D. T., & Ross, M. (1975). Self-serving biases in the attribution of causality: Fact or fiction? *Psychological Bulletin, 82,* 213–225.

Miller, D. T., Turnbull, W., & McFarland, C. (1989). When a coincidence is suspicious: The role of mental simulation. *Journal of Personality and Social Psychology, 57,* 581–589.

Miller, D. T., Turnbull, W., & McFarland, C. (1990). Counterfactual thinking and social perception: Thinking about what might have been. In M. P. Zanna (Ed.), *Advances in Experimental Social Psychology* (Vol. 23). San Diego, CA: Academic Press.

Miller, J. G. (1984). Culture and the development of everyday social explanation. *Journal of Personality and Social Psychology, 46,* 961–978.

Miller, M. (1993, December 20). The real Schindler. *Newsweek.*

Miller, N., & Brewer, M. B. (1984). The social psychology of desegregation: An introduction. In N. Miller & M. B. Brewer (Eds.), *Groups in contact: The psychology of desegregation.* New York: Academic Press.

Miller, N. E. (1941). The frustration–aggression hypothesis. *Psychological Review, 48,* 337–342.

Miller, R. L., Seligman, C., Clark, N. T., & Bush, M. (1976). Perceptual contrast versus reciprocal concessions as mediators of induced compliance. *Canadian Journal of Behavioural Science, 8,* 401–409.

Miller, T. Q., Heath, L., Molcan, J. R., & Dugoni, B. L. (1991). Imitative violence in the real world. *Aggressive Behavior, 17,* 121–134.

Minshull, M., & Sussman, M. (1979). *Strength of eyewitness testimony vs. strength of objective evidence in influencing jury decisions.* Paper presented at the annual meeting of the Midwestern Psychological Association, Chicago.

Mitchell, H. E. (1979). *Affective and informational determinants of juror decision making.* Unpublished doctoral dissertation, Purdue University (#209135).

Monteith, M. J., Devine, P. G., & Zuwernik, J. R. (1993). Self-directed versus other-directed affect as a consequence of prejudice-related discrepancies. *Journal of Personality and Social Psychology, 64,* 198–210.

Montgomery, B. M. (1988). Quality communication in personal relationships. In S. Duck (Ed.), *Handbook of personal relationship.* New York: John Wiley.

Moran, G., & Comfort, J. C. (1986). Neither "tentative" nor "fragmentary": Verdict preference of impaneled felony jurors as a function of attitude toward capital punishment. *Journal of Applied Psychology, 71,* 146–155.

Moreland, R. L. (1987). The formation of small groups. *Review of Personality and Social Psychology, 8,* 80–110.

Moreland, R. L., & Levine, J. M. (1982). Group socialization: Temporal changes in individual–group relations. In L. Berkowitz (Ed.), *Advances in experimental social psychology* (Vol. 15). San Diego, CA: Academic Press.

Moreland, R. L., & Levine, J. M. (1989). Newcomers and old-timers in small groups. In P. Paulus (Ed.), *The psychology of group influence* (2nd ed.). Hillsdale, NJ: Erlbaum.

Moriarty, T. (1975). Crime, commitment, and the unresponsive bystander: Two field experiments. *Journal of Personality and Social Psychology, 31,* 370–376.

Morrison, B. (1994, February 14). Letter from Liverpool: Children of circumstance. *The New Yorker,* pp. 48–60.

Morrison, S. E. (1965). *The Oxford history of the American people.* New York: Oxford University Press.

Morrow, L. (1992, December 14). The ruin of a cat, the ghost of a dog. *Time,* 24.

Morrow-Howell, N., Lott, L., & Ozawa, M. (1990). The impact of race on volunteer helping relationships among the elderly. *Social Work, 35,* 395–403.

Morton, T. L. (1978). Intimacy and reciprocity of exchange: A comparison of spouses and strangers. *Journal of Personality and Social Psychology, 36,* 72–81.

Moscovici, S. (1980). Toward a theory of conversion behavior. In L. Berkowitz (Ed.), *Advances in experimental social psychology* (Vol. 13). San Diego, CA: Academic Press.

Moscovici, S. (1985). Social influence and conformity. In G.

Lindzey & E. Aronson (Eds.), *Handbook of social psychology* (3rd ed.). Hillsdale, NJ: Erlbaum.

Moscovici, S., & Lage, E. (1976). Studies in social influence III: Majority versus minority influence in a group. *European Journal of Social Psychology, 6,* 149–174.

Moscovici, S., Lage, E., & Naffrechoux, M. (1969). Influence of a consistent minority on the responses of a majority in a color perception task. *Sociometry, 32,* 365–369.

Moscovici, S., & Zavalloni, M. (1969). The group as a polarizer of attitudes. *Journal of Personality and Social Psychology, 12,* 124–135.

Moskos, C. (1990). *A call to civic service.* New York: Free Press.

Moskos, C. (1991, August 5). How do they do it? *The New Republic,* pp. 16–21.

Moyer, K. E. (1987). *Violence and aggression.* New York: Paragon House.

Mugny, G. (1975). Negotiations, image of the other and the process of minority influence. *European Journal of Social Psychology, 5,* 209–228.

Mullen, B. (1986). Atrocity as a function of lynch mob composition: A self-attention perspective. *Personality and Social Psychology Bulletin, 12,* 187–197.

Mullen, B. (1991). Group composition, salience, and cognitive representations: The phenomenology of being in a group. *Journal of Experimental Social Psychology, 27,* 262–284.

Mullen, B., & Baumeister, R. F. (1987). Group effects of social self-attention and performance: Social loafing, social facilitation, and social impairment. In C. Hendrick (Ed.), *Review of personality and social psychology* (Vol. 9). Beverly Hills, CA: Sage.

Mullen, B., & Riordan, C. A. (1988). Self-serving attributions for performance in naturalistic settings: A meta-analytic review. *Journal of Applied Social Psychology, 18,* 3–22.

Murdoch, D. D., & Pihl, R. O. (1988). The influence of beverage type on aggression in males in the natural setting. *Aggressive Behavior, 14,* 325–335.

Myer, C. B., & Taylor, S. E. (1986). Adjustment to rape. *Journal of Personality and Social Psychology, 50,* 1226–1234.

Myers, D. G., & Kaplan, M. F. (1976). Group-induced polarization in simulated juries. *Personality and Social Psychology Bulletin, 2,* 63–66.

Myers, D. G., & Lamm, H. (1975). The polarizing effect of group discussion. *American Scientist, 63,* 297–303.

Myers, D. G., & Lamm, H. (1976). The group polarization phenomenon. *Psychological Bulletin, 83,* 602–627.

Myrdal, G. (1962). *An American dilemma: The Negro problem in American democracy.* New York: Harper & Row.

Nadler, A., Altman, A., & Fisher, J. D. (1979). Helping is not enough: Recipient's reactions to aid as a function of positive and negative information about the self. *Journal of Personality, 47,* 615–628.

Nadler, A., Fisher, J. D., & Ben Itchak, S. (1983). With a little help from my friend: Effect of single or multiple act aid as a function of donor and task characteristics. *Journal of Personality and Social Psychology, 44,* 310–321.

Nadler, A., Fisher, J. D., & Streufert, S. (1976). When helping hurts: Effects of donor-recipient similarity and recipient self-esteem on reactions to aid. *Journal of Personality, 44,* 392–409.

Nagel, I. H. (1983). The legal/extra-legal controversy: Judicial decisions in pretrial release. *Law and Society Review, 17,* 481–515.

Narby, D. J., Cutler, B. L., & Moran, G. (1993). A meta-analysis of the association between authoritarians and jurors' perceptions of defendant culpability. *Journal of Applied Psychology, 78,* 34–42.

Neimeyer, G. J., & Rareshide, M. B. (1991). Personal memories and personal identity: The impact of ego identity development on autobiographical memory recall. *Journal of Personality and Social Psychology, 60,* 562–569.

Neisser, U. (1981). John Dean's memory: A case study. *Cognition, 9,* 1–22.

Nelan, B. W. (1993, January 25). Serbia's spite. *Time,* 48–49.

Nemeth, C. (1986). Differential contributions of majority and minority influence. *Psychological Review, 93,* 23–32.

Nemeth, C. (1992). Minority dissent as a stimulant to group performance. In S. Worchel, W. Wood, & J. A. Simpson (Eds.), *Group process and productivity.* Newbury Park, CA: Sage.

Nemeth, C., Swedlund, M., & Kanki, B. (1974). Patterning of the minority's responses and their influence on the majority. *European Journal of Social Psychology, 4,* 428–450.

Neuberg, S. L. (1989). The goal of forming accurate impressions during social interactions: Attenuating the impact of negative experiences. *Journal of Personality and Social Psychology, 56,* 374–386.

Neuberg, S. L., & Fiske, S. T. (1987). Motivational influences on impression formation: Outcome dependency, accuracy-driven attention, and individuating processes. *Journal of Personality and Social Psychology, 53,* 431–444.

Newcomb, T. M. (1961). *The acquaintance process.* New York: Holt, Rinehart & Winston.

Newton, L. (1990). *Overconfidence in the communication of intent: Heard and unheard melodies.* Unpublished doctoral dissertation, Stanford University, Stanford, CA.

Nichols, K. A. (1974). Severe social anxiety. *British Journal of Medical Psychology, 74,* 301–306.

Niedenthal, P. M., Setterlund, M., & Wherry, M. B. (1992). Possible self-complexity and affective reactions to goal-relevant evaluation. *Journal of Personality and Social Psychology, 63,* 5–16.

Nisbett, R. E. (1968). Determinants of food intake in human obesity. *Science, 159,* 1254–1255.

Nisbett, R., & Ross, L. (1980). *Human inference: Strategies and shortcomings of social judgment.* Englewood Cliffs, NJ: Prentice-Hall.

Nisbett, R. E., & Wilson, T. D. (1977). The halo effect: Evidence for the unconscious alteration of judgments. *Journal of Personality and Social Psychology, 35,* 250–256.

Noel, J. G., Forsyth, D. R., & Kelley, K. N. (1987). Improving the performance of failing students by overcoming their self-serving attributional biases. *Basic and Applied Social Psychology, 8,* 151–162.

Noller, P. (1985). Negative communication in marriage. *Journal of Social and Personal Relationships, 2,* 289–301.

Noller, P., & Ruzzene, G. (1991). Cognition in close relationships. In G. J. O. Fletcher & F. D. Fincham (Eds.), Hillsdale, NJ: Erlbaum.

Notarius, C., & Markman, H. (1993). *We can work it out: Making sense out of marital conflict.* New York: G. P. Putnam & Sons.

Nowak, A., Szamrej, J., & Latané, B. (1990). From private attitude to public opinion: A dynamic theory of social impact. *Psychological Review, 97,* 362–376.

O'Connell, R. L. (1989). *Of arms and men: A history of war, weapons and aggression.* New York: Oxford University Press.

Ohbuchi, K., & Kambara, T. (1985). Attacker's intent and awareness of outcome, impression management, and retaliation. *Journal of Experimental Social Psychology, 21,* 321–330.

Oliker, S. J. (1989). *Best friends and marriage: Exchange among women.* Berkeley: University of California Press.

Oliner, S. P., & Oliner, P. M. (1988). *The altruistic personality: Rescuers of Jews in Nazi Europe.* New York: Free Press.

Olweus, D. (1984). Development of stable reaction patterns. In R. J. Blanchard & D. C. Blanchard (Eds.), *Advances in the study of aggression* (Vol. 1). San Diego, CA: Academic Press.

Opdyke, I. G., & Elliot, J. M. (1992). *Into the flames: The life story of a righteous gentile.* San Bernardino, CA: Borgo Press.

O'Rourke, D. F., Houston, B. K., Harris, J. K., & Snyder, C. R. (1988). Modifying type A behavior. In B. K. Houston & C. R. Snyder (Eds.), *Type A behavior pattern.* New York: Plenum.

Osborn, M., & Osborn, S. (1994). *Public speaking.* Boston: Houghton Mifflin.

Osgood, C. E. (1962). *An alternative to war or surrender.* Urbana: University of Illinois Press.

Osgood, C. E., Suci, G. J., & Tannenbaum, P. H. (1957). *The measurement of meaning.* Urbana: University of Illinois Press.

Osherow, N. (1988). Making sense of the nonsensical: An analysis of Jonestown. In E. Aronson (Ed.), *Readings about the social animal* (5th ed.). New York: W. H. Freeman.

Oskamp, S. (1991). *Attitudes and opinions* (2nd ed.). New York: Prentice-Hall.

Padawer-Singer, A., Singer, A. N., & Singer, R. L. J. (1977). Legal and social psychological research in the effects of pretrial publicity on juries, numerical makeup of juries, nonunanimous verdict requirements. *Law and Psychology Review, 3,* 71–80.

Paicheler, G. (1979). Polarization of attitudes in homogeneous and heterogeneous groups. *European Journal of Social Psychology, 9,* 85–96.

Parker, J. F., & Carranza, L. E. (1989). Eyewitness testimony of children in target-present and target-absent lineups. *Law and Human Behavior, 13,* 133–149.

Paternoster, R., & Kazyaka, A. (1988). Racial considerations in capital punishment: The failure of evenhanded justice. In K. C. Haas & J. A. Inciardi (Eds.), *Challenging capital punishment: Legal and social science approaches.* Newbury Park, CA: Sage Publications.

Patterson, G. R., DeBaryshe, B. D., & Ramsey, E. (1989). A developmental perspective on antisocial behavior. *American Psychologist, 44,* 329–335.

Paulhus, D. L., & Reid, D. B. (1991). Enhancement and denial in socially desirable responding. *Journal of Personality and Social Psychology, 60,* 307–317.

Paulus, P. B., Dzindolet, M. T., Poletes, G., & Camacho, L. M. (1993). Perception of performance in group brainstorming: The illusion of group productivity. *Personality and Social Psychology Bulletin, 19,* 78–89.

Pavelchak, M. A., Moreland, R. L., & Levine, J. M. (1986). Effects of prior group memberships on subsequent reconnaissance activities. *Journal of Personality and Social Psychology, 50,* 56–66.

Peele, S. (1988). Fools for love: The romantic ideal, psychological theory, and addictive love. In R. J. Sternberg & M. L. Barnes (Eds.), *The psychology of love.* New Haven, CT: Yale University Press.

Pelham, B. (1991). On confidence and consequence: The certainty and importance of self-knowledge. *Journal of Personality and Social Psychology, 60,* 518–520.

Pelham, B., & Swann, W. B., Jr. (1989). From self-conceptions to self-worth: On sources and structure of global self-esteem. *Journal of Personality and Social Psychology, 57,* 672–680.

Pennebaker, J. W. (1989). Confession, inhibition, and disease.

In L. Berkowitz (Ed.), *Advances in experimental social psychology* (Vol. 22). San Diego, CA: Academic Press.

Pennebaker, J. W., & Beall, K. S. (1986). Confronting a traumatic event: Toward understanding of inhibition and disease. *Journal of Abnormal Psychology, 95,* 274–281.

Pennebaker, J. W., Colder, M. L., & Sharp, L. K. (1988). *Accelerating the coping process.* Unpublished manuscript, Southern Methodist University, Dallas.

Pennington, N., & Hastie, R. (1986). Evidence evaluation in complex decision making. *Journal of Personality and Social Psychology, 51,* 242–258.

Pennington, N., & Hastie, R. (1988). Explanation-based decision making: Effects of memory structure on judgment. *Journal of Experimental Psychology: Learning, Memory, and Cognition, 14,* 521–533.

Pennington, N., & Hastie, R. (1992). Explaining evidence: Tests of the story model for juror decision making. *Journal of Personality and Social Psychology, 62,* 189–206.

Penrod, S. D. (1990). Predictors of jury decision making on criminal and civil cases: A field experiment. *Forensic Reports, 3,* 261–278.

Peplau, L. A., & Perlman, D. (1982). Perspectives on loneliness. In L. A. Peplau & D. Perlman (Eds.), *Loneliness: A sourcebook of current theory, research, and therapy.* New York: John Wiley.

Pepler, D. J., King, G., & Byrd, W. (1991). A social–cognitively based social skills training program for aggressive children. In D. J. Pepler & K. H. Rubin (Eds.), *The development and treatment of childhood aggression.* Hillsdale, NJ: Erlbaum.

Perdue, C. W., Dovidio, J. F., Gurtman, M. B., & Tyler, R. B. (1990). Us and them: Social categorization and the process of intergroup bias. *Journal of Personality and Social Psychology, 59,* 475–486.

Perlman, D., & Oskcamp, S. (1971). The effects of picture content and exposure frequency on evaluations of Negroes and whites. *Journal of Experimental Social Psychology, 7,* 503–514.

Perloff, L. S. (1987). Social comparison and the illusion of unique invulnerability to negative life events. In C. R. Snyder & C. E. Ford (Eds.), *Coping with negative life events: Clinical and social psychological perspectives.* New York: Plenum.

Perrin, S., & Spencer, C. (1981). The Asch effect—A child of its time? *Bulletin of the British Psychological Society, 33,* 405–406.

Peterson, C. (1988). Explanatory style as a risk factor for illness. *Cognitive Therapy and Research, 12,* 117–130.

Pettigrew, T. F. (1979). The ultimate attribution error: Extending Allport's cognitive analysis of prejudice. *Personality and Social Psychology Bulletin, 5,* 461–476.

Pettigrew, T. F. (1986). *Racially separate or together?* New York: McGraw-Hill.

Pettigrew, T. F. (1991, July 16). *New York Times,* p. 31.

Pettit, G. S., Bakshi, A., Dodge, K. A., & Coie, J. D. (1986). The emergence of social dominance in young boys' play groups: Developmental differences and behavioral correlates. *Developmental Psychology, 26,* 1017–1025.

Petty, R. E., & Cacioppo, J. T. (1986a). *Communication and persuasion.* New York: Springer-Verlag.

Petty, R. E., & Cacioppo, J. T. (1986b). The elaboration likelihood model of persuasion. In L. Berkowitz (Ed.), *Advances in experimental social psychology* (Vol. 19, p. 126). San Diego, CA: Academic Press.

Petty, R. E., Cacioppo, J. T., & Goldman, R. (1981). Personal involvement as a determinant of argument-based persuasion. *Journal of Social Behavior and Personality, 41,* 847–855.

Petty, R. E., Schumann, D. W., Richman, S. A., & Strathman, A. J. (1993). Positive mood and persuasion: Different roles for affect under high and low elaboration conditions. *Journal of Personality and Social Psychology, 64,* 5–20.

Peukert, D. (1987). *Inside Nazi Germany: Conformity, opposition, and racism in everyday life.* New Haven, CT: Yale University Press.

Phillips, D. P. (1983). The impact of mass media violence on U.S. homicides. *American Sociological Review, 48,* 560–568.

Phillips, D. P. (1986). Natural experiments on the effects of mass media violence on fatal aggression: Strengths and weaknesses of a new approach. In L. Berkowitz (Ed.), *Advances in experimental social psychology* (Vol. 19). New York: Academic Press.

Pihl, R. O., Smith, M., & Farrell, B. (1984). Alcohol and aggression in men: A comparison of brewed and distilled beverages. *Journal of Studies on Alcohol, 45,* 278–282.

Pihl, R. O., & Zacchia, C. (1986). Alcohol and aggression: A test of the affect-arousal hypothesis. *Aggressive Behavior, 12,* 367–375.

Piliavin, I. M., Piliavin, J. A., & Rodin, J. (1975). Costs, diffusion, and the stigmatized victim. *Journal of Personality and Social Psychology, 32,* 429–438.

Piliavin, J. A., & Piliavin, I. M. (1972). Effects of blood on reactions to a victim. *Journal of Personality and Social Psychology, 8,* 353–361.

Pittman, T. S., & Pittman, N. L. (1980). Deprivation of control and the attribution process. *Journal of Personality and Social Psychology, 39,* 377–389.

Platt, J. (1973). Social traps. *American Psychologist, 28,* 641–651.

Pliner, P., & Pelchat, M. L. (1986). Similarities in food preferences between children and siblings and parents. *Appetite, 7,* 333–342.

Plomin, R. (1989). *Nature and nurture: An introduction to human behavioral genetics.* Pacific Grove, CA: Brooks/Cole.

Plomin, R., Corley, R., DeFries, J. C., & Fulker, D. W. (1990). Individual differences in television viewing in early childhood: Nature as well as nurture. *Psychological Science, 1,* 371–377.

Polivy, J., & Herman, C. P. (1983). *Breaking the diet habit.* New York: Basic Books.

Polivy, J., & Herman, C. P. (1985). Dieting and binging. *American Psychologist, 40,* 193–201.

Poole, D. K., & White, L. T. (1992). *It happened two years ago: Question repetition and the eyewitness testimony of children and adults.* Paper presented at the annual meeting of the Midwestern Psychological Association, Chicago.

Prager, K., Fuller, D. O., & Gonzalez, A. S. (1989). The function of self-disclosure in social interaction. *Journal of Social and Personal Relationships, 4,* 563–588.

Pratkanis, A. R., & Aronson, E. (1992). *The age of propaganda.* New York: W. H. Freeman.

Pratkanis, A. R., & Greenwald, A. G. (1989). The cognitive representation of attitudes. In A. R. Pratkanis, S. J. Breckler, & A. G. Greenwald (Eds.), *Attitude structure and function.* Hillsdale, NJ: Erlbaum.

Pratkanis, A. R., Greenwald, A. G., Leippe, M. R., & Baumgardner, M. H. (1988). In search of reliable persuasion effects. III. The sleeper effect is dead. Long live the sleeper effect. *Journal of Personality and Social Psychology, 54,* 203–218.

Pratto, F., & Bargh, J. H. (1991). Stereotyping based on apparently individuating information: Trait and global components of sex stereotypes under attention overload. *Journal of Experimental Social Psychology, 27,* 26–47.

Pratto, F., & John, O. (1991). Automatic vigilance: The attention-grabbing power of negative social information. *Journal of Personality and Social Psychology, 51,* 380–391.

Prentice-Dunn, S., & Rogers, R. W. (1989). Deindividuation and the self-regulation of behavior. In P. B. Paulus (Ed.), *Psychology of group influence* (2nd ed.). Hillsdale, NJ: Erlbaum.

Pritchard, R. D., & Watson, M. D. (1992). Understanding and measuring group productivity. In S. Worchel, W. Wood, & J. A. Simpson (Eds.), *Group process and productivity.* Newbury Park, CA: Sage.

Pruitt, D. G. (1968). Reciprocity and credit building in a laboratory dyad. *Journal of Personality and Social Psychology, 8,* 143–147.

Pruitt, D. G., & Carnevale, P. J. D. (1982). The development of integrative agreements. In V. J. Derlaga & J. Grzlak (Eds.), *Cooperation and helping behavior and theory.* New York: Academic Press.

Pruitt, D. G., & Johnson, D. F. (1970). Mediation as an aid to face saving in negotiation. *Journal of Personality and Social Psychology, 14,* 239–246.

Pruitt, D. G., & Rubin, J. Z. (1986). *Social conflict: Escalation, stalemate, and settlements.* New York: Random House.

Pryor, J. B., Reeder, G. D., & McManus, J. A. (1991). Fear and loathing in the workplace: Reactions to AIDS-infected coworkers. *Personality and Social Psychology Bulletin, 17,* 133–139.

Pulkkinen, L., & Pitkanen, T. (1993). Continuities in aggressive behavior from childhood to adulthood. *Aggressive Behavior, 19,* 249–263.

Pyszczynski, T., Greenberg, J., Mack, D., & Wrightsman, L. S. (1981). Opening statements in a jury trial: The effects of promising more than the evidence can show. *Journal of Applied Social Psychology, 11,* 434–444.

Pyszczynski, T., & Wrightsman, L. S. (1981). The effects of opening statements on mock jurors' verdicts in a simulated criminal trial. *Journal of Applied Social Psychology, 11,* 301–313.

Quattrone, G. A. (1982). Behavioral consequences of attributional bias. *Social Cognition, 1,* 358–378.

Quattrone, G. A., & Jones, E. E. (1980). The perception of variability within in-groups and out-groups. *Journal of Personality and Social Psychology, 38,* 141–152.

Radelet, M. L. (1981). Racial characteristics and the imposition of the death penalty. *American Sociological Review, 46,* 918–927.

Rajecki, D. W. (1990). *Attitudes* (2nd ed.). Sunderland, MA: Sinauer.

Ransford, H. E. (1970). Isolation, powerlessness, and violence: A study of attitudes and participation in the Watts riot. In E. I. Megargee & J. E. Hokanson (Eds.) *The dynamics of aggression.* New York: Harper & Row.

Rattner, A. (1988). Convicted but innocent: Wrongful conviction and the criminal justice system. *Law and Human Behavior, 12,* 283–294.

Raven, B. H., & Kruglanski, A. W. (1970). Conflict and power. In P. Swingle (Ed.), *The structure of conflict.* New York: Academic Press.

Raven, B. H., & Rubin, J. Z. (1983). *Social psychology* (2nd ed.). New York: John Wiley & Sons.

Rawlins, W. K. (1982). Cross-sex friendship and the communicative management of sex-role expectations. *Communication Quarterly, 30,* 343–352.

Rawlins, W. K. (1992). *Friendship matters: Communication, dialectics, and life course.* New York: Aldine De Gruyter.

Regan, D. T. (1971). Effects of a favor and liking on compliance. *Journal of Experimental Social Psychology, 7,* 627–639.

Register, L. M., & Henley, T. B. (1992). The phenomenology of intimacy. *Journal of Social and Personal Relations, 9,* 467–482.

Reinisch, J. M., & Sanders, S. A. (1986). A test of sex differences in aggressive response to hypothetical conflict situations. *Journal of Personality and Social Psychology, 50,* 1045–1049.

Reisman, J. M. (1981). Adult friendships. In S. W. Duck & R. Gilmour (Eds.), *Personal relationships: Vol. 2. Developing personal relationships.* New York: Academic Press.

Reiss, M. J. (1984). Human sociobiology. *Zygon, 19,* 117–140.

Report of the National Advisory Commission on Civil Disorders. (1968). New York: The New York Times Company.

Reynolds, V., Falger, V., & Vine, I. (1987). *The sociobiology of ethnocentrism.* Athens, GA: University of Georgia Press.

Rhodewalt, F. T. (1986). Self-presentation and the phenomenal self: On the stability and malleability of self-conceptions. In R. F. Baumeister (Ed.), *Public self and private self.* New York: Springer-Verlag.

Rhodewalt, F., Morf, C., Hazlett, S., & Fairfield, M. (1991). Self-handicapping: The role of discounting and augmentation in the preservation of self-esteem. *Journal of Personality and Social Psychology, 61,* 122–131.

Rice, M. E., & Grusec, J. E. (1975). Saying and doing: Effects on observer performance. *Journal of Personality and Social Psychology, 32,* 584–593.

Richardson, D. R., Vandenberg, R. J., & Humphries, S. A. (1986). Effect of power to harm on retaliative aggression among males and females. *Journal of Research in Personality, 20,* 402–419.

Ringelmann, M. (1913). Research on animate sources of power: The work of man. In *Annales de l'Institut National Agronomique,* 2e serie—tome XII, 1–40.

Rodin, J. (1974). Effects of distraction on the performance of obese and normal subjects. In S. Schachter & J. Rodin (Eds.), *Obese humans and rats.* Hillsdale, NJ: Erlbaum.

Rodin, J. (1981). Current status of the internal–external hypothesis for obesity: What went wrong? *American Psychologist, 36,* 361–372.

Rodin, J., & Langer, E. (1976). Long-term effect of a control-relevant intervention. *Journal of Personality and Social Psychology, 35,* 897–902.

Rodin, S., & Salovey, P. (1989). Health psychology. *Annual Review of Psychology, 40,* 533–579.

Rogers, R. W. (1983). Cognitive and physiological processes in fear appeals and attitude change: A revised theory of protection motivation. In J. T. Cacioppo & R. E. Petty (Eds.), *Social psychophysiology.* New York: Guilford Press.

Rohsenow, D. J., & Bachorowski, J. (1984). Effects of alcohol and expectancies on verbal aggression in men and women. *Journal of Abnormal Psychology, 93,* 418–432.

Rokeach, M. (1968). *Beliefs, attitudes, and values: A theory of organization and change.* San Francisco: Jossey-Bass.

Rokeach, M. (1973). *The nature of human values.* New York: Free Press.

Rokeach, M. (1979). *Understanding human values: Individual and social.* New York: Free Press.

Romer, D., Gruder, C. L., & Lizzadro, T. (1986). A person-situation approach to altruistic behavior. *Journal of Personality and Social Psychology, 51,* 1001–1012.

Ronis, D. L., & Kaiser, M. K. (1989). Correlates of breast cancer self-examinations in a sample of college women: Analysis of linear structural variations. *Journal of Applied Social Psychology, 19,* 1068–1085.

Rosenbaum, M. E. (1986). The repulsion hypothesis: On the nondevelopment of relationships. *Journal of Personality and Social Psychology, 51,* 1156–1166.

Rosenberg, M. L., & Finley, M. A. (1992). The federal role in injury control. *American Psychologist, 47,* 1031–1035.

Rosenberger, C. (1993, February 1). Serbian tightrope. *National Review.*

Rosenman, R. H., Swan, G. E., & Carmelli, D. (1988). Definition, assessment, and evolution of the Type A behavior pattern. In B. K. Houston & C. R. Snyder (Eds.), *Type A behavior pattern.* New York: John Wiley.

Rosenthal, R., & Jacobson, L. (1968). *Pygmalion in the classroom: Teacher expectation and pupil's intellectual development.* New York: Holt.

Roskos-Ewoldsen, D., & Fazio, R. H. (1992). On the orienting value of attitudes: Attitude accessibility as a determinant of an object's attraction of visual attention. *Journal of Personality and Social Psychology, 63,* 198–211.

Ross, L., Amabile, T., & Steinmetz, J. L. (1977). Social roles, social control, and biases in social perception processes. *Journal of Personality and Social Psychology, 35,* 484–494.

Ross, L., Greene, D., & House, P. (1977). The "false consensus effect": An egocentric bias in social perception and attribution processes. *Journal of Experimental Social Psychology, 13,* 279–301.

Ross, L., & Nisbett, R. E. (1991). *The person and the situation.* New York: McGraw-Hill.

Ross, M., & Holmberg, D. (1992). Are wives' memories for events in relationships more vivid than their husbands'? *Journal of Social and Personal Relations, 9,* 585–606.

Ross, S. L., & Jackson, J. M. (1991). Teachers' expectations for black males' and black females' academic achievement. *Personality and Social Psychology Bulletin, 17,* 78–82.

Rowlinson, R. T., & Felner, R. D. (1988). Major life events, hassles, and adaptation in adolescence: Confounding in the conceptualization and measurement of life stress and adjustment revisited. *Journal of Personality and Social Psychology, 55,* 432–444.

Rubin, J. Z. (1980). Experimental research on third-party intervention in conflict: Toward some generalizations. *Psychological Bulletin, 87,* 379–391.

Rubin, J. Z., & Brown, B. R. (1975). *The social psychology of bargaining and negotiation.* New York: Academic Press.

Rubin, Z. (1970). Measurement of romantic love. *Journal of Personality and Social Psychology, 16,* 265–273.

Rubin, Z. (1973). *Liking and loving: An invitation to social psychology.* New York: Holt, Rinehart & Winston.

Rubin, Z., Hill, C. T., Peplau, L. A., & Dunkel-Schetter, C. (1980). Self-disclosure in dating couples: Sex roles and the ethics of openness. *Journal of Marriage and the Family, 42,* 305–317.

Rule, B. G., & Ferguson, T. J. (1986). The effects of media violence on attitudes, emotions, and cognitions. *Journal of Social Issues, 42,* 29–50.

Rusbult, C. E. (1987). Responses to dissatisfaction in close relationships: The exit-voice-loyalty-neglect model. In D. Perlman & S. Duck (Eds.), *Intimate relationships: Development, dynamics, and deterioration.* Beverly Hills, CA: Sage.

Rusbult, C. E., Verette, J., Whitney, G. A., Slovik, L. F., & Lipkus, I. (1991). Accommodation processes in close rela-

tionships: Theory and preliminary empirical evidence. *Journal of Personality and Social Psychology, 61,* 641–647.

Ryckman, R. M., Robbins, M. A., Thornton, B., Kaaczor, L. M., Gayton, S. L., & Anderson, C. V. (1991). Public self-consciousness and physique stereotyping. *Personality and Social Psychology Bulletin, 18,* 400–405.

Saks, M. (1981). *Small-group decision making and complex information tasks.* Washington, DC: Federal Judicial Center.

Saks, M., & Hastie, R. (1978). *Social psychology in court.* New York: Van Nostrand Reinhold.

Sales, S. M. (1972). Economic threat as a determinant of conversion rates in authoritarian and nonauthoritarian churches. *Journal of Personality and Social Psychology, 23,* 420–428.

Salovey, P., & Birnbaum, D. (1989). Influence of mood on health-relevant cognitions. *Journal of Personality and Social Psychology, 57,* 539–551.

Sampson, R. J. (1987). Urban black violence: The effect of male joblessness and family disruption. *American Journal of Sociology, 93,* 348–382.

Sanbonmatsu, D. M., Akimoto, S. A., & Biggs, E. (1993). Overestimating causality: Attributional effects of confirmatory processing. *Journal of Personality and Social Psychology, 65,* 892–903.

Sanna, L. J., & Shotland, R. L. (1990). Valence of anticipated evaluation and social facilitation. *Journal of Experimental Social Psychology, 22,* 242–248.

Sayers, S. L., & Baucom, D. H. (1991). Role of femininity and masculinity in distressed couple's communication. *Journal of Personality and Social Psychology, 61,* 641–647.

Schachter, S. (1951). Deviation, rejection and communication. *Journal of Abnormal and Social Psychology, 46,* 190–207.

Schachter, S. (1973). Some extraordinary facts about obese humans and rats. In N. Keill (Ed.), *The psychology of obesity: Dynamics and treatment.* Springfield, IL: Charles C. Thomas.

Schachter, S., & Rodin, J. (1974). *Obese humans and rats.* Washington, DC: Erlbaum/Halstead.

Schachter, S., & Singer, J. E. (1962). Cognitive, social, and physiological determinants of emotional state. *Psychological Review, 69,* 379–399.

Schaffer, K. F. (1981). *Sex roles and human behavior.* Cambridge, MA: Winthrop.

Schaller, M. (1991). Social categorization and the formation of group stereotypes: Further evidence for biased processing in the perception of group-behavior correlations. *European Journal of Social Psychology, 21,* 25–35.

Scheier, M. F., & Carver, C. S. (1987). Dispositional optimism and physical well-being: The influence of generalized outcome expectancies on health. *Journal of Personality, 55,* 172–210.

Scheier, M. F., & Carver, C. S. (1988). A model of behavioral self-regulation: Translating intention into action. In L. Berkowitz (Ed.), *Advances in experimental social psychology* (Vol. 21). San Diego, CA: Academic Press.

Scheier, M. F., Matthews, K. A., Owens, J., Abbott, A., Lebfevre, C., & Carver, C. S. (1986). *Optimism and bypass surgery.* Unpublished manuscript.

Scherwitz, L., & Canick, J. D. (1988). Self-reference and coronary heart disease. In B. K. Houston & C. R. Snyder (Eds.), *Type A behavior pattern.* New York: Plenum.

Schiffenbauer, A., & Schavio, S. R. (1976). Physical distance and attraction: An intensification effect. *Journal of Experimental Social Psychology, 12,* 274–282.

Schleiter, S. J., Keller, S. E., Bond, R. N., Cohen, J., & Stein,

M. (1989). Major depressive disorder and immunity. *Archives of General Psychiatry, 46,* 81–87.

Schlenker, B. R. (1986). Self-identification: Toward an integration of the private and public self. In R. F. Baumeister (Ed.), *Public self and private self.* New York: Springer-Verlag.

Schlenker, B. R. (1987). Threats to identity: Self-identification and social stress. In C. R. Snyder & C. Ford (Eds.), *Coping with negative life events: Clinical and social psychological perspectives.* San Diego, CA: Academic Press.

Schlenker, B. R., & Leary, M. R. (1982). Social anxiety and self-presentation: A conceptualization and model. *Psychological Bulletin, 92,* 641–669.

Schlenker, B. R., Soraci, S., Jr., & McCarthy, B. (1976). Self-esteem and group performance as determinants of egocentric perceptions in cooperative groups. *Human Relations, 29,* 1163–1176.

Schlenker, B. R., & Trudeau, J. V. (1990). Impact of self-presentations on private self-beliefs: Effects of prior self-beliefs and misattribution. *Journal of Personality and Social Psychology, 58,* 22–32.

Schlenker, B. R., Weigold, M. F., & Hallam, J. R. (1990). Self-serving attributions in social context: Effects of self-esteem and social pressure. *Journal of Personality and Social Psychology, 58,* 855–863.

Schlesinger, A. M., Jr. (1965). *A thousand days.* Boston: Houghton Mifflin.

Schlesinger, S. R. (1988). *Pretrial release and detention: The bail reform act of 1984.* Washington, DC: U.S. Department of Justice Bureau of Justice Statistics.

Schmidt, G., & Weiner, B. (1988). An attribution-affect-action theory of behavior: Replications of judgments of help giving. *Personality and Social Psychology Bulletin, 14,* 610–621.

Schneider, D. J. (1991). Social cognition. *Annual Review of Psychology, 42,* 535–557.

Schneider, S. G., Taylor, S. E., Hammen, C., Kemeny, M. E., & Dudley, J. (1991). Factors influencing suicide intent in gay and bisexual suicide ideators: Differing models for men with and without HIV. *Journal of Personality and Social Psychology, 61,* 776–788.

Schoen, R., & Wooldredge, J. (1989). Marriage choices in North Carolina and Virginia, 1969–71 and 1979–81. *Journal of Marriage and the Family, 51,* 465–481.

Schopler, J., & Matthews, M. (1965). The influence of perceived causal locus of partner's dependence on the use of interpersonal power. *Journal of Personality and Social Psychology, 2,* 609–612.

Schutt, R. K., & Dannefer, D. (1988). Detention decisions in juvenile cases: JINS, JDs, and gender. *Law and Society Review, 22,* 509–520.

Schutz, W. (1983). A theory of small groups. In H. H. Blumberg, A. P. Hare, V. Kent, & M. F. Davis (Eds.), *Small groups and social interaction* (Vol. 2). New York: Wiley.

Schwartz, S. H. (1975). The justice of need and the activation of humanitarian norms. *Journal of Social Issues, 31,* 111–136.

Schwarz, N., Bless, H., & Bohner, G. (1992). Mood and persuasion: Affective states influence the processing of persuasive communications. In M. P. Zanna (Ed.), *Advances in experimental social psychology* (Vol. 24). San Diego, CA: Academic Press.

Scott, W. A. (1957). Attitude change through reward of verbal behavior. *Journal of Abnormal and Social Psychology, 55,* 72–75.

Segal, M. W. (1974). Alphabet and attraction: An unobtrusive measure of the effect of propinquity in a field setting. *Journal of Personality and Social Psychology, 30,* 654–657.

Selye, H. (1976). *The stress of life.* New York: McGraw-Hill.

Senchak, M., & Leonard, K. (1992). Attachment styles and marital adjustment among newlywed couples. *Journal of Social and Personal Relationships, 9,* 221–238.

Sereny, G. (1974). *Into that darkness: An examination of conscience.* New York: Vintage Press.

Sereny, G. (1992). John Demjanjuk and the failure of justice. *New York Times Review of Books, 39,* 32–34.

Shanab, M. E., & Isonio, S. A. (1982). The effects of contrast upon compliance with socially undesirable requests in the foot-in-the-door paradigm. *Bulletin of the Psychonomic Society, 20,* 180–182.

Shanab, M. E., & O'Neill, P. (1979). The effect of contrast upon compliance with socially undesirable requests in the door-in-the-face paradigm. *Canadian Journal of Behavioural Science, 11,* 236–244.

Shanab, M. E., & Yahya, K. A. (1977). A behavioral study of obedience in children. *Journal of Personality and Social Psychology, 35,* 530–536.

Shanab, M. E., & Yahya, K. A. (1978). A cross-cultural study of obedience. *Bulletin of the Psychonomic Society, 11,* 267–269.

Shapiro, E. G. (1980). Is seeking help from a friend like seeking help from a stranger? *Social Psychology Quarterly, 43,* 259–263.

Shaver, P., & Hazan, C. (1985). Incompatibility, loneliness, and limerence. In W. Ickes (Ed.), *Compatible and incompatible relationships.* New York: Springer-Verlag.

Shaver, P., Hazan, C., & Bradshaw, D. (1988). Love as attachment: The integration of three behavioral systems. In R. Sternberg & M. Barnes (Eds.), *The anatomy of love.* New Haven, CT: Yale University Press.

Shaw, J. M., & Scott, W. A. (1991). Influence of parent discipline style on delinquent behavior: The mediating role of control orientation. *Australian Journal of Psychology, 43,* 61–67.

Shepperd, J. A. (1993). Productivity loss in performance groups: A motivation analysis. *Psychological Bulletin, 113,* 67–81.

Sherif, M. (1936). *The psychology of social norms.* New York: Harper & Row.

Sherif, M. (1958). Superordinate goals in the reduction of intergroup conflict. *American Journal of Sociology, 63,* 349–358.

Sherif, M. (1972). Experiments on norm formation. In E. P. Hollander & R. G. Hunt (Eds.), *Classic contributions to social psychology.* New York: Oxford University Press.

Sherif, M., Harvey, O. J., White, B. J., Hood, W. R., & Sherif, C. W. (1961). *Intergroup cooperation and competition: The Robbers Cave experiment.* Norman, OK: University Book Exchange.

Sherif, M., & Hovland, C. I. (1961). *Social judgment.* New Haven, CT: Yale University Press.

Sherif, M., & Sherif, C. W. (1973). *Groups in harmony and tension.* New York: Octagon Books.

Sherif, C. W., Sherif, M., & Nebergall, R. E. (1965). *Attitude and attitude change: The social judgment-involvement approach.* Philadelphia: Saunders.

Sherman, S. L., Hamilton, D. K., & Roskos-Ewoldsen, D. R. (1989). Attenuation of illusory correlation. *Personality and Social Psychology Bulletin, 15,* 559–571.

Shipler, D. K. (1986). *Arab and Jew: Wounded spirits in a promised land.* New York: Times Books.

Shotland, R. L., & Heinhold, W. D. (1985). Bystander response to arterial bleeding: Helping skills, the decision-making process, and differentiating the helping response. *Journal of Personality and Social Psychology, 49,* 347–356.

Showers, C. (1992). Evaluatively integrative thinking about

characteristics of the self. *Personality and Social Psychology Bulletin, 18,* 719–729.

Sibicky, M., & Dovidio, J. F. (1986). Stigma of psychological therapy: Stereotypes, interpersonal reactions, and the self-fulfilling prophecy. *Journal of Counseling Psychology, 33,* 148–154.

Sikes, M. P. (1975). *The administration of injustice.* New York: Harper & Row.

Silverstein, B., Perdue, L., Peterson, B., & Kelly, E. (1986). The role of the mass media in promoting a thin standard of bodily attractiveness for women. *Sex Roles, 14,* 519–532.

Simon, L. (1977). *The biography of Alice B. Toklas.* Garden City, NY: Doubleday.

Simonton, D. K. (1985). Intelligence and personal influence in groups: Four nonlinear models. *Psychological Review, 92,* 532–547.

Simonton, D. K. (1988). Presidential style: Personality, biography, and performance. *Journal of Personality and Social Psychology, 55,* 928–936.

Simpson, J. A. (1990). Influence of attachment styles on romantic relationships. *Journal of Personality and Social Psychology, 59,* 971–980.

Singer, J. E., & Krantz, D. S. (1982). Perspectives on the interface between psychology and public health. *American Psychologist, 37,* 955–960.

Sistrunk, F., & Clement, D. (1970). Cross-cultural comparisons of the conformity behavior of college students. *Journal of Social Psychology, 82,* 273–274.

Skowronski, J. J., Betz, A. L., Thompson, C. P., & Shannon, L. (1991). Social memory in everyday life: Recall of self-events and other-events. *Journal of Personality and Social Psychology, 60,* 831–843.

Sleek, S. (1993, November). People craft their self-image from groups. *APA Monitor,* p. 22.

Sleet, D. A. (1987). Motor vehicle trauma and safety belt use in the context of public health priorities. *Journal of Trauma, 27,* 695–702.

Slovic, P., & Fischoff, B. (1977). On the psychology of experimental surprise. *Journal of Experimental Psychology: Human Perception and Performance, 3,* 544–551.

Smeaton, G., Byrne, D., & Murnen, S. K. (1989). The repulsion hypothesis revisited: Similarity irrelevance or dissimilarity bias. *Journal of Personality and Social Psychology, 56,* 54–59.

Smith, C. A., Haynes, K. N., Lazarus, R. S., & Pope, L. K. (1993). In search of "hot" cognitions: Attributions, appraisals, and their relation to emotion. *Journal of Personality and Social Psychology, 65,* 916–929.

Smith, E. R. (1988). Category accessibility effects in simulated exemplar-based memory. *Journal of Experimental Social Psychology, 24,* 448–463.

Smith, E. R. (1990). Content and process specificity in the effects of prior experiences. In T. K. Srull & R. S. Wyer, Jr. (Eds.), *Advances in social cognition* (Vol. 3). Hillsdale, NJ: Erlbaum.

Smith, K. D., Keating, J. P., & Stotland, E. (1989). Altruism reconsidered: The effect of denying feedback on a victim's status to empathetic witnesses. *Journal of Personality and Social Psychology, 57,* 641–650.

Smith, M. C. (1983). Hypnotic memory enhancement of witnesses: Does it work? *Psychological Bulletin, 94,* 387–407.

Smith, P. B., & Bond, M. H. (1994). *Social psychology across cultures.* Boston: Allyn & Bacon.

Smith, R. E., Keating, J. P., Hester, R. K., & Mitchell, H. E. (1976). Role and justice considerations in attribution of responsibility to a rape victim. *Journal of Research in Personality, 10,* 346–357.

Smith, T. W., Allred, K. D., Morrison, C. A., & Carlson, S. D. (1989). Cardiovascular reactivity and interpersonal influence: Active coping in a social context. *Journal of Personality and Social Psychology, 56,* 209–218.

Smith, T. W., & Frohm, K. D. (1985). What's so unhealthy about hostility? Construct validity and psychosocial correlates of the Cook and Medley Ho Scale. *Health Psychology, 4,* 503–520.

Smith, W. P. (1987). Conflict and negotiation: Trends and emerging issues. *Journal of Applied Social Psychology, 17,* 641–677.

Sniderman, P. M., & Piazza, T. (1994). *The scar of race.* Cambridge, MA: Harvard University Press.

Snodgrass, M. A. (1987). The relationships of differential loneliness, intimacy and characterological attributional style to duration of loneliness. *Journal of Social Behavior and Personality, 2,* 173–186.

Snowden, F. M., Jr. (1983). *Before color prejudice: The ancient view of blacks.* Cambridge, MA: Harvard University Press.

Snyder, C. R., Ford, C. E., & Harris, R. N. (1987). The effects of theoretical perspective on the analysis of coping with negative life events. In C. R. Snyder & C. E. Ford (Eds.), *Coping with negative life events.* New York: Plenum.

Snyder, M. (1987). *Public appearances as private realities: The psychology of self-monitoring.* New York: W. H. Freeman.

Snyder, M. (1993). Motivational foundations of behavioral confirmation. In M. P. Zanna (Ed.), *Advances in experimental social psychology* (Vol. 25). San Diego, CA: Academic Press.

Snyder, M., Berscheid, E., & Glick, P. (1985). Focusing on the interior and exterior. Two investigations of the initiation of personal relationships. *Journal of Personality and Social Psychology, 48,* 1427–1439.

Snyder, M., & Cunningham, M. (1975). To comply or not to comply: Testing the self-perception explanation of the foot-in-the-door phenomenon. *Journal of Personality and Social Psychology, 31,* 64–67.

Snyder, M., & Swann, W. B., Jr. (1978). Hypothesis-testing processes in social interaction. *Journal of Personality and Social Psychology, 36,* 1201–1212.

Snyder, M., Tanke, E. D., & Berscheid, E. (1977). Social perception and interpersonal behavior: On the self-fulfilling nature of social stereotypes. *Journal of Personality and Social Psychology, 35,* 656–666.

Solano, C. H., & Koester, N. H. (1989). Loneliness and communication problems: Subjective anxiety or objective skills? *Personality and Social Psychology Bulletin, 15,* 126–133.

Solomon, S., Greenberg, J., & Pyszczynski, T. (1992). A terror management theory of self-esteem and its role in social behavior. In M. Leary (Ed.), *Advances in experimental social psychology* (Vol. 25). San Diego, CA: Academic Press.

Sommer, R. (1969). *Personal space.* Englewood Cliffs, NJ: Prentice-Hall.

Spacapan, S. (1988a). Social psychology and health. In S. Spacapan & S. Oskamp (Eds.), *The social psychology of health.* Beverly Hills, CA: Sage.

Spacapan, S. (1988b). Psychosocial mediators of health status. In S. Spacapan & S. Oskamp (Eds.), *The social psychology of health.* Beverly Hills, CA: Sage.

Spanos, N. P., Gwynn, M. I., Comer, S. L., Baltruweit, W. J., & de Groh, M. (1989). Are hypnotically induced pseudomemories resistant to cross-examination? *Law and Human Behavior, 13,* 271–289.

Spanos, N. P., Quigley, C. A., Gwynn, M. I., Glatt, R. L., & Perlini, A. H. (1991). Hypnotic interrogation, pretrial preparation, and witness testimony during direct and cross-examination. *Law and Human Behavior, 15,* 639–654.

Spence, J. T. (1985). Gender identity and its implications for concepts of masculinity and femininity. In T. B. Sonderegger (Ed.), *Nebraska symposium on motivation: Psychology and gender.* (Vol. 32). Lincoln: University of Nebraska Press.

Spivey, C. B., & Prentice-Dunn, S. (1990). Assessing the directionality of deindividuated behavior: Effects of deindividuation, modeling, and private self-consciousness on aggressive and prosocial responses. *Basic and Applied Social Psychology, 11,* 387–403.

Sporer, S. L. (1993). Eyewitness accuracy, confidence, and decision times in simultaneous and sequential lineups. *Journal of Applied Psychology, 78,* 22–33.

Sprafkin, J. N., Liebert, R. M., & Poulos, R. W. (1975). Effects of a prosocial televised example on children's helping. *Journal of Experimental Child Psychology, 20,* 119–126.

Stangor, C., & Lange, J. E. (1994). Mental representations of social groups: Advances in understanding stereotypes and stereotyping. In M. P. Zanna (Ed.), *Advances in experimental social psychology* (Vol. 26). San Diego, CA: Academic Press.

Stasser, G. (1992). Pooling of shared and unshared information during group discussions. In S. Worchel, W. Wood, & J. A. Simpson (Eds.), *Group process and productivity.* Newbury Park, CA: Sage.

Stasser, G., Kerr, N. L., & Davis, J. H. (1990). Influence processes and consensus models in decision making groups. In P. Paulus (Ed.), *Psychology of group influence* (2nd ed.). Hillsdale, NJ: Erlbaum.

Stasser, G., & Stewart, G. (1992). Discovery of hidden profiles by decision-making groups: Solving a problem versus making a judgment. *Journal of Personality and Social Psychology, 63,* 426–434.

Stasser, G., Taylor, L. A., & Hanna, C. (1989). Information sampling and unstructured discussions of three- and six-person groups. *Journal of Personality and Social Psychology, 57,* 67–78.

Stasser, G., & Titus, W. (1987). Effects of information load and percentage of shared information on dissemination of unshared information during group discussion. *Journal of Personality and Social Psychology, 53,* 81–93.

Stattin, H., & Magnusson, D. (1989). The role of early aggressive behavior in the frequency, seriousness, and types of later crime. *Journal of Consulting and Clinical Psychology, 57,* 710–718.

Staub, E. (1985). *The roots of evil: The origins of genocide and other group violence.* Cambridge, England: Cambridge University Press.

Steele, C. M. (1988). The psychology of self-affirmation: Sustaining the integrity of the self. In L. Berkowitz (Ed.), *Advances in experimental social psychology* (Vol. 21). San Diego, CA: Academic Press.

Steele, C. M., & Josephs, R. A. (1990). Alcohol myopia. *American Psychologist, 45,* 921–933.

Steil, J. M., & Weltman, K. (1991). Marital inequality: The importance of resources, personal attributes, and social norms on career valuing and the allocation of domestic responsibilities. *Sex Roles, 24,* 161–179.

Steil, J. M., & Weltman, K. (1992). Influence strategies at home and at work: A study of sixty dual-career couples. *Journal of Social and Personal Relationships, 9,* 65–88.

Steiner, I. D. (1972). *Group process and productivity.* New York: Academic Press.

Stellman, J. M., & Bertin, J. E. (1990, June 4). Science's anti-female bias. *New York Times,* p. 34.

Sternberg, R. J. (1986). A triangular theory of love. *Psychological Review, 93,* 119–135.

Sternberg, R. J. (1988). Triangulating love. In R. J. Sternberg & M. L. Barnes (Eds.), *The psychology of love.* New Haven, CT: Yale University Press.

Sternberg, R. J., & Gracek, S. (1984). The nature of love. *Journal of Personality and Social Psychology, 47,* 312–329.

Still, W. (1872/1968). *The underground railroad.* New York: Arno Press and the *New York Times.*

Stipek, D., Weiner, B., & Kexing, L. (1989). Testing some attribution-emotion relations in the People's Republic of China. *Journal of Personality and Social Psychology, 56,* 109–116.

Stone, G. S. (1979). Patient compliance and the role of the expert. *Journal of Social Issues, 35,* 34–59.

Stone, J., Aronson, E., Crain, A. L., Winslow, M. P., & Fried, C. B. (1994). Inducing hypocrisy as a means of encouraging young adults to use condoms. *Personality and Social Psychology Bulletin, 20,* 116–128.

Stoner, J. A. F. (1961). *A comparison of individual and group decisions involving risk.* Unpublished master's thesis, Massachusetts Institute of Technology.

Storms, M. D. (1973). Videotape and the attribution process: Reversing actors' and observers' points of view. *Journal of Personality and Social Psychology, 27,* 165–175.

Straus, M. A. (1991). Discipline and deviance: Physical punishment of children and violence and other crime in adulthood. *Social Problems, 38,* 133–152.

Strong, B., & DeVault, C. (1994). *Human sexuality.* Mountain View, CA: Mayfield.

Suls, J., & Sanders, G. S. (1989). Why do some behavioral styles place people at coronary risk? In A. R. Siegman & T. M. Dembroski (Eds.), *In search of coronary prone behavior: Beyond Type A.* Hillsdale, NJ: Erlbaum.

Sulthana, P. (1987). The effect of frustration and inequity on the displacement of aggression. *Asian Journal of Psychology and Education, 19,* 26–33.

Swann, W. B., Jr. (1984). Quest for accuracy in person perception: A matter of pragmatics. *Psychological Review, 91,* 457–477.

Swann, W. B., Jr. (1992, February). Seeking "truth," finding despair: Some unhappy consequences of a negative self-concept. *Current Directions in Psychological Science,* pp. 15–18.

Swann, W. B., Jr., Hixon, J. G., & De La Ronde, C. (1992). Embracing the bitter truth: Negative self-concepts and marital commitment. *Psychological Science, 3,* 118–121.

Swann, W. B., Jr., Pelham, B. W., & Krull, D. S. (1989). Agreeable fancy or disagreeable truth? Reconciling self-enhancement and self-verification. *Journal of Personality and Social Psychology, 57,* 782–791.

Swann, W. B., Jr., Stein-Seroussi, A., & Giesler, R. B. (1992). Why people self verify. *Journal of Personality and Social Psychology, 62,* 392–410.

Swann, W. B., Jr., Stein-Seroussi, A., & McNulty, S. E. (1992). Outcasts in a white-lie society: The enigmatic worlds of people with negative self-conceptions. *Journal of Personality and Social Psychology, 62,* 618–624.

Swim, J. (1994). Perceived versus meta-analytic effect sizes: An assessment of the accuracy of gender stereotypes. *Journal of Personality and Social Psychology, 66,* 21–36.

Switzer, R., & Taylor, R. B. (1983). Sociability versus privacy of residential choice: Impacts of personality and local social ties. *Basic and Applied Social Psychology, 4,* 123–136.

Sykes, C. J. (1992). *A nation of victims.* New York: St. Martin's Press.

Tajfel, H. (1981). *Human groups and social categories.* Cambridge, England: Cambridge University Press.

Tajfel, H. (1982). *Social identity and group relations.* Cambridge, England: Cambridge University Press.

Tajfel, H., Billig, M., Bundy, R., & Flament, C. (1971). Social categorization and intergroup behavior. *European Journal of Social Psychology, 1,* 149–178.

Tanford, S., & Penrod, S. (1984). Social influence model: A formal integration of research on majority and minority influence processes. *Psychological Bulletin, 95,* 189–225.

Tanford, S., & Penrod, S. (1986). Jury deliberations: Discussion content and influence processes in jury decision making. *Journal of Applied Social Psychology, 16,* 322–347.

Tavris, C. (1982). *Anger: The misunderstood emotion.* New York: Simon & Schuster.

Tavris, C. (1990, August). *Mismeasure of woman: Paradoxes and perspectives in the study of gender.* Master lecture presented at the annual meeting of the American Psychological Association, Boston.

Tavris, C., & Baumgardner, A. (1986). How life would be different. *Vogue,* 55–59.

Taylor, S. E. (1979). Hospital patient behavior: Reactance, helplessness, or control? *Journal of Social Issues, 35,* 156–184.

Taylor, S. E. (1981). The interface of cognitive and social psychology. In J. H. Harvey (Ed.), *Cognition, social behavior, and the environment.* Hillsdale, NJ: Erlbaum.

Taylor, S. E. (1983). Adjustment to threatening events: A theory of cognitive adaptation. *American Psychologist, 38,* 1161–1173.

Taylor, S. E. (1986). *Health psychology.* New York: Random House.

Taylor, S. E. (1989). *Positive illusions: Creative self-deception and the healthy mind.* New York: Basic Books.

Taylor, S. E. (1990). Health psychology: The science and the field. *American Psychologist, 45,* 40–50.

Taylor, S. E., & Brown, J. D. (1988). Illusion and well-being: A social psychological perspective on mental health. *Psychological Bulletin, 103,* 193–210.

Taylor, S. E., & Fiske, S. T. (1978). Salience, attention, & attribution: Top of the head phenomena. In L. Berkowitz (Ed.), *Advances in experimental social psychology* (Vol. 11). New York: Academic Press.

Taylor, S. E., Kemeny, M. E., Aspinwall, L. G., & Schneider, S. G. (1992). Optimism, coping, psychological distress, and high-risk sexual behavior among men at risk for acquired immunodeficiency syndrome (AIDS). *Journal of Personality and Social Psychology, 63,* 460–473.

Taylor, S. E., & Thompson, S. (1982). Stalking the elusive vividness effect. *Psychological Review, 89,* 166–181.

Tec, N. (1986). *When light pierced the darkness: Christian rescue of Jews in Nazi-occupied Poland.* New York: Oxford University Press.

Tennen, H., & Affleck, G. (1987). The costs and benefits of optimistic explanations and dispositional optimism. *Journal of Personality, 55,* 377–393.

Tennov, D. (1979). *Love and limerence: The experience of being in love.* New York: Stein & Day.

Tesser, A. (1988). Toward a self-evaluation maintenance model of social behavior. In L. Berkowitz (Ed.), *Advances in experimental social psychology* (Vol. 21). San Diego, CA: Academic Press.

Tesser, A. (1993). The importance of heritability in psychological research: The case of attitudes. *Psychological Review, 100,* 129–142.

Tesser, A., Campbell, J., & Mickler, S. (1983). The role of social pressure, attention to the stimulus, and self-doubt in conformity. *European Journal of Social Psychology, 13,* 217–233.

Tesser, A. & Collins, J. E. (1988). Emotion in social reflection and comparison situations: Intuitive, systematic, and exploratory approaches. *Journal of Personality and Social Psychology, 55,* 695–709.

Tesser, A., & Shaffer, D. (1990). Attitudes and attitude change. *Annual Review of Psychology, 41,* 479–523.

Tetlock, P. E. (1985). Accountability: A social check on the fundamental attribution error. *Social Psychology Quarterly, 48,* 227–236.

Tetlock, P. E. (1986). Is categorization theory the solution to the level-of-analysis problem? *British Journal of Social Psychology, 25,* 255–256.

Tetlock, P. E., & Levi, A. (1982). Attribution bias: On the inconsistencies of the cognition-motivation debate. *Journal of Experimental Social Psychology, 18,* 68–88.

Tetlock, P. E., Peterson, R. S., McGuire, C., Shi-jie Chang, & Feld, P. (1992). Assessing political group dynamic: A test of the groupthink model. *Journal of Personality and Social Psychology, 63,* 403–425.

Thibaut, J. W., & Kelley, H. H. (1959). *The social psychology of groups.* New York: Wiley.

Thompson, B., & Borrello, G. M. (1992). Different views of love: Deductive and inductive lines of inquiry. *Psychological Science, 1,* 154–155.

Thompson, S. Z., Cheek, P. R., & Graham, M. A. (1988). The other side of perceived control: Disadvantages and negative advantages. In S. Spacapan & S. Oskamp (Eds.), *The social psychology of health.* Beverly Hills, CA: Sage.

Thompson, W. C. (1989). Death qualification after *Wainwright v. Witt* and *Lockhart v. McCree. Law and Human Behavior, 13,* 185–216.

Thornhill, R., & Gangestad, S. W. (1994). Human fluctuating asymmetry and sexual behavior. *Psychological Science, 5* 297–302.

Time Almanac (1992). Washington, DC: Compact Publishing.

Toklas, A. B. (1963). *What is remembered.* New York: Holt, Rinehart & Winston.

Tonnesmann, W. (1987). Group identification and political socialisation. In V. Reynolds, V. Falger, & I. Vine (Eds.), *The sociobiology of ethnocentrism.* Athens: University of Georgia Press.

Tornstam, L. (1992). Loneliness in marriage. *Journal of Social and Personal Relationships, 9,* 197–217.

Train, G. J. (1983). War: Psychobiologic factors and communications between Einstein and Freud. *International Journal of Group Tensions, 13,* 42–48.

Treisman, A., & Souther, J. (1985). Search symmetry: A diagnostic for preattentive processing of separable features. *Journal of Experimental Psychology: General, 114,* 285–310.

Trenholm, S. (1989). *Persuasion and social influence.* Englewood Cliffs, NJ: Prentice-Hall.

Triandis, H. C. (1989). The self and social behavior in differing cultural contexts. *Psychological Review, 96,* 506–520.

Triandis, H. C. (1994). *Culture and social behavior.* New York: McGraw-Hill.

Triplett, N. (1898). Dynamogenic factors in pacemaking and competition. *American Psychologist, 9,* 507–533.

Trope, Y. (1983). Self-enhancement and self-assessment in achievement behavior. In J. M. Suls & A. G. Greenwald (Eds.), *Psychological perspectives on the self* (Vol. 2). Hillsdale, NJ: Erlbaum.

Trope, Y. (1986). Identification and inference processes in disposition attribution. *Psychological Review, 93,* 239–257.

Trope, Y., Cohen, O., & Alfieri, T. (1991). Behavior identification as the mediator of dispositional inference. *Journal of Personality and Social Psychology, 61,* 873–883.

Trope, Y., & Lieberman, A. (1993). The use of trait conceptions to identify other people's behavior and to draw inferences about their personalities. *Personality and Social Psychology Bulletin, 19,* 553–562.

Tuchman, B. (1978). *A distant mirror.* New York: Ballantine.

Turner, J. C. (1987). *Rediscovering the social group: A self-categorization theory.* Oxford, England: Basil Blackwell.

Turner, J. C., Wetherell, M. S., & Hogg, M. A. (1989). Referent informational influence and group polarization. *British Journal of Social Psychology, 28,* 135–147.

Tversky, A., & Kahneman, D. (1973). Availability: A heuristic for judgment frequency and probability. *Cognitive Psychology, 5,* 207–232.

Tversky, A., & Kahneman, D. (1974). Judgment under uncertainty: Heuristics and biases. *Science, 185,* 1124–1131.

Tversky, B., & Tuchin, M. (1989). A reconciliation of the evidence on eyewitness testimony: Comments on McCloskey and Zaragoza. *Journal of Experimental Psychology: General, 118,* 86–91.

Tybout, A. M., Sternthal, B., & Calder, B. (1983). Information availability as a determinant of multiple request effectiveness. *Journal of Marketing Research, 20,* 280–290.

Tyerman, A., & Spencer, C. (1983). A critical test of the Sherifs' Robbers Cave experiment: Intergroup competition between groups of well-acquainted individuals. *Small Group Behavior, 14,* 515–531.

Tyler, T. R. (1988). What is procedural justice? Criteria used by citizens to assess the fairness of legal procedures. *Law and Society Review, 22,* 103–134.

Tyler, T. R. (1990). *Why citizens obey the law: Procedural justice, legitimacy and compliance.* New Haven, CT: Yale University Press.

Tyler, T. R., & Schuller, R. A. (1991). Aging and attitude change. *Journal of Personality and Social Psychology, 61,* 689–697.

Tziner, A., & Eden, D. (1985). Effects of crew composition on crew performance: Does the whole equal the sum of its parts? *Journal of Applied Psychology, 70,* 85–93.

Vallone, R. P., Griffin, D. W., Lin, S., & Ross, L. (1991). Overconfident prediction of future actions and outcomes by self and others. *Journal of Personality and Social Psychology, 58,* 582–592.

Vallortigara, G. (1992). Affiliation and aggression as related to gender in domestic chicks. *Journal of Comparative Psychology, 106,* 53–58.

Van Kippenberg, D., de Vries, N., & Van Kippenberg, A. (1990). Group status, group size and attitude polarization. *European Journal of Social Psychology, 29,* 121–134.

Van Velsor, P. (1990). *Eating behavior: Externality and social influence.* Unpublished manuscript, University of Toledo, Toledo, Ohio.

Vaughn, D. (1986). *Uncoupling: Turning points in intimate relationships.* New York: Oxford University Press.

Veninga, R. L., & Spradley, J. P. (1982). *The work–stress connection: How to cope with job burnout.* New York: Ballantine Books.

Vinokur, A., & Burnstein, E. (1974). Effects of partially shared persuasive arguments on group-induced shifts. *Journal of Personality and Social Psychology, 29,* 305–315.

Vinokur, A., & Burnstein, E. (1978). Depolarization of attitudes. *Journal of Personality and Social Psychology, 36,* 872–885.

Visher, C. (1987). Juror decision making: The importance of evidence. *Law and Human Behavior, 11,* 1–18.

Vissing, Y. M., Straus, M. A., Gelles, R. J., & Harrop, J. W. (1991). Verbal aggression by parents and psychosocial problems of children. *Child Abuse and Neglect, 15,* 223–238.

Vlaander, G. P. J., & van Rooijen, L. (1985). Independence and conformity in Holland: Asch's experiment three decades later. *Tijdschrift Voor Psychologie, 13,* 49–55.

Walford, R. (1986). *The 120-year diet.* Los Angeles, CA: UCLA Press.

Wallach, M. A., & Kogan, N. (1965). The roles of information, discussion and consensus in group risk taking. *Journal of Experimental Social Psychology, 1,* 1–19.

Wallach, M. A., Kogan, N., & Bem, D. J. (1962). Group influence on individual risk-taking. *Journal of Abnormal and Social Psychology, 65,* 75–86.

Walsh, J. (1993, January 4). The butcher of the Balkans. *Time.*

Walster (Hatfield), E., & Festinger, L. (1962). The effectiveness of "overheard" conversations. *Journal of Abnormal and Social Psychology, 65,* 395–402.

Walster, E., Walster, G. W., & Berscheid, E. (1978). *Equity Theory and Research.* Boston: Allyn & Bacon.

Walton, M. D., Sachs, D., Ellington, R., Hazlewood, A., Griffin, S., & Bass, D. (1988). Physical stigma and the pregnancy role: Receiving help from strangers. *Sex Roles, 18,* 323–331.

Ward, C. H., & Eisler, R. M. (1987). Type A behavior, achievement striving, and a dysfunctional self-evaluation system. *Journal of Personality and Social Psychology, 53,* 318–326.

Warren, A., Hulse-Trotter, K., & Tubbs, E. C. (1991). Inducing resistance to suggestibility in children. *Law and Human Behavior, 15,* 273–286.

Wason, P. C. (1960). On the failure to eliminate hypotheses in a conceptual task. *Quarterly Journal of Experimental Psychology, 12,* 129–140.

Wason, P. C. (1968). Reasoning about a rule. *Quarterly Journal of Experimental Psychology, 23,* 273–281.

Watson, P. W., & Thornhill, R. (1994). Fluctuating assymmetry and sexual selection. *Trends in Ecology and Evolution, 9,* 21–25.

Watson, R., with D. Foote. (1986, July 7). Avenging angel. *Newsweek,* pp. 33–35.

Weaver, M. A. (1993, October 4). Bhutto's fateful moment. *The New Yorker,* pp. 82–119.

Webb, E. J., Campbell, D. T., Schwartz, R. D., Sechrist, L., & Grove, J. (1981). *Nonreactive measures in the social sciences* (2nd ed.). Boston: Houghton Mifflin.

Webster, T. M., King, H. N., & Kassin, S. M. (1991). Voices from the empty chair: The missing witness inference and the jury. *Law and Human Behavior, 15,* 31–42.

Wegner, D. M. (1986). Transactive memory: A contemporary analysis of the group mind. In B. Mullen & G. Goethals (Eds.), *Theories of group behavior.* New York: Springer-Verlag.

Wegner, D. M. (1988). Stress and mental control. In S. Fisher & J. Reason (Eds.), *Handbook of life stress, cognition, and health.* Chichester, England: Wiley.

Wegner, D. M. (1989). *White bears and unwanted thoughts.* New York: Viking/Penguin.

Wegner, D. M. (1993). Thought suppression. In M. P. Zanna (Ed.), *Advances in experimental social psychology* (Vol. 25). San Diego, CA: Academic Press.

Wegner, D. M., Lane, J. D., & Dimitri, S. (1994). The allure of secret relationships. *Journal of Personality and Social Psychology, 66,* 287–300.

Wegner, D. M., & Pennebaker, J. W. (Eds.). (1993). *Handbook of mental control.* Englewood Cliffs, NJ: Prentice-Hall.

Weinberg, A. (1957). *Attorney for the damned.* New York: Simon & Schuster.

Weinberg, A., & Weinberg, L. (Eds.). (1961). *The muckrakers.* New York: Capricorn Books.

Weiner, B. (1986). *An attributional theory of motivation and emotion.* New York: Springer-Verlag.

Weiner, B. (1991). Metaphors on motivation and attribution. *American Psychologist, 46,* 921–930.

Weiner, B. (1993). On sin versus sickness: A theory of perceived responsibility and social motivation. *American Psychologist, 48,* 957–965.

Weiner, B., Figueroa-Munoz, J., & Kakihara, C. (1991). The goals of excuses and communication strategies related to causal perceptions. *Journal of Personality and Social Psychology, 17,* 4–13.

Weiner, B., Perry, R. P., & Magnusson, J. (1988). An attributional analysis of reactions to stigmas. *Journal of Personality and Social Psychology, 55,* 738–748.

Weisse, J., Neselhof-Kendall, B., Fleck-Kandath, B., & Baum, A. (1990). Psychosocial aspects of AIDS prevention among heterosexuals. In J. Edwards, R. S. Tindale, L. Heath, E. Posavek (Eds.), *Social influence processes and prevention* (Vol. 1). New York: Plenum.

Weisz, C., & Jones, E. E. (1993). Expectancy disconfirmation and dispositional inference: Latent strength of target-based and category-based expectancies. *Personality and Social Psychology Bulletin, 19,* 563–573.

Welch, S., Spohn, C., & Gruhl, J. (1985). Convicting and sentencing differences among black, Hispanic, and white males in six localities. *Justice Quarterly, 2,* 67–80.

Weld, H. P., & Danzig, E. R. (1940). A study of the way in which a verdict is reached by a jury. *American Journal of Psychology, 53,* 518–536.

Wells, G. L. (1978). Applied eyewitness testimony research: System variables and estimator variables. *Journal of Personality and Social Psychology, 36,* 1546–1557.

Wells, G. L., Ferguson, T. J., & Lindsay, R. C. L. (1981). The tractability of eyewitness confidence and its implications for triers of fact. *Journal of Applied Psychology, 66,* 688–696.

Wells, G. L., & Gavanski, I. (1989). Mental simulation of causality. *Journal of Personality and Social Psychology, 56,* 161–169.

Wells, G. L., Leippe, M. R., & Ostrom, T. M. (1979). Guidelines for empirically assessing the fairness of a lineup. *Law and Human Behavior, 3,* 285–293.

Wells, G. L., Wrightsman, L. S., & Miene, P. K. (1985). The timing of the defense opening statement: Don't wait until the evidence is in. *Journal of Applied Social Psychology, 15,* 758–772.

Werner, C. M., Kagehiro, D. K., Strube, M. J. (1982). Conviction proneness and the authoritarian juror: Inability to disregard information or attitudinal bias? *Journal of Applied Psychology, 67,* 629–636.

West, S. G., Whitney, G., & Schnedler, R. (1975). Helping a motorist in distress: The effects of sex, race, and neighborhood. *Journal of Personality and Social Psychology, 31,* 691–698.

Wheeler, L., Reis, H., & Nezlek, J. (1983). Loneliness, social interaction, and sex roles. *Journal of Personality and Social Psychology, 45,* 943–953.

White, R. K. (1968). *Nobody wanted war: Misperception in Vietnam and other wars.* Garden City, NY: Doubleday.

Whyte, G. (1989). Groupthink reconsidered. *Academy of Management Review, 14,* 40–56.

Wicker, A. W. (1969). Attitudes versus actions: The relationship of verbal and overt behavioral responses to attitude objects. *Journal of Social Issues, 25,* 41–78.

Wicklund, R. A. (1975). Objective self-awareness. In L. Berkowitz (Ed.), *Advances in experimental social psychology* (Vol. 8). San Diego, CA: Academic Press.

Widom, C. S. (1992, October). The cycle of violence. *National Institute of Justice Research in Brief,* pp. 1–6.

Wiebe, D. J. (1991). Hardiness and stress moderation: A test of proposed mechanisms. *Journal of Personality and Social Psychology, 60,* 89–99.

Wiegman, O., Kuttschreuter, M., & Baarda, B. (1992). A longitudinal study of the effects of television viewing on aggressive and prosocial behaviors. *British Journal of Social Psychology, 31,* 147–164.

Wilder, D. A. (1986). Social categorization: Implications for creation and reduction of intergroup bias. In L. Berkowitz (Ed.), *Advances in experimental psychology* (Vol. 19, pp. 293–355). New York: Academic Press.

Wilder, D. A., & Shapiro, P. (1984). The role of outgroup salience in determining social identity. *Journal of Personality and Social Psychology, 47,* 177–194.

Wilder, D. A., & Shapiro, P. (1991). Facilitation of outgroup stereotypes by enhanced ingroup identity. *Journal of Experimental Social Psychology, 27,* 431–452.

Wilford, J. N. (1992, February 11). Nubian treasures reflect black influence on Egypt. *New York Times,* p. 29.

Williams, A. W., & Lund, A. K. (1992). Injury control. *American Psychologist, 47,* 1036–1039.

Williams, K. D. (1994). *The relationship between intentions to vote and actual voting behavior.* Unpublished manuscript, University of Toledo.

Williams, K. D., Harkins, S. G., & Latané, B. (1981). Identifiability as a deterrent to social loafing: Two cheering experiments. *Journal of Personality and Social Psychology, 40,* 303–311.

Williams, K. D., & Karau, S. J. (1991). Social loafing and social compensation: The effects of expectations of co-worker performance. *Journal of Personality and Social Psychology, 61,* 570–581.

Williams, K. D., & Williams, K. B. (1989). Impact of source strength on two compliance techniques. *Basic and Applied Social Psychology, 10,* 149–160.

Williams, R. B. (1989). The trusting heart. *Psychology Today, 23,* 36–42.

Williams, R. B., Jr., & Barefoot, J. C. (1988). Coronary-prone behavior: The emerging role of the hostility complex. In B. K. Houston & C. R. Snyder (Eds.), *Type A behavior pattern.* New York: Plenum.

Williams, R. B., & Williams, V. (1993). *Anger kills: Seventeen strategies for controlling the hostility that can harm your health.* New York: Random House.

Williams, S. S., Kimble, D. L., Covell, N. H., Weiss, L. H., Newton, K., Fisher, J. D., & Fisher, W. A. (1992). College students use implicit personality theory instead of safer sex. *Journal of Applied Social Psychology, 22,* 921–933.

Williams, W. M., & Sternberg, R. J. (1988). Group intelligence: Why some groups are better than others. *Intelligence, 12,* 351–357.

Williamson, G. M., & Clark, M. S. (1989). Providing help and desired relationship type as determinants of changes in mood and self-evaluation. *Journal of Personality and Social Psychology, 56,* 722–734.

Williams v. Florida, 399 U.S. (1970).

Wills, T. A. (1987). Help seeking as a coping mechanism. In C. R. Snyder & C. E. Ford (Eds.), *Coping with negative life events.* New York: Plenum.

Wilson, E. O. (1975). *Sociobiology: The new synthesis.* Cambridge, MA: Harvard University Press.

Wilson, E. O. (1978). *On human nature.* Cambridge, MA: Harvard University Press.

Wilson, G. (1981). *The Coolidge effect: An evolutionary account of human sexuality.* New York: Morrow.

Wilson, J. P. (1976). Motivation, modeling, and altruism: A person x situation analysis. *Journal of Personality and Social Psychology, 34*, 1078–1086.

Wilson, M. G., Northcraft, G. B., & Neale, M. A. (1989). Information competition and vividness effects in on-line judgments. *Organizational Behavior and Human Decision Processes, 44*, 132–139.

Wilson, T. D., Dunn, D. S., Kraft, D., & Lisle, D. J. (1989). Introspection, attitude change, and attitude behavior consistency: The disruptive effects of explaining why we feel the way we do. In L. Berkowitz (Ed.), *Advances in experimental social psychology* (Vol. 22). San Diego, CA: Academic Press.

Wilson, T. D., & Kraft, D. (1988). The effects of analyzing reasons on affectively-versus cognitively-based attitudes. (Unpublished raw data), cited in: Wilson, T. D., Dunn, D. S., Kraft, D., & Lisle, D. J. (1989). Introspection, attitude change, and attitude behavior consistency: The disruptive effects of explaining why we feel the way we do. In L. Berkowitz (Ed.), *Advances in experimental social psychology* (Vol. 22). San Diego, CA: Academic Press.

Winch, R. G. (1958). *Mate selection: A theory of complementary needs.* New York: Harper & Row.

Wolf, S. (1979). Behavioral style and group cohesiveness as sources of minority influence. *European Journal of Social Psychology, 9*, 381–395.

Wolfe, T. (1979). *The right stuff.* New York: Bantam Books.

Wollstonecraft, M. (1792). *A vindication of the rights of women.* Garden Grove, CT: World Library.

Wong, M. Mei-ha, & Csikzentmihalyi, M. (1991). Affiliation motivation and daily experience. *Journal of Personality and Social Psychology, 60*, 154–164.

Wood, C. (1978). The I-knew-it-all-along effect. *Journal of Experimental Psychology: Human Perception and Performance, 4*, 345–353.

Wood, W. (1982). Retrieval of attitude-relevant information from memory: Effects on susceptibility to persuasion and on intrinsic motivation. *Journal of Personality and Social Psychology, 42*, 798–810.

Wood, W. (1987). Meta-analytic review of sex differences in competence. *Psychological Bulletin, 102*, 53–71.

Wood, W., Wong, F. Y., & Chachere, J. G. (1990). Effects of media violence on viewers' aggression in unconstrained social interaction. *Psychological Bulletin, 108*, 137–147.

Woodall, K. L., & Mathews, K. (1993). Changes in and stability of hostile characteristics: Results from a 4-year longitudinal study of children. *Journal of Personality and Social Psychology, 64*, 491–499.

Worchel, P. (1961). Status restoration and reduction of hostility. *Journal of Abnormal and Social Psychology, 63*, 183–187.

Worchel, S., Coutant-Sassic, C. & Grossman, M. (1992). In S. Worchel, W. Wood, & J. A. Simpson (Eds.), *Group process and productivity.* Newbury Park, CA: Sage.

Worchel, S., & Shackelford, S. L. (1991). Groups under stress: The influence of group structure and environment on process and performance. *Personality and Social Psychology Bulletin, 17*, 640–647.

Wright, E. F., Luus, C. A. E., & Christie, S. D. (1990). Does group discussion facilitate the use of consensus information in making causal attributions? *Journal of Personality and Social Psychology, 59*, 261–269.

Wright, P. H. (1982). Men's friendships, women's friendships and the alleged inferiority of the latter. *Sex Roles, 8*, 1–20.

Wrightsman, L. S. (1969). Wallace supporters and adherence to "law and order." *Journal of Personality and Social Psychology, 13*, 17–22.

Wrightsman, L. S. (1987). *Psychology and the legal system.* Pacific Grove, CA: Brooks/Cole.

Wrightsman, L. S. (1991). *Psychology and the legal system.* (2nd ed.) Pacific Grove, CA: Brooks/Cole.

Wyden, P. (1979). *Bay of Pigs.* New York: Simon & Schuster.

Wyer, R. S., Jr., & Srull, T. K. (1986). Human cognition in its social context. *Psychological Review, 93*, 322–359.

Yakimovich, D., & Salz, E. (1971). Helping behavior: The cry for help. *Psychonomic Science, 23*, 427–428.

Youngstrom, N. (1991, November). Campus life polluted for many by hate acts. *APA Monitor*, pp. 22–24.

Zaccaro, S. J., & Lowe, C. A. (1988). Cohesiveness and performance on an additive task: Evidence for multidimensionality. *Journal of Social Psychology, 128*, 547–558.

Zaccaro, S. J., & McCoy, M. C. (1988). The effects of task and interpersonal cohesiveness on performance of a disjunctive group task. *Journal of Applied Social Psychology, 18*, 837–851.

Zajonc, R. B. (1960). The process of cognitive tuning in communication. *Journal of Abnormal and Social Psychology, 61*, 159–167.

Zajonc, R. B. (1965). Social facilitation. *Science, 149*, 269–274.

Zajonc, R. B. (1968). Attitudinal effects of mere exposure. *Journal of Personality and Social Psychology, 9*, 1–27.

Zajonc, R. B. (1985). Emotion and facial efference: A theory reclaimed. *Science, 228*, 15–21.

Zajonc, R. B., Heingartner, A., & Herman, E. M. (1969). Social enhancement and impairment of performance in the cockroach. *Journal of Personality and Social Psychology, 13*, 83–92.

Zajonc, R. B., & Rajecki, D. W. (1969). Exposure and affect: A field experiment. *Psychonomic Science, 17*, 216–217.

Zanna, M. P., & Rempel, J. K. (1988). Attitudes: A new look at an old concept. In D. Bar-Tal & A. Kruglanski (Eds.), *The social psychology of knowledge.* New York: Cambridge University Press.

Zebrowitz, L. A., Olson, K., & Hoffman, K. (1993). Stability of babyfaceness and attractiveness across the lifespan. *Journal of Personality and Social Psychology, 64*, 453–466.

Ziemer, G. A. (1972). *Education for death: The making of the Nazi.* New York: Octagon Books.

Zillman, D. (1971). Excitation transfer in communication-mediated aggressive behavior. *Journal of Experimental Social Psychology, 7*, 419–434.

Zillman, D. (1984). *Connections between sex and aggression.* Hillsdale, NJ: Erlbaum.

Zimbardo, P. G. (1969). The human choice. In W. J. Arnold & G. Levine (Eds.), *Nebraska Symposium on Motivation* (Vol. 17). Lincoln: University of Nebraska.

Zimbardo, P. G., & Leippe, M. R. (1992). *The psychology of attitude change and social influence.* New York: McGraw-Hill.

Zucker, G. S., & Weiner, B. (1993). Conservatism and perceptions of poverty: An attributional analysis. *Journal of Applied Social Psychology, 23*, 925–943.

Zuckerman, M. (1990). The psychophysiology of sensation-seeking. *Journal of Personality, 58*, 313–345.

Zuckerman, M., Mann, R. W., & Bernieri, F. J. (1982). Determinants of consensus estimates: Attribution, salience, and representativeness. *Journal of Personality and Social Psychology, 42*, 839–852.

Zuckerman, M., Miyake, K., & Hodgins, C. (1991). Cross-channel effects of vocal and physical attractiveness and their implications for interpersonal perception. *Journal of Personality and Social Psychology, 60*, 545–554.

Credits

(continued from copyright page)

PHOTO CREDITS

Chapter 1 p. 1, © 1991 Dan Lamont/Matrix International; p. 2, © 1992 Robert Holmes Photography; p. 4, © Leo Stone/Sygma; p. 8 (left), © Jerry Mennenga/Gamma Liaison; (right), © Evan Agostini/Gamma Liaison; p. 12 (top), © Douglas Burrows/Gamma Liaison; (bottom), © John Barr/Gamma Liaison; p. 16, © Douglas Burrows/Gamma Liaison; p. 19, © Bob Thomas/Gamma Liaison; p. 26, © P. Breese/Gamma Liaison; p. 29 (top), © Jeff Greenberg/Photo Edit; (bottom), © Alan Dorow/Actuality Inc. **Chapter 2** p. 42, © Mark Richards/PhotoEdit; p. 44, Photofest; p. 48, © Capitol Features/The Image Works; p. 50, © Tom McKitterick/Impact Visuals; p. 57, courtesy Richard Gill; p. 62, Reuters/The Bettmann Archive; p. 66, © Terry Ashe/Gamma Liaison; p. 69, © Amy C. Etra/PhotoEdit; p. 75 (top), © Rhoda Sidney/PhotoEdit; (bottom), © Vic Bider/PhotoEdit; p. 81, © Luc Novovitch/Gamma Liaison. **Chapter 3** p. 86, © Mary Kate Denny/PhotoEdit; p. 88, © Sygma Photo News; p. 92, © Billy E. Barnes/PhotoEdit; p. 94, Reuters/The Bettmann Archive; p. 100, © John Neubauer/PhotoEdit; p. 103, © Michael Newman/PhotoEdit; p. 104 (left), UPI/The Bettmann Archive; (center), Motion Picture and Television Photo Archive; (right), © Westenberger/Gamma Liaison; p. 118, NASA/The Image Works; p. 119, © Alex Quesada/Matrix International. **Chapter 4** p. 124, © Giboux/Gamma Liaison; p. 126, © Fred Ward/Black Star; p. 130, © Yvonne Hemsey/Gamma Liaison; p. 133, © Sygma Photo News; p. 134, UPI/The Bettmann Archive; p. 140, © Chip Hires/Gamma Liaison; p. 143, Motion Picture and Television Photo Archive; p. 155, © Joel Gordon 1992; p. 161, © Tony Freeman/PhotoEdit; p. 167, © Olympia/Gamma Liaison. **Chapter 5** p. 174, © Mark Richards/PhotoEdit; p. 176, © Jim West/Impact Visuals; p. 179, © 1993 Laurie Sparham/Matrix International; p. 181 (left), © Capitol Features/The Image Works; (right), The Bettmann Archive; p. 185, The Bettmann Archive; p. 190, © Cynthia Johnson/Gamma Liaison; p. 194, © Karen T. Borchers; p. 204, © Tony Savino/The Image Works; p. 206 (left), © Tony Freeman/PhotoEdit; (right), © John Pearson; p. 213, © D. Wray/The Image Works; p. 219, © Mark Richards/PhotoEdit. **Chapter 6** p. 224, © Mary Kate Denny/PhotoEdit; p. 226, The Bettmann Archive; p. 229 (top left), © Ilene Perlman/Impact Visuals; (top right), © Dan Habib/Impact Visuals; (bottom left), © Pugliano/Gamma Liaison; (bottom right), © Jacques Chenet/Gamma Liaison; p. 232, © Robert Brenner/PhotoEdit; p. 236, © Bob Daemmrich/The Image Works; p. 240, © Paul Conklin/PhotoEdit; p. 246, © Donna Binder/Impact Visuals; p. 254, © Bob Daemmrich/The Image Works. **Chapter 7** p. 262, © Dan McGlynn/The Image Works; p. 264, AP/Wide World Photos; p. 267, © Paul Conklin/PhotoEdit; p. 272, © Michael Newman/PhotoEdit; p. 279, © Gamma Liaison; p. 286, © Joel Gordon 1990; p. 289, © Capitol Features/The Image Works; p. 291, © Amy C. Etra/PhotoEdit; p. 293, © Gamma Liaison; p. 297, © Joel Gordon 1994; p. 302 (left), © CNN Pictures/Saba Press; (right), AP/Wide World Photos; p. 306, The Granger Collection. **Chapter 8** p. 312, © Joan Liftin/Actuality, Inc.; p. 314, © Billy E. Barnes/PhotoEdit; p. 317 (left), © Michael Newman/PhotoEdit; (right), © Mary Kate Denny/PhotoEdit; p. 323, Sygma Photo News; p. 331 (top), AP/Wide World Photos; (bottom), The Image Works; p. 332, Photofest; p. 334 (top), UPI/The Bettman Archive; (bottom), Bill Luster/Matrix International; p. 343, © Robert Fox/Impact Visuals; p. 347, © Tom McCarthy/PhotoEdit. **Chapter 9** p. 356, © J. Langevin/Sygma Photo News; p. 358, The Bettmann Archive; p. 359, © Sipa Press; p. 362, UPI/The Bettmann Archive; p. 363, © Patrick Piel/Gamma Liaison; p. 365, courtesy of Alexandra Milgram; p. 370, © Gamma Liaison; p. 375, UPI/The Bettmann Archive; p. 380, The Bettmann Archive; p. 383, © Tony Freeman/PhotoEdit; p. 384, UPI/The Bettmann Archive; p. 387, © Gamma Liaison; p. 390, © Chip Hires/Gamma Liaison. **Chapter 10** p. 396, © Mark Richards/PhotoEdit; p. 398, AP/Wide World Photos; p. 401 (top), © Charles Harbutt/Actuality Inc.; (left), © Renata Rotolo/Gamma Liaison; (right), © Joan Liftin/Actuality Inc.; p. 409, © Bob Daemmrich/The Image Works; p. 412, Reuters/The Bettmann Archive; p. 415, © Bob Daemmrich/The Image Works; p. 418, © David Toy with permission of Anne Yamamoto; p. 425, © Mary Kate Denny/PhotoEdit; p. 427 (left), The Bettmann Archive; (right), © Charles Harbutt/Actuality Inc.; p. 436, © Malcolm Denemark/Gamma Liaison. **Chapter 11** p. 444, © Joel Gordon; p. 446, UPI/The Bettmann Archive; p. 449, © Deborah Davis/PhotoEdit; p. 456, © Polly Brown/Actuality Inc.; p. 457, © Steve Allen/Gamma Liaison; p. 460, Motion Picture and Television Photo Archive; p. 468, Reuters/The Bettmann Archive; p. 472 (top left), © Jeff Greenberg/The Image Works; (top right), © Joel Gordon; (bottom left), © Rebecca Cooney/Actuality Inc.; (bottom right), © Joan Liftin/Actuality Inc.; p. 477, © Bob Daemmrich/The Image Works. **Chapter 12** p. 488, © Chris Tagaki/Impact Visuals; p. 490, © Allen Tannenbaum/Sygma Photo News; p. 492 (top), © 1989 Paula Allen/Matrix International; (left), © Jim Tynan/Impact Visuals; (right), © Esaias Baitel/Gamma Liaison; p. 495, © David Young Wolff/PhotoEdit; p. 498, © Enrique Marti/Impact Visuals; p. 504, © Arnold Kopelson/Motion Picture Television and Photo Archive; p. 510, © Karen T. Borchers; p. 513, © Michael Newman/Photo Edit; p. 520, © Zade Rosenthal/Motion Picture and Television Photo Archive; p. 523, © Joan Liftin/Actuality Inc.; p. 528, © Catherine Smith/Impact Visuals. **Chapter 13** p. 536, © James L. Shaffer/PhotoEdit; p. 538, The Bettmann Archive; p. 540, © Hazel Hankin/Impact Visuals; p. 546, © Joel Gordon 1991; p. 549, NYT Pictures; p. 557, © Robert Brenner/PhotoEdit; p. 565, © David James/Universal/Motion Picture and Television Photo Archive; p. 571, UPI/The Bettmann Archive; p. 577, Reuters/The Bettmann Archive; p. 581, © Mark Richards/PhotoEdit. **Chapter 14** p. 590, © John Neubauer/PhotoEdit; p. 592, © KTLA/Sygma Photo News; p. 597, © John Neubauer/PhotoEdit; p. 599, © UPI/The Bettmann Archive; p. 602, © Cindy Reiman/Impact Visuals; p. 606, © John Neubauer/PhotoEdit; p. 613, © Brian Palmer/Impact Visuals; p. 614, © Sygma Photo News; p. 625, Reuters/The Bettmann Archive; p. 626, © James L. Shaffer/PhotoEdit; p. 627, © John Neubauer/PhotoEdit; p. 634, © Joel Gordon. **Chapter 15** p. 642, © Dion Ogust/The Image Works; p. 644, © Richard Hutchings/PhotoEdit; p. 647, © Michael Newman/PhotoEdit; p. 651, © Elizabeth Crews/PhotoEdit; p. 653, © Tom McCarthy/PhotoEdit; p. 655, © Michael Newman/PhotoEdit; p. 661, © David Young Wolff/PhotoEdit; p. 665, © Donna Binder/Impact Visuals; p. 667, © Joel Gordon; p. 673, © Douglas Burrows/Impact Visuals; p. 681, © Robert Brenner/PhotoEdit; p. 683, © Tony Freeman/PhotoEdit. **Chap-

cial Psychology, 57, 1. Copyright © 1989 by the American Psychological Association. Adapted with permission. Fig. 7-8, adapted from R. E. Petty, et al., "Positive Mood and Persuasion: Different Roles for Affect Under High and Low Elaboration Conditions," Journal of Personality and Social Psychology, 64, 1. Copyright © 1993 by the American Psychological Association. Adapted with permission. Table 7-2, from P. B. Cronin and J. G. Rosa, "The Effects of Age Differences on Sexual Risk-Taking Behaviors, Attitudes and Justifications." Reprinted with permission of the author. **Chapter 8** Fig. 8-6, from B. Latané, "The Psychology of Social Impact," American Psychologist, 36, 1981. Reprinted with permission. **Chapter 9** Fig. 9-1, from Obedience to Authority by Stanley Milgram, figure 1, page 15. Copyright © 1974 by Stanley Milgram. Reprinted by permission of HarperCollins Publishers. Fig. 9-5, from Obedience to Authority by Stanley Milgram, page 154. Copyright © 1974 by Stanley Milgram. Reprinted by permission of Harper-Collins Publishers, Inc. Fig. 9-6, from Obedience to Authority by Stanley Milgram, figure 8, page 42. Copyright © 1974 by Stanley Milgram. Reprinted by permission of HarperCollins Publishers, Inc. **Chapter 10** Fig. 10-2, from R. L. Moreland, and J. M. Levine, "Group Socialization: Temporal Changes in Individual-Group Relations," in L. Berkowitz (ed.), Advances in Experimental Social Psychology, 15. Copyright © 1982 by Academic Press. Reprinted by permission. Fig. 10-6 and 10-7, from P. R. Laughlin, S. W. Vanderstoep, and A. D. Hollingshead, "Collective Versus Individual Induction: Recognition of Truth, Rejection of Error, and Collective Information Processing," Journal of Personality and Social Psychology, 61. Copyright © 1991 by the American Psychological Association. Reprinted with permission **Chapter 11** Page 450, FAR SIDE, copyright 1991 FARWORKS, INC./Dist. by Universal Press Syndicate. Reprinted with permission. All rights reserved. Table 11-1, from "Love as Attachment: The Integration of Three Behavioral Systems," by P. Shaver, C. Hazan, and D. Bradshaw, 1988, in R. Sternberg and M. Barnes (eds.), The Psychology of Love, by permission of Yale University Press. Copyright © 1988 by Yale University Press. Fig. 11-2 and 11-3, from L. Festinger, S. Schachterm and K. W. Back, Social Pressures in Informal Groups: A Study of Human Factors in Housing. Copyright © 1959 by Harper & Row. Fig. 11-4, from J. H. Langlois, L. A. Roggman, R. J. Casey, L. A. Riesner-Danner, & V. Y. Jenkins, "Infant Preferences for Attractive Faces: Rudiments of a Stereotype?," Developmental Psychology, 23. Copyright © 1987 by the American Psychological Association. Adapted by permission. Fig. 11-5, from E. Hatfield, J. Traupmann, S. Sprecher, M. Utne, & J. Hay, "Equity and Intimate Relationships: Recent Research," in W. Ickes (ed.), Compatible and Incompatible Relationships. Copyright © 1985 by Springer-Verlag. Reprinted by permission. Fig. 11-6 and Table 11-2, from R. J. Sternberg, "A Triangular Theory of Love," Psychological Review, 93. Copyright © 1986 by the American Psychological Association. Adapted with permission. Fig. 11-8, reprinted by permission of the publisher from "Vigilance to Violence: Tactics of Mate Retention in American Undergraduates" by D. M. Buss, Ethology and Sociobiology, 9. Copyright 1988 by Elsevier Science Publishing Co., Inc. **Chapter 12** Fig. 12-2, from "Hormonal Influences on Aggressive Behavior" by R. L. Conner and S. Levine, 1969, in S. Garattini and E. B. Sogg (eds.), Aggressive Behavior. Copyright 1969 by John Wiley. Reprinted by permission. Fig. 12-5 and 12-6, from "Attacker's Intent and Awareness of Outcome, Impression Management and Retaliation" by K. Okbuchi and T. Kambara, Journal of Experimental Social Psychology, 21, 321–330. Copyright © 1985 by Academic Press. Reprinted by permission. Page 515, figure from Aggression: A Social Learning Analysis by A. Bandura. Copyright © 1973 by Holt, Rinehart, & Winston. Reprinted by permission. Fig. 12-7, from "A Developmental Perspective on Antisocial Behavior" by G. R. Patterson, B. D. DeBaryshe, and E. Ramsey, American Psychologist, 44. Copyright © 1985 by the American Psychological Association. Reprinted by permission. Fig. 12-8, from "Sexual Arousal to Rape Depictions: Individual Differences" by N. M. Malamuth and J. V. P. Check, Journal of Abnormal Psychology, 92. Copyright 1983 by the American Psychological Association. Adapted by permission. **Chapter 13** Fig. 13-1, from "Distress and Empathy: Two Qualitatively Distinct Vicarious Emotions with Different Motivational Consequences" by C. D. Batson, J. Fultz, and P. A. Schoenrade, Journal of Personality, 55. Copyright 1987 by Duke University Press. Reprinted by permission. Fig. 13-3, based on "Group Inhibition of Bystander Intervention in Emergencies" by B. Latané and J. M. Darley, Journal of Personality and Social Psychology, 10 and "Bystander Intervention in Emergencies: Diffusion of Responsibility," by J. M. Darley and B. Latané, Journal of Personality and Social Psychology, 8. Fig. 13-5, from "The Reaction to Rape by American Male Bystanders" by H. Harari, O. Harari, and R. V. White, Journal of Social Psychology, 125. Copyright © 1985 by the Helen Dwight Reid Educational Foundation. Reprinted by permission. Fig. 13-6, from data provided in "Dependency and Fault as Determinants of Helping" by C. L. Gruder, D. Romer, and B. Kroth, Journal of Experimental Social Psychology, 14, 1978. Fig. 13-7, from "A Person-Situation Approach to Altruistic Behavior" by D. Romer, C. L. Gruder, and T. Lizzaro, Journal of Personality and Social Psychology, 51. Copyright 1986 by the American Psychological Association. Reprinted by permission. Fig. 13-8, based on data from "Motivation, Modeling, and Altruism: A Person × Situation Analysis" by J. P. Wilson, Journal of Personality and Social Psychology, 34, 1976. Fig. 13-10, from "The Help-Seeking Process" by A. E. Gross and P. A. McMullen, 1982, in V. J. Derlaga and J. Grezlak (eds.), Cooperation and Helping Behavior: Theories and Research. Copyright 1982 by Academic Press. Adapted by permission. Fig. 13-11, based on data from "Is Seeking Help from a Friend Like Seeking Help from a Stranger?" by E. G. Shapiro, Social Psychology Quarterly, 43, 1980. Fig. 13-12, from "With a Little Help from My Friend: Effect of Single or Multiple Act Aid as a Function of Donor and Task Characteristics" by A. Nadler, J. D. Fisher, and S. Ben Itchak, Journal of Personality and Social Psychology, 44. Copyright 1983 by the American Psychological Association. Adapted by permission. **Chapter 14** Fig. 14-1, from data provided in Affective and Informational Determinants of Juror Decision Making by H. E. Mitchell, 1979, unpublished doctoral dissertation, Purdue University. Fig. 14-3, from "The Elaboration Likelihood Model of Persuasion" by R. E. Petty and J. T. Cacioppo in L. Berkowitz, Advances in Experimental Social Psychology, Vol. 19. Copyright 1986 by Academic Press. Adapted by permission. Fig. 14-4, from data provided in "Effects of Kind of Question and Atmosphere of Interrogation on Accuracy and Completeness of Testimony" by J. Marshall, J. H. Marquis, and S. Oskamp, 1971, Harvard Law Review, 84. Fig. 14-6, from data provided in "Eyewitness Identification: Lineup Instructions and the Absence of the Offender" by R. S. Malpass and P. G. Devine, Journal of Applied Psychology, 66, 1981. Fig. 14-7, from data provided in Eyewitness Testimony by E. F. Loftus, 1979. Harvard University Press. Copyright 1979 by Harvard University Press. Fig. 14-8, from data provided in "Sentencing Disparity and Jury Packing: Further Challenges to the Death Penalty" by J. E. Jacoby and R. Paternoster, The Journal of Criminal Law and Criminology, 73. Copyright © 1982 by Sage Publications. Fig. 14-9, from data provided in "Racial Considerations in Capital Punishment: The Failure of Evenhanded Justice" by R. Paternoster and A. Kazyaka, in K. C. Hass and J. A. Inciardi

Name Index

Brown, D. L., 548
Brown, J. A. C., 304
Brown, J. D., 404, 661
Brown, R., 193, 362, 683, 700
Brownell, K. D., 676
Brownmiller, S., 150, 522
Brownstein, R. J., 350
Brunner, H. H., 15
Brush, S. G., 211
Bryan, J. H., 569
Bryant, F. B., 509
Buckhout, R., 618, 621
Bulman, R., 148
Burger, J. M., 162, 347, 350
Burgoon, M., 343
Burnett, A., 447
Burnstein, E., 317, 432
Burt, M., 151, 522, 524
Bush, M., 346
Bushman, B. J., 500
Business Week, 403
Buss, A., 497
Buss, D. M., 458, 460, 474, 475, 486
Buss, E., 497
Byrd, W., 529
Byrne, D., 453, 456, 457

Cacioppo, J. T., 238, 275, 280, 282,
    284, 288, 299, 347, 667, 668
Cahoon, D. D., 151
Cain, K., 687
Calder, B., 342
Callero, P. L., 572
Camacho, L. M., 425
Campbell, D. T., 237
Campbell, J., 323
Campbell, J. D., 317, 326
Cantor, N., 94
Cantrill, J. G., 342
Caplan, N. S., 511
Carducci, B. J., 343
Carli, L. L., 328, 329, 330, 456
Carlsmith, J. M., 290
Carlson, M., 497
Carlson, N. R., 502
Carmelli, D., 679, 682
Carnevale, P. J. D., 726
Caro, R., 242, 243
Carothers, L. E., 518, 519
Carranza, L. E., 625
Carroll, J. S., 611
Carver, C. S., 53, 59, 60, 658, 659
Casey, R. J., 461
Cassilth, B. R., 654
Castro, M. A. C., 581
Caswell, J., 150
Ceci, S. J., 623
Cha, J. H., 141
Chaiken, S., 288, 675
Chang, S., 437
Chanowitz, B., 256
Chapman, J., 202
Chapman, L. L., 202
Check, J. V. P., 522, 523, 524, 525
Cheek, P. R., 652
Chen, H., 137

Cheng, P. W., 143, 144, 164
Chesner, S. P., 556
Christian, M. A., 616
Christiansen, K., 501
Christianson, S. A., 616
Christie, S. D., 421
Chrvala, C., 329, 330
Cialdini, R. B., 69, 194, 343, 344, 345,
    346, 347, 348, 350, 351, 354, 546
Cioffi, D., 669, 670
Claire, T., 103
Clark, M. S., 467, 579
Clark, N. T., 346
Clark, R. D., 334, 354, 556
Clarkson, F. E., 214
Clary, E. G., 564
Clement, D., 331
Clifford, B. R., 615
Clore, G. L., 453, 457
Clymer, A., 270
Cogan, D., 654
Cogan, R., 654
Cohen, A. R., 291
Cohen, O., 144
Cohen, S., 647, 680
Coie, J. D., 498
Colder, M. L., 663
Cole, J. R. I., 732
Coleman, L. T., 196
Collins, J. E., 68, 70
Collins, R. L., 286
Colvin, C. R., 110
Comer, S. L., 619
Comfort, J. C., 603
Congressional Record, 270
Conner, R. L., 502
Contrada, R. J., 683
Cook, S. W., 191, 218
Cooley, C. H., 47, 58
Cooper, H. M., 500
Cooper, J., 291, 292, 432, 715
Cooper, L., 291
Cornell, D. P., 85
Cottrell, N. B., 410
Couric, E., 598
Courington, S., 657
Courtwright, J., 426, 436
Cousins, N., 654, 655, 672
Cousins, S. D., 49
Cox, M., 603
Crabb, P. B., 713
Cramer, R. E., 557
Crandall, C. S., 459, 678
Crano, W. D., 291
Creason, C. R., 343, 346
Crockenberg, S., 516
Crocker, J., 195, 196, 205
Crohan, S. E., 468
Cronin, P., 298
Crosby, F., 563
Crowley, M., 558
Croyle, R. T., 668, 669, 670, 691
Crutchfield, R. S., 324
Csikszentmihalyi, M., 61, 448
Cunnick, J. E., 680
Cunningham, J. A., 290

Cunningham, M., 341
Curran, F., 114
Current Biography, 244
Cutler, B. L., 597, 599, 612, 621, 626

Dafraniere, S., 624, 625
Dallek, R., 242, 260
Dambrot, F. H., 151
Dame, A., 682
Dannefer, D., 595
Danzig, E. R., 606
Darley, J. M., 109, 112, 113, 166, 201,
    279, 544, 549, 550, 552, 553, 554,
    555, 557
Davidson, W., 213
Davis, B. O., Jr., 360
Davis, J. H., 417, 422, 424, 629
Davis, K. E., 129, 131, 132, 133
Davison, A. R., 241
Dean, J. W., 126, 170
Deaux, K., 330
DeBaryshe, B. D., 515
Deffenbacher, K., 621
de Groh, M., 619
DeJong, M., 459
DeJong, W., 341
DeLamater, J., 402
De La Ronde, C., 71, 73
Delgado, J. M. R., 501
Della Femina, D., 518
Delongis, A., 649
Dempsey, C. B., 343
Dennis, A. R., 425, 441
DePaulo, B. M., 110, 577, 579
Derlega, V. J., 15
Desforges, D., 216
Des Pres, T., 664, 665
Deuser, P. S., 343
Deutsch, M., 316, 706, 721, 722, 725
DeVault, C., 471
Devine, P. G., 208, 209, 210, 620
Dexter, H. R., 597, 612, 626
Diaz, C. R., 510
Diehl, M., 425
Dillard, J. P., 343
Dimitri, S., 480
Dion, K. K., 461
Ditto, P. H., 668, 670, 672, 673
Dodge, K. A., 498, 528
Dodson, C., 617
Doll, J., 254
Dollard, J., 504, 505, 506
Doms, M., 331
Donnerstein, E., 189, 521, 522, 523,
    524, 525
Donnerstein, M., 189, 522, 523, 524
Doob, L., 504
Doris, J., 640
Dovidio, J. F., 185, 186, 198, 205, 542,
    546, 562
Dozier, J. B., 575, 588
Dragna, M., 557
Drickamer, L. C., 497, 499
Duck, S. W., 456, 478, 481
Dudley, J., 652
Dugoni, B. L., 520

Duhe, A., 155
Dunbar, R. I. M., 183
Duncan, T. E., 63
Dunn, D. S., 256
Dweck, C., 212, 213
Dyck, R. J., 509
Dzindolet, M. T., 425

Eagly, A. H., 214, 215, 250, 252, 268, 278, 285, 288, 328, 329, 330, 427, 428, 457, 461, 494, 558
Early, P., 338, 354
Ebbesen, E. B., 595, 631
Eccles, J. S., 97
Eckenrode, J., 655
Edelman, B., 678
Eden, D., 423
Edmonds, E. M., 151
Edney, J. J., 704, 732
Edwards, S. B., 501
Egeth, H., 626, 640
Eisenberg, N., 24, 25, 541, 568, 570, 581, 582
Eisenstadt, D., 190
Eisler, R. M., 680
Eitzen, D. S., 197, 198
Ekman, P., 279
Elkin, R. A., 291
Ellard, J. H., 156
Elliot, A. J., 210
Elliot, J. M., 575, 588
Ellis, A. L., 422
Ellison, K. W., 621
Ellsworth, P. C., 603
Elms, A., 364, 365, 366, 379
Ember, R., 123
Engell, D., 678
Enna, B., 213
Epps, J., 528, 529
Epstein, S., 649
Erber, R., 661
Eron, L. D., 504, 512, 517, 518, 519
Eskenazi, J., 303
Evans, R., 522, 523, 524
Ewing, C. P., 595

Fagenson, E. A., 715
Fairey, P. J., 317, 326
Fairfield, M., 81
Fanning, D., 646
Farber, J., 218
Farmaian, S. F., 415
Farquhar, J. W., 683
Farrell, B., 500
Fazel, M., 709
Fazio, R. H., 254, 257, 268, 291
Feeney, J. A., 451
Feinstein, J., 441
Feist, J., 404
Feld, P., 437
Felmlee, D., 470
Ferguson, T. J., 519, 621
Feshbach, S., 493, 525
Festinger, L., 58, 268, 289, 290, 295, 321, 327, 348, 404, 454
Fiebert, M. S., 481

Fiedler, F. W., 427, 429
Fifield, J., 652
Figueroa-Munoz, J., 152
Fincham, F. D., 154, 155, 156, 467
Finkelhor, D., 521
Finley, M. A., 686
Fireman, B., 388, 389, 390
Fischer, E., 471
Fischer, G. W., 206
Fischoff, B., 30
Fishbaugh, L., 329
Fishbein, M., 250, 251
Fisher, H., 472
Fisher, J. D., 577, 579, 580, 581, 582, 583
Fiske, S. T., 91, 94, 95, 98, 99, 105, 108, 110, 144, 161, 164, 167, 168, 192, 208, 216, 217, 223
Fitzgerald, F., 247
Fitzgerald, F. S., 44, 82
Fitzgerald, R., 603
Flanagan, T. J., 495
Fleck-Kandath, B., 297
Fleming, A., 226, 227
Fleming, J. H., 112, 113, 166, 279
Fletcher, G. J. O., 168
Flohr, H., 100, 196, 197
Flowers, M., 436
Flynn, J. P., 501
Foehl, J. C., 346
Folkman, S., 649, 675
Ford, C. E., 658
Forehand, R., 527
Forgas, J. P., 161
ForsterLee, L., 100, 282, 607
Forsyth, D. R., 153, 400, 402
Fortune, W. H., 641
Foss, R. D., 343
Franco, B., 150
Frank, M. G., 169
Frank, R. G., 687
Fraser, S. C., 340
Frazier, P. A., 149
Freedman, J. L., 290, 340, 520
French, J. R. P., Jr., 378
Frenkel-Brunswik, E., 183, 379
Frey, D., 161
Friedman, H. S., 654, 660
Friedman, L. M., 6, 7
Friedman, M., 679
Friedrich, L. K., 569
Fulford, J. A., 616, 620
Fuller, D. O., 481
Fultz, J., 541, 546, 557
Funder, D. C., 110
Funk, S. C., 657
Furnham, A., 161, 332

Gadow, K. D., 520
Gaertner, S. L., 185, 186, 562
Galley, D. J., 303
Gamson, W. A., 388, 389, 390
Gangestad, S., 458
Ganley, R., 456
Garcia, S., 457
Gatchel, R. J., 646, 656

Gavanski, I., 117
Geen, R. G., 410
Geffner, R., 370, 373
Gelles, R. J., 517
Gelman, E., 296
George, C., 518
Gerard, H. B., 58
Gergen, K. J., 416, 580
Gergen, M., 416
Gerrard, H. B., 316
Gerrard, M., 298, 300
Gest, T., 633
Geva, N., 710, 711, 713, 721
Gibbons, F. X., 62, 298, 300
Gibbs, N., 244, 245
Gibson, J. T., 383, 394
Giesler, R. B., 71
Gilbert, D. T., 111, 145, 146, 162, 179, 208, 255
Gilbert, S. J., 376
Gilovich, T., 94, 96, 123, 169, 172
Ginsburg, G. P., 432
Giuliano, T., 560
Glassman, R. B., 548
Gleicher, F., 272, 274
Glick, P., 76
Goeckner, D. J., 500
Goethals, G. R., 101
Goetz, T. E., 212
Gold, P. E., 616
Goldfarb, R. L., 595
Golding, J. M., 622
Goldman, M., 341, 343, 346, 350, 566, 567, 576
Goldman, R., 284
Goleman, D., 185, 237, 260, 547, 570, 571, 660, 661
Gonzalez, A. S., 481
Goodman, G. S., 622, 623, 624, 625, 626
Goodwin, D. K., 242
Goranson, R. E., 581
Gottman, J. M., 469
Gould, S. J., 210
Gouldner, A. W., 579
Gracek, S., 473
Graham, M. A., 652
Graham, S., 560, 561
Grammar, K., 458
Gray, R. A., 544, 545
Greenberg, J., 72, 605
Greenberg, M. A., 664
Greene, D., 167
Greene, E., 611, 619
Greenwald, A. G., 48, 54, 269, 280, 303
Griffin, D. W., 111, 112, 160
Gross, A. E., 577, 578
Gross, M. M., 370, 373
Gross, P. H., 201
Groth, A. N., 521, 524
Grove, J., 237
Grube, J. W., 232
Gruder, C. L., 269, 559, 572
Gruhl, J., 632
Grunberg, N. E., 652
Grusec, J. E., 569

Ketelaar, T., 11
Kexing, L., 141
Kiesler, C. A., 347
Kihlstrom, J. F., 94
Kilham, W., 372, 373, 374, 375
King, G., 529
Kitayama, S., 49
Kite, M. E., 214, 215
Kleck, R. E., 666
Klein, J. G., 107, 302
Klein, S. B., 54
Klimoski, R. J., 725
Knussmann, R., 501
Kobasa, S. C., 656, 657, 683
Kogan, N., 432
Kohnken, G., 615, 617
Kojetin, B. A., 279
Kolata, G., 459
Koltai, D. C., 162
Konecni, V. J., 595, 631
Korth, B., 559
Kowalski, R. M., 74
Kraft, D., 256, 257
Krahe, B., 151
Kramer, G. P., 611
Kramer, R. M., 705
Krantz, D. S., 646, 678, 686
Krauss, R. M., 706, 721, 722, 725
Kravitz, D. A., 412, 616
Kremer, J. F., 509
Kreutzer, J. S., 500
Krishan, L., 579
Krismer, K., 290
Kristiansen, C. M., 233
Krosnick, J. A., 239, 243, 254, 299
Kruglanski, A. W., 327, 378, 407, 408
Krull, D. S., 71, 145, 162
Kunda, Z., 58, 103, 118, 119, 120
Kunju, T., 150
Kurdek, L. A., 470
Kuttschreuter, M., 521

Lage, E., 333, 337
Lagerspetz, K., 494, 519
Laird, J., 622
Lamm, H., 431, 432
Landay, J. S., 304
Landis, K. R., 655
Lane, J. D., 480
Lang, A. R., 500
Lange, J. E., 179, 207
Langer, E., 256, 653
Langford, B. J., 544
Langford, C. C., 544
Langlois, J. H., 461
LaPiere, R. T., 249, 250
Larrieu, J. A., 569
Larsen, K., 330, 331
Larsen, R. J., 11
Lassiter, G. D., 288
Latané, B., 336, 337, 354, 413, 414, 549, 550, 553, 554, 555
Laughlin, P. R., 417, 418, 422
Lawler, E. J., 726
Lawrence, R. A., 651
Lawson, E. D., 712

Lawson, R. G., 274, 604
Lazarus, R. S., 147, 649, 675
Lea, J. A., 616, 620
Leary, M., 74
Leary, M. R., 450
Lefkowitz, M. M., 512
Lehman, D. R., 509
Leippe, M. R., 231, 269, 291, 292, 296, 303, 623, 626, 674, 685
Lemann, N., 147
Leonard, K., 452
Leone, D. R., 303
LePage, A., 496, 497
Lerner, M. J., 559
Lerner, R. M., 558, 562
Levenson, R. W., 469
Leventhal, G. S., 580
Leventhal, H., 271
Levi, A., 168
Levin, J., 223
Levine, J. M., 402, 405, 406, 407, 422, 423
Levine, S., 502
Levinger, G., 462, 463
Levinson, D. J., 183, 379
Lewin, K., 9, 10, 13
Lewis, C. E., 676
Lewis, D. O., 518
Lewis, L., 552
Lewis, L. D., 151
Liberman, A., 288
Lichtenstein, M., 192
Liebert, R. M., 246, 519, 534, 569
Lieppe, M. R., 621
Lifton, R., 386
Likert, R., 236
Lilly, T., 218
Lin, S., 160
Lindsay, D. S., 616, 617
Lindsay, R. C. L., 616, 620, 621
Lindskold, S., 722, 723, 724
Linville, P. W., 57, 206
Linz, D., 521, 525
Lipkus, I., 467, 468
Lippmann, W., 179
Lips, H., 178
Lipscomb, T. J., 569
Lisle, D. J., 256
Litman, C., 516
Lizzadro, T., 572
Lochhead, C., 270
Loftus, E. F., 612, 614, 615, 617, 618, 619, 621, 622
Loftus, G. R., 615
Loftus, J., 54
Logan, G. A., 105
Long, N., 527
Longo, L. C., 457
Lorenz, K., 497, 498, 499, 534
Lorge, I., 417
Lott, L., 563
Lovely, R., 518
Lowe, C. A., 426
Luginbuhl, J., 80
Lund, A. K., 686, 687
Lusk, E. J., 654
Luus, C. A. E., 421

Lynch, D. J., 679
Lynn, A. R., 239
Lytton, H., 494

Maass, A., 334, 354, 615
MaCauley, C., 207
Maccoby, N., 683
Mack, D., 605
Mackie, D. M., 215, 283, 432
Macrae, C. N., 179, 192, 277
Maddi, S. R., 656, 657
Made, V. A., 172
Magnusson, D., 512
Magnusson, J., 560
Maguire, K., 495
Maharukh, B. K., 151
Main, M., 518
Major, B., 138, 195, 196, 205, 330
Makhijani, M. G., 457
Malamuth, N. M., 512, 513, 514, 521, 522, 523, 524, 525
Malpass, R. S., 616, 620
Manion, A. P., 623, 626
Mann, L., 237, 372, 373, 374, 375, 415
Mann, R. W., 167
Mantel, D. M., 374, 376
Manuck, S. B., 680
Marcus-Newhall, A., 497
Mark, M. M., 509
Markman, H., 469, 471
Markus, H., 49, 52, 53, 55, 56, 58
Marlatt, G. A., 500
Marquis, K. H., 614
Marshall, J., 614
Marshall, P. S., 654
Martin, B., 412
Mathews, K., 680
Matsuda, N., 331
Matthews, M., 559
Mayseless, O., 327
McAdams, D. P., 448, 481
McAlister, A. L., 683
McAlister, H. A., 569
McArthur, L. Z., 138, 458
McAuley, E., 63
McCall, C. G., 343, 346
McCarthy, B., 75
McCauley, C., 404, 408, 432, 434
McCloskey, M., 617, 618, 626
McClure's, 227
McConahay, J. G., 186, 187, 188
McCoun, R. J., 628
McCoy, M. C., 426
McCue, M., 654
McDaniel, A., 164
McDevitt, J., 223
McFarland, C., 117, 555
McGill, A. L., 139
McGinnies, E., 137
McGrail, C. A., 150, 151
McGuire, C., 437
McGuire, C. V., 50, 52
McGuire, W. J., 30, 50, 52, 234, 276
McHan, E., 515
McManus, J. A., 235
McMaster, M. R., 557

McMullen, P. A., 577, 578
McNeill, W. H., 18, 696
McNulty, S. E., 110, 145
Medin, D. L., 94
Mednick, B. R., 518, 519
Medvec, V. D., 172
Meek, D., 629
Meeus, W., 374, 375
Mendolia, M., 666
Messo, J., 615
Meyer, A. J., 683
Miami News, 244
Miceli, M. P., 575, 588
Michelli, J., 622
Mickler, S., 323
Midlarsky, E., 569
Miene, P. K., 604
Milgram, S. L., 32, 237, 325, 326, 331, 332, 365, 367, 368, 369, 374, 377, 378, 379, 380, 385, 395
Miller, C., 654
Miller, C. E., 317, 324, 422
Miller, D. S., 654
Miller, D. T., 103, 117, 168, 555
Miller, J. A., 347
Miller, J. D., 141, 161
Miller, M., 134
Miller, N., 215, 326, 497, 504
Miller, N. E., 506
Miller, P. A., 541
Miller, R. L., 346
Miller, T. Q., 520
Mills, J., 579
Milne, A. B., 179, 277
Minshull, M., 621
Mitchell, H. E., 150, 600
Miyake, K., 460
Molcan, J. R., 520
Montano, D. E., 241
Monteith, M. J., 209, 210
Montgomery, B. M., 468
Moran, G., 597, 599, 603, 612
Moreland, R. L., 402, 405, 406, 407, 422, 423
Morf, C., 81
Morgan, D., 147
Moriarty, T., 562
Morris, K., 275, 288
Morrison, B., 551
Morrison, S. E., 305
Morrow, L., 304
Morrow-Howell, N., 563
Morton, T. L., 464
Moscovici, S., 323, 333, 335, 337, 431
Moskos, C., 218, 219
Mowrer, O., 504
Moyer, K. E., 493
Mugny, G., 333
Mullen, B., 59, 167, 168, 411, 415
Murdoch, D. D., 500
Murnen, S. K., 457
Mussen, P., 568, 570
Myatt, C. R., 500
Myer, C. B., 148, 149
Myers, D. G., 431, 432, 630
Myrdal, G., 197

Nadler, A., 577, 581, 582
Naffrechoux, M., 333
Nagel, I. H., 595
Nam, K. D., 141
Narby, D. J., 597, 599, 603
Nash, J. D., 683
National Advisory Commission on Civil Disorders, 511
Nauful, T., 622
Neale, M. A., 287
Nebergall, R. E., 278
Neimeyer, G. J., 53, 54
Neisser, U., 127
Nelan, B. W., 304
Nelon, M., 15
Nelson, D., 456
Nelson, S., 213
Nemeth, C., 333, 334, 335
Nesselhof-Kendall, B., 297
Neuberg, S. L., 91, 108, 109, 208, 216, 217
Newcomb, T. M., 453, 456
Newsweek, 89, 191, 205
Newton, L., 111
New York Times, 150, 177, 186, 211
Nezlek, J., 482
Nichols, K. A., 450
Nickerson, R., 39
Niedenthal, P. M., 57
Nietzel, M. T., 641
Nisbett, R. E., 10, 46, 49, 111, 141, 162, 204, 205, 212, 376, 677
Noel, J. G., 153
Noller, P., 451
Northcraft, G. B., 287
Norwood, M., 241
Notarius, C., 469, 471
Novick, L. R., 143, 144, 164
Nowak, A., 337
Nunamaker, J. F., 425
Nurius, P., 52, 55

O'Connell, R. L., 18
O'Connor, F. J., 621
O'Donnell, V., 246
Ohbuchi, K., 506, 507
Oleson, K. C., 544, 545
Oliker, S. J., 482
Oliner, P. M., 564, 565, 566, 567, 568, 571, 575, 576
Oliner, S. P., 564, 565, 566, 567, 568, 571, 575, 576
Oliver, P. V., 110
Olmstead, M. P., 678
Olson, K., 458
Olweus, D., 15
Omoto, A. M., 477
O'Neill, P., 346
Opdyke, I. G., 575, 588
O'Quin, K., 557
Orenstein, L., 564
O'Rourke, D. F., 682
Osborn, M., 286
Osborn, S., 286
Osgood, C. E., 722
Osherow, N., 295

Oskamp, S., 210, 212, 235, 238, 239, 242, 248, 249, 296, 614
Ostrom, T. M., 621
Ozawa, M., 563

Packel, E. W., 548
Padawer-Singer, A., 610
Paicheler, G., 334, 355
Paige, J. M., 511
Palmer, T., 80
Papageorgis, D., 276
Park, B., 179, 207
Parker, J. F., 625
Paternoster, R., 632, 633
Patterson, G. R., 515, 527
Patterson, T. L., 670
Paulhus, D. L., 237
Paulus, P. B., 425
Pearson, N. A., 494
Pelham, B. W., 64, 65, 71, 162
Peltonen, T., 494
Pennebaker, J. W., 30, 107, 662, 663, 664, 665, 666, 667
Pennington, N., 99, 100, 422, 605, 627
Penrod, S., 337, 422, 521, 525, 599, 621, 626, 627, 629, 724
Peplau, L. A., 449, 450, 466
Pepler, D. J., 529
Perdue, C. W., 198
Perlman, D., 239, 449, 450
Perloff, L. S., 298
Perrin, S., 330
Perry, R. P., 560
Peterson, R. S., 437
Petrovic, D. M., 503
Pettigrew, T. F., 185, 207
Pettit, G. S., 498
Petty, R. E., 238, 272, 274, 275, 280, 282, 284, 288, 299, 347, 413
Peukert, D., 383, 391
Pfeiffer, C., 652
Pfiefer, J. R., 557
Phillips, D. P., 520
Piazza, T., 190, 191, 223
Pierce-Otay, A., 456
Pihl, R. O., 500
Pike, S., 39
Piliavin, I. M., 557
Piliavin, J. A., 557
Pinto, A. J., 150
Pitkanen, T., 512
Pittman, N. L., 46
Pittman, T. S., 46
Platonow, E., 545
Platt, J., 702, 703, 705
Pliner, P., 675
Plog, A., 54
Plomin, R., 248
Poletes, G., 425
Polivy, J., 678, 679
Poole, D. K., 623
Pope, L. K., 147
Poulos, R. W., 569
Powell, B., 296
Powell, M. C., 579
Prager, K., 481

Subject Index

cross-race identifications, 616
definition, 612
estimator variables, 614
hypnosis, 619
misinformation effect, 617
reconstructive memory, 617
system variables, 614
testimony, 613, 621–623, 624–626
violence of crime, 615–616
weapon focus, 614–615

False consensus bias, 156, 166–167
Fear, in persuasion
anti-smoking campaign, 272
effectiveness of, 271–274
protection-motivation explanation, 274
Feinstein, Diane, 270
Field experiment, 27, 28, 34
Field research, 25, 26
Field study, 26, 27
Field survey, 27
Five-stage decision model of helping
bystander effect, 553–556
in emergencies, 549, 550–561
in long-term helping, 574–576
Focal set, 142–144, 164
Foot-in-the-door (FITD) technique, of
compliance, 339–344, 347, 350
definition, 340
limits of, 342–344
perceptual contrast hypothesis, 342
self-perception hypothesis, 341
Free riders, 413
Friendship, 480–483
gender differences in, 481–482
and the life cycle, 482–483
Frustration-aggression hypothesis, 504–510
displaced aggression, 505
Functional size, of lineup, 621
Fundamental attribution error, 156, 158,
161–162
and formation of stereotypes, 203–
205, 215
and multiple audience problem, 279
See also Correspondence bias

Gatsby, Jay, and the self, 44–46, 47, 51,
55, 57, 64, 73, 74, 82
Gender bias, and self-fulfilling prophecies, 97
Gender differences
in aggression, 494–495, 519
in attributions about rape, 151
in conformity, 328–330
in friendship, 481–482
in hostility, 680
in leadership, 427–429
in need for affiliation, 448
in need for intimacy, 448
in obedience, 373
in receiving help, 582
in social behavior, 6
in social loafing, 414
and stress, 651–652, 655
Gender identity, definition, 211

Gender roles, 52
definition, 211
Gender role stereotypes, 210–213
definition, 211
effects on children, 212
General adaptation syndrome, 646–647
Generalizability, 22, 28
Genovese, Kitty, 549, 553, 557
Goldstein, Baruch, 491, 493, 709
Goodall, Jane, 26–27
Graduated and reciprocal initiatives in
tension reduction (GRIT), 722–724
Group
cohesiveness, 402–403, 426, 436
decision making, 417–429
definition, 400
features of, 400
formation, 403–405
influence on behavior, 408–417
leadership, 427–429
membership, 405–407
norms, 402, 403
participation, 411, 412–414
polarization, 430–432, 630
roles in, 407–408
size, 423–426
Group-serving bias, 168
Groupthink, 433–437
conditions favoring, 433–434
definition, 433
preventing, 435
symptoms of, 434
Gun control, 496

Hardiness, 657–658
Hate crimes, 176–177
against African Americans, 176
Health
belief model, 670–673
effect of mood on, 653–655
and lifestyle, 673–681
social psychology of, 646
and social support, 655–656
and socioeconomic status, 662
and stress, 647–652
Health belief model, 670–673
Heinrich, Ingo, 362, 363
Helping behavior
biological explanations for, 547–548
characteristics of victim, 558–559,
562–563
definition, 540
effect of mood, 558
egoism, 541–542
in emergencies, 549–563
empathy-altruism hypothesis, 541–542
empathy-punishment hypothesis,
544–546
five-stage decision model, 550–561,
574–576
long-term, 549
motives for, 541–548
personality factors in, 564
situational factors in, 563–564
situation-specific, 549
Help-seeking, decision model, 577–580

Heritability, 248–249
Heuristic and systematic information
processing model (HSM), 288
Heuristics
availability heuristic, 114
definition, 113
processing, 288
representativeness heuristic, 115–116
simulation heuristic, 116–117
Hinckley, John, Jr., 106, 130–131
Hindsight bias, in social psychology
research, 30
Historians, view on violence, 14, 18
HIV infection. *See* AIDS
Homophobia, 218
Hormonal influences on aggression,
501–503
role of testosterone, 502–503
Horton, Willie, 301–302
Hostile aggression, 493
Hostility
and coronary heart disease, 680–681
gender differences in, 680
Human immunodeficiency virus (HIV),
297, 298, 300. *See also* AIDS
Hypnosis, and eyewitness testimony, 619
Hypothesis, 19, 21
definition, 19
testing, and confirmation bias, 163

Ideal self, 59
Illness
coping with, 667–670
and life stressors, 647–649
prevention, 681–687
social context, 662
Illusion of control, 112
Illusion of efficacy, 425
Illusion of invulnerability, and groupthink, 434
Illusion of unanimity, and groupthink, 435
Illusion of unique invulnerability, and
AIDS, 298
Illusory correlation, 201–202
Implicit personality theory, 103, 675
Impression formation, 100–110
accuracy in, 108–110
and attribution, 127
belief perseverance, 102
central trait, 102
definition, 100
mechanisms of, 105–107, 108
primacy effect, 101–102
Impression management, 74–82
manipulative strategies, 78
and self-esteem, 74–75
self-presentation, 74–75
Independent variable, 20, 21, 22, 26
Individual characteristics
correlational studies on, 25
role in social behavior, 11–13
Individuation, 179
Induced compliance, 291
Inferential adjustment, 144–146

Reward theory, of interpersonal attraction, 453
Righteous rescuers, 564
  personality factors, 567–568
  situational factors, 566–567
Robbers Cave experiment, 700–701, 714
Rogers, Will, III, 88, 89, 90, 111
Role schemas, 96
Role strain, 385–386
Routinization, in obedience, 383

Sadat, Anwar, and Egypt-Israeli peace accord, 133, 135, 139–140
Sanctioned aggression, 493, 519
Scapegoat, 183
Schema, 53, 54, 95–96, 99
  definition, 95
  event schemas, 96
  person schemas, 96
  role schemas, 96
Schindler, Oskar, 134, 135
Schindler's List, film, 217
Scientific explanation, definition of, 20
Scientific method, 19–20, 35
  steps in, 19
Self
  autobiographical memory, 54
  collective self, 48–49
  components of, 47
  definition, 47
  as doer, 47
  and Jay Gatsby, 44–46, 47, 51, 55, 57, 82
  in medieval society, 51
  and memory, 54–55
  as personal historian, 54
  as totalitarian, 54
Self-affirmation theory, and rationalization, 294–296
Self-awareness, 59, 60–61
Self-blame, and trauma, 148–149
  behavioral self-blame, 148–149
  characterological self-blame, 148–149
Self-censorship, and groupthink, 435
Self-complexity, 57
Self-concept
  components of, 48, 50–56
  cultural influences on, 48, 49
  definition, 47
  formation of, 58
  stability of, 58
  structure of, 58
  working self-concept, 52
Self-consistency, 68, 71, 74
Self-destructive behaviors
  counterproductive strategies, 79, 80
  primary self-destruction, 79–80
  self-handicapping, 79, 80–82
Self-disclosure, 463–464
Self-efficacy
  expectancies, 63–64
  and stress, 652
Self-esteem, 65–74, 80, 81
  and attribution, 150, 153
  discrepancies, 65–67
  and group membership, 405

and impression management, 74–75
and in-group bias, 195–196
internal influences on, 65–68
and obesity, 675, 678–679
and receiving help, 577, 580, 581–583
Self-evaluation maintenance (SEM) theory, 68–70
  bask in reflected glory (BIRG), 69
  comparison process, 69
  reflection process, 69
Self-focus, 59–60, 62, 63
Self-fulfilling prophecy, 96–97
  behavioral confirmation, 97–98
  and gender bias, 97
Self-fulfillment, and culture, 49
Self-guides, 59, 62–66
  actual self, 59, 64–66
  ideal self, 59, 64–66
  ought self, 59, 64–66
Self-handicapping, 79, 80–82
  and attribution, 153
Self-knowledge, 46, 51, 58, 77, 82
  methods used to gain, 46
Self-monitoring, 74–77
Self-perception theory, 293–294
  and FITD technique, 341
Self-persuasion, models of, 289
Self-presentation, 49, 74–75, 78, 80, 82
  management, 74–75
  strategies, 49
Self-regulation, 59–64, 65, 68
  factors influencing, 59–64
  self-focus, 59–60
Self-schemas, 52–53, 54, 55, 57, 58, 95, 96
  definition, 53
Self-serving bias, 118–121, 156, 167–168
Self-verification, 71, 73–74
Sequential lineup procedure, 620–621
Sexism
  cognitive roots of, 213–215
  definition, 178
  gender role stereotypes, 211–212
  historical roots of, 210–211
  male norm, 214–215
  social context, 211–213
  social roles theory, 215
Shah of Iran, overthrow of, 88
Sides, USS, 89, 90
Simulation heuristic, 116–117
Situation, definition, 10
Situational attribution, in covariation theory, 136, 137, 141
Slavery, and prejudice, 203
Sleeper effect, 269, 609
Social anxiety, 447, 450
  traits, 450–451
Social behavior, 5, 6, 9–13
  definition, 3
  effects of self-esteem on, 72
  Lewin's model, 10, 13
  role of individual characteristics, 11–13
  role of the situation, 10–11, 13
Social cognition, 11–13, 34
  definition, 11
Social comparison, 58, 404–405

Social comparison theory, and conformity, 327
Social compensation, definition, 414
Social context, 5, 10
Social desirability, 131, 132–133, 135, 137
Social exchange theory, of relationships, 464
Social facilitation, 408–409
Social identity theory, and stereotypes, 194
Social influence, 34
  and conformity, 323
  effect on behavior, 315
  and obesity, 677–678
  and persuasion, 265
  types of, 316
Social information processing view, 528
Social inhibition, 408
Social-interactional model, 515–516
Social isolation, 655
Socialization
  and aggression, 512
  in obedience, 380–382
Social judgment theory
  and discrepancy, 278
  latitudes, 278
Social learning theory
  and aggression, 512–513, 514–515
  and altruism, 568–570
Social loafing
  cultural differences, 414
  definition, 412–414
  free riders, 413
  gender differences, 414
Social norms
  and conformity, 318
  and racism, 191–192
Social penetration theory, 463
  self-disclosure, 463–464
Social perception, 11–13, 54, 90, 95
  definition, 11
  strategies and methods, 90–91
Social power, bases of, 378
Social psychologists, view on violence, 14, 16
Social psychology, 3–5
  approach to intergroup hostility, 17
  comparison with sociology, 16
  definition, 3
  of health, 646
  and related fields, 14–16, 18
  research in, 25–28
  sociohistorical perspective, 6–7
Social reality
  construction of, 90–91
  egocentric bias, 111
  story model approach, 99–101
  use of prototypes and exemplars, 94
Social relations, 34, 35
Social roles theory, 215
Social self, 47
Social situation, 13–16, 18
Social support, 655
Social trap, 702–705
  commons dilemma, 704–705
  prisoner's dilemma, 703, 705
Sociobiology, and aggression, 499